I0821695

THE HOLOCAUST IN CROATIA

THE HOLOCAUST IN CROATIA

IVO GOLDSTEIN AND
SLAVKO GOLDSTEIN

UNIVERSITY OF PITTSBURGH PRESS

PUBLISHED IN ASSOCIATION WITH THE

UNITED STATES HOLOCAUST MEMORIAL MUSEUM

This English-language edition has been translated from the original Croatian publication:

Ivo Goldstein and Slavko Goldstein, *Holokaust u Zagrebu* © 2001 by Novi Liber and Židovska općina Zagreb, Zagreb

Translated by Sonia Wild Bićanić and Nikolina Jovanović.

The authors gratefully acknowledge Steve Salemson for his assistance in the final preparation of the English-language manuscript.

This work is published with the support of the Jack, Joseph and Morton Mandel Center for Advanced Holocaust Studies, United States Holocaust Memorial Museum, and with the support of the Croatian Ministry of Culture. The assertions, arguments, and conclusions contained herein are those of the authors. They do not necessarily reflect the opinions of the United States Holocaust Memorial Museum.

Published by the University of Pittsburgh Press, Pittsburgh, Pa., 15260

Manufactured in the United States of America
Printed on acid-free paper
10 9 8 7 6 5 4 3 2

ISBN 13: 978-0-8229-4451-5
ISBN 10: 0-8229-4451-0

Cataloging-in-Publication data is available from the Library of Congress

Jacket photo: A Jewish inhabitant of Zagreb with the newly introduced Jewish star and the initial of the Croatian word for "Jew." Photograph, 1941. ullstein bild / The Granger Collection, New York — All rights reserved.

Jacket design by Alex Wolfe

CONTENTS

PART I. IDEOLOGICAL AND SOCIAL PREREQUISITES OF PERSECUTION

PART II. SPRING AND SUMMER OF 1941: EXCOMMUNICATION

PART III. SUMMER AND AUTUMN OF 1941: CONCENTRATION AND EXTERMINATION

PART IV. MOVING TOWARD FINAL ANNIHILATION, 1942–1943

PART V. TRYING TO SURVIVE

PART VI. EPILOGUE

PART I

IDEOLOGICAL AND SOCIAL PREREQUISITES OF PERSECUTION

1

A BRIEF HISTORY OF CROATIA

The territory of present-day Croatia was the home of Illyrian tribes when the Romans conquered it in the first century B.C., creating the provinces of Pannonia and Dalmatia, and subsequently most of the population was gradually Romanized. The Slavs and the Croats moved to the region by the end of the sixth century, when the age of the great migrations of peoples was coming to an end. At the beginning of the ninth century, a state was organized under the Trpimirović dynasty, replaced in 1102 by the Hungarian Arpad dynasty. In this way, Hungary and Croatia created a union that was to last until 1918, but within which Croatia always retained a degree of autonomy. In 1526, the Hapsburg dynasty was elected to the throne of Hungary-Croatia, and thus Hungary-Croatia became part of the huge Austrian Empire. At that time, the Ottoman Turks held large parts of Croatia, almost two-thirds, and much of the coast belonged to the Venetian Republic from even earlier times.

By the end of the seventeenth century, after it was gradually liberated from the Ottomans, the territory of Croatia acquired its characteristic horseshoe shape, and its borders have since changed very little. In those days, the territory inhabited by the Croats, which included parts of Bosnia and Herzegovina, was divided by state frontiers among the Hapsburg Monarchy, Venice, and the Ottomans. It was socially, culturally, and climatically heterogeneous, and had poor road connections. The National Revival began in the 1830s, but, due to prevailing conditions, it developed very slowly.

Croatia was peripheral to the Austro-Hungarian Monarchy, and was alternately governed from the two centers, first Vienna and then Budapest. When the Monarchy disintegrated in 1918, Croatia became part of a newly formed state of Yugoslavia, more by the dictate of conditions in general than by the will of its political leaders and people. Yugoslavia bridged the area from the Alps almost to the Aegean Sea, which had not been under a single administration since the fourth century. Life in the new state placed Croatia in a completely novel situation: the central-European environment, which had been very important for it, gradually eroded, and attempts were made to replace it by a new South Slav (i.e., Yugoslav) cultural and national self-awareness. National dilemmas were always in the foreground, both when ideas about separate nations or about a single Yugoslav nation were being promoted. At the same time, growing social stratification and the development of the proletariat led to class issues. Various solutions were offered to solve these problems, and totalitarian concepts, either right- or left-wing, gathered strength. As the Second World War approached, political development, especially on the international level, did not favor middle-class and democratic solutions.

Although after 1918 the very important ties with central Europe—especially Vienna and Budapest—waned as time passed, at first the Croatian economy did very well in the new community. Croatia was still a predominantly agricultural country (the population that depended on agriculture did not fall below 70 percent until the 1920s), but, all the same, its industry was much stronger than in the poorly developed eastern parts of the new country. Thus, Croatian industry, especially the wood industry, was assured of an internal market. The increased use of mechanization favored the processing industry and trade. Zagreb became a commercial and banking center, and Croatia, and Yugoslavia with it, was a country with good developmental potential, profitable businesses, and a basis for rapid growth. This led to more foreign investment in Croatia than in other parts of Yugoslavia. Until 1926, the Croatian economy expanded, and, until 1930, conditions remained relatively good. Despite these favorable circumstances and great profits, during the 1920s the workers' purchasing power was lower than in 1914. Zagreb and Croatia lagged behind most western- and central-European lands, but were better developed than most of the eastern and southeastern parts of Yugoslavia, or the other European countries farther to the south and southeast. Zagreb most of all, but other urban centers too, developed much like the urban centers in some other parts of Europe: Zagreb Radio began broadcasting, a Zagreb–Belgrade airline route was opened, and the development of a rich urban class with sophisticated tastes fostered greater art production that was partially influenced by the avant-garde currents of postwar Europe. Zagreb University also expanded after 1918, because it was now more difficult to study in the former Austro-Hungarian centers.

On the other hand, as a result of the Communist Party's success in elections for the Constituent Assembly, and because of the demonstrations and strikes that were spreading throughout the country, laws were passed in 1920 making it possible to imprison people for political ideas and activities. According to the Yugoslav government, "the freedom of public activities and writing remains untouched, provided that it does not insult the State and demoralize the people." Be that as it may, in the interwar period, thousands of people were arrested and tried in accordance with these and other laws, which later grew increasingly repressive, and scores of people were killed by police violence.

The assassination attempt on the life of Stjepan Radić, head of the Croatian Peasant Party, and his associates in the Belgrade Assembly in 1928, and especially Radić's death a month later as a result of the wounds inflicted, caused great unrest in Zagreb and in other parts of Croatia. For months the atmosphere remained tense, as a result of which, on January 6, 1929, King Aleksandar issued a manifesto abolishing the Constitution, dissolving the National Assembly, and banning all political parties of national, religious, or regional nature (because of the date, this was known as the "Sixth-of-January Dictatorship"). Laws were passed making the king the supreme state authority and establishing absolute royal prerogatives. The persecution of political opponents, including moderate middle-class politicians, increased.

At the same time, the state was administratively subdivided into nine units called *banovinas* without any ethnic, economic, or geographical justification. The banovinas were designed to annul the boundaries and continuity of historical and national provinces, and to impose Yugoslav national unity under the leadership of the ruling Serbian circles.

Things got worse in 1930, greatly influenced by the world economic depression: foreign capital was withdrawn from the Croatian economy, and Croatia did not receive the necessary financial aid from Belgrade, which signaled the beginning of the end of economic prosperity for Croatia's various regions. In 1931, after more than eighty years of unbroken economic growth and expansion, Croatia experienced a catastrophic financial crash. The brutal suppression of national freedom and identity led to extremist nationalistic reactions, which in Croatia gave rise to the activities of the Ustasha organization.

To decrease internal pressure, in 1939 the Belgrade government developed what was known as the Cvetković-Maček Agreement. In an attempt to solve the Croatian national question, the Prime Minister, Dragiša Cvetković, signed an agreement with the leader of the Croatian Peasant Party, Vladko Maček, establishing the Croatian banovina as an administrative unit and agreeing to found a joint government. Unfortunately, it turned out that this solution, although realistic and workable in some respects, came too late (and, in the long run, it was doomed to failure because it did not take the Muslim question into consideration). By that time, internal tensions and foreign pressure had mounted beyond the control of even an effective policy.

The Axis Powers attacked Yugoslavia in April 1941, and the Yugoslav army quickly capitulated. The Independent State of Croatia (ISC) was created on the territory of Croatia and Bosnia and Herzegovina, under the rule of the Nazi-Fascist Ustasha movement, which launched a policy of genocide against Serbs, Jews, and Roma (familiarly known as Gypsies). They also persecuted many Croats who opposed them, or might oppose them in any way. All this quickly led to an anti-Fascist resistance under the leadership of the Communist Party and Josip Broz Tito. The Partisan movement in Croatia and Bosnia and Herzegovina was unparalleled in Europe in its massive popular support and its level of organization, exceeded only by the one in occupied parts of the USSR. Skillfully combining broad anti-Fascist goals with their own social and national agenda, the Communists turned the Partisan units into an indigenous force that, after the Second World War, was in a position to impose its own government.

2

THE JEWS IN ZAGREB PRIOR TO 1941

In fourteenth- and fifteenth-century Gradec (the commercial part of the city, as distinct from the bishop's city of Zagreb), there was a small Jewish community that seems not to have consisted of more than a dozen families. In the 1450s, they were banished from the city and after that Jews were only occasional passers-through. They were forbidden from settling in north Croatia, even for a short time (unlike the coastal areas, where there was an important community in Split under Venetian rule, and another in independent Dubrovnik). It was not until the second half of the eighteenth century that Jews began to appear in some north-Croatian towns, usually for fairs and for trade in general. A regulation existed forbidding them access to the Zagreb fair on the grounds of being "dangerous for the citizens because of their swindling," but they continued to come nonetheless, and in 1769 and 1780 Zagreb merchants protested against the competition mostly of the Eastern Orthodox, but also of the Jews.[1]

In 1782, Emperor Joseph II issued the "Edict on Tolerance," which was applied in Croatia starting the following year, giving Jews the right to settle in all the lands of the Hapsburg Empire, and the first "tolerated" Jew came to Zagreb in 1786. His name was Jakov Stiegler, he came from Trebič in Moravia, and in 1787 he was issued with a residence permit. Like his fellows, he was a merchant, trading only in the goods permitted for Jews:

agricultural produce and secondhand goods. He was a peddler in Jastrebarsko (twenty-five kilometers southwest of Zagreb) and the surrounding villages, sold what he was allowed to, and bought what no one else did, even fir cones and acorns.[2]

Jewish settlement was slow because a long administrative procedure was needed to acquire a residence permit, and there were only nine Jewish families in Zagreb at the beginning of the nineteenth century. These were the conditions under which a Jewish religious community was established in Zagreb in 1806, and three years later the first rabbi arrived. It was a community of young people: according to the first census in 1809, only four of the fifty-two Jews were older than forty. Except for two families, the rest had only just moved in and were very poor.

The Zagreb Jewish Community mostly followed the general course of Jewish history in Europe, especially in the Hapsburg Monarchy. The first generation that moved to Zagreb was already strongly influenced by the enlightened ideas of Moses Mendelssohn. In 1839, the Zagreb and Varaždin Communities jointly submitted an application to the Croatian Parliament requesting social emancipation and fundamental economic rights: "Obstacles are placed before us to prevent us from making our livelihood, either by way of crafts or agriculture."

Many Zagreb and Croatian Jews took an active part in the revolutionary events of 1848–1849 on the side of Ban Josip Jelačić (1801–1859), who opposed some anti-Semitic incidents and supported civil rights for Jews. This was the beginning of the faster inclusion of Jews in the social life of the city and of Croatia in the following decades.

In the mid-nineteenth century, Croatian lands went through a period of rapid modernization, and this progress gradually brought the Jews civil rights. They finally got full civil equality in 1873, which opened up new perspectives and led to dramatic changes. The first generation that moved to Croatia mostly consisted of peddlers or village and small-town shopkeepers. In the next generation, having acquired a certain fortune, many moved to bigger towns and finally to Zagreb. The second and third generations went to university and established themselves in prestigious professions, mostly as doctors or attorneys, which became real "Jewish" professions in all of north Croatia. Although Jews made up less than 1 percent of the population in 1910, 17 percent of the attorneys, and as many as 25 to 26 percent of the doctors were Jewish. Many others became builders, architects, and artists. In many cases, the merchants developed into wholesale merchants and bankers, and the craftsmen into industrialists.

In comparison with Poland, Hungary, or Romania, the Croatian Jewish population was always relatively small. At the turn of the nineteenth century, there were only about 20,000 Jews in Croatia (3,237 of them in Zagreb); nevertheless, the Zagreb Jewish Community was by far the largest, richest, and most important in the country. At one point, at the end of the nineteenth century, the Osijek Community was larger and economically stronger, but generally, in the broader region from Vienna to Thessalonica, the Zagreb Community was equaled, but only in number, by the Jewish Communities in Belgrade (Serbia) and Sarajevo (Bosnia).

Between 1850 and 1941, Zagreb developed much more quickly than any other Croatian town in size, economic strength, culture, and scientific research, and the Jewish community in the city grew and developed faster than anywhere else in Croatia. In 1857, when Zagreb had 27,349 inhabitants, 625 (or 2.3 percent) were Jews. Some twenty years later, in 1880, Zagreb already had a population of 41,895, and twice as many Jews as before—1,285 (3.1 percent). At the turn of the century, Zagreb was twice as large as it had been twenty years earlier, with 79,282 inhabitants, but there were two and a half times more Jews—3,237. After the First World War (1921), when the population of Zagreb comprised 131,707 citizens, there were almost 6,000 Jews (5,970, or 4.6 percent). Just before the Second World War, in 1939, the Zagreb Jewish Community had 9,467 members. These were 8,712 (92 percent) Ashkenazim (Neologs), 8,712 (6.6 percent) Sephardim, and 130 (1.4 percent) Orthodox Jews.[3] In that year, Zagreb already had more than 250,000 inhabitants.

These numbers included only the members of the Jewish Community. However, other sources give different data. At the end of the thirties, David Levi, secretary of the Union of Jewish Communities in Yugoslavia (SJVOJ), said that the Ashkenazic and Sephardic Communities together had 10,175 members, and that there were another 130 members in the Orthodox Community, which meant that the Jewish Communities in Zagreb had a total of 10,305 members.[4] In 1929, the President of the Community, Hugo Kon, said that "there are about 12,000 souls in our community," and in 1931 he said that the "number of Community members has grown to about 13,000."[5] When he said "Community members" he obviously meant people who were Jews by birth, including those who did not pay Community dues, who played no active part in its work, who had married non-Jews, and others.

The importance of Zagreb's Jews for the history of their city grew rapidly once they were able to take an equal and complete part in civic life. This attracted increasing numbers of Jews to Zagreb, and the new arrivals gave further impetus to the multifaceted urban progress, strengthening the Jewish Community in the city in every way.[6] As Zagreb and its Jewish population grew and developed together, the history of all the Jews in Croatia was increasingly concentrated in Zagreb; what happened in Zagreb came to be representative of all the Jews in Croatia, and also partly of some outside it.

In 1867, a new synagogue was constructed in Praška Street, marking one of the crucial events in the life of Zagreb's Jews. The synagogue's characteristic architecture, monumental appearance, and location changed the appearance of the city's center and symbolized the important role of the Jewish community in city life.

Many Jewish societies were founded in Zagreb after the end of the nineteenth century: charities, women's groups, youth groups, choral societies, literary groups, and sports teams, and social activities burgeoned until 1940. The magazine *Židovska smotra* began publication in 1906, while the informative and political weekly *Židov,* the best and most influential Jewish paper in Yugoslavia at that time, was published from 1917 until the Second World War. Other papers were the cultural and political youth magazine *Gideon* (1919–1926) and its successor *Hanoar* (1927–1937), a magazine for children *Ha'aviv* (1922–1941), and the cultural magazine *Omanut* (1936–1941).[7]

Better life also brought new problems. The eternal question about the significance and meaning of Jewry, for centuries marked by enforced isolation or Orthodox self-isolation, now acquired new dimensions: could the Jews keep their traditional concepts of religious organization and religious-national determination in a society in which they had become equal citizens? These challenges evoked fundamentally different answers in Zagreb, as they did among all European Jews at that time. Integrationists prevailed in the Zagreb Jewish Community, as opposed to the isolationists. In the first confrontations between the Orthodox and the reformists in 1840, the reformists won. In the 1850s, it was decided to organize a single Community with a single administration, but with two houses of worship and two different rites. However, the reformists kept increasing in number and influence, and by 1941 Orthodox Jews constituted barely 2 percent of the Jews in Zagreb.

In the first half of the nineteenth century, the Zagreb Jews were closely tied to the lands from which they had come. They spoke their languages (usually Hungarian and German), were given traditional Jewish names (Abraham, Benjamin, Jošua, David, Sara, Rahela, Mirjam, Estera, etc.) or traditional German names (Hermina, Karolina, Matilda, Rudolf, Oskar,

Fani, Berta, Leopold, Maksimilijan, etc.). By the beginning of the second half of the nineteenth century, their names, too, began to reflect their integration into the Croatian environment: after 1850, names such as Josip, Ljudevit, Milan, Bogoslav, Slavko, Slavoljub, and Drago became more common.[8] Language assimilation took place rather quickly, and Croatian became the teaching language at the Jewish school in 1865. While only 30.3 percent of Croatian Jews gave Croatian as their mother tongue in 1880 (with 55.6 percent giving German and 11.7 percent Hungarian), some fifty years later, in 1931, Croatian was the mother tongue of 69.4 percent (for 14.2 percent it was German and for 10.6 percent Hungarian). In Zagreb, the language assimilation of Jews was even faster than the average in Croatia as a whole. In 1900, Croatian was the mother tongue of 54.1 percent of Zagreb Jews, and in 1931 it was the mother tongue of 73.6 percent (with 12.2 percent giving German and 7.5 percent Hungarian).

These numbers are an indirect indicator of how strong the assimilating current among the Zagreb Jews was. The middle and higher classes mostly supported assimilation. Members of the most distinguished and richest Zagreb Jewish families were not Zionists as a rule, although they participated in Community activities, especially in membership in the Hevra Kaddisha (a traditional institution of Jewish Communities for burying the poor and for social welfare). Although assimilation was never formulated as an ideology or a closed ideological system, its supporters very clearly expressed their basic views—they denied world Jewry as an organic whole. Before the First World War and between the wars, most assimilationists considered themselves part of the nation in which they resided, saying that they belonged only to the Jewish religion. In the 1920s, assimilationists gathered in the society Narodni rad (People's Work Society), which later got the additional name of "društvo židovskih asimilanata i anticionista u Hrvatskoj" (Society of Jewish Assimilationists and Anti-Zionists in Croatia). The object of Narodni rad was to "gather all Croatian and other Yugoslav citizens of the Jewish religion, regardless of political and party views."[9] In the second half of the 1930s, assimilationists belonged to the Klub zagrebačkih jevrejskih građana (Zagreb Jewish Citizens' Club).[10] Extreme assimilationists moved away from Judaism as a culture and nationality; some even discarded the religion, and some Croatized their names and surnames. In this way, they were part of an extinguished branch of Jewry: within a generation or two, with a significant percentage of mixed marriages, they lost any identification with Judaism. From 1941 to 1945, many of them were nevertheless persecuted, just like all the other Jews.

Community work under the influence of the integration/assimilation approach usually meant that members gathered to organize traditional Jewish philanthropic work to help the poor. However, Zionist ideas also spread among Zagreb Jews from the beginning of the twentieth century on, mostly among the middle class, while the poor remained at first apolitical. To different degrees, the Zionist movement championed the foundation of a Jewish state in Palestine, but it was a Jewish national revival too, similar to that undergone by other European peoples in the eighteenth and nineteenth centuries. Zionism was also a call to Jews to learn about their past, culture, and especially to learn Hebrew, and to use these foundations to build up their national self-awareness. The Zionists took power in the Zagreb Community with the elections for Community administrative bodies in 1920, and in the interwar period the Zagreb Jewish Community was the center of the Yugoslav Zionist movement. Nevertheless, before 1941, only about 200 Zagreb Jews confirmed their Zionism by self-sacrificing emigration to Palestine. Most of them preferred to offer moral and financial support to the Zionist movement.

The results of the 1935 elections show the balance of power within the Zagreb Community: the joint party of center and left Zionists won 73.8 percent of the votes, the party of the Revisionist Zionists (followers of Ze'ev Jabotinsky) 9.3 percent,[11] and the assimilationist party 16.9 percent.[12] It must also be remembered that quite a large number of assimilationists did not vote, or had already left the Community.

Despite the deep roots of Zagreb Jews in the economic and cultural life of the city, some barriers were very difficult to cross, let alone remove. Although they enjoyed nominal equality, the Jews were not on a par with non-Jews.[13] For a long time they had been considered a foreign body. At first, the language barrier had been the most prominent: the mother tongues of nineteenth-century immigrants to Croatia were usually Hungarian or German, languages whose use Croatian cultural circles fiercely opposed at that time in their ongoing and long-lasting struggle for national self-awareness. There was also a traditional mistrust of foreigners that sometimes grew to the proportions of xenophobia, combined with a deep-rooted prejudice against Jews as swindlers. Deepest of all was the religious mistrust, the consequence of surviving medieval beliefs that the Jews had killed Christ and that all Jews must pay for this forever.

Many Jews encouraged prejudice of this kind by self-isolation, which had various motives, from those based on traditional Jewish Orthodoxy to the desire to keep to themselves because of the prejudice and intolerance of the broader community. Still, in the long term, these barriers slowly fell or diminished. The growth and strengthening of the modern middle-class society in Croatia was tested, and is still tested, through the speed at which the Croatian majority regarded the Jewish minority as equals. Two opposing positions were constantly present in this process: one was intolerant and undemocratic, embracing authoritarianism, clericalism, traditionalism, and later also racism, while the other was liberal-democratic and progressive.

In the 1830s, and then again in 1848–1849 and at the end of the century, there were significantly more anti-Semitic incidents in Zagreb than anywhere else in Croatia. At the same time, middle-class public opinion and the strong institutions of the civil society at the end of the nineteenth and the beginning of the twentieth century made such acts less important, pushing them outside the main social currents.

The interwar period was a golden age for the Jews in Zagreb, Croatia, and Yugoslavia as a whole. As the report about the work of the Community written in July 1945 shows, the Zagreb Community was "not only in number, but perhaps even more in its activities and productive work in all fields of Jewish life, one of the most distinguished Communities in all of Europe. Some far larger Communities could not boast of as much active work as that performed by our Community."[14] There were many influential Jewish organizations—social, cultural, humanitarian, economic, sports-oriented—which worked equally within and outside the Jewish community. Some of them were Jewish institutions and were part of general Zagreb life. Increasing numbers of Jews participated in their intensive and multifaceted activities, and some of them were also joined by growing circles of other Zagreb citizens as well. As they developed and nurtured their Jewish identity, the Jews of Zagreb also took a greater role in the city and its overall life, which was a valuable contribution to Zagreb, a city with a strong multicultural European tradition.

"To write the whole history of the Zagreb Jews would be the same as to write the history of the city of Zagreb . . . and if one were to imagine Zagreb without Jews, it would be a dead and destitute city," wrote Lavoslav Šik in 1931.[15]

The establishment of the ISC was a severe rebuff, the eradication of everything of value that the Zagreb Jews, in cooperation with other citizens of Zagreb, had achieved in the preceding hundred or so years in the fields of politics, economy, and culture.

3

ANTI-SEMITISM IN THE THIRTIES

The Horror Begins

With hindsight, viewed from the end of the twentieth and beginning of the twenty-first century, events in various European countries in the early 1930s should have provided many reasons for deep concern. However, most Zagreb Jews, like many others in Croatia and in Yugoslavia and all over Europe, treated the indications that a new anti-Semitism was arising very casually.[1]

The anti-Semitic hysteria during and after the First World War had gradually subsided during the twenties, and there were very many fewer anti-Semitic incidents at the end of that decade and in the early thirties.

In 1930, the article "Numerus clausus" appeared in the Croatian Catholic seminarists' periodical *Luč* (The torch), which wrote favorably about the institution of a numerus clausus in Hungary, saying that its introduction was a reflection of the struggle between "Hungarian nationalism and immense Jewish capital." It also printed a detailed description, not unsympathetic to the perpetrators, of recent anti-Semitic outbursts that had taken place at the universities in Vienna, Krakow, Budapest, and elsewhere.[2] "It is natural that the excessive number of Jewish students in Hungary was likely to lead to frequent and violent clashes . . . anti-Semitism is flourishing, which is understandable, because the Hungarians, just like any other people, want to be masters in their own house." The magazine drew on all the usual stereotypes of the right-wing press (for example, it claimed that "belligerent Muscovite Jewish Bolshevism is flaunting itself in our regions also").[3] *Luč* was otherwise a very informative magazine with contributions about literature, art, social and political life in general—for example, on the same page on which it supported the numerus clausus, *Luč* gave a very accurate review of the assembly of the Jewish Academic Support Society.

Even earlier there had been some sympathy for anti-Semitism based on the racial theory. In 1925, the magazine *Nova revija vjeri i nauci* (New review of faith and science) of Makarska (fifty kilometers southeast of Split), edited by Professor Petar Grabić from the Catholic seminary, began to publish the fradulent *Protocols of the Elders of Zion* in installments.[4] The editors of the *Protocols* were M. Tomić and M. Butmi. Butmi was the Russian writer and polemicist who had published the *Protocols* in 1907. Tomić's comments left naive readers no doubt that the *Protocols* were an authentic document; he wrote about their "awful historical truth" and concluded by instructing his readers: "Important—Attention!" and adding, "Read this and pass it on to others to read!"[5] *Nova revija* had other articles that were either openly anti-Semitic or indirectly attacked the Jews,[6] but there were also articles that gave objective information about Jews and Jewry.[7] At that time, the Catholic Church took the position that the appearance of Christ had ended the historic and theological mission of Jewry and that the solution to the "Jewish question" was the conversion of Jews to Christianity. Thus, *Nova revija* took great pleasure in informing the public that a Central Committee of the Society for Helping and Converting Jews had been established in Rome, with the aim of "paving the way, through prayer, acts of mercy, and missionary work among the Jews, for conversion to Christ's true faith."[8] Contrary to *Nova revija,* the Zagreb liberal paper *Obzor* (Horizon) published information about the *Protocols* generally and clearly expressed the opinion that it was worthless forgery.[9]

During the Eucharistic Congress in 1930, the *Protocols of the Elders of Zion,* which had been published in Split and Šibenik the year before, appeared in Zagreb bookshops. This was the first complete edition of the pamphlet in Croatia and Yugoslavia. Tsvi Rothmüller reacted in *Židov* (The Jew) to the publication of the *Protocols*—he wrote that the "objective public will be able to distinguish between writing that is not serious and is dishonorably superficial, and integrity and honor. Jews shall not be led astray even by such documents of human wickedness. We believe in the progress of humanity, in the triumph of justice."[10] In answer to Rothmüller, Tomić published another article entitled "The Brazen Provocation of *Židov.*" He called all the accusations "careless and superficial" and aggressively claimed that the *Protocols* were authentic and had been "published not in revenge or to persecute Jews, but for the necessary self-defense of the state and the people from their hellish intention to subdue the whole world under the scepter of a ruler of Jewish blood."[11] At that time, at the beginning of 1931, Dr Bukić Pijade, an official of the Belgrade Jewish Community and of the Union of Jewish Communities of Yugoslavia, talked with General Petar Živković, the Prime Minister of the Royal Government, about the "printing and circulation" of this book. Živković was "surprised that such books as this can be published in our country" and promised to do all he could "to prevent any activity designed to spoil the harmonious relations between Jews and other citizens."[12]

Besides *Luč* and *Nova revija,* other anti-Semitic publications were published by people connected with the Catholic Church: "writers of Catholic leanings" published the monthly *Hrvatska prosvjeta* (Croatian Enlightenment) in which the book *Gog* (Florence, 1931) by the Italian writer Giovanni Papini (1881–1956) was reviewed. Papini was known for his attempts to "topple recognized authorities," and *Gog* was one of his lesser-known books.[13] The magazine gave a favorable account of the book's basic approach, which was an attack on the cosmopolitan civilization that could not lead to happiness. The book asked, how was the "downtrodden and debased Jew to avenge himself on his enemies?," and concluded that to do this "it was necessary to humiliate, shame, unmask, and bring down the ideals of the Goyim [i.e., non-Jews], and destroy values that were the life-blood of Christianity." Then it attacked Heine, Marx, Nordau, Freud ("according to him, even the most virtuous man and excellent gentleman is a villain, he is incestuous and a thief"), Einstein ("he claims that space and time are the same"), Lassalle, Disraeli, and other Jews. It concluded that "today's intellectual Europe is under the influence of the Jews. Born among different peoples, they devoted themselves to research in various fields. All of them, the Germans and the French, the Italians and the Poles, poets and mathematicians, anthroposophists and philosophers, they all have the same character and one single goal: to spread doubt about acknowledged truths, to destroy what is elevated, to besmirch what is pure, to shake the foundations of what is permanent, and to stone what people honor."[14]

The anti-Semitism of the twenties was partly the result of the rather large social gap which at that time still existed between Jews and non-Jews in some portions of Zagreb, Croatian, and Yugoslav society. In the thirties, this gap was obviously closing as the middle-class became increasingly aware that the Jews were equal citizens and should be treated as such. However, it was just at that point that Nazi propaganda was launched, accusing Jews of responsibility for everything that was going wrong. Anti-Semitism was a cheap and simple way to spread the Nazi ideology to other European lands, including Croatia and Yugoslavia. The "hard times effect"[15] ensured public support for anti-Semitism because, after the Great Depression of 1929, in the thirties people thought with nostalgia of the times when they had been richer and enjoyed greater security.

Anti-Semitic articles in the Croatian and Yugoslav press in the early thirties were minor in comparison with the texts that began to be published in 1933, and increased in number in the following years.

In 1932, a journalist under the pen name of "Danubiensis" wrote the article "Why Are the Germans Harassing the Jews?" in the Belgrade daily *Pravda* (Justice). It called the brutality of the German National Socialists a "cultural struggle," saying that all the Jews in the world ("and everywhere in the world") are against Christianity, and that Zionism "is just as dangerous and subversive for many states as Communism." *Pravda* was a pro-regime daily, which lent more significance to its assertions.[16] In the next few days, two prominent Belgrade Jews wrote very lucid and witty answers, one of which, by Leon Amar, *Pravda* would not publish. Amar wrote that "we must tell the authorities it is better to forecast evil than to heal it . . . They must not allow anyone to write whatever they like about Jews simply because they are Jews."[17]

The writer and publicist Ivan Nevistić (1899–1941) is a good example of the mistrust and hostility toward Jews in Croatia and Yugoslavia in the late twenties and in the thirties. At the beginning of the thirties, Nevistić became *Pravda's* Zagreb correspondent. He was dogmatically faithful to the "Yugoslav national line," which means to the ruling ideology—he criticized *Jutarnji list* (Morning paper) of Zagreb for having sided with the Austro-Hungarian authorities, and of "working against the interests of the integral Yugoslav nation."[18]

When writing about "Zagreb theater news," Nevistić said that a "person must simply ask in amazement what makes this a Yugoslav state and national theater. We are not against foreigners in principle, against the Germans and the Hungarians (most of them are Jews) . . . who do not participate in our cultural life at all and keep to themselves in an attitude of 'superiority.'"[19] Saying that a "relatively large number of male and female members of even the richest Jewish families of Zagreb" were Communists, he concluded that "by acting as they do, the Jews are giving strong grounds for anti-Semitism and it is they who are to blame for the development of a racist mood and opinion in our extremely tolerant national public."[20]

In October 1932, swastikas appeared on the building of the Jewish Community in Palmotićeva and on "some coffeehouses that were probably considered Jewish meeting-places, and on some Jewish shops." The police did not find the perpetrators.[21] Beginning in 1932, the rather well-known nationalistic theater, called the Society of Croatian Theater Volunteers, produced the comedy *The Prize* in Zagreb with "great success." It described the suffering of an honest peasant, and included the stereotypical Jew who had a hooked nose, and made many mistakes when he spoke.[22]

In earlier decades, Croatian anti-Semites had accused the Jews of being in alliance with the Germans or the Hungarians, partly because they spoke better German or Hungarian than Croatian. In the thirties, charges of this kind would have been completely out of place because Austria-Hungary no longer existed, and the younger Jewish generations had in the meantime learned Croatian. Accusations that the Jews had killed Jesus, that eternal argument of traditional Christian anti-Judaism, were at this time waning even on the level of folk narration. This objection sounded meaningless and old-fashioned in the sophisticated middle-class society of the thirties, and besides, many interwar anti-Semites were indifferent to Christianity. The new anti-Semites mostly insisted on the racial theory and in this, as in some other elements, their approach hardly differed from the anti-Semitism of the Nazis. Although the editorial of the first issue of *Mlada Hrvatska* (Young Croatia), a typical pro-Nazi magazine that came out from 1936 to 1938, claimed that "we will not confront the Jews with racial theories,"[23] this was only to pull the wool over the eyes of the police to avoid a ban. Every issue of *Mlada Hrvatska* was full of caricatures of Jews with large noses and other allegedly Jewish racial characteristics. *Mlada Hrvatska* was the first magazine in Croatia that presented, as part of a totalitarian Nazi-type ideology, an integral form of "modern" anti-Semitism based on the perception of Jewry as a racial problem.

The new wave of anti-Semitic incidents in Croatia and Yugoslavia started in about 1933, mostly under the influence of the growing Nazi propaganda. It was not by chance that one of the first such incidents connected with Croatia took place in April 1933 in Munich: the National Socialist paper in that city, *Völkischer Beobachter*, published, in Croatian and German, a call for a boycott of Jewish shops in Zagreb, in answer to the alleged Jewish boycott of German produce. The call was signed by "Croatian nationalists."[24] The text had obviously been taken from a leaflet handed out in Zagreb houses by unknown persons sometime earlier, during March, in which Croatian nationalists called "for the boycott of Jewish shops, doctors, and attorneys." The leaflet also threatened that "Our Zionists, those obedient servants of every foreign government, have been warned not to challenge us in this way again, because they will share the fate of their 'fellow-nationals' in Germany."[25] It seems that this leaflet was a relatively isolated occurrence, because the police report from November 1933 said that "we have no information that the Roman Catholic clergy are organizing any kind of activity for the boycott of the Jews," but that "clerics are probably talking against the Jews in private."[26]

In August 1933, Joel Rosenberger wrote in *Židov* that "we do not live on an isolated island . . . today various things that are happening in relation to the Jews outside the borders of Yugoslavia are being imitated here in a sufficiently noticeable degree. The newest line of resistance favors all people who have no moral backbone, no constructive stand in life, who want to and hope to rise politically or materially at someone else's expense." There is no doubt that the anti-Semitic leaflet already mentioned was one of the things that made Rosenberger react. At that time, leaflets calling for a boycott of Jews were stuck on houses several nights running in Kustošija, a northwestern Zagreb suburb. When it wrote about this, *Židov* advised "no panic, but it would be an even greater sin to ignore these cases as sporadic incidents . . . they are nothing new for Zagreb."[27] The following year, the prominent Jewish activist Tsvi Rothmüller, in an article about the position of Jews in Europe (entitled "Jewish Catastrophe"), declared that "Yugoslavia is still one of the countries least contaminated by anti-Semitism . . . here it is hardly necessary to talk about the onrush of the anti-Semitic torrent."[28]

At the beginning of 1934, news came from Daruvar that the parish priest Etinger, as commissioner of the Domagoj Society of Zagreb, was handing out a brochure titled *Why the Jews Are Persecuted in Germany,* which was full of accusations against the Jews and justified Nazi persecution.[29] In February, the Banal Administration banned the "dissemination and sale" of this booklet.[30]

In April 1936, *Židov* wrote that "leaflets were handed out in Zagreb on the eve of the Catholic and Orthodox Easter, calling for the boycott of Jewish merchants."[31] The police confiscated a large number of these leaflets in a bakery that sold matzoh for Passover! As the leaflets bore the signature of the Agricultural Cooperative (an organization of the Croatian Peasant Party), this organization published a denial in some Zagreb papers saying that it had "nothing to do with the published leaflet, which claims to mention an action that we organized, nor are activities of this kind part of our program."[32] In a by-the-way note, *Obzor* wrote about the "dark purposes of the anonymous publisher." In those days, the President of the Jewish Religious Community, Marko Horn, visited the office of the Attorney General, who convinced him that "measures have been taken to put an end to activities of this kind."[33]

A frequent technique of anti-Semitic propaganda was unscrupulous generalization, when something in which some Jews had in any way been involved was extended to cover all Jews. Thus, Jews were attacked as being Communists, but also as being capitalists, as being cosmopolitans, as being insufficiently patriotic, and so on. *Židov* wrote: "In our country, anti-Semites use two unethical methods of spreading hatred: unethical generalization and unethical specialization. When one Jew does something bad, they immediately blame the entire Jewish community. But for every news item of this kind, there are just as many news items about the same acts committed by non-Jews."[34] In 1935, the editors of *Židov* complained that the Zagreb press had attacked Jews for attending visiting performances by German theater companies, and saying that Jews should not and had no reason to watch performances in German. When Jews drew their own conclusions from this kind of writing and practically unanimously proclaimed a boycott of German performances, the same source criticized the Jews for not visiting performances of the highest artistic level for reasons known only to themselves.[35]

A frequent accusation against the Jews in Croatia was that they had flooded Masonic lodges. It is true that there were more Jewish Freemasons in Croatia than in Serbia, but many fewer than might be supposed from the size of the Jewish middle class, the usual source of Freemasons. Some estimates said there were proportionately the most Jews in the Osijek lodge "Future," of whose 79 members only 18, or 22.8 percent, could be identified as Jews from their surname. Interwar Freemason leaders denied the rumors about Jewish domination among the Freemasons.[36]

Members of the Croatian Cultural Academic Domagoj Society, "which is under the influence of and is owned by Catholic laymen," edited and published a series of books called the *Modern Social Chronicle*.[37] In 1935, it published the booklet *Jewish Freemasonry*, giving the names and occupations of lodge members in Zagreb and in five other Yugoslav towns, accusing them of "destructive activities" on the soil of the country whose democratic structure they were abusing. It also alleged that Masonic lodges were working to realize the eternal Jewish aspirations to rule the world and the nation in which they lived, and added: "the names and the occupations of lodge members show that these societies have gathered all who are the most powerful, influential, and great."[38] *Modern Social Chronicle* also published the booklet *Who Is Ruling Russia?—Jews.*

In the thirties, Nazi and Fascist supporters or sympathizers infiltrated the editorial boards of many existing papers, the crucial year for this being 1933. In that year, the editorial policy of, for example, *Hrvatska straža* (Croatia watch) changed significantly. At the same time the magazine *Hrvatska smotra* (Croatian review) was launched, which backed the introduction of the new European order by repeating Fascist and Nazi propaganda. In 1934, it published a panegyric to Benito Mussolini by Božidar Stari, who called himself a "Fascist": "We find a man who feeds his creative power with the basic forces of nature . . . just looking at any picture of Mussolini shows his outstanding vital force and energy, a concentration of will power."[39] It is true that this same *Hrvatska smotra* published an article about Zionism "which provides excellent insight into conditions in the Zionist movement," an article "to which we could easily add our signature," wrote the revisionist *Jevrejska tribuna* (Jewish tribune). However, the same issue of *Hrvatska smotra* also published a text stating that "the time of Jewish mastery in Europe has passed."[40]

In the mid-thirties, newspapers appeared in Croatia and elsewhere in Yugoslavia that concentrated on spreading anti-Semitism, and which shrank from nothing in attacking the Jews, however ludicrous the accusations might be. Modeling themselves on the German Nazis and on anti-Semites in other countries, as time passed their attacks on Jews grew increasingly violent and ruthless. These papers did not publish for very long—in most cases several issues only, and hardly ever longer than one year.

The basic idea of these articles was always more or less the same: in their ostensible support for Croatian economic and social interests, they used the methods of Nazi propaganda to blame the Jews for the bad economic conditions. "We shall not spare the intruders who are exploiting us everywhere . . . we shall demand equality in our land from the Jews, where they are guests and that is how they must behave," asserted the editorial board of *Mlada Hrvatska* in the editorial run in the first issue.[41] This fundamental thesis was followed by explanations of racial origin, Jewish character, inclination to swindling, etc.

There is no doubt that the editors of, and contributors to, these publications were ideologically close to the Ustasha movement, but some of them did not formally become members in the thirties. In most cases, these people did not rise to important positions in the ISC, but in their prewar texts and activities they certainly contributed to the development of extremist anti-Semitic views in a section of the population. First and foremost among them was Stjepan Buć (1888–1975), an MP for the Croatian Republican Peasant Party (HRSS) in the early twenties, who was expelled from the party because he did not agree with its moderate policy. After that he joined the Party of Rights, on whose ticket he was again elected MP in 1927. In the thirties, he unsuccessfully tried to renew the Party of Rights, and in 1938 he became editor-in-chief of the racist and anti-Semitic *Nezavisnost* (Independence). In June 1940, he founded the Croatian National Socialist Party. The liberal Zagreb magazine *Nova riječ* (New word) considered Buć the leader of "Zagreb racists," and it ironically called his followers "bućheads."[42] During the war, the Nazi secret service considered Buć "leader of the racist and anti-Semitic wing of Pavelić's party."[43]

As early as 1932, Stjepan Buć tried to prove that the Croats were of Germanic origin, and that the Slavs were an inferior element without any creative potential, incapable of founding a state.[44] This was only the beginning, a time in which the end goals were still to a certain extent hidden: in 1934, Buć expounded on the "racial theory of the national-social movement" in several magazines, using quotations from *Mein Kampf* as a foundation. He wrote that the "racial movement looks on practical life completely realistically, much more realistically than any of its opponents . . . only the racial man can have great social meaning."[45]

Another prominent member of anti-Semitic and pro-Nazi circles was Kerubin Šegvić. He expressed sympathies for Hitlerism and anti-Semitism in *Hrvatska smotra* as early as 1934.[46] Šegvić was the best known and most consistent advocate of the Gothic theory about the origin of the Croats, and *Nova riječ* ironically observed that Šegvić "stands above all other Zagreb racists," that he is a "racial Übermensch, a Goth by race."[47] *Nova riječ* also made fun of Šegvić by writing his name as "Cherubin Schegwitsch," and Buć's as "Herr Butsch."[48] Joe Matošić (1896–1966), the founder of *Danica,* soon began to write a large number of anti-Semitic articles in his paper. In the spring of 1933, he wrote: "Unfortunately, in Zagreb it is enough to have a hooked nose to become a manager in twenty-four hours, especially if the hooked nose is from Austria or Germany." At the same time, he published his very positive biography of Benito Mussolini.[49]

One of the first pro-Nazi publishing projects was *Naša gruda* (Our soil), a youth-movement paper addressing contemporary problems. Only two issues came out and both were banned, and soon thereafter the editor-in-chief Vladimir Singer emigrated to Vienna. There was anti-Semitism in the paper, but it was not pervasive, it was simply one of the vehicles used to promote the new pro-Fascist and pro-Nazi ideology. In the article "Italian Fascism and Hitler's National Socialism," Vladimir Mintas openly expressed sympathies for Mussolini and Hitler, writing that "Hitler's majority will abolish the Weimar Constitution, provide jobs for all the unemployed, disband the Communist Party, and finally banish all the Jews from Germany." He wrote that the "Jews are the leaders of the Marxist factor . . . in Austria it is the Jews who are at the head of the workers' movement." To oppose them, Hitler "organized his own movement in Germany that he wants to use, among other things, to disable the Jews." "Marxism is a growth and a boil . . . and among us it is the Serbs and the Jews who are spreading it."[50]

The newspapers *Istina* (Truth, with the subtitle "free and independent weekly") and *Nezavisnost* (Independence) appeared in April 1934 but only three issues came out. They never mentioned the Jews, but instead described the "arrogance of the immigrant from Vienna," and called for "unmasking the exploiter." In harsh words it attacked the engineer Semo Margel, an immigrant from Germany, who was said to have called "our language a 'Gypsy' language" during an altercation with passers-by in the center of Zagreb, and the landlord Simon Seligman, who had allegedly threatened his tenant.[51] Papers that were to come out in future months and years attacked the Jews very much more directly. It seems that tolerance for anti-Semitic outbursts slowly grew after 1933; the public simply considered this kind of behavior permissible.

Hrvatska gruda first appeared on February 1, 1936; three issues came out fortnightly. It promoted Hitler's *Mein Kampf*, and copied slogans directly from the National Socialist terminology—"the future of the Croatian People lies in preserving the blood and the soil." In international relations it completely sided with Germany and Italy, and was against Great Britain. Anti-Semitism was clearly expressed but not dominant, and it did not appear in the headlines. For example, the article "International Position" said that "today Jews, Communists, and Freemasons are fighting against Fascism," that "'freedom, equality, brotherhood' is a Jewish—Freemason lie tossed about among nations which could not understand its hypocrisy and realize that there is no equality in nature itself."[52]

Only days after the last issue of *Hrvatska gruda* came out, the publication of *Glas opozicije* (Voice of the opposition) began. Like *Istina,* it ostensibly defended the greater good of the people, and claimed that the Croats and the Serbs could not have the same goals. It expressed belligerent anti-Communism ("Communism is the hotbed of debauchery"), and in the article "Foreigners, Out," demanded that Markus and Šandor Dajč, allegedly "merchants from Budapest" and owners of leather shops, "should be enabled to move out of the country as soon as possible."[53] The following year another ten or so issues of *Glas opozicije* came out, without any strong anti-Semitic invective. Similarly to *Glas opozicije, Glas istine* (Voice of truth, free organ of public opinion), the only issue of which came out in April 1937, also promoted "indirect" anti-Semitism. Its basic goal was the "concord and unity of all Croats," and it attacked Danon, Dajč, and König.[54]

In April 1936, the first and only issue of the paper *Grudobran* (Bulwark) came out. It was dominated by overt hatred of Belgrade and the Serbs, demanding "punishment for all who are guilty," and only mentioning the Jews in passing—in a torrent of attacks on the hated Rudolf Bićanić, who had launched and was the main organizer of the Agricultural Cooperative, the paper claimed that he had "Jewish blood" and looked like a "Jew."[55]

Savremena senzacija (Modern sensation) appeared several weeks later, in May. Some issues had the heading "Special Edition against the Oppressors of the Croatian People." The paper emphasized that "only Jews who obey the laws of this people can be left alone, for all others, a fight to the death." Sometimes Jews are not specifically mentioned, but the basic message, conveyed by bombastic titles and subtitles, cannot be mistaken: "To Court with the Thieves!—Funk and Richter are plundering millions from the state."[56]

Hardly had the last issue of *Savremena senzacija* come out, when *Zagrebačka senzacija* (Zagreb sensation) appeared. In the first issue, printed in August 1936, the anti-Semitic harangues reached new levels: all the new paper wrote about were the Jews, and it spewed out torrents of hatred against them. One title read "Jews—Gangsters—Thieves," and the subtitle "We demand the gallows for all Jewish thieves—Herman Goldman, merchant in Jurišićeva Street, has swindled the state out of 731,492 dinars." Its first issue was confiscated, but the vitriolic hatred in the next issues did not abate. They deviously made no more mention of Jews, even though this was obviously whom they were writing about—"How the Newcomer Neiman Became Rich."[57] *Senzacija* was a poor and badly edited paper, full of spelling mistakes. Besides, it seems that those accused of being Jewish swindlers and criminals were not Jews at all, as there are no surnames Griesbach and Knaus on the lists of the Zagreb Jewish Community, and in any case, these are not typical Jewish names.

The profile of *Hrvatski slobodan narod* (Free Croatian people) was similar to that of *Senzacija*. The second issue demanded the arrest of Žiga Štern because the "sound of this name brings up a whole series of swindles, corruption, and other crimes. His name reeks of the cesspool of extreme wickedness." These words were not completely without foundation, because Žiga Štern (Stern), the owner of a tannery, really did pay his workers poorly, and they occasionally went on strike.[58] However, we must add that workers in firms that were not owned by Jews also went on strike for the same reasons, although *Hrvatski slobodan narod* did not mention those cases.[59]

Two especially notorious extremist papers in the thirties were the already mentioned *Mlada Hrvatska* and *Nezavisnost*, a Frankist paper that began publication in 1938. They promoted a very coherent pro-Nazi ideology adapted to Croatian conditions, with anti-Semitism as one of the key elements. The nuances in some of the articles are not important, because they sometimes simply reflected the author's personal prejudices and at other times were triggered by the occurrence of a specific event for which the Jews were blamed. According to *Nezavisnost,* the Jews were the "greatest evil in the Croatian economy." It was necessary to "secure the right to economic development, because up to now all the places have been taken by Jews." From issue to issue, *Mlada Hrvatska* printed the following slogan on its pages, as a kind of advertisement: "Conscious Croats buy only from Croats. Those who buy from foreigners are selling their homeland."[60] *Mlada Hrvatska* often ran anti-Jewish illustrations and cartoons—they were either taken over from the Nazi weekly *Der Stürmer* (which was edited by Julius Streicher, who, in 1946, was adjudged guilty of a crime against humanity) or were modeled after those in *Der Stürmer.* Both *Der Stürmer* and *Mlada Hrvatska* equated Bolshevism with Jewry.

It also promoted Fascism under the guise of "Croatian nationalism," glorified the "leader," mocked the Slavs, admired foreign imperialism, and wished the Germans would subjugate Switzerland, Denmark, and Czechoslovakia.[61] In several issues, one B. Marjanović expounded the theory of "racial purity." Letters by some readers claiming to be 100 percent-pure Aryans were published.[62] The most frequent claim in these papers was that Jews had very great world influence—"Jewry is an international organization that does not have, nor can it have, any love and feeling for the people among whom the Jews are living."[63] The article "Film Masters—Who Hold the Film Companies in their Hands?" counted the Jews in the Croatian film industry and concluded that they were to blame for everything that went wrong. Then the paper printed lists of Jewish doctors and expressed horror at the fact that some health institutions employed as many as 30 percent of them.[64]

The editors of these two papers were openly sympathetic to Nazi Germany and Fascist Italy. They called Hitler a "gigantic figure" and wished him a happy birthday with "Heil Hitler!." They justified the assassination of Minister Walter Rathenau (1867–1922), a Jew: "this is the end of all 'patriots' of that kind," concluded *Nezavisnost*. When writing about the annexation (*Anschluss*) of Austria to Germany in 1938, *Nezavisnost* maintained that "Austria had been reduced to having the Communists and the Jews as the main defenders of its so-called freedom."[65] The rabble-rousing propaganda of these papers coined all kinds of new words that had no meaning except to express hatred: "Jew-liberals," "Jew-usurers," "international Jews," "Jew-Freemasonry," "Jew-capitalists," "Jew-democrats," and also "Soviet Jew-Bolshevist government," "Jew-Marxism," "Jew-Marxists," and "Jew-Communists."[66]

The way in which some Croatian papers wrote, after 1933, about the Nazi persecution of the Jews in Germany clearly showed the different attitudes to the Jews in the late thirties and during the ISC. Zagreb's *Jutarnji list*, *Obzor*, and *Večer* (Evening) condemned the violence, because this was a logical result of their general democratic position. *Obzor* attacked the writing of *Nezavisnost* in strong terms, saying that it was "superficial, to say the least, to connect the racial origin of a people with their political interests," and wrote about the difficult position of the German Jews with a lot of sympathy.[67] Some right-wingers labeled those papers "Semitic."[68]

Although this anti-Semitic writing expressed a spirit of evil, it had no mass organized movement behind it nor was there any legal political party in Croatia with a clear anti-Semitic program. Until the establishment of the ISC, there were not even isolated acts of physical violence against Jews either in Croatia or in Yugoslavia. At that time, in the thirties, there was also another Croatia, one which clearly opposed the anti-Semitic rhetoric. In April 1938, Vladko Maček, president of Hrvatska Seljačka Stranka (HSS), by far the strongest and most influential Croatian political party, said that anti-Semitism is "an unusual and ridiculous phenomenon . . . there is no Jewish danger anywhere, this is only the hallucination of some circles. Therefore, anti-Semitism cannot exist among the Croats," and in another place, "We Croats do not hate the Jews."[69] Because of statements of this kind, *Vreme* of Belgrade accused Maček of acting in collusion with Jews and wrote that Dr Rudolf Bićanić, the main initiator and organizer of the Agricultural Cooperative, "is connected to certain Jewish circles."[70] Other extremist papers—*Nezavisnost*, *Grudobran*, *Hrvatsko pravo* (Croatian right)—also wrote that the HSS was closely connected to the Jews.[71]

However, there were also some completely different reports about the relationship between the HSS and the Jews. Outside Zagreb it was rumored that the HSS was connected to the printing and distribution of some anti-Semitic leaflets, to which Maček again reacted: "Today many people . . . are hiding under the gowns of the HSS, including some anti-Semites. The HSS is a movement that does not judge people either by faith or by origin, but by honesty and humanity. We measure Christians and Jews by the same scale."[72] The editorial board of *Židov* wrote, "We take special pleasure in learning that Dr. Vlatko Maček, who we already knew does not approve of anti-Semitic outbreaks and incidents, has put an end, we hope once and for all, to the false slogans spread by irresponsible elements."[73] There can be no doubt that Maček, contrary to his predecessor at the head of the HSS, Stjepan Radić, consistently condemned anti-Semitism and opposed its spread.[74]

There were reasons for Maček to go public: at the time when the above leaflets were printed, in the spring of 1936, a requiem mass was held in Slavonska Požega for Karlo Brkljačić, an M.P. of many years' standing and a prominent HSS member, who had been killed by an unknown person.[75] The procession that "moved from the church to the assembly hall broke the windows on the houses of some citizens who did not put out black flags. Besides windows of non-Jews, the windows on the houses of some Jewish citizens were also broken; and so were the windows on the Jewish temple."[76]

Nezavisnost broadened the list of alleged Jewish collaborators: the papers *Večer*, *Novosti* (News), and *Jutarnji list* were proclaimed "Jewish smut," under the "influence of international Jewry," *Jutarnji list* was called "Jewish," as was *Narodni Val*, said to be published with the help of Jewish capital by Vladimir Radić, son of the former HSS president Stjepan Radić (1871–1928). *Nezavisnost* wrote that the "Croatian bourgeoisie was partly Jewish in spirit" and that "it must banish Jewishness from its spirit, as well as from its worldly dealings."[77]

At the time when the anti-Semitic rhetoric in *Nezavisnost* and *Mlada Hrvatska* peaked (1938), *Smotra slavenske politike* (Slav policy review) of

Zagreb and *Podravske novine* (Podravina news) of Koprivnica (ninety kilometers northeast of Zagreb) wrote: "Spreading hatred of the Jews is growing increasingly obvious . . . this rhetoric has become truly inhuman . . . 'Croats' who have nothing at all in common with the honest national soul are screaming out against the Jews the most, and they are far worse than the worst Jew."[78] *Dom* (Homeland) of Zagreb, close to the HSS, wrote: "Attacks on the Jews, because they are Jews, is not in accordance with the principles of humanity or righteousness."[79]

In March 1939, the philosopher Albert Bazala, former rector of Zagreb University, gave a lecture about the problem of race. He clearly opposed the basic precepts of the racial theory, maintaining that it is "difficult to determine what races are and to delimit them" and also said that "a race cannot be purified by violence . . . but by self-refreshment. Not to amputate, but to strengthen from inside. Then, there will be no place for xenophobia, or hatred of foreigners."[80]

The liberal *Nova riječ* sharply criticized anti-Semitism and racism in Germany several times: "The most comical—would that it were only comical—idea used to defend this anti-Semitic plague and barbarism is that the Jews are a people of exploiters and that they are the main, or perhaps even the only, real bearers of capitalism." It pointed to *Nezavisnost* as the most notorious representative of anti-Semitism. In the editorial "The Jewish Fate," the editors of *Nova riječ* commiserated with the Jews for their suffering in the "new economic order" that was rapidly being created.[81]

The Catholic Church in Croatia maintained a very contradictory position towards the Jews, as did the Croatian public.[82] An unsigned editorial in the Đakovo weekly *Narodna obrana* was similar in content to the articles in *Luč, Nova revija,* and *Hrvatska straža.* The management and editorial board of the weekly were in the hands of the bishopric's seminary, and the editor was Professor Pero Ivanišić of the Đakovo Theological University. In an editorial, they backed Hitler as being right to target the Jews because they had greatly sinned against "German honesty," "which Hitler's followers call 'Germanic racial morality,' although it is in fact Christian morality." The Jews had started a worldwide outcry against Germany, even "our liberal press is whining about this 'persecution' in Germany, but it did not oppose the persecution of Catholics in Mexico. . . . The measures of the Hitlerites against Jews cannot be condemned . . . no people among whom they live will forgive the Jews if they go against the national interest and against what that people hold sacred. They want Jews as loyal compatriots, but not as grave-diggers and masters."[83]

On the other hand, there were also convinced anti-racists: in November of 1933, Professor Dr. Andrija Živković, at that time the best-known Catholic moralist, lectured in Zagreb about his impressions from a pilgrimage to the Holy Land, and spoke with a lot of sympathy about the local Jews and the Zionist movement in general.[84] Later, in 1938, Živković wrote an article in *Katolički list* (Catholic paper), "Racism in the Light of the Catholic World View and Life": "We do not mind a people wanting to take care of themselves in their own way . . . but we must say: there are values in life that are higher than the nation . . . racists claim that the biological difference between an Aryan and a Jew is greater than between the lowest human race and an animal, a claim that has no scientific grounds at all, a fact which we do not intend to prove at this time, and of which the intelligent reader will need no proof. The supreme ethical norm of racism, its criterion of what is good and what bad, is the interest of the race and blood—again, philosophically, completely wrong. Naturally, everything derived from this principle completely destroys morality and law. From the religious aspect, racism establishes a whole series of claims that have by no means been proved, nor can they be proved."[85]

Even before this article came out, and later too, *Katolički list* published articles that condemned racism from the biological, ideological, moral, and political perspective.[86] In March 1937, *Osservatore Romano* sharply criticized Hitler's speech in the German Parliament, especially the crucial slogan "blood and race": "it is a historical error to think that the racial theory contributes anything new or anything good. Race means separation, the racial theory leads to separation among people and prevents understanding among nations."[87] Canon Stjepan Korenić published a text in *Omanut* in which he clearly condemned Hitlerism because of its approach to race: "The mindless way in which these new Apostles have recently, in Germany, been denying the Old Testament and persecuting those who defend the Old Testament, shows that they do not hold either with God or with Christ."[88] *Narodna svijest* (National consciousness) of Dubrovnik, a weekly of the Popular Party (1925–1941) that in later years became a paper "within the framework of the Catholic press," published the article "The Error of Racism," saying that because "both Fascisms: the old form from the south and its younger partner from the north . . . have increasingly begun to go astray . . . a terrible downfall is in store for them. One of the most dangerous errors of Fascism is undoubtedly its monstrous, despicable racism: a horrible and hollow farce, [and] things have gone so far that even the Holy See had to raise its voice against them, with all the power of its infallible authority."[89]

On New Year's Eve 1938, Archbishop Alojzije Stepinac once more condemned racism in a sermon.[90] At the beginning of June 1938, the American Benedictine John LaFarge, one of the authors of the encyclical *Humani generis Unitas,* which was never published or used, visited Stepinac in Zagreb and obviously consulted with him about the contents of the encyclical, which was to have condemned racism and anti-Semitism more clearly than any other document. Later, in his memoirs, LaFarge called Stepinac a "convinced antiracist."[91]

However, in his own diary, parts of which were published as late as 1990, Stepinac wrote about the Jews in a different vein. On the dates of April 25 and 27, 1935, he wrote that "the Church can hope for nothing good either from the left or from the right," and that he "no longer believes in justice in this state ruled by the Freemasons and the Jews." As a relevant source about "Jewish rule everywhere," Stepinac mentioned the anti-Semitic pamphlet *Who Is Ruling Russia?—Jews,* advertised by the publisher as providing "irrefutable proof that Jews are really ruling Russia today, and that Bolshevism was only a device in the hands of a small group that wanted to seize power." This text even considered Stalin a "Jewish tool." The anonymous authors said that they "do not want to fan hatred against the Jews as such, but we consider it our duty to caution people that in Russia the Jews have managed to skillfully make use of Bolshevism to seize power . . . and today Russia is not ruled by the Slavs but by the Jews."[92] On November 5, 1940, the Archbishop wrote about the war that was already raging: "If Germany wins, there will be horrible oppression and destruction for small peoples. If England wins, the Freemasons and the Jews will retain power, and thus immorality and corruption will ensue in our countries. If the USSR wins, then the devil has gained power over the world as well as over hell. Where, then, can we raise our eyes but to You, O Lord?"[93]

Dr. Janko Šimrak, head of the *Hrvatska straža* consortium, stood out from the otherwise rather measured and balanced church hierarchy. The consortium included a weekly and a daily of the same name. Although he was not an editor, Šimrak had a decisive influence on the editorial policy of these papers: the public considered him the *éminence grise,* the "inspirer" of *Hrvatska straža.*[94] One of the main characteristics of the editorial policy was anti-Communism ("Communism is the greatest national evil"); they supported Italy and Germany because "they do not tolerate the Jews or the Communists or the cunning dangerous Freemasons." The article "Occupations of Jews in Vienna" quoted one Dr. Grohauser, who wrote about the above-average participation of Jews in commerce, among attorneys, bankers, the press, etc., and announced the "fall of Vienna and any other city where they hold everything in their hands, if we do not shake off this foreign slavery first." It presented the current troubles in Palestine very one-sidedly: "The Arabs are a very proud people . . . they realize what the loss of Palestine, and the increasing immigration of Jews, means for the Arab national interest. . . ." It wrote about "that Jew Trotsky" in an extremely negative context.[95]

The liberal *Zagrebačka smotra* (Zagreb review) wrote that *Hrvatska straža* had "recently become noted for its sharp racist views, although it keeps emphasizing its Catholic character."[96] *Hrvatski dnevnik* (Croatian chronicle) also attacked *Hrvatska straža* for anti-Semitism.[97] On the other hand, *Hrvatska straža* called its opponents "brothers of the Jews," and labeled the writing of the middle-class papers *Nova riječ* and *Jutarnji list* as "Jew-Marxist deception," characteristic of the "Jew-Marxist struggle," although Jews had not been mentioned in the article at all.[98]

A popular science text in *Merkurov vjesnik* (Mercury's herald) presented the ideas of Jean-Baptiste Lamarck and Charles Darwin about the origin of the world in a simple way. *Hrvatska straža* proclaimed those ideas "anti-Christian," and said that the text was written in the "Freemason-Marxist-Zionist spirit."[99]

Hrvatska straža even considered itself close (at least relatively) to the pro-Nazi *Nezavisnost.* Its editors commented on the disputes between *Nezavisnost* and some attorneys in the following words: "We think that this is not a time for everyone to pull in his own direction . . . the Croatian people require agreement and for everyone to work together . . . it took years and years for the people to achieve unity . . ."[100] It must be said that the outlook of both the weekly and the daily *Hrvatska straža* changed significantly, especially in relation to Belgrade, when the concordat between Yugoslavia and the Vatican failed in the summer of 1937.[101]

Luka Vincetić rightly noticed that "the texts in *Hrvatska straža* were 'now like this, now like that'—as required by any particular kind of pragmatism. The paper had contributions by journalists and associates with different world views, and the papers willingly expressed these differences of opinion."[102] At that time, and during the war, the Catholic Church in Croatia had a high degree of tolerance for individual deviation of its priests from general church policy, regardless of whether the deviation was for radical nationalism or for anti-Fascism.

In April 1938, as the persecution of Jews in Austria intensified, newspapers wrote about their difficult position with a lot of sympathy. *Hrvatska straža* concluded that they could not remain in their homeland, nor could they go to Palestine. The next year the paper attacked racism of any kind when it presented, with great approval, the main tenets of the book *Racism and Christianity,* written by five prominent Catholic priests at the incentive of the by-then-deceased Pope Pius XI. The book was clearly against the idea that "human races are so different that the lowest of them is further away from the highest than it is from the most highly developed animal species," that "all means must be used to preserve and cultivate the strength of the race and the purity of the blood," and that "all moral and intellectual human characteristics emerge from blood, as the bearer of racial characteristics." It also opposed totalitarian concepts whereby "man does not exist except through the state and for the state." One text even shows Hitler as above all a man who hates ("the Jews, socialists and France . . . in the final instance, intelligence").[103]

Perhaps Šimrak's attitude toward the Jews could in one word be defined as prejudice, which sometimes grew into intolerance. In 1937, Pope Pius XI wrote the encyclical *Mit brennender Sorge* (With burning concern) to the Germans, decisively condemning the Nazi racial theory, the "cult of idolatry" that substituted faith in the true God by a "national religion," and the "myth about the race of blood."[104] However, in his commentary, Šimrak distorted the meaning of the Pope's call for tolerance and interpreted it as saying that "foreigners in Croatia should honor the environment in which they are living," where the word "foreigners"—it is easy to conclude—refers to the Jews.[105] During the lifetime of Pius XI, Šimrak and those who thought like him, were still rather subdued in expressing views of this kind. In the daily *Hrvatska straža,* one M. Belčan wrote, at first with caution, that "love for our own people and homeland must not lead us astray, make us unjust to other peoples," but then he vehemently continued, "the first enemy, who has already sneaked in among us, is the depraved press . . . which hides hundreds and thousands of infidels of various kinds . . . Whoever is an enemy of the faith and of Christ is a traitor of the Croatian homeland . . . whoever spreads a teaching contrary to Christ's is not and cannot be a friend of Croatia and the Croatian people, because Croatia is a Catholic land."[106] If we add that Archbishop Stepinac said pornographic publications in Croatia were put out by the Jews,[107] it is clear who was targeted by the accusations in *Hrvatska straža,* edited and managed by Šimrak from 1929 to 1941. From a promoter of Catholic Yugoslavism in the twenties, in the thirties Šimrak evolved into a Croatian nationalist. However, it seems that he already had distanced himself in 1941 from the policy of the Ustasha regime in general, and in relation to the Jews in particular, because he spoke against the passage of the racial laws. At the beginning of 1942, Šimrak was appointed Greek Catholic Bishop of Križevci,[108] and in 1944 he donated a million kunas (i.e., Croatian currency introduced by the Ustasha government in 1941 and later replaced by the Yugoslav dinar) to the anti-Fascist movement through the organization *Narodna pomoć* (People's aid). The money was delivered by Šimrak's nephew Ivan, also a Greek Catholic priest, who joined the Partisans at that time. In the same year, Ivan was killed in an Ustasha ambush.[109]

Besides the weekly *Hrvatska straža,* the paper *Nedjelja* (Sunday, Zagreb, 1929–1945), put out by the Križari Society, and *Katolički tjednik* (Catholic weekly, Sarajevo), also inclined towards anti-Semitism, which gave rise to frequent polemics between them and other Catholic publications.

Nedjelja published a positive review of the anti-Semitic booklet *Jewish Freemasonry,* and, in the Easter issue, in a long article titled "The Problem of the Jews," it gave a detailed presentation of the editors' beliefs: "The problem" appeared in communities where there was "minimum direct contact between Jews and non-Jews." *Nedjelja* was in favor of the "Jews working, helping one another, keeping their religion and customs," envied the Jews because "all their children become gentlemen," and hated the Jews because they owned "shops, firms, banks, theaters, cinemas," etc. The anonymous author tried to justify this apparent hatred, because he wrote that "it is not the Jew's fault, the person's fault, it is the condition of the Jews," their "materialistic spirit." He accused Jews of eternally scheming against other peoples, he interpreted the First Jewish Revolt as an "attempt of the Jews to gain control over what was then the cultural world," the Bar Kokhba revolt as "a mere dream of world revolution," he attacked Spinoza for what he called creating a "teaching of pantheism," and Marx as the creator of the "Marxist movement." The article included photographs of "eight Marxist Jews" with the caption: "Look at these criminals, these beasts in human form, who pretend to be leaders of the proletariat." The text directly attacked the Jews for all the evil in Soviet Russia, saying that the "dictator Lenin was no more than a plaything in the hands of the Jewish Marxists Sverdlov, Zinoviev, and Trotsky."[110]

Katolički tjednik wrote that "the fact that the Holy See is rising against racial theories and racial hatred has created the impression that the church is, in its way, protecting the Jews. This is partly right, because the church is as a matter of principle against the ruthless and unjustified persecution of any people, including the Jews . . . If the Pope does not today speak about past Jewish guilt and Jewish sins, it by no means follows that he cannot see them . . . Long before today's anti-Semitism was born and before radical anti-Jewish political tendencies grew strong in Europe, which in places seem to have already obtained the character of pogroms, the Catholic press cautioned about the countless negative and destructive influences spread by the global Jewish plutocracy in their insatiable desire to master the world . . . Responsibility for this nevertheless belongs to Jewry as such. If the *sins of the people* exist in any case, then it is here." *Katolički tjednik* explained the current situation in relatively few words: racist anti-Semitism is a "ruthless and violent reaction to unscrupulous and unprincipled action." The text ends with the following words: "The Jews too must beat their breasts and sincerely say: we have sinned. They must fundamentally revise their ideals and seek, together with Christian peoples, a new and better solution. If they do not do this, things will only get worse for them."[111]

The Church was very critical of Fascism as well. According to Petar Grabić, the publisher and promoter of the *Protocols of the Elders of Zion,* Fascism was "based on paganism," Mussolini was "dangerously selfish," and his omnipotence in Italy was a "perilous concentration of all physical and spiritual might in one man."[112] In the text "Racist Deviations in Italy," *Hrvatska straža* quoted the *Osservatore Romano* of December 15, in which the Fascist racial laws were called "unjust as a measure," "an insult of one's neighbor," and which said, "we oppose hatred with the middle-class solidarity of Christian love and the view of humanity and life in the spirit of Christ's teaching." *Hrvatska straža* also published a sermon by Monsignor Giovanni Cazzani, Bishop of Cremona, saying that "the racial laws have reduced the Jews to a miserable position, which demands compassion."[113] Therefore, *Hrvatska straža,* and Petar Grabić in particular, did not consider it a contradiction to plead for the individual dignity of every Jew persecuted in accordance with racial laws on the one hand, and to consider that it was dangerous for Jews to have a strong influence of any kind on social events on the other. Kerubin Šegvić, who also flirted with Nazism in the thirties, stated in 1939 that the racial theory is "the most dangerous heresy recorded by the history of Christianity."[114]

The satirical paper *Koprive* (Nettles) exposed extremism and racism time and again.[115] The priest Milan Dobrovoljac (1879–1966), under the pen name of Žmigavec,[116] contributed the short poem "To an Unknown Zagreb Lady," in answer to a report that a lady had arrived in a spa with her dog and allowed it to bathe in the pool. A man protested, and, as he was a Jew, the lady answered, "If Jews can bathe with us, so can dogs" whereupon the man slapped her face. Žmigavec wrote:

And if you still think, fine dame,
That Jews and dogs are the same,
A Christian you may be,
But Christian love lack thee.
The teaching of Christ is no other
Than each is his neighbor's brother!
Every man to God is tied
Be he christened or circumcised.

In its reaction to the above report, published in *Židov*,[117] *Koprive* wrote that several years earlier it would not even have been necessary to mention the obvious fact about the equality of Jews. Žmigavec had previously published poems ("Poem—God Be With Us" and "The Palestinian Question") in which he showed Jewish history and the current situation in simple verses:

There's always been a Palestine,
It's the Jewish people's lifeline,
Land of Jewish sons,
Since the time of King Solomon.
Come, Jews, from far and wide
In the promised land abide.
But the Arab,
Looks askance,
Palestine
He won't renounce.

The old Jewish land is a place
Where strange things happen apace.
There various bad things befell
The sons of Israel . . .
If you think I insinuate
When these bare facts I state,
And if you do protest
I shall not be impressed.
My mother bade me always speak
For the side of the weak,
And every sufferer to support,
In words, at least, not to fall short,

This may not solve their plight
But comfort their spirit it might . . .[118]

Ernest Bauer (1910–1995), a writer and later a diplomat in the service of the ISC, in 1936–1937 wrote the booklet *Today's Germany,* published by *Matica hrvatska* (the central cultural institution in Croatia, founded in 1842). In it, he voiced his admiration for Hitler and praised National Socialism: "Mixing of the races is harmful to the state. The state must do all it can to preserve fresh and pure blood in marriages, and race must be at the center of all of life." He also gave a positive opinion of "racial and political measures" that "are designed to reduce to a minimum Jewish influence in public life."[119] Filip Lukas, at that time president of *Matica hrvatska,* obviously did not mind being the head of an institution publishing a pamphlet of that kind. In an exceptionally critical review of the book, *Hrvatski dnevnik* wrote that the "reader gets the impression that he is reading an official report of the German government."[120] *Nova riječ* considered that "*Matica hrvatska* made two massive mistakes in publishing Bauer's book: first, it broke with its cultural tradition of serving the search for truth and voluntarily gave itself to the needs of a particular political agenda, and second, by serving this agenda, it has debased itself by becoming a vulgar public-relations agency."[121] *Obzor* calmly concluded that "this booklet is unnecessary . . . and it is especially unnecessary for *Matica hrvatska,* which has its own viewpoint."[122] Bauer was a typical example of Jewish "self-hate": his mother, Gertruda, née Lazansky, was Jewish.[123]

In its reports about frequent anti-Semitic incidents, *Hrvatski dnevnik* of Zagreb wrote that the Jews "always knew of two things only: of hard and useful work of all kinds, both for their own and for the general good, and of real and true love for our common homeland . . . In today's social order they must be accorded full protection for their threatened personal and national feelings."[124]

Smotra slavenske politike of Zagreb opposed anti-Semitic propaganda: "Anti-Semitism means persecuting people—Jews. Attacks of this kind have run through human history as a shameful thread for centuries . . . The National Socialists planned to use anti-Semitism to ensconce themselves in our country and master it . . . Our Jews have usually repaid our people, and that is how we see them, at our side, whenever necessary."[125]

In the spring of 1938, the bust of the outstanding actor Josip Papić (1878–1928) was unveiled in the Croatian National Theater in Zagreb. Dubravko Dujšin, another great actor and leading man of the same theater, at that time director of drama, spoke about him with a lot of sympathy.[126] Jewish institutions organized guest performances in Zagreb (and Belgrade) of the Hebrew Habima Theater from Tel Aviv in 1938. They met with "outstanding success," and were a "great success, both with the public and with the critics." In Zagreb, the company was hosted by the Jewish Community.[127] Critics wrote that the "performance deserves to be seen by people who have not lost faith in the theater, in good theater,"[128] and that "art is a cult for Habima members,"[129] that "the Habima's acting turns a play into unparalleled art,"[130] that "theater has been elevated to the mystique of a cult,"[131] and that historical reconstruction was rendered with incredible "psychological power."[132]

Sometimes anti-Semites and the supporters of tolerance came into direct or indirect conflict. It is difficult to establish the number and strength of either side, but some examples may indicate general trends. At Zagreb University, the Frankists clashed with the leftists and with HSS members. The Frankists started to physically attack the leftists at the beginning of the thirties, and the violence peaked in 1937, when the first murder took place.[133] Tension between them and the HSS was especially strong at the Faculty of Medicine, where the students' club leaders in 1936 were HSS supporters. In the following months, some committee members sided with the Frankist faction, and in the 1938 club elections they put forward a ticket which they wanted to show as comprising HSS supporters. Their plans were thwarted when the HSS leaders published a statement in *Hrvatski dnevnik* to the effect that only people who voted for the leadership-approved ticket could be considered HSS supporters.[134] Then the Frankists began to threaten the Jews, Slovenes, Serbs, and others. A Frankist proposed that, at the annual membership meeting, they should discuss a motion to introduce a numerus clausus for Jews, even forbidding them from enrolling for the next two years because there were too many of them at the faculty already, but of course the HSS members opposed this. Then the so-called proclamation of the National Defense Committee of Croatian University Students was published. Its basic motto was, "Only Croat students have the right to decide who will lead their clubs. This is their moral right because the Croatian University was formed and is being supported by the Croatian people." Serbian, Jewish, and Slovenian medical students were warned not to attend the meeting. "Those who appear will come to a bad end, because the Croats will stop at nothing to preserve their rights."[135]

It was decided not to discuss the introduction of a numerus clausus provision at the meeting, but only to vote on the matter, to which the HSS supporters agreed. A total of 369 students had a vote, and they split into three groups. Those who were the most resolutely opposed refused even to vote, because they considered a numerus clausus to be "against the rules and against the beliefs of freedom and democracy." A second group (including HSS supporters) decided to vote "against," and the Frankists supported the introduction of a numerus clausus. The president of the election committee recorded the group which had refused to vote as having "abstained" from voting on this issue, so the final result was that 162 students supported the Frankist proposal, 107 were against, and 100 refused to vote. Considering that the general atmosphere was by no means pleasant and that the voting was public, the 60 percent refusal of the Frankist proposal was fairly high. The group that refused to vote included, besides Jews, most of the members of the newly elected club leadership, who had been elected by 207 votes to 162. The winning ticket, therefore, voted against, either by an open "no," or by clearly refusing to vote on the numerus clausus provision at all.[136]

Although not many written traces exist about the numerus clausus issue, it seems that it was imposed by extremist circles under the influence of growing anti-Semitism throughout Europe. Edo Lovrić, the rector of Zagreb University, attended the dance of the Jewish Academic Society and, in his welcoming speech, "praised the young people for their patriotic stand and guaranteed there could never be a Jewish question at the university under his leadership . . ."[137]

Other facts also give evidence of the relatively weak support enjoyed by the proponents of anti-Semitism: the anti-Semitic press was by no means as influential or important as the newspapers and magazines that defended the Jews. The most influential Croatian papers—*Jutarnji list,* very often *Novosti* and *Hrvatski dnevnik*—opposed the extremist press in no uncertain terms. The editors of *Mlada Hrvatska,* on the other hand, complained that people were avoiding them—although coffeehouses subscribed to their paper, they did not offer it to guests to read at all.[138]

Anti-Semitic incidents did not take place only in Zagreb and in Croatia, but in other parts of Yugoslavia as well. All of them reflected what was happening in other central-European countries and in Europe in general. Mounting anti-Semitism and increasing public pressure for rapprochement with Germany was felt in 1938 in Austria, Hungary, Rumania, and in a specific way in Poland, too. The desire and proposals to push the Jews out of economic life, the moves to introduce a numerus clausus, and even pressure to make them emigrate increasingly became part of those countries' policies.[139]

Male novine (Little newspaper) of Belgrade, from the first issue published in June 1933, continuously printed anti-Semitic articles. In September of that year, the Royal State Attorney in Belgrade banned the book *Why Germany Is Defending Herself from the Jews,* published by *Male novine.* The book was said to contain data from an unknown book by a certain university professor Kato. Although *Male novine* wrote "we are very far from defending Hitler's ideology in general, because we often do not agree with it . . . but we are especially interested in the attitude of Hitler's Germany toward the Jews," they also said that "the position taken by Germany toward the Jews is understandable."[140]

One of the characteristics of the clerical paper *Slovenec* (The Slovenian), published in Ljubljana, was anti-Semitism. In the article "The Jewish Question," it repeated allegations that the Jews dominated the financial market, Masonic lodges, published "shameful books," and participated in "revolutionary campaigning." Because of this, the paper asked: "Is it not every Catholic's duty to become an anti-Semite? Or can another solution be found for the Jewish question?" Although the anonymous author wanted to be "fair," and said "we must not attribute what many Jews are doing to all Jews," he concluded by offering a solution in the spirit of the clerical movement: "According to St. Paul (Romans, 11, 25), the Jews will become Catholics; this is how God Himself will solve the Semitic question."[141] Several days later, *Pohod* (Campaign), a paper put out by Yugoslav nationalists in Slovenia, published the article "Yugoslavia—Judea," saying that the "Jewish question is especially important for understanding the reasons for the great economic depression." It was "to a great degree caused by amoral methods . . . The Jewish race was especially prominent in this amoral boom . . . Before the establishment of Yugoslavia, we Slovenes were the purest part of the Yugoslav nation. Jewry did not fall on fertile ground among us . . . The Slovenian part of our nation must on no account allow Jewish penetration."[142]

The first anti-Semitic words in the Senate in Belgrade were spoken in 1933, when Senator Ivan Hribar, during a discussion about the budget, began by saying that he "has nothing against the Jews" in general, "doubtless there are good and honest people among them." However, it is crucial that "one fault is more developed among them than among other people—a desire to make as big and as easy a profit as possible." Thus, they "like best" to occupy themselves with commerce, which does not require "physical effort," and their "inborn clearheaded cunning" ensures them the advantage of great profits. Isak Alkalaj, Chief Rabbi of Yugoslavia, also a senator, reacted to Hribar's words in the Senate, but there was no public response.[143] Several months later, the Split attorney Ivan Majstrović, in the Senate, questioned "the immigration of Jews from Germany, as the native Jewish element in Yugoslavia is part of the Latin branch of Jewry, the Sephardim, against which we do not mean to raise any objections; the same cannot be said of the Germanic Jews, the Ashkenazim, who gradually came among us uninvited and unwanted as time passed and who have not only refused to assimilate into the native Slav population, they have always remained foreign to it in language, mentality and aspirations . . . They were the supporters of anti-national regimes, and, with rare exceptions, never showed any gratitude to the people among and with whom they live."[144] Majstrović emphasized that he spoke "only in my own name and I am not an anti-Semite, but . . ." It is quite probable that Majstrović was the author of the anti-Semitic brochure *Israel from the Fall of Jerusalem to the Conquest of the World,* which was published in Split in 1936 (but was signed only "I. M.").[145] Milutin Stanojević said in the Senate that he was an "enthusiastic supporter of Hitler's policy, although the only thing that does not fill me with enthusiasm is the fact that we [i.e., Yugoslavia] must feed refugees" from the Third Reich.[146]

In October 1933, the Union of Jewish Communities of Yugoslavia (SJVOJ) sent a memorandum to all its members warning them to be on their guard and to notify the Union if they noticed any occurrences of anti-Semitism.[147] Even without this warning from Belgrade, *Židov* noted that "anti-Semitic papers and publications have recently begun to sprout, one after another here too . . . Journalists and writers have begun to spread hatred against us—mostly on the German model . . . There is an appetite to ape Hitlerism."[148] *Malchut Jisrael* wrote similarly: "Anti-Semitism has no roots in Yugoslavia. The tolerance of the Yugoslav nation, known worldwide, and especially its Serbian part, never permitted any major excesses against other peoples or religions . . . Why have polemics recently appeared against the Jews from a certain source? . . . All this indicates an organized anti-Jewish campaign." Two years later, the same paper wrote that "during the last year [i.e., 1935], an anti-Semitic war cry, imported from abroad, has gained force in a certain but . . . an unimportant part of the Yugoslav press."[149]

Jugoslovenska reč (Yugoslav word), a paper that came out in Zagreb from 1932 to 1934, was in fact the paper of Jugoslovenska akcija (Yugoslav Action), a movement promoting unitary Yugoslavism, anticlericalism, and a kind of racial theory: "We Yugoslavs are one community by blood." When discussing "social and economic problems," it wrote that "capital is concentrated in the hands of egoistic non-Yugoslavs by race . . . who cannot have constructive feelings for our nation and state, but only attempt to place themselves above the state and above the entire nation." Attacks on the Jews were not direct, they were cloaked in the mist of the "problem of foreigners in our economy" ("the great majority of foreigners are completely unnecessary to us") and the like. The paper emphasized that "our people certainly have none of those barbaric anti-Semitic instincts, like the Germans. But the Jews' unseemly behavior might provoke the same reaction as any foreign element must, when it lives only as a parasite on the national body."[150]

Regardless of the claims made by local racists that they did not look to German racial theory for inspiration, everything indicates that this was, in fact, the case. In Croatia and Yugoslavia, racial theories could rest either on Croatian exclusiveness in relation to other South Slavs (K. Šegvić and S. Buć), or, as in the writing of *Jugoslovenska reč*, on the creation of a kind of Yugoslav-Slavic race. A certain Milan Rakočević was even more explicit than *Jugoslovenska reč*, when in *Sadašnjost* (Our times) of Ljubljana he wrote that the "pan-Slav idea can be implemented . . . through a union of blood, through a union of a shared view of the world and of human society . . . [for] the Slavs represent a real race."[151]

The Split paper *Pokret jugoslovenskih nacionalista* (Yugoslav nationalists' movement) was ideologically almost identical to *Jugoslovenska reč*.[152] In 1933, *Svoj svome* (Brother to brother), a paper promoting the political and economic independence of the Slavs, began publication in Zagreb with the slogan "Faith in God and Harmony among the Slavs." The main focus of this paper's articles was to denounce and vilify foreigners. The following year the paper moved to Sarajevo, and at the end of 1935 to Belgrade.[153]

Although the writings of *Jugoslovenska reč*, *Svoj svome*, or *Pokret* about the Jews cannot be compared with the fury the attacks found in *Nezavisnost* or *Mlada Hrvatska*, which appeared in the following years, these publications showed that all exclusive policies end in xenophobia, or anti-Semitism. The following incident, isolated at that point in time, confirms this: in 1933, a group of people affiliated with Mlada Jugoslavija (Young Yugoslavia) was walking through the streets of Zagreb carrying the Yugoslav flag and "among their cheers for Yugoslavia and the Royal House, several times used anti-Jewish slogans, rousing and inciting the mass to unsavory outbursts." At the assembly that was later held, they "appealed to Hitler and Goebbels." *Mlada Jugoslavija*, their group's periodical, called on "patriots" to fight against the Jews.[154]

A new stage in the transformation of the Yugoslav nationalistic movement into an anti-Semitic and pro-Nazi movement started in 1934, when the paper *Buđenje* (Awakening) began publication in Veliki Bečkerek (after 1935 called Petrovgrad, and, after 1946, Zrenjanin) in Vojvodina. After its eighth issue, it became the paper of the Yugoslav National Movement Zbor, a pro-Nazi organization led by the attorney Dimitrije Ljotić, who was already calling himself a supporter of Hitler (and even corresponded with him). In time, the paper's anti-Semitic campaign grew increasingly aggressive and articles with titles such as "Jewish Brashness," "The Kike Problem," and "The Kikes and the Revolutionary Movements in Russia" appeared; and, at a later date, "The Decisive Struggle against Jews and All International Gangs." After July, when the first issue of *Erwache* (Awake) came out, the two papers supported one another.[155]

By the beginning of 1936, the number and force of anti-Semitic outbursts had increased to such a degree that the central problem at the Sixth Congress of the SJVOJ in Belgrade, at the end of March, was anti-Semitism—in Germany, Poland and Russia, and also in Yugoslavia. In 1930, the prominent Jewish activist David Albala had written an article "Why the Jews Love Yugoslavia," in which he repeated "we love it" ten times, and gave answers such as: "We love it because its joy is our joy, its pain is our pain, its enemies are our enemies, its desires are our desires." The following year, in 1931, he again praised the position of "Jews in Yugoslavia." However, by 1936, everything had changed—at that point he said that he was "not used to anti-Semitism in Serbia . . . It is difficult to be a Jew in Yugoslavia. I wish many non-Jews could be Jews for only twenty-four hours and feel all the tragedy of our position, feel what it is like when people turn their heads and eyes from a Jew, when conversation dies down as soon as a person discovers that he is talking to a Jew."[156]

The only resolution coming out of the Sixth Congress of the SJVOJ in connection with anti-Semitism was: "The Congress is aware of the significance of the frequent anti-Jewish attacks that are taking place in our country without impediment, although they insult the fundamental principle of the equality of religious communities. The Congress emphasizes that anti-Semitism, as an expression of the darkest backwardness, cannot sway the feelings of civil uprightness and patriotic duty among the Jews of this country . . . The Congress considers that events of this kind, unknown among us until recently . . . have led to justified and immense dissatisfaction in our Jewish community, and it demands and expects all factions to respect full and real equality."[157] At that time, Braco Poljokan, the editor of *Jevrejski glas* (Jewish voice), wrote: "In fact, we do not know where we stand; are we Jews really equal citizens of this country or are we not?"[158]

Several days after the Congress, David Albala met with Prime Minister Stojadinović and informed him "about the organized anti-Jewish activities in our country, about the distress and dissatisfaction in Jewish circles . . . The Prime Minister expressed his clear disapproval . . . and resolutely stated that he would issue the necessary orders to prevent the anti-Jewish campaign in our country."[159] The paper *Židov* was not as direct, reporting only that a "representative of the Union" visited "some relevant state officials" who "formally promised that the anti-Jewish activities in our country would be stopped and prevented."[160] This news item was presented vaguely, without giving the names of the participants at the meeting, without their having assumed any specific obligations, and the results of the meeting were equally vague. That same year, the SJVOJ also failed to secure a ban on the distribution of the newly published *Protocols of the Elders of Zion.*

Several weeks later, *Židov* reported that "Prince Regent Pavle recently gave an audience to Dr. David Albala and expressed his sympathies for the Jewish people, showing full understanding for all their suffering and for their desires."[161] Less because of his inclination for the Nazis and their sympathizers, but more to keep Yugoslavia from getting involved in the war, which was rapidly approaching, Prince Pavle indulged the right-wingers and the Nazis.[162] Thus, this visit by Albala could not produce any results. Nevertheless, up until the eve of the war, Jewish activists considered the Prince a sincere supporter of democratic principles and the last barrier before the oncoming wave of anti-Semitism. Several months later, in the fall of 1936, although the Main Committee of the SJVOJ stated that the "anti-Semitic press is growing stronger," it had no new ideas about how to react except to "intercede whenever necessary with competent officials, to put a stop to anti-Semitic propaganda."[163]

In 1936, *Nova revija* of Makarska, the magazine that had published the *Protocols* between 1925 and 1928, advertised on its cover that the *Protocols* could be obtained from its management. The SJVOJ demanded the Ministry of Justice act according to the law.[164] However, the Ministry replied that "there are no grounds to take action . . . [as] it is not a criminal offence to publish an advertisement, nor has the book itself been banned . . . [and] as a translation from the French, it has not been banned from entering, nor from being distributed in, the country."[165] Only a month or two later, the hypocrisy of the authorities emerged again, when the Minister of Justice, Niko Subotić, tried to convince the Chief Rabbi of Yugoslavia, Isak Alkalaj, of his determination to "firmly order all organizations to stop all anti-Semitic incidents."[166]

At the end of 1937, two of the most highly placed officials in the SJVOJ—President Fridrih Pops and Secretary General Šime Spitzer—visited the Minister of Justice, Žika Simonović, and complained about the writing of various papers, especially *Balkan, Mlada Hrvatska, Erwache,* and *Sturm,* and about the "unhindered publication of a new edition of *The Protocols of the Elders of Zion.* The only report from the meeting was that "the Minister showed great interest in the arguments of the Union's representatives and promised to do all he could to comply with the Union's desires and requests."[167]

This was a time when prominent community members were calling for loyalty to the state, hoping that this was the best defense from growing anti-Semitism. In the fall of 1935, Chief Rabbi Gavro Schwarz ended his sermon in the Zagreb synagogue by advising his listeners to "fervently comply with their obligations to the state and to Jewry, and we will again be surrounded by respect as we always have been in many progressive states and in our glorious and beautiful Yugoslavia."[168]

Nazi propaganda spread throughout Croatia and Yugoslavia in various ways, beginning in 1933, soon after Hitler came to power. Groups of German students visited Germans outside the Reich, ostensibly to research the history, language, and culture of the German ethnic minority. Some members of one such group wore the swastika on their lapels in Zagreb in 1933, and in the village of Gorjani (where there was a German minority population) near Đakovo (in Slavonia), they handed out a leaflet with one of Hitler's speeches.[169]

The systematic cultural and social emancipation of the German minority in Yugoslavia began with the Kulturbund, the Swabian-German Cultural Alliance (Schwäbisch-Deutscher Kulturbund), founded in 1920 in Novi Sad. This was in fact a kind of belated national revival. In Zagreb, the German Support Society (Hilfsverein) was founded in 1929, to "support members of Germany, regardless of whether they belong to our society or not. Any discussion about nationality and religion is banned from the society, because its purpose is purely humanitarian." Several dozen German societies were founded in the thirties, mostly in Slavonia. At first they were by and large politically neutral, but between 1936 and 1939 people who called themselves Renewers took over the Kulturbund, and then other societies as well. These were young intellectuals who had come into contact with the ideas and activities of Hitler's National Socialist Party during their studies in Germany.[170] *Židov* began to warn against the consistent and well-organized National Socialist propaganda that was being spread through these legal German-minority "cultural" societies in Yugoslavia, generously financed from within the Third Reich, as early as 1933. At the end of 1935, the police discovered that youths were taking vows on the Hakenkreutz flag (i.e., a flag bearing the swastika) in Kulturbund branch offices, and swearing an oath never to marry Serbian, Hungarian, or Jewish women.[171]

From the beginning of 1936, the reports sent to Washington from the American Embassy in Belgrade described the Nazi propaganda, and the abundantly financed publications and other pro-Nazi activities in the country.[172] The National-Socialist *Der Weltkampf* (a monthly devoted to world politics, national culture, and the Jewish question) indirectly confirmed this in the article "The Struggle Against the Jews in Yugoslavia," in which it quoted *Buđenje* and *Erwache* and greatly praised the work of the Zbor Movement.[173]

In Zagreb, at celebrations for German minority day, the "speakers took the opportunity to rouse people against the Jews in the spirit of the Nuremberg laws" passed in 1935.[174] In 1937, the Schwäbischer Kulturbund in Zagreb was "managed in the National Socialist spirit and run by prominent supporters of Fascism."[175] In 1938, the police confiscated a circular letter printed in Zagreb by the Zagreb Hilfsverein, which discussed the "Jewish question" and in doing so exalted Hitler, and ended with the words "Heil Hitler." The police found that the "society has overstepped its field of work" and thus recommended that it be disbanded.[176]

The Anschluss of Austria to the Reich in March 1938 spurred the pro-Nazi activities of German societies. In 1939, the Kulturbund stepped up its aggressive promotion of Nazi ideology. The police, and especially the secret services, managed to keep up with these pro-Nazi activities, at least partly, but the justice department obviously reacted only occasionally. In an investigation in 1949, Branimir Altgayer, the prewar Kulturbund leader for Croatia and Slavonia, and leader of the German ethnic minority in the ISC, defensively stated that the Kulturbund "took care not to meddle in local and Yugoslav party matters, and in minor issues," but that it had in the "last years" before the war "worked on aiming and directing its members toward the National Socialist ideology and the main National Socialist precepts." In 1938, Altgayer was a guest at the National Socialist Party (NSDAP) Congress in Nuremberg.[177]

Nevertheless, some people claimed that "not the entire German element in Vojvodina looked on recent events (i.e., the Anschluss and the spreading of Nazism) with single-minded sympathy," and gave "several examples indicating friendly relations between the German population and the Jews."[178] These were not the only such examples: *Die Donau,* the paper of the German Catholic minority in Yugoslavia, wrote, "We resolutely refuse any worship of racism, although we otherwise honor the nationality we belong to and which we nurture."[179]

The paper *Erwache* came out in Petrovgrad, starting in 1936, as a "rebellious National-Socialist paper" and the voice of the Yugoslav National Movement Zbor. "The Jews are our misfortune!" and "You have been murderers from the very beginning" were only two of the many slogans it printed. The first was literally copied from *Der Stürmer: "Die Juden sind unser Unglück."* The article "Decisive Struggle Against the Jews and Other International Gangs," taken over from *Buđenje*,[180] said that the most important task of the Ljotić movement was the "implacable and uncompromising struggle against the Jews, and all international organizations founded and promoted by our own and international Jews." As these were by far the most aggressive anti-Semitic outbursts in Yugoslavia, at the end of 1936 the SJVOJ sued the *Erwache* editorial board. There is nothing to say why the SJVOJ did not react when the same text was published in *Buđenje* in the Serbian language somewhat earlier, but the reason was probably conformism: it seemed easier to the union to sue a paper published in German than one in Serbian, which was allegedly promoting Yugoslav patriotism. However, even the charges against the German paper failed; proceedings were "stayed with the explanation that the union did not have standing to file such charges, because the paper it sued had not attacked the Jewish faith in any way."[181] The court found that the law protects only Yugoslav "tribes," and the Jews were by constitution a religious, not an ethnic, minority. However, not wanting to simply free Milorad Mojić, the paper's editor, who was also associated with Dimitrije Ljotić, of any responsibility at all, the court sentenced him to a fine of 600 dinars and a suspended sentence of two years.[182]

In following years, Mojić and Ljotić remained true to themselves: when *Buđenje* stopped coming out, *Novi put* (The new way) was launched in Petrovgrad in 1937, and, in it, anti-Semitic attacks often grew into open threats: "Jews, do not let the people be your judges!" The Petrovgrad district attorney's office started an investigation into what were alleged to be anti-Jewish texts in *Novi put* and banned issues 5, 7 and 8.[183] *Novi put* claimed that it had a "Zagreb office," but reports from Zagreb were written in a strange mixture of Serbian and Croatian. The anti-Jewish accusations in these texts almost seem to have been copied from other Zagreb publications of a similar bent.

The last issue of *Novi put* came out in December 1938, and the first one of *Naš put* (Our way) appeared as early as March 1939. The unsigned article "A Warning to the Jews" said that "if the Jews, as a racial minority, will not adapt to the clearly defined racial majority, then they must at least stop aggravating the racial majority unless they want to provoke an inevitable reaction." At the end of the text, the editors added: "We are printing this article although we do not completely agree with it. Draconian measures, not warnings, are necessary against the Jews."[184] In the immediate prewar years, Ljotić and his collaborators published *The Protocols of the Elders of Zion* and other anti-Semitic texts.[185]

Middle-class politicians cautioned about the danger from extremists. In 1936, at the Belgrade Assembly of the Yugoslav National Community, Minister Đuka Janković demanded that Jews be "treated today as the dignity of every citizen demands and not be insulted." *Malchut Jisrael* wrote, full of hope, that this is "finally the first warning to the anti-Semitic press in Yugoslavia."[186] That same year, the League against Anti-Semitism was founded in Belgrade, under the slogan "A Brother Is Cherished, Whatever Faith He Practices." It upheld "democracy, and was opposed to reactionary political movements that promoted rule by force instead of people's right to freedom." Not much is known about this event, except that the attorney Miloš Lj. Stanković gave a speech and was "rewarded with an enthusiastic ovation."[187]

In March 1937, the M. P. Života Milanović (from the National Peasants' Club) demanded the suppression of the growing Hitlerite propaganda in Yugoslavia, because "our Fascists are threatening everybody in their papers . . . The Minister of the Interior should pay as much attention to this faction as he does to the Communist danger." Ascertaining that "Fascism is today centered in Vojvodina and in Zagreb" and that "today this group has several papers that are printed and distributed for free," Milanović asked himself: "Who is paying for all this? Who is paying for the various agitators, agents, district secretaries, entire trains, etc.?"[188] The secretary of Zbor answered Milanović: "Because the Jews are imbued with a ruthless capitalist sprit and are the promoters of Communist rage among the people, we therefore are against them."[189]

Balkan of Belgrade promoted an integral Yugoslavism and rigid anti-Communism, supported the creation of a Greater Serbia, and made anti-Semitism one of the fundamentals of its editorial policy. Some papers considered it the "center of anti-Semitic propaganda in regions south of the Sava river."[190]

In the editorial "My Opinion of the Jews," Krsta Cicvarić, the director of *Balkan,* wrote that "it would be best to send the Jews off to Mars or to Jupiter." Accepting that this was "physically impossible," and as he was against "pogroms and banishment," he proposed "placing the Jews under extraordinary laws, which would prevent the harm they are doing."[191] The prominent Croatian writer Miroslav Krleža often ridiculed Cicvarić and his papers, and once called him a counterpart of Kerubin Šegvić and Filip Lukas in Croatia.[192] For a long time after *Balkan* stopped coming out, "Cicvarićean" remained a synonym for the "lowest form of journalism."[193]

The Zagreb Jewish Community thought of suing *Balkan,*[194] but it seems that neither the Community nor the SJVOJ did so, probably fearing that this would only enrage the anti-Semites further. Still, there may have been some intercession, because *Balkan* was banned by a decision of the Minister of the Interior in 1939.[195] The next year it was succeeded by *Novi Balkan* (New Balkans) in which the priest Vaso Vujović defined the position of the Jews in contemporary Europe: "When the Jewish wedge in the body of the Slavic Mother Russia reached the heart of the great victim and caused her agony and her death in martyrdom, some European lands, frightened by the catastrophe of the old Slavic oak felled by the Semitic worm, became most seriously concerned for their own destiny. Woken by Fascism from their democratic slumber, they began to pluck, and are still plucking, Jewish thorns from their flesh . . . Due to Judaism in Europe, today her culture is Christian in name only, without anything of the Spirit of Jesus, without anything purely humane—today everything is in the spirit of dry law and bestial egotism. After killing Christ physically, the Jews have systematically been killing the spirit of His exalted and most selfless doctrine. In the Roman Catholic, so-called Western, culture, they have succeeded in this 100 percent."[196]

At that time, the Serbian Orthodox Church was one of the hotbeds of anti-Semitism.[197] At the beginning of 1937, the Serbian Patriarch Varnava, quoted in the German paper *Völkischer Beobachter,* said that he was "following the Führer's struggle against the world Bolshevist danger with sympathy . . . The struggle of Adolf Hitler against Bolshevism, which has yoked the Russian people, is motivated by idealism and has nothing to do with imperialist goals." *Glasnik* (Herald), the official paper of the Serbian Orthodox Patriarchy, also carried part of Varnava's speech at a congress of Russian bishops: "Earlier it was very difficult for me to speak in defense of Russia against Communism and the international Jews . . . I had to rely only on myself. But God has sent the German people a far-seeing Führer who represents the same opinion as the one I myself formed."[198]

As early as 1935, Bishop Nikolaj Velimirović of Žiča "paid his respects to the German leader . . . We are the children of God, people of the Aryan race charged by fate to be the main protagonists of Christianity in the world."[199] Later, he spoke of Hitler as protection from "Judeo-Bolshevism" and the corrupt West. Velimirović considered that not only Serbia was in danger from the Jews, but all of Europe, because the Jews "and their father the devil have managed, by slow and long-lasting poisoning of the spirit and the heart of European humanity, to turn it away from real respect for God and make it bow before the idol of culture . . . All the modern European slogans have been devised by the Jews, who crucified Christ: democracy and strikes, socialism and atheism, tolerance for all religions, pacifism and overall revolution, capitalism and communism."[200]

The right-wing Belgrade daily *Vreme* (Time) was under the influence of the pro-Axis politician Dr. Milan Stojadinović. In September 1940, in the weeks when the government was preparing anti-Semitic regulations, the paper began to publish many anti-Semitic texts. An article by the former Senator Dragoslav P. Đorđević kept alive the banal story about Jewish guilt for the outbreak, and then for fanning the war that was currently raging. It also published his rabble-rousing text, "An Ill-Fated Union: Freemasonry and Jewry, Their Goals, Development and Methods." Later, Đorđević wrote again, saying that "it is not strange people know nothing about the destructive force of Judeo-Masonry—nothing could be written about it for twenty years."[201]

Unlike *Vreme,* the main Belgrade daily *Politika* (Politics) remained attached to liberal-democratic principles and up until the war attacked Nazism.[202] Thus, the difference in the attitudes to Nazism and anti-Semitism, at that time characteristic of the Zagreb press, was similarly a mark of the Belgrade press, and generally of the press in all of Yugoslavia at that time.

"Anti-Semitism is the political persuasion of the mob. It is a disgusting contagious disease, like cholera—it cannot be explained or cured," *Malchut*

Jisrael happily quoted the book *Auch ein Wort über unser Judentum* by the famous German historian Theodor Mommsen (1817–1903).[203] Karl Kraus (1874–1936) of Vienna, a Jewish publicist, poet, and satirist, defined the phenomenon even more precisely and sarcastically: "Anti-Semitism is a serious disease of the majority people or religion, which is fatal for Jews."[204]

4

THE JEWS IN THE LIFE OF ZAGREB AND YUGOSLAVIA BEFORE 1941

From Dire Premonitions to Their Realization

Fascism was first mentioned in the Jewish press in 1926, when the editors of *Židov* observed that "hardly anything has yet been written on this subject." The paper's correspondent in Rijeka (at that time an Italian city on the Yugoslav border) did not consider that Mussolini's imperialism would affect the Jews in any special way. His conclusion was that the Fascists were representatives of the bourgeoisie, and since most Italian Jews belonged to this social class, he assumed that the Jews would "support Fascism openly."[1]

The Yugoslav Jewish press did not begin to write about Nazism until 1931, when *Židov* copied an article from the National Socialist paper *Völkischer Beobachter* about the future "National Socialist Legal Order," which forecast the future position of the Jews more or less in the way that was later inaugurated by the Nuremberg Laws of 1935. Obviously, the editors of *Židov* did not think that these ideas would be realized, but they nevertheless "presented these medieval thoughts of Hitler's supporters, so that our readers will always know how to be on the lookout for them."[2]

The first indications of future events, at that time still completely ephemeral, surfaced in Croatia several months later, in the summer of 1931. At that time, the Osijek ironmonger Ljudevit Scinicz printed a pamphlet that "ridicules and shames Jews and Jewry in the most inappropriate way," and called the Jews "*Saujuden*"—"Jewish swine." Scinicz was President of the Evangelical Church Community, and his son, a student in Graz, allegedly belonged to the local "*hakenkreutzler*" group. When the Osijek Jewish Community sued him, Scinicz offered a large financial compensation, but the Community refused the offer.[3]

At the end of March 1932, when the anti-Semitic wave in Germany had already begun to roll relentlessly forward, papers wrote in greater detail about the persecution and chaos in Rumania than about what was going on in Germany. At the end of April, during regional elections in Prussia, *Židov* wrote that "the world is waiting for the results with apprehension and curiosity," but "right now we are more interested in another Berlin . . . which has, in connection with the Jews, developed and is still feeding aggressive civil and religious assimilation." Therefore, at that time *Židov* still considered both assimilationists of a civil orientation and Marxists more dangerous.[4]

When Hitler became Chancellor at the beginning of 1933, *Židov* printed a short commentary describing the condition of the German Jews as "tragic"; it then quoted an article by the *Jüdische Rundschau* from Basel: "German Jews . . . must keep their calm and pride. Obviously, German Jews will marshal all their forces and energy to resist any attempt to divest them of their rights and destroy them financially." Trying to show that the assimilationism of the German Jews had contributed to their present plight, *Jüdische Rundschau* concluded that "Jewry can wage this struggle only if it is conscious and proud of its nationality. The times of assimilation and self-suppression have passed." *Židov* added: "If there are many such German Jews, as the Zionist movement expects, it will be easier for them to overcome the danger that is now threatening to ruin them." The writing of *Židov* shows that the Zagreb Community was keeping very careful watch over what was happening in Nazi Germany. As early as March 1933, S. Löwy wrote that the German Jews were facing a "'cold pogrom'—the social and economic decline of German Jewry," but no one suspected what was really going to happen. The paper wrote about the opinion in some German Jewish circles that the "German Jews must 'keep their dignity' and patiently wait for the victory of justice and righteousness, because soon the present transitory excitement will abate." The following week, after major pogroms ("like a wild torrent, the National Socialist regime is piece by piece destroying the heritage of. . . . emancipation"), it wrote in great distress that the "Jews in Germany are no longer equal citizens." Then followed new articles, which now had titles such as "The Middle Ages," and described the position of German Jews as hopeless, because they were "weak and persecuted." In April 1934, *Jevrejski list* entitled an article about events in Germany "Racist Madness in the Third Reich." One year after the event, people in the Zagreb Community began to talk about the "catastrophe of German Jewry in the year 1933."[5]

Soon after Hitler assumed power, and hearing the first reports about the persecution of Jews, Jews in Croatia started to think about boycotting Germany and German goods. A letter by Teodor Gros from Daruvar (in western Slavonia) shows that individuals were already doing so on their own initiative. On the institutional level, the first public mention of a boycott in Zagreb and in Yugoslavia was by members of the Makabi Jewish sports club at a protest rally on March 21, when they decided to "join a common front in solidarity with other Jews against the rabid Hitlerites . . . and as of today we will unanimously boycott German films, to show the oppressors the madness of their actions in the way they will feel most keenly." However, the owners of the Zagreb cinemas said they could not "boycott German films, because we have already signed contracts to show them and the contracts cannot be broken," and that they "have already paid for the films in advance." The owners considered that a Jewish boycott "would harm domestic film institutions and cinemas most of all." The central issue at the "Shekel" rally in April 1933 was a protest against the persecution of Jews in Germany. Aleksandar Licht demanded "the right to be bitter, just like the Poles and other Slavs . . . our protest is opposition against the incursion of shameful barbarianism." He concluded that "it remains for us to be pioneers and build ourselves a dry path through the waves to reach the shore of our deliverance." His final words "were lost in frenetic approval." Zagreb's non-Jews responded to the boycott poorly and indirectly.[6]

In 1933, Jews began to think about changing their German surnames, "because it is not fitting for Jews to bear names acquired from a nation that is now trampling the basic principles of Jewish human dignity in an unprecedented manner."[7] However, most people who Croatized their surnames in these and later years probably did so more to achieve complete assimilation within Croatian society than to protest against the Nazis.

In 1933, a flag with the swastika appeared on the German consulate on Starčevićev Square.[8] In February 1934, *Radničke novine,* under the control of the right wing of the workers' movement, wrote that "more and more people in Zagreb are enthusiastic about Hitler and the National Socialist regime . . . Exceptions of this kind are found among bankers, landlords, merchants, the poor, private employees, and even workers. In their enthusiasm, some of them used the swastika to decorate . . . all the public toilets in Zagreb. Some are already wearing a small swastika on their lapel . . ."[9] It was clear that nothing would ever be the same for the Jews of Zagreb and Croatia.

It seems that people were generally of the opinion that nothing could be done to improve the situation of the Jews in Germany, but that efforts should be made to transfer as many of them as possible to Palestine. Therefore, a "great protest rally" was held in Zagreb in May 1934 against the British policy in Palestine, specifically the small immigration quotas. Political rallies were also held in later years, but only one was aimed against the Nazi anti-Jewish pogroms.[10]

All this pressure on the Jews made some of them take radical action. In February 1934, the Association of Yugoslav Jews was founded in Subotica (Vojvodina), and issued a proclamation calling themselves "happy citizens of our dear homeland," and inviting "our brothers to foster honest, sincere and creative cooperation with our other Yugoslav brothers." They called for Jews to "work on the Yugoslav national ideology and culture . . . [and] to organize courses for learning the Yugoslav language."[11] The immediate reason for this initiative was probably the large number of Subotica Jews whose mother tongue, or the language they usually spoke, was Hungarian, and also the founders' ambition to show that they were "nation-builders." A similar initiative was launched several months later: in July 1934, a Belgrade Jew named Avram Lević, a former official in the Ministry of Finance and a banker in Milan, announced in the Belgrade paper *Štampa,* in his own name and in the name of a small group, the establishment of a Movement "for the Nationalization of Jews," allegedly in agreement with the *Narodna odbrana* ("National Defense"—a "national institution" in charge of promoting Yugoslavism as a unitary concept). These Sephardim-integrationists ("followers of Moses' religion, ancient inhabitants of Belgrade") rejected Zionism as an ideology and practice, and complained that most Yugoslav Jews opposed assimilation: "A large number of Jews, especially in the northern and western regions [i.e., they primarily meant the Ashkenazim] . . . do not even find it necessary to learn the language of the state, or to feel themselves members of the community to the degree that should be expected . . . They will either become loyal sons of this country, or will have only themselves to blame for all the adversities that may in the future befall them . . . Our Jews must, above all, be good Yugoslavs."[12] The opinion among Jews was that Lević had monopolized patriotism and by so doing had "exposed a vast majority of Yugoslav Jewry to slander," the supporters of Zionism first and foremost. Dr Jakov Čelebonović was another prominent integrationist in Belgrade, who became president of the Belgrade Jewish Community in 1932 after tight elections. One of his most important slogans was that "a Jew is a good Jew only if he is a good Yugoslav." He defined Jews as "Yugoslavs of Moses's religion." Like Lević, Čelebonović also considered that "Palestine may awaken sympathy, but Yugoslavia must be loved . . . A son has only one mother . . . [and] love cannot be divided, if it is sincere." Another important member of this group was Lazar Avramović of Belgrade, for a time SJVOJ treasurer, who was released from duty, in the words of his sympathizers, "because he is frugal and is not a Zionist," and "because he was, and still is, a real man of Šumadija." In a letter signed by A. Baruh, "Zionism" was identified with "nationalism," which he hated.[13] All the Jewish papers sharply attacked Lević's initiative and its proponents.[14]

All this happened in the months before the assassination of King Aleksandar in Marseille. Even after Aleksandar's death, representatives of the Jewish community regularly met with the highest state officials, but there was less and less cordiality and more and more wariness and fear at these meetings, at least on the Jewish side.[15] Even so, the Jewish community and its representatives carefully went through the motions expected of them. *Židov* very thoughtfully, in editorials, marked the twelfth birthday of King Petar II, the forty-third birthday of Prince Regent Pavle, also the birthday of "Her Majesty the Queen Mother Marija." At the Seventh Congress of the SJVOJ in April 1939, the President of the Union, Fridrih Pops, "first of all greeted Lieutenant Colonel Miodrag Tomić, representative of His Majesty the King," which was followed by "ovations to His Majesty the King."[16]

The hundreds of news items about persecution in Germany were followed in September 1935 by news about the introduction of the Nuremberg racial laws. In an editorial, *Židov* rightly concluded that their enactment "only served to provide with legal force a situation that has existed there since Hitler came to power." The only thing the paper could do was express its contempt for and bitterness toward the Nazis ("the new laws, more than anything else, prove the moral depravation and weakness of the National Socialist regime"), and continue to keep intact its pride in Jewishness and Zionism ("we can and will oppose anti-Semitism only through the national awakening of the Jewish people, the renewal of Jewry in the renewed Eretz Yisrael"). The presidency of the Zagreb Jewish Religious Community joined the protest of Jewish organizations in the rest of the country and abroad addressed to the League of Nations. In Zagreb, the Makabi Hall in

Palmotićeva hosted a "spontaneous" rally against the "anti-Semitic laws" in Germany. The revisionist Zionists warned people about Nazi danger much more clearly and directly—as early as September 1935, Ze'ev Jabotinsky said, and *Malchut Jisrael* reported, that "the Third Reich has started a war for the complete eradication and destruction of the Jews."[17]

In 1937, Aleksandar Licht provided another possible answer to the tide of Hitlerism in the booklet *On Hatred and On Redemption.* He wrote about the "superior being" who was in fact an "inhuman being," proving that the followers of Nazism fanned hatred. Licht did not forget the difficult position of Jews in Soviet Russia either, because the Soviet system "is just as far from a freedom-loving society." He concluded by saying: "Zionist strength is unbreakable: it is not for us to hesitate on our path: we will not stop—until we reach eternity."[18]

New ideas about a boycott spread through the world before the Berlin Olympic Games in 1936. In Jewish circles, there was an especially strong campaign against any Jew going to Berlin, so the announcement that Ivo Steinhart would go to Berlin as head of the swimming team, and Fischer, a member of the Zagreb Makabi, as a wrestler, upset people.[19]

In the summer of 1936, "because of the frequent anti-Semitic writing of a Zagreb paper (i.e., *Senzacija*) and also because of the appearance of various other anti-Semitic publications," the presidency of the Zagreb Jewish Community submitted several oral and written applications to the Attorney General's Office and the Police Administration, demanding in strong terms an end to this kind of writing. After this intercession, *Senzacija* was confiscated, and its further publication banned, although it continued to be circulated through secret channels. The Community representatives went to see Viktor Ružić, Ban (i.e., Governor) of the Sava Banovina, and wrote to the SJVOJ in Belgrade: "All these steps, and the promises we received, have to date been unsuccessful." The government's good will to put an end to outbursts of this kind often faced unexpected difficulties. The anti-Semitic papers frequently changed names and addresses, editorials were signed by editors with invented or borrowed names. For example, after it was banned, *Senzacija* changed its name to *Savremena senzacija,* and several times one Gjuro Horvat, a worker who had been fired from a Zagreb bandage factory, was credited as editor. In the Zagreb papers, Horvat strenuously denied any connection with *Senzacija* and its editor Milenko Matejić.[20]

Toward the end of the thirties, the police became increasingly suspicious of any and all Jewish activity. The first indications of these changes came in 1936, when a report to "state security" called the Zionists "extreme Jewish elements" who are "also members of the Jewish lodge B'nai B'rith." It gave the names of the heads of Zionist organizations in Zagreb and in other towns, and said that "the work of the B'nai B'rith lodge is being kept under discrete surveillance." The report concluded by proposing "a ban on all further work of the B'nai B'rith lodge in Zagreb" because it is "working illegally." The police report extensively quoted the anti-Semitic pamphlet *Jewish Freemasonry,* which had been published in Zagreb a year earlier. Although the report claimed that some of the conclusions in the book were "biased," it took over most of the facts as they stood, accusing the Jews of "snobbery" and of belonging to the "capitalistic class," and at the same time saying that "they are in sympathy with all left-wing activities, and this kind of upbringing in Jewish families resulted in twenty out of twenty-six commissars in the first period of Soviet Russia being Jews, and these were the ones who proved themselves the most bloodthirsty." B'nai B'rith and various other Zionist organizations contributed to confusion in the rigid minds of the police officers, and made some ridiculous claims that could have been taken over from Ze'ev Jabotinsky and his supporters—that the "Zionist organization is mostly composed of left-wing elements," and that the Zionists' work helps "subversive elements."[21] Apparently, however, at that time, or even later, the police took no repressive action.

At the beginning of 1938, the secret police heard that some Jews had met in Zagreb to discuss "what the Jews in Yugoslavia should do if the authorities take similar measures against them as those that are being introduced in some other countries. Allegedly, some people suggested that the owners of capital should take their capital out of the country while there was still time." An informer was sent to the next meeting, but as he did not hear any of the speakers—David Albala, Aleksandar Licht, and others—say anything aimed against state interests, he could not claim that "anyone had spoken about taking capital out of the country." The informer even attended meetings of the Židovsko narodno društvo (Jewish National Society), which inclined to Zionism but was completely benign from the perspective of state security.[22]

In March 1938, the Anschluss of Austria only served to exacerbate the charged atmosphere. Affected by the prevalent mood in Europe, and by the above event, in 1937, and especially in 1938, Milan Stojadinović's Yugoslav government abandoned its previous pro-French and pro-British foreign policy and gradually turned to Germany and Italy.[23]

In April 1938, only a month after the Anschluss, "tendentious news that some anti-Jewish laws are being prepared" began to spread among the public. The *Izvršni odbor* (Executive Committee) of the SJVOJ stated that it came from "well-known sources," obviously alluding to right-wing and pro-Nazi circles. The rumors were so intense that the Avala national news agency issued an official statement: "In connection with reports from various quarters that a special law is being prepared against the Jews in our country, relevant sources have informed us that all these reports are untrue, because there are no special reasons for a law of this kind."[24] This statement did not quell the unrest and prominent Jewish activists used every opportunity to ask high officials about their intentions. In May, Dr. David Albala visited the Minister of the Interior, Anton Korošec. After they "touched on all current questions, especially those affecting the Jewish community in Yugoslavia," Albala "brought back the best impressions from this visit." At the beginning of September, the Chief Rabbi of Yugoslavia, Isak Alkalaj, informed the IO–SJVOJ (Executive Committee of the SJVOJ) that "during a conversation at an official event, the ministers present most decisively rejected any idea of a special law against Yugoslavia's Jews."[25]

However, it was no longer a secret that Stojadinović's government was antagonistic to the Jews: in the summer of 1938, the German authorities decided to fire all Jews employed as representatives of German firms in Yugoslavia, and the Minister of the Interior said with pleasure that they had promised to replace them with "our capable people." However, instead of doing so, the Germans sent "their representatives" as replacements.[26]

In September 1938, Anton Korošec said that "in Yugoslavia . . . there is no Jewish question. In our country, Jews enjoy the complete protection of the law."[27] At the same time, Korošec was a patron of the paper *Slovenec,* which often published anti-Semitic texts. British diplomats reported from Belgrade that Korošec was "exceedingly anti-Semitic, and under his influence the Yugoslav government is increasingly showing anti-Jewish feelings." The British were especially concerned when the government on several occasions refused to extend the visas for Jews who were representatives of British firms.[28] The pro-government paper *Napred* began publication in Belgrade at that time, and wrote that "no anti-Semitic course could have any grounds in Yugoslavia, nor would the Constitution permit it." At the end of October, Dr. Bukić Pijade, member of the Executive Committee of SJVOJ, visited Prime Minister Stojadinović in his office and reported: "During a long conversation, Stojadinović said that the rumors being spread about preparations of a law about Jews in Yugoslavia have no grounds whatsoever . . . He is a personal friend of the Jews, he respects their work . . . [and] the government is not even thinking of interfering in, or in any way restricting, the civil equality of Jews in Yugoslavia." At that time, Minister Dr. Branko Kaluđerčić also vehemently denied rumors about preparations for "Jewish laws."[29]

In this atmosphere, during 1938, many Jews in Zagreb began to renounce Judaism, which had not happened in earlier decades. From 1914 to 1920, 122 people left the Jewish religion in Zagreb, an average of 20 a year.[30] The numbers did not change in the twenties either: 18 Jews converted to other religions in 1926 and in 1928.[31] When all the figures are added up, they show that 525 people left Judaism between 1911 and 1937 in Zagreb, and 132 people joined it, giving a proportion of 3.96:1.[32] According to some slightly different statistics, 396 Jews converted to Christianity between 1912 and 1932, and 129 people took the Jewish religion, making the proportion 3.07:1.[33] This shows a kind of conformism, indicating that people were convinced that it was socially more "desirable" to be a Christian than a Jew. Had it not been so, I suppose that the proportion of converts to Christianity and Judaism would have been about 1:1.

An average of twenty people left Judaism every year, although the numbers differed from one year to the next. At the end of the twenties and beginning of the thirties, there were fewer than average conversions, but after 1933 their number grew to about thirty to thirty-five a year. This confirms that the Jews were feeling more direct and indirect pressure from the strengthening of Nazism in Europe and of its supporters in Croatia, resulting in the increase in the number of conversions.

In 1938, the usual rhythm and number of conversions from Judaism was disrupted. In that year, by far the largest number of Zagreb, Croatian, and Yugoslav Jews renounced their religion. In all of Yugoslavia, 821 people converted, 580 Yugoslav citizens, and 241 foreigners.

Most of the conversions, 624, or 76 percent, took place in the Sava Banovina, where 429 Yugoslav citizens and 195 foreigners left the Jewish religion that year (the foreigners were refugees from Austria and Germany, most of whom had come to Zagreb and its surroundings, and they converted in Zagreb). A great majority of the 429 converts were from Zagreb, and the Chief Rabbinate in Zagreb gathered all the data and published them. This mass conversion took place within a very short time, in barely three months in the middle of the year.[34] There are also data about which religions the Jewish converts joined: 224 of them were registered in Catholic parishes. The Old Catholic Parish recorded ninety-six conversions, more than ever before or after.[35]

When this mass conversion began, *Židov* published a list of 229 Jews from Zagreb and 82 from other places who had renounced Judaism in 1938, by the time the paper came out.[36] They included many distinguished Jews and active Community members who inclined towards assimilation, such as Milan Marić, industrialist and Turkish Consul in Zagreb, a non-Zionist member of the Jewish Agency, and, through his wife, connected to the distinguished Alexander family.[37] Why did so many Jews convert in a period of several weeks, while before and after things were more or less as usual? Why did Zagreb Jews leave the Jewish religion proportionately more than Jews in other places in Croatia and Yugoslavia? There are no answers to these questions, and we can only guess:[38] in the deluge of dramatic news that had been engulfing Zagreb Jews from the early thirties onward, it seems that 1938 was the most difficult year. Disturbing reports kept following one another: in February, strong German pressure on Austria began, a plebiscite was held, the Anschluss took place in March, quickly followed by a wave of anti-Semitic violence in Austria. It must have been especially depressing that none of the European powers, or the League of Nations, even tried to counter this course of events. After the Anschluss, German might reached the borders of Yugoslavia, and Jewish refugees started to arrive from Austria, many of them passing through Zagreb, giving Zagreb Jews a preview of what might lie in store for them. At the same time, anti-Semitic pressure in Germany grew stronger than ever: many anti-Semitic laws were passed, on November 9 and 10, the "Night of Broken Glass" took place—the peak of the anti-Semitic campaign in Germany, when 177 synagogues were burned down, 7,500 shops destroyed, at least 91 Jews killed, and 30,000 Jews taken to concentration camps, where several hundred were killed. Enormous monetary damages were imposed on the Jews. In March, the Sudetenland crisis began: the Sudetenland Germans were allegedly demanding autonomy within Czechoslovakia, and, in September, the British and French governments agreed to hand Sudetenland over to the Germans. From the perspective of Zagreb, it was easy to gain the impression that Hitler's arrival was imminent. The terrible pressure, when people thought that they must do something to ameliorate their position, must have been very difficult to bear. There is no doubt that the mass conversions of Zagreb Jews in the summer and early fall of 1938 resulted primarily from the grave and alarming foreign-policy situation, the relentless advance of Nazism. Dr. Alfred Singer said that the "presence of refugees in Zagreb is causing panic among the Jews."[39] The ambassador and industrialist Aleksandar Sohr, one of the main defendants in the well-known "Našička" affair in the first half of the thirties (this was one of the greatest corruption scandals in the Kingdom of Yugoslavia), did what others were not capable of doing: in those months, he sold off all his considerable property, including a villa in Zagreb in Jurjevska Street, and moved with his family to Geneva.

However, the mass conversion to Christianity cannot be directly connected with any particular event, because most of Zagreb's Jews who abandoned the Jewish religion in 1938 did so before the Night of Broken Glass. Nothing much can be made from the brief conclusion of *Jevrejska tribuna:* "The reasons for this mass flight can be almost exclusively attributed to the tragic position of Jewry in Europe," or the conciliatory statement of the President of the Community, Marko Horn: "Although I do understand those who have changed to another religion because of the heavy burden of the present moment, and in fear of the most terrible atrocities, it still pains me . . ."[40] A year later, *Jevrejski glas* wrote that "this disproportionately high number of converts can be explained by the panic that developed in some regions in connection with rumors about the passage of anti-Jewish laws."[41]

It is true that various rumors began to spread through Zagreb and Yugoslavia in April 1938 to the effect that the government was preparing anti-Jewish measures ("news from different quarters that a special law against the Jews is being prepared in our country"), and the converts hoped that, as members of another religion, these laws would not affect them. This is suggested in the report of the IO–SJVOJ: "Learning from what is happening in the neighborhood, and afraid of the specter of poverty" they witnessed among the incoming refugees, "many of our Jews became concerned for their future and believed the rumors of various kinds, which had no foundation at all."[42]

At that time, *Novosti* of Zagreb, which usually supported the regime's policy, wrote that "Jews in Yugoslavia are living in fear of possible measures," but "no law about the Jews is being drawn up in our country." Then it cautioned that "our Jews should not, by any actual or potential behavior, hinder our new foreign policy, which is so successful and well conceived." The paper meant the policy of approaching or at least coordinating interests with Nazi Germany. *Novosti* considered that "this foreign policy of peace and friendship, and especially of good relations with those who are an important factor in our foreign trade, is having a positive effect on our overall home situation, and especially on the economic development of the country . . . The Jews know this. It is only necessary for their behavior to reflect this knowledge."[43]

In February 1939, the President of the Community, Marko Horn, said that "people have stopped leaving our community."[44] This was only partly true; 85 people left Judaism in 1939, and at least 100 in the following year.[45]

All Jewish organizations unanimously and without reservation condemned the renunciation of Judaism. The Jewish press published a list of Zagreb Jews who had renounced their religion, giving their full names, addresses, and occupations, so that no one could make a mistake and so that everyone knew who was to be ostracized. Everybody thought that the situation was alarming, and even the Federal Committee of the SCJ and the GO–SJVOJ (Board of Governors of the SJVOJ) discussed the problem. The Main Office members from Zagreb were the severest in condemning conversion: Lavoslav Šik demanded the introduction of "propaganda against conversion," and Joel Rosenberger was in favor of "isolating the converts." Even Oto Heinrich, who had been an assimilationist in the twenties, "advocated a firm stand against converts, because they are greatly to blame for many of the misfortunes of Jewry," and Makso Mautner, a prominent member of the Board of Governors and an industrialist, also an assimilationist, spoke about the "destructive work of the converts." Mautner said that "not enough influence is exerted on people to dissuade them from their intention of changing to another religion. Previously, the Community administration used to be more energetic and coped better under similar circumstances." Dragutin Rosenberg considered that "there is in principle no excuse" for converts.[46] *Jevrejski glas* wrote about the difficult times, and that "many of us cannot endure this martyrdom and desert in one way or another. We can understand this, but we do not justify it. There are people who do not have enough will and strength for great suffering, but such people must be condemned."[47]

The behavior of the President of the Community, Marko Horn, was more conciliatory, and he spoke about "the difficult times we are living in, which demand great sacrifices that some people willingly support, while others solve their problems by rejecting their Jewishness."[48] Alfred Singer was even milder: in his opinion that they had "left our community unnecessarily. I beg you to believe that we care for all these things with undiminished love, but reality and the difficulties we encounter must be considered . . . We have already gone through all this in history . . . We are a liberal community."[49] With one year of distance, the head of the Management Board, Lavoslav Steiner, said only that "last year a horrible specter swept over our heads."[50]

Joel Rosenberger probably best defined the attitude to converts at the

Seventh Congress of the SJVOJ: "If we criticize those who have fled from us like rats from a sinking ship, or scattered like chips when wood is being cut or whittled, then this not only expresses the alarm of a living organism against defectors and renegades, but also expresses our moral uprightness . . . No Jew has risen against the baptism of those who are leaving us because they are changing their religion and going to join others. This may be a matter of personal belief, but we are against lessening these people's responsibility for the animosity that their behavior is causing in the non-Jewish community, and we use this occasion to thrust them aside." At the same meeting, Lav Štern added: "We cannot allow and suffer the development of an unhealthy situation and permit people to gain the impression that life in our country is easier if a person has been baptized."[51]

"A ruthless struggle must be waged against these deserters and cowards," wrote the revisionist *Jevrejska tribuna,* quoting the views of like-thinkers from Czechoslovakia, but added: "These occurrences also mean a crystallization of the nation. What is rotten falls away; what is healthy remains."[52] The SJVOJ also reacted, stating that it would "take the renegades' behavior into account with contempt," and warning churchmen that "according to canon law, Jews may only be converted after several months of preparation, and even then only if the person has publicly renounced his/her wrong beliefs." In April 1939, the Zagreb Hevra Kaddisha requested the opinion of the SJVOJ Congress about how to bury converts,[53] and in the following year the Zagreb Community asked the Executive Committee of the SJVOJ for "instructions about what approach to take to refugees who have forsaken the Jewish religion."[54]

The Jewish press attacked converts violently and quite often, writing that conversion "leaves a bad impression on everyone. Many non-Jews talk about the flight from the Jewish community with contempt . . . We have received many letters from our subscribers." One of those letters said: "You should have stigmatized the shameful defectors and their motives long ago. I congratulate the Zagreb Jewish Community, to which someone offered to pay his religious tax for the next ten years [probably to assuage his bad conscience], but it refused [this probably alluded to the Turkish Consul Milan Marić, who had converted a month previously] . . . These people should be isolated publicly and privately. The Community will easily make up for the lack of funds, because in this situation we will all be glad to pay a higher tax."[55] The title in *Jevrejska tribuna* was very characteristic: "Deserters Are Worse Than Enemies."[56] In its "holiday letter" to Zagreb Jews on the eve of the high holidays in the fall of 1937, the Zagreb Chief Rabbinate wrote that "all those who flee from Judaism today, and seek shelter in other religions, are cowards. All who think that this opportunistic step will save their children and grandchildren, are short-sighted."[57] Jews had no understanding at all for their former co-religionists, although all those who converted must have had to make agonizing choices between the need to preserve their identity on the one hand, and the desire to obtain a secure place in society on the other. The editors of *Židov* wrote that the Serbian Orthodox Church hesitated to accept the new converts, and the Catholic Church also expressed doubts about their sincerity, so the converts were not made to feel welcome there, either.[58] That new converts wished to give voluntary contributions to the Jewish Community indirectly is proof of the difficult position they found themselves in and their wish to remain in contact with the Jewish community.

Sometimes conversion to Christianity (Catholicism) was accompanied by a change of surname, although this was not required. Even some Jews who remained loyal to Judaism changed their surnames to lessen the pressure of the Christian environment. For example, in October 1940, Slavko Rosenberg changed his surname to Radej, Skender Aleksandar Kleinkind to Klanjčec, Ivo Hermann to Hrlić, and Hermann Blühweiss to Bošnjak.[59] The Zagreb paper *Danica* published a list of about thirty surnames, "the Croatian national names to which Jews are changing their former foreign names," for example Izrael to Ilić, Herrenstein to Hoić, Reich to Raić, Stein to Kamenski, etc.[60]

Most who converted or changed their surname, or did both at once, probably believed that by doing so they would completely erase their Jewish past as far as the outside world was concerned but many of them were wrong. Radej, Klanjčec, Bošnjak, and Hrlić even converted in 1941, but they had to take back their old names after the establishment of the ISC. The first three were killed in the Holocaust, while Ivo Hermann-Hrlić was arrested, then released, and finally fled the country.[61]

In November 1938, the Community decided not to continue accepting the voluntary contributions of converted Jews, and to return money that it had received to the donors. These were not easy decisions to make, because as 169 taxpayers had converted, the Zagreb Community lost almost 10 percent of its income in 1938.[62] "It seemed that the mass renouncements might shake the foundations of our Community, so we had to increase our efforts a hundredfold and work very hard to retain our financial balance."[63] In addition, many members emigrated at that time ("especially to overseas countries"), and several members who paid high Community dues died, which decreased the Community's income by almost another 100,000 dinars, or almost 4 percent. In addition, the "grass roots have grown poorer."[64]

Nevertheless, the Community was too proud to accept one single dinar donated by converts. The Zagreb Community had generally not been very poor because, between 1930 and 1938, the number of religious-dues payers grew from 2,740 to 3,480. However, by the end of 1939 their number fell to 3,161. Some people were optimistic because 161 new taxpayers registered in the 1940 fiscal year, but this optimism was largely groundless because most of the new members were rather poor; and all together contributed less than 13 percent of what had been lost during the previous two years.[65] To make matters worse, at the same time, 186 people left the Community for various reasons.[66]

Stojadinović's government tried to develop and retain good relations with its dangerous neighbors—Fascist Italy and Nazi Germany. In January 1938, Stojadinović met with Hitler to convince him that "Yugoslavia will never, under any circumstances, enter into any kind of a pact or coalition against Germany," which Hitler countered by saying that "Germany wants nothing from the Balkans but an open door for its economy." Cooperation with Germany was strategically acceptable for Yugoslav policy-makers. As Foreign Minister and later Prime Minister Bogoljub Jevtić told British Ambassador Neville Henderson in 1934, "If we are made to choose, then there is no doubt at all whom we prefer, Italy or Germany. Germany recognizes Yugoslavia and will be willing to cooperate with us." In this unprincipled trading, the Jews could easily be used as small change.[67] On the other hand, Stojadinović told representatives of the ethnic Germans in Yugoslavia, "We do not want to interfere in relations within other countries, however, we reject the model in our country which is flirting with the introduction of a cult of the leader" (i.e., like the example of Nazi Germany).[68]

In January 1939, Stojadinović gave an interview to the Paris paper *Le Petit Parisien* denying that "anti-Jewish measures are being prepared in Yugoslavia," but then he to a certain degree refuted his words by saying, "as long as the Jews continue to provide proof of their loyalty . . . this will not be an issue. Therefore, the future, in fact, depends upon the Jews."[69]

Immediately after his appointment in February 1939, Prime Minister Dragiša Cvetković received the obviously worried three-member delegation of the SJVOJ (Fridrih Pops, David Albala, and Šime Spitzer). Cvetković "showed full understanding for the problems" and "in his democratic and humane way . . . convinced the representatives of the SJVOJ that the Jewish community in our Kingdom has no reason to be uneasy" or "concerned." Barely a month later, the Chief Rabbi of Yugoslavia, Isak Alkalaj, visited the Prime Minister, with whom he too had a "long, cordial conversation."[70] Rabbi Maurice L. Perlzweig, member of the board of the World Jewish Congress and one of the leading men in the Jewish Agency, arrived in Zagreb and Belgrade in April 1939 to "raise the spirits of the Jewish communities in Romania and Yugoslavia," and he also was received by Prime Minister Cvetković.[71] However, judging from the fact that *Židov* did not mention his visit at all, it seems that he had no success in "raising spirits."

All the Yugoslav Jews could do was wait and hope. In August 1939, an agreement was made between Dragiša Cvetković and Vladko Maček, which seemed to be a solution for the long-lasting crisis in the country. One of the things they agreed on was to found the Croatian Banovina (on the territory of Croatia and parts of Bosnia and Herzegovina), a move designed to satisfy the Croats. *Židov* published a headline at the top of the first page, "The Agreement Has Satisfied All the Requirements for the Complete Consolidation of Our State." In the first sentence it made clear, which was extremely unusual for that paper, that "we are assessing this event as loyal citizens of our country." Until then, the editors of *Židov* had unswervingly and vehemently opposed Jews publicly expressing loyalty of any kind to their narrower or wider homeland, considering that this was something that could never be doubted and that Jewish loyalty to the state was a given.[72]

The Cvetković-Maček government tried to sail a middle course between the already-warring sides, but in fact it increasingly gave way to German pressure. People realized that certain restrictive measures, on the German model, would have to be brought against the Jews. The more the highest state officials tried to convince Jewish representatives that there would be no anti-Jewish laws, the more suspicious, it seems, did the Jews become. Rumors about the drawing up of "anti-Jewish" laws grew more frequent: about twenty days before the formation of the Cvetković-Maček government, *Jevrejski glas* wrote that "Several foreign papers have published reports they received from Berlin, about the passing of an anti-Jewish law in Yugoslavia. In connection with this, we must say that all such news came from German sources; the competent authorities always denied it."[73] In January 1940, when Prince Pavle and his wife, Olga, visited Zagreb, *Židov* wrote that Pavle "has always, even in these difficult and ill-fated days . . . shown a sincere interest and warm sympathy for the Jews." Pavle had a "long talk" with the President of the Community, Marko Horn, and Chief Rabbi Schwarz, who said that there is "true equality among citizens" in the country. The Prince expressed his "warm interest in Jewish refugees and in those Jews who are suffering so severely in today's clashes."[74] Pavle retained a similar diplomatic tone several months later, when he was talking to the Chief Rabbi of Yugoslavia, Isak Alkalaj.[75]

At preparatory meetings for and at the Seventh Congress of the SJVOJ, held on April 23–24, 1939, in Belgrade, all these difficult issues and problems were hardly mentioned at all. The report of the Main Committee said that "the friendly relations that have always existed between the Jewish and non-Jewish population are becoming closer and more cordial from year to year . . . Sometimes the escalation of the organized anti-Jewish wave, which started to spread throughout the world, could be felt in our country. However, the traditionally progressive political views of the Yugoslav people prevented it from marring the peaceful life of Yugoslav Jews, and particularly of restricting their civil rights in any way." The "aim" of the Congress was to "tell all and everyone: the Jews in the Kingdom of Yugoslavia, notwithstanding their close links with this country and their loyalty to this state, are an integral part of the entire Jewish people, who are building a homeland for all the Jews in Eretz Yisrael."[76] Reality soon belied this excessively optimistic tone.

Several resolutions were adopted at the Congress: about solidarity with suffering Jews, about support for Jewish reconstruction in Eretz Yisrael, about support for young people, about the need to step up publishing activities, about standardizing the pronunciation of the Hebrew language, and about providing help to small communities. But nothing was said about right-wing extremism, anti-Semitism, or similar dangers that were facing Yugoslav Jews. Chief Rabbi Schwarz of Zagreb, speaking in the name of all the Yugoslav rabbis, placed a special accent on unity in the belief that "today the only constructive work for the future of Jews is the reconstruction of Eretz Yisrael," and those present "greeted his words with stormy applause." Very few delegates spoke about Nazism and its effects. One of them was Dr. Moša Švajger, who said that "a cry is wrung from our very being, a cry of desperation and a cry of accusation of all mankind, a cry of anguish: save us!," but he immediately added: "In our souls there is another cry, a cry of admiration for those who are in that small distant land . . . standing in the front line to build a Homeland for the suffering Jewish people." Lav Štern of Zagreb also spoke of the danger of Nazism, and his words reflected the thoughts of most of those present much better than Švajger's: "When we are asked, how long will it last?, what will happen afterwards?, we who know history must know the answer: never yet in history has anything like this lasted forever . . . In answer to the question, how long will it last?, my friend Gottlieb [the well-known writer and translator Hinko Gottlieb] gave the example of a soap bubble that floats high up and reaches it maximum volume, but at that moment explodes, deflates and falls . . . There is a dynamic internal force in the soap that stretches the membrane, the volume of the bubble, but the larger the bubble becomes, the weaker it gets, and the air resistance increases, until the bubble must burst, and it shall burst." The last words were followed by the "stormy approval and applause" of over two hundred people who were present.[77]

Despite the ominous signs, members of the Jewish community heartened one another and did all they could to convince themselves that there was hope The President of the SJVOJ, Fridrih Pops, said, in the introductory speech at the Congress, that many people in the country and abroad were "worried about our possible fate . . . Let us raise our heads and rely on our strength, in our glorious army, in our leaders, and we will continue to be masters and winners! I can follow these words up with only one cry, and that is: Long live the King! (Loud, long-lasting applause and enthusiastic shouts: Long live the King!), Long live Yugoslavia! (More ongoing applause)."[78] The activist of the Zagreb Community, Lavoslav Steiner, recognized the work of the Almighty, because "thanks to the understanding and great wisdom of our rulers, our country has remained neutral, and we hope and pray with our warm Jewish hearts to the Great Judge of Human Destinies that it will continue to remain apart, outside the whirlpool of the war."[79] Was this not a voice of indirect support for the highest Yugoslav officials in their unprincipled siding with the Nazis? Be that as it may, in the fall of 1938, the President of the Community, Marko Horn, almost as if he were trying to comfort the members of his community, said that "we are living in a happy country in which there are no pogroms."[80]

In the general debate at the Congress, Joel Rosenberger of Zagreb appealed for the "preservation of dignity," for Jews not to "grovel," and repeated that young Jews had said "if any evil comes to this soil of ours, into which we have such deep roots, we can be counted on." Lav Štern pleaded for the "Communities to assuage anxiety . . . and hysteria, and to spread a feeling of peace arising from confidence in our own value and our own strength." Rosenberger probably best formulated the mood of the delegates at the congress: "It is difficult to be a Jew, but it has never been and will never be anything shameful. Whether the Jewish name remains pure and can be worn with pride depends only on us."[81]

The prominent Zionist leader David Albala of Belgrade also took part in the debate. He said that the "time has come when even the most convinced assimilationists, the greatest doubting Thomases, who believe in nothing but reality, even they must today respect that small nest that is growing bigger and stronger every day, because they have realized that the little bit of gold one holds in one's hand, all this can today vanish and disintegrate; houses and property disappear . . . A financier, an unrealistic man, a believer in fantasies, asked me how things stand in Palestine, and could he, his wife, and his children go there. The time has come and you can all feel it . . . What if that little country called Eretz Yisrael did not exist? . . . For many people, this is today the only light on our Jewish horizon. And if that very modest Jewish hearth in Eretz Yisrael did not exist today, despite the Arabs' ongoing terror campaign, and despite the possible insincerity of the British government, and despite all the difficulties that they are placing before us in Eretz—if this Eretz did not exist, and in it the 400,000 to 500,000 people who are scratching and digging the soil with their bare hands and nails, not only for themselves, but for all of us—I ask everyone: what would happen today to the soul and the spirit and the heart and the feelings and the hopes of the Jewish people if this Eretz Yisrael did not exist? We created it, we and those who came before us, for these hard times that have today come and that may still be here tomorrow . . . But, believe me, nothing terrible will happen to us if we are aware of the moment that we are living in and if we always do our duty. Things may get harder. Perhaps some of us will suffer, but the people as such will not perish. The people will rise, the people will shine, and if the people shine, then all of us, even as we suffer and do not have enough bread or a roof over our heads, even then we will know that somewhere there is a land with a blue-and-white flag, with the banner of our ancient holy tribes and leaders, where not only the present, but also the future of our people is to be built."[82]

Yugoslav Jewish organizations represented only a small fraction of European Jewish organizations and activities. The most important event in this period was the Twenty-fourth Zionist Congress, held at the end of August 1939, in the very days when Nazi Germany was making the final preparations for the attack on Poland (on September 1). The Congress passed six resolutions, all of them concerned with the White Paper of 1939. The white paper was issued by the British government on May 17, 1939, and, after decades of Arab protests and revolts, it reduced the annual Jewish immigration quota to Palestine to 15,000 people; furthermore, after five years, no further immigration would be possible without Arab agreement. In this way, the Arabs could prevent the Jews from becoming a majority in Palestine. The very impassioned protests against the white paper make it even more obvious that the Congress did not mention the Nazi danger at all! This was not a case of political blindness, because between 1933 and 1938 the same people realized what was going on and warned about the danger from Nazism time and again. Was it resignation? Or was it the tactic of "not rocking the boat"? Or were all hopes directed towards the Palestinian future, because *Židov* optimistically announced that "the strength of our *halutzim* in Eretz will bring down the white paper and thus remove the obstacle that is standing in the way of our creating a great and free Jewish state in Palestine!"[83]

The main subject of the Jewish press in Croatia and Yugoslavia, which was mostly of Zionist persuasion, was Palestine. It analyzed conditions there in detail, and attacked the British government for its policy. Yugoslav Jews organized a petition and demonstrations in many Jewish communities when the British government published the white paper.[84] In May of that year, a "large protest meeting" of Zagreb Jews was organized against the white paper, and the Makabi Hall in Palmotićeva Street was packed with people. The editors of *Židov* considered this such an important event that they published a photograph of it, the only photograph of a political gathering of that kind in the entire twenty-five years during which the paper came out.[85] At that time, the Jewish press also kept a close watch on the progress of the Nazi movement and reported on anti-Semitic incidents in many European countries. However, it made hardly any mention of anti-Semitic episodes in Croatia and Yugoslavia at all. It seems that most Jewish papers and organizations did not want to react, out of fear and because of traditional Jewish caution, in order to avoid any public questioning of their loyalty to the state.

From this perspective, the evolution in the writing of *Židov* is interesting. At the beginning of the thirties, as in the twenties, it was usual to give a detailed description of every anti-Semitic incident and call its perpetrators to account (to give at least moral satisfaction, if nothing else). It seems that the attitude toward domestic anti-Semitism began to change about 1933 and 1934: at first, the editors rationalized by saying that if a swift and sharp reaction always followed these attacks, it gave them too much importance. They said that "for now, Yugoslav Jews do not have much reason for concern. All the same, we must not disregard the danger from the further strengthening of the virus of anti-Semitism."[86] In the second half of the thirties, *Židov* usually only quoted criticism of anti-Semitic incidents made by the liberal middle-class press. It published no commentary of its own, and hardly ever mentioned anti-Semitic episodes, whose number and violence were mushrooming. Even when they protested, Jewish representatives did so very obliquely. In articles about the extremist pro-Ustasha press in 1939, they used the term "Gothic press," which sounded scornful but certainly did not touch the crux of the matter. Even in the fall of 1938, and the spring of 1939, Yugoslav Jewish organizations maintained that their state was one of the few in eastern and central Europe where there was no anti-Semitism.[87]

In an editorial published several days before the war broke out, the revisionist *Jevrejska tribuna* wrote that three blocs existed: England and France, Germany, and finally Russia as the third, that they were all imperialistic, and that if "war and revolution break out in Europe, there will certainly be pogroms aimed at the Jews." It is difficult to guess who might perform these pogroms from the article, but it emerges that Germany and Russia were the ones to fear. The author concluded that the solution for the Jews was to be "pro-active," that "Jewish regiments should be formed in countries where there were a lot of Jews," but it did not make clear on whose side these units would fight.[88]

In the first wartime issue of *Židov,* which came out on September 8, both front-page articles wrote about the outbreak of the war from the perspective of how it would affect Palestine, without saying one word about who was the aggressor and who the victim, nor about who should be supported. It wrote about preparations for defense from air raids in Palestine, but nothing about who would attack. On the eve of the Jewish New Year, *Jevrejska tribuna* inventoried conditions in the Zionist movement, printed many New Year's greetings, but did not mention the war at all. In the next issue, *Židov* published Dr. Emil Königstädtler's article "Jews and the European War," which expressed fear that this war, by now a fortnight old, would be similar to that of 1914, "only the means of war have since been greatly perfected . . . therefore every Jew, as a human being, must from the bottom of his heart condemn any shedding of innocent blood." He started by writing that "two great democratic powers . . . England and France, had proclaimed war on Germany, which had attacked Poland," and then added: "But the heavy blows of fate in recent years have taught us, not only as humans, but also as Jews by nationality, to look on events through the eyes of politicians." *Jevrejski glas* took a neutral position as well: it complained that Jews were under attack from all quarters—some people attacked them because they were "warmongers," others for "pacifism," some because they were "undesirable and unreliable." "Jewish emigrants from Germany still talk about their German homeland with the longing of a son for his lost mother . . . It is not uncommon for Jews to continue feeling love for the country they live in even when this country ill-treats them."[89]

The poet and translator Hinko Gottlieb wrote in *Omanut* in a somewhat different vein. He concentrated on the fact that the Yugoslav government had announced its neutrality, and that "loyal citizens do not obstruct the plans of their government. But a *man* (emphasis H. G.), by his very nature, cannot be neutral . . . Governments can be neutral, but people are subjective and want to take sides. We have already chosen our side—we are for freedom, and against tyranny. We are for equality." The unsigned editorial "Optimism" contained a conversation with a Jewish refugee in Yugoslavia whose apartment and shop had been taken from him in his old homeland and whose wife had died of sorrow, and he said, "We have been reduced to such a level of poverty and misery that we can sink no lower." The author concluded that "our optimism is of the kind that Nietzsche called heroic optimism."[90] In May 1940, the President of the Zagreb Community, Marko Horn, said that the "situation is changing from day to day and for us it seems to be deteriorating"; he advised "everyone to do his duty, not to lose control and presence of mind . . . We must all gather around our Community, understand the weight of our responsibility, and keep the spirit of our compatriots alive."[91]

During those months, Jewish circles reacted in various ways. In February 1940, *Židov's* cultural and literary supplement published literary notes from Palestinian life: there was no allusion to Nazi Fascism, but there was criticism of the white paper.[92] When Germany occupied Denmark in April 1940, *Židov* found occasion to publish the text "The Jewish Tragedy Is Growing" at the bottom of the second page. At the beginning of May 1940, *Židov* published an editorial for the first time, "A Bloodstained Balance," which indirectly suggested that the main guilty party was the Nazis ("It is all the Jews' fault—this is the stereotype that a certain kind of propaganda keeps repeating."). The editorial was signed with the pen name Ben Ruben. In a series of pieces in later issues of *Židov*, the same author wrote about the Jewish tragedy in the past and present, but even then he did not mention the Nazis explicitly. At a mid-May intercity meeting of Kadima, the moderate Zionist youth organization, three political resolutions were passed, all in connection with Palestine, although by then Belgium, the

Netherlands, and Luxembourg had been attacked and the Jews there were in immediate danger.[93]

It seems that no Jew, even at his most pessimistic, could imagine the kind of catastrophe that was soon to befall them. They all feared that they were facing severe persecution, but they expected it to take the form of something "already experienced"—such as the pogroms in Russia at the beginning of the twentieth century. In the middle of September 1939, they thought that the main danger, should Poland be defeated (which was at that time more or less certain and inevitable), was that the Jews would be "declared members of an inferior race." At that time, *Jevrejski glas* printed what "some of Hitler's officials" had allegedly said, that "if there is a general war, all Jewish independent economic activities will be terminated, and the Jews will probably be sent to forced labor." At the end of 1939, the Zagreb Community "still had no complete picture about what had taken place" in Poland. "We know only that towns and villages have been razed, that millions and millions of Jewish men, women, and children have lost their houses and everything else . . ." Most of them had lived "poorly and miserably, and have now been forbidden to make even the poorest kind of living." The leaders of the Zagreb Community "cannot anticipate what kinds of tasks lie ahead for us. We are here not even contemplating the possibility that we might hold back our helping hand." On September 20, 1940, a full year after the beginning of the war, *Židov* discussed the "future of European Jews." It forecast that the "immediate prospect is a period of hostilities, and if Germany wins and during the first postwar years, a perspective of complete misery." Even then, there was no lack of optimism: in August 1940, *Jevrejski glas* from Sarajevo wrote about the current "martyrdom" of European Jews, but then concluded that "we realize that this suffering will come to an end."[94]

The Jews and Jewish organizations were not the only ones to underestimate the Nazis' will and readiness to commit an unprecedented crime. All democratic Europe, headed by Great Britain and France, believed as late as September 1938 that by signing the Munich Agreement, which sacrificed Czechoslovakia, they had achieved "peace in our time," as British Prime Minister Chamberlain put it.

In the fall of 1940, many people believed that Hitler's Germany would quite certainly soon win the war. Denmark and Norway had been occupied, Belgium, the Netherlands, Luxembourg, and France trampled, and the British had been forced into a humiliating retreat from Dunkirk. The Yugoslav government, torn apart by its own weakness and facing difficult internal problems, could not resist Hitler's pressure. It began by giving in on issues that it judged "cost" the least, and which would easily satisfy the Germans: it proclaimed two anti-Jewish measures (anti-Jewish laws were also passed in Rumania at that time). Furthermore, internal conditions throughout Yugoslavia were becoming increasingly unstable, as the economic situation was deteriorating and shortages of basic foodstuffs began to be felt. In the Kingdom of Yugoslavia, and in the Croatian Banovna, the government began to intervene on the market: some price-levels were fixed, hoarding supplies of the most vital goods was prohibited, and rationing was introduced. This gave rise to false hopes that state interventionism was a solution for establishing order in, and control over, economic life in the country. The government was especially keen to gain control over the cereals market and regulate consumption, so "people's bread" began to be sold starting on September 21, and in Split from October 8. The production of any other kind of bread was prohibited.[95] In this situation, when many people were worried about their bare existence, it was very easy to turn the Jews into scapegoats. At the plenary meeting of the Croatian Workers' Federation on June 28, 1940, in Zagreb, "there was a lot of talk about social reform," and some people proposed that the "Sterns and the Deutsches should donate their money, of which they have enough anyway" for the construction of small apartments. Other people advocated the nationalization of industry, so that "we do not work for the private interests of Stern and Deutsch, but for us, for our Croatian Banovina."[96]

At the beginning of September, "Jewish parents in Belgrade were surprised by a statement issued by the headmasters of grammar schools to the effect that their children, by order of the Ministry of Education, could not be enrolled at school; instead, their applications were accepted and they were told that they would be informed about the final decision later." In the SJVOJ, they thought (or perhaps hoped?) that this was a "misunderstanding," but this "assumption proved baseless." This was a clear sign that provisions of some kind were in preparation; SJVOJ representatives rushed to the offices of the top officials to see what could be done. "At all these meetings and talks, except at the audience with Minister Korošec, the Union was allowed to hope that the measures were the result of general conditions, and that they would be very mild, if they were even passed at all. In the meantime, these two Decrees have extinguished our hopes." Korošec confirmed that "he had indeed given the order for Jewish children who wanted to enroll in secondary school to have their names recorded for the time being, because the final decision about whether, and in what form Jewish children will be allowed to attend school, had not yet been made." The SJVOJ submitted an "application" to the Minister of Justice, Laza Marković, and informed him about the "unsatisfactory answer from the Minister of Education," and Marković promised the "full protection of the constitutionally guaranteed rights" of Jews. Thus SJVOJ representatives "hope that this quarter will do everything to prevent us, equal citizens, from being turned into second-class citizens." Sooner or later they stopped believing even in these promises, so the Chief Rabbi of Yugoslavia, Isak Alkalaj, went to see Prince Pavle. The SJVOJ had decided not to "burden the Prince Regent with this matter earlier" and to inform him of everything "only when all other means have been used and have given no results."[97] This meeting too was fruitless, although the Jews considered Pavle a sincere supporter of democratic principles and the last barrier to the rise of anti-Semitism—for example, it sent to all the highest state officials telegrams of greeting from the Seventh Congress of the SJVOJ in April 1939, but only to Pavle did it extend "expressions of the warmest gratitude for the protection of civil freedoms and equality, which the Jews of Yugoslavia enjoy under the rule of the Karađorđevićes."[98]

Although they did all they could through secret channels, the Jews avoided any public reaction to the announcements about the passage of anti-Semitic laws. It seems that their representatives had at least a vestige of hope that they would manage to do something through intercession, or they considered that publicly insisting on equality would be of no use. Thus, there was hardly any reaction at all in *Židov:* it published news about anti-Semitic decrees being drawn up only on the seventh page in the middle of a long article entitled "From Press Reports." On September 30, the presidency of the Zagreb Community concluded that "whatever happens, we must remain calm and dignified, but also ready for anything," and Chief Rabbi Freiberger "appealed to people to remain calm, which is so essential today."[99]

As the Jewish population prepared to suffer further decrees, at the beginning of September the Banovina Government passed the "Ordinance on the Mandatory Registration of Stores of Goods," with the purpose of trying to "bring out" hidden goods and prevent their hoarding for speculative purposes.[100] To create a public picture of how very efficient these measures were, the government decided to "publish a press release every time a speculator was sent to a detention center." In the prevalent atmosphere, when cheap demagoguery was used to demonstrate loyalty to the idea of social justice, it was easiest to act against Jewish merchants.

On the very day when the ordinance was published in the official gazette *Narodne novine,* the Zagreb merchants Vilim (sometimes called Vilko) Kardoš, Vjekoslav Gostl, and Julio Hochsinger were arrested. The first two were accused of hiding flour, the third of selling pasta for higher prices than the maximum. Three days later, they were sent to "detention" in the out-of-the-way village of Donji Lapac in Lika. They were tried in Zagreb *in absentia*—Kardoš was released, while the other two were sentenced to three months' detention.[101] In the meantime, several more merchants were arrested and sent to detention, some from Zagreb, some from other towns.

As announced, on October 5, the Yugoslav Government passed two laws in the form of decrees, "restricting the rights of Jews." They were signed by Dragiša Cvetković and Vladko Maček, then by the other ministers as well. The first law was called the Decree on Measures Concerning Jews in Performing Activities with Items for Human Consumption. It practically forbade the work of all wholesale food businesses owned or co-owned by Jews: "Wholesale shops . . . shall be subject to review if their owners are Jews."[102] A sentence of up to two years in prison and the draconian fine of up to 500,000 dinars faced those who broke the law. Jews who fictitiously transferred their businesses to non-Jews faced the same punishment. Commissioners were to be appointed in "industrial firms that produced items for human consumption."

The second law, the Decree on Enrolling Persons of Jewish Origin at Universities, University-Level Schools, High, Middle, Teacher Training, and Other Vocational Schools, introduced a numerus clausus for Jews. This meant that the number of Jewish students and pupils was to be reduced to the same percentage as that of the Jewish population in the total population. The measure was to be applied in the current academic year of 1940–1941, for the first grade of lower schools and the first year of university. This was a painful measure for the Jewish population, as Jews invested a lot in education and traditionally gave their children a good one. Although Jews represented only 0.46 percent of the total Yugoslav population, they constituted 4 percent of the students in commercial schools, 2.57 percent in grammar schools, and 1.51 percent in middle technical schools. A special problem was Zagreb University, where they were almost 16 percent of the enrollment at the Faculties of Medicine and Law.[103]

According to the testimony of contemporaries, the decree took effect one day after the deadline for the first enrollment period. In primary and secondary schools, instruction had already begun a month earlier, so there would have been no major problems there despite Minister Korošec's stipulation quoted above. Students who were enrolling at university were not officially informed (there were no postings, circular letters, etc.), but discovered through various channels that they must do so during the first enrollment period to avoid complications. In this way, all who wanted to were able to enroll without restrictions.[104] The decree was legally incomplete and this was probably done on purpose. There was no definition of who were considered to be persons of "Jewish origin." The further elaboration of the decree from 1940 concerning commerce stated that "even converts born of Jewish parents are to be considered Jews," and "foreigners of Jewish origin" could not enroll under any circumstances. Nevertheless, there was a way to sidestep the law, especially if there was reason for intercession: Article Two provided that "people of Jewish origin, whose parents have done meritorious deeds for the homeland, may, on approval of the highest school authority, enroll . . . regardless of the restriction."[105]

A report from the U.S. Embassy in Belgrade sent to Washington on October 7 estimated that the decrees were "passed under German pressure," and they will "probably be implemented without great enthusiasm and excessive strictness."[106]

Pursuant to the Decree on Measures Concerning Jews in Performing Activities with Items for Human Consumption, the "Colonial Goods and Foodstuffs" shop in Zagreb, founded in 1901, was closed at the beginning of November. Its owner was the already mentioned Vilko Kardoš, who had in the meantime returned from "detention" in Lika. Its inventory was handed over to the Naproza Supply, Sale and Consumption Cooperative (a cooperative of the Croatian Businessmen's Organization in Zagreb). The same happened to the shop of imported goods owned by Jošua M. Israel in Zagreb, and the shops of Marko Armuth and Alexander Richtmann in Sisak. To achieve complete control of the wheat market, the Banovina also liquidated the large Trgopromet firm from Osijek, headed by Marko Jurinčić, in which at least two of the four board members were Jews (Žiga Erdenji and Eugen Kohn).[107] Kardoš was not a major or rich merchant at all—the dues he paid to the Jewish Community between 1938 and 1940 placed him between 52nd and 59th place among the 625 Jewish merchants in Zagreb, so it is not clear how he could have hindered market relations.

The Banovina also took over the Osijek shop of Herman Šajn and Co., merchant in cereals, flour, and agricultural produce, which was renamed Poljoproizvod d.d. However, matters soon showed that it was not the Jews who were to blame for the difficulties on the food market: by the end of the year, a clash broke out between the bakers and the city authorities because the bakers tried to produce other kinds of bread whose prices were not maximized. Bread coupons or food coupons were introduced as an essential part of the new rationing system, whereby every household got a certain amount of rationed food. At the beginning of 1941, Ban Ivan Šubašić signed a decree about the production of bread containing 65 percent corn and 35 wheat flour, which the people called "šubašić bread."[108] All this showed that the decree prohibiting Jewish trade was pure governmental demagoguery. At a time when a large part of the population was on the brink of malnutrition and hunger, it was passed to demonstrate, on the one hand, that the government was ready to and could use radical measures to solve problems, and on the other, to accuse the Jews and make them responsible for the current situation. It is true that there was no increase of anti-Semitic pressure in the following months, especially from government circles, but even these two decrees fundamentally complicated the position of Jews in all of Yugoslavia.

When the decrees were published, the Executive Committee of the SJVOJ, in the name of Yugoslavia's Jews, immediately reacted by issuing a declaration: "One decree has prevented Jewish children, because they are Jewish, from attending secondary schools and universities. The other allows the authorities to exclude Jews from one branch of the economy, because they are Jews . . . This humiliates and insults all the Jews in our country . . . The Croatian and Serbian people have always treated us in the spirit of brotherhood and civil solidarity. Thus, we do not believe that these severe measures are in harmony with what the essential national character of this people has for centuries aspired to, because it, too, for many centuries suffered all the bitterness of slavery, violence, and deprivation of rights."[109] *Jevrejski glas* expressed "amazement, both our own, and that of all other citizens . . . [and] to the last moment we could not believe that the decrees would be passed."[110]

By this time, the public, not to mention the government, paid no attention to declarations of this kind.[111] It seems that the Jews were aware of their helplessness. "We Jews have no political power, despite the great efforts the National-Socialist press is making to show the existence of what it calls world Jewry as a major political power of the first order."[112] *Jevrejski glas* of Sarajevo wrote similarly: "In our country, Jews play a very modest role in every field. First, we are barely 0.5 percent of the population . . . [and] have no decisive say in any sphere of national life. Not a single statesman or politician is a Jew, and we are hardly represented in the press at all."[113]

Obviously, the decrees were not revoked after the declaration was published. However, "a certain number of grammar school principals, mostly in places south of the Sava and the Danube, quietly disregarded the school decree, while the solidarity of students and pupils with their Jewish colleagues was never an issue. In this latter, the Sava and the Danube did not represent a border."[114]

In his *Memoirs,* Vladko Maček wrote that the anti-Semitic decrees were passed at the proposal of Korošec, which the minutes of the IO–SJVOJ, already mentioned, also indirectly confirm.[115] Maček defended himself for supporting the anti-Semitic decrees by saying that he "also thought it necessary to intervene in the trade in foodstuffs, and especially in wheat, under those difficult conditions." However, Maček continued: "As soon as the proposal to change the publishing law came up on the agenda of the ministerial council, whereby no Jew would be allowed to own a printing house, I resolutely opposed it, stating that I would sooner open a government crisis than support this, or any other similar law with a Hitlerist-Nazi tendency."[116] In the second half of October (the report was written on October 22), information reached the U.S. Embassy in Belgrade that the "Government is under strong pressure, which it will obviously not be able to resist," to "bar Jews from participating in the film industry," and that it is "only a matter of time before other provisions are enacted" restricting Jewish participation in industry.[117] However, contrary to American expectations, the government did not decide to introduce new decrees.

Maček wrote his *Memoirs* after the war and was obviously not completely forthcoming. What he claimed was partly refuted by the writing of *Hrvatski dnevnik,* the paper of Maček's Croatian Peasant Party (HSS). *Hrvatski dnevnik* came out from 1936 to 1941 and was a good indicator of the changes in the HSS and of Croatian policy in general at that time. Until 1938, the paper unswervingly exposed anti-Semitism and all pro-Nazi ideas, in accordance with the general views of the HSS. The credit for this probably went partly to then editor Ilija Jakovljević (1898–1948), a liberal writer and publicist and later a prisoner in the Ustasha camp of Stara Gradiška (1941–1942). However, after 1938, and especially at the end of 1939, *Hrvatski dnevnik* steadfastly supported both the strategy and the specific activities of the Belgrade and Banovina governments, including the passage of the two anti-Jewish decrees. In an unsigned commentary dated October 6, a day after the decrees were passed, it admitted that "the government has not yet given any explanation for the decrees," but "the reasons . . . are known anyway . . . Among us, and in the rest of the world, the Jewish element is considered a special group that has its own ideals, different from those of other citizens. The Jews have long wanted to form their own nation-state. Even today they consider Palestine their homeland . . . As the Jewish element has not shown their homeland to be this country, it could not be entrusted with the care of supplying it under such delicate and difficult circumstances. Feeding the people is to be placed in the hands of those who will consider work of this kind a payment of their debt to their own homeland."

Commenting on the decree's introduction of the numerus clausus, *Hrvatski dnevnik* wrote that "a disproportion exists in the number of Jewish, Christian, and Muslim, students . . . After this decree, Croatian sons will no longer be left jobless, while their Jewish colleagues take positions in greater numbers than they merit." The ease with which *Hrvatski dnevnik* distinguished "Croatian sons" from Jews, who were allegedly working against the interests of the state, is very characteristic.

The basic conclusion of the commentary in *Hrvatski dnevnik* was that the two decrees "regulated" the position of the Jews. It added that "the decrees have the purpose of reducing Jewish influence on our economy and our cultural life to the proper measure and of preventing those, with capital, from being the decisive factor in supplying the population with foodstuffs, or being the hotbed of foreign ideas among our intelligentsia." It concluded that these two decrees "reflect concern for the vital interests of the common state and our three peoples, who come first who should give the community its identity." The commentary expresses the conformity and hypocrisy of the Croatian policy-makers then: it is completely unclear on what grounds the editors of *Hrvatski dnevnik* concluded that the Jews were not loyal, making it logical to ban them from selling food, and on what basis they concluded that the excessive influence of the Jewish intelligentsia was a "hotbed of foreign ideas" and harmful for the state, making it logical to restrict their enrollment in schools. The ultimate hypocrisy was the conclusion that passing the discriminatory decrees against Jews had not "abrogated their basic human rights." That this absurd contradiction did not worry the editors of *Hrvatski dnevnik* very much can also be seen from the very firm pronouncement that "other regulations, that may in future be passed . . . will not affect the basic rights of Jews either."[118] It is possible that *Hrvatski dnevnik* possessed information that a decree was being prepared about Jews as owners of printing houses, which Maček mentioned in his memoirs.

On October 10, *Hrvatski dnevnik* reacted, in two unsigned pieces, to the writing of "some foreign papers" on this subject. These texts also contradicted what Maček later wrote in his memoirs. The first one in *Hrvatski dnevnik,* entitled "Dr. Korošec and the Jewish Question," denied that Dr. Anton Korošec "is forcing the Jewish question, in which he is allegedly encountering opposition from some of his ministerial colleagues," and explained that "Korošec is the representative of the Slovenes in the common government, as it is well known that the Jews have never had any success in Slovenia. There was never a Jewish question in Slovenia. It only exists in Croatian and Serbian regions, so it is understandable that the main talks about this question were conducted between the Serbian and Croatian representatives, who reached complete agreement."[119]

Just under the first article came the second, "Two Voices about the Jewish Question in Our Country." In it, the editors commented on allegations from newspapers in Prague (*Vlajka*) and Warsaw (*Warschauer Zeitung),* papers from Nazi-occupied countries which presented pro-Nazi views. These claimed that the Banovina authorities took a "negative view" of the anti-Jewish decrees passed by the government in Belgrade and that they would not implement them. In its commentary, *Hrvatski dnevnik* claimed these statements were untrue, and called the misinformation in the foreign press the work of ill-meaning domestic informants, obviously people who "formally upheld the Agreement policy [i.e., the Cvetković-Maček Agreement of August 1939], but who in their heart still harbored the old hatred for Croatia and the Croats." The paper repeated the opinion expressed in the first text that "there has been no clash in Yugoslavia over the Jewish question, because both the decrees were passed with full support." Since the Warsaw daily supposed that the "Jews, with their well-known slyness, will very quickly relocate to Croatia all the firms that Jews are not allowed to manage," *Hrvatski dnevnik* answered that "in Croatia there is no such issue as Jews being considered meritorious for the state. This is a specifically Serbian problem . . . The Serbs have their warrior Jews and their descendents. The Serbs may proclaim someone meritorious for their state, but we have been the opposition for twenty years and will certainly not proclaim anyone who served the Belgrade regime meritorious for the state."[120]

This did not end discussions about the anti-Semitic decrees, and two weeks later the head of the Gospodarska sloga Agricultural Cooperative, Ljudevit Tomašić (1901–1945), at a meeting of the HSS district organization in Zagreb, directly accused the Jews: "You know that when the Croatian Banovina was created, the winter before and in the spring there was hunger in many parts of Croatia. And then some speculators, mostly Jews, began to speculate with food."[121] It is interesting that accusations of this kind did not appear at the time when "mostly Jews" were allegedly speculating with food, but only after the anti-Semitic laws were passed. Tomašić's statement and Maček's agreement to the passage of the anti-Semitic decrees are only two of the indications that the HSS policy was shifting to the right. This was not a premeditated move (especially not by Maček, who remained a convinced democrat), but an adjustment to internal and external conditions, conformity, and a desire for compromise; in it all, the Jews were only a small and unimportant victim.

The deteriorating position of the Jewish community could also be felt in other areas: issue 51 of *Židov,* at the end of 1940, was confiscated because it had a review of Chaplin's film *The Great Dictator,* about which *Židov's* American correspondent, Emanuel Newman, wrote in an extremely benign tone. There was no mention of the fact that Chaplin's character of Adenoid Hynkel was in fact meant to be Adolf Hitler, but the article did say that "the film has obviously not been made for entertainment only . . . It is a sarcastic and destructive caricature, with a special gift for comic distortion, [in which] Chaplin wants to show the monstrous abnormality of the most dangerous man in the world."[122] In February 1941, the SCJ distributed in the usual way the leaflet *Conditions in Palestine, Report no. 4,* which said that "war can indirectly be felt" in the country, and gave a condensed presentation of the ideas of David Ben-Gurion about the need to organize Jewish units in the British army. The office of the Ban of the Croatian Banovina considered that the "leaflet has impermissible content, because it violates the neutrality of our country." Thus, the Police Directorate was required to "take the most urgent measures against the leaflet's publisher and distributor," however, nothing was done because the person responsible, *Židov*'s editor-in-chief, Dr. Joel-Julije Rosenberger, who was to be interrogated, had taken his wife and children to Palestine and had "not yet returned, and no one knows when he will return."[123]

However unjust these anti-Semitic decrees were, in the report from 1945, the representatives of the Zagreb Jewish Community did not complain about them too strongly because, they said, "except for interning several Jews, and taking over some shops, nothing much was done against the Jews other than issuing these decrees. Obviously, they were passed more to satisfy political pressure, which Hitler was at that time putting on Yugoslavia, than to in fact do anything."[124]

The denunciations made by Lavoslav Ebenspanger of Zagreb are a good illustration of the incendiary anti-Jewish atmosphere at that time. At the end of 1940 or the beginning of 1941, he sent a letter to the Banovina Government "about the anti-Croatian policy in the Jewish Religious Community." Ebenspanger stressed that he was "worried in this difficult time for us Jews." He then said that "all the members of the Main Office, together with the head of the temple, Mr. Bernhard Grüner, have served every Belgrade regime and voted against the policies of Dr. Maček." He proposed that instead of Dr. Gavro Schwarz, "who gave speeches in favor of those policies . . . a man who feels himself to be Croatian should be made Chief Rabbi." Giving the example of several "Jews of Croatian nationality," and those who voted for the HSS, or were even members of that party, Ebenspanger insisted that it is "possible to conduct the proper national policy even in the Jewish Community . . . which would result in Croatian Catholics not being badly disposed toward the Jews." Since Ebenspanger considered the behavior of the Jews themselves to blame for the growing anti-Semitism and intolerance, he then proposed that the "Banovina authorities should use their authority at the next elections for the Jewish Religious 'Great Community' [Ebenspanger differentiated between the Ashkenazic Community and the two smaller ones, the Sephardic and Orthodox] to secure the election of men whose political work could not be criticized, and who stood at the side of the Croatian people and voted for the policies of Dr. Maček in 1935." The Banovina authorities, i.e., the Police Directorate, duly received and made note of the letter. The Directorate "will, from what has been said, take into consideration the frame of mind in part of the Jewish Community . . . and take whatever steps are necessary." But, again, it seems that nothing was done. Besides, there was no time, because no more elections for the heads of the Jewish Community were held.[125] Lavoslav Ebenspanger (born 1907) was an Orthodox Jew, unmarried, a cantor by profession but out of work and poor. It is not difficult to guess his motive for the denunciation to the police: hatred, envy, an attempt to secure a job in this way? Ironically, after this outpouring of Croatian patriotism, Lavoslav Ebenspanger was killed in the Holocaust.[126]

Despite all the unfavorable circumstances, the Main Office of the Jewish Community published a very successful financial report in the middle of 1940.[127] Then, as before and later, there was a lot of understandable self-deception in discussions within Community bodies. Two years earlier, a member of the Main Office, Oskar Heim, had optimistically concluded that "work in all fields, and accountancy figures, show the success and progress of our Community . . . [which] is moving towards the consolidation of its finances."[128] In 1939–1940, the Community had increased expenses for refugees and was burdened by the mass renouncements of 1938—"In this way, the Community lost its stability for a foreseeable period of time."[129] Although everyone knew this, no one mentioned that financial stability was maintained at the expense of the hard work of the Community members, and also by spending the money set aside for the construction of the Jewish hospital and the Jewish home.[130]

Wishing its members a happy New Year 5701 at the end of September 1940, the SJVOJ hoped that the past year was "the last in this ill-fated series of years," and informed them that "because of the uncertain days, we are entering the New Year with a lot of apprehension."[131]

The atmosphere was bad: the final sentence in the letter sent by Adela Weisz (1906–1978), later an activist of the Zagreb Community, in the name of the Association of Zionist Women of Križevci (a town sixty kilometers northeast of Zagreb), to the Yugoslav Headquarters of WIZO in January 1940, probably best describes those last months of peace: "One thing comforts us—our conscience is clean and we can assure you that we have not, despite everything, lost hope in a better future."[132] The report of the secretary to the Main Office of the Zagreb Community said the same in similar words: "The Zagreb Jewish Community, as long as circumstances allow, will continue to be a torchbearer and banner for the good and better future of all Jewry."[133] In his report of November 1940, the prominent Community activist and head of the Management Board, Lavoslav Steiner, tried to make the Jews face reality: "Although we have as yet been spared the hardship of war, nevertheless we can slowly but surely feel that difficulties are approaching. Facts must be faced, we must all be aware of how things stand in all their stark truth, as they are. Legal restrictions have been introduced in our country too, mild as yet, but we have been quite badly affected, and we never know where this vicious circle will end."[134] Steiner said that the "forecast for the future is blurred, unclear, because we do not know what tomorrow will bring" and considered that "on our thorny path it is of the utmost importance to preserve our morale and be harmonious. Concord saved our ancestors, it will also help us to overcome all difficulties."[135] The President of the Community, Marko Horn, at that time also spoke of "difficult times . . . I beg the councillors gathered here to work with the citizens, so that they do not panic, and remain on their jobs doing their patriotic duty." He also pleaded for the preservation of unity: "Today it is necessary for us all to gather round the Community, as the central point of events affecting us."[136]

Some events suggested that life was still running relatively smoothly. During the Christmas and New Year's holidays of 1940–1941, Makabi organized an excursion to Kranjska Gora in Slovenia. A dance for Jewish university students was organized on February 22, 1941, and, on March, 12 the Makabi fencing club registered twelve competitors for the championship of the Croatian Banovina. The Makabi Purim Ball was even announced for March 15, but as the last issue of *Židov* came out on March 7, we do not know whether this actually took place. In this last issue, the editors of *Židov* published a short announcement: "The paper will stop coming out for technical reasons." And that was all. It seems that the decision to stop publication resulted from the general pressure on the Jews in Zagreb. Because of this Ze'ev Glück, the editor-in-chief of *Židov,* went to Novi Sad and published several issues of the paper there, as the Hungarian occupiers allowed this for a time, but this did not last long.[137]

The atmosphere at the last match of the Makabi football club against *Ličanin* (a club from Zagreb), at the end of March 1941, was difficult. "Fights kept breaking out among the fans of the two teams, and this was soon carried to the field among the players." As Makabi won by one goal in the last minute, "there was no end to the joy." Then they all went to an inn owned by a friend of the players, where "we were all happy and joyful and behaved a bit wildly . . . as if we could feel that this was our last meeting."[138]

5

FROM EXCLUSIVE CROATIANHOOD TO USTASHA ANTI-SEMITISM

Ante Starčević's (1823–1896) ideology was to have an independent Croatian state outside the framework of the Hapsburg Monarchy. In his work to achieve this end, he was inspired by liberal democracy, and especially by the French Revolution, combining these ideals with the Croatian tradition of state law. He considered that, except for the Bulgarians, the Croats constituted the only "nation" in the entire area inhabited by the South Slavs, and that they were in fact a mixed population imprinted by the spirit of their ancient overlords, the early Croats, but this spirit had not yet managed to encompass them all. He linked exclusive Croatianhood with a struggle for general suffrage and considered religion the personal business of an individual. He envisioned an independent Croatian state as one achieving harmony between the state and society, the sovereignty of the Croatian people combined with the moral virtues and creative potentials of the individual. Josip Frank (1844–1911), a Jew who converted at twenty-four, became a member of the Party of Rights at the end of 1890 and gradually became its leader. The only program he managed to publish was the demand for Croatian state autonomy within the Hapsburg Monarchy. Therefore, he discarded Starčević's demand for complete Croatian independence, as well as his view that all the South Slavs were Croats. Frank acknowledged that a Serbian people existed in Serbia, but proclaimed the Serbs the greatest enemies of the Croats. Even before the First World War, Frank's supporters (who called themselves "Frankists") began to settle scores with political opponents violently, in the street, and introduced goon-squad politics as a method into Croatian political life.[1]

In their propaganda for an independent Croatian state, the Ustashe obviously claimed to be following the teaching of Starčević[2]—"the Poglavnik, Dr. Ante Pavelić, has realized Starčević's plans."[3] They tried to show Starčević as the forerunner and instigator of their totalitarian Fascist- and Nazi-inspired ideology, which was an obvious fabrication, as right-wing intellectuals had laid the ideological foundations for these theories in the 1930s.

Filip Lukas, geographer, geopolitician, university professor, and the then president of the Matica hrvatska, extolled Starčević, saying that with his "broad overview he had nationally united all the components of the Croatian people . . . had laid down ideals that will last as long as Croats exist."[4] Stjepan Buć wrote in a similar vein: "There is no Croatianhood outside Starčević's views! Anything lasting and valuable can only be built on the foundations of Starčević's teaching—everything else is a haze and leads to disaster!"[5] The magazine *Hrvatska gruda* wrote in a similar way: "There are no Croats or Croatia outside Starčević's teaching, there are only traitors!," and claimed that "Ante Starčević means complete reliance on blood and soil."[6]

On the other hand, they rejected Ljudevit Gaj's (1809–1872) policy of Illyrianism, and criticized Bishop Josip Juraj Strossmayer (1815–1905) for promoting Yugoslavism. They considered Strossmayer's views unacceptable partly because he was not a Croat by origin ("Strossmayer could not see, because having entered our national body along a horizontal cultural line, he did not instinctively feel that a people cannot voluntarily renounce their individuality").[7] Buć said that Gaj and Strossmayer were "real representatives of foreignness, of a society opposed to our blood and our interests."[8]

The left-wing intelligentsia would not allow this manipulation of Starčević's original ideas and the ideology of the state's rights.[9] In the poem "Planetorium," Miroslav Krleža called Starčević "the only lamp in the dense night,"[10] and praised him on several occasions, emphasizing his attachment to the ideals of the French Revolution.[11] August Cesarec wrote "The Son of the Homeland," an apotheosis of the revolutionary work of Eugen Kvaternik, Starčević's closest collaborator.[12] The liberal *Nova Riječ* wrote that *Nezavisnost* was suppressing fundamental arguments that showed Starčević was not anti-Semitic.[13]

In time, especially after the foundation of the ISC, the claims about the Ustashe being Starčević's ideological heirs became less convincing. The Ustashe themselves realized and admitted this, although some of them still called on Starčević and his ideology.[14] When Frane Milobar wrote the article "The Eightieth Anniversary of the Croatian Party of Rights" in March 1942 in *Hrvatska gruda,* saying that the party still "exists," Ustasha Intelligence did not share his opinion. An anonymous report said that "the Ustasha Movement should not in this way be called the continuation of an earlier party."[15] At the beginning of the war Blaž Jurišić edited Ante Starčević's *Selected Documents,* which were printed in 1943 but not put on sale until after the war because the Ustasha regime could not come to terms with the true Starčević: his deep-seated devotion to democratic principles and his obsessive hatred of the Germans.

Milan Šufflay was a lucid, educated, and remarkable man who was killed on a Zagreb street by operatives of the Yugoslav police in February 1931. In a collection of essays and articles, *Croatia Is the Light of World History and Politics,* Šufflay developed a historical and national mysticism in which the people possessed "self-hood" (i.e., a kind of process of acquiring cultural and national identity). He spoke of the "fateful boundary on the Drina along which the mighty Roman Empire had cracked in two . . . which was a spiritual and cultural boundary,"[16] and then went on to elaborate this thought: "The Croatian people passed through the Roman-Western melting-pot, the Serbian people through the Byzantine-Turkish one. Thus, the souls of the two peoples are different in their essence, although the languages are similar. To unify these peoples would mean to homogenize and destroy them. To centralize under these conditions would mean turning Croatia into a laboratory animal for experiments in vivisection. I consider that the Croatian nation, as a citizen of the great empire of Western civilization, has the right to raise its voice against any oppression . . . Anyone who knows history knows that the Yugoslav idea has no dynamic force. It is nothing in comparison with the powerful Croatian idea. In Croatia, the Yugoslav idea is nothing but a thin shell covering the seething Croatian national volcano: an insignificant trigger could lead to an eruption . . . For myself as a philosopher and free-thinking Croat, it is immaterial whether I am incarcerated in a small police prison or in any other prison or, having allegedly been set free, I emerge into the great dungeon in which—thank God, only temporarily!—the Croatian people are languishing!"[17] Although none of Šufflay's sentences show his connections with Ustasha plans for violence and slaughter, many Ustasha authors gladly quoted him, starting with Pavelić himself, who repeated Šufflay's above views in his brochure *From the Struggle of the Croatian People,* published in Vienna in 1931. Šufflay's idea about the "centuries-old boundary on the Drina" gained mythical proportions for many people who wrote about this problem, especially the extreme nationalists and pro-Ustasha intellectuals.[18]

Šufflay was obviously a specific combination of a leading scholar and a man influenced by mythologems. For him, national history was conditioned "by blood and soil first and foremost," that is, by "vital vigor, and after that by the climate and the topography of the land." He saw Croatia and its history as primarily a "reflection of the struggle between the Mediterranean East and West."[19] Some of Šufflay's other thoughts—such as "we Croats, even without a blood test, can well feel in our bones that the avaricious, petty-pinching Tzintzar blood that has been brewing in the Byzantine-Turkish cauldron for centuries is still more than alive in Belgrade today"[20]—were also an inspiration for some right-wing propagandists to continue developing ideas based on people's ethnic origin, which brought them very close to the prevailing racist theories of the Nazis.

Filip Lukas explained the concept of the "people's community," which was a literal translation of the term *Volksgemeinschaft,* taken from the Nazi ideology: "A people are in their spirit a mythical being, in which the biological is so closely entwined with the metaphysical that they serve as the foundation for spiritual and biological unity. Just as a people represent an ethnobiological species, they also represent a spiritual species. In this way a people become a community of blood, a community of necessity, but also a community of the spirit, and a community of freedom. This leads to a double link between individuals in a people, ties of the blood and ties of the spirit. This community comes most obviously to expression in the present generation, because it is imbued with the essence of all past ideals, which great individuals can bring to fruition in accordance with contemporary needs and the spirit of the time."[21]

In 1936, the ideologists of racism availed themselves of the fortieth anniversary of Starčević's death to promote their ideas and connect them with what was ostensibly Starčević's conceptual heritage. Thus it was very logical that when he wrote about Starčević, Filip Lukas in places made use of racial arguments—"Starčević, as an inheritor of our race, possessed all the ethnobiological and mental characteristics linked to it . . . Starčević was a person who knew how to condense the most essential prerequisites for our survival from the biology of our race." Sometimes he did not mention race, but used euphemisms instead: "As we honor the memory of

Starčević, we also honor ourselves in him, our ethnobiological and spiritual characteristics."[22]

Stjepan Buć was even more direct in emphasis on the racial element: "Starčević was the kind of person . . . who had all the attributes of the chosen race, a man of quality, he possessed in addition to a sharp, discerning outlook, also reliability, an uncompromising attitude, an absolute nation-building instinct and awareness . . . Starčević was the product of pure Croatian blood, and this blood gave direction to his total behavior and work. A man of mixed blood, on the contrary, has no character, is not consistent . . . Had Starčević, for example, had any foreign, nomadic blood—he would not have been Ante Starčević! . . . Starčević was a purebred Croatian man."[23]

Similarly to Buć, Božidar Murgić also thought that "Starčević by his racial characteristics opposed gentle, soft fighting methods . . . Pacifism is theoretically and philosophically a fine thing . . . [but] for us Croats, the following will be true as long as the world exists: *Si vis pacem, para bellum* [if you want peace, prepare for war]." Murgić said that "the final result of Croatian politics will be—the complete revival of Starčević's total national-political program, which rests on the reality of the historical continuity of the state, on the separate Croatian culture as the product of the soil and the blood of the people." He obviously adopted the phrase "blood and soil" from the National Socialist ideology. "Today, at a time when Europe is being ruled by strong warrior-like ideas of revolution and reform, Starčević is the contemporary interpreter of the Croats' wishes and feelings."[24]

Stjepan Buć even went a step further: he used data torn out of context, overemphasized, distorted, and even faked, to conclude that "Starčević's work is founded on the concept of race." Buć concluded by directly linking Starčević with Hitler: "Seventy years ago, Starčević emphasized the kind of racial ideas on which Adolf Hitler based his program for the rebirth and reorganization of German national life . . . Starčević, just like Hitler so many decades later, pointed out the value and cult of the chosen and high-quality national element on which our future life must be built."[25]

Buć's ideas brought the ideology of Croatian exclusiveness to the extreme—it grew into a typical Nazi ideology transplanted to Croatia: "The Croatian people will suffer neither a Communist nor a Judeo-shyster-usurious Croatia . . . Croatian nationalists consciously reject the idea that Croats are Slavic in origin and consider the Croats . . . a separate race . . . For them, from the perspective of blood, both 'christened' and pure Jews are Jews, because the blood of both is equally Jewish. Jews must be completely separated from the life of the people by the strictest prohibition of mixing blood. There is no room for them on the territory of our people."[26] Although this ideology did not have many followers before 1941, the ISC authorities eagerly applied it on the legislative as well as on the political and military-police levels.

In 1940, the future ISC Foreign Minister and Minister of the Interior, Mladen Lorković, published the book *The People and Land of the Croats,* in which he developed ideas typical of exclusive Croatianhood: he proclaimed all Bosnia and Herzegovina a Croatian land, saying that "there is room for non-Croats in Croatia only because Croats live outside it—in foreign lands. Given the economy and the social level and structure, there was room for six million inhabitants in Croatia in 1931. But since over two million non-Croats lived in Croatia, 1.75 million Croats had to live outside it." Sorrow over the emigration of Croats and attempts to return them to the country are the central ideas of the book. As Lorković included members of the "Islamic religion" among Croats, he was obviously referring to the Serbs when he said "non-Croats who entered Croatian lands that were emptied by the Turkish wars."[27] From these ideas to their realization through the mass pogroms of non-Croats in the ISC was not a long step.

During the existence of the ISC, many authors added to this ideological attitude. For example, Filip Lukas published a racial map of the Balkans in the collection of essays, articles, and speeches *The Croatian People and the Croatian State,* and discussed the racial components of some peoples. He concluded that the Croats and the Serbs represented opposite racial types, but that the Montenegrins belonged to the Croatian racial type. He sympathized with the Iranian-origin theory about the Croats, which implied that they were not Slavs, but reduced it to the level of political pragmatism and, in fact, falsified it. He was especially eager to prove that the Croats had nothing to do with the Russians: "There is certainly no racial homogeny among the Slav peoples, especially as there is no blood kinship between the Croats and the Russians."[28]

In the book of "national-political essays" *Croatian Vistas,* Julije Makanec (1904–1945) discussed the "malignant political power—Marxism . . . that appeared as an opposing and robust force on the battleground of modern nationalism." Makanec asked himself, "Will the understanding prevail . . . that every pure-blooded people are the bearer of divine life . . . a unique thought of God."[29]

Right from its beginnings in 1932–1933, the Ustasha movement, speaking through the paper *Ustaša—Herald of Croatian Revolutionaries,* was anti-

Yugoslav and fanned hatred of the Belgrade regime and its officials, and then of the Serbs. It explicitly stressed that "all means are allowed in the struggle for sacred goals, even the most terrible," and that the main means will be violence that also announced terror: "The KNIFE, REVOLVER, MACHINE GUN AND TIME BOMB, these are the idols, these are the bells that will announce the dawning and the RESURRECTION OF THE INDEPENDENT STATE OF CROATIA," said the editorial of the first issue of *Ustaša* in February 1932, signed by the Poglavnik—the Leader.[30] The knife, which was placed first in the order of weapons, became a kind of cult object (which developed into a mythology) in the following years, both among the Ustashe and among their Chetnik enemies.

The Principles of the Ustasha Movement, published abroad in June 1933 as the main program of the Ustasha organization, show a clearly developed ideological system close to Fascism and Nazism. "Something new had to come, something stronger and more capable of fighting Bolshevism, capable of defeating it. And this new thing springs from Fascism," wrote Pavelić in the mid-thirties in a book that was published in Zagreb in 1942.[31] In time, the Ustasha ideology took over parts of the Nazi and Fascist ideologies, with some details adapted to the specific case of Croatia. National exclusiveness was one of the basic ideas of *Principles,* but even *Ustaša,* which came out in exile, had no direct expression of anti-Semitism. There were at least two reasons for this: the first, that the Ustashe were confronting their main enemy, the Belgrade regime, against which they aimed all their ideological vitriol and hatred, and the second, that some people who considered themselves Catholics and Croats, but were Jews according to the racial theory and Nazi laws, had a very prominent role in the beginning of the Ustasha movement. These were the assimilationist Dr. Vladimir Sachs and Ivo Frank, son of Josip Frank and uncle of Eugen Dido Kvaternik. As far back as 1895, Ivo Frank had led the mob that demanded that the "Serb-Orthodox church banner" should be removed from the Orthodox Church on Preradovićev Square in Zagreb. However, early on, Frank split off from Pavelić.[32]

In October 1934, Pavelić wrote a programmatically important text titled *Decree.* It did not mention the Jews at all, its main characteristics being vengeful wrath against the Belgrade regime and a call to wait for the right moment to create the independent state of Croatia.[33] As time passed, Pavelić laid increasing emphasis on the importance of creating a Croatian state on totalitarian and exclusivist foundations in which the Croatian people would be the masters, which logically radicalized the attitude toward the Jews. Vladimir Židovec, an attorney, a prewar "sworn" Ustasha, and later the ISC Ambassador to Bulgaria, wrote his political autobiography in a Yugoslav investigative prison in 1948. Writing about Pavelić's attitude toward the Jews and the Serbs, he said that "the original plan, at least its cutting edge, was pointed against the Serbs in Croatia. The Jews were probably added when things peaked and at the height of Hitler's pogroms against the Jews, all the more so as capitalist Jewish circles in Croatia, at least most of them, did not show much sympathy for the struggle and the ideals of the Croatian people."[34]

In the thirties, connections between the Ustashe and the German Nazis and Italian Fascists grew stronger, and the Ustasha ideology was gradually developed at this time. It was a specific synthesis of Fascist and Nazi elements, adapted to reality in Croatia and Bosnia and Herzegovina. The Ustashe took their attitude to the Jews directly from German Nazism, since the Italian attitude to the Jews was considerably more temperate.[35]

Ivan Oršanić, editor of *Hrvatska smotra,* a paper that glorified the Nazi "new European order," wrote in 1939 that "blending into the new order must be psychologically, politically, culturally, and economically completely transparent and defined because this is not something that happens occasionally, it is the historic beginning of a new age."[36] These characteristics of the Ustasha movement achieved clear expression in the commentary to the *Principles of the Croatian Ustasha Movement,* published in 1942: "The ISC is totalitarian because . . . it has assumed total care for all classes of the people . . . It is totalitarian because it wants to control, lead, manage, and organize everything."[37]

When they took over some elements of the Nazi ideology, the Ustashe also adopted racist anti-Semitism. Pavelić's study *The Croatian Question,* of October 1936, sent to the German Foreign Ministry, clearly showed his desire to draw close to Nazism.[38] He focused on the "Serbian government, international Freemasonry, Jewry, and Communism" as the enemies of the Croatian liberation movement. Writing about the Jews, he said: "Today, almost all banking and almost all trade in Croatia are in the hands of the Jews. This could happen only because the state gave them privileges and because it used this to weaken the strength of the Croatian people. Jews greeted the foundation of the so-called Yugoslav state with great joy, because a Croatian nation-state would by no means suit them as well as did Yugoslavia—a state made up of various peoples . . . The empire of Judas lies in the muddle of peoples: here Jewry, as a financially strong element and ostensibly loyal to the state authorities, can grovel before them and secure the good will of the rulers . . . Yugoslavia developed as the Jews had anticipated, into a real 'Eldorado' for Jewry because of the corruption of public life in Serbia. They were very grateful to Belgrade for offering them protection by stealing capital from the Croatian people and using it to fight against Croatian liberation movements. On every occasion, Jews in Croatia showed in their own and noisy way their loyalty to Yugoslavism and to state unity, wanting to create the impression abroad that the Croats were satisfied with their fate. The entire press in Croatia is in Jewish hands. This Jewish-Freemason press incessantly attacks Germany, the German people, and National Socialism."[39]

Pavelić thought the same several years earlier, too, but expressed himself in a different way. The "political novel" *The Lovely Blonde,* which he started to write in October 1934 in the Turin prison, and which was first printed in 1935, was full of anti-Semitic invective.[40] The book is an example of bad literature, the transparently one-sided characterization of the figures being only one of its weaknesses. All the Croats are good, resolute, honest idealists, most of them poor, while the Serbs (who have the invented surnames of Kuršumlijević, Čevapović, Ugursuzović, Kalimegdanović, etc., which bring to mind the influence of their Turkish heritage) are dishonest policemen and oppressors. The central theme of the novel is the Croats' struggle for freedom. The Jews also play a role in Pavelić's storytelling, and while there is no explicit mention of Jews, the surnames Morgenstern, Blum, Greif, Donner, Rosenfeld, Freitag, Špicler, or the name Samuel, are clear enough to every reader. These Jews are rich or swindlers, or both, or importunate suitors. Greif is also a police informer who later gets just punishment—he is stabbed with a knife, a kind of punishment that was to become very characteristic in later years. All the Jews are described as "greedy," and as "devious servants" of the regime.

What Pavelić did not want to write or say publicly, he said in his inner circle. During interrogation in 1951, Ante Brkan, the "Poglavnik's aide" during the first period of exile, testified that Pavelić had said in 1934, in Turin, that "all enemies must be slaughtered, all Serbs, Jews, and Gypsies." Brkan had protested that this was "impossible, as 25 percent of the population in Croatian lands were Serbs, but Pavelić remained steadfast."[41]

In time, Pavelić became increasingly radical in public as well, and in a proclamation to the Croatian people on July 1, 1940, he said: "The greatest and most obvious injustice of England and France in their Versailles *diktat* was to create an unnatural and freak state, which was first named Yugoslavia by International Jews, and then also by the official bodies, but which is in fact Greater Serbia . . . The Freemason and Jewish France is already lying in the dust . . . Today, England and France, and Jewish democracy with them, have been completely defeated." He concluded his pamphlet by openly announcing measures that would follow the foundation of the Croatian state as he envisioned it: "In the Croatian state . . . Jews will not trade with all goods and with what the Croatian people hold sacred."[42] Only months later, in November, in a "message to the homeland," did he say that "Jews have been plundering the Croatian people for centuries, especially the little people . . . in the future, in the ISC, they will not be able to do this, because the Croatian economy and the education of youth will be in Croatian hands."[43] At the end of the year, in the brochure *What Pavelić's Croatian Ustashe Are Fighting For*, he proclaimed as hostile all the ideologies that he considered to be backed by Serbs, Jews, Communists, and the HSS (Croatian Peasant Party).[44] In the "New Year's Letter to the Croatian People," written "somewhere in Italy" on January 1, 1941, Pavelić did not mention the Jews, but in the anticipation of the victory of his ideas, he announced that "we shall have to pass through fire, blood, and violence, before the New Croatia is born."[45] The cult of the knife, and the obsession with blood and violence, soon reached the proportions of myth, creating fertile ground for the genocidal crimes of the ISC.

Ustasha ideas resounded in certain circles, especially among right-wing Croatian intellectuals, most of all in Zagreb. Right-wing students ("Frankists," who later mostly joined the Ustasha movement) gradually, in some places already by the mid-thirties, assumed leadership in various organizations, such as the August Šenoa Central Academic Society, later the Eugen Kvaternik Society, and in various professional faculty clubs. Starting in 1935–1936 and continuing in later years, graffiti appeared on Zagreb walls: *ŽAP—Živio Ante Pavelić* (Long Live Ante Pavelić).[46] At the end of 1937 and at the beginning of 1938, Ustasha supporters infiltrated other societies and institutions as well. They were active in Catholic organizations (Križari, Domagoj), and found supporters among the youth in Croatian Hero (*Hrvatski junak)* and at the University. Petar Milutin Kvaternik, brother of Slavko Kvaternik, was one of the heads of the Croatian Workingman (*Hrvatski Radiša).* Ustasha-oriented intellectuals also became increasingly influential in the central cultural institution Matica hrvatska, whose president, Filip Lukas, developed increasingly strong anti-Serb and anti-Communist views, and the Matica's magazine, *Hrvatska revija,* gradually renounced its earlier liberal orientation. Members of the August Šenoa Club, together with some members of the Ante Starčević

Cooperative, published illegal Ustasha papers under various names, which were immediately banned, and various right-wing groups at the university were also actively publishing.[47]

The escalation of anti-Semitic incidents and the increasingly pronounced anti-Semitic atmosphere in Croatia and Yugoslavia in the second half of the thirties were a prerequisite and indirect preparation for the genocide committed against the Jews in the ISC and in other parts of former Yugoslavia. Prewar anti-Semites found that the Ustasha regime and its policy provided an opportunity for fulfillment of their ideas. However, they were usually individuals or relatively small groups, not a widely organized social movement. Sometimes the promotion of anti-Semitism in a paper depended on the beliefs of the editor. While Joe Matošić edited and owned *Danica, Croatian Family Weekly for Town and Country,* there were expressions of sympathy for Hitler[48] and Mussolini, there was anti-Semitism, but there was no aggressive rabble-rousing. When Antun Pernić became editor in May 1938, the anti-Semitism in the paper gradually grew more and more aggressive.

Mile Budak, Jure Francetić, Josip Milković, Mladen Lorković, and others, later prominent officials of the Ustasha regime, returned to Croatia from exile in 1937 and 1938. The most influential among them, Budak, began to edit *Hrvatski narod* when he returned. The writing of this paper is a good example of how the stand of the Ustashe on the Jewish question changed and evolved.[49]

Hrvatski narod was a weekly for the better-informed and more educated readers. The editorial policy focused on opposition to the Belgrade regime (which indirectly grew into anti-Serbism), a clear anti-Communist position, and gentle criticism of the excessively "soft" policy of Vlatko Maček and his HSS. Obviously, Budak and his collaborators at *Hrvatski narod* refrained from fully presenting their real views in order to prevent the paper from being banned or incurring other problems (nonetheless, some issues were banned in 1940 and 1941). The editors made no secret of the fact that in the war that was already raging in Europe, their sympathies were on the side of the Axis Powers—"Fascism is not a sin."[50] The authors of articles expressed clear totalitarian predispositions: for example, Božidar Cerovski (1902–1947), who lived abroad at that time and returned to Croatia in 1941, wrote: "The interest of the individual must disappear before the interest of the whole!," which was no more than the Nazi code differently phrased: "Your people are everything, you are nothing."[51]

Jews also had their place within an ideological system of this kind, although anti-Semitism was not a key characteristic of the editorial policy of *Hrvatski narod* (as was the case with *Nezavisnost* or *Mlada Hrvatska*). Articles were printed showing the number of non-Croats in Croatian music institutions and at the Music Academy, pointing out that there many of these were Jews. There was special emphasis on the Jews being "foreigners." When the HSS won student elections at the Faculty of Forestry at Zagreb University, *Hrvatski narod* wrote that this was the result of "the help of international brigades," which was another name for Jewish voters. In the article "Several Thoughts on the Organization of Croatia," Budak wrote in favor of the well-being of the Croatian peasant. His condition was to be improved by creating a kind of ideal society based on Croatian rural values, which, of course, excluded the influence of foreigners. Budak wrote in horror that, allegedly, "the current commercial law has been written for converted and unconverted Jews, who call themselves businessmen but have never built anything anywhere, produced or created anything, not even a nickel, all they have done is increase the price of peasant produce." The paper also showed a double standard in reports from Palestine. When the Arabs were attacked, this was emphasized, but when the Jews were attacked, facts were ignored or only mentioned indirectly. Finally, news from Germany about the deportations of Jews was given without any commentary. The Jews were directly attacked for the first time in an article about the railway car factory in Slavonski Brod, whose workers were suffering because four Jews were allegedly exploiting them.[52]

Although *Hrvatski narod* expressed open dislike of the Jews, its writing did not veer into aggressive rhetoric. For example, the paper published an article about anti-Semitism from *Katolički tjednik* of Sarajevo, and added that it is a "fact that all effects have a cause, and this is also true of the anti-Semitic movement in nationalistic countries." *Katolički tjednik* had similar views as *Hrvatski narod*, so articles published there were happily reprinted. *Katolički tjednik* defined racist anti-Semitism as a "ruthless and violent reaction to an unscrupulous and unprincipled action [i.e., on the part of the Jews]."[53]

Hrvatska gruda, a weekly that began appearing in June 1940 (and only shared the name of its predecessor from 1936), had a similar profile to *Hrvatski narod*. It uncompromisingly supported what it considered were Croatian interests ("Croatia for the Croats!"), and fought against corruption.[54] It was against what it viewed as Serbian national interests, but in the first issues at least this did not turn into anti-Serb propaganda ("Provoking Croats in Dalmatia").[55] Gradually, as the war progressed, the editors sided more openly with the Axis Powers, and in July were already writing that "we Croats have always had close economic and cultural ties with the great German people, and we have also had good relations with the Italian people . . . ," and "All our national efforts at this moment can only be directed toward living in friendship . . . with our neighbors the Germans and the Italians." It is true that the editors sometimes distanced themselves from a general attack on the Jews: "We emphasize this Judeo-Zionist fabrication, but this is not the fault of other Jewish citizens, who themselves oppose the Zionist Jewish movement," although this was only an insignificant remark in a sea of anti-Jewish views.[56] The editors found the reasons for the "fall of the liberal capitalist economic system" in "Jewry, which was the main owner of major capital," and they advocated "a new type of state and social organization."[57] In the Middle Ages, "Jews engaged in an extensive amount of unethical activity . . . they oppressed miserable nations . . . sucked their blood," and the measures of the Hungarian kings and other medieval rulers against the Jews were completely logical and fully justified.[58] In another place, the editors attacked "Freemasonry" (but did not add the customary "Jews" in this context) which "caused so much evil to the Croatian people."[59] Consciously or not, they took over the Fascist-Nazi terminology: they wrote about the "living space the nation has created for itself"—a literal translation of Hitler's Lebensraum—and called this "the greatest wealth for which a nation is ready to make any kind of sacrifice."[60] "Capitalistic Judeo-Zionist Masonic lodges are to blame for today's war," or "the true guilty party for the war . . . is world capitalism that stands behind the democratic governments in England and the USA."[61]

In October, anti-Semitic attacks became more direct: "Most of the capital of the present economic system, forming an international, egotistical, and materialistic force, is today essentially grouped in the hands of international Jewry, and is one of the dangerous triad that enslaves peoples and states, creating economic hegemony over them."[62]

Both *Hrvatski narod* and *Hrvatska gruda* were printed at the Tipografija printing plant, which allegedly was owned by Jews.[63] Was this why neither paper was aggressively anti-Semitic? This can be accepted as part of the explanation, the other part being the wish of both editors to show their papers as middle-class, as "true Croatian publications" that were "fighting for the rights of man, Croats, and the Croatian homeland!"[64], but not to the detriment of other groups. This orientation of *Hrvatski narod* made German secret services suspect Budak of being ideologically incorrect. In a report from Zagreb to Berlin in 1941, the Gestapo wrote that "this also explains why Dr. Budak, in his recent speech in Karlovac, called National Socialism a ridiculous and pernicious movement."[65] The conclusions drawn by German intelligence, at least with respect to Budak's attitude toward the Jews, were somewhat hasty. At the same time, while he was pretending to be moderate in *Hrvatski narod,* Budak published the novel *The Blossoming Cherry Tree,* in which he clearly expressed anti-Semitic views: he wrote, for example, about "the stinking Jew Wetter who made no contribution . . . That dirty kike Wetter won't give a dime . . . He's plundered half of Croatia."[66]

The editorial policy of *Hrvatski narod* underwent a fundamental change after the establishment of the ISC. The paper became the main daily and the mouthpiece for the Ustasha regime. Articles about underhanded Jewish activities, "plots," "Freemasons," etc., of the kind in which the prewar extremist press abounded,[67] grew fewer and fewer and were replaced by systematic attacks and violent threats, ostensibly indirect but in fact a direct encouragement of genocidal crime. *Hrvatska gruda* lagged behind the speed and ferocity of *Hrvatski narod* only by a hair: the first anti-Semitic articles appeared on May 10 ("Jewish Incursion in the ISC," "The Dangerous Influence of the Worst Allied Triad: the English, Jewry, and the Freemasons"), and then the paper scrupulously reprinted all the anti-Semitic decrees and announcements.[68] However, the intensity of the anti-Semitic attacks in *Hrvatska gruda* never reached the level of those in other papers, nor did it use headlines to intensify the anti-Semitic campaign (although there were sometimes exceptions—for example, "Three Evils That Shall Be Completely Uprooted: Jewry, the English, and the Americans Are the Children of Satan and the Daughters of Israel").[69] Obviously, most of the credit for this restraint goes to the editor-in-chief, Ante Jedvaj, who saved some Jews from deportation in those months, and, it seems, unsuccessfully tried to save others, as well.[70]

In September 1940, the paper *Hrvatsko pravo* (which was full of anti-Semitic articles) published a letter allegedly written by a peasant, Stjepan Fuček from Đurđevac (110 kilometers. northeast of Zagreb). It contained sentences that provide a good insight into the views of people who would, several months later, either participate in or calmly watch the genocidal activities: "There are still people who turn their eyes to that 'glorious' Judeo-Masonic democracy, expecting it to save them. For every thinking person, it has become obvious in this war that democracy is totally rotten. It has helped the worst elements weave their way into the life of the people, and these are sucking their blood and plundering them . . . They acquired and are still acquiring immense fortunes, while the people go hungry . . . This evil has gained a foothold with us in Croatia, too . . . The Judeo-Masonic democracy has caused the present war, as well . . . The German people have risen and are smothering this poisonous serpent . . . God willing, soon it will be struck dead."[71]

PART II

SPRING AND SUMMER OF 1941

EXCOMMUNICATION

6

THE BEGINNING OF PERSECUTION

Public Incitement, the First Murders, and Plunder

In April 1941, a dark and tragic time began for many of the people living in the ISC, first and foremost the Jews. It is a period that is difficult to understand, even more difficult to explain, because the horrors that took place were so atrocious that anyone living at the end of the twentieth and the beginning of the twenty-first century finds it impossible to believe that such things could ever have happened. The rational approach of a historian may establish facts and the course of events, help understand circumstances; but it is left to the reader to explain to himself or herself what had in fact taken place, and why. Miroslav Krleža (1893–1981), probably the greatest Croatian writer of the twentieth century, wrote in 1945 that we would "need a new Shakespeare" to understand, at least in part, the immensity of the tragedies and the extent of the catastrophes that had befallen us. If we focus on the subject of this book, we must ask ourselves how it was possible for communities in which culture and civilization flourished—and Zagreb was undoubtedly one of them—to suddenly turn into scenes of mass crime and savagery? Or, to turn the question around, how was it possible for the otherwise traditionally cautious, even mistrusting, Jews to wait, as if deaf and blind, to be overtaken by mass death, despite the earlier warnings? In Zagreb, the full horror that was to come was presaged by the mass arrival of Jewish refugees from the Reich, which began in 1933 and increased after

1938. A year or two later, Zagreb and Croatian Jews were in flight or trying to escape, but for most of them the time of salvation had passed.

The generation that survived the Holocaust, and was already mature enough to understand all the horror of that event, did not have the need to offer any particular proof of what had happened. I belong to a newer generation, having been born thirteen years after the Second World War. What is necessary is the historian's scrupulous, professional approach, free of emotion and politically motivated allusions, an approach maximally based on simple facts. It is not enough to simply describe general trends. To help people understand what had happened, I believed that I had to show the fates of as many individuals as possible, so that individual tragedies could help in comprehending the terrible fate of all.

Anti-Jewish measures began to be implemented in Zagreb right after the establishment of the ISC, without a single day of respite. The speed with which they were put into effect and with which they quickly followed one another showed that they must have largely been planned and prepared in advance. German troops entered Zagreb on a Thursday afternoon, on April 10, and by the next morning, on Friday, April 11, the Gestapo had taken over the building of the Jewish Community at Palmotićeva Street 16. The treasury was sealed and the archives impounded. The money was never returned: 328,000 dinars in cash and about 500,000 dinars in bank deposits were taken. The plunder was confirmed in a document that the Gestapo pedantically handed over to the people in the Community, and which they signed.[1] Community officials were arrested at the same time (the former President Kon and his son, Chief Rabbi Schwarz, and his wife, main Community Secretary Klein and his wife, and two small children, and Chief Cantor Grüner and his wife and children) and so were the inhabitants of the building, about thirty of them. In a day or two, after the Gestapo had interrogated them, they were all released, although Klein was threatened with death on the spot; which was done in order to instill fear among the Jews.[2] The Gestapo moved into the building on Palmotićeva and remained there until October 1941, when a department of the ISC Ministry of Posts was moved there.[3]

In synchronization with the first German police measures against the Jews, the members of the German minority (the *Volksgruppe*) immediately started anti-Semitic activities and propaganda. In the first month of the ISC, they sometimes helped the Ustasha police arrest Jews, but their activities were mostly limited to Slavonia.[4] In Osijek, they published various papers—*Slawonischer Volksbote* (later *Grenzwacht*), *Neue Zeit, Volk am Pflug,* and others—which, like those published by the Ustashe, demanded the persecution of Jews.[5] On April 14, German youths set fire to the Osijek synagogue, and members of the German minority collected a "contribution" from the Osijek Jews and later took over Jewish shops.[6]

The Ustasha authorities began anti-Jewish activities only a day or two after the Germans. In the first days of the ISC this was mostly confined to plunder. First they broke into the Hevra Kaddisha building at Amruševa 8, and into the Community buildings in Petrinjska 7 and Amruševa 4.[7] The Hevra Kaddisha was ejected from its premises, as were other Jewish institutions. The sum of 400,000 dinars was taken from the Hevra Kaddisha treasury and another 500,000 dinars in bank deposits, about 300,000 dinars from the Keren Kayemeth treasury,[8] about 3,000,000 dinars from the EZRA (Aid) institute where Jews had deposited them.[9] In those days, plunder became so widespread that it slipped beyond the control of the authorities, so, on April 19, the *Doglavnik* (second in command) and Marshal Slavko Kvaternik announced that "Chetniks and various other thugs and bandits, calling themselves Ustashe, are entering houses and apartments and looting . . . I order the security forces to shoot such persons and looters on sight. I warn citizens that no one has the right to enter the homes of peaceful citizens without the proper approval of the legal authorities. I encourage citizens who are disturbed in this way by unauthorized persons to offer resistance on the spot."[10] This threat was obviously made to curb the arbitrary looting that had gone too far, but the plunder organized by the authorities continued systematically. In mid-May the Ministry of Transportation and Public Works moved into the house at Amruševa 8, which was owned by the Jewish Community.[11] At the same time the authorities began their planned activity of demanding a contribution in gold and other valuables.[12]

The first murder took place at the same time as the first robberies: immediately after the proclamation of the ISC on April 10, the Zagreb industrialist Artur Marić-Mayer, while trying to escape, was killed and robbed in Petrinja by his chauffeur of many years. While the motives for the murder are not completely clear; they were most likely primarily mercenary or to settle some kind of private score.[13] The factory owner Aleksandar Adler from Brod na Savi was killed between April 10 and 13, and later found with his throat cut in a wooded area beside the town. The circumstances and motives of the murder remained unknown.[14]

Only a day or two after arriving in Zagreb, the Gestapo arrested some fifty prominent Zagreb Jews and took them to Graz, where the center of the SD (Sicherheitsdienst) Einsatzgruppe for Yugoslavia was situated at that time. It seems that they were imprisoned in the Amtsgerichtsgefängnis court prison at Paulustorgasse 15. The arrestees included Hinko Gottlieb, poet and editor-in-chief of the Jewish cultural magazine *Omanut,* Aleksandar Licht, prominent attorney and Zionist leader, Lavoslav Šik, Judaic scholar, Dragutin Schwarz, prominent Zagreb surgeon, and members of the richest Zagreb Jewish families—Vlatko, Gustav and Robert Deutsch Maceljski, Slavko Mayer, and Branko Alexander. The attorney Pavao Fröhlich (1886) was also arrested; he was not a member of the Jewish Community but was a Freemason and declared himself a Yugoslav of the faith of Moses.[15] The Nazis interrogated them in detail about the Jews in the ISC.[16]

Josef Konforti's father-in-law Žiga Neumann was one of those arrested. With great persistence and with the help of good connections, the family managed to discover which prison he had been taken to. Konforti said, "We waited for hours in front of the prison entrance without knowing what to expect." When a truck appeared "they made a group of people get onto the truck. I recognized some of them, they were leading citizens. These were not young men capable of jumping into the truck, but middle-aged and elderly men. The soldiers forced them to climb up quickly and pushed them. Aleksandar Licht was one of the last to climb in . . . he climbed on the truck without losing any of his dignity. Both the soldiers and officials felt a kind of respect for him."[17]

Most of those imprisoned in Graz were released after a time, except for Mayer, who was never heard of again. Fröhlich's family got a letter dated January 14, signed by "Eng. V." (obviously one of the prisoners), saying that Fröhlich had been taken from the prison in Graz "in an unknown direction," but that he was "quite well" and that "there was no need at all to worry about him." The writer advised his wife Danica to take care of her health and of their small children, who were "so precious" for her husband. A month later, Fröhlich sent word from Dachau, but never again. It was not until September 1943, at the request of the Zagreb Chamber of Attorneys, that word arrived from Germany that he had died in Dachau on June 15, 1942, "of a weak heart and general weakness" and of "catarrh of the intestines."[18] Some of the Graz prisoners managed to escape and emigrate as soon as they returned, or not long thereafter, while others, like Lavoslav Šik, were later arrested again in Zagreb and then killed.[19] After that, until the spring of 1942, the Germans did not directly interfere in affairs concerning the Jews in the ISC. The Ustasha authorities ran everything independently, but nevertheless there was constant consultation between the Ustasha Security Service UNS and the offices of the SD (Sicherheitsdienst—Security Service) and the Gestapo in the ISC.

These first events frightened and horrified the members of the Jewish community. People were disorganized and disoriented, everybody reacting in the way that seemed best to him or her. Some simply stopped working, and closed their shops and businesses. This worried some of their non-Jewish employees, and on April 17, several trade-union groups of office workers and other employees held an urgent meeting to find a solution for people who were losing their jobs because of this.[20]

Some Jewish merchants thought that they should express loyalty to the new regime, but their attempts ended in failure. On April 16, *Hrvatski narod* published the warning that "it has come to our notice that some Jewish shops in the city center are placing swastikas in their shop windows. This is insolence . . . and will certainly not bring the desired benefit to their owners." The next day, "all Jewish shops are warned to immediately remove Croatian flags and flags of the German Reich from their shop windows . . . because all who are caught in this dishonorable activity will be subject to the gravest penalties."[21] Finally, regulations of April 30 prohibited such activities by law.

As soon as the ISC was created, anti-Jewish propaganda in the media and at public engagements became politically desirable behavior. Almost every day, texts threatening what would happen to the Jews were published. On April 20, the leading paper in the new state, *Hrvatski narod,* under the headline "The strictest measures must be taken against the Jews," reprinted the text of April 17 from *Deutsche Zeitung in Kroatien,* which ended with the words: "Without a solution to the Jewish question there will be no final peace in the southeast area. And it is also certain that these measures can never be severe enough."[22] Andrija Artuković, the new Minister of the Interior, was quoted in the *Deutsche Zeitung in Kroatien* to the effect that the ISC government would "soon solve the Jewish question in the same way that the German government has solved it," emphasizing that they would "act just as vigorously to make sure that racial laws are strictly applied as soon as possible."[23] At the end of April 1941, *Hrvatski radnik* wrote that "enemy blood that is foreign to Croatian blood runs in Jewish veins . . . The Croatian people must unite and together cast off the authority and influence of Serbs, Jews, and Marxists."[24] Only a day or two later, *Hrvatski narod,* writing about Jews and "Gypsies," claimed that "the will for self-preservation demands that the people of every state precisely define their relations with foreign racial communities, and especially with those that came as guests and passers-through, for short periods of time, and in many ways fatefully and negatively influenced the destiny of the people."[25] Hardly had three days passed from this text in *Hrvatski narod* when Pavelić himself made things completely clear in the same paper: "The Jewish question will be radically solved on the basis of racial and economic lines."[26] *Hrvatski radnik* was one of the most vitriolic leaders of hate-speech in its anti-Semitic rhetoric: in mid-May 1941, it published a text entitled "Throughout history the Jews have been considered the enemies of every people," saying among other things that "the Jew has nothing noble in him, nothing elevated . . . when the Jew penetrates or moves among Aryan peoples, his destructive influence is immediately felt," and it concluded with what was the most direct threat made by the Ustashe in print, that "no measures that are taken against the Jews can be inhuman, if we compare them with the immeasurable evil that Jewry has created in the world."[27] Similar statements appeared just as often during the next weeks and months. In the first issue of the renewed *Ustaša, The Herald of the Ustasha Movement for Croatian Liberation,* which came out on May 22, an article entitled "What the Poglavnik is doing . . ." said,

> For centuries the Jews have been sucking the blood of the Croatian people, for centuries they have mercilessly plundered and grabbed the Croatian national wealth. They have turned our lovely Croatian towns into little 'Jerusalims,' they have created harems in our Croatian houses where they have dishonored our Croatian daughters. No one dared put an end to this, and, what is more, so-called leaders cooperated with this group of leeches. Today this has come to an end. In one month, the Poglavnik has established everything necessary to throw the Jews out of the Croatian temple. The Jews are no longer masters in Croatia.[28]

In the next issue of *Ustaša,* three weeks later, in an article entitled "In the Ustasha State things must be done in the Ustasha Way," it said, "Yellow notices have appeared in the streets . . . Ustasha commissioners can be seen in various shops . . . no more hooked noses appear in coffeehouses . . . our peasant maidens are no longer slave-girls in the harems of various Grünhuts and Scheyers . . . there are no more Jewish 'ladies' with décolletés and painted in all colors in the centers of towns and on public promenades. The air seems to be cleaner, the lungs freer, the people have straightened their backs." This part of the text ends with threats that are by no means veiled: "No defiance will help the Jews, no so-called pride, no awakening, no pact-making with the Communists . . . The Ustasha hand reaches and will reach everywhere, wherever necessary." The unsigned author of the article even claims that this "hand will reach . . . anyone who defends the Jews and other enemies of the Croatian people. Let no one doubt this!"[29] At the beginning of June, *Hrvatski narod* wrote that the final goal of the Aryan state was "to get rid of the non-Aryan element, especially the Jews."[30]

The Jews were accused of all sorts of social evils: of "forcible abortions," of the fact that this "criminal business of destroying Croatian generations had taken root," and the guilty were found "mostly among Jews and other foreigners" who were "killing Croatian children with extreme lack of conscience and for purely selfish motives" and in doing so making immense amounts of money.[31]

The public harassment was becoming increasingly unbearable. On May 11 alone, the influential paper *Novi list* published seven articles exclusively about the Jews (other texts also mentioned Jews, but this was not their central subject), on May 13 the same paper published nine such articles, on May 14, six articles, on May 16, seven, on May 17, ten, and on May 18, eight. Therefore, one paper, in a mere six days, published a total of forty-seven such articles, or an average of eight a day! The incendiary tone was immediately obvious in the titles, for example on May 16 these were: "London rabble-rousers and the Jewish clique in Washington are equally guilty for the war," "5,000 Jews arrested in Paris," "Jews and English flee from Palestine," "List of pure-blooded Jews in Zagreb completed," "Legal intercession for Jews prohibited," "Ordinances of the Police Directorate in Sarajevo concerning the movement of Jews," and "Jews help rebels." The list compiled after 1945 for the needs of the State Commission for War Crimes, which is kept in the Croatian State Archives, recorded that in 1941 there were 367 ideological-incendiary anti-Semitic contributions in *Hrvatski narod* and *Novi list* alone, there were 123 such contributions in 1942, 74 in 1943, 20 in 1944, and "only" 5 in 1945.[32] This is a total of 589 contributions, and even this number is not complete for these two papers. According to this statistic, almost two-thirds of the anti-Semitic contributions (62.3 percent) were published in the first ten months of the ISC, and another 20.9 percent were published in the next year. It is understandable that the anti-Semitic charge of the media weakened as the war drew to its end—the "Jewish" problem had mostly been solved, and in time the

Ustasha regime had far more dangerous enemies to face, especially Tito's Partisans and their allies.

An important link in the well-organized and interwoven fanning of an incendiary atmosphere was to have taken place in the Maksimir Stadium (on the eastern side of town), where compulsory gymnastic exercise for secondary-school students was organized as of the beginning of May. During one of these sessions, Zdenko Blažeković, at that time an official of the University Ustasha Office in Zagreb, gave a speech that was "from beginning to end inflammatory against Serb and Jewish youth, and he invited all the Serbs and Jews present to move over and form a group on the opposite side of the stadium." This was a surprise for the young people present, but the Serbs and Jews were "followed to the other side first by members of the League of Communist Youth (SKOJ members), and then all the others."[33] This was, without a doubt, the clearest expression of solidarity with the Serbs and the Jews at that time in Zagreb and Croatia. Those who were there at the stadium, in testimony given at the end of the twentieth century, agreed that few people paid heed to Blažeković—everyone kept on talking, some even made a noise. Thus, even those who wanted to listen to him could not do so without difficulty, because the loudspeaker system was bad. When the order came for the Serbs and the Jews to move to the other side, "for a time people were indecisive, and then there was a general commotion."[34] Branko Polić said to his classmates, "I don't want any trouble, I'm going to the other side." Many from his class answered, "If you're going, so are we all."[35] "The children were tired, they reacted spontaneously." Some of the participants did not understand that individuals and groups were crossing to one side, and that others were following them; it seemed to them that "they had all fused together."[36] Branko Polić says that his class was near the exit to the stadium: "As we were at the side, we could see the commotion and we left the stadium without crossing over to the other side."[37] This ended the gymnastics session, and students went home although the program was supposed to go on.[38] From whatever angle we view the events in Maksimir Stadium, the Ustasha regime was shamed and their intention to drive a wedge between the students failed, although it had been carefully planned. But, as with so many times later incidents, public harassment was only the first stage in implementing a far-reaching plan. The very next day, on May 27, according to an prior arrangement, a group of 165 young Zagreb Jews were reported to the police and arrested. Ostensibly they were "going to do communal work," but in fact they left on a trip of no return.

Many anti-Semitic pamphlets were published with the direct or indirect support of the state. One of them came out in Osijek, written by a certain "St. Gabrijel" and entitled *The Kike and the Talmud or the Greatest Enemy of All the Non-Jews.*[39] It claimed that "Europe is being renewed. In this renewal, one of the main problems is to get rid of the Jewish question, which will be solved when the last Jew is gone from Europe." Then it concluded that "the Jews will soon disappear, because the providential swastika will swiftly mow them down, as can be seen on the title page."

Several Ustasha ministers competed in speaking out against the Jews (and also the Serbs) with virulence and hatred. On July 27 in Donji Miholjac, Foreign Minister Mladen Lorković said that "the Croatian people must cleanse themselves of all elements that are a calamity for them, elements that are foreign and alien to them, who corrode the healthy forces of the Croats, who have for decades pushed them from one evil into another. These are our Serbs and our Jews." Milovan Žanić, Minister-President of the Legislative Commission, spoke at a rally in Daruvar: "We Ustashe always said that heads will roll, the heads of those who are in our way, because we are now creating history for centuries and centuries to come." Aleksandar Seitz, chief secretary in the Prime Minister's office, told his listeners at a rally in Dugo Selo "Not to fear: the Serbs will never be back, nor will the Jews, nor will those who served them. There can be no more Serbs and Jews, there will be no more of them because the Croatian army and the Croatian Ustashe guarantee this."[40]

Pavelić and his close associates gave the tone that other members of the regime accepted, and which various papers followed. Anti-Jewish rhetoric became a normal form of public communication. On June 15 the Zagreb paper *Novi list* claimed in the article "The Croatian State—a guarantee of our national well-being" that the "Jews did not have any feeling or understanding for our Croatian needs, which is understandable because, although they live in Croatia, they remain on the fringes of the struggle and goals of the Croatian people in both mentality and feeling. For the Jews, Croatia was an object of exploitation, and that is how they behaved toward the Croatian people . . . Nothing can stand against the measures that must be undertaken to drive the Jews into their natural economic borders, allowing the Croat to become economic master in his own country."[41] *Novi list* also printed the lecture given in Zagreb by Vjekoslav Blaškov, Ustasha commissioner of the Zagreb Workers' Chamber, about the role of Jews in the relations between workers and capitalists. Blaškov demanded that the ISC be cleansed of foreigners, and speaking of the Jews he said, "It is they who have always been considered enemies of human society. There is no people in history among whom the Jews lived, which did not react against them."[42]

During those early months, in the spring of 1941, a lively song with a very attractive and catchy tune could be heard in Zagreb, in the very town center, in front of the synagogue on Praška Street and on Zrinjevac Square: "Zagreb is not a Jewish town, a Jewish town, a Jewish town, Zagreb is an Ustasha town, an Ustasha town, an Ustasha town, out with them, we won't have them."[43]

In the summer of 1941, about fifty former volunteers from the Spanish Civil War, who had returned to Yugoslavia through underground channels via France and Germany to organize a rebellion, passed through Zagreb with forged papers. These included Velimir Drechsler (whose nom de guerre when he joined the Communist Party was Marko Perić), who gave a very somber account of Zagreb in his memoirs. He conjured up an atmosphere of fear and mistrust, and mentioned meetings with Jewish friends who were wearing the yellow star, among them his mother whom he had not seen for many years.[44] Soon after he left to join the Partisans, his mother, Helena, was deported and ended her life in the Đakovo camp in 1942.[45] Similarly, some other of Drechsler's friends who were still in Zagreb hesitated and wondered whether to flee or not and whether there was still time to escape.

7

LEGAL DISCRIMINATION

The Third Reich as a Model

Anti-Jewish legal regulations were enacted parallel with the media campaign. During the first several weeks of the ISC, many anti-Jewish laws were passed and ordinances issued with few or no delays, turning the Jews initially into second-class citizens, and soon thereafter into a national and religious group that was completely stripped of its legal rights.

The Legal Provision for the Defense of the People and State, of April 17, was the foundation stone of an entire legal system that endorsed terror and defined the state institutions that were to implement it. It provided that anyone "who in any way violates or has violated the honor and vital interests of the Croatian people, or has in any way threatened the survival of the ISC or the state authorities, even if this act is no more than an attempt, is guilty of high treason" and "whoever is guilty of the crime in Point 1 shall be punished by death."[1] This legal provision also called for the foundation of "extraordinary people's courts," which in a legal provision of May 17 grew into summary courts. The Legal Provision on Summary Courts provided for only one sentence—death: "If the defendant is found guilty, the summary court shall sentence him to death by shooting. No legal remedy is permitted (against this sentence), and an appeal for a reprieve shall not have the power to stay the sentence." The sentence was to be carried out "within three hours after it was pronounced."[2] In December

1941, a legal provision was passed whereby "in less serious cases, the court may instead of a death sentence pronounce a sentence of imprisonment for no shorter than three years" (but even these "three-year prisoners" were deported to camps where many were killed).[3] The summary court that had jurisdiction in the area of the Zagreb court was proclaimed on May 27.[4] In the beginning, most of the victims of summary courts were Jews and Serbs, in protection of the "honor and interests of the Croatian people," but soon all who expressed any kind of dissatisfaction with the Ustasha regime were tried, as well as anyone suspected of Communist-party membership. The legal provisions of July 5 and 10 greatly extended and specified the list of transgressions subject to trial by summary court, including anyone "who in writing, printing, publishing, or circulating books or papers" denigrates the current order, speaks against the ISC, the Poglavnik, spreads communist propaganda, etc. Also, anyone who listens to banned radio stations (the first and foremost the BBC), or who spreads any news from banned radio stations.[5] Records in the Ministry of Justice and Religious Affairs refer only to cases that were not "solved" immediately, or those that in various ways entered the procedure of reprieve. There are more than one hundred of them, mostly from the later years of the ISC, and not a single one refers to Jewish prisoners. Jewish cases were solved by the Ministry of the Interior and some UNS services. Usually Jews were not even sent to the prisons under the Ministry of Justice and Religious Affairs, but to one of the camps administered by other services.[6]

In the first week after Ustasha rule was established, on April 18, the Legal Provision on Preserving Croatian National Property was passed, which annulled all legal contracts that had been made between Jews, or between Jews and other persons, in the two months before the ISC was proclaimed. Anticipating difficult times, some Jews had, in fact or in name only, sold their property or given it away to save at least some money or other kinds of property, which was forbidden by this legal provision.[7] On the following day, a provision was passed assigning commissioners to all Jewish firms. *Hrvatski narod* reported on this and similar measures aggressively, under titles such as "Passing urgent measures for Jewish firms," "Legal provisions concerning Jews," etc.[8] At this time, as a kind of informal pressure, notices appeared on some shops: "No Jews," "Jews Undesirable," "Aryan Shop—Jews Not Welcome."[9] The French Consul, G. Gueyraud, informed his government that diplomats in Zagreb took an extremely negative view of these developments.[10] This kind of pressure was already proving unbearable for some Jews, and Žiga Štern (Stern), owner of a leather factory and one of the richest Jews in Zagreb, committed suicide on April 21.[11] Around the same time, two women from the most distinguished Zagreb families also killed themselves: Jelka Benedik, née Deutsch-Maceljski, and Zlata Wolf, née Granitz.[12]

On April 30, the official gazette *Narodne novine* published three crucial anti-Jewish legal provisions at the same time, which effectively put Jews into a category outside the law, which exposed them to any kind of discrimination and stripped them of any legal or social protections: the Legal Provision on Racial Affiliation, the Legal Provision on the Protection of Aryan Blood and the Honor of the Croatian People, and the Legal Provision on Citizenship. The Legal Provision on Racial Affiliation defined who was of "Aryan" and who of "non-Aryan" descent. Jews were defined as "persons who have at least three ancestors twice removed (grandfathers and grandmothers) of the Jewish race. Grandfathers and grandmothers shall be considered Jewish if they are of the faith of Moses or if they were born in that faith." As for persons who had "two ancestors twice removed who are Jews by race," they were to be considered Jews if they belonged to the "faith of Moses" or if they had a "spouse who is a Jew," and if the "Ministry of the Interior, after considering a substantiated proposal of the Racial Political Commission, decides that they are to be regarded as Jews."[13] These provisions were not as complete in defining the term "Jew" as were the Nazis' Nuremberg Laws and Provisions that were later passed in Germany.[14] Exceptions were provided for, so that "the head of this state may, outside the provisions of this law, accord all the rights belonging to persons of Aryan descent to such persons who, before April 10, 1941 [the day when the ISC was founded], showed merit for the Croatian people, especially for their liberation, and these rights will also extend to their spouses and the offspring of such a marriage." Despite the "mildness" of the Ustasha provisions, on May 3 the German Ambassador, Sigfried Kasche, reported to Berlin that some "legal provisions deserve attention and recognition," in the first place those "about citizenship, Jews, and the protection of the blood (well harmonized with German legal regulations)."[15]

The separate Legal Provision on the Protection of Aryan Blood and the Honor of the Croatian People, which was passed on the same day, prohibited marriage between Jews and other persons of "non-Aryan" descent with persons of "Aryan" descent. It is true that Point 2 made it possible to apply for a "special marriage license" that could be issued by the "Ministry of the Interior after hearing the Racial Political Commission," but the number of such cases to reach the attention of the Ustasha administration was relatively small and was always refused.[16] The Roman Catholic Franjo Krajcar (1914), a locksmith's assistant, said that he had met the Jew Edita Schwabenitz (1924) "two years ago, and in time we grew to love one another so much that we cannot live without each other, so we decided to enter into holy matrimony and wed according to the rite of the Roman Catholic faith." They applied for a marriage license in August 1941. Branko Rukavina, commissioner in the Ustasha Head Office and a high official in the UNS, supported the application ("I know Krajcar to be an honest and conscientious Croat"). However, in October, Krajcar "withdrew his application." In June 1942, Krajcar requested that Edita and her mother Ilonka be released from a camp, but this request was not met. Ilonka allegedly ended her days in Đakovo, and Edita in an unknown place.[17] Nevertheless, there were some happy cases: in June 1942, Katarina Hollenberger, dressmaker, requested that her husband Josip, whom she had married in 1910, be declared officially dead because he had disappeared during the First World War on the Galician Front. She wanted to marry the Roman Catholic Franjo Oković in the Catholic Church, as she had been living with him since 1922. It seems that Katarina survived the war but she no longer appears in the documents of the Jewish Community, either under her old or her new surname.[18]

The same legal provisions prohibited Jews from having "extramarital sexual relations . . . with a female person of Aryan origin." The sentence for this was "imprisonment . . . in especially grave cases, especially in cases of raping a virgin, a death sentence could be pronounced." The authorities acted on these provisions very promptly—in July, Mirko Bihler (1885) and Ivka Magdić (1897) were arrested in Osijek "on suspicion of sexual relations between a Jewish man and Aryan woman."[19] In November, the traveling summary court sentenced Oskar Weiss to execution by firing squad because he "many times, to satisfy his physical lust, publicly undertook lewd acts in preparation to rape a fourteen-year-old and a fifteen-year-old girl, both of the Aryan race."[20]

Finally, the legal provisions "on the protection of Aryan blood and the honor of the Croatian people" prohibited Jews from employing an Aryan woman younger than forty-five (which was later elaborated in more detail in a separate legal provision), from hanging out "the Croatian state and national flag," or showing "Croatian national colors and emblems."[21] Several days later, *Hrvatski narod* wrote that "this legal provision was based on the German one . . . the German law mentions *deutsches oder artverwandtes Blut,* the Italian law *razza italiana,*" but instead of the term "blood" an expression much better suited to Croatian circumstances is used—"Aryan descent."[22]

The Legal Provision on Citizenship rounded off discrimination against the Jews. Point 2 of this provision defined who was a citizen of the ISC: "Only a person of Aryan descent who, by his behavior, has proved that he did not work against the desire for liberation of the Croatian people and who is willing to readily and faithfully serve the Croatian people and the ISC." Point 1 of the same provision stipulates that "a member of the state is a person who is under the protection of the ISC." In other words, a person who was not of "Aryan descent," i.e., a Jew or a Roma, could not be a "member of the state," was not "under the protection of the ISC," and was therefore outside any kind of protection and law, and exposed to any kind of arbitrariness and persecution. The formulation of Point 2 paved the way for persecution of all kinds against the non-Jewish population as well, which soon began to take place.[23]

Finding themselves in this position, Jews could not even help themselves by converting to Catholicism, as Serbs could, because the position of Jews was clearly defined by the provision on racial affiliation. *Hrvatski narod* gave a very precise explanation: "When we speak about Jews we do not mean members of the faith of Moses, but members of the Jewish racial community, because it is not religion that makes the essence of the Jewish community but their racial structure and biological heritage from the distant past . . . A baptismal certificate is not required because of religion. A baptismal certificate is the surest criterion that someone's grandfathers and grandmothers, ancestors twice removed, were members of the Aryan racial community, because at the time of our grandfathers Jews hardly mixed with Aryans at all."[24] The legislative bodies and the top Ustasha authorities never had any doubts on this point, but doubts obviously arose on the lower levels of authority. Thus, the Public Order and Security Directorate, in its ordinance of July 8, 1941, demanded that all "undesirable persons" who are "Greek-Easterners and Jews" should be transported "to Gospić," and specified that this also referred to Jews "who converted to the Catholic religion after April 10, 1941."[25] About twenty days later, on July 30, the Directorate repeated, with minor changes, that "in the interest of public security all Jews (converted or not) . . . and those imprisoned under suspicion of communism . . . are to be sent to the transit camp in Gospić."[26] It must be taken into account that the accusation of "communism" was made very easily at that time, and anyone could be so labeled practically without any proof.

On May 3, the Legal Provision on Conversion from One Religion to

Another was passed, which made it almost impossible to convert from the Jewish religion to Catholicism or Islam (all earlier legal regulations about the way of changing from one religion to another were abolished).[27] Also, the conversion of entire families from the faith of Moses to the Roman Catholic or Muslim faith did not mean that they were recognized as Aryans, and this right was withheld even from children whose parents or grandparents had done this earlier. These provisions were reconfirmed on July 3 in a circular saying that the conversion of Jews to Catholicism or Islam does not mean exemption from the Law on Racial Affiliation.

Exactly one month after the establishment of the ISC, on May 10, the ISC radio station and the state papers published the order of the Jewish Section of the Ustasha Police Directorate, that all "pure-blooded Jewish males from sixteen to sixty must report to the office of the Ustasha Police" in Bogovićeva Street by May 14.[28] In the meantime, "the registration of all pure-blooded Jews in Zagreb had been completed." On this basis, the Jewish Section of the Ustasha Police issued 3,500 documents called Jewish Identity Cards. Ezra Levi got number 393, Cezar Gaon was 3,182, Dragutin Rosenberg 3,494, Josip Abraham 124, Aleksandar Klein 1,914, etc. At the same time the Jews also had to register their property.[29]

On May 25, *Deutsche Zeitung in Kroatien* expressed the opinion of German political circles and representatives in Zagreb that the anti-Jewish measures undertaken by the ISC authorities to date should be commended, but they at the same time hoped that others would follow. The article concludes: "The Croatian people will not become independent until they solve the most urgent question of all—that of the Jews."[30]

In the following weeks, anti-Jewish legal provisions and other measures followed each other at such a rate that the victims had no time to recover from one blow before another, even more deadly, followed. "Jewish laws . . . had the purpose of finally destroying Jewry both materially and morally. People could not get their bearings about the direction in which this anti-Jewish policy was leading before Jews began to be herded into camps and the criminal plunder of everything that Jews owned was organized," says the report of the president of the Jewish Community, Glücksthal, written in July 1945.[31]

The noose was pulled tight gradually, but relatively quickly. After the accelerated passage of laws, the time came when Jews began to submit requests to be granted Aryan rights, to be freed from wearing the yellow insignia, etc., whose favorable solution could mean the applicant's return among citizens with all rights. However, in many cases, a paper of this kind meant nothing: the authorities could "temporarily" (for a month, three months, and so on) free the applicant from wearing the Jewish insignia. When this time passed, people were left to the mercy of the Ustasha Police and many fared badly. Even a temporary guarantee that they would not be evicted from their apartments, lasting for only several weeks, could be withdrawn, or some other institution could initiate the eviction. Finally, many who had "acquired Aryan rights" or were under "protection" of some other kind got caught up in one of the many roundups and were deported to a camp and killed there.

In comparison with the rest of Croatia and the whole of the ISC, in Zagreb the organization and implementation of anti-Jewish measures was of particular importance. Almost one third of all the Jews in the ISC lived in Zagreb, and the Zagreb community was absolutely and relatively much richer than the other Jewish communities in the ISC. Thus, Zagreb was the best testing-ground for the anti-Jewish aims of the Ustasha regime. Although the plans were carried out with the most precision in Zagreb, this did not preclude a lot of poor organization, improvising, contradictory orders, and arbitrary behavior. However, it seems that the authorities were fully aware of these instances of arbitrary behavior and even encouraged them, so as to make it almost impossible for the Jews to do anything. The separate instances of violence, the arbitrary behavior of individual Ustasha officials or ordinary Ustashe, did not result only from primitivism and the desire for plunder, but also from Pavelić's and Artuković's ambition to show themselves to the Germans as "more Nazi than the Führer." All the activities, whether directed against an individual or against hundreds of people, whether carefully organized or improvised, had the same goal: their purpose was to rob the Jews of all their possessions and then to kill as many of them as they could, and for this to cause as little public reaction as possible.

The genocidal "cleansing of the area" of Serbs had been prepared in advance, and later the more systematic persecution of the Jews was added to this, based on newly passed laws. In the spring and summer of 1941, people were killed *en masse* in many Serb villages, almost on their front doorsteps, usually without any effort to legally justify this in any way, but the Jewish genocide took place more gradually and rationally, in several stages. The model had obviously been found in the Nazi method that planned a phase of excommunication, an intermediary phase of concentration, and a final phase of extermination. The Ustasha regime began to carry out this last phase, the phase of the extermination of the Jews, as early as the summer of 1941. At that time, there were already death camps in Jadovno and on the island of Pag; by September, the Jasenovac camp began to be organized, and in Zagreb groups of Jewish hostages were shot during these months. It took the Nazis eight years to pass from the phase of excommunication to the phase of extermination (1933–1941), but the Ustasha authorities did this in less than four months (April–July 1941). There is no doubt that this did not take place only under the general influence of Third Reich policy, which the Ustasha ISC tried to follow in many things, but was also the result of direct German advice, which later became demands. Nevertheless, during this whole time, the Ustashas did a lot on their own initiative and much of their behavior was arbitrary.

8

WEARING THE JEWISH INSIGNIA

The only anti-Jewish measure introduced in the ISC before it was introduced in the Third Reich was the required wearing of the Jewish insignia. In some parts of the ISC, this began as early as the end of April, in others in May. Local Ustasha bodies decided what the insignias should look like, so they were not the same throughout the ISC.

A decree of May 22 ordered all Jews in Zagreb to wear the Jewish insignia. This at first consisted of two patches of yellow material of approximately five inches by three inches; one was to be worn on the left side of the chest, the other on the left side of the back. In the middle of each patch was the large black letter "Ž" (for *Židov* = Jew). How carefully the implementation of this decree had been planned can be seen from the fact that on May 16, six days before the decree was proclaimed, the Jewish Section approved "the purchase of 125 meters of ordinary yellow linen for the needs of the Jewish Religious Community,"[1] obviously for making the insignias.

To obtain a piece of fabric, all Jews had to report "for supervision" in alphabetical order between May 23 and 28 to the Ustasha Commission–Jewish Section at Bogovićeva Street 7.[2] The announcement said that "all Aryans must report any Jewish man or woman who does not obey this summons . . . to the Ustasha Police Commission." The final provisions were the usual: "Whoever does not answer the summons and does not wear the insignia in the prescribed place will be most severely punished." A day later, *Hrvatski narod* once more confirmed that "any Jewish man or woman who refuses to wear this insignia will be most severely punished."[3] In this way, the Ustashe indirectly admitted that they were not sure whether the provision about wearing the insignia would be consistently implemented. And, in fact, a lot of people did not obey. This was confirmed by the authorities themselves: in those days, while the Zagreb Jews were picking up the insignias, *Hrvatski narod* carried the warning from the Jewish Section that all Jews covered by the obligation to wear "the Jewish insignia, are obliged to wear it . . . It has been noticed that some Jews who picked up the insignias do not wear them. The most severe proceedings will be undertaken against them."[4] Glücksthal, the president of the Jewish Religious Community in 1945, said that the purpose of this insignia was to make the Jews "look ridiculous and make them an object of scorn, but it must be admitted that, despite all the animosity that some people felt [toward them], this attempt by the Ustashe was not fully successful."[5] The Gestapo report written in May 1942 also claims that "this measure had an effect contrary to what had been expected: there are innumerable cases when Jews who were wearing the insignia on the street or in the streetcar were approached by completely unknown people from all walks of life (citizens, peasants, even German officers and soldiers) who expressed sympathy. What is more, many Jews, especially old women and children, had their insignias removed by non-Jews."[6] Eugenio Coselschi, head of the Italian mission in Zagreb, also felt that the Croatian public was against this procedure, and that allegedly "even the Poglavnik" does not like the decree about the yellow star.[7] Berta Israel said that, in the first months after the decree was passed, the insignias had to be worn; after that, as the number of Jews in the city rapidly decreased, people, even the police, cared less whether Jews were wearing the insignia or not. Besides, no more arrests were being made in the streets.[8] Vera Fischer said that she did not wear the insignia: "I believe that there were more of us, because it was more dangerous to walk about wearing it than to disobey."[9] Some people attached the insignia to their coats, but held the coats over their arms.[10]

However, this could be very risky. Ljerka Magdić (from a mixed marriage, so she was not obliged to wear the Jewish insignia) was walking in town with her cousin Nada Weiss, who had the yellow insignia on the fur collar of her coat, but had clumsily covered it with her handbag. A young Ustasha in uniform came up to them, hit Nada roughly on the arm and said, "Move that bag, kike, and get off the sidewalk where you don't belong. Walk on the road!" The cousins had to do as he said.[11] Some fared even worse: the Požega merchant Vilko Braum was arrested for being on a train without the insignia, which he was hiding in the pocket of his spring coat.[12] In June 1941, a friend was helping Ida Roger-Schwarz to fasten the yellow band on her back in the street, when a police agent came up and took her to the police station in Petrinjska Street, where she remained for three days. After that, all her things were returned to her, but not the 7,000 dinars of her savings that had been so difficult to come by. She was told that she had to pay a fine of 5,000 dinars, although other people said that they had been fined 200 to 500 kunas. Ida did not survive the war.[13]

Wearing the insignia was a stigma that many people found difficult to bear. In the request to free him from wearing the Jewish insignia, Leopold Müller stated that this was a "brand of shame."[14] Many Croats understood this: Petar Grgec, Catholic writer and publicist, professor at the Archbishopric Classical Grammar School, in the winter of 1941–1942, took his hat off in the street to unknown Jews who were wearing the insignia. When his daughter asked him whether he knew those people, he answered that she could not understand "how much these people are suffering and how humiliated they are. When I pass them and that shameful mark, I feel a deep respect for their suffering and for those brave people." It is paradoxical and really sad that after 1945 this man was persecuted.[15]

It seems that some Jews who lived on the outskirts of Zagreb thought that the strict order to wear the insignia would not be consistently implemented. The local Ustasha organization informed the Jewish Section that there were a total of 153 Jews obliged to wear the insignia in the municipalities of the Zagreb District (Vrapče 18, Stupnik 7, Remete 2, Šestine 7, Brdovec 7, Kustošija 82, Sesvete 7, Stenjevec 23).[16] A report from Pisarovina shows that it had 12 "home" Jews and 34 émigrés.[17]

Since the racial criterion was decisive in deciding who had to wear the insignia, the first local regulations laid down that even babies had to be marked and baby carriages with the insignia could be seen in the streets. Even nuns and Catholic priests who were Jews by race had to pick up the insignias.[18] Vladko Maček himself claimed that he "did not see it with his own eyes, but had heard from eyewitnesses that even a nun who had been born Jewish had to wear the yellow patch on her habit on her way to church."[19]

The criteria for exemption from wearing the insignia, like the criteria for being granted Aryan rights, were very elastic. For example, Jakob Grünwald's application was refused although he had been decorated for courage in the First World War.[20] The request for exemption from wearing the insignia and for keeping his apartment, submitted by Mavro Löwenstein, an 80 percent war invalid (from the First World War), a lieutenant without an arm and a kidney, was "set aside." Whether this was done when the applicant had already been deported or not does not make much difference, because we do not know where Mavro Löwenstein ended.[21] Branko Fürst applied in December 1941 to not wear the insignia because his firm had been "Aryanized" and he had been told that his "further employment there would be impossible if he wore the Jewish insignia." How the request was resolved is not known, but Branko survived the war.[22] Mira Gostl was exempted from wearing the insignia at the request of the "sworn Ustasha" Stjepan Baričević, who, in May 1942, asked that she should remain in the former shop of Vjekoslav Gostl in Vlaška Street 33. Mira Gostl survived the war, but her father, Vjekoslav, was killed in Jasenovac.[23]

In spite of everything, a sense of humor could still be felt: there was a joke about the Jewish insignia among the Jews in Zagreb—the two letters "Ž," people said, were in fact short for *Žanićeva žena* (i.e., "Žanić's wife," referring to the wife of Minister Milovan Žanić, who was of Jewish origin: Alma, née Stöger).[24] A report of the Jewish Section gives another angle: it attacks Jews for making jokes about the Jewish insignia and "interpreting it as meaning 'Long live David's Star' (*Davidova zvijezda–živila*)."[25] At the end of May, the Intelligence Office informed the Jewish Section that "some Jews have even been noticed wearing these insignias with pride . . . and some even wear various kinds of decorations under them, which they got in the Austro-Hungarian army."[26]

As the days went by, there were fewer and fewer reasons for joking: on June 4, a new phase began when the patches started being replaced by a yellow badge.[27] Wearing this insignia—"a Jewish insignia in the form of a round tin plate"—was mandatory for all Jews over fourteen "when they are outside their homes . . . In its center there must be a capital letter "Ž," 1.2 inches long, 0.8 inches wide. This insignia is to be worn in a visible place on the left side of the chest." With this provision, all the "earlier ones went out of force," which meant that children no longer had to wear the Jewish insignia. Article 9 provided that "Jews by race, who are state and local government officials, while they are in active service, and Catholic priests, monks, and nuns, if they are wearing a habit, are released from wearing the Jewish insignia." This shows a kind of mitigation of the earlier regulations, but the number of people spared by the application of this article was negligible.[28] For example, the only church person I managed to discover who was a Jew according to the racial law was Zdenko Graf, son of Milan, born in Zagreb in 1921, who attended an Esperanto class in 1940. When he was ordained in 1946, he was christened Pavao.[29] Besides, the Ustasha authorities probably did not want to enter into conflict with the Catholic Church, because Archbishop Alojzije Stepinac had already demanded that "good Catholics who are of the Jewish race . . . should be taken into account."[30]

To distribute the badges, the Jewish Community made a special list of Zagreb Jews called the *Jewish Insignia Index*.[31] According to this list, Jewish insignias were issued to 9,087 people in Zagreb. The list does not include those who had in the meantime been granted Aryan rights, or who hoped they would be, those who had already fled to the sea or abroad, some prominent members of the Contribution Committee, etc. This means that more than 10,000 Zagreb Jews were to be included in the Ustasha-Nazi pogrom. The list included only some of the Jewish refugees from Germany, Austria, and Czechoslovakia who found themselves in Zagreb and its surroundings.

The list gives the impression that those on it were petrified and did all they could to avoid being issued the insignia. The head of a family entered on the list reported that the family members (usually wife and children) were "Aryans,"[32] that they had been "converted,"[33] or that they were "half-Aryans."[34] These definitions of status meant nothing to the Ustasha authorities: "Aryanism" had to be confirmed in a special procedure, and possible conversion to Catholicism had no meaning. As for the term "half-Aryan," this did not even exist in the legal terminology of the Ustasha administration.[35]

The Jewish badges produced in Zagreb through the Zagreb Jewish Community were sent to the surroundings of Zagreb and throughout the ISC: to Pisarovina (42 pieces), Ivanić-grad, Krapina (30), Dugo Selo (8), Križevci (24), Donja Stubica (5), Koprivnica (208), Suhopolje, Crikvenica (8), Našice (150), Belišće (100), Slavonski Brod (350), Dubrovnik (20), Podravske Sesvete, Garešnica (23), Ludbreg (48), Pakrac (105), Antunovac near Pakrac (6), Tuzla (206), Sarajevo (500), even to Omiš (20) and some other places.[36] The price per badge was 5 dinars, and the Jewish Section recommended to the competent institutions (e.g., Ustasha Office, District Council) in Garešnica, Pakrac, and Tuzla "not to charge more than 20 dinars per insignia."[37] The local authorities in Pisarovina even pressed urgently for more badges from Zagreb.[38] Vinkovci found their own craftsman and cancelled the order of badges from Zagreb.[39] The work was done very carefully: from Pisarovina they first sent 195 dinars and then 5 more dinars for the purchase of 40 badges, and they "returned two that had not been sold, since two of the émigré Jews have . . . allegedly fled to Italy."[40]

Some Jews found it impossible to pay the price of 20 dinars per badge, and the Jewish communities in those towns had to provide the money, which was an additional financial burden.[41] It seems that, in Zagreb, the Ustasha Police Directorate set a flat sum of 500,000 dinars, so the Board of the Jewish Religious Community decided that the insignias in Zagreb would cost 100 kunas each.[42]

9

REQUESTS TO NOT WEAR THE INSIGNIA AND BE GRANTED ARYAN RIGHTS

The Zagreb Jews tried to protect themselves in all kinds of ways practically from the early days of the ISC, but as the weeks and months passed, it became increasingly clear that what they in fact had to save were their lives. Regardless of whatever kinds of documents they possessed or that the Ustasha authorities gave them, or of the friends they had among the authorities, or of how much money they gave to anyone, no one could guarantee their survival. People managed to obtain residence and work "permits," but this did not help them. Bernard Biller, "an active civil servant," had Aryan rights, his parents Bernard and Rozalija, née Steiner, had "permits," but nevertheless they were sent to a camp from which they never returned. Their son, Bernard, and his wife, Elza, survived the war.[1] Vlatko Rosenberg from Zagreb was deported and killed in Jasenovac in 1941, although his son had "served in the Croatian army in Bosnia from the beginning of the war."[2]

Many people thought that converting to Catholicism would be a good and relatively simple way of saving their life. In June and July of 1941, hundreds of Zagreb Jews practically besieged parish offices in Zagreb and obtained baptismal certificates, but these provided no real security.[3] Obtaining Aryan rights proved safer—but not much—and in this the Ustasha authorities were extremely tight-fisted. By the autumn of 1941, about 2,000

Zagreb Jews had applied to Ustasha institutions for exemption from wearing the Jewish insignia, and for recognition of Aryan rights and permission to freely live and work in Zagreb. This included many who had converted to Catholicism even earlier. Thus, Zlata Petrović "most humbly" begged the Ministry to "exempt me from wearing the statutory insignia so that the insignia should not damage my husband's standing as a wood merchant, because I believe that I have fulfilled all the conditions to have exemption granted."[4] Maks Mautner, the founder and first secretary of the Zagreb Fair, requested exemption from all the provisions laid down for the Jews. The result of his application is not known, but this did not change his fate—he was killed in an "unknown place." His son, Dragan, a student, was already in Jasenovac in November 1941, and was killed in the branch camp in Feričanci.[5]

The request of Terezija Neustadt, née Donner, was met "because she was the sister of Julije Donner, a major who suddenly died of a heart attack in April 1941." It is not clear whether this was what saved her, or the fact that she was under the protection of the distinguished composer Rudolf Matz, the husband of her daughter Margita, or something else entirely.[6] The request of Ljerka Benedek, née Šarić, for her husband Rudolf was also granted, because he "had become an even more enthusiastic Croat and always worked for the good of Croatia" after he had met her, and Ljerka "was herself an ardent Croat." However, the administration did not hesitate to enter both Rudolf and Ljerka Benedek in the *Economic Reconstruction Directory*, to prevent them from saving Rudolf's property from confiscation by putting it in Ljerka's name. Rudolf Benedek's fate is not known.[7] In August 1941, the 68-year-old Lavoslav Reves married his thirty-year-old servant, a Croatian woman, in church, after which he requested exemption from wearing the insignia. His request was refused; what is more, the Ministry of the Interior demanded an "investigation to establish whether there are grounds for criminal charges, because the law prohibited a marriage of this kind." Unlike most other supplicants who had been refused, Reves survived the war.[8] The request of Klara Hönigsberg and her family shows that the criteria for exemption from wearing the insignia were strange, to say the least, and that confusion in this process was created both intentionally and unintentionally. They were freed "on the grounds of her acquaintance and cooperation with the late Šufflay."[9] By decision of Božo Cerovski, after the intercession of the Italian Embassy, Hansi Pšerhof was exempted on the recommendation of the secretary to the commercial attaché of the Italian Embassy, because "she speaks Italian, and must be able to move freely about town to make various purchases with my wife."[10] One of the few who were released from wearing the insignia, although this should not have been possible under the prevailing law, was Oto Ružinski (1882), whose mother was the sister of Josip Frank.[11] G. Gueyraud, French Consul in Zagreb, interceded with Mladen Lorković, Minister of Foreign Affairs, on behalf of the tennis champion Franjo Schäffer, who was in an Ustasha prison in July 1942. He managed to have Schäffer "exempted from wearing the insignia and all the laws on non-Aryans." The background of this move by the French diplomat was that Schäffer was married to one of Gueyraud's secretaries.[12] Mary Vuchetich, wife of Oton Vuchetich, Secretary of the American Consulate, was also Jewish. She was exempt from wearing the insignia after Vuchetich spoke to Božidar Cerovski.[13] However, even a diplomatic passport did not provide complete protection from harassment. In July 1941, a certain Mrs. Biljan, wife of a retired Army captain, reported Edita Stiasni, wife of the Consul General of the Republic of Honduras, when she saw her at the Dolac market without the Jewish insignia and outside the hours reserved for Jews.[14] The guard arrested Mrs. Stiasni on the spot, but she was later released. Soon after, she and her husband, Ljudevit, and the Consul Oto Orlik, also Jews, left the ISC with the help of old connections and bribes.[15]

Since many individuals and groups of Croats were working to save individual Jews and their families, on May 15 the Police Directorate sent an official letter to the Chamber of Attorneys "prohibiting attorneys from intervening in political matters, especially on behalf of Jews. Anyone who does not respect this will be held responsible and will suffer grave consequences."[16] However, it seems that this did not have any great effect, so Ante Pavelić personally issued a statement to the press on June 27, forbidding anyone "in accordance with the Extraordinary Legal Provision and Order of June 26 . . . from appealing their personal cases, in the form of intercession, to the Ustasha Head Office, because they will not be heard under any circumstances."[17] In those days, the papers were full of news of this kind: at the beginning of July, under the title "Enough interventions!," *Ustaša* wrote that "in connection with the Poglavnik's order, the Ustasha Head Office cautions all Ustasha officials that any intercession in personal matters is punishable by death. Ustashe must prevent this dishonorable practice with all their might and close, once and for all, the doors of their offices to those who do nothing but go to offices, despite the law and its provisions, and 'intervene' now for a Jew, now for a Serb, now for one uncle, now for another."[18] Such drastic and nervously repeated threats show that intercession was taking place and that it could probably not be stopped, because of corruption or personal acquaintance. The supplicants knew this too, and in many cases they turned to Pavelić himself, thinking to secure something they thought they could not through regular channels. Preserved documents do not generally show any trace of the Poglavnik or his office because the cases were referred to lower levels with obviously an oral recommendation only.[19] But here too there are exceptions: in September 1941, Pavelić himself granted Eleonora Feldmann (1923) of Zagreb "and her legitimate descendents, all the rights of persons of Aryan origin."[20] Also, in the case of the Justitz family, who are "known to him personally," he "begs" the Jewish Section to "solve all the requests favorably."[21] It seems that Pavelić's and Artuković's intercession was decisive in the favorable resolution of some other cases as well.[22]

Pavelić personally demanded that the Portuguese consul, "the Jew Aleksandar Ehrmann, be treated as the representative of Portugal in our country." All the same, this did not save Ehrmann from having to give the contribution.[23]

Many Ustasha officials made concessions to particular Jews because the ISC was the kind of state in which personal connections and money were often decisive, both among the high officials and with the Poglavnik himself. Thus the file of the Parodis, Italian citizens, says under the heading "connections: none," but with the addition that the wife was to be released from prison and that their property was not to be touched because the head supervisor of the Italian police in Croatia had intervened on their behalf.[24] During the first days of the ISC, the prominent Zionist activist and Zagreb attorney Aleksandar Licht was arrested, together with a large number of other distinguished Zagreb Jews. He managed to get himself set free, and then obtained documents and emigrated. The Jewish Section of the Ustasha Police Directorate did not have the authority to grant Aryan rights, but they confirmed that "no measures of compulsion" were to be taken against the distinguished conductor Milan Sachs and his wife. They were allowed to live in their apartment in Gundulićeva Street, "which no one shall take away or requisition," so that Sachs "could continue to work unhindered in the field of music, as a civil servant and conductor of the State Opera."[25] Sachs converted in July 1941, and after that, it seems, Eugen Dido Kvaternik himself interceded for him and his wife.[26] In the twenties and the early thirties, the Croat Marko Ožanić (1905) was a waiter in one of the leading Zagreb coffeehouses (Corso) and in a well-known restaurant

(Gradski podrum). Then he fled to Hungary, where he went to train in an Ustasha camp. He returned to Zagreb in 1941 and became manager of the restaurant in the Main Railway Station. Although he did not formally hold any public office, he was an "old Ustasha" and as such was considered a person with good connections in the Ministry of the Interior. At the end of May 1941, he "most warmly recommended" the request of Dragutin Kuh, also a waiter, for exemption from wearing the Jewish insignia. Despite his recommendation, the request was not granted and Kuh later ended his life in an "unknown" place.[27]

Some people entered the business of recognizing Aryan rights completely legally—on May 31, the Croatian Information Office advertised that it could obtain "all the necessary information on racial affiliation and proof of Aryan origin in Croatia and abroad," and that to do so it had "over 3,000 commissioners in all the important places."[28]

In September 1941, the Poglavnik's Office, where most of the requests were finally resolved, sent to the Public Order and Security Directorate (RAVSIGUR), to Eugen Dido Kvaternik in person, four lists of Zagreb Jews who could be granted Aryan rights or residence permits, and who were thus, for the time being, exempted from measures laid down for Jews.[29] Twenty-three Jews on those lists were granted Aryan rights, in three cases their families as well, and the remaining 400 got "residence and work permits," forty-seven of them together with their families, which made a total of over 500 people.[30] At the same time, the Poglavnik's Office sent a notification to the Jewish Section of the RUR informing them that those who had been granted "residence and work permits" were not exempt from wearing the insignia, however those who were "intended for Aryanization need not wear the insignia."[31]

Dozens of requests for recognition of Aryan rights were sent to the Jewish Section of the RUR, but most were refused. On the basis of over 400 filed and preserved requests, it can be seen that 138 people got Aryan rights, and 407 persons were refused. Thus, barely one quarter of the applicants (25.3 percent) got a favorable answer.[32] It must also be considered that only Jews who had any reason to hope for a favorable answer (because of connections, bribes, having left the Jewish religion long ago, mixed marriage, special merit, etc.) applied for Aryan rights or exemption from wearing the insignia. The great majority of Jews could hope for nothing. As time passed, the number of requests for granting rights decreased: in the summer of 1941 they were still being submitted, in the autumn they became very rare, and in 1942 the Jewish Section hardly received any at all.[33] Often, one official would grant something, and then another would refuse what had already been granted, and vice versa.[34]

Sometimes compromises were made: for example, temporary permits for exemption from wearing the insignia were issued, valid up to a certain date, or for one month, or two, and the like.[35] The engineer Oton Krušić (earlier Kraus), who had converted in June, was issued a permit to not wear the Jewish insignia until June 15, but in the middle of July it was not extended. It seems that Krušić had found a way of escaping from the city by that time and later lived in Turin.[36] Some requests were simply not answered at all.[37] According to a series of documents in the holdings of the RUR–Ustasha Police Directorate, Jewish Section, in time the policy of granting Aryan rights grew increasingly restrictive. While in May and June up to 40 percent of the requests for granting Aryan rights were met, in the next month or two this fell below 30 percent, and by August fewer than 10 percent of the applicants received a positive answer.

The archives do not include requests (for granting Aryan rights, for not wearing the insignia, for protection of an apartment, etc.) made by any members of two prominent and very rich Zagreb Jewish families, the Deutsch-Maceljskis and Alexanders (some family members spelled their name Aleksander). Most of the members of these two families remained in Zagreb and did not try to escape. In September 1941, Ante Pavelić, through the mediation of *Doglavnik* Ademaga Mešić, accorded Aryan rights to Erich Aleksander (1868), former head of the Middle Technical School, and his descendents, but this document cannot be found in any HDA archival collection.[38] However, not all the Alexanders got this kind of protection. Dr. Branko Aleksander, son of the Zagreb industrialist and banker S. D. Aleksander, was even sent to the Slano "death camp" on the island of Pag, from which he was the only Jew to be returned to Zagreb by urgent order, immediately released, and issued with a passport to leave the ISC.[39] However, Ines Aleksander (born in 1895), who converted in July 1941, had to request that Aryan rights be granted to her through the normal channels. The request was refused, and Ines later met her end in an unknown place. Her son, Miljenko (1921), was killed in Jasenovac, most likely before the end of 1941, and his father, Đuro (1894), was probably killed there too.[40]

Documents show that only two members of the large Deutsch-Maceljski family—Gustav and Vlatko—were granted Aryan rights.[41] At the end of May 1941, their brother Robert was on the list of those in the process of being granted Aryan rights (with an uncertain resolution), so he was not obliged "to pick up or to wear the Jewish insignia." The rest of the family did not get any formal document to save them from persecution ("permits" and the like), so did what they could to try to survive just like everyone else—by hiding with kind people, friends, and non-Jewish relatives. Despite the Aryan status that they had been granted, Vlatko Deutsch-Maceljski and his wife, Marga, were arrested in August 1942 and taken to the grammar school in Križanićeva Street, where the assembly point for Auschwitz was then located. On the intercession of an unknown person, they were released from Križanićeva and sent to the prison on Sava Road. It had been arranged for them to be released from there too, and it seemed that their connections and remaining money would save their lives. However, someone denounced them, claiming that a member of the Deutsch-Maceljski family was concealing some sort of property, so they were returned to their cell and then deported to Jasenovac and Stara Gradiška, from which they never returned.[42] Vlasta and Milan, Vlatko and Marga's children, were arrested in May 1943, at the time of great deportations, imprisoned on Sava Road, and were only freed when the equivalent of one hundred pounds in gold had been paid for them. Ultimately, however, many of the Alexanders and Deutsch-Maceljskis shared the fate of most of Zagreb's Jews. Wealth was no guarantee that anyone would be saved: the family of Lavoslav Steiner, vice-president of the Jewish Community, who gave almost 1,500,000 kunas in the contribution, were all killed: Lavoslav, his wife Elza, née Haas, and their daughter, Mira.[43]

The request of Vjekoslav Pilpel for exemption from wearing the insignia had, instead of the usual typewritten note, a recommendation in thick red pencil, "not to be approved for any reason because he is also a Freemason," which clearly shows that decisions about wearing the insignia were not made only according to legal, but also to other, criteria.[44] Archbishop Stepinac himself interceded for the exemption of Oto Laufer from wearing the insignia, and "warmly recommended" the request, but this did not help. Laufer was killed in a camp.[45] Even the favorable opinion of Lieutenant General August Marić did not help some people.[46] Bruno Prister wrote that his ancestors Emanuel and Eduard had "lived in Zagreb one hundred years ago" and that they were great Zagreb benefactors. The request was refused, but Prister survived the war by fleeing the city.[47] Many requests were co-signed by friends, some by heads of the firms in which the Jews were employed, and some were written by spouses, but usually none of this helped. Some requests were considered "meaningless because the named is in c.c." (i.e., a concentration camp) or were "placed a.a. as meaningless."[48] Even the annotation "out of date" might mean that the applicant was in concentration camp or had already been killed.[49] Many requests have the letters "a.a.," *ad acta,* which in fact meant the same as "out of date." On others, the seal and the annotation belong to different ISC institutions, which usually meant that the prisoner had ended his days in a camp during the time it took for the file to travel from one place to another.[50] The well-known architect Stjepan Gomboš also submitted a request for exemption from wearing the insignia, but, in December 1941, his request was "out of date" because he had in the meantime escaped from Zagreb.[51]

Even a favorable opinion given by the Poglavnik's Office did not always mean salvation, because sometimes the Ustashe took no notice of this document and sent the owner to a camp anyway. In May 1941, Bela Altstädter of Zagreb was on the list of recipients of Aryan rights, but in the summer he was thrown out of his apartment, and by the end of that year killed in Jasenovac.[52] In August 1941, the prominent attorney and Judaic scholar Lavoslav Šik was exempted from wearing the insignia. The procedure for Šik to obtain "Aryan rights" was under way and many prominent people interceded for him, but, despite that, he was deported to Jasenovac. He was released on Stepinac's intercession, but in 1942 was sent to Jasenovac again and once there was "immediately killed."[53] It did not help Šik that he had since 1918 been considered as "Croatian-oriented" (or, as a report of the Yugoslav police said, "a separatist"), and that he was known as the attorney of Croatian soldiers who had demonstrated on December 5, 1918, only five days after the establishment of the Kingdom of Serbs, Croats, and Slovenes.[54] The Ustashe considered that day "fateful," a "revolutionary campaign," and they called the people killed on that day the "first Croatian victims."[55] Pavelić personally founded the Fifth of December Battalion, thus marking the event. Šik's defense of the soldiers was an act of great civil courage, and to make the irony even greater, Šik did it all for free.[56]

Slavko Kvaternik personally protected the family of Dr. Oskar Stern and of his father-in-law, the banker Sigmund Pordes, and the family of Dr. Milan Schwartz (Emil's father, who took the name of Ariel Shomrony in Israel); he had been Stern's best man at his wedding in the synagogue in Praška Street in 1930. When Kvaternik fell in 1942, both families had to flee. Kvaternik also protected the three members of Šandor Braun's family. The Brauns had other protectors as well, Ivica Frković, Minister of Forests and Ores, Monsignor Augustin Juretić, a close associate of Archbishop Stepinac, and some others, but no one could keep them from being arrested in October 1942.[57]

On May 24, 1941, the Ministry of the Interior informed the Police Directorate that 202 Zagreb Jews "are not obliged to wear the Jewish insignia" and enclosed a list with the letter.[58] According to the provision that the Jewish question was not a religious but racial issue, all the others were refused regardless of the religion they belonged to.

The great struggle for exemption from wearing the insignia brought people into terrible situations and sometimes caused family dramas and rifts. The Osijek dentist Rudolf Woger, "an Aryan by descent, Roman Catholic by birth, a Croat by nationality," demanded that his former wife, Iva, a Jew, should not be "granted Aryan rights" because she had called him "a Christian-Catholic swine and beast." On the other hand, Iva claimed that her former husband had called her a "slut, a Kike pig . . . a cursed Kike."[59] The request for exemption from wearing the insignia submitted by the twenty-year-old Vitomir Krauth was also refused; he considered that "the tragedy of my life is that my ancestors are Jews and therefore so am I. I emphasize and underline that this is tragic because all through my existence, since I was a small child, I have always said and felt myself to be a Croat." None of this helped Krauth (or Kraut) and at the end of 1941 he was killed in Jasenovac.[60] The engineer Aurel Gorjan had a similar fate. In his own words, to wear the Jewish insignia would "subject him to the scorn of others." In November 1941, parcels in his name were sent from the Jewish Community to Jasenovac, but afterward no more were sent. He was probably killed at that time, and the entry on the List of Victims showing that he was killed in an "unknown place" is most likely wrong.[61]

10

A CHALLENGE TO LIVING

Dismissal from All Services

The legal provisions of April 30, 1941, which stripped the Jews of rights on the basis of race, were in the following days and weeks rapidly worked out in more detail and supplemented by new provisions and regulations—persecution soon began to take on specific forms. On May 6, the Legal Provision on the Prohibition of Employing Female Persons in Non-Aryan Households was passed, whereby "female persons of Aryan origin aged under forty-five" may not be employed in "Jewish households . . . if these households include male non-Aryans aged between fourteen and sixty-five, or if such persons spend longer periods of time in the household."[1] This provision was another safeguard to make sure that Jews would not have the opportunity for "extramarital sexual relations . . . with a female of Aryan origin," which had already been prohibited by the Legal Provision on the Protection of Aryan Blood and the Honor of the Croatian People. The purpose of these legal provisions was to show the public that rich and arrogant Jews would no longer be able to exploit Croatian women and men in any way, and to additionally humiliate the Jews and show them once again that they could never lead a normal life in the ISC. On May 16, this legal provision was amended by clauses about severance pay for servants who had to be dismissed. If the former employers could not afford the severance pay, this financial obligation was transferred to the Jewish Religious Community.[2]

There were many Croats who were not in favor of these provisions, despite what the Ustasha authorities had intended and hoped to show. The MUP NDH Collection in the Croatian State Archives has several dozen applications from maids requesting exemption from the above legal provision, but as a rule the answer was negative. It made no difference whether the "non-Aryan" employer or the "Aryan" employee submitted the request. Jagica Stipčić wrote that she was satisfied with her status in the Jewish family she worked for, and that she had to support her husband and child; Jelka Dubravec wrote that she had been working in Bela Altstädter's family for four years and that she was satisfied, that this law would make her lose her job, and she had old parents and winter was coming; Barica Rogina wrote that no one in the Jewish household had objected to her because of her religion and that her employers had always treated her like "family"; Rezika Cigan wrote that she would lose her livelihood because she had given "the severance pay she had received to her family, who were poor." Instead of severance pay in money, Marija Novak asked for some of the furniture from the apartment of her former employer, Dr. Beno Stein (who was by then already dead), but her request was refused because "the Police Directorate had started an investigation against her"; she was suspected of already having "secreted some of his property" earlier.[3] The worst situation was that of the forty-two year old Katarina Mesarić (close to the age limit of forty-five), who was a mother of three and who had been widowed in her thirties. The Jew David Schleien had found work for her in his house, given her money to prevent the seizure of her furniture when she fell into debt, and for the last three years had been feeding her and her two younger children in his home. Katarina said that the severance pay she had received "cannot by any means be a substitute."[4]

In accordance with an ordinance of the Ministry of National Economy of the ISC, on May 17 all Jews began to be dismissed from state employment. Zagreb University was to be a rare exception, at least for several months, because in that case "the problems of teaching had to be borne in mind, which would suffer if some of the teachers were dismissed before replacements were found. Thus, some of them could keep their jobs for the time being, until they had done their duty by training a successor and writing a text-book."[5] This provision referred primarily to the Serbs, because the percentage of Jewish teachers at the university was even smaller than that of Jewish students, and by then, in September, there were only a few Jewish professors left at the university. They were not all made to retire until January 1943—this happened to Stanko Frank (1883–1953) and Bertold Eisner (1875–1956), professors at the Faculty of Law. After the liberation in 1945, they were all rehired.[6]

People were also dismissed from private firms, and a permit issued by the Jewish Section RUR was necessary for them to remain at work. In June 1941, Josip Juvand got permission to employ Željko Biller, an optician's assistant, "because there was a shortage of Aryan experts." It soon became clear that the effort to procure this permit had been in vain, because several months later Biller met his end in Jasenovac.[7] In June, the Jewish Section allowed Dragutin Gliks "to work in the Ivo Restaurant as a dishwasher." However, this permit did not mean much because, by the end of the year, Gliks (Glücks) was killed in Jasenovac.[8] Albert Breuer got a permit to "keep his job of traveling salesman until further notice."[9]

This intimidation and the arrest and deportation of Jewish experts understandably had a negative effect on production. At the end of May, Ljudevit Gržanić, commissioner of the Zagreb Shoe Factory, requested that "the only experts in this factory, two Jews . . . be exempted from wearing the Jewish insignia . . . as it is very embarrassing if they wear it because of our connections with the German authorities, whose trust we have won."[10] At the end of August, nine owners of crafts firms (most of them metal workshops, cabinetmakers, and upholsterers) requested that Aleksandar Ehrenfreund, owner of the Zmaj firm, "be released, otherwise we, the undersigned, will have no livelihood because up to now we have worked exclusively for Mr. Ehrenfreund, who is the only expert in the company." Ehrenfreund was not set free, and in 1942 he died in Jasenovac.[11]

When Krešimir Meštrović, supervising commissioner in three Jewish firms, requested in June 1941 that Jewish traveling salesmen should not be dismissed because "this would not be well-advised in the interest of the firms, as they are experts and associates of many years' standing." The State Directorate of Economic Reconstruction gave him a negative reply, saying that "a possible short setback because of the replacement of traveling salesmen will not harm the State and economy as much as would Jews traveling around and agitating." Finally, they said that it "would be against the principles of state policy regarding the Jews, and would be politically and psychologically very awkward for Jews to move around as traveling salesmen."[12]

In June, the Našice tannin factory and steam sawmill dismissed eighty-nine Jews, but on July 1 there were still eighteen working in the central office in Zagreb, and another twenty-three in other places. The factory sent a request to the Jewish Section of the RUR asking for them not to be deported. In December, the factory was still employing thirty Jews, twelve in Zagreb, and requested permission for their "temporary employment."[13] On July 3, the Intercontinentale & Caro i Jelinek transport joint stock company informed the Jewish Section that they had dismissed eight of the sixteen Jews in their employ, but that those who remained were indispensable. The request was refused because the "reasons are not sufficiently justified."[14] Some Jews got permission to continue working, but the permit for the civil servant Cecilija Wilhelm was "valid until its cancellation."[15] In July, the engineer Robert Koller, owner of a mechanical workshop, requested permission to continue working. Koller's twelve workers supported the request, claiming that "he has always been a good and sincere friend, he helped us in good times and bad, and even when business was not going well he made sure we got our wages." But Koller was soon sent to Jasenovac where he met his end within a few months.[16] In September, Mijo Gavranović, owner of the Pokorny liqueur factory, who called himself an "Ustasha," submitted a request for his foreman, Aladar Stern, to be allowed to "work and move about freely" because "otherwise work might stop." Thus, Stern "temporarily kept his job."[17] He may have survived, but we can't be sure because he is not on the list of those who died nor of those who survived.[18]

Sometimes even the authorities admitted that many "Jews are indispensable in the economy." There are even requests or demands by some state institutions for the exemption of an expert from anti-Jewish measures or, even more, for his return from a camp after he had been sent there.[19] For example, in October 1941, the Ministry of Croatian Home Guards asked for the Jews David Papo and Oton Donerkeil, by then in camp, to be "returned to work in the UNITAS cotton factory until equally expert replacements are found" because the replacements at that time were said to be incapable. Neither was released from Jasenovac, and Papo ended his days there. The story about the suffering of Oton Donerkeil is rather unclear: in September 1941, his wife, Ruža, was informed that he had been sent "to Germany with a large number of Jews," which was possible because the Germans were demanding experts as well. In 1943 she found out that, in the meantime, Oton was said to have been "taken to Poland and that everyone in his group had been killed." However, the Jewish Community was still sending parcels to Donerkeil in Jasenovac at the end of 1943, so it is possible that he was there all the time. Be that as it may, Oton Donerkeil did not survive the war. In November 1943, Ruža Donerkeil was working in the soup kitchen of the Zagreb Jewish Religious Community and living in the village of Rača near Veleševci (about twenty kilometers southeast of Velika Gorica) and had converted to Christianity, but ultimately she too perished in an unknown manner.[20]

For the Jews who continued to work in their own firms for a time, business was made difficult and practically impossible in many ways. For example, the Jewish Section, in coordination with the postal service, discontinued phone service or did not allow Jewish firms to use the telephone.[21] In July, Bernard Moster's Chemical Factories only managed to keep their phone connection because of the request made by the commissioner and the intercession of higher authorities.[22] The Moster firm on Šubićeva Street stopped work in October 1941 due to impossible conditions, although the owner, Bernard Moster, had converted to Catholicism in July of that year.[23] At the beginning of January 1942, Bernard's brother Edmund and Edmund's wife, Klara, were deported, followed by his sister Julka (Julija) Haas,[24] who had also converted in July 1941. In July 1942, the Jewish Section received a request for Julka to be released from camp. The request was denied, but it is not certain whether Julka was even still alive at that time, because it seems that she ended her days in the Đakovo camp.[25] Klara was killed in Đakovo, and her husband Edmund in Jasenovac. Bernard Moster and his wife, Zora, saved themselves temporarily, but, in 1944, the Nazis caught them on Rab and sent them to Auschwitz.[26]

Probably by June or at the latest by July, the Economic Reconstruction Office compiled a list of economically indispensable Jews, but the Ustasha services deported people regardless of whether they were on this list or not. In the following months, it became clear that one of the reasons why the ISC economy was on the decline was because incompetent commissioners had been appointed to run the former Jewish firms, and because of the general lack of qualified workers.[27] In time, the Ustasha authorities realized this too, and at the end of 1942 they demanded from the Italian military and civil institutions the return of Jewish doctors and engineers who had fled to the ISC zone under Italian occupation. The Italian authorities refused, rightly fearing that these experts might be deported to camps.[28]

The Legal Provision on the Protection of the National and Aryan Culture of the Croatian People of June 4, 1941, forbade Jews from "participating in the work of social, youth, sports, and cultural organizations, and institutions of the Croatian people in general, and especially in literature, journalism, art and music, town planning, theater, and films."[29] This resulted in the intensification of purges based on the Ordinance on Establishing the Racial Affiliation of State and Local Civil Servants and Self-Employed Academic Professionals.

The Chamber of Attorneys waited until June 30, 1942, before removing their Jewish members, when fifty-one Zagreb attorneys and forty-three from other Croatian towns were struck from the list.[30] These were not all the Jewish attorneys by far—according to some statistics, there were at least seventy-three (and probably eighty-nine) in Zagreb alone. Some, like Lavoslav Šik, had by then already been killed, while others, like Rudolf Rodanić, had left by themselves. In any case, terminating their membership did not have any real meaning, because by then none of the Jewish attorneys were working any longer, and most of them were dead, had been deported, or had fled from Zagreb. The following year, in 1943, the Chamber of Attorneys showed all its legal precision when it was solving the matter of the property of Dr. Siegfried Perlberg, who had "when going to camp determined that, after his death, his legal library should be donated to the library of the Commercial Court." It seems that Perlberg was killed in Jasenovac.[31]

Jews were dismissed from other professional associations too: although the Zagrebian Society was neither anti-Semitic nor pro-Ustasha, but nurtured old Zagreb traditions and love for the city, by the end of June, "eighty-three members were dropped for racial reasons."[32] In August, the Society of State and Local Government Pensioners of the ISC asked the Ministry of the Interior whether they should "revoke the memberships of the Jews or whether they could continue to be members of the Society," since the "Society has neither a political nor a religious character." Although the Ministry's response is not recorded, there is no doubt as to its content.[33]

Some other institutions also tried to find ways of sparing Jews, or at least some of them, from the effects of anti-Jewish measures. At the beginning of June 1941, the Zagreb Chamber of Commerce asked the Ministry of Justice whether the "legal matters" that were prohibited between Jews and Aryans by the provision of April 18 also included "commercial matters," and got a positive answer.[34] In April and May, the Alliance of Monetary and Insurance Institutions several times requested guidance from the Ministry of Justice as to who was to be considered a Jew; they considered that "only a person who is of the Israelite religion" is a Jew, and claimed that "all financial business and the entire economy would collapse . . . if every client was to be asked to submit evidence that he or she is not a Jew."

The Ministry answered that the Legal Provision on Racial Affiliation must be implemented.[35]

On June 4, 1941, the authorities set up a Racial Political Commission at the Ministry of the Interior. Its structure included the Racial Political Council (which had at least nine experts: biologists, doctors, lawyers, etc.), Racial Political Office, and other "supplementary institutions." The Racial Political Commission had many tasks: "to draft bills and laws, legal provisions, and ordinances in the field of racial biology, racial policy, racial hygiene and eugenics . . . give their opinion on all such proposed laws, establish racial affiliation, especially in dubious cases," to maintain relations with similar institutions in other countries, etc. The members of the Racial Political Council had to be pure Aryans, and they worked in the greatest secrecy. Since their work was so important, the members were paid a sum determined by the Minister of the Interior.[36] The Ministry of Health did their part of the work with the utmost bureaucratic conscientiousness: they sent the Ministry of the Interior a proposal for the members of the Racial Political Council.[37]

In accordance with the Ordinance on Determining the Racial Affiliation of State and Local Civil Servants and Self-Employed Academic Professionals, of June 4, all civil servants had to fill in one of the forms of the Declaration on Racial Affiliation.[38] "Giving false information or concealing known facts will lead to a prison term of at least three months and loss of employment, that is, of eligibility to perform the job,"[39] says one of these forms. On the back are detailed instructions: "Under the heading for ancestors, only non-Aryan ancestors up to the third generation are to be given, not in name but by racial affiliation only, e.g., 'Father: Jew' or 'Grandmother: Gypsy' or 'One great-grandfather: Negro,' 'One great-grandmother: Jewish.' Only the closest ancestors of non-Aryan lineage are to be given. For example, if the father is a Jew, then the paternal grandfather and grandmother are not listed because it is obvious that the parents of a Jew are also Jews." The form says that "in addition to Jews, non-Aryans are in the first place to be considered Gypsies, Tartars, Kalmiks, Armenians, Persians, Arabs, Malayans, and Negroes." There is special emphasis that "no mention is to be made of the ancestors' religion, only of their race; if, for example, all the great grandfathers were Jews of Moses's faith, and the grandfather and grandmother were converted Jews, then only 'Father: Jew' is to be entered, because only racial affiliation is considered."

For the authorities, all these "racial" matters were very important only in the cases of Jews and Roma. Although the text of the provision also includes other groups and nationalities, they were basically unimportant and were included only to bolster the legal (in fact the "racial") correctness of the law. The case of Meržav Melkon (born in 1899), a naturalized Armenian who had already in Russia been assimilated into the Russian culture and who moved to Varaždin in 1922 and married a Catholic, shows this well. Melkon requested Aryan rights, and the Poglavnik's Office itself gave the opinion that "Armenians should be treated the same as Aryans, since the legal provision is primarily targeted against the Jews and Gypsies." Thus the Poglavnik's Office notified the Ministry of the Interior, "please inform the applicant that his application is meaningless, because he in principle already enjoys the legal position of an Aryan."[40]

11

THE ADMINISTRATIVE MACHINERY FOR IMPLEMENTING PERSECUTION

The Ustashe very quickly, in the first week after the proclamation of the ISC, established their power in almost the whole country, but they did not have a clear plan for organizing the state administration. There was hardly anyone with knowledge and experience of public administration among the Ustasha leaders, and they were in a hurry to get rid of everything old and establish the new order. The results were rash improvisations, constant reorganization, mixed competence, and organizational confusion that was not resolved in most ministries until the fall of the ISC. Parallel authority, characteristic of the great majority of dictatorships, created additional confusion: on the one hand, things were ostensibly legal with reliance on extremely strict, rapidly tailored laws that set up a dictatorship and state repression; on the other hand, there was a parallel line of arbitrary decision-making outside the law, the dictator's personal omnipotence above the law, oral commands and permission that were transmitted through the most trusted officials and which usually had the purpose of implementing illegal forms of violence.

After some initial improvisation, the ISC police machinery was more systematically organized than the other ministries. At the same time, it too undertook many activities outside the law. The Poglavnik, Pavelić himself, appointed the most responsible people in these services. In doing so, he at first predominantly relied on the Ustashe who had come to the country with him from exile. On the very day when he arrived in Zagreb, April 15, 1941, Pavelić appointed Eugen Dido Kvaternik Commissioner of Public Order and Security of the city of Zagreb; three days later, he appointed him Director of Public Order and Security for the whole ISC, and on May 4, State Secretary of Public Order and Security in the Ministry of the Interior of the ISC.[1] The Public Order and Security Directorate (RAVSIGUR) was established on May 7 by legal provision, to "introduce uniform organization and supervision over all the police services in the ISC."[2] By the same provision, RAVSIGUR was to consist of nine departments, some of which had authority in relation to Jews. In administrative organization, RAVSIGUR was formally a separate department in the ISC's Ministry of the Interior, and under its oversight, but in fact it acted largely independently from the very beginning. Dido Kvaternik, the head of RAVSIGUR, got authority, permission, and instructions for important decisions and actions directly from Pavelić.

As the central police institution of the whole ISC, RAVSIGUR initially worked through the existing local police force over which it had gained control. At the end of April, Marijan Nikšić was appointed head of the Police Directorate for the city of Zagreb. Nikšić had worked in the police force of the Kingdom of Yugoslavia from 1928, but had in 1938 declared himself in favor of the Croatian opposition and, after the establishment of the Croatian Banovina in 1939, became police chief in Šibenik and secretly expressed sympathy for the Ustasha movement.[3] On May 8, he signed ordinances about moving Jews and Serbs out of the northern parts of Zagreb and restricting their movements within the city.[4] Senior police adviser Dr. Ivan Brtivić was responsible for Jewish issues in the Zagreb Police Directorate. He too had been a police officer of long standing in the Kingdom of Yugoslavia; he had, just like Nikšić in 1938, begun to express sympathy for the nationalistic Croatian opposition. In April 1941, he immediately became senior adviser, then head of the Political Section in the Police Directorate of the city of Zagreb,[5] and was in this position when he initiated collecting the contribution.[6] It seems, however, that Eugen Dido Kvaternik did not have full confidence in men from the old police force, and he very soon began to create a parallel police—the Ustasha Police.[7]

On April 22, 1941, the pre-war Ustasha émigré Božidar Cerovski was appointed Ustasha Commissioner for Public Order and Security in the city of Zagreb. He immediately singled out some sections of the Police Directorate (Section I.b for espionage and the Frankists, Section I.c for the Communists) and formed an independent Ustasha Police Commission for the city of Zagreb, which quickly grew into the Ustasha Police Directorate of Zagreb.[8] The first public edict issued by the Ustasha Police was an announcement dated May 10, saying that "an Ustasha Police station has been formed at Bogovićeva Street 7, headed by Mr. Ivica Baraković" for the "primary purpose of supervising the Jews in the city of Zagreb." In this announcement and in a special public notification signed by Božidar Cerovski, all Jews "of the male sex aged sixteen to sixty" were invited "to apply at this station for records to be made."[9] In May 1941, there were jurisdictional disputes between the newly created Ustasha Police and the Police Directorate, so Marijan Nikšić resigned at the end of that month and Cerovski assumed almost all of his duties.[10]

From mid-May to mid-August of 1941, the Ustasha Police, through their Jewish Section at Bogovićeva 7, carried out the most drastic anti-Jewish measures in Zagreb (various prohibitions, arrests, deportations to camps). In June and July, the section head, Ivica Baraković, until 1941 an office employee in Osijek and an early member of the Ustasha movement, decided himself who was to be sent to camps or released to go home from the assembly point at the Zagreb Fairground.[11] More complicated cases, further investigations, and some intercessions and appeals, were referred to the Ustasha Police Directorate at Račkoga 9, where decisions were made by Božidar Cerovski.[12] Cerovski's immediate and only hierarchical superior was Eugen Dido Kvaternik.

Creating the Zagreb Ustasha Police was only the first step toward establishing a separate Ustasha police force, the bulky and omnipotent Ustasha Control Service. Pavelić himself announced the Provision on the Composition and Work of the Ustasha Movement of June 24, which established the Ustasha movement as the exclusive and only political body and organization in the ISC. He also announced the foundation of the Ustasha Control Service (UNS) that would "make sure that all Ustasha organizations and state institutions work in accordance with Ustasha principles, and that would oppose any work that may possibly be to the detriment of Croatian state independence."[13] After several weeks of preparation, the UNS was formed on August 16, and, a week later, Eugen Dido Kvaternik was appointed its head with the title Commander of Ustasha Control.[14]

The UNS consisted of four (later five) offices. The first office was the Ustasha Police Directorate (RUR), whose first commander was Vilko Pećnikar, also deputy commander of the entire UNS. This office had a bulky apparatus that branched throughout the state and had competence in all political matters, issued special ordinances and instructions to all state and Ustasha institutions, compiled secret personal card indexes, and ordered arrests and deportation to camps of Jews, Communists, Serbs, Roma, etc. The second UNS office was the Intelligence Service; the third was known as the Ustasha Defense and ran the concentration camps, with responsibility for their organization, maintenance, security, and the treatment of inmates; the fourth dealt with human resources; and the fifth, established subsequently, was the Poglavnik's security guard, responsible for security in general.[15] In his double role of director-in-chief of RAVSIGUR and control commander of UNS, Eugen Dido Kvaternik united both the services and in practice became the omnipotent chief of all the police, intelligence, and security services in the ISC—the "Croatian Himmler." After he was forced to resign under pressure from Pavelić in the early fall of 1942, UNS was abolished as a single institution in January 1943 and its services were divided among RAVSIGUR, the Ustasha Army (Ustaška vojnica), and other Ustasha institutions.[16]

In September 1941, the Ustasha Police Directorate, as the first UNS office, established its own Jewish Section headquartered at Vojnovićeva 31, which took over all the work of the earlier Jewish Section at Bogovićeva. Vilko Kühnel, a young lawyer from Bjelovar, a prewar member of the Ustasha movement and of the pro-Nazi German minority organization, was appointed its head. In documents about his national affiliation, he sometimes wrote "Croat" and sometimes "German."[17] Ivica Baraković, the earlier head of the city Jewish Section, became an official in Kühnel's section.

However, this did not give the desired centralization of "Jewish affairs" under the UNS. Ivan Britvić, from the Zagreb Police Directorate, continued to head activities connected to the contribution; the Ministry of Economy had primary responsibility for the "Aryanization" of Jews, followed by the independent State Directorate for Economic Reconstruction and the State Treasury; the City Housing Office was charged with taking over and distributing Jewish apartments in Zagreb; in some instances they were asked for their opinion on granting Aryan rights and other exemptions from anti-Jewish measures, but the final decision was made by the Poglavnik's Office; the Racial Political Commission in the Ministry of the Interior was tasked with defining affiliation to the Jewish race; the Ustasha Police Directorate sent people to camps, but so did courts, local police directorates, local Ustasha offices, county police etc., and only the Ustasha Defense administered the camps.[18] Sometimes there were disputes and clashes about authority and primacy among these institutions, but the UNS and its first office (RUR) were the most important. Thus, for example, when Ivan Britvić wanted to bring some deported Jews from Ilok back from camp, so that money and valuables could be collected from them for the contribution, a notice arrived from the Ustasha Police Directorate that "Mr. Britvić cannot grant permission for the return of Jews."[19] Since all this led to jurisdictional confusion, the RUR's Jewish Section demanded from RAVSIGUR that all requests for release from camp should go through RUR and its Jewish Section.[20] Nevertheless, all these hasty improvisations and reorganizations still did not slow down the "solution of the Jewish question." On the contrary, there was a constant "acceleration of solutions," from the initial excommunication to the increasingly frequent mass extermination, which was the purpose of much of the reorganization.

In the late summer and the fall of 1941, the Zagreb Jews who submitted individual complaints and requests were shuttled from the State Directorate for Economic Reconstruction to the Ministry of the Interior and its Racial Political Commission, from the city police in Đorđićeva to the Jewish Section in Vojnovićeva. Some of them looked for "connections" in the Ustasha Head Office, in the offices of the highest state officials, right up to the Poglavnik's Office. Being sent from place to place in this way was demeaning, and usually also disappointing and in vain. Judging from the memories of current officials in the Jewish Religious Community, in these direct contacts the heads of the two Jewish Sections, Baraković and Kühnel, were usually more moderate and somewhat more considerate than the ever-arrogant Britvić. Both Baraković and Kühnel obediently carried out all the anti-Jewish ordinances and measures, but nothing shows that they exceeded them in any way. Sometimes they were both even ready to "turn a blind eye" and approve an exemption, which cannot be said of Britvić. This can probably be explained by the difference in character between them, and perhaps also by the fact that Britvić, as a police advisor inherited from the old regime, had to prove his loyalty by being ruthless. When the contribution was at an end, the representatives of the Zagreb Jewish Community asked Kühnel to begin issuing passes to those who had fulfilled their obligation so that they could leave Zagreb. Kühnel really did begin issuing passes, for which he must certainly have had the approval of his superiors, Pećnikar or Dido Kvaternik. By that time most people had realized that the Jews in Zagreb could expect nothing but the worst and that they could save their lives only by escaping to other countries, best of all to Italy or the

Italian occupation zone, since it was already thought likely that Jews were in danger of being interned there, but not of being killed.

Kühnel issued passes to those who had fulfilled their contribution obligations on receiving a confirmation from the Contribution Committee. When news that passes were being granted spread throughout the city, people who wanted to emigrate literally began to besiege the Jewish Section. The Contribution Committee demanded that anyone who wanted to get a pass had to pay the complete welfare sum to be used for buying food and taking care of the camps.[21] Hinko Mann, secretary of the Contribution Committee, claimed that as many as 2,000 passes were issued in this way.[22] This is certainly an exaggerated number; Mann obviously wanted to emphasize his own importance. It is estimated that a total of about 2,000 persons escaped from Zagreb with passes. Many of them, probably most, bribed other state services or individuals to obtain the passes, and did not get them from Kühnel or Mann. "A blind eye was turned on our flight from Zagreb, toward the sea or to Slovenia, 'just for us to be gone,' but we had to leave all that we owned. And then 'hyenas' appeared with promises, from granting Aryan rights to salvation from being sent to a camp, and, luckily, they also provided real or forged passes that led to the path of salvation." This was how Vera Fischer remembered those days.[23] Some people even obtained passes without bribery, through friendly connections, such as Žarko Dolinar (1920–2003), a table-tennis champion (in 1954 he became world champion in pairs). He organized an entire network for the production of excellent forged passes for his Jewish friends, who saved themselves by escaping to Italy and even to other countries, for which he later became a Righteous Among the Nations. Several hundred Zagreb Jews, perhaps as many as one thousand, fled from the city illegally, without the proper documents.

All these can be only estimates: no individual person or service officially recorded how many passes they had issued to Jews because they were afraid that other services of the Ustasha regime might complain. Records show the existence of these passes only indirectly. Dezider Singer "made his contribution in the matter of Jewish donations for the needs of the ISC," and by doing so was probably able to get a pass (which the document, of course, does not mention specifically).[24] Some got permission to leave the ISC from the Economic Reconstruction Office and the State Directorate of Economic Reconstruction.[25] Documents granting permission to leave exist, but it is not certain whether refugees could use them only up to a certain point on the trip, and then had to go on without documents or use others. Some people had passes for Sarajevo, for Macedonia, for various other places. It is possible that these places were a starting point for salvation, for reaching the Italian occupation zone and continuing on to Italy.[26] Like many others, who did not hide that they were going to the Italian occupation zone, Dr. Oskar Fischer justified his departure to Novi Vinodolski and Sušak for "reasons of health and the need for sea bathing." Dr. Moric Levi testified: "Because of severe rheumatism, I am urgently in need of serious treatment, which has to be undertaken at the sea . . . in the Hrvatsko primorje."[27] On the advice of Dr. Ivo Petrić, Minister of Health, and Andrija Artuković, Minister of the Interior, Ivo Baraković issued a pass to the founder of the Contagious Diseases Hospital, Dr. Izidor Steinhardt and his family.[28] In June, Hinko Saphier also left Zagreb.[29] Although there was a lot of uncertainly and danger on these escape trips, this was still, other than leaving to join the Partisans, one of the few hopes for salvation.

As an energetic security commander, Eugen Dido Kvaternik did his best to introduce discipline in the UNS. Acts counter to commands were already being punished in August 1941—sometimes very strictly. His greatest efforts went into suppressing corruption and arbitrary plunder. In January 1942, Ivica Baraković was arrested for abuse of position because he had appropriated some plundered Jewish property. The Ustasha Disciplinary and Criminal Court withdrew his Ustasha membership, but he retained ownership of two Jewish firms (in Zagreb and Osijek), where he worked until the end of the war, when he fled abroad and all trace of him was lost.[30]

Vilko Kühnel remained head of the Jewish Section in the UNS and later in GLAVSIGUR until the spring of 1944. He was a multifaceted personality. In some individual cases, he mitigated the harshest measures and procedures, sometimes even going beyond his authority. Dijana Budisavljević wrote in her diary that in November 1941, Kühnel allowed her to send help, via the Jewish Community, to imprisoned women of the Orthodox faith and their children in Loborgrad and issued her with a pass to visit them, which no one else had permitted her to do.[31] On the other hand, Kühnel was the main organizer of the largest mass arrests of Zagreb Jews and their deportation to Auschwitz in August 1942 and May 1943, when exemptions and leniency were reduced to the minimum. He gave detailed information to Hans Helm, German SS police attaché in Zagreb, and his agents about the political opinions and conversations of high Ustasha officials in the Ministry of the Interior and elsewhere. When the Ustasha intelligence services found out about this, Kühnel was removed from GLAVSIGUR and, in the spring of 1944, was appointed superintendent of the economic section of the Main Police and Armed Services Command. He committed suicide in the last days of the war.[32]

Dr. Ivan Britvić remained in a leading advisory position in the Zagreb Police Directorate and then in the Ministry of the Interior ISC right up to December 1944. At the beginning of 1945, he managed to arrange a trip to Vienna on some business of a confidential nature, and he, his wife, and father-in-law were in Vienna when the war ended. On September 23, 1948, an UDB (Yugoslav Secret Police) agent reported that "Britvić is living in a country manor near Salzburg and is very well off" and that some émigrés had in quarrels accused him of "living so well because of the jewels and gold he had plundered in Croatia."[33] A year later, Britvić was in Argentina, from where he occasionally got in touch with his brother and other relatives in Croatia and invited them to visit him.

During an interrogation by the Zagreb UDB, after the British military authorities had taken him from a refugee camp in 1945 and handed him over to the Yugoslav authorities as a war criminal, Božidar Cerovski stated for the record: " . . . always the same emphasis on one goal—having their own state, and considering everything else of secondary importance . . . was catastrophic right from the beginning of the ISC," and "all the lawlessness, injustice, even crimes if you will, are the consequence of this mistake." He was sentenced to death and executed in January 1947.[34]

In the early fall of 1942, Pavelić forced Eugen Dido Kvaternik to resign from all his duties. It seems that this was the result of pressure because of the frequent displeasure of German and Italian representatives who complained of the chaotic conditions in the ISC. Internally, Pavelić blamed Dido Kvaternik for everything and made him a scapegoat, following which political terror was temporarily somewhat mitigated and, also temporarily, the mass liquidations in Jasenovac stopped. After Kvaternik, the directors of RAVSIGUR, then of GLAVSIGUR, were as follows, each for a short period: Ljudevit Zimperman, Filip Crvenković, Vladimir Jurčić, Danko Vidali, and Erih Lisak.[35] In 1943, Eugen Dido Kvaternik was banished to Slovakia, and after the war he went underground in Austria and Italy, until he managed to get to Argentina. He was killed in a traffic accident not far from Buenos Aires in 1962. After 1951, he occasionally appeared in political-historical discussions and wrote articles that were sometimes even repentant. The texts were very well written, erudite, and very critical of the totalitarian and dictatorial character of the regime and the mistaken state policy of the ISC. Reading between the lines, it can to a certain degree—albeit rarely—be felt that the author was aware of his personal guilt, which he blamed on his excessive devotion to, and belief in, Pavelić's policies, as well as his dutiful and complete implementation thereof, and which he subsequently called traitorous and criminal.

On the other hand, the public appearances of Pavelić and his most faithful followers during their "second exile" (after the war) show no trace of remorse, no admission of guilt. If, in fact, there were any crimes committed in the ISC, they attributed all responsibility and blame for them to Eugen Dido Kvaternik, whom they called a "psychopath," "abnormal," and "mad." And, in his texts, Kvaternik suggested that Pavelić was a serious psychopath.[36]

12

THE CONTRIBUTION

As early as mid-April, the Ustasha Police arrested about forty of the wealthiest and most distinguished Zagreb Jews (Julio König, Theodor Grünfeld, Dr. Josip Weissmann, Chief Cantor Bernard Grüner, and others), and did not release them from jail until they had agreed to organize the collection of a "contribution."[1] Soon after, during April 25–28, the Ustashe arrested another large group of well-known Zagreb Jews and interned them in the Kerestinec Camp. According to the testimony of an attorney, this was a group of about eighty Zagreb attorneys and other lawyers. They were released after fourteen days, then almost half of them were arrested again and taken back to Kerestinec, from there to the Gospić assembly camp, and then to Jasenovac.[2] This group, just like the first arrested in mid-April, was to have served as hostages for payment of the contribution. This was the usual procedure of the Ustasha regime, and similar things happened in Osijek, Bjelovar, and other towns. On May 13, Ivan Britvić summoned several prominent Zagreb Jews and ordered them to collect 1,000 kgs. of gold, or the equivalent value in jewels, money, or good securities, as the condition for their release. Britvić guaranteed that their lives, and the lives of other Zagreb Jews, would be spared in return for the gold. According to one post-war testimony, Britvić "placed a revolver on Julio König's chest and asked him to tell 'where the gold is.' König answered that he had no gold, especially not on him, to which Britvić replied, 'I'll release you and I order you to collect 1,000 kgs. of gold for the needs of the state, and when you have done so and handed over the gold, then the Jews will be treated with kid gloves.'"[3] According to another source, Britvić threatened that they would "all be shot if the ransom is not procured within three days."[4]

On May 8, before he summoned the Jews, Britvić had already received "an oral command from Kvaternik and Cerovski [at that time Ustasha police commissioner for Zagreb] that a Jewish committee should be organized." Britvić was obviously "in direct and permanent contact" with Kvaternik.[5] Josip Vragović also testified about the close contacts between Kvaternik and Britvić. Vragović had been head of the county police for the city of Zagreb in 1941, and while in prison in 1945 he claimed that it was Kvaternik who had ordered the imprisonment of the wealthy Jews.[6] It also seems that Kvaternik had arranged for the establishment of a contribution committee at a meeting held just between him and Julio König, even before Britvić's meeting with the group of Jews. After the war, Robert Glücksthal, then president of the Jewish Religious Community, claimed, "on the basis of what the other Committee members had said,"[7] that this was so. Britvić's play-acting with the revolver before the frightened Jewish notables was probably only an act put on to force the Zagreb Jews to collect the money and valuables quickly, although Kvaternik himself had already secretly arranged everything and informed König about it. This course of events, with Britvić acting publicly and Kvaternik arranging everything in the background, was confirmed in later months because Britvić did nothing without the agreement of his superiors. When the ransom was collected at the end of August, Britvić received an "order by telegram from Pećnikar, deputy director of UNS, granting him permission to sort and evaluate the valuables."[8] Kvaternik obviously also coordinated the anti-Jewish activities in Zagreb, and Cerovski, along with Joso Rukavina, Ivan Britvić, Vilko Kühnel, Ivo Baraković, and others, held important positions.[9]

News about the threats spread "through Jewish circles in Zagreb with the speed of lightning." Although the "very short deadlines for collecting the contribution were extended several times,"[10] the people who had been released and those who welcomed them back immediately organized themselves and established the so-called Contribution Committee, the Committee on the Matter of Contributions by Jews for State Needs, with an office at Draškovićeva 25. The Committee members were Julio König,

Dr. Josip Laufer, Dr. Juda Levi, Aleksandar Jelenić Hirschl, Hinko Mann, Egon Pollak, and Makso Borowitz; Aleksandar Piliš and Nikola Halasz worked in the treasury, Dr. Milan Brichta and Dr. Robert Glücksthal were lawyers, Robert Goldstein and Pavao Vogel kept the records, and Ignac (Ignjat) Weiss was the janitor.[11] The Committee soon had rather a broad circle of associates—allegedly volunteers, and also people who cooperated at the order of the authorities. The Zagreb Jews believed that giving this so-called invisible wealth could save their lives. Word spread that a receipt issued by the Contribution Committee to the effect that someone had fulfilled their obligations to the ISC would make it possible to get a passport or pass. It was soon shown that this was only partly true, but in those days the response was very good and the collection happened very quickly. Work began on May 15, when four people handed in just over one million kunas in money. The next day, sixty-five people gave almost nine million, and on the following day, 180 Jews handed in eleven million kunas.[12] By the end of May, more than fifty million kunas had been collected in money and valuables, which grew to one hundred million during June and in the following months.

The work of the Committee was very meticulous; each "contributor" got a receipt in three copies, and the Committee kept a large Contribution Book.[13] Whatever was collected was classed in categories: cash and securities, gold and jewels, foreign currency. Every day, everything that had been received was taken to the police in sealed bags and placed in a separate steel safe. However, civil servants soon began making new conditions and demanding other kinds of property. Soon, household and office furniture that had belonged to the "contributors" was furnishing offices in the Ministry of the Home Guard, the Marshal's Office, the Ustasha Army, a German general, the Police Directorate, Ustasha Police Directorate, and others.[14] The Committee got a precious dining-room suite of great antique value from the industrialist S. D. Aleksander, which was transported to Kvaternik's Marshal's Office.[15] Frequently Ustashe demanded cash or foreign exchange, and the Committee acquired this, too. Valuables obtained during the frequent police and other confiscations of Jewish property were also placed in the police safe.

On October 31, 1941, the Committee handed over to the Police Directorate in Zagreb the main report about the conclusion of the work, which had lasted for several months. It consisted of a collection of several documents: an accompanying official letter, two supplements, a report, and the statistics.[16] Hinko Mann and Aleksandar Piliš signed the documents in the name of the Contribution Committee, and it also bore the Committee's seal. The last document, "Comprehensive Survey of Contributions by Jews for the Needs of the State," is the most extensive, the most mundane, but also the most terrible. It is a very detailed and scrupulous list of everything that had been collected and handed over to the police and the other ISC services. It neatly lists the names, surnames, and addresses of the "contributors" (Supplement 15). The gold, jewelry, and gold coins were placed in 82 boxes and bags; there were 19 boxes of diamond jewelry, 4 boxes of pearl necklaces, 6 bags of gold napoleons, and there was 1 bag of gold ingots of the highest purity. For example, there were 680 gold watches, 223 pieces of gold and diamond jewelry, and 735 pieces of diamond jewelry.[17]

Much of the jewelry and other valuables was original artwork, which increased its value, and the state services estimated the total value at almost 160 million kunas (precisely 159,800,850 kunas). The Committee officially estimated the value of the treasure at 30 percent more, about 210,000,000 kunas.[18] During the six months of the existence of the ISC and the work of the Committee, the value of the kuna had already begun to fall rapidly, so the value of the diamonds was, as the Committee said, "abnormally high." The Committee called their estimate "modest," in other words, underestimated because of fear; they stated that the "gold and valuables collected are, in fact, worth much more than expressed in the estimate and entered on the books."[19] However, this statement was allegedly made "merely to pull the wool over the eyes of the authorities, who believed it because they were ignorant about the true value." After the war, one of the Committee members, Aleksandar Piliš, said that in actual fact the "value of the treasure that had been handed over was much smaller." He explained that it had been possible for him to give higher estimates because of the increase in the value of gold and the devaluation of the kuna, and by the "operation of calculating all the values on the basis of fourteen-carat gold." The whole report was styled and toned to "hide the actually smaller value of the contribution."[20] Be that as it may, the amount of money and treasure was vast: of the total value, 45.6 percent was gold, 35.6 percent cash, 18.5 percent foreign exchange, 0.2 percent furniture, and 0.1 percent securities.[21]

A "whole team of Jewish attorneys" was kept busy in the collection of the money and valuables, and in arranging the assignment of various kinds of papers, bank deposits, and so on.[22] The popular idea about the enormously wealthy Jews who would find it easy to pay the contribution is diametrically opposed to the reality that emerges from the dry documents. Many faced poverty after paying the contribution, especially as they no longer had a steady income. People handed over a lot of old family jewelry, often everything of value they had in the house, in the hope that by doing so they would save their lives and those of their family members. Thirty-three boxes were opened on January 19, 1942, in the presence of fourteen representatives of various state institutions (policemen, accountants, state treasury officials), two women who kept the records, and three members of the Contribution Committee: "Box number seventeen is now being opened, with the following contents: men's gold watches (30), all of fourteen-carat gold. Total weight about 788 grams." In the following days, several dozen boxes and bags were opened, savings accounts assigned, etc.[23] In later months and years, according to the proper procedure and with precise records, assets kept abroad were assigned—for example, on April 11, 1942, from the Deutsch-Maceljski family, $20,000 in gold, $42,000 in cash, 19,640 Swiss francs, and 2,680 British pounds.[24]

After the war, other Committee members, such as Robert Glücksthal, also claimed, probably because they were afraid that they might have problems, that "the Committee managed to hide and save a lot of the property owned by many people." Had the contribution not been made, they said, the Ustasha authorities would have broken into apartments and carried away the valuables themselves. There is no doubt that it was possible to save some of the property through a "voluntary contribution."

The pressure under which the Committee worked was terrible. Ivan Britvić mercilessly demanded daily reports from the members of the inner committee.[25] They returned from these meetings "very depressed, sometimes almost desperate." Julio König "cried and said that he could not endure it, and that he realized all the work was meaningless."[26] However, the police used other means of pressure too: at one of the meetings, Britvić demanded that some of the Jews should be summoned to make contributions again, claiming that he had information that the contribution they had paid was not the proper proportion of their wealth. It then turned out that the police had an informer: the cloth merchant Samuel Hahn. However, several months later, like some other informers, Hahn too was deported to Jasenovac, where he met his end before the winter of 1941.[27] Josip Bruckner allegedly also informed, leading to the arrest of some prominent Jews. He later fled to Spain.[28] Maks Šerf was also "in the confidential service of revealing people who engaged in forbidden trade and smuggled foreign exchange and gold." It seems that this activity enabled him to save himself, because he did not return to Zagreb.[29] Zdenko Šternberg claimed that when they met in the offices of the Jewish Community in August

1941, Freiberger asked him to keep his voice down because he was afraid of eavesdropping informers.[30]

Still, everybody did not give as much as the Committee estimated they should. Even the Committee members did not all react in the same way when Britvić, at the meeting at which he threatened them with a gun, ordered them to submit a list of all their property in the country and abroad. Several of them tried to hide some of their property, but the distinguished and rich Zagreb attorney Rudolf Rodanić reported everything that he owned, even what was in a Swiss bank, fearing that the police would find out about it through the Germans.[31] Rodanić transferred his Swiss gold to Britvić, but asked him to return his wife's gold, which had been confiscated during a search of their apartment. He felt that he had this right because his "wife was Aryan." Later, some of Rodanić's money (a total of 250,000 kunas) was handed over to the Jewish Community for the upkeep of the camps.[32]

Obviously, the Committee members, who had entered into this obligation least of all of their own free will, "were hated and defamed."[33] They found themselves between Scylla and Charybdis, and it was extremely difficult to resolve all situations in such a way that everyone would be satisfied. Rudolf Rodanić did all he could to avoid becoming a Committee member because "he found the situation most unpleasant," but he also claimed that several people told him that "the police were threatening the Committee members."[34] In 1945, David Akselrad also said that "all the Committee members worked with the best will under terrible pressure."[35] It seems that there was the most gossip about Hinko Mann: there were stories that he, and maybe some other Committee members as well, had benefited financially from the work of collecting the contribution.[36] This is very unlikely, because too many people were involved in the work, both Jews and non-Jews, so it would not have been easy to do. Later, Mann was also accused of getting rich by procuring passes for members of the Community. Although this kind of work was not regulated nor were proper records kept, as they were in the case of the contribution, it was too risky for a Community member to keep back money from sources of this kind. Had the Ustashe found out about it, or even only suspected it, Mann would probably not have survived.[37] According to his own testimony and that of others, Mann wanted the Ustashe to look on him as a very cooperative person. The accompanying letter that the Committee sent to the Police Directorate said that "the Committee members consider this work their duty" and that they would "in future be ready to accept other tasks to prove their loyalty to the State, which they consider their Homeland."[38] Mann did all he could to protect himself, but there is doubt that he also saved some Jews and some Jewish property. To safeguard this position, he obviously "dealt with parties who had fallen behind in their contribution rather energetically."[39] In connection with this problem, at the beginning of July, the Jewish Community informed the Jewish Section that some Jews were not willing to pay the Community dues, stating that they would not pay them because they had in the meantime converted to Catholicism. The Community therefore requested an authentic interpretation of the Legal Provision of Racial Affiliation. The Jewish Section replied that "all persons are required to pay the Community dues . . . regardless of whether and when they left the Jewish religion." In the case of a dispute, the Community was "authorized to collect the dues through seizure."[40]

In comparison to others, a higher percentage of members of the Contribution Committee survived the war: "All the Committee members tried to emigrate, and they did so at the first opportunity that presented itself," says a postwar report.[41] The Ustasha authorities issued those who were in Zagreb in the summer of 1941 identity cards, which stated that "the owner of this identity card is working in the interest and on the behalf of the state and the Ustasha authorities, and neither he nor his family nor his apartment may, under any circumstances, be touched, requisitioned, arrested, or taken to forced labor."[42] All the members of the Contribution Committee and of the Community Council were issued with certificates saying that they "have the right of unhindered work," and in July, seventy of them got passes to move freely through the city on Community business.[43]

But in many cases, guarantees of this kind did not help. In the fall of 1941, Ivo (Ivan, Hans) Hochsinger obtained a pass to travel "out of Zagreb, to Loborgrad, Gornja Rijeka, Osijek, and Đakovo and back" to coordinate work on caring for the Jewish inmates.[44] At the beginning of 1942, he was arrested and deported to Jasenovac. In June and July, additional food was regularly sent to him every week to Gređane (one of the Jasenovac farms), then he was moved to the main camp in July. He was killed in Jasenovac on November 20 of that year.[45] Dr. Josip Laufer, the Committee member second in importance, was later arrested and killed "in an unknown place." Josip Klein, who acquired foreign currency for the Committee on behalf of the Ustasha authorities, had "already allegedly been sent to camp" [to Jasenovac] at the end of October, when the report was written. Leo Tobolski, Teodor Grünfeld, and Aladar Merkler also met their end in Jasenovac.

Grünfeld, Merkler, and Klein did not live to see the end of 1941, while Tobolski probably lived a little longer.[46]

The fate of the administration staff and employees of the Jewish Religious Community of Zagreb was even worse. In October 1941, the Community Board sent a petition to the City Housing Bureau asking that institution to protect the property of eighty-nine administrative staff and employees of the Jewish Community, whose names and addresses they enclosed.[47] Since many of them were evicted from their apartments, deported, and killed in the following months, it is possible that the Ustasha services used this list of addresses as an excellent source of information. In 1941, David Atijas, a barber's assistant, was deported, but some were temporarily spared, even protected. When Armin Davidović, manager and shareholder of the Union Factory (now the Josip Kraš Chocolate and Biscuits Factory), was evicted from his apartment in Rapska Street, instead of an Ustasha moving in, the keys of the apartment were "allocated to his son Ivan Davidović, who was an employee of the Jewish Religious Community . . . and therefore neither his apartment, nor that of his parents, may be confiscated."[48] Despite all these guarantees, Armin Davidović was incarcerated in the prison on Sava Road on January 9, 1942, and then deported.[49] At the end of January 1943, Ivo Davidović was still in Zagreb, because he signed his name on various Community documents at that time, but it appears that he was deported in May of that year.[50] Alice Dukes, teacher in the Community school, was taken away and killed as early as 1941. Ruža (Rosa) Hacker (64), a Community employee, was deported to Stara Gradiška or Đakovo in February 1942, and there she disappeared because she had allegedly "helped Jews escape to Italy."[51] The Community secretary, Aleksandar Klein, was also almost killed: he was arrested in August 1941 and, after much intercession, released in November, but continued to be under close watch and had to report to the police twice a day.[52] All this shows that Community employees, at least those on the list of employees from the summer of 1941, were killed in the same or an even higher percentage than the Community members in general—almost 80 percent of them did not survive the war. The fact that they were in contact with the authorities, or that the authorities had precise data about them, only made it easier to deport them at the moment once the authorities chose to do so.

13

PLUNDERING JEWISH PROPERTY

Confiscating gold was only one of the methods used to plunder Jewish (and Serb) property that the authorities had their eye on. Since Croats held 50.5 percent of the shares in joint stock companies, the Ustasha authorities could justly claim that the ISC economy was "to a great measure in the hands of non-Croats." However, most of the shares held by non-Croats belonged to people who were citizens of Switzerland, USA, Germany, and Great Britain, and these, of course, could not be touched. In an attempt to justify the expropriation of Jewish property, a variety of lies were circulated: for example, on June 6, 1941, at a meeting with Hitler, Pavelić said that the Jews in Croatia were "very influential in all fields—in industry as much as 70 percent."[1] In actual fact, before 1941, Jews held 7 percent of the shares in joint stock companies, and 23 percent in commerce. The Ustasha authorities decided that industries had to be "made national," or "Aryanized," and that "non-national and non-Aryan elements—which meant the Jews—must be eliminated from the Croatian economy."[2]

At the beginning of May, a campaign began that was designed to bring great material benefit to the authorities. On May 2, they passed the Legal Provision on the Regular Operation of and the Prevention of Sabotage in Business Enterprises, which, in practice, was aimed exclusively at the Jews. The following day, the Bureau of Economic Reconstruction was founded, ostensibly to bring "order" to the economy. In its articles of incorporation, the Bureau was not anti-Jewish in character, but in practice its work was strongly anti-Jewish. It was founded to supervise the work of businesses and to manage them if necessary (had the owner left or the firm been seized), to buy and sell businesses, and generally to dispose of various kinds of nationalized (stolen) property.[3] Until its incorporation in the newly founded State Directorate of Economic Reconstruction, the Bureau was very active in the plunder of Jewish property.

The Jewish Section found various other ways of robbing Jews and coordinated some of these activities: on May 7, the Employees' Retirement Fund in Zagreb requested an answer from the Jewish Section to the question, "if employees who are Jewish lose their jobs, may they get back part of the deposit that they had paid in?" (which was the rule). The answer was that "no deposits may be returned without the approval of this Section."[4] The Jewish Section also informed the Employees' Savings and Loans Cooperative that "members who are pureblooded Jews may not withdraw deposits nor may loans to them be approved."[5]

New laws followed at the beginning of June. The Legal Provision on Marking Jewish Shops was passed on June 4, and next day saw the Legal Provision on Prevention of Concealing Jewish Property and the Legal Provision on the Obligatory Registration of Jews and Jewish Firms.[6] By May and June, about 800 commissioners had been appointed to Jewish businesses in Zagreb alone.[7] The first provision stated that "anyone who conceals Jewish property or the Jewish character of a firm . . . anyone who makes a legal contract for a Jew and in so doing deceives the other contracting party" was liable to face one to five years of imprisonment and confiscation of property.[8]

The second provision ordered Jews to report their property to the competent ministry within twenty days from the day when the provision entered into force, including property they had sold or given away after February 10, 1941. "Any disposal of Jewish property" was forbidden under the threat of imprisonment. Jews who did not "report their property or who kept it secret, completely or in part, will be punished by severe imprisonment from one to ten years and confiscation of property."

The "provision" was accompanied by an "ordinance on application" whose most important and longest part was two forms that had to be filled out for the "obligatory report of Jewish property."[9] The first form was for the "obligation to report property," the second for the "obligation to report Jewish firms, i.e., firms that are completely or partly owned by Jews." The forms were very well-designed and detailed, obviously on the Nazi model: they took up as many as seven pages in the Collection of Laws and Ordinances, and as many as thirteen pages as printed sheets. The first form required people to identify themselves, among other things, as to citizenship, place of origin, race of spouse and children, primary and secondary occupations, ownership and joint ownership. Separate forms were made out for attorneys, financial and legal representatives, business advisors, doctors, for registering real estate, for "engineers, builders, former public notaries and members of other free professions," for "mining rights," "leases and options," "patents and licenses," "copyright," "valuables" (with seven questions and five secondary questions), "participation in firms," "claims" (with twelve questions and secondary questions), "market value of tools, instruments, and equipment they own for performing their occupation," about "furniture, foodstuffs, clothes and other household property," and "other property that accrues from any other legal contracts." Finally, they had to make a "statement of debt" on the day when the provision entered into force, in which they had to "state the character of the debt and the racial affiliation of the creditor."

On July 12, 1941, the Zagreb Chamber of Industry "required all Jewish firms . . . to report as soon as possible," with the official letter giving a detailed explanation of what was considered a "Jewish firm."[10] At the end of August, the head of the State Directorate of Economic Reconstruction wrote to Mirko Puk, Minister of Justice, that "Jewish property was frequently being hidden." Since cases of this kind were under the jurisdiction of the regular courts, which could pronounce sentences of confiscation of property and imprisonment, and since these courts were "overburdened with work," the State Directorate proposed to the Ministry of Justice that the Directorate should take over from the regular courts the authority to sentence people to confiscation of property.[11] However, ideas of this kind became unimportant in the following months because the confiscation process had already gone much further.

The card index of firms kept by the Directorate of Economic Reconstruction showed that 1,456 firms were considered Jewish in Zagreb alone.[12] In the following months, many ISC services were engaged in the process of taking over Jewish firms, or clarifying whether a firm was Jewish or not. On May 20, Hugo Deutsch resigned from the management board of the Prof. Dr. Franjo Brössler Scientific Institute, and Ernest Fischer was "struck from membership of the supervision board, because his residence is not known." This was done because, according to the explanation given by the Ministry of the Interior and the Ministry of the National Economy in June 1941, the Institute had connections with "one of the most prominent factories in Germany" whose representatives, "if they realized that the Institute was a Jewish firm, might make it lose the privileged position that it enjoys thanks to its correct and conscientious work, so, in its business operations, the Jewish connection—except for ownership of the shares—was not obvious, nor was it generally known that there were any Jews in the firm."[13]

Germany provided the Ustasha authorities with direct help in the operation of "taking over Jewish property." Doglavnik and Marshal Slavko Kvaternik, Commissioner of the State Economic Commission, invited the lawyer Dr. Hermann Dzialas, Nazi "Aryanization expert" (i.e., specialist in the confiscation of Jewish property), to spend some time in Zagreb as professional senior advisor in the State Directorate of Economic Reconstruction. He was officially appointed by Ćiril Ćudina,[14] Head of the Directorate, "on the order of the Marshal [Slavko Kvaternik] and in agreement with Dr. Košak, Minister of Finance." Dzialas was to spend "several months working on the Aryanization of industries." Ćudina instructed the officials in the Directorate to offer "Dzialas unlimited help and to support him."[15] At the beginning of October, Dzialas sent Slavko Kvaternik a detailed report in which he generally praised the effects of "Aryanization," but also found some ineptness and disorganization.[16] Dzialas complained that he had not been allowed to see all the data and some other details about the work of the State Directorate, which in fact means that the Ustashe even tried to hide some of their activities from their German "professional senior advisors."

Certainly, senior advisor Dzialas did not complain of poor organization in the Ustasha state without reason. As in other fields, in the "Aryanization" of Jewish property, hasty improvisation and the overlapping of authority was widespread. After May 3, the Bureau of Economic Reconstruction in the Ministry of National Economy ran the "Aryanization" process. In the following weeks, the Bureau got much more work than an improvised ministry department was able or competent to handle, since the amount of property that had belonged to Jews or Serbs who had been deported or escaped was constantly increasing as the number of deportees increased. In addition, preparations had to be made to take over all the Jewish businesses and their property, which soon became one of the publicly defined political and economic goals. These activities fell within the jurisdiction of several other ministries besides the Ministry of the Economy (e.g., finance, justice, interior), so it was decided to merge some functions and raise them to a "higher level" of responsibility. For this purpose, two state directorates were created. The State Directorate of Reconstruction, founded on June 24, took over the property of the "emigrated population," temporarily managed it, and handed it over or sold it to new immigrants. The euphemism "emigrated population" mostly meant Serbs, who were by then being forcibly moved to Serbia, and there were plans for much greater, almost total deportation.[17] The State Directorate of Economic Reconstruction, on the other hand, was founded on July 1, and it took over all the other work of the former Bureau of Economic Reconstruction and greatly extended it. It had the responsibility for making a record of all Jewish property, taking over Jewish firms and Jewish property in general, and selling or entrusting it to others.[18] Thus, this Directorate was in practice usually known as "Jewish Reconstruction." The scope of this work can also be seen from the fact that this Directorate employed about one hundred people.[19] The similarity between the two state directorates did not end with their crypto-names ("reconstruction" instead of "confiscation" or "seizure"), their areas of responsibility often overlapped too, which led to more confusion instead of to better organization. The confusion was exacerbated by the important role the State Economic Commission had in managing nationalized property, which was under the iron fist of Slavko Kvaternik. He decided that nationalized craft firms should be handed over to the Croatian Workingman's Cooperative, and in August 1941 he issued an order for what had now come to be called Reconstruction: "I hereby inform the directorate that, without my approval, no ruling may be issued in accordance with the legal provisions concerning the property of persons who have left the territory of the ISC."[20] Vlado Košak, State Treasurer (Minister of Finance), said that the State Economic Commission was an "economic committee of ministers" responsible for decisions on economic matters and on nationalized property.[21]

To lessen this organizational confusion, on September 15, the two state directorates were combined into one, called the State Directorate of Reconstruction, which did all the work of the previous two.[22] Finally, on January 1, 1942, this Directorate was abolished as well, and all its work transferred to the Ministry of Crafts, Industry and Trade, Ministry of Justice and Religious Affairs, and the State Treasury. A separate department called the Nationalized Wealth Bureau was created as part of the Property, Credits and Debts Bureau of the State Treasury.

At the end of August 1941, by legal provision, the management of all

Jewish-owned buildings and property was transferred to town and district boards, which had the right to collect rent.[23] This gave rise, on September 25, to some minor amendments on procedure in the Legal Provision on the Preservation of Croatian National Property, of April 18.[24] Finally, on October 10, 1941, the Legal Provision on the Nationalization of Jewish Property and Jewish Businesses was passed, in which Jewish movable and immovable property was qualified as "state property." This was the beginning of plunder in the name of the state,[25] the legalization of confiscations that had already taken place, and at the same time an announcement of new ones. In certain cases, it was possible to avoid confiscation and even for owners to be paid compensation, but this happened very rarely. In practice, it was much more usual for regime officials to extort property arbitrarily and for their own use. Although voices were sometimes raised, decrying such acts as "unlawful," obviously the regime did nothing to prevent them but, on the contrary, encouraged them. The Germans and the Italians also "broke into Jewish apartments and shops and took whatever they could lay their hands on . . . The most valuable things were taken to furnish newly acquired apartments and institutions of the occupying forces. Railway freightcars full of goods were sent to Germany and Italy . . . Of course, by far, most of the looting was done by Ustashe." As for real estate, if it was not taken by the state, "it was sold," not at "the market price, but was given by favoritism to good Ustashe . . . Jewish businesses fared even worse."[26] Even before the end of June 1941, the German military command had taken Manfred Sternberg's office furniture, worth 30,000 dinars.[27] When outrageous pillage was tried in court—as, for example, in the case of Pavao Jurić and Marija Hancko, who looted Jewish apartments in Vukovar—there would be a regular court trial and the persons responsible would be found not guilty.[28]

The State Directorate of Economic Reconstruction, in an official letter of September 5, 1941, informed all the commissioners it had appointed that Jews must on no account be given severance pay, "which would in many cases be based on years of fictitious employment of the Jewish owner's friends and relatives, who never actually worked in the firm but cost it a lot in high salaries in order to get around existing regulations."[29] In September 1941, in a "very confidential circular letter," this Directorate informed "all town and district heads" that if their services discovered any "empty apartments, either because the owners have fled, disappeared, or been taken away, they should immediately take all measures for the preservation and assignment of the empty property." They were ordered to set up a "special committee" of several members that would include a representative of the authorities, a representative of the Ustasha organization, and a representative of the ethnic German national group (if it existed in that locality). There were also precise regulations that valuables (ready money, gold, foreign currency, etc.) must be placed in the "safe of the town government or the district office," that "clothes, shoes, and household linen should be appropriately stored in a safe place," and that furniture must immediately be listed and then sold at market value, "first and foremost to the families of those who were in any way actively fighting for the Homeland."[30] In October 1942, the National Economy and Traffic Committee estimated that in carpets alone the state took goods to the value of one billion kunas from the Jews.[31]

Although people who forced their way into apartments that the Jewish occupants had just left looted a lot of the property, some Jewish property did end up at auctions. At the end of October 1941, chattel "for sale . . . confiscated from the Jews and people who emigrated," was exhibited at the Zagreb Fair, in pavilion F, on the first and second floors. Buyers had to "show the circular letter and their identity card" and could only buy "for cash." The City Government, which acquired money in this way, informed the Prime Minister's Office that it had preemptive rights.[32] The State Directorate of Reconstruction gave its approval for civil servants in the Jewish Section RUR to "buy, for an appropriate price, twenty-three items of various fabrics that have been confiscated from Jews."[33] In August 1942, the Staff Command of the Ustasha Female Youth in Karlovac said that "in all towns, the Ustasha Youth got the clothes and shoes of Jews who had been removed" and that they hoped that the Karlovac City Government would act in a similar way and distribute "all goods and clothes to needy Ustasha youth."[34] In Karlovac, all the books from Jewish apartments were transported to the Ustasha Office and anyone who went there could take them.[35] In the summer of 1942, the grand prefect of the Grand County of Baranja in Osijek considered that "this is the chance for all workers' apartments to be supplied with furniture and objects from Jewish apartments."[36] The plundered goods were stored in a warehouse in Feričanci (near Valpovo in Slavonia), where the Ustasha authorities wanted to set up a modern farm, and "every day, Ustasha officers came to pick out carpets for their rooms, silk stockings and dresses that used to belong to Jewish ladies for the use of their mistresses and whores."[37] In the attic of a house in Garićgradska in Zagreb, where she had rented an apartment, Mila Kniewald-Mirković saw fine furniture and other things that were far beyond her landlady's means. When she asked the landlady where she had got those things, she replied angrily and avoided giving a direct answer.[38]

Some of the provisions passed in those months did not apply only to Jews, though they affected them, too. The Legal Provision on the Property of Persons Who Emigrated from the Territory of the ISC was passed on August 7, 1941, and provided that the State Directorate of Reconstruction "shall immediately begin procedures whereby the movable and immovable property of persons who have emigrated shall be proclaimed ISC property." This procedure began by placing such property under "security measures." If the owner, even after being summoned by the authorities, did not report in person within fifteen days, the State Directorate proclaimed that the property was now owned by the ISC. If the authorities so decided, it was possible for part of the property to be held in usufruct by the statutory heirs. There were no legal remedies against the decisions of the State Directorate.[39] The Legal Provision on Amalgamating the Property of Some Foundations and on Changing the Purpose or the Name of a Foundation, of August 16, 1941, provided that, in the case of "foundations in which achieving the purpose of the foundation has become impossible, legally or morally impermissible, or useless, the Ministry of Education shall issue a decision determining some other purpose of general use or shall amalgamate the property of such foundations with that of some other existing foundation."[40] In accordance with this provision, the Tilda Deutsch–Maceljski Foundation for the organization of summer hostels, which had between the wars sent several hundred needy children to the sea or the mountains every year, had its name changed in December 1941 to the Crafts School Students' Home. The main reason why this was done was to get hold of the hostels for Jewish children in Ravna Gora (twelve kilometers east of Delnice) and in Crikvenica, which were the property of the foundation.[41] However, this cunningly devised legal provision did not achieve the desired result: the Ustasha authorities could not lay their hands on either of the two properties. By the end of 1941, Ravna Gora was already in an unsafe region, communications were often broken, and, from October 1942, the area was under Partisan control. The Crikvenica property could not be used either, because, as a rule, the Italian occupation authorities did not allow Jewish property to be requisitioned.

In October 1941, Jewish firms began to be handed over to favorites of the regime. These included dozens of important industries and other companies,[42] but also Kajon Heim's newspaper stand in Branimirova Street[43] and the Corso Coffeehouse in Ilica.[44] During interrogation in 1947, Slavko Kvaternik said that "Jewish shops were primarily given to Ustasha émigrés, then to Ustashe in Croatia, and then to other people who were well known for their strong Croatian feelings."[45] For example, in only one issue in March 1942, *Hrvatski narod* published the notice "Firms for Sale," offering ownership of forty-nine firms that had almost all been the property of Zagreb Jews.[46] The following month, *Hrvatska gruda* offered twenty-two "Jewish" firms, seventeen of them in Zagreb.[47]

In these proceedings there were often cases when the activities of the Ministry of Justice and Religious Affairs overlapped with those of the State Treasury, and it seems that sometimes this even led to disputes; however, the basic goal was always achieved—the Jews were stripped of their property.[48] The Ministry of Justice was careful to comply with the law. For example, they annulled the contract whereby Marta Rajić, née Sauerbrunn, donated to her children Fedor and Ksenija, who were minors, the family house (one apartment) and land in Zvonimirova Street 99 in Zagreb, because she was "Jewish by origin, that is, non-Aryan." As Marta had married a Serb, Đuro Rajić, who had later become a Roman Catholic, the children were from a mixed marriage and in principle the racial laws did not apply to them. Nevertheless, the whole family was arrested in June 1941 and taken to the Zagreb Fairground, but soon released. Although their house in Zvonimirova was taken from them by the state, the family was allowed to remain there and, despite several house searches and other forms of unpleasantness, they managed to survive the war. However, Marta's mother, Elza Sauerbrunn, although she had converted, was taken to Auschwitz and never returned.[49]

It is paradoxical that the process of confiscating Jewish property took longer than it took the Ustasha regime to kill most of the Jews. This was a general characteristic of Ustasha rule, where the authorities often worked along two parallel lines: one was the ostensibly law-abiding line, which sometimes preceded but usually lagged behind the other line, which was always marked by violence and unlawful behavior. Someone who cared about the first, ostensibly law-abiding line, obviously wanted to effect this plunder in a legally impeccable manner, although—and this is the most paradoxical aspect of the entire procedure—in most cases, the owners had already lost their lives. On February 6, 1942, the Legal Provision on the Conversion of Nationalized Jewish Buildings and Building Sites into Money was passed, and their management was transferred to the State Treasury. By the same provision, Jews who were still in a position to do so had to hand over all their securities and bank deposit books, insurance policies, valuables, and items of artistic, cultural, and historic value.[50]

This entire process of "taking over" former Jewish property was deeply corrupt, because, as Slavko Kvaternik said in 1947, much of it was in fact motivated by various kinds of favoritism.[51] Even the parliamentary Treasury Committee could not keep silent about this, and, in June 1942, it sent a deputation to Poglavnik Pavelić to draw his attention to the corrupt and arbitrary behavior that attended the plunder of nationalized Jewish property. The deputation recalled Pavelić's speech to students, when he said that "they did not ask for their patriotism to be paid for in Jewish shops and Persian rugs." At that time, there was already clear proof that "shameless plunder was going on, because the nationalized Jewish firms with large stores of goods and raw materials were simply being sold off at low prices."[52] However, despite these complaints, nothing changed.

The Legal Provision on the Nationalization of Jewish Property of October 30, 1942, provided for the final confiscation of all Jewish property without any compensation or exceptions, and it covered the property of all who were still alive and those who had died after February 10, 1941 (which gave greater force to the decision of April 17, 1941).[53] Five full pages and nineteen articles of precise legal text made sure that there would be no ambiguity and no possibility for any kind of Jewish property not to be taken over by the state (special attention was paid to cases when property was involved in a lawsuit, etc.). The Ministry of the State Treasury, its State Property, Credits and Debts Department–Nationalized Wealth Bureau, issued a very detailed letter emphasizing in bold lettering that this legal provision had "inaugurated a radical change in the issue of Jewish property" because "there is no more Jewish property left. Everything that used to be Jewish property has, through the enactment of the above legal provisions, become the property of the ISC."[54] After March 1943, all Jewish firms and shops were placed on the market. The Ustasha authorities gave some of them to various state organizations, while the rest were bought by individuals close to the authorities for a minimum price. In July 1943, the German intelligence services circulated information about "Jewish women who flee from Croatia to Italy, get divorced, and marry Italian officials and officers, and who then immediately submit requests for nationalized Jewish property." The Germans suspected that these marriages were "only fictitious."[55] This intelligence report probably says more about the anti-Semitic hysteria in Nazi intelligence services than about what was really taking place, because no such case has been recorded in documents known to date. In July 1943, the Zagreb Jewish Community, in response to a query of the Ministry of Justice and Religious Affairs about the management of the Jewish Community's property, answered that "this Community has no property, except for the chattel in its office premises, and it is supported by the voluntary donations of individuals."[56]

Until the very end of the war, the Ustasha administration continued to devote thorough attention to the legal aspects of robbing the Jews:[57] on March 24, 1945, only about forty days before it fled from Zagreb, the Ministry of Justice and Religious Affairs sent a directive giving instructions about how to ensure "uniformity of procedure" in accordance with the law of October 30, 1942, and ordering that all changes of ownership should be entered in the cadastral registers. Although the wording is in dry and precise legal language, the intent of the directive's authors was obvious: by entering property in these registers, they wanted to ensure ownership in the postwar period as well.[58]

Some postwar estimates show that the ISC authorities robbed the Jews of property in excess of twenty-five billion dinars according to the prices of 1939. However, in 1945, only six billion dinars worth of this property was discovered, in real estate, without taking into account unrealized income. The above estimates only covered property that had been publicly registered and was known; it can never be ascertained how much unregistered property was stolen (family jewelry, art works, furniture, etc.) through looting after the owners of apartments and houses were deported or had fled. Some was found later. A considerable quantity of furniture from the Jewish Community was sent to the Kulturbund in Haulikova Street, and it was easy to identify it in June 1945. It included at least 101 chairs, almost thirty desks of various kinds, ten large cabinets (one with eight doors), a tiled stove, a gas stove, etc.[59] The Croatian Workingman's organization "took over and carted away all the furniture from the Jewish Orthodox Temple." In July 1945, this furniture was "stored in the courtyard garage in Petrova Street 5."[60]

A thorough and well-substantiated report to the State Commission for War Crimes estimates that, after 1945, the state managed to recover only about five billion kunas worth of Jewish property, and that "property to the value of about fifty billion kunas was dispersed throughout the ISC, about thirty-six billion in Croatia."[61] During postwar interrogation, Vlado Košak claimed that the Reconstruction Directorate alone "acquired Jewish facilities to a value of about five or six billion prewar dinars, mostly consisting of real estate and shops, while most chattel was looted and never reached the directorate. There were about three to four billion in valuables, and a further five to six billion prewar dinars in other movable property. The value of the movables was within the scale of the budget used for the needs of the ISC."[62] This means that the total value of the nationalized property was between thirteen and sixteen billion dinars.[63]

In Zagreb itself, about 1,200 buildings were nationalized, of which at least eighty were valued at over three million kunas (of these, over 90 percent were the property of Jews, the remainder being the property of Serbs).[64] It is estimated that in the total value of the "nationalized Jewish property and of others who emigrated," 65.1 percent was accounted for by buildings, 22.9 percent by commercial and crafts firms, 5.8 percent by industries, 3.6 percent by securities, and 2.6 percent by movable property.[65]

Košak said that "at the time of the persecution of Jews and their deportation to concentration camps, it was supposed that large amounts of Jewish valuables had been taken by the police authorities, and by the highest officials, including Eugen Kvaternik himself, but how he disposed of these and what kinds and amounts he handed over to Pavelić and his family, I do not know."[66] Košak told the truth, because records exist only about the police authorities robbing Jews, not about what happened to the spoils later. A good example is from 1942, at the time of deportations from Slavonia and Zagreb. At that time, the Ustasha Police Directorate sent their official, Dragan Albrecht, to Vinkovci to organize the operation, and among other things to "take the money and valuables of the evicted Jews," with the instruction that everything must be tidily recorded and handed over properly.[67] Košak said that "on one occasion, he asked Kvaternik where these Jewish valuables were and suggested that they should be given to the Reconstruction Directorate, to which Kvaternik replied that there had been certain small amounts, but that he had used them for the upkeep of the Jews in the camps."[68]

There is no doubt that the very highest authorities took part in stealing Jewish property. During the investigation in 1947, Slavko Kvaternik and Vladimir Košak mentioned the case of Lieutenant Colonel Mihovil Sertić, Quartermaster General in the Supreme Command of the Ustasha Army, claiming that he had laid his hands on millions. Sertić's biography shows that he must have been involved in some unsavory business, if not outright criminal activities: in March 1943, at the age of 33, he was pensioned, but later he became an SS major (Sturmbannführer), which in fact meant he had been rehabilitated.[69]

In 1947, during the interrogation of Mehmed Alajbegović, former ISC Foreign Minister, the interrogators said that his ministry had received valuables from the Nationalized Wealth Bureau. Alajbegović answered that this was not true, but that he knew of one case when someone got diamonds to travel to Spain on Pavelić's personal orders. He also said that "just over 1,000 kg. of gold was sent from the ISC to Switzerland before he had become foreign minister," meaning before May 1944. He had also heard that "a large amount of silver was supposed to have been sent to Switzerland in 1944, or even earlier," but did not know whether this silver had really arrived there.[70] Perhaps Alajbegović really did not know that in May and August 1944, the Croatian National Bank deposited 1,338 kg. of gold in the Swiss National Bank, and 2,750,000 Swiss francs in that and in two other banks.[71] "There is no doubt that 45 percent of the value that had been deposited in the bank was Jewish property. We will be able to establish how much Jewish wealth went abroad more exactly when the records are found about the valuables in the thirty-two boxes that were stored in the Franciscan Monastery located at 9 Kaptol Street, and were discovered at the beginning of 1946," Jareb concluded.[72]

Even their enormous contributions to the Ustasha authorities did not manage to save from persecution the members of two distinguished and very rich Zagreb Jewish families: Aleksander and Deutsch-Maceljski. Between the two world wars, the most prominent Alexander in the business life of Zagreb was Samuel (born 1862). He founded the First Croatian Oil Factory, Mirna Coal Mine, Portland Cement Croatia Factory (in Podsused, then a suburb of Zagreb), Danica and Titanit Chemical Industries, owned the Zagreb Brewery, and was cofounder and vice-president of the Zagreb Stock Exchange and the Zagreb Fair (from which today's Zagreb Fair, the *Velesajam*, developed). Samuel Aleksander was often called the "Nestor of Zagreb industrialists."[73] In his eightieth year, in compliance with the demand for the "obligatory registration of Jewish property," Samuel registered property having a total value of 15,840,222 kunas. It is very difficult to estimate how much this would be worth today. Two of the most important pieces of real estate—an apartment house at Žerjavićeva 12 and half an apartment house at Đorđićeva 7 (both in the center of Zagreb)—were at that time estimated at 1,200,000 and 550,000 kunas respectively, and together they made up only about 11 percent of Samuel's registered property. The most valuable item consisted of 32,909 shares, worth 7,404,525 kunas, in the Zagreb Brewery, in which Samuel was the majority owner. He also owned an important share of the Associated Zagreb Bank, Mirna Coal Mine Company in Zagreb, First Croatian Oil Factory, and some other smaller businesses. In the contribution, Samuel gave 1,700,000 kunas of the total of 68,000,000 (as was estimated at the time) given by the Zagreb Jews.[74] After that, the Alexanders were "magnanimously" recognized as having already given 278,000 kunas in gold and other valuables for the contribution (did someone deliberately hide the real numbers?), but even so, the following was later listed (and then taken): dinner and coffee table silver (90,000 kunas), a necklace with 127 pearls (35,000 kunas), an emerald brooch with diamonds (74,000 kunas), a diamond bracelet (75,000 kunas), two paintings by the famous Croatian artist Menci Clement Crnčić (12,000 kunas), a statue by the famous Croatian sculptor Ivan Meštrović (30,000 kunas), a gold box (25,000 kunas), a Persian lamb coat (12,000 kunas), paintings, etc. A lot of furniture of various kinds was listed in detail and taken, and the entry "other furniture" alone is valued at 70,000 kunas.[75]

In October 1941, the Committee on the Matter of Contribution by Jews for State Needs informed the State Directorate of Economic Reconstruction that S. Aleksander had assigned to them a sum of 1,700,000 kunas, which represented the monetary value of part of his shares, and which he paid out in cash. On October 28, 1942, in meticulously conducted proceedings, the ISC State Treasury, Property, Credits and Debts Department–Nationalized Wealth Bureau, "nationalized" Samuel's 10,587 shares in the Zagreb Brewery and 5,409 shares in eight other stock companies.[76] In October of that year, Samuel's account balance of 312,000 kunas in the Associated Zagreb Bank was also requisitioned.

In February 1942, Samuel and his wife were arrested and imprisoned at Sava Road, but UNS demanded that the Jewish Section of RUR release them, which was done.[77] His health impaired, the elderly Samuel and his wife then found refuge in Dr. Vranešić's private sanatorium in Zelengaj in Zagreb, a safe haven for some wealthy Jews and other endangered people who could afford to pay. He died there in relative peace on March 8, 1943, in his eighty-first year, and his wife, Ema, née Neumann, (1866–1952) survived the war.[78] Even after his death, the Ustasha administration did not leave Samuel alone: on June 21, 1944, Legal Subsection I inquired of the Workers' Insurance Subsidiary whether "Aleksandar Samuel is a natural or legal person," because he owes 123.5 kunas, which represented approximately 0.0008 percent of his prewar property. Earlier (in May), the Ministry of the State Treasury had been allowed to make good this debt from Aleksander's nationalized property. On July 28, 1944, the same Legal Subsection inquired with the City of Zagreb Police District "where is Aleksander Samuel of Zagreb at present located, is he a Jew, and is he said to have been taken to camp and on what date?"[79]

The other members of the numerous and branching Alexander family were also rich and, in 1941, reported their property, which was then taken from them. Some of them managed to escape from the ISC during the summer and fall of 1941 and scattered throughout the world, from Italy and Switzerland to the USA and Palestine. Of those who hesitated and remained in Zagreb, some died in Jasenovac and Auschwitz (Zlata, Oto, Đuro, Ines, and Miljenko Alexander, Zora Marić and others), others managed to survive various kinds of harassment and the war, including the painter Oskar Artur Alexander (1876–1953).[80] Zdenko Vinski and his parents, grandmother, and brother Ivo were exempt from wearing the insignia and were allowed to go on living in their apartment.[81]

The Deutsch-Maceljskis were an old Zagreb family. The first of the family to be born in Zagreb was Filip, in 1829. Their story was in fact a typical success saga: Filip became a wood merchant (in Vlaška Street), and his sons, Vilim, Albert, and Benko, continued to develop the business called Filip Deutsch and Sons, Wood Merchants and Forest Industry. They were very conservative businessmen and took no great risks: they took out no loans, the family did not enter any other business, nor did they found stock companies, like other Jews. Still, thanks to their ability and entrepreneurial flair, they managed to cover the entire process of wood production and sale, purchase several forests, and build a number of sawmills, such as the one in Turopolje (a region twenty kilometers south of Zagreb).

The family members were prominent benefactors and, from the end of the nineteenth century, donated wood and other necessities to many poor Zagreb families. In the first years of the twentieth century, the Deutsch family members were granted nobility and added the title "of Macelj" or Maceljski to their surname, because the forest on Macelj Hill (north of Krapina, near the boundary between Slovenia and Croatia) was the property of the company, and they owned a sawmill in nearby Đurmanec. At the end of the twenties, the younger family members left out the surname Deutsch, but the Ustasha authorities returned it, so the family was in 1941–1945 called Deutsch-Maceljski.

In 1913, the Deutsch-Maceljskis were the main founders of the Israelite Holiday Colony in Zagreb, which between 1915 and 1922 financed seaside holidays for about 300 children. In 1922, Albert Deutsch-Maceljski bought the Villa Antonia in Crikvenica for 2,000,000 crowns, had it reconstructed, and turned it into a holiday hostel with a clinic and playgrounds.[82] In 1938, Albert also built a summer camp on Ravna Gora near Delnice, at an altitude of over 800 meters, and donated it to the "holiday colony" because he considered that children needed the fresh mountain air.[83] Between 1924 and 1939, the foundation provided holidays for a total of 2,304 Jewish children, mostly from Zagreb.[84] Mrs. Deutsch occasionally organized donations of clothing, linens, and other things for Jewish children.[85]

In 1941, Charlotte (1863), Albert (1867), and his wife Matilda (Tilda) (1874), and his brothers Gustav (1882), Vlatko (1883), and Robert (1884), owned about ten houses and several pieces of land in the city center and surroundings (Bijenička). They also owned the Eden Hotel in Crikvenica (which was not used as a hotel but was bought in 1938 as a holiday house) and houses in Budapest. Most of this real estate could not be valued in the report to the authorities in June 1941. Several expensive cars (Cadillac, Plymouth, etc.) had already been requisitioned during the second half of June 1941. The property owned by Filip Deutsch and Sons, Wood Merchants and Forest Industry, was extremely valuable and worth more than 48,000,000 dinars, which the family members owned in fixed shares. They owned the large warehouse in Vrhovčeva (today part of Draškovićeva, the corner of Draškovićeva and Ulica kneza Borne, where the Sheraton Hotel now stands). After reporting their property in June 1941, the Deutsch-Maceljskis handed over much of their movable property to the Reconstruction Committee. It seems that this was a sum of at least 6,500,000 kunas, out of the total of 68,000,000 (estimated at that time) given by the Jews of Zagreb.[86] The obligatory registration of property included "a piano, fur coats, crystal chandeliers, and furniture that is not built-in."[87]

Robert Deutsch-Maceljski converted to Catholicism in July 1941.[88] He was a great art collector, and placed all his artworks, paintings, carpets, and antique furniture under the protection of the Croatian Museum. At the end of June, the Croatian Conservation Institute decided to begin "packing these items, so that they suffer as little damage as possible if they have to be taken to the cellar during an air raid." Vlatko and his wife, Marga, were deported to Jasenovac and Stara Gradiška in August 1942, Robert and his wife, Hilda, to Auschwitz in May 1943, from which they did not return. The rest of the family escaped deportation in various ways.[89] Gustav was married to an "Aryan," he had converted to Catholicism, and his children were christened as soon as they were born, so he was protected. Charlotte died in Zagreb on October 11, 1944, after an abdominal operation, while Matilda (Tilda) survived the war, remaining in Zagreb, where she died in 1946.[90]

The Ustasha authorities seized the property of the Honorary Chilean Consul, the industrialist Miroslav Sever (formerly called Emil Schwarz, and who had converted in 1938), explaining that they were treating him as they would any other Jew. However, on the intercession of the Italians and the Germans, Sever managed to leave Zagreb.[91]

The industrialist Manfred Sternberg (1892) left Zagreb at the beginning of April 1941 with his wife and two children. They traveled through Hungary and Austria and, in dramatic circumstances, on the afternoon of April 5, at the last moment crossed into Switzerland. The very next morning they would probably have been detained in Austria as travelers with Yugoslav passports, because on April 6 the Third Reich attacked Yugoslavia. After this escape and salvation, the whole family very soon went to the United States. Sternberg had houses in Ilica and on Jelačićev Square estimated at between eight and nine million dinars. No other property was reported to the Ustasha authorities, because Sternberg had already sold his shares, and of his movable property he took what he could with him, and gave the rest away or stored it somewhere.[92]

At that time, the craze for Jewish property attracted some people and institutions from whom this kind of behavior would certainly not have been expected under normal circumstances. One of the saddest examples is the letter that the central Croatian cultural institution—Matica Hrvatska—sent to the State Directorate of Economic Reconstruction on August 8, 1941, just a month after this institution for the "Aryanization" of Jewish property was founded. Matica Hrvatska wanted one of Sternberg's houses, so, in the name of the institution, its president, Dr. Filip Lukas; vice president, Dr. Blaž Jurišić; secretary of the economic board, Dr. Mile Starčević; and secretary of the literary board, Mirko Jurkić, signed a letter, which read as follows:

> Matica Hrvatska, which has, in the most difficult times, carried out its duty of faithfully serving its historic mission, now brought to fruition in the ISC, is now facing a time of new, greater, and much more demanding tasks. It intends to extend its publishing and other activities, found new organizational branches, and increase the part it plays in the development of a Croatian national consciousness based on cultural creativity, in which it has for a long time been restrained.
>
> To carry out this new work, Matica needs assets greater than the ones it presently has at its disposal. It does not yet have its own printing press, or a building to house it, which would also include the necessary offices and public rooms.
>
> The possibility now presents itself of obtaining suitable buildings on a site appropriate for Matica Hrvatska, as the oldest, most deserv-

> ing, and most distinguished Croatian society, which will shortly after the proclamation of the ISC enter the milestone year of its hundreth anniversary. This is a location in the center of Zagreb, at Jelačićev Square 15, which comprises the three-story house facing the square and its courtyard buildings, the property of the Jew Sternberg (formerly Prister), which property is mortgaged for three million kunas to the benefit of an un-named creditor.
>
> This property would answer our needs perfectly. Here, Matica could arrange rooms for its committees, secretaries, and offices, its archives and library, reading room and library for the local subcommittee, and a lecture hall; on the ground floor there could be an exhibition of Matica's books, designs, pictures and graphs, and a shop and office; in the courtyard, a printing house.
>
> According to our information, this property is not yet owned by the ISC.
>
> Convinced that, in this matter, as in others, the Directorate has the progress of our deserving educational society close to heart, we beg you to keep in mind the above needs of Matica Hrvatska when the property mentioned becomes owned by the ISC.
>
> For the homeland!

On August 23, the State Directorate replied to Matica, in a letter signed by "deputy state director Borić," saying "this building has not yet formally become the property of the ISC" but "the Directorate will certainly bear the needs and desires of Matica Hrvatska in mind and act in the manner which Matica deserves, considering its renown and role among our people and the task that awaits it in the future."[93]

The letter sent by the heads of Matica shows that they had very carefully gone over the rooms into which they wanted to move, informed themselves about the owners, and thought everything out well before writing the letter, but nothing shows whether any of the signatories asked themselves what would happen to the ten or so families who were still living in that large apartment house. In the end, Matica Hrvatska did not move into the house "of the Jew Sternberg" at Jelačićev Square 15. During all the time of the ISC, it remained in its building in Matičina Street, where it still is and has been without a break since 1887. It cannot now be established whether the signatories of Matica's letter of August 8, 1941, later realized how shameful their act was, or whether the Ustasha authorities decided that Matica was not an institution that "deserved" to be moved to larger premises on the main Zagreb square. After initial statements from both sides that "in the new age, Matica would get new, greater, and more demanding tasks," soon the mutual cordiality in the relationship between the Ustasha authorities and Matica decreased somewhat, although no public distancing ever took place. The celebration of Matica's centenary in the summer of 1943 was rather modest, and, in his address, its president, Lukas, emphasized that "all the demands concerning the national principle" for which Matica had fought "have been realized," that its work "in this direction has ended, and it has returned to cultural work only." This can obviously be understood as unconditional support for the establishment of the ISC, but also as distancing from some aspects of the current policy.[94]

Filip Lukas was sometimes even openly critical of the Ustasha authorities, as in the case of the Agreements of Rome.[95] As president, he tolerated different opinions and authors in Matica's publications to a somewhat greater extent than the Ustasha authorities thought desirable.[96] On the other hand, Lukas was a prominent advocate and ideologist of "exclusive Croatianhood" and "rigid nationalism" from 1928 until his death as an émigré in 1958; he wrote and edited various publications praising the ISC and Ustasha and Nazi ideology. In the centenary speech already mentioned, Lukas gave an evaluation of everything that immigrants had brought to Croatia. Of the "western group" of immigrants (Germans, Slovaks, Slovenians, Czechs, Hungarians) he wrote with sympathy ("most of them identified with the local population in good and in bad"), unlike the "eastern group" (Serbs), who "permanently remained foreign to the spirit of this people and the traditions of this land." Lukas saw nothing good in the immigration of Jews: he claimed that this "group of the population . . . with their migratory instinct, with foreign characteristics, and their religio-legal spirit, could not find their roots in the country, could not fit in with the people among whom they lived, and have therefore not taken over their national ideals. This understanding and their international connections in and of themselves mean a disintegration of the national idea."[97]

Blaž Jurišić (1891–1974), philologist and publicist, was in 1941 appointed head of the Croatian State Language Bureau, but he soon resigned both from this post and as a professor at the Faculty of Philosophy in Zagreb, in this way distancing himself from the rigid Ustasha measures in science and culture. The third signatory, Mirko Jurkić, the closest friend and best man at Blaž Jurišić's wedding, also distanced himself to a degree. The fourth signatory, Dr. Mile Starčević, was Minister of National Education in the ISC government in 1942–1943, but in the fall of 1943 he resigned because he did not agree with some of Pavelić's personal decisions, and retired.[98] Therefore, all four of them were people with strong personalities who did not hesitate to distance themselves from some aspects of the Ustasha idea, although they belonged to the movement with all their heart (Starčević), or widely supported it conceptually (Lukas), or at least sympathized with it for a time (Jurišić and Jurkić). During some periods of his life, Blaž Jurišić kept a very detailed diary, which was posthumously published in 1994. The book was edited by Biserka Rako, Jurišić's daughter, who thought that her father had in May 1945 destroyed or hidden his entries from the war period, which she could not find.[99] Perhaps one of the reasons why he did this was because these entries contained descriptions of the unsavory episode with his signature on Matica's letter of August 8, 1941. It is not impossible that some of the signatories—or at least Jurkić and Jurišić, and perhaps Lukas as well—were later ashamed of having signed. Still, the signatures remain as a sad reminder of a time in which evicting people from their homes, robbery, even committing crimes, suddenly became all too normal and accepted everyday occurrences, when the basic criteria of elementary human decency were too easily forgotten.

The Catholic Church obviously tried to keep aloof from these arrangements, but sometimes it was drawn in even against its wishes. In September 1941, the authorities requisitioned the Tuškanac building of the School Brothers Student Hall, a secondary-school institution, and assigned it to the Bulgarian ambassador, so the institution moved to Dežlićeva, to the former premises of the Jewish firm Zagorka owned by Armin Schreiner. At the turn of 1942–1943, the School Brothers had to leave Dežlićeva too, because the authorized state institution had in the meantime sold this "Aryanized" location to a third person. Thus, a request was sent to the State Treasury, Nationalized Wealth Bureau, for the institution to be assigned the use of a "nationalized" building (five locations in the city were mentioned) or "some other building." At more or less the same time, the School Brothers interceded with Poglavnik Pavelić, and he finally settled the matter by deciding that "until the house in Jurjevska [which had not been mentioned earlier] is handed over, the order . . . is to remain in its present premises."[100]

Very soon, in the summer months of 1941, the organized plunder of the offices of Jewish doctors began. At the same time, without any system, other offices were also broken into: young thugs in civilian clothes broke into Edo Neufeld's apartment and law office, which were on the same floor in Bauerova 12, and very quickly took away everything that could be carried.[101]

Looting was just one of the stages in solving the "Jewish question." Many Jews died soon after, because those who had robbed them made sure that the owners were deported and killed. Probably some of the new owners were still afraid that under some new circumstances—if the old owners survived—they could be deprived of their newly acquired property. However, the great majority of the old owners did not survive. Robbed of everything they had, completely impoverished, the Zagreb Jews in most cases no longer had the courage, or the means, to embark on unknown paths of escape from the ISC, on which there might possibly have been some chance of survival and salvation.

14

EVICTING JEWS FROM HOUSES AND APARTMENTS

The Zagreb Police Directorate issued a decree (which was posted in streets as an announcement) on May 8, 1941, saying that "all SERBS and JEWS" who live in the elite northern parts of the city have eight days to move to other parts of the city." The decree specified that they were to move "from the north side of Maksimirska Road, Vlaška Street, Jelačićev Square, from Ilica as far as Mitnica, and also from the city areas north of these streets."[1] This was one more way of making some of the Zagreb Jews homeless, especially those who were wealthier, and of robbing them of their property. The regulation, like all the rest, included a threat: "Anyone who does not comply with this decree shall be, after the expiration of the above deadline, FORCIBLY EVICTED at their own expense and PUNISHED in accordance with existing LEGAL PROVISIONS." And this is exactly what took place. Anyone who failed to move within the time limit was immediately evicted from his or her apartment and deprived of all property.[2] There were hardly any exceptions, although some Jews managed to go on living in smaller and more nondescript apartments and houses; the larger apartments and villas, however, were evacuated without exception. The authorities claimed that some of the apartments would be used to house "unemployed private employees and workers,"[3] but this did not happen. In March 1947, Slavko Kvaternik said that "all the members of the ISC government moved into Jewish villas and apartments in Tuškanac [Tuškanac was the quintessential choice neighborhood, the most sought after of them all]; Pavelić and his wife took no fewer than nine such villas for themselves." One of them had belonged to the industrialist Emil Sever.[4] Kvaternik himself moved into a furnished villa that belonged to a Jew unknown to him, who was "forcibly moved out."[5] This was the Tuškanac villa of the industrialist Oskar Fröhlich (converted in 1938), who escaped to Italy with his family in time.[6] The families of Vlatko and Robert Deutsch-Maceljski had twenty-four hours to evacuate their apartments on what was then Square N (today Trg žrtava fašizma /Fascist Victims' Square/) because the apartments were earmarked for Milovan Žanić, a member of the government, and Pavao Canki, state secretary in the Ministry of the Peasant Economy.[7]

Soon, in May, evictions of Jews in apartments south of the Ilica–Vlaška–Maksimirska line started as well. In the following weeks and months, evictions were formally and legally underpinned by the Legal Provision on the Evacuation and Occupation of Residential Premises for Reasons of Public Security of May 31, 1941, the Legal Provision on the Expropriation of Buildings for the Benefit of the State of June 9, and the Legal Provision on the Evacuation and Occupation of Residential and Business Premises for the Needs of Public Offices of August 11.[8] The first law allowed "police precincts to issue ordinances banning dangerous and undesirable persons from living and doing business in particular areas, in particular properties, buildings, and premises." They were to be turned out "without any notice or compensation," and no appeal "has the power to stay proceedings."[9] Under the second law, "any building, whether owned by a natural or a legal person, may be expropriated for the needs of the State. Land may be expropriated together with the building."[10] Under the third law, "police precincts may order that particular properties, buildings, and premises shall be evacuated to accommodate public offices, and may issue a decision ordering all persons to vacate them within a term of one month."[11]

Although the authorities very often called on the first of the three provisions, that about "dangerous and undesirable" persons, no reason was ever given why a particular person—in other words, a Jewish or Serbian man or woman—was "dangerous and undesirable." As a group, the three legal provisions on the "evacuation and occupation" of apartments enabled the Ustasha administration and military-police services to evict anyone from his or her apartment, anywhere, and at any time. However, despite the "broad" powers that they enjoyed, the authorities often acted on their own, contrary to the prescribed procedure. Most by far of the documents kept in the files of the Ministry of the Interior and of the Ustasha Police Directorate, Jewish Section, refer to cases from Zagreb—probably about 90 percent, perhaps more. It seems that the authorities in Zagreb, more than in other places, wanted to act according to ISC laws and regulations, whereas local authorities outside Zagreb cared much less about leaving any written record concerning dispossession from apartments and similar kinds of maltreatment.[12]

In Zagreb, a City Housing Bureau was founded on June 9 (some documents called it the City Government Housing Bureau in Zagreb), after the Legal Provision on the Evacuation and Occupation and the Legal Provision on the Obligatory Registration of Jews and Jewish Firms was passed, and it was put in charge of the implementation of these laws. It took over the management of the vacated Jewish apartments and allocated them to people who filed requests for apartments and who had the right to move in according to the criteria established by the Ustasha authorities.[13] From the very first day, this institution was buried in work. There were Ustasha émigrés who had returned to Croatia from abroad, and Ustashe who had come to Zagreb from other parts of Croatia, and all were in search of housing. Some of them were temporarily put up in hospitals or in the building of the Croatian Workingman's organization in Radišina Street.[14] On the other hand, even before the foundation of the City Housing Bureau, there were many empty Jewish and Serb apartments that urgently had to be assigned to someone, or which had already been occupied, and this had to be legalized by a formal paper issued by the administration. For example, Filip Baum reported that he had vacated his five-room apartment at Dežmanov Passage on May 12, Slavko Singer that he had "left his apartment on Sv. Duh" on May 15, Milan and Lili Singer had left "their own house on Nad Lipom Street 14" June 12, and Isak Abinun a "ground-floor house at Petrova 95" on June 18.[15] Milan and Lili Singer also reported that on June 20 they had "leased a three-room apartment in their house, with all the amenities, to Captain Nikola Čulek, who had brought permission from the Ustasha police."[16] The least wealthy of the above, Isak Abinun, moved to Kustošija after he was evicted from his house; he was soon arrested and deported, and was killed in Jasenovac by the end of the year. Milan Singer survived the war, but Lili and their children, Leo and Mira, ended their lives in Đakovo and Auschwitz. It seems that all the other people mentioned above survived the war. In 1941, the "industrialist" Filip Baum had to pay the Jewish Community dues of 3,500 kunas, and in the next year 7,000.[17]

There are no documents that specifically order the rather large number of evictions, especially those that took place right at the beginning. Indirectly, however, it can be ascertained that the evictions had taken place, obviously not in accordance with any prescribed procedure, perhaps even before such a procedure was laid down. In early July, Heinrich Freywald, an employee of the Jewish Community, requested permission from the Jewish Section to continue living in the Gajevo naselje housing estate (at that time on the outskirts of the city, today in its southwest, between Srednjaci and Staglišće), where he had moved after having to leave "his earlier apartment in Bauerova, since all Jews had been moved from that street."[18] It is difficult to determine whether this had really happened in "all of" Bauerova and whether "all the Jews" had been dispossessed, but documents show that Jews moved out of numbers 4, 5, 15, 16, 17, 28, and 29.[19] The apartment house at Bauerova 22 was evacuated, i.e., the "house was requisitioned," by ordinance of the Police Directorate of June 18.[20] By the beginning of July, the house at Vojnovićeva Street 31 was completely emptied because the Jewish Section of the RUR moved there and remained until the middle of 1942.[21]

Although no written documents to this effect exist, it seems that the Ustasha authorities were especially active in turning people out of the more easterly parts of the city, those lying east of Burze Square and Draškovićeva right down to Heinzelova. This area was known between the wars as the *Judenviertel* (i.e., Jewish Quarter, often pejoratively), because it had a higher percentage of Jews than other parts of the city—not because of any ghetto mentality, but due to a set of social circumstances, perhaps also to family connections ("buy a house from a Jewish contractor," etc.). It is impossible to say precisely how many Jews there were in that area, but according to lists of residents from the early thirties, six out of eight families in Martićeva 4 were Jewish, seven out of eight in Smičiklasova 18.[22] In June, Zlatko Lipa and his family (two children, ages three and five) moved out of their apartment on Burze Square to a "small apartment with two small rooms" in the Sigečica area. He asked Ivo Baraković, whose classmate he had been for three years at school, to issue him with an "authorization to use this apartment . . . so that he and his family can continue to live in peace." Baraković made a note on the request saying that "no authorization can be issued, but Lipa can continue to live there." They survived the war.[23] The attorney Makso Njemirovskij moved out of his apartment in Solovljeva Street and rented a flat in Hatzova Street.[24] In December 1941, Erna Pollak from Tvrtkova Street wrote, "Because I am Jewish, various people come to me from time to time and demand that I move out quietly, others threaten me. None of them have up to now been able to show me any kind of document . . . I would have left by myself, but I really have nowhere to go, nor do I have any money (five of us are living in a two-room apartment)."[25]

The third law, that concerning "evacuation and occupation" of August 11, began to be implemented as soon as it was passed, but was not strictly followed. The apartment in Ribnjak 8, from which the "Jew Balaš" had previously been evicted, was allocated to Ustasha Major Martin Markač, although the provision explicitly stated that the police authorities may order "removals" of this kind only "to accommodate public offices."[26] Even though the provision on dispossession does not say where the Jews were supposed to move, most of them went to the outskirts of the city—to Sigečica, Vrapče, Kustošija, Gajevo naselje, or Stenjevec.[27] This was what the authorities wanted, because on May 16, *Novi list* suggested that those who had moved from the northern parts of the city "should move to the southern parts of the city and must be under police supervision."[28] Rudolf Ungar and Ilka Fürst moved from the city center to Horvati, Albert Hiršler to Dugo Selo, and Alfred and Karlo Plan to Samobor.[29] However, by July 10, they were ordered to "move out of" these fringe towns as well.[30] Various Ustasha state services observed that the Jews were "moving out of Zagreb to the suburbs, where they want to escape the enforced measures," and the "inhabitants of the surrounding municipalities are rightly complaining about this." Some Jews (three in Šestine, seven in Kustošija, nineteen in Vrapče including Gajevo naselje, and five in Stenjevec) requested permission to remain at those addresses.[31] It seems that the answer they received was not in written form but of a different kind, because deportations from those urban areas started in September. There were exceptions in this trend: when Bela Altstädter was evicted from his apartment in Stančićeva Street, he moved to a one-room cellar apartment without conveniences in the nearby Vrbanićeva Street, the property of his brother Josip. But this was only the beginning of Bela's troubles, because he was soon deported to Jasenovac where he died by the end of the year.[32]

In October 1941, the main office of the Jewish Religious Community sent an application to the City Housing Bureau asking it to protect the property of members of the management board and employees of the Jewish Community, because they were "being evicted from their apartments, they often had to leave without notice, in one or two hours, in most cases without the right to take their furniture, appliances, and things with them."[33]

Although these activities seem to have been very disorganized and there was a lot of improvisation, they all nevertheless led to one final goal in keeping with the well-designed Nazi model: deportation–concentration–extermination. Jews were to be evicted from their apartments and concentrated in one part of the city, from where sending them to their final destination would be a mere logistical problem.

In December 1941, the Jewish Section of the Ustasha Police Directorate demanded from the Directorate of Economic Reconstruction to "*urgently* send a list of Jewish buildings in the city of Zagreb . . . for the accommodation of members of the Poglavnik's Bodyguard Battalion."[34] Even before this urgent request was sent, starting in August and increasing as the end of the year approached, dozens of men from this battalion moved into Jewish apartments. Among others, Ante Čašljar, Franjo Šredl, Ante Mišetić, Ivan Čapin, Ante Pezo, Marko Bajić, Dane Mikulić, Franjo Blažinčić, Martin Wolf, Marko Lončar, Mile Barešić, Stjepan Roščić, Nikola Orešković, Mirko Granić, Ambroz Leko, Josip Galić, Srećko Ivančić, Božo Đerek, Ante Nevistić, and Grga Grubišić moved into the apartments of Ruža Rosenbaum in Maksimirska, Blanka Steiner in Daničićeva, Franciska Beck in Stančićeva, Julije Hoffman in Erdedijeva, Rosa Santo in Petrinjska, Josip Feliks in Petrinjska, Zora Vijas in Palmotićeva, Elsa Spitzer in Petrinjska, Zora Fridrih in Jurišićeva, Leopold Weiss in Patačićkina, Ernestina Leko in Smičiklasova, Dr. Aleksander Gara in Radišina, Alfons Prister in Kačićeva, and Terezija Kerkaj in Ulica Kraljice Marije.[35] The villas in the northern parts of the city were valued the most and could go only to the highest-ranking officials of the Ustasha regime. Apartments in the less exclusive neighborhoods went to those who had lower Ustasha rank.[36]

Dispossession was only the first step toward further suffering. Of all the above who had been "moved out," only Dr. Gara and Ruža Rosenbaum survived the war;[37] Rosa Santo and Ernestina Leko do not appear on lists of victims, but neither are their names on the lists of survivors from 1945. All the others are on the lists of victims.[38] Gerda Schwarz was evicted from her apartment in Boškovićeva 8 "at the request of the Community for Trading in Livestock and Livestock Products," and Bela Reich from Deželićeva "for the needs of Chancellor Göring of the German Embassy."[39] It was obvious that even doctors would not be spared, especially those at such an attractive location as the apartment of Dr. Oton Frank on N Square.[40]

Many evictions were organized in this way, several hundred altogether, and the administration properly recorded them between August 1941 and the beginning of 1942.[41] From December 12, 1941, to April 1942, a new set of documents appeared, hastily filled in and saying only that, for example, "the apartment of Hermina Goldman, Račkoga 12, is allocated to Ivan Vrdoljak, member of the Poglavnik's Bodyguard Battalion. On the receipt of this order, Hermina Goldman and all who live in the apartment must vacate it." Several hundred Jewish apartments in the Lower Town were emptied in this way, and members of various Ustasha units or civil servants moved in.[42] Some of these documents say only that someone is moving into somebody else's apartment, for example into that "of the Jew Josip Löwy," but there is no clause that Löwy must move out. In most cases, this probably meant that the owner had already been deported or had fled from Zagreb. In some cases, no effort was made to register the owner at all; often, all it says is that the "Jewish apartment is empty."[43] A rare exception is the comment on the back of a document saying that "Second Lieutenant Mate Gudelj . . . did not get the apartment of the Jew Dr. Makso Strassmann in Reljkovićeva" because the "above is married to an Aryan and has a son who is a volunteer on the Eastern Front."[44]

When Klara Mandelsamen was evicted from her apartment in Tvrtkova in September 1941, Ensign Ante Duževič made her sign that she had "received from him all the clothes, except for three men's suits and one coat that belonged to my brother." Then follows a detailed list of what the new resident had taken over: all the furniture, etc., even down to "nine kg. sugar, eight kg. flour, one kg. candy, eighteen eggs, eight liters oil, four kg. washing soda . . . five kg. jam." Klara's husband, Adolf, was already in Jasenovac at that time, where he was killed in December 1941. Klara and her three children found shelter with a family, and at the end of 1941 they bought passes and all fled to Crikvenica. The son, Natan–Nino, soon joined the Partisans, and the Germans arrested Klara and her two daughters after the capitulation of Italy. All three of them survived the war under inhuman conditions in Rižarna Prison in Trieste.[45]

Records of requests for requisitioning furniture were kept very carefully. Hermina Bruckner from Baruna Filipovića Street was told to "hand over to the Ustasha Raić Franjo, to whom your apartment has been allocated, the bed linen and other things that you have taken, and which are necessary in the vacated apartment." She was killed in 1944.[46] In July 1941, Izabela Kohn was allowed to take from the sealed apartment of her daughter, Dr. Marta Fodor, in Vrhovčeva, "all the most necessary clothes for the above and for her two children, and then to seal the apartment again" (Marta Fodor and her daughters were in camp at that time).[47] However, Margita Schlesinger, "at present homeless," did not even get a reply when she requested permission to take at least the essentials from her apartment on Bukovac, out of which she had been expelled. Later, probably in 1943, Margita ended her days in Auschwitz.[48] In July 1942, Alica Blühweiss requested permission to take from her former apartment on Marulićev Square "the essential furniture and linen necessary for living," but on December 31 the request was declared "outdated." This probably meant that Alica was already dead, but archives do not show when and how she died; Alica's relative Miroslava Despot-Blis wrote down that she had been deported to Hungary, then to Auschwitz, which indicates that she was deported in August 1942.[49]

There were some exceptions to the general rule about evicting Jews from their apartments: the Jewish Section permitted Julija Singer to "live with her child in the cellar apartment in Maruševečka" (at that time a back street in Trešnjevka). Nothing is known about Julija Singer's further fate; she does not appear on the lists of victims or those of survivors.[50]

Often everything happened very quickly: on December 17, Ruža Rosenbaum and her daughter were evicted from their apartment in Maksimirska and they moved in with their seventy-eight-year-old relative Charlotta (Šarlota) Deutsch-Maceljski in Solovljeva, but only three days later Charlotta also was forced to move in with her son.[51] This was Charlotta's second "move": in June, she had been thrown out of her apartment in Jurišićeva.[52]

When they wished to evict people "according to the regulations," the legal vocabulary was at its most formal, which shows a high degree of cynicism, as, for example, when the UNS instructed the Jewish Section to "please move out the Jewess Dora Schrenger, who is in an apartment in the former Beogradska Street 5, which has been allocated to Ustasha Lieutenant Josip Mišlov." Dora Schrenger did not survive the war.[53]

Work on "moving out" ran parallel with work on "moving into" apartments, and all requests of this kind had to be submitted to the Housing Bureau of the City Government. Several hundred applications were filed, "requests for apartments" that were approved after the Jews had "moved out."[54] Some documents refer to a "list" or "record" of "free Jewish apartments," which obviously existed in the City Housing Bureau in 1942 but has not been preserved.[55] It was completely normal and usual for civil servants, and especially soldiers, to apply to the Jewish Section or to the City Government to be assigned an empty apartment.[56] The State Treasury demanded that "only the Housing Bureau of the City Government should do all the work on collecting and selling the property of Jews . . . who have been removed from Zagreb."[57] It seems that the work on "moving out" was finished in 1942, because in that year most of the reports refer to "making lists of chattel" in apartments that had already been "vacated," meaning apartments that Jews had left when they were deported or had fled.[58]

In December 1941, Rustem Biščević requested that he should be "allocated an apartment in which Jews live, and for them to be moved to my present apartment, which I was forced to rent from a Jewess." Biščević's request is a good description of the frenzy to find apartments and property, because he says that he had been to "at least eighteen addresses where Jews used to live or still do," and that he had "lost about forty days in searching for an apartment." He concluded that "a Jewish apartment could be allocated to me" and that he would "find most suitable an apartment in Martićeva 33 . . . or Đorđićeva 7."[59] At the beginning of 1942, Ivan Vraneković, employed at the State Information and Promotion Bureau, requested, because he was soon to be married, the "allocation of a suitable apartment because it is impossible for me to find one, and if possible, for me to buy the furniture from a former Jewish apartment that has been emptied." Vraneković's request was not met because the Jewish Section of the Ustasha Police, to which the request was sent, allegedly did not "have a suitable apartment at its disposal."[60] In this period, Major Herman Kadić, serving with the Ministry of the Croatian Home Guard, demanded that the Jewish Section "allocate me a complete three-room apartment from among the empty and available Jewish apartments, if possible near the Ministry of the Croatian Home Guard . . . I have no furniture, so would need some."[61] The Administrative Command of the Ustasha Youth requested allocation of the apartment "of the Jewess Anka Waldhauser in Zvonimirova 34" to the hostel for young workers because "the women workers are almost homeless." Anka Waldhauser did not survive the war.[62]

Keeping to what was then the proper procedure, from the end of 1941 to the beginning of March 1942, the Ministry of the Interior, in cooperation with the Ministry of Justice, "evacuated residential premises." A smaller number were to be evacuated in accordance with the provision of May 31 (Legal Provision on the Evacuation and Occupation of Residential Premises for Reasons of Public Security) and a larger number in accordance with the provision of August 11 (Legal Provision on the Evacuation and Occupation of Residential and Business Premises for the Needs of Public Offices). In these cases, apartments belonging to citizens of various nationalities in Zagreb and elsewhere in Croatia were "evacuated," but most of the apartments were owned by Jews, and were located in Zagreb. There are records of over 200 evictions of Zagreb Jews from their apartments in that period. Some names in the requests of the Ministry of the Interior had already appeared earlier, some were new, for example the apartments of Judita Bornstein in Ljubljanska, Bernard Rosenberger in Derenčinova, and Irma Kraljević in Tratinska. Judita Bornstein and Bernard Rosenberger did not survive the war, and nothing is known about Irma Kraljević.[63]

A document issued by the RUR's Jewish Section in March 1942, after the most extensive operation of evicting Jews during the winter of 1941–1942, states that there is still an "overall lack of apartments" which most "seriously affects . . . Ustasha officials and civil servants—Croats, who have recently moved to Zagreb."[64] This triggered a new wave of "moving people out" of apartments in May 1942, but this was a smaller operation because not many people were left to be evicted.[65] In July 1942, appetites were still not sated, because at that time the UNS demanded "a list of all Jews with flats" from the Jewish Section, and, eight days later, the list seems to have been delivered.[66] The hunger for apartments had not waned by September 1942: "people interested in apartments were sent every day" to Vilko Lehner at Fijanova 4, who had earlier been granted Aryan rights. Because of this, the Jewish Section instructed the City Housing Bureau to "immediately strike this apartment from the list of free Jewish apartments, since it cannot be disposed of"; nonetheless, Lehner's property was entered in the *Reconstruction Directory*.[67]

Documents of this kind do not give a complete picture of how broad the operation of "emptying apartments" was, primarily because Pavelić and his closest associates, who moved into villas in Tuškanac, obviously did not want to leave behind any written trace. Besides, many flats were taken by brute force.

Imbro Berger had an apartment on Pejačevićev (today Britanski) Square, from which the Ustasha police evicted him, his wife, and their son on April 19, 1941. The family found shelter with Imbro's brother in nearby Kačićeva Street, but six days later, on April 25, Captain Vid Katić of the Home Guard and his son, Second Lieutenant Dragutin Katić, came to his brother's apartment and threatened Imbro with a revolver, ordering him to hand over the keys to his apartment on Pejačevićev Square. The Berger family later moved to Ludbreška Street in Trešnjevka. Imbro was arrested on July 9, 1941, and sent to Jasenovac, where he met his death before October. Imbro's wife, Margareta, was sent to Stara Gradiška in August 1942, where she was killed on the same day, and at the same time their son, Milan, was deported to Auschwitz, from where he did not return.[68]

Many apartments were forcibly possessed after their owners had fled or been deported. Usually, the Ustashe arrested people at night, then sealed the apartment, and on that same night returned to loot it.[69] Marijana Freund was thrown out of her apartment in December 1941, but three days later she managed to procure a permit to return to it. When she returned, she discovered that "everything has been scattered around and the following are missing: three men's suits, one blouse, three pairs of woman's shoes . . . six towels . . . twelve handkerchiefs . . . four alarm clocks . . . woman's walking boots." Second Lieutenant Franjo Dodić and Ensign Mijo Karoglan of the Poglavnik's Bodyguard Battalion "entered the apartment in the evening and took away things, but did not sleep in the apartment." In 1944, Marijana Freund was deported from Rab to Auschwitz, together with her sons, Saša and Branko.[70] In other cases, people simply entered apartments, ordered the Jewish inhabitants to leave, and said that they were doing it with the permission of a certain "Marko Vujava, Ustasha."[71] In December 1941, the City Government in Zagreb informed Blaž Lorković, aide to the Poglavnik, that in many instances people were moving into apartments by force, and that only the City Housing Bureau may allocate the apartments. When city officials came to the newly occupied apartments, they were threatened with "a revolver, imprisonment, etc." There is nothing to show whether Lorković or anyone else did anything to stop this.[72] Obviously, the greed for the empty Jewish apartments also led to serious quarrels.[73] Some state services demanded subsequent legal verification of unlawful acts of entry that had already been committed, calling on laws and legal provisions, although earlier there had been no adherence to legal procedure. At the end of June 1941, RUR informed the City Housing Bureau that they had requisitioned "a formerly empty Jewish apartment in Karadžićeva, that they had properly painted it" and had then "placed it at the disposal of Ustasha General Vilko Begić, so we request that you assign this flat to him . . . Furthermore, we have requisitioned the Jewish house in Zvonimirova 2 for the needs of this Directorate, and request that you confirm this requisition as well."[74]

It seems that the City Housing Bureau tried to comply with the required procedure whenever this was possible. When it made the contract for Lav Alković to move into one of the apartments in Antun Gottlieb and Alica Landesmann's house in Mihanovićeva, the recently appointed manager of the building, the "Aryan" Hrvoje Stožir, took part in the proceedings.[75]

In May 1942, the Deutsch family was "moved" from their flat in Gundulićeva to Trešnjevka. Until 1941, their daughter, Lea Deutsch (1927), had been a famous Zagreb "child prodigy" (the actor Tito Strozzi wrote a play for her titled "Child Prodigy"), a multitalented actress and singer, and a star of the Croatian National Theatre, popular and beloved by all in Zagreb and wherever else she appeared. When the Deutsches were thrown out of their apartment, the Jewish Section informed the City Housing Bureau that the Deutsch family may take with them "the piano that is there, on which the famous Lea Deutsch, daughter of the above mentioned Jew Stjepan Deutsch, practices—the new tenant will certainly not need this item."[76] Lea Deutsch was deported to Auschwitz in May 1943, but died on the train.

In this operation of taking over apartments, people grabbed as much as their position allowed them to. While a soldier normally got one apartment, with sometimes two soldiers being accommodated in one larger apartment, Second Lieutenant Šime Korčulanić of the Poglavnik's Bodyguard Battalion took the apartment of Josip Steiner in Boškovićeva and the apartment of Franjo Weiser in Gundulićeva.[77] To make this "legal" operation go as fast as possible, the Ministry of the Interior usually compiled lists of Jewish apartments (and very rarely of "Orthodox" [i.e., Serb] apartments) "for Mr. Trobentar's records."[78] The impression is that someone who did not have insight into the documents of the Jewish Community and Ustasha services went from apartment to apartment and made lists of Jewish property.[79] How this was done can be seen from the order the Jewish Section gave to the Ustasha policeman Mato Bošnjak in March 1942. He was told to "investigate the corner of Lopašićeva and Klaonička and make a survey and list of Jewish apartments in that building." He had to work very quickly, because the "order expired in two hours."[80]

An anonymous report, written in the following months by a civil servant, shows that the provisions on "moving out" were implemented in a very rough manner and that arbitrary behavior that exceeded the regulations was frequent. The report says that "various things happen in Zagreb every day," about which the author is convinced "the authorities have no inkling. People get thrown out of apartments, which they must sometimes leave in ten minutes. In most cases they are not allowed to take even the bare essentials. There is a provision that only the City Housing Bureau may dispose of the apartments, but it seems that this provision is not always complied with, because various other institutions also empty apartments . . . Not long ago, a case took place in Mrazovićeva 3, two old people were thrown out of an apartment, he had a stroke, he was seventy-nine, his wife was about sixty-five."[81]

The quick changes of residents in apartments also brought other complications that had not been foreseen: for example, the gas company could not work properly and the danger of accidents increased, of which the gasworks warned the Jewish Section at the end of July 1941.[82] The Jewish Community tried to reach an agreement with some institutions that would at least allow the Jews to place their apartments at the disposal of the authorities themselves, to prevent the residents from being thrown out without anything at all, particularly without their clothes and shoes. Although Vilko Kühnel, head of the RUR's Jewish Section, was ready to support the proposal by the Jewish Community for a milder eviction procedure, this happened very rarely. Usually, Jews would not leave their apartments of their own free will, and, when they got evicted, it was too late for any kind of intercession.[83]

15

SALVATION FOR A GROUP OF DOCTORS

In Bosnia, syphilis was rampant, so at the end of 1941 the Ustasha authorities in Banja Luka founded the Institute for the Control of Endemic Syphilis.[1] It soon became obvious that Croatian doctors were not applying to go there, although they were being offered "appropriate remuneration" and were assured that every year of service there would count as two in the retirement insurance system.[2] As a result, the authorities (seemingly with the knowledge of Pavelić himself) spared from deportation at least eighty-one Jewish doctors from Zagreb, and, in the fall of 1941, sent them to the most isolated parts of Bosnia to control this disease.[3] Dr. Samuel Deutsch (or Dajč), one of the doctors who went to Bosnia, later remembered that Dr. Ante Vuletić, a dermatologist-venereologist who was an expert in hygiene, and his friend Dr. Miroslav Schlesinger, devised this scheme with the primary goal of saving some doctors and their families, and the lesser goal of treating syphilis victims and controlling the spread of the disease. In Bosnia, syphilis was not spread only by sexual contact but was also inherited, i.e., babies got infected during birth, breast-feeding, through personal contact, and by using contaminated tableware (there were frequent primary effects on the tonsils or the soft palate).[4] It took a considerable time for Vuletić (who was later proclaimed a Righteous Among the Nations) to negotiate the founding of the Institute to control this disease with the authorities, because, for a time, Pavelić would not agree.[5] Finally, the proposal was accepted, because his arguments were: "You have proclaimed that the Muslims are the flower of the Croatian nation, but this flower is being eroded by endemic syphilis. Instead of sending Jewish doctors to work camps, use them to root out syphilis in Bosnia. When they have done that, you can still send them to the camps."[6]

After several weeks of hesitation, Jewish doctors applied because this work obviously offered at least some hope of salvation. Only six of the twenty Jewish dermato-venereologists in Croatia were included in the project, but there were specialists in other branches of medicine, and most of the doctors were general practitioners. The first group of twenty-three doctors, put together by the Ministry of Health, left for Bosnia on August 8.[7] The second group, which arrived at the beginning of October, had thirty-two doctors, all of whom had previously gone through additional training at the dermato-venereological clinic.[8] Seventy-three doctors went to Bosnia in 1941, the following year three more; the Statistics of the Ministry of Health ISC show that a total of seventy-six Jewish doctors were engaged, twelve of them women.[9] The oldest was fifty-eight (born in 1884), the youngest twenty-seven (born in 1915), fifty-one were married, and eighteen were unmarried. When typhoid began to spread, at least thirty Jewish doctors worked to combat this, too (five of them got typhoid, but none died), because there was a general lack of doctors. They also performed other services: four were Home Guard doctors, two Ustasha doctors.[10]

In January 1942, three Jewish doctors served in the Home Guard, all from Zagreb; others were "called up for service," but the response kept growing weaker.[11] Some had already fled from Zagreb, many had been arrested.

The doctors who joined the anti-syphilis project soon heard about the mass arrests and deportations. At this time, the Partisan movement was growing stronger, and most doctors used the first opportunity to join it. In March 1942, the Zagreb Jewish Community knew where nineteen Zagreb doctors were stationed: four were in Tuzla, three in Travnik, two in Žepa, one each in Turbe, Banja Luka, Vareš, Teslić, Ljubija, Kotor Varoš, Bosanska Krupa, Pećigrad, Sanski Most, and Kakanj.[12]

Of the seventy-six doctors, no fewer than fifty-eight and no more than sixty-seven later joined the Partisans; the Germans or the Ustashe killed four, and three died working in Bosnia.[13] The pediatrician Ivo Spitzer contracted a very severe form of typhoid after a time in Bosnia and returned to Zagreb, where it took him a long time to recover his health. As one of the leading pediatricians in the city, he continued his practice and thus survived the war.[14]

The families of the doctors who went to Bosnia to treat syphilis were in principle protected and were even allowed to remain in their apartments.[15] A memo to this effect was sent to all the county police precincts,[16] but explicitly said that only "the most immediate family, i.e., wife, children, and parents of the doctor," was exempt from the "forcible measures," but not including "the family of the doctor's wife."[17] Some family members got permission to accompany the doctors to Bosnia,[18] but all requests of this kind were decided on a case-by-case basis, and family members were required to wear the Jewish insignia, which was a first step toward deportation.[19]

The deportations of August 1942 swept away the mother-in-law and nephew of the dentist Dr. Artur Reichl: Antonija (76) and Ruben (14) Pfeferman, who were members of the doctor's household and had earlier been granted protection. Somewhat later, Dr. Reichl himself disappeared.[20] Sometimes, as in the case of Dr. Emil Reich, the whole family was deported to a camp, even though the Ministry of Health demanded their release.[21] In August 1941, the well-known Zagreb orthopedist Dr. Edo Deutsch went to work in Tuzla in Bosnia. There, he was informed that his mother, Berta, had died in the Đakovo camp at the beginning of April 1942.[22] Later, Dr. Deutsch and his wife and sons, Velimir (1931) and Đurica (1935), joined the Partisans, but they were all killed by the Chetniks in the area around Brčko in 1944.[23] Dr. Teodor Grüner and his wife were arrested in Vareš at the beginning of 1942, under suspicion of cooperating with the "rebels" (i.e., the Partisans), but were released after someone interceded on their behalf. At the end of July 1942, Grüner pleaded on behalf of his parents, his younger sister Edita, and his wife's family. Although the Ministry of Health intervened for Grüner's mother-in-law in August 1942, only his parents managed to save themselves (his father was chief cantor and the only person in the Jewish Community who could conduct public worship after May 1943). His sister was deported to Auschwitz, despite the "protection" she enjoyed.[24]

Dr. Grüner was one of the few Jewish doctors sent to Bosnia of whom any trace at all can still be found in archives covering the second half of 1942—all the others had become inaccessible to the Ustasha authorities months earlier. Like Grüner, Dr. Miroslav Schlesinger and his wife, Dr. Marija, who were treating syphilis in Pećigrad (in Cazinska krajina), were also in communication with Zagreb. On August 24, 1942, at the height of the deportations from Zagreb, they requested that their mothers, Šarlota Schlesinger and Chaja Brandler, be allowed to join them in Bosnia. They stated that their mothers were guaranteed safety as family members of doctors, and "if they have already been taken to the mustering-point in Zagreb or to a transit camp . . . we request that the above-named be released and returned to their apartment." It is not known whether they got travel permits at that time or not, but the mothers did not join their children in Bosnia. The Schlesingers joined the Partisans in November of that year, and Marija Schlesinger became the legendary doctor of the Central Hospital attached to the Headquarters of the National Liberation Army of Croatia, located on Petrova Gora mountain in Kordun. During a German offensive, she managed to hide a group of wounded in a secluded underground dugout, concealed all trace of them at great personal risk, and managed to save them. Unfortunately, she became very ill and died in April 1943, and the Germans caught Miroslav and their daughter, Milena, in June 1943 and shot them. As for their mothers, Šarlota died a natural death in 1943 in her Zagreb apartment. In 1943, Chaja was being treated at the Hospital of the Sisters of Mercy in Zagreb, but nothing is known of her later fate.[25]

Some pro-Ustasha doctors were doubly pleased when the Jewish doctors went to Bosnia, which rid them of competition in Zagreb. It dispatched their competitors to places where no one wanted to go, and, at the same time, they could make use of whatever was left in the offices of the Jewish doctors, whose plunder the Ustasha regime had organized.

In the requisitions of Jewish property during the following months, the Reconstruction Directorate alone seized 121 instrument cabinets of various kinds taken from doctors' offices, 157 dentistry and instrument tables and desks, 36 heating apparatuses, 18 gynecological examination chairs, 17 dentistry and diagnostic X-rays, 19 quartz lamps, 16 dentists' chairs, 16 dental drills, 5 microscopes, and many other items, even including washbasins, towels, wall clocks, paintings, carpets, curtains, X-ray gloves, quartz spectacles, telephones, doctors' coats, suction pumps, probes, various kinds of laboratory equipment, etc.[26] It seems that some of these appliances and instruments ended up in Jasenovac.[27] True, this looting began while the Jewish doctors were still in Zagreb: the gynecologist Erich Rosenzweig was completely robbed as early as the summer of 1941, before he went to Bosnia to treat syphilis. When the doctors who were working for Camp Welfare came to ask him to donate medicines, they found him sitting in his empty office and he said, "You're too late, boys. Ankica Budak came yesterday and took the lot."[28] It seems that this looting really had been organized by Ankica Budak, secretary in the Ministry of Health and the niece of Minister Mile Budak.[29]

Dr. Karl Breyer's office in Jurišićeva Street 5 "was taken apart by the Ustashe" when Breyer was sent to camp in 1941, and his apartment was looted as well.[30] At its express wish, the Ustasha Youth Camp for the City of Zagreb moved into the house of dentist Mauricije Horn in Zvonimirova Street.[31]

Issue number four of *Vjesnik,* the internal paper of the newly founded health institute in Banja Luka, put out a detailed "statistical supplement" about the operation to control syphilis in Bosnia (with very informative tables), but without a single word about the doctors not being "Aryans."

Although the number of Jewish doctors in Zagreb had greatly decreased, in December 1941, there were still forty-five left, ten of whom worked for the Jewish Community. However, seventeen were "over sixty" or "over seventy" or had already retired.[32]

The anti-syphilis project was a chance for the Ustasha regime to win sympathy among the Muslims in Bosnia and Herzegovina. Nevertheless, it seems that the Ustashe sometimes thought it more important to kill Jewish doctors than to eradicate syphilis—they killed in cold blood twenty-five Jewish doctors who lived in Bosnia and Herzegovina before the war. They also killed Croatian and Zagreb doctors: Dr. Bogomir Hiršl (1866) was taken to Gospić in August 1941, from where he never returned.[33]

Still, as a rule, it was felt that doctors should be considered as a special group, and this was how they were indeed treated. When Jews were "moved out" of the town of Podravska Slatina in June 1942, and on other occasions, the "lack of doctors" was given as the reason for their more favorable treatment.[34] In November 1941, Mauricije Horn of Zagreb opened a dentist's office in Senj with the approval of the Ministry of Health, because "there is need of a dentist . . . although not a single Jewish doctor in the ISC has previously been granted this kind of approval." Later, Horn also joined the Partisans.[35]

There was a general shortage of professionals of all kinds, and the Ustasha government could not come to complete agreement about whether Jews who were professionals should be spared, or whether they too should be killed—this was true for doctors above all, but also for engineers and some other professions. Attempts were made to get back Jews who had fled to the Italian occupation zone and place them under Ustasha authority, and they instructed the Italian authorities to not "send to transit camps doctors, engineers, and other officials of the Jewish race who used to serve in our state," but to send them back from the areas of ISC under Italian occupation.[36] In March 1943, the Head Directorate of Health asked the Minister of the Interior to "re-examine the reasons . . . for imprisoning . . . all the doctors who have been sent to camps or prisons," and to place those who were not under suspicion "at the disposal of the Directorate," and those who had been found guilty "to work as doctors in camps."[37] For many Jewish doctors, interventions of this kind came too late, and, as far as can be ascertained, this particular intervention did not help anyone.

The Jasenovac inmates noticed that "doctors arranged their living quarters nicely. They were the most favored group in the camp, a kind of camp aristocracy. At that time, there were about twenty of them, mostly Jews."[38] However, out of eighty-six Jewish doctors in Jasenovac, only nine survived.[39]

The RUR Jewish Section took the stand that "no Jews whatsoever are to be employed by the state." The Directorate of the Main State Roads sent a letter to the UNS saying that "if Jewish engineers are to be allowed to work for the state, because of the lack of experts," then "protective identity cards should also be issued to the members of their families."[40] It seems that, in general, engineers and their families were not protected, although there were exceptions: engineer Milan Seligman from Karlovac was released from Jasenovac and exempted from wearing the insignia so that he could give his professional services to build a bridge across the river Kupa.[41] Viktor Hahn was taken to Jasenovac twice and then brought back, because he was irreplaceable as research laboratory head in the Kaštel pharmaceutical factory, which was how he survived the war.[42]

After the establishment of the ISC, attorney Nikola Tolnauer was arrested with the first group of Zagreb Jewish attorneys and taken to Kerestinec, and, after some of the prisoners escaped from there, to the prison in Sava Road. The management of the Našička Wood Company, Ltd., succeeded in procuring some kind of exemption for him—he continued to work in the firm—but after working hours, a policeman escorted him back to the prison on Sava Road. At the beginning of 1944, he was deported to Jasenovac and was killed in April 1945 during the breakout from the camp.[43]

In his memoirs, Gojko Nikoliš, head of the medical corps of the Supreme Command of the National Liberation Army of Yugoslavia, praised Jewish doctors in several places. Many of them joined the Partisans after they had gone to treat syphilis in Bosnia and Herzegovina. "My friends used to reproach me for being too kindly disposed to the Jewish doctors . . .

I am sure that I was not wrong. To put it simply, we had many of them in our midst and, with very few exceptions, they were very capable men, good organizers who would not put up with negligence, and I assigned them to responsible duties with a clear conscience."[44]

The ISC's Ministry of Health also commended the work of Jewish doctors. In December 1941, in connection with suppressing endemic diseases in Bosnia, it informed the State Information and Promotion Bureau that the doctors' "great devotion and love for the people became manifest, because they put all their efforts into this responsible task." There is no mention of the doctors being Jewish.[45]

16

OTHER FORMS OF PERSECUTION

By the summer of 1941, when mass deportations to concentration camps began, the first stage of anti-Jewish measures in the ISC had been more or less completed: laws had been passed excommunicating the Jews from society and completely stripping them of rights, their property had been plundered or prepared for plunder by regulations, they had been almost completely prevented from earning money and making a living, and by having to wear the Jewish insignia they were marked and humiliated. Many additional kinds of discrimination made their lives unbearable. They had to request permission for whatever they wanted to do, however insignificant. The provision of May 8, ordering Jews and Serbs to move out of the northern parts of the city, also introduced a curfew: "Serbs and Jews, who live in the city of Zagreb, may move about Zagreb only from 6:00 a.m. to 9:00 p.m." "Legal regulations" of this kind were usually simply the manifestation of brute force, but formally they were derived from the just as brutal Legal Provision on the Defense of the People and State. On May 30, *Novi list* published an inflammatory article entitled "By Their Behavior, the Jews Will Provoke Even Stronger Measures against Them." The article said that "Jews are forbidden to loiter in any public promenades and parks, and in the center of the city—for example, in Ilica, on Jelačićev Square, around the Main Railway Station."[1] The Jewish Section considered that "Jews like to go to these major thoroughfares, as if they wanted to 'demonstrate' how many of them there are in Zagreb." The article concluded with an open threat: "The insolent behavior of the Jews will soon provoke the enactment of a provision placing all of them in a strictly controlled part of the city."[2] It seems that the top authorities were already thinking seriously about this idea and that it was planned to concentrate Jews in the western parts of the city. Work on its realization began but never went far, because the mass deportations of Jews to camps that were soon organized made their ghettoization in the city meaningless. Rumors that Jews were gathering on Tomislavov Square and around the neighboring Main Railway Station probably started because on May 15 the Jewish Community got new premises at Tomislavov Square 4, so its employees and members kept coming there. A "police detective" had noticed this, and had written a report about it, but another police detective said that there was "nothing suspicious" about this concentration. The Ustasha authorities made good use of rumors of any kind to misinform the public, purposely adding oil to the fire. The pressure on the Jews increased every day: at that time, at the end of May, a group of 165 young Jews were arrested and sent to Danica Camp in Koprivnica, and then to Jadovno, where they were killed.

On April 22, Jews were forbidden to enter restaurants, coffeehouses, and inns; later the ban was extended to cinemas and theatres, and they could only go to the markets to buy food after 10:00 a.m. The implementation of such rigorous measures sometimes gave rise to new charges: under the title "Disgusting Speculation in Zagreb Markets," *Novi list* wrote that many of the stall holders kept their prices high, or did not come to the markets at all before ten o'clock, so that they could make money by selling to Jews, and that their attitude was: "If you won't buy at our prices you don't have to, take it or leave it; the Jews will come after ten and they'll pay whatever we ask."[3] But this is probably only partially true, for at that time there were already such great shortages that after "ten o'clock, all the food was already sold."[4]

In the meantime, Jews were prevented from moving around in the city in various ways. They were even banned from walking through parks, and from going to the town center. For example, Julije Hirschl, who moved to Kustošija, had to get a permit on July 30 to "pass the Ilica Tollhouse and go on to the city."[5] As "some Jews did not obey the strict ban on passing through and loitering in certain parts of the city," on June 4, the dental technician Teodor Herman, schoolboys Petar Klein and Hinko Gottlieb

(1926), and the craftsman Zdenko Lion were sent to a camp. All of them except Lion (whose fate is unknown) died in Jasenovac. Hinko received a parcel from the Zagreb Jewish Community at the beginning of November, and then all trace of him disappeared.[6]

To make it possible for them to go on functioning, the Ustasha authorities issued Jews with various kinds of permits. Viktor Kohn, business manager of the Ivo Restaurant, got a special permit "to buy foodstuffs on the market even before 10:00 a.m."[7] In June, in answer to the explicit inquiry of the Professional Cinema Association, the Jewish Section answered that "Jews may not go to cinemas, or to any other public place."[8] But, in July 1941, Ivan Färber got a permit to spend between 10:00 a.m. and 2:00 p.m. in the northern part of the city "on business"; the Fein-Pichler family were permitted to spend the time from 10:00 a.m. to noon and from 4:00 to 6:00 p.m. in the garden of the house in Ribnjak no. 2;[9] on July 11, Klotilda Guthard was allowed to "visit her husband's grave between 3:00 and 7:00 p.m.,"[10] Roza Gross was permitted to "be on Strossmayerov Square from 10:00 to 11:00 a.m.,"[11] and Ella Schlein to "cross Zrinjski Square on her way to and from work."[12]

Ordinances of this kind made it terribly complicated for Jews to move about the city: for example, there are no more than a few hundred meters between Trenkova 9 and Tomislavov Square 4, two addresses at which some of the Jewish Community services were located. However, as Jews were not allowed to cross Tomislavov Square (one of the central city squares), they had to take a roundabout way from Trenkova, passing under the railway line on Miramarska Road, and then walking over the pedestrian bridge that at that time crossed the Main Railway Station leading from the Steam-Mill area to the post office in Branimirova Street. Altogether, this is a distance of about one and a half kilometers, so instead of three minutes they had to walk for about twenty.[13] The case of Hinko Löwy (1880), prominent dermato-venereologist and medical historian, shows what happened to people who did not obey these orders. He defiantly walked across Tomislavov Square, wearing the "Ž" insignia and several distinguished Austro-Hungarian military medals that he had won in the First World War; for this he was severely beaten and had his medals torn off. Later, Dr. Löwy and his entire family perished in the camps.[14] It is true that a Jew could take off his insignia and walk through those forbidden zones, but the danger of having to show his identity papers or of being recognized was very great.

Oto Waldner had to procure a permit to continue living in his apartment in Fruškogorska, in Ljubljanica (at that time on the outskirts of the city).[15] At the beginning of June, the Ustasha Police Commission issued a proclamation forbidding Jews "to leave or travel from the territory of the city of Zagreb," so requests had to be submitted to the Jewish Section even to travel to nearby Stubičke and Krapinske Toplice.[16]

Besides "passes," which had to be obtained on practically every occasion, people also requested and were issued with residence and work "permits." These "permits" were a kind of compromise solution midway between being granted Aryan rights and being completely stripped of all rights. When a Jew had some kind of "merit" because of which he or she could be spared at least to some degree, but his request for being granted Aryan rights had been refused, he was issued with a "permit" that was supposed to allow him to continue working at his job and living in his apartment. Very many such "permits" were issued beginning in May 1941,[17] but they soon became useless because people started to be evicted from their apartments and lost their jobs *en masse,* and soon thereafter they began to be deported. There are no more documents about these permits to be found in later months and years. In the middle of November 1941, the Ministry of the Croatian Home Guard sent a notice saying that the "the identity cards issued to Jewish reserve officers decorated for courage in the world war, which allowed them to freely move about and work in the city of Zagreb, have been proclaimed invalid and will be withdrawn."[18]

The provision about the "protection of Aryan blood and honor," of April 30, 1941, proclaimed that all changes of "Jewish surnames made after December 1, 1918, are outside the law and they must revert to their original surname." Nevertheless, on June 4, the Legal Provision on Changing Jewish Surnames was passed, which additionally clarified these regulations and broadened them somewhat, and the Decree on Taking Back a Former Surname referred to "spouses and descendents" as well. No pseudonym was allowed, nameplates with the present name had to be changed within eight days, and people were given the same deadline to inform the competent authorities about the new (old) surname.[19] Josip and Chawa Korjan were forced to take back their old surname, Kohn, after long proceedings. The artillery major Zdravko Miroslav Miladinović became Mühlstein again.[20] Artur Polić went back to Pollak, and documents mentioned the attorney Rudolf Rodanić by his old surname Rosenfeld, too, although it is not clear whether he had to take it back and whether he did so.[21] In the summer of 1941, Polić's son Branko was issued a school report card for the seventh grade of grammar school in the name of Polić, but Pollak was added in brackets, just in case.[22] During this period, Vlasta Maceljski (in the twenties Deutsch-Maceljski) received a school graduation certificate in the surname of Deutsch only.[23]

A surprisingly small number of documents relating to the administrative procedures in which Jews took back their old surnames remain, probably because the people to whom this would have applied had either escaped or had been deported before their case came up. For example, Andrija Kraljević, formerly König, who converted in July 1941, was killed in Jasenovac in November or December 1941.[24] Surnames were changed right up until the end of the war: at the end of 1943, Aleksandar Glavaš and his daughter, Ingeborg, got the surname Hauptmann, and in February 1944, Želimir Muževič (1932) became Želimir Müller.[25]

However, the Ustasha regime was not completely consistent in that all through those years the Department of Religious Affairs in the Ministry of Justice and Religious Affairs allowed some Jews to change their "old" surnames to "new" ones. In 1941, Dragutin Fischer became Földi, Branko Stern became Šimek, and the Bergers became Gorans. Renata Kikinis became Renata Simeoni.[26] In 1942, Zvonimir (1899) and Eugenija Deutsch changed their name to Dainović, Jelka Kraus, née Muačević, who was married to a Jew, became Jelka Ivanović,[27] in May, Dr. Vladimir and Lili Schwarz became Crnek, the distinguished physicist Josip Goldberg became Letnik, Leo and Tomislav Drucker became Držić, and Marija Rosenblat changed her surname to Ružičić.[28] It seems that in most of these proceedings some or all the documents were antedated to make it seem that the first step had been taken before April 10, 1941. Anđelina Gentner, who married Mijo Gentner in 1929, took back her maiden name Modrovčić at the end of 1942.[29] Milan and David Eckstein from Sisak changed their name to Egić in 1940, and they managed to have this entered on their documents (in the parish office, etc.) in August 1942, despite the legal ban.[30] Even in 1945, Julija Rosenberg changed her surname to Vince.[31] Some people changed both name and surname. Erika Ivana Günther (1923) changed her name to Renata when she converted, and "she has the right to use this name."[32] As most of these people wanted to break off all relations with the Jewish community, it is very difficult to follow their later fate because the change of surname had obviously not been a guarantee of survival. Eugenija Deutsch-Dainović was deported to Auschwitz in 1943, and the list of victims shows her under her old surname of Deutsch. Jelka Kraus-Ivanović had to flee to Switzerland. There is no information about Zvonimir Deutsch.[33] At the beginning of 1943, the Jewish

Community sent mail to Dr. Goldberg under his new surname of Letnik, but in the list of survivors in 1945, and in all postwar activities, he was Goldberg again.

A decree of May 13, 1941, banned the ritual slaughter of animals and the selling of the meat of the same, obviously referring to kosher food.[34] Ten days later, on May 23, all Jews and Serbs were ordered to hand in their radio sets.[35] The main reason for confiscating radio sets was plunder, but added to that was fear that Jews might listen to "undesirable radio stations." This had been banned by the decree of the military court, but obviously it was felt necessary to additionally underpin these regulations. Some non-Jews also lost their radio sets at this time, Anđelka Biermann, née Drčić, an "Aryan," got back her radio set, which had already been allotted to a man called Šuprina. She was an "Aryan" woman married to a Jew, and the Jewish Section was displeased that her radio set had been returned, fearing that even those "who are in a mixed marriage will listen to the enemy, that is, to banned radio stations."[36]

The legal provision that ordered the change of surname also ordered that all Jewish shops must be marked with a piece of yellow paper "in an especially visible place with the words 'Jewish establishment.'" The RUR's Jewish Section ordered that Jews must not leave the territory of the city of Zagreb, reiterated that they must not frequent markets before 10:00 a.m., and stressed that they must shop only in Jewish establishments.[37]

After radio sets, on June 26, Jews had to hand in their cameras, cinéma cameras, and film projectors. A day later, on June 28, the Press Department of the Prime Minister's Office requested that the Jewish Section "hand over to us cameras confiscated from the Jews, at least five cameras of the following brands: Rolleiflex, Leica . . . all of them the most modern models, since this is most important for the needs of state propaganda."[38] The State Archives also asked for "equipment for a photo laboratory, furniture for one office, a large iron safe, and a typewriter," but they received the answer that the request "cannot be met because the material requested has been placed at the disposal of the State Propaganda Bureau."[39] In its letter to the RUR's Jewish Section, the Ustasha Head Office claimed that it "does not have enough typewriters at its disposal" and asked to be given "a list of private Jewish persons who have one."[40]

The decree on handing over cameras was accompanied by an order forbidding Jews of both sexes to "bathe in the public baths on the Sava river, and to loiter near them."[41] The exclusive goal of these measures was to further humiliate the Jews. The day after the decree was issued, *Hrvatski narod* printed a text under the incendiary title "Despite the Ban, Jews Are Still Bathing in the Sava River."[42]

Another form of humiliation took place without being made public: the Jewish Section informed the Jewish Community in June 1941 that "it has come to our notice that your papers and stamps still have Hebrew names . . . In future you shall leave them out."[43] The Community obeyed, and after that Hebrew characters did not appear on the letterhead.

The Legal Provision on the Protection of Aryan Blood and the Honor of the Croatian People of April 30 also forbade a man or a woman of the Jewish race from marrying an Aryan. As someone had in the meantime concluded that "Jews and other non-Aryans are not obeying, and are trying to thwart regulations by converting to Catholicism or Islam, and under the mask of Catholicism or Islam they contract marriages that are against the regulations before the religious authorities," in October an "amendment" of the text was published. In it, anyone who enters into a marriage of this kind "shall be punished by at least six months of harsh imprisonment and loss of citizenship and national affiliation," and for a civil servant "at least six months of harsh imprisonment and loss of service."[44]

At the end of August 1941, the Jewish Religious Community of Zagreb requested from the RUR's Jewish Section that they be allowed to celebrate the Jewish New Year and Yom Kippur (September 22 and 23 and October 2) in the synagogue in Praška. This request was refused.[45]

17

THE WORK OF THE JEWISH RELIGIOUS COMMUNITY IN ZAGREB

The very day after they assumed power, the Ustashe seized and sealed the building of the Jewish Religious Community in Palmotićeva Street This meant that the Community's activities, and the way they had been carried out for decades, were also terminated. The activities of the societies and foundations which were housed in the building also came to an end or were drastically changed. All Community accounts were blocked. Neither the school nor the nursery school could continue working where they were, and publishing activities died out completely. "All the work done previously was annulled, all the flourishing life of prewar times was trampled underfoot and ended," said a report from 1945.[1]

Hardly any of the many and thriving Jewish activities in prewar Zagreb remained. A partial exception was the continuing work of the Humanitarian Society, a mixed Croatian-Jewish charity association that had been founded in 1846 by Jacques Epstein, and whose first members included Ljudevit Gaj, Josip Jelačić, and other renowned Croats of that time. To prevent the more drastic involvement of the Ustasha authorities, Vladimir Cesar replaced Dr. Milan Schwartz, the president for many years, and the Society continued to function as before, as a "society of distinguished Zagreb citizens working in solidarity, without distinction of religion or social class." They helped persecuted Jews, and also Croats and Serbs who fled to Zagreb from the Italian occupation zone or for other reasons. The work of the Society was extremely restricted because the residents of the house where the center was located and which was its property, most of them Jews, were deported, and Ustasha functionaries moved into the apartments and were extremely irregular rent-payers. In addition, rents were paid at a time of inflation and "the work of the Society went almost unnoticed in the great social needs of that time."[2]

When the activities in Palmotićeva ended, an institutional vacuum ensued that had to be filled in. On April 16, the Jewish Community, Hevra Kaddisha, and the Chief Rabbi's Office requested permission from the Police Directorate to "take from the sealed rooms, under supervision, printed forms, stamps, registry books, and other essential books, and we will continue to work either in one of our offices that have not been confiscated or in an empty apartment that we will find for this purpose."[3] On May 16, the Jewish Section of the RUR issued an oral decision allowing the work of the Jewish Religious Community in Zagreb (ŽBOZ) to continue, and it was allowed to use the above name. "How much greater and graver the catastrophe that had befallen Jewry would have been had the Community not started to work, and had it not immediately begun to help people, is unimaginable," says a postwar report.[4] It no longer worked in Palmotićeva, but on May 15, the Community moved to Tomislavov Square 4, into much smaller rooms owned by the Friedfeld Foundation.[5] "The lawyer Dr. Drago Rosenberg systematically and quietly organized the work of the Community with new people and in the new venue. He took the smallest room for his own office, and all the other rooms were like a beehive full of associates and volunteers working at full pace."[6]

The 1945 report says that the decision to allow work to be resumed came after the "intervention of the Community administration."[7] It seems that the favorable decision of the Ustasha authorities had been expected, because the eleven-member Community Council was constituted on May 14, 1941, on approval of the Jewish Section, and consisted of Dr. Hugo Kon, Lavoslav Steiner, Dr. Dragutin Rosenberg, Rikard Kohn, Professor Aleksa Semnic, Albert Baum, Dr. Miroslav B. Schlesinger, Julio König, and Dr. Žiga Neumann. Dr. Hugo Kon was reelected as president. It was also simultaneously decided that the Sephardic and Orthodox communities should join the (Ashkenazic) Jewish Religious Community, so Cezar Gaon represented the Sephardim in the Council, and Leon Hessel the Orthodox Jews (later, he and his family reached Palestine via Italy).[8] Aleksandar Klein became secretary. At that time, the Community administration had a staff of twelve: Rudolf Buchwald, Herman Bresslauer, Eugen Kohn, Josip Abraham, Zlata Goldschmitt, Irena Engel, Ida Mandolfo, Lorant Levi, Zora Haberfeld, Robert Veith, Robert Stein, and Andrija Pick.[9] Of all the activists, two were especially noteworthy: the President of the Community, Hugo Kon (1870–1943), and the Zagreb Chief Rabbi, Miroslav Šalom Freiberger (1903–1943), who was a religious teacher, Hebrew scholar, translator, lawyer, doctor of theology, prolific writer, and the spiritual leader of the Zagreb Jews. "The wisdom and equanimity of the former, the skill and practical consistency of the latter, even his diplomatic skill, were irreplaceable," the Community members remembered with sadness in 1945.[10]

For a time, the Sephardic and Orthodox communities continued to work in their own rooms. When the Sephardic Community united with the majority Ashkenazic Community, sometime in the middle of May, the Ustasha authorities confiscated the former's premises in Karadžićeva 3, and just over a month later handed them over to the Jewish Community to serve as a synagogue.[11] The authorities did not confiscate the premises of the Orthodox Jewish Community in the courtyard of Duga Street 32 until September. The furniture and inventory remained the property of the Jewish Religious Community and were moved to Trenkova 9, where it rented rooms. At first, most of the space there was taken by the school. The Social Department and Camp Welfare were in the ground floor, the Chief Rabbi's Office and synagogue on the second floor. Services were held regularly, on holidays, Fridays and Saturdays in the morning and evening.[12] At first, they were conducted by Chief Rabbi Gavro Schwarz, and when he died in February 1942, they were taken over by Chief Rabbi Miroslav Šalom Freiberger and Chief Cantor Bernard Grüner.[13]

The somewhat longer existence, if only formally, of the Sephardic and Orthodox communities was probably due to the authorities not considering them especially important, or perhaps just less dangerous.

In June, the Jewish Section allowed the Community to "continue its normal transactions with the Postal Savings Bank in Zagreb," and the Hevra Kaddisha to "continue its transactions with the same bank." At that time, the accounts that had earlier been blocked, with almost 500,000 kunas, were reopened.[14] A few days later, approval arrived for the Jewish Community to dispose of its twelve other current accounts, with the Jewish Section as "co-signatory."[15] A telephone "under RUR control"[16] was installed in the offices on Tomislavov Square and in Trenkova 9, despite the fact that only several days later, at the beginning of July, the Jewish

Section was ordered to "cut off all telephones owned by Jews . . . since censors still encounter telephone conversations that are in code or whose content is against our interests."[17]

In public documents, the Jewish Section confirmed that the Jewish Religious Community of Zagreb was working "on the orders and under the control of the state authorities."[18] In 1941, the minutes of every meeting of the Community Council recorded that it was "being held with approval of the Jewish Section of the RUR."[19] The relations between the two institutions became completely absurd, because in July, the Jewish Community requested that the Jewish Section order Jews to report their new addresses after they had been evicted from their apartments. The Community had to keep its records up to date so that it could collect dues and meet its financial obligations to the state.[20] The Jewish Section replied that Community dues "must be paid by all persons covered by the provisions on racial affiliation who had been members of the Community on September 1, 1940," and that the Community "must inform its members" that it will be impossible to decrease the community tax.[21]

The school was also allowed to continue working. Teaching was resumed on June 9, after a two-month break. In July, a "holiday course" was organized from 8:00 to 10:00 a.m., obviously for children to make up for what they had missed.[22] Since Jewish children were forbidden to go to secondary school, and in July the request of the Jewish Community to open a secondary school was refused,[23] a day center was opened for secondary-school children in Trenkova. This day center was supposed to provide the children with a secondary-school education, so that they could later, if this became possible, pass exams in what they had lost in regular schooling. The Community kept tidy records of who attended the day center. Željko Deutsch from Križevci was accepted at the end of 1941.[24] However, most of the children were later taken to a camp and killed there.[25]

It seems that the Ustasha authorities even allowed the publication of a "children's paper for young Jews in the ISC." In June, the Jewish Community informed the Jewish Section that it had begun preparations to publish *Židovski glasnik* (Jewish Herald), the official paper of the Jewish Religious Community of Zagreb, and *Židovski dječji list* (Jewish Children's Paper). At the end of July, the "material for the first issue was finished," but the *Herald* never came out.[26] The Ustasha authorities allowed the Jewish Community to carry out some activities: e.g., in July 1941, they allowed them to collect "religious dues from Jewish firms." However, the real reason for this was pecuniary, because if it had no money, the "Community would not be able to meet the obligations that were required," claimed the Community representatives.[27]

The Community Council held its first meeting after the proclamation of the ISC on May 22, at which it made preparations to organize survival under the new conditions. The most immediate task was to help those who had already suffered in the Ustasha onslaught, and people who would soon find themselves in a similar or worse position. At the meeting of September 30, 1941, the councilors euphemistically stated, "We resumed our work in the second half of May of the current year on approval of the competent authorities. Because of changed conditions, our activities developed in two directions: within the limitations imposed by the new circumstances, we tried to continue the activities that the Community had always carried out, and, at the same time, we began to most urgently address problems we faced under the new regime, and the views it held about the solution of the Jewish question."

The foundation of various committees was planned at the meeting of May 22: financial and legal, school, social, religious, productive work, evictions, burying the dead, caring for the sick, providing for the Lavoslav Schwarz Old People's Home, collecting religious and social taxes, the children's day-care center, and care for those who had converted were all on the agenda.[28] They began to be dealt with immediately after this date. On June 4, at the second meeting of the Community Council, the Women's Social Section was founded, with the following members: Hilda Klein, Julija König, Marija Neumann, Stabka Frank, Marta Schulz, Helena Kabiljo, Slavica Gowelb (Gewoelb), Terka Njemirovski, and Dr. Oton Pollak.[29] Existing material shows the lists of members of the other committees and Community employees only in part. The list of officials from June 18 contains Gizela Kohn-Fuchs (head of the elementary school), Eugen Mandel (cantor), Mira Kaufer (teacher), Isak Hendel (cantor), Bernard Grüner (chief cantor), Josip Basch (training cantor), Dr. Moric Levi (secondary-school religious teacher), Dr. Samuel Romano (secondary-school religious teacher), Dr. Miroslav Freiberger (rabbi), Mirjam Weiller (head of the nursery school), Greta Weiss (teacher), Ruža Schlesinger (teacher), Geza Lang (janitor), Isak Baruh (deputy rabbi), Alice Dukes (teacher), Hani Flesch (teacher), Nisim Konfino (teacher), and Elvira Reich (teacher).[30] Documents show that as many as seventy people were engaged in various kinds of work in the Community by the end of July, and they were all issued with passes.[31] Most of the planned committees were founded during those weeks. On the approval of the authorities, a soup kitchen was opened at Preradovićeva 29 on July 23, in what had been the Jewish Academy Canteen.[32] At that time, it served only lunch, with a capacity of about 250 servings.

Many of these activities existed only on paper. The Community started some of them with the best of intentions—and usually in vain—to do something to mitigate the horror: "It was all naïve, and I don't know whether any of it was realized at all," said Stjepan Steiner.[33] The Productive Work Committee was designed to plan, organize, and hold courses at which Jews would "train as quickly as possible for household jobs, or as tailors to sew, or to work leather, wood, metals, to engrave glass, or learn house crafts," because "many of them will no longer be able to perform their professions of attorney, merchant, or broker."

Some activities were invented so as to justify the increased number of community staff that the Ustasha authorities issued with certain papers, which provided them with some kind of protection. The protection was minimal, because it only covered working hours; at other times, the Ustashe could arrest, intern, and kill employees. But at that time, even this poor protection was better than none.

Mass deportations to camps made it necessary to establish and give priority to the service called Camp Welfare, and the poor state of nutrition and health also demanded the establishment of a special committee for health protection.[34]

Two doctor's offices were established that provided free examinations for all who could not afford to pay. One of them, for children, was run by the pediatrician Dr. Gustav Jungwirth, and the other, for adults, by Dr. Leo Wilf.[35] Jungwirth was soon included in the operation of treating syphilis in Bosnia.[36] Later, Dr. Isak Heršković was appointed Community doctor, but the office stopped working in August 1942, when Dr. Heršković was deported.[37]

All these activities required money, so the Religious Dues Assessment Committee was instituted in May. All Jews, former and present Community members, who had converted or still belonged to the Jewish faith, had to pay religious dues. A memo in June informed them how much they had to pay, and they had the right to "appeal [the sum] in writing within a term of eight days," but the "appeal did not have the power to defer payment." Anyone with religious and social dues outstanding from preceding years was even threatened with seizure, and anyone who would not pay the religious dues was threatened with "enforced payment."[38] The cards printed in the second half of May 1941, to record who had been issued the Jewish insignia, already included the following entries: "proposal" (of religious dues), "assessment," "appeal," "after appeal," "second appeal," and "final assessment."[39]

To enable the Council members and Community employees to move about freely, on May 27, the Jewish Section provided them with identity cards. Thus, Dr. Kohn was allowed to be out until 11:00 p.m. and could live in the Schwarz Home in Maksimirska, while the Community secretary Aleksandar Klein got a permit to live at Bogišićeva 2. Klein's permit explicitly says that any seizure of his effects must immediately be terminated.[40] The RUR's Jewish Section made a list of sixty-one "employees of the Jewish Religious Community and their apartments," which other Ustasha services were to exclude from any kind of persecution.[41]

In allowing the Jewish Community a degree of freedom and autonomy of work, the Ustasha authorities were to a certain extent following their Nazi models. The German authorities demanded the formation of Jewish Councils (*Judenräte*) in the large Jewish ghettoes in occupied Poland in 1939–1941, to which prominent members of the local Jewish community were usually elected. These Jewish Councils were given the role of mediator: they conveyed the orders and demands of the occupation authorities to the Jewish population, and they represented the Jewish community in dealings with the occupying powers. Council members enjoyed a degree of (temporary) safety and some other relief, but when the mass deportations to death camps started in 1942, they were taken away and killed together with the other members of their community.[42] Jewish Communities did not stop working in other countries allied with Germany, either (e.g., Hungary, Slovakia, Bulgaria, parts of Romania). When the German troops occupied Hungary in the spring of 1944, Eichmann continued to communicate with the Hungarian Jews largely through the Jewish Community in Budapest and through some of its representatives. Jewish Councils in ghettoes tried, and sometimes temporarily managed, to at least mitigate somewhat the hardships suffered by their members. On the other hand, there were cases when Council members helped the Nazi authorities to the detriment of their community in order to save their own lives, which Hannah Arendt considers "undoubtedly the darkest chapter in the overall tragic story."[43] Nothing like this has been recorded in the work of the councilors and other officials of the Zagreb Jewish Community in 1941–1945. On the contrary, under conditions that it is no overstatement to call impossible, there is no doubt that the Jewish Religious Community of Zagreb, with the greatest self-sacrifice, tried everything it could, sometimes successfully, to help at least some of its members in the greatest distress, and even managed to save some of them. The Ustasha authorities obviously thought, and perhaps they had gotten this advice from the Germans, that it would be easier to control the surviving Jews in Zagreb and in other places in the ISC if the Jewish Community continued to exist.

For a very short time, perhaps for a month or two, the Community officials lived under the illusion that they would be able to maintain some kind of a public and religious life for Jews even under the Ustashe. Soon their main and almost only concern became Camp Welfare: the attempt to help the growing number of deportees to survive. They worked on this with amazing persistence, despite constantly growing difficulties. During the first months, Dezider Abraham was in charge of Camp Welfare, and, on the medical side, doctors Ivo Löw, Zdenko Löwenthal, and Stjepan Steiner. Food was collected in houses, Jewish doctors donated medicine and sanitary materiel, the Community staff packed food parcels, put together emergency medical stores and took them to the prisoners at the Zagreb Fairground, later to Zavrtnica.[44] "Finally, we went to Dr. Mile Budak [nephew of the minister of the same name]. He gave us all the medicine, bandages, and instruments he had," said Dr. Stjepan Steiner.[45]

The only positive circumstance in the work of the Community, at least to a degree, was the financial aid it received from abroad, although the Ustasha authorities paid special attention to this too, and did their best to strictly control it. When the ISC was established, all connections between the Jewish Religious Community of Zagreb and the most important international Jewish organizations, directly or through the Alliance of Jewish Religious Communities in Belgrade, were severed. As these international organizations (most of all the American JOINT) were ready to offer a degree of material aid to the persecuted Jews, the Zagreb Community established indirect links with neutral Switzerland via Italy, and with representatives of Palestinian Jews in Istanbul, in neutral Turkey, through the Jewish Community in Budapest. Some Zagreb Jews who had managed to escape to Switzerland played an especially important role in this; outstanding among them was the Zionist leader Dr. Aleksandar Licht. Existing documents do not show exactly how much money arrived through these channels, but they do show that the parcels the Zagreb Community sent to the camps, and the upkeep of the Lavoslav Schwarz Old People's Home, were mostly funded from those sources. The donators preferred the money not to be sent to individuals, but to an institution in which they rightly had confidence. The Ustasha authorities tolerated this because it gave them complete control over the money inflow, as well as an indirect benefit (the conversion of precious foreign currency, the plunder of parcels that were sent, etc.). All these were additional reasons why the Ustasha authorities allowed the survival of the Jewish Religious Community of Zagreb, and why this institution could maintain a small number of its severely truncated activities to the end of the war. Very similar circumstances led to the survival of the Jewish communities in Hungary and Slovakia, which, in the last phase, received considerable aid from the International Red Cross, as well.[46]

How strict a watch the Ustasha authorities kept over the international aid sent to the Zagreb Jewish Community can well be seen from the travels of Aleksander Klein, Community secretary, who in March 1942 went to Ljubljana "to reach an agreement to aid refugees." "Geza Farbak, deputy head of the RUR's Jewish Section, accompanied him on this trip," obviously to keep Klein under surveillance day and night.[47] Besides, some members of the regime may have thought that they could use the existence of the Community for propaganda purposes, and boast of their allegedly more liberal attitude to the Jews to foreign guests and representatives (for example, those from the Vatican).

As the life of most Jewish communities in Croatia—meaning the ISC—had practically died out by the autumn of 1941, and the Zagreb Community was still kept alive in various ways, it increasingly began to care for all the persecuted Jews of Croatia and Bosnia and Herzegovina. A good example of this is a memo the Zagreb Community sent to all the communities in the ISC on May 21, 1941, saying, "We wish to inform you that our Community has continued its regular work, with the permission of the competent authorities. Since it has also been charged with the support of refugees in the territory of Croatia [here again, meaning the ISC], we beg you to support our work with all your might."[48]

In the following months, the Zagreb Community corresponded most frequently with the Sarajevo and Osijek communities. From Sarajevo, Judge Srećko Bujas, commissioner for the Jewish Sephardic Community, sent word to Zagreb as early as June 8 that the "Community entrusted to me is at present in such a situation that it cannot participate in any aid." At the beginning of August, small sums of money were nevertheless sent from the Sephardic and Ashkenazic communities in Sarajevo,[49] to which the Zagreb Community replied that this was not enough by far. It appealed to Sarajevo to take the request seriously "because otherwise our Community will not be able to care for the members of your Communities in the camps," by which they meant prisoners in Jadovno and on Pag.[50]

Bujas came to Zagreb on about June 20, and he and the Community secretary, Aleksandar Klein, discussed "many mutual questions and problems." It was necessary to take care of the "many Jewish poor in Sarajevo," And they also wanted to help Jewish emigrants from the Third Reich who were coming to Sarajevo and its surroundings, into "our needy region."[51] Several days later, it could be seen what this looked like in practice. The Zagreb Community gave Bujas 20,000 kunas, part of which was spent to supply 150 Jewish emigrants, traveling via Sarajevo to Mostar, with "food and other things they needed to continue the journey."[52]

In July, the Zagreb Community informed the Dubrovnik Community that there were 117 German Jews in Gacko, in Herzegovina, who were penniless, hungry, and wretched. Since it was not possible to contact them from Zagreb, the Community sent 10,000 kunas to Dubrovnik, and the Dubrovnik Community bought food and immediately sent it to Gacko.[53] In September, Branko Milaković, commissioner of the Sarajevo Ashkenazic Community, who "did a lot for our community in his work and efforts,"[54] came to Zagreb. At the end of September, 30,000 kunas were sent from Zagreb to Sarajevo, "which were to be used in agreement to the best effect."[55]

When Jewish men and women from Sarajevo were sent to Jasenovac and to Loborgrad sometime later, money began to be sent from Sarajevo to Zagreb because the Zagreb Community "was in a difficult financial situation due to its great expenditures for Loborgrad (and Jasenovac)."[56] In the first half of November 1941, the Zagreb Community negotiated with the Jewish Section of the RUR about important issues connected with the Sarajevo Jews, such as the organization of Jewish societies that were to merge with the Sephardic Community, and about Jewish property. Despite the good will and great efforts, even "helped by the Jewish Section," it was clear that "no general and underlying solution could be reached," because the Ustasha regime had already decided what it wanted to do with the Sarajevo Jews.[57] Only several days later, at the height of sweeping arrests and deportations, the commissioners of the Sarajevo Jewish communities described the dramatic events, "the tragedy that has befallen the Jewish community of Sarajevo," and begged the representatives of the Zagreb Community to look into this "Sarajevo problem, to call it that, since it is the most urgent issue at present and to devote all your attention and all efforts exclusively to it," to "inform us on a daily basis about everything that you are doing, both in this problem of ours and in other general and special issues of Jewish communities."[58] Drago Rosenberg wrote to concerned relatives in

Sarajevo that "I certainly do not need to assure you how worried I am for all Sarajevo Jews, and how much we are trying to do and are doing for them, but as you can see, without any real results, although those we turn to sincerely want to help." Hugo Kon and his associates were obviously doing their best, and once more they sent relatively optimistic messages to Sarajevo, saying that they would talk to commissioner Maks Luburić "in connection with the Sarajevo Eastern-Orthodox prisoners interned in Jasenovac," but had "not yet managed to do so."[59] In addition to all the informal contacts, Kon and Klein also wrote an official letter to the Jewish Section of the RUR in which they "describe the desperate situation of the Sarajevo Jews" and "beg for urgent intercession for an improvement of conditions."[60] The Zagreb Community also received several official letters every day about events in Sarajevo, and, in the following months, played an important role in organizing help for Sarajevo's Jewish men and women interned in Loborgrad, Đakovo, and Jasenovac. A meeting was organized in Zagreb in early December between the representatives of the Zagreb and Osijek communities and the commissioner of the Sarajevo Community to coordinate attempts to help prisoners and try to stop further deportations. But all these efforts achieved no real results.[61]

The Jewish Section approved the Community sending doctors to the camps on Pag and on Velebit to treat inmates who were seriously ill, to inoculate prisoners preventively, and to improve hygiene, so that "contagious diseases do not spread from there."[62] In August, the Zagreb Community informed the Karlovac Community that "its twenty-eight members in Jadovno and on Velebit were healthy and that they were all right," that they would send them "additional food," but that the Karlovac Community was to "send them the necessary sum."[63] This was one of the few instances of misinformation, although not intentional: all the people on the list were by then already dead or were killed a day or two later and thrown into the nearby karst pit. The Zagreb Community also cared for Jews from Slavonski Brod, and asked the authorities to send some of the interned members of this community home.[64] When a considerable number of Jews arrived in Crikvenica in October 1941 and had no money for their upkeep, the Jewish Section demanded that the Zagreb Community support them.[65]

On June 3, the Zagreb Community informed other communities that it was no longer able to continue supporting Jewish refugees from the Reich in the entire ISC by itself, and that it had assigned the support to some of their centers in other religious communities: in Bosanski Šamac (30 people), Derventa (98), Ruma (153), Lipik (64), Banja Slatina (74), Daruvar (88), Tuzla (12), Donji Lapac (6), and Sarajevo (100). A total of 625 people were left in the care of other communities, but the Zagreb Community, together with some smaller communities, continued to care for refugees in Pisarovina (30), Draganići (178), Kerestinec (160), and Zagreb (about 450), for a total of some 818 individuals. Another document shows that, after the establishment of the ISC, the Zagreb Community had 1,800 Jewish refugees from Austria, Germany, and Bohemia in its care.[66]

At one of the following meetings, on July 31, the Community Council said that "some Communities have not taken our call to make contributions for some of the camps seriously enough," so the Zagreb Community was "forced to send greater amounts to some camps so as to prevent our inmates from going hungry." The refugees in Zagreb got increased support, and they were also given two meals a day in the soup kitchen.[67]

A great number of activists were arrested, and this very quickly weakened the Community so much that it could no longer function, either in departments or as a whole. At the meeting of July 31, it was established that only four of the eleven Council members were still in Zagreb.[68] Some had managed to escape, but most had been deported. For example, one of the deportees was Lavoslav Steiner, vice-president of the Community, former stationery wholesaler, who was killed in an "unknown place," and so were his wife and daughter.[69] One of the eleven Council members, Professor Aleksa Semnic, his wife, Sofija, and their daughter, Rut, were taken to Pag, whence none of them returned.[70] As people disappeared, others replaced them in the Community services, at least on paper. Thus, Chief Rabbi Gavro Schwarz and Miroslav Šalom Freiberger took over part of the administrative work in the Community.

In the following months and years, the Zagreb Community devoted its primary efforts to helping those who had been taken to camps.

PART III

SUMMER AND AUTUMN OF 1941

CONCENTRATION AND EXTERMINATION

18

MASS ARRESTS AND TRANSIT CAMPS

As soon as the Ustashe took power, they began to arrest Jews. In the first weeks, and until the end of May, prominent and influential members of the Jewish community were usually arrested individually.

The Gestapo carried out the first group arrest in the middle of April, when about fifty distinguished Zagreb Jews were sent to Graz. There they were interrogated, and several days later most were sent back to Zagreb, but at least two were kept in Graz.

The second group arrest of Jews was carried out by the Police Directorate of the City of Zagreb on April 27 and 28, when seventy-nine Jewish attorneys from Zagreb were sent to Kerestinec Camp.[1] Several of them were released and sent home individually after intercession in May, several were kept in camp (for example, Dr. Ivo Kuhn, who was a Communist), and sixty-one Jewish attorneys were released on June 10 in connection with the contribution.[2] The Zagreb Chamber of Attorneys and its president, Dr. Ivo Politeo, interceded on their behalf, but they were not released until some of them had made payments for the contribution, and others firmly committed themselves to doing so.[3]

Similarly, in early May, about forty wealthy and influential Zagreb Jews, who had been arrested individually in April, were released from prison so that they could take part in the contribution.

The first mass arrest of Zagreb Jews, which marked the beginning of a journey of no return, took place between May 27 and 29, when 165 youths aged between eighteen and twenty-one were arrested. They were summoned to report for public work to be carried out in Koprivnica, and came to the police station of their own accord. The summons even specified what kind of clothes they should bring. They were sent to Danica Camp in Koprivnica on May 31. The Jewish Section sent a letter to the Ustasha Office in Koprivnica saying that "we have sent you the first group of Jews," which shows that they were already planning further group arrests and deportation.[4] At the beginning of July, the youths were transported as a group from Koprivnica to Jadovno, near Gospić, where all but ten were killed.

In May, only a small group of the highest authorities—Pavelić, Dido Kvaternik, and some of their associates—probably had a more-or-less clear picture of what they would do with the Jews. The Ustashe in general and the police officials could not yet know, but many indications made them suspect that the worst was being planned. This can be illustrated by the following story. Eighteen-year-old Željko Šrenger, a half-Jew, replied, as did many young boys, to the summons to register for public work, happy to get it over with as soon as possible during the summer months. In the Jewish Section in Bogovićeva, an Ustasha official called Šuprina was making a list of those who had applied. Šuprina was a friend of Šrenger's mother's family, and when he noticed Šrenger, he sent him home, roughly ordering him never to come there on that business again. In so doing, he saved his life.[5]

There were no mass arrests of Jews in Zagreb during the first three weeks of June. At about this time, Stjepan Vukovac, ISC State Secretary and Assistant Minister of the Interior, told Vladimir Židovec, Ustasha official from Karlovac, that "although only some individual incidents have taken place to date, everything indicates that Dido Kvaternik and various other 'top brass' are getting ready for a real war of extermination against the Serbs and the Jews."[6] Vukovac's suspicions proved true, and a new wave of arrests began on June 21, on the largest scale so far. First, all the male members of the Jewish Makabi Sports Club in Zagreb and some other young Jews were arrested, about 200 in all. Three days later, the Jewish members of a left-wing trade union, the Alliance of Banking, Insurance, Commercial, and Industrial Clerks (SBOTIČ), were arrested. Young Jews were arrested in Karlovac, for example, on June 27, as part of a carefully planned campaign—any organized resistance had to be nipped in the bud, and the authorities rightly supposed that young people might well offer resistance. One of the sources on which arrests were based was the list of Jewish students at Zagreb University compiled by the Jewish Section. It included 14 law, 10 philosophy, 6 agronomy, 44 technical, 11 business school, 5 veterinary, and 29 medical students, a total of 119.[7]

Panic broke out among Zagreb Jews at the end of June: no one could be sure that they would not be arrested. Then came the days when "whole families were taken away."[8] Most of them—men, women, and children alike, no difference was made among them—were taken directly to the Zagreb Fairground, along with Jews from other parts of the ISC.[9] This was the place where the Student Center stands today, a triangle formed by Sava Road in the west, and two railway lines in the north and south. The location was carefully chosen: isolated enough to be easy to control and guard, and linked by an industrial line to the main railway network, to make it easy to deport prisoners. The use of the industrial line had previously been arranged with Croatian Railways.[10] Most of the internees were placed in what used to be the Pavilion of the French Republic, with some in the two neighboring ones. At first they slept on the bare ground, until, on June 27, straw was brought for them.[11] Railway boxcars stood on the line all the time, and when it was decided that enough prisoners had been collected, they would load them into the cars at night and take them away. Prisoners in other pavilions did not know what was going on, especially at night, because they were not allowed to move from their pavilions.[12]

The Zagreb Fairground was a mustering point, a temporary transit camp in which a selection for further processing was made among the interned Jews: most of them were sent on to real concentration camps, to Danica or Gospić, to Pag or Jadovno, later also to Jasenovac. Sometimes *Volksdeutsche,* members of the ethnic German community, stood beside the Ustasha guards at the camp entrance from Sava Road, just as they did two months later in front of Zavrtnica Camp.[13] In her memoirs, Zdenka Novak described the atmosphere as follows: "Our first stop was the Zagreb Fairground. A young Ustasha sat at the entrance and made threatening gestures to hurry us up into the large hall . . . A soldier in Ustasha uniform made us clean the floor, mumbling something against the Jews . . . [and] gradually the hall filled up and became crowded. There were a lot of young people, among them some young couples that we knew. Everyone had brought a small backpack, because they had been told to prepare to go to a work camp, but no one knew where or when. Ironically, facing us was the French Pavilion with a large inscription: *Liberté, Egalité, Fraternité.* Several more Ustashe arrived and a table was set up for them with several chairs, for a kind of commission that was to decide our fate . . . The names of those who could return home were called out—people in mixed marriages, those with certain professional skills, and people who were seriously ill and who had medical certificates to that effect. The atmosphere was distressing and full of apprehension. The tension grew when Baraković arrived, as he was to make the final decision for each individual."[14]

Some people were taken from the Fairground to the Ustasha Police Office in Račkoga Street 9, where the proceedings were certainly stricter,[15] while others already had valid passes to leave for other countries or go to coastal towns in the Italian zone of occupation; most of them were allowed to leave. Ante Jedvaj, commissioner in her father's factory, noticed Zdenka Novak in the great crowd at the Fairground, and, with the consent of Baraković, because she was said to be ill, he took her home and thus saved her. Jedvaj promised that he would save Fritz Brichta, the husband she had just married, in the same way the next day, but he did not keep his word—or perhaps could not keep it.[16] Accompanied by an Ustasha, Zdenka managed to see Fritz and her parents once more at the Fairground, but only to say good-by, because the Ustasha kept hurrying her up—"hurry up, hurry up, or you'll stay here too"—and they were taken away to camps from which they never returned.[17] Dr. Stjepan Steiner was released from the Fairground because, as a doctor, he was on the list to go to Bosnia and Herzegovina for the syphilis-treatment program.[18]

Those who were not released were already mistreated at the Zagreb Fairground. The members of an Ustasha battalion in training were billeted there, and, according to the testimony of Dr. Oto Radan, they used the prisoners for various jobs and in so doing mistreated them.[19] The attorney Dr. Robert Farkaš, at that time sixty-one years old, described this mistreatment in more detail. He was one of the prisoners who cleaned out latrines and scrubbed floors in the rooms where the Ustashe were billeted. As he carried dirty straw out to the rubbish heap, an Ustasha swore at him and hit him with his rifle stock. They all worked until 9:00 p.m. and were then ordered to relieve themselves because no one would be let out of the hall at night. If anyone tried to get out, the Ustashe threatened to shoot him.[20] They were given no food at all, but relatives and friends were allowed to bring them some. The Jewish Community was especially active in this kind of work, and regularly supplied the internees at the Zagreb Fairground with food, blankets to sleep on, and other necessities.[21]

The great wave of mass arrests in June was timed to coincide with the specific psychosis that followed June 22, the day when Germany and its allies attacked the Soviet Union. At that time, rumors were spreading through Zagreb that a general uprising was being planned against the ISC on June 28, the Serb Orthodox holiday of Vidovdan.[22] Poglavnik Pavelić exploited this psychosis to issue the Extraordinary Legal Decree and Order on June 26, in which he greatly extended the legal grounds for all kinds of persecution in the ISC and, in particular, legalized the mass arrests of Jews and their deportation to concentration camps. "In view of rumors that plans have allegedly been made to persecute one part of the population in Croatia on the twenty-eighth of this month, I order that anyone who spreads rumors of this kind shall be tried by the court-martial."[23] Since the "Jews are spreading false reports with the purpose of disturbing the population, and are using their well-known speculations to hinder and obstruct supplying the population, we consider them collectively responsible and shall therefore treat them accordingly and place them, in addition to implementing penal and correctional measures, in open-air prison camps . . . Finally, I call on each and every citizen to forego intercession of any kind in personal or material matters before any state or any similar authority, because all intercession will be regarded as sabotage and also subject to proceedings by the court-martial. Anyone who considers that the law or his interests have been infringed on in any way may always apply in writing to any competent authority or to the Prime Minister's Office, without paying a tax."[24] This text was ordered to "be published for three days running on the front page of all papers and broadcast for three days running, three times a day, on the radio, and put up as posters in all towns." In the whole of the ISC, this was a new signal for further mass arrests and deportation to camps, which, as was soon shown, also included women and children.[25] The anti-Jewish campaign was spread through the media too, the main slogan being, "There is no room for Jews in the ISC."

At that time, on June 29, *Hrvatski narod* wrote that the Zagreb City Government's "competent market institutions" had established that "Jews are still hindering the supply of the population with foodstuffs, sabotaging and obstructing normal supply." The City Government was "for the last time calling on such Jews to stop this, because if not, . . . the most severe measures are being prepared."[26] It is not clear what "the most severe measures" meant, because arrests and deportations were already being carried out, although mass killings had not yet begun. However, the text titled "The Last Moment of Reckoning," published in *Ustaša* on July 3, only several days later, leaves little doubt about the further intentions of the authorities: "Ustasha-ruled Croatia wishes to square accounts with the Freemasons first and foremost, and to square accounts with plundering

Jewry . . . We know them well . . . those Jews . . . we know their lairs, we know their shelters, we know their activities, we know their storehouses and their stores . . . We know and we will exterminate them . . . And let no one be horrified, let no one weep over their fate, let no one ask why and how . . . The Ustashe know what they are doing, how they must do it and why, and the Croatian people, especially the small Croatian people, will, in the near future, realize clearly and precisely why this was done."[27]

Parallel to the announcement of forthcoming drastic measures, the State Directorate of Economic Reconstruction was making a list of those Jews indispensable for the economy, and in July it sent twenty-six names to the Public Order and Security Directorate. As some people who were on the list had already been "taken for forced labor," and the same happened to others in the following months, the extent to which these lists were any use, or whether they even reached other Ustasha services, remains open.[28] At the end of August, the same State Directorate compiled a list of thirty Jews who are "not at present needed," and requested that "the scheduled measures be taken against these persons."[29]

Even when there was some kind of an announcement that an individual would be arrested, few people decided to try escaping because it was clear that the Ustashe would vent their rage on the immediate or extended family or on Jewish hostages. It was difficult, almost impossible, to escape at the last moment. I have recorded only one such case: when the German army entered Kravarsko (forty kilometers south of Zagreb) in 1943, they forced their way into a Jewish house in the village and took away four members of the Schwabenitz and Švarcenberg families, but Berta Israel, née Švarcenberg, grabbed her six-year-old daughter, Lea, and escaped through the back door to her neighbors' house, where she dressed her daughter and herself in peasant clothes so that the Germans would not recognize them.[30] During arrests, one or two policemen usually came to the person's home and demanded that he or she accompany them to the police station or to the transit camp, which is what happened to Egon Berger.[31] A Gestapo officer came to the apartment of the attorney Pavao Fröhlich, who was arrested with about fifty other Jews, and politely asked him to accompany him for "interrogation"—from which he never returned.[32] However, there were cases, such as that of Lavoslav Steiner, where "a policeman left a message at his apartment saying that he, his wife, and eighteen-year-old daughter were to report to the Zagreb Fairground that afternoon."[33] Zdenka Novak described how "on June 27, in the morning of that black Friday, two men came to inform my parents to get ready to leave for work camp;

they gave them a few hours' time. My father could not decide what to do . . . but, after much agonizing and hesitation, he finally decided to prepare backpacks and wait for them to come and get him. His fear of the threat of the death penalty in case of disobedience prevailed, and so my parents and my sister, Mira, were taken away that afternoon."[34] The Ustasha policemen came for the Braun family in Đurđevac: they were arrested at 3:00 a.m., immediately taken by train to Zagreb, and from the railway station straight to prison.[35]

Often, the odds of arrest or salvation depended on mere chance. On an August day in 1942, Ustasha policemen suddenly came to the apartment of Vlatko Deutsch-Maceljski at 11:00 a.m. and arrested him and his wife, Marga. Their children, Velimir and Vlasta, were saved because they happened to be listening to Radio London in the neighboring apartment, since no radio sets were allowed in Jewish apartments.[36]

Many arrests were not so "civilized." When the Ustashe surrounded the house of the Israel family at 6:00 a.m., one of them went in and demanded that Milan Israel accompany him. When his wife, Berta, asked, "Why are you taking my husband away?," he gave her a short answer, "We're taking him for interrogation." Milan never returned home.[37] Sometimes, the Ustasha services gave the order, "Tonight, all the Jews on this list are to be discreetly arrested and taken to camp."[38] At other times, arrests were made in the street, in broad daylight. Leopold Israel (1877) lived in Sokolgradska Street (in Trešnjevka). In August 1941, he left home for a short time on some errand, as usual wearing the Jewish insignia. He was probably arrested on the nearby main street, Tratinska, and his family never found out how and where he met his end. Since most of the Jews arrested in those days were deported to Jasenovac, this was probably what happened to sixty-four-year-old Leopold as well.[39] These surprise street arrests, with no announcement or any subsequent information, were probably worse than being taken from the house, because the uncertainty drove the family crazy.

In those days, at the beginning of July 1941, the Jewish Section received reports with increasing frequency that Jews had "left their apartment, and no one knows where they have gone." Often, the people who filed these reports did not know whether the residents had fled or had been deported. For example, in July 1941, the commissioner in the Lyon i Marberger Cardboard Works reported the disappearance of Gjuro Marberger, about whose fate nothing was ever discovered.[40] Blanka and Josip Lackenbach were probably deported, because it is recorded that they ended their lives in an unknown place.[41] Suzana Büchler and Albert Breyer probably managed to escape, because they survived the war.[42] Some people escaped in a dramatic way or in great secrecy, as for example Miroslav Spitzer-Španić, who fled without anything about his fate being known in the Zagreb Community. Although he returned to Zagreb in 1945, those who compiled the lists of victims thought him dead. Only in 1948, when he emigrated to Israel, did they learn that he had survived.[43]

Prisoners at the Zagreb Fairground began to be deported in the night of June 22–23, in a train with shuttered empty freight cars. About 200 Jews were loaded into them, Makabi members and the young men who were arrested first, on June 21. They were taken to Gospić,[44] and from there most were deported to the Pag, Jadovno, or Velebit camps. By the end of June, three or four more such transports had left, taking a total of at least 800 people.

On July 16, *Novi list* published the article "The Evacuation of Jews from Zagreb" [*sic!*], claiming that the "Jews had tried to evade the regulations about Jews." Because of this, wrote *Novi list,* "the authorities have recently started taking thorough and radical measures against them, so about 200 more Jews were sent to forced labor on July 12, in addition to earlier transports, and this practice will continue" because this is the only way "to cleanse Zagreb of Jews."[45] In the second wave of July arrests, carried out by the end of the month, some 700 more people were arrested and deported.[46] In the July arrests, the first large transport set off from Varaždin on July 12, because all the Varaždin Jews had been arrested and were sent via the Zagreb Fairground to Gospić. Varaždin was then proclaimed the first town "cleansed" of Jews—which is how the Jewish Section sent the information to *Hrvatski narod.*[47] Božidar Gregl, commissioner of the Ustasha Police for the Grand County of Zagorje in Varaždin from July to December 1941, organized and carried out the deportations from Varaždin in person. Later, in the fall of that year, he was in charge of the Loborgrad concentration camp for a time.[48] After that, Jews from other towns in the ISC were brought to the Zagreb Fairground: first from Bjelovar and Koprivnica, then from Našice, Sarajevo, and Travnik.[49] A total of 2,500 Jews, both from Zagreb and other places, passed through the Zagreb Fairground, so that in June, July, and August, Zagreb was the key transit point for Jewish transports in the ISC.

On the last day of July, Mirko Vutuc signed a memo in the name of the Ustasha Police Directorate demanding that the competent authorities "imprison, in the interest of public security, all Jews (whether converted or not) under suspicion of communism, and send those against whom there is no evidence, on the grounds of which they could be tried by court-martial, to the transit camp in Gospić."[50] This was the bureaucratic foundation for new arrests and deportations that took place several days later.

At the beginning of August, Poglavnik Pavelić said that the "Jews had robbed and exploited the Croatian people, had always been in the service of enemies of the Croats, had openly supported our enemies. Even now, the Jews serve the enemies of Croatia and its allies. Now, as always, the Jews are on the side of the Serbs, Russians, and English . . . The Jews are open allies of the Serbian Chetniks, who are fighting under the red Bolshevist banner . . . And even so, there are wretches in Croatia who speak in favor of Jews and say, 'he was one of us,' 'he has merit,' 'he gave his support.'"[51] With these words, Pavelić announced a major new wave of arrests. Preparations for them began at the latest on August 2, when the Jewish Section of the RUR demanded that the Police Directorate arrest "all Jews whose family members are owners or employees of the following firms," and then followed the names of nineteen Jews or their firms.[52] During that whole month, but especially on August 6, several hundred Jews were seized in Zagreb (according to some estimates, about 800, to others about 1,000).[53] However, at this time, transports no longer passed through the Zagreb Fairground but through a new transit camp in the eastern part of the city, in Zavrtnica.

Although documents do not show why the transit camp was moved to Zavrtnica, the Zagreb Fairground probably became unsuitable because it was in the city center and everything took place in plain view of a great many people. The freight cars were loaded practically before the eyes of the public, because there was nothing but a railway embankment several meters high separating the fairground from the houses in Crnatkova Street. The people who lived on the higher floors of Crnatkova could easily see what was going on at the Zagreb Fairground and were strictly forbidden to look out of their windows, whose blinds had to be drawn day and night.[54] In addition, for their journey south, the freight cars full of deported Jews had to pass through the Main Railway Station itself, in full view of passengers and passers-by on the platforms. People in town knew about the bad conditions at the Zagreb Fairground, as the letter of protest sent by Archbishop Stepinac shows. It is true that he did not specify any location from which people were being "deported to transit camps," but his letter to Pavelić of July 21 leaves no doubt that he was primarily thinking about the Zagreb Fairground.[55] Stepinac cautioned Pavelić that "we have heard from several sources that here and there non-Aryans are being inhumanely treated during deportation to transit camps, and in the camps themselves . . ." and he said that measures of this kind could be implemented "showing . . . human and Christian concern for old men and women and innocent children and those who are ill." Stepinac proposed that prisoners should be allowed "to bring with them the basic necessities . . . enough food . . . medication . . . be allowed to correspond with their families . . . not be transported in crowded sealed boxcars."[56] The Ustasha authorities did not pay any attention to his suggestions about "mitigating the procedure." On the contrary, each new stage of anti-Jewish measures in 1941 brought harsher treatment, but, in August, attempts were made to at least keep this partly hidden from the Zagreb public.

Instead of the Zagreb Fairground, a new mustering point was organized in what had been the Kristalum warehouses ("community for the textile trade") in Zavrtnica. The location was carefully chosen—walls isolated the building from the outside world. At that time, Zavrtnica was an industrial zone practically on the fringe of the city, where relatively few people lived. To conceal the columns of arrested people from the public, many were brought to the warehouse in trucks,[57] and an industrial railway track led to the warehouse as well. The train only had to cross nearby Heinzelova Street to reach the city outskirts, which kept the entire operation far from curious eyes. On August 11, an agreement was made with Croatian Railways about the "use of the industrial track beside the Moster Factory in Heinzelova between numbers 50 and 58." It was agreed that "Jews [who, for the most part, were those being brought to Zavrtnica from other parts of northern Croatia] are to be transported in closed railway cars if possible, and the transports should arrive at the Zagreb station by morning trains."[58]

The internees in Zavrtnica were treated much more harshly, and people were released from there only on rare occasions, and with strong connections. Some doctors were set free because they had applied to go to Bosnia and Herzegovina to treat syphilis.[59] When a highly placed official demanded the release of Levin Schlenger because he was very ill (progressive paralysis), he was not released, or was released only temporarily, because he ended in an "unknown place."[60] On September 20, Eugen Dido Kvaternik interceded for Josip Hercer to be released from Zavrtnica, and for two other Jews to be "exempted from all measures." We do not know whether Hercer was released, because he too ended in an "unknown place."[61] Sometimes intercession by the highest-ranking Ustasha officials did help, but, more often, as in the cases of Schlenger and Hercer, the intended protégé met his end all the same. Moric and Rifka Levi, a husband and wife, obtained a recommendation from Doglavnik Ademage Mešić to travel to the Croatian Littoral. Although Mešić's intervention helped part of the Alexander family, it did not help Moric Levi, because he was killed in the following months, apparently in Jasenovac, although Rifka survived the war.[62]

No one seems to have been killed in Zavrtnica, although the guards threatened death all the time. The food was bad and scarce, people slept in stifling rooms and were not allowed to open the windows. In those days, at the height of the arrests and deportations to Zavrtnica, Pavelić said, "As for the Jews, I can say that soon this issue will finally be resolved. The problem of the Jews is very serious. In Zagreb alone there were 18,000 of them, now hardly 4,000 remain, and these too will be sent to forced labor or concentration camps."[63] Intentionally or not, Pavelić's figures were wrong, as there were about 12,000 Jews in Zagreb in 1940. But he was not wrong when he said there would be new deportations, which took place only a few days later. The augmentation of the number of Jews in Zagreb may have been for propaganda reasons: at the beginning of May, *Hrvatski narod* claimed that "if we include half-Jews and the wives and children of Jews, there are over 20,000 Jews in Zagreb."[64] In September, the prisoners from Zavrtnica were deported east by train several times (to Jasenovac), sixty prisoners to a freight car. As one transport was sent, new prisoners arrived. "On September 10 at noon, mothers, children, wives, and sisters began to arrive, and to their horror they found an empty courtyard, and the prisoners already in the rail cars. All we could do was send them our final greetings by waving our arms, and they cried and sobbed, clutching at their heads and hair . . . The Ustashe drove the women and children away from the tracks with the butts of their rifles," one of the prisoners recounted.[65] "Some women fainted."[66]

At the end of September, a new wave of arrests began (according to Josip Abraham, the so-called Fifth Group), when about 700 Jews were detained. Some of the arrests took place in the Zagreb suburbs, because on September 15, the County District in Zagreb informed the Jewish Section that "there have recently been frequent acts of sabotage," "the intellectual instigators being . . . opponents of the present system in our state, among which we must certainly count Jews." Thus, it is "necessary, in the interest of public order and tranquility, to remove all Jews from the surroundings of the capital city of Zagreb. The majority of the Jews are in the municipalities of Kustošija, Vrapče, and Stenjevec, while the municipalities of Šestine, Remete, Stupnik, and Brdovec have about ten each." Finally, "we beg you to address this issue most energetically, and thus cleanse this district of Jews."[67] It seems that the Jews in the areas surrounding Zagreb were mainly arrested and deported in the wave of roundups during the second half of September, because records exist for at least eight of them.[68] Many others were probably affected as well, several dozen and perhaps as many as a hundred, because they never appeared in later records. The attorney Dr. Josip Laufer, a member of the Contribution Committee, was deported and later killed, although he submitted documents that should have allowed his release.[69] The command of the transit camps in Jasenovac reported that 199 Jews were sent to their camps from Zagreb on September 20.[70]

After they were deported from Zavrtnica in September, more than 1,500 Jews were sent to camps, most of them to Jasenovac. They were told that they were "going to work," to "build embankments to dry out Lonjsko polje."[71] During the August and September arrests, a small number of Jews were temporarily placed in the prison in Sava Road, from which women and children were sent to Stara Gradiška and later to Đakovo, and men to Stara Gradiška, that is, to Jasenovac.[72]

By the end of September 1941, more than 3,000 Zagreb Jews had been murdered, deported, or simply arrested in Zagreb. It became clear that it was difficult to avoid arrest there. To save their lives, Jews had to keep well hidden or escape. Only a few felt safe, and even this safety was an illusion.

Assimilationists were not spared, either. One of the best-known was Mirko Breyer, a distinguished scholar of the history of Croatian literacy and a publicist. He had been accorded Aryan rights and was exempted from wearing the Jewish insignia, but he was nevertheless taken to Stara Gradiška at the age of 78, where he was interned for six months and then released in April 1942. He was later imprisoned twice more.[73] While he was in camp in March 1942, he wrote the poem "In the Transit Camp," which, although without any literary merit, impressively conjures up sorrow for lost freedom and youth.[74] He was in Zagreb at the end of the war, and died there at the end of 1946. The prominent philosopher and university professor Pavao Vuk Pavlovac-Pavlović, and his mother, sixty-nine-year-old Janka Wolf, née Granitz, although she had converted as long ago as 1900, were in mortal danger. Janka was taken to prison in Sava Road, from which her son's students had her released. The family then had to move from their apartment in the city center to a small house in Ludbreška Street (in Trešnjevka). Pavao, although a man in his prime, was suspended and then pensioned.[75] These are the stories that had a happy ending. Hundreds of people who had before the war considered themselves, and been thought of by others, as assimilated, perished, including some of the most distinguished and richest (members of the Alexander and Deutsch-Maceljski families).

Another characteristic case was that of Oskar Sachs, former attorney in Zlatar, who moved to Zagreb when the ISC was founded, to Jurjevska Street 20 in the northern part of the city. As he had been involved in transferring money to the Ustashe in Italy in the thirties, Pavelić had personally guaranteed him safety and "Aryan rights." Nevertheless, an Ustasha functionary had his eye on Sachs's apartment and he was deported. He managed to return home, sued in court to get his apartment back, and even converted in April 1942, but finally he too was taken to Stara Gradiška and killed there in April 1943.[76]

After the mass deportations in September, relative calm set in until about the end of the year. Jews in Zagreb were in most cases arrested individually, and there were no more mass arrests until the beginning of 1942.

19

CONCENTRATION CAMPS, SUMMARY COURTS, AND HOSTAGES

Immediately after the establishment of the ISC, the Germans encouraged the Ustasha authorities to organize concentration camps of their own.[1] In some places, groups of ethnic Germans collaborated openly in these activities (for example, at the Zagreb Fairground, in Osijek and elsewhere). This kind of cooperation between the Ustasha police and the equivalent bodies of the Third Reich followed right after the visit of Eugen Dido Kvaternik and several of his close associates to the SS Main Office at the end of May and the beginning of June 1941. SS-Obersturmbannführer Willy Beisner, the first SS police attaché in the ISC, whom Dido Kvaternik called a personal friend in his memoirs, accompanied the delegation. In June 1941, the German Ambassador in the ISC, Siegfried Kasche, reported that Kvaternik and his associates had spoken to Gruppenführer (Major General) Gottlob Berger, chief of the SS Main Office, and other high-ranking SS officers. One of the agreements they reached was that 200 young Ustasha policemen would train in various SS units.[2] Kasche continued his report by saying he was sorry he had not been given advance notice of these talks; as "the Croats are not a Germanic people," he considered that such close contacts between the Ustashe and the SS were "a mistake."

The first activities of RAVSIGUR and the Ustasha Police on June 3 and 4, immediately after the Ustasha Police delegation returned from Germany, clearly show that Kvaternik and his associates had been given detailed advice on the organization of concentration camps and preparations for the "final solution of the Jewish question," which was at that time a top priority for the highest SS officials. In actual fact, however, the camp system in the ISC had begun to be formulated six weeks earlier, in the second half of April 1941.

The first stage in the development of the camp system, which was still a kind of improvisation, was the formation of transit camps, "mustering points," or "camps for emigrants." These were provisional accommodations for large groups of arrestees, usually on the fringes of towns, in outdoor or indoor areas, empty factories, schools, sometimes even in synagogues. At first, most of the prisoners were Serbs and Jews, later joined by Croatian Communists and other anti-Fascists. After spending two or three days in these temporary transit camps—in Zagreb these were the prisons on Petrinjska Street and Sava Road, and the Zagreb Fairground and Zavrtnica—prisoners were usually sent in larger groups to concentration camps intended for the more permanent stay of internees or for quick liquidation. All these activities were largely improvised, badly organized, often disorganized. Since almost 1,000 Jews were taken from the Zagreb Fairground to Gospić and neighboring camps in the last days of June, on July 2, after the deportations, the State Directorate of Reconstruction issued the Instruction on the Foundation of Emigration Offices . . . their organization and work and the procedure during arrests for sending to concentration camps. This "instruction" gave detailed directives that "transit camps must have drinking water and lighting, even petroleum lighting . . . [and] there is to be no smoking in transit camps."[3]

Concurrently with the formation of the various transit camps came the foundation of the first concentration camps. The first large camp in the abandoned halls of the failed Danica chemical factory was opened near the village then called Koprivnički Ivanec near Koprivnica. This was Danica Camp, and a branch of the Koprivnica-Hungarian border railway line entered the grounds of the former factory. The first large group of prisoners were Serbs: 504 men from the Grubišno Polje district, already in rather bad condition and beaten. They arrived in Danica Camp on April 28.[4] Two days later, the first transport of prisoners from Zagreb arrived, which included Jews. The largest group of Jews was the 165 youths from Zagreb arrested at the end of May, about whom we have already written. At the beginning of July, they were sent on to Gospić.

The Danica Camp administration, "either on purpose or because of the primitive form of keeping records," never knew the exact number of internees.[5] On May 18, the camp was said to have 1,007 prisoners; on June 30, there were 2,175. By the middle of July, there were a total of 2,656 internees in Danica Camp according to some testimonies, and as many as 5,600 according to others. After the war, camp treasurer Martin Kokor stated that of these 5,600 inmates, 3,000 were Serbs, about 1,000 were Croats, just over 600 were Jews, and about 400 were Roma.[6] Most of the Jews were from Zagreb, and there were smaller groups from Bjelovar and its surroundings, from Karlovac, Koprivnica, later also from Sarajevo.

Second Lieutenant Martin Nemec, Ustasha commissioner for Koprivnica, was the organizer and first commander of Danica. He was a former Koprivnica merchant, and a former Ustasha émigré who had been abroad from 1933.[7] A report of the camp administration from June 30 says there were eighty-nine Ustasha guards.[8] When Nemec was badly hurt in a traffic accident at the end of June, he was replaced by Nikola Herman, the new Ustasha commissioner for Koprivnica and new commander of Danica. The camp administration was directly subordinate to the central RAVSIGUR office in Zagreb, from which it received orders and to which it submitted reports. Eugen Dido Kvaternik, the head of RAVSIGUR, and Mijo Babić, later commander of all the concentration camps in the ISC, took part in the preparations for the foundation of Danica Camp and visited it, probably for talks and inspection.[9]

When the prisoners arrived in the camp they were all thoroughly searched and ill-treated in various ways. The Ustasha guards took away their valuables, money, and food provisions, and if anyone complained, he was immediately beaten. Beatings were also frequent during various kinds of roll calls, inspections, and individual interrogations.[10] Every day, the inmates were taken for physical labor: filling in anti-tank trenches around Koprivnica, leveling roads, and so on. Their food was extremely bad, and there was not enough of it, but relatives were allowed to send food parcels from which the Ustasha guards took a lot for themselves during inspection; however, although usually "reduced," the parcels did reach the internees. Milan Radeka remembered that the Jews not only got individual parcels, but that food and other supplies were sent to them, as well. This aid was organized and financed by the Zagreb Jewish Community through the Jewish Community of Koprivnica, with the approval of the Jewish Section of the Ustasha Police Commission for the City of Zagreb. Some of the Jews were placed in separate accommodations, but they were treated equally badly.[11]

There was no mass killing in Danica. Former internees very often speak loosely about numbers, so they sometimes mention as many as "about 200 people killed in the camp and its surroundings,"[12] but Radeka, who spent six weeks in Danica, knew of only about three people killed in the camp and several more outside the camp, during work.[13]

The first transport from Danica to Gospić took place on June 30. A record of transfers shows that by July 15, "1,960 prisoners were taken to Gospić, and seventy-six people were released and escorted to Zagreb" (according to other testimonies, more than 200 were released).[14] On July 8, Eugen Dido Kvaternik issued an order to all county and town police stations saying that "in cases when the interests of public security demand removing undesirable persons from their place of residence, all Eastern Orthodox and Jews (even those who converted to the Catholic religion after April 10, 1941) are to be sent to Gospić and placed at the disposition of the County Police Directorate there, and are not to continue being sent to Danica Camp in Koprivnica. Catholics and Muslims are not to be sent to Gospić."[15] After the Germans attacked the USSR on June 22, waves of mass arrests swept through Zagreb and the entire ISC. By the end of June and in July, Danica Camp could obviously no longer admit nearly as many prisoners as were being arrested, and it was not a camp designed for killing people. However, the above order clearly indicates the genocidal character of the group of camps centered in Gospić. By the end of July, all the Jews in Danica were sent to Gospić, with the exception of a few who were released. A somewhat larger number of "Orthodox" prisoners was released, some were deported to Serbia (for example, Orthodox priests), but most were sent to Gospić, as well. Danica Camp continued to exist until the spring of 1942 with a much smaller number of internees, and then it was closed down.

About 150 Zagreb Jews and roughly 400 Jewish emigrants from the Third Reich, who had found themselves in the environs of Zagreb after the proclamation of the ISC, passed through Kerestinec Camp. The camp was founded by the Police Directorate for the City of Zagreb on April 19, 1941, in the Kerestinec manor house and estate, eighteen kilometers from Zagreb, in the direction of Samobor. The commander and guards were former Zagreb policemen and some former "defense guards" (members of the prewar Peasant Defense) from the surrounding area. The camp administration kept careful records about the prisoners, who were divided into three separate groups: "Serb-Yugoslav," "Jewish," and "Communist."[16] The first list, from April 21, has sixty prisoners, most of them Serbs from the civil service of the Croatian Banovina.[17] Soon another 100 or so prominent people from Zagreb and the surroundings were brought in small groups, most of them Serbs. Almost all were released or sent to other camps in the following weeks. The arrival of the group of 79 Jewish attorneys, already mentioned, was recorded on May 1.[18] The "Communist" division was established on May 22, when the first large group of Communists was brought from Lepoglava and the Zagreb prisons in Petrinjska Street and Sava Road, and by the end of June their number had grown to just over 100.[19]

The Zagreb Jewish Community also had to care for the Jewish emigrants from the Third Reich who had not managed to get visas to travel further and leave Yugoslavia before April 10, 1941. These were accommodated in refugee camps in Draganići (near Jastrebarsko), in Pisarovina, in Slavetić Castle (also near Jastrebarsko), in Samobor, and in Zagreb itself. On June 27, the first group of about 140 men, women, and children from Samobor was brought to Kerestinec, followed by some more groups, for a total of 400 individuals. On June 20, all of them were transported from Kerestinec to a joint camp for Jewish emigrants near Sarajevo, from which they were later sent to German camps. None of them are known to have survived the war.[20]

On the whole, prisoners in Kerestinec were treated much better than in other camps in the ISC. Food could regularly be brought to them and they could receive short visits, and on Sundays, they could talk to their visitors for longer periods without the presence of the guards. There was relatively little mistreatment and brutality. The prisoners could spend four hours a day in the fresh air, usually in the courtyard or under guard around the manor house, and they could even play volleyball. In the first days of July, 119 prisoners were recorded as Communists, 44 as "Jews," 21 as "Serb Orthodox," and there were 40 "Catholics."[21] The Communists also included 26 Jews, so that the total of 224 prisoners included 70 Jews, almost one-third (31 percent).

On Saturday, July 5, a "green Thomas," a police van, came to Kerestinec from Zagreb with several policemen, and hurriedly took away ten Kerestinec prisoners. The selection of the prisoners, and the way in which they were taken away without any explanation and in nervous haste, worried the other internees: all ten belonged to the most distinguished and best-known Kerestinec intellectuals. Their wives and other family members, who persistently made the rounds of police and Ustasha institutions in Zagreb over the following three or four days, trying to get any kind of information, were treated gruffly and sent away. The families of the ten men were extremely distressed, as no one would or could tell them where they had been sent and where they were. Even Božidar Cerovski, Director of the Police Directorate for the City of Zagreb, nervously told one of his close acquaintances that he knew nothing, and not to ask him any more, because it was outside his area of responsibility, and not to come to him any more, because it could only harm him.[22]

On the Thursday morning of July 10, Zagreb awoke to find itself plastered with large posters and the morning papers all carried the same public notification: "On July 4, 1941, the dead and mutilated body of police officer Ljudevit Tiljak was dragged from a pond near Radnička Road (southeastern suburb of Zagreb)" and "the following (here followed the names of the ten men taken from Kerestinec Camp), as the intellectual instigators of this crime, were handed over to the senate of the Traveling Summary Court, who sentenced all ten of them to death. The sentence was carried out on July 9 by shooting." The names of the executed men, their place of birth, age, occupation, and religion were listed in the following order: Božidar Adžija, Ognjen Prica, Ivo Kuhn, Zvonimir Richtmann, Ivan Korski, Viktor Rosenzweig, Alfred Bergman, Sigismund Kraus, Otokar Keršovani, and Simo Crnogorac. Of the ten, Kuhn, Richtmann, Korski, Rosenzweig, Bergman, and Kraus were Jews.[23] This was the first warning, and it was broadly publicized, that the Ustasha authorities had opted for the most drastic form of political terror, that is, killing people by arbitrary selection, without any legal procedure, investigation, or guilt. The choice of the executed men showed that the elites of the "undesirables" would be struck down first, and their religious (or ethnic) composition allowed people to suspect that genocide was being planned against the Jews.

The behavior of the Ustasha authorities in the days preceding the execution, and especially Cerovski's statement that it was all "outside his area of responsibility," indicate that the top people in the Ustasha hierarchy were in the process of making the final decision about increased terror and genocidal killings. It was certainly no chance that all this coincided with the beginning of mass liquidations in the camps on Velebit and on Pag. Even more broadly, one notices concurrence with the first genocidal actions carried out by the *Einsatzgruppe* in the occupied parts of the USSR. There is no doubt that the top ranks of the Ustasha regime knew about the German plans for mass killing from the time they first began.

Three days later, in the night between July 13 and 14, the Communist prisoners of Kerestinec Camp, in agreement with their underground Party leaders in Zagreb, attacked the camp guards, disarmed them, and escaped from the camp. Eighty-nine inmates took part in the escape, two from the "Serb-Yugoslav" and one from the "Jewish" part of the camp, and the other eighty-six from the "Communist" part.[24] In the report he sent to Rome about the breakout from Kerestinec, the representative of the Italian government, Raffaele Casertano, wrote that the "Chetniks and the Jews" tried to escape.[25] Dr. Edo Neufeld said that the prisoners in the Jewish part of the camp had no advance knowledge and that they were surprised by the Communists' nocturnal breakout. There were about forty Jewish prisoners, most of them re-arrested Jewish attorneys from Zagreb, and they could not make up their minds quickly about whether to join the escapees or not, so they stayed in the camp. After a brutal investigation headed by Dido Kvaternik himself, on July 15, they were all sent via the Zagreb Fairground to Gospić, and then on to other camps, from which none of the twenty-eight attorneys returned alive, except the witness Neufeld.[26]

The eighty-nine fugitives included about fifteen Jewish Communists. Communist task groups from Zagreb did not meet them at the prearranged place due to bad organization by their local committee. Confused and not knowing what to do, the fugitives waited in the nearby Obrež forest too long, and most of them were caught in the mass pursuit organized by the Ustasha Police. In fights with the police, thirty-one fugitives were killed and forty-four were taken prisoner. Several days later, all of them were brought before the Traveling Summary Court, sentenced to death, and shot in Dotrščina.[27] Of the forty-four, five were Jews (Isak Katan, Hugo Kon, Ljudevit Kon, Ernest Rado, and Israel Steinberg), while Lavoslav Koričan, Izidor Perera, Israel Osias, Elijas Singer, and Uri Šnetrepl were killed earlier, in the fighting after the breakout.[28] Only fourteen fugitives managed somehow to avoid recapture, and in various ways they all joined the Partisans, but only seven of them survived the war.[29]

In the days and weeks that followed, there were many public announcements about Summary Court sentences of execution by shooting of named individuals and small groups, and unnamed hostages who were shot en masse. When a task group of the Zagreb Communists threw bombs from the Botanical Gardens at a unit of the Ustasha University Army on August 4, 98 "Jews and Communists" were immediately shot on the same day as "accessories and intellectual instigators," and 87 more on August 6.[30] After a bomb was placed in the Main Post Office in Zagreb on September 14, 50 "Jews and Communists" were shot.[31] The names of the people who were killed in these three incidents of repression, the greatest that took place in the city of Zagreb, are not known, but more than half of the victims of mass murders of this kind were always Jews—sometimes even as many as two-thirds—so it seems realistic to assume that about 150 Jews lost their lives. The names of the 21 Jewish men and women who were shot in retaliation for the attack near the Botanical Gardens are known, however, and also the names of 4 more who were shot in retaliation for the attack on the Main Post Office. One of the hostages shot in reprisal for the Botanical Gardens attack included seventeen-year-old Verica Gross.[32] Adela Neumann also lost her life in one of the mass shootings.[33]

On August 25, the Summary Court passed the death sentence, and the execution was carried out on the same day, on one "Ivan Ferber, a brush maker from Zagreb, a Jew, for anti-state and anti-Ustasha propaganda, because he said that the ISC was not any kind of a state, but a den of rogues."[34] It seems that many Jews were shot by Summary Court decisions, and it also seems that not all the sentences have been preserved.[35] The papers wrote about some of the executions: "Bela Roth and Ašer Eškenazi were shot" because they had allegedly "faked the jubilee issue of ISC stamps by reprinting them,"[36] and fifty-three-year-old Oskar Weiss because he had "publicly undertaken lascivious acts in preparation for raping two Aryan girls."[37] The press did not leave any doubts about what was being planned. At the beginning of August, an article titled "Another Warning" appeared in *Ustaša* after the shooting of "189 Jews and Communists" (after the Ustashe were attacked at the Botanical Gardens). Claiming that those who had been executed had in fact been "accomplices of the Communists who had attacked the ISC regime," the article concluded by saying that this shooting "should be a last warning to everyone. If anyone, from any side, dares to attempt any other obstruction of our Ustasha work of building the Croatian state, he will pay even more terribly and painfully."[38] The threat was soon carried out: on September 11, when fifty "Jews and Communists" were taken for execution from the prison in Sava Road, as retaliation, because a Zagreb Communist Youth task group had killed Ustasha Police informer Ivan Majerhold.[39] In those days, several groups of prisoners were shot at Rakov Potok (twenty kilometers southeast of Zagreb), among them a considerable number of Jews.[40]

The quasi-legal foundation for killing hostages was not created until October 2, 1941, in the Legal Provision on the Procedures in the Case of Communist Attacks When the Culprit Is Not Found.[41] In practice, this meant that before this date, according to the criteria of Ustasha law, every sentence passed by the Traveling Summary Court to shoot in retaliation unnamed "Jews and Communists" who were hostages was illegal. Of course, the above legal provision itself was a gross violation of the basic norm of all legal systems, where individual guilt is the only criterion for punishment. It also contravened international conventions and laws of war, which prohibit shooting hostages. At the Nuremberg trials in 1946, Field Marshal Wilhelm Keitel, Head of the General Staff of the German Wehrmacht, was sentenced to death for war crimes and crimes against humanity, especially those committed by ordering the shooting of hostages.[42] In the fall of 1945, during pretrial interrogation in Zagreb, Aleksandar Benak Jr., a high-ranking official in UNS and RAVSIGUR, described the procedure for making a decision to shoot hostages after the legal provision of October 2, 1941, was passed. "Repression and retaliation were carried out as follows: the district police submitted a written proposal to the Head Directorate (RAVSIGUR, or from the beginning of 1943, GLAVSIGUR) . . . On the basis of this proposal, the Head Director in person decided whether there would be any retaliation or not, and on its scope and method . . . The police precinct then submitted a written proposal with a description of the future hostages, whose number exceeded that which had been decided on, which the police official, and sometimes the head of the political section, personally submitted to the Head Director; he wrote a short order in pencil on the proposal itself, more or less as follows: *to be carried out,* and he chose the individuals. The other necessary implementation orders were issued on the basis of the above order."[43] The "other necessary implementation orders" included, "if necessary," the signature of the president of the Traveling Summary Court, who neither saw nor gave a hearing to the people who had been sentenced to death.

By the end of September 1941, many Jews in Zagreb—certainly more than 200—had been shot as hostages in mass reprisals after Summary Court sentences. Ivan Vignjević was president of the Traveling Summary Court for the Zagreb district throughout the war, until 1945. On September 28, 1942, Canon Augustin Juretić reported about him from the Vatican to Dr. Juraj Krnjević, Vice-President of the Government of the Kingdom of Yugoslavia in London, in the Report on Conditions in Zagreb and Croatia, "Judge Vignjević of the court-martial has by now sentenced 1,200 people to death." In a letter of December 3 of the same year, also to Krnjević, Juretić said that "Vignjević . . . recently celebrated his 1,500th death sentence."[44]

20

DEATH CAMPS ON MOUNT VELEBIT AND PAG ISLAND

Genocide

The final stage of the Holocaust in the ISC—mass killings—began when the Gospić–Velebit–Pag Island camp system was established in June 1941. This camp system was planned and directed from the central RAVSIGUR office in Zagreb, and its operations were under the immediate command of the County Police Directorate in Gospić. It consisted of one prison, one camp, and several improvised mustering points and transit camps in Gospić itself, two camps on the island of Pag, and two on Velebit Mountain. The main sites of mass killings were the Jadovno Camp on Velebit and the Slana Camp on Pag Island. People were not sent to these camps for political reasons, but for racial, religious, and ethnic ones.[1]

During only two summer months, from June 21 to August 21, about 2,500 Jews from all parts of the ISC disappeared in the Gospić–Velebit–Pag system of camps, including about 1,000 from Bosnia and Herzegovina. At least 300–350 citizens of Zagreb are known to have been killed there, but their number was certainly greater. In many cases, it is impossible to discover the exact place where someone was killed.[2] Research is difficult because often only the total number of Jews in a camp is given, not their names. And if names do exist, there is usually no information about where the prisoners came from, only in some cases their place of birth. Thus, most of the time, only indirect methods can be used to establish the approximate number of Jews from Zagreb in a camp, and the approximate number from other parts of the ISC or from other European countries. If we compare the number of people who were deported from the Zagreb Fairground to Gospić at the end of June and during the first half of July, with the number who arrived in Kruščica, Loborgrad, Jasenovac, or Stara Gradiška, from where they could send word, then almost a third of the total number of Jews killed in the Gospić–Velebit–Pag camps probably came from Zagreb.[3]

Fewer than one hundred Jews survived the men's camps of Jadovno and Slana; they were spared either because an Ustasha official interceded for them in person, or they were in a mixed marriage with an "Aryan," or simply by chance. Most of them were killed later, in other camps. Only about fifteen are known to have survived the entire war, seven of whom gave detailed testimony.[4] In their fundamental parts, these testimonies are supplemented and confirmed by contemporary Ustasha documents, statements of Jewish, Serb, and Croatian internees who survived, memories of eyewitnesses, postwar court files from trials for crimes committed, the reports of two Italian Army sanitary inspections from September 1941, and postwar findings of several expert commissions and two groups of speleologists. The many facts that all these documents share give a more-or-less clear picture of how the inmates were treated, their fate, and the character of the camps. Ante Zemljar contributed greatly to knowledge about the Pag Camps,[5] and Đuro Zatezalo about Jadovno Camp in an unpublished monograph of the same name.[6]

Gospić Transit Camp

In the first days of June, immediately after the Ustasha Police delegation returned from Germany, Eugen Dido Kvaternik began to work on the organization of the camp system in the ISC. On June 4, he made Božidar Cerovski commander of the Ustasha Police, which was authorized to organize group arrests and deportations to camps. At the same time, Mijo Babić was appointed commander of all the concentration camps in the ISC.[7] Kvaternik immediately sent Babić to Pag and to Gospić to find locations for new camps. Kvaternik appointed Stjepan Rubinić, prewar traveling salesman from Jastrebarsko and afterwards Head Ustasha Commissioner for the districts of Kostajnica, Dvor na Uni, and Bosanski Novi, director of the County Police Directorate in Gospić. His orders were to "found a camp in Jadovno and carry out temporary supervision over the camp on Pag."[8] During UDB (Yugoslav Secret Police) interrogations in Zagreb in

1947, Ljubo Miloš said, "From conversations I had with Luburić and other Ustasha officers, I know that Pavelić ordered Kvaternik to do so, because Pavelić was very interested in the camps.[9] Rubinić's first assistant, Dragan Pudić, said that he was "in the Gospić Camp from its founding, i.e., from June 18, 1941," so that date can be taken as the beginning of the operation of the whole system.[10]

The first group of about 200 Zagreb Jews was transported from the Zagreb Fairground to Gospić on June 23. They spent one night in the Sokol Building, where the Ustasha headquarters were located, and on the second morning two groups were singled out: about twenty-five to thirty men were sent to Jadovno by truck, and a somewhat larger group of men, including Dr. Oto Radan, was sent on foot by road to Karlobag, about forty kilometers away, and then on to the camps on the island of Pag. They were bound to a long chain running lengthwise, to which the men were attached in pairs transversally by wire. On the way, they suffered severe hunger and thirst, and occasionally the Ustasha guards beat them with the butts of their rifles. The peasants in the villages they passed through were not allowed to, or did not want to, give them water. The first transport of women prisoners followed the men along the same road, and the first rape took place at Baške Oštarije (a village on the Velebit mountain).[11]

From June 18 to August 23, 1941, Gospić was the administrative center of a large camp system and the main reception point from which prisoners were sent on to Velebit or Pag. Some were kept in Gospić itself. In the hearing at his trial in 1941–1942, Rubinić said that he "received masses of prisoners every day," that he did not have enough men for "that job (which) caused so much concern" so he did "the best he knew how and could." The prisoner transports flowed in from the whole territory of the ISC every day by train, truck, horse cart, and even on foot, and all were received by Rubinić himself or his assistant Janko (Ivica) Mihalović. All the prisoners had to be recorded individually by name, and then the Ustasha had to decide where to send then.[12] The lists have not been preserved—they were probably destroyed on purpose when the Ustasha Police were withdrawing from Gospić with the surviving inmates on August 23, 1941. According to a later statement by Rubinić, the lists had 28,700 incoming internees.[13] The vast majority were Serbs, then about 3,000 Jews, not more than 1,000 Croats and Bosnians (mostly Communists), and an unknown but not very great number of Roma.

The prisoner transports to Gospić increased in number and frequency after the order issued by the Public Order and Security Directorate on July

8, mentioned above, whereby "all Eastern Orthodox and Jews are to be sent to Gospić, and no longer to Danica Camp in Koprivnica."[14] The group of about 165 Zagreb Jewish youths came to Gospić from Danica Camp on July 10 and were immediately transported by truck to the village of Trnovac, and from there, on foot, chained together, to Jadovno Camp.[15] Dr. Edo Neufeld was brought to Gospić from Zagreb on July 15 or 16 with a group of 28 Jewish attorneys, former Kerestinec prisoners.[16] The transport had a total of about 600 people, Serbs and Jews; besides the men, there was a fair number of women and a small number of children. They were first placed in the District Court prison, where they joined about 2,000 prisoners already there, mostly Serbs. Then, Neufeld and a group of about 400 Jews spent fourteen days in the building and yard of the Gospić cinema and, finally, about another two weeks in the sheds of the Ovčara sheep farm (today a pheasant-breeding farm), about three kilometers outside Gospić. The number of prisoners kept there fluctuated greatly, although it was usually kept to between roughly 1,000 and 1,600. At all these locations, the men and women prisoners were exposed to systematic robbery, they were overcrowded in extremely unhygienic conditions, hungry, humiliated in every way, and many were physically mistreated. Several times, Neufeld wrote down that the Serbs in the Gospić transit camps were usually treated more roughly than the Jews, and considerably more roughly than the imprisoned Croatian Communists. Every day, he saw transports, usually several, of 50 or more men tied by wire in pairs to a long chain running lengthwise, already exhausted and beaten, being taken to Velebit. On one occasion, a column of about 600 exhausted and beaten Jews and Serbs were being taken through the town and he saw townspeople at the windows of the houses clearly showing their outrage and dissent, and "occasionally we saw an old woman wiping tears from her eyes."[17]

At that time there were individual killings of prisoners in Gospić itself, but no group killings. Every day a mass of at least 4,000 internees crowded the town. They were kept for a short time in various kinds of improvised reception and mustering points at the railway station, in the cinema building and yard, in the former hotel, or in the Sokol Building, and were soon sent on to other destinations. They stayed relatively the longest at the Ovčara sheep farm, which was planned as a work camp for prisoners who were needed for various kinds of work in Gospić itself. Most of the prisoners in Ovčara were Jews, many of them from Zagreb. Under heavy guard the inmates were taken every day to clean streets, for roadwork, to do various kinds of farm work, sometimes on the deserted fields of the Serb population who had fled or had been deported. Conditions and hygiene were inhuman in the overcrowded camp, the food was extremely meager, but sometimes during outside work internees came into contact with the local population, from whom they could get some food. Sometimes aid also arrived from the Jewish Religious Community in Zagreb, but the Ustasha guards always "took their pick" first. The internees lived in a constant nightmare of humiliating abuse and arbitrary terror, usually initiated by the camp commander, Dragan Pudić, known as "Paralysis," allegedly a mental patient.[18]

In the old building of the District Court prison, known as Štik, the prisoners were treated much more brutally. Vlado Mađarević, who passed through the prison in Lepoglava and the Danica and Jastrebarsko Camps, said that "nowhere was as terrible as Gospić."[19] The crowded prison usually had 2,000 or more prisoners, usually the ones the Ustasha Police had singled out for further interrogation or special treatment. There were by far mostly Serbs, but also a small number of Croatian Communists and Jews. The same building housed the County Police Directorate. Some of the women prisoners testified, all of them agreeing, that they "often heard cries for help at night from cells where the Ustashe were beating and torturing people," and then suddenly all the lights would go out and from the windows they could see bodies of people who had been beaten to death being carried away.[20]

Ante Rukavina, an old member of the Croatian Peasant Party from the village of Trnovac near Gospić, who had also spent a short time in the Gospić prison, confirms this in even more detail. Branko Cetina, eighteen years old at the time, said that he witnessed "scenes of torture that are incomprehensible to a normal person."[21] Maca Gržetić testified that the Ustashe "tried to set the (imprisoned) Croats, Serbs, and Jews against each other. Occasionally, they incited them against one another," but they did not manage to provoke the quarrels or fights they desired. Had they done so, thought the witness, the Ustashe would have used them as an excuse to punish or kill the prisoners for rioting.[22]

However, the treatment of the prisoners who were taken from Gospić to Velebit or to the island of Pag was the most brutal. In the second half of July and in early August, "there were many of these transports, several in the morning and several in the afternoon."[23] The prisoners who were taken from the prison yard by truck were additionally beaten with rifles as they were loaded onto the trucks and then "tied with wire to make sure that no one would even try to escape."[24] The truck and later the boats for Pag were crammed, the prisoners tortured by hunger and thirst and ill-treated in various ways, so that some died on the way to the camps.[25]

The prisoners who were sent from Gospić to Jadovno or Karlobag on foot, usually in groups of 50 or more, were always tied in pairs by wire and attached to a long chain. "This sad column of people walked down the middle of the road, tormented and exhausted by traveling, hunger, and thirst, and at the side the Ustashe were constantly beating them with their rifle stocks, swearing at them and making them sing. Who could, walked; who could not, was mercilessly killed. I know that the local people were horrified by what they saw. I remember one of my relatives crying when she looked at those exhausted people, but she had a daughter who was an Ustasha sympathizer who screamed with joy. They both knew that the people were being taken to be killed.[26]

Today it is difficult to determine the degree to which the cruelty during the transports was part of a system devised to break any potential resistance among the victims, and to what degree it was an expression of individual vicious instincts fanned by the shameless ideology of hatred.

Slana and Metajna Camps

Mijo Babić, the newly appointed commander of all the camps in the ISC, visited some parts of the island of Pag right after his appointment, and at a meeting with several local officials decided on the locations for two concentration camps: a camp for women at the edge of the village of Metajna, and a camp for men on the barren rocks of Slana Point. Canon Don Joso Felicinović (1889–1984) from Pag attended the meeting; he was a prewar collaborator of the Ustasha movement and one of the leading men in establishing ISC authority on the island of Pag. In his manuscript, *Personal Memories,* from 1978, he wrote that "Mijo Babić, the main organizer of the Pag Camp, had promised that people would be treated well in the camp and it would only be a 'cleansing and correctional' institution. He told me that the internees would build a road on Pag, from Povljana to Lun . . . He deceived me bitterly! He lied to me," because "Slana became an Auschwitz–Dachau in miniature, a camp in which innocent men, women, and children were killed in all kinds of bestial ways."[27]

It seems that Babić was preordained for this kind of work, and had started preparations while still an émigré. In March 1929, in Zagreb, he killed Toni Schlegel, head of a publishing and printing firm and editor-in-chief of the Zagreb daily *Novosti,* allegedly a supporter of the dictatorship of

King Alexander.[28] The prominent publicist Josip Horvat (1896–1968) said that Schlegel's murder "announced the apocalyptic future." Several months later, Babić placed explosives in a police barracks and killed a policeman. As early as 1932, he declared in the Ustasha papers that, in the struggle for the Croatian state, the "self-sacrifice, revolvers, bombs, and the sharp knives of Croatian Ustashe will play the main role, they will clean and cut everything that is rotten from the healthy body of the Croatian people, so that it never returns."[29] When Babić was killed in a clash with the first insurgents in Herzegovina on July 3, 1941, Vjekoslav Maks Luburić, also a prominent Ustasha émigré, "the most infamous representative of Ustasha terror," replaced him as commander of all the camps.[30]

The first internees to arrive in Slana in a small boat from Karlobag were a group of 30 Jews from Zagreb, among them Dr. Oto Radan. This was on June 25, 1941, which can be taken as the founding date of Slana Camp.[31] Radan was the only one of that group who survived in Slana for almost two months, from the first to almost the last day of the camp's existence. On the next day and during the following days, new larger groups of prisoners arrived, at first only Jews, then increasing numbers of Serbs and a small number of Croatian Communists. The members of the Zagreb B'nai B'rith lodge were also brought, and almost the entire Makabi football team.[32] The Ustashe engaged nine boats for transport, and in his statement in 1945 and again in 1987, Šime Brnin Maržić from Pag estimated that he and his father Brne, in his father's boat *Sv. Josip* [St. Joseph], transported about 3,000 men and women prisoners to Slana and Metajna over a period of forty days.[33]

Slana Camp covered about twelve and a half acres in a rocky valley on an uninhabited Pag promontory, about five kilometers from the nearest hamlet of Metajna and almost the same distance from the lighthouse of Sv. Kristofor (St. Christopher). Even today, there are no possibilities for any kind of a normal life on this barren rocky ground, directly exposed to the stormy *bura* wind from nearby Mount Velebit, without good water, and without any vegetation. There were no habitations, no camp organization, no provisions for the camp to function when the weather grew cold, especially in winter. The first groups of internees slept on the cold rocks beside the sea, under the open sky. During the burning daytime heat, they built watchtowers for the Ustasha guards and improvised habitations for the prisoners.[34] Then they built the approach road to the camp from Metajna. They worked for ten to twelve hours a day, the work was exhausting and accompanied by ill-treatment, which became crueler as the days passed.[35]

All they got for breakfast was lime tea, for lunch and supper potato soup with two or three beans, without any flavoring. During work, the inmates collapsed from weakness and exhaustion, which provoked further mistreatment and beatings; later, they were killed where they fell as a warning to others. Hygiene was appalling: latrines under the open sky, about thirty meters from the barracks. Soon, dysentery appeared. Two prominent track-and-field athletes of the Zagreb Makabi Sports Club, Pali Klein from Osijek and the Austrian émigré Vili Kaiser, who came to Zagreb in 1938 (one of the best four-hundred-meters runners in Yugoslavia), tried to escape. Klein was killed in the attempt, and Kaiser lost his bearings as he tried to swim across the Velebit Channel at night, was caught, and the next day was shot in front of the assembled inmates.[36]

The men's camp in Slana was divided in two parts, Serb and Jewish, between which all communication was prohibited. "From the very beginning, the treatment of the Serbs was much worse than ours," said Dr. Oto Radan, and Emerik Blum confirmed this.[37] The Jews in Slana could not receive visitors, but they did receive censored mail, occasionally their families sent them sparse food parcels ("reduced" by the guards), and they received some aid from the Jewish Community in Zagreb, which made a great effort in this respect but usually with little success. The internee Zlatko Weiller estimated that they got about 500 to 700 calories a day each, and that this was systematically premeditated to make "the grueling work and the poor food liquidate us in a short time . . . people melted away before our very eyes."[38] At least 1,800 calories a day are needed to survive under hard physical labor.

It seems that Weiller's suspicions about the calculated purpose and character of Slana Camp were right. At that time, the SS-Einsatzgruppen and some other bodies of the Third Reich had begun to carry out the "final solution" in the conquered regions of the USSR, but there was as yet no developed "death industry" system, which was started in the late fall of that year. In the summer of 1941, the leaders of the SS were still discussing various "possible solutions" (*Lösungsmöglichkeiten*). One of them was called *Vernichtungsernährung* ("destructive nutrition"): killing by starvation and exhaustion, which Zlatko Weiller experienced. Working out this "possibility," the main creator and implementer of the anti-Jewish measures in the Reich, Reinhard Heydrich, anticipated the "total evacuation of all the Jews to the East." Once there, placed in camps under harsh conditions, "in great work colonies, separated by gender, Jews will build roads in these (eastern) regions, and a great majority will perish in the natural way; the others, who are obviously the most resilient, will have to be exposed to suitable special treatment" (he used the terms *entsprechend behandelt* and *Sonderbehandlung*).[39] This was a formula that the commander of the Pag Camps and the commander of the Thirteenth Ustasha Battalion, Captain Ivan Devčić, known as Pivac, one of the veteran Ustasha émigrés,[40] made use of to a large degree in Slana.

As the prisoner transports to Slana increased in frequency and number during July, and the area of the camp became small, on July 3, 1941, Commander Devčić began to implement a "special procedure": on that day, a group of 55 older men in the Jewish part of the camp were singled out, taken from Slana, and never seen again.[41] They were killed most cruelly somewhere on Velebit and thrown into a pit, as the Ustasha Jerko Fratrović said during a UDB interrogation in 1952.[42] After this first group liquidation, larger or smaller groups of internees were regularly taken away, usually at night and predominantly from the Serb part of the camp, which the new transports after July 10 had made considerably more populous than the Jewish part. During the next month, as a prisoner transport arrived in the camp, a similar number of internees would be sent off to execution sites under cover of darkness. Surviving inmates and former guards estimated that the Jewish part of the camp was usually kept to between 200 to 400 internees, and the Serb part to about 800 to 2,000. Oto Radan said that, almost every night, the inmates listened with horror and fear to the machine-gun fire from the execution sites on nearby Furnaža, above Karlobaški Malin and in Slana Cove.[43] The citizens of the town of Pag (some ten kilometers away) also heard the gunfire, despite the Ustashe's efforts to keep them in the dark. They heard a lot about the horror that was going on in Slana in various ways. Don Joso Felicinović wrote how Anđelka Maržić of Pag, wife of Josip Maržić, owner of the boat *Sv. Josip,* told him "one evening in the greatest secrecy that her son Šime was transporting . . . internees from Slana Camp to another place called Furnaža in his boat, where a trench had been dug on a plateau and that [the Ustashe] were killing them there . . . Mrs. Maržić begged me to intercede for her son to be released from this work, because he would go mad. She also said that "men and women were usually taken on foot from Slana Camp to Furnaža, there they were killed and thrown into a trench that had already been prepared."[44] Almost all the boat owners who transported prisoners to or from Slana in the summer of 1941 made statements to the Commission for War Crimes in 1945 and 1946. Their testimonies can be counted among the most reliable descriptions of how prisoners were treated and a source of data about their approximate number and their fate.[45]

The first group of internees in the women's camp of Metajna consisted of several Jewish women brought from the Zagreb Fairground and on the way separated from their husbands, who were taken to Slana. Then followed women students and Makabi athletes.[46] At first they were not mistreated. They made shirts for the Ustasha prison guards in Slana (who lived in Metajna) and were allowed to buy food from the villagers. The first larger transport of 275 Jewish women, some of them with children, arrived in the middle of July, also from the Zagreb Fairground. The internee Nada Feuereisen, who survived, told about it at great length and in detail only three years after the event.[47] They lived in three houses and the adjacent barracks on the edge of Metajna. They did not do any work, but the food was extremely meager, and they were treated increasingly badly as the days went by. Instances of rape and the individual killing of prisoners who resisted or tried to escape from the violence grew in number.[48] After a large transport of Serb women and children were brought to Metajna at the end of July, Nada Feuereisen estimated that about 600 Jewish women and 78 children were taken to Slana in fishing boats.[49] Here "the real torture began . . . Even as we disembarked, the Ustashe beat us, kicked us, swore at us most horribly." The older women and mothers with children were placed in a large barracks, while the others had to make do with the bare rocks under the open sky. Women died of hunger and thirst. Hygiene was severely lacking and dysentery soon developed. The women prisoners saw the men prisoners going to work, but were not allowed to contact them.[50] Camp Commander Devčić Pivac allowed them to bathe in the sea, but when they did so they had to walk naked before him and the guards. Devčić chose one woman from Zagreb, called Brajković, to "do him a favor," and when she refused, she disappeared, although an order existed for her to be sent to Zagreb because someone had interceded.[51] In *Personal Memories,* Don Joso Felicinović wrote that during his first visit to the abandoned Slana Camp at the end of August, he found "a piece of cardboard on the wall of the main Ustasha barracks on which records were kept of the women and girls raped in the camp, with their names and the dates, and by which Ustasha."[52]

Jure Kunkera from Novalja on the island of Pag worked in Zagreb, in the Löwy firm at 3 Svačićev Square. At the beginning of August, he was bringing two cases of food and various necessities from Zagreb for his employer's sons, who were imprisoned in Slana, but when he reached

Karlobag, his relative, the Ustasha Ante Kunkera, told him not to even try delivering the cases, because the Löwys were no longer alive.[53] Aleksandar (Aleksa) Semnic and Teodora Dežma, teachers at the Second Classical Grammar School in Zagreb, and Dr. Pšerhof and his wife, also ended their days in Slana. The Milinovs, owners of the Dubrovnik Hotel in Zagreb, who were Serbs, first had to watch, bound, as the Ustashe raped their daughter, and then all three of them were killed. The only prisoner in Slana who received a visit was Milan Fuks from Zagreb, whose common-law wife, a hat maker from Marićev prolaz, found her way to the camp by some miracle and they were allowed to spend several minutes together outside the wire in the presence of a guard. The following day, Milan Fuks was the first of the prisoners whose names were called to join the group taken for liquidation on Furnaža.[54]

In July 1941, about 150 soldiers of the Italian border guard (*Guardia alla Frontiera*) were stationed in Pag and in Novalja, under the command of Captain Paolo Bertoli. In February 1946, his superior, Colonel Pietro Fioretti, testified that Bertoli was very well aware of what was going on in Slana Camp and reported about it to his superiors, which Ante Zemljar and Don Joso Felicinović confirmed from their personal experience. In some cases, Bertoli interceded on behalf of some Serbs from Pag to not be persecuted, but on the whole he was very restrained about what was going on in Slana, as the Staff of the Second Army had commanded him not to interfere in any way.[55] At that time, there was a large Italian garrison with several thousand soldiers in Gospić. The imprisoned Zagreb attorney Dr. Edo Neufeld described several occasions when Italian officers or soldiers helped save some Jews and a group of Serb children, but when Neufeld had the occasion to ask an Italian commander for official protection for the whole camp, he "refused with regret."[56] The Italian officers had been instructed that the Italian army must behave "as a guest and a friend in a friendly country" (i.e., in the ISC), which meant that they could not interfere in what the Ustasha authorities were doing.

The Italians' behavior changed in the first days of August. In July 1941, a rebellion broke out in some parts of the ISC, and spread rapidly because of the Ustashe's mass crimes against the Serb population. German and Italian intelligence and their military and diplomatic representatives were quite well informed, and soon began to criticize the Ustasha authorities because their "senseless persecution of the Serbs" was causing "damage to the Croatian state" and "creating chaos." This went against the interests of Germany and Italy, which needed their armies elsewhere, and not tied up pacifying the ISC.[57] On July 28, 1941, the *carabinieri* command in Zadar reported that the "repression against the Orthodox Serbs seems to have become even more bloody after the Italian troops left Gračac" (a town in the Lika region, fifty kilometers from Gospić).[58] Soon "word spread through Gospić every day that the Italian Second Army, which was stationed in the region as an allied army, would assume command over this territory as well as control over the civilian administration."[59] Vlado Singer, head of Ustasha intelligence at that time, got confirmation of these rumors from his intelligence officers, and warned his government that the Italians were preparing to reoccupy Zone B, that is, the entire coastal region and its hinterland. Eugen Dido Kvaternik gave a vivid description of the dismay among the leaders of the Ustasha government when a telegram for Pavelić arrived on August 16 from Mussolini, in which the Italian leader officially demanded urgent reoccupation "because of measures of military security that cannot be deferred."[60] During the hearing mentioned above, on October 29, 1941, Rubinić described how, after this news reached them in August, "a degree of panic broke out . . . in Gosipć and its surroundings" among his men (policemen and Ustashe).[61] Sadly, the greatest victims of this panic were all the surviving internees in Jadovno and most of the internees in Slana.

Zone B included the entire area of the Gospić–Velebit–Pag Island camp system. According to the Agreements of Rome of May 18, 1941, on delimitation of territory between the Kingdom of Italy and the ISC, this zone went to the ISC but with the permanent presence of the Italian army. An additional agreement allowed the Italian army, for reasons of security, to assume complete control over this zone if necessary, including civilian authority. At first, Pavelić and his government tried to resist, but they had no choice—they had to bow to the Italian demands. This entailed the urgent retreat of the Ustasha army from the area and the evacuation or liquidation of the concentration camps.[62]

If Slana had originally been planned as a camp of "destruction by starvation and exhaustion," when its evacuation was announced, it grew into a camp of direct killing by the quickest methods, into a real death camp. Don Joso Felicinović considers that most of the internees were killed in these last days before the evacuation.[63] Pag fisherman Vladimir Kustić described how he was out fishing on the calm sea in the Zaton area in the night between August 14 and 15, "when suddenly the quiet night was broken by long bursts of machine-gun fire mixed with ghastly screams from Furnaža."[64] The statements of some of the perpetrators at their trial in Zadar in 1952 indicate that about 800 prisoners were killed on Furnaža on that night. Ustasha Colonel Juco Rukavina brought Rubinić an order from Dido Kvaternik "that the office of the (police) directorate, the camp and all the Ustashe . . . must move from Gospić . . . to Jastrebarsko." Rubinić had to carry out a very complex operation, according to his own statement at his hearing at the end of October that year: "I was alone with several of my closest collaborators facing this enormous job of evacuation, and moving the camp gave me great trouble because it had about 4,000 people, as they had also burdened me with the embarkation and evacuation of the prisoners from the island of Pag.[65]

And so, on about August 23 and several days later, the camps on Pag and in Gospić were liquidated. Rubinić said that "moving the camps gave me the most trouble with . . . the prisoners from the island of Pag" because they had to be evacuated urgently, and he had no means of transport from Karlobag to Gospić at his disposal. Later during the hearing, Rubinić vividly described the chaos and grabbing of any form of transport that went on in Karlobag, where some Ustashe seized the "official bus to transport their families and other civilians, while I needed that bus and other means of transport most." According to Rubinić, it was because of this "chaos" that some of the internees were killed on the way; they had been shipped from Slana to Karlobag but never arrived in Gospić. These were the groups of people who were thrown into Kijevac pit near Karlobag, Jasenovac pit above Križac Bay (not far from Karlobag), and Bliznica and Badanj pits not far from the village of Stupačinovo (near Baške Oštarije).[66]

About 400 prisoners arrived in Gospić from Pag, mostly from the women's camp. Together with about 2,000 more from the Gospić prison and about 1,500 more from Ovčara Camp, they were sent by train first to Jastrebarsko and then, in later days and weeks, farther on to Jasenovac (the men), Kruščica, Loborgrad (women and children), and to other camps.[67] Almost all later lost their lives in other camps in the ISC and in Auschwitz. To the best of our knowledge, only 3 Jewish women prisoners from Pag survived the entire war (Nada Feuereisen and Anica Ehrenfreund-Polić, who gave statements, and Salčika Engel), and only 6 men from the Jewish part of Slana Camp (Dr. Oto Radan, Dr. Branko Aleksander, Dr. Robert Farkaš, Zlatko Weiller, Emerik Blum, and Dr. Pavle Löw-Levković).

When the Ustashe evacuated Slana in great haste on August 21, they left behind a deserted camp. The ten or so people from Pag and the surrounding villages who had reason and courage to go to Slana and Furnaža in the following days were horrified and appalled by the still visible traces of the crimes that had been committed there.[68] "The trenches have been covered with five to twenty centimeters of earth and stones . . . The main trench is about fifty meters long, four wide, and two to three deep. It has six extensions full of bodies . . . : men, women, and children are in the main trench," wrote Don Joso Felicinović, and beside the text drew a sketch of the trench with the extensions and the distribution of the victims.[69] They found ten mass graves on the stretch from Metajna to the lighthouse of Sv. Krištofor (almost ten kilometers).[70] Two sanitary-disinfectant commissions of the Italian Army went to Slana on September 3 and 22, 1941. Both submitted detailed reports to the Military-Health Directorate of the Fifth Army Corps. The second commission, headed by army doctor Santo Stazzi, photographed the remains of the camp and the two mass graves discovered above Slana Bay and near Karlobaški Malin. For sanitary reasons, the commission exhumed and burned the 791 bodies in those two graves, among them 293 women and 91 children, ages five to fifteen.[71]

As usual, there is most disagreement about estimating the number of victims of the Pag camps. The lowest estimate, given by the commander of the Italian garrison, Captain Bertoli, is 4,000 victims. The estimate given by boat-owners is the highest—15,000 dead. Zemljar considers that the "number cannot be definitely established" and that "there were many more victims at Slana" than the number of bodies found.[72] Emerik Blum mentions about 10,000 Serbs killed and just over 1,000 Jews. Don Joso Felicinović mentions a total of 12,000 victims,[73] about 4,000 of them women and children. There were probably close to 1,500 Jews killed, about one-third of them from Zagreb.

Jadovno

If Slana Camp was organized to implement the idea of *Vernichtungernährung,* in other words, killing by starvation and exhaustion, the purpose of Jadovno Camp was, from its very beginning, the direct physical liquidation of prisoners. This is even suggested by its location in the deep forests of the Velebit massif, on an inaccessible plateau without any approach roads or paths, at an altitude of 1,200 meters, completely isolated from the outside world, twenty-two kilometers from Gospić and six-and-a-half kilometers from the nearest hamlet of Jadovno, which gave the camp its name. On a plateau of 90 by 180 meters, the camp was surrounded by a double oval belt of barbed wire four meters high, heavily guarded with machine-gun nests, a thick forest without any paths, and deep karst pits of ill-omened purpose.[74] The isolation of the camp was complete: unlike all the other camps in the ISC, no one in Jadovno ever received any of the many letters and parcels sent to them, no one was allowed to contact the outside world from Jadovno. Between July 7 and August 22, 1941, the Zagreb Jewish Community several times demanded, proposed, and begged to be allowed to send parcels to Pag and Jadovno via the Red Cross. The Red Cross Society of the ISC accepted the proposal, the Jewish Section of the RUR from Zagreb issued a permit on July 23, the Public Order and Security County Directorate in Gospić confirmed receipt of a large number of parcels by official letter of August 11. Some parcels arrived in Slana, but not a single one came to Jadovno. In August, the Zagreb Jewish Community informed the Karlovac Community that "twenty-eight of its community members are in Jadovno on Velebit, they are healthy and well," that they would "send them additional food," but that the Karlovac Community must "send the money." However, this information was outdated, because that group of people from Karlovac had in the meantime already been killed.[75] At the request of the Zagreb Jewish Community, on July 21 and 25, 1941, the Jewish Section of the RUR issued a permit to the physician Dr. Milivoj Schwarz to travel to Gospić and take medicine and food for the Jews imprisoned on Pag and in Jadovno (obviously, there had been plans for other doctors to go too, to help the seriously ill, to preventively vaccinate the prisoners so that "no contagious diseases spread from there").[76] It is not clear whether Dr. Schwarz ever arrived in Gospić, but he certainly never got to the camps on Pag and in Jadovno. No one but the innermost circle of Ustasha authorities was ever allowed to see Jadovno Camp.

Stjepan Rubinić, the newly appointed director of the County Police, founded Jadovno Death Camp in June 1941.[77] The location was determined by people who knew the ground and conditions better, Jurica Frković, chief Ustasha commissioner for Lika and Grand Prefect for Gacka and Lika, and Juco Rukavina, commander-in-chief of the Ustasha Army.[78] As fighters in the Velebit Uprising in 1932,[79] which had partly taken place in that very section of Velebit, they were both well acquainted with the area around Jadovno. They placed the Seventeenth and Twenty-second Companies of the Ustasha Lika Battalion at Rubinić's disposal for guard duty in Jadovno.[80]

The first inmates arrived in Jadovno on June 24, 1941. They were Zagreb Jews from the first group of about 200 people who had been taken to Gospić from the Zagreb Fairground during the night of June 22–23. In Gospić, thirty of them, better able to work, were singled out, loaded on a truck with rolls of barbed wire, and taken to Jadovno.[81] This first group cleared the area of the camp on the plateau and surrounded it with barbed wire. Several days later, other groups started to arrive, increasing in frequency and size. Two barracks were built for the Ustasha guards, and the prisoners at first slept under the open sky. Only later were they allowed to build themselves shelters covered with branches of fir and beech, and ferns, which they called dwellings. They were up to two meters high and there was room for about thirty people under each. The dwellings were arranged in the shape of a horseshoe, with the Jews housed separately, the far-more-numerous Serbs separately, and several dozen Croats, political opponents of the Ustasha regime, in one dwelling.[82] The food was even poorer than on Pag or in the Gospić prison. Branko Cetina described how, on the day after they arrived in the camp, the Ustasha guards gave his group pieces of wood ten by twenty centimeters and several axes, and ordered them to make themselves bowls for food. Every day, a small amount of mash and drinking water was placed in them, and they ate using their hands because they had no spoons.[83] For a short time, the prisoners were taken from the camp to clear a forest path and cut trees, until four prisoners from the Serb part of the camp fled into the forest (among them Branko Cetina) and managed to get away. After that, Luburić forbade outside work, and during the investigations against "Rubinić and his companions" he wrote in the file on November 5, 1941, "Since there were not many guards . . . I ordered more men to be sent, and the late Mijo Babić sent them to Gračac and Gospić for that purpose."[84]

It seems that it was just after Luburić's visit to Jadovno and the arrival of the new guards that the killing of the prisoners, which had already started, intensified. According to some testimonies, at one time there were about 3,000 prisoners in the camp, and Božo Švarc estimated that the highest number was 4,000.[85] As new transports kept arriving with growing frequency, especially during the second half of July and in the first days of August, one of the Ustasha commanders—Second Lieutenant Bešlić, Rude Ritz, or Dragan Pudić—would every evening call out or simply choose groups of internees, who were taken from the camp under heavy guard, usually to the pit on Grgin Hill, about one-and-a-half kilometers distant. After an hour at the most, the internees in the camp heard long bursts of machine-gun fire from that direction, and there was no doubt about what was happening to those who had been taken away.[86] It seems that some groups of prisoners did not even reach the camp because they were killed en route and thrown into the Šaran pit, between the village of Jadovno and the camp. The group of 165 Jewish youths from Zagreb who were sent from Koprivnica to Gospić on July 10, and then straight on to Jadovno, were, except for ten of them, killed several days after they arrived at the camp. They were bound together with wire, thrown into the pit on Grgin Hill, some of them still alive, and then the Ustashe threw hand grenades down into the pit after them.[87]

Although the Ustashe wanted as few people as possible to know about the killings, terrible stories about Jadovno soon began to spread through Velebit villages and throughout the region. Stjepan Kosović from Lički Novi, at that time a boy of twelve, said, "We usually drove the livestock to the Novoselo area. There I saw the Ustashe leading columns of bound prisoners in the direction of the village of Trnovac almost every day. There were columns in the morning and in the afternoon, in the mornings around three or four, in the afternoons around two or three . . . Some people were well-dressed and carried suitcases; they looked like gentlemen. But there were also very many who were almost naked and barefoot, all they wore were a shirt and pants. At that time, I did not know who the people were. I found out in the village, when people said that they were Serbs and Jews being taken to Jadovno, to be thrown into the pits and ravines.[88] Don Joso Felicinović found out about Jadovno in the following way: "A poverty-stricken woman from Velebit, from the surroundings of Jadovno near Gospić, asked me if it was a sin to keep the clothes of people who had been killed and thrown into a pit. That was how I found out that innocent victims were being killed in the camps in my homeland."[89] Edo Neufeld reckoned that Jadovno Camp was liquidated in the first days of August, because "it is a fact that there had been no sign of life from any of these people after the beginning of August 1941, and this was when the Ustashe brought us (i.e., the inmates in Ovčara) several cauldrons and kitchen pots, saying that they were things from Jadovno because the camp had been abandoned."[90] Ustasha Lieutenant Pudić, the commander of the Gospić Camp, removed some people he knew, Serbs from Bijeljina (in northeastern Bosnia), from the transport for Jadovno, because "nothing good was in store for them there," and one of Pudić's assistants told Milan Relić, who was saved, some details about how prisoners in Jadovno were thrown "down a ravine."[91]

Immediately before the mass liquidation started, Rubinić's assistant, Ustasha Second Lieutenant Janko (Ivica) Mihalović, probably because he knew what was going to happen, ordered ten Jewish prisoners from Jadovno to be taken back to Gospić to sweep the streets. The choice was not made by chance, as all ten of them had gone to grammar school with Mihalović in Zagreb. Eight were later killed in other camps, but Saša Blivajs and Božo Švarc survived the war.[92] Because of intercession and through the connections of his wife, as his was a mixed marriage, Bela Hochstädter also returned to Zagreb from Jadovno and survived the war.[93] At the personal intercession of Ivica Baraković on July 2, Rudolf Berković returned and six days later got a permit to move about Zagreb freely.[94] There is no information about any other Zagreb Jews returning from Jadovno. After spending thirteen days in the camp, before mass liquidation began, Ante Rukavina and thirty other Croatian prisoners were sent back to the Gospić prison. Ten of them were released from prison and sent home, while twenty-one were taken to the camp in Jastrebarsko.[95]

By the middle of August, when Juco Rukavina told Rubinić about Kvaternik's order for all the remaining prisoners from Pag, Gospić, and Jadovno to be immediately sent to Jastrebarsko because of the imminent Italian reoccupation of the entire region, Jadovno Camp no longer existed. All its internees had already been killed and thrown down the bottomless karst pits in the area surrounding the camp—most of them down the Šaran pit on the path from the camp to Jadovno village. A witness, a local inhabitant, said that the moaning of the victims could be heard from one of the pits for several more days, and then everything went silent.[96] Some of the pits, from which came "a pungent and overpowering stench characteristic of the later stages of decaying flesh," were discovered by an Italian military-sanitary inspection on September 4, 1941, and the report about them was signed on September 6 by the doctor of the Fifth Army Corps, Vittorio Finderle, and the director of the Military-Health Directorate of the same corps, Colonel Dr. Muzio Fiorini.[97] On the basis of the findings of several postwar commissions and two groups of speleologists, and of the testimony of some local inhabitants and the confessions of some of the perpetrators, Zatezalo counted eighteen such pits.[98] Most of them were the graves of Jadovno internees who had been killed.

The victims from the "auxiliary" camp near Stupačinovo village were thrown down several of these pits closer to Baške Oštarije. During the stage of mass liquidations, probably as early as the second half of July, the Ustasha garrisons from Baške Oštarije and from Karlobag, with the knowledge of and at the order of Luburić, established another temporary camp not far from Baške Oštarije, which served as a transitory station for liquidation.[99] Several months later, Maks Luburić said that prisoners brought from Gospić were "handed over to our guards" at Oštarije and that "our men took them and robbed them of all they possessed."[100] Only one man of those who had been thrown down the pits managed to save himself—Serđo Poljak, from the village of Šibuljine under Velebit. He was killed in 1942, fighting as a Partisan against the Ustashe, but before that he gave a detailed account.[101]

As a refugee in Switzerland in December 1943, Dr. Edo Neufeld testified that "horrible tales were being told in Gospić itself about how that camp had disappeared."[102] At the Zagreb Red Cross, people already knew on August 22 that "the Jewish camps in Gospić and its surroundings had allegedly been closed down."[103] Horrific rumors about the fate of the inmates spread through Zagreb, especially when news about the findings of the Italian inspectors on the island of Pag and on Velebit became known at the beginning of September.[104] A year later, in Stara Gradiška, Rubinić himself and some Ustashe from the Jadovno garrison told Ilija Jakovljević and some Jasenovac prisoners various details about the liquidation of Jadovno Camp.[105]

The sudden liquidation of Jadovno Camp led to a dispute among the top Ustasha officials. Rubinić claimed that "because it was not suitable to have a camp in Jadovno, he had moved this camp, again with the knowledge of Director Kvaternik, to the Maksimović Sheep Farm in Gospić," thus referring to the thirty or so Croatian prisoners and about fifteen Jews who really were returned to Gospić before the liquidation of the camp.[106] Eugen Dido Kvaternik, on the contrary, maintained that "Rubinić moved the camp from Jadovno to Gospić . . . at his own initiative, without informing me about it first."[107] Luburić claimed that "the liquidation of Jadovno had been decided on because it was difficult to bring food, construction materials, etc., there" and that "it is most inappropriate to talk about these things," but he accused Rubinić very strongly of insubordination and especially of looting and arbitrary behavior, and he "repeatedly told Mr. Kvaternik that he would not collaborate with him (Rubinić)."[108] Rubinić defended himself by saying that they were "against him" in Gospić because he had been appointed "police director in the heart of Lika, although I am not from Lika."[109]

On the order of Eugen Kvaternik, Juco Rukavina arrested Rubinić and his associates Mihalović and Pudić on September 13, 1941, in Jastrebarsko and Slavetić, where they were in command of temporary camps for prisoners brought from Gospić. Pudić and Mihalović, however, were soon released. At the trial before the Ustasha Penal and Disciplinary Court, which lasted for several months, about twenty more Ustasha officers and high-ranking officials were heard besides Kvaternik and Luburić, whose statements have already been quoted. These included Grand Prefect Jurica Frković, Commander of the Ustasha Army Juco Rukavina, and head of the Jewish Section Vilko Kühnel. The sentence was pronounced on January 29, 1942, and Rubinić was punished by being "stricken from Ustasha membership" for, "as County Police Director in Gospić, arbitrarily moving the camp from Jadovno to Gospić," and for "treating the prisoners incorrectly as commander of the camps (in Gospić and Slavetić), entering into amorous relations with them."[110] After the sentence, Rubinić was sent to Stara Gradiška, where he spent almost a year as a very privileged prisoner who lived and ate together with the Ustasha command. Ilija Jakovljević described Rubinić (whom he ironically calls the Exalted) in great detail and very vividly in the book *Concentration Camp on the Sava*. This book is the most moving and best-written personal testimony from the Jasenovac complex of camps. Rubinić often complained to, and confided in, Jakovljević, sometimes describing his "meritorious work" in Gospić and Jadovno in great detail.

After his release from Gradiška, Rubinić was not taken back into the Ustasha organization, but was given two Jewish commercial firms. Very little was known about him, and there is even an entry in the card index of the War Crimes Commission in 1945 that he had been "allegedly killed by the Ustashe." Later, he was found: on October 17, 1948, a Yugoslav secret agent sent information that Rubinić was often seen in the company of Ustasha émigrés in Salzburg, especially with Vjekoslav Blaškov, and that "he was last seen in Salzburg between September 12–25 in the Grossglockner coffee house . . . After that, all trace of Rubinić disappeared." Rubinić was "financially very well off, so Hotko and Kovačević think that he lives somewhere in Austria or Germany in complete seclusion."[111]

The First Croatian Armored Regiment informed the Public Order and Security Directorate in Zagreb that on August 20, 1941, "2,000 Jews were sent by train to Zagreb" from Gospić, and that, on the following nights, "the next shipments will be sent, also of Jews."[112] Although it is completely untrue that the transports contained only Jews, because they contained at least five times more Serbs than Jews, the document does confirm the dates when the Gospić–Velebit–Pag system of camps was closed down, and indirectly it also confirms Rubinić's statement that about 4,000 men and women inmates were sent back.

As usual, there are widely varying estimates of the number of victims. Zatezalo wrote about more than 40,000, while Peršen considered that the "number of victims in the whole group of Gospić camps might have been between 15,000 and 25,000."[113] It seems that the number that Rubinić told Jakovljević in Stara Gradiška was closest to the truth. It has already been said that Rubinić and his assistant Mihalović recorded by name all the prisoners who were brought to Gospić. In Stara Gradiška, Rubinić told Jakovljević that he recorded a total of 28,700 prisoners.[114] Taking into account that about 4,000 prisoners left Gospić at the end of August, and that some had been released earlier, this leaves 24,000 victims who disappeared in the camps on Velebit, Pag, and in Gospić itself. These included about 2,500 Jews, perhaps one-third of them from Zagreb, but also from Varaždin, Sarajevo, Koprivnica, Križevci, Travnik, Zenica, Karlovac, Tuzla, and many other Jewish communities in the ISC. The "Dotrščina" list, which is incomplete, has the names of 222 Zagreb Jews killed in Jadovno, and another 75 in the Pag camps.[115]

Kruščica Camp, near Vitez in central Bosnia, was organized in August 1941 on an abandoned Serb estate, which had served as an internee camp even during the Croatian Banovina (1939–1941). According to some testimonies, about 3,000–4,000 people passed through it, while according to others as many as 5,000, about 90 percent of them Jews and the others Serbs. Kruščica was a temporary transit point, because the camps in Gospić, on Pag, and in Jadovno had been closed down, and Jasenovac, Đakovo, Loborgrad, and the others had not yet been established. The camps in Jastrebarsko and Slavetić played a similar temporary role at the end of August and in September 1941. The Zagreb Community mostly financed aid to the prisoners.[116] As soon as it was possible to move them, this was done. On October 1, 250 men were transported to Jasenovac, and some time later, women and children were sent to Loborgrad.[117] There were Zagreb Jews in this camp too, but there are no records of any of them being killed there, although it seems that about one hundred Serbs were killed, and at least two Sarajevo Jews.[118]

21

THE APOGEE OF TERROR

Jasenovac

A lot has been published about Jasenovac Concentration Camp: 1,106 books, 1,482 memoirs and research papers, and 108 collections of documents had come out by the year 2000.[1] Nevertheless, many people believe that research is still not complete and that an objective picture about the Jasenovac group of camps has yet to be presented.[2] The reason is the long years during which this subject, in itself traumatic and made more so by any one-sided approach, was used for political ends and underwent relentless manipulation. Bitter disagreements about the number of victims, never definitively established, dominated and are still dominating discussions loaded with personal and ethnic feelings, blocked by hard political prejudice that has at times been even morbid. Irresponsibly exaggerated numbers are used in the attempt to prove that Jasenovac was a camp in which everything focused exclusively on killing, a gigantic and terrible death factory whose very size turns it into an indictment against a whole people. Deceiving cover-ups suggest that Jasenovac was mostly a work camp and a legally established institution for imprisoning confirmed opponents of the regime, which not only is disingenuous, but a shameful effort to whitewash the genocidal policy of the Ustasha ISC.[3] Both these one-sided approaches obscure the real picture of Jasenovac.

The Jasenovac camps were an execution site and grave for more than half the Jewish victims during the existence of the ISC and for more than one-third of the Zagreb Jews who disappeared in the Holocaust in 1941–1945.[4] Although this book is primarily concerned with their destiny, this destiny cannot be separated from the general conditions in those camps or from the destinies of their Serb, Roma, Croatian, and other fellow-prisoners. It is true that the numbers of victims have not yet been conclusively established, but a comparative analysis of the accessible documents and publications gives a rather clear general picture of what went on in the Jasenovac camps and also their character.

The main and most exhaustive published materials are three books by Antun Miletić, which consist of 629 documents and twenty-six detailed documentary supplements. The documents are chosen to show various aspects of the basic character of the Jasenovac camps and also their diversity, and the various periods through which they went. Miletić's bafflingly confused system for categorizing the documents, not easily negotiated, and some arbitrary comments in the foreword and afterword, may be no more than a calculated smoke screen that allowed this basic and indispensable book to be published under unfavorable circumstances.[5] No one has as yet even attempted to dispute either the selection or the authenticity of the documents in Miletić's books. Anyone who wants to prove anything about Jasenovac makes extensive use of Miletić's voluminous treasury—ranging from Franjo Tudman to Milan Bulajić—but most of them take from it only what supports their own political preconceptions.

Parts of the second edition of Mirko Peršen's book *Ustaša Camps* are to date the most universal and the more-or-less most realistic description of various aspects of the functioning of Jasenovac, unfortunately without sufficient reference to sources and with some less important weaknesses carried over from the first edition in 1966. Most of the individual testimonies in the collection *Memories of Jews of Jasenovac Camp* are very credible and precise. Ilija Jakovljević's book *Concentration Camp on the Sava* is the best written and most moving personal testimony of a surviving internee. The general picture is significantly completed by some historiographic works (e.g., by Mihael Sobolevski, Narcisa Lengel-Krizman, Petar Strčić, Davor Kovačić, and others), the unpublished manuscripts of Dijana Budisavljević and Nikola Nikolić, and a critical reading of memoirs and books (e.g., by Egon Berger, Vladimir Carin, Ante Ciliga, Đorđe Miliša, Nikola Nikolić, and others) with careful attention to points of convergence and difference in their descriptions of the same events and situations.

Jasenovac I and Jasenovac II

The Jasenovac group of camps was named after nearby Jasenovac, a small municipal center of about 1,200 inhabitants on the left bank of the Sava river facing the mouth of the Una, about 110 kilometers southeast of Zagreb. The official name of the entire complex was Ustasha Defense–Command of the Jasenovac Transit Camps. In documents and literature, names such as Jasenovac Transit Camp, Jasenovac Concentration Camp, and Jasenovac Transit and Work Camp are often used.[6] From the end of August 1941 to April 22, 1945, it was the central and by far the largest system of concentration camps in what was then the ISC. It was also the largest camp system in Europe during the Second World War in which mass killings took place without the direct participation of the German Nazis.

The system consisted of five separate camps designated by the Roman numerals I to V. Jasenovac I was near Krapje village, on the bank of the Sava, about ten kilometers northwest of Jasenovac village. Jasenovac II was near Bročice village, about six kilometers northeast of Jasenovac, near the Novska road. The central and by far the largest camp, Jasenovac III, was on the edge of Jasenovac village, on the large estate and industrial plants of the entrepreneur Ozren Bačić and his family, who had, as endangered Orthodox, emigrated from the ISC in the spring of 1941. Jasenovac IV was not established until early 1942, in Jasenovac itself, as a small work camp in what had been a little leatherworks (known as the Leatherworks). In early 1942, the former prison in Stara Gradiška was also turned into a multipurpose concentration camp and attached to the system as Jasenovac V.[7]

During investigations in 1947, Ljubo Miloš, one of the most notorious Ustasha commanders in Jasenovac, claimed in the UDB prison in Zagreb that Eugen Dido Kvaternik had ordered the foundation of the Jasenovac camp system, probably in mid-July 1941.[8] It is most likely that Kvaternik decided on this location because it was much more accessible and had better internal communication than the Gospić–Velebit–Pag system, and had other advantages as well. The thirty or so industrial plants and auxiliary buildings already constructed on the Bačić estate (brickyard, sawmill, mill, electrical power plant, chain factory, leatherworks, locksmith's, sheds, haylofts, warehouses, etc.) were suitable for a camp economy and other needs; an industrial railway line led to the very center of the complex, it was situated in a plain that made it easy to keep watch over the camp and its surroundings, and the proximity of the large Stara Gradiška Prison could serve, and later did serve, as a supplementary part of the whole system.

There are indications that Jasenovac III was originally planned as a work camp with large and cheap production potentials for the needs of the Ustasha Army and the camp system itself, while the more distant and secluded Jasenovac I and II were gotten ready for a combination of work and death camps right from the beginning. As the administrative procedure for taking over the Bačić plants and adapting them for camp purposes lasted several months, until November all the prisoners were transported to Jasenovac I and II, that is to Krapje and Bročice.[9]

Jasenovac I and Jasenovac II were camps for men only, in the beginning for Serbs and Jews only, somewhat later to be joined by small groups of Croats. Preparations for construction began on July 24, 1941, at the latest, when the Land Reclamation and Water Regulation Directorate ordered timber "for building wooden barracks in Jasenovac"; on August 9, 10, and 12, it ordered "trimmed timber and chipboard for building barracks" and "the construction of thirteen wooden barracks in Jasenovac."[10] It was to these barracks, surrounded by guardhouses and barbed wire, that the first larger groups of Jasenovac inmates came at the end of August. They included Zagreb Jews and other prisoners who had survived the camps on Pag and in Gospić, and who arrived in Krapje on August 23 "after two days of traveling into the unknown."[11] On the same day, *Hrvatski narod* reported that "the barracks in Lonjsko polje have just been finished and will serve for the accommodation of workers who will begin work immediately." No mention was made of what kind of "workers" these were to be, but *Hrvatski narod* promised the "regulation of the course of certain rivers, tributaries, streams, and underground rivers, and drainage of the vast flood areas of Lonjsko polje."[12]

The prisoners of Jasenovac I and II really did build flood-protection embankments along the rivers Strug, Lonja, and Sava, but as they were starving, beaten, forced to use the most primitive tools, and worked on waterlogged ground, under the torrential fall rain, their work was very inferior. "We had to run to the embankment, which was very muddy. The holes and ditches beside the embankment were already full of water and mud. We had to carry earth fifty to 100 meters. The clay could no longer be transported because the ground was very slippery and we had to carry it on shovels. Woe to anyone who got stuck in the mud. They would beat us every step of the way, raining anywhere from five to twenty-five blows on our bare bodies. On the very first day we brought five dead and three badly wounded back to the camp . . . Heveš from Sarajevo threw himself under a train on the third day, it was just passing by when we had to cross the tracks. A little later, Dr. Vita Kajon, director of the former City Savings Bank in Sarajevo, poisoned himself."[13] Even ISC state officials showed how severe the conditions were: engineer Görlich, technical adviser at the Ministry of Transportation and Public Works, at a meeting of the Economic Committee of the Croatian National Parliament in June 1942, said that "we got the camp in Jasenovac, but there has been little success. The workers are no good and there are fewer of them every day," and a member of the same committee, Hundrić, added that he had "watched the prisoners working, and some dug using spades while other carried the earth in their bare hands."[14]

The earliest document from those days about transporting people to Jasenovac was dated September 11, 1941, and signed by Eugen Kvaternik, who ordered "fifty Communists and Chetniks from Bijeljina . . . sent to Jasenovac transit camp."[15] In September, transports also arrived from Zavrtnica in Zagreb; Egon Berger arrived in a transport of several hundred Jews from Zagreb on September 11, and on September 20 another 199 Jews arrived, also from Zavrtnica.[16] Internees were then brought from the transit camps of Kruščica near Travnik, Vukovar, Đakovo, and elsewhere.[17] In Jasenovac II, in two barracks for Jews and one for Serbs "that were for a maximum of 400 beds, they crammed over 1,300 prisoners in each," so that "it was not possible to lie down, people sat and dozed all night."[18] Oto Breyer also remembered that two-thirds of the internees were Jews and one third were Serbs, and so the privileged prisoners—the camp foremen who assigned men to work places—were "two Jews, Diamantstein and Spiller, and one Serb, whose name I don't know."[19] When he was being interrogated in the UDB prison in Zagreb in 1947, Ljubo Miloš stated that in early October 1941, at the order of Luburić, he personally made a list of the internees in Krapje and Bročice, and that there were at least 4,000, perhaps even 5,000 prisoners at that time.[20] Transports continued to arrive, but the number of prisoners in Jasenovac I and II did not increase significantly. With hunger and beatings, the spread of illness, and "harder and harder work, our resistance began to weaken"[21] and more and more people died, and soon the first group liquidations also began.[22]

The garrisons in Jasenovac I and II were part of the Ustasha Thirteenth Battalion and the Lika Battalion, which had previously done the same duty in Slana and Jadovno Camps. Second Lieutenant Ante Marić was commander of Jasenovac I, Second Lieutenant Ivan Rako of Jasenovac II.

They had both previously been officers in the command of Slana Camp on Pag, and, before that, Ustasha returnees who had emigrated in 1933. The security commanders and other officials in those early days of the Jasenovac camps were also people tested in Jadovno and Slana: Second Lieutenants Vjekoslav Ile, Ivica Brkljačić, Anton Remenar, Maks Očić, Ustasha returnee Božo Đerek, Junior Second Lieutenants Matijević and Karla, Lance-Sergeant Prpić, etc.[23] They simply transferred the methods they had used in Pag and Velebit to Krapje and Bročica.

On October 7, 1941, Maks Luburić gave a speech in Krapje Camp, "good in style, sophisticated in content." He did not threaten, he flattered his listeners, most of them Jews, saying that "in the past the Croats had lived in harmony with the Jews and that the Croats had not forgotten Dr. Frank, that it was not the will of the Ustashe and of Zagreb to treat the Jews badly." But, said Luburić, "a certain Dr. Büchler wanted to found a Communist republic somewhere on Mount Plješivica, and the Ustashe will know how to deal with attempts of that kind." Later, the internees heard that eighty-three prisoners had been killed because of alleged connections to the supposed Dr. Büchler.[24]

All who survived the first months in Jasenovac mentioned hunger as the most relentless torture: "Hunger destroyed even that light doze we would drop into just before dawn."[25] Breakfast was "a little warm water," lunch "several beans without any fat or flour," and "supper was like lunch." Sometimes, instead of beans for lunch they got "two or three boiled potatoes . . . we all had just one wish—to eat our fill. Our greatest desire was bread . . . this was the main thought for all the prisoners."[26] Egon Berger, who lived through forty-four months of Jasenovac, said, "To eat my fill, that was the thought that followed me all through my camp life."[27]

Peasants from the surrounding villages saved Vladimir Carin from the worst hunger several times, they "slyly winked, carefully caught the moment when the Ustasha guards were looking the other way, and threw ears of corn along the road from their carts . . . Hidden in the bushes, we would ravenously shell them."[28] In a statement given in 1945 and again in 1971, Albert Maestro "wishes to especially say" that the "civilian population of Jasenovac and Krapje villages tried to help us inmates with food on every occasion, although this put them in danger . . . I feel the need and duty to thank them, in my own name and in the name of many who are now dead, for the comfort and food they secretly gave us to ease our hunger, and in this way they really did prolong the lives of some people until they got the chance to save their lives themselves by escaping."[29]

To still their terrible hunger "people ate grass and leaves, but these were very difficult to digest . . . From time to time we would find cabbage roots or turnips, carrots, or something else in the ground." The prisoners ate, as a special treat, a dog that had been run over by a peasant cart, and there were also cases of scatophagia—prisoners removing undigested beans or the like from the feces in the Ustasha latrine.[30] People began to die of starvation in October 1941: Zagreb engineering student Ivo Dirnbach was sick with dysentery. He was tormented by terrible hunger and he somehow acquired a pot of beans. "The doctor came up to him and told him he must not eat that because he was too ill, but Dirnbach begged him in a tearful voice saying that he wanted to die full. He ate the beans and put an end to his torment."[31]

People worked all day. The prisoners had to come back to the camp for lunch, "so tired that we could hardly lift out feet, yet we had to sing on the way back." Since the worksite was about three kilometers away, they walked about twelve kilometers every day. They worked every day, conditions became very bad due to the autumn rain and Ustasha ill-treatment, and "those who were weaker were completely exhausted, some got serious bloody diarrhea, and if they did not manage to stop it in several days, they died."[32]

Beating was part of the camp ritual: after one beating, only thirteen internees out of twenty survived.[33] Vladimir Carin described his own severe beating in detail.[34] The cold and the lack of vitamins and hunger made the prisoners' legs swell, their eyesight deteriorated, they got wrinkles. Before dying, they "became a mask from which only their eyes protruded." The prisoners could tell how long someone would last just by looking at them—two, three days. "People died easily and in full consciousness." Before he died, engineer Erich Neumann (1906) divided his property among his friends, and those were his last coherent words. "Several minutes later, he began fantasizing that he would be going to Bucharest by plane and that he did not care to remain here. The next day, he was dead." In the winter of 1941–1942, about twenty people died every day just of hunger and exhaustion.[35] Probably around the New Year's Day 1942, Zagreb wholesale merchant Geza Marton (48, who had converted to Catholicism in 1938) was waiting in line for lunch. It "seems that he lost his balance from weakness and cold and when he bent over the cauldron he suddenly fell inside. Two other prisoners from the line pulled him out of the hot cauldron and threw him to the side. He was dead."[36] At first, "dying left a painful impression; later, we did not experience death so badly . . . we were ready for it every day."[37]

From the very first days, when the transports from Gospić and Zavrtnica started leaving for Jasenovac, the Jewish Community in Zagreb tried to help the prisoners. It sent a large number of parcels and some money through the Red Cross directly to Jastrebarsko, where the transports from Gospić sometimes waited for several days. Oto Breyer saw the Ustashe keep a large Red Cross delivery for themselves.[38] Still, many parcels, some probably after being "taxed," reached those to whom they were addressed, and some addressees were ready to share what they had received with others. On April 11, 1942, Đuro Medić made a statement before Nedić's Commissariat for Refugees and Displaced Persons in Belgrade, saying that "we got no food at all from the Ustasha authorities in Jastrebarsko, and we Serbs and the Croats were fed by the Jews who received parcels from home, and they also bought food for money."[39] When Vladimir Carin arrived in Jasenovac II (Bročice), he still had some walnut pie that Rabbi Freiberger himself had given him in Zavrtnica, which did a little to ease the first hungry days for him and several other inmates.[40] Five Serb prisoners from Bijeljina, who were in Bročice in early September, stated on April 13, 1942, in Belgrade, that "the Jews who were in the same camp received food from their Jewish Communities, and they took a little of that and gave it to us."[41] This confirms that the efforts of the Zagreb Jewish Community, despite the strict isolation of Jasenovac Camps I and II, were not completely in vain. Some of the plentiful deliveries sent by the Community did manage to reach the prisoners in September 1941, which eased their suffering for a very short time but could not affect their subsequent fate. According to Oto Breyer, "on about September 20, all the prisoners had their money taken from them, and anything valuable, and after this followed a period of torture and ill treatment of prisoners at work and in the camp itself."[42]

At the end of October, about 1,000 Jewish men between the ages of sixteen and sixty were arrested in Sarajevo and sent in groups to Jasenovac I and II. Regularly informed about this from Sarajevo, the Zagreb Jewish Community tried to intervene. "We described the situation to the head of the Jewish Section [Vilko Kühnel], but we realized that nothing could be done about it," said President Kon and Secretary Klein in Sarajevo, reporting on the result of their intercession. "These internees will probably be placed in a camp in Jasenovac and share the fate of the other internees."[43] New transports soon arrived from Sarajevo and from Visoko, and the Zagreb Community was informed about them all and sought ways to help.[44]

To neutralize the reports of hunger, sickness, and killing in the camps, at some time in late September or early October 1941 the Ustasha authorities tried to convince representatives of the Zagreb Jewish Community that "a reservation will be organized for Jews in which all Croatian Jews will be accommodated. This reservation is to cover about 50,000 acres of land (just over 20,000 hectares or more than 200 km^2) with eleven deserted Orthodox villages, somewhere near Jasenovac. There, the Jews are to have their self-government under the supervision of a state official." These proposals were, of course, never serious. Nevertheless, in mid-October, the Jewish Community made a study about founding a "special Jewish colony." In the accompanying information, they requested that "sending Jews to camps should stop immediately . . . requisitioning Jewish apartments should stop . . . conditions in the camps should be made bearable . . . all people who are ill, old, and women with small children should be released."[45] There are no records showing that the authorities ever considered these documents seriously, and the gloomy tone of the letters sent from the Jewish Community of Zagreb in October and November indicates that the leading people in the Community no longer had any illusions about what was going on in Jasenovac, but were still "clutching at straws" to at least improve what they could.

According to the statement of Ljubo Miloš, the first mass liquidation of prisoners took place in late October or early November 1941, in Jasenovac I: "Luburić ordered Lieutenant Remenar, who was at that time camp quartermaster, to liquidate Krapje Camp by starvation. Remenar began to carry out the command, but this led to a prisoner rebellion. Since the rebellion took place at night, the guards opened fire and a large number of prisoners were killed on the spot. After the rebellion, in reprisal, Luburić brought the Traveling Summary Court to Jasenovac, headed by Judge Ivan Vignjević, who sentenced about one hundred prisoners from Krapje Camp to death. Luburić shot them in person. In my opinion, this was the first mass murder of prisoners in Jasenovac and Krapje, and, to the best of my recollection, this was also the only liquidation where some attempt was made to provide legal grounds. All later liquidations were carried out without any preceding investigation, trial, or anything of the kind. I think that there were several more trials, but these were only individual cases."[46] The memories of surviving prisoners do not contradict Miloš's description, but they look on the first mass murder in a somewhat different light: for example, Oto Breyer claims that it was "a rebellion that the Ustashe had stage-managed" so as to find justification for mass liquidation.[47]

In October and November, "it rained without stopping for three weeks. In the barracks, water rose above the edges of the bottom beds. Several prisoners died in each barrack every night."[48] Finally, the Sava broke through the weak and unfinished embankments. "The camp protruded from the immense amount of water like an island from the sea. The Ustashe could do nothing but move us somewhere else."[49] Jasenovac Camps I and II were abandoned between November 14 and 16, and all the surviving prisoners remembered that the move was a real ordeal. Of about 3,000 to 4,000 prisoners in both camps, only about 1,500 arrived in Jasenovac III,[50] and Leon Koen thinks that "about 2,000 to 2,500 completely exhausted inmates were moved to Jasenovac III–Brickyard."[51] They were temporarily accommodated in the Brickyard building because the barracks for the prisoners were still being built.[52] On that first night in the Brickyard, "50 prisoners from the Jasenovac II group died because they had been so badly beaten on the way that they simply collapsed."[53] The gravediggers, who later removed traces from Jasenovac III, said that they had buried 1,200 bodies in Jasenovac II.[54] They encountered horrifying scenes in the barracks of Krapje Camp: about 550 unburied frozen bodies that had been locked in there and left after the camp was abandoned.

Winter 1941–1942: Death Camp

"Luburić himself directed the move of Camps I and II and the organization of Camp III," said Ljubo Miloš, who was at that time appointed commander of the prisoners' work service in Camp III.[55] In September 1941, Luburić spent ten days "getting acquainted with" the camp in Sachsenhausen-Oranienburg near Berlin,[56] from which he returned with some new ideas, especially about "founding work facilities in the camp."[57] Sachsenhausen, founded in 1936, was one of the three largest concentration camps in the Third Reich, through which about 200,000 prisoners passed by 1945—German Jews and political opponents of the regime, anti-fascists from occupied lands, and Soviet prisoners, of whom more than 100,000 died or were killed in the camp itself. It had several industrial plants where the prisoners, numbering about 25,000, worked for the needs of the German army.[58] Siegfried Kasche, envoy of the Third Reich in the ISC, claimed that "Captain Luburić made plans for building the (Jasenovac) camp while he was still in exile. After he had toured the German installations, these plans were improved."[59]

Modeling himself on Sachsenhausen, Luburić obviously planned to use the Bačić plants in Jasenovac to establish a similar combined-type camp: production for army needs and the isolation and liquidation of the "undesirables." However, there had not been time to adapt the Bačić plants by the end of 1941, nor had the entire area been prepared to receive a large number of prisoners.

The position of the Jasenovac camp system, and especially Jasenovac III, was very carefully chosen: part of the camp, including Stara Gradiška Prison added later and the Bačić plants, did not have to be built anew. Because of the proximity of the Sava and the Una rivers, and the very inaccessible and flooded area of Gradina, it was practically unconquerable from the south, and the Veliki Strug canal afforded rather good protection from the north. The camp site was in the middle of the marshy Lonjsko polje, called Mokro polje (Wet Field). In March 1942, one of the inmates mentioned, as an essential characteristic, that the camp was "on marshland and inaccessible, and escape from it was impossible," and that "this was an area that already held the plants of Bačić and Co."[60] The Partisans never dared to attack the camp because they estimated that, even if they managed to overcome the very strong Ustasha units, saving the inmates would be difficult. "We, the Slavonian Partisans, wanted to liquidate that accursed Pavelić slaughterhouse in Jasenovac more than anything. But wishes were one thing, and the possibility of doing anything something else."[61] The Ustashe could defend the camp relatively easily, and help could arrive very quickly by rail from not-too-distant Zagreb and Sisak. Jasenovac was also a very good choice because it was easy to transport prisoners there: a railway line already existed, and the camp was centrally placed in relation to the important Jewish communities between Karlovac and the Danube, which the Ustashe planned to deport. The camp was also near important concentrations of the Serb poulation in the Banija and Kordun regions, in northern Bosnia and western Slavonia.[62]

Floods and incessant rain during the first half of November threatened Jasenovac III, as well. On November 13, the Ustasha Police Directorate sent a telegram informing the Great County of Vrhbosna "that no one is to be sent to Jasenovac Camp until further notice."[63] Probably under the pressure of this situation and the arrival of about 1,500 survivors from the abandoned Camps I and II, on November 14, Luburić and Miloš carried out the first slaughter of a large group of prisoners in Jasenovac III Camp and "from that day on, mass killings continued."[64] When the second group of prisoners from the abandoned Jasenovac II, among them Leon Koen, arrived "at front of the gates of the main camp, there was a great heap of four to five hundred dead there. Semi-nude skeletons were piled one above another. In the morning, the Ustashe made the camp prisoners throw them in a cart and take them across the Sava by ferry, where they were buried in a common trench. Most of them were Serbs and older Jews, including many distinguished ones. I remember that these included Rabbi Ham Moše Nisim Papo."[65]

These methods very quickly put an end to the "excess" of prisoners, and probably the danger of flooding also abated, so, on November 18, the Sarajevo County Police sent notice that they were sending "to Jasenovac concentration camp" 116 people with a standard accompanying list of names and personal data. Under the heading of "religion," these included 47 "Greek Eastern," 39 "Roman Catholic," 17 "Islam," 10 "Jewish," and 3 "Jewish Roman-Catholic." However, 11 of the "Roman Catholics" had markedly Jewish surnames (Papo, Stern); obviously, they were Jews who had converted to Catholicism but who were nevertheless considered Jewish according to the laws passed on April 30, 1941. This is the first document showing that women also were sent to Jasenovac—on this occasion, twenty-three. The political qualification of these people is absurd—107 were recorded as "*com.*" (Communist) and 9 as "*čet.*" (Chetnik)—because the list clearly shows that entire Serb and Jewish families were included, which means that the criterion was religious and racial, not political.[66]

In coming days, transports of people arrested all over the ISC arrived at Jasenovac III in increasing numbers. The quasi-legal grounds was Pavelić's Legal Provision on Deporting Undesirable and Dangerous Persons to Enforced Detention in Assembly and Work Camps, passed on November 25, 1941, whereby "the decision to send a person to enforced detention . . . shall be made by the Ustasha Police as a branch of the Ustasha Security Service," and " . . . there shall be no legal remedy nor appeal to the administrative court" against this decision, and "the detention in transit and work camps may not be less than three months nor more than three years."[67] According to the testimony of Ljubo Miloš, after that day "two kinds of prisoners came to Jasenovac. The first were sent in accordance with regular RAVSIGUR decisions, which included the duration of their term in camp . . . The second kind were the mass transports sent from almost all parts of the ISC. These prisoners came without any decisions, possibly only with a list of names."[68] Miloš claimed that "Luburić ordered that there should always be about 3,000 prisoners in the camp, because this number was in most cases sufficient to satisfy all the needs of the work service . . . There were cases when there were as many as 5,000 prisoners in the camp, but this could never last long because in such cases the 'excessive' were liquidated . . . This liquation of 'excess' prisoners was carried out constantly from the foundation of the camps, right up to the last day of their existence . . . When the number of prisoners was satisfactory, new prisoners were usually accompanied by Matković,[69] who decided how many people would be sent to the camp, while the others were taken straight for liquidation."[70]

This went on, almost incessantly, from mid-November 1941 to March 1942. The greatest liquidation of the "excess" prisoners took place on Christmas Eve and Christmas Day 1941. With certain unimportant differences, all the Jasenovac III survivors remember it. On Christmas Eve, Luburić gave another of his hypocritical speeches to the prisoners, "Well, I had to break off my Christmas holiday because I found out about injustice in this camp . . . so I came here to make order. I was in Đakovo and there I gave the order for preparations to be made to receive old and sick prisoners from Jasenovac. All the rest of you will make up the work camp."[71] Many believed this to be a Christmas present for the internees, and, in answer to Luburić's call more than a thousand, hurried to the Administrative Registry Office to apply for "transfer" to Đakovo. Berger and Carin describe how those who applied were greeted by machine guns in front of the Administrative Registry Office and "1,200 people died in an incredibly short time." The other witnesses say that this took place on the first or second day of Christmas and that the prisoners who applied for Đakovo were taken out of the camp and liquidated there.[72] After that, "going to Đakovo" was a black-humor euphemism for liquidation. During the postwar investigations, Ljubo Miloš claimed that there could have been up to 500 victims of that slaughter.[73] People heard some Ustashe say that those Jews were killed on Christmas Night "in honor of Christ."[74] One of the men killed in this way was Milan Israel of Zagreb.[75]

During this period, in late 1941 and early 1942, the number of Serbs began to exceed the number of Jews and very quickly there were several times more Serbs in the camp. In retaliation for a group of Partisans breaking into the town of Karlovac, on November 25, over 300 prisoners were sent to Jasenovac, some 260 Serbs and the rest mostly Jews. As far as is known, almost no one from that group was ever heard of again, and, according to some testimonies, most were liquidated immediately on arrival.[76] In January 1942, the largest group, consisting of about 1,500 Zagreb Jews, was brought to Jasenovac (and Stara Gradiška).[77] According to Jakov Kabiljo, "Jews from all parts of the ISC were brought in the spring, but individuals and smaller groups, families, came later, in the summer. In the spring, fewer than 10 percent of the great number of young and old people who had arrived by the end of 1941 were left."[78]

In general, the winter of 1941–1942 was the worst period for the prisoners in all the forty-four months of the existence of the Jasenovac camp system. At first, just after the camps were founded, people worked on the Sava embankment, which "exhausted the prisoners so much that they died in great numbers, or, when they grew quite weak and could not work any more, they were simply killed." As the percentage of Jews was highest in the camp in 1941, it seems very logical to conclude that great numbers of them died in the above way.[79] "Luburić in person determined the amount of food distributed to the prisoners . . . It can clearly be seen that the prisoners' nutrition and health were purposely kept at the bare minimum," said Ljubo Miloš.[80] "That year, the winter was unprecedented," described Jakov Kabiljo. "The snow was high, and the temperature kept decreasing from mid-December. The prisoners dragged themselves around the camp without food, half-naked and barefoot, unshaven and dirty. There was no water because it had frozen, so people did not wash at all. The dirt resulted in disease (typhus) that killed many prisoners. Many people also died of cold . . . It is not known how many people died every day, or disappeared, but it is enough if I say that about 120 prisoners were grave-diggers . . . who carried the dead out, buried them, threw them in the Sava . . . (and) they were not allowed any contact with the other prisoners so as not to give away what they had seen and what they had to do. That is why the grave-diggers were liquidated every two–three months . . . and they kept changing them."[81] Gabrijel Winter, a private clerk from Zagreb, who drove a horse-drawn cart that transported goods in and out of Jasenovac, and thus managed to escape, testified that the group of grave-diggers was headed by "Dudo Bararon, a Jew from Tuzla, his coat unbuttoned so that his revolver could be seen. Besides Danon, he was the most notorious member of what was known as the 'D' Group that dug trenches for the dead, and they too killed alongside the Ustashe and photographed the victims"—but not even they escaped death, because "no living witness of those terrible deeds was allowed to survive."[82]

The Ustasha authorities in Zagreb were not completely impervious to the horrific tales that were spreading about Jasenovac or to the objections of the Catholic Church and the Italian and German representatives. Thus, Dido Kvaternik brought an international commission to Jasenovac on February 6, 1942, but this was an obvious ploy of which even the commission members must have been aware, because not one of them spoke a single word with any of the prisoners. To give the visitors a good impression of the camp, prior to their visit, new beds and bedclothes were sent to the camp surgery and infirmary from Zagreb. Before the commission came, apples were placed on the bedside tables, which never happened before or after. For days before the arrival of the commission, the prisoners were made to tidy up the camp, and got better food for three days. All the inmates got colored armbands with numbers: yellow for the Jews, blue for the Serbs, red for the Croats, green for the Muslims. They were strictly forbidden to talk to the commission members and told to answer any question only by, "I am number so and so, you can get data from the administration." Those who did not look too bad were put to bed to "act like patients, and it seems that some, who were completely exhausted, were killed to prevent the commission from seeing them in that condition."[83] Siegfried Kasche, the German ambassador in Zagreb, later said that "there is good reason to reject as unfounded all the rumors that are spreading about Jasenovac," because the camp leaves "a completely irreproachable and good impression." Kasche added that "at the moment, there are about 1,000 prisoners, among them about 75 percent Jews. The rest are Roma, Serbs, and Communists."[84] It is not known how the discrepancy between this number and that mentioned by Ljubo Miloš (3,000 to 5,000 prisoners) arose: it is possible that Kasche was misinformed, but it is also possible that the camp authorities killed as many as two thirds of the prisoners who looked "bad" and who were not to be seen by the visitors.

After this visit, articles appeared in the Zagreb press, such as "Jasenovac Is Neither a Place of Torture Nor a Health Resort" and "Jasenovac Is Not a Sanatorium Nor Is It a Torture House."[85] They wanted to create the impression that treatment was strict but just, and that the prisoners were doing good work with great enthusiasm (the title "A Firm Will for Honesty"). The author claimed that "three types can be seen among the Jews. The first throw themselves into their work and do all they can to improve their temporary position and forget everything else. The second remain faithful to themselves: they seek a warm place, take up work quickly when someone is coming, laugh disrespectfully right in people's faces and pretend that it is all nothing. The third are serious, they look in front of them with vacant faces in which the shadow of broken resistance can be seen." The text ends with the conclusion that Croats in small villages live worse than these prisoners do.

After this visit by the commission, the prisoners who were "acting" like patients in the surgery and infirmary were thrown out of bed, the temporarily improved food was reduced to the old starvation level, and everything returned to what it had been.

Although under the strictest order to maintain silence, the gravediggers did tell their fellow-prisoners something of the brutality they had witnessed. We do not quote these indirect descriptions because they have no confirmation, except for one, the testimony of Albert Maestro, a chance eyewitness, whose detailed testimony about camp conditions can generally be included among the most sober and most measured. His statement was taken down and witnessed in October 1945, when his memories were still vivid: "On Christmas Day 1941, the Ustashe ran into the Serb barracks yelling, mallets in their hands. As soon as they entered, they began to hit the inmates and tie their hands together with wire. The long column of prisoners with a heavy escort, headed by this group of Luburić's men, went to the eastern exit. About 300 meters from the camp, a trench had already been dug, long and narrow, for these prisoners. At that time, my shift on the main gate had ended and I went into the new Farm Barracks, from where I could see what was going on. Although I was so shaken that I thought that I would break down mentally and physically, something in me kept telling me that I must endure. I wanted at least one witness to such atrocities to survive . . . The prisoners were brought there and made to stand in a line on both sides of the trench. They were ordered to turn and face the trench, and from behind them the Ustashe hit each on the head with a mallet. They fell unconscious, and then the butchers finished them off with knives. I noticed that some of the prisoners tried to get hit as soon as they could so as not to watch the others being butchered."[86]

The Year 1942

Conditions for some Jasenovac prisoners improved in the spring of 1942, and this was not due only to better weather. "From my arrest in 1941 to April 1942, I could not send word to anyone outside the camp, nor could the other prisoners, so that people outside did not know whether I was alive, or where I was,"[87] but "at the end of March 1942, permission came for prisoners to write (postcards) and receive parcels."[88] "You can imagine our joy when the first parcels and replies from families began to arrive . . . True, they took away all the best things from the parcels, but any small amount of food that they left meant a lot to us."[89] In the Zagreb Jewish Community, there is precise evidence about the postcards that arrived from Jasenovac and about the parcels sent there after June 1942.[90]

During the winter 1941–1942, a system of selection among the prisoners was gradually adopted. Those who were skilled in some crafts or in any needed profession were sent to the camp production plants, workshops, and the farm, where the prisoners received relatively better treatment. Many from these groups survived several years of camp life, but, in the end, they did not escape the fate of most of the other prisoners.[91] A second group consisted of younger and healthier prisoners without desirable professional skills, who were given various kinds of physical work; under the cruel conditions of building the embankments along the Sava in the winter and spring of 1942, they died quickly, while those who did other kinds of work (loading and unloading, farm work, and the like) survived longer.[92] The third group were the older and weaker people, who were assigned to "Group C" together with the other unnecessary and "undesirable" prisoners, and were later sent to a special part of the camp called "Three C," in which people starved to death very quickly or ended up on mass execution sites.[93]

According to some original Ustasha plans, Jasenovac III was to become the center of weapons production for the ISC army, and, with that in mind, Luburić organized a drafting office where some very ambitious building plans were made for the construction of large factory plants.[94] Almost none of this was realized, but the existing Bačić plants did start operations, mostly in spring 1942, and, by the end of 1944, they employed an average of 3,000 inmates. The brickyard, sawmill, chain factory, tool shop, and ceramics and gunsmith's workshops produced goods for external customers, while the electrical power plant, carpenters, cobblers, tailors, smithy, mill, leatherworks, car repair shop, construction unit, joiners, builders and technical draftsmen mostly worked for the needs of the camp and the Ustasha garrison, which, together with the surrounding defense system, amounted to about 1,500 soldiers.[95] There was also the rag hut, where the inmates had to search the clothing of prisoners who had been killed or had died to find any jewelry, money, or other valuables they had sewn into their clothes. This was how, in 1942, Adolf Schwarzenberg found the clothes of his wife, Sida, who had lost her life in Stara Gradiška.[96] There was also a thriving farm with cowsheds, a pigsty, a butchery, an icehouse, and a bakery, and occasional "mobile farms" in Feričanci, Gređani, Jablanac, Bistrica, Mlaka, and elsewhere.

In some of these plants, there were a lot of Jews, since they were able to supply craftsmen and professionals in many fields, especially the Jews from Bosnia. Jews also outnumbered the other prisoners in Jasenovac IV, the small separate camp in the former leather factory in the village of Jasenovac itself. Established in January 1942, it employed up to 200 inmates and produced leather items for the ISC army until early 1945. According to survivors, there was the least amount of mistreatment and killing of prisoners in this camp for three years, but, in the end, in April 1945, almost all were killed except for eleven who saved themselves in the breakout.[97]

Stara Gradiška Prison was reorganized into a "transit and work camp" and assigned to the Jasenovac system as Jasenovac V by decision of the Ministry of the Interior of February 17, 1942.[98] It developed into a kind of supplementary plant, a smaller replica of Jasenovac III in almost every aspect. During 1942, it cooked for a daily average of about 3,000 prisoners. Of these, about 850 men and about 300 women worked in permanent production plants and other workshops and on the camp farm. At this time, until October 1942, major transports for mass liquidation also came to Stara Gradiška from time to time.[99] Stara Gradiška differed somewhat from Jasenovac III in that it had relatively more political prisoners, Croatian women and men, and women and children who were mostly Serb.[100] There were relatively fewer women in Jasenovac III, where separate quarters for women existed from the beginning of 1942.

In a memo dated December 30, 1941, RAVSIGUR informed all the Grand Counties that "the commanders of transit camps must not and will not accept one single person in camp without a decision issued by the Ustasha Security Service, Office I, about sending him or her to camp."[101] The county police adhered to this memo, but the units of the Ustaša Military and the Ustasha Defense did not. Right up until October 1942, many waves of new prisoner transports, without any decisions or accompanying papers of any kind, kept arriving at Jasenovac and Stara Gradiška. But, by 1942, and especially in 1943, the proportion of prisoners sent on the basis of administrative decisions, with specific sentences of up to three years, increased, although this did not constitute any kind of dependable defense from Ustasha arbitrariness and killing in the camps themselves. The "three-year prisoners," people sentenced to camp for three years by the Ustasha Police, were treated especially harshly. Allegedly, in June 1942, a transport of about 300 "three-year prisoners" arrived at Jasenovac and was immediately sent on to Gradina, "where the Gypsies killed them."[102] In 1942, on August 22 and 23, "three-year women prisoners" arrived in Stara Gradiška, among them Margareta and Stela Berger from Zagreb, and it seems that they were killed on the same day.[103] The brothers Jakov and Edo Präger were arrested in the street in Zagreb, then taken to the prison in Sava Road, then to Jasenovac, where they were killed as soon as they arrived, allegedly because the guards had found money hidden in their socks.[104] The UNS card for Ruža Singer from Kutina—"religion: RC/ until 1941 Jewish"—says that she was "arrested on June 27, 1942, during the cleansing of Jews from Kutina and its surroundings" and that "she was sent to Stara Gradiška Camp for three years by decision No. 39295 of Office I"; it was later added on the card that "by UNS, Office I, decision No. 86139, of September 24, 1942, word was sent that the above died in camp on July 29, 1942."[105] There is evidence that some prisoners were killed even after the order came for their release.[106] Nevertheless, quite a large number of prisoners sentenced to shorter terms were released from camp according to the regular procedure after their term was over, but these hardly ever included Jewish men or women. There were no Jews in the first amnesty for forty-nine prisoners, which was "read out on February 22, 1942, before the lined-up internees,"[107] nor in later amnesties, which by 1945 covered at least 500 prisoners.

From January 23–31, 1942, a conference was held in the German Embassy in Zagreb at which "the Croatian government expressed its readiness to move to Serbia all the persons demanded," and that "in cases of transfer from a camp, the members of the (more immediate) family would also be transferred," but "detainees may take with them to Serbia only such things as they have with them in camp."[108] In accordance with this decision, the first group of about 450 Serbs was transported from the ISC to Serbia on March 30, 1942, among them thirteen internees from Jasenovac and Stara Gradiška.[109] Then followed several such transports.[110] In June 1942, a "total of 1,200 persons arrived in Zemun for the Viking work drive. All were from the Croatian camp of Jasenovac."[111] Viking was the code name for enforced transportation of detainees to Germany, mostly to work in the war industry and in agriculture to make up for increasing labor shortages. According to Ustasha Major Ante Vrban, about 10,000 men and women prisoners, mostly Serbs but also Croats and Muslims, were taken from the Jasenovac system to work in Germany.[112] The last large group of about 600 prisoners was taken from Jasenovac to Germany on February 18, 1945, among them some old inmates from 1941 and 1942, who were liberated on May 5 in Linz by the American army.[113] The Ustasha authorities never included Jews in these transports, nor would the Germans have accepted them.

Concurrently with the occasional release of a relatively small number of prisoners, most mass liquidations of large prisoner transports to Jasenovac III and Stara Gradiška took place throughout almost all of 1942. On March 31, 1942, the Army Headquarters issued a command saying, among other things, "If an attack on the Home Guards or Ustashe, land or rail postal communications, or state institutions takes place near a village, the said village shall be searched and all the persons (female and male, old people, and children) from all the homes in which no men are found (escaped) shall be taken to concentration camps as hostages. The houses, livestock, wheat, and everything else shall become state property."[114] A notice to all concerned was issued by the Poglavnik's Headquarters, No. 400, dated April 27, 1942, saying that "the command of the Ustasha Control Service has informed us that the Jasenovac transit and work camp can receive an unlimited number of prisoners."[115] After this, on May 20, the Supreme Army Command instructed all available regiments to round up, by order of the Ustasha Control Service of May 16, No. 24789, "all the Gypsies in their area and in agreement with the competent county district send them to Jasenovac."[116] From the reports submitted by the county districts, it follows that at least about 10,000 Roma were sent to Jasenovac during the following month as part of this action.[117] They were temporarily accommodated in camp "Three C," where all their belongings were taken from them. Then they were liquidated to the last person, most of them in Granik and Gradina, in a most brutal manner that many publications describe in the most atrocious detail.[118]

After the winter of 1941–1942, Jasenovac and Stara Gradiška camps received the most prisoners in June and July 1942. At that time, in addition to the arrival of Roma, mass transports also came from areas in the Prijedor, Dubica, Gradiška, Bosanski Novi, and Banja Luka Districts "cleansed" during the German-Ustasha offensive on Mount Kozara. From lists of names, many researchers consider that at least 68,000 civilians were rounded up and deported from the areas around Kozara. The Jasenovac camps became graves for many thousands of them, probably up to 15,000. In the Bosanska Dubica municipality alone, which suffered the most, there is a list of 5,523 names of people who disappeared during Ustasha reprisals, mostly in Jasenovac and Stara Gradiška.[119] For many more, Jasenovac and Stara Gradiška were transit stations in which they were robbed, starved, and tortured, but their lives were spared. "The Jasenovac Transit Camps Command recently sent 155 railway cars of Kozara refugees to the area of the Požega District, which is about 10,000 people. In answer to my request by telegraph to Ustasha Major Luburić, sending those refugees to the territory of this district has been discontinued," say the records of the Slavonska Požega County District of August 30, 1942.[120] About 6,000 people from Kozara were similarly transported to the Daruvar area, several thousands via Zemun, to work in Germany.

More than 10,000 Kozara children under twelve remained in the Jasenovac III and Stara Gradiška camps, and in a temporary camp near Sisak. Their parents had been killed or sent to work in Germany, where children of their age could not go. Very quickly, word reached Zagreb about the terrible suffering of these children: they were starving, very many were ill, many died. The persistent Dijana Budisavljević, an Austrian woman married to a prominent Zagreb surgeon and university professor, managed through her connections with high German military representatives in Zagreb to obtain a permit to visit the children's hospital and other quarters for children in the Stara Gradiška Camp on July 9 and 10. The terrible scenes, much worse than anything that had been heard in Zagreb, horrified her.[121] She galvanized all her acquaintances and connections, threatened to go public, and managed to coerce the senior German officers to obtain Pavelić's agreement to release the Kozara children from Jasenovac Camp. With the help of the Croatian Red Cross, the Catholic Caritas, and several civil servants in the Social Welfare Department of the Ministry of Public Administration, about 7,000 Kozara children were placed in hospitals, homes for deaf and dumb, and other children in various institutions, in camps in Jastrebarsko and Gornja Rijeka, and in private homes. Almost as many children, probably about 5,000, died of disease and hunger or were killed in the Jasenovac camps.[122]

The concentration camp in Đakovo was liquidated between June 15 and July 7, 1942. Between 2,400 and 3,200 Jewish women and children were transported to Jasenovac III and left in front of the Brickyard. For days, the locked railway cars stood on the track and people in them died *en masse* of heat, hunger, and thirst. Finally, the survivors were "ferried across the Sava, where they were killed."[123]

German military commanders in the ISC and their intelligence officers used various channels to complain about the Ustasha terror against the Serbs, which was making things difficult for them: it increased the chaos and incited armed rebellion. There is no doubt that this was one of the reasons why Pavelić forced Eugen Dido Kvaternik to resign in September 1942. However, in September and October, Luburić and the units of his Ustasha Defense continued to round up and deport residents of Serb Orthodox villages in the broader environs of Jasenovac. On September 20, 1,008 captives were brought to Jasenovac from the villages of Vinska, Vrela, Velika Brusnica, Mala Brusnica, Donji Klakar, and Gornji Klakar. The duly supplied list shows that these were mostly women, older men, and children, twenty-three of whom were babies less than one year old, the youngest only four days.[124] The previously "quiet and loyal villages" Crkveni Bok, Ivanjski Bok, and Strmen got their turn on October 13, and about 1,000 people were sent to Jasenovac. By order of Luburić and under the command of Ljubo Miloš, the villages were completely razed.[125] It seems that this was the last straw for the German military representatives, because it all took place near the Zagreb-Belgrade railway line, which they had under heavy guard. Glaise von Horstenau, the main German army representative in the ISC, immediately went to Crkveni Bok and the neighboring devastated villages. He demanded that Pavelić punish very strictly "his faithful followers whom [he, i.e., Horstenau,] called criminals, murderers, and tyrants."[126]

This time, Pavelić had to give in. Luburić and Ljubo Miloš were dismissed, placed under investigation and imprisoned (which was in fact a farce because they were soon released and appointed to similar duties).[127] Before this, Luburić had enough time to remove some of the evidence: the relevant part of the records was burned, a "Group D" of grave-diggers was liquidated, the prisoners of the compromising Camp III C and the camp itself were liquidated. At that time, Jewish men and women who did not work in the camp production plants, hospital, or farm were also liquidated.[128] Dr. Pavao Spitzer, a prisoner and doctor in the prisoners' hospital in Jasenovac III in 1942, testified in 1945 before the People's District Court in Zagreb: "On November 20, 1942, Ivan (Hans) Hochsinger was taken from his camp quarters (barracks) by the guards who always took prisoners to be liquidated, and he never returned. I know that he was liquidated because at that time, about 200 prisoners were liquidated every day, and Ivan Hochsinger was taken on the last day . . . We know that these were liquidations because the things belonging to the deceased were returned to the storehouse and because the Ustashe immediately afterward told how each of the prisoners had behaved during liquidation, especially those who were better known or if the behavior had been in any way unusual."[129] In a completely independent testimony of April 25, 1945, Oto Breyer also claimed that "the last major liquidation in 1942 in Camp III took place on November 17, 18, and 19, when the Ustashe went into the barracks every evening and picked out the Jews . . . and at night sent them to Gradina and killed them all there . . . and so, in those three days, killed about 700 to 800 Jewish prisoners."[130]

In the list of names in the book *Jasenovac: War Victims According to Data of the Statistical Bureau of Yugoslavia,* there is a year of death beside almost every name. Although incomplete, the list shows that about 90 percent of the Zagreb Jews in Jasenovac were killed or died in that camp system in 1941 and 1942. The data about Jewish victims from the entire territory of the ISC is similar.

In the fall of 1942, the number of male Jewish prisoners in Jasenovac and Stara Gradiška was "smaller every day." Dominik Mandić claims that, in those months, "there were some Jews left in Jasenovac, but they suffered terribly and were on the decline."[131] In early 1943, there were about 1,800 Jewish men left in Jasenovac III, IV, and V, but "at the end of 1942, there was not a single Jewish woman or child in any Ustasha camp. There are only several younger women in Stara Gradiška, who work in the tailor's shop," said Albert Maestro.[132]

In January 1943, Miroslav Šalom Freiberger wrote in a letter that the Zagreb Community was taking care of "600 prisoners who write regularly, but do not have anyone left." According to Freiberger, "the fewest of them are from Zagreb, hardly 5 percent, all the rest are from the provinces"; this means that about thirty were from Zagreb.[133]

The "Peaceful Years" and the End

The year 1943 and the first months of 1944 were, relatively speaking, the most peaceful period in the Jasenovac camps. Considerably fewer transports arrived and there were by far fewer mass liquidations. "In that year (1943) they made us organize a group of 'dilettantes,' a music group and a football section. This was done to deceive the public. They forced us to write home for books for the library, which never existed."[134] The camp band was said to be of very high quality, and the football team of hungry inmates was very weak but it still had to play against the Ustasha garrison team. It was all a sad farce, because, at the same time, punishment was introduced for disobedience, and people had to walk about, even at work, for several days in shackles and chains. If someone did not do his best at work or other activities, the whole group was punished and did not receive parcels for up to a month, so the Ustasha garrison feasted on the parcels that arrived.[135]

The Ustasha Control Service was disbanded on January 21, 1943, by Pavelić's decision, but nothing changed in Office III, which was in charge of all the camps, except that it became part of RAVSIGUR. Luburić was replaced as the head of Office III by his deputy, Stanko Šarac, who had obviously been instructed to ease conditions in the camps. New commanders were also installed in Jasenovac and Stara Gradiška, but all belonged to the old group of Jasenovac officers. Luburić, who had to go "underground" temporarily because the Germans were demanding his extradition, in fact remained the real commander of Ustasha Defense from his refuge in a village near Lepoglava.[136] On June 28, 1999, in his defense at the main hearing before the County Court in Zagreb, Dinko Šakić claimed that "as camp commander, in questions of camp and prisoner security, he was directly subordinate to the commander of the First Brigade of the Ustasha Defense,"[137] which means that Luburić continued to keep much of his earlier power over the Jasenovac Camps.

With the same Ustasha garrison in command, great uncertainty continued for the Jasenovac internees; any Ustasha could beat or kill any prisoner, for any real or invented reason. In the jargon of the Ustasha guards and officers, this was called "kill for guilt" or "simply kill."[138] A Zagreb barber named Stern was "simply killed" on a whim. Miro Krein, a veterinary student from Krapina, was killed "for guilt" because he was said to have eavesdropped while the Ustashe were listening to news on the radio.[139] Attorney Dr. Ivo Gavrin, son of the Zagreb Chief Rabbi Dr. Gavro Schwarz, was killed by an Ustasha during a dispute because Gavrin had dared object to an order. Zagreb sculptor Slavko Bril worked in the pottery workshop from 1942, and died of tuberculosis in the camp hospital in the fall of 1944. When Zagreb oculist Dr. Marko Bauer died of typhoid in Camp III, the Ustashe decided to play a joke: they summoned his wife to come and visit him, saying that he was very ill. When she arrived, the camp administration told her that she had come too late and that her husband had already died. Shocked, she started too vociferously to demand to see her husband's dead body or his grave, so the Ustashe killed her.[140]

Zagreb Jew Ljudevit Stolzer was Pavelić's school friend. On an earlier occasion in 1929, when Pavelić had been in danger from the Yugoslav police, Stolzer had hidden him in his apartment. When Stolzer and his whole family were transported to Jasenovac in January 1942, Pavelić ordered them to be given privileged treatment. The Stolzer family lived in a house in Jasenovac village, and Stolzer worked as a scribe in the municipality. On the night of September 24, 1943, allegedly at the demand of someone in the Zagreb Gestapo, a group of Ustashe surreptitiously surrounded the house in which the Stolzers lived and killed the entire family without firing a bullet.[141]

Srećko Tkalčić was group leader in the camp kitchen for a time. The inmates respected him, especially the camp doctors, because he gave better food when someone was ill or had been beaten and needed it. Perhaps he was reported, because the Ustashe accused him of being a "secret leader of Jews who are planning a camp rebellion." As the Ustashe were leading him beside the "ghostly lake" he broke away and jumped in. They pulled him out and took him to Gradina to be liquidated.[142] In *Sećanja Jevreja,* the camp survivor Josip Erlih described the death of Ivan Volner of Zagreb in May or June 1944. Volner was leader of the camp building group. He played the accordion well "and was in the camp band. The Ustashe knew him and on one occasion, without the knowledge and permission of the camp command, took him to Dubica to play for them. He played until the Ustashe got drunk. Then, in drunken wantonness, they simply slit his throat, and sent word to the camp that he had been killed while trying to escape." According to Erlih, the camp commander, Dinko Šakić, carried out a sketchy investigation in which he killed two prisoners in rage, and sent several inmates from Volner's group of builders and from the camp band to Zvonara, the notorious camp prison and place of torture, from which most of them never returned.[143] In his defense before the County Court in Zagreb in 1999, Dinko Šakić did not deny that the "Volnar case" had taken place, but "this happened before the time of my command [he was camp commander from July 2 to October 1, 1944] and there was no investigation, shooting, or sending inmates to Zvonara because of that."[144]

Accused of helping a group of prisoners prepare for escape, the young Zagreb doctor Dr. Gustav Leimdörfer (1916), foreman of the camp prison in Jasenovac III, was killed in Gradina on October 24, 1944. He was a very selfless man, ready to take risks if necessary to help sick and healthy prisoners, respected by the inmates and the medical staff. His death was a definite indicator that there were to be no exceptions, that few would survive.[145] A total of seventy-seven Jewish doctors and twenty-four dentists were killed or died in the Jasenovac camps, among them twenty-four doctors and eleven dentists from Zagreb.[146]

In the main hearing of June 24, 1999, Šakić claimed that he had "done a lot for" an Ivan Heinrich of Slavonski Brod, "and that his close relatives Milan and Mirko Hirschl, who were Jasenovac prisoners, were set free."[147] At the hearing on June 25, 1945, Miroslav Majstorović-Filipović said that Heinrich had many connections in the German command, from which he had acquired some weapons for Luburić, so "he interceded to have several Jews set free from the camp."[148] However, the list of 170 Jasenovac internees amnestied in July 1944 for Pavelić's birthday (14 July), at the time of Šakić's command, has no Hirschl and not a single Jew.[149] The lists of male prisoners to be released from camp because their prison sentences had expired also contain no Jewish surnames. The list of 101 women internees whose sentences had expired in the first half of 1944, and the list of thirty-one women internees whose sentences were soon to expire, contain three who could, from their surnames, have been of Jewish origin.[150]

One of the few Zagreb Jews known to have been freed from the Jasenovac camps was the sculptor Viktor Samuel Bernfest, married to an "Aryan." It seems that he was released because Zagreb ophthalmologist Dr. Vilko Panac, Bernfest's brother-in-law, operated on a relative of Ante Pavelić and some other senior Ustasha officials for double cataracts.[151] Dr. Ivo Spitzer, one of the leading Zagreb pediatricians, was rewarded for saving the child of a high-ranking Ustasha official in the fall of 1944 by the release of his son-in-law, Adolf Schwarzenberg, who had been in Jasenovac since the summer of 1942.[152] The prominent Judaist Lavoslav Šik was released from Jasenovac in early 1942, after the intercession of Stepinac, but was soon arrested again, deported to Jasenovac, and immediately killed.[153] It was almost impossible for Jews to leave Jasenovac in the legal way. *Incomplete List*, a record of prisoners probably made in the late summer or early fall of 1944, contains a total of 3,502 prisoners, among them 748 surnames that could be Jewish. A witness wrote on the list itself that seventy-six of the prisoners had been "released," but only one of them was a Jew, which is an obvious disproportion, as 21 percent of the prisoners were Jews, but they constituted barely 1 percent of those released.[154]

There was a saying among the Ustashe: "Not a single Jew from the camp must survive, because the Jews will be the most relentless witnesses against the Ustasha movement."[155]

About 300 prisoners managed to escape from the camp complex during the four years, some of them in the final breakout, but many more lost their lives in such attempts. Camp security was very tight, there were many Ustasha patrols, and it was difficult to swim across the Sava to escape to the Bosnian side. Only ninety-five Jews managed to escape, one-third of them in the breakout on April 22, 1945. During 1942, when there were by far the most Jews in Jasenovac, only five managed to escape.[156] Albert Maestro fled in August 1943, when the Partisans attacked a group of internees and guards who were out cutting wood.[157]

Several dozen Jewish men and women were saved when internees and captured Partisans were exchanged for Ustasha and German officers and soldiers who had been captured by the Partisans. According to German sources, about 2,000 captives or prisoners were exchanged in this way on both sides from September 1942 to April 1945. According to Partisan sources, the number was 800 on each side.[158] At least half of these were internees and captured Partisans from the Jasenovac camp system. The Partisans always gave priority to arrested Communist Party members and other anti-fascist activists and captured Partisans, and these included Jews. The first such exchange for Jasenovac prisoners was carried out on September 23, 1942, near Okučani. The captured Mirko Vutuc, vice director of RAVSIGUR (the director at that time was still Eugen Dido Kvaternik), and Karl Wagner, head of the Nova Gradiška County Police, were exchanged for thirty prisoners who were sent to the Partisans. These included one Jewish woman, Olga Kohn, who later married Hebrang.[159] In the increasingly frequent later exchanges, there were always some Jewish women or men, but always fewer than 10 percent, because many of those whom the Partisans asked for were no longer alive.

In 1943–1944, the Jasenovac camps had increasingly varied groups of prisoners who were treated in different ways. Although individuals and small groups were still occasionally killed, even captured Partisans were no longer killed as a matter of course but were kept for exchange or were sent to work in Germany.[160] Selection was also made among the captured Home Guard deserters: some were sent to work in Germany, some were dressed in Ustasha uniforms and sent straight off to join Ustasha fighting units, and some groups were killed.[161] In 1943, Jasenovac V (Stara Gradiška) had about 1,100 male prisoners serving time sentences, mostly politically suspect Croats and Bosnians, about 200 Jewish men (mostly qualified workers) and rather more Serbs on the farms, and about 700 to 800 women and children.[162] In Jasenovac III and IV, there were an average of about 5,000 internees in the camp workshops and farms at that time, at least 1,000 of them Jews.[163] In mid-1943, there was a total of only about 2,600 Jewish men still alive in Jasenovac and Stara Gradiška.[164]

In 1943, the prisoners were generally treated better and the prison food improved somewhat, but the interrogations in the camp penal system (Zvonara in Jasenovac III and Kula and the so-called Gagro Hotel in Jasenovac V) remained just as cruel. Few prisoners came out alive, because they were systematically starved to death.[165] In Jasenovac III, there was a separate barracks, and in Jasenovac V separate cells for Ustasha soldiers under punishment. They had privileged treatment: they ate with the Ustasha garrison, and some proved their loyalty by participating in the supervision and ill-treatment of the other inmates.[166] Still, even they could not be sure of their fates: Luburić ordered a group of his killers, called the Black Arm, to kill Vlado Singer, the first chief of Ustasha intelligence; Dragutin

Hadrović, the Grand Prefect of Banja Luka; and several other Ustashe in Jasenovac, who were not to their liking.[167]

The International Committee of the Red Cross did not send its representative, Julius Schmidlin, to Zagreb until the end of 1943. He failed in his attempts to procure promises from the representatives of the Ustasha authorities, among others from Andrija Artuković, that conditions for the remaining Jews in the ISC would improve. In the spring of 1944, Schmidlin got permission to visit the Jasenovac complex. During the entire visit, he was accompanied by agents of one of the Ustasha intelligence services and by Dr. Milutin Jurčić, secretary of the ISC Ministry of the Interior. Before Schmidlin's arrival, Jasenovac was specially prepared and improved. Perhaps due to conformism and fear, and perhaps also because the International Committee of the Red Cross had rather ambiguous relations with the Nazis, Schmidlin's report is a transparently whitewashed presentation of conditions in the Jasenovac complex. When Schmidlin left the camp and returned to Zagreb, conditions in the camps immediately deteriorated again. In June, Schmidlin submitted a list of proposals to enable the efficient work of the International Committee of the Red Cross: he demanded a list of imprisoned Jews with all relevant data, to be regularly informed about transfers, deaths, and hospitalizations, the participation of internee commissioners in the organization and distribution of aid, all according to the principles of the Convention on Prisoners of War. It is obvious that any such attempt was wishful thinking and had no results: in the fall of 1944, the International Committee of the Red Cross stopped sending parcels to Jasenovac because they could not rely on the Ustasha representatives, nor could they get guarantees that the Zagreb Jewish Community would be allowed to take part in distributing aid.[168] The desire of the International Committee of the Red Cross to help the imprisoned Jews reached as far as Nahum Goldmann, president of the World Jewish Congress.[169] As the end of the war approached, Schmidlin's chances of doing anything weakened, and, in early March 1945, he returned to Switzerland.[170]

At the beginning of 1944, Luburić returned to Zagreb from his refuge near Lepoglava. His Ustasha Defense quickly grew to division size, even larger, and through it Luburić resumed direct command over the Jasenovac camp system. He discharged camp commanders who had introduced a more moderate regime and appointed new ones, and through them "Luburić brought back to the camps the old regime from 1942," so there "was new mass killing, slaughter, and strangling, with the goal of extermination."[171] In 1944, conditions for the men and women inmates kept deteriorating, and, after September, "the worst period in our life in Jasenovac began . . . Mass liquidations of women and men were an everyday occurrence. In the fall of 1944, our camp for women in Jasenovac always had about 500 to 1,000 prisoners, because new transports arrived every day, and every evening 100 to 200 women were called up for liquidation."[172] The same was taking place in the men's camp Jasenovac III. "From the end of September to the New Year 1945, every night, 200 or more prisoners were taken away to Granik or Gradina, where they were killed and thrown into the Sava. Every day, new prisoners arrived, and the number did not diminish."[173]

When the agony and decline of the ISC began, the Jasenovac camp system was completely exposed to the whims of Luburić and his men, who were increasingly becoming Pavelić's main and most reliable support. When he was settling scores with the more moderate faction in the Ustasha leadership, headed by Ministers Vokić and Lorković, "Poglavnik Ante Pavelić ordered General Luburić to prevent this coup, but without spilling blood," so the current Jasenovac commander, Dinko Šakić, and some other Jasenovac Ustasha officers were ordered to come to Zagreb from August 26 to September 11 to "carry out the action."[174]

With the arrival of new prisoners, the number of internees in Jasenovac III "rose from 2,500 to 8,000 in one month alone [September]" and when "the mass killing stopped at the end of 1944, of the 8,000 prisoners, only 1,800 were left in the camp, not counting those who were brought in during the day and killed on the same evening, because their number cannot be known, even approximately. In the opinion of the internees, about 14,000 men, women, and children were killed during this liquidation in 1944."[175] The only ones spared were the "prisoners in the various industrial plants and the farm, because they were still needed."

The fall liquidations were an attempt to remove all Jewish women and men with the exception of experts of this kind. "At that time, Camp Forewoman Pina [Pina Vlah] said that the Ustashe had ordered that no Jewish woman should survive. Among us, in the workshops, we watched over comrades of Jewish origin, saying that they were 'Aryans.' The young Jewish woman Stela Polak was the last we said that about . . . In late fall, her name was called out when we were on our way back from the laundry. She was very brave, she did not cry . . . The Ustashe themselves, those who were present at her liquidation, spoke of her heroic death. She shouted out slogans and would not stand still to be hit with the mallet, but had to be held to have her throat cut."[176] Selma Grünwald was killed in Jasenovac in October 1944, and Nada Friedländer in Lepoglava as late as March 1945.[177]

In September 1944, the Partisans attacked Banja Luka and the camp in Stara Gradiška found itself in the danger zone. "There was turmoil in this camp (and) immediately the main criminal, Luburić, appeared there . . . on September 22 we were summoned to line up and about 400 Serbs were singled out straight away, bound with wire, and the night swallowed them all."[178] The following day, September 23, about 650 to 700 inmates, most of them Croats and Bosnians and some Jews, were sent on foot to Jasenovac, which was thirty-six kilometers away. "On the way, people began to fall under the weight of their meager possessions, in the mud, hungry and exhausted . . . and the (Ustasha guards) finished them off. About 200 people disappeared like this on the way from Gradiška to Jasenovac."[179] Most of the remaining inmates from Stara Gradiška were then sent to the Lepoglava Camp and Prison. By the spring of 1945, only about seventy prisoners remained in Stara Gradiška (thirty-five men and thirty-five women) who were needed by the Ustasha garrison. These did not include any Jews. When the Ustashe began to liquidate the last inmates during the final retreat on April 23, some managed to hide, some to escape, and seven men and three women prisoners thus saved their lives.[180]

According to an incomplete list, probably compiled in the late summer or early fall of 1944, there were a total of 3,502 prisoners in Jasenovac, among whom 748 names and surnames can be recognized as Jewish.[181] Although the title says that it is the "list of the parquet-making workshop," the anonymous compiler claims that it is a list, although incomplete, of prisoners from the entire camp. Of those 748 people, the witness claims that 11 escaped, and he knows that 89 were "liquidated" or died. After the war, Adolf Fridrih estimated that there were 1,800 Jewish prisoners still alive in Jasenovac at the end of 1944, but there were probably not that many.[182]

Following the mass fall liquidations, after the New Year 1945, there was a temporary lull in Jasenovac. When the last transport of 600 Jasenovac prisoners was sent to work in Germany on February 18, about 1,200 men and about 700 women remained in Jasenovac III.[183] Camp IV (Leatherworks) still had 147 inmates.[184] There were about 700 Jewish men (there were no more Jewish women), and the Zagreb Jewish Community "believed that they at least would return home," but in the last wave of slaughter the Ustashe killed "many remaining Jews, about 650 of them."[185]

The last wave of liquidations began in March and culminated in April 1945. In January 1945, the main Ustasha Defense forces and their commanders were with Luburić, whom Pavelić had given the task of organizing the defense of Herzegovina and Sarajevo. Enraged by their imminent retreat, they sent various groups of prisoners (Home Guard deserters and rebels, Partisan collaborators, etc.) to Jasenovac "from the field." A full trainload of prisoners also arrived from Lepoglava, which had to be evacuated. All these groups were liquidated on the day of arrival or a day or two later.[186] The Ustasha leaders were now doing whatever they could to hide and obliterate all traces of the mass liquidations, and the "old" prisoners were assigned outside work, burning bodies and camouflaging graves. They passed columns of exhausted, thin German soldiers who were tiredly dragging themselves westwards.[187] "The breath of freedom was close, but we were approaching ever closer to death."[188]

The Ustashe began to evacuate the main Jasenovac camp on April 19, 1945. On that day, they first sent off to Zagreb the prisoners of two small camp units who they considered would be useful to them during their further retreat: eleven women and men prisoners from the medical staff of the Ustasha hospital, and about fifteen of the best mechanics and other skilled workers from the Quick Assembly car repair shop. Some managed to escape during the chaotic retreat, and the Partisans freed the rest when they captured the entire transport near Maribor.[189] A Home Guard officer took Doctor Arnold Schön in his company's truck and released him in front of the house of Schön's friend in Šenoina Street in Zagreb, where he hid until the arrival of the Partisans.[190]

On the same evening, April 19, the Ustashe evacuated the medical staff and patients from the prison hospital, headed by Dr. Leon Perić, ostensibly for "transfer to Sisak," and liquidated them that same night.[191] A much larger group of prisoners was taken from the barracks of Camp III the following night, also for "transfer to Sisak," and liquidated on the other bank of the Sava in Gradina. "Panic broke out among the prisoners, and about a hundred of them hanged themselves in the barracks and workshops in despair."[192]

On the following morning, all the remaining male prisoners from all parts of Jasenovac III (it is reported that there were exactly 1,073) were shut in the Brickyard building and kept there under heavy guard. On that evening, April 21, they watched from the windows as the many Ustashe marched the entire women's camp to liquidation. The eyewitnesses, Ješua Abinun, Jakob Danon, and others, all said that there were "760 women and young girls," Josip Engel said that there were "about 700," Jakov Finci that there were "about 800," Adolf Fridrih estimated their number at "almost 900." They left with amazing bravery, "sending greetings to their comrades and saying goodbye to them" and "threw away their things and sang, stepping out to meet death with dignity."[193]

In the men's camp, everyone realized that it was their turn next and on that night made the final decision to escape, as they had planned long ago. Wary of possible informers, only a small circle knew about the plan until the last moment. On April 22, at exactly 10:30 a.m., organized groups of internees, armed with carpenter's knives, hammers, and pieces of wood, attacked the Ustasha guards. They managed to wrest two guns and a machine gun from them. According to plan, when the student from Sinj, Ante Bakotić, shouted, "Forward, comrades, charge! . . . we jumped out of the windows and doors of the three-story building in which we had been shut and charged the camp gate on the Novska side. Leading to it was an open space about 150 meters long, without any kind of shelter from bullets. The Ustashe immediately started to shoot with rifles and machine guns, and some of them threw bombs into the crowd."[194]

About 600 prisoners took part in the breakout. Perhaps almost 200 managed to get out of the camp, but many were cut down by fire from the protective bunkers when they were already outside the wire. The Incomplete List of Jasenovac Camp Prisoners Who Survived the Breakout of April 22, 1945, lists eighty-four names.[195] If we add the survivors from the Quick Assembly works and the medical staff from the Ustasha hospital, about ten Stara Gradiška prisoners who were saved, and several unlisted fugitives from the Leatherworks, a total of just under 120 men and, at most, 7 or 8 women probably managed to save themselves from the Jasenovac camps at the last moment. These included just over 30 Jews, but fewer than 10 from Zagreb.[196]

J. Grossepais-Gil, Egon Berger, and Vladimir Carin gave a moving account of the breakout from the camp and the ten or so days of wandering through the surrounding forests before coming upon the Yugoslav Army.[197] Earlier, a small number of internees had escaped from a transport by making a hole in the wooden floor of the railway carriage. They found themselves in Moslavina, where they ran into Germans and Ustashe. Eight of them were arrested and brought to Zagreb. Escorted by four Home Guards dressed as Ustashe, during the night between April 24 and 25, 1945, Lavoslav Koričan and seven other prisoners visited his sister and her family in Trešnjevka. Just before dawn, the guards made them leave and the eight were never seen alive again.[198]

After the breakout from Jasenovac III, about 460 prisoners remained in the camp, those who had not joined the escape out of fear, resignation, exhaustion, or in a mistaken hope of survival. In a rage, the Ustashe killed most of them that same day. No one knows how many of them tried to hide in the camp, but they too perished, mostly in the following days when the Ustashe mined and blew up all the prisoners' barracks that had not been destroyed in three air raids at the beginning of April.[199] According to existing evidence, only three of the prisoners who had hidden in the camp escaped alive.

The report of the Yugoslav State Commission for Establishing War Crimes, which was sent in German to the International Military Tribunal in Nuremberg on December 26, 1945, says that Jasenovac III "existed until April 1945. Before the Yugoslav Army liberated it, the Ustashe destroyed the entire camp, all the buildings and records, and killed the surviving inmates, except for fifty who saved themselves by escaping or hiding."[200] This number is obviously too small, because approximately twice as many survived the breakout alone.[201]

Alarmed by the morning gunfire and blasts from Camp III, two kilometers away, on April 22, the prisoners of Camp IV (Leatherworks) prepared to escape that same evening. The brothers Ervin and Oto Moser from Zagreb and the Sarajevo chemist Avram Demajo prepared a vial of cyanide for each prisoner to poison himself with if the Ustashe caught him.[202] Late in the afternoon, they managed to noiselessly kill and disarm two Ustashe who entered their rooms. With the first dusk, according to an advance plan, all 147 "leatherworkers" crowded the exit gates together and scattered in all directions towards the Sava and the woods. As the Ustashe were on the alert and had increased the number of guards because of the morning events in the Brickyard, a great majority of the prisoners did not manage to get through. The camp foreman and the main planner of the breakout, engineer Silvio Sesi Alkalaj, poisoned himself so as not to fall into the Ustashe's hands. Only ten prisoners escaped, among them seven Jews. They all went through several days of extreme duress, hiding and hungry and walking through the forests, until they managed to join Partisan units.

Before the final retreat on May 1, the Ustashe set fire to everything that remained in the camp and many houses in the village. According to the report of the Forty-Fifth Division of the Yugoslav Army of May 2, 1945, "during the night between April 30 and May 1, the First Company of the Third Battalion of the Twenty-fourth Brigade crossed the river Sava east of Jasenovac . . . and thus entered Jasenovac, which the enemy had deserted after setting fire to it."[203]

Jews and Jewish Victims in Jasenovac

After the late fall of 1941, and the days of improvisation and disorganization in Jasenovac I and II Camps, the Ustashe tried to organize Jasenovac III much better, modeling themselves on German concentration camps. The camp commander "commanded the military units that secured the camp and guarded the prisoners during work and liquidation," the work-service commander was in charge of "work in the camp itself, food for the prisoners, accommodations, health, etc. . . . The prisoners' main representative was the camp forean . . . [who had] a broad field of duties because the heads of work service did their work through him."[204]

"Internal management" was established in the camps, run by the prisoners and headed by the camp foremen (*logornik*). In the larger camps, Brickyard and Stara Gradiška, there were also group leaders (*grupnik*) in charge of particular workshops and other departments, who were subordinate to the camp foremen. Within the general framework of Ustasha command, the camp foremen only had authority in the work service and in auxiliary prisoners' services. They assigned work tasks directly or through group leaders, distributed prisoners to barracks or work units, placed prisoners on the sick-list, and picked prisoners for special groups and jobs. They had no say about the prisoners taken in the mass transports, who were liquidated immediately on arrival, nor about some special groups of internees. It was usual for the Jasenovac camp system to have five or six camp foremen at the same time: there were camp forewomen in the women's sections of Jasenovac III and V, camp foremen in the men's camps III and V, foremen of Jasenovac IV and the Quick Assembly car repair shop, and for a time the internee who was head of the hospital and medical service also enjoyed the status of camp foreman.

Twenty-two prisoners performed the duty of camp foreman between the fall of 1941 and May 1945, six of them Jews.[205] Of the Jewish camp foremen, the Zagreb "private clerk" Bruno Diamantstein in Jasenovac III, the Zagreb traveling salesman Herman Spiller in Jasenovac V, and, to a somewhat lesser degree, Bernhard Wiener (camp foreman in Jasenovac III after Diamantstein's death), were notorious and ruthless Ustasha collaborators. Until the Ustashe killed them too, they enjoyed great privileges, moved freely outside the camp, received pay, and mistreated the prisoners mercilessly. On the other hand, camp foremen engineer Silvio Alkalaj (Jasenovc IV), Dr. Gustav Leimdörfer (hospitals and surgeries), and Maks Samlaić-Somlei (Quick Assembly) showed consistent solidarity with their inmates, and survivors spoke of them only in the best of terms, as people who helped and saved lives whenever they could.[206] To some extent, the same can be said—for better or worse—of the other sixteen camp foremen and forewomen.

When the system of "internal management" was established in Jasenovac III in the fall of 1941, Jews were in a great majority in the camp. There were relatively many highly skilled Jewish prisoners, because it was precisely these that the Ustasha authorities had arrested and deported in the summer and fall of 1941. And so, in the beginning, Jews "had priority. They worked in offices, kitchens, warehouses, they were suppliers, took all the 'better posts,' in short . . . Jews were the second authority. But, it must also be said that there was a limited number of such 'good posts.'"[207] A great majority of Jews in the Jasenovac camps shared the fate of most of the other internees, and, from the early spring of 1942, except for the Roma, constituted proportionally the largest number of those liquidated. Thus, the number of Jews in the "better posts" gradually decreased, and "it also became evident that it was not good to be the 'second authority.' After they learned more than was desirable, these 'in authority' were regularly removed—in the only way that people in the camp got removed."[208]

Some Jews curried favor and "collaborated" with the Ustasha command and thought that by doing so they would save their lives. In more than 600 documents brought by Miletić, and in various memoir books and records, about ten such people are mentioned by name: the "informers" Steiner, Felbauer, Sohr, Polan, the grave-diggers Danon and Baranon, the looters Katan and Pajtaš, the collaborator Begović, the criminals Diamantstein, Spiller, and Wiener.[209] Sigismund Städler Bobi, former correspondent of the left-wing press in Spain, was a very active Communist Party member before the war. After the Ustashe arrested him twice, they sent him to Jasenovac as an *agent provocateur*, and when he was of no more use to them, they killed him in 1942.[210]

"The time of Spiller's and Diamantstein's camp management [from November 1941 to July 1942] is remembered as the most terrible by all who survived it," remembered former inmate Dr. Mladen Iveković,[211] and Sado Koen also testified about this period, saying that they "made life a real hell" and that we "Jews incurred the hatred of the other prisoners because of such fiends and bandits in gloves."[212] However, there were also several "Serb and Croat villains . . . [who] helped the Ustashe and the prisoners' management in that bloody work."[213] During his interrogation, the former Franciscan Miroslav Filipović-Majstorović, Jasenovac Camp Commander, went furthest in accusations against the Jewish camp foremen. He claimed that "Diamantstein, Spiller, and others" were "bullies, real tyrants in the camp, who did more evil, spilled more blood, than any camp Ustasha." Allegedly some Ustashe later told Filipović that "when the first camp was being built, they killed thousands and thousands of Jews by making them work."[214] Ante Ciliga also presents a number of accusations against the Jews in Jasenovac.[215]

Although Diamantstein sometimes managed, if not to save the lives of some people then at least to postpone their deaths,[216] the prisoners nevertheless described him as "infamous,"[217] as "a good servant to bad masters," as "merciless to other prisoners," as a person who treated other prisoners "inhumanely,"[218] "as a man without character who sold others to make his own life easier, and in this way tried to prove to the Ustashe that they had loyal servants even among the prisoners."[219] Berger added that "there were Diamantsteins of this kind during the entire time of the camp's existence, and it was immaterial to us whether they were called Spiller, Steiner, or Polan."[220] The Jewish prisoners considered Spiller's cruelty to be even worse, because he personally beat the inmates and was "a very evil man."[221] Spiller "tortured the prisoners and killed them for 'keeping back' one potato, for several grains of corn."[222] Berta Israel claims that she saw Diamantstein in the company of Maks Luburić, when they came to the rooms of the Jewish Community on Tomislavov Square. They were on intimate terms, on a first-name basis.[223]

Before the Ustasha command appointed them, the first camp foremen in Jasenovac III and V, Diamantstein and Spiller, had already held similar roles in the Pag Camp in Slana and in Krapje and Bročice. In time, they grew so close to some of the Ustasha commanders that they joined them, with the help of some Roma, in the organized and systematic plunder of gold from murdered and living prisoners. "During searches, which they also carried out on their own initiative, they found the few gold coins that some prisoner had sewn somewhere in his clothes."[224] It is not known who informed against them about all this, or who ordered the strict investigation and the severe sentences that were carried out. First, the foremen's families were killed; then, Diamantstein and Spiller, were killed in the cruelest way, as well as their two Jewish collaborators and several Roma and Ustasha accomplices, one of whom was the brother of Luburić's deputy Matković:[225] first they were beaten and stabbed, then they were dragged before the inmates and publicly shot.[226]

Bernhard-Ladislav Wiener (or Viner) from Varaždin succeeded Diamantstein as camp foreman, and even gave a speech when the Ustashe killed Diamantstein and four other prisoners. In December 1942, the Jasenovac Camp Command confirmed that Wiener, his wife, Elizabeta, and sons Vladimir and Miroslav, were "of good conduct in every way." It seems that the entire family converted to Catholicism at that time. In 1942, Vladimir Wiener was even enrolled in the Jasenovac school. Despite all this, Ljubo Miloš testified that Wiener was liquidated in 1944, together with his wife and children.[227]

The atrocities of these few Jewish informers and collaborators are sometimes used in making generalizations about the behavior of Jews in the Jasenovac camp system. Such generalizations are inappropriate, as are all generalizations about entire peoples and ethnic groups. The most sweeping statements of this kind were in the testimonies of about fifteen Serbs who were freed from Jasenovac and Stara Gradiška in spring 1942 and sent to Belgrade. In April 1942, they made statements before the Commissariat for Refugees and Displaced Persons of Nedić's government. First, they spoke about the Jews in Jasenovac favorably and neutrally, then, under obvious pressure, they began to make new statements and said the worst things about Jews in general. Vojislav Prnjatović's statement that "A Jew remains a Jew, even in Jasenovac Camp . . . selfish, sly, without solidarity, parsimonious, underhanded, and an informer"[228] is not authentic, but was either manipulated or fabricated. It is this statement that Franjo Tuđman usually quotes in the *Horrors of War* as the main argument for bolstering anti-Semitic insinuations.[229]

In 1964, the Federal Statistics Bureau of SFR Yugoslavia carried out the most extensive research into the victims of the Jasenovac camps, but the results were kept secret for a long time because they did not suit the political and propagandistic claims at that time. It was not until 1998 that the Bosnian Institute, seated in Zurich and Sarajevo, managed to publish the materials. This list gives, by name, a total of 59,188 victims, 49,602 of them in Jasenovac, 9,586 in Stara Gradiška.[230] The caution that "this list is not complete" appears on every page, and this is easy to establish by consulting some partial but reliable municipal or other local records. The list gives 9,044 victims as "Jewish," but the entries were made according to religion. Jews who had converted to Catholicism in 1941 or earlier were entered as Croats, and—judging from the pronounced Jewish names, surnames, and parents' names—there were at least another 3,000 Jews. The incomplete nature of the list is most obvious in the case of the Roma, of whom it contains only 1,471, and it also gives 33,944 Serbs, 6,546 Croats, 949 Muslims,

194 Slovenes, 105 persons of other nationality, and 6,850 "nationality unidentified." If this list is taken as a starting point and is increased by about 40 or 50 percent at the most (this increase results from comparison with some reliable albeit partial records), we approach the number of 80,000 to 90,000 victims of the entire Jasenovac system, the number also reached by Vladimir Žerjavić.[231]

Research into, and analysis of, the total number of Jasenovac victims exceeds the scope of this book, so the authors will for the present, until newer and more precise records are produced, accept Žerjavić's research as the most appropriate starting point. However, his number of 13,000 Jewish victims of the Jasenovac system must be corrected, because Žerjavić did not take some groups of Jewish Jasenovac victims into account: Jews who had converted to Catholicism before 1941 and their descendents were not recorded as Jews anywhere, but they nevertheless suffered according to racial laws; the women and men from the liquidated Đakovo Camp, who were executed in Jasenovac; and, finally, Jewish refugees from other countries, quite a large number of whom were also killed in Jasenovac. All the same, in answer to the question, "Is it possible to establish the number of victims of the Jasenovac camps?" we concur with the distinguished Croatian historian Ljubo Boban, who said, "doubtless, this would be very difficult, and could never be completely precise."[232]

In any case, whichever number is accepted as being more or less exact, there is no doubt that more than half the Jewish Holocaust victims in northern Croatia and Bosnia and Herzegovina were killed in the Jasenovac system of camps. The number is probably very close to 17,000, in addition to several hundred Jews from abroad and from other parts of the former Yugoslavia.[233] A significant number of prisoners and victims were Zagreb Jews—their number is impossible to establish precisely, because the percentage of Zagreb Jews kept changing in relation to the total number of imprisoned Jews, and so did the percentage of Jews in relation to the total number of prisoners. For example, prisoner Egon Berger claims that there were about "700 Jews" and about "600 Serbs" on September 11, 1941, but that "new groups kept arriving."[234] According to one list with the names of 1,454 Jewish internees in Jasenovac (probably not complete), obviously compiled at the end of 1941, 805, or 55.4 percent of them, were from Zagreb.[235] Another list of internees, made at about the same time, has 269 Jews, 53 of them from Zagreb (19.7 percent); the majority are from Sarajevo (184, or 68.4 percent).[236] In early November 1941, the Jewish Community of Zagreb claimed that about 4,000 Jewish men to whom they were sending aid were imprisoned in Jasenovac.[237] This means that there were certainly more Jews, because a considerable number of prisoners were not entered in the registers of the Zagreb Jewish Community. Besides, the "constant liquidations, transfers from one camp to another, cases of individual release, escapes, and exchanges"[238] make it that much more difficult to establish even an approximate number of Jews in the Jasenovac system of camps, and thus, also, the final number of Jewish victims.

Based on analyses of eyewitness testimonies, various documents, and demographic statistics, the conclusion is that about 4,000—maybe even 4,500—Zagreb Jews were killed in the Jasenovac system of camps between 1941 and 1945.[239]

22

ON THE WAY TO EXECUTION

Loborgrad and Đakovo

Loborgrad Camp was organized in an evacuated old people's home run by the Social Welfare Society in Hrvatsko zagorje, on the road from Zlatar to Lobor.[1] At the beginning of 1941, it had housed about sixty old people, but, around September of 1941, doctors from Camp Welfare were ordered to inspect the building and estimate how many Jewish women and children it could accommodate. They were headed by Božidar Gregl (1893), Ustasha Police Commissioner for the Grand County of Zagorje in Varaždin, whose father was an ethnic German and whose mother, Terezija, née Schlesinger, was Jewish (his mother had converted to Catholicism at the age of eighteen). "The manor house was in a very run-down state, half of the roof was missing, many doors and windows were broken, and part of the floor was missing. We measured the usable rooms and decided that they could accommodate between 150 and 180 people. Then Gregl pointed a machine gun at us and instructed us to say that 400 to 600 persons could be accommodated, so we did."[2] Later, representatives of the Zagreb Jewish Community agreed that the buildings were "suitable" for receiving as many as 800, and finally about 1,300 women and children were placed in the manor house. After the inspection, the building started to be converted.[3] On September 29, the Jewish Section of the RUR issued Ašer Kabiljo, an activist of the Jewish Community in Zagreb, a permit to "travel to Zlatar and back, and to stay in the surroundings and procure food and material to repair and renovate Loborgrad."[4] The Community undertook to provide food for the prisoners. On October 1, its representatives came to Lobor to "get everything ready for sleeping accommodations and food."[5] At the beginning of October, the transports started out from Kruščica. After spending a short time in Slavonski Brod, where they were met by "representatives of the Zagreb Jewish Community who provided the first food for them," on October 5–7, 1941, the women and children arrived in Zagreb. "The transports spent a considerable time in Zagreb, so that besides providing them with all the food they needed while they were here, we could also supply them with everything they would need for the further journey to Lobor. In cooperation with the Red Cross, all the women were cleaned, deloused, and bathed."[6] After that, according to some data, between 1,500 and 1,700 Jewish women and children were accommodated in the camp, along with about 300 Serb women and children.[7] The differences in the estimated numbers of internees are partly the result of the steady arrival of new prisoners, and of the great number of people who died of typhoid. Nineteen Zagreb Jews came to Loborgrad directly from Zagreb on October 2, nine men and ten women. The men were craftsmen, glaziers, carpenters, and mechanics who were to help in the construction of the camp.[8] At the beginning of November, ten Jewish women arrived from the camp in Slavetić, which had been closed down.[9] Ten more women came on December 15.[10] Around New Year's Day, typhoid appeared, and soon reached epidemic proportions. The number of prisoners then began to decrease, although some recovered.[11] On the list of 1,032 women prisoners, 210, or 20.3 percent, were Jewish women from Zagreb, while the most Jewish women were from Sarajevo. The list also included a small number of Serb women.[12] There were at least 220 children under the age of sixteen in the camp; the camp commander, Vilko Heger, said that the camp had over 300 children.[13] In June, he said that there were "1,025 prisoners,"[14] but he probably did not include the almost 300 children, which means that he estimated the number of prisoners at about 1,300.

Since the Loborgrad Camp was overcrowded, in November 1941, a branch camp was founded in Gornja Rijeka near Križevci.[15] It had just over 300 prisoners—at first only Jewish women and children.[16] In April, there were plans to leave "the healthy women who could work in Loborgrad, and to put the old women who could not work and the children in Gornja Rijeka," but it seems that this idea was abandoned because of the danger of transmitting contagious diseases.[17] The Serb women were released from

Gornja Rijeka in May 1942, and the "seventy-three Jewish women who were there were sent back to Loborgrad."[18] In August of that year, they were taken to Auschwitz, together with all the other Loborgrad men and women prisoners.

In Loborgrad, the "accommodations were terrible, the manor was neglected, it had no windows nor any sanitary facilities." At the end of October 1941, not long after the camp was established, the camp commander demanded that the "number of internees be reduced to 800" because "there is an average of eighty people per room, the building had too few latrines, the kitchen is too small, the bathroom cannot be used."[19] People slept on boards laid down in the rooms.[20] The Community regularly, "at least twice a week, or eight times a month," sent food by truck directly from Zagreb to Loborgrad, and, every day, supplies also came to the railway station in Zlatar-Bistrica, and were taken by truck from there to Loborgrad. The Community especially had to beg for, and find ways to procure, gas, tires, and inner tubes.[21] In this way, "the camp was supplied with everything it needed." This included mouse traps, brooms, nails, washing powder, boots, eyeglass frames, medicines, millet for gruel, salami, jam (for which a 20 percent luxury tax had to be paid), spaghetti and various kinds of pasta, lard, salt, beans, barrels of oil, sugar, tons of potatoes, vinegar, onions, milk (from the nearby villages), and smoked meat.[22] In May 1942, the Croatian Workingman's Cooperative sold the Jewish Community 600 kgs. of lump sugar for the Loborgrad Camp.[23] During April 13–30, 1942, the daily milk supply was an average of 167 liters,[24] which meant about 15 centiliters per prisoner per day. However, as 31,000 liters of milk were delivered to the camp during the 300 or so days during which it existed, the average daily supply was, in fact, barely 100 liters. A total of 51 tons of flour came to the camp, 6.5 tons of pasta, 16 tons of semolina, 13 tons of lard, 46.5 tons of various kinds of vegetables, etc.[25]

Zagreb and Zlatar merchants earned quite a lot from these orders, and so did merchants in other places (e.g., in Varaždin, Petrinja).[26] A lot of money was used to buy medicine.[27] The bills kept in the Croatian State Archives (there is no way of knowing whether all the bills have been preserved) show that, all together, the Zagreb Jewish Community paid more than 7,100,000 kunas for food, other necessities, and transport during the time of the camp's existence.[28] In January 1942, the Jewish Community acquired, and the Red Cross distributed, sanitary napkins for about half the 3,600 Jewish prisoners in Đakovo, Loborgrad, Gornja Rijeka, and Stara Gradiška.[29]

White barley coffee was provided three times a week, but only those "who had tickets for that day" could get milk. The daily bread ration was fifteen decagrams, or just over five ounces. Only the men, the eighteen women bakers, and women who did physical labor, "for which the administration issues special tickets," got thirty decagrams of bread a day. "The law forbids giving more than the above amounts of bread."[30] As a rule, there was only black barley coffee for breakfast, and for supper, cumin soup, brown roux soup, or linden tea. Lunch always consisted of only one dish: millet gruel with meat sauce, corn mash with fried onions, pickled turnip with millet and smoked meat, beef soup with pasta, etc.[31] Thanks to the efforts of the Zagreb Community, 786,000 meals were supplied in Loborgrad and Gornja Rijeka Camps.[32]

The prisoners themselves are the best witnesses about conditions in the camps. On January 12, 1942, "Irena, Liza, and Beba" wrote from Loborgrad asking the Petrović family in Podsused (at that time a suburb of Zagreb) to "send a thick exercise book with hard covers in the next parcel . . . and paper, and a pencil."[33] Women also asked for headscarves, shoe polish, candles, matches, brushes for mud, cigarettes, stockings, warm underwear, shirts, and food (sugar, lemons, "something sour," jam, oranges, "the gherkins were good, thanks!").[34] It is no longer possible to find out who "Irena, Liza, and Beba" were, but there is little doubt that they shared the fate of all Loborgrad's other internees in Auschwitz. It was probably in those winter months that Roza Altarac of Zagreb asked, via the Jewish Community, Stefa Lorger at Pantovčak 2 to send her "an old pair of size 38 shoes, an old warm dress, and a pair of gloves."[35] The Zagreb Jewish Community received orders from the Loborgrad prisoners and forwarded them, using a printed form, to family and friends who were still free. Hinko Berger from Begov Han (Bosnia) got a message from Magda Kraus, who was

> in the camp for interned Jews in Loborgrad, and she asks us to tell you that she needs the following: *garters, size 38 sports shoes, skirt and jersey, warm coat, warm underwear, soap, toothpaste and toothbrush, candles, dry food* [the words in italics are written in pencil on the printed form]. Please sew a patch of linen with the exact name on each of these items, then sew all the items in a linen bag with the exact name and surname of the recipient, and place of residence. Please send this parcel to our address.
>
> We especially underline that it is strictly prohibited to put food and

letters in the bag. Our internees and the Community, which is caring for them, will both suffer consequences.

Please confirm the receipt of this notice.

JEWISH RELIGIOUS COMMUNITY IN ZAGREB
CAMP WELFARE DEPARTMENT
Trenkova 9[36]

The guards in Loborgrad belonged to the Kulturbund and were often very cruel. Camp Commander Heger, despite some positive efforts, "behaved like an animal."[37] Any "sexual intercourse shall be strictly punished, and anyone suspected shall be handed over for further proceedings to the Ustasha police," threatened the administration. The Jewish Section "many times ascertained that there have been intimate relations among prisoners" and said "it was all the fault of the camp commander."[38] Prisoners were not permitted to change beds, and especially to change rooms, without permission of the administration. Because of "repeated insubordination," prisoner Hedi Tudiover (Hedwiga Tudiower from Vienna) did not get food for two days in March 1942.[39] The children were treated more leniently: Vilko Heger ordered little Saša Friedrich and two of his companions to be shut up in the attic because of some childhood prank. But sometimes Heger showed some humanity, as when he allowed the Friedrich family to obtain a coffee mill: little Saša came to ask him, because his mother Mina thought that he would get permission more easily than she would.[40]

The prisoners were often woken up at night, ordered to "line up," and then had to spend several hours standing in the courtyard, lightly clothed and without shoes, regardless of the weather.[41] The latrines could only be used at a precisely predetermined time, only for four hours during the daytime; at other times, the prisoners used small buckets in the rooms, which always got too full, and their contents often spilled in the rooms and corridors.[42]

On their arrival, during the first days of October 1941, the women's health was very bad. The doctor, president of the Social Welfare Society, who was still in the manor at that time, described them as follows: "The wretched women had a helpless dumb stare, drawn faces, sunken eyes, dry wrinkled skins that were peeling as a sign of the horrors and misery they had been through, and a latent pathological fear. The diagnosis for almost all was vitamin deficiency, due to which their teeth and hair were falling out . . . all the prisoners also suffered from amenorrhea. Psychiatric diagnosis: pathological fear and psychoneurosis."[43]

In the following months the general condition of the prisoners and their children worsened. In December, a typhoid epidemic broke out—at the end of 1941, there were "six women with the symptoms of enteric typhoid fever" in the camp. Some of the patients were sent to hospitals in Zagreb, but, despite that, nine-year-old Brankica Fried and fifteen-year-old Meri Eškenazi died on December 31, 1941, and January 1, 1942, respectively, in the Hospital for Contagious Diseases.[44] By the beginning of February, 100 people were ill, and by around March 20, about 350. At the end of March, the epidemic "abated," and by the end of April the number of patients even began to decline: while there had been 142 on April 13, by April 21 their number decreased to 82, and by the beginning of May, to 77. In May, there were about 1,300 people in the camp, seventy of them suffering from typhoid and about 160 convalescents. At the end of June, there were twenty-seven typhoid patients; in July, there were no more newly ill, and only twelve patients.[45]

The patients were placed in what was known as the "patients' room." People in the camp were convinced—and this showed itself to be true—that whoever entered the room would never leave it. Healthy prisoners and children were not allowed in. Little Saša Friedrich could only look at his ill mother from the door, she waved to him, and that was the last time he saw her.[46] Later, word spread among the prisoners that the patients in that room had been given a lot of potatoes, which were in short supply for others, as extra food. It is very dangerous to eat potatoes and other heavy food in cases of enteric typhoid. By giving the patients potatoes, the camp administration had consciously or unconsciously contributed to their speedier demise.

The Jewish Section was informed about the typhoid epidemic, but did nothing.[47] It seems that Camp Commander Heger made more efforts: during the first half of 1942, disinfection was carried out with 57 kilograms. of phenol (carbolic acid), 94 liters of Lysol, and 1,070 kilograms of lime, and about 299 people were deloused.[48] According to the testimony of prisoner Anica Ehrenfreund-Polić, Heger went to this trouble because of his pathological fear of contracting typhoid himself. This was why he sent some of the patients to Zagreb hospitals, and the Zagreb Community did all it could to help: by their own efforts, the Community members "managed to suppress a serious epidemic of typhoid fever and improve the health and morale of the imprisoned women and children."[49] The Jewish

Section estimated that the typhoid death toll was about 9 percent,[50] but it seems that the percentage was much higher. The typhoid survivors looked terrible—in the three months that her son had not seen her, Zeev Glück's mother had lost twenty-three kilograms, her hair had gone completely gray, and her son only recognized her by her voice.[51]

The Jewish Community sent doctors from Zagreb, and, until the beginning of July 1942, doctors also went of their own accord to treat typhoid. Sometimes a pharmacist also came, and the camp had two permanent women doctors[52] and a dentist, who did over 1,000 examinations, fillings, extractions, and other dental work.[53] It seems that word spread that they worked well, so peasants from the surrounding villages also began to ask for their help.[54] In the late spring of 1942, the Jewish Community, and even the Jewish Section, attempted to procure vaccines to prevent a dysentery epidemic.[55]

Occasionally, the administration of Loborgrad Camp made it possible for their prisoners to be treated at Zagreb hospitals. While the transports were still passing through Zagreb in October 1941, Jewish Community representatives "managed, unfortunately only for a very small number of the most serious patients, to have them taken out of the transport and placed in a hospital."[56] At the beginning of November, Palomba Levi "was released from the camp for women prisoners for reasons of health" and returned to her son in Sarajevo, with the Zagreb Community advancing travel expenses for Mrs. Levi and her attendant.[57] Zlata Frankl was admitted to the Hospital for Contagious Diseases for typhoid, and, when she recovered, the hospital director, the distinguished epidemiologist Dr. Fran Mihaljević (after whom the hospital was later named), released her from hospital but did not return her to Loborgrad.[58] A total of sixty-one patients were sent to hospital.[59]

At the end of October, twenty-one-year-old Zagreb dressmaker and former Loborgrad prisoner, Palomba Kabiljo, née Alkuser, who was pregnant, spent four days in the Šalata Hospital in Zagreb. She was diagnosed with "disorders connected to pregnancy" (*molimina graviditatis*). The fact that she was placed in Šalata, and not in any of the gynecological wards or in the Petrova Maternity Hospital, indicates that she probably had some connections. Her husband, Avram, had already been deported to Jasenovac in 1941, and sent word from there for the last time in November 1942. Palomba again spent four days in the hospital at the end of November, and was "released because there is not enough room, and since she is due to give birth on December 4, 1941, we recommend that she stay in Zagreb and come to the institution to give birth," said the letter the hospital sent to the Police Directorate, so Palomba stayed in Zagreb. By saying that she was due at the beginning of December, the doctor deliberately lied, probably in the hope that the police would not make Palomba go back to Loborgrad so far-advanced in pregnancy. The doctor really did help, and Palomba gave birth to her son Isak undisturbed on January 15, 1942. The doctor could not have been as many as forty days off about when she was due, nor could Palomba have given birth to a healthy child so long-overdue. She was released from the hospital and she and her child lived in an apartment in Vlaška Street. In July 1942, the Šalata Hospital billed Palomba for hospital fees, and, as she obviously had no money, the Jewish Community paid for her. However, her happiness was short-lived because the Ustasha authorities seem to have known where Palomba was living. At the beginning of August, she and the baby were arrested and taken to the school in Križanićeva, and she was deported on August 13, 1942, and subsequently killed in Auschwitz. In January 1943, Palomba's father, Bencion Alkuser, from Bitola (in Macedonia), inquired about her, but the Zagreb Community could only tell him that she had been "sent to a work camp somewhere in Germany." Somehow, a Zagreb woman, Jozefina Ambrož, took charge of her son, Isak, from the Križanićeva mustering point, and he was christened in September 1942. The Jewish Community helped with the upkeep of the child in various ways; he survived the war, and, in 1945, he was no longer with Mrs. Ambrož but with his grandfather Isak Kabiljo.[60]

Other prisoners were also released from camp and sent for "surgical procedures."[61] Bjanka Levi was released from Loborgrad to give birth in Zagreb, but with the instruction that "after delivery, she is to return to camp," and it was the same for other women at term.[62] It seems that the Jewish Community managed somehow to obtain permission for Bjanka to remain in Zagreb after her baby was born, in one of the old people's homes, in a "shelter for old people and children." Her documents go together with those for the child Danko Levi, so this seems to have been Bjanka's son. He was given permission to "stay in the hospital for about ten days for blood treatment" and then to continue living in Zagreb.[63]

To avoid any misunderstandings, the Jewish Section of the Ustasha Police Directorate cautioned the General Hospital of the Sisters of Charity in Vinogradska that patients sent from camps "for treatment cannot, under any circumstances, be released from the hospital to freedom without a written order from this Section."[64] It was very rare indeed for patients to get permission to leave the hospital, that is, to be released for home care and into the care of the Jewish Community.[65] In November 1941, Bea Abinun and Julija Brück (from Ruma in Vojvodina, Serbia) were permitted to "permanently move to the area of the city of Zagreb," but these documents (in the same handwriting) carry the added note, "returned to Lobor on December 24, 1941."[66] Berta Pollak and Helena Schreiber were placed in the old people's home in Rapska Street.[67] The Loborgrad Camp Command demanded a report and other documents from the Zagreb Community about the movements of former prisoner Franciska Blau. In November 1941, she had been released from Loborgrad to Zagreb for "home care under medical supervision" and was staying with Artur Löwenstein in Erdödyjeva Street. Then she got a pass from the Ustasha Police, Jewish Section, to travel to her brother, T. Weiss, to Budinščina, "where she is now on home care."[68] About thirty, if not more, other Loborgrad prisoners of all ages, even children, were similarly released and got permission to live in Zagreb, mostly in old people's homes of the Jewish Community. Their stay was strictly supervised by the Ustasha services, which meant that they had been saved from death only temporarily. For a small number, there are records that they were killed in camps—for example, Mirjam Berger, Elizabeta Fodor, and three-year-old Mirica Kuh. In other cases, we can usually assume that this was what happened, because all the homes, except that in Stenjevec, were closed after the deportations in May 1943. Data for the Jewish women do not exist: they were not from Zagreb, so their names would not appear on lists of Jewish victims from Zagreb. They do not appear on lists of victims who came to Zagreb, either (in many cases, there is no information about where they came from).[69]

There were also some happy moments in the increasingly tragic fate of the Loborgrad prisoners: during the spring of 1942, an anonymous man brought to the rooms of the Jewish Community on Tomislavov Square a parcel, in which the employees found a two-year-old girl. Little Dina had been sent by her mother, Blanka Büchler, a Loborgrad prisoner, with the message to hand her over to her cousin Blanka Sitzer Fürst. As Blanka Sitzer had to flee as well, she left the child in the care of a Zagreb family, Beritić, with whom Dina lived to the end of the war. She was an orphan, because her father, Dragan, an attorney, was killed in Jasenovac in 1941, her mother was deported together with the other Loborgrad prisoners, and her maternal grandfather and grandmother, Milan and Elza Brodarić, were also killed (there is no information about Dragan's parents).[70]

It seems that, starting in May 1942, some of the healthy Loborgrad prisoners did farm work for the "surrounding peasants, because most of the men had been called up."[71] Despite everything, a school was organized in the camp in May, and, in June, also a kindergarten for children ages three to seven.[72]

The administration tried to "maintain hygiene in the interests of the prisoners." At the beginning of March 1942, there was an order given that all the rooms should be thoroughly cleaned and disinfected, and, at the end of March, the district doctor inspected the outhouses and latrines and "found that everything had been done according to the demands of the commission twenty days earlier." In May, the camp informed the superiors in Zagreb that "the construction of the new outhouse will not be finished for two to three months," and the bad condition of the outhouses and wells were also mentioned in August, a short time before the liquidation of the camp.[73] A memo in June 1942 prohibited cooking in the rooms, water was to be thrown only in the drainage channels, and "it is forbidden to empty chamber pots in the channel, under the threat of strictest punishment." Drinking water could be drawn from only one well, while water from the second well was used only for bathing, and from the third, only for cooking and washing clothes. Water from the stream had to be boiled before use. The second well began to be used around April 1942, and, before that, it seems that there was generally not enough water, even for cooking and baking bread.[74]

Death was common. In a notice of March 30, 1942, the administration ordered the infirmary to, "after every death, hand over to the Administration an exact list of all the remaining valuables and property of the deceased."[75] After the death of each prisoner, the camp commander sent a notice to the Jewish Section of the RUR; for example, he informed them that between April 25 and May 4, "there have been no deaths in the camps in Loborgrad and Gornja Rijeka."[76] One report says that about 200 people died in the camp, but the list of deaths in Loborgrad has only ninety-five names, nine of them of Jewish women from Zagreb and their children.[77] After several months, "the Serb women were released and sent home from the camp." In March 1942, the Zagreb Jewish Community requested from the Jewish Section and other competent institutions that the Jewish orphans in Loborgrad be "released to the care of the Religious Community in Zagreb," but the answer was that "for special reasons, at least at present, the proposal cannot be complied with . . . therefore, the Jewish Community is directed to care for the welfare of these children . . . if it wishes to, by arranging to feed and care for them in the camp itself."[78] In March, Dragan Albrecht, an advisor in the Ministry of the Interior, visited the camp and "issued orders concerning the camp." It seems that he did nothing to "combat typhoid," as the accompanying official letter says, because he did not know how to do so. It is much more likely that he was making preparations for deportation, because this was what he did in August and September in Vinkovci, where he was "head of the activities concerning the removal of Jews."[79]

In early August, representatives of the Jewish Section of the RUR came to the Loborgrad Camp together with a German commission to inform the prisoners that "as of this moment, you have been taken over by the German Reich." The prisoners had to hand over any valuables that they still possessed and all their clothing and shoes, except for the most indispensable.[80] The women and children were placed in transports that arrived from Zagreb and were deported to Auschwitz in August, together with the internees from Križanićeva Street. In March 1943, the official version in the Zagreb Community was still that they had been "taken to a work camp abroad, we do not know which," and, in internal letters, they only wrote "Poland."[81] A small group of Croatian women were taken to Stara Gradiška. Only about fifty women were left for the most necessary work, and some more Jewish women arrived. On October 6, they were finally all sent to Jasenovac, and only two of them were released.[82] According to information obtained from people in the Jewish Community in 1945, "only about five or six children" of those who had been interned in Loborgrad were saved.[83]

In addition to Lobor (and Gornja Rijeka), a camp was also organized in Đakovo.[84] It seems that it had up to 3,800 prisoners, mostly Jewish women and children, most of them from Sarajevo, and also from Slavonski Brod and Bosanski Brod, Nova Gradiška, Požega, Zenica, Zagreb, Lipik, Pakrac, Travnik, and other places. Some transports set off from Sarajevo at the end of November 1941, and the communities in Slavonski Brod and Zagreb tried to organize accompaniment and aid.[85] On the list of women and children who arrived in the camp on February 26 and March 6, 1942, of a total of 1,073 people, 274, or just over one-quarter, were from Zagreb.[86]

As in the case of Loborgrad, very many necessities of various kinds and food arrived from outside the camp. The First Croatian Oil Factory in Zagreb sold oil for the prisoners, and other firms joined in as well.[87] A shipment of twenty kg. of the pesticide Cyclone B (in German, Zyklon B) arrived from Zagreb, obviously for disinfection.[88] Among the preserved bills, there is a disproportionately large number for medicines.[89] The Jewish Community in Osijek organized the supply of Đakovo Camp until its liquidation in June 1942, and the Ustasha regime financially exploited them to the maximum.[90] There was hunger in the camp before it was closed down, and daily rations were reduced to two or three potatoes.[91] Then, the Zagreb Jewish Community asked to take over supplying the prisoners, but the request was denied because it had obviously already been decided to liquidate the camp.[92]

There was no mass killing in the camp itself, but there were beatings and starvation. Hygiene was appalling, and, in January 1942, a commission gave advice about what to do—but no action was taken.[93] It is therefore not surprising that as many as 800 prisoners succumbed to the typhus epidemic in May 1942. Of the 569 identified camp victims buried in the Jewish cemetery in Đakovo, there are at least fifty-seven Jewish women from Zagreb (16.1 percent of the total number).[94]

The camp was closed down in June 1942, when the women and children were transferred to Jasenovac, where all of them were killed with extreme cruelty.[95]

In the concentration camps in Loborgrad and in Đakovo, the Jewish women and their children were, in fact, without suspecting it, only awaiting their death sentences from the top Nazi or Ustasha authorities. The Loborgrad women and children were taken to the gas chambers of Auschwitz, and those from Đakovo met their death in Jasenovac. These camps were like the "ordinary" concentration camps in the Third Reich, such as Theresienstadt, where internees lived in a kind of waiting room prior to being sent to the death camps in Poland.

23

A NEW KIND OF CORRESPONDENCE

Requests for Release from Camps

Many Zagreb Jews were arrested in the street during one of the numerous raids, or else policemen came to their apartment and took them away "for interrogation." In most cases, their families knew nothing or had only some unconfirmed information about their whereabouts and about what was happening to them. People were figuratively torn apart and were driven crazy by the lack of any solid information. When they found out that camps had been organized and that their loved ones were there, a specific kind of correspondence developed between the Ustasha authorities and the families of the arrestees—requests for release from camp.

Right from the beginning, when the group of 165 Zagreb youths was taken away, despite the reassuring explanations of why this had been done, families obviously began to fear the worst. On May 30, a former colonel in the health service, Viktor Ružić, begged for his son, Branko, to be released, because "I have no other family and he is my only reason for living." His request was accompanied by the recommendation of Lieutenant General Vladimir Laxa, commander of the land forces, pointing out that both the Ružićes "had converted to the Catholic religion" (although their request for conversion was filed with the Parish of St. Blaise in Zagreb on May 22, so there had not been time for even a very formal and short ceremony!).

The request was approved, probably because of Laxa's intercession, and Branko Ružić was released. Viktor Ružić survived the war, but Branko's fate is not known, as he is neither on the list of survivors nor on the lists of victims.[1] Saša Blühweiss (Blivajs), another member of that group, was also released, and he too survived the war.[2]

In July, Elza Reis submitted a request for her son Gjuro to be sent home from Koprivnica, saying that he was ill; however, Gjuro was killed in Jadovno at about that time, and later Elza herself lost her life in an unspecified place.[3] At the end of August, Žiga (Sigismund) Schotten (Šoten) requested the release of his son Branko, who had been, said the father, taken from Jadovno to Pag together with other Zagreb youths. On July 18, when Branko was already in camp, Žiga and his wife, Olga, converted to Catholicism, and they put down Branko's name for conversion too. But Branko was killed in July or, at the latest, at the beginning of August, and the father and mother later ended their lives in an unknown place.[4] Someone added the word "refused" on the requests for release from camp submitted for Pavao Berenji, Ivan Koller, and Ignac and Zoltan Boroš. However, it made no difference whether requests of this kind were formally refused or accepted—in the meantime, all the above were killed in Jadovno.[5] At the beginning of July, the Zagreb Jewish Community requested an amelioration of living conditions for the youths in Danica Camp, but this was pointless because they were by then already in Jadovno.[6] Finally, on September 20, 1941, the forty-one undersigned parents of these youths personally begged the Minister of the Interior for the "children to be returned to their families." The parents claimed, rather unconvincingly, that "our children left home with great joy to do students' work service, because they were told that they would work and return home after eight weeks." At the time when the parents wrote the request, they already knew that the Jadovno Camp had been shut down and there was no one there any more, so they hoped that the children were either in the newly built Jasenovac Camp, the establishment of which they had heard of at that time, or that they had been "sent from Jadovno to Pag." The request was still circulating among various Ustasha services during the first half of October, without any answer.[7]

When some indirect or random information awoke the hopes of family and friends that the worst had not happened, a particular ambience developed. When Jews were deported to Gospić and to the surrounding camps, Ustasha propaganda vehemently claimed that "they are going to Lika . . . to [Mount] Velebit . . . for forced labor . . . They are going to build roads and tunnels."[8] Although it became clear as time passed that the prisoners in Jadovno and Pag were not doing any kind of work, but were being killed, rumors continued to circulate for many months that they had escaped from camp and had already joined the Partisans, that they were safe but could not send word so as not to give away their whereabouts, etc. "Accounts of the Holocaust show that often even the Jews themselves did not want to believe, although they could see what was going on."[9] In the case of the Jadovno group, apparently the Ustashe themselves encouraged stories about the prisoners still being alive, because it seems that they removed the prisoners from the camp under the pretext of taking them to Pag, and then threw them down one of the nearby pits. After the war, the peasants in the surrounding hamlets told that the moans of the dying could be heard from the pits for days.

Requests for release of the Jadovno group from camp are the first and the last in which euphemisms such as "going for work duty" and the like are used. In October 1941, doubt about any favorable outcome is clearly expressed in a document for the first time, when housewife Rozalija Kremer inquired about her seventeen-year-old daughter, Bela, known as Beluška, who had been taken to the prison in Petrinjska on July 1, and then to a camp. "To the best of my knowledge, she is not in any of the existing camps . . . so I am wondering whether she is still alive." Bela was killed in 1941, probably in Dotrščina.[10]

When the 165 youths were arrested in Zagreb at the end of May, many people believed the official explanation that they were "being taken for work," so requests for their release did not begin in any great number until July and August. However, when mass arrests of Jews began on June 21, many people already suspected that this was not any kind of "taking for work" or the like, so requests were immediately submitted in the following days, such as the one for "Oton Mermelstein to be returned to work; he was taken to the Zagreb Fairground on June 21 and did not return from there." Mermelstein (1905) was killed in an unknown place.[11] On July 9, the knitwear company Zenit asked the Jewish Section to "temporarily postpone the detention of Mr. Alfred Eisenstädter," but Eisenstädter did not survive the war either.[12] During the first days of July, Branko and Vladimir Vilković, owners of a shop at Ilica 13, were "temporarily exempted" from deportation. Vladimir survived the war, but nothing is known about Branko.[13] On July 14, the technical goods shop in Nikolićeva requested that Josip Haas should be given an "exception from the measures undertaken against the Jews, because he is very necessary," but the request was not "approved" and Haas was killed in Jasenovac by the end of the year.[14] On July 9, the Farmabion biochemical laboratory requested "the release of the owner of the firm, Dr. Milan Farkaš," who was also killed in Jasenovac by the end of that year.[15] The commissioner of the Lacquers and Paints Factory was especially skilled in using euphemisms. In July 1941, he wrote that "engineer Ivan Brichta, technical manager, has been relieved of duty as of the end of September, but since it is his duty to train his successor, who is a Croat, we request that he be issued with a certificate until then, so that no one bothers him." Ivan Brichta very soon fled to Ljubljana, and later joined the National Liberation Struggle.[16] An inclination for using this kind of language can also be seen in the official letter of the Chamber of Attorneys from 1943, which claims that Dr. Siegfried Perlberg, "when he was leaving for camp, instructed" what was to happen to his property "after his death."[17] At that time, Perlberg was already dead.

Due to the general state of fear within Jewish circles that spread through Zagreb at that time, many Jews rightly feared that they would be taken away, so they interceded on their own behalf. On June 24, Zoltan Weil asked the Jewish Section to "please exempt me from potential forced labor," substantiating his request with a document issued by his firm in which he was the only "engineer." Although his file says that "preventive protection cannot be approved," Weil survived the war.[18] On June 30, the Jugo-petrol firm requested postponement in interning Stjepan Peći so that he could bring to a conclusion some very important work in connection with importing equipment from Germany. It seems that the intercession succeeded, because Peći survived the war.[19] On the other hand, when Lavoslav Steiner, vice-president of the Jewish Community and the largest paper and cardboard wholesaler in the State, requested from the Jewish Section on June 27 exemption from reporting to the Zagreb Fairground, all his arguments—both professional and medical—were disregarded because "he is a Jew, and a Freemason" (Steiner was a member of B'nai B'rith, and probably also a Freemason). Steiner ended his days in Jasenovac; at the beginning of November the first parcel was sent to him. His wife Elza and his daughter Mira did not survive the war either.[20]

In July, eighty-two-year-old Franciska Beck, who was seriously ill, requested that her daughter, Ivana Haas, be "freed from a potentially planned eviction because I have no one to help me." Dragutin Ebenspanger requested the liberation of his daughter, Elly, who was taken to the Zagreb Fairground on July 8, and on July 12 "transported we do not know where," adding that he was "a serious pulmonary invalid." Franciska Beck and Ivana Haas were deported in 1943. Elly Ebenspanger was killed in 1942, and her father did not survive the war, either.[21] At that time, eighty-six-year-old Izabela Kohn, "a citizen of Germany," requested the release of her fifty-year-old daughter, Dr. Marta Fodor, and her daughters Anamarija and Elizabeta (ages 18 and 8), who had already been "taken to an unknown place."[22] It is possible that Marta and her daughters were released at that time, but Marta and Anamarija perished in a "German camp" in 1942, while the younger daughter, Elizabeta, survived and in August 1945, returned to the Jewish faith in Zagreb. Izabela Kohn did not survive either, but she probably was not deported but possibly died a natural death.[23]

Many people acquired various certificates about a serious health condition, which the authorities, at least at first, took into account and sometimes even recognized. As doctors obviously issued these certificates quite frequently, especially to delay eviction from an apartment or deportation, the Ustasha authorities threatened the doctors in an official letter to the Medical Chamber, saying that "any doctor who issues a certificate without an objective medical finding will be most strictly punished."[24] At the beginning of September 1941, a certain Dr. Rakulić was appointed to determine which Jews in the Srebrnjak Sanatorium were fit for transportation to Zavrtnica, and which were not.[25] The sculptor Slavko Bril was not saved from deportation to Jasenovac at the beginning of 1942 either by the fact that he had converted to Catholicism in July 1941 or by his health. He was seriously ill with tuberculosis and had a broken leg in a plaster cast, but nonetheless he was loaded in a railway car on a stretcher because the doctor on duty had proclaimed him "fit for transportation." In 1942, Bril worked in the Jasenovac pottery, and he died in the prison hospital, according to some sources in 1943, and to others, in 1944.[26] Mihajlo Bauer and Avram Kabiljo were deported from Zagreb in 1941 and ended their days in camp. At the time of deportation, Mihajlo's wife, Regina, was pregnant, and she already had a child of three. Avram's wife was in the last stages of pregnancy.[27]

The Jewish Section also received letters that were inspired by other motives, some sincere while others were pretexts. In a letter dated July 9, the commissioner of Union, Deutsch, and König Confectionaries and Chocolate Factory, claimed that the cashier, Draga Gerber, a Jewish woman, "was taken from her apartment after work hours" and that she had not "managed to hand over the keys to the safe nor to turn in her accounts." Thus, he requested that "Draga Gerber be allowed to do this as soon as possible." We do not know whether Draga returned the keys or turned in her accounts, but it is a fact that her life ended in an unknown place.[28] Some people worded requests for a particular Jew to be spared from deportation in a very specific way: "We would not even lift our finger for this Jew if we knew of any Aryan expert," but "Ladislav Gissingen is the only expert for reception and transmission tubes in the State," wrote the First Croatian Radio Factory. Even this explanation did not help, because, by the end of the year, Gissingen ended his days in Jasenovac.[29]

After the end of August, tens, and then hundreds, of requests for release from Zavrtnica transit camp suddenly appeared.[30] Some were written with pathos or flattery, some are restrained and factual, some desperate and despairing, some irresistibly sad and touching. Eleven-year-old Sofija Singer, a "daughter," in an unskilled hand begged for her father Leopold (Lavoslav) Singer (1884), who "has been completely deaf for the past thirty years," and with a heart defect, to be released from Zavrtnica. "Mommy is completely impossible without him, and I, as a child, am helpless . . . I have many reasons to fear for my Daddy . . . I have no one to help me." It would appear that someone was moved by the letter from this child, and a recommendation arrived for Singer to be "temporarily released." It is not clear, however, whether Singer really was released—it seems that the recommendation arrived too late and that he had already been deported to Jasenovac. He never sent word from Jasenovac, and, for this reason, no parcel was ever sent to him, which means that he was already dead in October, or at the latest in November.[31]

Leopold Singer was a "craftsman who made amusing paper goods . . . paper masks and the like." Soon after the proclamation of the ISC, he had no more work. The Singers belonged to the lower classes of Zagreb Jews: all they had in valuables were 3,600 dinars in cash, two wedding rings, four silver tablespoons, six silver coffee spoons, and a "contraption for making paper masks, which has not been used for many years and is rusty." The family was thrown out of its apartment in Bauerova in about June or July and moved to what was then the outskirts, to Hvarska Street in Sigečica. The mother, Eugenija (1895), was arrested in Daruvar in 1942 and killed in Stara Gradiška. Where and when Sofija died is not known, but she did not survive the war either. It is paradoxical that on the List of Victims from Zagreb, her nationality is given as "Croatian."[32]

In the fall of 1941, requests for release from Jasenovac began to pour in, hundreds of them, and this went on for months. Then, at the turn of the year, requests for release from Loborgrad and Đakovo appeared, and, finally, in August 1942, for release from the mustering point in Križanićeva Street.[33] For example, Sofija Deči from Zagreb requested the release from

Stara Gradiška of her eighty-one-year-old and ill mother, Berta, from Slavonska Požega, who had been deported at the end of 1941. As an argument, the daughter said that all six of Berta's children had become Catholics, and that her own family had done this as far back as 1915.[34] The UNS also received a request for Dragica Hercer and her children to be released from camp, but the answer was that "Dragica Hercer cannot be released for special reasons, and since the children cannot be separated from the mother, the recipient should inform the supplicant that the request cannot be met."[35] Around the fall of 1941, there were increasing numbers of requests which show that those who had lodged them did not even know in which camp those for whom they were interceding were located—which made the requests even more futile. Hundreds of requests, just as, several months earlier, requests for exemption from wearing the Jewish insignia, or for being granted Aryan rights, flooded Ustasha state institutions, providing them with legitimacy and a reason for existing, but which proved to be mostly ineffectual.

If chances for a favorable solution had still existed when requests were submitted for Aryan rights or exemption from wearing the Jewish insignia, the requests for release from camp were as a rule fruitless, and the great majority were not even considered.[36] If a request for release from camp had any writing on it at all, then this was "not approved," "refused," "refused by higher order," "no decisive (justified) reasons are given for release from camp," "no real reasons are found for meeting the request," "there are no preconditions on the grounds of which the request can be met," or "more important reasons must exist for the request to be complied with." Sometimes, simply nothing was done at all and things were "put off for three months" because the case was being dealt with by some other service, for example, UNS or MUP.[37] Even when someone wanted to meet a request, as in the above case of the little girl Sofija Singer, who asked for her father Leopold to return home, sometimes it was too late.[38] Slavka Baselli became pregnant by Šime Lion, who was Jewish. Before they managed to get married, Šime was deported to Jasenovac. The case moved an unknown official in the Ustasha Police Directorate to carry out a small study. On one hand, he found that the child had obviously been conceived before the racial laws banning marriages between Jews and non-Jews entered into force, so there were no obstacles for Slavka and Šime to be married on those grounds. On the other hand, he claimed that Šime's possible conversion to Catholicism had no meaning, because the Jewish question was racial, not religious. Finally, the request for Šime's release from camp, and any possibility for the couple to be married, was refused, although the parish priest of St. Peter's Parish in Zagreb, obviously with the desire to help, confirmed that Šime and Slavka had been living together and were engaged. Šime never returned from Jasenovac.[39]

In this endless mass of victims, some people were released from camp on various grounds, but these rarely included Jews.[40] The many state services kept watch on one another to prevent any of them from becoming too compliant—thus, the Jewish Section demanded a list of released internees from the commanders of Loborgrad and Gornja Rijeka Camps, which would show by whose order this had been done.[41]

Toward the end of 1941, the number of requests for release from camp waned, and, in the following years, there were hardly any. The supplicants realized that it was to no avail. In 1942, a new kind of correspondence appeared: the Jews who had fled to the Italian zone, and on to Italy and other countries, sent dozens of letters to the Zagreb Jewish Community every day, asking after their family and friends. More or less at the same time, the Ustasha authorities permitted the prisoners to send home short messages, which were allegedly a "reward for good behavior."

24

MIXED MARRIAGES AND "HONORARY ARYANS"

By the laws and other provisions of the ISC, Jewish men and women in mixed marriages, half-Jews, Jews who had been granted Aryan rights or who enjoyed "protection" for various reasons, were to be exempted from racial laws and protected from any persecution. Most of them survived the war, but many were persecuted in various ways. They all lived in fear of being killed, and some were. Not one person from these groups was certain of surviving.

In the summer of 1941, the painter Ivan (Ivo) Palčić (1892–1969), born in Novalja on the island of Pag, requested Aryan rights for Ruža, allegedly his wife, who was Jewish. The request was co-signed by several Croats, but this did not help; it was refused, and Ruža was later deported and killed.[1] In July 1941, Eugen Janušić, a Croat and "Aryan," requested exemption from wearing the insignia for his wife, Dragica, née Hirschl (1896), "who has always felt herself Croatian." In October, a note was added to the request, without any further explanation, that Janušić had "taken back the papers, withdrawn his request." It is possible that the request had become meaningless because Dragica had in the meantime been deported and ended her days in an unknown place.[2]

There was quite a lot of "flexibility" in applying the provisions about Aryan rights, and people in mixed marriages were treated in different ways.

In principle, members of mixed marriages were guaranteed protection, but nonetheless some of them were killed. Even some Jewish women married to "Aryans" were killed, although they were considered "safer" than Jewish men married to "Aryan women." Sidonija Petelinšek, née Blau, married to the Croat Albin, who had a daughter, Vanda, by that marriage, died in the Đakovo Camp in June 1942.[3] Jewish women married to "Aryans" almost always became Catholics before having a church marriage (which was the only legal form of marriage in interwar Yugoslavia), and children born in these marriages, although half-Jewish (which means that they could be considered "half-Aryan"), were usually exempt from arrest, at least in 1941. On the other hand, when the husband was a Jew and the wife "Aryan," the procedure varied. A certain number of men were spared because they used various kinds of connections, especially if the children of such marriages had been christened in the Catholic Church and were therefore Catholics.[4] But, for example, Izidor Levi was sent to Slana Camp on the island of Pag as early as the end of June 1941, and then killed in Jasenovac, although his wife was Aryan.[5]

The case of Milivoj Šenwald (Schönwald, born 1906) from Zagreb can be seen as characteristic.[6] He stated that he was the "illegitimate child of a Jewish woman" who had neglected him, so he was "brought up by a peasant family in the Catholic spirit," that he did not "know his father's name, but I heard that he was a Catholic." Šenwald was married to an Aryan woman, had a baptized child of nine and considered himself "an indomitable Croat, who had publicly voted for the Croatian Peasant Party." Šenwald's request for exemption from wearing the Jewish insignia was refused, and in the summer of 1941 he was deported to Pag; by the end of 1941, he had lost his life in Jasenovac.[7]

Emil Kohn (twenty-eight), married to the Croat Anka, née Turković, and a father of two children ages two-and-a-half years and nine months, who worked for the Siodd Warehouse and Shipping, was fired on July 30. In this way, he "lost his livelihood." At the end of September, Siodd received an official letter from the Ministry of Crafts, Industry, and Trade saying that "if Emil Kohn is indispensable . . . you may keep him," and it is possible that he did return to work. He obviously had some money, because he regularly paid the Community dues until the end of 1942 (he had to pay the minimum sum of 350 kunas for 1941, 700 kunas for the next year). However, in the long run this did not help, and Emil Kohn was deported, probably in May 1943. It appears that his wife was killed too, although she was "Aryan." Nothing could be found out about the fate of their children.[8]

The request of Milan Katz (1888) from Sveti Duh to not wear the insignia was refused, although he had already converted to Catholicism in 1923 and was married to an "Aryan," Marija, née Horjak. He even had a certificate from the parish priest that he was an "exemplary Catholic," and he said that one of his two daughters belonged to the university Ustasha units. In July, his radio set was confiscated. Finally, Milan Katz disappeared in an unspecified camp, but his daughters were saved. Zlata fled to Italy, and Nada, who lived to see the liberation, inscribed her name on the list of surviving members of the Jewish Community in 1945.[9]

In 1941, Zvonimir Fürst Galeković was "taken to a concentration camp" and was killed in Jasenovac at the end of that year, but his wife, Olga, and their children, as "Aryans," survived the war.[10]

During the First World War, Herman/Ljudevit Švarcenberg had been taken prisoner by the Russians. In Russia, he married a Russian woman, Vasilka, and returned to Croatia, to Daruvar, and they had four children. Herman and his sons, Boris Maks and Vilim, were killed in camps, while the sisters, Sonja (1926) and Lidija, survived by joining the National Liberation Struggle.[11]

David Baruch (1904) and his wife, Lucija, née Dianić-Orač, who was Croatian, owned shops that sold materials in Tkalčićeva Street and on Kaptol. It seems that he and his son, Rafael (1936), had fled to Italy by the beginning of June 1941, while his wife and daughter, Lea-Lenka (1939), remained at home. On June 6, his wife handed over cessions in the value of 100,000 kunas to the Contribution Committee.[12] David returned to Zagreb, probably thinking that he would not be persecuted since he was in a mixed marriage, but the Ustasha services soon arrested him. In prison, he was tortured and became mentally ill, and was sent to the Psychiatric Hospital in Vrapče. At the beginning of January 1941, he converted to Catholicism. In 1943, he was released from hospital, although he had not been cured, because the family paid someone. Soon he attacked his wife with a knife, sending her to the hospital for two months. David was arrested again, sent to Jasenovac, then returned to the Psychiatric Hospital in Vrapče. In September or October 1944, an Ustasha unit under the command of Ljubo Miloš got him out of the hospital and he was never seen again. His son, Rafael, although he and his sister became Catholics in 1941, spent eight months in Jasenovac, but was released. Lucija filed for divorce at the beginning of 1944, just before her husband's death, because it was a way of increasing her chances and the children's for survival, and remarried soon thereafter. Thus, Lucija and the children survived the war.[13]

Jewish men and women in mixed marriages, or who had "connections" in the government, and half-Jews, had greater chances of surviving. Even as late as July 1942, the Fourth Office UNS first gave the order for fifteen Jews in Zagreb to be arrested, but to "find out whether these Jews have Aryan rights or any other kind of special protection, whether they are in a mixed marriage with an Aryan person, and are there any children in this marriage. If a person fits none of the above cases, these Jews must be detained and sent to transit camps."[14] But, despite some extenuating circumstances, the position of persons in mixed marriages was never quite safe. At the time of deportations in August 1941, Catholic husbands and Catholic wives from Osijek begged that their non-Aryan spouses be protected.[15]

Although it had been agreed during preparations for deportations in May 1943 that "honorary Aryans, people from mixed marriages and half-Jews" would not be deported, this agreement was not followed to the letter.[16] Even people who had been granted "Aryan rights" suffered: the entire Büchler family, the husband, Leo, wife Zora and children Zvonko and Zlata (born 1925), were granted Aryan rights because Leo did work on "transporting and moving" for the Naval Command. All the same, the husband and wife were killed, while Zvonko survived the war and Zlata later joined the Partisans.[17] Edo Funk was shot in 1944 although he had Aryan rights.[18] In the same year, the "honorary Aryan" Aleksandar Klein also disappeared.[19]

Dragutin and Hinko Weiller were granted Aryan rights by the "generosity of Poglavnik Pavelić." In November 1941, they thanked him heartily and concluded the letter with the words, "in readiness for the Poglavnik and the homeland." Dragutin met his end in an unknown place, but Hinko seems to have survived the war, by escaping from Zagreb.[20]

Julija Katz wrote to Andrija Artuković in person; she said that she had "had to wait six years to get a job because I emphasized that I was a Croat," what is more, "an ardent Croat." After "I welcomed the arrival of the ISC, I lost even the little that I had previously had: my job. I was fired because I was Jewish. Now I am a Catholic with tuberculosis and old parents, who used to depend on my miserable pay . . . I beg you to protect my life . . . so that, if I cannot get any kind of a job from the State, at least my parents and I do not have to suffer in Croatia, like I suffered as a Croat in Yugoslavia." Julija Katz's request for Aryan rights was granted, but later she and her parents, Ignac and Eta, ended their lives in a camp.[21]

It seems that Jewish women married to Serbs were treated more strictly. Regina Kovačević, wife of a major from Zagreb, and Vera Georgijević, wife of an attorney from Zagreb, were not exempt from wearing the Jewish insignia. There is a note on both the requests, stating "not granted," without any explanation. This probably would not have happened to them had they been been married to Croats.[22] Persons born in a Croatian-Jewish marriage had a much better chance of avoiding persecution than those born in a Serb-Jewish marriage. Despite great difficulties, Vera Georgijević survived the war, and it seems that Regina Kovačević did as well.[23]

Nevertheless, the families of mixed marriages—the spouses and children—lived in constant fear. Ivana Forenbacher, née Rosskamp, told how they listened in fear to the engine of every car that passed through Deželićev prilaz, fearing that it would stop in front of their house. During the deportations in May 1943, the Rosskamp family slept in the homes of their good friends, the Šalić family. The Rajić family, too, whose father was Serb and mother Jewish, found shelter in safer places during the deportations, and avoided living in their own home.[24]

25

CARE FOR THE INTERNEES AND FOR THE SURVIVAL OF THE JEWISH RELIGIOUS COMMUNITY

The clearest announcement of plans to completely annihilate Zagreb's Jews was the commencement of demolition of the central Zagreb synagogue in October 1941. For three-quarters of a century, the fine synagogue in today's Praška Street, in the very heart of the city, had been one of the landmarks of Zagreb and the symbol of Jewry in the city. Thus, its total destruction (as opposed to some kind of a conversion) had a symbolic meaning.

Zagreb's mayor, Ivan Werner, a well-known prewar Zagreb butcher, explained the decision to pull down the synagogue in *Hrvatski narod*[1]: "This decision was made because the temple does not comply with the general plan regulating the layout of the city of Zagreb." However, Werner did not decide the fate of the synagogue by himself—it was a decision made at the top state level. Leonardo Grivičić, who did not have any important political function but was a very influential man and close to Poglavnik Pavelić, informed Chief Cantor Grüner of what was being planned just one day in advance. Grüner was allowed to take the Torahs from *Aron Hakodesh* before seven o'clock in the morning on the very day when demolition began, and, in this way, eight Torahs were saved from destruction.[2] Demolition began on October 10, and lasted all through the winter, and by the spring of 1942, the area in Praška Street was completely cleared. All that was found after the war was one of the capitals that had supported the gallery, which Ivo Kraus, a member of the Council of the Jewish Community and who worked in the district attorney's office, had brought to the Community building in Palmotićeva 16.[3] As Chief Rabbi Schwarz watched the demolition from nearby, he said, according to David Levi, "They are pulling down the building bricks and stones . . . that is all. A building built of bricks and stones is not important. What is important is the building built of morality and ethics that we carry within us. They can demolish our synagogue, they can even kill us . . . but no enemy can destroy the building that we are carrying within us."[4] Chief Rabbi Schwarz did not live to see the temple's complete destruction, as he died on February 7, 1942, and was buried in the Mirogoj Cemetery. Although the Ustasha authorities had imprisoned and harassed him, and he was in poor health anyway, suffering from diabetes, it seems that what affected him most was sorrow for the Jews who had lost their lives and for the destruction of the synagogue.[5]

According to Amiel Shomrony, Archbishop Stepinac spoke in the cathedral about the ongoing demolition of the synagogue. Some people got the text "in writing." "The house of God, whatever religion it belongs to, is a holy object, and whoever lays hands on it will pay with his life. In this world and the next, he will be tormented." Stepinac also added that this was being been done by the "Ustashe and their leaders."[6]

There were no mass arrests at the end of 1941, but the police frequently arrested individuals: thus, Egon Spitzer, a clerk at Jadransko osiguravajuće društvo (an insurance company), was arrested on November 8 and ended in an unknown place (probably in one of the Zagreb prisons or in Jasenovac).[7] On November 24, another ten people were deported, mostly members of the Fuchs family—Vera (1889), Jelena (1889), Saša (1921), Ivo (1927), Marta (1927)—and the Wertheimer family—the mother Regina (1893), together with her daughters Mira (1916) and Marta (1924). The Wertheimer family lived in Masarykova, and the father, who was a locksmith, had been deported to Jasenovac earlier. No member of either family survived the war.[8]

The Legal Provision on Conducting Undesirable and Dangerous Persons to Forced Internment in Transit and Labour Camps was enacted on November 26, and formally legitimized the camp system. Although the text of the provision does not specifically mention the Jews, they could be included in its implementation in various ways: they could easily be proclaimed "undesirable and dangerous" as potential "saboteurs," as persons who had violated various Ustasha provisions, as "persons without citizenship, etc." What this looked like in practice can be seen by an example from

Virovitica (130 kilometers northeast of Zagreb). The Proposal for Enforced Internment in a Camp, filled in by the local County Police Precinct, says that "in accordance with the UNS order . . . Josip Emanuel Štern, as a Jew, is deemed undesirable for public order and security."[9]

This legal provision also laid down that "no legal remedy or appeal to the administrative court is possible against the decision of the Ustasha police for enforced internment in transit or labor camps."[10] At the same time, the UNS Command sent a directive to all the grand counties and to the Police Precinct of the City of Zagreb with precise instructions about how to implement the provision. UNS tightly controlled all activities, and the provincial services were left with very little maneuvering space.[11] How important the authorities considered this provision can also be inferred from the fact that it was amended and supplemented twice, although not significantly, in February 1942 and in January 1945.[12]

On the grounds of this or other provisions, and even before they were passed or regardless of them, by the late fall of 1941, almost half the Jews in Zagreb, Croatia, and Bosnia-Herzegovina had been arrested and deported to camps, and many of them killed.

To allay the tragedy that was growing worse by the day, in the summer of 1941, the Zagreb (and Osijek) Jewish Community founded a special institution called Camp Welfare, which had its own funding. The Ustasha authorities demanded that all aid should go through Welfare and through the Jewish Religious Community in Zagreb, obviously to allow complete control.[13]

The Ustasha authorities intended for Jewish religious communities, in particular the Zagreb Community, to care for all the Jewish prisoners in the camps. The communities also had to help the many members and their families who had lost their income and livelihood. They had to supply the transports traveling to the camps from various destinations, most of which passed through Zagreb. All this was a great burden, both financially and in human resources, which the Community Council and staff met with admirable persistence.

There were three main sources of funding: first, the dues paid by Community members, which were already insufficient by the summer and early fall because most members had been plundered, and many had already been deported to camps or had fled from Zagreb; second, requests were submitted to the Ustasha authorities to unfreeze Community bank accounts and to assign the Community part of the assets from the contribution, an appeal to which the authorities were deaf until 1942, releasing only minimal and completely inadequate amounts; and, third, aid sent by Jewish organizations and individuals from neutral countries (e.g., Switzerland, Portugal, Turkey) and from Hungary and Italy, small amounts of which began to arrive at the end of 1941, and which, by the summer of 1942, became the most important source of community funds and the key to maintaining Camp Welfare and other humanitarian community activities.

The Ustasha authorities ordered that everyone who was a Jew by race, according to the Legal Provision on Racial Affiliation, had to pay community dues or a tax to the local Jewish Community. As most of the Jews soon lost their permanent sources of income, had their bank accounts frozen and the rents they collected blocked, many of them could no longer pay this tax. The Ustasha commissioners who took over the management of Jewish firms hardly ever paid the full amount, although this contravened the Legal Provision of July 3, 1941, whereby Jewish religious communities were allowed to collect community dues from all Jewish firms in the same amount as before. Communities submitted many requests and applications for permission to use the money in frozen bank accounts for the upkeep of the camps, or for part of the contribution. They considered that any part of the contribution they received could be regarded as an advance on the final settlement of financial issues in connection with Jewish property. At first, the authorities did not consider these requests at all, and later they processed them very slowly and with great reservations, so that the Jewish Religious Community in Zagreb spent its last financial reserves on Camp Welfare in the fall of 1941.

The situation was made somewhat easier by the fact that families and the Community itself could send aid to prisoners through the Croatian Red Cross, which also provided a small amount of aid. The Ustasha Police Directorate authorized the Red Cross to receive parcels for imprisoned Jews and to forward them to the camps, and to provide food for transports that were on their way to Gospić and which stood for a short time on railway sidings in Zagreb. Starting in mid-July 1941, the Society began to send a large number of parcels to Gospić, Jadovno, and Pag. The Jewish Section of the Ustasha Police issued couriers with passes,[14] which the Ustasha Police Directorate in Gospić confirmed. However, in a letter to the Ustasha Police Directorate in Zagreb, dated August 22, the Croatian Red Cross Society protested that it had received many complaints because a large number of the parcels had not been delivered to the recipients. It proposed that arrangements should in future be made to "enclose delivery notes in each parcel on which the recipient would confirm receipt of the parcel." At the same time, it requested permission for prisoners to send postcards, because "under the Geneva Conventions, prisoners have the right to write to their families once or twice a month on open Red Cross postcards. The content of these postcards may only be of a personal nature, and may contain up to twenty-five words." These requests were not met, and the Red Cross parcels that arrived in the camps continued to be looted.[15] An anonymous report sent from the Ustasha administration confirms this, stating that "food from the parcels is sold to the local population and to prisoners who still have the money to pay for it." The Red Cross received information that "the going price for one loaf of bread was 100 to 150 kunas, a piece of cellophane-wrapped cheese, 100 kunas." The senders were aware that the parcels were being looted, "but all the same we kept on sending them, hoping that some of the things would nevertheless reach the internees."[16] It must be said that the Loborgrad Camp administration, in a notice, recommended that prisoners ask "their family and friends who send them parcels to wrap them up tightly," because the "Zlatar post-office has complained that most of the parcels arrive in very shabby condition" and that the "contents of the parcels go bad quickly or fall out."[17]

The Communist organization People's Aid also helped internees. In Zagreb it had an underground city committee and a well-organized and large network of secret activists and supporters, of which the organizers and leading activists were members of the Communist Party of Croatia. Before April 1941, People's Aid helped Communist prisoners in Yugoslav prisons and their families, and from the summer of 1941 onward it began to help other members of the anti-Fascist resistance. As these included some Jews after 1941, People's Aid helped them, especially if they had been arrested, and also helped their endangered families. It collected and distributed food, clothes, medicine, sanitary, technical, and other materiel. In Zagreb, People's Aid collected 3,384,000 kunas between August 1941 and August 1942 alone. Most of the money and other kinds of aid went to camp internees or for the needs of Partisan units, and only a small part was spent for the needs of the organization itself.[18]

The Zagreb Jewish Community sent twenty crates of "additional food" to Kruščica as early as September. At the same time, it also sent twelve crates of "additional food" to Jasenovac.[19] In the fall of 1941, the Zagreb Community received about forty requests from Jews from Bijeljina who were imprisoned in the "camp for Jewish internees in Krapje" for winter clothes and shoes, blankets, and the like,[20] so it sent a special truck of clothing parcels to Jasenovac in November. Allegedly, Luburić himself had allowed this, and the Community official Robert Stein accompanied the shipment. The Community had made a list of 400 internees who were to receive the parcels, and Stein was to oversee the distribution.[21] After November 1941, large amounts of food and sanitary materiel were sent to Jasenovac. The list included just over 150 kinds of medicine.[22] Members of the Zagreb Jewish Community "sent hundreds and hundreds of parcels to their relatives and friends," but the Ustashe "handed only the most pathetic remains over to the prisoners."[23] According to Egon Berger, in November and December 1941, "thousands and thousands of parcels suddenly began to arrive. We saw them, but we did not know whom they were for, because the Ustashe had torn off all the addresses. Many of the addressees were certainly already dead. People who sent such parcels . . . will probably remember the great hope and joy they experienced when packing them, and the Ustashe ate everything."[24] Ante Ciliga described sending aid as follows: "Some of the forms of Jewish solidarity that I saw in Jasenovac seemed unbelievable and fantastic to me. The only outside aid that came systematically, constantly, and in an organized way to the camp, was for Jews, sent through the Jewish Religious Community in Zagreb. Every week, the Community collected parcels for individuals, and made up its own parcels for Jews who had nothing sent to them from outside. It sent these individual parcels, and also two or three large crates, by rail to Jasenovac station, accompanied by a man specially employed for that job, a Catholic-Croat. The aid was sent every Thursday, so that the goods could be distributed in the camp on Friday for the Sabbath."[25]

About 1,000 women prisoners in Loborgrad got parcels from the Zagreb Community between December 24 and 31, which included bags of candy, toys, and books for the children.[26] Parcels traveled to Loborgrad every week, with just under 400 sent on December 17 alone.[27] The Community sent 102 tubes of toothpaste, 51 toothbrushes, hair clips, face and hand cream, beds for children, a cradle, and a swing to Loborgrad.[28]

The Jewish Community sent parcels to other internees as well—to the "Orthodox" women in Loborgrad, and to Croats in Jasenovac.[29] Some imprisoned Croats got their first parcels from Jewish communities, especially from the Zagreb Community.[30]

During the first months after the establishment of the ISC, while there were still relatively many Jews in Zagreb and while they still had money, the Zagreb Jews sent parcels individually and on their own initiative. As time passed, this work was increasingly taken over by the Jewish Community, which paid for the transport of the parcels out of its own resources.

For example, between December 1941 and September 1943, it sent 27 parcels to Stara Gradiška to Vladimir Aladar Eckstein (1896–1943?) from Zagreb.[31] Rudi Adanja got 81 parcels from the end of April 1942 to April 1945, Meir Kasorla (from Visoko, in Bosnia) as many as 107 in the same period.[32] The only question is, how many parcels did Eckstein, Adanja, and Kasorla really receive, and how many were never delivered to them?

Because of the great expense involved in sending parcels and aid to those who needed them, "there were often days and weeks when our limited assets were almost depleted, especially at the end of 1941 and during the entire first half of 1942."[33] At the beginning of September, the Community informed state institutions that it had no more money and it sent the first official letter to the State Directorate of Economic Reconstruction requesting the unfreezing of bank accounts and assignment of funds from the contribution.[34] At the beginning of November 1941, the Community informed the Jewish Section that its funds were "completely exhausted . . . we have no available assets or source of income." It wrote that it had sent requests and applications to institutions at various state levels to free money from the contribution for its use, or to unfreeze its bank accounts, but it did not "even know whether the requests had been considered." It claimed that the requisitioned buildings were estimated at over 7,000,000 kunas, and that the frozen bank and savings accounts contained another 4,500,000 kunas. This was without taking into account the contribution.[35] At the beginning of December, the Community wrote to the State Directorate of Reconstruction requesting money for the upkeep of inmates in Loborgrad, Đakovo, and Jasenovac, again saying that "our funds are completely exhausted." It needed 2,820,000 kunas a month.[36] The Jewish Religious Community of Zagreb asked the Directorate of Reconstruction to permit a more favorable assessment of Community tax for Jewish firms in 1942, saying that conditions were the same in all the communities in the ISC.[37]

In the winter of 1941–1942, the Community sent a circular letter: "WINTER IS HERE . . . so the men and women prisoners in all the camps urgently need winter clothes, shoes, and underwear. Please bring whatever you can most urgently to Camp Welfare, Trenkova 9. Furthermore, prisoners who have no one left to care for them need a continuous supply of food. If you can donate foodstuffs in kind, hand them over to Welfare; if you cannot, we beg for a monetary contribution so that these prisoners may get additional food as well."

In April 1942, at the demand of the Jewish Section, the Nationalized

Wealth Bureau at the State Treasury paid the Jewish Religious Community 6,500,000 kunas from the funds of Jewish nationalized money for "the upkeep of the Jewish camps."[38]

Despite all the self-sacrifice and efforts of the Community heads, some people were dissatisfied with the work of the Community. At the end of 1941, Leopold Pick, a refugee from the Reich, wrote to some aid organizations abroad "seriously insulting and defaming the Community and Secretary Klein."[39]

It the summer of 1941, it was already becoming clear that the ruined, robbed, and persecuted Zagreb Jews could no longer even take care of themselves, let alone of all the unfortunates from Zagreb, Croatia, and Bosnia-Herzegovina in the camps in Croatia. The Croatian Red Cross was controlled by the Ustasha authorities, and only as much help as the Ustashe allowed could be expected from that quarter. All this affected the atmosphere in the Community. At meetings in May, people were still calmly discussing what to do and how to work in the future, but, by the end of 1941, the meetings became depressing. One Community Council meeting dragged on for five hours over two days, December 15 and 19, and the only subject of discussion was the camps and internees and how to help them.[40]

The Community also had to pay hospital bills for poverty-stricken Jews, which the Hevra Kaddisha had done before 1941. From the summer of 1941 on, patients were as a rule sent to the Sisters of Charity Hospital in Vinograd Road.[41] As the Community had little money, it paid for minimal health services for them, for "third-class" treatment. "If there is no room in the third-class section, please place Mr. Altman in the second-class section, but only until a place in the third-class section becomes available," said a letter from the Community to the hospital management.[42]

The Jews became destitute, escaped from Zagreb in large numbers, and even more of them were deported en masse, and all this took place suddenly, so the Community budget for the second half of 1941 became unrealistic. It seems that a document reflecting the new conditions and forecasting the Community tax in 1942 was not created until the end of 1941.[43] There were 1,502 taxpayers in 1941, who were also expected to pay the tax in 1942. Of these, 638 members (42.5 percent) belonged to the lowest income bracket and were to pay a "religious tax" of 350 kunas; the next bracket had 370 members (24.6 percent), who were expected to pay 700 kunas. If we add to these two groups the 11 members who paid considerably less than 350 kunas (100, 150, etc.), then 1,019 (67.8 percent) of the 1,502 taxpayers in 1941 were to pay a minimum tax, since, at the end of 1941, the Community management considered that these people were living at an existential minimum. We must also add the 292 taxpayers who did not pay any dues at all in 1941, mostly because of poverty. As many as 204 (69.9 percent) of them were expected to pay 350 kunas in 1942, and another 72 members (24.7 percent) were to pay 700 kunas, which were also minimum amounts. In 1942, taxpayers were expected to pay larger sums than in 1941 because of increased expenses and inflation, so their tax was accordingly increased from 350 to 600 kunas, from 700 to anywhere between 1,000–1,400 kunas, etc. Eight new taxpayers were expected to pay 1,200 kunas in 1942, which placed them in the lowest bracket. Another eight were expected to pay 2,400 or more kunas, and only one 6,000 kunas, so the new taxpayers in 1942 could obviously not bring the Community any significant financial "injection." All this means that the Zagreb Jewish Community had 1,794 taxpayers at the beginning of 1942, of whom 1,303, or 72.6 percent—almost three quarters—were living in poverty.[44] In 1941, 416 taxpayers (23.2 percent) were assessed between 1,050 and 7,000 kunas (and, in 1942, upward of 1,500 kunas), which placed them in a middle-income bracket. Only 75 taxpayers (4.2 percent) were to pay from 8,400 to 350,000 kunas in 1941, and could be considered rich.

Receipts showing the payment of Community dues have not been preserved, so it is not possible to work out how much money the Community actually did receive from that source. If all the 1,502 taxpayers paid everything they owed, the Community would have collected about 4,328,350 kunas in 1941. This sum was not enough for even two months of sending parcels and keeping up the camps, because, in December 1941, the Jewish Community estimated that it needed an average monthly sum of 2,820,000 kunas for this work.[45]

The community tax for Albert, Gustav, Matilda (Tilda), Robert, and Šarlota Deutsch-Maceljski was assessed at between 21,000 and 350,000 kunas each, for a total of 826,000 kunas, but not one of them paid anything. It seems that the Deutsch-Maceljskis were robbed of everything they had by the end of 1941, because in the spring of 1941, they had given money and other valuables worth at least 6,500,000 kunas for the contribution, so the above sum should not have been a problem for them. In the thirties, Eugen Radovan was one of the richest men in Zagreb, and he had converted to Catholicism long ago and was in a mixed marriage.[46] Radovan's Community tax was assessed at 49,000 kunas, but he did not pay either. These nonpayments alone brought the Community a deficit of almost 900,000 kunas, which was more than 20 percent of the annual budget.[47] Remarks were entered on the list of taxpayers, for example, that Berta Adler paid only 225 kunas instead of 700, Klementina Lachmann paid 400 instead of 1,400 kunas, Slavica Lausch only fifty instead of 350, Slavko Schmidek only 4,000 instead of 7,000, etc. The word "Bosnia" was written beside some names, which means that these people had been included in the work on suppressing syphilis (for example, Dr. Arpad Hahn), the word "absent" stands beside some names (Zlata Friedman), beside others it only says "Jasenovac" (Felix and Leopold Schwabenitz). Zlata Friedmann was killed in an unknown place; both the Schwabenitzes ended their days in Jasenovac, as did Leopold's younger brother Marko.[48] Some people did not pay the tax because they had no more money or considered that they could not spare any without endangering their own existence. Thus, it is dubious whether the tax assessment made at the end of 1941 and the beginning of 1942 can be used as a basis for speaking about "poor," "moderately wealthy," and "wealthy" Zagreb Jews, when the entire community had obviously suddenly become penniless.

A list exists of 118 Community members who complained of the tax assessment for 1942.[49] It seems, however, that this list is not complete, because there are numbers from 2 to 162 beside the names, which means that a longer list of at least 162 names had existed. Since the complaints were resolved at the beginning of March 1942, it is possible that the people missing from the list had, in the meantime, been deported or fled from the city. Only nine of the complaints were "partially resolved": people who together were to pay 28,200 kunas, now had to pay 5,200 kunas less. Oskar Kunetz's tax was decreased from 400 to 150 kunas, Mazalt Samokovlija's and Herman Spitzer's from 500 to 380 kunas, and Blanka Stern's from 500 to 400 kunas.[50] Some people, such as Ladislav Stern, did not complain but were exempted from paying even the minimum Community dues for 1941 and 1942 because they were receiving monthly support from the Community treasury—but even this was only temporary, because Stern ended his days in Jasenovac in June 1942.[51] Later, in June 1942, Aranka Müller was exempted from paying Community dues for 1941 and 1942, of 300 and 1,200 kunas respectively, because the house that supported her was "nationalized, and she has no income from it."[52] When it rejected complaints, the Community often referred to the decision of the Jewish Section of the RUR of January 27, 1942, stating that complaints about Community tax may not be accepted.[53] The reason for that was "the upkeep of the Jewish prison camps."

One of the complainants was Nelly Bauer (1878), owner of a house in Bauerova. She said that she could not pay the tax of 12,000 kunas because

"I have no income, as the house and store have been taken from me, and I have not been getting anything from them for several months." Nelly Bauer and her daughter Mira survived the war, but her husband Robert and her other daughter, Nada, were killed.[54]

Zlata Hiršl (1911) was to pay the minimum tax of 350 kunas, but reported "My circumstances are today such that my small income does not cover even the barest necessities . . . I am at the point at which I will have to appeal for someone else's help." Zlata Hirschl was deported to Auschwitz in 1943.[55]

By that time, many Community members had already requested and received financial aid, and, as the months went by, this happened increasingly often. Gizela Keler wrote to the Community in July 1942: her husband and son, who had supported her, had been deported to a camp. When her husband was arrested, "the commission immediately came and made a list of all my belongings and strictly forbade me to sell any of them. Since I have no ready money . . . I am forced to ask for financial aid." It seems that Gizela did not survive the war.[56] Olga Fürst Galeković also asked for help at that time: in 1941, her husband, Zvonimir, had been "taken to a concentration camp. Since I have no job or source of income, I cannot feed myself and my children." Zvonimir did not return from camp, but Olga and the children, as "Aryans," survived the war.[57] Sixty-eight-year-old Artur Glück asked for an increase in support "to at least 500 kunas a month," because "the price of all foodstuffs has gone up terribly, and I cannot live . . . I receive no help from anyone in the world; those who gave to me before have disappeared." It seems that Artur's wife, Henrietta, and daughter, Alma, were deported before him and did not return, and Artur also ended in a camp.[58] After October 1941, Riki (Rifka) Grünberger, née Papo, and her son, Bernard, ate at the soup kitchen and got a monthly allowance for the rent. Rifka sold what they had in the house to meet their other needs. In July 1942, she had nothing left to sell, so she requested an increase in Community aid. Her husband, Alojz, had already been deported and killed, and later, Rifka and Bernard also ended their days in an unknown place.[59] Even doctor Julija Gross and her small daughter, Edita, were forced to eat at the soup kitchen. Her husband, Herman, a doctor, had been deported to Jasenovac, and she had been thrown out of her apartment "and had in this way lost all my property and the possibility of making money." Herman and Julija were killed, but it seems that Edita survived the war.[60] In bad Croatian, twenty-nine-year-old Bela Feldman also asked for help: "As a Polish emigrant, since I have lost any kind of livelihood. In the hope that you will do something for me. Consider my request. I thank you in advance and remain respectfully yours."[61] Jelisava Glesinger asked for a "suitable sum to buy glasses, because I have no money to buy them."[62] In September 1942, Gustav Grünwald asked for "extraordinary aid" so that he could "pay my rent on the fifteenth, my shoes are being repaired, my raincoat has been pawned, I do not have a single kuna of income, and my daughter, who helped me for a year, is in a camp." Gustav was deported in May 1943.[63]

In this situation, Jewish old people's homes, which had been founded in Zagreb, were increasingly becoming shelters for the poorest, not a place for taking care of the old and the ill. Seventy-eight-year-old Terezija Kastl was admitted to a home after she had been thrown out of her apartment in July 1942, and was "ready to pay a certain sum for my upkeep in the home." Terezija's husband, Ignac, had died in 1928. Terezija did not survive the war, her son, Dragutin, was killed in Jadovno in 1941, and Dragutin's wife, Draga, née Salzer, was killed later.[64] Vilma Kalman from the surroundings of Daruvar asked in 1942 for her daughter, Suzana (1934), to be admitted to the Home for Women Apprentices and Old Women, because, as I "rent my apartment, I must not and cannot have my child with me." The daughter was "yesterday thrown out" of Jurjevska 45, where she had lived until then. Vilma along with her husband, Josip, and little Suzana, were all killed.[65]

The Jewish Religious Community in Zagreb needed foreign aid to cover the growing expenses. In the summer of 1941, and then twice more in 1942, the Community Secretary, Aleksandar Klein, traveled to Budapest to arrange for aid from the local JOINT office, which did indeed promise the money.[66] What is more, it seems that a JOINT representative had already come to Zagreb in July 1941, because the Jewish Section considered "the money transfers that would arrive in this way necessary and desirable."[67] To the best of our knowledge, neither Klein nor the Jewish Community got much, only the value of about 2,000 United States dollars paid in Hungarian pengős. Later, small sums arrived several more times, but did not cover even one-third of the most urgent needs. In March 1942, Klein traveled to Ljubljana "to arrange for aid for the refugees."[68] Dragutin Rosenberg[69] and Dezider Abraham[70] traveled to "Hungary, Italy, and Switzerland" on the same business. All this was far from enough, and, at the beginning of 1942, the Zagreb Community turned to Jewish and other organizations in Switzerland, initially to Dr. Alfred Silberschein, who was the head of RELICO—Relief Committee for the War-Stricken Jewish Population—which was located in Geneva.[71] Thus, on one occasion, 1,200 boxes of various kinds of food—sardines, sugar, macaroni, canned goods—were sent to the camps through the International Red Cross.[72] As a "Swiss organization," RELICO partly "covered" the activities of JOINT. An intermediary was found, a Swiss businessman who brought financial aid to the Zagreb Jewish Community. At the same time, on three occasions, JOINT sent aid directly through the International Red Cross, "large and fine shipments" of various medicines, especially those that could not be obtained in Zagreb, and most of this was forwarded to the camps.[73] One of the shipments ("eleven crates of pharmaceuticals") arrived at the address of the Croatian Red Cross in July 1943, and was distributed to the camps through the Zagreb Jewish Community.[74] In a short survey of wartime events, the Association of Jewish Communities of Yugoslavia accorded special recognition to Mr. Kelert, Swiss Consul in Zagreb at the time of the ISC, who secretly brought money to the Zagreb Jewish Community from representatives of international Jewish organizations in Turkey.[75] A certain amount of aid also came from the Italian Jewish organization DELASEM—Delegation for the Assistance of Jewish Emigrants—which chiefly helped Jewish refugees in Italy and in the Italian occupation zones. Ante Ciliga wrote that Jewish prisoners in Jasenovac told him in 1942 that the money used for sending parcels to Jasenovac came to Zagreb via Budapest, "mostly from Jews in America and England."[76]

According to some accounts, this was how the Jewish Community was able to send very large amounts of clothing, medicine, sanitary goods, and about 50,000 to 51,000 food parcels (which also contained tobacco) to Jasenovac, Stara Gradiška, Lepoglava, and some other camps.[77] If the number of 50,000–51,000 food parcels is correct, and it seems to be, the Jewish Community sent an average of twenty-five to thirty parcels to the camps every day during the four war years, including Sundays and holidays.[78] The parcels were "expertly put together and prepared . . . [and] careful records were kept about sending them." Although the parcels had to conform to certain specifications, the Community received information from "various people who were free and people who had been released from camp, who were not Jewish . . . that food which had to be cooked was taken from the inmates in Stara Gradiška and they only got the prepared food. Then, information arrived that everything was taken away from the imprisoned women but cakes . . . [so] we changed the contents of the parcels according to this information." When the Community sent suits and men's underwear to Jasenovac, they heard that "the Ustashe took 90 percent for themselves."[79]

However much the Ustashe stole from the parcels, no one doubts that it was "only the food from these parcels that kept the internees alive. Without them, they would all have starved to death long ago. Besides, the parcels had a moral effect on the unfortunate prisoners, as almost the only contact from the outside."[80]

Letters kept in the Jewish Community archives clearly show camp conditions: the postcards, which were strictly censored (which was confirmed by a stamp), had the printed reminder that "writing is a reward for good work and conduct" (sometimes with the addition; "and gives the right to receive parcels"). There was usually also a reminder that "communications" may be written "in Croatian and German, up to twenty words."[81] The internee Berger claimed that the addition "writing and receiving parcels are rewards for good conduct" was in reality a more or less ingenious attempt to hide the fact that many internees were already dead. It was necessary to convince people outside the camp that some prisoners were not writing because they had not behaved "properly" and "well."[82] It was also a way for the Ustasha services to avoid endless inquiries about the fate of family and friends.

The Loborgrad Camp administration, where conditions were much better than in Jasenovac, also issued an additional notice to prisoners that "postcards may only be written in pencil, up to twenty words."[83] These regulations were modeled on those introduced in Germany. The Loborgrad Camp commander copied and translated German regulations about the treatment of war prisoners, which were to serve as a "standard" for everyone.[84] All the messages were strictly censored: when Vilko Heger, commander of Loborgrad, asked for "instructions as to whether I must censor all the mail . . . because a member of the Jewish Community cannot be controlled without censorship," the Jewish Section of the RUR informed him that "you must always check that mail."[85]

On the postcards, people sent thanks for parcels they had received, sent greetings to family and friends, and asked questions: still, the bottom line is a feverish hope for their own survival and the survival of those dearest to them. On June 30, 1944, Vlado Eckstein wrote from Jasenovac to Zlata and Emil Petrović that he was "healthy. Two months without news from you. I would be grateful for a parcel." In the next letter, he wrote, "I'm healthy. How are you? Do you remember me?"[86]

Since the Community kept careful records about parcels sent to individuals and about when they had written from camp, "anyone who did not send word for three to four months was erased from the card index, and, sadly, in most cases, this corresponded with how things really were."[87]

In November 1942, Zlata Petrović requested permission "to take care of . . . Lea Grünfeld, who is a minor . . . who was taken to Stara Gradiška camp with her parents." She explained her request by saying that "the child is a Roman Catholic, and I wish to continue bringing her up in that spirit."[88] Zlata Petrović, née Grünfeld (1910), who offered her help in such an unselfish way, converted to Catholicism in May 1941. Her husband Emil was a Croat, which was why they could help in this way.[89]

Most of the meals prepared in the soup kitchen were distributed free of charge; only a small number of people had to pay a symbolic price. In the beginning, 300 lunches and suppers were cooked a day. Later, the number fell to 150, because there were fewer and fewer Jews in Zagreb. It seems that about 334,000 meals had been served by the end of the war in May 1945.[90]

After the rooms in Palmotićeva 16 were closed, the kindergarten was reopened in Mirjam Weiller's apartment in Palmotićeva 20 in June 1941. It operated at that address with ten to fourteen children until April 15, 1942, when the police came to arrest headmistress Weiller and she killed herself. Several months later, a day center for twelve small children was opened, headed by Dragica Kohn.[91]

A secondary school was started there, too, for students from first to sixth grade (from eleven to sevnteen years of age). During the 1940–1941 school year, classes were attended by 247 children, and there were 7 teachers. Jewish children were evicted from other schools, so ninety-five students enrolled at the beginning of the 1941–1942 school year and Miroslav Šalom Freiberger assembled a new group of five volunteer teachers. At the end of that school year, however, there were only 43 students left in the school, and in the fall of 1942, the number of students fell to 16.[92]

Despite all the difficulties, in the fifth and sixth grades (students ages fourteen to sixteen), the curriculum was very intensive and of a high level. The subjects included religious instruction, Croatian, German, Italian, French, Hebrew, history, and geography. The students' maturity and knowledge were admirable, especially taking into account that this was during wartime. School essays written in Croatian included "Development and importance of plays," "Importance of the main characters in Shakespeare's play *Hamlet*," "The contents of Sophocles' *Antigone*," "The contents of Demeter's *Teuta*" [Dimitrije Demeter, 1811–1872, was a well-known Croatian writer], and Dubrovnik as a literary center in the seventeenth and eighteenth centuries; in German, "The quintuple iambic verse in classical literature," "Schiller's work as I like it," and "Lessing as poet and thinker"; in French, "Use of the subjunctive," and "Analysis of Paul Verlaine's poem 'Spring promenade.'"[93]

There were 283 Jewish students at Zagreb University during the 1940–1941 school year, but after the establishment of the ISC, Jews were forbidden to enroll, though "those who have been granted honorary Aryan rights may exceptionally enroll." In this way, thirty-two Jews enrolled in the fall of 1941, but no information exists for 1942–1943 and later years.[94]

PART IV

MOVING TOWARD FINAL ANNIHILATION, 1942–1943

26

IN THE NEW YEAR

A New Wave of Persecution

Dr. Hugo Kon, President of the Zagreb Jewish Community, wrote to Poglavnik Pavelić in December 1941: "I am writing to Your Excellency to beg you to receive me and allow me to describe to you in person the conditions in Jewish Communities and among the Jewish population in the ISC. I am wholly convinced that the Jewish question can be solved in a way to suit high state interests and also to satisfy the most elementary needs of the Jews and Jewish Communities in the ISC."[1] Dr. Kon was a distinguished person, for many years a municipal senator, and president of the Jewish Religious Community from 1920 to 1935, and again starting in the summer of 1941. He had been at school with some of the top people in the Ustasha government, but nonetheless, no answer came from Pavelić's office. Everything that had already been done, and what was to be done in the following weeks and months, was a painfully clear message.

In press statements and in international contacts, Pavelić left no room for doubt. At a meeting with Italian Foreign Minister Count Galeazzo Ciano in December 1941 in Venice, he said that the ISC had "started to solve the most urgent problems, in the first place the Jewish question," and of the 35,000 Jews when the Ustashe came to power there were now (in December) no more than 12,000."[2]

By the beginning of 1942, the Jewish population in Zagreb and Croatia was on the road to extermination. After the new wave of deportations in January 1942, about half the Zagreb Jews were gone, and many of them had already been killed. Those who had not fled from the city woke up every day fearing arrest and deportation. At that time, twenty-one-year old Vera Zoričić, née Schwabenitz, hid and slept in Zagreb stairways. Her parents and sister had been evicted from their apartment in September 1941, and later they fled to Slovenia. Vera was taken in by the Sirovatka family until she obtained documents that enabled her to escape.[3]

Some families disappeared. The Benčić-Schwabenitz family: the father, Aleksandar (1890), a merchant, and the son, Milan (1924), were arrested in October 1941 and deported to Jasenovac, where all trace of them was lost; the mother, Sidonija, née Brecher (1897), and the daughter, Verica (1923), were imprisoned in Petrinjska Street in December 1941. Later, Sidonija died in the Đakovo Camp, and all trace of Verica is lost.[4] The fate of the Levi family was the same: the father, Sadik, ended in Jasenovac before the end of 1941; the mother, Roza, and children Emica and Danko, had already been deported to Loborgrad.[5] They were all killed, together with the other Loborgrad prisoners, in the fall of 1942 in Auschwitz. In 1941–1942, Roza was pregnant, but there is no information about whether the baby was born, nor what happened to it later.[6]

At the very beginning of 1942, on January 8, a new "hunt for Jews" was organized in Zagreb. All the arrestees were brought to the prison in Sava Road, which quickly filled up with new prisoners, so the ones already there were taken to the Zagreb Fairground. On the first day, January 9, there were at least 120 Zagreb Jews in the Sava Road prison, according to a list that has been preserved.[7] At the Zagreb Fairground, the men were separated from the women and children, and trains deported the men to Jasenovac and the women and children to Stara Gradiška and Đakovo. Estimates are that about 1,500 Zagreb Jews were arrested and deported in that January wave.[8]

Some complete families disappeared in the January deportations. For example, the Lions lived in the city outskirts, in Borongajska Road. The father, an innkeeper, died before the war. The brother, Šime, was deported to Jasenovac in the fall of 1941, where he was soon killed. The rest of the family was arrested on January 9 and registered in the prison in Sava Road on that day. The mother, Berta, and the sisters, Hermina and Ružica, died in Đakovo or Jasenovac, while the brothers, Slavko, Dragutin, and Herman, were killed in Jasenovac by 1944 at the latest.[9]

The arrests and deportations in early 1942 also struck families without a father, for the first time. The Lions were only one of many examples. Vera Fischer, Melita Gross (later Njemirovski), Rut Rechnitzer, and their mothers fled immediately before the deportations in January and thus saved their lives.[10]

It was becoming increasingly clear that children must be saved, too. Furthermore, many children were orphaned, and guardians had to be found for them. At that time, Jakob Pick from Gundulićeva found shelter for little Jakob Levi. On January 15, 1942, the Jewish Community asked him, as prearranged with a Community employee, "Ruža Hacker, to hand little Jakob over to Mrs. Ruža Kršić, who will take care of him. We also ask you to provide all the correct information about the child and the parents." It seems that Jakob survived, but his father, Juda, mother, Sida, and brother, David, were killed "in an unknown place."[11] On January 14, Josip Horvat, retired head of the State Railways Directorate, informed the parish office that he was "taking care of and bringing up Smiljan (13) and Marijan (9) Steiner, replacing the parents who were in concentration camp."[12] Josip Horvat had a typically Croatian surname but he was of Jewish origin: in the summer of 1942, he and his wife fled to Hrvatsko Primorje, then he spent time in the Kraljevica and Rab Camps, and finally joined the Partisans. The Horvats survived the war.[13] The two little Steiners also survived the war, but their parents did not. In the following months, and during the first half of 1943, many Jewish children were given over to the care of Croatian families, and in this way the lives of most of them were saved. Only after liberation in 1945 did the issue of their permanent guardians arise, and efforts were made to discover the identities of those whose true identity was unknown.[14] The Zagreb Archbishopric also saved children during those months, and placed some Jewish children with Croatian families in Ludbreg (100 kilometers northeast of Zagreb, near Varaždin).[15]

After the Wannsee Conference, and based on conclusions reached at that time, in early February 1942, the Nazis informed the Ustasha authorities that the Jews from the ISC must be sent "east," and that the Third Reich services were ready to organize their transport.[16] Even before this, regardless of the Nazis' plans, the Ustashe showed their own initiative in solving the "Jewish question" via renewed deportations. In January, the Legal Provision on Competence in Solving Jewish Questions was passed,[17] placing the Ministry of the Interior in charge of Jewish affairs and dissolving the Racial Political Commission. Nevertheless, confusion about authority over the Jews and disorder in "solving the Jewish question" remained. For example, services attached to the Ministry, such as UNS, arrested and deported Jews, whereas the State Directorate of Reconstruction wanted to keep some of them at work to maintain production.[18]

Poglavnik Ante Pavelić convened the first (and only) session of the Croatian National Parliament in February 1942.[19] Completely contrary to the tone predominant in his statements during the first months of the ISC, in his formal speech, Pavelić was not especially harsh when talking about the Jews. It seems that he considered the Jewish question a thing of the past. All he said was that former Yugoslavia had been ruled by, among others, "Freemasons and Jews . . . The ISC has already made sure . . . that foreigners who held almost all industry and commerce in their hands, who cared only for their own wealth . . . are prevented from further work."[20] Andrija Artuković, Minister of the Interior, had the task of settling scores with the Jews. Explaining the role of "international Jewry," Artuković said that the Jews wanted to "cause dissent among political parties, cause dissent among classes, denigrate the authorities, and kill leaders, because everyone must obey them, and those who do not must be drowned in blood . . . The Jews have two hands that work for them, similarly to the New York gangsters, these are the Communists and the Freemasons. The ISC . . . by taking a decisive and healthy step, has solved the so-called Jewish question . . . This necessary step of cleansing is justified not only from the moral, religious, and social aspect, but also from the national and political aspect, because international Jewry has forged an alliance with international Communism and Freemasonry, and is even today attempting to destroy the Croatian people."[21] Artuković's claim that the "Jewish question has been solved," one of the most direct acknowledgements of Ustasha genocide of the Jews, was greeted with cries of approval—"Hear, hear!"

At the Parliamentary session on the following day, Minister of Justice Mirko Puk gave the reasons for the racial laws and other anti-Jewish measures. "The community demands, and as an organized community the state itself demands, the removal of elements that disturb and spoil the peace and survival of the community and the state . . . to remove their harmful influence on the Croatian national community . . . The Jews have been expelled from all public and government services and their private contracting activities in the economic field have been curtailed, marriage between Jews and Aryans has been forbidden . . . It is a proven fact that Jews are a race that works only in its own private interests, not in the interests of the community, so the Jews had to be excluded and eliminated from all public and private life. Since blood is a factor in all this, it was necessary to do away with the transfer of Jewish blood to members of the

Aryan race." Not needing to express himself in a falsely learned way, Puk also gave a very simple explanation of the plunder of Jewish property. He claimed that it was "the property of the Croatian people anyway, which these leeches have taken from them, so it is completely justified that the property be returned to the community it had been taken from."[22] The general atmosphere in Parliament did not differ from the tone of Artuković's and Puk's speeches. When Slavko Kvaternik was announced as a speaker, someone shouted, "Long live the Marshal!," and someone else, for some reason, shouted "Death to the Jews!" The context does not make it clear whether this was an outburst of hatred to insult or attack Kvaternik personally, whose wife was the daughter of Josip Frank, or whether it was pure coincidence. *Narodne novine,* the official gazette of the regime, correctly reported that outburst as well.[23]

The atmosphere in the parliamentary committees was somewhat different, and a "parliamentary opposition" could be felt in some of them. For example, some members demanded the punishment of all who had "illegally appropriated the property of either the Jews or the Serb Orthodox."[24]

Dr. Kon, President of the Jewish Community, desperately tried to do something. Using the session of the Croatian National Parliament and the anniversary of the foundation of the ISC, on April 7, he sent another letter to Poglavnik Pavelić (after the one he had sent in December the previous year) through Marko Došen, Speaker of the Parliament:

> The Jews are in a desperate state, both materially and morally.
>
> Throughout this year during which the ISC has existed, measures have been implemented that completely solved the Jewish question by totally excluding Jews from political, economic, social, and cultural life in Croatia. The Jews have lost their jobs, not only in state and local government institutions, but also in private firms, they have lost their shops, workshops, and industries, they cannot work as free professionals, their houses and other property have been taken from them, most of them have lost their apartments, machinery, and instruments, even their clothes, linen, and so on.
>
> All the Jews have left are their bare lives, and these they mostly spend—if they have not died, which has also happened to many of them—under the worst conditions in camps . . .
>
> The imprisonment of thousands upon thousands of Jews in group camps has broken up what people have always found the most sacred,

> what has always been the center and focus of self-sacrifice, giving, a feeling of togetherness, and duty.
>
> Men have been separated from their wives, children from their parents. The family has been destroyed.
>
> Life, food, and health in these camps are totally miserable, and everyone suffers, especially children and adolescents, old men and women over fifty, and also a great number of serious invalids, so that the death toll in the camps is increasing . . .
>
> . . . It will be a glorious act, an act pleasing to God, if Your Excellency, to mark celebrations for the first anniversary of the proclamation of the ISC, shows the grace of disbanding the Jewish group camps and releasing the prisoners to freedom . . .

Someone in the Ustasha hierarchy added the note "no intercession" on Kon's letter, and this was the only response.[25]

The police and intelligence forces of the Ustasha state provided another answer. Fearing diversions, attacks on the army and police, and similar disorders during celebrations of the first anniversary of the ISC, they arrested a certain number of Zagreb Jews to use as potential hostages, but, since nothing happened, all of them were released several days later.[26] This release was only temporary, however, and every day the police unexpectedly appeared at apartments to arrest people. On April 15 the police came to the apartment of Mirjam Weiller, head of the Jewish kindergarten. She asked for permission to go to the bathroom, where she took poison and ended her own life.[27] Even then, on the ISC's anniversary, the authorities showed their anti-Semitism: the Prime Minister's Office decided that, during the celebrations "Croatian citizens of the Catholic, Muslim, Croatian-Orthodox, and Protestant religion may hang out flags" but that "Jews are forbidden to."[28]

The anti-Semitic campaign did not die out during 1942, and the Ustasha regime engaged many people and a lot of energy in this work. At the beginning of 1942, UNS and the State Propaganda Department demanded all the data about Jews in Zagreb, about their "movements and activities to date, and especially about their criminal offences" from the Jewish Section of the RUR.[29] This was obviously done to step up pressure, especially through the anti-Semitic exhibition in May 1942 in Zagreb. The exhibition was a climax for the entire campaign. Minister of the Interior Andrija Artuković, German Ambassador Siegfried Kasche, representatives of the German and Italian armies and of the Italian and Slovakian governments attended the opening. A lot of propaganda material was displayed, photographs of the synagogue in Praška being demolished, and so on. The basic concept of the exhibition was that the "Jewish Question has been solved." *Hrvatska gruda* wrote about the opening of the exhibition that "an end has come to Jewish mastery, because the Poglavnik has issued many orders with this in mind, which are gradually being implemented."[30]

Every schoolchild had to visit the exhibition, and so did "all civil servants." Nazi and anti-Semitic films were also shown. The exhibition later toured Karlovac, Zemun, Vukovar, Dubrovnik, and Sarajevo.[31]

The exhibition consisted of six parts:

1. Jews in ancient times. Examples that prove that Jews behaved even in ancient times the same way they do today, and how they wormed their way into the lives of other peoples.
2. Jewish settlement in Croatian lands from the destruction of Jerusalem in AD 70 to the Edict of Tolerance in 1782.[32] What they did in Croatia, how they slowly but surely enchained the Croatian people.
3. Jews in Croatia from 1782 to 1918. The sudden strengthening of Jews in Croatia. How they wormed their way into the nobility, how they Jewified Croatian public life.
4. The Jews as allies of Croatian oppressors in 1918–1941. How and why the Serbs and the Jews equally oppressed the Croats. The Croatian economy in Jewish hands.
5. Days of freedom. How Ustasha Croatia has solved the Jewish question.
6. Jews in other countries. The USSR is in the grip of Jewry. The English nobility is mixed with Jewish blood. Jews head the USA; their politics and economy are ruled by Jews.[33]

"Zagreb citizens showed very great interest in the anti-Jewish exhibition," wrote *Nova Hrvatska*. The paper considered that the exhibition was one more incentive to intensify the anti-Semitic campaign.[34] Other papers and magazines wrote affirmatively about the exhibition as well.[35]

A month or two later, Ustasha propaganda fabricated another lie about the Jews. In September 1942, an exhibition was mounted at the Zagreb Fairground of products made by internees in Jasenovac, under the title "One Year of the Ustasha Defense Transit Camps." The exhibition was organized to show that Jasenovac was no more than an exemplary work camp. For the occasion, an "original barracks, used for accommodating camp prisoners," was built and surrounded by barbed wire. Some products of the prisoners' work were exhibited: ceramics, soap, glue, brushes, honey, jam, fruit, vegetables, etc. All this, as the texts in the captions and in the papers professed, was supposed to suggest that Jasenovac production was of great importance for the ISC. In the article "Prisoners build Sava embankment," *Hrvatski narod* wrote that "their earlier work had been politics—our present policy is work," and added, "For years, the Jews, Freemasons, and various other similar groups lived at the expense of the Croatian people. They sucked from their living tissue, wanting to exploit Croats to the maximum. . . . Prisoners who used to amass money and make use of the bloody calluses of the Croatian worker, are themselves today working, working systematically, and in this way paying back the Croatian people, whom they exploited for years."[36] Ustasha propaganda systematically tried to create the impression that Jasenovac was a kind of correctional institution. *Ustaša* printed a comment, half jokingly: "We have seen that black-marketeering is the richest profession. So, a mother might say, 'My son must get rich, therefore he will become a black marketeer!' A rich profession! We heard that they have built their own special sanatorium—Jasenovac."[37] The following "explanation" was also printed: "Many people ask, What is Jasenovac?, Where is Jasenovac?, What is it like in Jasenovac?, and so on. We will give some explanations . . . Concerning the Jews: Jasenovac is a strict gymnastics school that provides free education and care for all those who are somewhat corpulent and gives a 'slim line' to people who until recently (due to obesity) tortured themselves by taking plundered money from the till. Training is organized by professions and is free, and lasts for an unlimited time . . . Concerning us: Well, that is the simplest! Jasenovac is a collection of the 'most honorable' big shots from the former Yugoslavia, may it rest in peace. Who is right?!"[38]

At the end of the year, the booklet *The Anglo-Saxon World* was published, in which German Count Michael Alexander Soltikow wrote the first part, "England," and Hans Schadewaldt the second part, "America." The pamphlet attacked all the values of these countries, and constantly harped on the "decisive role" and "control" Jews had over them.[39]

An event that took place in June 1942 exemplified the anti-Jewish hysteria of those months. At that time, the parliamentary Committee for Treasury Affairs interceded for the release from prison of Arnold Bauer, former owner of the oil factory in Podravska Slatina, who continued to manage the factory even after he had been dispossessed. The committee president, Fran Milobar, professor at the Zagreb Faculty of Law and in the twenties a prominent member of the Croatian Party of Rights, considered that Bauer's deportation would greatly harm the state. In answer to the comment of some committee members that he was interfering with the "Jewish question," Milobar answered that the committee cared about "state interests . . . We are not defending a Jew but state property. Why should we be afraid to protect Jews? Today, whoever wants to prove himself a great Croat speaks out against the Jews." Although this remark remained within the walls of the parliamentary meetings room, Milobar's words spoken in public were certainly an expression of personal courage, completely out of keeping with the current practice in ISC state bodies.[40]

At that time, in mid-1942, the Zagreb Jewish Community had a large staff of sixty-one. All of them were protected, at least in principle, and so were fifty-five members of their families.[41] At the beginning of 1943, the number of employees decreased to thirty-five. The Community continued to exist, but its members were dying. In 1942, the Chief Rabbi's Office still performed some weddings: Julija Kaufer was released from Loborgrad Camp to marry Željko Drucker.[42] The Drucker family obviously had some connections among the Ustasha authorities, but this did not help the newlyweds—they ended in an unknown place.[43] In the same year, Dr. Teodor Grüner and Matilda Berger also got married.[44] In the spring of 1943, just before the first deportation, Šalom Freiberger sent a report on entries in the Register of Births to the Zagreb City Government. At the beginning of the century, the Register of Births in the Jewish Community had up to one hundred entries a year, in the thirties it had about eighty, in 1942 there were seventeen entries, and in 1943 not a single one.[45]

By the spring of 1942, almost all Jewish communities in the ISC had in fact ceased to exist or were run by appointed commissioners (e.g., in Karlovac, Našice, Sarajevo). Starting in May 1942, the Jewish Religious Community in Zagreb "carried out central supervision over all Jewish religious communities in the country."[46] In May and June 1942, the Zagreb Community wanted to take over the supply of the Đakovo Camp and of the kitchens and camps in the Mostar District, but this was refused.[47] At the beginning of 1942, the Zagreb Community assessed the community tax for the other communities, e.g., for Križevci.[48]

In the spring and summer of 1942, as the Jewish communities throughout the ISC disappeared, registers of births, marriages, and deaths were brought to Zagreb from the communities in Bjelovar, Brod, Čepin, Dalj, Daruvar, Doboj, Donji Miholjac, Đakovo (camp), Hrvatska (Srijemska) Mitrovica, Ilok, Karlovac, Kutina, Ludbreg, Nova Gradiška, Orahovica,

Osijek, Pakrac, (Slavonska) Požega, Sarajevo (Sephardic community), Slatina, Sisak, Tuzla, Valpovo, Virovitica, Visoko, Vukovar, and Zenica.[49] The Dubrovnik registers were taken away, the Bihać, Brčko, and Đakovo registers were "destroyed"; the Ruma registers were destroyed by "irresponsible people." The Doboj and Vinkovci registers "disappeared," those from Zavidovići were "burned," those from Derventa and Zvornik "were sent but did not arrive," those from Hrvatska (Srijemska) Mitrovica were "partly destroyed."[50] "Archives" arrived from Bijeljina, but not the registers.[51]

In June 1942, the Chief Rabbi's Office in Zagreb took over all these archives and registers from the Jewish Section. Then, it informed the competent institutions that the registers from Bjelovar, Ludbreg, and (Slavonska) Požega were complete, and those from Zenica and Hrvatska (Srijemska) Mitrovica incomplete. It also took over the registers of the Jewish communities in Slavonski Brod, Bosanski Brod, and Tuzla, but they disappeared after the mass deportation from Zagreb in May 1943.[52] In July 1943, the Community Board said that many of these registers "probably got lost . . . during moving." This happened, for example, to the books from Ilok and Vinkovci.[53]

In the following months, the Chief Rabbi's Office began to get requests from various Ustasha and Nazi services to check data in the registers of births, marriages, and deaths. In February 1943, the Jewish Section of the RUR received information that Robert Reiner was not "entered in the registers at the Chief Rabbi's Office."[54] At the end of March, the Ministry of Justice and Religious Affairs demanded that Freiberger enter Izrael Jozef Wiedmann (1936), son of David and Ruža, née Gelb, in the Community registers.[55] It is difficult to say whether this demand was a case of cynicism or bureaucratic pedantry, because little Izrael and his brother, Josip (1939), were killed several months later in Auschwitz, while their father, David (1892), had been killed a year earlier in Jasenovac. There is no information about the mother, Ruža.[56]

Between the great deportations in January and August 1942, the UNS did not stop arresting small groups and individuals. In January 1942, a list was compiled of twenty-two Jews, mostly women, who were to be "sent to camp," and against whom the Public Order and Security Directorate "has nothing in particular." After the Zagreb Jewish Community interceded, eight were struck from the list, and, at the end of February, fourteen Jewish men and women were sent to Jasenovac.[57] In the meantime, on February 12, seventeen Zagreb Jews were deported to Jasenovac, and, during the first days of March, another twelve.[58] On March 28, eighty-six Jews were deported from Zagreb to Jasenovac and Stara Gradiška;[59] at the end of April, another twenty-eight were sent to the same destinations.[60] At the beginning and in middle of May, another eleven, then ten, then three, and finally two.[61] In all, 183 people were deported between February and May; and these were probably not all, but only those recorded in the archives of the Jewish Section of the RUR.

In June 1942, the six members of the Löwy family from Komin (or Sv. Ivan Zelina, 30 kilometers northeast of Zagreb) were arrested and brought to Zagreb, with the explanation that they provided "a refuge for Communists and a center of enemy propaganda, and it is high time that they are removed from Sv. Ivan Zelina." As early as August 1941, the local Ustashe from Komin had informed the competent services in Zagreb that "someone has been paid to intercede on behalf of Löwy . . . He is walking around Zagreb completely free." Löwy was relatively wealthy, so he was to pay 10,000 kunas in dues to the Zagreb Community in 1942, and it is possible that plunder was the main reason for this arrest.[62]

In mid-June, the arrests were stepped up. As far as documents show, 193 Jewish men and women were sent from Zagreb prisons to Jasenovac and Stara Gradiška between June 18 and August 18.[63] Since Jews were kept in Zagreb prisons before deportation, on July 6 there were forty Jews in the Zagreb County District.[64] Dr. Natan Policer (1864) and Mirko Ilić (1873) were sent from Zagreb to Jasenovac in June or July 1942. Ilić was born in Kutina, and his name did not indicate a Jewish origin, but he ended his life in camp, just like his wife, Matilda, née Stern. Dr. Policer (Politzer), a resident in Kutina, was a very fine doctor who had worked in Croatia from the end of the 1880s. He continued to work in the Jasenovac clinic for a time; his last postcard was written on October 14, and, by the end of 1942, he was dead. The Jewish Community sent him parcels from Zagreb on November 4 and December 9, 1942, and continued to do so up to April 1943 in the hope that he was alive.[65] Records that have been preserved show that almost 400 Jews were sent from Zagreb to Jasenovac and Stara Gradiška between the two great deportations in January and August 1942.

Since the transit camp in the school in Križanićeva Street (from which prisoners were deported to Auschwitz, according to an Ustasha-Nazi agreement) had already started operating in the first half of August, the criteria according to which some prisoners were sent to Jasenovac instead of to Križanićeva are not clear. Obviously, these were two parallel activities, where arrangements for deporting Jews to the Jasenovac camps had been made earlier. Because of this, for many people who were taken away in August 1942, it is impossible to say whether they were liquidated in Jasenovac or in Auschwitz.

Unlike the summer and fall of 1941, in 1942 it was very difficult for Jews to move to the city outskirts, where they had earlier felt safer. In April 1942, the Jewish Section cautioned that Jews moving "from Zagreb to places near it have an undesirable detrimental effect on the local population."[66] When some Jews wanted to move to Samobor, the Jewish Section would not consent because "there are enough Jews in Samobor already" and their moving would "cause unnecessary protests from the local population." It is possible that people wanted to move closer to safety by moving to Samobor, because Samobor was near the border with Slovenia, ruled by the Italians. However, Adolf Schwarzenberg's family did manage to move from Zagreb to Samobor, but they were all deported in the summer of 1942 and no one survived.[67]

In June 1942, a new tragedy struck the Jews of Zagreb, Croatia, and Bosnia-Herzegovina. Typhus was spreading through the Đakovo Camp and the nearby town, and the camp became a burden to the Ustashe, so they decided to "relocate" it, that is, liquidate it. The Minister of Health, Ivo Petrić, urged the "relocation" or "closing down" of the Đakovo Camp, proposing "improved and increased food for the prisoners . . . This ministry has undertaken extensive measures to harness all available forces to check the spread of these epidemics in the northern parts of the country."[68] Someone decided to close down the Đakovo Camp in the simplest way: the women and children were locked up in freight cars, and, over the following days, one train of five to eight cars went to Jasenovac every day.

"Not one single child or woman from the Đakovo Camp came to Jasenovac Camp alive. Surviving internees testified that word spread through the camp in those days that for almost a whole week, several cars came to a track beside the Sava River every day. In the evening, the Ustashe would open the cars, ferry the people in them across the Sava, and there they slaughtered them and threw the bodies in the river. There are no eyewitnesses to this terrible massacre of 3,208 Jewish women and children. It was the Ustashe themselves who did the slaughtering, and Roma (i.e., Gypsies) buried them or threw them in the Sava. Then, the Ustashe slaughtered the Roma as well. It is true, however, that not a single woman or child who had been in Đakovo Camp could ever be found anywhere . . . This was to date the most terrible massacre of Jews, also terrible because there were many small children, some of them born in the camp itself, such as Leon Abinun (3/7/1942) and Mosko Papo (3/16/1942)."[69]

On June 13, Jakob Maestro wrote from Osijek to Split that "one day earlier, a transport of 540 women was taken away [from Đakovo] to an unknown place, the younger and healthy ones . . . The women were not taken to Čitluk (a place in Herzegovina), as we had hoped, but, it seems, to Jasenovac. There are indications that they will be selected for another transport and taken to Germany." Another fact caused additional confusion, and awoke hope: "all were first deloused."[70] On June 16, Jakob Maestro wrote another letter to Split, this time with much less optimism. "Another transport is leaving tomorrow, also with about 550 women. The difference is that now women are being sent regardless of age, even those who can hardly stand on their feet. It seems that at the end, Đakovo will be liquidated. The commander says that he also asked about the old and the ill, but it did not help—he must obey orders and send them all away. Understandably, this is very worrisome for us. The increased death toll in recent days, the uncertain fate of our old women and of hundreds who are ill, we all look on this pessimistically, even catastrophically. The Jewish Religious Community in Zagreb is surprised, the Jewish Section in consternation [!], but powerless to stop the course of events."[71]

The Zagreb Community, although "surprised," still hoped that everything would somehow turn out all right. Never suspecting what was going on, on July 7 and 14, it sent about 120 food parcels and other necessities to Jasenovac, to the former Đakovo women and children prisoners.[72] During the first days of September, people in the Zagreb Community suspected what had happened: perhaps they already knew the full truth. They informed families that "at the time, the competent authorities instructed us that they have all been relocated to Jasenovac, however, they had not contacted us from there."[73] There is no doubt that, at the beginning of 1943, Hugo Kon and Miroslav Šalom Freiberger knew what had happened, as they gave concerned relatives the following information: "Greta Vajs was in Đakovo Camp, from where she and the other women were taken to an unknown place when that camp was closed."[74]

27

DEPORTATIONS IN AUGUST 1942

Very early in the spring of 1942, the Germans expressed their dissatisfaction with what they considered to be the large number of Jews still alive in the ISC, despite the Ustashe's drastic measures. That summer, the Reich Security Main Office in Berlin directly included the ISC in its activities through Section IV B 4, in charge of "Jewish affairs." This was preceded by a report on the "status of Jews in the ISC," written in May 1942 in the Gestapo office in Zagreb. Coldly and rationally, the report described the reprisals, deportations, and mass killing of Jews north of the demarcation line between Italy and Germany in the ISC. It accused the Ustasha authorities of senseless cruelty ("the prisoners could not bathe for weeks and months"). "Very many Jews have simply disappeared . . . It remains unclear why so many human lives were destroyed and are still being destroyed, when there is a need for cheap labor." This criticism by the Germans that mass killings were being carried out without any rational reason cannot be understood other than as pure cynicism.[1] The general conclusion was that the "Jewish question" had been "solved" to a high degree in the German sphere of interest, but the Nazis found that the Ustasha authorities had nevertheless not been thorough enough. The report said, which was true, that a certain number of Jews had been spared from arrest and deportation thanks to personal and family connections, corruption, and the intercession of the Catholic Church in Zagreb for Jews in mixed marriages and their children, and for some individuals.

The deportations of Jews in August 1942 and May 1943, in which the Germans took an active part, were a new kind of German interference in life in the ISC. They soon applied pressure for the removal from office of Eugen Dido Kvaternik, and Pavelić readily complied. In August and September 1942, German officer Hans Ott organized the first exchange of captured Partisans and Germans, independent of the Ustasha authorities. Pavelić had to soften his policy toward the Serbs because of German pressure, and when the main Partisan forces penetrated into western Bosnia and Kordun in November of that year, the Germans realized that they had to act more forcefully, so what became known by the Partisans as the Fourth Enemy Offensive—which the Germans named Weiss I and II—began on January 20, 1943.[2]

In the spring of 1942, Hans Helm, the German police attaché in Zagreb, informed the ISC government that the Nazi forces wanted to organize the "relocation" or "evacuation" of the remaining Jews in the ISC to the eastern parts of the Reich.[3] Preparations were coordinated with the corresponding forces in the ISC, which received direct instructions from the Germans. The very term "evacuation," which the Ustasha authorities now began to use, had obviously been taken from the Germans, who used the expressions *Aussiedlung* or *Evakuierung*.[4] "Evacuation" became a euphemism for deportation: until then, the Ustasha terminology had been very clear and they spoke of "sending the Jews to camps," and so on.[5] Hauptsturmführer Franz Abromeit from Eichmann's Section IV B, an expert in this kind of work, came to Zagreb from Berlin as a representative of the Reich Security Main Office (RSHA). From then on, the ISC police-intelligence services were under direct pressure to improve the procedure of capturing and deporting Jews. The local government in the surroundings of Zagreb seconded this pressure: at the end of July, the County District in Pisarovina (thirty kilometers south of Zagreb) demanded the "evacuation" of Jews because some were fleeing to Slovenia, and others were "a burden on the local population."[6]

It seems that the Jewish Community got word that deportations were being prepared. Clinging tightly to a straw of salvation, on July 2, 1942, President Hugo Kon and Secretary Rosenberg proposed to Minister of the Interior Artuković that "Jews whose duties and tasks do not keep them in Zagreb, and who have not been granted protection and allowed to live freely in Zagreb, should be settled as a group on a provincial agricultural estate . . . The illustrious Cathedral Chapter of Zagreb has agreed to place its estates in Sesvetski Kraljevec, or in Varaždinske Toplice, at our disposal for this purpose." The Jewish Section of the RUR agreed with this request in principle,[7] but there was no chance for it to be realized, and no reply ever came from Artuković or anyone else. Besides, the fate of the remaining Zagreb and Croatian Jews had already been decided.

Another census of Jews was made between July 29 and 31, 1942. Dido Kvaternik ordered Joso Rukavina, then head of the Ustasha Police, and Vilko Kühnel, head of its Jewish Section, to arrest all the Jews in Zagreb except those in mixed marriages. On August 3, the Prime Minister's Office sent a letter placing Ivan Tolj in charge of the "concentration and accommodation of evacuees in temporary transit camps," and Vilko Kühnel in charge of "organizing railway transports."[8] Kühnel was also placed in charge of the "activities for evacuating Jews from the territory of the ISC."[9]

Preparations for arrests were thorough. It was necessary, among other things, to create an inflammatory atmosphere in which the public would find the deportations easier to accept. At that time, at the beginning of August 1942, an employee at the Press Section of the Ustasha Police Directorate, a man named Ivančević, sent a memo to all newspaper editors saying that "it is necessary to start writing about the Jews again. The articles must connect them with the uprising on Kozara (a mountain in northwest Bosnia where Partisan units were strong), etc., and emphasize that it was almost exclusively Jews who incited the rebels who have been arrested.[10] For this purpose, at the beginning of next week, newspaper editors will receive material with exact information, names, and so on. Until this material arrives, one or two more general articles can be written, which will show the activities of Jews as leaders of Partisan units and as political commissars in Soviet Russia."[11] It did not take long for the directive to start being carried out: on August 7, *Hrvatski narod* published an unsigned article on page three, "Two Main Responsibilities of the Ustasha Movement." The article quoted Pavelić's rabble-rousing words against the Jews in 1940: "Until now, for centuries, the Jews have plundered the Croatian people . . . [but] in the future, in the ISC, they will not be able to do this."[12] The journalist concluded his article by declaring that "this message shows the genius of that great man, because he foresaw everything exactly . . . The Ustasha movement has banished all enemies from Croatia."[13] The article further declared that one of de Gaulle's associates was a Jew, and printed the message of President Roosevelt to the Jews.[14]

After the ground had been thus prepared, about 1,200 Jews were arrested in Zagreb from August 8 to the night of August 12–13 August (Josip Abraham estimated that about 1,700 Jews were arrested and deported in this wave).[15] The Security Police for the City of Zagreb and the Grand County of Prigorje made the arrests. The police came at night to the apartment of Home Guard Captain Ivan Kampuš, whose wife, Štefanija, née Stern, was of Jewish origin. They took away Štefanija's relatives, thirty-four-year-old Dragutin Zeisler and his mother, Malvina, née Glesinger, who were all members of the same household. Then Kampuš showed himself to the Ustasha policemen in his Home Guard uniform, and demanded ambulance transport for Malvina's sisters, seventy-nine-year-old Lotika Glesinger and eighty-two-year-old Eugenija Stern, née Glesinger, because they were old and ill, and practically bed-ridden. The policemen, who realized that they would have to carry them to the car, accepted these arguments and left the old women in the apartment.[16] Eugenija died a natural death about a month later, on September 20, and Lotika survived the war.[17]

All those arrested were taken to the transit camp in the east wing of the school in Križanićeva Street, where they were placed in the classrooms, which were empty because of the school holidays. The guards prevented all contact with the outside world, even through the windows of the neighboring buildings which were barely twenty meters away.[18] About 400 of the 1,200 or so arrestees were released, mostly old people, doctors, and members of their families.[19] Vanda Stern, née Breyer, tried to kill herself in Križanićeva, but she was "saved" and taken to camp, where all trace of her was lost.[20]

The logistics concerning the prisoners' stay in Križanićeva were very well organized. The Zagreb Jewish Community was ordered to deliver food (potatoes, beans, oil, and flour) to feed the internees. It obtained 4 tons of flour, 1 ton of beans, 300 liters of oil, and 200 kilograms of sugar, which were also intended to "feed the transports passing through [i.e., those that were not from Zagreb] during the evacuation of the Jews."[21] The Jewish Section arranged with the State Railways Directorate for a total of five or six transports on August 13 and 24, from Zagreb (departing from the Zlatar-Bistrica station, used for the deportation of the Loborgrad prisoners), and on August 16, 20, and 27 from Osijek. Preparations for the last transport, which was supposed to depart on August 30, were to await "later notice," but this transport was cancelled because "the evacuation of Jews from ISC territory to Germany has already been completed."[22] On August 14, the Jewish Section sent word to Osijek that "a transport of 1,000 people must be ready for departure and everything organized for August 15, according to earlier instructions. Money sent. Transport to leave on Saturday night."[23]

On August 7, Eichmann's deputy, Sturmbannführer Rolf Günther from Berlin, informed Abromeit in Zagreb that seven freight trains had been arranged with the ISC authorities, starting on August 13, for transporting Jews from Croatia via Maribor to Auschwitz, each transport traveling for two days.[24] On August 18, between the two transports from Zagreb (the first left on August 13, the second on August 24), the UNS Technical Section insisted that the Jewish Section "deliver the addresses of all the remaining Jews in Zagreb with the utmost haste," and consider this "matter extremely urgent!" The Jewish Section replied that it couldn't give any information because "recently, many Jews have left the city of Zagreb illegally, and many have been sent to camps without this section being informed."[25]

Ivan Kampuš described the deportations from the Main Railway Station in Zagreb. For several days he knew nothing about his relatives Dragutin and Malvina Zeisler, who were taken from the apartment they had all shared. Then, one day, while walking in the city, he heard people saying, even shouting, to one another: "They're transporting the Jews from the Main Railway Station." Without telling anyone, he went to the station, and on one of the distant tracks he saw a freight train full of people. Only one door on each of the cars was open, and even this was chained so that no one could get out. Kampuš, just like everybody else who came, managed to get to within about ten meters from the cars. The guards, who did not behave violently, did not let them get any closer. Many of them seemed upset as well, or at least embarrassed. A great number of people came to exchange messages and farewells with the prisoners, and, as the people on the platform called out names, the person called would appear at the door of the railway car. In one of the cars, Kampuš found his relatives, Dragutin and Malvina, and managed to exchange a few words with them. Everyone was crying, the prisoners in the cars and the people standing on the platform. After Kampuš had spent about two hours near the cars, the guards ordered all the visitors to leave the station. Only then did the train set off, but none of the visitors could see this. Ivan Kampuš never heard from his relatives again.[26]

The close cooperation between the Ustasha authorities and the German representatives lasted from August 13 to the end of the month. Although the State Railways provided the trains, the German police force organized the guards and all the rest in connection with the transports. The Nazis took the arrested Zagreb Jews, and the Jewish internees from the camps in Loborgrad and Gornja Rijeka, from Zagreb to Auschwitz; to these were added the internees from Tenja, and all the Jews by then arrested in other places in the ISC. Most of the Jews were from Sarajevo, as that city was "cleansed" of Jews. The Jewish Section informed the State Railways "to bill the State Treasury of the ISC for the costs of transport from the place of embarkation to the place of debarkation."[27] At the demand of the Germans, and according to an earlier agreement, the Ustasha authorities were to pay these expenses.

The prisoners were taken from Križanićeva School to the Main Railway Station, less than a kilometer distant, by day and "in full view of all the citizens." The historian and Franciscan, Dominik Mandić, who was living in Rome at that time, said that "the citizens of Zagreb expressed great sympathy for the deportees as they were being taken away, because they were transported to the station in trucks."[28] On August 22, the Italian Ambassador in Zagreb sent a report to Rome saying that the Jews were being deported to "an unknown destination in the East." The Italian intelligence services reported that "the last mass arrests of Jews weighed heavily on the people of Zagreb and gave rise to very unfavorable comments . . . To express their disagreement, many people went to the prisons and took food to the prisoners."[29] Allegedly, Minister of the Interior Andrija Artuković personally supervised the transports.[30]

Doctor Iso Fröhlich and his wife, Ljubica, née Lichtenberg, were taken from the prison in Sava Road to Auschwitz, and Community official Emil Feigenbaum and temple supervisor Samuel Singer were also deported.[31] It seems that the following were taken away at that time: Drago Bachrach (converted in 1938), manager of the sawmill in Turopolje (a town twenty kilometers southeast of Zagreb); shop assistant Josip Deutsch (1885) and his wife, Adela, and son, Reno; Vatroslav Mayer (1896) and his wife, Blanka, and children, Željko and Rajka; Elza Sauerbrunn (1880), widow of Moric, Ignac Sauerbrunn (1893) and his wife, Šarlota, and children Mavro and Leo;[32] and engineer Armin (1870) and Frida (1882) Friedmann.[33] Some inmates of the six old people's homes were also arrested and deported. The Community doctor, Dr. Heršković, and his whole family were taken away. After Heršković was taken away, the clinic of the Jewish Community was impounded and no one provided medical services within the Community any longer.[34] Five-year-old Lela Frankl was taken from Loborgrad, although her mother, Zlata, did all she could to save her: "An arrangement was made with a railway worker to take Lela out of the transport when the train passed through Zagreb, however, the transport did not pass through Zagreb but bypassed the city and went directly to Auschwitz . . . [and] for a long time Zlata lived with the illusion that her daughter was at a work camp, and, later, that she was one of the children saved from Auschwitz."[35]

Some of the deportees managed to send word back once or twice, "and then never again any word or trace." Julio Sternberg of Osijek was in a transport that traveled through Austria, and on August 22 he somehow managed to send a postcard to his son, Željko, in Italy, saying only that he was going to "Uncle Paderewski."[36] According to the testimony of survivors from the next transports to Auschwitz or Birkenau, eight months later, not one person from the first group survived until 1943.[37] It seems that death came very quickly: according to the Auschwitz list of victims, which includes the date of death, most of the deportees were killed in September or October.[38] According to this list, of the sixty-one Croatian Jews on it, two were killed immediately on arrival in Auschwitz, on August 20: Eugen Weiss (Vukovar, 1911) and Hinko Weinberger (Varaždin, 1898). Ignac Weiss (Trnjani, near Slavonski Brod, 1914) and Oton Deutsch (Zagreb, 1912) were gassed on August 31.[39] Fifty-one people were killed in September and October. Willy Breuer (Vukovar, 1890) and Milan Schwarz (Virovitica, 1905) were killed only a day after Weiss and Deutsch, on September 1, Dragica Sovari (Virovitica, 1907) on September 2, Nada Rosenberg (Osijek, 1909) on September 3, Želimir Mayer (Zagreb, 1924) on September 4, Božidar Milanović (Zagreb, 1922) and Eizik Goldenberg (Ilok, 1920) on September 6, Johana Stern (Ilok, 1922) on September 9, Irma Weiss (Trnjani, near Slavonski Brod, 1912) on September 10, Imre Ehrlich (Donji Miholjac, 1906) on September 11, Dragica Pollak (Slavonski Šamac, 1921) on September 13, Emil Gross (Zagreb, 1927) and Hana Stern (Ilok, 1924) on September 14, Vera Gombos (Osijek, 1924), Maks Rosenberg (Grgurevci, 1910), and Heskel Goldenberg (Ilok, 1922) on September 15, Reno Deutsch (Zagreb, 1926) on September 17, Ernst Neufeld (Koprivnica, 1902), Erik Pollak (Slavonski Šamac, 1916), and Leo Erlich (Donji Miholjac, 1926) on September 18, Aleksandar Ehrenfreund (Dalj, 1922) and Ankica Preger (Pitomača, 1920) on September 19, Salamon Ehrenfeld (Ilok, 1925) on September 21, Ariel Fischer (Osijek, 1925) on September 23, Lazar Stern (Ilok, 1899) and Lea Sauerbrunn (Zagreb, 1928) on September 26, Renka Rosenfeld (Vukovar, 1919) and Ružica Spitzner (Đakovo, 1914) on September 27, Mirko Salamon (Osijek, 1920) on September 29, Marko Steiner (Ilok, 1919) and David Franzos (Ilok, 1942) on September 30, Leo Schön (Osijek, 1900) on October 1, Josip Schuller (Osijek, 1903) on October 5, Adolf Stein (Osijek, 1901) on October 7, Georg Stein (Ruma, 1920) and Vilim Forstner (Srijemska Mitrovica, 1900) on October 9, Eduard Ferber (Novska, 1912), Branko Fürst (Koprivnica, 1888), and Milan Steiner (Vukovar, 1925) on October 10, Ilija Goldstein (Osijek, 1923) on October 11, Josefine Sara Schmalzl (Zagreb, 1887) on October 14, Nikola Ehrlich (Harkanovci, 1913) on October 18, Stjepan Spitzer-Španić (Zagreb, 1898) on October 22, Leopold Bauer (Osijek, 1923) on October 24, Otto Weiss (Trnjani, near Slavonski Brod, 1916) on October 26, and Milan Preger (Pitomača, 1921) on October 27.[40] Only Mirko Schäffer (Đurđenovac, 1917) lived a little longer, but even he survived only until December 1, 1942.[41] Nothing more was heard about Irma Sternberg; her husband, Julio, was still alive in October, but was killed soon thereafter.[42]

There was no reliable information about the fate of the deportees, and various rumors circulated. It seems that no one had the strength to face the truth. Representatives of the Zagreb Community informed people who made inquiries that they had, "according to unofficial information . . . been taken to a work camp in Silesia."[43] Some people thought that the transports had, in fact, gone "to Hungary." For example, the List of Victims says that Alica Blühweiss was deported to "Hungary."[44] The rumor about "Hungary" may be partly true, because some transports may really have traveled via Čakovec or Koprivnica, and then via Budapest, Miškolc, Košice, and Krakow to Auschwitz.

On March 23, 1943, Dr. Richard Korherr, chief SS statistician, submitted to the office of SS Reichsführer Himmler an appendix (of seven pages) to the report about the "final solution of the Jewish question," in which he numerically summed up everything that had been done in this field up to the end of 1942. According to this report, a total of 4,972 Jews were deported from the ISC to camps in Poland in four large transports during the month of August.[45]

Dominik Mandić said that, in August 1942, "almost all the Jews from Zagreb and other places were moved to Poland and Germany; even small children."[46] About a month later, in September, Pavelić met with Hitler in the Ukraine and very clearly stated that the "Jewish question is practically solved in a large part of Croatia."[47] Pavelić was quite right, because the ISC territory under Ustasha and German control, except for the city of Zagreb itself, really was "cleansed" of Jews.

The husband and wife Bertold (1867) and Malvina Jünker also disappeared in this deportation.[48] They lived in a rented apartment in the city center (Nikolićeva Street). In April 1943, their maid, Rozika Mlinarić, said that "after the Jews were taken away, I went on living in the apartment for a short time. However, their belongings were removed from the apartment as state property, and the landlady rented the apartment to another tenant, and so I suddenly found myself in the street." Rozika asked the court for five months' wages to be paid to her from the impounded property, as the Jünkers had stopped paying her. The landlady, Anka Engelsfeld, submitted a request to the State Treasury (Nationalized Wealth Bureau) saying that "the Jünkers left ISC territory not long ago" and that the rent they owed should be paid from the property they left, including interest and court costs.

In August 1942, a small number of Zagreb Jews were spared because of connections, intercessions, and the presence of international diplomats and representatives of other organizations. In a letter from 1943, Miroslav Šalom Freiberger wrote that, after August 1942, only the "remains of the remains of Zagreb Jews" were left in Zagreb. Most of them were caught up in the last wave of mass deportations in May 1943.

28

SAVING THE CHILDREN, HIDING IN HOSPITALS

The Jews remaining in Zagreb did all they could to save themselves, and were constantly trying to find new ways to do so. At the end of August, a police informer sent word that a certain Anny Körner from Zvonimirova Street "was sending Jews across the border for money." Marked "*geheim*" (secret), this short report was translated into German and sent to the Gestapo. It is not known whether Anny really did send Jews across the border, but she was not Jewish.[1]

Some people managed to find shelter in Zagreb hospitals. Zlata Kellert (1892) was admitted to the Sisters of Charity Hospital on August 8 with the very unusual diagnosis of "cystitis–cholecystitis–polyarthritis." "Cystitis" is an inflammation of the bladder, "cholecystitis" an inflammation of the gall bladder, and "polyarthritis" a general inflammation of the joints. She was released five weeks later, on September 15. Even more mysterious are records of the treatment of Zlata Frankl (1909) and Margita Böhm (1895), who were also hospitalized at the Sisters of Charity on August 4 and 16, and were diagnosed with "cholecystitis acuta postgripposa" and "dysenteria acuta," respectively. They were released on September 1 and October 1, as "cured."[2] "Post-influenza inflammation of the gall bladder" does not mean anything, and "dysentery" could mean simple diarrhea. In the first two cases, there are no indications of surgery, essential in serious cases. The relative youth of the patients, and the probability that the above diagnoses were in fact meaningless, indicate what had really happened: Zlata Frankl had been marked for deportation in Križanićeva, but Dr. Bronislava Prašek interceded for her with Dr. Herškovič, who invented a diagnosis so that she could be transferred to the Sisters of Charity Hospital in Vinogradska. The following day, the doctor released her from the hospital and she hid with the Prašeks. For the other two women, going into the hospital was obviously a way of avoiding deportation, because they were admitted during the very days when mass arrests of Jews were organized in Zagreb, and released when the immediate danger had passed. It is also odd that the hospital discharge forms for Frankl and Böhm do not mention the hospital in which they had been cared for. That it was the Sisters of Charity Hospital can only be seen from the bills that the Jewish Community paid to that hospital. In the end, however, Zlata Kellert did not survive the war.

Taking refuge in hospitals was quite common. Olga Schaeffer was in the Psychiatric Hospital in Vrapče (the western suburb of Zagreb) beginning in 1930. When he was preparing her for conversion in 1942, the hospital priest, Karlo Bubanić, said that "she is almost cured now, but continues to live in the hospital because of the present circumstances." Olga survived the war, and in 1945 was living in an apartment in Đorđićeva Street.[3] German refugee Norbert Thumin-Landau somehow found shelter in 1941 in the same hospital, although he was not ill at all, and managed to survive the war.[4] Nada Weiss (1924), who suffered a complicated arm fracture while riding a bicycle in the summer of 1942, was placed in Merkur Hospital by her uncle, Stjepan Magdić, who was a Catholic. Thanks to Dr. Benković, Nada was kept in the hospital longer than necessary, and thus avoided being deported (which her parents, Drago and Gizela, did not manage to avoid).[5]

People provided shelter for children, too. At the end of 1942, Dominik Mandić wrote that "friendly neighboring families in Croatia and Zagreb hid and saved several small children."[6] Mihajlo Bauer was deported in 1941, and his wife, Regina, née Gold, was taken away in August 1942. Their children, four-year-old Leon and seven-month-old Ljerka, were then taken in by relatives, the Roman Catholics Stjepan and Marija Bauer in Bogišićeva Street. Mihajlo and Regina did not survive the war, but their children did.[7] Ladislav (1938) and six-month-old Nadica Deutsch, the children of Antun and Ružica, née Kohn, and Lea Kohn (1935), daughter of Aleksandar and Katinka, née Strenger, were brought from Vinkovci in September 1942, or someone got them out of Loborgrad, and they were placed with Dragica

Jureković (née Kohn) in Vlaška 70d. "The parents of all three children are somewhere in the camps." Dragica "took the children in just as they were, without clothes or shoes," but she could not feed or clothe them, so she received aid from the Jewish Community. Ružica was killed, so were the Strengers, and there is no information about Antun Deutsch, but all three children survived the war living with Mrs. Jureković.[8] In August 1942, seven-month-old Isak Kabiljo was given into the care of "Roman Catholic housewife" Jozefina Ambrož from Ilica 132, after his mother, Palomba, was deported to camp. Jozefina took care of the child although she was "penniless."[9]

Two-and-a-half-year-old Tamara Schwarz (born on November 15, 1939) arrived somehow in Zagreb from Vinkovci in July 1942, after her parents, Pavao/Pali and Kornelija, were taken to Jasenovac with the other Vinkovci Jews.[10] No one knows who sent Tamara from Vinkovci, who took care of her in Zagreb, or what happened to her later.

Aleksandar-Saša Friedrich (1933) and his mother, Mina, née Taubman (1905), were in 1941 deported to Slana Camp on Pag, then to Kruščica, and, finally, to Loborgrad. Mina's husband and Saša's father, Julius, was deported to Pag, then to Jasenovac, where it seems he was killed during the breakout in April 1945. Mina got typhoid at the beginning of 1942 and shortly thereafter died in the "patients' room" in Loborgrad Camp, as did many other imprisoned women. Soon after his mother's death, one of the camp guards placed little Friedrich in a truck and brought him to Zagreb, leaving him in front of the house of his uncle Leopold, who was protected because he was in a mixed marriage. Saša soon developed symptoms of typhoid and was admitted to the Contagious Diseases Hospital. When he recovered, he returned to his uncle, who hid him in the convent school in Deželićev Prilaz. He was there until the end of the war, although he was arrested in May 1943 and transferred to the prison in Sava Road, but, thanks to a bribe, he was returned to the school, again, escaping death by the skin of his teeth.[11]

Documents show that many children were given into care and hidden, but their true number cannot be established. At the end of August 1942, the Ministry of Registration, and Minister Lovro Sušić himself, demanded that the church authorities find homes for refugee children. After that, Archbishop Stepinac sent a letter to Catholics, encouraging them to show Christian charity and help all who were in trouble. In a second letter, he ordered parishes to organize care for orphans and children from areas stricken by hunger.[12] These were Catholic and Serb Orthodox children, and

Jewish children as well, mostly orphans and children who had no one to care for them after the offensive on Mount Kozara in June and July 1942, when many Serb villages in the area were destroyed and almost the entire population was taken to camps or relocated.

On January 30, 1943, the priest of St. Peter's Parish informed the Archbishopric Clerical Office that "several parishioners have come to me, who have taken in children brought to Zagreb from places from which parents were taken either to camps, or to work, and no one knows anything about the parents, nor how old the children are, and no one knows whether they have been christened, and which religion they belong to." Most of the above were probably Orthodox children, but the same principles applied to Jewish children. The Archbishopric Clerical Office instructed him to "apply the instructions given in *Katolički list*."[13]

There were other ways of finding shelter, too. On August 5, 1942, Elza Hiršl placed her five-year-old daughter, Biserka, in the Orphanage of St. Theresa of Jesus on Vrhovac (which is today next to the Carmelite Convent). In doing so, she was helped by an associate of Archbishop Stepinac, a customer in her shop. She never found out his name; all they had was a telephone number. Biserka was in the orphanage at the height of the deportations, until August 27. The same person found shelter for her mother in the suburbs, in Kustošija, in a small house with a vineyard. When the immediate danger had passed and they obtained documents with false names, mother and daughter traveled to Dubrovnik, were interned in Kampor Camp, and survived. At that time, the Carmelite Orphanage on Vrhovac only took in girls, and it sheltered sixteen Jewish girls during the war. Like Biserka Hiršl, the following were also saved from the deportations of August 1942: Elza and Nada Bek, Karla-Dragica Haas and Ilonka Schmidt.[14] Boys were sheltered in St. Joseph's Orphanage in Hrvatski Leskovac, near Zagreb (which was also beside a Carmelite Convent). Đuro Engelsrath (1935) from Rijeka was placed there on July 28, 1942, and he, like the little Jewish girls on Vrhovac, also survived the deportations. His father and grandfather had by then already been killed, and his mother, Elizabeta, fled to Tangiers (in Morocco). For a time, Đuro was hidden in Donja Stubica with his maternal grandfather, David Kutscher, who handed him over to Zora Hafner in Zagreb, and she took him to the Carmelites. "Returned to his aunt on July 6, 1945," says the booklet kept in the Carmelite Convent in Hrvatski Leskovac.[15]

All children were not so lucky. In July 1942, six-year-old Aviva Pfeiffer was admitted to one of the Jewish old people's homes in Zagreb. Her parents, Aleksandar and Helenka, had already been sent to camp in 1941, whence they never returned. Aviva was apparently deported in August 1942.[16]

Lavoslav Stern was traveling with his wife, Milka, and son, Božidar (1937), and was taken off a train in 1942 and immediately sent to Jasenovac, from where he did not return. Milka and Božidar came back to Zagreb and then hid in a cellar in Bauerova Street. At her parents' behest, Milka's niece and Božidar's cousin, Ljerka Magdić, went to Milka, begging her to hand Božidar over to them, in order to save him. Božidar had blonde hair and blue eyes, and his Jewish origin was not obvious. Milka did not want to be separated from the child: "Where I go, so will my child." It seems that they were both deported in May 1943.[17]

Eight little girls were lodged in the old people's home in Boškovićeva in November 1941,[18] but it is impossible to discover what happened to them later.

Discovering the happy or tragic fates of children is made much more difficult, or even impossible, by the fact that orphans were often moved, many were christened, and some got false names or a completely new identity.

During the first months of 1942, the Jewish Agency launched a broad effort to save several thousand Jewish children from Hungary and neighboring countries and send them to Palestine. The Palestinian Office in Budapest supplied the Zagreb Community with fifty permits for children.[19] Representatives of the Catholic Church also took an active role in this work, and the telephone in the Archbishop's Palace was used in the negotiations with Budapest.[20] People from various services, and individuals in Budapest and Istanbul, corresponded extensively with Zagreb and were to take care of the children on the trip. The Istanbul office of the Jewish Agency for Palestine coordinated the whole undertaking, and the Swiss Consulate in Zagreb was also very intensively engaged.[21]

It appears that, at first, the representatives of the Zagreb Community did not believe that it was possible to save the children, or that it was completely legal, and asked the Ministry of the Interior of the ISC to approve the emigration of children whose parents had already been deported to camps. The Ministry indicated that it would give a positive answer, and requested information about the children. The Community collected data about those who were eligible for evacuation and cared for them until they left. It was not easy to find children, either in Zagreb or in other Croatian towns, because some had already been deported, others had escaped, and still others had been hidden. Guardians and parents were afraid to send their children off into the unknown; they thought it safer to take care of them themselves. The Community representatives were also extremely suspicious of the Ustasha authorities; nevertheless, in mid-May 1942, they supplied them with the names of eighty-seven children and nine people to accompany them, giving the towns in which they resided but not their addresses. The list was also sent to Istanbul to the organizational headquarters of the entire operation. This was in fact only a preliminary list of children interested in evacuation, and contained the names of ninety-six individuals, not just the fifty that Budapest and Istanbul had demanded, as the Zagreb Community could not be sure whether some of them would be deported or would escape while they were waiting for departure. The forebodings of the Zagreb Community proved themselves to be justified, as weeks and months passed in bureaucratic procrastination.[22]

The number of children on the list kept decreasing; in the early fall of 1942, it was reduced to thirty-five names, then to twenty-five, and then to only twenty; on January 15, 1943, there were only fifteen names left on the list, and, by the end of the month, only twelve.[23] Many had in the meantime been deported or had fled. The identities of other children, who had in the interim been found and assigned for emigration, were carefully hidden from the Ustasha authorities, and their addresses and other data were not put on the list. The protests of Jewish organizations in Budapest and Switzerland to Zagreb over the constant decrease in the number of children on the list did not engender any results.[24] Freiberger and Kon wrote to Budapest on January 14, demanding precise answers to the questions: "When will the children leave?"; "What must they take with them (the minimum)?"; "How much may they take with them (the maximum)?"; "May someone accompany the children as far as Turkey?; if not, may they be escorted as far as Budapest?" Three days later, they thanked Otto Komoly in Budapest for his efforts,[25] and two days later the procedure for getting passports was started.[26] On January 22, a telegram arrived from the Jewish Charitable Organization HICEM confirming a list of fourteen travelers.[27] [HICEM was founded in 1927 in Paris, the name being an acronym of the names of its three founding organizations: HIAS (Hebrew Immigrant Aid Society), ICA (Jewish Colonization Association), and EMIG (Emigration Direct).] But there was a hitch in obtaining Hungarian transit visas, and the by now completely desperate Freiberger and Kon demanded answers to letters they had sent almost two months earlier to the people in charge in Geneva. They begged them to hurry up and finish with all bureaucratic red tape as quickly as possible.[28] On January 28, HICEM informed them that the passports for the children had been approved, and that they were urgently interceding to get the Hungarian visas. Three days later, confirmation of the Hungarian visas arrived.[29] On February 3, word was sent from Budapest that the "pictures have been sent" and that "departure must be hurried up."[30]

While the transport was being organized, Miroslav Šalom Freiberger also asked the Catholic Church to intervene. Vatican diplomats and Archbishop Stepinac talked to high ISC officials, which very probably contributed to the children getting passports, although the authorities did all they could to make their departure difficult until the last moment.[31] In this way, finally, on Sunday, February 7, 1943, eleven young boys and girls set off for Palestine, among them eleven-year-old Ruben Freiberger, son of Miroslav Šalom.[32] Chief Rabbi Freiberger was named to go with the children as an escort, to save himself, but he refused.[33] In Budapest, Jewish children from Hungary and Slovakia were given the names from the original list of Jewish children from the ISC, most of whom were no longer free or alive. Very probably, the certificates were sold.[34] Five days after leaving Zagreb, the children arrived in Bucharest on February 12,. From there, a telegram was sent to the Jewish Community in Zagreb, saying that they were "all well, and that they have continued their journey."[35] Marija Bauer, who had lived in Istanbul for a long time and was one of the key people in the operation to save Jewish children, hoped that she would see her grandson, Fedor-Feđa Frank, among the children, but another child arrived under his name.[36] "One of the boys, however, said that he was Feđa Frank. Mrs. Bauer shouted that he was not Feđa, but the boy shivered and repeated the name: Fedja Frank."[37] Apparently, little Fedor was killed in the Zemun Camp; his father, Makso, had been killed in Kerestinec in 1941.[38] Finally, the children arrived in Palestine after a journey of sixteen days. News about them reached Zagreb from Marija Bauer. Some letters even came after May 1943, when Kon, Freiberger, and others had already been deported.[39]

One of the last actions undertaken by Hugo Kon and Miroslav Šalom Freiberger, just before their own deportation in May 1943, was an attempt to organize another children's transport. On January 28, the two of them sent a list of twenty-eight names to Budapest, including that of Lea Deutsch and some children from the Kalderon family from Bitola, who were in the old people's home in Dužice.[40] Interest in this new transport was greater than in the previous one: conditions in Zagreb were deteriorating, hopes of surviving in the city were declining, and people grabbed at any hope of salvation. Moreover, it seems that few people believed that the children would ever reach safety in Palestine when the first transport was being organized. After its success, hopes of salvation grew, and the heads of the Zagreb Community proposed a new transport of "forty-five children." In a letter of February 9 to Drago Rosenberg in Vicenza, Kon and Freiberger wrote that they were "working on securing approval for a new list of children for emigration."[41] However, nothing came of this initiative, even though Freiberger asked the people in "Budapest to try to get approval as soon as possible." They wrote again on February 11, begging to include Feliks Deutsch on the list, too, although he was over sixteen, and telegrams were exchanged.[42] Most of the children slated for evacuation to Palestine, such as Lea Deutsch, Isak, Pinhas and Stela Kalderon, Ljerka and Željko Dreissiger, Amalija and Josip Herzberg, and others, were sent to Auschwitz in early May 1943.

Thus, the "massacre of the innocents" became the "saddest chapter in the massacre of the Jews in Croatia." A postwar report says that "nothing could have been done to save them, although we did everything imaginable."[43] Several dozen saved children are not "nothing," but this is a pathetically small number compared with the hundreds and thousands who were killed.

When it became clear that no new children's transport would depart from Zagreb itself, in March 1943, an initiative was launched in the Kraljevica Camp to send the children from there to Palestine.[44] At the beginning of May, a list with the names of about seventy children was sent to Zagreb and Budapest from Kraljevica. The information that a new children's transport might be organized also reached the camps in the surroundings of Dubrovnik: "In the spring of 1943, people in the Lopud Camp began to talk about the children going to Palestine. Lists were even made, but the parents were too suspicious to part from their children. Soon, all talk of this stopped."[45] The deportations from Zagreb in May 1943 prevented the organization of the transport, because the Zagreb Community was to have been the organizer. Soon, nothing more could be done even without the Zagreb Community, because the Kraljevica prisoners were transferred to Rab, Italy capitulated in September, and the children were sent to other places to be saved, not to Palestine.[46]

29

THE AGONY ON THE EVE OF THE LAST DEPORTATION

Danijel Crljen published the *Principles of the Ustasha Movement,* and also wrote a commentary, in 1942 in Zagreb. This text can be considered the Ustasha government's official stand on the Jewish question and it sums up all the anti-Jewish accusations they had made in public. The Eleventh Principle is: "God and the Croats—Only members of the Croatian people may decide about the Croatian state and national affairs," and to this Crljen added the commentary: "Tenacious and destructive, sly and exceedingly adept, enemies of all peoples except their own, the Jews attach themselves to the bodies of all peoples like dangerous parasites, suck their juices, and destroy them economically, politically, culturally, and morally . . . In the field of culture, they use all the means at their disposal to promote decadence and debase public standards. They turn music into savagery, painting into a travesty of real art, theatre into an exhibition of stupidity and obscenity. In the field of morals, they play the most destructive role in obliterating all healthy forces, thwarting every honest effort and praiseworthy aim." The idea about the "decadent Jews" who spoil healthy art concepts was a direct borrowing from Nazi ideology.

Crljen also described the treatment of the Jews since the foundation of the ISC: "The basic focus on the development and progress of the Croatian people demanded the quick and vigorous cleansing of these treacherous parasites from the Croatian national body. This was the only real way to remove their dangerous influence on our public life and their mastery in our economy and business. The sad days of the recent past are gone, leaving open wounds on the Croatian body, which are slowly healing, and painful memories in our hearts, which pale as the days go by."[1]

Crljen's ideological foundation and approach are very similar to those given in the *Protocols of the Learned Elders of Zion.* To the best of our knowledge, the State Information and Propaganda Bureau published the first edition of the *Protocols* in the ISC in 1942, which says a lot.

Other publications in 1942 also created the impression that the Jewish question had more or less been solved. *Hrvatska gruda,* in the article "No More Jewish Danger," wrote that immediately after the proclamation of the ISC "many laws were passed which erased Jewish influence from economic and public life. But since this was not enough, Jews were removed from the entire territory of the Croatian state. Thus, the Jewish danger in Croatia has been completely eliminated."[2] Ivo Bogdan wrote that the Croatian state had been under attack from both external and internal enemies, these were "Jews, Freemasons, and Communists," and they were capable of destroying the Croatian people. Ustasha Croatia had to resist these threats with "courage, determination, and political vision."[3] In May and June of 1942, *Ustaša* wrote the following in the semihumorous column "In Several Lines": "It is true that there are no more Jews in Croatia, but a new Jewish sect has appeared among Christian souls," and, "true, the Jews stripped us of all we had and left us high and dry. But thank God, now there are no more Jews."[4] Population figures were given in Petar Pekić's book, *The Origin of the ISC,* published in 1942. He wrote that the ISC had almost 5,000,000 Croats, 1,250,000 Serbs, etc., but not a single Jew. Pekić did not write what had happened to the Jews, but he obviously considered that there were none left, or he planned for that to be the case. He wrote in a very positive tone about the "provision for preserving Croatian national property of April 19." According to Pekić, "the legal provisions on racial affiliation, on the protection of Aryan blood and the honor of the Croatian people, and on citizenship, are revolutionary."[5]

Although intensive Ustasha propaganda was very clear about the "Jewish question" in the ISC being completely solved forever, especially after the deportations in August 1942, the police services knew that this was not so. They persisted in their attempts to find Jews who had gone into hiding, and in keeping the others under control. At the beginning of September

1942, UNS instructed the Jewish Section to include the Jew Milan-Emil Bačić (Bachrach) in its index. As Bačić and his daughter, Zora, are not on the list of victims, it seems that they both survived the war.[6] Despite its great ambitions, at the end of October 1942, UNS had to admit that it could not establish even the approximate number of free Jews in Zagreb and the entire ISC. They knew that at least 800 Jews were living in mixed marriages. Counting the Jews was additionally complicated by the fact that quite a lot of them had come to Zagreb illegally from other Croatian towns and villages, without reporting to anyone.

On October 21, the three members of the family of Šandor Braun, landowner and sawmill owner, were arrested in Đurđevac (120 kilometers northeast of Zagreb, near the Hungarian border). They were transported to Zagreb by train, to the prison on Trg N. Due to the intercession of some highly placed official in the ISC government (probably Slavko Kvaternik), they were not sent to Jasenovac, as would have been expected, but to the prison in Sava Road, from which they were deported to Auschwitz in May 1943.[7]

In mid-October 1942, a new phase began in "solving the Jewish question." The ISC authorities, to give the impression that they were underlining "Croatian sovereignty," confirmed the provision about stripping Jews of citizenship. In the name of the ISC government, Minister of Finance Vlado Košak told Siegfried Kasche, German ambassador in Zagreb, that the ISC was ready to pay thirty Reichsmarks to Germany for every Jew deported from ISC territory "as a contribution to German efforts in the final solution of the Jewish problem."[8]

At this time, the work of the Zagreb Community was increasingly reduced to sending information to family and friends about the fate of prisoners, sending parcels to internees, caring for the old and infirm in Zagreb, and to an activity that can only be inferred from fragmentary information—intercession with various people to save the remaining Zagreb and Croatian Jews from deportation and death.

For a long time, until the spring of 1943, the Community had cared for a group of about 126 refugees from Austria, Poland, and Czechoslovakia, who had at the beginning of the war fled from Samobor to Čapljina (in southern Herzegovina), and then, in the fall of 1942, were placed in Kupari (near Dubrovnik) by the Italian authorities. There were very many quarrels among the members of this group, and some of them reported others to the Zagreb Community for embezzlement.[9]

At the beginning of 1943, the Community sent many desperate letters to several hundred Zagreb addresses, begging the recipients to pay the Community dues. It seems that it sent out five kinds of letters.

The first kind was sent to people who had paid regularly until then: "you, dear Sir (Madam), did your duty and paid tax last year . . . We thank you for this, and we implore you to increase your contribution as you deem fit, and as you are able."[10] There were also expressions of special gratitude, for example, to Vera and Alfred Carnelutti, who were not Jews: "We thank you warmly for the complete understanding that you showed for our most needy . . . May God's blessing be the reward for your goodness."[11]

The second form, which seems to have been sent more often, went to those who had remained deaf to requests in 1942, and even in 1941. "Up to now you have, unfortunately, not helped in the way that would correspond with our needs and expectations. You have not shown your willingness to help us with even a partial payment of your Community dues."[12] Characteristically, this letter, unlike some of the others, emphasized that "the Jewish Religious Community in Zagreb, as you know, is working under the supervision of the Main Directorate of Public Order and Security."

It is plausible that some people did not give money to the Jewish Community, fearing that their names would end up on the Ustasha-Nazi deportation list more easily if they were recorded in the Community archives. Thinking that this might be the reason, the Community heads apparently tried to encourage people to pay their dues by mentioning Ustasha supervision over Community work. One wonders whether the Community heads were, in fact, discouraging potential contributors by publicly acknowledging that the Ustashe were in complete control.[13] Another possible reason for not paying Community dues could have been fear of a different kind: conformism etc., as suggested by the addresses of some of the nonpayers who lived in Medveščak, Voćarska, Petrova, on Srebrnjak, Gajdekova (on Šalata), on Ribnjak, in Novakova, Vinogradska, all areas which Jews should have vacated by the order of May 8, 1941. However, judging from the amount of the Community tax, most of these people were of very modest means, so it is possible that they had been allowed to remain in their houses and apartments simply because no one was interested in them. Some (although not many) who had "done their duty and paid tax to the Community" also lived in the northern part of the city—in Vramčeva (on Šalata), and on Ksaverska Road.[14] It is obvious that fear was not the only, perhaps not even the most common, reason for not paying.

Paying or not paying Community dues was not crucial in avoiding deportation, although it seems that those who paid the Community tax stood a better chance of survival. Of the 125 nonpayers whose fate could be established with some kind of certainty (out of a total of 133), as many as 78, or 62.4 percent, were killed, and it seems that 47 were saved. On the other hand, of the 58 who "did their duty and paid tax to the Community," and whose fate could be established, 31, or 53.4 percent, were killed and 27 survived.[15]

Records show the names of 133 people who did not pay Community dues in 1942, and probably not in 1941, either. Only some of them, perhaps three, might be considered well-off: these were Ilija Weiss-Vitković from Kučerina and Slavko Walder from Gajdekova, who were each supposed to pay 3,500 kunas in 1941, and 7,000 kunas in the following year, and Eugen Radovan, who was to pay 49,000 kunas in each of those years.

Statistics show that some Zagreb Jews still had a little money left in 1941, but in time they all became destitute. Of the 133 nonpayers in 1942, as many as sixty-seven had still paid part of their dues in the preceding year, 1941, and the rest were too poor even then to pay. Most of the partial debtors paid what they could in 1941, and in 1942 they could no longer pay anything. Hinko Slavić Schwarz paid the full Community dues in 1941 in the amount of 28,000 kunas, but in 1942 he did not pay anything. Even better examples are the well-known building contractor Ignac Deutsch (1867–1952) from Martićeva and Oskar Kikinis from Krajiška. They overpaid the Community dues for 1941: Deutsch paid 37,200 kunas instead of 35,000, and Kikinis gave more than double, paying 3,770 kunas instead of 1,750. But, in 1942, neither of them paid anything. The example of Ervin Stein from Kranjčevićeva shows how people had to watch every penny. In 1941, he paid 320 kunas of the 350 due, and in 1942 he paid nothing. Moise-Mosko Danon paid only 100 kunas in 1941 instead of the assessed 350, and in 1942 he paid nothing. Vojko Fischer paid exactly 416 kunas in 1941 instead of 350, but in 1942 he paid nothing. The conductor Milan Sachs was to pay 700 kunas in 1941, but he paid only 400, and in 1942 he paid nothing. In 1941, sums that individuals paid into the Community treasury were still entered in the Card Index of Jews Forced to Wear the Insignia; in the following year, entries were a rarity, and, from 1943 to the end of the war, no more entries were made on the cards.[16]

The following example illustrates how the payment of Community dues was enforced: on January 6, 1943, Kon and Freiberger wrote to Adolf Heim-Hrlić, who had hidden in the Franciscan Monastery in Samobor. "During your last visit to us you promised to pay, within the next few days, the outstanding Community tax of 3,500 kunas for 1942. As more than a month has passed since then, we feel free to remind you of your promise." Adolf Heim and his wife, Siga, survived the war.[17]

A special letter was sent to members of one of the richest prewar Zagreb Jewish families—to Albert, Gustav, Matilda (Tilda), Robert, and Šarlota Deutsch-Maceljski, whom the Community had "contacted several times with the request and invitation to help in our difficult work. All our efforts have been fruitless. Not only have you not paid the assessed tax, you have not even paid a part of it to show your good will . . . Your family is one of the oldest in our Community. Its members held honored positions in it, and your contributions have helped support much good work. Today, when our worries are the greatest and when every bit, even the smallest amount, is more precious than ever, you have completely turned your backs on us."[18] The outcome of this correspondence is not known. The Community was not quite right in saying that the Deutsch-Maceljskis had not helped, because the family members paid at least 6,500,000 kunas of the total of 68,000,000 (as was the estimate at that time) paid by the Zagreb Jews in the contribution in May and June 1941.[19] After that, their other property was taken away from them, too. By the end of 1942, the Deutsch-Maceljskis had been completely impoverished, and even if they had given anything it could not have been much. Besides, it is not certain that these letters reached any of the Deutsch-Maceljskis (or any other Zagreb Jews), because not one of them lived at their known addresses—everyone was in hiding.[20]

Aleksandar Fröhlich-Frelić (1860–1943) came from a family of moderate means and always lived simply. He gave much of what he earned for charity, and was known as the "pauper king" and the "greatest pauper in Zagreb." In 1929, he opened the Charity Home at Klaićeva 10 and was its president. However, the Ustasha regime robbed him of everything, including his pension. In 1941, the Jewish Community assessed his dues at 3,500 kunas, much less than the sum Frelić had paid the Community in preceding years. Frelić did not pay even this small sum, but only 800 kunas, so the Community administration sent him an unusual letter: "Last year, by sending us a small payment in lieu of your assessed tax, you certainly wanted to show us that you have not lost sight of our worries, despite your own. We thank you for this! But you must understand, dear Sir, that in such difficult times we ask for more." At that time, Frelić was helping the family of his son-in-law, Artur Polić, who was in the Kraljevica Camp, as well as three of his sisters, and had taken in his niece, Zlata Mizler, who had arrived from Novi Sad and had no income of any kind. Frelić soon died, in March 1943, and his wife, Ernestina, was deported in May.[21]

Some rich Zagreb Jews did pay their dues to the Community. Zora Marić, née Alexander, and the prominent attorney Rudolf Rodanić-Rosenfeld paid 105,000 kunas each in 1941, or 300 times the tax paid by most of the Community members.[22] However, Zora's wealth soon disappeared, and at the end of 1942 and beginning of 1943, she lived in complete destitution in the Kraljevica Camp. She was then transferred to the Italian camp on the Island of Rab, and stayed there after it was closed in September 1943, following the armistice with Italy; however, in 1944, she was caught by the Nazis and deported to Auschwitz.[23]

The third form seems to have been sent most often, to people who had "paid part of the assessed dues last year." The Community "thanks you for the good will you have shown . . . We are sure that the rest was not paid only by oversight, because we cannot imagine that you would stop paying because you lack interest in the concerns that we all share equally. We therefore beg you to decide by yourself on the dues you will pay the Community this year, according to your means, and even more according to your heart, feelings of solidarity, and understanding of our troubles."[24] Engineer Viktor Hahn received a letter to this effect at the beginning of February, and answered: "I found everything that you wrote in your esteemed letter completely justified, and I tried to assess my annual tax as highly as my restricted material circumstances allow. I would like to say that I send at least one parcel of food or other necessities at my own expense weekly, through Camp Welfare."[25] Hahn estimated the value of the parcels he sent as eight times greater than the dues he was supposed to pay.

The fourth form was sent to people who "had not been entered on the list of taxpayers last year through carelessness or by chance, so on whom no tax had been assessed." After describing its difficult financial circumstances, the Community expressed its belief that "as you sit beside a warm stove and at a full table, you will not forget people for whom every ounce of meat, cheese, or jam, every piece of fruit, means more than we can imagine."[26]

The fifth form was sent to Jews "in the provinces" (in Sisak, Bjelovar, Križevci, Jastrebarsko, Zavidovići, Daruvar, Osijek, Metković), even to some who had converted, whom the Community had not previously asked "for help." But "now all our sources have been exhausted, and we will not be able to keep up our work at the previous level if everyone does not help us."[27] At least seven letters with requests for payment of Community dues were sent to the doctors in Bosnia and Herzegovina who were still in the service of the ISC, and whose address the Community knew.[28]

The authorities were aware of everything that was going on in the

Community. No one hid this, and in the circulars it sent to its members at the beginning of 1943, the Community administration emphasized that all its activities were coordinated with the Head Directorate of Public Order and Security–Jewish Section. In January and February 1943, UNS was closed down and part of its affairs, among others the Jewish Section of the RUR, were taken over by RAVSIGUR, later renamed GLAVSIGUR.[29] Of course, the "coordination" mentioned above was not true coordination but a case of various ISC services meddling in every Community activity. For example, at the beginning of 1942, the Jewish Section of the RUR informed the Zagreb Community that the "appeals of your Community members because of tax assessment . . . will not be accepted . . ." and that "everyone included in the Legal Provision of Racial Affiliation" must pay tax.[30]

"Coping" under these circumstances was very exhausting for the people in charge of running the Community, and everything pointed to an inevitable end. Miroslav Šalom Freiberger's letter of January 12, 1943, to attorney Dr. Marko Leitner in the Osijek Community, best shows the desperation in the Zagreb Community and among the Zagreb Jews. To begin with, Freiberger wrote that "months have passed" since the Osijek Jews had sent them "any news. We know nothing about you, and on the other hand, you certainly do not know of our work, our anxieties and our pain." The organized life of Jewish communities in Croatia had died out long ago, and personal connections died out, too. In addition to caring for 220 old women and men, continued Freiberger, the Zagreb Community sent about 150 parcels to camps every day. The difficulties the senders experienced in putting together each parcel seem in time to have become equal to the amount of desperation they felt every time any of the prisoners stopped sending word. Because of this, Freiberger asked Leitner to urgently send word of how much he can contribute, because "who, while sitting beside a warm stove and full table, can take the responsibility of decreasing food for the hungry or parcels for the prisoners?" Leitner sent Freiberger 10,000 kunas, although there are "very few Jews left in Osijek, they are in difficult material conditions . . . but we will do our duty to the end."[31] The Community estimated that, at this time, the minimum value of one parcel was 350 kunas.[32] Therefore, the Osijek contribution was equivalent to the value of thirty parcels, which was hardly enough for one daily consignment.

There was a soup kitchen during all these months and years, right up to the end of the war. One report says that it served about 350 free meals a day.[33] According to another report, 12,837 meals were served in November

1942, which is an average of 418 a day (not more than 449, not fewer than 402).[34] Considering the circumstances, the food was quite varied and of high energy value. At that time, thirteen people worked in the kitchen, two of them men.[35] Some of the destitute came to the kitchen and ate there. Every day food was sent to the six old people's homes,[36] and, if possible, even to people who had been arrested and were awaiting deportation in one of the Zagreb prisons. It was very difficult to supply the soup kitchen. In January, the Community got 5,000 kilograms of potatoes for feeding the old people's homes; however, the 1,000 kilograms of beans that were "to come from Kutina in the same railway car" did not arrive for a whole month and a half.[37] Until the end of 1942, meat could be bought without food coupons; after that, not. The Community administration did all they could to buy meat, but this was "impossible." In February, they managed to buy 1,400 kilograms of fresh horsemeat for the camp prisoners. Kon and Freiberger also asked for "lard," of which "we got none at all during the last three months."[38]

On March 2, 1943, Hugo Kon and Ivo Davidović wrote to Town Mayor Ivan Werner (the same who had signed the order to demolish the synagogue in the fall of 1941) and "kindly begged him to increase the monthly shipment of food" to 3,000 kilograms, in the first place potatoes that "are the main food," and lard, oil, and flour. The allotment of potatoes for the soup kitchen had been decreased from 2,000 kilograms to 600.[39] The outcome of Kon's and Davidović's request is not known.

There was no lack of meticulous paperwork, and every day, reports were sent to the soup kitchen about the number of residents in the old people's home in the city, with every change reported in writing. On February 10, there was a request to "send light mashed food to Josip Vogel, who is seriously ill."[40] The Community, usually Hugo Kon and Miroslav Šalom Freiberger in its name, also organized the delivery of meals from the soup kitchen to the old people's homes scattered throughout the city.[41] Nevertheless, not everybody was satisfied with how this was done—who was fed at home and who was not, which led to problems and disputes.[42] Some of those who frequented the soup kitchen were required to take food to the homes or had other duties.[43]

Medicines arrived from Switzerland, but irregularly. On January 30, 1943, Kon and Freiberger wrote to RELICO, complaining that they had not received a medicine shipment for two months,[44] and two weeks later they telegraphed HICEM requesting that month's shipment. They also asked for medicines from some other organizations in Geneva. It seems that a time came when acquiring medicine abroad was replaced by buying it from a domestic producer. On April 12 and 19, and even at the beginning of the new deportations, on May 3, 1943, the Community submitted an order to its permanent supplier, the Pliva Factory, for various quantities of interphan pills, tubes of ointment, tranquilizers and sleeping pills, piramidon (used with high temperatures and as a painkiller), disinfectant soap, chamomile, Protamin Zinc insulin, calcium, antihistamines, and yellow petroleum jelly to prevent bandages from sticking to burns.[45] The medicines were distributed in the homes, given to the remaining Jews in Zagreb, and sent to camps: "We also put medicines, vitamins, flour, brown sugar, and other food in every parcel."[46]

In February 1943, Freiberger made great efforts to provide matzo at the Zagreb Commune for Passover. He received answers from the Jewish communities in Genoa and Trieste that the ministry forbade the export of even minimum quantities.[47] He also sent a letter of request to Geneva, Rome, and several addresses in Budapest and in Subotica, but the outcome of this action is not known.[48]

Despite seemingly insurmountable difficulties, help for the camp prisoners was never discontinued. Financial conditions improved when the Community began to receive help from abroad in 1942.[49] In that year, food parcels were sent to the Jasenovac internees every two weeks, later every ten days, and at the beginning of 1943, the Jewish Community sent some prisoners one parcel a week.[50] Even in March 1943, when deportation was literally hanging over the heads of Zagreb Jews, the Zagreb Community, through its Camp Welfare, sent "additional food, medicines, if necessary, clothes and shoes" to Jasenovac and Stara Gradiška, up to 450 parcels a week, or up to 1,800 a month.[51] On March 30, and then again on April 18, 1943, it ordered "500 kilograms of bacon for the internees for April," and "200 kilograms of Trappist cheese for the internees for May," the same amount as in all the preceding months.[52] At the end of April, following the ongoing extensive correspondence with commissioners of the Jewish Communities in Sarajevo, it claimed that it sent 900 parcels a month to the Sarajevo Jews alone, but that it had problems because "the Sephardim have many prisoners with the same name and surname," which creates confusion.[53]

The Ustasha authorities made sending parcels to the camps difficult. The regular and detailed inspection of each parcel was additionally complicated by the long list of banned goods. For example, tobacco and tobacco products were not allowed, and on January 18, 1943, the Zagreb Community wrote to the Ustasha Defense Office, at Ustasha Control, begging for permission to send tobacco. It received a positive reply, but then it had to secure permission from the State Monopoly Directorate for these cigarettes to be acquired and bought, because the sale of cigarettes was rationed.[54] It seems that subsequently the prisoners got cigarettes.

Even then, Kon and Freiberger thought of many things: at the end of March, the Jewish Community sent to the Kraljevica Camp over eighty books for primary and secondary school and for religious instruction, over 200 notebooks and drawing pads, and other school materials. "Please consider this a contribution from our Community, and sell it to those who can afford to pay, for the benefit of the poor," was the message from Zagreb for the Kraljevica internees.[55] At that time, it also promised the Kraljevica internees to "try to acquire the alcohol, bandages, and balms that you asked for, but these are difficult to get."[56] It is not known whether the alcohol and bandages ever went to Kraljevica.

The Community also organized "support" for people who had no income at all. In March 1943, Camp Welfare included a tailor's workshop, whose forewoman was Ana Flesch.[57] Through it, the Community supplied many members, both those in camp and those who were free, with clothes. At the beginning of March, the Community premises in Trenkova were broken into, and the thieves took "thirty men's shirts, sixteen women's blouses, eighteen pairs of men's pants, twelve warm vests, etc., fifteen meters of linen, forty-five meters of various cloth, thirty meters of lining, twelve pillow cases" and "various clothes, worth about 100,000 kunas."

At that time, Kon and Freiberger did the very important, albeit very unpleasant, job of corresponding with people who inquired about the fate of family members or friends. In March 1942, Sunhula Sides from Skopje (Macedonia) inquired after her daughters, Ora (Zlata) Heršković, married to Adolf, office employee in the Astra shoe factory, who lived in Babonićeva, and Sara Weiss, married to Vilko, traveling salesman, who lived in the former Beogradska. Ora was evicted from her apartment and lived nearby, in unsuitable basement rooms, while Sara moved away of her own accord to her mother-in-law's in Vrapče. As Ora was very ill, the Jewish Community found accommodations for her at Jarun (a southeast suburb), and undertook to "keep an eye on her health." Ora was killed in an unknown place, but Sara and her daughter, Helga, survived the war.[58] In January 1943, the Community informed Šua Kasorla in Visoko (in central Bosnia) that his son, Meir, had been sent to Jasenovac, and that they knew nothing about his wife and children. Subsequently, they informed him that Meir was receiving one parcel from the Jewish Community every week. At the end of 1943, Meir was alive, but he did not survive the war.[59] In February of that year, they informed Bencion Alkuser in Bitola (Macedonia) that his "little grandson is placed with Mrs. Jozefina Ambruš in Ilica 105 in Zagreb," and that his daughter had, "together with the others, been sent on August 13 to a camp in Germany, we do not know which." The formulation "a camp in Germany, we do not know which," used to describe the destination of those who were deported in August 1942, was repeated many times in Freiberger's and Kon's letters.[60] In an administratively stilted way it hid the tragedy of individual fates. There is no doubt that in February 1943, people in the Zagreb Community absolutely knew that those deported to Germany could still be alive only by a miracle.

Iso Poljokan, who was in Split in February 1943, asked about his father, Moise (1875), and brother, Albin (1900). In November 1941, they had been taken to Jasenovac, but the only information the Community could provide was that "they are not sending word."[61] The Community could inform family and friends about the condition of the internees only if these internees sent postcards to the Zagreb Community and asked for help, as this was the only record that the Zagreb Community had.[62]

Unlike the case of the Jasenovac prisoners, usually the only information that came from Zagreb about deportees was that "we know nothing about the Jews who have been sent to work camps in Germany."[63]

There were unpleasant moments in this correspondence with family members. Kon and Freiberger answered the letter of Estera Pinto from Sarajevo, who was in Dubrovnik in October 1942. They denied the charge that they were "illegally appropriating the money of the poor," that is, that they were spending for other things money that Jews were sending from abroad for family and friends in the camps. "We are convinced that you, too, know what our Community did and what it is doing for the prisoners and camps, and the troubles it is going through to feed and supply hundreds of poverty-stricken and miserable people, who include more of your acquaintances and relatives than of ours . . . Most of our efforts go for people from Bosnia and Herzegovina."[64] A lot of effort went into answering the demands and administrative requirements of the Workers' Insurance Subsidiary.[65]

Even in April, Freiberger and Kon reported about the fate of the Loborgrad prisoners to their relatives in the Ferramonti di Tarsia Camp; they also informed Dr. Petö in Ada (Vojvodina) about the fate of the Weitzenfeld family from Srijemska Mitrovica. A parcel sent from a camp in

Dubrovnik was properly forwarded to a prisoner in Stara Gradiška. They asked Albina Pick from the old people's home in Boškovićeva Street to pay the "living costs outstanding for the month of April . . . and in future to pay in advance at the beginning of the month, without special invitation."[66] It is fascinating how many different and very demanding tasks those two Community activists did only several weeks before the deportations, when rumor was already spreading through Zagreb that all the Jews would be arrested. All we know is based on the Community archives, which have been only partially preserved—part has obviously disappeared. For example, sometimes postcards requesting information about camp prisoners have a remark in Kon's or Freiberger's hand, e.g., "does not send word" or "has not sent word." Someone certainly must have written the answers to these postcards, but these have not been preserved.[67]

In the first days of April 1943, the Community even reported an insignificant break-in to the Police Precinct—the third one, in fact—which had obviously been "committed by the same person," without "any real damage" in the rooms in Trenkova Street 9. Was this an expression of confidence in the Ustasha Police, or simply an attempt to deal with every incident, however meaningless?[68]

In March or April 1943, the Racial Policy Department of the Ministry of the Interior required the Jewish Community to supply it with a list of Jews who had been granted Aryan rights, but it is not possible to establish whether this was merely part of the preparation for deportations in May. To comply with this demand, and to compile the list, Freiberger and Kon wrote a letter requesting "the illustrious Addressee to please send the Community the list of Jews who have been granted Aryan rights, together with the date and the number of the file."[69] It would appear that this list was never compiled, as the deportations cut off work on it.

On April 18, several days before he was deported, Freiberger wrote to "Drago" (obviously to Dragutin Rosenfeld in Palestine) saying that "death is taking its toll incessantly and tirelessly." He asked Drago to answer him because "we are always happy when we get a letter from old friends, who are now so few."[70]

30

FINAL ANNIHILATION

The Deportations of May 1943

Despite the enormous and self-sacrificing efforts the Community officials made to keep the Jews alive, all their work was becoming increasingly pointless because the ring around the remaining Jews was tightening every day. On March 22, Dr. Hugo Kon and Dr. Miroslav Šalom Freiberger sent a letter to Vladimir Šipuš, Director of Internal Administration at the Ministry of the Interior ISC, begging for information about which state institution was in charge of the work of the Jewish Religious Community.[1] The UNS and the Ustasha Police Directorate that belonged to it, together with the Jewish Section, had been abolished at the beginning of 1943, and the Ministry of the Interior and the newly formed GLAVSIGUR had not yet allocated the work they had taken over. There was no reply to the letter, either because the Ustasha authorities considered that replying was no longer necessary, or because the new deportations overtook the letter.

At the beginning of 1943, the Germans very carefully and thoroughly began to plan the last deportation of the Croatian Jews. All the activities were coordinated with the Ustasha authorities and directed through the German Ambassador to the ISC, SA Obergruppenführer Siegfried Kasche. On January 19, there was a meeting at the office of the Directorate of Public Order and Security, attended by the Director, Filip Crvenković,

Vilko Kühnel, and SS Hauptsturmführer Franz Abromeit representing the German side.[2] They decided "to undertake action to finally cleanse Croatia of all Jewish elements, regardless of age, sex, and confession." There were even plans to first concentrate all the Jews in Jasenovac and Stara Gradiška, and then deport them to death camps in Poland. This plan was soon abandoned, and they agreed to transport the prisoners directly to "Germany" because the Nazis considered "Croatia has no suitable camp for concentrating all the Jews."[3] They also agreed not to deport "honorary Aryans, people of mixed blood, and half-Jews." It is not clear whether a different arrangement was later made and why this agreement was not honored, because very many people from all three categories were deported in May 1943. Furthermore, they decided at the meeting to "reduce intercession to the minimum," to place "Crvenković in charge of them," and "not to take intercessions made to lower bodies into account."[4] All the same, some exceptions were made, because Ester Nir, née Deutsch, said that she and her family had already been loaded in a railway car destined for Auschwitz when an order arrived from some quarter to let them go home, so the whole family was saved by a miracle.[5] Ten-year-old Saša Friedrich was also arrested and sent to the prison in Sava Road, but was released the next day at the intercession of his uncle, obviously accompanied by a bribe.[6] The decision whereby only Crvenković would deal with intercessions also meant that there was a person with whom some kind of an arrangement could be made. Crvenković personally ordered the release of Vlasta and Velimir Deutsch-Maceljski from the prison in Sava Road only a few days before the May deportations, after the family of Vlasta's fiancé, Zvonimir Urbić, gave Crvenković 100 British gold sovereigns.[7]

As agreed, the Ustasha authorities then organized another census of Jews in Zagreb. This included people who had previously been spared: people in mixed marriages, people of "Jewish origin who had exceptionally been granted Aryan rights,"[8] and people who had earlier enjoyed special privileges because of their functions in the Jewish Community or Camp Welfare. At the beginning of February, Siegfried Kasche informed the Foreign Ministry in Berlin that "preparations for the new Jewish action in Croatia will be completed by the end of the week. Transports of smaller groups of twenty to 150 people will follow by district, since there is no suitable camp for concentrating all the Jews." Deportations of "about 2,000 Jews" were planned. The Germans took a very firm stand right from the beginning, because "emigration must be carried out regardless of the money and foodstuffs secured for each person." They considered that the action would begin "in the middle of March,"[9] but preparations obviously dragged out, so the deportation did not start until the beginning of May.

As agreed, during individual arrests at the end of January exceptions were no longer made, as they had been in earlier years and months. Ernest Wolf, who carried food to the old people's home in Lovranska Street, was arrested at this time, along with his wife, Margareta, née Lang, who was five-months pregnant. Hugo Kon and Miroslav Šalom Freiberger filed a request with the Police Precinct for the City of Zagreb to release the Wolfs from prison and to "approve their conveyance to our old people's home." This had no effect, because the very next day Kon and Freiberger ordered the soup kitchen to "send food to the detained Ernest and Margareta Wolf every day." The Wolfs' fate is unknown; it seems that they were not from Zagreb, so there is nothing about them in the ŽBOZ records.[10]

During the first days of March, word spread throughout Zagreb about preparations for new arrests and deportations, as "posters summoning all Jews to report to public security offices" were put up all over the city. Archbishop Stepinac sent letters to Pavelić, protesting the arrests of Catholics of Jewish origin. On several occasions, more forcefully than ever before, the Vatican representatives in Zagreb interceded for all the Jews (including those who had remained in the Jewish faith).[11]

The "representatives" and "leaders" of the German ethnic minority in Zagreb took part in the arrests. The report of a member of this group, sent on March 16, 1943, shows how this worked in practice. The police informer alleged that he had entered an "Aryanized" firm in Miramarska Road "by order of the German military command," and that he had found "in rooms that not everybody can enter . . . five full-blooded Jews, sitting with cups of real coffee and smoking the most expensive cigarettes" (considering the existing shortage of coffee and cigarettes, this allegation was designed to be especially irritating). He then said that the "typical face of Moric Fischer" can be seen in a fashionable shop, the face of a Jewish woman, "Sara," in another, and that one can see the "typical Jewish butcher Oskar Hafner" at the market. They all sell their wares for "a lot of money."[12] However, no list of Zagreb Jews includes anyone named Moric Fischer or Oskar Hafner.[13] Thus, these denunciations should be seen as a way to rob someone, or as an attempt to find enemies where none existed. Members of the German ethnic minority participated in arresting Jews in other towns as well, for example in Našice.[14] The German ethnic group enjoyed a privileged status in the ISC and often behaved as if they were above the law, thus sometimes even generating backlash from the ISC authorities.[15]

In April 1943, the Nazi and Ustasha police received information that a considerable number of Jews, as well as some distinguished left-wing intellectuals (Miroslav Krleža among them), were hiding in the Vranešić Sanatorium for Mental Diseases on Zelengaj 37. Most of them seem to have been wealthy people who could afford to pay the sanatorium fees.[16] The police obtained a list of sanatorium patients, but, as with other lists, this one is also full of incorrect and unreliable information, such as "engineer Hirschl" and "engineer Stern, Civil Servants' Cooperative, Zagreb." To the end of the list, the Nazi officials added fourteen names, eleven of them from Zagreb, saying that these were "real Jews, with no evidence that they were in a mixed marriage." As the information in the list is incomplete, the exact identity of most of the people on it could not be established. Ruža Rothstein, née Schwabenitz, was in the sanatorium at the beginning of 1942, and in April of that year, she fled the city with forged documents.[17] Vanja and Šarlota Deutsch-Maceljski and Vera Rosenberg also found shelter at Vranešić for a time. The conductor Milan Sachs is known to have spent some time in the sanatorium, but his name does not appear on this list.[18] Despite all the deficiencies of the list, some Jews were deported from the sanatorium at the beginning of the following month: Slavko Neumann, Vilim Pick, Greta Spitzer (1905), and engineer Rudolf Steiner. It seems that engineer Ivan Hermann and Marko Schlesinger, "smuggler of foreign currency," were also taken away.[19] Of the fourteen people added to the list later, Šandor Fürst and Julio Gross were killed.[20]

The atmosphere of fear of imminent deportation is also reflected in the passes issued by the Jewish Community on April 14, 1943, which confirmed that Blanka Mayer and Jozefina Markus were employed in the soup kitchen, "so we beg the authorities not to arrest the above-mentioned and take her away, nor to disturb her in any way."[21] Never before or after did the Community administration issue passes of this kind. The fear was justified, because at least six of the thirteen kitchen employees were deported in May, including Blanka Mayer. There is no information about Jozefina Markus.[22] Some male Community employees also got employment certificates during the first days of April "for the needs of registration with the army," although it was completely clear that not one of them had been called up for military service.[23] This, too, was obviously issued as a document that might afford some measure of protection from arrest.

The "last great hunt for Jews" in Zagreb started on May 3, 1943. This time, the Gestapo took part in the arrests and deportation of Jews even more directly than in August 1942, and Hauptsturmbannführer Franz

Abromeit, representative of Eichmann's Office IV B, personally directed operations. "Policemen come to their apartments at night, while they are sleeping peacefully, and catch them without any regard for age, social status, or whether they had converted. Some of the older ones die of terror," reported Apostolic Visitator Giuseppe Ramiro Marcone from Zagreb to Rome.[24] "About 1,700 Jews (once more entire families)" were caught in Zagreb and about 300 more in other towns.[25] They were concentrated in several locations in the city—in Trenkova 9, in the prison in Sava Road, and elsewhere—and were handed over to the Germans and immediately transported to Auschwitz.[26] Šandor Braun, estate owner from Đurđevac, his wife, Elly, née Mautner, and son, Boris (1920), were deported to Auschwitz from Sava Road, where they had been imprisoned since October 21, 1942. Through their connections in official bodies, the Brauns had already been issued with ISC passports that would have gotten them out of prison, but to get out they also needed visas for Italy, to which they could then travel after being released. Boris Braun heard that the visa was to be approved on the very day that he and his parents were deported to Auschwitz. Obviously, the Nazis and the Ustasha services that organized the deportations in May 1943 worked faster than the people who were trying to help the Brauns.[27]

The deportees included Robert Deutsch-Maceljski and his wife, Hilda, and Bela (1873) and Mici (1880) Ernst, who had, in August 1942, sent word to their nephew Mirko Mirković in the Fürstenberg concentration camp that his parents had been deported. Now the same happened to them.[28] As everything was done by night, the Ustasha Policemen even went to the boarding school in Deželićev Prilaz for ten-year-old Saša Friedrich. The nun told them that there was no one of that name there, but they returned the next night and this time took Saša away. He was later released.[29]

The then seventy-three-year-old President of the Community, Hugo Kon, and his wife, son, and daughter-in-law, and Chief Rabbi Miroslav Šalom Freiberger with his wife, were also deported. Freiberger and Kon continued working in the Community until the last moment. On April 30, they sent letters to the camp in Kupari, on May 2, they co-signed a letter to Kupari for the last time and issued an order to the soup kitchen to "serve the following meals on May 3" to the annexes of the old people's homes.[30] The next day, on May 3, only Kon signed letters to Osijek, to Split, to the camp in Postira on Brač, and ordered medicines from the Pliva pharmaceutical factory. After that, silence.[31] No one answered the postcards that arrived in the following days asking for information about the fate of family members.[32] On May 6, the Jewish Community sent a letter with the information that the two employees in the soup kitchen would "acquire and cook food for the Jewish prisoners in the Sava Road prison," but it does not have either Kon's or Freiberger's signature, or, which was usual in recent months, the signatures of both of them. This letter had no signature at all.[33]

The inmates of the old people's homes in Boškovićeva, Draškovićeva, Trenkova, Dužice, Rapska, and Lovranska were also arrested, and the homes ceased to exist. Only the old people's home in Stenjevec remained. The German report shows that about thirty women, ages sixty to ninety were deported from "an apartment in Boškovićeva."[34] Current and former Community employees were also arrested: cook, Frida Bauer; Community clerk Lorand Löwy; probably also Cantor Eugen Mandel and tax collector Ernst Richter.[35]

Gizela Stern (1879) was arrested on May 4, 1943, and, according to some witnesses, shot at Dotrščina. Some people testified that at that time, Anka and Antun Freiberger, the chief rabbi's parents, were shot at Rakov Creek. This is probably misinformation, because there were no mass shootings at those two execution sites at that time. It is much more likely that all three were deported to Auschwitz with all the other Jews in May 1943.[36]

Both Miroslav Šalom Freiberger and Hugo Kon knew that the arrests would start, but they "waited at home with dignity for the criminals who came to arrest them." Archbishop Stepinac offered to save Freiberger, but Freiberger would not save himself while the members of his Community were being deported.[37] One of the many who were arrested and deported to Auschwitz was child actress Lea Deutsch, together with her mother and brother, Saša. Lea had been converted in June 1941.[38] Lea's father, Stjepan, was saved because Dr. Vilko Panac at the Ophthalmological Ward of the Sisters of Charity Hospital hid him and some other Jews. Even at that time, some people hoped that the women and children would be left alone, and especially that famous people, such as Lea, would be spared. Lea died in transit, because the journey in the railway cars to Auschwitz was terrible.

Other people besides Freiberger and Kon were informed that arrests were imminent, but apparently most did not believe that it would really happen to them, as there had been rumors of this kind earlier, yet no arrests had taken place.[39] The Rosskamp family found shelter with friends.[40] Vlasta and Velimir Deutsch-Maceljski spent the critical night in the laundry room in their cellar.[41] On May 4, Nada Weiss, who had been hiding in a relative's apartment in Radišina, was taken away as the last of her family;

her brother, Branko, was killed in Jadovno and her parents, Drago and Gizela, were deported in August 1942. Three detectives came for nineteen-year-old Nada, and three more guards were waiting in front of the house.[42]

In those days, terrible fear and feelings of helplessness reached their peak: even half-Jewish Ljerka Magdić, her mother, Jelka, née Stern, and her father, Stjepan, a Catholic Croat, had three rucksacks packed at that time, and even during the time of earlier round-ups, in case they were deported, despite the "protection" of the mixed marriage. Stjepan Magdić was ready to go with them.[43]

In August 1942, deportations had been organized from Zagreb, Osijek, Sarajevo, and other towns and regions in the ISC. The May 1943 deportations mostly included Zagreb Jews only, because there were hardly any left elsewhere in the ISC. In August 1942, the Ustasha agents in most cases had not arrested people based on lists of Jews, but had gone from house to house and asked the concierges whether any Jews lived there. In May 1943, people were arrested according to precise lists, as a rule at night. This was another fundamental difference from August 1942, when people were arrested during the day.[44] During the 1942 deportations, it had still been possible to find shelter in a hospital, but, in May 1943, this was much more difficult to do. Chaja Brandler, Salamon Hochstädter, Oskar Scheiber, and Berta Dorner were admitted to the Sisters of Charity Hospital at the end of April and beginning of May, and it seems that they only pretended to be ill to avoid deportation. Hochstädter (61) was admitted on April 28 with the diagnoses of "haemoptysis" (coughing up blood from the lungs) and "Tbc pulmonum non aperta" (latent pulmonary tuberculosis). He was released at the end of May, as his condition had "improved." Although he escaped from the police during the first wave of arrests, Hochstädter did not survive the war. It seems that Scheiber and Dorner were also arrested at that time, because they were killed in an "unknown place," while Chaja Brandler's fate is unknown. Ladislav Deutsch was at the Contagious Diseases Hospital in Rockefeller Street at the time of the deportation, and the hospital billed the Jewish Community for his treatment. The Community replied that "they could not pay the expenses because the Community had not sent him to the hospital." Deutsch survived the war.[45]

In May 1943, the Ustasha services were more rigorous than in August 1942 and they searched for Jews in hospitals. Dr. Maks Spiller and Olly Spiller, née Stein, were taken from the Sisters of Charity Hospital and "nothing was heard from them until December 1945."[46] On May 3, "the police authorities" took seventy-one-year-old Charlota Münzer from the same hospital, where she had been really or fictitiously treated from July 29, 1942.[47] She had been admitted to the hospital only several days before the August 1942 deportations, but, after the May 1943 deportations, she ended her days in an unknown place. Her son, Albert, had already been killed in Jasenovac.[48] However, some stories about people who hid in hospitals did have a happy ending. Emigrant Leo Braff (1896) was in the pulmonary ward of the Sisters of Charity Hospital from August 1942. It is not clear whether Braff was really ill, because the Jewish Community paid all his hospital bills very promptly, whereas for others, payment was sometimes several months late due to lack of funds. In March 1943, Braff was "the only dependent of the Jewish Community in the Sisters of Charity Hospital," and he stayed there at least until the end of September 1943, so it is possible that he financed his hospital stay himself. Braff survived the war.

It seems that all the deportees were taken to the prison in Sava Road. Boris Braun remembered that he and the other prisoners left that prison on May 4, were taken on foot along the railway embankment through Šarengradska and Brozova, past the Western Railway Station, and were placed in cattle cars on the industrial railway track close to Vodovodna Street. The Ustashe were in charge of them until then, at which time the SS, who were standing beside the cars, took over. "The cars were immediately bolted. For a time we stood there, then set off. In Maribor, they let us all out to relieve ourselves, and in Vienna, the Jewish Community provided bread and some tins. After that, nothing."[49]

Edita Armuth, who survived Auschwitz, testified that of the seventy-five people in the railway car, twenty-five died and twelve went mad after six nights and five days of transport to Auschwitz.[50] Boris Braun said that they set off on May 4 and arrived on May 7, which means that he remembered the journey lasting a shorter time. However, the effects for the travelers were no less terrible: when they began to get off the train, an SS soldier standing there ordered the twenty-three-year-old Braun, whose striking physique and youth singled him out, to pull the bodies out of the car and help those who could not get off without assistance.

In the meantime, the prisoners were lined up in three columns: one consisting of women and children, another of younger, stronger men capable of hard work, and the third of all the other men. When Braun finished carrying the dead bodies and those who could not walk, or who could hardly walk, out of the cars, he wanted to join the third column, where his sixty-three-year-old father was standing. At that moment, an SS soldier asked about the people who had thrown the dead bodies out of the cars. Braun and some others answered, and they were told to join the second column.

Out of more than one thousand deportees who had set off from Zagreb to Auschwitz, only about fifty men entered the work camp, according to Braun. He heard nothing about the other men, women, and children, but soon realized that they were obviously no longer alive.[51]

At the height of the deportations, on May 4, Aleksandra Montag, née Printz, requested the annulment of her marriage to Viktor Montag, which had been celebrated in 1940 in the Old Catholic Church, because she had been "a Roman Catholic since birth." It is difficult to understand what had happened. Obviously, this was some kind of a ruse to trick the authorities, because all the Montags were members of the Jewish Community. Their plan worked, because the parents and their son, Želimir, were reunited in the USA after the war.[52]

News about the deportations reached as far away as Ankara, from where Ilija Šumenković, the Yugoslav Ambassador to Turkey, informed his government in London with considerable delay that the remaining Jews in Zagreb and other towns were in great danger because the Ustasha authorities intended "to banish them all, down to the last remaining Jew, to an unknown destination, allegedly in Poland."[53] Considerable correspondence started flowing from Istanbul and Jerusalem to London and Rome. Some people even believed that the Zagreb Jews had been temporarily kept in Jasenovac, and that they could still be saved.[54] German intelligence found out about this diplomatic correspondence, and, as late as July 1943, obviously not knowing that their countrymen and the Ustashe had already finished the work, sent instructions "to make every effort to evacuate these Jews to the east quickly," including "Rabbi Freiberger and a functionary called Kon."[55]

All this information was completely inaccurate or out-of-date. "Three deportees managed to send word to Zagreb from somewhere . . . and after that, there was no more news about these people."[56] In August, Nada Weiss (1924) sent word from Auschwitz on a camp postcard containing the permitted twenty words in German. "She wrote that she was well, that she was working in the nursery-garden, and we are to think of her and send her food parcels." A parcel was immediately sent to Nada from Zagreb, but was soon returned, torn and completely empty except for a pair of shoes.[57] Only later did people learn the full truth about the fate of Nada Weiss and the great majority of the other prisoners. According to some witnesses, Miroslav Šalom Freiberger protested at the entrance to the concentration camp about the inhumane treatment of the members of his community, and was immediately killed in front of everybody.[58]

In those months, the Catholic Church, and Archbishop Alojzije Stepinac in person, were trying to save the remaining Zagreb and Croatian Jews more actively than ever before. At the same time, the Nazi services were engaged in carrying out their deportations more aggressively than ever. The Ustashe cooperated with the Germans very zealously, so, obviously, intercessions in general, even when made by high church dignitaries, could achieve no significant results. An additional reason for the Ustasha and Nazi fervor in this work was the arrival in Zagreb of Reichsführer Heinrich Himmler on May 5. The Ustasha and the Nazi services wanted to show him their efficiency.[59] It is paradoxical that many individuals and institutions became engaged in trying to save the Zagreb and Croatian Jews at a time when they had, in fact, already been destroyed.

On April 14, in an atmosphere of desperation before the imminent deportations, Freiberger sent a letter—or one of many letters—to the Cathedral Chapter of Zagreb, asking the Church to try to save the inmates in the old people's homes and the children. Three days later, a meeting of the Chapter was held, at which it was decided that "we will keep to our earlier decision to meet your request . . . to accommodate the old people and children in the deserted stables of the Chapter estate." This would be done on condition that the "state authorities approve."[60] One notices that the meeting was held on April 17, and the letter signed by Canon Lector Monsignor Lovro Radičević was written and probably sent on May 15, and that the Jewish Community received it two days later.[61] In the time that had elapsed, almost a month, Freiberger and a large number of other Zagreb Jews, including many old people and children, were deported. Would a faster reaction from the Chapter have given them a greater chance of salvation?

The letter of May 15 reveals another dilemma: were there plans to shelter children on the Chapter estate, too? Perhaps these were the forty-five children that Kon and Freiberger wrote about in February, whom the Jewish Community wanted to send to Palestine.[62] After the deportations of May 3, all this, of course, became purely academic, as these children were no longer in Zagreb in the care of the Jewish Community. This does not mean that all of them were deported. Records show that some church institutions hid some Jewish children at that time. Marija Rigler was placed in the Orphanage of St. Theresa of Jesus on Vrhovac (beside the Carmelite Convent) from March 28 to July 19, 1943.[63] Quite possibly, some other children were hidden in this way, but it is difficult to find out about them, and some very small children were hidden without documents.

The May 1943 deportations covered five small old people's homes in Zagreb, but the largest one in Stenjevec was exempt. Why the Ustasha and Nazi authorities did not deport the old people from Stenjevec can only be guessed at. The thoroughness with which they prepared and carried out the May 1943 deportations precludes any mistake. These Jews were saved thanks to Archbishop Stepinac, who, in response to the Jewish Community's plea to save the "old people and children," made great efforts to prevent their deportation. He did not manage to save the children, and he saved only some of the old people: the residents of the Stenjevec home survived, while those of the other five homes were taken to Auschwitz. It seems that saving the Stenjevec Jews was a small concession made by the ISC authorities, who wanted to show that not all the requests from church dignitaries for the salvation of Jews were fruitless. On the other hand, the Chapter hesitated in doing anything contrary to the wishes of the Ustasha authorities, and twice stated in a short letter to the Jewish Community that the old people could be placed on their estate, but only if "the state authorities approve."[64]

In his report to Berlin in December 1943, German Ambassador Siegfried Kasche could, without any fear of being wrong, say that the "Jews and Freemasons have already been removed from Croatia."[65]

PART V

TRYING
TO
SURVIVE

31

CONVERTING TO CATHOLICISM

When the ISC was founded, Jews soon became aware they would lose all their rights and be persecuted, but few of them imagined that they would be killed. Months passed before they realized what was actually going on in the Jadovno and Pag death camps. This partly explains why such a large number of Jews in Croatia and Bosnia and Herzegovina, and also in Zagreb, waited at home to be taken to execution sites. Considering the circumstances, a relatively small number of them used one of the two opportunities they had to save their lives: to join the Partisans, where they could fight against persecution honorably, or to flee into the occupied and annexed areas under the Italian or—in fewer cases—the Hungarian government. Theoretically, they could have survived by joining the Chetnik movement, which had an anti-Croatian and anti-Muslim, but not anti-Jewish, program.[1] However, no Zagreb or Croatian Jew is known to have ever chosen that path, although indeed at least ten Jews from Zagreb fell into Chetnik hands during the war and were killed.

During the first months of the ISC, Zagreb Jews hoped that converting to Catholicism would be enough to save them, and some of them showed themselves to be quite naïve. On August 8, 1941, Ladislav Kerschner informed the Jewish Section of the RUR that he and his wife had been accepted into the Roman Catholic Church[2] and asked "to be left alone and to be exempted from wearing the insignia." When they converted, they got a baptismal certificate, which persuaded the naïve that they would not fall under any anti-Jewish government measures. It soon became obvious that those who had converted, just like those who had kept their Jewish religion, were equally candidates for deportation.

In the document Renunciations of Judaism in 1941 in the Archives of the Zagreb Jewish Community, 3,518 people were listed as having renounced the Jewish religion. They did not all renounce it in 1941, and the section Year of Renunciation also lists some prior years. Twelve individuals converted before 1900 (the earliest conversion dates from 1885), another 37 before 1910, another 92 between 1910 and 1919, another 117 between 1920 and 1929, 94 between 1930 and 1937, as many as 166 in 1938, 70 in 1939, and 65 in 1940. The fact that those who had converted several decades earlier asked the Community to confirm their renunciation shows that they hoped having such a document would save them. If we subtract those who converted before 1941, the above figures show that 2,877 people renounced their Jewish religion in that year, which was almost one-third of the Zagreb Jewish Community.[3] Unfortunately, in 1941, no one recorded the exact dates of the conversions, so there is no way of telling how many took place before April 10 and how many after. The Renunciation document shows that there were about 1,685 conversions before July 31, and another 1,192 after. Up to that date, the book includes detailed information about the individuals who converted—address, property status, and income—while after that date, only the letter "*p*" was added to the name (meaning *pokršten* = converted). The reason for keeping statistics in this way can be surmised: the person who entered the information in the register either no longer had the patience, or the time, or was afraid to enter the address and property status in case someone in authority, getting his hands on the book, might use the information for blackmail, robbery, or deportation. It is also possible that the change was due to a combination of these.

In May 1941, RUR asked the Catholic parish offices, Evangelical and Orthodox communities, and the Islamic Religious Community for information about former Jews who had joined their communities. The lists they got contained the names of 1,156 Jews who had converted before May 1941. Most priests gave reports based on the year of conversion; some, like St. Blaise's Parish in Primorska Street and the Evangelical Community, had records from the end of the nineteenth century. The Evangelical Community had only a list of persons who had converted before mid-1938; the rest of the list was probably lost. Some, however, like St. Peter's Parish, reported 253 conversions, but did not mention the year when they took place.[4] An insignificant number of people who had converted from the Jewish religion to another religious group died before 1941. These lists provided the Ustasha Police with the names of only 62 Jews who had converted to another religion in 1941.[5] Of these 62 converted Jews, 4 converted to the Orthodox Church, which is 6.5 percent (much less than between 1931 and 1937, when 25 of the 91 converted Zagreb Jews opted for the Orthodox Church, which represented 27.5 percent).[6]

We do not know whether the Ustasha authorities required the religious communities to continue sending lists of converted Jews after May 1941. They may no longer have been interested in who had converted and who had not, because the newly adopted Racial Laws treated the Jewish question as a racial issue, and not as a religious one.

The documents kept in the Archbishopric Archives in Zagreb mainly confirm the information in the Renunciations book and provide additional explanations. From the beginning of 1941 until April 10, Zagreb parishes submitted only seven requests for conversion. This number corresponded with the average for the interwar years, when about twenty people a year renounced the Jewish religion, and five to six people a year converted to the Jewish religion.[7] But, after April 10 and until the end of that month, there were twelve Jewish applications in only twenty or so days, and in May at least ninety.[8] In June, 232 Zagreb Jews applied to be converted.[9] This situation peaked in July, when 1,200 people are known to have converted, and it is more likely that there were 1,370 of them.[10] This general atmosphere of massive "flight" from the Jewish religion is well illustrated by the fact that on July 12, 70 Jews asked to be converted in the Holy Family Parish Office in Držićeva Street, on July 15, another 30, and on July 21, 19 more.[11]

In these calculations, we must bear in mind that some applications were submitted in one month and resolved in the following—the statistics show the month in which the applications were resolved—but this does not significantly affect the total numbers. The Church reacted fast to the large number of conversions. On June 11, 1941, Archbishop Stepinac appointed Canon Milan Beluhan spiritual guide to the Committee for Assisting Converts to Catholicism in Zagreb.[12]

The number of conversions fell in August 1941 to around 400.[13] In September, the Archbishopric Clerical Office received 229 Jewish applications for conversion from the Zagreb parishes.[14] During this month, the number of Orthodox who sought conversion to Catholicism exceeded the number of Jews several times over. Only a month or two earlier, it had been the other way around: many Jewish applications and an insignificant number of Orthodox. Till the end of the year, the number of conversions gradually decreased, with between 500 and 600 Zagreb Jews converting from the beginning of October to the end of December.[15] All this shows that the numbers in the Renunciations registry (which lists 2,877 Jews who converted in 1941) are practically identical to those in the documentation of the Archbishopric Clerical Office, which registered between 2,800 and 2,900 conversions. The exact number of converted Jews is not known, because the registry does not give all the names, but, in many cases, only that of the head of household.

In 1942, the number of converted Jews continued to fall. According to information given by the Archbishopric Clerical Office, seventy-six Zagreb Jews converted during that year. In 1943, only three conversions were registered.[16]

Before the war and in the first days of the ISC, the leaders of the Zagreb Jewish Community retained the old, strict attitude to converted Jews: contempt and rejection. By the end of May, a Department for Converted Jews was founded in the Community, which shows that the attitude toward people who renounced the Jewish religion had slowly started to change in the Zagreb Community. If there was not yet any understanding for them, at least someone took care of them. At that time, Jews started visiting the parish offices en masse, so the Community Board held a meeting on July 31, 1941, and decided that "converted Jews may not be members of any committee of this Community . . . Converted Jews may be buried in the Jewish section of the Mirogoj Cemetery only if they have a family tomb there . . . All support will be withheld from converted Jews."[17] In December 1941, the Community Council decided "to suspend all support to the refugee camp in Banja Luka, because many refugees have renounced the Jewish religion." At the same time, it decided that, due to a constant increase in prices, the donations to refugees in other locations should be increased.[18] During the war years, the Community softened its attitude toward converted Jews, and, at the beginning of 1943, Miroslav Šalom Freiberger asked the converted Jews to pay Community dues, emphasizing that the Zagreb Jewish Community "in its work, pays no attention to whether someone is a member of our religious community."[19]

The stories of those who converted in 1943 and later are characteristic. Veronika Rosenfeld (1917) arrived in Zagreb in May 1942 with her son, Ivica (1934), and daughter (1938), whose name has not been recorded and who had been christened in Kragujevac (Serbia). In September 1943, she wanted to christen Ivica as well, because, as an "artist, she traveled here and there, and had no opportunity to have her son christened. She has been in Zagreb for some time already, but she was ill and could not have her child christened." There is no information about the further destiny of Veronika and her children.[20] Ladislav Steiner (1900) converted and convalidated his marriage in September 1943.[21] The last conversion during the war was that of eighty-seven-year-old Ivana Rosskam (Rosskamp), which took place in May 1944. The old lady fled from Zagreb to her daughter in Vukovar, and then they both fled to Tuzla (in Bosnia) to Ivana's granddaughter, who was protected as a doctor's wife. Some time after that, Ivana was sheltered in a convent. At the beginning of 1944, the nuns brought her to Zagreb and handed her over to her son, Rikard, who had converted in 1918, was married to a Croat, and had Aryan rights. Ivana was "very ill" and aware that her end was near. Her family was afraid of burying her in the Jewish cemetery, so the priest said she could be buried in the Christian part of the cemetery if she converted. Ivana, practically on her deathbed, was secretly converted at home, and the priest wrote in the annexed file that "she has been instructed in the most important religious truths."[22]

Some people, whose Jewish background may be assumed from their names, converted to Catholicism from other Christian communities. In July 1944, Kornel Saffer (Šaffer) was received into the Catholic Church from the Greek Eastern Orthodox Church, as was Miljenko Erny (1933), son of Vladimir, a month later.[23] A month or so after that, student Miroslav Eckert, son of Gotfrid and Maria, née Samac, a Lutheran, converted to Catholicism.[24]

The Catholic Church had an established routine for accepting new believers. When a Jew expressed a desire to convert, the parish priest forwarded the application to the Archbishopric Clerical Office, which generally gave its approval. This was in accordance with the instruction from the Vatican that "the Catholic Church shall not accept any adult under its wing who seeks to join it, or return to it, unless he/she is completely aware of the importance and consequences of the step he/she is about to take."[25] In April 1941, Jews still wrote long explanations about why they wanted to convert. Ivan Klein (1911) was, according to the parish priest, an "honest man . . . intelligent, who had gone to university, studied canon law, and therefore knows a lot about the Catholic Church . . . I made a threat, and I will keep to it, that unless he learns well . . . I will not marry him."[26] As time went by, the explanations grew shorter and more basic. There were several simple formulations that justified conversion. The new believer, according to the parish priest, showed that "he/she is familiar with the Catholic religion, and that he/she has a pure and sincere desire to become a Catholic," or that "he/she was brought up as a Catholic," or that "he/she learned all the necessary prayers, even though with difficulty, as he/she does not speak Croatian well," or that "he/she was touched while attentively listening to the religious truths."[27] Jews married to Catholics had to undergo the same procedure.[28]

It is obvious that many times the priests looked the other way and paid little attention to the strict rules for conversion, i.e., to whether people knew the catechism well and whether they accepted the religious truths, as canon law required.[29] In many cases, whole four-member (the mother and three daughters of the Eisenstädter family) or even five-member families (the Sage and Müller families)[30] converted, so all the members could not be expected to be well informed about the new religion. Elza Sauerbrunn (1880) was even "convinced the Catholic religion is the one and only right religion in which she can find peace and salvation for her soul." Nevertheless, she died in Auschwitz.[31]

Šarika (Sara) Štefica Sarfati "has problems remembering her catechism because she is weak-minded, but she knows the most important truths." Šarika did not survive the war.[32] The reason why Elza Glück, née Adler, did not submit her application to join the Catholic Church until February 1942 was, as explained by the parish priest, that "she would have done it earlier but she was very ill" (Elza did not survive the war), while Mavro and Dragica Weinberger, claimed the parish priest at the beginning of 1942, had been preparing for baptism since "last year in the fall" (nevertheless, they were killed in 1944).[33] Eta Mandolfo was "baptized privately as a child, but was not registered in the baptismal registry book."[34]

That these affirmative phrases hid completely different reasons can be seen in the case of Mira and Marta Wertheimer, who were, according to the parish priest, "well-instructed in the Catholic Religion. They were imprisoned three months ago . . . have been released now, and want to join." Like many others, the Wertheimers did not save their lives by converting, for neither Mira nor Marta, nor their parents Mavro and Regina, survived the war.[35] Fanika Spitzer and her daughters, Johana and Sofija, were converted in February 1942. Fanika's husband, Albert, was in a "camp at the time and could not be converted."[36] By then, Albert was already dead, killed in Jasenovac, and Fanika (Frida), Johana, and Sofija were killed in "an unknown place."[37] The Ungar family had a similar destiny: the mother, Zlata, had her sons, Vilim (1926) and Branko (1931), converted in April

1942, and their father, Jakov, a merchant, was deported to Jasenovac and "his destiny was unknown for a long time."[38] Jakov was killed in Jasenovac, and neither Zlata nor her two sons could escape death even by converting—in August 1942, they were taken to Auschwitz.[39] Jakov (1879) and Srećko (1921) Donner converted, but were killed, probably in Dotršćina.[40] The whole Cohen family also converted. Despite this, the father, Iso (1896), was killed in Jasenovac in 1941, the son, Fedor (1929), in Auschwitz in 1942, and with him probably his mother, Flora-Fani.[41]

Many camp internees believed that conversion was their last hope. Žiga Schotten filed an application for the conversion of his son, Branko, in July 1941, at which time Branko had already been in a camp for over a month, and was killed at the latest in August.[42] In 1944, the Daruvar Parish Office asked permission to convert Boris Maks Švarcenberg (1926), "who had learned about the religion while in the Jasenovac Camp and practiced the Catholic religion." Boris Maks was from Daruvar. Though from a mixed marriage (his mother was Russian), conversion did not help him, and he did not survive the war.[43]

There were, however, stories with a happier ending. Seventy-four-year-old Claudi Bondy, widow, converted in September 1942, while her son, Ivan, was in a "camp." Claudi was deported, and Ivan somehow survived the war.[44] Tilda Hirschler and her daughter, Stanka, sought to convert to Catholicism, and Tilda's husband was "in captivity in Germany, and would convert as soon as he returns." Both Tilda and Stanka survived the war, and Hugo Hirschler returned home.[45]

The story of Gertruda-Truda (1924) and Zora (1929) Dirnbach is an exception. They renounced membership in the Jewish Community and were converted at the beginning of June 1941. Their mother, Maria (Marija), an Austrian Catholic, had converted to Judaism in 1922 when she got married. In the mid-thirties, however, she divorced her husband, Samuel, and returned to her original Catholic religion after the Anschluss in 1938, sensing that things might turn bad in Yugoslavia. When converting the Dirnbach sisters, the parish priest was well rewarded for backdating the certificates of baptism to March 1941. The night after she was baptized, Zora went to her family in Osijek, where her sister and mother joined her a month later. The family was considered Catholic now, and despite some minor problems all three survived the war.[46]

"Conversions were done for money, and for large sums at that," claims Ljerka Magdić.[47] There is no reason not to believe that statement, although it is also clear that, in some or many cases, no payment was made, as the converted did not have money. The richest and most prominent Jews also converted—Rudolf Rodanić did so in July, his wife Elvira, née Lesković, about a month earlier, in June 1941, and by doing so survived the war.[48] Husband and wife Robert and Hilda Deutsch-Maceljski converted also, and so did their daughter Vanja.[49] Vanja was saved by escaping to Palestine, but her parents were deported to Auschwitz in 1943.[50]

The list of prisoners in the Italian camp in Kraljevica is a good indicator of whether and to what extent conversion provided a greater hope for salvation, as it mentions the religion beside the name. Out of the 1,185 Jews interned in Kraljevica, 614 (or 51.8 percent) declared themselves as "Israelites," 538 (or 45.4 percent) as Roman Catholics, and 33 (or 2 percent) as members of other religions (7 Greek Catholic, 10 Protestant, 7 Orthodox, 2 Muslim, 2 with no religion, 5 with no record). There were 627 Zagreb Jews, which is 52.9 percent of the total number. Of those, 353 (or 56.3 percent) declared themselves to be Roman Catholics, 266 as "Israelites" (42.4 percent), and 8 (1.3 percent) as belonging to other religions (4 Greek Catholic, 3 Protestant, and 1 Muslim). When the number of converted Jews from Zagreb is compared with the number who were not from Zagreb but were also in Kraljevica, there are significant differences: among those who were not from Zagreb, 348 (or 62.4 percent) remained Jewish, 185 (or 33.2 percent) declared themselves Roman Catholics, and 25 (or 4.4 percent) were members of other religions or were not religious. This means that among the Jews in Kraljevica, there was a much larger percentage of converted Zagreb Jews than converted Jews from other places in Croatia. This also means that Jews who renounced the Jewish religion had a greater chance for survival, because about 30 percent of the Zagreb Jews converted in 1941, and over half of the Zagreb Jews in the Kraljevica camp were converts. Therefore, a proportionately larger number of converted Jews were saved.[51]

At the very beginning of the ISC, toward the end of April and beginning of May, many married couples who were both Jewish, or where only one spouse was Jewish, annulled their civil marriage so that they could get married in church. They submitted their applications to the Ministry of the Interior, which approved the cases rapidly and then had the church confirm them, because that was the only way for them to get married in church.[52]

A special category were women who had converted to Judaism when they got married and later converted back to Catholicism, such as Kristina Rosenberg, née Breznik, Marija Taussig, née Štir, Marija Lustig, née Šerbec, Dragica Müller, née Pustaj, Dragica Hochstädter (Laurenčić), Anita

Sachs-Kobilschek, née Janceković, Ivka Švicer, née Kovačić, and Marija Brussler, née Grahek.[53] Bara Weiss, née Dojčić, returned to Catholicism together with her daughter, Mira.[54] Tugomila Sasson asked for "forgiveness from church punishment for leaving the Roman Catholic religion and converting to the Israelite religion, as well as for marrying in a non-Catholic temple and before a non-Catholic clergyman, and for raising her children in a non-Catholic Religion." She also asked the Roman Catholic Church to accept her two children, Ingrid (1936) and Solvega (1937).[55]

Some people thought that they would avoid a terrible fate by renouncing their so-called or real Jewish parents. Greta (Zita) Neumann (1911) claimed that her mother, Marija Neumann, née Rakarić, was a Catholic who had been adopted by a Jew, Marin Werner, and had therefore converted to Judaism. Her mother then lived in a common-law marriage with the Catholic Josip Zdunić and the "fruit of that relationship were two daughters and a son." As she was entered in the registry books according to her mother's religion, Greta became Jewish. The common-law marriage ended in 1918, and Marija met Aleksandar Neumann, a Jew, who adopted her three children. In June 1941, Greta converted to Catholicism. In a court trial that lasted from the end of 1942 to February 1943, Greta and her brother, Franjo (1912), were proclaimed the illegitimate children of Marija Neumann, née Rakarić. Therefore, they officially lost all connections with Judaism and, so they thought, had escaped from the danger of being deported. Nevertheless, Greta Neumann was killed in an "unknown" place, and there is no information about Franjo.[56] Rudolf Blüth (1896) initiated proceedings to proclaim him the illegitimate child of Regina, née Taussig, and, by the end of 1941, he successfully brought them to a close. This, however, did not help him, as he was killed in an unknown place. His sixteen-year-old son, Erich, was also killed.[57] Rudolf's sister, Štefica, was proclaimed illegitimate in the same proceedings, and she survived the war and remained a member of the Zagreb Jewish Community.[58] In 1942, four-year-old Stanko Glas also went through a similar process, during which it was found that "Franjo Glas from Zagreb is not the father of the registered child," but that he was the "illegitimate child of Hedvega Glas, née Papiga."[59] There were other similar cases during those years, but, as people wanted to leave as little evidence as possible in the documents, we can only guess at many of the details of the stories.

Jewish children left to the care of Croatian families after their parents were deported were usually christened. Eight-month-old Isak Kabiljo was christened in September 1942, after his mother had been deported a month earlier, and his father a year before that. The same was done with Smiljan (1929) and Marijan (1933) Steiner, and Leon (1938) and Ljerka (1942) Bauer, whose parents were in camps at the time. Each application said that "the parents expressed a desire for their children to be baptized, and that the children's grandparents want the same," or some such phrase. However, it is difficult to believe that the parents were in the situation to say anything.[60]

Many church people tried to help the Jews. In doing so, some parish priests resorted to small tricks. At the beginning of July 1941, the Archbishopric Clerical Office sent a circular letter warning all deans that "some parish offices issue converted Jews with certificates stating that they have honorary Aryan rights." The deans were instructed to inform the parish offices they are not authorized to do so.[61] It is possible that in the first months of the ISC, some individuals in the Ustasha administration in charge of deportations really did believe that parish priests could issue such certificates.

The parish priest in St. Peter's Parish Office in Zagreb, Dr. Josip Lončarić, addressed the Archbishopric Clerical Office in mid-June 1941, asking for directions about how to marry an Aryan and a Jew. He understood that the "state does not accept" such marriages, but people come to him, "Catholic men and women who have known the Jewish parties for months and would like to get married, but are afraid of the state authorities and their persecution." The priest said that "while it was possible, while still close to the tenth day of April, to save these people from problems, which are obviously unjust, in the case of marriage we backdated the day of the wedding to make it appear that they had gotten married before April 10. We cannot do that any more." After discussing this at their meeting, the Archbishopric Clerical Office answered that they "can give no interpretation . . . because we have received no instructions on the matter from the state authorities. We leave it to the discretion of each parish priest to do what he thinks best. The state authorities have not held anyone liable for marriages performed after April 10. In any case, this religious authority will, when the time comes, try to mitigate the legal provisions regarding such marriages."[62]

The church authorities rarely acted without the consent of the civil authorities. And the ISC authorities rarely directly confronted the actions of the Church, especially if these actions did not challenge the basic goals of the governing structure. Thus, in September 1942, the chaplain in the Psychiatric Hospital in Vrapče (a western suburb of Zagreb) asked instructions for christening a Jew, Olga Schaeffer, and the Archbishopric Clerical Office replied that "from our side there is no objection for her to be christened . . . but this religious body cannot take responsibility for her christening before the civil authorities." The fact was that Olga Schaeffer had no documents, and the Clerical Office advised the priest to "take matters up with the city council."[63]

On some occasions, a Jew who had been recently converted died, and his/her family tomb was in the Jewish cemetery. In such cases, Catholic priests did not want to officiate at the funeral. Rabbi Freiberger talked to Cardinal Stepinac about this in the spring of 1942. It seems that they agreed that "a place should be determined for burying such people, and if any are to be buried in the Jewish section, a priest must officiate." Canon Kamilo Dočkal was assigned to write more detailed instructions about this, which were sent to all parish offices in Zagreb.[64] He considered that "as a general rule, converted Jews should be buried in the Roman Catholic cemetery . . . In exceptional cases, in cases of a family tomb, they may be buried in the Jewish cemetery. In such cases, a Roman Catholic priest will lead the deceased to the family tomb, where he will bless the place in which the Roman Catholic is to be buried . . . Members of different religions may bury their deceased in a similar way in the Roman Catholic cemetery."[65]

When the Zagreb and Croatian Jews reached safety, some renounced the Catholic religion and returned to Judaism. There were a few such examples, although many fewer than the other way around during the previous years. The first recorded reversions happened as early as July 1943 in Vela Luka (on the island of Korčula), when eight Zagreb Jews converted back: the four-member Klein family (Eugen, Heda, and the children, Petar and Dagmar), Leon and Olga Hirschsohn, and Melita Gross and Oskar Rösler.[66]

Zenfira Engel christened her son, Boris, right after he was born in December 1944 "only because I had to . . . as I am a Jew and my husband Antun (who was killed in Jasenovac) was also a Jew." On June 26, 1945, Boris renounced the Catholic religion in St. Mark's Church in Zagreb, and, in the summer of 1945, his mother "had him entered in the registry books of the Jewish Religious Community."[67] In the summer of 1945, the Jewish Community in Zagreb created a form for reverting to the Jewish religion: the returnee had to notify the parish office in which he had been christened that he was returning to the Jewish religion and to submit that paper together with his application. Then his reversion would be registered in the Community registry books. On several occasions in August and September 1945, the Jewish Community sent the parish offices letters with a list of a total of 112 returnees to the Jewish religion.[68] However, the number of returnees was much larger: the List of Survivors, created in the summer of 1945, was supplemented with the list of those who had returned to the Jewish Religion—there were a total of 626 in Zagreb, and it must be taken into account that many of them had not lived in Zagreb in 1941.[69] After this, people reverted individually. Henrieta Papo, née Adler, returned to the Jewish religion on November 1, 1945. The whole Hohnenwald family returned to Judaism in Feričanci (near Valpovo in Slavonia) on the same day.[70] However, in 1946, a total of 102 Community members converted back in the Zagreb Chief Rabbi's Office, seventy-eight of whom were from Zagreb, and the rest from other places. Of the 102, ninety-six reverted from Roman Catholicism, two from Eastern Orthodox, and two from the Old Catholic Religion, one from Lutheranism, and one from the Islamic Religious Community.[71] Some returns followed a very complicated procedure: in June 1946, the three-member Eremić family authenticated their statements about reverting to the Jewish religion in the Yugoslav General Consulate in Zurich. These statements were sent to the Zagreb Jewish Community, which then sent them to St. Anthony's parish office, where the Eremićs had been christened.[72]

It seems, however, that there were more returns to the Jewish religion than those registered in the Jewish Community Archives. In October 1945, Egon Bader from Virovitica asked the Zagreb Community to send him "four forms to complete regarding my return to the Jewish religion. Under occupation, during the ISC, I was forced to convert to the Roman Catholic faith and I would like to revert, together with my family. In any case, there are more families like that here, so please send additional forms so that I can distribute them."[73] At the same time, after the war ended, there were also reversions in the other direction, from Judaism to Catholicism: widow Lea Hamberger, housewife, "having the right intent," was christened at the end of July 1945.[74]

The words "conversion to Catholicism" do not cover all renouncements of the Jewish religion, as sixteen Jews who converted to Islam—two of them were Jews who married Muslims—were registered in the Muslim Religious Community in Zagreb at the beginning of May 1941 (of the sixteen, two later renounced Islam).[75] Merchant Mavro Rechnitzer (1880) converted to Islam in 1941 and became Mehmed, but was killed nevertheless.[76]

32

TO STAY PUT OR ESCAPE?

When Ustasha persecution began, "many Jews simply did not want to leave, did not understand what was happening."[1] "We could not believe it, we would not accept that it was true."[2] In some cases, the instinct to escape, to save one's life, mixed or clashed with the hope that their Croatian friends and neighbors of many years' standing would manage to protect them. A good number of Jews hoped that their reputation and good position in their community (town, neighborhood, village, etc.) would be a sufficient guarantee of salvation. Many had become relatively wealthy in recent decades and they hesitated to leave their wealth behind. They remembered the poverty of their own or earlier generations, the constant moving triggered by the wish to make a fortune, or at least to create the basis for a normal middle-class life. Now, having achieved this, it was difficult to leave it all. The very wealthy Sida and Adolf Švarcenberg (they owned a house in the center of the city, in Jurišićeva Street, and an apartment in nearby Martićeva) decided that they would "rather go to Mirogoj [i.e., the town cemetery] than emigrate," although the whole family got passports to leave for Split, in other words, for Italy. Their property was soon sequestered and they moved to nearby Samobor, and, in the summer of 1942, were deported to Jasenovac. Adolf was one of the few Jews who were released from Jasenovac, but Sida was killed. Their daughter, Zlata

Mondschein, her husband, Ivo, and her ten-year-old son, Milan Bornstein (from her first marriage), were also killed.[3]

Some people couldn't make up their minds until the last moment. "Some obtained passes, but did not leave in time."[4] When Edo Čango (Ödon Csango) sent his son, Bruno, to Karlovac and on to salvation in the Italian zone in May 1941, one of his friends accused him of being "disloyal to others," saying that Jews "must obey the authorities if they want to survive" and that he himself would send his sons to report to the Ustashe. Bruno and his sister, Noemi Čango, made it to Palestine, but the parents, Edo and Vilma, were deported from Budapest in 1944.[5]

Albert Baum, leader of the assimilationist current in the Zagreb Community in the thirties, claimed that "all Zagreb knows me and nothing can happen to me," especially as his wife, Zora, née Frank, was a distant relative of Josip Frank. When Albert and his wife spent four nights sleeping on the bare ground at the Zagreb Fairground in June 1941, he changed his views.[6] He was taken off the train to the Gospić Camp at the intercession of an unknown person and he and his wife were sent home. Soon they fled abroad. The case of Geza Frank, also a distant relative of Josip Frank, did not have as happy an ending. Geza returned from Split to Zagreb after the establishment of the ISC, believing that he was safe because Ante Pavelić had been a junior clerk at his law office. Only a month later, he ended his life in Pag, and his son, Saša, was killed in Jasenovac in November or December 1941. Saša's wife, Stanka, née Hertmann, and their three daughters fled to Switzerland and survived the war.[7]

"Hinko Levi and his oldest son, Aurel, got passes, but they would not leave."[8] Dr. Hinko Löwy (Levi) was a distinguished dermato-venereologist and medical historian.[9] He, his son Aurel, and daughter, Amalia, were arrested at the very beginning of 1942 and on January 9 he was imprisoned in Sava Road. His wife, Marija, and other son, Karlo, were also deported. The whole family perished in the camps.[10] Even sadder is the story of the Schwarz family: the father, Oskar, married to a non-Jew, said "If others are going, so shall you" and then made his son, Aleksandar, join the other 165 youths going to "work" in Koprivnica in May 1941. Aleksandar was killed in Jadovno, and the father was later killed in an unknown place.[11] When Leopold Israel was arrested and taken to camp in August 1941, his son, Milan, courted arrest as well so as to be able to help his father. Milan was arrested on September 10, and neither he nor his father returned from camp.[12]

Vlatko Deutsch-Maceljski would not flee, because he thought he would not be able to leave the city with faked documents, as many people in Zagreb knew him because of his charity work. Besides, he hoped that people who owed him a favor would get him out of trouble. On one occasion, Ustasha Colonel Jedvaj, whom he had helped with money and food in the thirties, saved him.[13] Vlatko and his wife, Marga, née Rosenbaum, were deported in August 1942 all the same.

Otto Müller, a doctor from Crnatkova, was rather naïve; his lodgers, a married couple, broke the house rules, so Müller decided to terminate their lease. They reported him to the police as a Jew, and Müller, as an "honest and upright man who has never had any dealings with the police, or with courts" turned directly to Ivica Baraković and Poglavnik Pavelić.[14] Müller, who was also called Miljević, very quickly lost any illusions he may have had when his request to not wear the insignia was refused. In January 1943, he worked as a doctor in the home in Rapska, and managed to survive the war.[15]

Dr. Miroslav Duić–Deutsch treated several distinguished Catholic priests, and he and his family converted in the summer 1941 to save themselves. When Archbishop Stepinac advised him to apply for treating syphilis patients in Bosnia, he took his advice, and that was how he was saved. Later he joined the Partisans.[16]

Poorer people hardly dared to think about escaping, because this took money: bribes had to be paid for passes, money was necessary to live in places where one could not earn it, and so on. Katica and Vera Fischer, a mother and daughter, sold their upright piano in the summer of 1941 to survive, and when they escaped from Zagreb at the beginning of 1942, they had just about enough money to live outside their home for six months.[17] Because more of the wealthier people escaped, a proportionately greater number of wealthy Jews arrived in Rab.[18] Alfred Pal said that Singer from Varaždin arrived in the Rab Camp with as many as 150 suitcases, which Pal and several of his friends carried from the boat to the camp barrack for a small fee.[19]

Of the 70 richest Jews—those who were supposed to pay Community tax in excess of 10,000 kunas in 1941 and 1942—who were still in Zagreb at the beginning of 1943, 35 were killed, and the other 35 seem to have survived the war. This means that exactly 50 percent of the richest survived. Of a total of 121 who paid a smaller sum, who the Community heads knew were less wealthy, almost two-thirds (78, or 64.5 percent) were killed, and the proportion of those deported in May 1943 (about 1,500–1,700) to the number who remained living in Zagreb even after that (about 800) is roughly the same.

Once a Jew was arrested, the family had one reason less to run; if the father had been arrested, the mother often did not dare escape alone with the children. In other cases, the family wanted to stay closer to the arrested member to help him or get him out. "The families of the 165 youths who were taken away at the end of May often remained in Zagreb waiting for their sons, and were themselves taken away."[20] There are many examples of solidarity leading to the demise of all. Licika Polak, née Berger, of Bjelovar, got typhoid in Loborgrad and was moved to one of Zagreb's hospitals. When she got better, the doctors tried to persuade her to escape from the hospital, but she refused because "she could not leave her mother and sister in Loborgrad," so returned there. Not one of the three survived the war.[21] In the winter of 1942–1943, Katica Fischer wanted to return from the safety of Split to her parents, Mavro and Julija Klein, in Zagreb, because "they are old and there is no one to take care of them." Her family in Split barely managed to dissuade her from doing that.[22]

Many cases show that hope often dies last. The Jews who arrived in the transit center at Zavrtnica in Zagreb in September 1941 did not know what was in store for them, and thought, "Forced labor for a time, this is not so terrible!"[23] Dr. Stjepan Steiner said that, from the end of June to the beginning of September 1941, the prisoners at the Zagreb Fairground and in Zavrtnica were frightened, but convinced that they were going to a work camp. But, in September, when the Jasenovac Camp was opened, people began to realize what was going on.[24]

Nevertheless, for a time, this self-delusion or deluding of others continued. Many people took part in it, intentionally or unintentionally. In the summer and autumn of 1941, when the Community officials were supplementing the card index of Jews who had to wear the insignia, beside the name of Isak Abinun, who was killed in Jasenovac not long after, they added the euphemistic note that he had "traveled to camp."[25] In short, "for a long time people did not want to believe that going to camp in fact meant going to death."[26]

Some people were even aware of the mortal danger, but as they were for one reason or another convinced that there was nothing they could do, they did not want to burden their families with this nightmare. Making children face this horror was certainly the most difficult. Teacher Mira Levi remembered the little boy Klein, who was the first to complete his assignment in her class in the Jewish school. Then, his little sister knocked at the door and called him: "Brother, come quickly, grandfather and grandmother are waiting down on the street. They have put pillows and mattresses on the cart. We're going to camp, hurry!" Klein and his family were never heard of again.[27] They were probably Ivan (11) and Eva Klein (8) and their grandfather, Samuel (1878) and grandmother Olga (1887), who seem to have been deported to Auschwitz or some other German camp in 1942. Ivan's and Eva's father, Mikša, had been killed in Jasenovac by the end of 1941, and their mother, Frida, was killed in an unknown place.[28]

Some people had a presentiment of what was in store for them and that there was no more hope. When he was "leaving for camp," probably in the fall of 1941 (because the Jewish Community sent him a parcel in November), attorney Dr. Siegfried Perlberg decided what was to become of his property "after his death." If, at the beginning of 1942, anyone still had any illusions, Lavoslav Šik, who was at that time released from Jasenovac for a short period, must have made them change their minds. After his return to Zagreb he said, "Whoever can, should escape at once. Do not stay here for one day longer."[29]

Finally, the question arose: Where to seek refuge? In the first months after the establishment of the ISC, there was often nowhere to run if a person or a family did not have a pass to leave the city. If the potential escapee could not hope to reach the Italian zone, or to escape from the country, or to reach the Partisans, it was best to remain in Zagreb or to go there, however paradoxical this may seem. It was extremely risky for Zagreb Jews to go to smaller Croatian towns or to villages, as anyone could notice them in a small unknown community and then, depending on his sentiments, report them. In Zagreb, it was possible to intercede for a friend, a relative, or for oneself; it also was easier for people to hide, and some help could be gotten from the Jewish Community. Besides, during the early months, Jews from smaller towns in the ISC came to Zagreb. At the beginning of 1942, Gizela Keller came to Zagreb from Vukovar and settled in Kustošija.[30]

About 500 Jews were caught trying to escape from Zagreb, at varying distances from the city, most of them in trains. Two large groups of about fifty fugitives were returned from Karlovac, and many people were arrested in Samobor, attempting to escape to the border region of Slovenia, which was annexed by Italy.[31] Jakov Präger and his wife, Adela, did not manage to get to Split and were brought back to Zagreb; later, Jakov was killed in Jasenovac, but Adela reached Split on her second attempt.[32] Factory owner Stjepan Spitzer-Španić (1898) and his mother, Tinka, née Neumann, were taken off the train in Karlovac in 1942 and were both killed—Stjepan in Auschwitz in October, and his mother at an unknown time and place.[33]

Lavoslav Stern and his wife, Milka, and five-year-old son, Božidar, were taken off the train in 1942 in Plase (on the border between the ISC and Italy, near Rijeka),[34] and Lavoslav was immediately taken to Jasenovac, whence he did not return. Milka and Božidar also met their ends in camp, probably in May 1943.[35]

Trying to save oneself often became a real adventure. When he heard about the coup on March 27, 1941, Zagreb attorney Lujo Weissman went to Belgrade and was there on April 6, at the time of the German attack. He hid in the interior of Serbia, and placed himself at the disposal of the forces of General Simović. Since he knew many languages, he listened to the news on foreign radio stations at the army headquarters and wrote reports about it. After the capitulation of the Yugoslav army on April 17, he traveled via Užice, Sarajevo, and Mostar to Trsteno near Dubrovnik. When conditions settled down a little, he wanted to return from Dubrovnik to his relatives in Zagreb. News about the Ustashe's roundups of Jews stopped him at the Plitvice Lakes (one hundred kilometers south of Zagreb), which were under Italian control, and he went to Sušak. There he obtained a passport and Portuguese and Spanish visas, and went to Italy. From Rome he traveled to Lisbon, and from there to New York, where, after 1944, as Lujo Goranin, he accompanied the prominent Croatian opera singer Zinka Kunc on the piano at a charity performance to raise funds for the Partisans.[36] Piroška Kornfein and her mother fled from Zagreb to their family in Grubišno Polje (ninety kilometers east of Zagreb), and when the arrests began in 1942, a poor woman named Ana Markoja hid them. Later, mother and daughter fled to Hungary, where they "somehow survived in incessant fear and danger, fighting for at least a bed and to earn enough for food."[37] Mordo/Marko Altarac, suspecting that trouble lay ahead, went from Zagreb to Tuzla several days before the establishment of the ISC. About two months later, in the second half of May, when it became more difficult for Jews to leave Zagreb, Mordo's friend, by now the sworn Ustasha Zvonko (surname unknown), acquired documents in typical Muslim names and surnames for Mordo's wife, Regina, née Kohen, and three-year-old daughter, Mira. Thus, the family was reunited in Tuzla, which was still quiet. Soon they had to escape from there, too, so Regina, in a chador and veil, fled to Sarajevo with little Mira, and then to Split, and Mordo joined the Partisans. After much trouble, going to Korčula and the El Shatt refugee camp, in May 1945, the entire family returned to Zagreb in an army truck.[38]

One of the questions in a survey completed by Yugoslav Jews in the late seventies and early eighties was, "How did you survive the Second

World War?" "Of the ten possible answers given in the questionnaire, few people chose only one. Their fates had taken them through prisons run by the occupation forces, through concentration camps, and through underground hiding places; they had fled from the authorities and used assumed names, many had joined the National Army of Liberation . . . Many of the respondents checked answer eleven ("other"), describing the various unforeseeable kinds of suffering and salvation that brought them to 1945, as if by a miracle."[39] In 1971, the 674 members of what was then the Jewish Community in Zagreb born before 1930 filled in a questionnaire about the various places they had been during the war: in camps (239, or 35.5 percent), in the National War of Liberation (238, or 35.3 percent), in hiding (147, or 21.83 percent), in prison (143, or 21.2 percent), refugees (97, or 14.4 percent), confined (86, or 12.8 percent), doing forced labor and "other" (58, or 8.6 percent), prisoners of war (38, or 5.6 percent), and in resistance movements in other countries and Allied armies (10, or 1.5 percent).[40] These figures included many Jews who had moved to the city after 1945, and a person could give more than one answer.

One of the ways of trying to survive, at least for girls, was to marry an "Aryan" or a person outside Croatia. Some stories had happy endings, but more did not. In March 1943, Zora Schönwald (28), a Roman Catholic who was at that time living in Zagreb, wanted to marry Ivo Fröhlich, who was somewhere in Italy or on territory under Italian occupation, where an "Italian curate was giving him religious instruction." Documents do not show whether this was a love match or only an attempt to save a life. If it was the Ivo Fröhlich from Hercegovačka Street (and not someone else), and this seems to have been the case, then Zora wanted to save her life by a fictitious marriage. She did not manage to do this, and ended her days in an "unknown place." Giovanni-Ivan Fröhlich returned to Zagreb in 1945 and soon married the girl he had been engaged to before the war.[41]

In December 1942, Josip Novak and Rut-Vera Podvinec were married in St. Peter's parish office in Zagreb; she was "the daughter of Jewish parents," but had first converted to the Old Catholic and then to the Roman Catholic Church. The Ustasha Police received an anonymous report that Novak had married a "non-Aryan," with the allegation that "Novak had given the parish priest in Trnje 30,000 kunas to marry them," which was a lie, because the marriage had been performed in St. Peter's parish office in Vlaška Street. An investigation was started, Novak was interrogated and he unconvincingly claimed that he did not know it was impossible to marry a person of that kind. The priest was not much more convincing, claiming that he did not know Rut was of Jewish origin, and that "he is very careful to make sure the betrothed couple are both pure Aryans."[42] At that time, Vera's mother, Frida, was also living in Novak's home. The upshot of the investigation is not known, but the final outcome was that Frida survived the war, while Rut-Vera was taken to a camp, from which she did not return.[43]

33

ESCAPE

After the ISC was established, it became increasingly difficult for Jews to escape. In 1941, even in 1942, people usually fled to the Italian occupation zone that stretched along the Adriatic coast and into the part of Slovenia annexed by the Italians. It will never be possible to discover the actual proportion of successful and unsuccessful escapes, because the unsuccessful cannot tell their tale. Some people were lucky and got away with legal passes: the Jewish Section of the RUR and other ISC institutions began to issue travel passes in the summer of 1941 to people who had fulfilled their obligations for the imposed contribution and paid tax to the Jewish Community. It is impossible to say how many of these passes were issued, because many were semilegal and illegal, obtained through bribery or skillfully forged. In 1944, Drago Rosenberg said that 12,000 Yugoslav Jews fled to Italy, Hungary, and Bulgaria. Most of them were from the ISC, with a minority from occupied Serbia and other parts of former Yugoslavia.[1]

In the summer of 1941, people were already aware that Jewish refugees in areas under Italian occupation and in Italy did not face death. Chances of survival were also much better in Hungary and Bulgaria, and in the areas annexed by Hungary (Bačka, Baranja, Međimurje), than in the ISC. It was relatively easier for Zagreb Jews to reach the Second Italian Occupation Zone (Zone B), since it was formally part of the ISC, so no passport was needed to travel there, simply a pass, which was somewhat easier to acquire or forge.

When the Agreements of Rome on Delimitation between Italy and the ISC were signed in May 1941, the Accord on Matters of Military Significance Referring to the Adriatic Coastal Area was also signed. This was an agreement to divide the ISC coastal area not annexed by Italy, together with a rather broad hinterland, into two zones. The zone nearer the sea was called the demilitarized zone (later the Second Zone). It included Gorski Kotar, all of Lika, a good part of Herzegovina, and all the coastal areas and islands that were formally part of the ISC. The Ustasha authorities were not allowed to have any military facilities, fortifications, or military bases there after August 1941, nor their own police force. The rest of the belt, up to the agreed-on demarcation line between the Italian and German armies in the ISC, was called the Third Zone (it included the band from Karlovac across Bihać, Bugojno, and Prozor to Bileća and Čajniče on the border of Bosnia and Serbia). In this zone, the powers of the Ustasha authorities and their police and army were somewhat restricted, as well.[2]

At first, the Italian authorities were afraid of a great population influx (not only of Jews) from the interior of Croatia into the relatively poor coastal areas, and, in the spring and early summer of 1941, they returned some fugitive Jews to territory under Ustasha control, especially those who came to Sušak. Only at the end of the summer, after they discovered what was going on in the Ustasha camps on Pag and on Velebit, did the Italian authorities stop sending the fugitives back. After that, a large number of Zagreb Jews saved their lives by escaping to these territories. According to the most conservative estimates, about 1,300 Jews, mostly from central Croatia and Zagreb, fled to Hrvatsko primorje, most of them finding shelter in Crikvenica (according to other estimates, there were as many as 1,500 Jewish refugees in that town). For a time, the Italian authorities continued to find it difficult to bear Jewish presence in the annexed areas, but they no longer returned Jews to areas under Ustasha rule but to the occupied Zone B. At the end of October, they returned 131 Jews from Sušak to Crikvenica, and later another 19. None of them had any means of support.[3] Many fewer ISC refugees went to the Novi Vinodolski District, where there were 67 Jews in May 1942; at that time, all four members of the Zagreb Grünhut family went to Novi Vinodolski.[4] Some smaller groups got permits to settle in other nearby places in Zone B: in Bakar, Kraljevica, Senj,[5] Hreljin, Skrad, Moravice, and elsewhere.

In November 1941, Zagreb dentist Mauricije Horn opened an office in Senj.[6]

The Ustasha authorities in these towns complained to the services in charge of the Jewish question in Zagreb that the Italian military was simply ignoring civilian ISC rule in this area and was acting at its own discretion in the case of the fugitive Jews. The Italians allowed the Jews to live in Crikvenica and did not require them to contact the Ustasha authorities for permission to ignore wearing the Jewish insignia or other requirements.[7] In March 1942, the Jewish Section of the Ustasha Police Directorate in Zagreb informed the Crikvenica County District that "all the Jews on your territory shall in future be obliged to wear the special Jewish insignia." Obviously, this Ustasha provision was not being complied with in Crikvenica, and this was how it continued "in the future." The Ustasha authorities did not manage to impose this regulation, and even in July, "many Jews in Crikvenica do not wear the prescribed badges." Fifty-six badges were ordered from Zagreb and arrived in August, but apparently this had little effect.[8] The general Ustasha policy was to prevent Jews from reaching areas under Italian control; they considered that Jews "should be returned to where they had come from," but, after August 1941, the Italian occupation authorities no longer agreed to this.[9]

Jews did not feel quite safe even in Zone B, which although under the occupation of the Italian army and military authorities was formally still part of the ISC. Because of this, some people used various illegal means to leave Hrvatsko primorje and try to reach areas annexed by Italy or, better still, reach Italy itself, where it seemed that their lives at least were safe. Although tolerant of all fugitives in occupation Zones B and C, for quite a long time the Italian authorities considered Jewish refugees undesirable in some annexed areas (Zone A, the so-called Provinzia Lubiana) and in Italy itself. Thus, the Italian army command in Sušak complained to the Ustasha authorities in March 1942 that "many Jews managed to escape and are still trying to leave Croatia secretly and reach the Province of Ljubljana."[10]

In 1941, some Jews from Serbia fled to the Adriatic region, too, and at first the Italian authorities did not welcome them, and demanded that the Germans keep them in Serbia. Later, when it became clear what was happening to these people in German-occupied Serbia, the Italian authorities began to "transfer all the undesirable elements to concentration camps in Italy."[11]

Zagreb Jews sought salvation in very different ways. Hinko Halpern fled to Novo Mesto in Slovenia, to the zone annexed by Italy, with his wife and his parents-in-law. The Italians deported them to Ljubljana, and, after October 1941, they were in Sedico near Belluno in northern Italy. In February 1944, the Germans caught them and some other Zagreb Jews there and transported them all to Auschwitz, from where only Hinko returned.[12] Ljudevit (1862) and Gizela Veith (1872), who lived in Preradovićeva Street, tried to escape to the Italian occupation zone or Italy despite their advanced age, but were caught in Karlovac, sent to prison, and then returned to their Zagreb apartment. At the time of the August 1942 deportations, they left their apartment, hid with friends, and were admitted to the old people's home of the Jewish Community in Rapska Street in September.[13] From there, they were deported "in an unknown direction" in May 1943, and nothing more was heard of them.[14] In July and August 1941, bank clerk Ernest Büchler (1885) fled from Zagreb, via Karlovac, to Ogulin and Otočac (in Lika), where he, according to a police report, "tuned pianos." The police caught him without a pass in Krasno village on Velebit mountain, so he was returned to the Zavrtnica Camp in Zagreb, and, in September, sent to Jasenovac, from where he did not return.[15] Merchant Adolf Hahn was deported to Jasenovac in 1941, from where he managed to escape after six months and hide in Zagreb. From Zagreb, he fled to the Hungarian border, where he was caught and returned to Zagreb. He was shot in 1942 in Dotrščina.[16]

Vlasta Urbić, née Deutsch-Maceljski, and her brother, Velimir, tried to cross into Hungary near Varaždin at the end of March 1943. The guide who was to take them across tricked them and left them at the border. The police ambushed them there, arrested them, and took them back to Zagreb, where they spent about a month in the prison in Sava Road.[17]

The flight of Jews to areas under Italian rule created a new occupation of "smugglers" and "black marketers." There were people who, for large sums of money, sold documents in an Aryan name with the photograph of the Jew buying them. These papers had all the necessary stamps and signatures, both of the Ustasha and of the Italian authorities. If they had a pass for Zone B, Zagreb Jews usually traveled by train via Karlovac to Plase on the border between the ISC and Italy. Many fewer traveled to Sušak, because this required a (much more expensive) passport for Italy, and a small number traveled to Split. As has already been said, the Italian authorities accepted Jewish refugees in Zone B after August 1941, but they controlled refugees traveling to Zone A and to Italy very strictly. In Zone A, fugitives without documents, and those who were discovered with faked documents, were sent to Italian prisons and concentration camps for refugees, or were returned to Zone B. However, at various levels, the Ustasha authorities, and especially representatives of the Third Reich, persistently demanded the return of the fugitive Jews. These demands led to ongoing diplomatic correspondence and disagreements, first between Italy and the ISC, and then to even more serious differences between the highest-ranking Italian and German diplomats. The fate—life or death—of about 5,000 fugitive Jews, among them about 2,000 from Zagreb, was being decided through this very extensive diplomatic correspondence in 1942 and the first half of 1943.

The German representatives in Sušak registered complaints with the Ustasha authorities, demanding that the ISC government take steps to return the Jews from areas under Italian control to areas under Ustasha and German control.[18] When the Nazis began to participate in solving the "Jewish question" in the ISC more directly in the spring of 1942, they soon realized that their "work" in cooperation with the Ustasha authorities on territories under Ustasha control would be relatively easy, but that they would have difficulties in arresting and deporting some 5,000 Jews who lived or had found shelter in the part of the ISC under Italian control.

They had originally planned to "collect" these Jews during the first deportation of Jews from the ISC to Auschwitz in August 1942. Some Italian commanders in the occupied area of Zone B, even of Zone C, already opposed this in preliminary contacts, suspecting that these deportations led to death. According to a German report, the local Italian commander in Mostar told the German representative that this action (arrest and deportation) was "contrary to the honor of the Italian army."[19] At the last moment, on July 30, 1942, the *chargé d'affaires* in the German Embassy in Zagreb, von Troll, telegraphed the Foreign Ministry in Berlin that the deportations of Jews from the ISC would begin on August 10, and that it had been planned for these to be immediately followed by deportations from Zone B, but that this had met with opposition from the Italian occupation authorities, so steps should be taken through diplomatic channels in Rome to ensure that they could proceed according to plan.[20]

The Italian diplomats stretched out negotiations on purpose and waited until August 21 to inform Mussolini, who wrote "*nulla osta*" ("nothing against") in his own hand in the margin of the document, thus, in principle, agreeing that 5,000 people should be sent to their deaths.[21] However, the Italian military commanders in Zone B did not recognize Mussolini's general remark as a direct order, and continued to avoid cooperating in plans to do that. General Mario Roatta, Commander of the Second Italian

Army in charge of the entire area of Zones A, B, and C, said on October 16, 1942, in talks during his stay in Zagreb, that he had recently received instructions from Rome to prepare handing over the Jews in Zone B to the German armed forces, but that he had sent an answer to Rome saying that he considered the German armed forces not competent to take charge of them, and that he was now awaiting a reply from Rome.[22]

At that time, some refugee Jews in Zone B got wind of these negotiations, in which their very lives were being decided, and, through various connections, dramatically appealed to the Italian commanders. In the name of a group of Zagreb Jews who had found shelter in Hreljin, Dr. Aleksandar Goldstein wrote an admirably composed and very detailed application in excellent Italian to General Roatta in person. In it, he described what was happening to the Jews in the ISC and how they had fled to the territory under Italian control, and ended by pleading for them not to be extradited to their deaths ("If the decision to extradite us to the Croatian authorities is carried out, this will be tantamount to a death sentence, because everyone knows what we can expect as soon as we are handed over to the Ustasha authorities in Karlovac").[23] At that time, the Italian Foreign Ministry in Rome received an alarming letter from General Piêche, Italian *carabinieri* commander in the occupied areas of the ISC. He said that Jews being deported from the German-controlled zone of the ISC were already being gassed during transport in sealed railway cars, and that the "decision to extradite them is the equivalent of a death sentence, and, if implemented, would cause very negative comments in the army and among the Muslim and Orthodox population, who are afraid that they might be exposed to the same treatment in the future, while today they stand under our flag with confidence."[24] Under the impact of all this information, the Italian Foreign Ministry and the army command reached a decision that Jews from the occupied zones should not be handed over to German police or military forces. This made Mussolini compromise: he no longer insisted on extradition, but ordered that all the Jews in these zones be interned in camps, and the German Ambassador in Rome, von Mackensen, informed his ministry in Berlin about this on October 8, 1942.[25]

The Italian occupation authorities immediately implemented Mussolini's order, but in a way that was not too harsh, and which some people called "liberal confinement." The largest camp in the northern Adriatic was in Kraljevica, and in the south most of the Jews were on the island of Korčula and in the towns of Korčula and Vela Luka. These places are often referred to as camps in the literature, but there was a huge difference between conditions in camps and conditions under confinement. Often, people were accommodated in empty hotels (such as the Slavija, Palace, Olevan, and Kovačić in Hvar), with Italian soldiers merely seeing that they did not leave the buildings at night or go to other parts of the town during the day. In the town of Korčula, they had complete freedom of movement inside the town, but were not allowed to leave it without a permit, which could be obtained for medical treatment, for taking school exams in Split, and so on.[26]

Veterinarian Božidar Steiner, although confined in Vela Luka on Korčula, moved freely all over the island and did his job.[27] Industrialist and merchant Rudolf Berger and his wife, Elizabeta, found shelter in Vela Luka in the house of their son-in-law, Dinko Vučetić.[28] The Grudar (Grünfeld) and Sever families lived a completely normal life in their villas in the town of Korčula, and the Zagreb families Bjelinski, Kereškenji, Piliš, Haas, Rendeli, and some others also found shelter in the town.[29]

Moric Danon, who was in Vela Luka in the first months of 1942, said that at that time the "young Jewish men and women, who are accommodated in buildings in which groups of young Zionists had been trained before the war, are starving. Some are managing somehow, others have turned into skeletons. They have become just like those scarecrows in the fields, on which old clothes hang on sticks." The internees on Lopud were also "more hungry than full."[30] The prisoners in Kupari "had poor food," and they "fried the rind of Parmesan cheese and boiled rice" on the terrace.[31]

Other people thought that the food and health conditions were bearable: Đorđe Ivković said that "the Jewish collective in the town of Korčula was very homogeneous and they helped one another. I maintain that there was no hunger. The Italians gave food coupons to all the Jews, too." Ivković said that "it was difficult for people who had no money." It was like that "at first, but later, about every month, a courier from the Vatican arrived bringing money donated by some American Jewish organizations, through the Vatican, with the knowledge of the Italians." This made it possible to live "reasonably well."[32]

There were smaller camps on Brač—in Sumartin, Postira (where Dragan Zvijezdić-Stern from Zagreb spent some time),[33] Milna and Nerežišća, in the town of Hvar, and in the surroundings of Dubrovnik—in Gruž, Kupari (in the Kupari Hotel complex), and on Lopud. In all of these places, there were people from Zagreb: Bruno Bjelinski came to Split and Korčula, Professor Branka Akerman came to Dubrovnik and Kupari with her mother and daughter.[34] In the first months after the establishment of the

ISC, "there were hundreds and hundreds of Jews from Zagreb, Belgrade, and Sarajevo in Split. Some found a way to make money, but most of them were forced into idleness, tormented because the Germans were winning and advancing on all fronts. We all lived waiting for something to change, but no one knew what the change would be."[35]

Zagreb doctors, who had been sent to Mostar to work on the elimination of syphilis (Dr. Gustav Jungwirth, Dr. Arpad Hahn, dentist Oskar Stern, Dr. Bela Kohn), came to Kupari with the Mostar Jews. Later they all joined the Partisans.[36] In 1942, Krešimir and Vladimir Rendeli of Zagreb were in Baška Voda.[37] Some Zagreb internees were politically very active. In Vela Luka, the brothers Fedor and Boris Njemirovski were accused of collaboration with the Partisans, and were taken to the Italian prison in Šibenik. Aleks Joelić was head of the Jewish organization of the Communist Party of Croatia in Vela Luka, which was linked with the local Party organization.[38]

In the first days of November 1942, a camp was opened in Kraljevica for Jewish refugees whom the Italian occupation authorities had gathered from Novi Vinodolski, Crikvenica, Selce, Senj, and other places in which the Jews from the ISC were hiding from Nazi persecution. "They gathered all of us Jews in Hreljin and took us to Kraljevica. They came early in the morning and banged on the door very forcefully. Quick, they shouted, you're going to Italy. They did not let us pack anything, but said that the things would follow us . . . I began to cry, it seemed to me that it was all over, that they would hand us over to the Ustashe in Karlovac. Then an Italian officer came up to me and asked me in surprise: 'Why are you crying so hard, woman? We're not sending you to your deaths, but to Italy.'" said Zlata Goldstein.[39] The Ustasha authorities agreed to the founding of the Kraljevica camp, but Pavelić himself demanded that the Jewish refugees from ISC territory should renounce in writing their Croatian citizenship and all their property.[40]

According to the preserved list, there were 1,185 Jews in Kraljevica Camp, of whom 627 (52.9 percent) were from Zagreb (it is possible that some of the people who gave their place of residence as Selce, Crikvenica, or somewhere else, were also from Zagreb, but the number of these is negligible).[41] There was a somewhat smaller percentage of Zagreb children: according to the list of those fed by the children's kitchen in the camp, 43 (39.1 percent) of the 110 children were from Zagreb.[42] The first camp commissioners were Dr. Vladimir Vranić, Herman Schossberger, and Arthur Lothe from Zagreb. "The Italian military authorities were, in fact, only supervisors, who in a rather ideal way allowed these commissioners to organize the camp according to their discretion."[43]

Externally, Kraljevica really did look like a prison camp, because the Italians had previously used it to intern about 800 Partisan collaborators and the families of Partisans from Gorski Kotar and Primorje. The internees lived in wooden barracks (women and children) and horse stables (men), surrounded by barbed wire. There were guardhouses and permanent guards at the gate. There was also a prison for disciplinary violations, but the "proceedings were humane, without any harassment, and the main demand made by the Italians was that people should work . . . There was not a single instance of beatings or violent behavior in the camp." No one wore the Jewish insignia. People could leave the camp, but only to go to the immediate surroundings. Sunbathing by the sea was possible only along a narrow strip of beach, so the internees were literally lying on one another.[44] They organized the kitchen, clinic, and even the cultural life and entertainment.[45]

However, there was another side to the story: the food was bad and in short supply. The Italians did not prevent people from buying extra food, so some people ate better, and those who had no money ate worse. But everyone agreed to give money for the children's kitchen. One of the most distinguished internees was Hinko Gottlieb, prewar editor-in-chief of the magazine *Omanut,* a fine poet, and the best translator of Heine into Croatian. He became very angry when people who had money did not want to give any for the children. Still, "there were very few such misers."[46] At the beginning of July 1943, the heads of the municipality in Crikvenica asked the Zagreb Caritas for help, because their area had "a lot of poor children who have very little to live on and are literally starving . . . Besides, many refugees with young and stunted children have moved into the town, and as there is no food the children wait for the Italian solders to give them some."[47] Most of the children mentioned were probably Serbs, because, in July 1943, the Jewish children were already in the camp on Rab, but it is possible that some Jewish children had also been hidden with poor Croatian families in Crikvenica.

There was a lot of illness in the camp.[48] According to some people, the atmosphere was bad, too. The internees allegedly accused one another of cowardice during life in areas under Ustasha rule, and also of financial corruption; they were divided among those who had converted and those who had not.[49] These differences became most obvious during religious services. Jewish services were conduced by Filip Boran, while the Catholics regularly went to mass.[50] Branko Polić does not remember these disputes. He said that they might have taken place, but that they were in essence completely insignificant.[51]

German intelligence officers thought that these conditions were almost idyllic, and they claimed that "the Jewish Committee has good relations with the Partisans in the Kraljevica Camp," that "the Jews lead a good life and enjoy great freedom," that "because of corruption in the Italian camp command, they can be absent from the camp for several days, etc."[52] This shows that the Germans kept very careful watch over conditions for Jews in the Italian camps, all for one very transparent reason:[53] in the spring of 1943, they demanded "that the Jews from Kraljevica Camp be sent to Poland. Because of this, the Italians proclaimed the Jews prisoners of war, thus making their deportation impossible."[54]

This German-Ustasha pressure became especially intense in the spring of 1943, when the second great deportation of Jews from the ISC to Auschwitz was organized, but the Italian occupation authorities in Zones B and C resisted this even more strongly than in 1942. This led to the decision to relocate all the Jews, scattered throughout Zone B, to the newly formed Kampor Camp on the island of Rab. The Jews on the Island of Korčula, which belonged to the annexed Zone A, were a partial exception.

There are several explanations as to why the Italians decided to concentrate all the Jewish refugees on Rab. According to one, the Italians wanted to show the Germans that they were "doing something" and that they were beginning to treat the Jews more rigorously, in order to reduce Nazi pressure. According to another, the Italian army high command already suspected that they would soon have to capitulate before the onslaught of the Americans, British, and their allies, so they wanted to remove the Jews to a place out of reach of Ustasha or German intervention, and thus assure a better image for postwar life. Apparently, General Roatta himself told some Jews on one occasion that the Rab Camp was a "submarine on which the interned Jews could submerge themselves under the sea while the war is on, and surface again after the war and thus save their lives."[55]

Departures from the Kraljevica Camp to the camp on Rab took place between July 5–15, 1943. Transport was by fishing boats, each for about one hundred people. The barracks commanders and the other prisoners who performed duties of any kind in the Kraljevica Camp had to go last, so as to properly hand the camp over to the Italian command. The Rab Camp was a real camp, called Campo di concentramento per internati civili di guerra Arbe. It was on the southeast part of the island, between Kampor village and St. Eufemija Bay, six kilometers from the town of Rab. There was a Slovene camp nearby, set up in July 1942, for Slovene and some Croatian Partisans, Partisan sympathizers, and members of their families.

Some imprisoned Croats and Slovenes considered that the Jews had privileged treatment when they came, and that "the occupying army greeted the Jews very warmly." The comments were that this was "how it is with people who have money," and that the "Jewish international will reimburse Italy for everything."[56] However, the Jews did not have any special privileges, because their money and valuables had been taken away from them, just as from everybody else.[57] "We had to hand over our money, that is, Italian currency, liras, for which people got coupons for buying in shops."[58] On the other hand, Branko Polić said that "no money or valuables" were taken away on Rab "because they had been taken away long before, in any case."[59] Polić considers that the impression that Jews were treated better than Slovenes and Croats was due to the fact that bitter weather and bad conditions in the camp had made life very difficult during the winter of 1942–1943, but in July 1943, when the Jews arrived, conditions were better because it was summer, and the discipline imposed by the Italian administration and guards had slackened.[60]

The Jews were accommodated in brick and wood ground-floor barracks that had previously been built by the prisoners of the Slovene camp, and families could stay together, although the food was bad and some people were "hungry all the time."[61] Other people said that the "food was better than in Kupari" but that the "general situation was depressing."[62] Water was a special problem, as there was not enough for drinking and washing. It was turned on only three times a day, or was brought by tanker trucks. The latrines were just holes dug in the ground, and they were near the barracks, so the camp stank.[63] Nevertheless, there was time for the orchestra that had been organized in the Kraljevica Camp to continue working in Kampor as well: it consisted of three accordions, seven violins, and one trumpet.[64] Children were born, too, such as Jakov Finci (September 30), whose family had fled from Sarajevo.

The Jews organized themselves. The writer Ervin Šinko (Franjo Spitzer), who moved to Zagreb after the liberation in 1945, became camp foreman. There were some 3,500 to 3,600 Jewish prisoners in Kampor. During the two months there, between forty and fifty of them died, eight from Zagreb.[65]

When Italy capitulated on September 8, 1943, on that day and the following one, the prisoners of the Rab Camp freed themselves.[66] They disarmed the Italian guards and formed the Jewish Partisan Battalion, consisting of 243 volunteers from the camp itself, which soon reached the mainland and joined the Partisan forces. At that time, many of the earlier Italian occupation troops in Zones B and C surrendered their weapons to units of the Partisan National Liberation Army, which suddenly grew stronger and liberated almost all the Adriatic islands and most of the east-Adriatic coast. German and Ustasha units managed to keep only the towns of Rijeka and Sušak, Zadar, Šibenik, and Dubrovnik, and their immediate surroundings. However, the German army soon got reinforcements and launched a strong offensive for control of the coast and islands, which posed a great danger to the Jews who had remained on Rab. As the German units progressed, the Nazi services demanded the "immediate arrest of all the Jews who are now in Dubrovnik . . . There is to be no shooting, the entire area is to be cleansed of Jews, and they are to be taken to the camp in Zemun." Faced with danger of this kind, in the fall of 1943, the Partisans, in a very complicated operation, evacuated almost all the prisoners of the former Jewish camp on Rab, 3,151 of them, including 1,812 noncombatants.[67]

This was one of the greatest and most successful actions to save Jewish internees during the entire Second World War, and the only instance of a whole camp being freed in such a way. The men and women internees who were capable of serving in the army, and in auxiliary army services, joined the National Liberation Army, while most of the others were distributed throughout the rural areas under Partisan control in Kordun (Viktor and Adela Schwabenitz and Ruža and Biserka Rothstein spent some time in Budačka Rijeka, about twenty kilometers south of Karlovac, where the peasants provided them with food),[68] in Lika, and in Banija. A small group of about twenty were, at their own request, placed aboard a Partisan motor yacht in Sv. Juraj (below Mt. Velebit) and transferred to Vis, then to Bari in Italy, after which most of them went to the U.S. These included the Pick family from Zagreb.[69] Immediately after the liberation of the Rab Camp, about 200 Jews applied for transport to Bari, for which they waited on Rab for three months. During embarkation, great attention was paid to who was on the evacuation list. Seventy-year-old Ana Reich from Karlovac was not on the list because she hadn't known that she needed to apply. However, during embarkation, she clutched the boat railing tightly and would not allow herself to be torn away. When the boat set off, someone shouted, "Throw the old gal inside," and so Ana arrived via Bari at the El Shatt refugee camp in Egypt and survived the war.[70] At the Headquarters of the National Liberation Army of Croatia, there were negotiations with the British military representatives about transporting to Italy around 7,900 elderly Jews from Rab, at that time located around Topusko, but finally the British said that they had no airplanes they could set aside for this purpose. Of the total of 1,812 Jewish noncombatants evacuated from Rab, 1,671 survived the war on Partisan territory, fifteen died a natural death, and 126 were killed, mostly during Ustasha-German attacks on Partisan territory. Of the 1,339 former Rab internees who joined National Liberation Army units or their auxiliary services, 119 were killed in combat by the end of the war, and 17 died, while the rest survived.[71]

About 200 former Kampor internees (exactly 204), mostly elderly and ill, did not apply for evacuation from Rab in September and October and remained on the island. For months, the Allies discussed how to help the refugees who had been relocated to central Croatia or had remained on Rab, and how to transport them from Croatian territory.[72] While these fruitless discussions were going on, the German forces disembarked on Rab in March 1944,[73] and the Gestapo started rounding up Jews on the island. The population was told that hiding Jews was a "crime against the Reich," which was punishable by death. Most of the remaining Jews on Rab were arrested during the next three days. Only a few managed to hide: a girl in someone's house; a family from Mostar in the Monastery of St. Anthony; and two married couples, the Hoffmanns from Prague and the Mittlers from Zagreb, with a family that, several months later, took them to the Karlovac hospital, where the distinguished Zagreb internist, Dr. Pavao Hercog (Herzog), kept them until the end of the war, thus saving them.[74] All those arrested were taken by boat to Rijeka, then by truck to Trieste, and finally to Auschwitz, from where hardly anyone returned. The only one of that group known to have survived was Edita Armuth (1922) of Zagreb.[75] However, Branko Polić says there were some other survivors: Edita's relative, Heda Sinberger, née Armuth, also survived (she lives in Jerusalem), and so did Mira Wollner (who lives in Paris), and the sisters Lilly Seferović and Lucy Kadribegović, née Pressburger, from Austria, who had acquired Yugoslav citizenship before 1941 by fictitious marriages to Muslims.[76]

Some Jews lived or spent a long time in the areas annexed by Italy, but were not saved. Most of them were caught in October 1943 when the Ustashe and Germans came to Split, and 121 of them, of whom at least 4 were from Zagreb, were deported to the Sajmište Camp in Zemun.[77]

Quite a few Zagreb Jews reached Italy in various ways and traveled on from there. Fifty-three Jews born in Zagreb passed through the Ferramonti di Tarsia Camp (in southern Italy, in the Cosenza Province, near the village of Tarsia) between 1941 and 1943, making up 6.2 percent of the total of 853 Yugoslav Jews there.[78] One of them was David Levi-Dale of Zagreb, a prominent Jewish activist and publicist, who, in the seventies, remembered that this was not a "death camp" but that it "divested a person of human dignity; wherever one looked, there was barbed wire and *carabinieri*."[79] At the end of 1942, Elsa Spitzer and her fourteen-year-old daughter, Anni, were in Vicenza. They had been thrown out of their apartment in Petrinjska Street in Zagreb at the end of 1941, then fled to Italy where they heard that Elsa's husband, Marko, and son, Miro, were in Jasenovac and in Stara Gradiška, and that the husband had escaped from camp. This was totally false, as both Marko and Miro were already dead by the end of 1941, and the mother and daughter returned to Zagreb after the war.[80] Gabriela (Ela) Deutsch and her three small sons, Pavel (1935), Branko (1936), and Đorđe (1938), found shelter in the small town of Malo, seventeen kilometers northwest of Vicenza. Ela's husband, Josef, was arrested on September 16, 1941, and four days later deported to Jasenovac, from which he did not return. Gabriela and her sons left Zagreb on September 23, on the second day of the Jewish New Year (Rosh Hashanah), and, as they were Orthodox Jews, she first had to ask the rabbi for permission to travel on such an important holiday. After the capitulation of Italy in September 1943, the Deutsches fled south and hid in the villages on Gran Sasso Mountain (about ninety kilometers northeast of Rome), where they were when the Allies arrived, and then they went to Palestine.[81] About ten Zagreb Jews hid in the small town of Calestano, about thirty kilometers south of Parma, including Ferdo Eichorn and his wife, Antonija Geiger-Eichorn, and Zlata Friedmann.[82] Josef-Buki Konforti, his wife, and parents-in-law hid in the town of Bellaria (about fifteen kilometers northeast of Rimini).[83]

The story about the dangerous, uncertain, and often adventurous journey to safety of about one hundred Jewish orphans from Austria and Germany, which lasted for four years, is well known and moving. Fleeing to Palestine from Nazi persecution, at least some of them arrived in Zagreb in October and November 1940,[84] but did not manage to leave the city before the Germans invaded Yugoslavia, at which point their journey east was blocked. However, in June, the whole group, under the leadership of Joško Indik from Zagreb (later in Israel, Josef Itai), managed to reach the part of Slovenia annexed by Italy (around Vrhnika). They subsequently crossed into Italy, and, in 1943, to Switzerland, where they stayed until the end of the war, when they all went to Palestine.[85] In March 1943, when they were in Nonantola (near Modena), they communicated with the Zagreb Community.[86]

After spending some time in Slovenia with the group of children led by Indik, Aleksandar Licht also went to Italy for a time. In the fall of 1943, after many difficulties, he reached Switzerland, spent two months in a refugee camp, and later, thanks to the sculptor Ivan Meštrović, established temporary residence. Using his widespread connections in the Jewish diaspora, Licht, during his stay in Switzerland, did a lot of work on organizing help for the remaining Jews in Croatia.[87]

A certain number of Jewish families, almost 200 people from Zagreb and other parts of Croatia (also including some Serbs and Croats, mostly anti-Fascists), hid during the war in the village of Aprica near Sondrio, in Sondrio Province, on the Swiss border. The local population called them all "*Zagabri*." They included the Neufeld family: the father, Edo, an attorney, his wife, Albina, and daughters Lea and Vera. There was also Judita Hercler, who inquired about her relatives in the Zagreb Jewish Community without much success. After the capitulation of Italy, the Germans came to the region, so one night they all crossed the mountain to Switzerland.[88]

Still, everyone who escaped to Italy was not so lucky. Margherita Bergmann "was taken to camp by the Germans from Montalto delle Marche (north of Ascoli in central Italy), and no more was ever heard of her again."[89]

Some Zagreb Jews reached Spain and Portugal. The Spanish authorities issued them with valid documents to travel overseas, usually to South America and South Africa. Enrico, son of Feliks and Blanka Singer from Zagreb, was born in August 1942 in Madrid, from where the family went to London. They settled there, and Enrico changed his name to Cvi (Zvi).[90]

In Italy, Spain, and in Zagreb itself, selling forged visas and passports for money, valuables, or other interests became a thriving trade. The Uruguayan Consulate in Zagreb played a prominent part in this, and the Spanish Consulate was also active. Aleksandar Ehrmann, Honorary Consul of Portugal, issued visas at his own discretion, probably because he was a Jew himself.[91] Portugal allowed rich Jews, who had to prove their wealth, to stay temporarily in Portugal until they left for other countries. As soon as they reached Italy, and especially the Iberian Peninsula, new possibilities opened up before the Jews: for example, Bolivia and Honduras accepted craftsmen. The United States sometimes issued entrance visas to people who had an affidavit, a letter of guarantee, from a prominent and wealthy American citizen; they also had to have at least $5,000.[92] Some

Jews from Croatia, and Bosnia and Herzegovina, managed to reach Switzerland from Italy ("We know of 700, but it seems there were more"), or Palestine (800), or the U.S. (1,000), while a certain number "reached Africa and other Allied countries." According to the State Commission for War Crimes, "about 3,000 to 3,500 people, Jews by race but not also by religion, could have saved themselves in this way."[93]

The Germans captured some Jews as Yugoslav soldiers in the April war of 1941. Twenty-seven officers spent the war in the Osnabrück prison camp.[94] Some of them sent word to Zagreb. On January 1, 1943, Alfred Müller wrote to Šalom Freiberger, hoping for some information about his numerous relatives "about whom I have no news." Freiberger replied that all his family members were certainly in one of the camps in the country or abroad, but that he knew nothing specific about their fate.[95] The Osnabrück prisoners collected money—at the end of 1942, they sent 7,800 kunas to the Zagreb Community, and, in April 1943, they sent 6,800 Reichsmarks for camp internees and for the rescue of children.[96]

As soon as they were brought to Germany, in April and May 1941, some of the war prisoners thought it would be better for them to return, believing that they stood a better chance in Croatia, or even that they might manage to escape from the train taking them home. Eugen Dido Kvaternik was president of the reception commission for captured Croats, and he informed all who wanted to return, and all other Jews in captivity, that the Ustasha authorities did not want them.[97] Gustav Gavrin (1906–1976), son of Chief Rabbi Gavro Schwarz, spent the war in German captivity, and returned to Zagreb in May 1945 with the Partisans.[98]

Several dozen Zagreb Jews survived as war prisoners in Germany and returned to Zagreb after the war. These included Hinko Abeles (1896), Moritz Alkalaj (1900), Bruno Anhalzer (1894), Mosko Atijas (1887), Bernard-Dov Basch (1915), Geza Bruckner (1901), Ernest Dajč (1908), Haim Gaon (1908), Lavoslav Glesinger (1901), Hugo Hirschler (1893), Izrael Kamhi (1911), Oskar Kaufer (1910), Željko Lederer (1909), Desider Morgenstern (1887), Adolf Rothmüller (1901), Dr. engineer Josip Drechsler (1903), engineer Miroslav Špicer (1900), Dr. Zvonko Novak (Mattersdorfer), Ivo Frõhlich (1915), Marijan Hirschl (1912), Professor Vojko Kiš, and others.[99]

There were also Jews from Zagreb in Buchenwald; these included Mavro Gross (1884), Branko Kahotfer (1921), Dr. Bela Kohn, Emil Lichtenberg (1913), Julio Linenberg (1902), Jozef Mancini (1926), Milan Mazel (1919), Fedor Rozaj (1911), Leopold Sačer (1910), Franjo Spiler (1911), and Velimir Spitzer (1928)

To the best of our knowledge, their fates were very different: Rozaj reached South America, Kohn and Linenberg returned to Zagreb, but Linenberg's health was very poor because he had been subjected to some medical experiments. Mavro Gross died in camp in April 1944.[100]

Jewish prisoners of war in Fürstenberg were engineer Tibor Preisz, Branko Rajić, Mirko Mirković, and also many Jews from other parts of Croatia, such as Hinko Hofmann from Sisak, and Yugoslavia (Vojvodina, Sarajevo). There was no special harassment of the Jews, they only had to sleep in a separate part of the barracks.[101]

A very small number saved themselves from Auschwitz and Birkenau, only a few Croatian or Zagreb Jewish men and women,[102] among them Edita Armuth, Boris Mautner, and Boris Braun.[103] Braun saved himself by applying as an electrician (although he was an agronomy student), so he spent the first three weeks with a group of electricians in Birkenau, and was then transferred to Auschwitz. About a week after he arrived there, two SS soldiers came to the group and told them that they were founding a new camp nearby and were looking for volunteers. No one knew whether they were telling the truth or wanted to entice the men to willingly report for liquidation. Braun had only several second to decide, opted to apply, and was saved. Of the seven electricians from the group who remained in Auschwitz, not one survived. The new camp was called Jawozno, and conditions there were better than in Auschwitz. Five of the seven who came to Jawozno survived; Braun was one of them.

Chemist Edi Bier also survived Auschwitz. On one occasion, he was transferred to Sachsenhausen Camp, where he joined a group of experts who forged money for the Nazis. He survived the war and returned to Zagreb.[104] The following survived in Jawozno: Izak Kalderon, Ivica (?) Jungwirt, the Weiss brothers from Virovitica, Rosenbaum from Vojvodina, who as a lawyer knew excellent German and was a clerk. All the Jawozno garrison knew Braun: he was useful to them because he worked well—for example, he made reading lamps for the SS, and in return they would give him bread. Some were even treated him decently. At the beginning of 1945, the camp was evacuated and all the prisoners were sent to Buchenwald.[105]

A girl whose name Ljerka Magdić forgot, but whose story she remembered well, also returned from Auschwitz: the girl testified about gas chambers, and "she was all swollen up from the injections the Nazis gave them to stop their periods, so that they could make sexual use of them better."[106]

34

JOINING THE PARTISANS

A Way to Save One's Life and Maintain Human Dignity

When organized resistance to the Ustasha and occupying forces began in Croatia and Bosnia and Herzegovina in July 1941, many Jews capable of fighting, including those from Zagreb, were already in prisons and camps. Nevertheless, by the end of the year, 224 Jews from Croatia and 388 from Bosnia and Herzegovina joined Partisan units, urban task groups, or other forms of organized resistance. As the Communist Party was the main organizer of resistance in the ISC in 1941, most of the first Jewish resistance fighters were Communists or had previous connections with the Communists. They joined the Partisans at least as much because of their political views as to save themselves from the dangers of Ustasha persecution. Among them were fifteen former International Brigade members from the Spanish Civil War with combat experience, and several dozen political activists used to organizing revolutionary and political work; these soon became prominent resistance fighters in underground urban task groups and the first Partisan units in the forests (Pavle Pap, Ilija Engel, Robert Domany, Pavle Goranin, Samuel Lerer, Adolf-Drago Steinberger, Vilim Drechsler, Gustav Perl, Josip-Pepo Polak, Vojko Hohšteter, Menahem-Mento Papo, Vladimir Majder, and others).[1] Jelka Schwabenitz (1919) was also a Communist sympathizer; in the summer of 1941, she fled with forged documents to Sarajevo, where her boyfriend was waiting for her. She was soon arrested, but managed to escape from prison and join the Partisans. In 1942, she was caught by the Chetniks, who killed her after first brutally torturing her.[2] Barely a quarter of the Jews who joined the anti-Fascist movement right at the beginning lived until the end of the war. Sixteen Zagreb Jews were awarded Memorial Medals for joining the uprising in 1941, and several Memorial Medal holders moved to Zagreb in later years.[3]

Josip and Stjepan Engel constructed an underground radio station in Tuškanova Street in Zagreb, which was allegedly used on July 4, 1941, to broadcast the proclamation of the KPJ Central Committee calling the "people of Yugoslavia to rise in arms." The story is not completely convincing, and was obviously played up by post-war Communist historians. The meeting of the inner circle of the Politburo of the KPJ Central Committee, at which the decision to start an uprising was made, ended on July 4 at 6:00 p.m. in Belgrade, and the proclamation was written after that.[4] Therefore, it is quite impossible for the Engels to have read this "call for an uprising" as early as July 4, so they probably read an earlier Central Committee proclamation. This radio station was obviously not very powerful, because very few witnesses heard it. The Ustasha police and intelligence services must have heard the proclamation, but they did not know where it had been sent from, or who had sent it. Available documents show that the Ustasha services did not suspect the Engels of Communist activities at all at the beginning of July. On July 9, five days after the call was allegedly broadcast from their radio station, the Engels, as Jews, had to leave their apartment in Tuškanova, so they requested permission to move to Jelašićeva 10, to the Gajevo settlement. The request was granted, and the Engels moved to their new address. But the Ustasha Police were already looking for them on July 17 and 18,[5] and by the end of July, they were arrested and later deported to Jasenovac, where they were killed. It would appear that Josip was still alive at the beginning of November, because the Jewish Community sent a parcel addressed to him.[6] Their sister managed to save herself by escaping to Hungary.[7] It seems that the Engels were simply caught up in the mass deportations of Zagreb Jews organized at that time.[8]

Robert Domany and Adolf-Drago Steinberger, a commander and a political delegate in the first Partisan units in south Kordun, were killed on April 3, 1942, victims of Chetnik betrayal. They were thrown to the bottom of a karst pit near Plaški, and their bones were found and buried in 1966.[9] The brilliant biologist Pavao Wertheim (1911), an assistant professor at the Faculty of Natural Sciences and Mathematics and member of the Communist Party, was killed in one of Zagreb's prisons in 1941.[10] Pavle Pap, member of the KPJ Central Committee from 1940, was in Zagreb during the first months after the establishment of the ISC and organized the actions of the first youth task groups. In August 1941, Pap was ordered to go to Split and help the local Communists organize an uprising. He helped form the first seven Partisan units, in which he was to have been political commissar, but was soon captured in an Italian carabinieri ambush and shot in Skradin near Šibenik.[11] One Zagreb task group of twenty young fighters, SKOJ members, was led by Haim Friedman and worked in the Sava Road area. Friedman was killed fighting against Ustasha policemen in November 1941.[12] Vojko Hohšteter joined the Partisans as a Communist in 1941. He was deputy commander in several brigades and fought in some of the most important Partisan battles. In the battle on the Neretva, in March 1943, when an enemy (Chetnik) bullet pierced his ear, eyewitnesses reported that he coolly said, like a real Zagrebian, so that everyone could hear, "Damn him, he can shoot well!" He was killed in the Oborovo battle, southeast of Zagreb, in May 1944.[13] Moša Albahari was a prominent Communist Party member at Zagreb University. He was sent to organize an uprising in Istria and Hrvatsko primorje. In July 1942, he was wounded and captured by the carabinieri, taken to Rome, sentenced to death, and shot in November of the same year.[14]

In August 1941, Elias-Ilija Engel was one of the first fighters in the Partisan detachment on Žumberak (a mountain twenty kilometers west of Zagreb), then, for almost three years, operations officer at the Supreme Command of the NOV of Croatia [the NOV, or National Liberation Army, was the name taken by the Partisan units], head of auxiliary background services, and finally department head at the Supreme Command. He was killed by a bomb in an enemy attack in May 1944.[15]

The following Zagreb Jews, and Jews who lived in Zagreb before leaving to join the Partisans, were proclaimed National Heroes: Robert Domany, Adolf-Drago Steinberger, Samuel Lerer, Ilija Engel, and Pavle Pap.[16]

Vilim Schwarz, known as Barba, came to Drvar (western Bosnia) with a group of Split fighters and worked as a photographer-reporter attached to the Supreme Headquarters. After the German parachute attack of May 25, 1944, when the Germans tried to liquidate Tito, he was killed on the Drvar–Oštrelj road trying to save his photographic equipment.[17]

In 1942 and up to September 1943, a further 452 Jews from Croatia and Bosnia and Herzegovina joined Partisan units and their auxiliary services, but most Jews joined the Partisans only after the capitulation of Italy in

September 1943.[18] Just as with their reactions to the Ustasha-Nazi genocide, which had been clearly announced in advance, people left it until too late to join the Partisans. There were many reasons for this, mostly to do with family: in the beginning, before the Partisan movement grew in strength, it was inconceivable for entire families to leave for Partisan-controlled territory, and if just one member capable of fighting went, this increased the danger for any undeported family members who remained. The Ustasha regime had precise lists of Jews and carefully supervised their movements, restricting them by means of a curfew, forbidden zones, and special permits. Any unexplained disappearance could be interpreted as flight abroad or to join the Partisans, and the result could be the death of the fugitive's immediate and extended family, or of other Jewish hostages. Finally, Zagreb and other towns could be left when joining the Partisans only by using underground connections. These were highly secret, which made it extremely difficult, especially for people who had no previous contacts with the leftist revolutionary movement, which included the majority of the Jews. A certain number of Jews in Croatia and Bosnia and Herzegovina are known to have left to join the Partisans on their own, but were caught and killed on the way.[19] Dr. Ivo Löw, for example, came across Chetniks who allegedly handed him over to the Germans in return for ammunition, and the Germans shot him.[20]

Only after the Partisans managed to create a unified liberated territory under their control in the second half of 1942, did some Jews begin to join the them with their whole families, including small children. Families with children were certainly a burden for Partisan units in some areas, but there are no known instances of refusal to accept them anywhere in Croatia or Bosnia. The only incident of this kind took place in 1941, in Bosnia, when the command of the Kalinovik Partisan Detachment (forty kilometers southeast of Sarajevo) refused to accept a group of about twenty young Sarajevo Jews with the explanation that "they didn't need city slickers," i.e., bourgeois, in Partisan ranks. Most of this group did manage to reach the Italian occupation zone in various ways, and later joined the Partisans in Dalmatia and Hrvatsko primorje.[21]

After racist humiliation and deadly persecution under Ustasha rule, after comparatively insignificant but nevertheless degrading discrimination in the Italian zone, among the Partisans the Jews were no longer persecuted victims. They got back their human dignity, the feeling that they were equal to everybody else. In practice, this was additionally confirmed by Partisan documents—thus, the KP Croatia's Regional Committee for

Dalmatia stated it in its platform in September 1941: "The Fascist aggressors, with the help of the Ustashe, have introduced the uncultured so-called 'new order' into our country, meaning anti-Semitism, the murder, robbery, mockery, and persecution of Jews. It is our duty to resist terror and persecution of the Jews."[22] In the fall of 1943, the Secretary's Office of the ZAVNOH (which had, at that time, already begun to constitute itself as a new government emerging from the anti-Fascist movement), circulated a letter signed by the secretary, Dr. Pavle Gregorić, warning that "any action against an individual or group of Jews that shows any degree of enmity or hatred against them will be subject to investigation and strict punishment."[23]

Among the Partisans, the Jews were distributed throughout fighting units and auxiliary services, according to their age and capabilities. Especially numerous and successful was their participation in the Partisan medical corps. Most of the Jewish doctors who had gone to Bosnia to treat syphilis in 1941 joined the anti-Fascist movement when it appeared and grew strong in their regions. In 1942, there were as many as forty Jews among the total of seventy-three doctors in the entire Partisan medical corps. After the capitulation of Italy in September 1943, Jewish doctors liberated from Italian concentration camps joined the Partisans, so that, by the end of the war, the Partisan medical corps in the ISC had almost 200 Jewish doctors and about 400 medical staff (pharmacists, veterinarians, medical students, qualified or trained nurses, etc.).[24]

The majority of Jews joined the Croatian Partisans after the capitulation of Italy, when the Italian concentration camps were freed: 1,203 Jews from Croatia and 868 from Bosnia and Herzegovina joined between September 1943 and the end of 1944. By far, most Jewish men and women joined the Partisans from the Rab concentration camp: at the time of the capitulation, on September 8 and 9, the internees disarmed the Italian guards and part of the garrison themselves, and, with the confiscated weapons, they formed the Rab Partisan Jewish Battalion, consisting of 243 volunteer internees. Somewhat later, another 448 former Rab internees were mobilized or voluntarily joined Partisan combat units, and 648 joined various auxiliary services on liberated Partisan territory.[25] However, the fate of some people was very unusual. Ernest Fischer (1903–1986) of Zagreb went to Montenegro in 1941 and immediately joined the Partisans (where he used the name of Velja Fijolić). The following year, he was tricked and captured by the Chetniks, then handed over to the Italians, and, after the capitulation of Italy, he rejoined the anti-Fascist movement.[26]

The Rab Jewish Battalion could not survive as a separate unit because none of the commanders or the fighters had the necessary military training or combat experience. They were also afraid that the enemy would find out about the battalion's existence and movements, and strike at it with special ferocity. Thus, the Supreme Command of the NOV of Croatia, as early as October, attached the battalion to the NOV's Seventh Banija Division, and distributed its members throughout the units of this division. The other volunteer and mobilized Rab internees were dispersed in a similar way. Of the 1,339 Partisans from the former Rab Camp, 119 were killed in action by the end of the war, and 17 died.[27]

The evacuation and accommodation of the noncombatant internees on liberated Partisan territory was not easy, but it was nevertheless in most cases successful. ZAVNOH recommended that People's Liberation Committees should "do everything in their power to help the Jews in the way of food and accommodations, and also transport . . . Special care must be taken with children, old people, and those who are ill." The first plan was to send the noncombatant Jews to Partisan-held territory in Slavonia, where it would be easier to feed them because "there is room for 20,000 people in Slavonia," but, in most cases, this had to be given up because of the difficulties of transport. Only one group of 250 people managed to reach Slavonia, and another group of about 230 people was "distributed in various places in Gorski kotar, Pokuplje, and Lika." Between 1,500 and 2,000 Jews were established in the villages of Kordun and Banija.[28] Even ZAVNOH admitted that there was generally "no exact or any other information about the refugees scattered throughout all the districts."[29]

"The material status of the Jews is rather poor, because, during the constant flight from the enemy, many of them lost the property that they had taken with them, so only one-third has enough to live on. Another third sometimes has enough to live on, and the final third does not have enough to live on at all. Until now, those who were richer helped those who were poorer, but now even this is no longer possible," said the ZAVNOH Social Department in a report from April 1944.[30] When they were on their way to Banija, they were advised to "try to find work with the peasants and do something, because today, in these difficult times, people look askance at those who do nothing although they are capable of working, yet ask to be fed, while, at the same time, the people themselves and those fighting against the enemy do not have enough food. Many Jews are capable of some kind of work, but they have not yet begun to do so. In this sense, committees have received instructions to primarily try to employ Jews capable of work on farms or in workshops."[31] Complaints of this kind can at least partly be explained by differences in cultural patterns and behavior—most of the Jews were from urban environments, as opposed to their largely rural surroundings. Still, antagonism of this kind never greatly escalated. For a time, a group of Chetnik sympathizers looted Jewish refugees passing through Kordun, somewhere in Kordunsko Zagorje. In the summer of 1944, the People's Court tried the robbers.[32]

Despite all the difficulties, and considering the circumstances, the employment and integration of Jews in the Partisan movement and among the population on liberated territory was successful. In its conclusion, the above report said that the "Jews in the Glina District have mostly started to work in the fields."[33] Many Jews managed to pay back the accommodations and food that they got: by knitting, sewing, nursing the wounded and the sick, various kinds of repairs, cooking, even holding courses for the illiterate and taking part in cultural activities. In Banija, Dr. Gustav Jungwirth took care of children. Dentists Miro Kaiser of Zagreb and Hugo Drucker of Sarajevo had a clinic in Glina.[34] In April 1944, the ZAVNOH Economic Department had a meeting, at which they concluded, "There are many professionals of various kinds among the Jews. They should be charged with writing reports about various sectors . . . They should be sought out, included in work . . . We do not have enough people who could be merchants . . . the Jews Frank and Adler should be considered . . . Feliks Hirschl has gone to Pokuplje."[35]

When the enemies conducted offensives, the Jews fled together with everyone else, and later returned to the gutted villages. In the summer of 1944, they began to receive aid from international Jewish organizations through the Allies, so conditions improved somewhat. Of the 1,812 Jews evacuated from Rab, 126 were killed, and 15 died by the end of the war, during the following eighteen months. Some were in the refugee camp in Topusko in May 1945.[36] At the time of liberation, there were 44 Jews in Glina, 8 of them from Zagreb.[37]

Besides the large group from Rab, several hundred Jewish families joined the Croatian Partisans in Dalmatia in the fall of 1943, retreating before the German-Ustasha offensive. About 130 young people joined combat units, and the noncombatants were accommodated in the Partisan-held hinterland. Some of them, 122, were later evacuated with other refugees via Bari to the large, well-known refugee camp in Egypt (El Shatt). About 300 Jews are estimated to have been in El Shatt, among about 28,000 evacuated Dalmatians. Several dozen were from Zagreb.[38] At the same time, a group of 117 Jewish volunteers from Bari, liberated from the Italian Ferramonti concentration camp after the capitulation of Italy, joined the Dalmatian Partisans.[39]

Some Jews came into conflict with the radical and often rigid criteria of revolutionary Communism, and the Partisans killed them. Usually there is no written record about why they were killed. There is hardly any mention of these events in the extensive postwar memoir and historiographic material. Thus, on the threshold of the twenty-first century, a researcher can rely only on verbal testimony or on several short archival records. However, one thing is certain: the rigid criteria of revolutionary Communism accorded no special privileges to Jews because the Ustashe and the Germans had persecuted them, nor was there any trace of aversion or hatred because they were Jews.

Slavko Hirschl-Herak and Milan Singer, "Italian confidants" in Kraljevica Camp,[40] "disappeared" when the Partisans arrived after liberating Kampor. Obviously someone had reported them for collaboration, and it is a question as to whether the report was checked, let alone proved. Singer's wife, Anny, also disappeared, but their child, who had an unusual physical anomaly, polydactyly (six fingers and toes), survived.[41]

Nineteen-year-old Helga Heim of Zagreb left Zagreb in August 1941, and was in the camps in Kraljevica and on Rab. At one time, the slogan "death to Helga Heim" appeared on the wall in the Kraljevica Camp. Helga had a camera, which was conspicuous in the camp, and she took a lot of photographs. According to the internees, she was extremely beautiful, and Italian officers came from as far away as Trieste just to look at her. After she joined the Partisans, she was shot in Klasnić in Banija in December 1943 or January 1944. According to one explanation, she had been accused of "whoring" with Italian officers in the camp, while according to another, a Partisan commander whose attentions she had rejected was behind it all, accusing her of being a spy and having her shot to get revenge.[42]

At the beginning of the war, dentist Dr. Leo Wilf worked in the clinic of the Zagreb Jewish Community, then fled to join the Partisans, arrived in Drvar, and there treated the teeth of Josip Broz Tito and the entire Supreme Command. At that time, Wilf's wife, Irena, née Neufeld, was an English interpreter at the Supreme Command, and by the nature of her work had daily contacts with the British officers present. In their free time, the Wilfs played cards with the British, and the British carried and brought back letters that Irena sent to Bari to her parents, Dr. Filip and Antonija. The Partisans found all this suspicious and they proclaimed Dr.

Wilf and his wife to be British spies, without any real investigation, and shot them.[43] It seems that the decision to liquidate them, after someone had denounced them, was made at the top level of the Partisan movement. It probably was made by Aleksandar Ranković, who, according to the testimonies of Gojko Nikoliš, Milovan Đilas, and Koča Popović, who knew the workings of the Supreme Command very well, asked Josip Broz Tito for approval of all sensitive decisions.[44]

In 1944, Artur Dečko Bresslauer of Vinkovci, from the Eighth Kordun Brigade, was shot in the surroundings of Topusko. According to one version, he had been accused of buying or selling foreign currency from the British; according to another, he had kept pieces of gold given to him and his brother by their parents (his brother, Pajo, was killed in the Partisans, while his parents and his fifteen-year-old sister, Greta, had been killed in Jasenovac in 1942).[45]

There is somewhat more information about the case of Dr. Đuro Fišer. At the end of 1943, he was a doctor in the hospital of the First Lika Military Area. He was shot "for unethical and irresponsible behavior in treating the wounded," but, unofficially, because he did not help a wounded man in the middle of the night due to tiredness. He was sentenced by the Military Court; later, someone said that the sentence had been pronounced by a Jew-hater. Fišer was posthumously rehabilitated.[46]

A prewar SKOJ member, Slavko Weiss (1920) of Karlovac, was a brave combatant of the first task groups in Karlovac as early as the summer of 1941; in the winter of 1941–1942, as commissary of a Partisan company, he was distinguished by his courage in the defense against an Ustasha offensive in Pokuplje and north Kordun (the areas around Prkos and Sjeničak); in November 1942, as battalion commissar in the Fourth Kordun Brigade, he was the first to enter Slunj under fire at the head of his unit. Several days later, he was executed in Slunj by the sentence of an improvised court attached to the Supreme Command of the NOV of Croatia, for allowing fighters from his battalion to help themselves to new boots from the impounded Ustasha warehouse, contrary to the instructions of the Supreme Command. The famous Partisan commander and later Town Mayor of Zagreb, Veco Holjevac, called this a "senseless decision," all the more so as the members of the Supreme Command got boots of this kind for themselves.[47]

As the end of the war approached, the Partisan movement, under the leadership of the Communist Party, paid less and less attention to its earlier democratic proclamations and statements while increasingly preparing for a society on the Soviet model, significantly marked by authoritarianism and totalitarianism. Probably the crucial event in this process was the liberation of Belgrade in October 1944, after which a wave of mass retributions was launched throughout Yugoslavia, and which did not wane until the summer of 1945. Accordingly, the intelligence services began to assume a different attitude toward the Jews. When they joined the Partisans, people felt sorry for them and accepted them as victims; later, some officers and intelligence officers began to find certain Jews suspicious. They thought, usually without any evidence, that the Jews were hostile to the Communist struggle and that they cooperated with the British intelligence services. The reasons for suspicion were extremely thin: some Jews, just like the Wilfs, knew English and had contacts with members of Allied missions attached to Partisan detachments. They immediately came under suspicion, all the more so as no one knew what they were talking about. Thus, knowing English could in some cases prove lethal.

As early as July and August 1944, OZNA claimed that Dr. Dezider Julius, at that time director of the Banija Military District hospital, had protected some Jewish women guilty of various misdemeanors, only because they were Jewish—"He asked for this to be overlooked and did all he could to have the matter hushed up. It seems that this is a case of Jews helping Jews, that is, they are helping one another to the detriment of other people," concluded the report writer.[48] People complained that Julius gathered "several Jews in the hospital, and they are constantly making plans and whispering and they showed great joy and an unusual mood" when they heard that Winston Churchill had allegedly called "King Peter the legal King of Yugoslavia." The investigator recommended that the "abovementioned Jews should be scattered to other places, so that they cannot help one another in an organized way at the expense of the Narodno Oslobodilacka Borba (National Liberation Struggle)."[49]

In a bimonthly report during the second half of December 1944, the OZNA commission in Glina reported that Alfred Weiss, previously discharged from several duties, at that time catering officer at a course for policemen in Glina, "had said that Jews are being disparaged . . . Thanks to their capabilities, no one could do anything to them, since the Jews were prepared to perform even the smallest duties just to survive . . . He said that the Jews in Serbia are not as disparaged as they are here . . . that Jewish families got aid from Italy in dollars, but that ZAVNOH kept the dollars, and paid the Jews in kunas."[50] In January 1945, the same OZNA commission in Glina reported that "the activities of the English Intelligence Service are growing increasingly stronger, and a special reason for this is that they help their people financially, Zina Pengov and many Jews."[51]

Pavao Breyer (1904), born in Križevci, was a student in Zagreb and then owner of a bookshop in Masarykova Street, specialized in acquiring books from abroad. He was active in the Communist movement, was a co-defendant during the trial against Josip Broz Tito in 1928, but was set free at the time. He continued his underground Communist activities, was arrested several times, and, at the beginning of 1936, was sentenced to one year in prison. In a report to the Comintern in 1938, Tito said that Breyer had "comported himself well" for years, but that he is now "selling books by Ante Ciliga [a controversial figure in the Communist movement at that time] in his bookshop, and other Trotskyite writing." At that time, a Communist's biography of this kind was enough to draw extreme suspicion. In 1941, Breyer fled to Italy, but in 1943 returned and joined the Partisans. He was executed in 1944, according to some people on Vis, in the immediate vicinity of the Supreme Command. Breyer spoke excellent English, liked to spend time with the members of the British military mission, and he had probably been groundlessly accused of being a British spy.[52]

Dr. Bela Kohn (1900), head surgeon and manager of the Seventh Banija Division hospital, almost had a similar fate. In 1943, a peasant came to him and asked him to teach someone there what he knew, so that he could be replaced if he died. Kohn answered that the skills he had took six years to acquire and he could not teach anyone overnight. The peasant reported him to the Partisan organization, saying that he did not want to cooperate, and they began to think of drastic measures. Fortunately, an educated Partisan commissary soon arrived, a prewar teacher, who calmed things down, luckily for Dr. Kohn and his patients.[53] It seems that such incidents were more frequent in the Banija area than in other places.

Between September 15, 1944, and January 2, 1945, 198 people were liquidated on the Sixth Corps territory (which was in Slavonia, centered on Papuk). No official record was made of any of the liquidations. The victims included two Jews, under numbers ninety-seven and one hundred. Mišo Rehnicer from Osijek was executed for holding "meetings with Jews in Kometnik [a village near Voćin, in western Slavonia] and writing down decisions reached at those meetings. He is involved with distributing to Jews money given by the English. He is suspected of working for the Intelligence Service." Ladislav Heller from Rumljani was a "Partisan in Zagorje, where he was captured and taken to Hungary." From there, he returned to the Partisans and "asked the corps commander to send him to

Hungary, because he had a connection there and could be of more help. He brought some letters from Hungary and boasted about them. He is suspected of being an Intelligence Service agent."[54]

At the end of the war, there were 2,339 Jews from Croatia and Bosnia and Herzegovina in Partisan units; 804 had been killed. In Croatia alone, 1,737 Jews took part in the anti-Fascist struggle, 325 were killed, ninety of them from Zagreb.[55] This means that in both Croatia and Bosnia and Herzegovina, every fourth Jewish survivor participated in the anti-Fascist struggle.

Almost another 2,000 noncombatant Jews, who had survived the war on Partisan-liberated territory, returned home with the Partisans. So, out of the just over 9,000 Jews who survived the Holocaust in what was then the ISC, about one-half were saved as members of anti-Fascist Partisan units or because they lived on liberated territory. In other words, about ten percent of the total prewar Jewish population participated in the anti-Fascist struggle or actively helped this struggle while living on Partisan-held territory. This was proportionately the largest Jewish participation in resistance movements in Axis-controlled parts of Europe, and also proportionately the largest number of Jews saved by anti-Fascist resistance.

Even then, the Jewish people were proud of the part they had played in the anti-Fascist movement. Six-year-old Mira Altarac started first grade in the El Shatt refugee camp. On "one of my father's photographs, I proudly wrote letters I had just learned: 'My Daddy is a Partisan!'"[56]

PART VI

EPILOGUE

35

THE LANGUISHING OF THE REMAINING JEWS

The May 1943 arrests and deportations of Jews in Zagreb and in the ISC were the last that took place on a large scale, although individual arrests continued until the end of the war. In June 1943, the German services laid down the following procedure: "Arrested Jews are to be handed over to the Croatian police . . . [and] placed in the police prison in Zagreb in Sava Road . . . until their transport to Germany."[1] In July, Ernest Gustović, desk officer in the Public Order and Security Department of the Zagreb Police Directorate, reported that twenty-one Jews were in the Sava Road prison "awaiting transport to Germany." Gustović asked when the Jews would be deported, and was told that he would be informed within ten days.[2] No one knows when these people were deported and whether this was the same as the one mentioned by witnesses after the war, who said that another group of about twenty people were taken to Auschwitz from Zagreb in the fall of 1943.[3] In March 1944, the Ustasha Army captured about eighteen Jewish men and women near Otočac (in Lika) and took them to Zagreb. It seems that Archbishop Stepinac pleaded for their safety in vain, because none of them are on the lists of survivors, and six are known to have been killed.[4]

From May 1943 until the end of the war, the Ustasha authorities and the Nazis found, arrested, and deported approximately 100 Jews throughout the ISC, not counting the 400 or so they caught at the end of 1943 and the beginning of 1944 on territory that had formerly been under Italian control. The greatest mass crime in this period took place in September 1944, when a group of Ustashe led by Ljubo Miloš broke into the Psychiatric Hospital in Vrapče on the pretext that healthy Jews, Communists, and Serbs were hiding among the inmates. It seems that someone in the government, in circles close to Miloš, had grown tired of ignoring the fact that hospitals had become safe havens for the persecuted. Miloš and his group singled out and listed 106 patients, and shut them up in a special pavilion. About twenty days, later they were all taken away in a police van, by night, to an unknown location; according to some people, they were shot in Stupnik or Rakov Potok, southwest of Zagreb, while according to others, they were deported to Jasenovac or to Dachau.[5] Not one of the deportees was ever seen alive again. Judging by the names and surnames, the 106 included 37 Jews. It seems that most of the Jewish victims really were healthy and that they had only simulated some kind of mental disorder. The dates when they were admitted suggest that 31 of these Jews were "simulating" illness, although it is possible that the stress of war really had turned some into mental patients. David Baruch became mentally ill after torture in an Ustasha prison.[6] The people who had simulated mental disease and were killed, included Sidonija Geiger, a prominent piano teacher in the school of the Croatian Music Institute, who had been hidden in Vrapče by her colleague, Melita Lorković, also a pianist.[7] Ella Abeles and Jelena (Ilonka) Funk found refuge in Vrapče in January, and even as late as July, 1944. Sixteen-year-old Ivo Scheiber was also taken from the hospital.[8] It seems that only six of the arrested Jews really were mentally ill. But even the serious patients, such as Rozalija Fuchs (1879) and Alice Fischer (1906), who had been in Vrapče since 1923 and 1928, were taken away and killed because they were Jewish.[9]

Izidor Stern had a stroke before the war. He became a serious mental patient when his sons, Drago and Mladen, were taken to Jasenovac, from where they did not return. He was taken to the Vrapče Psychiatric Hospital, where he soon died.[10]

After he had been in hiding for a long time, landowner Albert Schwabenitz (1880) was captured by SS troops in July 1943, in Kravarsko (near Velika Gorica), where he lived. The rest of the family had already fled abroad or joined the Partisans. In Zagreb, Schwabenitz was handed over to the Ustasha authorities and in October shot in Dotrščina.[11] At the same time, the SS troops also arrested Josip Schwarzenberg in Kravarsko, and he too was handed over to the Ustasha prison in Petrinjska, from where he was taken to Dotrščina and shot.[12]

Julio and Zlata Kollman were arrested in September 1943. For a time they were in prison in Sava Road, then they were shot at Rakov Potok.[13] Edo Funk was arrested around July 1944 and for a time he was in the Gestapo prison, then all trace of him was lost (at about that time, his wife, Jelena-Ilonka, was taken to an unknown place from the Vrapče Psychiatric Hospital).[14] Dragica and Mavro Weinberger were taken to the Gestapo prison on Square N. in November 1944, and then to Germany, from where they did not return.[15] Viktor Hafner from Palmotićeva was hanged in retaliation in Sveti Ivan Zelina on October 4. Bank clerk Oto Fuchs, from Gajdekova, and lawyer Koloman Schneller were shot as hostages in retaliation for an attack on German and Ustasha officers near Donja Stubica at the very end of 1944. Dragica Glasenhardt was arrested at the end of 1944 and shot in February 1945.[16]

After the establishment of the ISC, prominent prewar Zionist activist Nikola Tolnauer was arrested with the first group of Zagreb Jewish attorneys and taken to Kerestinec, and then, after some of the prisoners fled, was transferred to the prison in Sava Road. The management of Našička d. d. (a joint stock company), where he worked, arranged for some kind of exemption for him—he continued to do his job in the firm, but after working hours a policeman took him back to the prison. Someone remembered seeing him as late as the beginning of 1944, but he was deported to Jasenovac and killed during the attempted breakout from the camp in April 1945.[17]

Several days before the end of the war, another tragedy took place, under somewhat unclear circumstances. A group of about forty men, women, and children, said to be from Bohemia, Germany, and Banat (today in northeast Serbia), all or most of them Jews, were disguised as circus members and were living in today's southeast Slovenia, on the border of Croatia. As they had horses and carts, which the Nazis needed for their retreat to Germany, these were requisitioned. Then they transferred the people to ISC territory and handed them over to an Ustasha unit in the border village of Marija Gorica (near Zaprešić, thirty-five kilometers northwest of Zagreb). For a time, the group was imprisoned in the village, but they could contact the villagers. The older villagers remember that the group had some "educated people," and even that they staged performances for them. During the night of April 24–25, 1945, the Ustashe slaughtered the whole group (except for a woman and her child, who were by chance in another house), a total of forty-three people. As the village was liberated several days later, the local authorities very quickly exhumed the bodies and placed them in a common grave, on which the following names were inscribed: Max

Bamberger (1900), his wife and two children, Robert Frans (1911), Wilhelm Friedrich (1922), Mariška Friedrich (1943), Marta Hartmann (1880), Albert Hartmann (1880), Adelheid Hedel (1941), Hilla Hedel (1942), Albine Levy (1889), Lision Schmiedt (1929), Siegfried Schmiedt (1942), Elvira Schmidt (1906), Frieda Schmidt (1926), Ronald Schmidt (1924), Julius Schmidt (1902), Sofie Schmidt (1928), Karl Schmidt (1932), Juliška Schmidt (1942), Ella Stein (1915), and twenty people with the surname Winter: Mendi (1941), Linda (1942), Berta (1880), Reinboldt (1919), Willi (1944), Schamie (1939), Lotte (1925), Hedwig (1883), Karl, Georg (1900), Berta (1900), Josef (1891), Frieda (1900), Amanda (1900), Alfred (1933), Kundi (1932), Marie (1932), Adolf (1936), Anna (1933), and Alcis (1893).[18] Even at the beginning of the twenty-first century, people in the village of Marija Gorica and its surroundings have not forgotten this crime.

After the last mass deportations in May 1943, it was obvious that the interest of the Ustasha authorities in finding, arresting, and deporting Jews waned. Partly, this was because very few Jews still remained under Ustasha rule, and they were mostly under various kinds of protection. Besides, there was nothing left to take away from the Jews, because everything had already been taken in 1941 and 1942. It is also possible that the Ustasha authorities felt that the mass deportations of Jews were causing popular dissatisfaction.[19] Probably the most important factor was the definitive reversal of the war in favor of the anti-Fascist coalition on all the fronts in 1943, which made some people in the Ustasha hierarchy slowly begin to change their political plans and behavior. Right after the May 1943 deportations, the German intelligence services claimed that the "Croatian authorities undertook this action only to perform a task they had been charged with, without caring much about doing it efficiently. At the same time, however, they were implementing it in such a way that it is making the Germans unpopular in Croatia." Since even old women from the old people's home in Boškovićeva, some of whom had been bedridden for several years, were taken away, "this kind of evacuation is a burden on Germany in every way."[20] At that time, the Germans often complained to the Ustashe that they were not thorough enough in persecuting and killing Jews. Even after the deportations in May 1943, the Germans claimed that Jews in Zagreb "felt safe because they have good connections or still have enough assets to assure their protection."[21] "We cannot understand that, despite the constant emphasis on our common struggle, the Croatian state is still protecting and supporting so many Jews," said the report.[22]

Even after the May 1943 deportations, the Nazis complained that in these arrests the "number of arrested Jewish men is minimal," and that Jews can "still be seen in Zagreb, completely healthy."[23] In June 1943, the German intelligence services made a list of eighty-five Jews, twenty-six of whom were allegedly still living in Zagreb (some of them were in fact living in Bjelovar). Strangely, the list was very superficial, perfunctory, and some of the people on it had at that time already joined the Partisans, which is why it is difficult to establish how accurate it is. For example, it mentions only the surname "Schwarz," or a "frau Fröhlich who is hiding in Zagreb illegally."[24] Due to such incomplete data, only six people on the list of twenty-six can be identified with certainty. It seems that even the Nazis were not efficient, because only two of those six were killed, while the other four (Hinko Justitz, Albert and Gustav Deutsch Maceljski, and Oskar Winkler) were protected on various grounds and survived.[25]

"Frau Fröhlich" was an Austrian refugee, seventy-five-year-old Irma Fröhlich of Vienna, who fled to Zagreb to join her brother, Ignac Lauš, one of the owners of the Corso Coffeehouse in Gundulićeva. When her brother was deported, Irma had to find other accommodations, and she was taken in by Viktorija and Mila Kniewald in their rented apartment in Garićgradska Street. At the beginning of 1944, Mila Kniewald took Irma by carriage through the Ilica tollhouse to Samobor, from where Irma left for Partisan territory, where she soon died of typhoid.[26]

The German intelligence agent's views about the mild treatment of the Jews by the Ustasha regime after the summer of 1943 were an exaggeration. The most serious crime committed against the Jews in that period, the removal and killing of at least thirty-seven Jews from the Psychiatric Hospital in Vrapče, was committed by the Ustashe, not by the Germans. In any case, the Ustashe were not inactive. In a report from July 1943, the UNS claimed that a certain "Jew Vesely is probably still in Zagreb," that he is "very dangerous" and "on good terms with the Vatican Embassy." It is not possible to find out to which of the two "Jews Vesely" in Zagreb this referred, but both David Vesely and Karl Vesely were killed under unknown circumstances, one of them obviously even after the great deportations in May 1943.[27]

At the same time, the Nazi services searched for the remaining Jews with undiminished zeal. A German intelligence officer said that "a Jew called Konti, who has not been registered with the police, is living in a cellar in Deželićeva with the janitor . . . and engages in Communism." This was probably a false report, because there is no such surname on the lists of Zagreb Jews.[28] At that time, there was also a report that a certain

Branko Barković was in fact a Jew who used to be called Berges, and was living in Andrilovačka Street in Ferenščica. This person did not exist on the lists of the Zagreb Community either.[29] The Nazis sometimes reported real people. Heda Stern (whose husband, Žiga, killed himself immediately after the establishment of the ISC) and her daughter, student Renata Neumann, had been to prison but were released by the Ustasha authorities. The German intelligence officers were rightly afraid that they might both "soon leave Zagreb." This happened, and the Ustasha services later reported that "they had not yet been able to find them." Mother and daughter fled to Italy, where, after the war, Heda worked for the US Army in tracking down Ustasha war criminals who were trying to escape overseas via Italy.[30] In July, German intelligence services reported that the Jews "Jelinek, Steiner, Schwarz, Milivoj Hirschl, and many others" had been meeting every day "for several weeks" in Biankinijeva 19. It is possible that these were the dentist Dr. Jelinek, the doctor Dr. Milan Schwarz, and the veterinarian Dr. Milan Steiner, all three of whom survived the war in Zagreb.[31] Milivoj Hirschl was from Ivanić Grad (forty kilometers east of Zagreb), from a mixed marriage, and was not on the lists of the Zagreb Jewish Religious Community.[32] Because of denunciations of this kind, the German services concluded that it was necessary to "launch a general action against Jews who are still in Croatia."[33]

The newspapers of the German ethnic minority blended with and reinforced the atmosphere of anti-Jewish rhetoric. For example, their yearbook (*Jahrbuch der Deutschen Volksgruppe im Unabhängigen Staate Kroatien*) for 1944 had a short article called "Jewish Power Politics" (*Jüdische Machtpolitik*) by Professor Dr. Klaus Wilhelm Rath, from Göttingen. It claimed, using an academic vocabulary but no arguments, that the British ambition for predominance in Europe was spreading Jewish influence.

Even in February 1944, following up an anonymous report written in pencil but in good handwriting and in fluent German, the Germans reported that "Russian Jews" met every day in the Corso Coffeehouse in central Zagreb between 4:30 and 8:00 p.m., and that their leader was the dentist "Amper Heinrich." But the services of the Ministry of the Interior of the ISC were obviously in no hurry, and did not inform the German Embassy until June that "investigations have shown that Russian Jews do not meet in the Corso Coffeehouse." The dentist was not called Heinrich, but Hinko, and, at that time, he had an office in Ilica. He survived the war.[34]

In May 1944, the Nazi services, on the basis of reports by some members of the German ethnic group, informed Berlin that "investigations into the number of Jews who have remained in Croatia give a devastating picture, although the report only included some Jews." The picture was found to be so "devastating" (*erschütternd*) because allegedly "many Jews still, as before, hold positions of authority in the state and in the economy, camouflaged as usual (as Catholics) . . . Among others, about 180 Jewish doctors are still working." The Germans thought that the Jewish "influence is very great" and that they "spread hatred" against the Germans among the population.[35] The Nazi services had obviously greatly exaggerated the situation, because only a small number of Jews were still left, and they could certainly not have a "great influence." There is no doubt that the number of 180 doctors said to be still working on Ustasha-controlled territory was exaggerated, probably tenfold or more. As late as September 1944, the Sicherheitsdienst commander in Croatia was informed that "all the Zagreb Jews are plotting together to sabotage the existing regime and the German military authorities, regardless of whether or not they enjoy Aryan rights or live in mixed marriages, using the system of sending reports and receiving orders through individual couriers."[36] Obviously many reports, such as the one mentioned above, were false or were in fact simply the fruit of the anti-Semitic hysteria[37] that developed in some Nazi services, and especially in Hitler himself, at the beginning of the agony of the Third Reich.

Besides giving estimates of conditions, the German services also undertook specific action against individuals. In June 1944, they complained that the vet Milan Steiner, who lived in Preradovićeva with his wife, Hansi, had been reported for "listening to enemy radio stations." The police came, "impounded the radio set and arrested Steiner," but several days later he was set free again. "Allegedly, he said that he could arrange everything." They also reported Zdenko Merkadić, a Jew from Slavonski Brod, and Marga Dragić. However, Merkadić was never on the lists of Zagreb Community members, nor was Marga Dragić.[38] In July, the Nazis demanded that the Ustasha authorities establish the "racial affiliation of Mario Marić and Roman Šovari," and, as they have jobs, "with what justification." In September 1944, the Ministry of the Interior, General Racial Policy Section, sent a letter to the Embassy of the Reich saying that Mario Marić, son of Milan, was a half-Jew, and that Roman Šovari was "protected." Roman Šovari (Šovary) survived the war.[39]

A special aspect of the work of the Nazi services was investigating pedigrees, so as to establish with complete precision who was a Jew, and who was not. This work intensified as the Nazis stepped up their engagement in deporting Jews from the ISC. In March 1943, the German Embassy showed an interest in the genealogy of Rudolf Hohenberg (1881), a Roman Catholic. Miroslav Šalom Freiberger answered that the register only had a Bela Hohenberg for that date, "both of whose parents were of Moses's faith. It is possible that Bela Hohenberg took the name Rudolf when he converted, which the Jewish Community registers do not show." There was no Rudolf Hohenberg in the Jewish Community records in 1941 nor in later years.[40] In July 1943, the "Sicherheitspolizei" from Trg Kulina Bana asked the Jewish Community to look in the registers of the Visoko Jewish Community (in Central Bosnia) for data about the parents of Simon Kornfeld. The Zagreb Community replied that the "notebook has been lost."[41]

The Familienforschungsinstitut (Genealogical Research Institute) from Graz inquired about some Croatian Jews, long dead. This was obviously a Nazi institution that was supposed to discover who was or wasn't a Jew. As early as July 1941, it inquired about Michaela Šoštarić from Jesenje, near Krapina (fifty kilometers north of Zagreb).[42] It seems that its interest grew as the end of the war approached. At the beginning of 1943, it asked whether the books of the Sisak Jewish Community between 1846 and 1852 showed the birth of Emil Herzka, son of Samuel and Regina. Chief Rabbi Freiberger answered that there was no such entry, but that Samuel Herzka is on the list of Sisak Jews for 1859.[43] The same institute asked the Archbishopric Clerical Office which parish the villages of Rogoža and Stupovača belong to (to the Kaniška Iva parish near Garešnica, about one hundred kilometers east of Zagreb), and then asked for someone's genealogy again.[44] Freiberger helped some people as much as he could. In a long letter to the Ministry of Justice and Religious Affairs, dated April 18, 1943, only two weeks before his own deportation, he maintained that, on the grounds of positive legal regulations, Liesel Reimann (1924), born in the marriage of a Jew and a woman of no confession, who "returned to the Roman Catholic Church" in 1938, cannot be considered Jewish.[45]

After Freiberger's deportation, Community officials continued doing the same kind of work. In the summer of 1943, they sent some birth certificates from the books of the Osijek Chief Rabbi's Office to the Ministry of Justice and Religious Affairs and the General Racial Policy Section.[46] At the end of that year, that Section received the birth and/or marriage certificates of Marija Hochstädter, Helena Sulzbach, Isidor Schlesinger from Osijek, Alfred Schlanger from Zemun, and Edo and Ernestina Deutsch from Vukovar.[47]

About 800 Jewish men and women married to Aryans, and the children of such marriages, remained In Zagreb after the deportations in early May 1943. Most of them had suffered from the anti-Jewish measures because they had lost their apartments or other property, but they were, as a rule, exempt from deportation. Stepinac and other church representatives interceded for some of them, the Ustasha authorities tolerated others.[48] Many tried to be as invisible as possible: for example, Irena Korda and her family survived "on the outskirts of Zagreb, in Trešnjevka, with false documents," and from 1943 lived in the same house with people in a mixed marriage, and were thus protected.[49] Some of them hid in the city and were mostly "without funds," while "others were unregistered and lived under conditions that the normal human mind cannot even understand." The Community fed and clothed them. Sometimes, some of them were hidden in one of the city hospitals at the Community's expense. There were also women with children of various ages; the Community took care that the children were clothed and got additional food, and some even attended private schools.[50] In November 1943, the Jewish Community sent the International Red Cross a list of nineteen children under the age of thirteen who were in Zagreb, and who "depend completely on what they get from us . . . all these children are very poor . . . some live with their parents, some with strangers." As a precaution, the Jewish Community did not send the Red Cross the addresses at which the children lived, but begged for "the things to be sent to us when they are being distributed, and we will forward them."[51] For almost three years, Zlata Frankl hid in the apartment of the Prašek family, from August 1942, when she was saved from the transit camp in Križanićeva, to the end of the war. When the Ustashe inspected the apartment during raids, Zlata hid in a recess behind the hall wardrobe; luckily, the Ustashe did not move the wardrobe.[52]

Ašer Kabiljo's family, his wife, Rahela-Shelly, and son, Alfons-Alfi (1935), survived the entire war in Zagreb, although they were all taken to the Ustasha prison on Square N. and to the Zagreb Fairground several times, but each time they were set free because someone interceded for them. Little Alfi was just one month short of finishing the first grade of the Jewish school when the school shut down after the wave of arrests and deportations in May 1943. In the fall, the Jewish Community nevertheless issued him with a certificate that he had graduated from first grade. He continued his regular schooling at the normal school in Zagreb, and had no more problems.[53]

About 800 Jews survived in Zagreb, and another 150–200 Jews were saved in the other parts of the ISC under Ustasha control, mostly by chance or because of the outstanding ingenuity of the Jews themselves or the people around them. In 1943, some state bodies began to adopt a more lenient attitude. For example, from time to time, the ISC State Council requested that ministries send them lists of people "who are not of Aryan origin, and are employed as state officials." In January 1942, the Ministry of the Croatian Home Guards had considered it necessary to explain that a "Jew has no right to serve in the army . . . and that, in the case of Jews, the legal provision defining who is a Jew is relevant, because it is a question of race and not of religion."[54] In 1943, the same ministry, whose name was changed in 1942 to the Ministry of the Armed Forces, sent a list of "non-Aryans" accompanied by a letter saying that all those on the list were "good and worthy officials and true patriots, and all of them not only deserve to serve, but are necessary in the Croatian army." The list that was attached to this document has not been preserved, but probably included some doctors who later either joined the Partisans or were killed.

In 1943, the Ministry of the National Economy reported that it employed Milan Švarc and Otokar Grabarić, both of whom had converted to Catholicism in 1938. Before the war, Grabarić (Vinkovci, 1907) was an attorney in Zagreb, and at some point had changed his surname of Grünbaum to Grabarić. The letter from the ministry said that Grabarić "has never worked against the good of the Croatian people but has, on the contrary, always recognized and stressed that he is a Croat." Nevertheless, in 1941, Grabarić had to give to the Contribution, and he also had to acquire a pass to move about the city. Both Švarc and Grabarić survived the war, but they did not register with the Jewish Community again.[55]

When Hugo Kon and Šalom Freiberger were deported at the beginning of May 1943, "the others were in great consternation, not knowing at first whether the Community would be allowed to and able to continue its work. After we calmed down several days later and found our bearings, we regrouped and continued to work where our predecessors had stopped," said Robert Glücksthal in July 1945.[56] On May 8, the Jewish Community sent a very unusual letter to the Ministry of the Interior. It was unsigned, and the contents were twofold: it was a combination of an appeal and a report. The Community begged "for its nine employees to be allowed further unhindered work." However, a comparison between those who were killed and those who survived shows that of these nine, four had, in the preceding days, been taken to Zagreb prisons, and, in the meantime, had probably been deported. Ultimately, they were killed in Auschwitz. The senders of the request were making a last desperate attempt to save them.

The second aspect of the letter is a kind of report about past work ("Camp Welfare has sent parcels with additional food to various camps . . . The soup kitchen fed Jews who were entitled to free food because of poverty"). There was no mention at all of the hundreds of Jews who were at that time being arrested and deported. Instead, the letter proposed a convoluted way, for the Community to continue working, consisting of five institutions: the Community Office, Registry Office, Camp Welfare, Soup Kitchen, and Office for Issuing Medicine.[57] On the same day, May 8, Archbishop Stepinac sent a letter to Minister of the Interior Andrija Artuković, demanding the unhindered work of the Jewish Religious Community in Zagreb.[58]

The result was that the Community resumed work, engaging a minimum number of people headed by Oskar-Ašer Kišicky and Dr. Robert Glückstha1.[59] They kept a soup kitchen in Zagreb, fed the old people in the Brezovica home, and sent parcels to camps. The Head Directorate of Internal Policy at the ISC Ministry of the Interior supervised the Community's work. Since the building at Trenkova 9 had been summarily appropriated, Camp Welfare moved to Tomislavov Square 4.[60]

Religious services could no longer be held in Trenkova, and the temple furniture was stored in "a carrier's warehouse." As Freiberger had been deported in May 1943, the only remaining person with religious training was Chief Cantor Grüner. There was hardly any religious work at all in Tomislavov Square. "From a small, cramped room, with improvised furnishings and the saved Torahs, linked by immense pain because of everything that had befallen our community . . . the prayers and thoughts of those who remained went out to those who were dying in groups in the camps."[61]

The first letter that anyone from the Community sent after the deportation of Freiberger and Kon was dated May 6, when the Jewish Community sent the information that two of the soup kitchen employees would "buy and cook food for the Jewish prisoners in the Sava Road prison."[62] The next letter was sent on May 14, eight days later, when some Jews in Italy were informed about the fate of their relatives in camps.[63] The first letter has no signature, the second is signed with an illegible initial. It was not until the end of the month that the Community began to send prompt answers to the many letters received. At the beginning of June, the correspondence normalized, but was signed with only an illegible initial, probably Ašer Kišicki's. At that time, David Alkalaj wrote from the Osnabrück military prison camp and personally thanked Ašer for the information.[64] It was not until the letter to the Committee for Aid to Jews in Hungary (Magyar Izraeliták Pártfogó Irodája), dated July 11, that Kišicky and Glücksthal both signed for the first time, with typed surnames and initials, just as Kon and Freiberger had always done until two months earlier.[65]

At the beginning of June 1943, the Split Jewish Community asked the Zagreb Community to "tell us whether you are still caring for the camps, as you had been doing until the beginning of May, that is, have there been any changes in this and since when?" Refugees on the island of Hvar asked a similar question.[66] The Jewish Community sent its first letter to the International Red Cross on June 8, giving information about the fate of some people.[67]

On May 7 and 19, Marija Bauer from Istanbul wrote to Freiberger and Kon, thinking that they were still in Zagreb. She did not begin to address her letters to Kišicki and Glücksthal until July.[68] On May 21, Isak Altarac wrote to Hugo Kon from Osnabrück (addressing him as "Dear Uncle," probably to help the letter pass the camp censors more easily); he did not yet know that Kon had been deported. It was not until June 22 that a letter was sent to him with the greeting "Dear friend," saying that "Hugo is here no more, because he was taken away with his other relatives in an unknown direction at the beginning of May."[69] Altarac later corresponded in a similar way with Ašer Kišicky, trying to help his relatives and friends in Jasenovac.[70]

Kišicky and Glücksthal did other kinds of very different work, too. As we have seen, they had to cooperate with various Ustasha and Nazi services in establishing the "racial" origin of people. Only several days after the mass deportations, on May 14, one of them issued Ivana Fussmann (1920) with a certificate saying that she was single and could get married.[71]

Kišicky and Glücksthal, and the other "members of the Jewish Community," were under the strict surveillance of the German services, and, in May 1943, the Foreign Ministry in Berlin informed Hans Helm in Zagreb that there were attempts to acquire money for "Jews who are in Croatia illegally, so that they can escape to Palestine." The information was true in the sense that money came to Zagreb from Budapest, but it was to be used exclusively for sending parcels to the camps. By that time, no one was even thinking about organizing transports to Palestine.[72] Documents show that just under 100,000 kunas were sent to the Community at the end of August 1943 from Budapest through bank accounts.[73] This was more or less enough for one month of parcels to the camps. The amount of administrative work, the volume of letters and receipts that have been preserved about this one bank transaction, is so great that this procedure was very difficult to repeat. There is no proof that money ever again arrived from the same source in a similar way.

Although Kišicky and Glücksthal were exposed to mistreatment and were not sure that they would live to see the next day, neither met with understanding when they had to explain the position of the remaining Zagreb Jews to Jewish organizations abroad. Glücksthal wrote that some "people in Budapest do not acknowledge that we are members of the same family."[74] This was probably due to the completely unjustified suspicions that they were both collaborating with the Ustasha authorities. After the war, the Federation of Jewish Communities of Yugoslavia accorded them full credit. "The Community . . . under the current circumstances, worked in the only way possible. This is certainly thanks to Dr. Robert Glikstal, engineer Đuro Kastl, and Ašer Kišicki, who contributed to the common cause while exposing themselves to the greatest danger . . . Of the 115 Jewish Communities in prewar Yugoslavia, only the one in Zagreb functioned to the very end."[75] All three survived the war as protected members of mixed marriages, and remained at the head of the Zagreb Jewish Community until 1946.

Sending parcels to camps was one of the main Community activities. A great problem was that much of the food and other necessities sent to the prisoners was systematically looted. The case of Sipura Papo well illustrates this. In April 1943, she wanted to send a parcel from the camp in Kupari, via the Zagreb Community, to her son, Eliezer, in Jasenovac. Instead of food, the parcel that reached the Zagreb Community contained coal![76] To prevent acts of this kind, the Jewish Community did what it could to arrange for the Jasenovac Camp administration to send back receipts that the parcels had been delivered. The Jewish Community would send a letter informing the Jasenovac administration that "today we sent 14 paper bags with 125 food parcels," and would enclose a list of prisoners who were to receive the parcels. A letter would then arrive from Jasenovac, for example: "We acknowledge receipt of a food transport consisting of 14 paper bags with 125 food parcels for prisoners here, which were received in good condition and distributed to the recipients according to the list." On another occasion, the camp manager, Captain Brkljačić, confirmed the receipt of "16 paper bags with a total of 139 food parcels for the prisoners, which we received properly and distributed to the recipients according to the list."[77] However, these letters were dated November and December 1943. It seems that, prior to that time, no such confirmations arrived from the Jasenovac Camp.

At this time. the correspondence between the Jewish Community and the Jasenovac Camp administration became very intensive. For the Christmas holidays of 1943, the administration wanted to put up trees for the Roman Catholics and "Croatian Orthodox," so they asked the Jewish Community to help them obtain decorations. The Jewish Community, obviously as a quid pro quo, asked permission for the Jewish prisoners to celebrate the holiday of the "candles," Hanukkah, which started on December 22.[78]

In 1944 and 1945, the Zagreb Community sent parcels "most abundantly," but it is ironic that internees who needed help received more of it because there were fewer of them as each day passed. From the beginning of 1945 to the middle of April, during seventeen weeks, the Zagreb Community sent Rudi Adanja and Meir Kasorla seventeen parcels each.[79] They contained smoked meat (bacon), cheese, jam, some fruit (probably apples), lemons, etc.[80] The last parcel was sent to Rudi Adanja on April 18, only four days before the prison break and the disappearance of the camp.[81] The prisoners who had spent months and years in the camp needed more and more help to keep alive. Selma Grünwald sent word from Jasenovac for the last time on October 13, 1944, dentist Ljudevit Friedländer from Lepoglava on March 6, 1945, and his wife, Nada, also from Lepoglava, as late as March 20. None of them survived to the end of the war.[82]

The remaining Jews in Zagreb lived in a kind of lethargy, waiting for liberation and hoping that they could avoid deportation. The plentiful correspondence with Ustasha institutions died out, and hardly anyone fled the city.

Mavro Klein (1870) escaped deportation in May 1943 because he was in the Sisters of Charity Hospital from mid-February, where he had undergone surgery for cancer. When he was released from the hospital in the summer of 1943, he was completely alone, because his wife, Julija, and sister-in-law, Berta Schwarz, had in the meantime been sent to camp, and his daughter and granddaughter had fled from Zagreb earlier. Soon his health deteriorated, and he was admitted to the hospital again. In November, he wrote to his relatives in Osijek: "Everyone has left me. I have no news from anyone . . . Aunt Julča sends no word, and neither do her children." "Aunt Julča" was his wife, Julija, but, being careful, Mavro did not want to write this, although he was probably aware that he would never see her again. Mavro Klein died on January 16, 1944. A relative, dentist Josip Osvald, married to an "Aryan," organized his funeral, and, on a cold January day in 1944, was the only mourner to see Mavro Klein into his grave.[83]

Ida and Antun Lang and their daughter, Ines, Old Catholics, wanted to convert to Roman Catholicism in December 1944, and begged for recognition of their civil marriage. Antun had converted to the Old Catholic religion in 1942. Ida, née Sotinski, had for many years previously been married to a Jew, whose name is not mentioned. Her first husband and her son from that marriage had obviously been killed in the persecutions, but Ida had no documents to prove the death of her first husband, so the whole procedure became complicated. However, the entire family survived the war.[84]

There were anti-Semitic outbursts in the media at this time, too, but the accusations were completely different than in 1941. Speaking on Radio Zagreb in December 1943 about the Partisans, Director of Propaganda Matija Kovačić said that, in prewar Croatia, "the Communists had mostly been Jews and other non-Croats." He tried to convince his listeners that "relatively speaking, there were probably the fewest Communists among the Croatian people before the war of any country in Europe!" Accusing Tito, he said that his "main adviser, his main controller, was the Jew Moša Pijade."[85] Moša Pijade (1890–1957) of Belgrade was a prominent prewar Communist and political prisoner, and during the war he really was one of Tito's closest collaborators.[86] He was a favorite target of anti-Semitic Ustasha attacks. At the turn of 1944 to 1945, a poster appeared all over Zagreb claiming that the "head of the Belgrade police and the most influential man of the Belgrade Soviet was the Jew Moša Pijade!" Tito's minister Andrija Hebrang was accused of "living in a common-law marriage with a Jewess," which was not true because Hebrang had married Olga Kohn in Slunj in December 1942.[87] They also claimed that Tito's army had "thousands of Jewish political commissars." The headlines and subtitles on the poster suggested that "Tito means the mastery and rule of the Jews," and "whoever fights for Tito, fights for the Jews." The most interesting detail is the claim that "Tito returned to the Belgrade Jews their apartments and shops, which had been taken from them, and threw the Serbs out into the street!." It seems that the writers of the poster had become panic-stricken, and they suddenly began to feel compassion for the Serbs who had wanted to plunder Jewish property.[88]

Much more aggressive and direct were the editors of *Hrvatski radnik:* under the tile "Facts Speak for Themselves," in an issue from June 1944, the paper wrote that "Today, after three years of bloody fighting by our people, we feel stronger than ever, largely because we have purged our people of the Jewish poison that now has no chance of spreading defeatism and despair."[89]

Kišicky and Glücksthal felt how unsure their position was in October and November 1944, when they almost lost their lives. For months, the Jewish Community had taken care of two Sarajevo Jews, Jakica-Jakov Gaon and Moric Katan-Levi, who had escaped from a transport to Jasenovac. Two of Gaon's children had been left in the transport, and so had Katan's wife. The Community managed to supply them with forged documents using false names, and they packed parcels for the camp internees in the Community. When an Ustasha recognized one of them in the street one day, the police burst into the Community office and detained Kišicki and Glücksthal and six other Community employees. Both the men from Sarajevo were hanged on October 28 near Čulinec (on the eastern outskirts of the city), together with eighteen other hostages, in retaliation for Partisan sabotage. Although sentences of the Traveling Summary Court do not exist either for Gaon or for Katan, it seems that the police arrested them and kept them in prison because they were accused of having "slaughtered innocent Croats in Bosnia." On the same day, but in another place, in Sv. Nedelja near Samobor, Milan Spitzer, who had allegedly acquired the fake documents for Gaon and Katan, was hanged in retaliation for some other Partisan actions. Three of the six Community employees arrested at that time—Antun Engel, Samuel Romano, and Viktor Wolf—were deported to Jasenovac, from where they did not return.

When Gaon, Katan, and the others were arrested, the Community stopped work, the rooms were closed, and one of the rooms was even sealed. It seems that Kišicky and Glücksthal were released from jail only thanks to the intercession of Julius Schmidlin, the representative of the International Red Cross Committee. On November 6, the Community got a permit from the City of Zagreb Police Precinct to continue working.[90]

The practice of taking Jews hostages and then shooting them had mostly been discontinued after about the end of 1941. However, it was resumed at the end of 1943, and continued right up to the end of the war. The Ustasha Police arrested people they considered Communists or Partisan supporters, but only some of them had ties to the Jewish Community. It is possible that some of them were arrested as Jews, but were then not deported to Jasenovac but accused of Communist activities so that they could be shot when the need arose for retaliation "against Communists and rebels." Radovan Reicherzer hid in Zagreb during the war. As an active Communist, he was arrested in May 1943 and shot in retaliation in December 1943. Zagreb housewife, Lili Ivanek, née Grünbaum (1902), born in Szent Gothard, and her husband "cooperated with the National Liberation

Movement" and sent food to the Partisans. She was shot in August 1944. Tina Atijas (1919), active in the Anti-Fascist Women's Front, was arrested and shot in December of the same year. Hermina Bruckner was arrested in December 1944 for alleged cooperation with the Partisans and shot in retaliation for an attack on German and Ustasha officers near Donja Stubica (thirty kilometers north of Zagreb) before the New Year.[91]

As the end of the war approached, the Ustasha services became increasingly less efficient. A case in point was that of Branimir and Erna Ljubičić (Erna was Jewish), who lived quietly in Zagreb during the war. They hid the valuables of some Jewish families (including seven paintings), and were reported for this on December 30, 1944 by their neighbor, Franjo Pustajec. Hearing of the denunciation, and fearing a visit from the police, Ljubičić gave the valuables to other people. On May 1, 1945, six days before the Ustashe fled Zagreb, two policemen came to Ljubičić's apartment and searched it, but apparently did not find anything that interested them, so they left the Ljubičićes alone.[92]

Barica Bulić, who was living in the apartment of Adolf Binenfeld, met "the former owner of my present apartment" in Gajeva Street in Zagreb at the beginning of March 1945, and Binenfeld said to her, "Yes, you are enjoying what belongs to someone else now, but not for long, because it will soon come to an end. I left my apartment peacefully, but you will all have to scurry down the stairs." Bulić reported Binenfeld to the Poglavnik's Bodyguard Battalion that same day (she obviously had good connections among the authorities), and the Battalion Commander, Mijo Bzik, forwarded the report to Lieutenant Colonel Viktor Tomić, former head of the Fourth Department UNS and at that time head of the Reports Department of the Ustasha Army. It seems that Tomić, one of the most violent Ustasha policemen, did nothing but forward the report, thirteen days later, to the City of Zagreb Police Precinct, however nothing came of it. In earlier years, an "outburst" of this kind by a Jew would have been mercilessly punished, but now things had changed. It seems that Adolf Binenfeld survived the war.[93]

At that time, on March 10, 1945, Pavelić made a speech in the Croatian Workers Chamber, but the cutting edge of his attacks had obviously become blunted and he no longer mentioned the Jews. Instead, he blamed the "Bolshevist hordes" or the "Belgrade Bolshevists" for the decline of his state.[94]

At the very end, on May 3, 1945, the Chamber of Attorneys suddenly thought that they should act: its president, Milan Pavelić (an attorney in

Zagreb before and after the war), requested the repeal of the Legal Provision on the Ban on Misappropriation of April 18, 1941 (which he—purposely or not—misquoted, as its exact title was Legal Provision on the Preservation of Croatian National Property), and pointed out the legal complications and difficulties that its application led to, although these had not bothered him during the preceding four years.[95]

The Legal Provision on Equalizing ISC Citizens With Regard to Racial Affiliation shows that the Ustashe themselves were aware of their activities during the past four years. This was literally passed at the last moment, on May 5, 1945, only two days before their flight from Zagreb. It provided that "all legal provisions according to which ISC citizens are differentiated with regard to racial affiliation, and all other regulations issued on the basis of these legal provisions, shall lose legal force."[96] On that day, newspaperman and publicist Josip Horvat wrote that the repeal of these laws "will not now save anyone, nor resurrect the dead."[97]

36

THE OLD PEOPLE'S HOME

From Maksimirska Road to Brezovica

The ninety-seven residents of the Lavoslav Schwarz Old People's Home were simply evicted from the premises in Maksimirska Road immediately after the establishment of the ISC. By order of April 14, 1941, of the Ustasha Head Office in Zagreb, by noon of the following day they had to "empty the whole home . . . in such a way as to take with them the private property of individuals and leave all the rest of the inventory for the use of the German army," which moved into the building. Several people, the most seriously ill, were allowed to remain in the cellar of the building for several more days, after the Community interceded on their behalf.[1] The residents who had family in Zagreb moved in with them, and, in May, the Jewish Community managed to find accommodations for the others in several apartments: in Rapska Street and in Boškovićeva 3, in what used to be the Home for Women Apprentices attached to the Central Jewish Station for Productive Social Aid. Ferdo Singer, who ran the Home, and his wife, Irena, managed to organize life even under these difficult circumstances, with the invaluable help of Đuro Harandi and head nurse Marija Bučar.[2]

In June 1941, Harandi persuaded Zagreb merchant Capek to lease to the Jewish Community two isolated houses in the suburb of Stenjevec. At the beginning of July, the Jewish Section approved the relocation of fifty-two residents there. The Community managed to gather the money and it paid the lease for two years in advance.[3] For the next year and a half, the life of the sixty or so residents was relatively bearable: given the circumstances, food, hygiene and nursing were at a high level. The Jewish home was hidden under the name of the Red Cross Home for Old People.

The old and infirm in Stenjevec were not the only ones under the care of the Jewish Community. In Zagreb, and even more in other Croatian towns, there were elderly Jews who had been "released from transit camps because of old age and infirmity, and whose entire belongings had been taken," so the problem arose of feeding them and providing for their other basic needs. From the summer of 1941 to the end of 1942, all the old Jewish men and women in Croatia were "assigned, usually by the UNS, to the care" of the Jewish Community in Zagreb, which placed them in old people's homes. The reports of the Jewish Religious Community in Zagreb to the UNS in February and March 1943 show that it provided for just over 200 people in various locations in Zagreb. There were about forty people in the home at Boškovićeva 3 from May 1941 to May 1943. At the beginning of 1943, there were forty-one residents in the rented house at Rapska 57. Another home was opened at Trenkova 9, in rooms on the third floor that had previously housed the secondary-school day center, and, at the beginning of 1943, it had twenty-nine residents. A small house at Lovranska 15 was also rented, which had eleven residents at the beginning of 1943. An apartment at Draškovićeva 25 had seven residents, and Dužice 18 (a street in Trešnjevka, the prolongation of Dobojska up to Ljubljanska) had twenty-three. The largest home was that in Stenjevec, with sixty-seven residents.[4] The Community had great problems acquiring beds and bed linen when it moved to three new locations, which shows how difficult conditions had become.

At the beginning of April 1943, the soup kitchen was sending thirty-six meals to Boškovićeva, six to Draškovićeva, twenty to Dužice, eleven to Lovranska, thirty-nine to Rapska, and twenty-six to Trenkova, for a total of 138 meals a day. The number of residents was somewhat larger, but some of them were so ill that they did not eat, or ate something different.[5] Their number kept changing, and on April 4, four fewer meals were sent to Dužice, sixteen in all, because a day earlier three old women had been sent to Stenjevec, and on that day seventy-five-year-old Malvina Jungwirth died. A week later, Marijana Atijas also died.[6] For these five homes (not counting that in Draškovićeva, about which there are no figures), the Jewish Community spent 34,500 kunas a month for breakfast and overhead expenses alone (because lunch and supper were recorded as the expenses of the soup kitchen).[7]

Because of the rise in food costs, on February 1, 1943, the Community was forced to raise the charge for food, which the residents paid as a contribution toward their upkeep. Some paid 1,500 kunas a month, while most of them paid 2,000 kunas. "This was not an easy decision to make, but if you do some simple calculations yourselves, you will see that you could not live more cheaply anywhere, and that this amount does not cover what we spend on accommodations, food, heating, and light,"[8] said the letter which the Jewish Community administration sent to the residents.

The several dozen who did not pay anything at all because of poverty were asked to "realize how unfair it is for you to spend, even though it is very little, for your personal needs or for additional food, while making no contribution for the basics, which are accommodations, heating, light, and food." They asked them "to inform the manager how much you have decided to pay, and he will collect your payments on the first of every month."[9] Later, some residents of Lovranska and Trenkova submitted requests for their living costs to be decreased or cancelled—only one of the twelve requests was not met, and only two people were exempted from paying any living costs at all.[10] The residents of Boškovićeva were not insensitive to the general situation, and, at the turn of 1942 to 1943, on the death of two of their number, they collected the sum 600 kunas and "donated it for charity."[11] On the other hand, the Community administration also tried to improve the life of the residents with small gifts: for Purim, at the end of March 1943, six of them got 100 kunas each.[12]

The homes had no servants in the real sense. "Every resident, regardless of whether he or she contributes anything to living costs, must help in the work." At the end of 1942, the Community administration admonished Herbert Thockus, saying that it was his duty to carry wood in two old people's homes.[13] At the very beginning of 1943, the Community administration wrote that "in all the homes, the worries are of a general nature, but the home in Rapska is a cause for special concern . . . because of a lack of discipline and little consideration for everything having to do with the Community." It is impossible to tell what happened from the document, except that during the move from Rapska to Stenjevec, some residents "took towels and duvet covers, which are Community property, with them."[14]

In a letter from November 1942, Kon and Freiberger informed the residents that the UNS had ordered that everyone must have authorization in writing before leaving the home.[15] On March 5, 1943, the Community administration "noticed that the residents of the home in Boškovićeva go around town too much." They cautioned that "residents are allowed to leave the home only for the most important reasons."[16] Possibly these were measures of precaution before the announced wave of arrests and deportations. On March 17, Julija Klein got written permission "to be absent for one afternoon" because of the "illness of her husband," Mavro, who was in the hospital at the time. Julija Klein was deported in May 1943.[17]

The correspondence between the Jewish Community and various state services took place on several levels, and a lot of it was about the old people's homes.[18] In February 1943, the Jewish Community gave the Jewish Section a list of residents in all six old people's homes in Zagreb.[19] The Ustasha authorities demanded precise records about the people in the homes, which the Jewish Community regularly supplied, because this was a condition for the homes continuing to exist. In November 1942, the Ustasha authorities allowed Ivana Kohn, Hermina Popper, Adela Heim, and some other old people to be placed in the Stenjevec home, as there was no more room in the other homes in the city.[20] In January 1943, Vilko Kühnel, head of the Jewish Section, personally allowed some "infirm Jews to be placed in the old people's home in Stenjevec."[21] On January 5, the Jewish Community assured the Head Directorate of Public Order and Security that it would admit to the home, and provide for at its own expense, Emil (1869) and Ženi (1880) Reich.[22] Around the same time, the UNS handed over to the Community Isak and Sara Kalderon, who were placed in the home in Dužice.[23] It seems that the sisters Julija Klein and Berta Schwarz were admitted to Boškovićeva at about this time; they had lived in a small house in Gajevo naselje from 1941, after being evicted from their apartment in Dukljaninova Street.[24]

Ustasha Control was also notified about the relocation of residents. Kon and Freiberger informed the UNS that Ruža and Felicija Klugmann had been moved from the home in Rapska to that in Dužice.[25] When the Jewish Community sent Rifka Grünberger and Jeanet Samek to the old people's home in Rapska Street on February 1and April 1, it instructed the home management to "register them with the police precinct immediately."[26] The deaths of David Stern, Ivana (Johana) Spiegler, Malvina Jungwirth, and Marijana Atijas were properly registered with the City of Zagreb Police Precinct, and also that Albert Pollak had been sent to the Srebrenjak sanatorium on about April 27 due to a serious illness. The Ustasha services were also informed that Katarina Braunstein had become "gravely ill," that she "needed constant care," and that she had thus been moved from the home in Rapska to that in Trenkova, and that Irma Mušić had been moved in the opposite direction. How sure the authorities were that they had everything under control can be seen from a letter of April 17, in which the Head Office of the City of Zagreb Police Precinct committed German Jew Verständig Heinrich to the care of the Community, and two weeks later he was sent to Auschwitz, together with all the others.[27]

All the old men and women, except for those in Stenjevec and some individuals from the other homes, were taken to Auschwitz at the beginning of May 1943. The epilogue was a letter the Jewish Community sent to the Zagreb Gasworks on 27 May: "Please disconnect the gas meters in our following former homes: in Boškovićeva and in Trenkova."[28]

The home in Stenjevec was in the immediate neighborhood of the German *Eisenbahnen-Sicherheitsdiens*t (Railway Security Service). In the summer of 1943, Nazis from the service entered the home and arrested the seventy-two-year-old manager, Singer, and three other adults and two children (eight and thirteen years old) who were, it seems, deported to Auschwitz, from where only one child returned. Then thirteen residents, whose ages ranged from sixty-five to eighty, were taken away, and released after intercession.[29] After that, Sturmführer Schuckart, head of the Sicherheitsdienst, ordered the home to be evacuated within ten days, otherwise all the residents would be deported to Germany. It seems that this took place in November 1943.[30] At that time, the representatives of the home, finding themselves "facing an almost hopeless task, appealed to Archbishop Stepinac," testified Amiel Shomrony, personal secretary of Chief Rabbi Freiberger until the Chief Rabbi's deportation. The Archbishop offered them accommodations in the church estate in Brezovica, about ten kilometers south of Zagreb.[31]

The relocation of the old people's home to Brezovica was neither quick nor simple. They were housed in one of the rather dilapidated farm buildings belonging to the manor house, which had to be adapted and have two rooms added to accommodate the fifty-eight residents, so "a lot of money and great effort had to be invested in acquiring material." One wing of the building already housed the Carmelite Convent.[32] Valent Klancir, co-owner of a Zagreb ironmongery, helped by supplying the "necessary goods partly for free, and partly for much lower prices."[33] In this way, conditions were created for the old people from Stenjevec to be sent by truck to Brezovica on December 8, 1943.[34] The Jewish Community, i.e., Jewish organizations in Switzerland, financed their accommodations, as suggested in a letter from the Cathedral Chapter: "For your Community, at its own expense and with the approval of the state authorities, to accommodate old people and children." It seems, however, that the Church provided part of the money. Although it looked as if they had probably been saved, for the following sixteen months the residents still lived in daily fear that the deportations might eventually sweep them up as well. Some of them died before the war ended, and some others were later admitted to the home.[35] In May 1945, fifty-two residents of the home in Brezovica were alive to greet the final liberation from fear.

37

THE CATHOLIC CHURCH, ARCHBISHOP STEPINAC, AND THE JEWS

Much has been written and discussed concerning Archbishop Stepinac and the role he played, both during his lifetime and for many years after his death, right down to the present. Implicit in all of this was the broader subject of how the Catholic Church in Croatia, and Stepinac himself, related to the Ustasha regime. The subject has been viewed from multiple perspectives, leading to differing conclusions. Various people have given completely contradictory and irreconcilable assessments of Stepinac's attitude toward the Jews, and that of the Church in general.

"Alojzije Stepinac could be called a man of high moral principles, strong passions, and a narrow political horizon. He was fanatically pious, endlessly loyal to the Catholic Church, and hated Communism intensely. He was a brave man."[1] The conduct of the Catholic Church in Croatia, and of Stepinac himself, was unswervingly bound to the stand taken by the Vatican and the Catholic Church as a whole, towards Nazism and Fascism, but not all the Vatican archives concerning these events have yet been opened to the public. Archbishop Stepinac was able to decide about some problems on his own initiative and in accordance with his own beliefs, but he was above all a faithful representative and follower of the Vatican.[2]

When Pope Pius XI signed a concordat with the Italian State in 1929, in an outburst of enthusiasm he publicly called Mussolini a "man sent to us by Providence." Still, both Pius XI and Pius XII were deeply aware that a totalitarian regime could not be "taken lightly." After 1929, many German bishops loudly criticized the racist and religious teaching of Nazism, and took the position that a Catholic could not be a Nazi. On the other hand, Rome looked on Nazism as the strongest barrier to the onslaught of Communism. In March 1937, Pius XI published the encyclical *Mit brennender Sorge,* intended for the Germans, in which he condemned racism and accused the Nazi authorities of spreading "a wealth of mistrust, discord, hatred, false accusations." He concluded that he "can see threatening storm clouds of a destructive war gathering on the German horizon."[3] On the other hand, several days later he published another encyclical, *Divini Redemptoris,* in which he condemned Communism in even stronger and more direct terms, calling its principles "in their essence inimical to faith in any form," and supporting the introduction of church social teaching as a counterweight to Communism and "immoral liberalism." Thus, it was Pius XI who paved the way for the Vatican's international policy in the coming period: Nazism and Fascist totalitarianism were errors, mistakes, and dangers, but it was heathen totalitarianism that was the main deadly enemy of religion and the Church.

In June 1933, the Vatican signed a concordat with Hitler's government, which had just been established, but, during the next three years, it sent about thirty notes of protest to Berlin because of infringements of this concordat. State Secretary Eugenio Pacelli, the future Pope Pius XII, who was later accused of sympathies for Nazism, composed most of them. The tone of these notes was far from cordial. Pacelli was horrified by the dictators' demands for the total subjugation of their citizens, demands for the Church's subjugation as well, and he also found the racist doctrine on which Nazism was founded hateful. On the other hand, he admired authoritarian political ideas that laid emphasis on traditional values, such as a harmonious family life and social discipline, which both Nazism and Fascism incorporated. Therefore, when he became Pope in March 1939, Pacelli's criticism of Nazism was visibly more restrained than that of his predecessor. In September 1938, Pope Pius XI himself had ordered three Jesuits to compose the encyclical *The Unity of the Human Race,* with the purpose of condemning Nazi racism and anti-Semitism more clearly than ever, but the encyclical was never published or used.[4]

The new Pope Pius XII had been papal nuncio in Germany for many years, spoke German fluently, and had a high regard for German music and culture. Although he found the Nazi racial theory repulsive, he considered, even more decisively than Pius XI, that Soviet Communism, not Nazism or Fascism, was the number one enemy of the Church.[5] Right until the last moment, to the last day in August 1939, Pacelli, in vain, broadcast public appeals on the radio and sent a large number of diplomatic messages to the governments of the Third Reich, Poland, Italy, and the western powers, in which he "beseeched them in the name of God" to "persevere in negotiations" and not go to war, saying that "nothing will be lost in peace, but everything could be lost in war."[6] He wanted to remain neutral in the war, but this "balanced" stand was difficult to maintain. In June 1940, he was still sending confidential messages to Hitler, Mussolini, and Churchill, offering himself as a mediator "for a just and honorable peace,"[7] until he realized that no agreement was possible while Hitler was in power in Germany. "The basis of all his activities was a timid indecision that kept increasing, and a highly polished diplomacy in which pondering over every detail seemed to paralyze action," so he earned the epithet of the "diplomaticizing pope," unlike the "temperamental pope," Pius XI.[8]

All the illogical and paradoxical aspects of papal policy achieved expression most strongly in the way in which the Vatican related to the Nazi genocide of the Jews. Right down to the Second Vatican Council (in 1961–1965), the accepted Catholic view was that the historical role of Judaism as a religion had, in fact, ended with the coming of Christ, because religious teaching founded on the Old Testament had become incorporated in the Christian religious idea. In this way, the Jewish religion, which had in its time been charged with guarding the idea of one God and announcing the coming of the Messiah, had, therefore, lost its reason for existence. This was why God was punishing those who persisted in their loyalty to this outdated faith, because they were collectively guilty of the death of Jesus. In practice, this meant that when Jews were persecuted, it was impossible to defend a Jew as the member of a religion, but one could and had to defend a Jew as a human being, because this meant honoring the basic commandments. This was, of course, an extremely ambiguous position, because religion is an essential part of the Jewish identity: how could a person's Jewish religion be separated from his/her complete physical and mental existence?

For a long time, Pius XII remained silent in the face of the growing news about the Nazi persecution and mass killing of Jews. One of the ways in which his silence was accounted for was by saying that he was convinced that publicly censuring the Nazi genocidal policy would not help the Jews. According to this theory, the Nazis would just extend their persecution of Jews to Catholics as well, and the Church, just like the Jews in Germany, Poland, and the rest of occupied Europe, would pay the price for this sort of papal act. In addition, in December 1942, Pacelli explicitly told the *chargé d'affaires* of the American mission in the Vatican that he could not condemn Nazi crimes and at the same time remain silent about those committed by the Bolshevists. Finally, at the end of 1942, the Pope gave in to the growing pressure, and, in his Christmas speech, called on all people of good will to bring society back to the rule of God. "This is our duty" also "to the hundreds of thousands of innocent people who have been killed or were condemned to a slow death, sometimes only because of their race or their origin." The Allies considered the Pope's message mild, roundabout, and cryptic, while Germany and Italy felt that the Pope had stopped pretending to remain neutral and had unambiguously condemned the Nazi crimes. In mid-October 1943, in occupied Rome, about 3,000 Roman Jews found shelter from Nazi deportation in the Vatican, with the Pope's approval, and several hundred more in Roman monasteries and churches. But even then, despite demands from his curia, Pius XII would not publicly condemn the Nazi violence "that was taking place under the walls and before the eyes of the Vatican," which German Ambassador Weizsäcker, in a report of October 28, considered the most favorable circumstance in an otherwise unsuccessful action.[9]

The Catholic Church in Croatia was in an even more sensitive position than the Catholic Church as a whole. Croatian bishops were dissatisfied with the position of the Church in the Kingdom of Yugoslavia. For quite a long time, Archbishop Stepinac accepted Yugoslavia as a state, with the hope that equal religious and national relations could gradually be achieved in it, but he kept experiencing disappointments in this regard. It seems that his disappointment was the most bitter when, in 1937, the Belgrade government, under pressure of the Serbian Orthodox Church, renounced the concordat with the Vatican, which had already been signed. Archbishop Stepinac took this as a sign that, in the Kingdom of Yugoslavia, the Catholic Church would never achieve the status to which it claimed a right.

The Church as a whole traditionally considered that the Croatian national idea and the Catholic religion were closely bound, with complementary and intertwined goals. Because of this, they deemed that the Croatian people, and the Catholic Church as an organization, were bound closely and inseparably. When the ISC was established as the national state of the Croatian people, the Church judged that one of the essential national goals had been accomplished, and that this in itself fulfilled some of the wishes of the Church. In addition, the Ustasha authorities announced that the ISC was a Catholic state, and many people assumed that the Catholic Church had reason to be very pleased.

When mass demonstrations began on March 27, 1941, in Belgrade and other towns, against Yugoslavia joining the Tripartite Pact, and pro-British officers carried out a coup, Archbishop Stepinac was extremely upset. He wrote in his diary: "Taken as a whole, the Croats and the Serbs are two different worlds . . . which will never come together except by a miracle of God. The schism (i.e., Orthodoxy) is the greatest curse of Europe, almost greater than Protestantism. They have no morals, no principles, no truth, no justice, no honesty."[10] Obviously, Stepinac considered religious differences at the foundation of all other differences, and also the main source of trouble in Yugoslavia.

On that very same day, he sent a letter to the clergy of the Zagreb Archbishopric recommending that they "pray to the Lord to bless the young King and help him in his reign, to spare our Croatia and the whole State from the horrors of war, and to enable its people to work for their progress and development in peace, freedom, and justice."[11] Does this contradict what he said about "Orthodoxy as the greatest curse of Europe"? At first glance, yes; in principle, no. To pray for the head of the state, whatever and whoever he is, is an expression of the traditional loyalty of the Catholic Church to the state.

Had he not nursed sympathies for the ISC, Archbishop Stepinac would probably not have been so quick to call on Slavko Kvaternik, starting on April 12. In the meantime, he also blessed the founding of the state. Only four days later, on April 16, the first day after Pavelić's arrival in Zagreb, Stepinac visited him and expressed loyalty to the new regime. On April 28, he sent a letter to his bishops to mark the establishment of the Croatian state, saying that this was "the most momentous event in the life of the Croatian people . . . an ideal dreamed about and wished for from time immemorial," and concluded: "Must we emphasize that the blood has begun to run faster in our veins, that our heart has begun to beat with more life? No reasonable person can censure this . . . because the finger of God incised love for one's own people in human beings and it is God's commandment!"[12] At that time, however, the synagogue in Osijek had already been demolished (April 14), the basic legal provision legalizing the worst kind of political terror had been passed (April 17), as well as several discriminatory legal provisions against Jews and Serbs, and the shameful rabble-rousing campaign in newspapers and on the state radio had already gathered momentum. Everyone could clearly see that the leaders of the newly established state had started off on a path that essentially differed from the ethical heritage of Christianity and a just society. In general, Archbishop Stepinac was obviously enthralled by the fact that the Croatian state had been founded, and considered that it must be given absolute support. At the beginning of June, *Katolički list,* the weekly that presented the views of the Zagreb Archbishopric, wrote that "Providence wanted to reward the Croats' faithfulness to the Church of God . . . by the greatest gift that a people can receive: an independent, sovereign state."[13]

For too long, Archbishop Stepinac considered that all the things that he protested were simply "mistakes," and, in November 1941, when he criticized the stand taken against the Orthodox and spoke about conversion from Orthodoxy to Catholicism, he said that "we do not blame the Government of the ISC for these mistakes . . . We do not want to present them as part of the system, but as acts of rogue elements who were not aware of their great responsibility and of the consequences of their actions."[14] In 1941, *Katolički list* welcomed the banning of some newspapers and "correspondence" columns in them, saying that these were advertisements placed by pimps, a "moral quagmire." It also welcomed the removal of "shameless pictures and statues from Zagreb shops" (these were innocent advertisements with pictures of women in very modest bathing suits), and the "friezes of naked men and women" from some buildings in Zagreb, the product of "Freemason effrontery." It demanded "police intervention to remove various female representations from the street and from public places." It supported Minister Mile Budak when he spoke in September against cursing in public, although they were very well aware that he was the author of the slogan, "Run, curs, across the Drina!" (the Drina river was the border between the ISC and Serbia, and this slogan symbolized the genocidal policy against the Serbs).[15]

Even in May 1943, Archbishop Stepinac repeated some of the contentions of *Katolički list,* saying that "the Croatian Government has not done as much evil as the Serbs claim, and it did a lot of good," that it was resolutely fighting against abortion, that it had abolished Freemasonry, passed ordinances against blasphemy, etc. He also counted among the "good things" done by the Croatian government its "strict ban on all pornographic publications, which were first and foremost published by Jews and Serbs!"[16] These were extremely sweeping statements: was it only Jews and Serbs who published "pornography," which is what they called illustrated magazines such as *Svijet* that came out in Zagreb, and other similar magazines, which had photographs of women in bathing suits and underwear? All the complaints of Archbishop Stepinac to the Ustasha authorities, especially in the early days of the ISC, were more like instructions for corrections within the system. In the letter quoted above, which he wrote at the demand of the Vatican, Stepinac enumerated and very extensively documented everything that the Catholic Church in the ISC had done by May 1943 to help the persecuted Serbs and Jews. However, his overemphasis of some marginal aspects of the Ustasha regime seems like self-justification for remaining silent for too long about the horrendous crimes that overshadowed any potential marginal (and sometimes questionable) positive aspects.

The church leaders, like Archbishop Stepinac himself, despite their satisfaction had some reservations about the regime right from the beginning. They knew that in a regime modeled on the current German or Italian models, the Church was in danger of becoming an instrument of the state, that it enjoyed various privileges on the one hand, but that its freedom was restricted on the other. Totalitarian regimes make the state absolute, and no institution, including the Church, may act outside the strict control of the secular authorities. Stepinac and the Church leaders knew of the difficulties and doubts of the Church in Germany and Italy. The Church interpreted the proclamation of the ISC as a "Catholic state" to be an announcement of the danger that the State might subjugate it.

The Catholic Church was nowhere near unanimous in its interpretation of, and relation to, the war and the conflicting parties. Seventy-five Catholic priests in Croatia and Bosnia and Herzegovina took part in the war on the side of the Partisans: fifty-two of them were Croats and all the rest, except for two, Slovenes. Forty-three priests, including eighteen Croats, were killed as Partisan collaborators, and of the remaining twenty-five, all but three were Slovenes.[17]

Some church people very quickly expressed their disagreement, even their opposition to the regime. Only days after the establishment of the ISC, Canon Pavao Lončar called Pavelić a "spiritual pauper," said that "priests cannot be Ustasha officers," etc. This was a reaction to the more or less hidden intentions of the Ustasha regime to subjugate the Church and use it for its benefit. Someone reported Lončar, and in August 1941 he was tried by the Travelling Summary Court, which sentenced him to death, and then commuted the death sentence to twenty years in prison. Lončar was released from Lepoglava at the end of 1943.[18] "Franjo Richter, a Croatian parish priest in Stubica, near Zagreb, refused to celebrate a ceremonial *Te Deum* in his church for Pavelić on his name day. The Ustashe arrested him, took him straight to Jasenovac, and killed him as soon as he arrived in camp."[19]

At a June 10–12, 1941 meeting in Zagreb, the Franciscan Provincial Ministers decided that no Franciscan may be a member of the Ustasha movement. Miroslav Filipović-Majstorović was expelled from the Franciscan Order in July 1942, after a dispute lasting several months, because he had acted as military chaplain without permission, because of his arbitrary links with the Ustahas, because of participating in units that massacred Serbs, and for assuming the office of one of the commanders of the Jasenovac Camp.[20] Nevertheless, for a long time, many in the Church ignored the worst acts of state terrorism, because they did not consider it important to take a public stand. Some Catholic priests even took active part in the Ustasha movement, as collaborators or even officials, mostly on lower and local levels. Their number is difficult to establish, but it was certainly much greater than the number of those engaged in the war on the Partisan side.[21]

Perhaps most church people would have agreed with what the prominent Franciscan Dominik Mandić wrote from Rome to his Provincial Fra Mijo Troha in Zagreb during the second half of June 1941, but their views remained a subject of private correspondence and conversation: "If you come into contact with the present rulers in the Croatian homeland, advise them to be just and noble in everything they do: to not return evil for evil, not persecute the innocent, not support hatred . . . They must not do anything to others that they would not want others to do to the Croatian people. Advise them especially to avoid religious persecution of the Serbs and the Jews. The Catholic Church has never approved, nor does it approve today, of persecuting people who live in good faith as members of other confessions. Forcible proselytizing among people of other religions also cannot be approved. The external marking of members of other religions must especially be publicly condemned."[22] Mandić then wrote to the Pope and the Croatian Franciscan Provincials, urging that they "caution believers and people in power not to do any injustice to Serbs or Jews," and adding that "Franciscans may not participate in the persecution of Serbs and Jews, or in requisitioning their property, fixed or movable."[23]

On the other hand, in May 1941, the Sarajevo *Katolički tjednik, nepolitički list za katoličku obnovu* (Catholic weekly, a nonpolitical paper for Catholic renewal), which presented the views of the *Križari*,[24] began to publish in installments the book by the Austrian parish priest Gaston Ritter, *Jewry and the Shadows of the Antichrist.* This was a notorious anti-Semitic pamphlet based on the *Protocols.* This appeared in a series of twenty-three installments, until the end of October 1941, by which time many Sarajevan and Bosnian-Hercegovinian Jews were already in Jasenovac.[25] Announcing the series, the editors said that *Katolički tjednik* had always considered that "Jewry, with its secret insurgent goals, was the greatest danger not only for the Catholic Church, but for the entire human race . . . We have already written about the secretly organized world of Jewry as of a negative feature, the most negative in the world."[26] The editors further claimed that "in evaluating the anti-Jewish movement in the world, to get a proper perspective, one must keep several important facts in mind. Undeniably the Jews . . . with their mercantile talents, have managed to impose themselves on states, governments, and rulers, as financiers, as secret masterminds, and sometimes even as open bloodthirsty dictators . . . The Jews, who pushed Europe and the whole world into an abyss—a religious, moral, cultural, and economic abyss—developed an appetite to conquer no less than the whole world. They worked hard at this. The strong ties of a secret organization bound them inexorably . . . This uniformity is manifested primarily as hatred for the Church and Christianity . . ."[27] Thus, it is not surprising that all the anti-Jewish provisions passed by the Ustasha authorities in June were greeted with sympathy, especially that about freeing the development of the national and Aryan culture from Jewish influence.[28]

Katolički tjednik clearly sided with the Nazis: after the successful German parachute landing on Crete, which seemed to have formed a "German-European fortress," the editorial board wrote that "we are one step closer to the goal of a stronger and healthier society."[29] An anti-Bolshevist and anti-Semitic text, which was also published in installments, claimed that the goal was a "Germany without Jews" (or a "Germany freed of Jews"), and that these would be "happy days." Then it wrote with open sympathy that the "text had been written when no one in Germany had even suspected what was in store for the Jews."[30] This was written in July, when it had already become clear "what is in store for the Jews" in the ISC, of which everyone in the ISC was very well aware by the spring of 1942. At that time, *Glasnik Sv. Ante,* a magazine from the central-Bosnian town of Visoko, writing about the anti-Semitic exhibition in Zagreb, said that the Talmud taught "that God had created non-Jews in human form only so that they could serve Jews day and night," and that "throughout history, the Jews 'worked' and 'created,' observing this teaching." However, "even work of this kind had to end one day. National movements that nurtured a fighting spirit discovered that Jews were working among other peoples in this way, and warned these people of the danger that threatened to completely destroy the best and most positive forces among them if such work was allowed to continue. The Croatian people have also settled accounts with Jewish work of this kind and exposed it—under the leadership of the Ustasha movement—in all its dissembling and destructive force, which the Jews have wielded among the Croatian people. The exhibition "The Jew" shows us most clearly the workings of the Jews during the historic struggle of the Croatian people. This is a document of the times, which clearly proves to the Croatian people what the Jews did in Croatia and what their intentions for the future were . . ."[31]

Despite the sympathies that Stepinac had for the new authorities, the first disagreements came about quickly. On April 23, 1941, in the incendiary atmosphere that preceded the passage of the "racial laws," Archbishop Stepinac wrote a letter to Minister of the Interior Andrija Artuković "on the occasion of the announced passage of anti-Jewish laws." He cautioned about "good Catholics who are of the Jewish race and who have converted from the Jewish religion and law and persuasion . . . There are even some among them who have distinguished themselves as good Croatian nationalists. I consider that it would be important, in passing the necessary laws, to take converts of this kind into account."[32] Therefore, the laws are "necessary," but they must not apply to Jewish converts to Catholicism.

Even this very early document shows the ambivalent position of the Church and Stepinac himself—in principle he did not oppose the passage of racial laws that he calls "anti-Jewish," but simply opposes some aspects and their completely rigorous application. The Archbishop protested again a month later, on May 22, in a similar vein. He wrote to Artuković and said that he had been told that "these laws had to be proclaimed for reasons that are beyond our control, but their application in practice will not be cruel. Despite this, we see that new and stricter provisions follow almost every day, which affect the guilty and the innocent equally." It is not clear which Jews the Archbishop considered "guilty." In the same letter, defending Jewish converts to Catholicism, he wrote that "many of them converted long before the persecution of the Jews, therefore, at a time when for them, from the material aspect, conversion was a minus."[33] Did Archbishop Alojzije Stepinac in this way not indirectly accept the claims of anti-Semitic propaganda that the Jews had been privileged in Croatia and interwar Yugoslavia?

This prejudice was probably at the root of Stepinac's arguments in the same letter of May 22, in which he implicitly justified racial ("anti-Jewish") laws, and explicitly agreed that they should be selective and that the procedure should be less harsh: "It is completely obvious that everyone will approve the desire of a State to be governed by the sons of its people, and to remove all harmful influences that corrode the national organism. Everyone will certainly approve the attempt to keep the economy in national hands, to not allow a non-national and anti-national element to amass capital, or foreign elements to decide about the State and the people. But to take away any possibility of existence from members of other peoples or other races, and to brand them with the stamp of shame, this is an issue of humanity and a question of morality. And moral laws do not hold true only for the life of the individual, but also for the state administration."[34] For this reason, Stepinac included in the letter that the "provision about wearing the Jewish insignia . . . should not be implemented" and that he "will be forced to caution Jews of the Catholic faith not to wear those badges, so as not to cause difficulties and create a scene in church."[35] He also added that "those who know say that the racial laws are not implemented with such severity and such speed even in Germany itself" (which in this case is true, because Jewish stars were not introduced in the Reich as obligatory until September 1, 1941). What was probably the essence of Stepinac's stand can be seen in the sentence that in fact sums up the entire above letter: "In connection with the above, I beg you, Mr. Minister, to issue the necessary orders for the Jewish and other similar laws (measures against the Serbs, etc.) to be implemented in such a way as to honor every person and human dignity."[36] It remains completely unclear how Stepinac thought it possible to reconcile discriminatory laws against entire peoples while, at the same time, honoring the "person and dignity" of every member of these groups. Nevertheless, this irreconcilable contradiction—irreconcilable from the aspect of logic, ethics, legal theory, and practical implementation—was often present in Stepinac's letters and other public appearances right up to the end of 1942 or the beginning of 1943. In a letter to Artuković in March 1942, Stepinac repeated the hypothesis about the "privileged" Jews, or about permissible punishment for the "injustice that the Jews had committed," but this time he emphasized that "it is insupportable for people who are innocent as individuals to be persecuted."[37]

The Archbishop's letter of May 22 probably contributed to the law of June 5, 1941, exempting some Jews from wearing the yellow insignia: those who were married to "Aryans," some public figures, church people and the clergy if they were in uniform.[38] Stepinac also protested against the proclamation about "Jews as the disseminators of alarming news" about June 26 [i.e., when Pavelić issued the Extraordinary Legal Decree and Order—see Chapter 18],[39] but this time he did not condemn the regime either, only some of its actions. The Archbishop did not protest the fact that inherently unchristian laws were passed in the name of "higher goals." *Katolički list* did not protest against these laws either, but it did approve the removal of "pornography." These double standards are not easy to explain, even less to justify. In any case, his condemnation of what the Ustasha regime was doing was exceedingly mild, considering the crimes to which it referred.

Nevertheless, misunderstandings and mistrust clearly existed between the Church and the State, and this could not be hidden. In July 1941, the Minister of Justice and Religious Affairs, Mirko Puk, warned Stepinac that Slovene priests posted in Croatia "are almost, without exception, disseminating criminal propaganda against our state." They usually claim that "it will last for two or three months at the most, then it will fail and Yugoslavia will return." From several sources, Puk was informed that some people said "His Excellency Stepinac is saying the same." The minister "does not, of course, believe or consider important the claims concerning your person," but he threatened that "if I receive any more reports of a similar kind, I shall be forced to round up all the Slovene clergy and place them in a concentration camp, and have the summary court try those who were especially conspicuous in making these statements." This was a threat indirectly addressed to the Archbishop himself, and to the entire Church. Both Puk and the heads of the Ustasha regime believed that the Church must be its obedient servant or face the consequences. This, and not just sympathies with the ISC as such, was another reason why Stepinac probably did not dare to protest more forcefully against Ustasha violence and crimes. The situation was rather similar to that of Pope Pius XII. In a diplomatically composed answer, Stepinac rejected the accusations in Puk's letter and wrote that "if anyone is sincerely happy because of the freedom of the Croatian people," it was he.[40]

The Archbishop was right when he wrote in one of his letters (on July 21, 1941) to Poglavnik Pavelić that "almost no one can be found with the nerve to inform you about them [i.e., about the 'inhuman acts against non-Aryans'], so it is all the more so my duty to do it myself."[41] Stepinac, however, did not protest against the passage of racial laws as such. It seems that Bishop Janko Šimrak of Križevci, probably on behalf of Stepinac, interceded with Slavko Kvaternik against passage of the racial laws, but Kvaternik replied, just as other Ustasha officials had done to Stepinac, that nothing could be done because this was a "concession that must be made to the Germans."[42]

In the letter to Pavelić of July 21 mentioned above, in which he protested against the "inhuman and cruel treatment of non-Aryans," simply by using the word "non-Aryan," Archbishop Stepinac in fact accepted the Ustasha's racial terminology. And, furthermore, "I hear from many sources that occasionally non-Aryans are inhumanly and cruelly treated during deportation to transit camps, and in the camps themselves; what is more, that even children, old people, and those who are ill are not spared from treatment of this kind." Even on this occasion, Archbishop Stepinac did not question the deportations as a matter of principle, but pleaded for them to be carried out "humanely": the procedure must be corrected, but its essence is not challenged. Stepinac proposed to Pavelić the introduction of "some particulars to mitigate the procedure: a) for people to be sent to camp in such a way as to allow them to first deal with essentials, to arrange for their most urgent obligations both to their families and their jobs; b) for transport not to be in crowded sealed railway cars, especially to distant places; c) to give internees enough food; d) to provide those who are ill with medical treatment; e) to allow them to receive shipments of the most necessary food, and permit them to correspond with their families."[43]

Archbishop Stepinac interceded for many people and groups, often without success, but many times successfully. At the very beginning of 1942, he wrote to the Vatican State Secretary, Cardinal Luigi Maglione, begging him to intercede with the Italian government to receive 200 children of Jewish origin from Zagreb, ages seven to seventeen, mostly orphans, who were living miserably "because of anti-Semitic laws." The letter of January 20, 1942, from Father Tacchi Venturi to Cardinal Maglione, shows that this diplomatic initiative had no success.[44] Dr. Ladislav Bodnar (1896), a Jew from Vienna who had converted to Catholicism in 1919, was arrested in Zagreb in September 1941 and deported to Jasenovac. The Archbishopric Clerical Office and the Vatican interceded to get Bodnar released from camp and supply him with documents to go to Brazil. The correspondence went on for months, and it seems that no one in the Church knew that Bodnar was already dead by the end of 1941.[45] At the request of Helena Marof, at the end of 1942, Stepinac interceded for Vlatko-Vladimir Rosenberg from Zagreb, but, almost a year later, in September 1943, he received a letter from the Ministry of the Interior saying "we inform you that so far the fate of the above-mentioned could not be established." Rosenberg had been killed in Jasenovac in 1941.[46] The Archbishop also intervened on behalf of Ivan (Hans) Hochsinger, but apparently word reached Jasenovac the day after Hochsinger was killed.[47]

According to Amiel Shomrony, who was unsuccessfully working to have Archbishop Stepinac proclaimed a Righteous Among the Nations, the Archbishop gave Miroslav Šalom Freiberger, as help for poor Jews, "large amounts of money every month . . . Before this, the Jews came to Kaptol (the part of Zagreb where the archbishopric was located) for financial aid; this, however, became dangerous, because whenever the authorities saw Jews gathering in one place, they would pick them up in the street, and there were also people who followed and robbed them."[48] In another place Shomrony claimed that the Archbishop "distributed money every month to refugees from Hitler's lands, at first to those who had converted, then regardless of religion, and finally to the poor Jews of Zagreb."[49]

When the demolition of the synagogue in Praška Street began in October 1941, Archbishop Stepinac, also according to Amiel Shomrony, gave a speech in the cathedral, of which "some people got a written copy": "A House of God, of whatever religion, is holy, and whoever touches it will pay with his life. Both in this world and in the next, he will be punished." The Archbishop added that this had been done "by the Ustashe and their leaders."[50] This was a very strong speech, powerful words that were rather unusual for Stepinac in 1941. They are essentially very different, almost contrary, to his otherwise gentle criticism of the racial laws, and there is no other confirmation of them, except in Shomrony's *Testimonies*. The driving force behind this speech may have been fear for the position of the Catholic Church itself, because if "a house of God of any faith" is touched, that constitutes an attack on every religious community.

In the resolution of the Croatian Bishops' Conference of November 18, 1941, the Catholic bishops "begged the Poglavnik" for the "protection of personal and civil freedom and the return of property into the rightful possession and ownership . . . of Jews, or the descendents of Jews, who are no longer even considered Jews after their religious conversion to the Catholic Church." They also requested that "State authorities not hinder Catholic priests who would, in accordance with their spiritual duties, wish to attend to former Jews, today Catholics, in places of internment and camps, for their spiritual needs."[51] Krišto considers that "the Church's insistence on converts of the Jewish nationality, faith, or race was not the selfish and narrow-minded salvation of 'its' flock, while neglecting non-Catholics. On the contrary, unable to protect innocent Jews, the Church made use of its right to protect Catholics, irrespective of racial or any other affiliation."[52] Unfortunately, this conciliatory tactic was unsuccessful, because most of the converts were not exempt from persecution and the proportion of those killed was almost equal to that of Jews who had kept their religion. Only members of mixed marriages and their descendants were spared to any significant degree. Krišto's way of justifying the stand of the Church and of Archbishop Stepinac himself is historiographically uncritical and unconvincing,[53] especially in light of the fact that relatively more persecuted Jews were saved when high church dignitaries openly, energetically, and in a principled manner opposed this persecution—as in France (especially the Archbishops of Toulouse and Lyon), the Netherlands, Italy, and Denmark, and for a time even in Germany itself.[54] Catholic bishops in Slovakia strongly opposed Nazi demands for extensive deportations and thus saved the lives of many converted Jews. The Orthodox Metropolitan Stefan in Sofia publically protested the impending deportation of Bulgaria's Jews. When, for other reasons, the deportation was suspended, 11,343 Jews from recently annexed portions of Macedonia and Thrace had already been shipped out.[55]

In the winter of 1941–1942, Archbishop Stepinac received some members of the Jewish Community who brought before him a fugitive from Jasenovac, "a man named Hahn, a merchant from Trešnjevka" (the western part of Zagreb), who had lost about twenty kilograms in several months and was severely beaten and wounded. Hahn showed Stepinac his wounds and told him about what was going on in Jasenovac. "The Archbishop's face grew darker and darker until tears started to run down his cheeks," said one of the members of the Jewish Community. When Hahn had finished, Stepinac said: "I have already demanded that Pavelić put an end to these atrocities in the camps, but he kept convincing me that what is being said about the camps is not true. Now, no one will be able to convince me."[56] As for traveling salesman Gustav Hahn (1896), who lived at Tratinska 13, he and his children, Armand and Alice, were later killed in an unknown place.[57] At that time, thanks to the Archbishop's efforts, the well-known Zagreb attorney, vice-president of the Zagreb Jewish Religious Community, and Judaic scholar Lavoslav Šik was temporarily released from Jasenovac.[58]

Stepinac could have obtained firsthand information about Jasenovac at that time: his personal secretary and the secretary of the papal nuncio visited Jasenovac, together with other diplomats and journalists, in February 1942.[59] Obviously, under the influence of everything he had learned, the Archbishop's view of the Jewish—that is, the "racial"—question, in time evolved. When rumors about arrests and deportations again began to spread through Zagreb in March 1942, Archbishop Stepinac wrote to

Artuković and protested the arrests. "It is necessary to prevent irresponsible elements from breaking not only the Christian law of love for one's neighbor, but also the basic natural law of humanity."[60] In October that year, in a well-known sermon, he asked "What, before God, are the races and peoples on earth? It is important to ask ourselves this at a time when class, racial, and ethnic theories have become the primary subject of discussion." He answered as follows: "All the peoples and races were created by God. In reality, there is only one race, God's race . . . Therefore, the Catholic Church has always condemned, and continues to condemn, any injustice and violence committed in the name of class, racial, or ethnic theories."[61] Archbishop Stepinac was more critical in this case, because the issue concerning races was part of religious teaching, and it was the same when he criticized the demolition of the synagogue. In all cases of principle upheld by the entire Church, which even the Ustasha regime would find it difficult to deny, Archbishop Stepinac felt that he could speak more clearly and criticize more directly.

In November 1942, the Archbishop wrote to Minister Puk in connection with the Legal Provision on the Nationalization of Jewish Property, passed on October 30, saying that he had "received some questions from Jews (both converted and not converted) who are in mixed marriages with so-called Aryans, asking what will become of their property."[62] About ten days later, the State Council informed the Archbishop that the issue was being "studied by the Ministry of the State Treasury," which would "draw up a proposal on how to regulate this issue for the State Council." This letter also shows Stepinac's evolution from 1941: he no longer wrote "Aryans" and "non-Aryans," but championed the cause, at least indirectly, of both converted and unconverted Jews.

In the meantime, at the end of February 1942, Archbishop Stepinac received Poglavnik Pavelić, members of the Croatian Parliament, and other guests in St. Mark's Church in Zagreb. He made a short speech to fit the occasion, rich in pathos and formalism, addressing the Poglavnik ("At this time, when that ancient symbol of Croatian statehood, the Croatian Parliament, is moving along the glorious trail from the past, and wishes, together with you, the Head of the ISC, to invoke the blessing of God the Creator upon its work, I, as representative of God's Church, cannot keep silent . . .), and also containing sentences that could be taken as a mild warning to the authorities ("May the Parliament pass laws that are just: where the burdens are equal, may so also be the rights! May it pass laws that are possible, so as not to place on people burdens which they cannot carry").[63] In a situation where he could have expressed much clearer criticism, Stepinac failed to do so. Still, in that same period, he sent Pavelić a letter in which he clearly informed him that the clergy was not allowed to take part in politics, and that he would not allow political activities within the church orders.[64]

In time, Archbishop Stepinac gradually grew increasingly critical of the Ustasha authorities. In February 1943, when seven Catholic priests (Slovenes by nationality), were killed in Jasenovac, Stepinac wrote to Pavelić that "Jasenovac as a whole is a shameful blot on the reputation of the ISC."[65] When the new census of "non-Aryans" was announced in March 1943, the Archbishop sent a very well-substantiated and energetic demand to Pavelić to "protect the most basic right to life of those subjects of the ISC who have, since the time of its establishment, become members of the Catholic Church." He continued by asking "in the name of humanity," somewhat less decisively, "do not allow any other subjects of our state to suffer unjustly."[66] Later, at the sermon for the anniversary of the enthronement of Pope Pius XII, on March 14, 1943, Stepinac said that "we have not remained unaffected by the groans of serious men and the screams of helpless women, threatened in their homes just because they do not conform to the theories of racism. How could we continue to remain silent? . . . The Church can obviously not condone measures that violate basic human rights."[67]

In June 1943, Bishop Petar Čule of Mostar informed Stepinac that the priest Ivo Guberina had given a "threatening and bloodthirsty speech in Mostar. It would have been unpleasant if even the most fanatical lay nationalist had spoken like that . . . our enemies will say that the Church condones that slaughter."[68] After that, Stepinac banned Guberina from "performing any kind of clerical duty, including celebrating mass."[69]

Informing Pope Pius XII about the meeting of the Croatian bishops in November 1941, Archbishop Stepinac began by writing about the "issue of converting the schismatics," and as the second point said that the "episcopate has also discussed the issue of all those who are suffering so much at this time." He also mentioned that they had sent a letter to the head of the state "demanding humane treatment of Jews, if that is still possible given the German presence," and "especially for those who have recently converted and descend from converted parents and ancestors."[70] The Archbishop always felt it important to show the Vatican that he was caring for the Jews, and, in May 1943, he sent "some documents that show how much we have done for the Jews" to Rome, which the Vatican acknowledged.[71]

Quite a lot of what Stepinac and his associates did or tried to do for individual Jews during the war has not been documented, but something can still be learned from the memories of survivors. For example, before the deportations in May 1943, the Švarcenberg and Israel families fled from Kustošija (a western suburb of Zagreb) to Kravarsko (a village some thirty kilometers south of Zagreb) in a car that came for them from Kaptol.[72] Greta Gjanković, a Jewish woman married to the prominent Croatian doctor Professor Gjanković, whose first husband had been Adolf Bresslauer, went to implore Archbishop Stepinac to issue her son, Dan (1925), with a fake birth certificate making it appear that Gjanković, not Bresslauer, was his father; in this way, as the child of a mixed marriage, Dan would be saved. Stepinac did what she asked, and Dan Bresslauer became Dan Gjanković.[73]

The Papal Chancery in Rome very early joined in the attempt to mitigate the Ustasha treatment of Jews, or to save the Jews. In August 1941, the representative of the Italian Jews asked the Vatican State Secretary, Cardinal Maglione, for the Holy See to intercede in favor of the Jews in Croatia, who are being imprisoned and ill-treated "without any reason" (the letter does not mention killings).[74] At the end of November 1941, the Zagreb Jewish Community wrote to a Father Weber in the Vatican to inform the Holy See about "hundreds of men, women and children . . . who are confined in Italy." The Community had been informed that the father was "taking care of them."[75]

From the beginning of the war, the Vatican was very well informed about what was going on in Croatia from various sources: from Jewish circles, from its own diplomacy, and from the Catholic Church in Croatia and other countries (e.g., Slovenia). It was especially aware of how the authorities were treating the Serbs and the Jews. Throughout the war, the Vatican was reserved in its relations with the ISC authorities: it did not recognize the ISC, and it sent a permanent legate to Zagreb but retained diplomatic relations with the royal Yugoslav government in London, thus recognizing Yugoslav continuity.[76] In July 1942, the Apostolic Visitator in the ISC, Giuseppe Ramiro Marcone, wrote to Rome that "in recent months, the Croatian authorities, faced with demands for news about Jews, have maintained an inexplicable silence . . . My secretary finally lodged a complaint, after which he began to receive some answers." The Vatican did not condone the Italian policy of preventing Croatian Jews from passing from the Italian occupation zone in the ISC to territory annexed by Italy on the east Adriatic coast, or to Italy itself, and strongly opposed forcing Croatian Jews who had fled in this manner to "return to Croatia." The

Vatican also demanded better conditions in Kampor Camp on Rab, and the prevention of handing over internees to the Ustashe or the Germans.[77] It instructed its diplomats in Zagreb to intercede with the Ustasha authorities in favor of Jews, which they regularly did,[78] although usually with no success.

The diary of Marcone's secretary, the Benedictine Giuseppe Masucci (1906–1964), which includes his service in Croatia, was posthumously published in Madrid in 1967. Masucci wrote that he "incessantly protested" against the persecution of the Jews. He wrote about Eugen Dido Kvaternik in the worst light, calling him a pathological criminal.[79] Kvaternik told Masucci that, in Croatia, the Jews had committed "300,000 abortions, rapes, and deflorations of young girls, etc." And when almost all of Zagreb was covered with posters in February 1942, ordering all Jews to register with the police, Miroslav Šalom Freiberger asked Masucci to intercede. Masucci went to Kvaternik and it seems that he at least persuaded him to spare Jews in mixed marriages.[80] However, as there were no important arrests and deportations from Zagreb in those months, Masucci's whole story must be viewed with some reservations. Since rumors that the Ustasha authorities would arrest the remaining Jews and hand them over to the Nazis increased over time, during the first days of August 1942, Archbishop Stepinac advised Šalom Freiberger to write to the Pope in Rome and ask him to intercede for the Croatian Jews who were facing deportation.[81] On this occasion, like many times earlier, Marcone and Masucci contacted high Ustasha officials, beginning with Eugen Dido Kvaternik. The success of these negotiations is doubtful, because almost 5,000 Jews were arrested and deported in August 1942, and few were spared, mostly those who were "under protection" or in mixed marriages.[82] As on other occasions, Freiberger thanked the Holy See for its efforts.[83]

The many intercessions by Archbishop Stepinac and via Vatican diplomacy in the spring of 1943, when they tried to save the remaining Zagreb Jews, and especially Stepinac's sermons, in which he condemned the Ustasha crimes more forcefully than ever before, led to a growing general conviction that Archbishop Stepinac was a friend of the Jews and thus an opponent of the regime.[84] Perhaps he also became much more critical because at the end of 1942 or beginning of 1943, the Germans (or the Ustashe) killed his brother, who had worked with the local Partisan detachments in the village of Krašić in the mountain of Žumberak (thirty-five kilometers west of Zagreb) as a member of the National Liberation Committee.[85] When Archbishop Stepinac gave another sermon in October 1943, which could be interpreted as open opposition to Ustasha policy, word about his stance spread further, to various circles and to many European countries. In November, there were rumors in Zagreb that the Archbishop had been arrested.[86]

In March 1944, the Archbishop's secretary, Ivan Šalić, interceded on behalf of eighteen "Jews by race," mostly women and children, caught by the Ustasha army around Otočac and brought to Zagreb (this was a group of internees from Rab: the Schrenger and Kraus families, and others). For the first time, Archbishop Stepinac, directly or indirectly through a subordinate, explicitly interceded with the Ustasha authorities to release Jews regardless of religion, and, if it was not possible to release the adults, the Archbishop's secretary offered that the Zagreb Archbishopric Caritas would at least take over care for the children.[87] The intercession apparently produced no results, because none of these people are on the lists of survivors, and there is credible information that six were killed, including seventeen-year-old Berurija Šrenger, allegedly in Auschwitz, and Zlata and Hinko Šrenger, allegedly in Jasenovac.[88]

There are documents about Catholic Church institutions saving Jewish children: at least two cases are known of the Zagreb archbishopric placing Jewish children in Croatian families in Ludbreg (near Varaždin, ninety kilometers northwest of Zagreb).[89] Quite a few Jewish orphans in Zagreb were placed in Catholic families, baptized, and thus saved, but their number cannot even approximately be ascertained.

In July 1944, Canon Nikola Borić, director of the Archbishopric Records Office, interceded with the Police Directorate for the City of Zagreb for Edo Funk, who was in the Gestapo prison. "It seems that he was imprisoned only because he is a Jew by race. But although he is a Jew by race, he has Aryan rights, so has been wronged. We beg the above, if possible without delay, to issue a certificate about his honorary Aryan rights, on the basis of which he could be released." Borić's intercession had no effect.[90] His behavior was similar to that of the highest church officials: on the one hand, he consistently worked for the salvation of every life, especially that of innocent people, while on the other, he accepted the terminology of the Ustasha regime, and thus indirectly also the arguments on the basis of which Jews were deported.

While it tried to help those who were in danger, the Church nevertheless tried to avoid acts of direct confrontation with the regime. In May 1943, a request arrived from the parish office of Gaćište (about fifteen kilometers east of Virovitica) for Stjepan Hrnčić to marry Ema Šajber, "who is of Jewish nationality," and who had "in 1941 converted to the Catholic religion . . . There is no obstacle to this marriage in canon law." However, the Archbishopric Clerical Office replied that "permission from the Ministry of Justice and Religious Affairs is necessary for a marriage between an Aryan man and a non-Aryan woman."[91]

When the Jewish Community asked the Church to help save the residents of Jewish old people's homes and Jewish children in April 1943, the Zagreb Cathedral Chapter gave permission "for the old people and children to be put up in the deserted stables of the chapter farm," but only on condition that "the state authorities approve."[92]

During the war, Archbishop Stepinac also tried, and sometimes managed, to protect some Serbs and other persecuted people. The Church Caritas found homes for several thousand Serb children who had lost their parents in the spring of 1942 during the Ustasha-German "cleansing actions" in Bosnia. However, for too long, the Archbishop deluded himself that the crimes of the Ustasha regime were only the excesses of irresponsible people in the field, and some conniving individuals in power, not the fruit of a totalitarian ideology and part of a planned state policy. Thus he never completely condemned the Ustasha ideology or regime, nor distanced himself from the ISC. There are many reasons for this, but cowardice was not one of them, because Archbishop Stepinac was a brave man. The Ustashe kept declaring themselves fervent Catholics and Archbishop Stepinac, despite all their "mistakes and sins," considered them part of his flock—Catholics and Croats—who might still be persuaded to stop doing evil. For a long time, he sought to find at least a vestige of good in them, and he found it in the fact that they had banned "pornography" and swearing, and that they prohibited abortions under threat of the death penalty. He never stopped including in their favor the establishment of the ISC, which the Archbishop supported as an idea to the very end. When the Partisans, led by the Communists, appeared and grew stronger, Archbishop Stepinac uncompromisingly saw them as the main enemies. He was always much more open and forceful when condemning Communism and Communist crimes than when he condemned Ustasha crimes and the Ustasha ideology. Between antipathy for Communism and antipathy for the atrocities of the Ustasha ISC, antipathy for Communism was always stronger, because the Archbishop considered that it was possible to improve the Ustasha ISC, but not Communism.[93]

In 1946, Archbishop Stepinac was tried on trumped-up accusations of being a war criminal, the spiritual instigator of the genocidal persecution of the Serb population in the ISC.[94] In books written for the broader public in Yugoslavia in later decades, these accusations were even broadened, and Archbishop Stepinac was stigmatized as the main ideologist of the Ustasha movement and of the genocide of the Serbs, which was, of course, baseless propaganda.[95]

Alojzije Stepinac was a man who faced many dilemmas during a painful time, when it was not easy to find clear answers, and often he did not find them.[96]

In late July 2016, as this English-language edition was headed to press, the Zagreb District Court overturned in its entirety the 1946 guilty verdict handed to Archbishop Alojzije Stepinac.

38

WHO IS RESPONSIBLE?

After the Gestapo implemented some initial anti-Jewish measures in the ISC in April 1941, between May 1941 and the summer of 1942, the Germans stood back and let the Ustasha authorities independently organize and carry out the persecution of the Jews. There is no doubt that the main instigator in this period was the Poglavnik, Dr. Ante Pavelić. As in many less important matters, he also provided the general guidelines for "solving the Jewish question." "It seems that decisions were made *in camera:* in talks between ministers, state secretaries, and representatives of the Ustasha Head Office on the one hand, and, on the other, Dr. Ante Pavelić, who kept a tight rein on everything. He made all political and personnel decisions himself."[1] Although Pavelić usually wanted to give the actions of the Ustasha authorities a semblance of legitimacy, his frequent and extremely incendiary anti-Jewish public statements were the basis for the increasing ruthlessness of his closest associates. The lower ranks of the Ustasha movement and police officials, on the other hand, took Pavelić's excesses as a good indicator that the regime at least tacitly supported any anti-Jewish activity, however cruel.

During investigations in the UDB prison in 1947, Slavko Kvaternik spoke generally about Pavelić and his responsibility for the persecution of the Jews, saying that "Pavelić did not initiate the persecution of the

Jews, it resulted from the demands made by the Germans, although it was the Poglavnik who explained it. He is guilty of permitting it, because he wanted to hush up the fact that his wife was of Jewish origin . . . and, finally, because the Germans knew about his obligations to the Italians and could publicly discredit him at any time if he did not go along."[2] Vladimir Židovec, a more analytical and intelligent witness to these events, considered that Budak's rabble-rousing slogans, such as "Flee, curs, across the Drina!," and Nikšić's statement[3] in May 1941 that "in our revolution, we will wade knee-high in blood," in fact expressed "the spirit and thoughts of Dr. Ante Pavelić, and of the Ustasha movement as he envisioned it, formed it, and brought it to life . . . It is that same spirit that spoke through acts of bloodshed." Židovec thought that this was the only plan that Pavelić brought back with him from emigration when he returned in 1941, the only "plan that had been conceived and prepared in advance." "He did not bring any ideas about the state, about work in it, about people who would be suitable for real constructive work, unless we count his plans about autocracy, Machiavellism, and a policy of manipulation, which ideas in themselves were in fact part of a plan."[4] As the first months of the ISC went by, "the people who criticized what was going on (i.e., political terror, poor choice of people in authority, etc.) usually supposed that all these things were happening without the knowledge of Dr. Pavelić, and looked on him as some kind of a last hope. They thought that many people had managed to worm their way to the top and do various stupid and improper things because Dr. Pavelić knew so little about the people and the circumstances, having spent twelve full years as an émigré."[5] Of course, this was the comforting self-deception of the gullible or the hypocritical fellow-travelers of the regime, the kind of people who are often found in dictatorships. According to Ljubo Miloš, some Ustashe had, while still émigrés on the Lipari Islands, "spoken with Pavelić about how to root out the Serbs in Croatia . . . how they themselves would incite revolts among the Serbs if the Serbs did not revolt of their own accord, so that they would have an excuse to liquidate them."[6] On the basis of his frequent meetings and transactions with Pavelić, General Glaise von Horstenau characterized the Ustasha leader as "insincere, mendacious, and evil."[7]

During postwar investigations, Ante Moškov said that Pavelić had "taken (or sanctioned) a rigid anti-Jewish stand only to gain maximum approval of the Germans, although he had espoused earlier, while an émigré, a completely different stance towards the Jews, at least as far as could be concluded from what he said." Still, added Moškov, "there is no doubt that the anti-Jewish propaganda that had developed in Zagreb before the war was very important for the kind of solution of the Jewish question that Pavelić had in mind. His interests coincided with those of certain financial and economic competitors of the Jews."[8]

Many high-ranking Ustasha officials worked closely with Pavelić in planning and implementing the persecution of the Jews. There is no record of any ISC government member or Ustasha Head Office member opposing any of the anti-Jewish measures as a matter of principle, although attempts were made—sometimes successfully—to tone down some of the measures or to allow exceptions in some cases. Few of these officials decided to resign: in June, Stjepan Vukovac, ISC state secretary and assistant minister of the interior, realized that "Dido Kvaternik and various other important 'bigwigs' were preparing a real war of extermination against the Serbs and the Jews." When the mass arrests and killing began, Vukovac "was retired at his own request" on June 28, as reported by *Hrvatski narod*.[9]

The racial laws of April 30, 1941, were the legal foundation for the genocide of the Jews in the ISC. At his interrogation in September 1945, Dr. Đuro Vranešić claimed that Dr. Milovan Žanić, Minister-President of the Legislative Commission, and Ivan Oršanić, influential Ustasha ideologist in the Banal Palace, permitted him in April 1941 to see the draft of the racial laws which, they said, Pavelić had drawn up himself. Vranešić "got the impression that the laws were too radical" so he advised "using as a model the racial laws in Germany, Italy, and Hungary that already existed, and to interest Professor Boris Zarnik at the Faculty of Medicine in the whole matter, because I knew he worked on racial matters." Žanić and Oršanić were interested in toning down the laws to make it possible to except their wives, who were of Jewish and half-Jewish origin. According to Vranešić, Professor Zarnik reworked and professionally improved the texts with this in mind, and this improved version, in the form of three complementary laws, was handed over to the Ministry of the Interior for further editing, and on April 30 was published as the fundamental laws of the ISC.[10] On April 26, *Hrvatska gruda* published the statement of Minister of Justice Mirko Puk, announcing that "a law about Jews will come out in a day or two,"[11] and on the day when the racial laws were made public, *Novi list* carried an interview with Puk. In answer to the question what had served as a model for the laws, Puk mentioned the German law "because it is the most complete," but "our best legal experts and biologists also took part in the drafting of this important law."[12]

Ante Pavelić, Andrija Artuković, Mile Dumandžić, and Mirko Puk signed the legal provisions on "racial affiliation" and the "protection of Aryan blood and the honor of the Croatian people."[13] In education, newspapers, and scientific and cultural institutions, these laws were put into operation through the Legal Provision on the Protection of the National and Aryan Culture of the Croatian People of June 4, 1941, also signed by Minister Mile Budak in addition to Ante Pavelić and Milovan Žanić.

Many facts show that all the leaders of the Ustasha regime endorsed the passage of the racial laws. At his interrogation in May 1945, Mile Budak said that "all the laws about non-Aryans were written by a committee of experts at the Poglavnik's order; we did not discuss the laws themselves, but we often talked about the material that the laws treated. All the government members were anti-Semitic, a result of our experience that the Jews in Croatia had always carried out an anti-Croatian policy and supported regimes of that kind."[14] In March 1947, Slavko Kvaternik said that "all the government members signed the legal provision on Jews, as did I, and we all considered it absolutely necessary to do so, feeling that we had in some way been forced to pass it."[15] At Slavko Kvaternik's trial in 1947, a witness testified that Kvaternik had been "thrown out" of a government meeting because he had raised his voice against the President of the Legislative Commission, Žanić, in connection with the racial laws. The witness probably wanted to help Kvaternik, but Kvaternik himself did not use this in his defense, so the validity of the statement is doubtful.[16]

While in a Yugoslav prison in 1946–1947, Kvaternik said that the "racial laws" of April 30 were "the first laws passed, which best show the character of currying favor with the allies . . . The formulation of these laws was not as far-reaching as, for example, that of the German laws, because in that case they would have applied to many of the highest Ustasha functionaries, or rather to their wives and families . . . but this made their implementation all the more cruel, for the same reason, because these people wanted to ingratiate themselves with the Germans and show themselves to be even more anti-Semitic than the Germans themselves."[17] When the Legal Provision on the Protection of the National and Aryan Culture of the Croatian People was passed on June 4, as an elaboration of the basic racial laws, a German secret service report subsequently claimed that "Mile Budak edited the law, but at the last moment he decided to put off its passage for several days, during which time it lay on his desk. The law was passed on the initiative of his associates."[18]

The following high-ranking officials also played an important part in the anti-Jewish persecution: Milovan Žanić, President of the "Legislative

Commission" in the Poglavnik's Office, cosignatory of laws and various anti-Jewish provisions; Mirko Puk, Minister of Justice and Religious Affairs, cosignatory of the provision on sending people to camps; Mile Budak, cosignatory of one of the most brutal racial laws; and Andrija Artuković, who issued many anti-Jewish ordinances as Minister of the Interior. Jozo Dumandžić, Minister of Registration, and Lovro Sušić, Minister of the National Economy, were also cosignatories of these laws. During the first months of the ISC, Mile Budak, Mirko Puk, Mladen Lorković, and other prominent Ustashe made many rabble-rousing speeches, which played an important role in creating an atmosphere condoning mass slaughter.[19] The Ustasha top ranks were in complete agreement about the anti-Jewish activities, and there were no significant nuances in their attitude toward the Jews—the later excuses made by some Ustashe and their sympathizers about this or that high Ustasha official "protecting" or "saving Jews" are completely out of place. It is true that almost everyone had "his" Jew, for whom he interceded and who managed to survive to 1945, but they did not react to the killing of thousands of other Jews, and some even readily took part in it. Only after May 1943, after all the "cleansing" and great deportations, did some Ustashe on certain occasions became reticent about persecuting and killing the rest of the Jewish population, on which the Nazis insisted. Based on this, the postwar "second Ustasha émigrés" and revisers of history tried to create the false impression that Jews had generally been "protected" in the ISC.[20]

The main organizer and general administrator of all the anti-Jewish persecution from May 1941 to September 1942 was Eugen Dido Kvaternik, the head of the ISC's Public Order and Security Directorate, and commander of Ustasha Control. As Ante Pavelić's closest associate, a man who enjoyed his greatest confidence from the days of Ustasha emigration until the summer of 1942, Dido Kvaternik discussed and made all major decisions personally with Pavelić practically every day. Pavelić gave him maximum authority and support for everything he did through the two police institutions he directed. He was looked on as the "symbol of Ustasha terror in the ISC."[21]

In May and June 1941, Dido Kvaternik and several of his closest associates went to Germany and talked to some of the leading figures in the Nazi police force.[22] Their actions when they returned to Croatia were a close copy of the German model. In his memoirs, which he titled *Memories and Observations,* Kvaternik emphasized his close cooperation and personal friendship with SS-Sturmbannführer Willy Beissner, the first German police attaché in the ISC, who performed this duty from April 1941 to April 1942. However, later in the text, Kvaternik called Hans Helm, Beissner's successor after April 1942, and Glaise von Horstenau, the German military envoy in Zagreb, his "sworn enemies," thus implying that he did not humble himself before the German representatives.[23] Glaise von Horstenau, on the other hand, considered Dido the "pathological son of the pathological marshal."[24]

During interrogations in 1947, Ljubo Miloš said that Eugen Dido Kvaternik "ordered the creation of the first concentration camps," that "Dido issued the order for mass arrests and the killing of Serbs, Jews, and other citizens, but my conversation with Luburić showed that the order originated with Pavelić."[25] Židovec also considered that the "measures against the Jews, so terrible and cruel . . . were invented and designed by the brain of Dido Kvaternik, a hellish figure."[26] Stjepan Vukovac talked to Židovec about Dido Kvaternik "as about a madman and maniac. He is mesmerized by his insane view of the *revolution* that must be carried out, and he obviously enjoys great powers because he can do as he likes and is, in fact, the real master in the Ministry of the Interior." Židovec himself said that he had never met Kvaternik personally, but that what others said had given him the impression that he was a "clever and intelligent young man, but obviously a maniac." Ante Moškov told Židovec that both he [i.e., Moškov] and "his friends, already in the thirties . . . noticed and were convinced that Dido Kvaternik was not normal, but was insane."[27] For the few writers who, as former émigrés, remained faithful to Pavelić after the fall of the ISC, the main culprit for the crimes committed in the ISC was always Eugen Dido Kvaternik. They called him a "madman," "sadist," "sick criminal," and so on.[28] However, Jere Jareb, who, it seems, had some personal sympathies for Kvaternik, or at least held a more benevolent view, wrote in the afterword to Kvaternik's *Memories and Observations* that "creating Ustasha Defense and camps under the command of Vjekoslav (Maks) Luburić was, in fact, outside the authority of Eugen Kvaternik," because Luburić, and Viktor Tomić, "carried out commands issued directly by Pavelić."[29] In this case, several dozen witnesses convincingly refute Jareb, because they prove from their own experience that, in 1941, Dido Kvaternik issued the main orders for the establishment and organization of all the major Ustasha concentration camps in the ISC, whereas Luburić did not begin to show more of a will of his own until the end of 1941 in Jasenovac, probably because of his direct contacts with Pavelić.

On the other hand, as a postwar émigré, Dido Kvaternik strongly accused Pavelić of having "consciously created and sustained a state of chaos."[30] In September 1958, Kvaternik wrote that it "is a notorious fact, which we cannot deny, that grave offences were also committed by the Croatian side during the last war, which were morally a sin, legally a crime, and politically insane."[31] He admitted that "for seventeen months, the writer of these lines was the pawn of a despot, transmitting his orders."[32] This "despot" was, of course, Pavelić himself, according to Kvaternik the man who caused and directly ordered all the evil committed during the time of the ISC, the main culprit for "the ISC not conducting a policy in the basic Croatian interests, which were set aside because of the criminal instincts of a Quisling and a traitorous despotic state."[33] Still, when writing about the persecution of the Jews, Dido Kvaternik in fact defended and hushed up the crime in which he had personally taken part, and of which he was one of the main initiators and organizers: "Nevertheless, quite a large number of Jews from the territory of Croatia were saved."[34] In a letter to Jere Jareb of April 3, 1960, Kvaternik even claimed: "I do not yet want to write about how many Jews we in the police saved, and in what way. But the number is very great."[35] A more suitable word for Kvaternik to use would have been "spared" instead of "saved." Because who was it that the UNS and Dido Kvaternik had to "save" the Jews from, if not from themselves?

Ante Moškov testified that "Pavelić made very subtle use of the fact that Dido Kvaternik's mother came from a Jewish family (Frank), so that Dido, certainly to show that no *racial* links impacted his behavior, wholeheartedly carried out all Pavelić's instructions and suggestions, and most resolutely, clearly, and publicly emphasized his hatred for every Jew. Because of this conspicuous emphasis . . . many people concluded that Dido acted of his own accord, regardless of Pavelić."[36] Vladimir Židovec, another well-informed witness to these events, saw Kvaternik as "a fanatic of the Ustasha revolution" and "Pavelić's favorite." As was to be expected, and as Pavelić rightly foresaw when he appointed him head of the police, Dido "immediately obeyed without hesitation" Pavelić's order to put the anti-Jewish laws into practice.[37]

However, not everything can be reduced to psychology and the mutual confidence and friendship between Dido and Pavelić. His own statement shows that Eugen Dido Kvaternik realized that the role of police chief would "mean his political death." At the end of the summer 1942, Pavelić forced Kvaternik to resign and emigrate to Slovakia. Kvaternik "raged against Pavelić" and considered himself Pavelić's political victim. He thought that he had been putting Pavelić's ideas into practice, and that once he had realized them, Pavelić had simply discarded him. In 1944, Dido Kvaternik allegedly told Drago Čubelić that "he knew the Jewish opinion of the ideals of the Croatian people and he was aware of the role they had played in Croatian political life during the last decades [meaning that the Jews had very negative opinions about 'the ideals of the Croatian people']. He was especially aware of the lethal danger for the Croatian people from the Serbs . . . He knew that this question *must be solved for the future of the Croatian people and state, and that someone must sacrifice himself and implement these odious but necessary measures!*" Kvaternik said that he had "pushed into the background . . . what will happen to me, knowing that I must now *sacrifice myself for the higher and historic interests of the Croatian people and state.*"[38] This type of self-justification was obviously very widespread among the more intelligent of the direct organizers and commanders of the mass crimes, because Ljubo Miloš spoke to Vladko Maček in Jasenovac in a similar vein, and so did Stjepan Rubinić to Ilija Jakovljević in Stara Gradiška.[39]

Although many people accused him of mostly using that other "informal" system of command, so that his men could behave without restraint when persecuting Jews, it seems that Kvaternik did try to keep things under control. When he considered that some people had gone too far, he acted. On February 9, 1942, Ustasha policemen Stjepan Crnogaj, Henrik Geršik, Branko Randić, and Vladimir Valent were each sentenced to "three years imprisonment in Jasenovac transit work camp" for "abuse of position . . . lack of discipline, roughness, violence, and inhumane treatment while acting in their official capacity."[40] At the same time, in January and February 1942, Ustasha émigrés Nikica Jasinski and Šime Frleta, Ustasha Second Lieutenant Ante Šnjarić, and Ustashe Ivica Baraković, Đuro Mehinac, and Franjo Nemet were in the Ustasha Police prison in Sava Road in Zagreb, under investigation.[41]

It seems that Vjekoslav Luburić's position with Pavelić was similar to Kvaternik's, although his rank in the Ustasha hierarchy was much lower. Ljubo Miloš said that Luburić "reported to Pavelić personally about conditions in the camps and about the Jews interned there." Obviously, Luburić was right in his frequent boasts to many people that he had "permission from the highest authority for everything I do."[42] Miroslav Filipović-Majstorović, the commander of the Jasenovac Camp, said that "only Maks Luburić could order the mass killing of prisoners." He, too, got orders from Luburić "in person or indirectly through Matković, who was his deputy, for the liquidation of Serbs."[43] Many camp survivors and other eyewitnesses testified that Luburić was not only in command in Jasenovac and Stara Gradiška, but that he even carried out cruel killings in person, serving as an example and incentive for other Ustashe. He behaved in the same way in the mass liquidations in Hrvatski Blagaj (forty kilometers south of Karlovac) in May, around Donji Lapac (Lika) in July, and in the villages of north Kordun in December 1941.[44]

Pavelić, Kvaternik, and Luburić were three levels of the genocidal crimes in the ISC: Pavelić was the main instigator, Kvaternik the planner and organizer, and Luburić the primary and cruel executor. As relations between Pavelić and Kvaternik gradually cooled starting in the late fall of 1941, Luburić's role grew more important. With only a short interruption in 1943, Pavelić kept sending him on confidential and delicate missions, and, at the same time, Luburić advanced up the Ustasha hierarchy. He was the person in whom Pavelić had the most confidence, although starting in the summer of 1941, all of Croatia and Bosnia and Herzegovina already knew that Luburić was the organizer and perpetrator of the cruelest measures and atrocities. Pavelić's increasingly close relations with Luburić, and his discarding of the more rational Kvaternik, prove that the Poglavnik had no qualms about cruelty in the implementation of genocide—on the contrary, he favored it. Finally, in his last order on May 5, 1945, Pavelić appointed Luburić commander-in-chief of all the armed forces of the disintegrating ISC.[45]

Pavelić alternately broadened and narrowed down the circle of collaborators he consulted when making important decisions, according to circumstances. Vladimir Košak, certainly the greatest economic and financial expert among the highest Ustasha officials, said that he, as Minister of the State Treasury, was never invited to take part in working out the laws on the nationalization of Jewish property. In his opinion, at that time Pavelić consulted only the "politically strong" ministers such as Andrija Artuković and Dido Kvaternik. Košak bitingly compared Pavelić's political style with the notorious "Italian *omertà*."[46] He also said that Pavelić convened government meetings "most unwillingly."[47]

In this statement, Košak alluded to a kind of dual system of ruling. One line was considered legal and legitimate and was mostly realized by government ministers, the other parallel line was inherently illegal, illegitimate, and, finally, criminal. Mile Budak explained this very precisely. At his interrogation in May 1945, he said that "some Ustasha functionaries, who were responsible directly to the Poglavnik . . . carried out a system of terror irresponsibly and independently of us. I spoke about these persecutions with Glaise von Horstenau, the German general in Croatia, who condemned, as I did, this kind of behavior by these irresponsible elements, such as Dido Kvaternik."[48] Budak very strongly insisted on the dual nature of Ustasha rule: "To any question you ask me about persecution, mass slaughter, torture, and any kind of ill-treatment, and especially about destruction and devastation against people and their property in Croatia, I can only answer the following: there were some people who worked not only parallel with, but against the intentions of all the members of the government, and who were not subject to any ministry. At their own discretion, they did whatever they wanted to, answering to no one except, I suppose, the Poglavnik."[49]

According to some other testimonies, Budak himself, at least partly, belonged to "that other" system, against which he spoke so vehemently. After giving his well-known rabble-rousing speech outdoors on July 13, 1941, in Karlovac, Budak spoke at a party for about fifty chosen guests in the Franciscan monastery. He was "able to speak openly about something that is now more than topical . . . about what will, in fact, happen to the Jews and the Serbs in our state . . . You are intelligent people and I need not spell it all out, it will be easiest to explain things with a story from our Ustasha emigration. It took place once when I was touring Ustasha camps. Conversation turned to the Serbs and the Jews, and to how they were behaving in our homeland, and how to solve this question once we returned home. One of our good Ustashe then said the following to me: 'When we return home, then you, Doctor, will certainly be a minister and represent the authority of the Croatian state. I will be a Croatian soldier and represent the Croatian fighting spirit. What shall we, Croatian soldiers, expect and demand from you, ministers and representatives of the Croatian government? Nothing but the following: when we soldiers are in the field somewhere, acting against the Serbs and the Jews, then you, as representatives of the state, will have to come and see what happened. All we expect is that you will *always come half an hour too late*.' There: that is the whole secret and the answer to your question," concluded Budak, at that moment "unusually elated," and "obviously feeling at home in the mission meted out to him by Providence," said eyewitness Vladimir Židovec. To make sure that the Italian and German military representatives present understood him, so that "none of his ideas are lost to future generations," Budak himself "translated his speech first into Italian, and then into German."[50]

Mile Budak's behavior after the establishment of the ISC will be easier to understand if some facts from his life are considered. He spent a long time as an émigré, but he was not on the Lipari Islands. He experienced a personal tragedy: in April 1940, his wife died under unclear circumstances. "He was persecuted and imprisoned in Yugoslavia . . . Suddenly, his wife was gone, and he still felt young and reborn. There was no more persecution, all of a sudden he achieved high state positions and, in fact, thought himself the most important figure in the new state, and that he was a messenger sent directly by God! This made him become completely unbalanced and he was no longer capable of reasoning in the way of the normal human brain!," said Vladimir Židovec, repeating what he claimed Stjepan Vukovac had told him with "particular contempt."[51]

During the "second emigration" after 1945, even the former radicals in the Ustasha government "avoided in any way they could talking about the measures against the Jews." "They prefer not to talk about this, and if they can manage to avoid doing so, they do," said Židovec.[52] And if they had to say anything about those measures, then they all, those who had remained free and those who had ended up in prison, almost unanimously stressed that the introduction of racial laws and genocide had resulted from "German pressure and demands." Slavko Kvaternik maintained that the first persecution of the Jews took place in Osijek, encouraged and organized by the "aggressive German ethnic minority in Osijek," joined by local elements who wanted to "plunder and lay their hands on Jewish apartments and shops." It is as if these events had surprised the top Ustasha authorities and "rushed" them to enact racial laws.[53] At his trial, Kvaternik said that the policy of the Ustasha regime toward the Jews depended on Pavelić, and his alignment with the opinion of the German Embassy, and that Pavelić "used the Germans as an excuse" for passing the racial laws.[54] Allegedly, when Bishop Janko Šimrak of Križevci intervened with Slavko Kvaternik against the passage of the racial laws, Kvaternik answered that he was not in a position to do anything because it is a "concession that must be made to the Germans."[55]

The Ustashe came to power exclusively by the design of the German occupiers, charted in Hitler's Directive 25 (Weisung 25) of March 27, 1941.[56] They would never have come to power if Hitler, angry because of the coup that brought down the Yugoslav government, a signatory to the Tripartite Pact, had not decided in this that "Yugoslavia must be broken up as soon as possible" and its territory shared out among the Axis Powers. Croatia was to have been the exception with "guarantees of autonomy." Therefore, the ISC cannot be looked on as a sovereign state, a member of the Axis coalition such as Hungary, Rumania, or Bulgaria. It was under a special kind of occupation, in which the German and Italian occupiers did not take over all responsibility, but by dividing the country into their respective spheres of interest they maintained control and kept careful watch that the general political orientation of the ISC never strayed from the ideological and strategic aims of the Axis Powers.

The German Army stationed an *Einsatzgruppe* in Zagreb to supervise the implementation of the genocide of the Jews and propose specific measures to the Ustasha authorities, which the Ustashe were more than willing to carry out. Many officials behaved in this way, and the top leaders set the tone: in early June 1941, Pavelić talked with Minister Ribbentrop, and then with Hitler himself, near Salzburg. Pavelić only hinted to Ribbentrop that the "laws against the Jews" had already entered into force, and that the "Jews will be increasingly pushed aside." It seems that Ribbentrop made no comment on this. In his talks with Hitler, the Jews were not mentioned at all. It seems that both sides were completely clear about the attitude and future proceedings against the Jews, and that neither of them had to persuade the other of what to do and how to act. Other matters were discussed quite exhaustively: for example, the position of the German minority in the ISC, which soon got a privileged status, relations with Italy, etc.[57] There were several reasons for the Ustashe's hurry in the implementation of anti-Jewish measures. Among other things, by persecuting and killing Jews, the Ustashe wanted to show their gratitude to the Germans for bringing them to power, and to allay German suspicions that they were still more closely allied with the Italian Fascists. In June 1941, someone from the German secret services estimated, contrary to other reports, that the government was mostly "anti-German," "Jewish," "under the strong influence of Freemasons and the clergy, mildly anti-Communist." The only person named as a German friend was "Minister Artuković" with his followers, who were, "in any case, rather isolated."[58]

Pavelić and his collaborators often contacted various representatives of the Third Reich. Edmund Veesenmayer, special envoy of the German Foreign Minister, was in Croatia during the crucial weeks of April 1941. He came back several more times (the last at the beginning of 1943) and each time, he and Pavelić discussed important "state matters."[59] Sometimes, very rarely, Nazi advisors came on longer guest visits to ISC institutions. In the matter of "taking over Jewish property," the Ustasha authorities got direct help from Dr. Hermann Dzialas, "Aryanization" expert, who, in 1942, spent three months as advisor at the State Directorate of Economic

Reconstruction at the invitation of Slavko Kvaternik.[60] Often, the German Ambassador in Zagreb, Siegfried Kasche, arranged these contacts.[61] During postwar investigations, in answer to whether he personally or the German leaders had officially opposed the ISC government measures against the Jews and Serbs, Kasche replied that he had "no right to take steps of that kind, nor any order . . . In Jewish questions, I interceded in many individual cases, but not in general."[62] Kasche said that "as regards the Jewish question, it is possible that it was negotiated by Heydrich and Dido Kvaternik [when they met in Berlin in May 1941]," but that he "knows nothing about it."[63] Dido Kvaternik himself told Kasche that the "governmental area in Zagreb will be cleansed of inhabitants inimical to the state, Jews and Serbs." Then, Lorković told him that the "Jewish and Serb population will be marked with yellow and white insignias."[64] Kasche said that "on the one hand, the Croatian measures against the Jewish population surpassed by far what I knew about German measures at that time (interning them, seizing property), and, on the other hand, there were very many honorary Aryans created on the basis of family relations between Ustasha leaders and Jewish families."[65]

The Ustashe later tried to justify themselves by claiming that they did not persecute Jews, that they protected them from the Germans, but these statements are completely without foundation. They might possibly be true only for the beginning of 1943 in some cases, and for the period after May 1943 more generally, when the Nazi services showed greater enthusiasm for persecuting and killing Jews than the Ustashe did. The Germans complained that deportations "are being carried out in a form that creates antipathy against Germany among the Croats," and that, after the deportations in May 1943, some Jews "certainly remained in Zagreb because they had good connections or still had enough assets to ensure protection."[66] But whoever accepts Ustasha justifications of this kind forgets, or would like to forget, that in 1941 and 1942, during the period when the majority of the worst crimes were committed, the Ustasha authorities showed extreme enthusiasm and brutality in the rapid application and implementation of anti-Jewish measures.

The speed with which the Ustashe began to persecute and kill Jews during the first year of the ISC was not only the result of closeness between the Ustashe and the Nazis, and the Ustashe's desire to show that they were close to the Nazis. Another factor was that the Ustashe were drunk with the absolute power that they had gained overnight, and they thought that they could do whatever they liked. This was the reason for the speed in the looting, and the brutality in the genocide. In about the middle of May 1941, State Secretary Veršić said to Vladimir Židovec that "instead of reason prevailing, pure madness is increasingly setting in . . . Things are developing in a fatal, insane, tragic direction."[67] In most cases, the perpetrators of cruelty and brutality of a degree that is difficult to imagine were from among the several hundred Ustasha returnees from emigration. Their rage was at least partly the result of their terrible frustration after seven years of internment on the God-forsaken Lipari Islands north and northwest of Sicily: "No work, constant persecution by the Italians, a black future without any promise ahead, all this led to nervous breakdowns among many of the prisoners, and there was a lot of scheming, dissatisfaction, accusations, expressions of disagreement, and even threats against their Italian guards."[68] Like any group of rigid revolutionaries, these were relatively young people in whom imprisonment, seemingly hopeless for a long time, awoke extreme hatred and dreams of revenge. When they returned to Croatia in 1941, they were angry with everything and everyone, like uncaged beasts.[69] Most of them came from poor village families, often in remote areas where life in itself was cruel. Their behavior and life outlook were far removed from the values of middle-class culture. These people became Pavelić's main support in the implementation of premeditated political and genocidal terror, which was confirmed by Luburić in his statement of November 5, 1941: "Our men and camps were always led by former émigrés. Camp commanders were always émigrés."[70]

All this often led to unprecedented cruelty and sadism: in Jasenovac, the Ustashe even used to kill prisoners by ramming a wooden peg down their throats with their rifle butts.[71] During the public execution of camp foreman (Kapo) Herman Spiller in Jasenovac, an Ustasha shot him in the head with two bullets, but Spiller "continued writhing." Then another Ustasha came up and "slit his throat with a dagger, and then, in front of everyone, licked the bloody knife with his tongue. Later, in front of the administration building, he said: 'Jewish blood gives strength, it is good to take in a little of someone else's blood from time to time!'"[72]

German military, police, and diplomatic representatives never restrained the Ustashe in their anti-Jewish measures, but in 1941 and 1942 they were very often horrified, as Captain Hefner of the intelligence office wrote, by the "criminal atrocities" being implemented.[73]

During postwar interrogations by the UDB and in court trials, most of the high-ranking Ustasha functionaries admitted the criminal character of the Ustasha regime, some even describing it very faithfully and in detail, but they tried to diminish or hide their own role while placing all the blame on Pavelić (Slavko Kvaternik, Budak, Košak, Moškov, Cerovski, Perčević, Servatzy, and others). A certain number of former high ISC dignitaries in the "second emigration," after 1945, took similar positions (the most pronounced example being Eugen Kvaternik). The immediate perpetrators of the mass crimes behaved very differently before the investigators and in court. Some of them admitted everything, probably under police pressure and torture, and described the cruelty of the crimes and their part in them in detail (e.g., Fra Filipović-Majstorović, A. Vrban); others claimed that they knew nothing and had not been there. One of the most exhaustive statements made by a perpetrator was that of Ljubo Miloš, in 1942 commander of the Jasenovac III Camp. His recounting was detailed and precise, accurately admitting his personal guilt but, at the same time, attempting to justify his actions. There were many witnesses against Miloš, so he had no way to wriggle out of it. While in investigative detention in 1947, he described how he had "killed three Jews for the first time; they had made contact with their homes by correspondence, so Luburić ordered me to shoot them. I shot them with a rifle in front of all the other prisoners from the camp work service. Another time, Luburić ordered me to liquidate a Jew who was involved in an affair concerning gold," etc. After the war, Miloš was generally considered one of those most guilty of having committed atrocities in Jasenovac.[74]

Ustasha genocide of the Jews was the result of various factors. Its main masterminds were Pavelić and his most radical followers, who arrived from abroad in April 1941. The brutal activities that started on the very first day created an atmosphere in which crime became possible, justified, and even desirable. In the country itself, there had been some educated extremists, few in number, who had more or less openly announced and indirectly set the stage for what was to happen. Both groups had the clear intention of establishing a totalitarian state, organized on the models of Nazi Germany and Fascist Italy, ethnically as "pure" as possible, so racial laws and the mass killing of Jews were a logical part of this program. Some high-ranking Ustashe did not at first suspect that mass murder would be committed against the Jews, but the violent policy that began to be implemented from the first day must have opened their eyes very quickly, certainly within several weeks. As part of the top Ustasha leadership, they must have been aware that they were assuming at least indirect responsibility. The mass killings of Jews was public—proclamations about shooting Jewish hostages were posted on walls, deportations to camps and "moving out" or evicting people from apartments took place before people's eyes. At the lower administrative echelons of the Ustasha movement and government, many officials and members, realizing the criminal nature of the regime, distanced themselves from it and either resigned their position or terminated their membership in the Ustasha movement. At the higher levels of the central government, there were very few such cases (such as the resignation of Assistant Minister of the Interior Stjepan Vukovac in June 1941).

The Ustashe planned for the ISC to be created as a "pure Croatian living space" that would enable the existence of a "pure Croatian nation." A precondition for this was to "cleanse it" of Serbs and Jews, who were proclaimed the "greatest enemies of the Croatian people," so "there is no place for them in Croatia." They tried to give the whole system a character of legality, starting with orchestrated political propaganda in the press, on the radio, and in the speeches of Ustasha officials, right up to creating a special legal framework, which was criminal in character, and corresponding institutions.[75] Soon after the establishment of the ISC, these activities, together with organized procedures based on them, finally led to mass terror as an integral part of state policy and its system. It is not completely clear whether the genocide of the Jews happened because the Ustashe were inherently anti-Semitic, or whether they became anti-Semitic by consistently conceptualizing and realizing the idea that Jews, as a foreign element, "have no place in Croatia." It is true that, during the first half of the thirties Ustasha ideology saw as its main opponent the Belgrade regime, and in the Serbs, a "disruptive factor." But the speed and "good organization" of the Jewish genocide, the systematic nature of the plunder, deportation to camps, and killings—when compared with the mass killing of Serbs in their homes—support the view that the genocide of the Serbs was much more improvised, founded on the basest of feelings, something visceral. On the contrary, the genocide of the Jews was much more cold-blooded, and its most obvious facet was a desire for unlimited plunder. The example of the Third Reich, and the presence of its representatives on ISC territory, had a significant effect on anti-Jewish activities. In other Third Reich-allied countries, which had a greater or lesser degree of autonomy, there was also a strong Nazi presence to influence their behavior toward the Jews (in Italy, Hungary, Romania, Bulgaria, Slovakia, and the unoccupied part of France). All these governments independently introduced various anti-Jewish measures, some of them very rigorous (e.g., Romania, Slovakia), but when the Nazis demanded the deportation of Jews to SS death camps, these governments refused, some a little later (Slovakia), some by making alternate arrangements (Bulgaria), and some adamantly and right to the end of the war (Finland, Denmark, Italy). Only the Ustasha authorities in the ISC did not resist at all; on the contrary, for a long time they carried out mass anti-Jewish actions on their own initiative. Only during the last phase did they become more passive, to some degree, but still cooperated with the Nazis to the very end.

It must always be borne in mind, however, that at least some of the Jews from ISC territory, more than twenty percent, managed to save themselves in various ways, that the Ustasha crimes against the Serbs were much more massive, and those against the Roma even crueler and more radical than against the Jews.

39

REVISIONISM IN CROATIA

The Case of Franjo Tuđman

In the last decade of the twentieth century, Croatian political life, historiography, journalism, the media, school textbooks, and public life in general were very strongly influenced by attempts to deny or at least to tone down and hush up some uncontested facts about the Ustasha-governed Independent State of Croatia during the time of the Second World War. This was a specifically Croatian variant of revisionism.[1]

Revisionism appeared in Croatia in 1989–1990 as a belated historiographic view and a deviant sociopolitical approach. In contrast to what was usual in Western countries, the new post-1990 political authorities in Croatia tolerated and encouraged it, and, to some degree, even incorporated it in their political program. It was characterized by and founded on fetishism of the state and an obsession with the idea of Croatian statehood. Everything that had, throughout history, acted in the direction of Croatian state independence was regarded in the most positive light and uncritically overemphasized, whereas any weakness or culpability was exonerated or at least minimized. Revisionists of this kind even went to the lengths of suppressing and avoiding facts, in both directions, and sometimes went as far as outright fabrication and lies. In this context, the Ustashe's Independent State of Croatia suddenly appeared in a relatively positive light, despite its Nazi-Fascist foundations, its unreserved political and military support of historic Evil, and the genocide and other crimes committed under its wing. On the other hand, the weaknesses and culpability of both Yugoslav states, and especially crimes committed in their name, were shown with such absolute stringency and so widely generalized that they became arguments for an unyielding nationalistic policy and, if possible, something to use as justification or at least qualification for Ustasha crimes.

In relation to the Jews, Croatian revisionists developed several theses, most of whose variants were based on manipulating facts or on outright lies. It is true, they said, that the ISC had passed racial laws under Nazi pressure, but these laws had not been implemented; Jasenovac was allegedly not a death camp, but only a work camp and penitentiary to which only legally convicted opponents of the regime were sent; in the ISC, claimed the revisionists, the greatest number of Jews were saved, proportionately, of all the countries in Europe; the Ustasha movement had allegedly never been anti-Semitic. The lies went so far as to cast doubt on whether there had ever been any genocide of Jews in the ISC at all: the Report of the Commission for Establishing War and Post-War Crimes, founded by the Croatian Parliament, shows that, after seven and a half years of work (from February 1992 to September 1999), this commission had managed to establish that only 331 Jews by religion and 293 Jews by nationality had been "war victims." The section about Jasenovac mentions 2,238 victims, but gives neither their religion nor their nationality.[2]

However, historians and publicists have established that over 30,000 Jews were killed during the genocide carried out by the ISC from 1941 to 1945, and only between 8,000 and 9,000 survived the war. Only 5,000 of 25,000 Croatian Jews survived the war. In other words, 76 percent and 80 percent of the Jewish communities in what are today Croatia and Bosnia and Herzegovina were killed.

There are many reasons for Croatian revisionism, but three are basic.

First, during the forty-five years of Communism, the issue of Ustasha rule and the ISC was very rarely addressed in an analytically sane manner. The approach was usually generalized with *a priori* evaluations that were often exaggerated and expressed in boring propagandistic phraseology. At the same time, there was the strictest embargo on any mention of Partisan and Communist war and postwar crimes. When political and social democratization at the end of the eighties made this possible, there was an eruption in the other extreme. The media reveled in sensationally exposing Partisan and Communist crimes, which were used as material for xenophobic and political propaganda and incitement, while Ustasha crimes were at the same time shrouded in an artificial fog of qualifications, justification, and silence.

Second, Croatian revisionist historiographers are usually not motivated by scholarly research into the more recent past, but by political goals. At the very least it may be said that they approach their work with political prejudice in line with the ruling policy in 1990–1999. As a rule, their political outlook is right-wing or extremely right-wing, and one of its basic characteristics is the avoidance of dealing fittingly with crimes committed by the Ustasha authorities during the ISC. There is also the influence of extremist Croatian political émigrés who never broke off with the Ustasha movement and ideology. The party that came to power in 1990—the Croatian Democratic Union (HDZ) under the leadership of Franjo Tuđman—proclaimed the "reconciliation of Ustashe and Partisans," because one of the foundations of their political program was to overcome any division among Croats. It was therefore necessary to dissociate the Ustasha movement from the odium of having been a faithful Nazi-Fascist ally and the perpetrator of the worst kind of genocide and crimes against the civilian population during the Second World War, and to provide the Ustashe with at least some kind of legitimacy for participating in Croatian development in the predominantly democratic European environment. This was shown to be impossible without radically revising history and denying or faking facts.[3]

And third, Croatian revisionist historiography was partly a reaction to the escalation of Serbian nationalism and revisionist historiography in the eighties. A reinterpretation of history, different from the ruling dogma, provided one of the main arguments to underpin the claim that the Socialist Republic of Serbia, and the Serbs in general, had been at a disadvantage in Yugoslavia. The new approach was a form of mystification that accentuated the cult of self-sacrifice and obsession with the past. It was based on an approach that the writer Dobrica Ćosić (who in the nineties was president of Yugoslavia) had already begun to formulate in the late sixties and had continued to develop: "In today's world, the Serbian nation is probably best known for their great sacrifice and suffering for freedom, which is the ideological substance of Serbian collective spirituality and ethics."[4]

Interest in previously forbidden subjects arose in Serbia and among the Serbs, too. One such subject was the Chetnik movement, the negative image of which, based on Communist historiography, the Serbs wanted to reinterpret. In September 1986, the Belgrade daily *Večernje novosti*[5] published the unfinished text of a document called the "Memorandum," written by the Serbian Academy of Sciences and Arts. The Serbian establishment for the most part reacted unfavorably to this text, but the authority of its authors and the Memorandum's nationalistic charge overpowered tepid official criticism. The document began by analyzing the Yugoslav crisis in detail and then outlined what was, in fact, the national program for a Greater Serbia. It openly accused Tito of willfully weakening Serbia, it spoke about nationalism that "came from above," alleging that other Yugoslav nations were developing their ethnic identities with the blessing of "higher circles," but that the Serbian nation was forbidden to do so. It called all the others "anti-Serbs" because they supported or tolerated Albanian protests in Kosovo. It claimed that a disgraceful program of assimilation was being implemented in Croatia with the final goal of Croatizing the Serbs. The basic idea underlying the Memorandum was that the Serbian nation was a kind of primary entity within Yugoslavia with special rights that surpassed all the usual political and geographical divisions. "The integration of the Serbian nation and their culture in all of Yugoslavia is essential for the survival of that nation." It recommended strengthening the Yugoslav federation, but, from the perspective of the nineties, the wish for "integration" may also be interpreted in a different way, i.e., the desire to create a Serbian state in all areas inhabited by Serbs.

At the same time, by no means inadvertently, another Belgrade paper published an article by the historian Vasilije Krestić, university professor and member of the Belgrade academy, entitled "Concerning the Origins of Genocide Against the Serbs in the ISC." He was the first to give a complete formulation of what is called the genocidal nature of the Croats: "It is quite certain that the origin of genocidal acts against the Serbs in Croatia should be sought . . . in the sixteenth and seventeenth centuries, when the Serbs began to settle Croatian lands."[6] He then gave many examples of Croatian-Serbian disputes in Croatia during the second half of the nineteenth and in the early twentieth century, always blaming the Croats and imputing a Croatian wish to destroy the Serbs. Serbian authors who belonged to this movement considered that the very great number of Serbs killed by the Ustashe in 1941–1945 made the Croats collectively guilty, and that the Croatian nation was genocidal in character. These efforts to prove the genocidal nature of the Croats focused on the camp in Jasenovac. In 1946, it was claimed that 46,000 people had been killed there. In following decades, estimates about the number of victims grew, and numbers of 600,000–700,000 were even officially given, but a very exhaustive analysis in the sixties of the victims of Jasenovac and Stara Gradiška could not bring more than 59,000 names to light. If victims whose names could not be found were added to these, this research would bring us closer to establishing the real number of victims. However, these results were not made available to the public because they differed from the generally accepted opinion. Scrupulous demographic and historical analysis shows that about 83,000 people were killed in Jasenovac.[7]

Expanding the already inflated numbers, they claimed that 700,000 Serbs alone had been killed. One anthropologist stated that "a minimum of 700,000 victims were buried in the area of Jasenovac and Gradina."[8] In February 1990, the prominent Serbian politician Vuk Drašković, leader of the Serbian Renewal Movement (Srpski pokret obnove, SPO), stated that Jasenovac was "forty times bigger then Mauthausen."[9] The number of victims subsequently rose to a million, then it was claimed that it would be "very difficult to deny that more than 1,110,929 men, women and children were killed in Jasenovac."[10] It was concluded that "it will never be possible to discover" the exact number of victims.

As the eighties drew to a close, incendiary articles in the Serbian press increased in number. Various journalists used the Memorandum as a starting point to try to prove, on the basis of data taken out of context, exaggerated, distorted, and even fabricated, that the Serbs had been "cheated," "short-changed," "killed," "destroyed even after the genocide," and, finally, that they were eternal winners in war and losers in peace. All this led to theories about a worldwide anti-Serb conspiracy.

This "newly composed history" might have remained no more than a specific cultural phenomenon had the passage of time not shown the politically volatile nature of these "scholarly" evaluations, especially after Slobodan Milošević came to power in 1987. A year or two later, they began to be used to justify the wars of conquest started by Serbia, Montenegro, the Yugoslav National Army, and some of the Serbs in Croatia and Bosnia and Herzegovina in 1991–1993. The repetition of such views had undertones of menace, the claim being that the Serbs deserved the greatest credit for the existence of Yugoslavia but that Yugoslavia had treated them unjustly. The Serbs had allegedly liberated all the other Yugoslav peoples, and what they had gotten in return was exploitation, genocide, and the break-up of Serbia. In Serbia, the conviction grew that whatever they did to "pay themselves back" was justified. Vindictive rage for 1941, the year "that had never been repaid," began to awaken.[11]

Franjo Tuđman was the key person in Croatian revisionist historiography. His historical writing was extensive and covered a relatively wide range of subjects, his ambition being to provide a broad historical synthesis, and he was well acquainted with facts about some parts of Croatian political history. His book *Bespuća povijesne zbiljnosti* (*Horrors of War*), published in 1989, lies at the very foundation of Croatian revisionism. Much of the text airs personal quarrels and provides pedantic political and gossipy disputes, but the book is dominated by two really important themes: an analysis of mass violence and crimes committed in the name of religion, nation, or state throughout history (for which Tuđman coined the rather suitable new word *zlosilje,* a combination of *zlo* [evil] and *nasilje* [violence]), and contesting the "Jasenovac myth" in connection with implications about the genocidal nature of the Croatian people.

In his broad analysis of *zlosilje,* Tuđman often gets entangled in contradictions: he "condemns genocidal acts and their perpetrators in general," yet shows excessive understanding and resigned acceptance of such atrocities because "violence, hatred, crime, and revenge are indivisible, a composite part of the individual and the nation as the highest form of human community." Thus, he draws conclusions that come close to directly justifying crimes of *zlosilje.* "When a movement or nation, a state or an alliance of states, a religion or ideology, is faced with an adversary which it considers a threat to its survival, or the main obstacle to its predominance, it will do everything and use any means to overcome and even destroy this adversary if it cannot bend him to its will in any other way."[12] Tuđman is aware of how contradictory his views about such crimes are and he tries to resolve them, but in so doing he creates new problems. For Tuđman, "genocidal acts and changes" that are "caused by a long history of inter-ethnic conflict that is difficult to reconcile . . . always have dual consequences. On the one hand, they inevitably deepen historic rifts, fan inter-ethnic hatred, and encourage the desire for revenge . . . On the other, they lead to ethnic homogenization within a nation, to greater balance between ethnic composition and state borders, and this may have positive effects on future development because it decreases reasons for new violence and grounds for new clashes and international turmoil."[13] In the light of some of Tuđman's later political moves and his behavior in some situations, sentences of this kind, rather thickly scattered throughout the *Horrors of War,* do not sound benign. At the very least, they indicate that he conceptually lagged behind the spiritual and political approach of the modern world to which he wanted to belong. They show that he had no understanding at all of modern European ideas about where a better life for all nations is sought, in going beyond "inter-ethnic conflict that is difficult to reconcile," i.e., ideas which totally reject, and vehemently condemn, finding any kind of justification for, or positive "consequences" from, violent "genocidal acts" committed in the name of such "inter-ethnic conflict."

To provide arguments for his thesis that nations have suffered from and inflicted genocide on other nations since biblical times, and that this is the inherent destiny of nations, Tuđman often uses the example of the Jews. Inclined to generalization and poorly thought-out parallels, he easily conflates the Nazi Holocaust and Israeli violence toward Palestinians, "What can this small step from Nazi-Fascism to Judeo-Nazism teach us?!"[14] There are some eighty pages about Jews in the *Horrors of War*, with too many misquotations of sources that Tuđman obviously did not know, and on the basis of which he drew superficial and dubious conclusions. He already showed his ignorance of source material in the very beginning when he misunderstood, mistranslated, and misinterpreted the basic Jewish understanding of the Holocaust—the symbolic word "Shoah."[15]

Tuđman's *Horrors of War* does much to refute the myth about 700,000 victims in Jasenovac and the genocidal nature of the Croats, but in places he goes to the other extreme. His unilateral choice of data unacceptably reduces to a bare minimum the number of total victims, especially Serbs, claiming that "in fact only several thousand (probably 3,000–4,000) prisoners of the Jasenovac camp were killed, mostly Gypsies [Roma], followed by Jews and Serbs, and also Croats."[16] He uses a strange "distribution of guilt" to indirectly decrease Ustasha responsibility. In this way he suddenly shows the Jews, except as Jasenovac victims, also as co-culprits in the crimes.

On pages 316–20 of the first Croatian edition of the *Horrors of War*, Tuđman describes the behavior and role of Jews in the Jasenovac camp. His choice of sources is completely one-sided and he relies exclusively on the evidence of three released Jasenovac prisoners who said that the Jews had generally held a privileged position in the camp, that the "camp administration was run by Jews (and) they were the inner authority in the camp," that there were "links between the camp administration and the Ustasha administration," that Jewish camp officials had "participated in the killing" and "were greatly responsible for 'selection,' i.e., for singling out prisoners for 'liquidation' and partly even its implementation." They claimed that in Jasenovac Jews had participated in the liquidation of Roma, and that the "organization of liquidating (Gypsies) in Gradina was also entrusted to a group of Jews"; the "Serbs, in addition to being killed by the Ustashe, were also killed by the Jews," who "constantly and skillfully intrigued against the Serbs." In the introduction, Tuđman says that these claims by the three alleged witnesses "give a rather faithful picture." He then quotes an ugly generalization, which he attributes to Vojislav Prnjatović, whom he considers the main witness, "A Jew remains a Jew, even in Jasenovac Camp. In the camp, they retained all their faults, which under such conditions became even more obvious. Their main characteristics were selfishness, cunning, no solidarity, stinginess, slyness, and informing on their fellow prisoners." Only here and nowhere else on four pages covered with quotations of this kind does Tuđman distance himself somewhat, in one single sentence, which is in itself not unambivalent: "This claim by Prnjatović seems excessive, we might say it shows an anti-Semitic stand, but some other witnesses said similar things, too."

These pages of the *Horrors of War* (316–20) are an extreme example of Tuđman's revisionism, and they are also very characteristic of revisionist historiography in general: First, the author starts from an advance thesis, which is usually politically inspired, and then looks for and selects arguments to substantiate it. Second, sources and arguments that uphold the advance thesis are not verified but are taken as they stand. Third, sources and arguments that refute the advance thesis, even if they are convincing and numerically predominant, are systematically ignored and concealed, and are mentioned only if it is possible to challenge them. Fourth, individual cases and examples are indiscriminately used for arbitrary generalizations about large groups of people, even entire nations. Fifth, revisionist historiographers do not even shrink from falsification.

Including fabrication, all five components of revisionist historiography can be found in Tuđman's characterization of Jews and Jewish behavior in Jasenovac. No one has ever yet written about this aspect of the *Horrors of War,* perhaps no one has ever yet noticed it, so we will give detailed arguments to substantiate it.

Vojislav Prnjatović's statement, which Tuđman refers to most often, is probably a fake, and Prnjatović quite certainly did not write its most sensitive parts. If he signed it, which he probably did not, then he did so under extreme pressure.

On March 30, 1942, Prnjatović and twelve more Serbian prisoners released from Jasenovac were deported from the ISC and arrived in Belgrade on the following day. This was the first group of prisoners released under an agreement signed between the Serbian collaborationist government of Milan Nedić, the ISC government, and the Germans.[17] On April 9, 1942, Prnjatović made an exhaustive statement before the Commissariat for Refugees and Displaced Persons of Nedić's quisling government in Belgrade, in which he gave a detailed and, it seems, very objective description of general conditions and some events in Jasenovac Camp. In the statement, there is not a single word or fact that would throw a bad light on the behavior of the Jewish prisoners.[18] Between the 9th and 13th of April 1942, the other twelve former Jasenovac prisoners, who had arrived in Belgrade together with Prnjatović, also made statements before the Commissariat. Antun Miletić's collection of documents, *Jasenovac Concentration Camp,* quotes the statements of the twelve former prisoners on forty-two pages.[19] Again, they say nothing against the Jewish prisoners in Jasenovac. On the contrary, in many places they speak of how the Jews suffered together with the Serbs, and in some places they mention their solidarity with, and the help they offered, their Serbian fellow-prisoners.[20]

However, two days later, on April 15, everything suddenly changed. Nedić's collaborationist government was in contact with the administrative headquarters of the authorized German commander for Serbia and was trying to persuade the Germans to help Serbian prisoners in Ustasha camps in the ISC in the name of "humanity and mercy."[21] The statements of the former prisoners were being used as arguments. Someone in the Nedić administration probably thought that the arguments would hold more weight with the Nazis if they were peppered with anti-Semitism. Thus, all thirteen former Jasenovac prisoners, who had made statements between April 9 and 13, were summoned to the Commissariat to make additional statements, this time only about Jews. Twelve of them, all except Prnjatović, signed a supplementary record on April 15.[22] It is not clear whether Prnjatović refused to sign or whether he did not even answer the summons to appear before the Commissariat. The record signed by the twelve former inmates begins by stating "the fact that from the very beginning, the Ustashe had been . . . more tolerant of the Jews than of the Serbs." It goes on to claim that "the Jews make maximum use of the positions they hold in the camp administration to make things as easy as possible for themselves and their fellow Jews, often to the detriment of us Serbs," and that "there were even Jews who helped the Ustashe in their many crimes against the Serbs." These claims are substantiated by two cases when Jewish group leaders in the electrical workshop and on a farm favored Jews over Serbs, a case when "a Jew known as Boris, and whose surname we do not know," reported to the Ustashe that the Serb Joco Čolaković had some money, which was against regulations, and, finally, the description of how "a Jew that everyone knew as 'the Bulgarian,' and whose surname was Hason," and an Ustasha, who were both drunk, joined in the cruel murder of a young Serbian man.

All this was obviously not anti-Jewish enough. Thus, someone subsequently put together a much more exhaustive *Report on the Organization, Work, and Life in Jasenovac Concentration Camp* and signed it in the name of Vojislav Prnjatović, or forced Prnjatović to sign it.[23] The report has twelve sections, one of which is entitled "Jews."[24] This section contains extremely abusive generalizations about Jews, among others that "hardly any of them are clean and tidy" and that "they are a hotbed and source of lice and dirt," so that their death rate is greater than that of the Serbs. There is also the general conclusion, quoted in the *Horrors of War* in its entirety, that "The Jew remains a Jew, even in Jasenovac Camp," etc.[25]

This *Report,* allegedly by Prnjatović, is not credible for several reasons: First, important parts of it do not correspond with Vojislav Prnjatović's earlier statement and with the statements of the twelve other former Jasenovac prisoners, made between April 9 and 13, 1942. Second, all the other reports and their signatures, made by former Jasenovac prisoners in the Commissariat for Refugees and Displaced Persons before and after this one, are properly certified, but this *Report* is not. Third, the term *Židov* is used for Jew in eighteen places in the Report, never *Jevrej.* Prnjatović was a Serb born in 1904 in Sarajevo, who grew up and lived in Sarajevo where Serbs (as in Belgrade) exclusively used the term *Jevrej* and never *Židov.* In his statement of April 9, 1942, Prnjatović only spoke about *Jevreji,* not once about *Židovi.* Why should he, several days later, change the vocabulary he had used since his childhood? It is much more probable that the Report, or at least the part about the Jews, was written by someone else. Fourth, in Jasenovac, Prnjatović was friendly with Sarajevo Jews. One of the most reliable witnesses, Albert Maestro of Sarajevo, wrote his memoirs in 1945; in them he called Prnjatović a "friend" and mentioned him as a possible witness for some details.[26] Finally, the fifth argument probably speaks for itself: Prnjatović was released from Jasenovac on March 30 and arrived in Belgrade the following day, as he said in his earlier statement and in one place in the Report. However, the bottom the Report is dated "March 11, 1942, Belgrade."[27] On March 11, Prnjatović was still in Jasenovac. Until the outbreak of the war, he had been secretary of the Chamber of Commerce in Sarajevo, and it is quite unbelievable that this kind of man would have made such a serious mistake in dating a document of this nature.

Tuđman noticed this contradiction in dates but he did not insist on it, he just mentioned it in one sentence in a footnote: "It is a pity that when he was dealing with the documents, Miletić did not try to explain the obvious discrepancy in dates."[28] There is not a breath of doubt about the document itself, which is obviously not credible and is at least partly faked. Tuđman uncritically took over a problematic document and, without properly distancing himself, presented it as the main indicator for the behavior of Jews in Jasenovac, which is completely in keeping with revisionist historiography.

For a deeper analysis of the fakes that Nedić's Commissariat for Refugees and Displaced Persons produced, we need insight into the signed originals and other documents from this commissariat. At present, these are not accessible to us, but we will make an effort to find an occasion to study them in the future.

The second of Tuđman's three sources is one item from the statement of Branko Popović, one of the first thirteen Serbian prisoners freed from Jasenovac. Allegedly, he had seen a Jew whom they called "the Bulgarian" participate in the cruel murder of a young Serbian man, and this was later included in the supplementary report with twelve signatures, quoted above, made up on April 15, 1942, in the Commissariat for Refugees and Displaced Persons of Nedić's Serbian government.

The third source for Tuđman's description of the behavior of Jews in Jasenovac is the book of memoirs by the controversial politician and apologist Ante Ciliga (1898–1992), *Through Europe Alone during the War (1939–1945)*. The subject of Jews obsessed Ciliga: almost a quarter of this 580-page-long book about the author's unusual odyssey through war-torn Europe is devoted to Jews and Jewry. On two pages, Tuđman passed on some of Ciliga's views founded on observing Jews in Stara Gradiška (part of the Jasenovac concentration camp complex) and in Jasenovac, where Ciliga had been imprisoned from December 1941 to December 1942.[29] Among other things, Tuđman quoted Ciliga's words that the Jews in Jasenovac were under the influence of Moses's teaching "that, as the chosen people, they were allowed things that nobody else was allowed," so other people envied and hated them, but in fact they are "the unhappiest people on earth . . . victims of their own pretensions and those of others," and they caused their tragedies themselves. "Moses's most extreme commandment . . . God commands you to exterminate others and take their place, because you are the chosen people" is always alive in Jews, it is the root of their "ruthless and overbearing self-assertion" which tells them "you are killing others to save yourselves and your group." Thus, the Jews in Jasenovac, said Tuđman quoting Ciliga, "took the initiative in preparing and provoking not only the individual but also the mass slaughters of non-Jews, Communists, Partisans, and Serbs."

Tuđman did not express any reservations about these and similar claims, but he probably did realize how absurd they were. He refrained from quoting Ciliga's even more fantastic hallucinations, which no one but he out of thousands of witnesses ever saw, such as "Killing each other was a general thing among the prisoners. It was not only Jews who killed non-Jews, non-Jews also killed Jews. And they killed one another . . . But in all the groups, including the Ustashe, I noticed some feeling of unease, some hesitation, some excuses, some signs of a bad conscience. However, there was not a trace of this among the Jews . . . Their movements, the expression on their faces, their eyes, tone of voice, all their ruthless self-assertion said: kill, have one or thousands of non-Jews killed to save one single Jew; this is not only egotistically but also morally justified . . . Moses is much stronger in them than they allow us to know. This is the central point of the drama."[30]

In expert circles, Ciliga is known as a "writer of fables." He writes smoothly, in places his style is literary, but too often his vivid imagination carries him away, usually to justify some of his problematic acts or to show himself as far-seeing, brave, and above all excellently informed in every situation. Ciliga is the only man in the world who knew that Stalin had proposed to the enthusiastic Ustasha leader Ante Pavelić that, with some conditions, the USSR would recognize the ISC in its borders. According to Ciliga, it had already been decided to formulate an agreement of this kind in Marshal Tolbukhin's headquarters in 1944, and it is not clear why the negotiations (via Switzerland) were broken off at the last moment.[31] Only Ciliga knew about the intimate secrets of a Zagreb lady who was both Tito's and Pavelić's mistress and who "acted as a mysterious liaison between Pavelić and Tito during the war, to the satisfaction and acknowledgement of both."[32] Allegedly, the Communist Party of Yugoslavia worked against Ciliga through none other than Ante Nikšić, at that time Minister of the Interior in Pavelić's government, but in fact a Communist agent since long before the war. The Party was after Ciliga's head during the war as well as after, when he was in exile, but luckily for Ciliga, another "secret agent" was working on his behalf and saved him. This was Konrad Klaser, Gestapo head for Zagreb and Croatia, who was, in fact, a Jew and was working for Josip Broz Tito; just before the war ended, Klaser got into his car in Zagreb and drove himself off to join the Partisans.[33]

These fables by Ciliga, and others of a similar kind, may be good material for second-rate spy novels, but in memoirs they are clear evidence that their author is neither a serious nor a reliable witness. Too often, Ciliga's uncontrolled imagination led to obvious contradictions, especially when he lightly made judgments about politics, about individuals, and about entire nations. Thus, "by its origin, Pavelić's party was philo-Semitic, a 'Jewish party' in Croatia." Lower down on the same page it became "an old Germanophile party," and, somewhat later, "Anglophile," with a prominent "group of Catholic Anglophiles" composed of "intellectuals and non-Ustasha factions" who controlled the editorial board of the main Ustasha ideological paper, *Spremnost* (subtitled *The Thoughts and Guidelines of Ustasha Croatia*). They used the paper to promote "a decisively pro-Allied line" and held positions of overwhelming influence in the "legal framework of Pavelić's regime," but this regime was still "terrorist at its top, anarchistic in its middle, and primitively patriarchal in its foundation."[34] It is even more difficult to reconcile Ciliga's drastic contradictions about Jews in Jasenovac and Jews in general. "Jews are a people with the broadest interest in everything, they are the most sensitive about general problems of truth and justice, but at the same time they are the most egocentric and most egotistical people in the world."[35] On the one hand "it is difficult to imagine . . . a stronger and greater argument for anti-Semitism than this one offered by the Jewish group in Jasenovac," while, on the other, "some of the forms of Jewish solidarity that I encountered in Jasenovac seemed to me incredible, fantastic . . . like a story from *A Thousand and One Nights* . . . It was impossible not to admire this expression of self-sacrifice and solidarity. The Jewish people are constantly staggering under the weight of Moses's Law of being the chosen people, but at the same time this ambition to be the chosen opens up broad horizons and encourages them to great deeds. *Noblesse oblige.*"[36] At the end of the 130-page-long chapter "Jasenovac: People in the face of death" ("Jasenovac: Ljudi pred licem smrti"), "after all the terrible memories . . . [Ciliga] thought once again of those bright examples that were not wanting in this place that showed human suffering and misery at its worst," and gave three "fine examples" that represent three ethnic groups of prisoners. In the first place, he gave the example of the Jew Dr. Pavle Spitzer, head of the camp hospital. One of the most notorious Ustashe, Vjekoslav Maks Luburić, ordered Spitzer "to give a lethal injection to a Serb who was ill." Although camp rules called for a death penalty for refusing an Ustasha order, Spitzer publicly and resolutely, to Luburić's face, answered that he had "sworn to help everyone who was ill without discriminating . . . and never to administer to anyone under the guise of medicine something that might be detrimental to his health," so he could not go against his oath and refused to obey Luburić's command.[37]

Tuđman is probably the only post-1945 European historian who quotes from Cililga's fairy-tale memoirs without making any reservations or distancing himself. What is more, in the *Horrors of War* he omits everything positive that Ciliga wrote about the Jews and quotes only his negative judgments. He also passes over hundreds of testimonies and thousands of documents that show the solidarity of the great majority of Jewish prisoners with other prisoners, and the allegedly "privileged treatment" that ended in the annihilation of all Jewish prisoners. Tuđman chooses only three obviously problematic sources and quotes even them selectively, to suggest and generalize an extremely unfavorable overall picture of the Jews in Jasenovac.

It is this part of the *Horrors of War* that provoked the most public indignation, especially among Jews. Under the pressure of criticism from American and Western European Jewish and state organizations and representatives, Tuđman publicly apologized to the leaders of the American Jewish B'nai B'rith organization, removed all anti-Semitic invective from the abridged American edition of his book, and reduced it in the most sensitive parts of the fifth Croatian edition.[38] This did not nullify the negative consequences of Tuđman's revisionism. In the nineties, many of his followers among Croatian journalists and apologists slavishly took his views from the first editions of the *Horrors of War*, developed them, and made abundant use of them in their defense of the Ustasha ISC, with their implicit tinges of anti-Semitism.

Tuđman's responsibility for the promotion of Croatian revisionist historiography is coupled with his even greater responsibility as the main patron of the corresponding revisionism in politics and public life. To this, Tuđman opened the door in his statement at the First HDZ (Hrvatska demokratska zajednica) Convention in February 1990, saying that the "ISC had not only been a Fascist creation but also an expression of the centuries-old desire of the Croatian people for an independent state." In the first place, this statement is extremely ethnocentric. If it were true that the ISC really had been the "expression of the centuries-old desire of the Croatian people," then it would have brought all the other peoples in Croatia, in the first place Serbs, Roma, and Jews, against whom that state committed genocidal crimes, into confrontation with Croatian historical memory and the Croatian people in general. The statement opened up an impassioned public dispute about the true character of the ISC. Realizing the dangers inherent in the ambiguity of his statement, Tuđman, in later denials, distanced himself from any links with Nazism and the Ustasha ideology, but he never publicly distanced himself from widespread attempts to design the identity of the Croatian state, of which he was president, in the spirit of his statement. This was done through the name of the Croatian currency, the kuna, which had been the name of the currency in the ISC during 1941–1945, and was reintroduced in 1994. The complete military terminology, the terminology in government documents, the new names for state institutions—even the Croatian Sabor (parliament) got back its ISC name, Croatian National Sabor—were another sign of continuity with the ISC. Monuments and memorials, 2,964 in all, for fighters killed in the National Liberation Struggle of the Second World War and for victims of Ustasha and Nazi-Fascist terror, were destroyed, desecrated, or removed.[39] Streets, army barracks, and some institutions in various towns were named after Ustasha officials and army commanders. Notorious Ustasha songs became part of the folklore in celebrations and other events. The term "Ustasha-Home Guard Army" or the "ISC Army" was increasingly replaced by the term "Croatian Army," while the earlier term for the other side, "National Liberation Army," was usually replaced by "Yugo-Communist units" or "Yugoslav Army," or, most frequently, "the Partisans."

After the elections on January 3, 2000, when the HDZ party led by Tuđman was defeated and the opposition coalition came to power, the situation changed significantly. Even so, much more effort will have to be expended before consciousness of real events and relationships during the Second World War prevail among the Croatian public.

In the spring of 2000, Bolta Jalšovec, a member of the moderate Croatian Social-Liberal Party (HSLS) and vice president of the Croatian Parliament, spoke at a commemoration for the Ustasha and Home Guard prisoners massacred on Bleiburg Field and on the Way of the Cross. He called them the "Croatian Army," and somewhat ambiguously indicated that they were the foundation of today's Croatia.[40] There is no doubt that the victors in the war committed a war crime by the massacre of these prisoners, but, in his oratorical enthusiasm, the vice president of the Croatian Parliament should not have forgotten that Vjekoslav Maks Luburić was its supreme commander in its last battles and at the moment of surrender, and that he had before that been in command of all the concentration camps in the ISC.[41]

Under the influence of this kind of psychosis, revisionist terminology crept into serious and respected lexicographic books that have otherwise nothing to do with revisionism, so even the *General Croatian Lexicon* calls the ISC Army the "Croatian Army." This lexicon mentions Jasenovac Concentration Camp in two places on a total of two lines, while the Way of the Cross takes up thirty-five lines, which is completely unsuited to the otherwise very condensed style of the book.[42] The two-volume *Croatian Lexicon* is a similar case. The general entries are lexicographically correct (e.g., "Ustashe," "ISC," "Pavelić"). In the "Bleiburg" entry, the ISC army did not become the "Croatian army" but remained "Ustasha-Home Guard units," but this entry takes up as many as 148 lines, while only two and a half lines are devoted to Jasenovac Concentration Camp. The other Ustasha camps are not mentioned at all, not even Jadovno, but there is an entry for the "Jazovka pit" (thirty-nine kilometers southwest of Zagreb, into which the new Communist authorities threw about 400 members of Ustasha, Home Guard, and other quisling units in May 1945) with an illustration and about ten lines of text, and the "Way of the Cross" has twenty-six lines.[43]

Jere Jareb's book *Half a Century of Croatian Politics* is a very specific form of revisionism. Jareb was professionally the most qualified historian among the postwar ISC-oriented émigrés. His analyses of relations in this state and among its leaders are precise and competent, obviously based on thorough research and numerous testimonies of surviving Ustasha émigrés, and he did not refrain from saying that "an extremely totalitarian system was introduced" in the ISC. Still, when he had to write something about the crimes it had committed, Jareb resorted to a singular use of euphemisms and ambiguity; instead of using the word "crime," which anyone can understand, he wrote that the "Ustasha movement introduced Balkan political methods in Croatian politics for the first time." According to Jareb, "Croatian soldiers, equally the Ustashe and the Home Guards . . . are the most glorious creation of the past war" in which "Ustasha military formations, with rare exceptions, fought and acted as a regular army," and only the "Ustasha Defense, as a police formation, and some Ustasha militias and units, created in the first months of the young state as police-military bodies, did not behave like an army . . ."[44] The reader needs a lot of effort to understand that this "mist" hides an indirect confession that crimes had been committed, too. Jareb was somewhat clearer when he wrote about the "attitude toward the Jews," but, again, he avoided explicit mention of killing, genocide, and the Holocaust: "In this respect, the Ustasha authorities behaved unreasonably and with extremism. It was impossible to save all the Jews because of German pressure, but the Croatian side could have treated them more humanely and correctly. It is certain that the number of

Croatian Jews who survived this war could have been much greater. Such a policy could certainly have been nothing but beneficial for Croatia's reputation."[45] And at the same time, in a detailed footnote, he tried to decrease the number of Jewish victims in the ISC.

Aleksa Benigar claimed that the "state administration in the ISC did a lot of good. It focused on internal state organization in the spirit of the *Principles of the Ustasha Movement,* which contained nothing contrary to religious and ethical teachings . . . The unparalleled enthusiasm of young Croats to preserve their own state was the best plebiscite that the Croatian people ever had. During the first two months, hundreds of millions of kunas were invested in great public works . . . the government took measures to improve public morality . . . there was a ban on begging, vagrancy, and fornication." Benigar even supported the death penalty for abortion, which he mentioned as a "strict measure." After this, he wrote about "administrative flaws" and mentioned racial laws, "similar to the Nazi anti-Jewish laws . . . the racial element played an important role in this provision, because it placed Jews and Roma outside the law, and was inhumane toward the Orthodox Serbs."[46]

Marijana Cota wrote a book in connection with the trial of the former Jasenovac Camp Commander Dinko Šakić (held in Zagreb in 1999), claiming that only people who deserved it were sent to Jasenovac and other camps, and that there was no killing except "executions in retaliation, which were at that time in accordance with existing laws of warfare." "There were no 'death camps' in the ISC, and this also includes Jasenovac . . . Jasenovac was a work and transit camp with intensive production for both civilian and military needs of the ISC."[47]

In their many postwar publications, émigré supporters or followers of the Ustasha movement did not usually have the courage to face the real nature of the Ustasha regime; even in 1991, some people maintained that summary courts worked according to the law, that "all countries in the world had summary courts and extraordinary laws for the defense of their security during the Second World War . . . ISC citizens and inhabitants who had broken the laws of the state were imprisoned in Jasenovac and other transit camps, and so were some others for security reasons."[48]

In the book *The Creation of the Jasenovac Myth,* Josip Jurčević was generally reasonable in his denial of all the exaggerated estimates of the number of Jasenovac victims, used for ideological and political propaganda, and particularly for creating a belligerent attitude among the Serb population of Croatia, Bosnia and Herzegovina, and Serbia in the eighties, but in so doing his approach was not original.[49] On the other hand, Jurčević usually implicitly, and in some places explicitly, denied or tried to hush up the genocidal intent and criminal character of the Ustasha camps, especially Jasenovac, and in this way provided a false or understated picture of the Ustasha regime in the ISC. Quoting arbitrarily and selectively, Jurčević suggested that Jasenovac was a work camp only, not a place designed for mass extermination.[50] When he wrote about the women's and children's camp in Loborgrad, Jurčević said that it had a primary and secondary school and a kindergarten, as if this made conditions in the camp easier.[51] He generally mentioned "difficult camp conditions" in passing, without saying anything more about them, nor about the fact that almost all the women prisoners and their children died in Auschwitz.

The prominent mathematician Josip Pečarić, a professor at Zagreb University, wrote *The Serb Myth About Jasenovac,* in which he analyzed the "genesis of the Serb myth about Jasenovac," devoting special attention to the writing of the prominent Serbian revisionist Milan Bulajić and his followers. Pečarić's primary goal was not to explain what really happened in Jasenovac and the ISC during the Second World War, but to contest Bulajić's claims. Pecarić contrasted Bulajić's indirect accusations that the Croats are a "genocidal" people by writing about two centuries of Serbian anti-Semitism, and described the Sajmište and Banjica Camps in Belgrade, and in this way gave Bulajić "tit for tat."[52] In answer to Bulajić's accusations of Ustasha collaborationism, Pečarić maintained that "most of the Serbian people collaborated with the Germans." He generally made a great effort to prove collaboration and crimes in Serbia during the Second World War and thus put in perspective or minimize ISC collaboration and crimes.[53]

Pečarić uncritically accepted as completely true views that were endlessly repeated publicly in Croatia during the nineties, and which were not true and were easy to disprove. For example, he claimed that, unlike the behavior of the Serbian people and the Serbian Orthodox Church, the "behavior of high church circles belonging to the Catholic Church in Croatia was completely different, and Archbishop Stepinac raised his voice against Nazi and racist policy, helped and saved Jews and Serbs, and was known as a friend of the Jews."[54] The chapter about Archbishop Stepinac in this book has shown that the reality was much more complex.[55] Probably to prove the "democratic nature" of the Ustasha regime, Pečarić claimed that "in the ISC, the Jewish Community in Zagreb functioned and was the only one in Europe that worked all through the war."[56] Pečarić simply does not know facts, because the Jewish Community in nearby Budapest also worked throughout the war, and part of the international aid that came to the Zagreb Community arrived via the Budapest Community. The Jewish communities in Bulgaria, Rumania, and Belgium worked all through the war as well, and a reduced Jewish Community even worked in the Theresienstadt Camp right up until the end of the war.[57]

One would have expected the excellent mathematician Pečarić to be careful when quoting numbers, but he uncritically adopted all those that supported his existing political prejudices. Having read the completely unfounded writing of one Jakov Gumzej in the newspapers, he concluded that these texts "confirm the cruel reality that most Croatian Jews were killed in Serbia!"[58] There is probably no claim as absurd as this offered by Gumzej and Pečarić, because the SS deported just under 200 Croatian Jews to the camp in Zemun (mostly from Dalmatia in the fall of 1943, but not a single Jewish internee from Jasenovac or Stara Gradiška, as Pečarić suggests). As Gumzej and Pečarić included the 340 Jews in Zemun and about 200 from the Drina region among "Croatian Jews," it seems that about 700 to 750 Jews from the ISC were killed in camps in Serbia. Additionally, manipulating the numbers, Gumzej and Pečarić claimed that "only about 10,000, not 30,000, Jews were killed in the ISC." Even if we were to accept this drastic minimization, this would not show how Josip Pečarić, a university professor of mathematics, worked out that the 750 Jews killed in Serbia constitute a "majority" of the 10,000 killed in the ISC, which would then, in this strange computation, be a "minority."[59] In great detail, Pečarić discussed the "well-known reports" of Vojislav Prnjatović, although even the date of "March 11, 1942" at the end of the second report should have warned him that it was a fake (as described in the preceding pages of this chapter). Pečarić accused the Commission of the Yad Vashem Museum in Jerusalem, which names the Righteous Among the Nations, of being under the influence of the Greater Serbian claim about the "genocidal nature of the Croatian people," and said that "this Greater Serbian policy is also being implemented by some Yugo-nostalgics in Croatia," who can be found "among the Croats," and even among the "Croatian Jews." This is why, claims Pečarić, the Commission will not proclaim Archbishop Stepinac a Righteous Among the Nations, i.e., grant him recognition for having saved Jews.[60] However, just like other revisionists, Pečarić will not accept that Stepinac, among other things, simply does not meet the conditions for being proclaimed a Righteous Gentile, because he did not endanger his own life while saving Jews during the Holocaust, which is one of the two basic conditions.

In nine places in the book, Pečarić wrote that Himmler "personally had to come to Croatia in 1943 because he was dissatisfied with the 'solution to the Jewish question,' and that he achieved a death-rate of 75 percent of all Croatian Jews," i.e., that "Himmler demanded that all the Jews be taken to camps."[61] One chapter is even called "Avoiding Mention of Himmler's Visit to the ISC," but contains absolutely nothing to clarify this title.[62] Pečarić does not know, or will not accept, that when Himmler came to Zagreb on May 5, 1943, he simply could not have demanded that "all the Jews be taken to camps," because, at that time, the Ustasha and Nazi services were just completing that "work" in the last of the many deportations of Croatian Jews. Before the deportations in May 1943, the Ustashe and the Germans had, without Himmler's help or direct influence, deported or liquidated about thirty thousand Jews from Croatia and Bosnia and Herzegovina. As his only interest was to gain political points, Pečarić probably considered these facts minor details that were not even worthy of mention.

Pečarić entitled one of the chapters in his book "Jasenovac as a Station in the Way of the Cross," but in this entire five-page-long chapter he wrote about the subject that is its title in the last two paragraphs only. In the first of these, he quoted Antun Miletić, who said that "cleaning up" Jasenovac lasted until 1951. However, he did not quote Miletić from his original book, but from a text by Ljubica Štefan. In the second paragraph, he wrote about engineer Ante Biluš's statement that his father Marinko had been in Jasenovac from the end of May to the middle of December 1945. This fact is not disputable: work on clearing up the demolished camp buildings continued for quite a long time after the war and was carried out by Stara Gradiška prisoners, but this is not proof that Jasenovac was a "station on the Way of the Cross" after the war, or that it was renewed as a camp.[63] All of this shows that Pečarić did not know the material he was writing about well enough, that he did not know the "craft of the historian," and that his political beliefs prevented an objective perception of the past. Thus, his books are only a shade better in quality and value than those by Bulajić, whom he attacked with so much passion and energy. Pečarić's editor said that his book is a "journalistic work . . . written in a popular style . . . The author mostly uses a picturesque style and irony . . . Readers who want more detailed information will reach out for books by Žerjavić" and others.[64] This evaluation touches the very essence of the problem, but one wonders why an eminent historiographic institution such as the Croatian History Institute ever published the book.

Jure Krišto's books provide the most thorough attempt to refute some previously dominant theses and reshape the opinion about the criminal character of the ISC. In accordance with his general view, Krišto made no attempt to hide his desire to decrease the number of Jewish victims and thus decrease the magnitude of the Ustasha genocide of the Jews. He arrived at a distorted picture of the fate of the Jews in the ISC by misconstruing the stands of other authors and the meaning of documents, and by ignoring facts that were not in his favor.[65] Characteristic of Krišto's method of quoting is the way in which he presented Vladimir Žerjavić's demographic analysis. According to Krišto, Žerjavić said that "just under 20,000 Jews had been killed in the ISC, including those who were killed in military operations,"[66] but Krišto ignored, intentionally or not, the fact that Žerjavić said this number of Jews had been killed on ISC territory, while another 7,100 had been deported to camps in Germany and occupied Poland and killed there.[67] Therefore, when it suits him, Krišto says that the genocide of the Jews was committed under German pressure; elsewhere, by manipulating the numbers he avoids including in his calculations Jews who were killed abroad by joint Ustasha-Nazi efforts.

Krišto's firm demands for "re-evaluation" are either a hasty excursion into material that he does not know well enough, or will not analyze more deeply, or an attempt to score easy and petty political points. Krišto wrote that Josipa Paver and her collaborators in the Dotrščina Project established that "5,293 people from Zagreb and its surroundings were killed in all the camps on the territory of the former Yugoslavia." Then he continued: "Considering that a large percentage of the Jews who ended up in camps and were killed came from Zagreb and its surroundings, current historiographic assessments require revaluation."[68] However, it would have been more accurate to write that the Dotrščina Project verified the names, and, as far as possible, the time of death, for 5,293 people from Zagreb in the camps in Yugoslavia, and this differs essentially from what Krišto wrote. The scrupulous authors of Dotrščina could not establish the time of death of 1,594 people from Zagreb, so they singled them out in a separate section. They also established that 1,141 people from Zagreb were killed outside Zagreb in retaliation, by firing squads and in other ways, and that another 1,852 were killed in camps outside Yugoslavia. He also avoided mentioning that Josipa Paver said that "the number of names established so far cannot be considered final. We have at our disposal a large number of names of people for whose death there is not sufficiently reliable data." Without any reservations, she concluded that the "number of names for people from Zagreb, with data about how they met their death, will increase significantly,"[69] but Krišto did not mention this other essential part of the summary.

Krišto admitted the "Ustasha authorities were quick to pass racial laws and anti-Jewish measures," but he immediately added that "anti-Jewish legal measures were a general occurrence in the middle of 1941 in countries under Axis domination."[70] He obviously said this to minimize the Ustashe's responsibility. He also developed the notion that Ustasha officials protected Jews because of family ties, and added that "Pavelić had personal reasons to oppose Nazi orders, at least at the critical moment, when his own wife, who was of Jewish origin, was threatened, along with the wives of several of his top collaborators."[71] This was a pure fabrication, because Krišto gave no arguments to confirm that Pavelić opposed "Nazi orders . . . at the critical moment," and, in any case, Pavelić's wife was not Jewish.[72]

As for the camps, Krišto wrote that "one need not be psychic to conclude that life in the camps was not only unbearable, but that there was mistreatment and torture of all kinds, and also liquidations of prisoners."[73] This shows that Krišto placed the "liquidation of prisoners" in a context to make it appear that this "liquidation" was one possible fate of camp internees, not by far the prevailing one. It is true that Krišto accepted Narcisa Lengel-Krizman's view that Jadovno, Pag, and Jasenovac were "death camps" or "camps of destruction," but then, to somewhat temper this view, he added Mihael Sobolevski's remark that these camps "are waiting for a more complete, detailed, and objective study."[74] Sobolevski did not make this remark to question the term "death camp" or the fact that the camps were places of mass atrocities, but Krišto presented Sobolevski's words in such a way as to make his readers conclude as much.

When he wanted to substantiate some of his arbitrary views, Krišto sometimes used arguments that he probably knew were incorrect, such as, for example, that the "Ustasha authorities deported the Jews who were incapable of working (i.e., old people, women, and children) to Italian zones."[75] On the contrary, the truth is that the Ustashe and the Nazis particularly demanded that Jewish refugees to the Italian zones should be returned to the ISC so that they could be "evacuated to the East."[76]

Krišto's revisionism peaked in his assessment that the "ISC policy toward the Jews was unexpected . . . Archbishop Stepinac was the greatest defender of Jews, not only in the ISC, but in the whole of Europe," and that "a few Jews joined the Communists in armed resistance."[77] As we have described in many places in this book, Stepinac did, in fact, intercede for the salvation of individual Jews and groups of Jews, but there were many more decisive and successful "defenders of Jews" in Europe and in the

Catholic Church than Stepinac. On the other hand, the several thousand Jews who fought with the Partisans or were saved by the Partisans as civilians, Krišto dismisses as "a few." Besides, Krišto forgot that, for most Jews, joining the Partisans was not an ideological commitment (at least at first) but a commitment to survival. In any case, at the time when the Jews joined the Partisan movement, even the Partisans had not publicly declared themselves as Communists.

Petar Vučić's book, *Jewry and Croatianhood,* is a pretentious "contribution to research into the Croatian-Jewish relationship." The author of this quasi-intellectual discussion writes not only about the relationship between the Croats and the Jews, but tries to describe and characterize the Jews themselves. Although he wants to leave an impression that his work is serious and scientifically founded, this is a shallow, undisguisedly anti-Semitic pamphlet.

The book says very little about the subject that is its title, and much more about "Jewry" itself. A slave to stereotypes, Vučić explained alleged Jewish collective character traits: "racism," "arrogance," "hatred," "cruelty," "immorality," "depravity," "perversion," "desire for wealth," and "desire for power." To prove all these "character traits," Vučić based himself on the anti-Semitic pamphlet *Jews and Catholics* by H. de Vries de Heekelingen, printed in Zagreb in 1941.[78] Finally, in Vučić's opinion, Jews find it "difficult to forget insults and any evil done to them." Of course, in comparison with the Jews, the Croats, "in the opinion of the Croats themselves, forget insults and evil done to them all too easily."[79]

This kind of attitude toward Jews was directly or indirectly taken from Otto Weininger's anti-Semitic pamphlet *Gender and Character* and from the notorious *Protocols of the Elders of Zion.* To leave no doubt about his attitude, Vučić quoted both of these sources in great detail as relevant literature, and supported their arguments.[80] Listing all the alleged "Jewish characteristics," Vučić built the foundations for one of his basic theses: he asks himself, "is it thus strange that with ideas like these, which, *nota bene,* formed the political atmosphere in pre-World War II Europe, that the Holocaust happened? No, what is more, it would have been strange if it had not happened."[81] In another place, he said the same in somewhat different words: there is "Jewish shared guilt for the traumatic pogroms," and the people who carried these out were simply, "because of their overreaction to Jewish nationalism, in legal terms, guilty of exceedingly justifiable self-defense."[82]

Vučić did not mention that the Ustashe and the Nazis had committed genocide against the Jews in the ISC, all he wrote about in places were the "traumatic pogroms" committed by "various peoples against the Jews during history."[83] It is therefore not surprising that Vučić repeated the trite and completely incorrect claim of the Ustasha-nostalgics that the "racial laws were implemented in the ISC, but much later and much more leniently that the Germans demanded."[84]

Vučić's assessments of the Jews are the most monstrous accusations that appeared in Croatia after 1945. Through them, he also denies the Holocaust, although he does not devote any special attention to this subject.[85]

Except for Tuđman's *Horrors of War*, none of the revisionist books mentioned, or the long list of those that have not been mentioned, in and of themselves had any important public resonance in Croatia in the nineties. However, taken all together, because of their number and the persistence in repeating revisionist stereotypes, they constituted important support for political revisionism concerning the Ustasha ideology and the ISC. This led to the downplaying of Ustasha crimes, even a kind of broad tolerance for the crimes committed in the name of a favored political idea, which embedded itself in one area of Croatian political life. The consequences have not yet been undone and are being overcome very slowly.

40

JEWS IN THE USTASHA STATE ADMINISTRATION

Several people who considered themselves Catholics and Croats, but were Jews according to racial theory and Nazi laws, played a very prominent role in the early days of the Ustasha movement. When Pavelić emigrated from Yugoslavia in 1929, his "first step as an émigré was to forge links with the small Frankist group in Vienna (Croatian Émigré Committee), whose president, Ivo Frank, was the son of Josip Frank,"[1] a Jew on his father's side. Attorney Vladimir Sachs, one of the best-known converted Jews, who had as early as 1910 publicly supported the view that the "Jews are not a people but Croats of Moses' religion," gave important financial aid to this group, and through it to Pavelić as well. Sachs also considered that the Jews should renounce their religion so as to blend completely into the Croatian ethos. Both Ivo Frank and Sachs parted ways with Pavelić very quickly. Eugen Dido Kvaternik, Josip Frank's grandson, was Pavelić's closest, and one of his most devoted, collaborators from 1933 onward.

Vlado Singer (1908), born in Virovitica,[2] introduced Dido Kvaternik to the Ustasha organization. Singer was a converted Jew who considered himself Croatian. From 1929 to 1933, during his studies in Zagreb, he was the main organizer and "central person of clandestine student nationalistic groups," while publicly he was a student leader in the Kvaternik Society. In 1932, he organized demonstrations against King Aleksandar, and the next year he launched and edited *Naša gruda*, the first Ustasha paper in the country. After the second issue came out, he had to emigrate and he joined Pavelić in Italy. Despite everything he did for the Ustasha movement, in 1941 Singer's fellow fighters arrested him, temporarily imprisoned him in the Sava Road prison, and then deported him to Stara Gradiška, where he was killed in 1943. In 1946–1947, while in a Yugoslav prison, Slavko Kvaternik accused Pavelić of Singer's death. He said that Singer had been killed for saying that "it was easy for Pavelić, living in Italy, but difficult for the Ustashe on the Lipari Islands," and that Singer was "dangerous" because he knew Pavelić from his days as an émigré and "had a great influence on, and enjoyed the sympathies of, young people." Many people said that Singer was one of the few people who spoke openly about Pavelić's failings[3] and he was a "thorn in Pavelić's side."[4]

Ante Moškov added to the story about Singer in his prison statements—he said that Singer had been arrested in September 1941, immediately after the explosion in the Zagreb post office, under the false and, at first glance, incredible accusation of collusion with the saboteurs, particularly with Vilim and Nada Galjer. Those who were more realistic said that Singer was criticized for his support of Galjer, because they had earlier been acquaintances. Some people later said that Eugen Dido Kvaternik told them he had arrested Singer himself on the orders of Pavelić, and sent him to Jasenovac.[5] However, Dido wrote very commendably about Singer in several places in his memoir notes written in Argentina and, when he enumerated the victims of Pavelić's intrigues and crimes who had been unjustly killed, he usually placed Singer first: "The deaths of Vlado Singer, Ante Vokić, Karamarko, Farolfi, Tomašić, and so many other Croatian patriots will, through the centuries, remain part of the bloody testimony of Pavelić's despotism."[6]

Singer enjoyed privileged treatment in Jasenovac for a time and shared Dr. Vladko Maček's room. They had long conversations, sometimes concerning politics, about which Singer wrote a detailed report that reached Pavelić himself. The report, which presented facts correctly and without flattery, shows that even in prison Singer remained faithful to the basic Ustasha ideas. After this, Pavelić told Vilko Pečnikar, a person in his confidence (and a future general), that "Singer's arrest is only temporary and he will be released after spending some time inside, but will not be able to hold office of any kind for a time because of the Germans." During the first months of the ISC, Singer had been head of the Office II UNS (intelligence service).[7]

Although the testimonies of high ISC officials rarely mention that Singer was a Jew, everything indicates that this was why Pavelić had Singer imprisoned and later killed. He probably feared German objections to him having a person of Jewish origin in a high state position, and it is possible that some Germans even did make this kind of a complaint. Pavelić's animosity toward Singer might also have played a role in the decision to arrest him. Finally, it seems that the immediate reason for his murder came when Singer "sent Pavelić a report from Jasenovac about the conditions there, with specific data, thinking that Pavelić knew nothing of what was going on. However, Pavelić handed the report over to Luburić and the result was Singer's death."[8]

Slavko Kvaternik was married to a half-Jew, Dido Kvaternik had Jewish blood, and other Ustashe were also Jewish or had wives of Jewish origin. Milovan Žanić's wife, Alma, née Stöger, was Jewish. Vilko Lehner, Robert Vilček, David Karlović, Ljubomir Kremzir, Oktavijan Svježić, Viktor Gutman, David Sinčić, Ernest Bauer, and Ivo Korsky were also Jews by origin.[9] The Ustasha diplomat Ernest Bauer had a Jewish mother.[10] Vladimir Židovec thinks it "interesting that the measures against the Jews . . . were devised by the brains of people who had personal links with Jewry." With these words he was primarily referring to the fact that Dido Kvaternik was a quarter-Jew, and that the wife of "Dr. Ante Pavelić was half-Jewish." He also said that the "wife of Ivan Oršanić and the wives of various other people were Jewish."[11] In 1947, Slavko Kvaternik also stated that the "wives of Pavelić, of Kvaternik himself, of Budak, Žanić, Oršanić, Pavičić, Perčević, etc., were Jewish, or had Jewish blood or Jews in the family."[12] There were many errors or facts that were impossible to verify in these off-the-cuff remarks. For example, Budak's wife, who was not Jewish, died before 1941, and Budak never remarried.

None of the Ustasha officials mentioned above, who had Jewish ancestors, any longer considered themselves Jewish either by nationality or by religion, nor did their wives consider themselves Jewish. Except for Vilko Lehner (1909), none of them, nor their wives, were included in the *Economic Reconstruction Directory,* which means either that the Ustasha authorities no longer considered them Jewish or that they had connections at the very top. Lehner, who was granted Aryan rights, was the senior commercial official in the Ministry of the National Economy, and had no important property.[13] David Karlović (1885–1946), university professor and prewar Party of Rights member, had already withdrawn in 1941; he spent the war in Switzerland, but was nevertheless pensioned off in 1943 in the last wave of retiring Jewish professors.[14] The parents of the lawyer and prewar Ustasha activist Ivo Korsky (1918) had converted, and he did not consider himself Jewish by nationally or religion. Korsky loyally served the apparatus of the Ustasha state throughout the war, and later, as an émigré, continued his activities in the Ustasha movement.[15]

Oktavijan Muci Svježić (1916–1947?) used to be called Frischmann and was ridiculed in Jewish circles in the late thirties for denying his Jewish origin.[16] Although he claimed, during postwar investigations, that he had spent more time on sick leave than at work, Svježić played an important part in various top-level Ustasha activities. During the war, he performed various responsible duties: he was close to Eugen Dido Kvaternik, and for a time was Dido's secretary in the UNS, and he was a "close friend" of Nikola Francetić, brother of the notorious Jure, with whom he was also on good terms. Svježić was one of the key figures in maintaining the Ustasha position in eastern Bosnia in 1942, a man of outstanding "skill." At the beginning of 1945, Maks Luburić appointed him commander of the Filipović Army Barracks in Sarajevo, after which he was appointed President of the Summary Court Martial in Sarajevo, and finally was promoted to major. He returned to Zagreb in 1945 and lived in the city for two years, hiding under an assumed name. In 1947, he was arrested, accused, condemned to death, and shot.[17]

Ustasha émigré, official, and Junior Second Lieutenant Ljubomir Kremzir was also a Jew by origin. Kvaternik confirmed this in his memoirs and commended him for his excellent behavior during the trumped-up trial against Dr. Vladko Maček in 1930 in Belgrade, when "all the fabrications of the rulers of Greater-Serbia collapsed thanks to . . . the martyrdom of a Croatian Jew."[18] Kremzir himself claimed, during the war, that "his whole family was under the protection of the Poglavnik"—three of seven brothers were Ustashe, and one of them (Srećko) was also an "Ustasha returnee," as was Kremzir himself.[19] However, Pavelić's protection was only of partial help to Kremzir: it saved his sister, Zlata Glück, from deportation when she was sent to the transit camp in Križanićeva on August 13, 1942,[20] but it did not save his aunt, Antonija Spiller, who was deported.[21]

After the war, the Jewish origin of prominent Ustashe or their wives was a frequent and popular subject for members and sympathizers of the Ustasha regime, either in emigration or during prison interrogation. Right up to the present, revisionist historians persistently revisit this subject, as if it could lessen the Ustashe's crimes against the Jews. There was even a false rumor that Mara Pavelić's mother was Jewish. Ante Moškov said that

"Mara told an American officer in America after 1945—explaining that she was not against the Jews—that she had Jewish relatives in America, and that her sister there was married to a Jew."[22] Branko Polić said that Mara's sister really was married to a Jew, Weinberger.[23]

At his interrogation in May 1945, Mile Budak said, "we tried to help a lot of Jews who were on the Croatian side . . . however, it is true that many were killed despite our attempts to protect them, but neither I nor other government members can be held responsible for this, because it was done by special Ustasha officials, who answered directly to the Poglavnik."[24] Pavelić himself had favorites among the Jews:[25] he arranged for the owner of the villa in Tuškanac, into which he moved, to escape to Switzerland without any problems. In the summer of 1941, his in-laws, the Weinbergers, were issued passports and reached America via Switzerland. For years, he protected Aleksandar Klein, who bought cloth for Ustasha uniforms in Hungary. However, Klein mysteriously disappeared just a few days after he was granted Aryan rights in 1944, perhaps because he "knew about Mara Pavelić's machinations with silver, and he also made certain acquisitions for Mara and her husband, the Poglavnik." Therefore, Pavelić secretly helped a number of Jews because of financial or other benefits.[26] However, publicly he showed himself adamant: in a newspaper statement on June 27, 1941, he forbade anyone from coming to the Ustasha Head Office to intercede against the anti-Jewish provisions passed a day earlier.[27] And when Hugo Kon, President of the Jewish Community, personally asked Pavelić in April 1942, for the anniversary of the proclamation of the ISC to "show clemency, close down Jewish group camps, and free the prisoners," someone wrote on Kon's appeal "no intercession," and that was the end of it.[28]

At his trial in 1947, Slavko Kvaternik said that his life's experience had taught him to be "grateful to Jews, because when I was interned for two years [in 1934–1935, after the assassination of Yugoslav King Aleksandar I in Marseille], none of my friends took any notice of me, but some Jews did." Kvaternik was telling the truth when he gave a "whole lot of evidence" that he had "helped" individual Jews and "interceded" for them with Pavelić during Ustasha rule.[29] However, when the investigator asked Slavko Kvaternik in 1947 how he had personally experienced the passage of the racial laws and how they had been experienced by "Žanić, Pavelić, and the others of you who had Jewish or half-Jewish wives," Kvaternik answered very simply, trying to prove that there had, in fact, been no special attitude toward the Jews: "None of us in the government completely agreed with the passage of the Jewish provisions, at least not in that form, but this was required of us, so we had to do it."[30]

Thus, the story that the Ustasha authorities nurtured some special attitude to the Jews is completely absurd. Even if all the claims about the Jewishness of the Ustashe and their wives were correct, this would do nothing to alter the reality of the criminal character of the Ustasha regime, or diminish in any way the magnitude of the Ustasha genocide of the Jews. Since the Ustasha regime was directly or indirectly guilty of the death of over 30,000 Jews, the fact that the lives of several faithful collaborators and half-Jewish wives were spared cannot mitigate this. From another aspect, if the wives of some high Ustasha officials were indeed Jewish or half-Jewish, how could their husbands have ordered or participated in the genocide of their wives' people? How could Milovan Žanić have cosigned the racial laws, and how could Eugen Dido Kvaternik have been one of the most steadfast organizers and executers of anti-Jewish persecution and mass slaughter?

Like Kvaternik, every high Ustasha official could say in his defense that he had saved some Jew. Even the notorious Ivan Britvić made exceptions: the Polić-Frelić family heard that Britvić had praised the humanitarian activities of Aleksandar Frelić, President of the Charity House. Therefore, Aleksandar and his daughter Dana went to see Britvić in mid-June 1941 to request the discharge of Frelić's son, Miroslav, and son-in-law, Artur, who were in prison in Petrinjska Street. Britvić was moved and immediately ordered Miroslav to be set free (which happened), but he said that he could not release Artur as well, because he (Britvić) had superiors he had to think about. Nevertheless, Artur was released about a fortnight later, on July 4. It is not known whether Britvić or someone else engineered that release, because various people promised to help in setting Artur free.[31] Ustasha diplomat Ernest Bauer, a half-Jew, asked Miroslava Despot, née Bliss, who was in a mixed marriage, what he could do for her. She had the courage to say to him, "Never let me set eyes on you again!"[32]

This principle of private "connections," family and acquaintance, that could save someone's life was well documented by Živan Kuveždić, minister in the ISC governments (1943–1945), a prominent prewar HSS member, originally a peasant from the surroundings of Šid (in Vojvodina, 110 kilometers west of Belgrade). After extradition in 1948 he was interrogated, and when asked, "Are Gypsies and Jews not people who have the right to live too, since according to what you say you saved only Serbs and Croats, and approved the liquidation of Gypsies and Jews?," he replied, "I only saved people who turned to me, and no Gypsy or Jew ever did, so I could not save them, all the more so as I did not know them, neither their names nor where they were."[33]

Discussing the percentage of Jewish blood in some Ustasha officials and their wives in order to to diminish the Ustasha crimes[34] is as inappropriate as trying to justify the Ustasha authorities by saying that the Germans forced them to slaughter the Jews. Had the Ustasha authorities really wanted to protect the Jews, they could at least have procrastinated—even if they could not have avoided any action at all—as did the authorities in some other European countries: Italy, Denmark, Finland, France, Belgium, Bulgaria, Hungary, even Slovakia, and, in its way, Romania. In its theoretical ground-laying and in practice, the Ustasha regime was overtly racist and anti-Semitic—the only glimmer of light in this tragedy was the fact that many Croats (the majority, even) opposed both the theory and the practice by political action during the thirties, and with arms during the war. Many of them even tried to help their persecuted Jewish friends and neighbors directly. The Germans participated in the deportation of the Jews from the summer of 1942 to the end of 1943, but even these activities were implemented in close cooperation with the Ustashe. However, by then the Ustasha authorities had done most of the work themselves.

41

THE USTASHE, THE CROATS, AND THE JEWS

The relations in this triangle were by no means simple.[1] In the prewar years, there was a noisy minority in Zagreb that clearly expressed its anti-Semitism. It was supported by a smaller part of the middle class, some workers and craftsmen, and some church circles. The majority of the middle class rejected anti-Semitism in theory and in practice, and, from time to time, publicly expressed their views. Intellectual discussions about anti-Semitism obviously did not reach the population at large, but people were not indifferent to the problem. It seems that very diverse feelings mixed on the level of everyday practice: the difference in religion and nation, and opposition to Jewish merchants, led to antagonism against the Jews, while, on the other hand, the traditional Croatian multiculturalism and multiethinicity, and the tolerance that resulted from it, encouraged cooperation. Because of all this, and also because of traditional conformity and fear, many people in Zagreb adopted the maxim, "I don't know anything, I haven't seen anything," although the persecution and deportations of Jews were taking place before their very eyes.[2]

As the years passed, the divergent elements that influenced the attitude toward the Jews increased or decreased, appeared or disappeared: anti-Semitism grew stronger or weaker depending on conditions in Croatia, in Yugoslavia, and also in Europe and the world. When the Ustasha genocide of the Jews and others began in 1941, some Croats readily took part, but a large number actively or passively resisted this behavior. "Some Zagreb people . . . greeted the Germans with bouquets of flowers and oranges," but "Ljubo Majer, who always was and has remained up to the present a great Croat, burst into tears," said Vlado Prašek, and then he emphasized, "This popular enthusiasm quickly deflated when the first posters appeared about shootings and about opponents and innocent hostages who had been hanged."[3]

As everywhere in Europe, Third Reich policy set an example and incentive for the persecution and killing of Jews in Croatia and Zagreb, and it was this policy that generally played a decisive role in the ISC and on which the ISC depended for its existence. The Germans brought to power a group that they knew would be very similar to them in ideology and practice (conversely, had Maček and the HSS come to power, as some people wanted and planned, there would have been no persecution of the Jews, or else the Nazis would have had to organize it themselves by force). However, the local population was more sharply differentiated on this issue than in most other occupied countries or countries influenced by Nazi Germany: there were relatively more local participants in the crime, and relatively even more local people who resisted the criminals. Andrija Artuković and Eugen Dido Kvaternik were not alone in organizing the killing—"The deliberate and calculated planners of the slaughter were Pavelić himself and his closest circle (Budak, Lorković, Puk, Dido Kvaternik, etc.), organizers in the field were people such as Gutić, Luburić, V. Tomić, etc., while the many killers were themselves often unconscious tools in the hands of the real culprits, blinded by racial and other theories."[4]

On the other hand, the prominent anti-Fascists Slavko Komar and Ivan Šibl did not throw bombs themselves or join the Partisans. In a speech in Glina in February 1944, the distinguished writer Vladimir Nazor (1873–1948) answered the question "Why did I join the Partisans?" by saying that he had been moved to do so by the "inhumane persecution and extermination of Jews, who are people just like we are, and—which is the main reason—I was moved to do so by the ill-treatment and slaughter of the Serbs, who are our brothers in blood and with whom we have been living together for so many centuries."[5]

One of the more important features in the internal organization of every Nazi-Fascist satellite was the existence of racial (anti-Semitic) laws: they existed in Germany and (in a milder version) in Italy, and in other countries that joined the Tripartite Pact. The Ustasha authorities accepted these laws without even the slightest pressure—they did so with enthusiasm, and then with the same fervor began organizing the plunder of Jewish property, and later mass deportations and murder. When the Nazis began to participate in this genocide as well, much later, the Ustashe were their very devoted collaborators.

The restrictions on Jews introduced by the Yugoslav authorities before the war were, in some circles in Yugoslavia and in Croatia, greeted with approval and intensified the anti-Semitism, but they were not an essential factor in the later genocide.

The Ustasha movement did not have a majority following among the Croats, and not all Ustashe participated in anti-Semitic propaganda or in other anti-Jewish activities. Nevertheless, there is no doubt that the perpetrators of crimes against the Jews belonged to the Ustasha movement and that this movement was the main organizer of all genocidal activities in the ISC. The perpetrators of the crimes were also, at least indirectly, under the influence of prewar anti-Semitic outrages, and traditional anti-Semitic views that surfaced in Croatia more or less often, and with greater or lesser force.

Archbishop Alojzije Stepinac was only one of the symbols in the by-no-means-simple relations between the Croats and the Croatian Jews during the Second World War. Flight to join the Partisans or to territory under Italian control gave the greatest chance of salvation; there, Jews met Croats who wanted to help them, and who often saved their lives. There were some who even endangered their own lives by doing so, which the Jews recognized. By the summer of 2004, ninety-six citizens of Croatia had been proclaimed Righteous Among the Nations (a person who saved Jews during the Holocaust, and by doing so endangered his/her own life).[6] For example, Pavao Horvat, who had leased a hotel in Karlovac, actively helped Zagreb Jews escape to Karlovac, hid them in his hotel, and then sent them on to the Italian occupation zone. In this way, he saved the lives of several Zagreb Jewish families. Horvat was later arrested and interned in Dachau until the end of the war. He was proclaimed Righteous Among the Nations in 1965. Dragutin Jesih, the parish priest of Ščitarjevo (near Velika Gorica), and the lexicographer Mate Ujević, also became Righteous.[7] Some people helped in other ways: in early 1943, Hugo Kon and Miroslav Freiberger wrote in a letter of gratitude that Dr. Ivo Šalek, assistant in the University Clinic, helped inmates of the old people's home in Boškovićeva Street "many times and unselfishly . . . and refused to take any kind of reward."[8]

However, a considerable number of Croats in areas under Ustasha rule continued to be indifferent to the suffering of Jews. For example, in June and July 1941, the citizens of Zagreb could see Jews being loaded into railway cars at the Zagreb Fairground. Except for youth demonstrations at the Svetice Stadium, there was no expression of civil disobedience (strikes or the like, which happened in the Netherlands and Denmark); the only people in the city who showed a clear reaction to the terror were members of underground Communist groups. Everything was being done overtly, in an intentionally public way. Many people will say that it was impossible to do anything because the Ustashe would have continued to treat the Jews in the same way, and the protesters would have suffered. All the same, this was conformity, the comfort of false neutrality, turning the head away, sticking it into the sand, in a way that can be humanly understood but that was nevertheless cowardly. Sadly, many people in Zagreb directly or indirectly participated in the genocide.

The situation in Zagreb did not essentially differ from conditions elsewhere. It is impossible to generalize: many documents that cannot be doubted show that Ivo Baraković and Vilko Kühnel (Kinel), already mentioned, sometimes helped Jews, although they were high Ustasha officials and probably "good Ustashe." It is not clear whether they were "good men" or were simply not fanatical anti-Semites, but, in some cases, exit visas to areas under Italian control could be obtained through them. On the other hand, in June 1941, Baraković organized the first mass deportation of about 800 Zagreb Jews to Gospić and the surrounding camps, although he also sent about 400 of them home at that time. Kühnel's "goodness" had another side; he was definitely a man with two faces. He was of German origin, but he wore an Ustasha uniform. As head of the Jewish Section of the UNS, he was in constant contact with the Germans. In personal dealings with the representatives of the Jewish Community, he was courteous and usually forthcoming, and in certain cases he was sometimes helpful, but in August 1942 and May 1943 he was in direct charge of the most massive deportation of Jews and handed them over "exactly according to the lists" to the German authorities, who then sent them to Auschwitz.[9] These accusations of the State Commission for War Crimes were confirmed by the Open Orders of July 27, 1942, no. 47830, issued by the UNS Command, appointing Kühnel head of the "action for evacuating Jews from ISC territory."[10] This probably took place as an immediate aftereffect of the German report from May 1942, which led to German pressure on the Ustasha services to improve the system of catching and deporting Jews. Obviously, Kühnel had done his work thoroughly and according to instructions in the deportations of August 1942, because his connections with German intelligence later became even firmer. When the Ustasha authorities wanted to remove him from office, saying that he was "incompetent and has too many connections," the Germans decided to protest sharply.[11]

Jews sometimes had acceptable relations with some policemen, and quite a few policemen and police agents warned Jews whenever raids were being organized. Some of them did this for money, others simply from feelings of friendship and humanity. These policemen sometimes turned a blind eye to the escape of a Jew, or pretended that they did not know where someone had hidden. A man she did not know, obviously a member of the Ustasha movement and a frequent customer in her grocery shop in Ilica Street in Zagreb, told Elza Hiršl that deportations were in the offing, which saved the lives of Elza and her daughter, Biserka.[12]

On the other hand, attorney Dr. Ivan Britvić, who was head of the political department of the Police Directorate, was in most cases ruthless despite his education, and the fact that he had personally known some Jews before the war. He kept the strongest pressure on the Jewish Community when the payment of the contribution was being enforced. Some of his policemen copied him, and did their best to take Jews into custody, so that they could move into their houses that very same evening and appropriate the property that remained.

In the cellar of the Ustasha prison in Račkoga Street, "Ustashe came in and beat the prisoners from the moment of arrest until they left the cellar. The policeman Vrkljan did this especially often."—this apparently referred to Ante Vrkljan, a police detective in the Zagreb political department.[13] In the summer of 1941, Ivica Starčević, head of the President's Office of the Ministry of the Home Guards, sent a letter to Minister Artuković asking to be consulted when Aryan rights were being granted to Jews from Međimurje, Slavonska Požega, and other places, because he "knows them all."[14]

Sometimes, personal motives determined which Jew to deport, and which not to. In 1940, one Ivan Vrkljan embezzled the considerable sum of 1,400,000 dinars from the Trgopromet Ltd. firm. The manager, Eugen Jenö Kohn, found out about the embezzlement, but did not want to take Vrkljan to court. Instead, he tried to solve the matter peaceably, that is, he demanded that Vrkljan return the money without any public controversy and scandal. Vrkljan answered that "Pavelić will come, and then he will settle accounts with him." At the end of May 1941, Kohn was arrested, and somewhat later a police escort allegedly took him to Gospić, where all trace of him was lost. At the same time, Vrkljan became an official in the Ustasha Police and an Ustasha captain.[15] In May 1941, war invalid Franjo Patarčec, from Tkalčićeva Street, reported Jewish shopkeeper Jakob Kohn, claiming that "on April 30, 1940, when I was buying denatured alcohol in his shop, he hit me on the head twice, and I still suffer the consequences, and he did that because I complained that he keeps raising the price of the alcohol by 25 paras." Patarčec requested that the "above Jew should be taken to task and that I should be paid for my medical treatment . . . and also for pain and suffering and the humiliation." Jakob Kohn ended his days in an unknown camp.[16] Branko Zadobošek, owner of a "car rental agency," said that the "Jew Krešimir Hirschl drove my car into a deep ditch and almost completely ruined it; he promised to pay for the damage, but never did . . . He was even rude and disrespectful . . . and is in any case a criminal type." Zadobošek demanded that Hirschl should be "condemned to forced labor, and I should receive his salary, as creditor." There was no one called Krešimir Hirschl in the Jewish Community in 1941.[17] Distinguished industrialist Milan Marić, Honorary Turkish Consul, was also denounced, but when the war broke out he was in Belgrade, whence the Turkish Ambassador sent him to safety in Istanbul on the first plane.[18] According to a report that reached the police, secondary school teacher "Viktor Haumer, a great supporter of Yugoslavia, a Jew and married to a Jew, gave bad marks to pupils who would not join the Yugo-Sokol [an organization that promoted pan-Yugoslav unification and identity]" and he held "short confidential conversations with suspicious people around Jelačić Square." Haumer, who was in fact called Heumer, ended in Jasenovac in 1941, and his wife, Roza, and sister were killed in Stara Gradiška and Đakovo in 1941 and 1942.[19] Carpenter's assistant Ivan Novačić denounced Mario Purec, who had "made a good financial career, of course, at the expense of the blood-stained and sweaty calluses of the Croatian People." Mario Purec had to wear the Jewish insignia, but, as his wife and daughter were Aryans, he managed to survive the war.[20]

Police clerk Ivan Lasić informed the Jewish Section in June 1941 that Zagreb merchant Emil Klein was refusing to wear the Jewish insignia; whether because of this denunciation or something else, Klein ended up in Jasenovac by the end of the year at the latest, and was soon killed.[21] In an unskilled hand, a "man from Varaždin" wrote to the Zagreb police that when he was "in Zagreb, I saw that all the Jews are wearing the insignia but not Plavetić the barber, who is a Jew and until recently used to be called Blau . . . He insulted and cheated a lot of people, so had to flee from Varaždin."[22] No one with this name and surname existed in the records of the Jewish Community. In April 1942, one Josip Lomota from Lekenik (a village on the Zagreb-Sisak road), asked for the "Jews to be removed from the area of the Lekenik municipality, as they have been removed from other places . . . since they are a danger to us all."[23] In April 1942, fourteen employees of the Zagreb firm Kaveks complained to the Jewish Community that the owner had "employed the Jewish woman Mila Kraus in his office not long ago. Since that day, there have been disputes among the workers because the above keeps terrorizing them all the time for all kinds of petty reasons . . . Please employ any means to remove the above from the firm, all the more so as we consider that, as such, there is no place for her among Croatian workers."[24] There is no information about whether Mila survived the war or not, or whether she was Jewish at all, because she is not mentioned either in the *Jewish Sign Index, List of Victims,* or in any other documents. Some people with the surname Kraus were considered Croats and Catholics: in 1941, Božidar Kraus, later prosecutor at the trial of Archbishop Stepinac, was proclaimed a "pure Aryan."[25] The cases of Mila Kraus and of the alleged barber Plavetić show the anti-Jewish atmosphere of which some people made use.

There were many such denunciations at that time, not only to acquire property but also to show one's political correctness to the authorities.[26] Olga Knapp reported Edo (Egon) Fürst for insulting her and for not wearing the Jewish insignia. Fürst ended up in prison and was later killed in Jasenovac.[27] An anonymous report from that time, obviously written by someone close to the authorities, said that "there are various denunciations, almost always without any foundation, which clearly shows their purpose. The commissioners in some firms use this as a way to get rid of the owner, so that they can do as they like in the firm."[28] In November 1941, some people even suspected Jews of "spreading Communist propaganda" when they met in the Community premises at Trenkova 9.[29]

In some cases, people wanted to use the new conditions to right old and painful injustices: Kristina Kolarek of Varaždin, the illegitimate child of a house maid and Zagreb attorney Franjo Ernst, "who is very rich, and has so far not paid me anything," begged the authorities to do something to ensure her livelihood. Franjo Ernst survived the war, changing his surname to Erić.[30]

Ordinary people behaved in very different ways: in July 1941, at the time of the great deportations, a Zagreb Jew who worked in a warehouse was greeted every day by his boss with the question: "Haven't you been arrested yet?" But, apart from him, "all the employees were very tolerant."[31]

In 1941 and later, ethnic Germans, known as *Volksdeutsche,* were often leaders in the persecution of Jews. Representatives of the German National Group in Đakovo, helped by the testimony of the local Ustasha Camp, secured the abolition of Aryan rights of the Jew Tibor Löbl and his mother, because he had "served in all the Serbian regimes" and was said to owe "large sums for grain to some Croats and Germans from Đakovo."[32]

On the other hand, there were an even greater number of touching attempts to save some Jews: in March 1943, the peasants from the surroundings of Jastrebarsko (thirty kilometers southwest of Zagreb) asked the Ministry of the Interior to grant Aryan rights to their local merchant, Srećko Breyer, because the Breyers were "upright citizens, good Croats." This was followed by the signatures of 142 peasants, mostly in bad handwriting, and the very favorable opinion of the local parish priest about Breyer.[33] About ten citizens of Podravska Slatina signed a petition for granting Aryan rights to Justina Bauer.[34] In August 1941, seventy-two peasants from Dolič, near Krapina (fifty kilometers north of Zagreb), three of them illiterate, requested that the "five-member Klein family be released from camp and returned home and allowed to have a permanent and peaceful life."[35] Sixty-nine peasants from Remetinec (today in southwest Zagreb) and its surroundings requested the release of Aleksandar Šandor Löwy from Jasenovac, and the Ustasha Luka Markulin, "aware of the Ustasha oath," claimed that "Šandor Levij [*sic*] is worthy of freedom." However, Šandor ended his days in Jasenovac.[36] Seventy-four peasants from Vrbovec (forty kilometers east of Zagreb) requested that their praiseworthy merchant, Dragan Štern, be released from Jasenovac.[37] And seventy-three peasants and craftsmen from Šestine signed a petition for the local merchant, Vilim Schönauer, which did not help him.[38] At the end of May 1941, some people from Zagreb signed a petition for Viktor Juhn to be granted Aryan rights, and then at the end of July a petition to release Adolf Schwarz from camp, but both attempts were in vain: in 1942, Juhn ended his days in an unknown place, and, by the end of 1941, Schwarz had been killed in Jasenovac.[39] Several "Croatian musicians and artists" pleaded for the composer and music critic Žiga Hirschler, who was deported to Jasenovac in September 1941, among them one of the leading composers, Boris Papandopulo, and the internationally famous conductor Lovro Matačić. Although the Jewish Section demanded the release of Hirschler from camp at the end of October, it was all in vain. Whether

Hirschler was already dead when the request for his release arrived is not known, because the Jewish Community sent him his first and last parcel in November.[40] In September 1941, historian Rudolf Horvat circulated a petition to release Arpad Stern of Gradec (near Vrbovec, forty kilometers east of Zagreb) from camp. It was signed by as many as 132 inhabitants of Gradec, but this did not help.[41] Dragutin Horvat of Zagreb made the same request for Vladimir Fuchs, his platoon commander in the Yugoslav army in 1940. Horvat said that "God Himself sent us Fuchs as platoon officer." Fuchs also ended his days in Jasenovac.[42]

Kustošija merchant Josip Švarcenberg was arrested for deportation twice. When the local people of Kustošija heard of this, they came to the Ustasha Office [i.e., the seat of the local Ustasha organization] both times and did not go away until Josip was released.[43] When the Ustashe came to raid an apartment building in Švearova Street, the concierge, who knew that Zlata Frankl was hiding in the apartment of the Prašek family, shouted up the stairwell to warn the Prašeks and Zlata: "A doctor lives here with her son, there is no one else in the apartment."[44]

Some people devised original ways of trying to get prisoners out of prison. When Hilda Atijas, née Eisenberg (1911), was imprisoned in Sava Road in February 1942, Vilko Sakušek (1916) and Vladimir Marhofer (1912) asked in St. Blasius' Parish Office in Zagreb for the annulment of her marriage, contracted in 1939 to Rafael Atijas, because they said it was only a marriage on paper. They claimed that Hilda had married Atijas to obtain citizenship, because her father was a citizen of Romania.[45] Sakušek testified that the marriage between Hilda Eisenberg and Rafael Atijas was one of convenience, and that he, Sakušek, loved Hilda and wanted to marry her, which was confirmed by his best friend, Marhofer. The arguments seemed very convincing, which is probably why Hilda was released from prison. As a Jew, Atijas could not have achieved similar results. It seems, however, that Sakušek and Hilda did not get married, but that Hilda tried to escape from Zagreb after her release from prison. She lost her life under unclear circumstances while escaping from Zagreb, apparently when Partisans ambushed her not far from Jastrebarsko, while she was riding in a cart. Rafael Atijas was still in Zagreb at the beginning of 1943, and it seems that he survived the war.[46]

A Franciscan tertiary, Rafaela Elizabeta Gustetić (1884–1962), interceded for a Jew in September 1941, saying that he was "worthy of recommendation."[47]

Some people gave money. In 1943, the co-owner of a hardware store in Zagreb, Valent Klancir, provided goods "partly for free, partly at considerably lower prices," when the building on the archbishopric estate in Brezovica was being adapted into a home for Jewish old people.[48]

The people in Trsat, Sušak, Crikvenica, and in other places of Hrvatsko primorje and Gorski kotar, were clearly hostile to the Fascists and the persecution of innocent people.[49] The testimony of Aleksandar Goldstein's family, who had hidden unregistered with Kata Miloš and her son, Drago, in Hreljin, is moving. One day, a poster in Italian appeared not far from the house, saying that anyone harboring unregistered people in their homes will be shot. To his mother's question, "What shall we do, Drago?," the son answered, "We won't register them."[50]

42

ON THE NUMBER OF JEWISH VICTIMS IN ZAGREB AND CROATIA

Statistical and demographic research during the last fifty years has provided the basic facts about the genocide of the Jews in the ISC and, as part of it, on the territory of what is today Croatia. All relevant scholarly publications now accept these facts overall, with possible inconsequential deviations. When numbers appear that are significantly different, they are either the result of ignorance or of the wish to promote interests that do not belong to the realm of science.[1]

Lists by name of members of Jewish communities exist: before the war there were some 38,000–39,000 Jews on ISC territory, including those who had converted but who were treated as Jews according to the racial laws. Only about 9,000 of them survived the war. The numbers are similar by region: only 4,000 out of 14,000 Jews in Bosnia and Herzegovina survived, just under 30 percent, and about 5,000 out of about 25,000 Jews in northern Croatia, Slavonia, and Srijem survived, or about 20 percent. It was somewhat better in Dalmatia, but there were only about 400 Jews there before the war, 250 of whom survived the war. The survivor lists for the City of Zagreb in 1946 show 2,214 people.[2] Which means that between 75 and 80 percent of the Jewish population was killed in the ISC between 1941 and 1945—only one Jew out of five in what are today Croatia and Bosnia and Herzegovina lived to see the liberation in 1945.[3]

Classical genocide of the Jews was committed in the ISC and in Zagreb. This can be proved in many ways, in the first place by the percentage of victims. The sex of victims from the Zagreb area provides the same conclusion: a sample of 2,454 Jews listed in the Dotrščina Project, with surnames from A to K, has 51.8 percent men and 48.2 percent women, while the ratio between men and women among Croats and Serbs in the same sample is 85.2 to 14.8, or even 85.3 to 14.7.[4] This means that almost six times more men than women were killed among the Croats, and, surprisingly, among the Serbs, while the ratio among the Jews is almost 1 to 1. These numbers show that in Zagreb, Croats and Serbs were mostly killed because they were considered a potential or a real ideological, political, or military threat to the regime, while the Jews were killed simply because they were Jews—in genocidal murder, where the sex and age of the Jewish victims were immaterial. This analysis provides another characteristic fact. Although the column about participation in the anti-Fascist movement was not consistently filled, and was left empty for many people, statistics show that 55.4 percent of the executed Croats were members of the anti-Fascist movement, somewhat fewer, 41 percent, of the executed Serbs, but only 5.7 percent of the executed Jews.[5]

The number of Zagreb Jews killed has not yet been precisely established. The data and estimates made immediately after the war differ, and even in later years, research did not yield precise data. In a 1947 official letter to the State Commission, Community Secretary David Levi gave an assessment of the total number of Jews killed. He started from the estimate that there had been somewhat more than 12,000 Jews in Zagreb before the war, including 1,000 who had converted. He said that 7,500 Zagreb Jews were deported to camps and were killed there, that about 500 "died in exile," about 400 "died or were killed in refugee camps," approximately another 400 were "killed individually in Zagreb during the occupation," and, finally, that in 1943–1944 about 200 were "taken from Rab and were killed." This means that about 9,000 Zagreb Jews were killed, which is about 73–74 percent of the prewar community.[6] Until there is more precise research, this number will have to be accepted. Many texts written for the public at large say that about 2,000 of the 11,000 prewar Zagreb Jews lived to see the liberation in 1945.[7]

Scrupulous research has not yet confirmed these numbers. The Dotrščina Project, so far the best and most extensive investigation into Fascists' victims in Zagreb, carried out in the Archives of Croatia (today the Croatian State Archives) during 1985–1986, records a total of 18,627 names,

6,399 of which have been recognized as Jewish. This is far fewer than the number in the report of the State Commission and of the representatives of the Jewish Community, whose estimates include up to 9,000 victims. How did the difference of as many as 2,600 victims come about? Josipa Paver, one of the main researchers in Dotrščina, distanced herself, saying in 1986 that the "number of established names with data about Zagreb victims will increase considerably."[8] Unfortunately, the Dotrščina Project was completed in the mid-eighties but subsequently never updated, although additional research had been planned.

The *List of Victims* book, the original of which is in the Jewish Community in Zagreb, gives 7,492 Jewish victims of "Fascist terror" in Zagreb. This alphabetical list only goes down to the surname Weiss, as the remaining pages have been lost. Comparing the *Jewish Sign Card Index,* which often has the remark "camp," etc., in the margins (which means that the person was killed), with the *List of Survivors* shows that the part of the list that disappeared (i.e., from Weiss to the end of the alphabet) should have had at least 151 more victims. The *Card Index* has no remarks about the fate of 285 people, and these do not appear on the *List of Survivors* either. Thus it is impossible to tell whether they were killed or were saved. There would certainly have been fewer people of unknown fate had the part of the *List of Victims* from Weiss through Ž been saved. For now, we may assume, because it is impossible to arrive at a more precise number without fundamental archive research, that about 70–75 percent of these 285 people on the card index were killed, which is about 200: this number corresponds to the percentage of Zagreb Jews killed as a whole. Therefore, about 350 more names should be added to the *List of Victims.* Adding 7,492 and 350 gives 7,842 people, i.e., the number of about 7,800–7,900 Jewish victims listed by the Jewish Community in Zagreb immediately after the war. In later years it was established, especially in cooperation with the Yad Vashem Museum in Jerusalem, that several hundred more people did survive the war, after all: now the column "Remarks" on the *List of Victims* contains the comments "alive," "survived the war," "died in the USA," or "died in Israel," beside the names of 646 people. It seems that the number of about 7,200 victims in the *List of Victims* is thus conclusive, but this is not a list of all the Jewish victims in Zagreb.

The final result of the Dotrščina Project, with the total of 6,399 Jewish victims in Zagreb, can immediately be corrected. The scrupulous Dotrščina researchers did not want to include a victim if no data could be found about him/her, at least the year of deportation or, for example, that the person had ended in a "Polish camp" (however undefined this designation may be). There are almost 800 such cases on the *List of Victims,* the original of which is in the possession of Jewish Community in Zagreb. Since these people "disappeared" during the war, we can consider them dead and Holocaust victims. Furthermore, archival sources that were not taken into consideration in the Dotrščina Project show the fate of some of them. For example, the Collection of the Croatian State Archives, Jewish Section RUR, records that Hilda Engelsrath and Frida Grossman were sent to the camp in Stara Gradiška. Since the Jewish Community in 1945 did not know to which camp these two women had been deported, and where they had been killed, the *List of Victims* gives no other information beside their names, so they were not included on the Dotrščina list.[9] The *List of Victims* also gives the names only of Otto (29) and Rene Deutsch, without either time or place of death, but they are nevertheless included on the Dotrščina list because they appear in the *Sterbebücher von Auschwitz,* as they were killed in Auschwitz on August 31 and on September 17, 1942.[10] The *List of Victims* compiled in the Jewish Community is not without its failings: although it seems to have been made by mechanically copying the *Jewish Sign Card Index* and other preserved lists in the Community, this was not so: by mistake, twenty-two people on the *Index* were simply left out, with surnames from Pažur to Peroš. The index cards show that twelve of them had been killed, one (Stjepan Peći) is known to have survived, and there is no information for the remaining nine.[11] The names of 270 Jewish children from Zagreb, killed in the Holocaust, were also published. To this list was added another compiled on the basis of documents in the Yad Vashem Institute in Jerusalem, with the names of thirty-nine Jewish children from Croatia, sixteen of them from Zagreb.[12] Most of these names already appear on the *List of Victims,* and the small number of new names requires additional verification. This is not all, as it is necessary to look at each case individually. For example, Jelena (Helena) Engel died at 66 in August 1944 in the home in Stenjevec. Before that, she was "persecuted, thrown out of her apartment, and imprisoned."[13] The head of the kindergarten, Mirjam Weiller, drank poison when the police came to her apartment to arrest her.[14] Both Helena Engel and Mirjam Weiller should be considered victims of terror.

Scrupulous researchers consider that lists of this kind have been completed when the identity of 90–95 percent of the victims is established by name. The Dotrščina Project and the *List of Victims* both arrived at the approximate number of 7,200 victims. However, there may have been as many as 9,000 victims, because there were many newcomers in Zagreb, or people who had been traveling through and were caught in Zagreb by the war; there were also many converts and people in mixed marriages. Many of them are not on the lists of the Jewish Community in Zagreb, nor were they later shown as Jewish victims. Thus, probably between 8,000 and 9,000 Jews were killed in the Holocaust in Zagreb. Additional careful research will be needed for these numbers to be made more precise, and the lists more complete.

It is easier to establish numbers for the immediate surroundings of Zagreb, because it was easier to keep abreast of things that took place in small towns and establish the number of victims: for example, seven of the twenty-five Jews in Donja Stubica were saved, ten of the twenty-two in Jastrebarsko and its surroundings, four of the fourteen in Sv. Ivan Zelina and its surroundings, and three of the thirteen in Velika Gorica and its surroundings.[15] Therefore, of a total of seventy-four Jews, twenty-four or almost a third were saved (32.4 percent).

A reliable way to establish the number of Jewish victims is to collect data about the number who were arrested and killed in particular Ustasha-Nazi actions. In the two or three years after the end of the war, the State Commission for War Crimes estimated that about 6,000 Zagreb Jews were taken from Zagreb to camps in seven actions of mass arrest (one in June 1941, two in July 1941, one in August–September 1941, one in January 1942, one in August 1942, and the last in May 1943). In his report to the State Commission, Community member Josip Abraham gave a precise list of all the mass arrests with the numbers of deportees—a total of 7,650 Zagreb Jews. However, in another place he estimated that about 8,000 Jews had been taken from Zagreb.[16] The difference between the State Commission's estimate and the one Abraham gave to this Commission arises primarily from the fact that the State Commission estimated that 500 Jews had been deported in August 1942, whereas Abraham estimated it had been as many as 1,700. The State Commission's estimate seems too low, and Abraham's number of 1,700 probably included Jews from other Croatian towns who were deported via Zagreb at that time. There are also small differences in the number of deportees from Zavrtnica in August and September 1941. These numbers show that over 7,500 Zagreb Jews were deported during the war. Since only a small number survived life in the camps, this means that there were about 7,500 camp victims.

In his statement mentioned above, David Levi estimated that about 400 Jews had been "killed individually in Zagreb during the occupation."[17]

Other estimates put this number as high as 500. These were people killed as hostages, or by the Ustasha authorities in retaliation to set an example. They usually were shot in Dotrščina (northeast of Maksimir Forest) and in Rakov Potok (near the old Zagreb–Karlovac Road).[18] As a rule, the Ustasha authorities left no record of the shootings, so only a small number of the names of people killed at these locations has been established. At least seventy-eight Jews were shot in Dotrščina in 1941, some after being sentenced by the summary court, fourteen in the following year, another twelve in 1943. Therefore, at least 102 Jews were shot in Dotrščina during the war.[19] At least seven Jews were shot in 1941 in Rakov Potok, and at least another five during the next two years. This means that the name, place, and at least approximate time of death has been established for 114 Jews.[20] For example, Marko Schlesinger (1896) was arrested in August 1941 and was probably shot several days later in Dotrščina.[21]

The discrepancies are not large, but are usually very difficult to correct. The differences result from the limited amount of research, the very diverse and broad body of material that is often lacking in data, and some incorrect facts. Finally, there is the most sensitive question: who is to be considered a Jew? During decades of life in Croatia, many Jews left the Jewish religion and converted to Catholicism (or, to a much lesser extent, to Orthodoxy or even Islam), many changed their surnames by Croatizing them,[22] and many were no longer members of Jewish communities. Thus, they no longer considered themselves Jewish, nor did it seem that they had any reason to. Still, many were killed in the Ustasha-Nazi genocide because of their Jewish origin. There is no reason for statistics to keep showing them as Croatian, Serbian, etc., rather than Jewish. These Jewish victims are the most difficult to identify and additional work and time will be necessary before researchers can establish more-or-less final numbers.

The *Economic Reconstruction Directory,* kept in the Croatian State Archives, is a list of people the Ustashe and the Germans considered Jewish. The lists in the Jewish Community include the people who considered themselves Jewish. As the Ustashe and the Germans killed people during the Ustasha-Nazi genocide because they considered them Jewish, regardless of whether the people considered themselves Jewish or not, the *Reconstruction Directory* is also relevant for any research into Jewish victims. However, it too has one fundamental failing: it lists only people who were employed or had any kind of property (housewives, pensioners, people of private means, etc.), not students, pupils, or children. Furthermore, it also lists Croatian men and women and members of other nationalities who were married to Jews. The reason for this was obviously to avoid property being hidden by being in the name of, or being placed in the name of, the spouse.

Another problem in establishing the fate of Jews, especially those who were deported during the second half of 1942 and in 1943, was that almost no one at all was left to bear witness. In a considerable number of cases, the *List of Victims* in the Jewish Community in Zagreb has the comment "Jasenovac," "Pag," or "Jadovno" added to the name for those killed in 1941, but for those killed later it much more often says "unknown" or the space is left empty. The place of death for twelve of the 113 Zagreb Jews who did not survive the war, but were still in the city at the beginning of 1943, and were obliged to pay community tax, is known only to a certain extent. For some of the twelve, the *List of Victims* says, for example, "Zagreb," and for others it says only very generally "Germany" or "Auschwitz." For the remaining 101, the column "place of death" says "unknown" or nothing at all.

A special problem was the mass deportation organized in August 1942, because prisoners were sent to both Jasenovac and Auschwitz at almost the same time, and they were very quickly liquidated. As no complete lists of those killed and those who died exist for either camp, but only partial lists, in many cases the place of death for this great deportation (August 1942) is only guesswork. Nevertheless, for some victims it can be established indirectly.

Two such cases are those of Drago Bachrach, sawmill manager in Turopolje, and Dora Bošan. For Bachrach, the columns "time and place of death" in the *List of Victims* have "unknown 1942," and for Dora Bošan only "unknown." However, both were killed in Auschwitz, on September 25, 1942, and on October 23, 1943, respectively. Both are listed in the *Reconstruction Directory.*[23] The *List of Victims* says nothing about the place of death of Oton (1912) and Reno (1926) Deutsch, Želimir-Željko Mayer (1924), or Lea Sauerbrunn (1928), but they were killed in Auschwitz on August 31 and on September 4, 17, and 26, 1942.[24] The *List of Victims* gives no data about the place and time of death of the Renos' parents, Josip (1885), a salesman, and Adela, of Željko's father, Vatroslav (1896), and sister, Rajka, of Lea's father, Ignac (1893), mother, Šarlota, and brother, Mavro, but they were most likely deported in August 1942 as well.[25] The *List of Victims* says only that Željko's mother, Blanka, was killed in Dachau in 1943.[26] According to the *List of Victims,* industrialist Stjepan Spitzer-Španić (1898) was killed by the Ustashe in 1941, but it seems that he was in fact killed in Auschwitz on October 22, 1942.[27]

In a letter from May 1945, the Community heads described how the documents were filled in during the war. They wrote, almost apologizing for not gathering data about the deaths of their members, that "all our difficult and hard work focused only on keeping alive the people who remained here or were unhappily in camps, so we neglected to work on statistics and do similar administrative work which would, in any case, have been somewhat dangerous in case of searches performed by the former criminal authorities, who did all they could to exterminate us."[28]

The lists of victims contain only some of the many refugees from the Third Reich or other European countries who were in the broader city environs in April 1941. They show that nineteen refugees from the Reich, Hungary, and Romania were brought to Danica Camp in early June. Walter and Ladislaus Berenyi, Bela Fischer, and other former citizens of Vienna disappeared without a trace, and have not been recorded on any list of victims.[29] Hans Sachs, also a refugee, lived in the Vrapče hospital starting in April 1941, but an Ustasha unit, under the command of Ljubo Miloš, arrested him in September 1944, took him away, and nothing more was ever heard of him.[30]

This was the fate of most other foreign refugees as well, and today it is difficult to determine their exact number. It is certain that a higher percentage of refugees was killed than of Zagreb and Croatian Jews, as they did not know the language, did not know their surroundings, and most of them had no money, so it was much more difficult to save them. One of the few exceptions may have been German refugee Norbert Thumin-Landau, who spent the war in the Psychiatric Hospital in Vrapče.[31] Ljudevit and Gizela Fürstenthal arrived in Zagreb from Austria in 1940. Ljudevit was taken to camp, from which he did not return, but Gizela managed to survive the war by finding shelter somewhere in Zagreb.[32] These cases show that all the refugees from other countries, who happened to be in Zagreb and its surroundings and were then killed, should be added to the total number of people killed in the Holocaust in Zagreb and environs, because they were either killed by the Ustashe or were deported by the Germans with the help of the Ustasha authorities. It is impossible to discover how many of them there were, probably several hundred.

To show the unreliability of some sources, and how different sources give different final figures, I give examples from the list of victims of the Jasenovac camp, which was made for internal use by the Federal Bureau of Statistics of Yugoslavia in Belgrade in 1992, entitled *List of War Victims 1941–1945—Ustasha Camp of Jasenovac,* and was published as a reprint by the Zurich–Sarajevo Bosniac Institute in 1998.[33] This book enumerates 8,121 Jewish victims in Jasenovac and 923 in Stara Gradiška, for a total of 9,044. Of this number, 3,218 victims were from Croatia, 5,417 from Bosnia and Herzegovina, 261 from Vojvodina, 117 from Serbia, 20 from Slovenia, 5 from Macedonia, and 3 each from Kosovo and Montenegro. This is a considerably smaller number of Jewish victims than the one that is generally accepted, even considerably smaller than Žerjavić's estimates, which are themselves somewhat too low. Thus, I compared the list of Zagreb Jews who were killed in Jasenovac, with surnames beginning with the letters "A" and "B," in the Dotrščina Project and in the book *Jasenovac:* Dotrščina gives 290, *Jasenovac* 84. However, in *Jasenovac,* the column for nationality gives "Croat" for 14 Zagreb Jews, whereas Dotrščina gives these people as Jewish victims. There is no doubt that Dotrščina is right, because the surnames of the victims, their age, and the place and time when they were killed clearly show that they were Jews. Jewish Community documents also show this. The dubious nature of the *Jasenovac* data is also shown by the fact that of six Zagreb Jews with the surname Goldstein, who were Jasenovac victims, three are entered as "Jews" and three as "Croats." The "Croats," Zvonko, Armin, and Albert, were born in 1923, 1892, and 1882 (they were thus 18, 59 and 49 years old at the time of death), and they were all killed in 1941. It is therefore difficult to believe that they were killed as Croats, anti-Fascists, or opponents of the regime of any kind. Of the eight Kaisers (Kajzers), six were entered as Croats, and the column "nationality" remained empty for two. All nine of the killed Kahans were entered as Croats, which is practically impossible, because this is a typical Jewish surname. Six of the ten Kalderones were proclaimed Croats, four without nationality. Even people such as Wolfgang Kafka (1901–1944) and Izrael (1922–1941) and Lavoslav (1880–1941) Kahan (father and son) appear as Croats in the book *Jasenovac.* Andrija Kraljević-König was entered as Hungarian, and he is known to have been a Jew. Finally, to make the paradox of entries of this kind complete, even Lavoslav Šik, a prominent Judaic scholar and activist of the Zagreb Jewish Community, is entered as Croatian by nationality.

Furthermore, the book *Jasenovac* mentions seventeen Croats who do not appear at all in Dotrščina, and who were obviously Jewish. Finally, twenty-nine Zagreb Jews killed in Jasenovac, according to the book *Jasenovac,* are not mentioned in Dotrščina at all, either among the Jewish or the non-Jewish victims. The opposite is also true: as many as 235 Zagreb Jews who were killed in Jasenovac, according to Dotrščina, are not mentioned in the book *Jasenovac* at all. This means that in the letters A and B alone, the two projects overlap only 55 names, which is less than 20 percent. It is immediately obvious that Dotrščina is an incomparably more studious and precise research project, and that *Jasenovac* is full of printing errors, misspelled surnames (Baner instead of Bauer, Bresslaner instead of Bresslauer, etc.) and, as shown in what we said about Lavoslav Šik being entered as a Croat, sometimes completely incorrect information. The authors of *Jasenovac* wanted first and foremost to establish the number of victims, but working in this way they were obviously not on the right path.

The Croatian State Archives have a *List of War Victims 1941–1945* compiled by the Commission for Listing Victims in 1964.[34] This list gives 7,489 victims of Fascism in Zagreb, with the nationality "Jew" for 3,217. However, the data base is identical to the one used for the book *Jasenovac*. The *List of War Victims* even repeats the mistakes I pointed out in *Jasenovac*. About 980 people, such as the already mentioned Kalderon, Kraljević, Goldstein, and others, are entered as Croats (and sometimes as Hungarians), when there is, in fact, no doubt that they were Jews. This number includes only people who have characteristic Jewish surnames, and who, given their age, could hardly have belonged to the anti-Fascist movement. It may therefore be taken that the *List of War Victims—Zagreb* contains at least 4,200 names of Zagreb Jews. However, it is often very uncertain how exact this information is and whether it can be confirmed and compared with the *List of Victims* of the Jewish Community and the Dotrščina Project.

According to the *List of Victims—Zagreb*, nine members of the Havaš family from Zagreb were killed in Auschwitz in 1941, which is obviously a mistake. It is true that Auschwitz Camp was founded in the spring of 1940, but the death camp on this location dated only from the beginning of 1942. There were never any transports to Auschwitz from Zagreb prior to August 1942. The *Jewish Insignia Index* contains only Leo Havas-Hirschl (1887), who was "unmarried" and was deported "to Germany," but in 1942.[35]

The Dotrščina Project includes the names of 6,399 Zagreb Jews. Most of them were killed in Jasenovac, 1,783, or 27.9 percent, and if we include the 287 people killed in Stara Gradiška, the total is 2,070, or 32.3 percent. According to Dotrščina, 828 people (12.9 percent) were killed in Auschwitz, 400 in Zagreb and in its broader environs (Rakov Potok and Dotrščina), 242 disappeared in Đakovo, and 222 Zagreb Jews perished in Jadovno. Ninety Zagreb Jews were killed in combat in the NOB, 75 on Pag,[36] and 65 died in Loborgrad. A total of 147 people were killed in other locations in Croatia, and another 219 elsewhere abroad. This means that the circumstances of death are known for only 4,290 Zagreb Jews, which is exactly 67 percent of those entered as Jews in the Dotrščina Project. In other words, the place and manner of death of every third Zagreb Jew are unknown. In some cases, such as those of Drago Bachrach and Dora Bošan, it was possible to discover their place of death, but for many others this will probably always remain unknown.

However, the Dotrščina Project does record that 85 Jews (1.3 percent) were killed in a "Polish camp," and that 288 (4.5 percent) were killed in a "German camp." It remains unclear what the people who supplied the information for this project, who wrote it down, and who finally processed it, meant by "Polish" and "German" camps. All the "industrialized death" camps with gas chambers for mass liquidation (Treblinka, Sobibor, Majdanek, Chelmno, Oswieczim-Auschwitz) were in the part of Poland that the Third Reich did not annex in 1939, but placed under the German occupation government. There were many other concentration camps on Third Reich territory (in Germany from 1933, with Austria and the annexed parts of Bohemia, Poland, France, and Slovenia), but they worked for the German war industry; the internees in them were also starved, ill-treated, and selectively killed, but there were no gas chambers for mass liquidation, such as those found in Dachau, Buchenwald, Bergen-Belsen, Ravensbrück, Theresienstadt, and others. Most of the Zagreb Jews deported in the direction of Poland and Germany were killed in Auschwitz, with a relatively smaller number in camps on Third Reich territory, so the numerical relations about these places of death in the Dotrščina Project are not precise. Besides, the people who gathered and processed the information could not know to which of the many camps a victim had been deported, and in which he/she met death. Only people who survived could testify: in October 1943, Wehrmacht soldiers arrested Mavro and Ella Gross and their daughter, Mirjana, in Savski Marof (near Zaprešić, twenty kilometers west of Zagreb), not far from the Slovenian border. They had been hiding there for a long time; the mother and daughter survived imprisonment in Ravensbrück, but the father died in Buchenwald.[37]

If we limit statistics only to victims whose place of death is known, then 41.6 percent of Zagreb Jews were killed in Jasenovac (1,783 of 4,290), and 48.3 percent (2,070 of 4,290) in both Jasenovac and Stara Gradiška, which is almost every second. This kind of calculation shows that 19.3 percent (828 of 4,290) Zagreb Jews were killed in Auschwitz, and 28 percent (1,201 of 4,290) in all the "German" and "Polish" camps.

For the final results about where Zagreb Jews met their death, it is not crucial to clarify what was meant by "German" and "Polish" camps: it is much more important that even such studious and detailed research as the Dotrščina Project could not establish the manner and place of death for as many as 1,736 people (27.2 percent), whose place of death statistics are given as "unknown." It would thus be much more important to discover where these 1,736 people were killed, and, as total data about the final destinations of deportees exist, some approximations are possible. Almost 5,000 Zagreb Jews were sent to Pag, Jadovno, Jasenovac, and other camps in Croatia in the deportations of 1941 and 1942, while some of them lost their lives in Zagreb. Almost 3,000 Zagreb Jews were taken to Auschwitz and other camps in today's Germany and Poland in the deportations during the second half of 1942 and in 1943. As the Dotrščina Project lists a total of 2,070 victims in Jasenovac and Stara Gradiška, and a total of 1,201 victims in "German" and "Polish" camps, it seems that the proportions between the various places of death have been more or less determined. In other words, we can safely say that close to 50 percent of Zagreb Jews were killed in Jasenovac and Stara Gradiška, close to 30 percent in Auschwitz and other German and Polish camps, and 20 percent in other places, mostly in Zagreb and elsewhere in Croatia. Thus, it is logical to assume that 50 percent of the victims whose place of death is "unknown" were killed in Jasenovac and Stara Gradiška, and the corresponding proportions in other places of death. This means that another 800–900 Jews listed in the Dotrščina Project, whose place of death is not known, lost their lives in Jasenovac and Stara Gradiška—in other words, that close to 3,000 Zagreb Jews listed in the Dotrščina Project were killed in Jasenovac and Stara Gradiška. By this calculation, the number killed in Auschwitz and other "German" and "Polish" camps climbs to about 1,700 (30 percent of the 1,783 victims killed in an "unknown" location, about 500–550 victims, added to 1,201). However, these numbers are not final, because they must be increased by the almost 2,500 who were not included in the Dotrščina Project, and who were killed in Zagreb or were from Zagreb. If we continue to use the above calculation, then 4,000 Zagreb Jews, perhaps as many as 4,500, were killed in Jasenovac and Stara Gradiška, and at least about 2,500, perhaps as many as 3,000, in Auschwitz and other German and Polish camps.

If Vladimir Žerjavić's calculations that about 13,000 Jews were killed in Jasenovac are accepted, this leads to the conclusion that about 30 to 35 percent of all the Jews killed in the Jasenovac Camp Complex were from Zagreb. This is somewhat more than the percentage of the Zagreb Jewish

Community in the total Jewish population in the ISC—some 10,000 to 12,000 thousand out of 40,000, which makes about 25 to 30 percent.

Can these figures be challenged? The most important objection to Žerjavić's figures is that they were obtained from lists of victims in which Jews largely did not declare themselves as Jews. Looking through the *List of Victims—Zagreb,* which gives 3,217 Jews, I deduced that the list has at least another 980 Jews, usually included as Croats or people without nationality. This can be seen from their characteristic Jewish surnames (and first names), the large number of women among them, and their age, which means at least 30 percent more (in this case, exactly 30.5 percent more). If this percentage is used to increase Žerjavić's 13,000 Jewish victims in Jasenovac, then the estimate is that about 17,000 Jews were killed in Jasenovac, which is almost the same number as that already mentioned in the literature.[38] I believe that further research will lead to even more precise results, but I do not think that possible differences in the number of victims will be so great as to affect the general picture of the death toll of Zagreb Jews in the Holocaust.[39]

43

A NEW BEGINNING?

Just as the requests for release from camp in 1941 and 1942 showed a desperate hope that the request would be met, so the postwar correspondence of the Zagreb Jewish Community with many addresses in Yugoslavia and abroad showed a desperate hope that the search for family and friends would have a happy ending. Hundreds of letters arrived at, and were sent from the Jewish Community in Zagreb in Croatian, German, and English, and some in French and Italian. It seems that one of the first jobs the Community tackled after liberation was updating and supplementing the evidence about war victims, which, after September 1945, served to a great extent as the official document about who had disappeared.[1]

In most cases, the news was bad, as in that of Vladimir (1913) and Zdenko (1917) Wasserthal. "Both were taken to camp in 1941, from where they have not yet returned, so they are probably no longer alive." It seems that both had already been killed in Jasenovac in 1941.[2] Matilda Fogel, née Levi, received information that "her husband, Juda Herš Fogel, and children Moric, Rafael, and Rašela, were, as Jews, taken by the Ustasha and German authorities to internment camps during the years of 1941–1943, and it seems that the criminals killed all of them there."[3] "The Jewish Religious Community confirms that Fani Gold, née Weiss, Sabina Gold, Regina Gold (married name Bauer), and Emil Freiwald lived in Zagreb until 1942. As they disappeared from Zagreb without a trace at the same time that Zagreb Jews were being taken to camps, it is probable that the above-named were taken to a concentration camp."[4] Arnold Frid in Varaždin was informed that "Heda Alkalaj from Sarajevo was in Loborgrad Camp until 1942, and was transferred to Germany from there. Since no one from that group returned, she is probably no longer alive."[5] Requests for information also arrived from abroad: Dorry Schonau from London asked about Mariana Kohn and her daughter, Eva, about whom she had no information after 1941, not long after they arrived in Zagreb from Vienna. She was informed that they had both been deported in 1942 "in the direction of Hungary, and all trace of everyone who was on that transport was lost."[6]

Even in October 1945, the Zagreb Community wrote to Split that "we know nothing about people who are still in Auschwitz . . . Auschwitz Camp was completely evacuated in January, except for people who were sick and were left in the hospital, but we do not believe they are there any longer." As people in Split were obviously claiming that there were still some survivors in Auschwitz, Zagreb informed them that "unfortunately, your information is wrong."[7]

There were also stories with a happy ending. Bela Frank from Novi Sad had no news about his son, Ivan (1925), "for over a year and a half." In December 1945, he was told by the Novi Sad Jewish Community that someone in Zagreb had found, in a Palestinian newspaper, a list of people who had been saved, and that his son was on it. The Zagreb Community confirmed the happy news, and sent him all the necessary information.[8]

Some people began a new life, but still under the strong influence of the tragedy. Ruben Freiberger (1932), Miroslav Šalom's son, whose parents had been killed in Auschwitz, lived in Kibbutz Shar Ha'amakim (fourteen kilometers southeast of Haifa). Ruben's uncle, knowing that the boy's parents were no longer alive, wrote a letter to the Zagreb Community: "In the spring of 1945, he finished the fourth grade of primary school and is continuing his schooling in the kibbutz. He has completely adapted to the new environment and the new way of life and feels good in this community."[9]

The Zagreb Community also worked on establishing the fate of members of the Zagreb and other Jewish communities in Croatia who had disappeared, in order to resolve many property issues. In August 1945, Arnold Grossman, Eugen Kon, and Vladimir Stastny of Zagreb stated that "they personally knew that Adolf Friedländer and his wife, Ivana, née Bröder, Paula Schlesinger, née Bröder, Greta Schlesinger (married name Friedländer), Anika Schlesinger, Izidor Perera, Nada Perera, née Friedländer, and Mirko

Friedländer had been taken to the Jasenovac and Stara Gradiška camps in 1942. Since the above have not reported back until now, they are probably no longer alive. We are prepared to repeat our statement at any time under oath in court." The Community clerk added that the "Jewish Religious Community in Zagreb officially confirms that the above signed their statement by their own hand."[10] Confirmation of this kind was still being issued as late as 1952, when Štefanija Štern, for the purpose of "regulating her child's allowance," was issued with a confirmation that "Milan Štern, son of Karlo, born in 1897 in Zagreb . . . who lived in an apartment at Klaićeva 62, was taken away by the Ustashe in May 1943 to an unknown camp and never returned."[11] In the same year, the secretary of the Zagreb Community confirmed that Berlin refugees Alfred (1891), Charlotte (1898), and Rudolf (1921) Weissman had been taken "by force" from Zagreb in June 1941 "by the Ustasha authorities to an unknown destination and were never again heard of."[12]

Officials of the Jewish Community of Zagreb even testified that some Belgrade Jews were no longer alive.[13] Informing families about the fate of their loved ones, in some cases, consciously or unconsciously, the Jewish Community adopted the Nazi-Ustasha terminology: it claimed that Josefina Grünwald from Koprivnica had been imprisoned in Loborgrad and that later the "Loborgrad prisoners were 'relocated' to Germany," but then added that "no one from that group returned, so she is probably no longer alive."[14]

Most of the very small number of Jewish foreign citizens who had survived the war in the greater Zagreb region and in Croatia could not take care of themselves after the war. In Zagreb, sixty-four-year-old Richard Löwenherz and his wife, Dagmar, refugees from Coburg, survived the war; they were probably left alone because Dagmar was not Jewish.[15] German refugee Norbert Thumin-Landau was still in the Psychiatric Hospital in Vrapče two and a half years after liberation, in October 1947, because he had nowhere to go. After that, attempts were made to place him in the old people's home in Zagreb. [16]

It was especially difficult to find homes for orphaned children. In May 1945, child refugee Milka Nahod (obviously she was named later because *nahod* means "orphan") was living with the Bradač family in Tomislavov Square.[17] In July 1945, ten-year-old Danko Flesch was living with Draga Schmidlehner in Ludbreg, and the Jewish Community requested that he be asked "whether he knows the names of his parents, and is he the brother of Dankica Flesch, eight years old, who has been placed with Mrs. Rosa Tkalec."[18] The Jewish Community also asked the Golubić bookshop in Ludbreg to "inform us if you know the names of the parents of the boy

Željko Mosez, who has been placed with you . . . We also beg you to send us any other information about the boy that you may have."[19] Little Batja Scher, daughter of Vukovar Rabbi Israel Scher, was in Vukovar at the end of 1945. Her whole family had been taken to camp, and no one returned. Their former servant, Mirjana Nikolić, took care of the little girl all through the war, "doing the hardest work, she fed and clothed the child from her earnings." The Zagreb Community "learned from reliable sources that the child is in very good hands, so that we do not want to take her away, all the more so that the child wishes to stay, and Mirjana wants the keep the child with her until we can find relatives, who are said to be living in Palestine or America."[20] At the end of 1945, Nada Goldberger (1934) from Vinkovci, who was in the Children's Home in Šestine (a northern suburb of Zagreb), became the ward of Štefica Rosbroj, née Schwabenitz, of Zagreb.[21]

At a meeting of the Community Board in the summer of 1945, Lavoslav Glesinger asked for data to be collected about children, and for the children to be returned to any surviving relatives: "Gathering data about these children is often met with the greatest resistance, because many people will not separate themselves from these children, whom they have grown to love as time passed, so often the authorities must intervene to drag such children from their hiding places. It is especially difficult in the case of very small children, because they do not even know their own names, and there are cases when even the adoptive parents do not know the children's names." Glesinger gave the example of a Jewish innkeeper, a First World War invalid, who lived in the environs of Đakovo or Podravska Slatina. He managed to avoid persecution himself and at the same time save three children from the Đakovo camp. He also found homes for a large number of Jewish children from that camp with non-Jewish families, who lived in the vicinity. Glesinger proposed that someone should go to Đakovo to investigate matters, and as for the general situation, to undertake certain activities independently, but to coordinate with the authorities as much as possible.[22]

In practice, there were also some unpleasant situations. The Jewish Community sent a letter to the already mentioned Franciscan tertiary Rafaela Elizabeta Gustetić. She lived in an apartment in Bogišićeva Street and, according to the testimony of contemporaries, took care of a large number of children during the war: "We heard that you have a little Jewish girl, an orphan, whom we wish to care for. Please hand over the child, together with her effects and documents, to the bearers of this letter without delay, they are our employees Ignac Weiss and Lovro Kereš. If the child has no documents, please tell us the exact names and surnames of the child and her parents. If you do not comply with our demand, we shall immediately undertake the most rigorous steps to have the child handed over."[23] However, they were not always so rough. Everyone knew that they could do only very little to decrease the tragedy, and there was, as a rule, much more consideration and mutual respect than the letter to Mrs. Gustetić suggests.

The Zagreb Community searched for children throughout Central Croatia and Slavonia. Jews in small towns and villages were sent a kind of circular letter with questions. At the end of 1945, Jews from Našice, Orahovica, and Vrpolje (in Slavonia, east of Slavonski Brod) sent word that they "do not know of any Jewish children who have not been provided for in our town or the immediate surroundings."[24] Despite all attempts, there is no doubt that all the children were not found. Some children discovered that their adoptive parents were not their natural parents, but their names and origin could not be discovered for certain, and, even in 2000, some were still searching for their real identity and family.[25]

The first postwar task of the Community was to take care of the survivors, because "most returnees have no personal property whatsoever," said many Community documents. On May 22, 1945, the Community appointed Elsa Frey and Gertruda Kohn to "collect all kinds of clothes and shoes in the name of the Community, to distribute to the returnees."[26] Mira Gavrin, daughter-in-law of the late Chief Rabbi Gavro Schwarz, "got free lunch and supper from the Jewish Community for herself and her children."[27] In June 1945, Oton Glikstal in the village of Kordunsko Zagorje (twenty-five kilometers south of Karlovac) received 40,000 kunas.[28] Greta Goldman asked for help, because there was no one to take care of her: "My brothers, who used to support me, have been killed. I suffer from a severe inflammation of the joints and chronic colitis, so that I am incapable of any kind of work. I am sending doctors' certificates to prove this."[29]

All who had returned from camp had to be taken care of, too. Irena Fuchs (1911) survived her internment in Auschwitz, and in August 1945 the Jewish Community asked "all the military and civilian authorities to help her in every way."[30] The Jewish Community issued Frida Fuhrmann, who had also returned from camp, with a certificate "requesting all competent people and other authorities to give her the necessary support and do all they can to help her to go to Klagenfurt (in Austria), where she has family."[31] Mira Glik from Zagreb returned from Auschwitz, so the Jewish Community begged "all the authorities to help her in every way in her search for her family."[32]

A home for returnees was opened at Haulikova 6 as early as May.[33]

Thirty-five returnees were soon accommodated there under "rather spartan conditions," where they were, if necessary, given breakfast, and children given other food as well to make them stronger. "We provide vitamins, condensed milk, Ovomaltine, and any necessary medication, send those who are ill to doctors, and offer all of them legal advice."[34] In July 1945, the Community asked the Red Cross for "a certain amount of condensed milk, if possible sweetened, considering that returnees, children, old people, and those who are ill, for whom the milk is intended, are unfortunately unable to supply themselves with sugar."[35]

On May 22, the Community received "six handkerchiefs, two pairs of shoes, three pairs of men's socks, two shirts, one petticoat, and one spool of thread" from Mrs. N. Smolej of Zagreb, and for this it "expressed its warmest thanks."[36] The next day, the Community asked the Leather and Textile Directorate to issue a permit for it to acquire 300 pairs of shoes, because returnees are arriving "from various parts of the country, and they are naked and barefoot."[37]

Oskar Quitner and Hermina Nemlich stayed in Tone Dasović's house in Švica (seven kilometers west of Otočac, in Lika) from September 1943 to January 1944. Then they had to flee before the onslaught of the German offensive, and they "left all their things with Dasović." At the end of 1945 and the beginning of 1946, a correspondence began between the Local People's Committee in Švica and the Jewish Community for "two men's suits, three women's mackintoshes, twelve women's dresses, five pairs of panties, and two pairs of shoes" to be sent to Zagreb, because neither Oskar nor Hermina "have anything to wear."[38]

At the beginning of June 1945, the Community sent Šandor Deutsch to Miramarska Road to acquire wood shavings to fill mattresses.[39] In August, the Community got eighty straw mattresses from the Red Cross. In October, before the coming of winter, the Community asked the Red Cross for one hundred blankets and one hundred sheets, and got twelve eiderdowns with covers, and eighteen blankets.[40] In December 1945, the Community was "taking care of about 600 people, whom we feed, dress, for whom we secure accommodations to the best of our ability in reception centers and medial aid in our own clinic and dentist's office. They include fifty-seven university students, thirty-six secondary school pupils, and forty-five children under the age of ten." In its requests to the Red Cross, it said that "the greatest concern are the completely exhausted children and old people, whom we cannot supply with the dietary food that the doctor prescribed, simply because we do not have money to buy such food."[41]

On May 17, the Merkur Sanatorium admitted thirty-three-year-old Egon Berger, who had survived Jasenovac, for treatment.[42] In September 1945, twenty-one-year-old Anjuška Kraus, who had survived Auschwitz, was admitted to the tuberculosis ward of the Sisters of Charity Hospital.[43]

Community activities slowly started to be renewed: by the end of June, the Community administration returned from the address in Tomislavov Square to Palmotićeva Street 16, occupying the ground floor.[44]

However difficult the problems of these people were, at least they had survived.

The usual phrase that peace always "heals the wounds of war" is not applicable in the case of the Jewish population of Croatia and Bosnia and Herzegovina, or in the case of the Zagreb Jews. These wounds, that were the consequence of losing three-quarters to four-fifths of their number, cannot ever be patched up. The Holocaust left a lasting imprint on their past, present, and future. This is true even of the younger Community members, born many years after the war, who are aware of what happened to their grandmothers and grandfathers and their families.

In California, Hilda Singer, née Freiberger, sister of Rabbi Miroslav Šalom Freiberger, waited apprehensively for news from her parents, sister, and brother. In July 1945, she again wrote to her parents, Antun and Anka, from Beverly Hills, saying "how wistfully I long for news from you, but nothing till now. Maybe something may come someday. Please inform me as soon as possible if you need anything. I am working in one of the biggest trading companies as an accountant, but when you come here we will open a store again." Hilda wrote a letter to her brother, Miroslav, asking him to "send his new address." She wrote to her sister, Ljubica Freiberger, "If I knew how you and all of our family were . . . when you come here I will make sure I find a nice place for you and we will enjoy life. We should forget everything sad that happened."

Although Hilda Singer wanted to forget "everything sad that happened," it was not possible. She did not receive any of the longed-for answers to her letters.

None of her family in Zagreb were alive. Her brother, Miroslav Šalom Freiberger, and his wife, Irena, were killed in Auschwitz in the spring of 1943. Her parents, Anka and Antun, and sister, Ljubica, died in an "unknown place."

Hilda could never forget.

NOTES

Abbreviations and Acronyms Used in Notes

AHA	*Antisemitizam, Holokaust, Antifašizam*
BP ŽHH	Baza podataka o Židovima žrtvama Holokausta u Hrvatskoj (Database of Jewish Holocaust Victims in Croatia, archival collection)
BVBH	Banska vlast Banovine Hrvatske (Office of the Ban of the Banovina of Croatia, archival collection)
CGK	Centralna gradska komisija (Central Municipal Commission)
ČSP	*Časopis za suvremenu povijest,* Zagreb (Journal of Contemporary History)
DKM	Dosjei konfiscirane mase (Dossiers of Confiscated Property, archival collection)
GLAVSIGUR	Glavno ravnateljstvo za javni red i sigurnost (Headquarters for Public Order and Security, Ustasha Police)
GO	Glavni odbor (Board of Governors)
HAZ	Historijski arhiv u Zagrebu (Historical Archives in Zagreb)
HBL	*Hrvatski biografski leksikon* (Croatian Biographical Dictionary)
HDA	Hrvatski državni arhiv (Croatian State Archives)
HDS	Hrvatski državni sabor (Croatian Parliament)
HDZ	Hrvatska demokratska zajednica (Croatian Democratic Union)
HRSS	Hrvatska Republikanska Seljačka Stranka (Croatian Republican Peasant Party [name of the HSS prior to 1925])
HSS	Hrvatska Seljačka Stranka (Croatian Peasant Party)
HZ	*Historijski zbornik,* Zagreb (Historical Review or Review of History, Zagreb)
IHP	Institut za hrvatsku povijest (Institute for Croatian History)
IBO	Izraelitska bogoštovna općina (Israelite Religious Community)

IO	Izvršni odbor (Executive Committee)
ISC	Independent State of Croatia (See NDH)
JA	*Jevrejski almanah,* Beograd (Jewish Almanac, Belgrade)
JIM	Jevrejski istorijski muzej, Beograd (Jewish Historical Museum, Belgrade)
JNA	Jugoslavenska narodna armija (Yugoslav People's Army)
JO	Jevrejska općina (Jewish Community)
JOINT	Jewish Joint Distribution Committee
JOO	Jugoslavenski olimpijski odbor (Yugoslav Olympic Committee)
JP	*Jevrejski pregled,* Beograd (Jewish Journal, Belgrade)
JVO	Jevrejska vjeroispovjedna općina (Jewish Religious Community)
JRZ	Jugoslavenska radikalna zajednica (Yugoslav Radical Union)
KAZ	Kaptolski arhiv u Zagrebu (Ecclesiastical Archives in Zagreb)
KH	Keren Hajesod (United Israel Appeal [Keren Hayesod])
KK	Keren Kajemet (Jewish National Fund [Keren Kayemet])
KP	Komunistička partija (Communist Party)
KPH	Komunistička partija Hrvatske (Communist Party of Croatia)
KPJ	Komunistička partija Jugoslavije (Communist Party of Yugoslavia)
LE	*Likovna enciklopedija,* t. 1–4, Zagreb (Encyclopedia of Art, vols. 1–4)
ME	*Muzička enciklopedija,* t. 1–3, Zagreb (Encyclopedia of Music, vols. 1–3)
MINORS	Ministarstvo oružanih snaga NDH (Ministry of the Armed Forces of the Independent State of Croatia)
MPB	Ministarstvo pravosuđa i bogoštovlja (Ministry of Justice and Religious Affairs)
MUP	Ministarstvo unutarnjih (unutrašnjih) poslova (Ministry of the Interior)
NAZ	Nadbiskupski arhiv Zagreb (Archdiocesan Archives of Zagreb)
NDH	Nezavisna Država Hrvatska (Independent State of Croatia)
NDS	Nadbiskupski duhovni stol (Archdiocesan Spiritual Board, archival collection)

NK	Nogometni Klub (soccer club)
NOV	Narodnooslobodilačka vojska (National Liberation Army)
OZN (OZNA)	Odjeljenje za zaštitu naroda (Department of National Security)
PF	Pravni fakultet (Faculty of Law)
PGZ	Poglavarstvo grada Zagreba (Administration of the City of Zagreb)
PP	*Povijesni prilozi,* Zagreb (Historical Contributions)
PTS	Poglavnikova tjelesna bojna (Name of the Poglavnik's Personal Unit)
RAVSIGUR	Ravnateljstvo za javni red i sigurnost (Directorate for Public Order and Safety)
RELICO	Relief Committee for the War-Stricken Jewish Population
RH	Republika Hrvatska (Republic of Croatia)
RSUP	Republički sekretarijat unutrašnjih poslova (Secretariat of the Interior of the Republic of Croatia)
RUR	Ravnateljstvo ustaškog redarstva (Directorate of the Ustasha Police)
SAD	Sjedinjene Američke Države (United States of America)
SBDZ	Savska banovina, Državna zaštita (Sava Banovina, State Security, archival collection)
SCJ	Savez Cionista Jugoslavije (Zionist Federation of Yugoslavia)
SDS	Služba državne sigurnosti (State Security Service)
SBUO	Savska banovina, Upravno odjeljenje (Sava Banovina, Administrative Division)
SJOJ	Savez jevrejskih opština (općina) Jugoslavije (Association of Jewish Communities in Yugoslavia)
SJVOJ	Savez jevrejskih vjeroispovjednih opština (općina) Jugoslavije (Association of Jewish Religious Communities in Yugoslavia)
SK	Savez komunista (Communist League)
SKOJ	Savez komunističke omladine Jugoslavije (League of Communist Youth of Yugoslavia)
SRH	Socijalistička Republika Hrvatska (Socialistic Republic of Croatia)
UDB	Ured Državne Bezbednosti (Office of State Security [after 1945, Yugoslav Secret Service])

UNS	Ustaška nadzorna služba (Ustasha Surveillance Service [Ustasha Secret Service])
USIKS	Ustaški stegovni i kazneni sud (Ustasha Disciplinary and Criminal Court)
ZAVNOH	Zemaljsko antifašističko vijeće narodnog oslobođenja Hrvatske (Antifascist Council of the Croatian National Liberation)
ZHP	Zavod za hrvatsku povijest (Institute for Croatian History)
ZKRZ	Zemaljska komisija za utvrđivanje zločina okupatora i njihovih pomagača (Zemaljska komisija za ratne zločine) (State Commission for Investigation of the Crimes Committed by the Occupying Forces and Their Supporters)
ŽAPD	Židovsko akademsko potporno društvo (Jewish Academic Assistance Society)
ŽBOZ	Židovska bogoštovna općina Zagreb (Jewish Religious Community of Zagreb)
Žid. odsj.	Židovski odsjek (Jewish Department)
ŽOZ	Židovska općina Zagreb (Jewish Community of Zagreb)
ŽVO	Židovska vjeroispovjedna općina (Jewish Religious Community of Zagreb)

2. The Jews in Zagreb Prior to 1941

1. Matasović, "Dva prosvjeda," 107–9.

2. Schwarz, *Povijest,* 8 ff.; see also Goldstein, "Zagrebačka židovska općina."

3. Freidenreich, *The Jews*, 48.

4. *Jevrejski narodni kalendar* for the year 1938–1939.

5. *Židov* 40 (1929); 37 (1931).

6. Kovač and Domaš, *Jewish Heritage.*

7. Völkl, "Die jüdische Gemeinde von Zagreb"; Völkl, "Zur Judenfeindlichkeit in Kroatien"; see also Goldstein, *Židovi u Zagrebu.*

8. Schwarz, *Povijest*, 56.

9. *Židov* 14 and 18 (1922); *Nova Evropa* 9–10 (1922): 280–83.

10. HDA, Collection 144, SBUO, box 283, 1725/II/1936.

11. The revisionists promoted capitalism, in contrast to the left-wing Zionists. They demanded a "revision" of the relationship with Great Britain, which, in their opinion, should have declared itself more positively and clearly in favor of creating a Jewish state in Palestine, which was then under British mandate. In the struggle for establishing a Jewish state, they championed the most militant methods, and the later Jewish terrorists in Palestine sprang from among them. They were never strong in

Croatia and Yugoslavia—see, HDA, group Contemporary History Institute—group XXIV, 1938, inv. no. 138.

12. *Židov,* 48a, 49, and 50 (1935).

13. A paraphrase of the basic idea of the article Gross, *Ravnopravnost.*

14. HDA, Collection ZKRZ GUZ, no. 306, box 15, 3874.

15. Šik, "Zagrebački Židovi u privredi."

3. Anti-Semitism in the Thirties

1. See in general, Völkl, "Zur Judenfeindlichkeit in Kroatien." This chapter is presented in more detail in Goldstein, *Židovi u Zagrebu*, 379–447.

2. *Luč* 3–4, year 25 (December 1929): 132–33; see also *Luč* 7 (1930); *Jevrejski glas* 9 (1930).

3. *Luč* 6, year 24 (February 1930): 200.

4. About Grabić, see Matijević, *Slom politike*, throughout

5. Butmi and Tomić, *Krvave osnove ili Protokoli sionskih mudraca*; *Nova revija vjeri i nauci* 1, year 4 (Makarska 1925): 70–81; Butmi and Tomić, *Krvave osnove ili Protokoli sionskih mudraca*, 73; it is interesting that *Nova revija* 4 (1927) ended its presentation of the *Protocols* with the twentieth meeting, whereas the original manuscript had twenty-seven meetings. The reasons why the *Protocols* were not carried in their entirety are not known; see also *Jevrejski glas* 34 (1930).

6. Vidi primjerice, *Nova revija vjeri i nauci* 2 (1925): 218; 1 (1926): 77; 2 (1926): 173–74; 1 (1927): 97; 2 (1927): 188, 215.

7. *Nova revija vjeri i nauci* 1, year 9 (Makarska 1932): 90.

8. *Nova revija vjeri i nauci* 2, year 5 (Makarska 1926): 187.

9. *Obzor*, August 28, 1928.

10. *Židov* 19 (1931).

11. *Nova revija vjeri i nauci* 1, year 10 (Makarska 1931): 75–78.

12. *Židov* 8 (1931).

13. *Encyclopaedia Britannica*, 17:289.

14. *Hrvatska prosvjeta* 1–2 (Zagreb 1932).

15. Staub, *Roots of Evil*, 35–51.

16. *Pravda* (Belgrade), August 10, 1932; *Židov* 32 (1932); about the orientation of *Pravda*, see, EJ 6, 581.

17. *Pravda* (Belgrade), August 12 and 15, 1932; *Židov* 34 (1932).

18. *Pravda* (Belgrade), December 8, 11, and 24, 1932.

19. *Pravda* (Belgrade), April 28, 1931; see also Nevistić's contributions in *Pravda* (Belgrade), December 10, 1932.

20. *Pravda* (Belgrade), December 20, 1935.

21. *Židov* 40 (1932).

22. *Novosti* (Zagreb), October 18, 1933; *Židov* 43 (1933).

23. *Mlada Hrvatska* 1 (1936).

24. "Hrvatski nacionalni bojkot Židova," *Völkischer Beobachter*, April 18, 1933; Freidenreich, *Jews of Yugoslavia*, 185.

25. HDA, fund 145, SBDZ, box 135, 9494/1933; see also *Hrvatski narod,* April 18, 1941.

26. HDA, fund 145, SBDZ, box 146, 30336/1933.

27. *Židov* 37 and 38 (1933).

28. *Židov* 4 (1934).

29. DAZ, fund A. Licht attorney's office, 75, 369, 370.

30. *Službeni list Banske uprave Savske Banovine*, February 15, 1934; *Jevrejski glas* 8 (1934).

31. *Židov* 16 (1936); the news was also carried by *Jevrejski glas* 16 (1936).

32. *Jutarnji list* (Zagreb), April 9, 1936; *Obzor* (Zagreb), April 9, 1936; *Židov* 15 (1936).

33. *Židov* 23 (1936).

34. *Židov* 24 (1934).

35. *Židov* 42 (1935).

36. Nenezić, *Masoni u Jugoslaviji*, 606–8; Radenić, *Bene berit*, 37–38; see also Mužić, *Masonstvo u Hrvata.*

37. "Židovska masonerija"; about these circles see Vincetić, "Antisemitizam u hrvatskoj katoličkoj štampi do Drugoga svjetskog rata," 63.

38. "Židovska masonerija," 31.

39. *Hrvatska smotra* 1 (1934).

40. *Hrvatska smotra* 5 (1939); *Jevrejska tribuna* 23 (1939).

41. *Mlada Hrvatska* 1 (1936).

42. *Nova riječ* (Zagreb), July 28, 1938; about Buć, see Petranović, *Istorija Jugoslavije*, 142; about Vilder, see EJ 8, 495.

43. About Buć, see Krizman, *Ante Pavelić i ustaše*, in various places; HBL II, 409–10; Stuparić, *Tko je tko u NDH*, 52–53; HDA, fund SDS RSUP SRH, 013.0.52, folder Dr. Mile Budak, from the archives of H. Helm, 132.

44. *Jutarnji list* (Zagreb), August 7, 1932.

45. *Hrvatska smotra* 3 (1934): 89–94; *Danica* 130 (1934).

46. *Jevrejski list* 17 (1934).

47. *Nova riječ* (Zagreb), July 28, 1938. For the senseless and politicized thesis with the wish to deny the Slavic nature of the Croats and make them part of the Germanic world, see Goldstein, *Hrvatski rani srednji vijek*, 23–24; about Šegvić, see Stuparić, *Tko je tko u NDH*, 378.

48. *Nova riječ* (Zagreb), April 21, 1938, and July 28, 1938.

49. *Danica* 74, 80 (1933); *Židov* 15 (1933); about Matošić, see Glavina, *Neobjavljeni novinski napis.*

50. *Naša gruda* 1 (1933); about Mintas, see Stuparić, *Tko je tko u NDH*, 278.

51. *Istina, slobodni i nezavisni tjednik* 1–3 (1934).

52. *Hrvatska gruda* 1, (1936).

53. *Glas opozicije* 1 (1936).

54. *Glas istine* 1 (1937).

55. *Grudobran* 1 (1936).

56. *Savremena senzacija* 1 (1936).

57. *Zagrebačka senzacija* 1–8, year 1 (Zagreb, 1936).

58. Testimony of Branko Polić; *Knjiga umrlih ŽOZ*; Žiga Štern was one of the

richest Zagreb Jews and certainly many people in Zagreb did not like him because of his behavior—see, e.g., *Zagrebačka smotra* 23 (1934).

59. *Hrvatski slobodan narod* 2, year 1 (Zagreb, 1937).

60. *Mlada Hrvatska* 1 (1936); 33 (1937); 2 (1938); and so on. The "Frankists" were radical nationalists and in 1941 most joined the Ustasha movement. They got their name from their former leader, Josip Frank (1844–1911). About Frank, see chapter 5.

61. See, *Nezavisnost*, in various places; Jelić-Butić, *Ustaše i NDH*, 48; *Nova riječ* (Zagreb) carried by *Židov* 16 (1938).

62. *Nezavisnost* 4–7, 41, and 42 (1938).

63. *Nezavisnost* 7, 19, and 30 (1938); compare also the articles entitled "Judeo-Communist Lies about Spain," "Judeo-Communist Offensive Against Germany," *Nezavisnost* 26 (1939).

64. *Mlada Hrvatska* 2 (1936); 13 (1937); 3 (1938); *Nezavisnost* 14 (1938).

65. *Nezavisnost* 4, 9, 12, 31 (1938); 28 (1939).

66. *Nezavisnost* 19, 21, 41 (1938); 12 (1939); *Mlada Hrvatska* 1, 10 (1936); 3 (1937); 13–14 (1938).

67. *Obzor* (Zagreb), May 14, 1938.

68. *Danica* 80 (1933); *Židov* 15 and 37 (1933).

69. See *Židov* 18 and 19 (1938); *Narodne novine* (Zagreb), April 24, 1938; *Vreme* (Belgrade), May 7, 1938; *Jevrejski glas* 16 (1938).

70. *Vreme* (Belgrade), May 7, 1938; *Jevrejska tribuna* 19 (1938); *Židov* 19 and 20 (1938).

71. *Nezavisnost* 10, 15, and 28 (1938); *Grudobran* 1 (1936); *Hrvatsko Pravo* (Zagreb), August 31, 1940.

72. *Obzor*, April 24, 1936; *Židov* 8 (1936); *Jevrejski glas* 18 (1936).

73. *Židov* 18 (1936).

74. About Radić's anti-Semitism, see Goldstein, *Stjepan Radić i Židovi*.

75. Maštrović, *Karlo Brkljačić*.

76. *Židov* 17 (1936).

77. *Nezavisnost* 32 and 39 (1938); 14 and 15 (1939); *Mlada Hrvatska* 6 (1936).

78. *Smotra slavenske politike* 80 (Zagreb), June 15, 1938; *Podravske novine* 17 and 21 (1938).

79. *Dom*, February 7, 1938; see also *Zelinske novine*, Sv. Ivan Zelina, February 4, 1939.

80. *Pravda* (Belgrade), March 10, 1939.

81. *Nova riječ* (Zagreb), April 21, 1938; June 23, 1938; June 28, 1938; August 11, 1938; November 24, 1938.

82. See in detail, Goldstein, "The Catholic Church in Croatia and the 'Jewish Problem,' 1918–1941," *Eastern European Jewish Affairs* 33, no. 2 (Winter 2003): 121–34.

83. *Narodna Obrana, list za prosvjetu, gospodarstvo i društveni život* (Đakovo), April 8, 1933. Under "the persecution of Catholics in Mexico," *Narodna Obrana* and later also *Nedjelja* meant the presidential term of Plutarch Elĭas Calles (1928–1934), whose policy was "militantly anti-clerical"—he limited the number of church officials and banned church schools. In return, the church boycotted public events. In 1929, conditions calmed down to a certain extent—see *Encyclopaedia Britannica*, micropaedia, 2:748, 859–60; macropaedia, 24:48.

84. *Židov* 47 (1933).

85. *Katolički list* (Zagreb), August 18, 1938.

86. Vincetić, "Antisemitizam u hrvatskoj katoličkoj štampi do Drugoga svjetskog rata."

87. After *Malchut Jisrael* 9 (1937).

88. *Omanut* 10 (1938).

89. *Narodna svijest* (Dubrovnik), January 11, 1939.

90. *Židov* 1 (1939).

91. Passelecq and Suchecky, *L'Encyclique cachée*, 80; LaFarge, *Un Américain comme les autres*, 201–2; see in detail, Goldhagen, *Moral Reckoning*, 107 and throughout.

92. *Tko vlada u Rusiji?–Židovi*, 23, 32; "Židovska masonerija," 33.

93. "Dnevnik A. Stepinca," *Danas*, Zagreb, 8/7 and 9/26/1990.

94. *Nova riječ* (Zagreb), April 21, 1938.

95. *Hrvatska straža, tjednik za katolički dom* 17, 41, 43, and 50 (1937); 10, 17, 19, and 28 (1938).

96. *Zagrebačka smotra* 20 (1934).

97. *Hrvatski dnevnik* (Zagreb), October 30, 1937, and April 28, 1938.

98. *Hrvatska straža, tjednik za katolički dom* 5, 12, 15, 16, 18, 27, 30, and 39 (1937); 1 (1938); *Hrvatska straža, dnevnik*, January 12, 1939.

99. *Merkurov vjesnik* 1–2 (Zagreb, 1932); *Hrvatska straža, dnevnik*, January 24, 1932; *Židov* 5 (1932).

100. *Hrvatska straža, tjednik za katolički dom* 18 (1938).

101. *Hrvatska straža, tjednik za katolički dom* 41 (1937).

102. Vincetić, "Antisemitizam u hrvatskoj katoličkoj štampi do Drugoga svjetskog rata," 59, 64.

103. *Hrvatska straža, dnevnik*, January 15 and 19, 1932; April 28, 1938; July 15 and 20, 1939.

104. Duffy, *Sveci i grešnici*, 261.

105. *Židov* 33 (1938); *Hrvatski dnevnik*, August 4, 1938; *Hrvatska straža, dnevnik za katolički dom*, August 5, 1938.

106. Hrvatska straža, tjednik za katolički dom 17 (1938).

107. Krišto, *Katolička crkva i Nezavisna Država Hrvatska*, 2:269; see also Goldstein, *Holokaust u Zagrebu*, 564.

108. About Šimrak, see Matijević, *Slom politike katoličkog jugoslavenstva*, in various places; Matijević, "Poticaji i organiziranje," 221; Stuparić, *Tko je tko u NDH*, 382; HDA, fund SDS RSUP SRH, 301886, folder S. Kvaternik, shorthand record from the main hearing (testimony of Mario Maričić), 319; Kisić-Kolanović, "Podržavljenje imovine Židova u NDH," 436; NAZ, fund Presidial Documents 143 (1941), 136 (1942).

109. Petešić, *Katoličko svećenstvo*, 142.

110. *Nedjelja* 8, 17, and 51 (1935).

111. Katolički tjednik 13/1939.

112. *Nova revija vjeri i nauci* 6, year 9 (Makarska 1932): 530–32.

113. *Hrvatska straža, dnevnik*, December 16, 1938, see also *Jevrejska tribuna* 46 (1938); 2 (1939).

114. *Hrvatska straža, dnevnik*, February 26, 1939.

115. *Koprive* 35 and 37 (1938).

116. About Dobrovoljac, see HBL 3:448.

117. *Koprive* 34 (1938); *Židov* 36 (1938).

118. *Koprive* 23 (1936).

119. Bauer, *Današnja Njemačka*, 37, 51; about Bauer, see Stuparić, *Tko je tko u NDH*, 27–28.

120. *Hrvatski dnevnik* (Zagreb), March 7, 1937.

121. *Nova riječ* (Zagreb), March 20, 1937.

122. *Obzor* (Zagreb), March 9, 1937.

123. Testimony of Branko Polić. The European model for this kind of "self-hate" was Otto Weininger (1880–1903) from Vienna, converted, whose pamphlet *Sex and Character* (*Geschlecht und Charakter*, 1903) served as a useful foundation for anti-Semitic propaganda at the time of Hitler. Weininger, *Pol i karakter*; about Weininger, see Abrahamsen, *Mind and Death*. See also Lessing, *Jüdischer Selbsthass*.

124. *Hrvatski dnevnik* (Zagreb), July 28, 1936.

125. *Smotra slavenske politike* (Zagreb) 85, October 1, 1938.

126. *Židov* 15 (1938); *Jevrejska tribuna* 15–16 (1938); JP 3–4 (1983); *Jevrejski glas* 14–15, 24 (1938).

127. *Jevrejska tribuna* 7 (1938); *Jevrejski glas* 7 (1938); minutes from the twenty-fifth meeting of the Executive Committee of the SJVOJ, February 17, 1938, 33, JIM.

128. *Večer* (Zagreb), February 8, 1938.

129. *Obzor* (Zagreb), February 9, 1938.

130. *Novosti* (Zagreb), February 11, 1938.

131. *Hrvatski Dnevnik* (Zagreb), February 10, 1938.

132. *Jutarnji list* (Zagreb), February 10, 1938.

133. EJ 5, 367.

134. *Hrvatski dnevnik* (Zagreb), November 15, 1938.

135. I could not find the original text of the proclamation in the archives, but it was printed in *Spremnost* (Zagreb) 11, May 10, 1942.

136. *Židov* 46 (1938).

137. *Jevrejski glas* 6 (1938).

138. *Mlada Hrvatska* 3 (1936).

139. Ben-Sasson, *History of the Jewish People*, 958.

140. *Male Novine* (Belgrade), June 5, 1933; *Židov* 26 and 46 (1933); *Zašto se Nemačka brani od Jevreja*, fund 145, SBDZ, box 158, 24989/1933, p. 5, 28, HDA.

141. *Slovenec* (Ljubljana), January 15, 1933.

142. *Pohod* (Ljubljana), January 17, 1932; see also *Pohod* (Ljubljana), April 22, 1933.

143. Radenić, *Bene berit*, 55.

144. *Malchut Jisrael* 8 (1934).

145. Minutes from the third meeting of the Executive Committee of the SJVOJ, June 4, 1936, JIM, Belgrade, 8 9; *Malchut Jisrael* 1 (1934) saw Majstrović's interpellation as "symptoms of an organized anti-Jewish campaign." *Jevrejski list* and *Malchut Jisrael* also gave Majstrović's name as Majstorović.

146. *Jevrejski list* 6 (1934).

147. JIM, box 30, SJVO to all Jewish communities, no. 4772, October 29, 1933; Freidenreich, *Jews of Yugoslavia*, 185.

148. *Židov* 38 and 45 (1933).

149. *Malchut Jisrael* 1 (1934); 1 and 12 (1936).

150. *Jugoslovenska reč* 1, 8, and 21–22 (1932); 52–53 (1933); about Domaink, see HL 1, 259.

151. Rakočević in *Sadašnjost* (Ljubljana), June–July 1939.

152. *Pokret jugoslovenskih nacionalista* 1 and 2 (1933).

153. *Svoj svome* 1–4 (1933–1934); 10–11, 14, and 15 (1936).

154. *Židov* 38 (1933).

155. *Buđenje* 1, 2, 4, 5, 10, and 23 (1934); 3, 16, 18, 19, 22, 38, 42, and 44 (1935); 22 (1936). See *Srpska konzervativna misao* 25, 47, 70, 77; Petranović, *Istorija Jugoslavije*, 141–42.

156. *Jevrejski glas* 36–37 (1930); minutes from the first meeting of the Executive Committee of the SJVOJ, April 15, 1936, p. 2, JIM.

157. *Spomenica Saveza jevrejskih opština Jugoslavije*, 58–59; *Židov* 14 (1936).

158. *Jevrejski glas* 12 (1936).

159. Minutes from the first and twelfth meetings of the Executive Committee of the SJVOJ, April 15, 1936, p. 2, and February 11, 1937, p. 6, JIM.

160. *Židov* 15 (1936).

161. *Židov* 8 and 17 (1936).

162. For more about Pavle's behavior, which exhibited rather a lot of sympathy for the right wing and for pro-Fascist and pro-Nazi views, see Hoptner, *Yugoslavia in Crisis*, in various places.

163. *Židov* 36 (1936); minutes from the third meeting Board of Governors of the SJVOJ, August 30, 1936, p. 3, JIM.

164. Minutes from the third meeting Executive Committee of the SJVOJ, June 4, 1936, p. 7, JIM.

165. Minutes from the sixth meeting Executive Committee of the SJVOJ, August 26 and 31, 1936, pp. 3–4, JIM.

166. Minutes from the eighth meeting Executive Committee of the SJVOJ, October 19, 1936, p. 1, JIM.

167. Minutes from the twenty-third meeting Executive Committee of the SJVOJ, January 5, 1938, p. 2, JIM.

168. *Židov* 41 (1935).

169. HDA, fund 145, SBDZ, box 146, 27797, 28637/1933; Geiger, *Nijemci u Kraljevini SHS*, 214–15.

170. Geiger and Jurković, *Što se dogodilo s folksdojčerima*, 37–39; Geiger, *Nijemci u Kraljevini SHS*, 205, 207; Scherer and Straka, *Kratka povijest podunavskih Nijemaca*, 46.

171. *Židov* 51 (1935); 1 (1936); *Jevrejski glas* 47 (1935) wrote in the same tone as *Židov*.

172. National Archives, Washington, D.C., Microfilm Publications, Microcopy 1203, roll 4.

173. *Der Weltkampf* 160 (April 1937).

174. *Jevrejski glas* 20 (1937).

175. *Slobodna Riječ* (Zagreb), August 28, 1937.

176. HDA, fund 144, SBUO, box 353, 5402/II/1938; about the "Judenfrage," in the supplemented *Der Auslandsdeutsche*, 275–76; Geiger, *Nijemci u Kraljevini SHS*, 210–11.

177. Geiger and Jurković, *Što se dogodilo s folksdojčerima*, 38; Geiger, "Saslušanje Branimira Altgayera," 581, 583.

178. Minutes from the extraordinary meeting of the Executive Committee of the SJVOJ, March 31, 1938, p. 46, JIM.

179. See *Die Donau*, end 1939, March 15, 1940. The last years of the paper *Die Donau* were not available to me, so I had to access them via reports in *Jevrejski glas* 2 and 15 (1940).

180. *Buđenje* 22 (1935).

181. Report on the work of the Executive Committee, February 14, 1937–January 23, 1938, contribution, minutes from the twenty-fourth meeting Executive Committee of the SJVOJ, January 17, 1938, p. 2, JIM; *Jevrejski glas* 5 (1940).

182. Minutes from the twelfth meeting Executive Committee of the SJVOJ, February 11, 1937, pp. 6–7; minutes from the eighth meeting Board of Governors of the SJVOJ, February 1, 1940, p. 3, JIM; *Židov* 49 (1936); *Jevrejski glas* 3 and 5 (1940).

183. *Novi put* (Petrovgrad) 1–7 (1937); 1 (1938).

184. *Naš put* (Petrovgrad) 3 and 4 (1939).

185. Tomić, *Jevrejsko pitanje*, 3; Milosavljević, *U tradiciji nacionalizma*, 189.

186. *Malchut Jisrael* 12 (1936).

187. *Jevrejski glas* 42 (1936).

188. *Židov* 10 (1937).

189. *Politika* (Belgrade), February 13, 1937.

190. *Balkan* 287 (1938); *Balkan*, October 21, 1936; *Nova riječ* (Zagreb), July 28, 1938.

191. *Balkan* 286, 287, 331, 332, and 333 (1938).

192. Krleža, *Deset krvavih godina*, 486.

193. Anić, *Rječnik hrvatskoga jezika*, 101.

194. Minutes from the meeting of the Administrative Committee the JVO in Zagreb, January 20, 1938, JIM.

195. *Jevrejski glas* 10 (1939).

196. *Novi Balkan* (Belgrade) 8, July 7, 1940.

197. For more detail, see, "Anti-Semitism in Serbia" in *Human Rights and Transition*, 260–82.

198. *Völkischer Beobachter*, January 4, 1937; *Glasnik, službeni organ srpske pravoslavne patrijaršije* 1–2 (1937): 33–34, owned by the Holy High Synod, Belgrade 1937.

199. Vuković and Bojović, *Pregled srpskog antisemitizma*, 45; Štefan, *From Fairy Tale to Holocaust;* Štefan, "Antisemitizam u Srbiji za vrijeme Drugoga svjetskoga rata," 309–10; all give other examples of anti-Semitism in Serbia.

200. Velimirović, *Iznad Istoka i Zapada*; Velimirović, *Kroz tamnički prozor*, 200, 299; for more detail, see Đorđević, *Srpska konzervativna misao*, 21–23.

201. *Vreme* (Belgrade), September 22 and 25, 1940, and October 21, 1940; *Jevrejska tribuna* 32 (1940).

202. In Serbia there were at that time also many unswerving opponents of

racism—e.g., Nedeljković, *Rase i rasizam*, wrote that ethno-psychological science knows of no pure race.

203. *Malchut Jisrael* 21 (1936).

204. About Kraus, see *Encyclopaedia Judaica*, 10:1243–44.

4. The Jews in the Life of Zagreb and Yugoslavia before 1941

1. *Židov* 31 (1926).

2. *Židov* 6 (1931); see also *Jevrejski glas* 5 (1932).

3. *Male novine, tjednik za savremena pitanja* (Osijek) 230, August 1, 1931; I could not discover how the case was resolved.

4. *Židov* 12, 16, 20, 31, and 39 (1932) (in issue 20: "There is no doubt that Hitler will rule Germany tomorrow. There is no need for any deep discussion to show how dangerous this is for German Jews"); *Jevrejski glas* 11 (1929).

5. *Jüdische Rundschau* (Vienna), January 31, 1933; *Židov* 5, 9, 11, 12, and 13 (1933); *Jevrejski list* 21 (1934); paper on the annual financial statements for 1933 of the JVO in Zagreb submitted to the meeting of the Main Office on October 30, 1934, JIM.

6. *Židov* 13, 15, and 20 (1933); 42 (1935); *Jevrejski glas* 13 (1933); *Malchut Jisrael* 29 (1936); "Shekel" rallies were traditional meetings of Zionist societies at which money was collected for the settlement and development of Palestine (the shekel was the monetary unit in Palestine in Biblical times).

7. *Židov* 38 (1933).

8. *Židovi na tlu Jugoslavije*, 176; *Jews in Yugoslavia*, 107.

9. *Radničke novine,* year 5, 5 (Zagreb), February 2, 1934.

10. *Židov* 20 and 21 (1934).

11. *Židov* 7 (1934).

12. *Štampa* (Belgrade), July 15, 16, and 19, 1934.

13. *Židov* 27 (1932); *Jevrejski glas* 28 (1934); *Štampa* (Belgrade), August 23, 1934.

14. *Štampa* (Belgrade), July 17, 19, and 22, 1934, and August 1, 5, 7, 10, 11, and 12, 1934; *Židov* 8 and 14 (1933); 29, 30, 31, and 34 (1934); *Malchut Jisrael* 15 (1934); *Hanoar* 6–8 (1933): 218; Freidenreich, *Jews of Yugoslavia*, 103–4.

15. See Goldstein, *Židovi u Zagrebu*, 317–29.

16. *Židov* 37 (1935); 18 (1936); 2 (1939); see also *Malchut Jisrael* 32 (1935); minutes from the meeting of the Committee for Religious Affairs of the JVO in Zagreb, April 14, 1937, and August 11, 1937; minutes from the Seventh Congress of the SJVOJ, April 23 and 24, 1939, p. 25, JIM.

17. *Židov* 39 and 40 (1935); *Malchut Jisrael* 33 (1935); minutes from the meetings of the Main Office of the ŽVO in Zagreb, September 26, 1935, JIM.

18. Licht, *O mržnji i o izbavljenju*, 20–21, 40.

19. *Židov* 29 (1936); *Malchut Jisrael* 29 (1936).

20. *Židov* 33 (1936); see also *Zagrebačka senzacija* (Zagreb), year 1, 1 (August 1936).

21. HDA, collection 145, SBDZ, box 20, 42–44/1936.

22. HDA, collection 145, SB, Confidential Documents, 2677, 5366/1938.

23. See Hoptner, *Yugoslavia in Crisis*, 117–19, and elsewhere; Petranović, *Istorija Jugoslavije*, 163 and throughout.

24. Minutes from the twenty-seventh Executive Committee meeting of the SJVOJ, 20. April 20, 1938, p. 49, JIM.

25. Minutes from the extraordinary meeting and the thirty-first Executive Committee meeting of the SJVOJ, May 6, 1938, and September 8, 1938, p. 60, 77, JIM.

26. HDA, collection 144, SBUO, confidential files II, 61994/1938.

27. *Židov* 37 (1938); *Jevrejska tribuna* 37 (1938).

28. Ristović, *U potrazi za utočištem, Jugoslovenski Jevreji*, 40–41.

29. *Židov* 40 and 44 (1938); *Jevrejska tribuna* 43 (1938); *Jugoslavenski list* (Sarajevo), November 22, 1938.

30. *Židov* 13 (1920).

31. *Novosti* (Zagreb), August 7, 1926; *Židov* 3 (1927); *Židov* 8 (1929); HDA, collection 252, RUR, J. Section, 27309.

32. *Hrvatski narod* 2 (1939).

33. *Glasnik SJVO* 3 (1933): 196–200; *Knjiga prijelaza.*

34. *Židov* 20 and 48 (1939); *Jevrejska tribuna* 22 (1938), in June it published the names of twenty-six people who had converted; see also *Jevrejska tribuna* 45 (1938).

35. HDA, collection 252, RUR, J. Section, 27309.

36. *Židov* 40, 49, and 51 (1938). It is impossible to establish the exact numbers. *Židov* 48 (1939) wrote that it was 430 people in Zagreb only. *Židov* 40 (1938) published a list of 229 people, and it is logical to ask why the names of the other 200 were not published as well at the same time. *Jevrejska tribuna* 45 (1938) published a list of 286 names of people from Zagreb and other places, on which the names from *Židov* were repeated.

37. About Marić, see Mirnik, *Obitelj Alexander ili povijest jedne zagrebačke obitelji*; Mirnik, "Obitelj Alexander ili kratka kronika."

38. In 1999 and 2000, I made inquiries about these renouncements of the Jewish faith among older members of the Jewish Community (I could not find anyone who had renounced at that time). It is typical that no one could remember anything in detail, except that the atmosphere was threatening and people thought that this move might in some future situation protect them.

39. Minutes from the meeting of the Main Office of the JVO in Zagreb, November 17, 1938, JIM.

40. *Jevrejska tribuna* 45 (1938); minutes from the meeting of the Main Office of the JVO in Zagreb, November 17, 1938, JIM.

41. *Jevrejski glas* 22 (1939).

42. Report of the SJVOJ's Executive Committee on its work from the last meeting of the Board of Governors to the present, November 28, 1938, p. 105, JIM.

43. *Novosti* (Zagreb), October 11, 1938.

44. Minutes from the meeting of the Main Office of the JVO in Zagreb, February 23, 1939, JIM.

45. HDA, collection 252, RUR, J. Section, 27309; secretary's report on the annual financial statements for 1939 submitted to the meeting of the Main Office of the JVO in Zagreb, May 21, 1940, and to the meeting of the Council June 13, 1940, JIM.

46. Minutes from the sixth meeting of the SJVOJ's Board of Governors, November

28, 1938, p. 100; minutes from the meeting of the Main Office of the JVO in Zagreb, November 17, 1938, JIM.

47. *Jevrejski glas* 27 (1940).

48. Minutes from the meeting of the JVO Council in Zagreb, September 22, 1938, JIM.

49. Minutes from the meeting of the Main Office of the JVO in Zagreb, November 17, 1938, JIM.

50. Report of the head of the Management Board as an introduction to the general debate about the budget for 1940, held at a meeting of the Main Office of the JVO in Zagreb, November 16, 1939, JIM.

51. Minutes from the Seventh Congress of the SJVOJ, 4/23–24/1939, p. 61, 69, JIM; Ristović, *U potrazi za utočištem, Jugoslovenski Jevreji*, 80.

52. *Jevrejska tribuna* 45 (1938).

53. Minutes from the Seventh Congress of the SJVOJ, April 23–24, 1939, p. 53, JIM.

54. Minutes from the seventeenth meeting SJVOJ's Executive Committee, May 16, 1940, p. 40, JIM.

55. *Židov* 50 (1938); 43 (1939).

56. *Jevrejska tribuna* 45 (1938).

57. JIM, collection ŽOZ, reg. no. 5288, sign. K-8-4-3.

58. *Židov* 49 and 51 (1938).

59. *Narodne novine* (Zagreb), October 9, 1940. Jews Slavicized/Croatized their surnames relatively often, e.g., Julijan Spitzer of Osijek became Kraljević in 1918, according to *Jug* (Osijek), February 5, 1918.

60. *Danica* 21 (1938).

61. *Kartoteka židovskog znaka*; *Popis žrtava*; *Spiskovi preživelih*.

62. *Židov* 48 and 50 (1938); 48 (1939); Freidenreich, *Jews of Yugoslavia*, 110, speaks imprecisely of "about 200,000 dinars."

63. Secretary's report on the annual financial statements for 1938 submitted to the meeting of the Main JVO Office in Zagreb, April 27, 1939, and the meeting of the JVO Council, May 11, 1939, p. 61, JIM.

64. Paper of the head of the Management Board; Minutes from the meeting of the JVO Presidency in Zagreb, March 21, 1940; secretary's report on the annual financial statements for 1939 submitted to the meeting of the Main Office of the JVO in Zagreb, April 18, 1937, p. 94, JIM; Report of the head of the Management Board as an introduction to the general debate about approving the budget for 1939, JIM.

65. Tax sheets, Records of JVO 1939, JIM.

66. Minutes from the meeting of the Main Office of the JVO in Zagreb, April 15, 1935; Report of the head of the Management Board as an introduction to the general debate about bringing the budget for 1938; secretary's report on the annual financial statements for 1939, submitted to the meeting of the Main Office of the JVO in Zagreb, May 21, 1940, and the meeting of the Council, June 13, 1940; *Otpisi ex offo akt* 565 (1940), JVO in Zagreb, JIM.

67. Hoptner, *Yugoslavia in Crisis*, 117–19, 136; Ristović, *U potrazi za utočištem, Jugoslovenski Jevreji*, 30–31.

68. Scherer and Straka, *Kratka povijest podunavskih Nijemaca*, 46.

69. *Židov* 4 (1939).

70. *Židov* 8 and 13 (1939); *Jevrejski glas* 8 (1939); see also Ristović, *U potrazi za utočištem, Jugoslovenski Jevreji*, 52.

71. Ristović, *U potrazi za utočištem, Jugoslovenski Jevreji*, 42; minutes of the third meeting of the SJVOJ's Executive Committee, July 4, 1939, p. 67, JIM; about Perlzweig, see *Encyclopaedia Judaica*, 13:298.

72. *Židov* 36 (1939); see also commentary in *Jevrejska tribuna* 3 (1939); and minutes of the seventh meeting of SJVOJ's Executive Committee, November 30, 1939, p. 100, JIM.

73. *Jevrejski glas* 30 (1939).

74. *Židov* 3 (1940); minutes of the meeting of the JVO Presidency in Zagreb, February 20, 1940, JIM.

75. Minutes of the sixteenth meeting of the SJVOJ's Executive Committee, May 9, 1940, p. 34, JIM.

76. *Židov* 16 (1939); minutes of the Seventh Congress of the SJVOJ, April 23–24, 1939, p. 24, JIM.

77. *Židov* 17 and 18 (1939); minutes of the Seventh Congress of the SJVOJ, April 23–24, 1939, p. 22, 73, JIM.

78. Minutes of the Seventh Congress of the SJVOJ, April 23–24, 1939, p. 25, JIM.

79. Report of the head of the Management Board as an introduction to the general debate about approving the budget for 1940, held at a meeting of the JVO's Main Office in Zagreb, November 16, 1939, p. 154–55, JIM.

80. Minutes of the meeting of the JVO Council in Zagreb, September 22, 1938, JIM.

81. Minutes of the Seventh Congress of the SJVOJ, April 23–24, 1939, p. 30, 61–62, JIM.

82. Minutes of the Seventh Congress of the SJVOJ, April 23–24, 1939, p. 89–90, JIM.

83. *Židov* 36 and 38 (1939). *Halutz* is Hebrew for a pioneer, i.e., an early immigrant to Palestine.

84. *Židov* (April–December 1939), in various places.

85. *Židov* 21 (1939).

86. *Židov* 24 (1934).

87. *Židov* 37 (1938); 8–15 and 50 (1939).

88. *Jevrejska tribuna* 30 (1939).

89. *Židov* 37–38 (1939); *Jevrejska tribuna* 32–33 (1939); *Jevrejski glas* 38 (1939).

90. *Omanut* 9 (1939).

91. Minutes of the meeting of the JVO Presidency in Zagreb, May 21, 1940, JIM.

92. *Židov*, "Kulturni i literarni prilog," 4, no. 4 (1940); in general about Yugoslav interest in Palestine, see Pelesić, "Bliski istok 1940."

93. *Židov* 16 and 18–20 (1940).

94. *Židov* 38 (1939); 38 (1940); *Jevrejski glas* 34–35 (1939); 27 (1940); report of the head of the Management Board as an introduction to the general debate about drawing up the budget for 1940, held at a meeting of the Main JVO Office in Zagreb, November 16, 1939, p. 154–55, JIM.

95. Šute, "Položaj i obilježje trgovine u Banovini Hrvatskoj," 195, 200; see also "ordinance on the obligation to report hidden stores of goods" in *Jevrejski glas* 29 (1940).

96. *Jevrejska tribuna* 19 (1940).

97. Minutes of the twenty-second and twenty-fourth meetings of the SJVOJ's Executive Committee, September 9, 1940, pp. 75, 83, 84, JIM.

98. Minutes of the Seventh Congress of the SJVOJ, 4/23–24/1939, p. 9, JIM.

99. *Židov* 39 (1940); minutes of the meeting of the JVO Presidency in Zagreb, September 30, 1940, JIM.

100. *Narodne novine* (Zagreb), September 11, 1940; see in more detail in Šute, "Položaj i obilježje trgovine u Banovini Hrvatskoj," 142 and throughout.

101. *Hrvatski dnevnik* (Zagreb), September 12, 15, and 16, 1940, and October 15, 1940. It is typical that all of them, Kardoš, Gostl, and Hochsinger, were arrested in the summer of 1941, in the first waves of arrests of Jews in Zagreb, and that all three perished in 1941 and 1942 in Jasenovac. The same happened to Kardoš's brother Zlatko, while his parents, Zlata and Ernest Kardoš, were killed later, in an "unknown place," probably in the deportations of August 1942 or May 1943. See, *Popis žrtava lišenih života.*

102. *Službene novine* (Belgrade), October 5, 1940; see also HDA, collection ZKRZ GUZ, no. 306, box 10, 442–43 and the supplement to the minutes of the twenty-fourth meeting SJVOJ's Executive Committee, October 9, 1940, p. 84–87, JIM; facsimile in *Židovi na tlu Jugoslavije*, 178; *Jews in Yugoslavia*, 109; *Jevrejska tribuna* 32 (1940).

103. The statistics were again given in *Židov* 41 (1940).

104. Testimony of Professor Dr. Fedora-Feja Frank, Ivana Forenbacher, née Rosskamp, and Professor Dr. Mirjana Gross; *Jevrejska tribuna* 32 (1940).

105. *Židov* 44 and 46 (1940); *Službene novine* (Belgrade), October 5, 1940; *Narodne novine* (Zagreb), October 9, 1940; see also HDA, collection ZKRZ GUZ, no. 306, box 10, 440.

106. National Archives Washington, D.C., Microfilm Publications, Microcopy 1203, roll 16, image 0203.

107. Šute, "Položaj i obilježje trgovine u Banovini Hrvatskoj," 196. See tax sheets in minutes JVO 1939, JIM.

108. Šute, "Položaj i obilježje trgovine u Banovini Hrvatskoj," 197, 200–203, 206–8.

109. Minutes of the twenty-fourth meeting of the SJVOJ's Executive Committee, October 9, 1940, p. 88–89, JIM; see also *Židov* 41 (1940); *Jevrejski glas* 31 (1940).

110. *Jevrejski glas* 31 (1940).

111. *Židov* 41 (1940).

112. *Omanut* 1 (1939).

113. *Jevrejski glas* 31 (1940).

114. JP 7–12 (1990).

115. Minutes of the twenty-second meeting of the SJVOJ's Executive Committee, September 9, 1940, p. 75, JIM.

116. Maček, *Memoari*, 140–41.

117. National Archives, Washington, D.C., Microfilm Publications, Microcopy 1203, roll 16, image 0211.

118. *Hrvatski dnevnik* (Zagreb), October 6, 1940.

119. *Hrvatski dnevnik* (Zagreb), October 10, 1940.

120. *Hrvatski dnevnik* (Zagreb), October 10, 1940.

121. *Hrvatski dnevnik* (Zagreb), October 24, 1940.

122. *Židov* 51 (1940); HDA, Collection 155 (BHKB), 9065/1941, box no. 77.

123. HDA, Collection 155 (BHKB), 10296/1941, box no. 78. See also chapter on Freiberger, Rothmüller, and Rosenberger.

124. HDA, Collection ZKRZ GUZ, no. 306, box 15, 3722.

125. HDA, Collection 155 (BHKB), 2057/1941.

126. Minutes of the meeting of the Assessment Commission of the JVO in Zagreb December 12, 1933; complaint against the religious tax for 1937, supplement to minutes of the meeting of the Main Office of the JVO in Zagreb, August 12, 1937, p. 133, JIM; minutes of the meeting of the JVO's Management Board in Zagreb, April 8, 1937; HDA, Collection 1076, Reconstruction, box 735, 213/5, file for Lavoslav Ebenspanger–15/2; Goldstein, *Židovi u Zagrebu*, 511–12.

127. *Židov* 26 (1940).

128. Minutes of the meeting of the Main Office of the JVO in Zagreb, April 19, 1938, JIM.

129. Secretary's report on the annual financial statements for 1938, submitted to the meeting of the JVO's Main Office in Zagreb, April 27, 1939, and the meeting of the JVO Council on May 11, 1939, p. 61, JIM.

130. Which can only be concluded indirectly from the paper submitted by the head of the Management Board, supplement to the minutes of the meeting of the JVO Presidency in Zagreb, March 21, 1940, JIM.

131. Savez jevrejskih opština Jugoslavije, *Spomenica povodom pedesetogodišnjice Doma staraca Saveza jevrejskih opština Jugoslavije* (fascimile), 215.

132. Altarac Hadji-Ristić, "Veliki humanist Adela Weisz."

133. Secretary's report on the annual financial statements for 1939, submitted to the meeting of the Main Office of the JVO in Zagreb, May 21, 1940, and the meeting of the Council on June 13, 1940, JIM.

134. Report of the head of the Management Board as an introduction to the general debate on drawing up the budget for 1941, held at the meeting of the Main Office of the JVO in Zagreb, November 12, 1940, JIM.

135. Report of the head of the Management Board as an introduction to the general debate on drawing up the budget for 1941, held at the meeting of the Main Office of the JVO in Zagreb, November 12, 1940, JIM.

136. Minutes of the meeting of the JVO Presidency in Zagreb, June 13, 1940, JIM.

137. *Židov* 3, 5, 9, and 10 (1941); JP 7–8 (1973); Domaš, "Zeev Glück."

138. JP 11–12 (1972); Joško, "Naša posljednja utakmica."

5. From Exclusive Croatianhood to Ustasha Anti-Semitism

1. Matković, *Čista stranka prava.*

2. See, for example, the articles in *Ustaša* signed by Milivoj Karamarko: "Sljub Starčević-Pavelić," *Ustaša* 17, November 23, 1941; 18, November 30, 1941.

3. *Hrvatska gruda* 85 (1942).

4. Lukas, *Starčević,* 28; see also Lukas, "Starčević," 7 and throughout.

5. Buć, *Temeljne misli*, 31.

6. *Hrvatska gruda* 1 (1936).

7. *Hrvatska smotra* 11–12 (1940): 565; Ante Oršanić (1909–1959), journalist, brother of Ivan, was the editor in chief of the daily *Nova Hrvatska* and occasionally also wrote long anti-Semitic articles—see for example, *Hrvatski narod*, October 21, 1941, *Nova Hrvatska*, September 20, 1942.

8. Buć, *Temeljne misli*, 12.

9. Gross, *Povijest pravaške ideologije*, 3.

10. Krleža, *Balade*, 139–42.

11. Lasić, *Krležologija*, in various places.

12. Frangeš, *Povijest hrvatske književnosti*, 301, 437.

13. *Nova Riječ* (Zagreb), June 11, 1938.

14. Došen, *Ante Starčević*; Oršanić, *Duh starčevićanstva.*

15. *Hrvatska gruda* 82 (1942); HDA, Collection 248, UNS, folder I-A-II 377, file no. 22.

16. Šufflay, *Hrvatska*, 58.

17. Šufflay, *Hrvatska*, 58.

18. See, for example, the contribution by F. Lukas in Draganović, *Povijest Bosne i Hercegovine*, 62 and throughout. See also Goldstein, *Granica na Drini.*

19. Šufflay, *Ocjena*, 123.

20. Šufflay, *Hrvatska*, 51.

21. Lukas, *Starčević*, 7.

22. Lukas, *Starčević*, 5, 7, 28.

23. Buć, *Temeljne misli*, 5, 6, 21; it is a paradox that Starčević's mother was of Serbian origin, i.e., she was of the Orthodox faith.

24. Murgić, "Hrvatski nacionalizam," 94, 99–101.

25. Buć, *Starčević*, 25, 30.

26. *Hrvatsko pravo* (Zagreb), September 1, 1940.

27. Lorković, *Narod*, 219; Stuparić, *Tko je tko u NDH*, 237–39.

28. Lukas, *Hrvatska*, 51.

29. Makanec, *Hrvatski vidici*, 192–94.

30. *Ustaša, viestnik hrvatskog ustaškog oslobodilačkog pokreta*, February 1932; see also, *Ustaša, Dokumenti*, 55. About the beginnings of the Ustasha movement and the Ustasha exile, in detail, see Jelić-Butić, *Ustaše i NDH*, 19, 34; Matković, *Povijest Nezavisne Države Hrvatske*, 23–38.

31. Pavelić, *Strahote zabluda*; *Ustaša, Dokumenti*, 110; see also Steinberg, *All or Nothing*, 26–27.

32. About the activities of Ivo Frank, see Krizman, *Ante Pavelić i ustaše*, in various places; Gross, *Izvorno pravaštvo*, 817–18; HBL 4, 381–82; Jelić-Butić, *Ustaše i NDH*, 19, 34; see also HDA, Collection 145, SBDZ, box 146, 28251/1933; about these individuals, see, Goldstein, *Holokaust u Zagrebu*, 619–25.

33. Krizman, *Ante Pavelić i ustaše*, 187 and throughout.

34. HDA, Collection SDS RSUP SRH, 013.0.56; Židovec, *Moje sudjelovanje u političkom životu*, 138; about Židovec, see Stuparić, *Tko je tko u NDH*, 435.

35. See, Jareb, "Ustaški pokret."

36. *Hrvatska smotra* 11–12 (1940): 565; Ivan Oršanić (1904–1968), brother of Ante, was commander of the Ustasha Youth in the ISC and one of Pavelić's most trusted collaborators—see Stuparić, *Tko je tko u NDH*, 302–3.

37. *Načela hrvatskog ustaškog pokreta*; *Ustaša, Dokumenti*, 87.

38. It was not filed with the ministry until the beginning of 1941; it was printed in that year in Germany, and in 1942 in Zagreb in the book *Pavelić Ante (Dr. Ante Pavelić) riješio je Hrvatsko pitanje*; *Ustaša, Dokumenti*, 95–109; see also Krizman, *Ante Pavelić i ustaše*, 235 and throughout.

39. Krizman, *Ante Pavelić i ustaše*, 241; *Ustaša, Dokumenti*, 104.

40. Pavelić, *Liepa plavka*.

41. HDA, Collection SDS RSUP SRH, 013.0.3, study by an unknown author under the penname of Dizdar, *Ustaštvo i NDH*, 53; Brkan (1892–?), in the thirties, one of the organizers of the Ustasha movement in Dalmatia, later he parted ways with Pavelić on the issues of settling scores with "enemies" and handing Dalmatia over to the Italians. In 1941, he went to Zadar and withdrew from politics, refusing Pavelić's offer to come to Zagreb. In 1951, he was interrogated by the State Security Service in Zadar, see HDA, File SDS no. 301531.

42. Krizman, *Ante Pavelić i ustaše*, 332–34.

43. *Ustaša* 24 (Zagreb 1942); *Ustaša, Dokumenti*, 120.

44. Pavelić, *Za što se bore Hrvati*.

45. See facsimile in Krizman, *Ante Pavelić i ustaše*, 337.

46. Testimony of Mirko Mirković.

47. Jelić-Butić, *Ustaše i NDH*, 43–44; Matković, *Povijest Nezavisne Države Hrvatske*, 39.

48. *Danica* 17 (1938).

49. About the circumstances of Budak's return to the country, see Boban, "Nekoliko izvještaja"; Krizman, *Ante Pavelić i ustaše*, 301 and throughout.

50. *Hrvatski narod* 13 (1939); 1 (1940).

51. Kisić-Kolanović, *Vojskovođa i politika, Sjećanja Slavka Kvaternika*, 15, 282; *Hrvatski narod* 50 (1940).

52. *Hrvatski narod* 5, 26, 36, 42, 46, and 47 (1939); 51a (1940); see also Krizman, *Ustaše i Treći Reich*, 2:373.

53. *Hrvatski narod* 8 (1939); *Katolički tjednik* 13 (Sarajevo), March 26, 1939.

54. *Hrvatska gruda* 6 (1940).

55. *Hrvatska gruda* 6 (1940).

56. *Hrvatska gruda* 8 and 9 (1940).

57. *Hrvatska gruda* 17 (1940); 32 (1941).

58. *Hrvatska gruda* 17 (1940).

59. *Hrvatska gruda* 10 (1940).

60. *Hrvatska gruda* 16 (1940).

61. *Hrvatska gruda* 8 (1940); 34 (1941).

62. *Hrvatska gruda* 20 (1940).

63. Tipografija was managed by Dragutin Schulhof.

64. *Hrvatska gruda* 15 (1940).

65. HDA, Collection SDS RSUP SRH, 013.0.52; file Dr. Mile Budak, from the archives of H. Helm, 87.

66. Budak, *Rascvjetana trešnja*, 3:30; see in detail also in HDA, Collection SDS RSUP SRH, 013.0.52; File Dr. Mile Budak, from the archives of H. Helm, 86.

67. Exceptions to this were, for example, the article about the "Judeo-Freemason-Serbian Clique in Interwar Sports" or quoting anti-Semitic statements by some well-known figures from European history—*Hrvatski narod* 65, April 18, 1941; 81, May 4, 1941.

68. *Hrvatska gruda* 45, 46, and 69 (1941).

69. *Hrvatska gruda* 77 (1941).

70. See pages about Jedvaj in this book.

71. *Hrvatsko pravo* (Zagreb), September 1, 1940.

6. The Beginning of Persecution

1. HDA, Collection ZKRZ GUZ, no. 306, box 10, 82; box 15, 3807–3808, 3873; *Zapisnici 1941*, Archives ŽOZ.

2. HDA, Collection ZKRZ GUZ, no. 306, box 15, 3807–3808, 3817; testimony of Dr. Teodor Grüner.

3. HDA, Collection ZKRZ GUZ, no. 306, box 15, 3804–3805.

4. Geiger, "Saslušanje Branimira Altgayera," 599–600; in general, about the Germans in Croatia during the Second World War, see Geiger and Jurković, *Što se dogodilo s folksdojčerima*, 45–54.

5. Geiger, "Saslušanje Branimira Altgayera," 599–600; Geiger, "Nijemci Đakova i Đakovštine u Drugom svjetskom ratu," 404.

6. Fišer, *Židovi u Osijeku*, 426; Geiger, "Saslušanje Branimira Altgayera," 600–602; Geiger, "Nijemci Đakova i Đakovštine u Drugom svjetskom ratu," 404.

7. Hevra Kaddisha is a religious charity that has existed in Jewish communities since ancient times. It helps the poor and others who find themselves in trouble, keeps up graves, and provides a dignified burial for every deceased community member.

8. Keren Kayemeth (often with the addition "LeIsrael") was the name of the Jewish National Fund that collected money "to buy and acquire land in Palestine, which will remain the inalienable wealth of the Jewish people"—*Židov* 24–25 (1918).

9. HDA, Collection ZKRZ GUZ, no. 306, box 10, 82; box 15, 3875; Collection 252, RUR, J. Section, 29119; *Zapisnici 1941*, Archives ŽOZ.

10. *Ustaša, Dokumenti*, 150.

11. HDA, Collection 252, RUR, J. Section, 29119.

12. Vidi str. 162–72.

13. Stuparić, *Tko je tko u NDH*, 256; Mirnik, *Obitelj Alexander ili povijest jedne zagrebačke obitelji*, 44; Radovi ZHP 28, 107–108.

14. *Hrvatski list* (Brod na Savi), May 1, 1941.

15. Testimony of Nada Rajner, née Fröhlich; Mužić, *Popis masona*, 311; Mužić, *Masoni u Hrvatskoj*.

16. HDA, Collection ZKRZ GUZ, no. 306, box 10, 62.

17. Konforti, *Od 6. aprila 1941*, 431.

18. Testimony of Nada Rajner, née Fröhlich; private archives of the author.

19. HDA, Collection ZKRZ GUZ, no. 306, box 10, 148; box 15, 3817.

20. *Hrvatski narod* 65, April 18, 1941.

21. *Hrvatski narod* 63, April 16, 1941; 64, April 17, 1941.

22. *Deutsche Zeitung in Kroatien*, April 17, 1941; *Hrvatski narod* 67, April 20, 1941.

23. *Deutsche Zeitung in Kroatien,* April 20, 1941; *Hrvatski narod* reprinted this statement, April 22, 1941; and *Hrvatski list* (Osijek), April 23, 1941.

24. *Hrvatski radnik* 16 (Zagreb), April 30, 1941.

25. *Hrvatski narod*, May 3, 1941.

26. *Hrvatski narod*, May 6, 1941; *Ustaša, Dokumenti*, 171; in general on the terror over the Jews, see Jelić-Butić, *Ustaše i NDH*, 178–84.

27. *Hrvatski radnik* 18 (Zagreb), May 15, 1941.

28. *Ustaša* 1 (Zagreb), May 22, 1941. "Jerusalim" is the Serbian form of the name "Jerusalem," while the Croatian form would be "Jeruzalem"; this was used to suggest that the interests and activities of the Jews were similar to those of the Serbs.

29. *Ustaša* 2 (Zagreb), June 13, 1941.

30. *Hrvatski narod* 43, June 4, 1941.

31. *Novi list* 49, June 17, 1941.

32. HDA, Collection ZKRZ GUZ, no. 306, box 10.

33. Lengel-Krizman, "Revolucionarni omladinski pokret u Zagrebu u toku rata," 143–44; on Blažeković, see Stuparić, *Tko je tko u NDH*, 42.

34. Testimony of Professor Fedor Rajić, PhD.

35. Testimony of Branko Polić.

36. Testimony of Professor Fedor Rajić, PhD.

37. Testimony of Branko Polić.

38. Testimony of Professor Fedor Rajić, PhD.

39. St. Gabrijel, *Civut i Talmud ili najveci neprijatelj svih Nežidova*; HDA, Collection ZKRZ GUZ, no. 306, box 10, 286, 521.

40. *Hrvatski narod*, June 24, 1941.

41. *Novi list* 47, June 15, 1941.

42. *Novi list* 58, June 26, 1941.

43. *Jutarnji list*, October 23, 2000; testimony of Vera Zoričić, née Schwabenitz.

44. Perić and Drechsler, *Doživljaji*, 153–58.

45. *Popis žrtava lišenih života.*

7. Legal Discrimination

1. *Zakoni, zakonske odredbe, naredbe NDH, I*:15; *Hrvatski narod* 18, April 18, 1941; *Ustaša, Dokumenti*, 149; Peršen, *Ustaški logori*, 28.

2. *Zakoni, zakonske odredbe, naredbe NDH, I*:288–91; *Ustaša, Dokumenti*, 182–83; Miletić, *Koncentracioni logor Jasenovac*, 1:50–51; Jelić-Butić, *Ustaše i NDH*, 159–60; Matković, *Povijest Nezavisne Države Hrvatske*, 155–57.

3. *Narodne novine,* 12/13/1941; *Zakoni, zakonske odredbe, naredbe NDH, I*:1038.

4. *Zakoni, zakonske odredbe, naredbe NDH, II*:2, 3; For an exhaustive study of the summary courts, see: HDA, Collection MUP SRH, box 45, 013.1.22, *Specijalni sudovi u NDH 1941–1945*.

5. Jelić-Butić, *Ustaše i NDH,* 161–162; Peršen, *Ustaški logori,* 29–30.

6. HDA, Collection 218, MPB NDH, Justice Department, box 417–419.

7. *Zakoni, zakonske odredbe, naredbe NDH, I*:20; *Narodne novine* 6, April 19, 1941; *Hrvatski narod* 66, April 19, 1941; *Ustaša, Dokumenti,* 149; HDA, Collection ZKRZ GUZ, no. 306, box 10, 531.

8. *Hrvatski narod* 18, April 19, 1941.

9. HDA, Collection ZKRZ GUZ, no. 306, box 10, 83.

10. Krišto, *Katolička crkva i Nezavisna Država Hrvatska,* 2:37–39, 54–55, 57, 260–61.

11. Testimony of Branko Polić; *Knjiga umrlih ŽOZ.*

12. Testimony of Vlasta Urbić, née Deutsch-Maceljski; *Knjiga umrlih ŽOZ*; Horvat, *Zapisci iz nepovrata–Hrvatski mikrokozam*, 242.

13. *Narodne novine*, April 30, 1941; *Zbornik zakona i naredaba NDH*, 42; *Zakoni, zakonske odredbe, naredbe NDH, I*:109–12; *Ustaša, Dokumenti*, 160–63 Miletić, *Koncentracioni logor Jasenovac*, 3:16–19; Peršen, *Ustaški logori*, 33; Matković, *Povijest Nezavisne Države Hrvatske*, 155, generally about the persecution of Jews, 161–62 and throughout.

14. *Encyclopaedia Judaica*, 12:1281.

15. Krizman, *NDH izmedu*, 27.

16. For example, see HDA, Collection 223, MUP NDH, II A 33795/41, 32638/41, 32829/41, 33187/41, 40263/41, 44039/41, 49039/41, 53248/41; Collection 252, RUR, J. Section, 29619, 29685.

17. HDA, Collection 252, RUR, J. Section, 29619; *Popis žrtava lišenih života.*

18. NAZ, skupina NDS 7188/1941.

19. HDA, Collection 252, RUR, J. Section, 27913.

20. *Hrvatski narod*, November 28, 1941; *Ustaša* 23 (Zagreb), December 7, 1941.

21. *Narodne novine*, April 30, 1941; *Zbornik zakona i naredaba NDH*, 43–44; *Zakoni, zakonske odredbe, naredbe NDH, I*:113–15; *Ustaša, Dokumenti*, 163–64.

22. *Hrvatski narod*, May 3, 1941; *Ustaša, Dokumenti*, 166.

23. *Narodne novine*, May 1, 1941; *Zbornik zakona i naredaba NDH*, 42; *Ustaša, Dokumenti*, 160; HDA, Collection ZK RZ GUZ, no. 306, box 10, 445.

24. *Hrvatski narod*, May 3, 1941; see also *Ustaša, Dokumenti*, 165, 167.

25. Miletić, *Koncentracioni logor Jasenovac*, 1:52; Peršen, *Ustaški logori*, 81.

26. Miletić, *Koncentracioni logor Jasenovac*, 1: 69–70.

27. *Narodne novine*, May 4, 1941.

28. HDA, Collection 252, RUR, J. Section, 27430.

29. HDA, Collection 252, RUR, 27372, 27727; *Novi list* 18 (Zagreb), May 16, 1941.

30. *Deutsche Zeitung in Kroatien*, May 25, 1941; HDA, Collection ZKRZ GUZ, no. 306, box 15, 3727.

31. HDA, Collection ZKRZ GUZ, no. 306, box 15, 3874.

8. Wearing the Jewish Insignia

1. JIM, Collection ŽOZ, without reg. no.

2. *Hrvatski narod*, May 22, 1941; *Ustaša, Dokumenti*, 173; HDA, Collection ZKRZ GUZ, no. 306, box 10, 423, 428; Collection 252, RUR, J. Section, 27431.

3. *Hrvatski narod*, May 23, 1941.

4. *Hrvatski narod*, May 29, 1941.

5. HDA, Collection ZKRZ GUZ, no. 306, box 15, 3875.

6. HDA, Collection ZKRZ GUZ, no. 306, box 10, 63–64.

7. Kišić-Kolanović, *Podravljenje imovine Židova*, 433.

8. Testimony of Berta Israel, neé Švarcenberg.

9. Testimony of Vera Fischer.

10. Testimony of Vlasta Urbić, née Deutsch-Maceljski.

11. Testimony of Ljerka Magdić.

12. HDA, Collection 252, RUR, J. Section, 27391, 27392, 27746, 27531.

13. HDA, Collection 252, RUR, J. Section, 28882; *Popis žrtava.*

14. HDA, Collection 252, RUR, J. Section, 29351.

15. Grgec-Tusun, *Uspomena*; on Grgec, see Stuparić, *Tko je tko u NDH*, 138–39.

16. HDA, Collection 252, RUR, J. Section, 27477, 27978.

17. HDA, Collection 252, RUR, J. Section, 27373.

18. HDA, Collection ZKRZ GUZ, no. 306, box 10, 146.

19. Maček, *Memoari*, 160.

20. HDA, Collection 252, RUR, J. Section, 27966.

21. HDA, Collection 252, RUR, J. Section, 29054; *Popis žrtava*; for cases of placing applications for exemption from wearing the sign *ad acta*, see also 28193.

22. HDA, Collection 252, RUR, J. Section, 28457.

23. HDA, Collection 252, RUR, J. Section, 29455; *Popis žrtava.*

24. Testimony of Branko Polić.

25. HDA, Collection ZKRZ GUZ, no. 306, box 10, 323.

26. HDA, Collection 252, RUR, J. Section, 27134.

27. *Hrvatski narod*, June 22, 1941; HDA, Collection ZKRZ GUZ, no. 306, box 10, 459.

28. *Narodne novine* 43, June 4, 1941; HDA, Collection ZKRZ GUZ, no. 306, box 10, 459–60.

29. *Opći šematizam*, 89, 744; testimony of Dr. Andrija Lukinović; testimony of Vera Fischer.

30. Krišto, *Katolička crkva*, 2:34; HDA, Collection 416 (Politeo), 222.

31. Archives ŽOZ. It is not known who initiated compiling this list; it may have been the Ustasha authorities in order to get a better sense of the Jews in Zagreb.

32. See, for example, Djuro Schwarz, Elizabeta Schwarz, Julio Schwarz, Lavoslav Schwarz.

33. For example, Julio Schwarz, Klara Schwarz.

34. Miroslav Schwarz.

35. Of course, there were exceptions, especially when they wanted to do someone a favor; see for example, HDA, Collection 252, RUR, J. Section, 29839.

36. HDA, Collection 252, RUR, J. Section, 27373, 27374, 27460, 2746 8, 27568, 27570, 27588, 27617, 27636, 27733, 27761, 27792–27794, 27800, 27851, 27925, 27977, 28036, 28037, 28181, 28292, 28342.

37. HDA, Collection 252, RUR, J. Section, 27744, 27792, 27851, 27854.

38. HDA, Collection 252, RUR, J. Section, 27958.

39. HDA, Collection 252, RUR, J. Section, 27528, 27606.

40. HDA, Collection 252, RUR, J. Section, 28120.

41. HDA, Collection 252, RUR, J. Section, 27445.

42. *Zapisnici Vijeća ŽOZ 1941*, Archives ŽOZ. In those days the Yugoslav dinar was converted to the Croatian kuna at the rate of 1:1, so the names of the two currencies were often used interchangeably in documents.

9. Requests to Not Wear the Insignia and Be Granted Aryan Rights

1. HDA, Collection 252, RUR, J. Section, 29270; *Popis žrtava*; *Spiskovi preživelih.*

2. NAZ, group NDS 318/1943.

3. More on this in chapter 31, "Conversion to Catholicism."

4. HDA, Collection 223, MUP NDH, 1099; II–A, 12420; *Popis žrtava.*

5. HDA, Collection 252, RUR, J. Section, 28110; *Popis žrtava*; *Secanja Jevreja*, 254; JIM, Collection ŽOZ, reg. no. 4866, sign. K-66–1-1/1–56.

6. Testimony of Branko Polić; HDA, Collection 252, RUR, J. Section, 27448; *Popis žrtava*; *Knjiga umrlih.*

7. HDA, Collection 252, RUR, J. Section, 27071; *Imenik Ponove*, 119.

8. HDA, Collection 223, MUP NDH, 109 9–1109, 1163, 1253, 1419, 1520, 1613; II–A, 12420, 12483, 21966, 26418, 39127, 45864, 51702; *Kartoteka židovskog znaka*; *Popis žrtava.*

9. HDA, Collection 252, RUR, J. Section, 27279.

10. HDA, Collection 252, RUR, J. Section, 27353.

11. HDA, Collection 252, RUR, J. Section, 27232.

12. Ristović, *U potrazi za utočištem, Jugoslovenski Jevreji*, 81.

13. HDA, Collection 252, RUR, J. Section, 27262.

14. HDA, Collection 252, RUR, J. Section, 27510; Ristovic, *U potrazi za utočištem*, 258.

15. Orlik and Stiasni had permission to remain in their apartments; HDA, Collection 252, RUR, J. Section, 27423, 27424.

16. *Novi list* 18, May 16, 1941.

17. *Novi list* 60, June 28, 1941.

18. *Ustaša* 3, July 3, 1941.

19. HDA, Collection 252, RUR, J. Section, 28184, 28185, 28189, 28252.

20. HDA, Collection Poglavnikov vojni ured, bb.

21. HDA, Collection 252, RUR, J. Section, 28415.

22. HDA, Collection 252, RUR, J. Section, 28070, 28072.

23. HDA, Collection 252, RUR, J. Section, 28885; *Knjiga kontribucije.*

24. HDA, Collection 252, RUR, J. Section, 29779.

25. HDA, Collection The Poglavnik's Military Office, bb.

26. NAZ, group NDS 8066/1941; HDA, Collection 252, RUR, J. Section, 28834.

27. *Jutarnji list* (Zagreb), January 22, 1929; HDA, Collection 252, RUR, 27183; File SDS no. 310155; *Popis žrtava*.

28. *Hrvatska gruda* 48 (1941).

29. See, e.g., HDA, Collection 252, RUR, J. Section, 27275–27276.

30. HDA, Collection 252, RUR, J. Section, 28642, 28644, 28646.

31. HDA, Collection 252, RUR, J. Section, 28705.

32. Out of a total of approximately 400 applications, Aryan rights were requested for one, or in some cases for two or more people; thus, there were just over 400 applications for a total of 545 people requesting Aryan rights.

33. HDA, Collection 252, RUR, J. Section, 27071–27133, 27135–27145, 27148, 27151, 27153–27157, 27160–27237, 27239–27251, 27258–27259, 27262, 27267–27270, 27275–27279, 27283–27286, 27288–27289, 27294, 27297–27304, 27328, 27333, 27335–27341, 27343–27347, 27350–27351, 27353–27355, 27361–27367, 27371, 27376–27380, 27382, 27387–27388, 27396–27397, 27400–27404, 27408, 27410–27415, 27420, 27426, 27428, 27433, 27435, 27437, 27448–27449, 27456, 27462–27463, 27465, 27467, 27469, 27474, 27476, 27478–27480, 27482, 27485, 27487, 27502, 27505–27506, 27512, 27533, 27552, 27562–27563, 27565, 27567, 27569, 27571, 27574–27575, 27577, 27579–27581, 27586, 27599, 27612, 27614, 27619, 27634, 27645, 27648, 27651, 27654, 27660, 27669–27671, 27679–27680, 27686–27687, 27693, 27718, 27724, 27726, 27738, 27742–27743, 27751, 27766, 27775, 27789–27791, 27795, 27797–27798, 27819, 27824, 27826–27827.

34. See, e.g., HDA, Collection 252, RUR, J. Section, 27933, 28025, 28042.

35. HDA, Collection 252, RUR, J. Section, 27347, 27486, 27541, 27812, 27866, 27911, 27936, 28060, 28167, 28269, 28327, 28343, 28434, 28513, 28523, 28613, 28767, 29028, 29274, 29275, 29330.

36. HDA, Collection 252, RUR, J. Section, 27271; NAZ, group NDS 6062/1941; *Popis žrtava*.

37. See, e.g., HDA, Collection 252, RUR, J. Section, 27920, 27930, 27932, 28090.

38. The photocopy of the document reproduced here is kept in the family archives of I. Mirnik; on Mešić, see Stuparić, *Tko je tko u NDH*, 265–66.

39. Testimony of Vlasta Urbić, née Deutsch-Maceljski; statement of Dr. Oto Radan, in Zemljar, *Haron i sudbine*, 117.

40. HDA, Collection 252, RUR, J. Section, 27917; NAZ, group NDS 10531/1941; Mirnik, *Obitelj Alexander ili povijest jedne zagrebačke obitelji*, 28, 99, 122; BP ŽHH, ŽOZ; *Kartoteka jasenovačkih zatočenika*.

41. HDA, Collection 223, MUP NDH, box 300, no. 30068; it contains a list of Jews who were granted Aryan origin.

42. Testimony of Vlasta Urbić, née Deutsch-Maceljski.

43. *Knjiga kontribucije*, 68.

44. HDA, Collection 252, RUR, J. Section, 27225.

45. HDA, Collection 252, RUR, J. Section, 27226. Stepinac's recommendation did not help in some other cases either; see 27616.

46. HDA, Collection 252, RUR, J. Section, 27272; about Marić, see Stuparić, *Tko je tko u NDH*, 256.

47. HDA, Collection 252, RUR, J. Section, 27363; *Spiskovi preživelih*.

48. HDA, Collection 252, RUR, J. Section, 27335, 28909.

49. HDA, Collection 252, RUR, J. Section, 27540, 27729, 27880–27882, 27884, 27914, 28139.

50. See the case of Samuel Spitzer from Varaždin, whose wife even pleaded for his liberation in the Poglavnik's Office, but in the meantime he was killed in Jasenovac; HDA, Collection 252, RUR, J. Section, 28164.

51. HDA, Collection 252, RUR, J. Section, 27520; about Gomboš, see *Likovna enciklopedija Jugoslavije*, 1:462–63.

52. See, HDA, Collection 223, MUP NDH, box 300, no. 30068; *Dotrščina projekt*; DAZ, Collection GPSUZ, 8567/41.

53. HDA, Collection 252, RUR, J. Section, 28381; Shomrony, "Svjedočenja, Gdje je Freibergerova biblioteka?."

54. On December 5, 1918, spontaneous demonstrations broke out in the center of Zagreb opposing the establishment of the new state and protesting the bad social conditions. In the clash between former *domobran* (Home Guard) units and the police, several people were killed or wounded.

55. *Ustaša* 5, August 3, 1941; 23, December 7, 1941.

56. Pallua, "Te sam ljude poznavao"; HDA, Collection 144, SBUO, box 216, 21307/1931.

57. Shomrony, "Svjedočenja, Gdje je Freibergerova biblioteka?"; testimony of Dr. Dragan Stern and Boris Braun.

58. HDA, Collection 223, MUP NDH, box 300, no. 30068.

59. HDA, Collection 223, MUP NDH, 1278/II–A, 29128.

60. HDA, Collection 252, RUR, J. Section, 27462; *Popis žrtava*; JIM, Collection ŽOZ, sign. K-66–1-1/1.

61. HDA, Collection 252, RUR, J. Section, 27571; *Popis žrtava*; *Kartoteka jasenovačkih zatočenika*; JIM, Collection ŽOZ, reg. no. 4866, sign. K-66–1-1/1–56.

10. A Challenge to Living

1. *Narodne novine*, May 6, 1941; HDA, Collection ZKRZ GUZ, no. 306, box 10, 451; *Zakoni, zakonske odredbe, naredbe NDH, I*:161–63.

2. *Narodne novine*, May 16, 1941; HDA, Collection ZKRZ GUZ, no. 306, box 10, 453; *Zakoni, zakonske odredbe, naredbe NDH, I*:296.

3. HDA, Collection 252, RUR, J. Section, 27464.

4. HDA, Collection 223, MUP NDH, 1270, 1304, 1311, 1357, 1365, 1398, 1423, 1429, 1432/A-II, 28047, 33989, 34178, 35181, 35916, 37424, 39169, 39319, 39651.

5. *Novi list*, September 14, 1941.

6. Šidak, "Sveučilište za vrijeme rata i okupacije od," 176; Barbić and Pavić, *Pravni fakultet u Zagrebu III*.

7. HDA, Collection 252, RUR, J. Section, 27295; *Popis žrtava*.

8. HDA, Collection 252, RUR, J. Section, 27363; *Popis žrtava*.

9. HDA, Collection 252, RUR, J. Section, 27341.

10. HDA, Collection 252, RUR, J. Section, 27403; also, similarly, 27424, 27436, 27473, 27538, 27559, 27560, 27609, 27610, 27650, 27736.

11. HDA, Collection 252, RUR, J. Section, 28049; *Popis žrtava.*

12. HDA, Collection 252, RUR, J. Section, 27722.

13. HDA, Collection 252, RUR, J. Section, 28145, 28616.

14. HDA, Collection 252, RUR, J. Section, 27685. See also other cases, 27695, 27698, 27715, 27772.

15. HDA, Collection 252, RUR, J. Section, 27771.

16. HDA, Collection 252, RUR, J. Section, 28709; *Popis žrtava.*

17. HDA, Collection 252, RUR, J. Section, 28160.

18. *Popis žrtava*; *Spisak preživelih.*

19. HDA, Collection 252, RUR, J. Section, 28632.

20. HDA, Collection 252, RUR, J. Section, 28392; HDA, Collection 252, RUR, J. Section, index, 7315; NAZ, group NDS 6428/1941; *Popis žrtava;* JIM, Collection ŽOZ, reg. no. 5381, sign. K-66–5-1/1–72, 1–75; sign. 65–4-1/1–10.

21. HDA, Collection 252, RUR, J. Section, 27828, 27968.

22. HDA, Collection 252, RUR, J. Section, 27763.

23. NAZ, group NDS 10601/194.

24. HDA, Collection 223, MUP NDH, 3594/II-A, 5616.

25. HDA, Collection 252, RUR, J. Section, 29608; NAZ, group NDS 10424/1941; *Popis žrtava.*

26. Testimony of Branko Polić; *Popis žrtava.*

27. Jelić-Butić, *Ustaše i NDH*, 131.

28. HDA, Collection General Administrative Commission with the Command of the Second Italian Army, 15387.

29. *Narodne novine*, June 4, 1941; HDA, Collection ZKRZ GUZ, no. 306, box 10, 455; *Zakoni, zakonske odredbe, naredbe NDH, II*:40.

30. Archive of the Chamber of Attorneys in Zagreb, facsimile in *Bilten ŽOZ* 12 (1989).

31. HDA, Collection 218, MPB NDH, Department of Justice, box 417, file Dr. M. Sabalić. Whether by chance or not, the preserved documents the Ministry of Justice sent to the Croatian State Archives include a file sleeve with the name of Dr. Perlberg, but it is empty. There is also nothing in the folder entitled *Brisanje odvjetnika iz popisa* (Striking attorneys from the list), although it can be seen that some files had been placed into it in 1941 and 1942, and again in 1945; *Kartoteka pripadnika židovske zajednice u Zagrebu.*

32. *Zagreb* 5–6 (1942): 115.

33. HDA, Collection 223, MUP NDH, 1307/II-A, 34071.

34. HDA, Collection 218, MPB NDH, Department of Justice, box 28, 31602/1941.

35. HDA, Collection 218, MPB NDH, Department of Justice, box 28, 19761, 19762, 30169/1941.

36. *Narodne novine*, June 4, 1941; *Zakoni, zakonske odredbe, naredbe NDH, II*:51; HDA, Collection ZKRZ GUZ, no. 306, box 10, 456–7.

37. Collection 223, MUP NDH 1196/II A 15016/41.

38. *Zakoni, zakonske odredbe, naredbe NDH, II*:105–17; *Ustaša, Dokumenti*, 201–2; Jelić-Butić, *Ustaše i NDH*, 101–2.

39. Documents I. Goldstein.

40. HDA, Collection 223, MUP NDH, 1580/II-A, 49862.

11. The Administrative Machinery for Implementing Persecution

1. Stuparić, *Tko je tko u NDH*, 224–25.

2. *Narodne novine*, May 7, 1941; Jelić-Butić, *Ustaše i NDH*, 185; Hory and Broszat, *Der Kroatische Ustascha-Staat*, 185.

3. Stuparić, *Tko je tko u NDH*, 296–97.

4. *Hrvatski narod*, May 9, 1941.

5. HDA, Processed and micro-photographed records 301990, 1–2.

6. For a detailed description of the contribution, see chapter 12 in this book.

7. Kobsa, "O organizaciji ustaškog aparata vlasti za provođenje terora u tzv. NDH," 247.

8. Kobsa, "O organizaciji ustaškog aparata vlasti za provođenje terora u tzv. NDH," 247; Stuparić, *Tko je tko u NDH*, 68.

9. *Hrvatski narod* (Zagreb), May 11, 1941.

10. HDA, 013.047, SDS, box 21; Stuparić, *Tko je tko u NDH*, 296–97.

11. HDA, Collection ZKRZ GUZ, box 45, 2753; Novak, *When Heaven's Vault Cracked*.

12. HDA, Collection 252, RUR, J. Section, 27887.

13. *Hrvatski narod*, June 24, 1941; Jelić-Butić, *Ustaše i NDH*, 107, 111–12; on the foundation of the UNS, see Miletić, *Koncentracioni logor Jasenovac*, 3:43–44.

14. Stuparić, *Tko je tko u NDH*, *224*–25.

15. Jelić-Butić, *Ustaše i NDH*, 185; Hory and Broszat, *Der Kroatische Ustascha-Staat*, 86.

16. Hory and Broszat, *Der Kroatische Ustascha-Staat*, 87.

17. HDA, MUP RH, General records 316342, box 133.

18. For more details about the responsibilities of these and other Ustasha and state institutions, see the preceding three and the next four chapters of this book.

19. HDA, Collection ZKRZ GUZ, no. 306, box 10, 339–341.

20. HDA, Collection 252, RUR, J. Section, 28284.

21. HDA, Collection ZKRZ GUZ, no. 306, box 10, 108.

22. HDA, Collection ZKRZ GUZ, no. 306, box 10, 107.

23. Testimony of Vera Fischer.

24. HDA, Collection 252, RUR, J. Section, 28077.

25. HDA, Collection 252, RUR, J. Section, 28078.

26. HDA, Collection 252, RUR, J. Section, 27590 and elsewhere.

27. HDA, Collection 252, RUR, J. Section, 27739, 29668.

28. HDA, Collection 252, RUR, J. Section, 27710. Ivo Petrić had a great respect for his former boss; testimony of Dr. Teodor Grüner; on Steinhardt, see Romano, *Jevreji zdravstveni radnici Jugoslavije*, 93.

29. HDA, Collection 252, RUR, J. Section, 27727.

30. HDA, ZKRZ-GUZ 2753/45 i MUP RH, spis II-91, box 150, 738.

31. *Dnevnik Dijane Budisavljević*, 18, 25.

32. HDA, MUP RH, general records no. 316342, boxes 133 and 306, ZKRZ-CGK, box 723.

33. HDA, Processed and micro-photographed records 301990, pp. 1–7, 306. ZKRZ-ZK, box 528 i 291, GUZ 7685/46.

34. HDA, SDS SRH 013.0.47, box 21; Stuparić, *Tko je tko u NDH*, 67–68.

35. Stuparić, *Tko je tko u NDH*, 75, 175, 234, 416, 431.

36. Kisić-Kolanović, *Vojskovođa i politika, Sjećanja Slavka Kvaternika*, in various places, especially 263.

12. The Contribution

1. HDA, Collection ZKRZ GUZ, no. 306, box 15, 3817.

2. HDA, Collection ZKRZ GUZ, no. 306, box 15, 3701–3702, 3817.

3. HDA, Collection ZKRZ GUZ, no. 306, box 10, 96.

4. HDA, Collection ZKRZ GUZ, no. 306, box 10, 193, 272; Lipa, in "Židovska općina," also writes about the contribution.

5. HDA, Collection ZKRZ GUZ, no. 306, box 10, 23, 191.

6. HDA, Collection ZKRZ GUZ, no. 306, box 10, 23, 191.

7. HDA, Collection ZKRZ GUZ, no. 306, box 10, 276.

8. HDA, Collection ZKRZ GUZ, no. 306, box 10, 23.

9. HDA, Collection ZKRZ GUZ, no. 306, box 15, 3732–3733.

10. HDA, Collection ZKRZ GUZ, no. 306, box 10, 276.

11. HDA, Collection 252, RUR, J. Section, 27701, 27996.

12. *Knjiga kontribucije*, 1–246.

13. *Knjiga kontribucije.*

14. HDA, Collection ZKRZ GUZ, no. 306, box 10, 149.

15. HDA, Collection ZKRZ GUZ, no. 306, box 10, 279.

16. HDA, Collection ZKRZ GUZ, no. 306, box 17, 5018–5091; report also in HDA, Collection MUP SRH, 013.0.65, 78–111.

17. HDA, Collection MUP SRH, 013.0.65, 123–139.

18. Kisić-Kolanović, "Podržavljenje imovine Židova u NDH," 451, assesses that the value of this property was 106,500,000 kunas.

19. Paver and Strčić, "Tisuću kilograma zlata"; Strčić, *Kontribucija.*

20. HDA, Collection ZKRZ GUZ, no. 306, box 10, 197.

21. Kisić-Kolanović, "Podržavljenje imovine Židova u NDH," 452.

22. HDA, Collection ZKRZ GUZ, no. 306, box 10, 105. An assignment is a legal transfer of assets, a document whereby one creditor cedes his assets and assigns them to another.

23. HDA, Collection ZKRZ GUZ, no. 306, box 10, 118, 155–174, 277.

24. HDA, Collection ZKRZ GUZ, no. 306, box 10, 24–42, 130.

25. HDA, Collection ZKRZ GUZ, no. 306, box 10, 105, 275.

26. HDA, Collection ZKRZ GUZ, no. 306, box 10, 277.

27. HDA, Collection ZKRZ GUZ, no. 306, box 10, 104–106; *Popis žrtava.*

28. Testimony of Branko Polić.

29. HDA, Collection 252, RUR, J. Section, 28020.

30. Testimony of Professor Dr. Zdenko Šternberg.

31. HDA, Collection ZKRZ GUZ, no. 306, box 10, 188–190.

32. HDA, Collection 252, RUR, J. Section, 28925.

33. HDA, Collection ZKRZ GUZ, no. 306, box 10, 107.

34. HDA, Collection ZKRZ GUZ, no. 306, box 10, 189–190.

35. HDA, Collection ZKRZ GUZ, no. 306, box 10, 272.

36. HDA, Collection ZKRZ GUZ, no. 306, box 10, 118, 121.

37. HDA, Collection ZKRZ GUZ, no. 306, box 10, 120–121.

38. HDA, Collection ZKRZ GUZ, no. 306, box 17, 5021.

39. HDA, Collection ZKRZ GUZ, no. 306, box 10, 103–122, 194.

40. HDA, Collection 252, RUR, J. Section, 27732.

41. HDA, Collection ZKRZ GUZ, no. 306, box 10, 280.

42. HDA, Collection ZKRZ GUZ, no. 306, box 10, 369–372; Collection 252, RUR, J. Section, 29878, 29879.

43. HDA, Collection 252, RUR, J. Section, 27280, 27372, 27488–27496, 27954, 28714–28719.

44. HDA, Collection 252, RUR, J. Section, 28558.

45. District People's Court for the City of Zagreb, R 1410/19 45, records of Mirjana Gross; JIM, Collection ŽOZ, reg. no. 4868, sign. K–66–3–1/1–14, 1–16, 1–18, 1–20, 1–27; JIM, Collection ŽOZ, reg. no. 4869, sign. K–66–4–1/1–14, 1–17.

46. HDA, Collection ZKRZ GUZ, no. 306, box 10, 194, 277; Strčić, *Kontribucija*; *Popis žrtava*.

47. JIM, Collection ŽOZ, without reg. no. and sign.

48. HDA, collection MUP RH III-24, 857.

49. *Popis žrtava*; JIM, Collection ŽOZ, sign. K-65–4-1/1–122; JIM, Collection ŽOZ, without reg. no. and sign.

50. JIM, Collection ŽOZ, without reg. no. and sign.

51. HDA, Collection 252, RUR, J. Section, 29298; *Popis žrtava*.

52. HDA, Collection 252, RUR, J. Section, 29154. Klein traveled to Budapest, Ljubljana, and to Italy several times in the following months, under the supervision of the UNS and accompanied by Ustasha policemen, to establish connections with some international Jewish organizations and raise money for the Camp Welfare Fund of the Zagreb Jewish Community. In May 1942, he managed to escape while in Italy and get to Switzerland, and thus survived the war.

13. Plundering Jewish Property

1. Krizman, *Ante Pavelić i ustaše*, 485.

2. Jelić-Butić, *Ustaše i NDH*, 131.

3. *Zakoni, zakonske odredbe, naredbe NDH, I*:50.

4. HDA, Collection 252, RUR, J. Section, 27368.

5. HDA, Collection 252, RUR, J. Section, 27508.

6. *Zakoni, zakonske odredbe, naredbe NDH, II*:73, 75, 79; *Ustaša, Dokumenti*, 195–97.

7. Kisić-Kolanović, "Podržavljenje imovine Židova u NDH," 442.

8. *Narodne novine*, June 5, 1941; *Zbornik zakona i naredaba NDH*, 142; see also HDA, Collection ZKRZ GUZ, no. 306, box 10, 298.

9. *Narodne novine*, June 5, 1941; *Zbornik zakona i naredaba NDH*, 142–51; *Ustaša, Dokumenti*, 198–200.

10. *Hrvatski narod*, July 13, 1941; see also HDA, Collection ZKRZ GUZ, no. 306, box 10, 436.

11. HDA, Collection 218, MPB NDH, Department of Justice, box 28, 50976/1941.

12. HDA, Collection 1076, Reconstruction, card index DKM; see also Kisić-Kolanović, "Podržavljenje imovine Židova u NDH."

13. HDA, Collection 223, MUP NDH, 1099, 1161, 1264, 1475/II-A, 12415, 20872, 27623, 43427.

14. Stuparić, *Tko je tko u NDH*, 83–84.

15. HDA, Reconstruction, box 1810, personal documents.

16. HDA, Collection MUP SRH, 013.0.65, Part III, 202–218.

17. *Zakoni, zakonske odredbe, naredbe NDH, I*:195.

18. *Zakoni, zakonske odredbe, naredbe NDH, I*:50, 252.

19. HDA, Collection 1076, Reconstruction, Index of personal papers.

20. Kisić-Kolanović, "Podržavljenje imovine Židova u NDH," 440.

21. HDA, Collection MUP SRH, 013.0.49, Part II, 179.

22. *Zakoni, zakonske odredbe, naredbe NDH, I*:1096; Kisić-Kolanović, *Židovska imovina*, 441.

23. *Narodne novine*, 115, 8/30/1941; HDA, Collection ZKRZ GUZ, no. 306, box 10, 464.

24. HDA, Collection 218, MPB NDH, Department of Justice, box 28, 1602/1941.

25. *Narodne novine*, 149, 10/10/1941; HDA, Collection ZKRZ GUZ, no. 306, box 10, 466–467; *Ustaša*, 17, Zagreb 10/26/1941; see also Kisić-Kolanović, "Podržavljenje imovine Židova u NDH," 438–439.

26. HDA, Collection ZKRZ GUZ, no. 306, box 16, 4888–4923.

27. HDA, Reconstruction, "P," box 99 (703).

28. HDA, Collection 218, MPB NDH, Department of Justice, box 28, 2753/1942.

29. HDA, Collection 1076, Reconstruction, Secretary's office TI 176/1941.

30. HDA, Collection 1076, Reconstruction, Secretary's office TI 197/1941.

31. Kisić-Kolanović, "Podržavljenje imovine Židova u NDH," 444.

32. HDA, Collection 237, Head Directorate of Propaganda, box 4., 5137/1941.

33. HDA, Collection 252, RUR, J. Section, 28508.

34. HDA, Collection ZKRZ GUZ, no. 306, 2–45, box 10, 134.

35. Lasić, *Autobiografski zapisi*, 186.

36. HDA, Collection 252, RUR, J. Section, 29766.

37. Kolar-Dimitrijević, "Sjećanja veterinara Zorka Goluba," 172.

38. Testimony of Mila Kniewald-Mirković.

39. *Narodne novine* 158, October 21, 1941; Kisić-Kolanović, "Podržavljenje imovine Židova u NDH," 438.

40. *Zakoni, zakonske odredbe, naredbe NDH, IV*:288.

41. HDA, Collection 218, MPB NDH, Department of Justice, box 33, I 159, 91227/1941.

42. HDA, Collection 252, RUR, J. Section, 28299, 28301, 28315–28317, 28349,

28356–28366, 28375–28378, 28400–28402, 28404–28405, 28407, 28411–28414, 28425, 28427, 28546, 28548, 28550, 28557, 28564, 28829, 29011.

43. HDA, Collection 252, RUR, J. Section, 28354.

44. HDA, Collection 252, RUR, J. Section, 28401.

45. HDA, Collection MUP SRH, 013.0.65, part II, 41.

46. *Hrvatski narod* 389, March 29, 1942.

47. *Hrvatska gruda* 93 (1942).

48. HDA, Collection 218, MPB NDH, Department of Justice, box 28, 4375/1942.

49. HDA, Collection 218, MPB NDH, Department of Justice, box 28, 44449/1942; collection 1076, Reconstruction, index DKM, file of Marta Raić, 924/5; *Kartoteka židovskog znaka*; testimony of Professor Dr. Fedor Rajić; NAZ, group NDS 8046/1942.

50. *Narodne novine* 31, February 7, 1942; HDA, Collection ZKRZ GUZ, no. 306, box 10, 469–471.

51. HDA, Collection MUP SRH, 013.0.65, II dio, 41.

52. Kisić-Kolanović, "Podržavljenje imovine Židova u NDH," 442, 448.

53. HDA, Collection ZKRZ GUZ, no. 306, box 10, 472–76.

54. See also text *Zakonske odredbe*; HDA, Collection 218, MPB NDH, Department of Justice, box 28, 2083/1942.

55. HDA, Collection MUP SRH, 013.0.65, Part III, 104, 105, 310, 311.

56. JIM, Collection ŽOZ, sign. K-67–1-1/1–239, 1–243.

57. *Narodne novine*, November 10, 1942; May 26, 1943; October 29, 1943; July 4, 1944; January 20, 1945; HDA, Collection ZKRZ GUZ, no. 306, box 10, 478–82.

58. HDA, Collection 218, MPB NDH, Department of Justice, box 28, 20807/1944, 7192/1945.

59. JIM, Collection ŽOZ, reg. no. 4864, sign. K-63–1-1/1–167, 1–168, 1–215, 1–292.

60. JIM, Collection ŽOZ, without reg. no.

61. HDA, Collection ZKRZ GUZ, no. 306, box 16, 4888–4923.

62. HDA, Collection MUP SRH, 013.0.65, Part II, 22.

63. Kisić-Kolanović, "Podržavljenje imovine Židova u NDH," 444.

64. HDA, Collection HDS, Treasury Committee, Committee information of 5/15/1942; Kisić-Kolanović, "Podržavljenje imovine Židova u NDH," 447.

65. HDA, Collection HDS no. 1371, Report of the Nationalized Wealth Bureau of September 15, 1943; Kisić-Kolanović, "Podržavljenje imovine Židova u NDH," 452.

66. HDA, Collection MUP SRH, 013.0.65, Part II, 19; about Košak, see Stuparić, *Tko je tko u NDH*, 199.

67. HDA, Collection 252, RUR, J. Section, 29059.

68. HDA, Collection MUP SRH, 013.0.65, Part II, 19.

69. HDA, Collection MUP SRH, 013.0.2: *Historijat ustaškog pokreta i NDH*, by S. Kvaternik and V. Košak, 355; on Sertić himself, see HDA, File SDS no. 322336; Vjesnik MINORS-a; HDA, Index ZKRZ, no. GUZ 7121-SKO-DK 10/14/1946, zh. no. 12672, 12714.

70. HDA, Collection MUP SRH, o 13.0.56; File Dr. Mehmed Alajbegović, interrogation record, 104–5; on Alajbegović, see Stuparić, *Tko je tko u NDH*, 4–5.

71. Jareb, *Zlato i novac.*

72. Jareb, *Zlato i novac,* 359; according to Professor Dr. Stjepan Steiner, Ivan Krajačić, a high-ranking Communist official, sent the boxes that were discovered in 1946 to Josip Broz Tito, and Steiner and other officers from the escort spent "days counting the gold coins, partly cleaning them of earth and packing them in rolls and making lists." Dr. Steiner thought that they were "sent to the National Bank, but he was not sure."

73. About Samuel Aleksander, see HBL, I:71–72. Until the First World War, Samuel signed his name as "Alexander," and after 1918 as "Aleksander," thus the differences in orthography; it was the same for certain other family members.

74. *Knjiga kontribucije.*

75. HDA, Collection 1076, Reconstruction, Index DKI, file of Samuel Alexander—15/2; Documents of I. Mirnik.

76. HDA, Collection 1076, Reconstruction, Index DKI, file of Samuel Alexander—15/2; Documents of I. Mirnik.

77. HDA, Collection 252, RUR, J. Section, 28913.

78. Mirnik, *Obitelj Alexander ili povijest jedne zagrebačke obitelji.*

79. HDA, Collection 1076, Reconstruction, Index DKI, file of Samuel Alexander—15/2; Documents of I. Mirnik.

80. Mirnik, *Obitelj Alexander ili povijest jedne zagrebačke obitelji.*

81. HDA, Collection 252, RUR, J. Section, 28370.

82. *Židov* 4–5 (1920); 30 (1922); 22 (1923); 51 (1924); 23 (1925); 11, 22, and 25 (1926); 30 (1927); 28 (1928).

83. *Židov* 39 (1939).

84. *Spomenica izraelske ferijalne kolonije u Zagrebu prigodom dvadesetpetogodišnjice opstanka društva.*

85. *Židov* 25 (1926).

86. *Knjiga kontribucije.*

87. HDA, Ponova (Reconstruction), "P," box 61 (665).

88. NAZ, group NDS 10072/1941.

89. *Popis žrtava.*

90. JIM, Collection ŽOZ, reg. no. 5289, sign. K 8a-1–6/2; testimony of Vlasta Urbić, née Deutsch-Maceljski; *Knjiga umrlih.*

91. Ristović, *U potrazi za utočištem, Jugoslovenski Jevreji,* 258–59; testimony of Sonja Budak née, Rešetar.

92. HDA, Collection 1076, Reconstruction, "P," box 99 (703); Index DKM, box 440, 1152; testimony of Lucija Rosenberg, née Sternberg.

93. HDA, Reconstruction, J. Section, no. 34420, of August 12, 1941.

94. Jelić-Butić, *Ustaše i NDH,* 209.

95. *Hrvatski leksikon,* 2:79. The Agreements of Rome of May 18, 1941, between the ISC and Mussolini, were the first great blow to Croatian national feelings. Almost all of Dalmatia was ceded to Italy, along with much of Hrvatsko Primorje and a small part of Gorski kotar, although the population of all those regions was about 90 percent Croatian.

96. Lasić, *Krležologija,* 3:176–77.

97. Lukas, *Ličnosti*, 236; Jelić-Butić, *Ustaše i NDH*, 138–39.

98. Stuparić, *Tko je tko u NDH*, 176–77, 243, 365–66.

99. *Dnevnik Blaža Jurišića*, 6.

100. NAZ, Collection Presidial documents 57/1943.

101. Testimony of Dr. Lea Prašek, née Neufeld.

14. Evicting Jews from Houses and Apartments

1. *Hrvatski narod*, May 10, 1941; *Ustaša, Dokumenti*, 172–73; HDA, Collection ZKRZ GUZ, no. 306, box 10, 322. The "*mitnica* (toll-house) in Ilica" or the "*Ilica mitnica*" was located where the last streetcar stop in Črnomerec is today, in the northeast part of the city.

2. HDA, Collection ZKRZ GUZ, no 306, box 10, 147.

3. *Novi list* 18, June 15, 1941.

4. Testimony of Sonja Budak, née Rešetar.

5. HDA, Collection MUP SRH, 013.0.65, Part II, 41; Kisić-Kolanović, "Podržavljenje imovine Židova u NDH," 444; *Jevrejska tribuna* 38 (1945).

6. Testimony of Branko Polić.

7. Testimony of Vlasta Urbić, née Deutsch-Maceljski; about Canki and Žanić, see Stuparić, *Tko je tko u NDH*, 64–65, 433.

8. *Zakoni, zakonske odredbe, naredbe NDH, IV*:227–30. On June 5, the Ordinance on the Implementation of the Legal Provision . . . for Reasons of Public Security was issued, which very precisely defined all situations that might arise. It was signed by Andrija Artuković and Mirko Puk; HDA, Collection 218, MPB NDH, Department of Justice, box 29, 31888/1941.

9. *Zakoni, zakonske odredbe, naredbe NDH, II*:24–26.

10. *Zakoni, zakonske odredbe, naredbe NDH, II*:162–64.

11. *Zakoni, zakonske odredbe, naredbe NDH, IV*:162–64.

12. The preserved material in HDA, Collection 223, MUP NDH, shows that some local authorities also wanted to be "legally" correct, for example in Vukovar.

13. Circular letter no. 7720-Prs-1941. of June 9, 1941; DAZ, Collection GPSUZ.

14. Later, in 1945, Radišina Street became Božidara Adžije Street, and since 1991 it has been named Kneza Mislava Street; on the accommodation of Ustashe in hospitals, see testimony of Professor Dr. Stjepan Steiner.

15. DAZ, Collection GPSUZ, 392/41, 421/41, 448/41, 646/41.

16. DAZ, Collection GPSUZ, 448/41.

17. *Kartoteka židovskog znaka*; *Popis žrtava*; see list of Jewish Community dues, JIM, Collection ŽOZ, reg. no. 4973, sign. K-64–2-1/1–26.

18. HDA, Collection 252, RUR, J. Section, 27418, 27419, 27674, 27801.

19. DAZ, Collection GPZ, 17654/1–3/1941, 16824/2/1941, 9859/1941, 14743/2/1941, 13278/7/1941, 9690/1941, 10376/6/1941.

20. HDA, Collection 252, RUR, J. Section, 28200; DAZ, Collection GPZ, 170/2/1941.

21. HDA, Collection 252, RUR, J. Section, 27576, 29714.

22. DAZ, Collection of law office A. Licht, attorney's office, bills for dues.

23. HDA, Collection 252, RUR, J. Section, 27441; testimony of Vera Zoričić, née Schwabenitz.

24. HDA, Collection 252, RUR, J. Section, 27442. See similar cases in 27443, 27444, 27447, 27458, 27459, 27461, 27525, 27561.

25. HDA, Collection 252, RUR, J. Section, 28462.

26. HDA, Collection 223, MUP NDH 2995, I A 3892.

27. HDA, Collection 252, RUR, J. Section, 27359, 27594, 27597, 27600, 27614, 27627, 27653, 28200, 28390.

28. *Novi list* 18 (Zagreb), May 16, 1941.

29. HDA, Collection 252, RUR, J. Section, 27475, 27708, 28083, 28957.

30. HDA, Collection 252, RUR, J. Section, 27632, 28611.

31. HDA, Collection 252, RUR, J. Section, 28159.

32. DAZ, Collection GPSUZ, 8567/41; *Popis žrtava.*

33. JIM, Collection ŽOZ, without reg. no. and sign.

34. HDA, collection MUP RH III-24, 415, 417. The Poglavnik's Bodyguard Battalion was not a fighting unit or a real military unit, but one that it was an honor to belong to. Almost all the more prominent earliest Ustashe belonged to it, under condition that they had spent a certain time in one of the Ustasha military training camps abroad or that they had been abroad at least twice as messengers or couriers.

35. HDA, Collection 223, MUP NDH 2995, 3006, 3007, 3041–3043, 3076, 3077, 3080, 3115, 3116, 3136, I A 3892, 3894, 4250, 4275, 4277, 4459–4461, 4476, 4635, 4640, 4786, 4787, 4856; collection 252, RUR, J. Section, 28463. In his text, Servatzy gives the names of some thirty-five of the most important Ustasha officials and members of the Poglavnik's Bodyguard Battalion, which do not include any of the above mentioned—see the study of V. Servatzy in Krizman, *Ustaše i Reich*, 2:431.

36. Pezo was a *dorojnik*; Barešić a *dovodnik*; Orešković, Mikulić, Ćapin, Granić, and Nevistić *čarkari* who became émigrés in 1933; Galić, Ivančić, Đerek, Šredl, Bajić, and Lončar were *čarkari* who arrived in camp in 1934; Blažinčić, Grubišić, and Čašljar were *čarkari* who joined up among the last, in 1935. The *dorojnik*, *dovodnik*, and *čarkar* were the lowest Ustasha military ranks. Mišetić, Wolf, Roščić, and Leko were never in Ustasha camps; see Krizman, *Pavelić i ustaše,* 555–58.

37. *Knjiga umrlih*; Testimony of Vlasta Urbić, née Deutsch-Maceljski.

38. *Popis žrtava*; *Spiskovi preživelih.*

39. HDA, Collection 223, MUP NDH 3044, 3045, I A 4462, 4463.

40. HDA, Collection 223, MUP NDH 3952, I A 6725.

41. See, HDA, Collection 223, MUP NDH 2032, 2644, 2927, 2929–2931, 2933–2939, 2950, 2951, 2976, 2979, 2981, 2991, 3000–3005, 3216–3218, 3238, 3239, 3242, 3257, 3266, 3269, 3270, 3272, 3273, 3283, 3301–3312, 3566, 3578, 3720–3722, I A/157–159, 288,293, 339, 393, 438, 442–444, 446, 569, 681, 682, 684–687, 689, 690, 692–694, 696, 2095, 2141, 2645, 2997, 2642, 3419, 3404, 3405, 3420, 3431, 3535, 3663, 3752, 3792, 3887, 3888, 3890, 3891, 3918, 3922–3924, 3927, 3928, 3940, 3943, 3945, 3958, 4003, 4005, 4007, 4049, 4142, 4162, 4164, 4233, 4268, 4270–4274, 5255–5257, 25691.

42. HDA, collection MUP RH III-24, 405, 409, 411, 419, 421, 423, 425, 427, 429, 449, 455, 515, 527, 545, 551, 555, 671, 757, 761, 763, 765, 767, 777, 779, 783, 789, 793, 799,

803, 817–828, 851, 869–878, 881–908, 911–918, 923–934, 939–942, 945–950, 953, 959–962, 977–992, 995, 999, 1005–1010, 1015–1024, 1027, 1033, 1039, 1047–1050, 1053, 1057, 1063, 1069–1072, 1075–1088, 1091–1096, 1103–1108, 1111, 1115, 1121–1124, 1129–1136, 1139–1144, 1147–1154, 1157–1160, 1163, 1167–1172, 1175–1178, 1185–1196, 1199–1204, 1207, 1211–1218, 1221–1230, 1233–1256, 1259–1264, 1269–1290, 1293–1306, 1309–1364, 1367–1386, 1389–1408, 1415–1418, 1421–1432, 1435–1438, 1441, 1445, 1447, 1453–1488.

43. HDA, collection MUP RH III-24, 407, 431–434, 443, 447, 453, 457–476, 479–484, 487–514, 517–526, 529–542, 547, 553, 557–654, 659–664, 667, 677–680, 683, 689–710, 713–734, 737, 741–746, 749–754, 773, 795, 797, 801, 805, 807, 809, 829–836, 841–848, 853, 859, 867, 935, 943, 951, 963–966, 969, 975, 993, 1003, 1011–1014, 1025, 1031, 1035, 1041, 1051, 1055, 1061, 1065–1068, 1089, 1099–1102, 1109, 1155, 1231.

44. HDA, Collection MUP RH III-24, 839–840.

45. HDA, Collection MUP RH III-24, 441; testimony of Natan-Nino Mandelsamen.

46. HDA, Collection MUP RH III-24, 549; *Popis žrtava.*

47. HDA, Collection 252, RUR, J. Section, 27709, 29609.

48. HDA, Collection 252, RUR, J. Section, 28384; *Popis žrtava.*

49. HDA, Collection 252, RUR, J. Section, 27915; *Popis žrtava*; estate of M. Despot.

50. HDA, Collection 252, RUR, J. Section, 29352; *Popis žrtava*; *Spiskovi preživelih.*

51. HDA, Collection 252, RUR, J. Section, 28598, 28599; HDA, Collection 252, RUR, J. Section, Index, 8166.

52. HDA, Reconstruction, "P," box 61 (665); HDA Collection 252, RUR, J. Section, 28922.

53. HDA, Collection 252, RUR, J. Section, 28691; *Popis žrtava.*

54. See HAZ, Collection GPZ, inventory books for 1941 and 1942.

55. HDA, Collection 252, RUR, J. Section, 29884.

56. HDA, Collection 252, RUR, J. Section, 28926, 28938, 28973.

57. HDA, Collection 252, RUR, J. Section, 28828, 29858.

58. See HAZ, Collection GPZ, inventory books for 1942.

59. HDA, Collection 252, RUR, J. Section, 29063.

60. HDA, Collection 252, RUR, J. Section, 931/1942.

61. HDA, Collection 252, RUR, J. Section, 28825, 29067.

62. HDA, Collection 252, RUR, J. Section, 29121.

63. HDA, Collection 218, MPB NDH, Department of Justice, box 29, 98066, 98067/1941; 545, 548, 845, 846, 1332, 1334, 1739–1743, 2463, 2464, 2680–2682, 2868–2871, 3099–3110/1942.

64. HDA, Collection 252, RUR, J. Section, 29060.

65. HDA, Collection 252, RUR, J. Section, 29441, 29442, 29467, 29468, 29472, 29473, 29483, 29504, 29505, 29507, 29508, 29510, 29511, and elsewhere.

66. However, it has not been preserved in the HAD Collections—HDA, Collection 252, RUR, J. Section, 29707.

67. HDA, Collection 252, RUR, J. Section, 29884; Collection 1076, Reconstruction, index DKM, file of Vilko Lehner—697/3.

68. Testimony of Dr Teodor Grüner; HDA, Collection 487, MINORS, Pension Bureau, personal pensions, 194.

69. HDA, Collection ZKRZ GUZ, no. 306, box 10, 150.

70. Testimony of Branko Polić; BP ŽHH, ŽOZ; HDA, Collection 252, RUR, J. Section, 28592; *Popis žrtava.*

71. HDA, Collection 252, RUR, J. Section, 28222. This was probably Marko Filip Vujeva, Ustasha returnee, see Kvaternik, *Sjećanja i zapažanja,* 65, 99, 329.

72. HDA, Collection 252, RUR, J. Section, 28559.

73. HDA, Collection 252, RUR, J. Section, 28920.

74. DAZ, Collection GPSUZ, 1319/41; on Begić, see Stuparić, *Tko je tko u NDH,* 29–30. Office III UNS, the command of the Ustasha Defense headed by Maks Luburić, moved into Zvonimirova 2.

75. DAZ, Collection GPSUZ, 164/41.

76. HDA, Collection 252, RUR, J. Section, 29282.

77. HDA, Collection 223, MUP NDH 2894, 2935, I-A 3267, 3534, 3782, 3936. Korčulanić was one of the first Ustashe in Dalmatia and became an émigré as early as January 1933—Krizman, *Pavelić i ustaše,* 555; HDA, file SDS no. 301531, p. 6.

78. The number of evicted Orthodox, that is Serbs, at least according to the inventoried and inspected part of the Collection, is ten and more times smaller—see e.g., the example of Teodor Panić from Deželićeva—HDA, Collection 223, MUP NDH 3046, I A 4114, 4291, 4464.

79. The Collection includes a list of seventy apartments and several houses in the city center (Ilica, Jurišićeva, Krešimirov Square, Branimirova, etc.) and in Trešnjevka—HDA, Collection 223, MUP NDH, box 300, 30068.

80. HDA, Collection 252, RUR, J. Section, 29065.

81. HDA, Collection ZKRZ GUZ, no. 306, box 10, 130.

82. HDA, Collection 252, RUR, J. Section, 27874.

83. HDA, Collection ZKRZ GUZ, no. 306, box 10, 115–116, 197.

15. Salvation for a Group of Doctors

1. *Zakoni, zakonske odredbe, naredbe NDH, II:*300–304.

2. See *Zakoni, zakonske odredbe, naredbe NDH, II:*303.

3. HDA, Collection 252, RUR, J. Section, 28017, 28266, 28658—see list of fifty-one doctors, also—29171.

4. Testimony of Professor Dr. Stjepan Steiner.

5. O. Deutsch in Romano, *Jevreji zdravstveni radnici Jugoslavije,* 112, 178; *Bilten ŽOZ,* 38 (1995).

6. Testimony of Professor Dr. Stjepan Steiner; the Ustasha regime had a special policy of winning over the Muslims in Bosnia and Herzegovina—they were proclaimed "the flower of the Croatian nation," and Bosnia was proclaimed "the heart of Croatia"—see in more detail, Tomashevic, *War and Revolution in Yugoslavia,* in various places.

7. Banja, L. "Statistički dodatak," 36, gives the number of twenty-five doctors.

8. Testimony of Professor Dr. Stjepan Steiner.

9. Banja, L. "Statistički dodatak," 37. The figures differ somewhat, depending on source, but this does not basically change the picture as a whole; other sources, less reliable, mention eighty-one doctors.

10. Banja, L. "Statistički dodatak."

11. HDA, Collection 252, RUR, J. Section, 28810.

12. JIM, Collection ŽOZ, reg. no. 4973, sign. K-64–2-1/1–22, 1–23.

13. JP 1–2 (1970); Lengel-Krizman, "Prilog proučavanju terora u NDH," 7; Levental, "Lekari"; Romano, *Učešće lekara Jevreja*, gives the best summary of the reasons for initiating the project and its course; Najfeld, "Sećanje iz vremena drugog svetskog rata"; on the merits of Ante Vuletić, see JP 7–8 (1977).

14. Testimony of Ljerka Magdić.

15. HDA, Collection 223, MUP NDH, 3510/II-A, 2570; Collection 252, RUR, J. Section, 27986, 28056, 28107, 28666, 29184, 29222, 29429.

16. HDA, Collection 252, RUR, J. Section, 29078.

17. HDA, Collection 252, RUR, J. Section, 29570.

18. HDA, Collection 252, RUR, J. Section, 27942, 27953, 27956, 27957, 28657, 28737.

19. HDA, Collection 252, RUR, J. Section, 27895.

20. HDA, Collection 252, RUR, J. Section, 29810.

21. HDA, Collection 252, RUR, J. Section, 28745.

22. HDA, Collection 252, RUR, J. Section, 29485.

23. Testimony of Branko Polić; Romano, *Jevreji zdravstveni radnici Jugoslavije*, 178.

24. HDA, Collection 252, RUR, J. Section, 28762, 29806, 29807, 29864; *Popis žrtava*—see also Greta, Mišo, and Stela Berger, Grüner's sister-in-law, brother-in-law, and mother-in-law, respectively.

25. JIM, Collection ŽOZ, reg. no. 4857, sign. K-62–3-1/1–136, 1–157; Romano, *Jevreji zdravstveni radnici Jugoslavije*, 190–91; testimony of Branko Polić.

26. See, *Popis preuzetih stvari židovskih ordinacija* (List of Items Taken Over From Jewish Doctors' Offices).

27. Kolar-Dimitrijević, "Sjećanja veterinara Zorka Goluba," 164.

28. Testimony of Professor Dr. Stjepan Steiner; on Rosenzweig, see Romano, *Jevreji zdravstveni radnici Jugoslavije*, 189.

29. Units of the Yugoslav Army captured and executed her in 1945 in Slovenia.

30. JIM, Collection ŽOZ, without reg. no.

31. HDA, Collection 252, RUR, J. Section, 28882.

32. HDA, Collection 252, RUR, J. Section, 28572.

33. Romano, *Jevreji zdravstveni radnici Jugoslavije*, 153.

34. HDA, Collection 252, RUR, J. Section, 29836, 29857.

35. HDA, Collection 252, RUR, J. Section, 28374; Romano, *Jevreji zdravstveni radnici Jugoslavije*, 183.

36. HDA, Collection 223, MUP NDH, 4276/I-A, 10521.

37. HDA, Collection 223, MUP NDH, 6081/minister's office, 708.

38. Kolar-Dimitrijević, "Sjećanja veterinara Zorka Goluba," 163–64.

39. Romano, *Jevreji zdravstveni radnici Jugoslavije*, 83, 154, 155, 157; *Popis žrtava*.

40. HDA, Collection 252, RUR, J. Section, 29904.

41. HDA, Collection 252, RUR, J. Section, 28477.

42. Šternberg, "Doprinos Židova," 235.

43. Testimony of Saša Tolnauer.

44. Nikoliš, *Korijeni, stablo, pavetina*, 652; about some doctors, see Steiner, "Sjećanje na Židove liječnike u NOB."

45. HDA, Collection 237, Head Directorate of Propaganda, box 4, 6425/194

16. Other Forms of Persecution

1. *Novi list*, May 30, 1941.

2. HDA, Collection ZKRZ GUZ, no. 306, box 10, 323.

3. *Novi list* 44, June 12, 1941.

4. Testimony of Ljerka Magdić.

5. HDA, Collection 252, RUR, J. Section, 27521, 27652, 27829, 28179, 28230.

6. HDA, Collection 252, RUR, J. Section, 27287; *Popis žrtava*; *Kartoteka jasenovačkih zatočenika.*

7. HDA, Collection 252, RUR, J. Section, 28064; see also 28416.

8. HDA, Collection 252, RUR, J. Section, 27385, 27678.

9. HDA, Collection 252, RUR, J. Section, 27341.

10. HDA, Collection 252, RUR, J. Section, 27640; see also 27641.

11. HDA, Collection 252, RUR, J. Section, 29156.

12. HDA, Collection 252, RUR, J. Section, 29736.

13. Testimony of Professor Dr. Stjepan Steiner.

14. Testimony of Professor Dr. Stjepan Steiner; *Popis žrtava.*

15. HDA, Collection 252, RUR, J. Section, registry book 1251, registry book 1261, registry book 1263.

16. *Hrvatska gruda* 50 (1941); HDA, Collection 252, RUR, J. Section, registry book 2049–51, 27704, 27705.

17. HDA, Collection 252, RUR, J. Section, Index.

18. HDA, Collection 252, RUR, J. Section, 28339.

19. *Zbornik zakona i naredaba NDH*, 43–44; *Zakoni, zakonske odredbe, naredbe NDH, II*:54; HDA, Collection ZKRZ GUZ, no. 306, box 10, 458; *Narodne novine* 43, June 4, 1941; see also HDA, Collection 223, MUP NDH, 1263/A-II, 27622.

20. NAZ, group NDS 357/1942.

21. HDA, Collection 252, RUR, J. Section, 28830, 28925, 29172.

22. Documents of Branko Polić; testimony of Branko Polić.

23. Testimony of Vlasta Urbić, née Deutsch-Maceljski.

24. HDA, Collection 252, RUR, J. Section, 28675; NAZ, group NDS 8350/1941; *Popis žrtava*; JIM, Collection ŽOZ, reg. no. 4866, sign. K-66-1-1/1–67.

25. NAZ, group NDS 10684/1943, 1200/1944.

26. NAZ, group NDS 2980, 3552, 3679, 7694/1941.

27. Testimony of Branko Polić.

28. NAZ, group NDS 1968/1941; group NDS 356, 1189, 4799, 5591, 5897, 6615/1942.

29. NAZ, group NDS 202/1943.

30. NAZ, group NDS 6964, 6965/1942.

31. NAZ, group NDS 896/1945.

32. NAZ, group NDS 5995/1943.

33. Testimony of Branko Polić; *Popis žrtava*; *Kartoteka židovskog znaka*; *Spiskovi preživelih*.

34. *Zakoni, zakonske odredbe, naredbe NDH, I*:219; This was a proclamation that kosher laws were illegal, that is, the laws on the ritual cleanliness and suitability of food and drink for human consumption.

35. *Hrvatski narod*, June 24, 1941; HDA, Collection ZKRZ GUZ, no. 306, box 10, 426.

36. HDA, Collection 252, RUR, J. Section, 28271, 28285a.

37. HDA, Collection ZKRZ GUZ, no. 306, box 15, 3727.

38. HDA, Collection 252, RUR, J. Section, 27499.

39. HDA, Collection 252, RUR, J. Section, 27500.

40. HDA, Collection 252, RUR, J. Section, 27760.

41. *Hrvatski narod*, June 25, 1941; HDA, Collection ZKRZ GUZ, no. 306, box 10, 434.

42. *Hrvatski narod*, June 26, 1941.

43. HDA, Collection 252, RUR, J. Section, 27323.

44. *Narodne novine* 162, October 25, 1941.

45. HDA, Collection 252, RUR, J. Section, 28013.

17. The Work of the Jewish Religious Community in Zagreb

1. HDA, Collection ZKRZ GUZ, no. 306, box 15, 3874; *Zapisnici 1941*, Archive ŽOZ.

2. Kolar-Dimitrijević, "Prvo dobrotvorno društvo," 73.

3. JIM, Collection ŽOZ, without reg. no.

4. HDA, Collection ZKRZ GUZ, no. 306, box 15, 3874; *Zapisnici 1941*, Archive ŽOZ.

5. HDA, Collection ZKRZ GUZ, no. 306, box 15, 3874; *Zapisnici 1941*, Archive ŽOZ.

6. Levental, "Sećanje na medicinski rad."

7. HDA, Collection ZKRZ GUZ, no. 306, box 15, 3875.

8. Testimony of Vera Zoričić, née Schwabenitz.

9. HDA, Collection: NDH, inv. no. 27372; Sobolevski, "Zagrebačka židovska općina od 1941"; *Zapisnici 1941*, Archive ŽOZ.

10. HDA, Collection ZKRZ GUZ, no. 306, box 15, 3875.

11. HDA, Collection 252, RUR, J. Section, 27389, 27409.

12. HDA, Collection 252, RUR, J. Section, 27324, 28099; Collection ZKRZ GUZ, no. 306, box 16, 4478; *Zapisnici 1941*, Archive ŽOZ; Sobolevski, "Zagrebačka židovska općina od 1941."

13. HDA, Collection 252, RUR, J. Section, 27255, 27324, 28099; HDA, Collection ZKRZ GUZ, no. 306, box 10, 92, box 15, 3876, box 16, 4478; Sobolevski, "Zagrebačka židovska općina od 1941."

14. HDA, Collection 252, RUR, J. Section, 27292, 27317, 28045. Demands of this kind were repeated in later months as well—same source, 28859.

15. HDA, Collection 252, RUR, J. Section, 27553, 27583.

16. HDA, Collection 252, RUR, J. Section, 27429, 27454.

17. HDA, Collection 252, RUR, J. Section, 27631.

18. HDA, Collection 252, RUR, J. Section, 28848.

19. *Zapisnici 1941*, Archive ŽOZ.

20. HDA, Collection 252, RUR, J. Section, 27894.

21. HDA, Collection 252, RUR, J. Section, 27893, 27921.

22. HDA, Collection 252, RUR, J. Section, 27318, 27587.

23. HDA, Collection 252, RUR, J. Section, 27924.

24. HDA, Collection 252, RUR, J. Section, 28761.

25. HDA, Collection ZKRZ GUZ, no. 306, box 15, 3875.

26. HDA, Collection 252, RUR, J. Section, 27265, 29154; *Zapisnici 1941*, Archive ŽOZ.

27. HDA, Collection 252, RUR, J. Section, 27316.

28. *Zapisnici 1941*, Archive ŽOZ.

29. HDA, Collection 252, RUR, J. Section, 27448, 27489, 27491–27493, 28099; *Zapisnici 1941*, Archive ŽOZ; Sobolevski, "Zagrebačka židovska općina od 1941."

30. HDA, Collection 252, RUR, J. Section, 27372.

31. HDA, Collection 252, RUR, J. Section, 27954.

32. HDA, Collection 252, RUR, J. Section, 27453, 27892; *Zapisnici 1941*, Archive ŽOZ.

33. Testimony of Professor Dr. Stjepan Steiner.

34. HDA, Collection 252, RUR, J. Section, 27446, 27589; *Zapisnici 1941*, Archive ŽOZ; Sobolevski, "Zagrebačka židovska općina od 1941."

35. Levental, "Sećanje na medicinski rad"; only several bills for orders for the clinic have been preserved, e.g., codeine—JIM, Collection ŽOZ, sign. K-65–4-1/1–11, 1–12, 1–17, 1–18; *Zapisnici 1941*, Archive ŽOZ.

36. Romano, *Jevreji zdravstveni radnici Jugoslavije*, 183.

37. HDA, Collection ZKRZ GUZ, no. 306, box 15, 3876.

38. JIM, Collection ŽOZ, sign. K-65–4-1/1–185.

39. *Kartoteka židovskog znaka.*

40. HDA, Collection 252, RUR, J. Section, 27372; Sobolevski, "Zagrebačka židovska općina od 1941."

41. HDA, Collection 252, RUR, J. Section, 30062.

42. Ben-Sasson, *History of the Jewish People*, 1026–27.

43. Arendt, *Eichmann*, 117.

44. Testimony of Professor Dr. Stjepan Steiner.

45. Testimony of Professor Dr. Stjepan Steiner; Romano, *Jevreji zdravstveni radnici Jugoslavije*, 178. Dr. Mile Budak (1903–1961), the minister's nephew and a doctor—Stuparić, *Tko je tko u NDH*, 55.

46. Laquer, *Terrible Secret*, 58–60.

47. HDA, zbirka MUP RH III-24, 1179.

48. JIM, Collection ŽOZ, reg. no. 4859, sign. K-65–1-1/1–172.

49. JIM, Collection ŽOZ, reg. no. 4859, sign. K-65–1-1/1–158, 1–159, 1–163, 1–164, 1–171.

50. JIM, Collection ŽOZ, reg. no. 4859, sign. K-65–1-1/1–172.

51. JIM, Collection ŽOZ, reg. no. 4859, sign. K-65–1-1/1–170.

52. JIM, Collection ŽOZ, reg. no. 4859, sign. K-65–1-1/1–165, 1–168.

53. JIM, reg. no. 2983; Tolentino, *Fašistička okupacija*, 204–5; Ristović, *U potrazi za utočištem, Jugoslovenski Jevreji*, 115–16.

54. JIM, Collection ŽOZ, reg. no. 4859, sign. K-65–1-1/1–148, 1–145.

55. JIM, Collection ŽOZ, reg. no. 4859, sign. K-65–1-1/1–147.

56. JIM, Collection ŽOZ, reg. no. 4859, sign. K-65–1-1/1–64, 1–71, 1–105.

57. JIM, Collection ŽOZ, reg. no. 4859, sign. K-65–1-1/1–8, 1–85.

58. JIM, Collection ŽOZ, reg. no. 4859, sign. K-65–1-1/1–59, 1–60.

59. JIM, Collection ŽOZ, reg. no. 4859, sign. K-65–1-1/1–58, 1–75.

60. JIM, Collection ŽOZ, reg. no. 4859, sign. K-65–1-1/1–52.

61. JIM, Collection ŽOZ, reg. no. 4859, sign. K-65–1-1/1–1, 1–11.

62. HDA, Collection 252, RUR, J. Section, 27793.

63. HDA, Collection ZKRZ GUZ, no. 306, box 15, 3872.

64. HDA, Collection 252, RUR, J. Section, 27596.

65. HDA, Collection 252, RUR, J. Section, 28270.

66. JIM, Collection ŽOZ, without reg. no.

67. *Zapisnici 1941*, Archive ŽOZ.

68. *Zapisnici 1941*, Archive ŽOZ.

69. *Popis žrtava.*

70. Testimony of Vera Zoričić, née Schwabenitz; *Popis žrtava.*

18. Mass Arrests and Transit Camps

1. Neufeld, "Svjedočanstvo preživjelog."

2. Komarica, *Kerestinečka kronika,* 257–59.

3. Komarica, *Kerestinečka kronika,* 255–56.

4. See the official letter in HDA, Collection 252, RUR, J. Section, 27148. The inordinate suffering and fate of this group of young people from Zagreb is described in detail in: Lengel-Krizman and Sobolevski, "Hapšenje."

5. Testimony of Professor Dr. Željko Šrenger.

6. Židovec, *Moje sudjelovanje u političkom životu*, 31, 33. Vukovac came into conflict with Eugen Kvaternik and expressed his disagreement with the regime as early as June, so he retired and was pensioned, see Stuparić, *Tko je tko u NDH*, 424.

7. HDA, Collection 252, RUR, J. Section, 27517a.

8. Here I paraphrase Fischer, "Židovska pučka škola."

9. HDA, Collection ZKRZ GUZ, no. 306, box 11, 645, 648; Collection 252, RUR, J. Section, 27498; Dizdar, "Logori," 99–100.

10. HDA, Collection 252, RUR, J. Section, 28000.

11. HDA, Collection 252, RUR, J. Section, 28372.

12. Testimony of Professor Dr. Stjepan Steiner.

13. Testimony of Professor Dr. Stjepan Steiner.

14. Novak, *When Heaven's Vault Cracked*, 35–36.

15. HDA, Collection 252, RUR, J. Section, 27887.

16. Ante Jedvaj was a private employee from Zagreb, a clerk in Merkur, a pre-

war "Frankist" (according to allegations of the State Commission for War Crimes), member of the Croatian National Parliament in 1942, publisher of the weekly *Hrvatska gruda,* commissioner of the Zagreb and Osijek steam mills, "silent partner" in the former Jewish firm Steiner Lavoslav Wholesale Paper Merchant, which he and others bought in 1943 from the Croatian Workingman's Cooperative. After the war, he was proclaimed a war criminal and shot; HDA, Collection ZKRZ, ZH 7057; Collection MUP RH, I-28, 624–625; IV-6, 18; *Spomen-knjiga povodom obljetnice uspostave NDH* (Zagreb 1942). It seems that this was the same Ante Jedvaj who on one occasion helped Vlatko Deutsch-Maceljski to avoid arrest. This was his way of returning a favor, because Vlatko had helped Ante financially in the thirties; testimony of Vlasta Urbić, née Deutsch-Maceljski (all the witness remembered was the name Jedvaj).

17. Novak, *When Heaven's Vault Cracked*, 37–38.

18. Testimony of Professor Dr. Stjepan Steiner.

19. Peršen, *Ustaški logori*, 96.

20. Peršen, *Ustaški logori*, 91; testimony of Professor Dr. Stjepan Steiner.

21. Dizdar, "Logori," 99–100.

22. Peršen, *Ustaški logori*, 78.

23. *Narodne novine* 61, June 27, 1941; HDA, Collection ZKRZ GUZ, no. 306, box 10, 314, 462, 463; Miletić, *Koncentracioni logor Jasenovac*, 1:47–49.

24. *Narodne novine*, June 27, 1941; *Ustaša* 3 (Zagreb), July 3, 1941; *Ustaša, Dokumenti*, 203; Krišto, *Katolička crkva*, 2:68–69; HDA, Collection ZKRZ GUZ, no. 306, box 10, 314; Sobolevski, "Zagrebačka židovska općina od 1941."

25. Peršen, *Ustaški logori*, 78.

26. *Hrvatski narod*, June 29, 1941; see also HDA, Collection ZKRZ GUZ, no. 306, box 10, 430.

27. *Ustaša* 3 (Zagreb), July 3, 1941.

28. HDA, Collection 252, RUR, J. Section, 27543, 29185.

29. HDA, Collection 252, RUR, J. Section, 28015.

30. Testimony of Berta Israel, née Švarcenberg.

31. Berger, *44 mjeseca u Jasenovcu*, 7.

32. Testimony of Nada Rajner, née Fröhlich.

33. HDA, Collection 252, RUR, J. Section, 27513; *Popis žrtava.*

34. Novak, *When Heaven's Vault Cracked*, 37.

35. Testimony of Boris Braun.

36. Testimony of Vlasta Urbić, née Deutsch-Maceljski.

37. Testimony of Berta Israel, née Švarcenberg.

38. HDA, Collection 252, RUR, J. Section, 29704.

39. Testimony of Berta Israel, née Švarcenberg.

40. HDA, Collection 252, RUR, J. Section, 28065.

41. HDA, Collection 252, RUR, J. Section, 27768.

42. HDA, Collection 252, RUR, J. Section, 27756, 27757.

43. HDA, Collection 252, RUR, J. Section, 27756, 27850, 29588, *Popis žrtava*; see also in 28883; testimony of Branko Polić.

44. Peršen, *Ustaški logori*, 96; Zemljar, *Haron*, 40, 146.

45. *Hrvatski narod*, July 16, 1941; *Novi list*, July 16, 1941; HDA, Collection 252, RUR, J. Section, 28089.

46. HDA, Collection ZKRZ GUZ, no. 306, box 15, 3732.

47. HDA, Collection 252, RUR, J. Section, 28089; *Hrvatski narod*, July 16, 1941; *Hrvatski list*, July 31, 1941.

48. HDA, MUP RH, II-93, 1255–1352.

49. Testimony of Professor Dr. Stjepan Steiner; Dizdar, *Logori*, 99.

50. HDA, Collection MUP SRH, 013.0.65, 62; about Mirko Vutuc, see Stuparić, *Tko je tko u NDH*, 424.

51. *Ustaša* 5 (Zagreb), August 3, 1941.

52. HDA, Collection 252, RUR, J. Section, 27983.

53. HDA, Collection ZKRZ GUZ, no. 306, box 10, 86; box 15, 3272, 3731–2, 3751–3, 3817.

54. Testimony of Professor Dr. Stjepan Steiner.

55. Krišto, *Katolička crkva*, 2:77–78.

56. Krišto, *Katolička crkva*, 2:77–78.

57. Kornfein, "I u paklu."

58. HDA, Collection 252, RUR, J. Section, 28000.

59. Testimony of Professor Dr. Stjepan Steiner.

60. HDA, Collection 252, RUR, J. Section, 28068, 28822.

61. HDA, Collection 252, RUR, J. Section, 28169; *Popis žrtava*. It seems that some other people were also released, obviously because they had connections—28151, 28152, 28154, 28215, 28180.

62. HDA, Collection 252, RUR, J. Section, 29668.

63. *Neue Ordnung in Kroatien* (Zagreb), August 24, 1941; Jelić-Butić, *Ustaše i NDH*, 181.

64. *Hrvatski narod*, May 11, 1941.

65. Testimony about Zavrtnica, see Kornfein, "Crno sjećanje na 'Zavrtnicu,'"; memories of Adolf Fridrih in Savez jevrejskih opština Jugoslavije, *Sećanja Jevreja na logor Jasenovac*, 26–28, 83; Berger, *44 mjeseca u Jasenovcu*, 7–8; Dizdar, "Logori," 99.

66. Kornfein, "I u paklu."

67. HDA, Collection 252, RUR, J. Section, 28161.

68. See list of thirty-four Jews, some of whom "went away on a trip," and some of whom were left alone; HDA, Collection 252, RUR, J. Section, 28173.

69. HDA, Collection 252, RUR, J. Section, 28171, see also 28172.

70. HDA, Collection 252, RUR, J. Section, 28207.

71. Dizdar, "Logori," 90; HDA, Collection ZKRZ GUZ, no. 306, box 15, 3773, 3817.

72. HDA, Collection ZKRZ GUZ, no. 306, box 15, 3731, 3754.

73. HDA, Collection 223, MUP NDH, box 300, no. 30068 (for recognition of Aryan status); on Breyer in general, see HBL, 2:302–3.

74. Miletić, *Koncentracioni logor Jasenovac*, 3:104.

75. *Istupi iz židovstva 1941*, Archive ŽOZ; Dobronić, *Splet sudbina*, 101; Dobronić, "Ignjat Granitz."

76. HDA, Collection ZKRZ GUZ, no. 306, box 15, 3735, 3819; NAZ, group NDS 5513/1942.

19. Concentration Camps, Summary Courts, and Hostages

1. See order of the German 49th Army Corps Command of April 30 in Miletić, *Koncentracioni logor Jasenovac*, 3:9–11.

2. S. Kasche's telegraph report quoted in Hory and Broszat, *Der Kroatische Ustascha-Staat*, 71.

3. Miletić, *Koncentracioni logor Jasenovac*, 3:24–28.

4. Peršen, *Ustaški logori*, 67–68; Dizdar, *Teror okupatora*, 35.

5. On the organization of the camp, see HDA, Collection 252, RUR, J. Section, 27315.

6. Horvatić, "Logor Danica u Koprivnici," 45–49; Dizdar, "Logori," 88; Dizdar, *Ljudski gubici*; Peršen, *Ustaški logori*, 67–75; see also HDA, Collection ZKRZ GUZ, no. 306, box 10, 567–9.

7. Stuparić, *Tko je tko u NDH*, 291.

8. Peršen, *Ustaški logori*, 70.

9. Peršen, *Ustaški logori*, 68.

10. There are rather a large number of statements and memoirs by former inmates of Danica Camp. The richest in detail and, it seems, the most measured, is the account of Milan Radeka (1898–1982), Orthodox religious teacher and prominent intellectual from Karlovac (Radeka, *Neka sjećanja*), which was published in full only recently.

11. Radeka, *Neka sjećanja*, 54; Lengel-Krizman and Sobolevski, "Hapšenje."

12. Horvatić, "Logor Danica u Koprivnici," 45–49; Dizdar, *Logori*, 88; Peršen, *Ustaški logori*, 67–75; see also HDA, Collection ZKRZ GUZ, no. 306, box 10, 567–9.

13. Radeka, *Neka sjećanja*, 49.

14. Horvatić, "Logor Danica u Koprivnici," 46; Dizdar, "Logori"; Peršen, *Ustaški logori*, 71.

15. Miletić, *Koncentracioni logor Jasenovac*, 1:52; Peršen, *Ustaški logori*, 81.

16. Komarica, *Kerestinečka kronika*, 261–62; Krizman, *NDH između*, 144; Dizdar, "Logori," 90.

17. Peršen, *Ustaški logori*, 53.

18. Neufeld, "Svjedočanstvo preživjelog."

19. Komarica, *Kerestinečka kronika*, 13–14; Dizdar, "Logori," 91.

20. Dizdar, "Logori," 91.

21. Dizdar, "Logori," 92.

22. Komarica, *Kerestinečka kronika*, 123–35; Neufeld, "Svjedočanstvo preživjelog," 2.

23. *Hrvatski narod*, May 10, 1941; *Ustaša*, 4 (Zagreb), July 19, 1941; Peršen, *Ustaški logori*, 58.

24. Dizdar, "Logori," 90–92; Komarica, *Kerestinečka kronika.*

25. Krizman, *NDH između*, 145.

26. Neufeld, "Svjedočanstvo preživjelog."

27. The Ustasha papers wrote about the escape from Kerestinec; *Hrvatski narod*, July 18, 1941; *Ustaša* 4 (Zagreb), July 19, 1941; see also *Dotrščina projekt*, HDA, 25.

28. *Dotrščina projekt*, HDA, 27–29; Komarica, *Kerestinečka kronika*, 207–11; Šibl, *Zagreb 1941*, 405–10.

29. Komarica, *Kerestinečka kronika.*

30. *Hrvatski narod*, August 5, 1941, and August 7, 1941; Krizman, *Ante Pavelić i ustaše*, 509.

31. *Novi list*, July 11, 1941; *Hrvatski narod*, August 7, 1941, and September 22, 1941; see also Collection ZKRZ GUZ, no. 306, box 10, 438, 439, 546–8; box 15, 3734–3736. For more on how decisions about retaliation were made and implemented and how the victims were selected, see also in box 15, 3767; see also "Ustaše su ubijale javno, svjedočanstvo."

32. Testimony of Professor Dr. Mirjana Gross; *Dotrščina projekt*, HDA, 27–29.

33. *Kartoteka židovskog znaka.*

34. *Ustaša* 10 (Zagreb), September 7, 1941.

35. *Hrvatski narod*, June 29, 1941, July 11, 1941, August 26, 1941, and November 28, 1941; *Ustaša* 3 (Zagreb), July 3, 1941; *Ustaša* 4 (Zagreb), July 19, 1941, *Ustaša* 10 (Zagreb), September 7, 1941; *Ustaša* 23 (Zagreb), December 7, 1941; HDA, Collection MUP RH, box 45, 013.1.22, Special courts in the ISC 1941–1945, 47, 50, 88.

36. HDA, Ustasha Police Announcement no. 7396/41; *Dotrščina projekt*, HDA, 23; *Ustaša* 3 (Zagreb), July 3, 1941.

37. *Hrvatski narod*, November 28, 1941; *Ustaša* 23 (Zagreb), December 7, 1941; *Hrvatska gruda* 75 (1941).

38. *Ustaša* 6 (Zagreb), August 10, 1941.

39. Šibl, *Zagreb 1941*, 220.

40. Testimony of Lea Goldstein and Vera Gerovac-Blažević, who were at that time in the prison in Sava Road.

41. *Narodne novine*, October 2, 1941; Kobsa, "O organizaciji ustaškog aparata vlasti za provođenje terora u tzv. NDH," 232–33.

42. Hilberg, *Destruction of the European Jews*, 686, 1070.

43. Šibl, *Zagreb 1941*, 84.

44. Boban, *Hrvatska u arhivima izbjegličke vlade*, 163, 173; Stuparić, *Tko je tko u NDH*, 416.

20. Death Camps on Mount Velebit and Pag Island

1. Memo of RAVSIGUR from July 8, 1941, Peršen, *Ustaški logori*, 81; Miletić, *Koncentracioni logor Jasenovac*, 1:52.

2. For more on the author's estimates, see chapter 42.

3. HDA, Collection ZKRZ GUZ, no. 306, box 11, 1096–1098, 1174–1227, 3797–3798.

4. These were Dr. Aleksandar-Saša Blühweiss (Blivajs), Dr. Robert Farkaš, Dr. Bela Hochstädter, Dr. Oto Radan, Božo Švarc, Zlatko Weiller (all from Zagreb), and Emerik Blum from Sarajevo.

5. Zemljar, *Haron i sudbine.*

6. Zatezalo, *Jadovno.*

7. Stuparić, *Tko je tko u NDH*, 16–17, 67–68.

8. The records of the Ustasha Penal and Disciplinary Court have a large file about the trial of Stjepan Rubinić for the liquidation of Jadovno Camp, held from October 1941 to February 1942. The witnesses included Vjekoslav Luburić, Eugen Dido

Kvaternik, and others, and the file is a fundamental contribution to the picture about what had gone on in the Gospić-Velebit-Pag system of camps in the summer of 1941; HDA, MUP RH II-91, box 150, USIKS 337/41, files from 738 to 868—see record about the hearing of Rubinić on October 29, 1941, USIKS 337/41, 804.

9. Miletić, *Miletić, Koncentracioni logor Jasenovac*, 2:1012.

10. HDA, USIKS 337/41, 817.

11. Testimony of Oto Radan, in Zemljar, *Haron i sudbine*, 40–42.

12. Švarc, "Kako sam preživio."

13. Jakovljević, *Konclogor na Savi*, 328.

14. Miletić, *Koncentracioni logor Jasenovac*, 1:52.

15. Statement of Dr. Aleksandar-Saša Blühweiss (Blivajs) of October 30, 1987, from Zatezalo, *Jadovno*, 193–94; Švarc, "Kako sam preživio," 5.

16. See chapter 19.

17. Neufeld, "Svjedočanstvo preživjelog."

18. Neufeld, "Svjedočanstvo preživjelog."

19. Zatezalo, *Jadovno*, 246.

20. Testimonies of Terka Gojmerac, Ana Fajdić, Jelena Basarić, Marica and Milica Vujnović in Zatezalo, *Jadovno*, 170–71, 180. On conditions and maltreatment in the Gospić prison, see also excerpts from the files on Stevo Simić and Đuro Medić in the Commissariat for Refugees and Displaced Persons in Belgrade, from April 1942 in Miletić, *Koncentracioni logor Jasenovac*, 1:214–15, 230–31.

21. Zatezalo, *Jadovno*, 179, 181.

22. Peršen, *Ustaški logori*, 84.

23. Statement of Ana Fajdić of September 13, 1947, HDA Karlovac, Archival Collection Center Gospić, box 120/47, quoted in Zatezalo, *Jadovno*, 171; statement of Đuro Medić in Miletić, *Koncentracioni logor Jasenovac*, 1:231.

24. Testimony of Ante Rukavina, in Zatezalo, *Jadovno*, 179.

25. Among the many witnesses who described these transports with a high degree of concurrence, the testimony of Radomir Vidas from Novalja is outstanding in precision and convincing presentation; in July 1941, as a Home Guard soldier, he was going home on leave from Otočac, and by chance joined a truck carrying prisoners from Gospić to Karlobag—statement from 1945, quoted in its entirety in Zemljar, *Haron i sudbine*, 142–44.

26. Statement of Mićo Jelača, at that time a mobilized Home Guard driver in Gospić, in Zatezalo, *Jadovno*, 201–2; similarly, also Neufeld, "Svjedočanstvo preživjelog"; Oto Radan in Zemljar, *Haron i sudbine*, 41; Branko Cetina in Peršen, *Ustaški logori*, 92; and many others in Zatezalo, *Jadovno*.

27. J. Felicinović, *Lične uspomene*, 1, 3. This important document has for unknown reasons remained unpublished to the present. It is retold in detail by Kustić, "Dobri duh otoka Paga"; also quoted in several places by Zemljar, *Haron i sudbine*, and by Ostojić and Sobolevski, "Pakao u kamenoj pustinji." The original, of which the author of this book has a photocopy, is the property of Don Živko Kustić.

28. King Alexander abolished the constitution on January 6, 1929 (the new regime thus became known as the "Sixth of January Dictatorship"), dissolved the National

Assembly, banned all political parties, and started to eliminate political opponents—see, Goldstein, *Croatia*, 121–22.

29. *Ustaša*, October 1932, 3; Stuparić, *Tko je tko u NDH*, 16–17; on Schlegel's murder, see Horvat, *Živjeti u Hrvatskoj*, 300–302.

30. Lengel-Krizman, "Prilog proučavanju terora u NDH," 10; Stuparić, *Tko je tko u NDH*, 62–63, 90, 240–42; Miletić, *Koncentracioni logor Jasenovac*, 2:1012.

31. Zemljar, *Haron i sudbine*, 42.

32. Peršen, *Ustaški logori*, 98–99.

33. Zatezalo, *Jadovno*, 222; Zemljar, *Haron i sudbine*, 174, 202.

34. Peršen, *Ustaški logori*, 95–102.

35. Testimony of Dr. Oton Radan in Zemljar, *Haron i sudbine*, 52–63; testimony of surviving inmate Josip Balaž-Joža in Zemljar, *Haron i sudbine*, 80–82, 89–94; statements of Ante Bukša, Duje Bilić, Ivan Škuca, and others in Zatezalo, *Jadovno*, 215.

36. Peršen, *Ustaški logori*, 98–99; Zemljar, *Haron i sudbine*, 60–61.

37. Zemljar, *Haron i sudbine*, 72, 155.

38. Testimony of Zlatko Weiller in Peršen, *Ustaški logori*, 97; Zatezalo, *Jadovno*, 148.

39. Hilberg, *Destruction of the European Jews*, 405.

40. Stuparić, *Tko je tko u NDH*, 90.

41. Peršen, *Ustaški logori*, 96; Oto Radan in: Zemljar, *Haron i sudbine*, 113.

42. Zemljar, *Haron i sudbine*, 114.

43. Zemljar, *Haron i sudbine*, 71–72.

44. Felicinović, *Lične uspomene*, 5; Zemljar, *Haron i sudbine*, 174, 202–3.

45. Ostojić and Sobolevski, "Pakao u kamenoj pustinji"; Zemljar, *Haron i sudbine*, 161–74, 201–14.

46. Peršen, *Ustaški logori*, 98–99.

47. Testimony of Nada Feuereisen of September 8, 1944, in Bari, given in its entirety in Zemljar, *Haron i sudbine*, 132–36; Zatezalo, *Jadovno*, 219–20.

48. Testimony of Nada Feuereisen, an inhabitant of Metajna, Jela Lončarić, and an Ustasha guard in Metajna, Josip Datković, who later joined the Partisans, and also of Ivan Festini, innkeeper in Pag, see in Zatezalo, *Jadovno*, 218–22.

49. Testimony of Nada Feuereisen, in: Zemljar, *Haron i sudbine*, 135.

50. Testimonies of Nada Feuereisen, in Zemljar, *Haron i sudbine*, 134–36, and of Anica Ehrenfreund-Polić, in Peršen, *Ustaški logori*, 100.

51. Testimony of Nada Feuereisen in Zemljar, *Haron i sudbine*, 135. The story could not be confirmed, because the ŽOZ archives have no data about a woman with the surname of Brajković. Perhaps it is a mistake or she may not have been Jewish (possibly a Serb?).

52. Felicinović, *Lične uspomene*, 20.

53. According to the recorded statement of September 18, 1945, quoted in Zemljar, *Haron i sudbine*, 116.

54. Data about Dežma, Semnic, the Pšerhofs, Milinovs, and Fuks according to the testimony of Dr. Radan in Zemljar, *Haron i sudbine*, 58–60, 116–17.

55. Felicinović, *Lične uspomene*, 19; Zemljar, *Haron i sudbine*, 31–36.

56. Neufeld, "Svjedočanstvo preživjelog," 3.

57. See, for example, the reports of the German intelligence branch in the ISC of August 7, 1941, in Hory and Broszat, *Der Kroatische Ustascha-Staat*, 85, 100–101; and statements of the Italian envoy Casertano of August 6, 1941, in Krizman, *NDH između*, 142.

58. Miletić, *Koncentracioni logor Jasenovac*, 1:65.

59. Neufeld, "Svjedočanstvo preživjelog," 3.

60. Kvaternik, *Sjećanja i zapažanja*, 131–32; Krizman, *NDH između*, 150–51.

61. HDA, MUP RH, file II-91, USIKS 337/41, 804.

62. Hory and Broszat, *Der Kroatische Ustascha-Staat*, 73–74; in detail, Krizman, *NDH između*, 149–61.

63. Felicinović, *Lične uspomene*, 19.

64. Ostojić and Sobolevski, "Pakao u kamenoj pustinji," 7.

65. HDA, MUP RH, file II-91, box 150, USIKS 337/41, 806.

66. Confession of perpetrator Luka Barješić during his trial in Zadar in 1952, statement of the boat owner Vinko Barić from Barić Drage before the Military Court of the Lika District Command in July 1945, and of others, and the findings of the Italian military-sanitary inspection of September 6, 1941, according to Zatezalo, *Jadovno*, 269, 283–85.

67. Testimonies of Nade Feuereisen in Zemljar, *Haron i sudbine*, 135, and Anica Ehrenfreund-Polić, according to Peršen, *Ustaški logori*, 100; estimates on the number of those who were returned in Zemljar, *Haron i sudbine*, 132, 160.

68. Testimonies of Pavao Lovrić, Ivan Lončarić, Vilko Markovina, Duje Bilić, Ante Fabijanić, and other, in Zemljar, *Haron i sudbine*, 163–74.

69. Felicinović, *Lične uspomene*, 21.

70. Zemljar, *Haron i sudbine*, 22.

71. Photocopies of the complete originals, translations of the reports of both the commissions, and reproductions of photographs in Zemljar, *Haron i sudbine*, 222–53; Peršen, *Ustaški logori*, 101–2, the text of the reports is also brought by Ostojić and Sobolevski, "Pakao u kamenoj pustinji."

72. Zemljar, *Haron i sudbine*, 129–32, 161; Zemljar, "Relativnost."

73. Zemljar, *Haron i sudbine*, 196; Felicinović, *Lična sjećanja*.

74. Description of the camp according to Zatezalo, *Jadovno*, 183–85, 188; Peršen, *Ustaški logori*, 89–90; the already quoted statements of Božo Švarc, Saša Blivajs, Bela Hochstädter, Branko Cetina (see index); visits by the author in 1992 and 1997.

75. HDA, Collection ZKRZ GUZ, no. 306, box 15, 3872; see also statement by Dr. Oto Radan on the arrival of the "reduced" parcels in Slana in Zemljar, *Haron i sudbine*, 57; correspondence in: HDA, Collection 252, RUR, J. Section; see also Zatezalo, *Jadovno*, 256–60.

76. HDA, Collection 252, RUR, Ž. section, 27793.

77. Record from the hearing of Stjepan Rubinić on October 29, 1941, MUP RH, file II-91, USIKS 337/41, 804.

78. Stuparić, *Tko je tko u NDH*, 121–22, 351.

79. In the fall of 1932 a group of Croatian émigrés attacked a police station in the Lika village of Brušani. The police made great efforts to catch the perpetrators. Most were arrested, some fled abroad. Police repression against the local population additionally poisoned relations. This event is known as the Velebit Uprising and members of the Ustasha movement considered it the formal birth of their organization—see also, Goldstein, *Croatia*, 125–26.

80. Miletić, *Koncentracioni logor Jasenovac*, 1:16.

81. Statement of Dr. Bela Hochstädter from March 1946 in Peršen, *Ustaški logori*, 90; statement of Oto Radan in Zemljar, *Haron i sudbine*, 41–42.

82. Description of the camp according to Zatezalo, *Jadovno*, 189–90 and the statements of the prisoners Božo Švarc, Dr. Saša Blivajs, Dr. Bela Hochstädter, Ante Rukavina, Jakov Ratković, and Mićo Jelača in Zatezalo, *Jadovno*, 192–204; statements of Dr. Bela Hochstädter, Božo Švarc, and Branko Cetina in Peršen, *Ustaški logori*, 89–92.

83. Peršen, *Ustaški logori*, 92.

84. HDA, Collection MUP RH, file II-91, box 150, USIKS 337/41, 814—statement of Vjekoslav Luburić.

85. HDA, Collection ZKRZ GUZ, no. 306, box 11, 645–655; Zatezalo, *Jadovno*, 192.

86. Zatezalo, *Jadovno*, 191.

87. Freundlich, "Tragedija"; Lengel-Krizman and Sobolevski, "Hapšenje,"; HDA, Collection ZKRZ GUZ, no. 306, box 10, 148.

88. HDA Karlovac, box Jadovno, according to Zatezalo, *Jadovno*, 205.

89. Felicinović, *Lične uspomene*, 5.

90. Neufeld, "Svjedočanstvo preživjelog," 3.

91. Miletić, *Koncentracioni logor Jasenovac*, 1:230.

92. Švarc, "Kako sam preživio"; Freundlich, "Tragedija"; Peršen, *Ustaški logori*, 91.

93. Peršen, *Ustaški logori*, 91.

94. HDA, Collection 252, RUR, J. Section, 27613; *Popis žrtava* proclaimed Berković dead, but according to the testimony of Branko Polić, Berković and his family arrived in Spilt and then went to the United States.

95. Statement of Ante Rukavina in Zatezalo, *Jadovno*, 196.

96. HDA, Collection ZKRZ GUZ, no. 306, box 10, 148.

97. Photocopy of the original report (*Izvještaj o privremenim grobljima u našoj zoni—Cimiteri provvisori della nostra zona*) in Zemljar, *Haron i sudbine*, 222–30, Croatian translation 234–44.

98. Zatezalo, *Jadovno*, 270.

99. Zatezalo, *Jadovno*, 238–44.

100. Statement of Luburić at the trial against Rubinić on November 5, 1941, HDA, MUP RH, II-91, box 150, USIKS 337/41, p. 814.

101. Zatezalo, *Jadovno*, 209–11.

102. Neufeld, "Svjedočanstvo preživjelog."

103. HDA, Collection 252, RUR, Ž. section, 28631.

104. Jakovljević, *Konclogor na Savi*, 57.

105. Jakovljević, *Konclogor na Savi*, in various places, especially 53–60. In the thirties, Ilija Jakovljević was a prominent publicist and newspaper editor of liberal views. The Ustasha regime imprisoned him in Jasenovac for eight months.

106. Record of October 29, 1941; HDA, MUP RH, file II-91, box 150, USIKS 337/41, p. 804.

107. Record of November 6, 1941; HDA, MUP RH II-91, box 150, USIKS 337/41, p. 811.

108. Record of November 5, 1941; HDA, MUP RH, file II-91, box 150, USIKS 337/41, p. 814.

109. Record of October 29, 1941; HDA, MUP RH, file II-91, box 150, USIKS 337/41, p. 805; Stjepan Rubinić was born in Jastrebarsko in 1909, and prior to 1941 was a traveling salesman employed in Zagreb.

110. HDA, MUP RH, file II-91, box 150, USIKS 337/41, p. 858.

111. HDA, ZKRZ ZK, Collection 306, box 291, 301990, p. 8.

112. Miletić, *Koncentracioni logor Jasenovac*, 3:47.

113. Zatezalo, *Jadovno*, 220; Peršen, *Ustaški logori*, 102.

114. Jakovljević, *Konclogor na Savi*, 328.

115. On the number of Jewish victims, see chapter 42.

116. JIM, Collection ŽOZ, reg. no. 4859, sign. K-65–1-1/1–86.

117. JIM, Collection ŽOZ, reg. no. 4859, sign. K-65–1-1/1–143, 1–144, 1–146, 1–161.

118. HDA, Collection ZKRZ GUZ, no. 306, box 11, 1096–1098; see *Dotrščina projekt*, HDA; Trninić-Šević, "Jom Kipur"; Savez jevrejskih opština Jugoslavije, *Sećanja Jevreja na logor Jasenovac*, 69; Peršen, *Ustaški logori*, 102–4; the most detailed description is in Lengel-Krizman, "Prilog proučavanju terora u NDH," 10–11.

21. The Apogee of Terror

1. Mirković, *Objavljeni izvori i literatura*.

2. For comments on, and a survey of, the most relevant publications, see Strčić, "Jasenovac i ratni zločin," 41, 80–82.

3. On the exploitation of the Jasenovac tragedy for political purposes, see Goldstein, "Upotreba povijesti." Characteristic of obsessive exaggeration and manipulation with Jasenovac victims are the many papers and five books by Milan Bulajić, and for manipulation by cover-up, the book by Franjo Tuđman, *Bespuća povijesne zbiljnosti*.

4. See chapters 21 and 42.

5. Miletić, *Koncentracioni logor Jasenovac*, vols. 1–3.

6. Miletić, *Koncentracioni logor Jasenovac*, 1:21–22.

7. Miletić, *Koncentracioni logor Jasenovac*, 1:20–22; Peršen, *Ustaški logori*, 123; Savez jevrejskih opština Jugoslavije, *Sećanja Jevreja na logor Jasenovac*, 117–27; Kovačić, "Zapovjednici," 100–104.

8. HDA, 013.2.30, Ljubo Miloš File, 1; Miletić, *Koncentracioni logor Jasenovac*, 2:1012.

9. Miletić, *Koncentracioni logor Jasenovac*, 1:215–16, 2:617–18; Peršen, *Ustaški logori*, 140–44; Savez jevrejskih opština Jugoslavije, *Sećanja Jevreja na logor Jasenovac*, 141–42; Berger, *44 mjeseca u Jasenovcu*, 28–29.

10. HDA, Collection of the Ministry of Transportation and Public Works ISC, no. 219, Land Reclamation and Water Regulation Directorate, Registration Office, 1791; for more detail on this subject, see Kevo, *Počeci logora Jasenovac*, 473–80.

11. Testimony of Zlatko Weiller, in Peršen, *Ustaški logori*, 129; Kevo, *Počeci logora Jasenovac*, 480–82.

12. *Hrvatski narod*, 8/23/1941.

13. Testimony of Albert Maestro in Savez jevrejskih opština Jugoslavije, *Sećanja Jevreja na logor Jasenovac*, 121.

14. Kevo, *Počeci logora Jasenovac*, 487.

15. Miletić, *Koncentracioni logor Jasenovac*, 1:81.

16. Berger, *44 mjeseca u Jasenovcu*, 11–12; HDA, Collection 252, RUR, Ž. odsj., 28207.

17. JIM, Collection ŽOZ, reg. no. 4859, sign. K-65–1-1/1–143.

18. Albert Maestro and Leon Koen in Savez jevrejskih opština Jugoslavije, *Sećanja Jevreja na logor Jasenovac*, 121, 140.

19. Miletić, *Koncentracioni logor Jasenovac*, 2:897–98.

20. HDA, 013.2.30, Ljubo Miloš File, in *Elaborat o radu Uredu*, 3:11, 78. Miloš speaks about 5,000 prisoners in Jasenovac I and II, during interrogation he mentioned 4,000; see also Miletić, *Koncentracioni logor Jasenovac*, 2:1014.

21. Berger, *44 mjeseca u Jasenovcu*, 13.

22. More or less the same descriptions of conditions and treatment of inmates in Jasenovac Camps I and II, in Peršen, *Ustaški logori*, testimony of Zlatko Weiller, Ivan Činčurak, Vladimir Carin, and Ante Milković, 129–38; Adolf Fridrih, Jakov Atijas, Leon Koen, and Jakov Kabiljo in Savez jevrejskih opština Jugoslavije, *Sećanja Jevreja na logor Jasenovac*, 28–33, 75, 84–85, 141.

23. HDA, 013.2.30. Ljubo Miloš File, 55–56, 110, 111; Kovačić, "Zapovjednici," 100–104; Krizman, *Ante Pavelić i ustaše*, list of émigrés, 556–57.

24. HDA, Collection ZKRZ GUZ, no. 306, box 15, 3775; this was the testimony of Đuro Schwarz, which was also provided by *Bilten ŽOZ* 38 (1995).

25. Carin, *Smrt je hodala četveronoške*, 38.

26. Berger, *44 mjeseca u Jasenovcu*, 11–15.

27. Berger, *44 mjeseca u Jasenovcu*, 60–61.

28. Carin, *Smrt je hodala četveronoške*, 68–69.

29. Albert Maestro in Savez jevrejskih opština Jugoslavije, *Sećanja Jevreja na logor Jasenovac*, 118.

30. Berger, *44 mjeseca u Jasenovcu*, 11, 13, 38; Peršen, *Ustaški logori*, 168; Ciliga, *Sam kroz Europu u ratu*, 252.

31. Berger, *44 mjeseca u Jasenovcu*, 17, 51; *Popis žrtava*; at the beginning of November, the Jewish Community still thought that Dirnbach was alive, because they sent parcels addressed to him at that time, see JIM, Collection ŽOZ, reg. no. 4866, sign. K-66–1-1/1–67.

32. HDA, Collection ZKRZ GUZ, no. 306, box. 15, 3774, 3789; Berger, *44 mjeseca u Jasenovcu*, 11.

33. Berger, *44 mjeseca u Jasenovcu*, 22.

34. Carin, *Smrt je hodala četveronoške*, 69–72.

35. HDA, Collection ZKRZ GUZ, no. 306, box 15, 3775, 3784–3785; *Popis žrtava.*

36. Berger, *44 mjeseca u Jasenovcu*, 37; *Popis žrtava*; *Jevrejska tribuna* 45 (1938); in November 1941, Marton was on the list of the Jewish Community for sending parcels, see JIM, Collection ŽOZ, reg. no. 4866, sign. K-66–1-1/1–67.

37. Berger, *44 mjeseca u Jasenovcu*, 12.

38. Miletić, *Koncentracioni logor Jasenovac*, 2:896.

39. Miletić, *Koncentracioni logor Jasenovac*, 1:231.

40. Carin, *Smrt je hodala četveronoške*, 35.

41. Miletić, *Koncentracioni logor Jasenovac*, 1:241.

42. Miletić, *Koncentracioni logor Jasenovac*, 2:897.

43. The numbers differ from letter to letter, some mention 2,000 arrested men, see JIM, Collection ŽOZ, reg. no. 4859, sign. K-65–1-1/1–91, 1–115, 1–121.

44. JIM, Collection ŽOZ, reg. no. 4859, sign. K-65–1-1/1–93, 1–97, 1–104, 1–116, 1–117.

45. HDA, Collection ZKRZ GUZ, no. 306, box 10, 112, 279; box 17, 4926–4936.

46. HDA, 013.2.30, Ljubo Miloš File, 57–58, also 11–12; Miletić, *Koncentracioni logor Jasenovac*, 2:1054, 1077; Tuđman, *Bespuća povijesne zbiljnosti*, 324–26, tries to prove that the total numbers of Jasenovac victims in Ljubo Miloš's statement are faked, i.e. that someone had subsequently written the numbers in by hand in two crucial places. However, Tuđman does not deny the validity of the other parts of Miloš's description, which he considers are "statements of a man who was aware that he had participated in *incredible* (underlined by Tuđman) crimes in a lost war, and was, before his death, confessing to what he knows and what his–probably awakened–consciousness allows." Miletić gives a detailed account of the relevant parts of Miloš's interrogation in prison (Miletić, *Koncentracioni logor Jasenovac*, 2:1010–23) and parts of Miloš's *Study on the Work of Office III* (Miletić, *Koncentracioni logor Jasenovac*, 2:1051–89). Considering that Ljubo Miloš's testimony is essentially in agreement with the preserved documentation, and with the statements of surviving prisoners, it may be considered credible, except in the estimated number of victims and some playing down of his personal responsibility. It is an important source for information about the management structure of the Jasenovac complex, about its purpose, general characteristics, and functioning.

47. Miletić, *Koncentracioni logor Jasenovac*, 2:897.

48. Carin, *Smrt je hodala četveronoške*, 46.

49. Testimony of Ante Milković, in Peršen, *Ustaški logori*, 138.

50. Miletić, *Koncentracioni logor Jasenovac*, 1:20, 224.

51. Savez jevrejskih opština Jugoslavije, *Sećanja Jevreja na logor Jasenovac*, 141.

52. Albert Maestro in Savez jevrejskih opština Jugoslavije, *Sećanja Jevreja na logor Jasenovac*, 122.

53. Jakov Kabiljo in Savez jevrejskih opština Jugoslavije, *Sećanja Jevreja na logor Jasenovac*, 87.

54. Albert Maestro in Savez jevrejskih opština Jugoslavije, *Sećanja Jevreja na logor Jasenovac*, 123; Peršen, *Ustaški logori*, 139–40.

55. HDA, 013.2.30, 64; Miletić, *Koncentracioni logor Jasenovac*, 2:1061.

56. Statement of Vjekoslav Luburić in a record from November 5, 1941. HDA, MLUP RH, file II.91, USIKS 337/41, 813.814; *Dnevnik Dijane Budisavljević.*

57. HDA, 013.2.30. Ljubo Miloš File, 10, 64; Miletić, *Koncentracioni logor Jasenovac*, 2:1061.

58. *Encyclopaedia Judaica*, 14:597–98.

59. Miletić, *Koncentracioni logor Jasenovac*, 1:170.

60. Miletić, *Koncentracioni logor Jasenovac*, 3:705.

61. Miletić, *Koncentracioni logor Jasenovac*, 3:705–9: Strčić also gives a detailed discussion of the possibilities of liberating Jasenovac, "Jasenovac i ratni zločin," 61–63, 95–96.

62. More about this in Peršen, *Ustaški logori*, 122.

63. Miletić, *Koncentracioni logor Jasenovac*, 1:93.

64. Savez jevrejskih opština Jugoslavije, *Sećanja Jevreja na logor Jasenovac*, 122.

65. Leon Koen in Savez jevrejskih opština Jugoslavije, *Sećanja Jevreja na logor Jasenovac*, 141–42; the word "ham" is an abbreviation of "haham," title of a Jewish theologian with the highest education, similar to "doctor of theology."

66. Miletić, *Koncentracioni logor Jasenovac*, 1:95–97.

67. *Narodne novine* 188, November 26, 1941; *Ustaša, Dokumenti*, 215–16; Miletić, *Koncentracioni logor Jasenovac*, 1:98–100.

68. HDA, 013.2.30. Ljubo Miloš File, 73; Miletić, *Koncentracioni logor Jasenovac*, 2:1070.

69. Ivica Matković was the head of the General Department of the Jasenovac Camp Command, and later camp commander; see Stuparić, *Tko je tko u ISC*, 261.

70. HDA, 013.2.30, Ljubo Miloš File, 69–70, 78–79; Miletić, *Koncentracioni logor Jasenovac*, 2:1066: this account of liquidating 'excess' prisoners above the number of 3,000 to 5,000 is confirmed by all the testimonies about Camp III in Savez jevrejskih opština Jugoslavije, *Sećanja Jevreja na logor Jasenovac.* See also Peršen, *Ustaški logori*, 145.

71. Berger, *44 mjeseca u Jasenovcu*, 46, 52; also the testimony of Dr. Teodor Grüner, as recounted by his father, Chief Cantor Bernhard Grüner.

72. Jakov Kabiljo in Savez jevrejskih opština Jugoslavije, *Sećanja Jevreja na logor Jasenovac*, 90; Carin, *Smrt je hodala četveronoške*, 109–10; Miletić, *Koncentracioni logor Jasenovac*, 2:904, 1102.

73. HDA, Collection MUP SRH, 013.0.56, Part II, 47.

74. Testimony of Dr. Teodor Grüner, recounted by his father, Chief Cantor Bernhard Grüner.

75. Testimony of Berta Israel, née Švarcenberg.

76. Letter of Danica Kos, née Mamula, in the possession of the author of this book; testimony of Brana Majder, who was set free from the group before it was transported; testimony of Vukašin Žegarac about liquidation in Jasenovac, in Miletić, *Koncentracioni logor Jasenovac*, 1:225.

77. See chapter 26.

78. Savez jevrejskih opština Jugoslavije, *Sećanja Jevreja na logor Jasenovac*, 88.

79. Savez jevrejskih opština Jugoslavije, *Sećanja Jevreja na logor Jasenovac*, 29, 33.

80. HDA, 013.2.30, 68–69; Miletić, *Koncentracioni logor Jasenovac*, 2:1065–66.

81. Savez jevrejskih opština Jugoslavije, *Sećanja Jevreja na logor Jasenovac*, 87.

82. Miletić, *Koncentracioni logor Jasenovac*, 1:556; Savez jevrejskih opština Jugoslavije, *Sećanja Jevreja na logor Jasenovac*, 87.

83. Berger, *44 mjeseca u Jasenovcu*, 52–55; Carin, *Smrt je hodala četveronoške*, 118–21; Albert Maestro and Jakov Atijas in Savez jevrejskih opština Jugoslavije, *Sećanja Jevreja na logor Jasenovac*, 77, 127–28; on the arrival of the commission, Ljubo Miloš, HDA, 013.2.30, 15–16.

84. Miletić, *Koncentracioni logor Jasenovac*, 1:172.

85. *Hrvatski narod*, February 10, 1942; *Spremnost*, March 3, 1942; article by Dr. Hermann Proebst in Miletić, *Koncentracioni logor Jasenovac*, 1:174–77.

86. Albert Maestro in Savez jevrejskih opština Jugoslavije, *Sećanja Jevreja na logor Jasenovac*, 124–25; on the same subject, also Ljubo Miloš: "In the beginning, liquidations were carried out by shooting; later, this was discontinued and an ax or mallet was used" (HDA, 013.2.30, 79).

87. Jakov Danon in Savez jevrejskih opština Jugoslavije, *Sećanja Jevreja na logor Jasenovac*, 20.

88. Oto Breyer, see Miletić, *Koncentracioni logor Jasenovac*, 2:907.

89. Adolf Fridrih in Savez jevrejskih opština Jugoslavije, *Sećanja Jevreja na logor Jasenovac*, 41.

90. HDA, 013.2.30, Jasenovac File.

91. Peršen, *Ustaški logori*, 140–44; Miletić, *Koncentracioni logor Jasenovac*, 2:1113–17; Berger, *44 mjeseca u Jasenovcu*; Carin, *Smrt je hodala četveronoške.*

92. Leon Maestro in Savez jevrejskih opština Jugoslavije, *Sećanja Jevreja na logor Jasenovac*, 112.

93. Isidor Levi in Savez jevrejskih opština Jugoslavije, *Sećanja Jevreja na logor Jasenovac*, 65–66; Miletić, *Koncentracioni logor Jasenovac*, 2:1106–9.

94. Miletić, *Koncentracioni logor Jasenovac*, 1:171–72, 2:903.

95. Miletić, *Koncentracioni logor Jasenovac*, 2:1066, 1069.

96. Testimony of Ljerka Magdić.

97. Savez jevrejskih opština Jugoslavije, *Sećanja Jevreja na logor Jasenovac*, 13–15, 91–92, 162; Berger, *44 mjeseca u Jasenovcu*; Peršen, *Ustaški logori*, 228–32; statement of Stojan Lapčević, in Miletić, *Koncentracioni logor Jasenovac*, 2:963–64.

98. Kovačić, "Zapovjednici."

99. Jakovljević, *Koncolor na Savi*, 106–7, 268–69.

100. HDA, 013.2.30, Ljubo Miloš study, 81–82; Peršen, *Ustaški logori*, 232–33.

101. Miletić, *Koncentracioni logor Jasenovac*, 1:116.

102. HDA, Collection ZKRZ GUZ, no. 306, box 11, 774; see also the testimony of Gabrijel Winter in Miletić, *Koncentracioni logor Jasenovac*, 3:227.

103. Testimony of Dr. Teodor Grüner.

104. Testimony of Andrija Präger.

105. Miletić, *Koncentracioni logor Jasenovac*, 1:347–48.

106. The material about Jasenovac is very extensive, very different in character, and of varying reliability. See, e.g., HDA, Collection ZKRZ GUZ, no. 306, box 11, 645–55.

107. Miletić, *Koncentracioni logor Jasenovac*, 1:170.

108. Miletić, *Koncentracioni logor Jasenovac*, 1:152.

109. Miletić, *Koncentracioni logor Jasenovac*, 1:219, 228, 235, 248.

110. Miletić, *Koncentracioni logor Jasenovac*, 1:378–80.

111. From the report of the police attaché to the German Embassy in Zagreb of July 13, 1942, in Peršen, *Ustaški logori*, 182.

112. Miletić, *Koncentracioni logor Jasenovac*, 2:1054.

113. Peršen, *Ustaški logori*, 182.

114. Miletić, *Koncentracioni logor Jasenovac*, 1:259; Peršen, *Ustaški logori*, 155.

115. Miletić, *Koncentracioni logor Jasenovac*, 1:269–70; Peršen, *Ustaški logori*, 155.

116. Miletić, *Koncentracioni logor Jasenovac*, 1:290–91.

117. Peršen, *Ustaški logori*, 156–59.

118. The most detailed accounts of the slaughter of the Roma can be found in Nikolić, *Jasenovački logor*, 257–72; and Nikolić, *Jasenovački logor smrti*, 242–64.

119. Numerical data according to Peršen, *Ustaški logori*, 159–60.

120. Miletić, *Koncentracioni logor Jasenovac*, 1:431.

121. HDA, Dijana Budisavljević's diary, manuscript, date July 10, 1942; Jakovljević, *Koncologor na Savi*, 107.

122. HDA, Dijana Budisavljević's diary, manuscript, July 11, 1942; Peršen, *Ustaški logori*, 272–79, 281–82, 288–90

123. HDA, 013.2.30, Ljubo Miloš File, 85; Albert Maestro in Savez jevrejskih opština Jugoslavije, *Sećanja Jevreja na logor Jasenovac*, 128.

124. Miletić, *Koncentracioni logor Jasenovac*, 1:462–81.

125. Peršen, *Ustaški logori*, 161–64; also see HDA, 013.2.30, 27–28.

126. Broucek, *Ein General in Zwielicht*, 166–69.

127. Stuparić, *Tko je tko u ISC*, 241, 276. In more detail, HDA, 013, Ljubo Miloš File and Luburić File.

128. Miletić, *Koncentracioni logor Jasenovac*, 1:26–28, 2:1108–10.

129. People's District Court for the City of Zagreb, record from December 19, 1945, no. R1410/45, document in the family archives of Professor Mirjana Gross; on Ivan Hochsinger, see Miletić, *Koncentracioni logor Jasenovac*, 2:1113.

130. Miletić, *Koncentracioni logor Jasenovac*, 2:910.

131. Miletić, *Koncentracioni logor Jasenovac*, 1:489.

132. Savez jevrejskih opština Jugoslavije, *Sećanja Jevreja na logor Jasenovac*, 129.

133. HDA, Collection ZKRZ GUZ, no. 306, box 16, 4481.

134. Sado Koen in Savez jevrejskih opština Jugoslavije, *Sećanja Jevreja na logor Jasenovac*, 174.

135. Savez jevrejskih opština Jugoslavije, *Sećanja Jevreja na logor Jasenovac*, 103–4.

136. Miletić, *Koncentracioni logor Jasenovac*, 1:26–28.

137. County Court in Zagreb, records from July 28, 1998, no. VK-242/98-190, 6.

138. Jakovljević, *Koncologor na Savi*, 268; on the cruelty and arbitrary behavior of some of the Ustashe towards the inmates, Ljubo Miloš, HDA, 013.2.30, 74–75.

139. Nikolić, *Jasenovački logor smrti*, 194, 195, 201.

140. Nikolić, *Jasenovački logor smrti*, 235–36; Romano, *Jevreji zdravstveni radnici Jugoslavije*, 150; on Bril see in *Enciklopedija likovnih umjetnosti*, 1:501.

141. Nikolić, *Jasenovački logor smrti*, 202; statement of Jakob Danon in Miletić, *Koncentracioni logor Jasenovac*, 3:533, 1119–20, mentions Stolzer's wife, Fibijana, and son, Vivijan, with the note "killed by the Ustashe in Jasenovac Camp."

142. Nikolić, *Jasenovački logor smrti*, 196.

143. Adolf Fridrih in Savez jevrejskih opština Jugoslavije, *Sećanja Jevreja na logor Jasenovac*, 48, 278–79.

144. County Court in Zagreb, records from the main hearing of June 28, 1999, docket no. VK-242/98-190, 9.

145. Nikolić, *Jasenovački logor smrti*, 194–95, 201; Romano, *Jevreji zdravstveni radnici Jugoslavije*, 155.

146. Romano, *Jevreji zdravstveni radnici Jugoslavije*, 117, 149–70.

147. County Court in Zagreb, records from the hearing of June 24, 1999, docket no. VK-242/98-190, 4.

148. Miletić, *Koncentracioni logor Jasenovac*, 2:1033–34.

149. Miletić, *Koncentracioni logor Jasenovac*, 3:383.

150. Miletić, *Koncentracioni logor Jasenovac*, 3:362–64.

151. *Novi Omanut* 29–30, 9.

152. Testimony of Ljerka Magdić.

153. See chapter 9.

154. *Nepotpuni spisak zatočenika sabirnog logora Jasenovac III.*

155. Jakovljević, *Konclogor na Savi*, 114.

156. Romano, *Jevreji Jugoslavije*, 189–90; Peršen, *Ustaški logori*, 189–93.

157. JP 1–2 (1988).

158. Broucek, *Ein General in Zwielicht*, 36; in some exchanges, the Germans and Ustashe traded more than one prisoner for their higher-ranking officers, which may explain the difference in numbers.

159. Miletić, *Koncentracioni logor Jasenovac*, 3:212–13, 1:432–36; Peršen, *Ustaški logori*, 183–89.

160. See letter by the authorized German general in Croatia in Miletić, *Koncentracioni logor Jasenovac*, 2:751–52.

161. Savez jevrejskih opština Jugoslavije, *Sećanja Jevreja na logor Jasenovac*, 49.

162. Note by Dr. Zvonko Tkalac in Miletić, *Koncentracioni logor Jasenovac*, 2:877–88; Savez jevrejskih opština Jugoslavije, *Sećanja Jevreja na logor Jasenovac*, 134–35.

163. *Nepotpuni spisak zatočenika sabirnog logora Jasenovac III.*

164. HDA, Collection ZKRZ GUZ, no. 306, box 10, 89–90.

165. Jakovljević, *Koncologor na Savi*, 163–65; Savez jevrejskih opština Jugoslavije, *Sećanja Jevreja na logor Jasenovac*, 167–68, 279; Peršen, *Ustaški logori*, 209.

166. Jakovljević, *Konclogor na Savi*, 53–60, 135; Peršen, *Ustaški logori*, 142; Maček, *Memoari*, 167.

167. Stuparić, *Tko je tko u ISC*, 147, 359; Miletić, *Koncentracioni logor Jasenovac*, 2:855–56.

168. Ristović, *U potrazi za utočištem, Jugoslovenski Jevreji*, 188; Peršen, *Ustaški logori*, 215–16; also see in detail, Favez, *Das Internationale Rote Kreutz und das Dritte Reich*, 371.

169. Ristović, *U potrazi za utočištem, Jugoslovenski Jevreji*, 185–86.

170. Ristović, *U potrazi za utočištem, Jugoslovenski Jevreji*, 188; Favez, *Das Internationale Rote Kreutz und das Dritte Reich*, 373.

171. Miletić, *Koncentracioni logor Jasenovac*, 2:856–58; Savez jevrejskih opština Jugoslavije, *Sećanja Jevreja na logor Jasenovac*, 175.

172. Nada Sálamon's memoir notes, according to Peršen, *Ustaški logori*, 209.

173. Adolf Fridrih, in Savez jevrejskih opština Jugoslavije, *Sećanja Jevreja na logor Jasenovac*, 49.

174. Testimony of Dinko Šakić, County Court in Zagreb, docket no. VK-242/98, from June 24, 1999, 5, and from June 28, 1999, 4–5.

175. Adolf Fridrih in Savez jevrejskih opština Jugoslavije, *Sećanja Jevreja na logor Jasenovac*, 49–50.

176. Nada Salamon's memoir notes, according to Peršen, *Ustaški logori*, 209; also Miletić, *Koncentracioni logor Jasenovac*, 2:952, where the List of Women Prisoners in Jasenovac Camp includes Stela Polak, with the note that she "died on December 8, 1944."

177. JIM, Collection ŽOZ, reg. no. 4864, sign. K-63-1-1/1–249.

178. Savez jevrejskih opština Jugoslavije, *Sećanja Jevreja na logor Jasenovac*, 176; Peršen, *Ustaški logori*, 264.

179. Savez jevrejskih opština Jugoslavije, *Sećanja Jevreja na logor Jasenovac*, 176; Peršen, *Ustaški logori*, 264.

180. Peršen, *Ustaški logori*, 264–65.

181. *Nepotpuni spisak zatočenika sabirnog logora Jasenovac III.*

182. Savez jevrejskih opština Jugoslavije, *Sećanja Jevreja na logor Jasenovac*, 50.

183. HDA, Collection ZKRZ GUZ, no. 306, box 10, 89–90; Miletić, *Koncentracioni logor Jasenovac*, 2:1115.

184. Carin, *Smrt je hodala četveronoške*, 180; Miletić, *Koncentracioni logor Jasenovac*, 2:1116.

185. HDA, Collection ZKRZ GUZ, no. 306, box 10, 89–90.

186. Savez jevrejskih opština Jugoslavije, *Sećanja Jevreja na logor Jasenovac*, 196–97; Carin, *Smrt je hodala četveronoške*, 178–79; Berger, *44 mjeseca u Jasenovcu*, 91–92; Miletić, *Koncentracioni logor Jasenovac*, 2:1114.

187. Carin, *Smrt je hodala četveronoške*, 174–77.

188. Josip Erlih in Savez jevrejskih opština Jugoslavije, *Sećanja Jevreja na logor Jasenovac*, 281.

189. Savez jevrejskih opština Jugoslavije, *Sećanja Jevreja na logor Jasenovac*, 67, 144, 146, 156, 159; Peršen, *Ustaški logori*, 220; Miletić, *Koncentracioni logor Jasenovac*, 3:538.

190. Savez jevrejskih opština Jugoslavije, *Sećanja Jevreja na logor Jasenovac*, 247–48.

191. Savez jevrejskih opština Jugoslavije, *Sećanja Jevreja na logor Jasenovac*, 282; Nikolić, *Jasenovački logor smrti*, 232; Romano, *Jevreji zdravstveni radnici Jugoslavije*, 157.

192. Miletić, *Koncentracioni logor Jasenovac*, 2:991, 1115.

193. Savez jevrejskih opština Jugoslavije, *Sećanja Jevreja na logor Jasenovac*, 197, 283; Miletić, *Koncentracioni logor Jasenovac*, 2:1115; Peršen, *Ustaški logori*, 217.

194. Savez jevrejskih opština Jugoslavije, *Sećanja Jevreja na logor Jasenovac*, 53, 148,

152, 197–98, 283; Peršen, *Ustaški logori*, 218–20; Miletić, *Koncentracioni logor Jasenovac*, 2:991–92, 1115–16.

195. Miletić, *Koncentracioni logor Jasenovac*, 2:971.

196. Romano, *Jevreji Jugoslavije*, 189–90; Savez jevrejskih opština Jugoslavije, *Sećanja Jevreja na logor Jasenovac*, 198.

197. Grossepais-Gil, "Bekstvo iz logora Jasenovac"; Berger, *44 mjeseca u Jasenovcu*; Carin, *Smrt je hodala četveronoške*.

198. Korda, "Povratak iz Jasenovca," 49–50.

199. Savez jevrejskih opština Jugoslavije, *Sećanja Jevreja na logor Jasenovac*, 51; Miletić, *Koncentracioni logor Jasenovac*, 2:1116.

200. Miletić, *Koncentracioni logor Jasenovac*, 2:998, 3:718.

201. Detailed descriptions of the flight and salvation in Berger, *44 mjeseca u Jasenovcu*, 94–102; and Carin, *Smrt je hodala četveronoške*, 180–87; Savez jevrejskih opština Jugoslavije, *Sećanja Jevreja na logor Jasenovac*, 15–17, 107–10, 113–16; Peršen, *Ustaški logori*, 228–32; record about the testimony of Stojan Lapčević of May 10, 1945, in Miletić, *Koncentracioni logor Jasenovac*, 2:963–65.

202. Savez jevrejskih opština Jugoslavije, *Sećanja Jevreja na logor Jasenovac*, 15; Carin, *Smrt je hodala četveronoške*, 181.

203. Peršen, *Ustaški logori*, 221.

204. Ljubo Miloš on camp organization, HDA, 013.2.30, 66.

205. Sobolevski, "Židovi u kompleksu koncentracijskog logora Jasenovac," 106–7.

206. About Diamantstein and Spiller, see especially Miletić, *Koncentracioni logor Jasenovac*, 3:721–22; about Wiener and other camp foremen, in HDA, 013.2.30, 66, in the Ljubo Miloš File; about Alkalaj in Savez jevrejskih opština Jugoslavije, *Sećanja Jevreja na logor Jasenovac*, 14–15, and the statement of Stojan Lapčević in Miletić, *Koncentracioni logor Jasenovac*, 2:963–65; about Samlaić in Savez jevrejskih opština Jugoslavije, *Sećanja Jevreja na logor Jasenovac*, 66, 145, 155. Only Samlaić survived.

207. Jakovljević, *Konclogor na Savi*, 113.

208. Jakovljević, *Koncologor na Savi*, 113.

209. Miletić, *Koncentracioni logor Jasenovac*, 2:872, 911, 1063; Savez jevrejskih opština Jugoslavije, *Sećanja Jevreja na logor Jasenovac*, 28–29, 164–165, 240; Berger, *44 mjeseca u Jasenovcu*, 25.

210. Kolar-Dimitrijević, "Sjećanja veterinara Zorka Goluba," 161; according to *Popis žrtava*, Städtler was killed at an "unknown" site.

211. Miletić, *Koncentracioni logor Jasenovac*, 2:872.

212. Savez jevrejskih opština Jugoslavije, *Sećanja Jevreja na logor Jasenovac*, 165.

213. Testimony of Dr. Mladen Iveković in Miletić, *Koncentracioni logor Jasenovac*, 2:872.

214. HDA, Collection MUP SRH, 013.2.86, 5; about Filipović, see Kovačić, "Zapovjednici," 107–11.

215. See, Ciliga, *Sam kroz Europu u ratu*, 280 and throughout.

216. HDA, Collection ZKRZ GUZ, no. 306, box 15, 3777, 3782.

217. Savez jevrejskih opština Jugoslavije, *Sećanja Jevreja na logor Jasenovac*, 28–29.

218. Peršen, *Ustaški logori*, 97–98.

219. Berger, *44 mjeseca u Jasenovcu*, 25.

220. Berger, *44 mjeseca u Jasenovcu*, 25.

221. Savez jevrejskih opština Jugoslavije, *Sećanja Jevreja na logor Jasenovac*, 240.

222. Testimony of Dr. Mladen Iveković in Miletić, *Koncentracioni logor Jasenovac*, 2:872.

223. Testimony of Berta Israel, née Švarcenberg.

224. Savez jevrejskih opština Jugoslavije, *Sećanja Jevreja na logor Jasenovac*, 165.

225. *Popis žrtava*; Peršen, *Ustaški logori*, 97–98.

226. Kolar-Dimitraiajević, "Sjećanja veterinara Zorka Goluba," 173–74; testimony of Dr. Mladen Iveković in Miletić, *Koncentracioni logor Jasenovac*, 2:872; Ljubo Miloš in Miletić, *Koncentracioni logor Jasenovac*, 2:1063.

227. Peršen, *Ustaški logori*, 144; Miletić, *Koncentracioni logor Jasenovac*, 1:182–83; Kolar-Dimitrijević, "Sjećanja veterinara Zorka Goluba," 165, 174; NAZ, Group NDS 2143/1943; Ciliga, *Sam kroz Europu u ratu*, 339.

228. Miletić, *Koncentracioni logor Jasenovac*, 3:115.

229. Tuđman, *Bespuća povijesne zbiljnosti*, 316–20.

230. *Jasenovac—Žrtve rata prema podacima Statističkog zavoda Jugoslavije*.

231. Žerjavić, *Opsesije i megalomanije oko Jasenovca i Bleiburga*, 72; Žerjavić estimates that some 48,000 to 52,000 Serbs, 13,000 Jews, 12,000 Croats, and 10,000 Roma were killed in Jasenovac.

232. Academician Ljubo Boban in an interview to the weekly *Danas*, April 26, 1988; according to Strčić, "Jasenovac i ratni zločin," 53.

233. About the number of Jewish victims, see chapter 42

234. Berger, *44 mjeseca u Jasenovcu*, 9–10.

235. HDA, Collection Ustasha Commission for the Town and District of Koprivnica, 1019–55.

236. Miletić, *Koncentracioni logor Jasenovac*, 3:77–92.

237. JIM, Collection ŽOZ, without reg. no. and sign.

238. Sobolevski, "Židovi u kompleksu koncentracijskog logora Jasenovac," 107.

239. See chapter 42.

22. On the Way to Execution

1. In general about Loborgrad, see Dizdar, "Logori," 94–95; Peršen, *Ustaški logori*, 279–281; in more detail, see Lengel-Krizman, "Prilog proučavanju terora u NDH," 12–21.

2. Testimony of Professor Dr. Stjepan Steiner; Gregl was not popular among the Ustashe: Ljubo Miloš greeted him with gunfire in the Jasenovac Camp, when he came to take over administration by order of Dido Kvaternik; see HDA, SDS File no. 301815-B. Gregl. On October 23, 1942, the Ustasha Penal and Disciplinary Court in Zagreb sentenced Gregl to seven months of strict prison and loss of Ustasha membership because he had abused his position in Varaždin and raped a Jewish woman; see HDA, MUP RH, II-93, 1255–1352; Gregl emigrated in 1945, and allegedly became a collaborator of the Yugoslav secret police, OZN. In 1948, he tried to organize the kidnapping of Mate Frković, former Ustasha Doglavnik and Minister of the Interior (Nikolić, *Pred vratima domovine*, 181–82).

3. HDA, Collection 252, RUR, J. Section, 28218, 28274, 28372, 28373.

4. JIM, Collection ŽOZ, sign. XII-3–5.

5. HDA, Collection ZKRZ GUZ, no. 306, box 10, 110; Collection 252, RUR, J. Section, 28275; see also JP 11–12 (1974); JIM, Collection ŽOZ, reg. no. 4859, sign. K-65–1-1/1–143.

6. JIM, Collection ŽOZ, reg. no. 4859, sign. K-65–1-1/1–143.

7. In October, Camp Commander Vilko Heger spoke of "around 370 Orthodox," but in December he sent a list with 236 Orthodox prisoners; see HDA, Collection 252, RUR, J. Section, 28281, 28577. The numbers about interned Jewish women differ: in October, the Jewish Religious Community in Zagreb said that there were "about 1,400 women and children" in the camp, and in December, the State Directorate for Food claimed there were about "1,700 Jewish women and children." In May 1942, the Jewish Section estimated that there were about "1,300 persons" (HDA, Collection 252, RUR, J. Section, 28485, 28507.).

8. HDA, Collection 252, RUR, J. Section, 28218.

9. HDA, Collection 252, RUR, J. Section, 28307.

10. HDA, Collection 252, RUR, J. Section, 28661.

11. HDA, Collection 252, RUR, J. Section, 28807.

12. HDA, Collection, Ustasha Commission for the Town and District of Koprivnica, 1056–1073.

13. HDA, Collection Ustasha Commission for the Town and District of Koprivnica, 1070; Collection 252, RUR, J. Section, 28281. The archive collection for Loborgrad includes a German list of 227 women with the surnames from Katz to Neumann; see HDA, Collection 248, UNS, Collection Transit and Work Camps in the ISC, Transit Camp Loborgrad, Statements of Jews in the camp.

14. HDA, Collection 252, RUR, J. Section, 29625.

15. Lengel-Krizman, "Prilog proučavanju terora u NDH," 13, 21–23.

16. HDA, Collection 248, UNS, Collection Transit and Work Camps in the ISC, Transit Camp Loborgrad–Gornja Rijeka. The list of prisoners, a partial one from no. 67 to no. 263, contains 197 names to which another fifty-one were subsequently added, for a total of 248 names. The first sixty-six places could have had another ten to twenty additional names (mostly of family members), which gives about 300 to 350 woman prisoners. See also, Lengel-Krizman, "Prilog proučavanju terora u NDH," 21; these numbers differ from the number of "about one hundred older women" mentioned for Gornja Rijeka by Lengel-Krizman, "Logori za Židove u NDH," 99; Peršen, *Ustaški logori*, 281–82; Dizdar, "Logori," 89–90.

17. HDA, Collection 252, RUR, J. Section, 29193, 29258.

18. HDA, Collection 252, RUR, J. Section, 29353.

19. HDA, Collection 252, RUR, J. Section, 28281, 28588.

20. Testimony of Saša Friedrich.

21. HDA, Collection 252, RUR, J. Section, 29058, 29118.

22. HDA, Collection 248, UNS, Collection Transit and Work Camps in the ISC, Transit Camp Loborgrad, Bills, I–II.

23. HDA, Collection 252, RUR, J. Section, 29389.

24. HDA, Collection 248, UNS, Collection Transit and Work Camps in the ISC, Transit Camp Loborgrad, Bills, group V, 10, 21.

25. As calculated by Lengel-Krizman, "Prilog proučavanju terora u NDH," 18.

26. HDA, Collection 248, UNS, Collection Transit and Work Camps in the ISC, Transit Camp Loborgrad, Bills, III–IV, 27, 30; VII, 18; Collection 252, RUR, J. Section, 28470.

27. HDA, Collection 248, UNS, Collection Transit and Work Camps in the ISC, Transit Camp Loborgrad, Bills, V, V group, 2, 2–4; V group, 10, 51–60; V group, 11, 2–4.

28. An idea can be got about the magnitude of this sum from the fact that workers from the surrounding villages, who worked on the construction and maintenance of Loborgrad Camp, were paid 9 kunas an hour. An egg cost 3 kunas, a kilo of meat 42 kunas, a kilo of plum jam 60 kunas; Lengel-Krizman, "Prilog proučavanju terora u NDH," 18, claims that it was a sum negligibly smaller than 6,158,000 kunas.

29. HDA, Collection 252, RUR, J. Section, 28842.

30. HDA, Collection 248, UNS, Collection Transit and Work Camps in the ISC, Transit Camp Loborgrad, Announcements and Circulars.

31. HDA, Collection 252, RUR, J. Section, 29170, 29311, 29427, 29538, 29678.

32. HDA, Collection ZKRZ GUZ, no. 306, box 10, 94; Vasiljević, *Sabirni logor Đakovo.*

33. Archive ŽOZ.

34. Archive ŽOZ.

35. HDA, Collection ZKRZ GUZ, no. 306, box 11, 1096–1098, 1059–1062.

36. JIM, Collection ŽOZ, no reg.

37. Shomrony, "Svjedočenja, Gdje je Freibergerova biblioteka?"; see also: Shik, "Ratni zločinac."

38. HDA, Collection 252, RUR, J. Section, 29192.

39. HDA, Collection 248, UNS, Collection Transit and Work Camps in the ISC, Transit Camp Loborgrad, Announcements and Circulars; about H. Tudiower, who was one of the prisoners in Danica Camp, see HDA, Collection 252, RUR, J. Section, 27960.

40. Testimony of Aleksandar-Saša Friedrich.

41. Lengel-Krizman, "Prilog proučavanju terora u NDH," 14.

42. HDA, Collection ZKRZ GUZ, no. 306, box 11, 2235; Lengel-Krizman, "Prilog proučavanju terora u NDH," 14.

43. Lengel-Krizman, "Prilog proučavanju terora u NDH," 13; amenorrhea is a discontinuation of the menstrual cycle for various reasons, among the prisoners obviously due to malnutrition, stress, etc.

44. JIM, Collection ŽOZ, reg. no. 4870, sign. K-65–2-1/1–74; see also HDA, Collection 252, RUR, J. Section, 28760, 28851.

45. HDA, Collection 25 2, RUR, J. Section, 28639, 28693, 29070, 29235, 29265, 29312, 29623, 29626, 29631.

46. Testimony of Aleksandar-Saša Friedrich (born 1932).

47. HDA, Collection 252, RUR, J. Section, 29059.

48. HDA, Collection 252, RUR, J. Section, 29733.

49. HDA, Collection ZKRZ GUZ, no. 306, box 11, 1096–1098.

50. HDA, Collection 252, RUR, J. Section, 29235.

51. Domaš, "Zeev Glück."

52. HDA, Collection 252, RUR, J. Section, 28309, 29366, 29594.

53. HDA, Collection 252, RUR, J. Section, 29677.

54. HDA, Collection 252, RUR, J. Section, 29630.

55. HDA, Collection 252, RUR, J. Section, 29300.

56. JIM, Collection ŽOZ, reg. no. 4859, sign. K-65–1-1/1–143.

57. JIM, Collection ŽOZ, reg. no. 4859, sign. K-65–1-1/1–109.

58. Testimony of Dr. Vlado Prašek.

59. Lengel-Krizman, "Prilog proučavanju terora u NDH," 15.

60. HDA, Collection 248, UNS, Collection Transit and Work Camps in the ISC, Transit Camp Loborgrad, Bills; HDA, Collection 252, RUR, J. Section, 28245, 28279; *Spiskovi preživelih*; *Popis žrtava*; JIM, Collection ŽOZ, reg. no. 4870, sign. K-65–2-1/1–34; JIM, Collection ŽOZ, sign. K-62–6-1/1–246, 1–249; JIM, Collection ŽOZ, no reg. no.; JIM, Collection ŽOZ, sign. K-67–1-1/1–124; JIM, Collection ŽOZ, reg. no. 4872, sign. K-60–7-1/1–1; NAZ, Group NDS 9274/1942.

61. HDA, Collection 252, RUR, J. Section, 28323, 29856.

62. HDA, Collection 252, RUR, J. Section, 28876, 29041, 29160.

63. JIM, Collection ŽOZ, reg. no. 4870, sign. K-65–2-1/1–45 do 1–47.

64. HDA, Collection 252, RUR, J. Section, 29179.

65. HDA, Collection 252, RUR, J. Section, 29180, 29273.

66. JIM, Collection ŽOZ, reg. no. 4870, sign. K-65–2-1/1–1, 1–17.

67. JIM, Collection ŽOZ, reg. no. 4870, sign. K-65–2-1/1–3 do 1–72.

68. JIM, Collection ŽOZ, reg. no. 4870, sign. K-65–2-1/1–11, 1–12.

69. JIM, Collection ŽOZ, reg. no. 4870, sign. K-65–2-1/1–3 do 1–10; *Popis žrtava.*

70. *Bilten ŽOZ* 38 (1995); JIM, Collection ŽOZ, without reg. no.; *Popis žrtava.*

71. HDA, Collection 252, RUR, J. Section, 29312.

72. HDA, Collection 248, UNS, Collection Transit and Work Camps in the ISC, Transit Camp Loborgrad, Announcements and Memos.

73. HDA, Collection 252, RUR, J. Section, 29235, 29312, 29755.

74. HDA, Collection 248, UNS, Collection Transit and Work Camps in the ISC, Transit Camp Loborgrad, Announcements and Memos.

75. HDA, Collection 248, UNS, Collection Transit and Work Camps in the ISC, Transit Camp Loborgrad, Announcements and Memos.

76. HDA, Collection 252, RUR, J. Section, 28691, 28723, and elsewhere, 29312.

77. HDA, Collection ZKRZ GUZ, no. 306, box 11, 1096–1098, 1059–1060, box 15, 3877; Lengel-Krizman, "Prilog proučavanju terora u NDH," 16; *Dotrščina projekt.*

78. HDA, Collection 252, RUR, J. Section, 29053.

79. HDA, Collection 252, RUR, J. Section, 29059.

80. HDA, Collection ZKRZ GUZ, no. 306, box 13, 2235; Lengel-Krizman, "Prilog proučavanju terora u NDH," 20.

81. JIM, Collection ŽOZ, sign. K-65–4-1/1–149, 1–164; on deportation to Auschwitz and on the fate of the deportees, see in several places, e.g., chapter 26.

82. Peršen, *Ustaški logori*, 281.

83. HDA, Collection ZKRZ GUZ, no. 306, box 15, 3878.

84. The most complete information about the camp is provided by Vasiljević, *Sabirni logor Đakovo*; see also Lengel-Krizman, "Prilog proučavanju terora u NDH," 23–31; Peršen, *Ustaški logori*, 282–86.

85. JIM, Collection ŽOZ, reg. no. 4859, sign. K-65–1-1/1–61 do 1–65.

86. HDA, Collection Ustasha Commission for the Town and District of Koprivnica, 961–76; Vasiljević, *Sabirni logor Đakovo*, 166–85.

87. HDA, Collection 248, UNS, Collection Transit and Work Camps in the ISC, Transit Camp Đakovo, Bills, IV group, 8, 8; 9, 2; HDA, Collection 252, RUR, J. Section, 28490.

88. HDA, Collection 248, UNS, Collection Transit and Work Camps in the ISC, Transit Camp Đakovo, Bills, IV group, 8, 4.

89. HDA, Collection 248, UNS, Collection Transit and Work Camps in the ISC, Transit Camp Đakovo, Bills, IV group, in various places.

90. HDA, Collection ZKRZ GUZ, no. 306, box 10, 94; Vasiljević, *Sabirni logor Đakovo.*

91. Lengel-Krizman, "Prilog proučavanju terora u NDH," 28.

92. HDA, Collection 252, RUR, J. Section, 29529.

93. HDA, Collection 252, RUR, J. Section, 28883.

94. The *Dotrščina projekt* gives the names of sixty-five Jewish women and children from Zagreb who died in Đakovo. HDA, Collection ZKRZ GUZ, no. 306, box 10, 570–640; Vasiljević, *Sabirni logor Đakovo*, 189–211.

95. HDA, Collection ZKRZ GUZ, no. 306, box 10, 570–640. See also HDA, Collection Ustasha Commission for the Town and District of Koprivnica, 981–1018; HDA, Collection 252, RUR, J. Section, 28693; HDA, 013.2.30, File Ljubo Miloš, 85.

23. A New Kind of Correspondence

1. HDA, Collection 252, RUR, J. Section, 27145; *Spiskovi preživelih*, 327; NAZ, group NDS 5274/1941; about Laxa, who obviously belonged to the more liberal part of the Ustasha hierarchy, see Stuparić, *Tko je tko u NDH*, 231–32.

2. HDA, Collection 252, RUR, J. Section, 27902; *Spiskovi preživelih.*

3. Elza Reis was in the Kraljevica Camp, later on Rab: it seems that she did not apply for evacuation, so the Germans probably deported her to Auschwitz in March 1944; Testimony of Branko Polić.

4. HDA, Collection 252, RUR, J. Section, 28049; NAZ, group NDS 10503/1941; *Popis žrtava.* See requests elsewhere too: Collection 252, RUR, J. Section, 27241, 27764, 27820, 28049, 28233, 27964, 28130, 28135, 28678.

5. HDA, Collection 252, RUR, J. Section, 27274, 27370, 27466; *Popis žrtava.* See also 27296, 27713, 27832, 27899–27900, 28055, 28074.

6. HDA, Collection 252, RUR, J. Section, 27592, 27592a.

7. HDA, Collection 252, RUR, J. Section, 28233.

8. *Novi list* (Zagreb), August 4 and 9, 1941.

9. Steinberg, *Deutsche, Italiener und Juden*, 74.

10. HDA, Collection 252, RUR, J. Section, 28382; *Popis žrtava.*

11. HDA, Collection 252, RUR, J. Section, 27427; *Popis žrtava.*

12. HDA, Collection 252, RUR, J. Section, 27668.

13. HDA, Collection 252, RUR, J. Section, 28100; *Popis preživelih.*

14. HDA, Collection 252, RUR, J. Section, 27683; *Popis žrtava.*

15. HDA, Collection 252, RUR, J. Section, 27770; *Popis žrtava.*

16. HDA, Collection 252, RUR, J. Section, 27834; Šternberg, "Doprinos Židova," 233–34.

17. HDA, Collection 218, MPB NDH, Justice Department, box 417, file of Dr. M. Sabalić.

18. HDA, Collection 252, RUR, J. Section, 27707; *Spiskovi preživelih.*

19. HDA, Collection 252, RUR, J. Section, 27542; *Spiskovi preživelih.*

20. HDA, Collection 252, RUR, J. Section, 27513; *Kartoteka jasenovačkih zatočenika.*

21. HDA, Collection 252, RUR, J. Section, 27748; see also 28535; *Popis žrtava; Spiskovi preživelih.*

22. HDA, Collection 252, RUR, J. Section, 27968; HDA, Collection 252, RUR, J. Section, Index, 1784, 2302.

23. *Kartoteka židovskog znaka*; *Popis žrtava*; *Spiskovi preživelih*; JIM, Collection ŽOZ, reg. no. 4860, sign. K-60–5-1/1–163.

24. HDA, Collection 252, RUR, J. Section, 27666.

25. HDA, Collection 252, RUR, J. Section, 28076.

26. NAZ, group NDS 10732/1941; Levental, "Sećanje na medicinski rad"; on Bril, see Ivanuša, "Židovi—likovni umjetnici"; JIM, Collection ŽOZ, reg. no. 4869, sign. K-66–4-1/1–17. According to Nikolić, *Jasenovački logor smrti*, 201, he died in the camp hospital in 1944.

27. NAZ, group NDS 9805/1942; *Popis žrtava.*

28. HDA, Collection 252, RUR, J. Section, 27737; *Popis žrtava.*

29. HDA, Collection 252, RUR, J. Section, 27864; *Popis žrtava.*

30. See request for release from Zavrtnica, HDA, Collection 252, RUR, J. Section, 28029, 28057.

31. HDA, Collection 252, RUR, J. Section, 28150; *Kartoteka jasenovačkih zatočenika.*

32. *Dotrščina projekt*; *Popis žrtava*; *Popis žrtava Zagreb*; *Kartoteka židovskog znaka; Imenik Ponove*; HDA, Collection 1076, Ponova, DKM, box 834, 1100/4.

33. HDA, Collection 252, RUR, J. Section, 28122, 28124–28127, 28137, 28235, 28254–28257, 28259–28262, 28267, 28290, 28452, 28458, 28489, 28512, 28736, 29197–29211, 29791.

34. HDA, Collection 223, MUP NDH, 3246, 3248, 3594, 4025, 4343/II- A, 5606, 5607, 5616, 5627, 5632.

35. HDA, Collection 252, RUR, J. Section, 29557.

36. HDA, Collection 252, RUR, J. Section, 28038, 28051.

37. HDA, Collection 252, RUR, J. Section, 27437, 27498, 27677, 27702, 27734, 27808, 27810, 28194, 28961, 29010, 29012, 29129, 29136, 29240–29244, 29246, 29247, 29281, 29514, 29516.

38. HDA, Collection 252, RUR, J. Section, 28150.

39. HDA, Collection 252, RUR, J. Section, 28282; *Popis žrtava.*

40. On release, e.g., from Jasenovac, see chapter 21.

41. HDA, Collection 252, RUR, J. Section, 28934.

24. Mixed Marriages and "Honorary Aryans"

1. HDA, Collection 252, RUR, J. Section, 27310; *Popis žrtava*; Palčić spent all the war in Novalja. He was a bohemian and lived alone all his life. It seems that he really had married Ruža, although it is not possible to establish when or where, so the marriage may have been only fictitious. On Palčić, see *Enciklopedija likovnih umjetnosti*, 3:621.

2. HDA, Collection 223, MUP NDH, 1099; II- A, 12420; *Popis žrtava.*

3. See, e.g., HDA, Collection 252, RUR, J. Section, 29826; *Popis žrtava.*

4. Lengel-Krizman, "Prilog proučavanju terora u NDH," 4–7; Lengel-Krizman, "Logori za Židove u NDH," 91–94.

5. HDA, Collection 252, RUR, J. Section, 29580; *Popis žrtava.*

6. HDA, Collection 252, RUR, J. Section, 29297.

7. HDA, Collection 223, MUP NDH, 1349/23073, 33187; *Popis žrtava.*

8. Reconstruction, DKM card index, box 458, 4081/1; JIM, Collection ŽOZ, without reg. no.; *Popis žrtava*; *Kartoteka židovskog znaka.*

9. HDA, Collection 252, RUR, J. Section, 28852; *Kartoteka židovskog znaka*; *Popis žrtava*; *Istupi iz židovstva 1941*, Archive ŽOZ; *Spisak preživelih*; testimony of Branko Polić.

10. JIM, Collection ŽOZ, reg. no. 4872, sign. K-60–7-1/1–30; *Popis žrtava*; *Kartoteka židovskog znaka.*

11. Testimony of Ljerka Magdić; Romano, *Jevreji Jugoslavije*, 499.

12. *Knjiga kontribucije.*

13. NAZ, Group NDS 768/1942, 205/1944; *Kartoteka židovskog znaka*; *Dotrščina projekt*, HDA, 26; testimony of Rafael Baruch.

14. HDA, Collection 252, RUR, J. Section, 29704.

15. Krišto, *Katolička crkva i Nezavisna Država Hrvatska*, 2:211–12.

16. HDA, Collection ZKRZ GUZ, no. 306, box 10, 89; box 15, 3732; Krizman, *NDH između*, 559–60; HDA, Collection MUP SRH, 013.0.65, part 3, 223–24.

17. HDA, Collection 252, RUR, J. Section, 27751; *Popis žrtava*; Romano, *Jevreji Jugoslavije*, 336.

18. See chapter 36.

19. This is not the same person as Aleksandar Klein, secretary of the Jewish Religious Community in Zagreb, who fled to Switzerland via Italy in May 1942.

20. HDA, Collection 252, RUR, J. Section, 28528; *Popis žrtava.*

21. HDA, Collection 252, RUR, J. Section, 27786; *Imenik Ponove*; *Kartoteka židovskog znaka*; *Popis žrtava.*

22. See cases: HDA, Collection 252, RUR, J. Section, 27181, 27197.

23. Testimony of Vlasta Urbić, née Deutsch-Maceljski.

24. Testimonies of Ivana Forenbacher, née Rosskamp, and Professor Dr. Fedor Rajić.

25. Care for the Internees and for the Survival of the Jewish Religious Community

1. *Hrvatski narod,* October 12, 1941; Krizman, *NDH između,* 46.

2. Testimony of Grüner's son, Dr. Teodor; about Grivičić, see Stuparić, *Tko je tko u NDH,* 140–41; according to the testimony of Ljerka Magdić, immediately after the establishment of the ISC, a notice was hung in the window of Grivičić's shop in Ilica 10 saying, "No dogs or Jews allowed."

3. Testimony of Mirko Mirković.

4. Levi, *Nedoživljeni jubilej.*

5. *Knjiga umrlih ŽOZ*; testimony of Dr. Bernard Grüner and Branko Polić.

6. Shomrony, "Svjedočenja, Gdje je Freibergerova biblioteka?"; in the eighties and nineties, Shomrony (formerly Emil Schwarz, secretary to Miroslav Freiberger) was the main supporter of proclaiming Archbishop Stepinac "Righteous among the Nations," see *Bilten ŽOZ* 44–45 (1996); *Glas koncila* (Zagreb), April 21, 1996.

7. HDA, Collection 252, RUR, J. Section, 28857.

8. HDA, Collection 252, RUR, J. Section, 27428; *Popis žrtava*; *Spiskovi preživelih.*

9. HDA, Collection MUP SRH, 013.0.65, 64, 67.

10. *Narodne novine,* November 26, 1941; Miletić, *Koncentracioni logor Jasenovac,* 1:98–100; *Ustaša, Dokumenti,* 215–16; see also HDA, Collection ZKRZ GUZ, no. 306, box 10, 302, 538; HDA, Collection 218, MPB NDH, Department of Justice, box 33, I 155, 92859/1941.

11. HDA, Collection 218, MPB NDH, Department of Justice, box 33, I 155, 92859/1941.

12. *Narodne novine,* February 27, 1943, and January 13, 1945; see also HDA, Collection ZKRZ GUZ, no. 306, box 10, 303–4.

13. HDA, Collection 223, MUP NDH, 13520/3095/42.

14. HDA, Collection 252, RUR, J. Section 27784, 27814, 27848, 28631.

15. Lengel-Krizman, "Prilog proučavanju terora u NDH," 9.

16. HDA, Collection ZKRZ GUZ, no. 306, box 10, 129, 151.

17. HDA, Collection 248, UNS, Collection Transit and Work Camps in the ISC, Transit Camp Loborgrad, Announcements and Memos.

18. Lengel-Krizman, *Organizacija i rad*; Lengel-Krizman, "Narodnooslobodilački pokret u Zagrebu," 48–49.

19. JIM, Collection ŽOZ, reg. no. 4866, sign. K-66–1-1/1–77 do 1–83.

20. JIM, Collection ŽOZ, reg. no. 4971, sign. K-63–3-3/1–140.

21. HDA, Collection 252, RUR, J. Section, 28371; JIM, Collection ŽOZ, reg. no. 4866, sign. K-66–1-1/1–67.

22. JIM, Collection ŽOZ, reg. no. 4866, sign. K-66–1-1/1–50.

23. HDA, Collection ZKRZ GUZ, no. 306, box 10, 87–88.

24. Berger, *44 mjeseca u Jasenovcu,* 31.

25. Ciliga, *Sam kroz Europu u ratu,* 305.

26. JIM, Collection ŽOZ, reg. no. 4866, sign. K-66–1-1/1–7, 1–11.

27. JIM, Collection ŽOZ, reg. no. 4866, sign. K-66–1-1/1–71.

28. JIM, Collection ŽOZ, reg. no. 4866, sign. K-66–1-1/1–72.

29. JIM, Collection ŽOZ, reg. no. 4866, sign. K-66–1-1/1–1, 1–35, 1–55.

30. Lengel-Krizman, "Prilog proučavanju terora u NDH," 9.

31. *Kartoteka jasenovačkih zatočenika*; see also Miletić, *Koncentracioni logor Jasenovac*, 1:199.

32. *Kartoteka jasenovačkih zatočenika.*

33. HDA, Collection ZKRZ GUZ, no. 306, box 10, 93, box 15, 3877.

34. JIM, Collection ŽOZ, without reg. no.

35. HDA, Collection 252, RUR, J. Section, 28507; JIM, Collection ŽOZ, without reg. no.

36. Miletić, *Koncentracioni logor Jasenovac*, 1:103–4.

37. HDA, Collection 252, RUR, J. Section, 28609.

38. HDA, Collection 252, RUR, J. Section, 29332.

39. *Zapisnici 1941*, Archive ŽOZ.

40. *Zapisnici 1941*, Archive ŽOZ.

41. JIM, Collection ŽOZ, reg. no. 5386, sign. K-65–6-1/1–1 to 1–51.

42. JIM, Collection ŽOZ, reg. no. 5386, sign. K-65–6-1/1–2.

43. JIM, Collection ŽOZ, reg. no. 4973, sign. K-64–2-1/1–26.

44. To better appreciate these figures, see note 28 in Chapter 22.

45. Miletić, *Koncentracioni logor Jasenovac*, 1:103–4.

46. Testimony of Branko Polić.

47. JIM, Collection ŽOZ, reg. no. 5386, sign. K-65–6-1/1–71, 1–72; JIM, Collection ŽOZ, without reg. no.

48. *Kartoteka židovskog znaka*; *Popis žrtava*; testimony of Vera Zoričić, née Schwabenitz.

49. JIM, Collection ŽOZ, reg. no. 4973, sign. K-64–2-1/1–25.

50. JIM, Collection ŽOZ, reg. no. 4973, sign. K-64–2-1/1–24.

51. JIM, Collection ŽOZ, reg. no. 4973, sign. K-64–2-1/1–15; testimony of Ljerka Magdić.

52. JIM, Collection ŽOZ, reg. no. 4973, sign. K-64–2-1/1–1.

53. JIM, Collection ŽOZ, without reg. no.

54. JIM, Collection ŽOZ, without reg. no.; testimony of Branko Polić; *Popis žrtava.*

55. JIM, Collection ŽOZ, without reg. no.; *BP ŽHH*, ŽOZ.

56. JIM, Collection ŽOZ, reg. no. 4872, sign. K-60–7-1/1–42; *Spiskovi preživelih.*

57. JIM, Collection ŽOZ, reg. no. 4872, sign. K-60–7-1/1–30; *Popis žrtava*; *Kartoteka židovskog znaka.*

58. JIM, Collection ŽOZ, reg. no. 4872, sign. K-60–7-1/1–26.

59. JIM, Collection ŽOZ, reg. no. 4872, sign. K-60–7-1/1–25; *Kartoteka židovskog znaka*; *Popis žrtava.*

60. JIM, Collection ŽOZ, reg. no. 4872, sign. K-60–7-1/1–24.

61. JIM, Collection ŽOZ, reg. no. 4872, sign. K-60–7-1/1–28, 1–29.

62. JIM, Collection ŽOZ, reg. no. 4872, sign. K-60–7-1/1–25.

63. JIM, Collection ŽOZ, reg. no. 4872, sign. K-60–7-1/1–23; *Popis žrtava*; *Kartoteka židovskog znaka.*

64. JIM, Collection ŽOZ, reg. no. 4872, sign. K-60–7-1/1–41; *Kartoteka židovskog znaka*; *Popis žrtava; Knjiga umrlih.*

65. JIM, Collection ŽOZ, reg. no. 4872, sign. K-60–7-1/1–40; *Popis žrtava.*

66. HDA, Collection 252, RUR, J. Section, 27352, 27793; *Zapisnici 1941*, Archive ŽOZ; Ristović, *U potrazi za utočištem, Jugoslovenski Jevreji*, 184.

67. HDA, Collection 252, RUR, J. Section, 27554.

68. HDA, Collection MUP RH III-24, 1179.

69. HDA, Collection 252, RUR, J. Section, 28575, 29153, 29154.

70. HDA, Collection 252, RUR, J. Section, 29153.

71. HDA, Collection 252, RUR, J. Section, 29153; Ristović, *U potrazi za utočištem, Jugoslovenski Jevreji*, 184.

72. HDA, Collection ZKRZ GUZ, no. 306, box 10, 93; box 16, 4687–4770.

73. HDA, Collection ZKRZ GUZ, no. 306, box 10, 93.

74. JIM, Collection ŽOZ, reg. no. 5386, sign. K-65–6-1/1–315.

75. *Spomenica Saveza jevrejskih opština Jugoslavije 1919–1969*, 89.

76. Ciliga, *Sam kroz Europu u ratu*, 305.

77. HDA, Collection ZKRZ GUZ, no. 306, box 10, 94.

78. HDA, Collection ZKRZ GUZ, no. 306, box 15, 3877, box 16, 4479.

79. HDA, Collection ZKRZ GUZ, no. 306, box 15, 3877.

80. HDA, Collection ZKRZ GUZ, no. 306, box 15, 3877.

81. Archive ŽOZ.

82. Berger, *44 mjeseca u Jasenovcu*, 64.

83. HDA, Collection 248, UNS, Collection of Transit and Work Camps in the ISC, Transit Camp Loborgrad, announcements and memos.

84. HDA, Collection 252, RUR, J. Section, 29153.

85. HDA, Collection 252, RUR, J. Section, 29625.

86. Archive ŽOZ. The letter of June 30, 1944, seems to have been the last that Vlado Eckstein sent from Jasenovac, and he did not survive the war: the Dotrščina Project gives incorrect information that he was killed in 1941 in Jasenovac.

87. HDA, Collection ZKRZ GUZ, no. 306, box 15, 3877.

88. Archive ŽOZ.

89. In 1960, Zlata contacted the Jewish Community in Zagreb, claiming that she was "Jewish" and that she had converted to Catholicism in 1941 to save her life. At that time, in 1960, she was living with her sister, because it seems that in the meantime her husband had died. There are no records about her renunciation of the Jewish faith in the *Book of Renunciations,* but it is possible that a mistake may have been made, and it may have been Zlata Petrić and Berta Petrić who converted in 1938. However, she claimed that she had gotten married in 1937 and converted in May 1941; see Archive ŽOZ for 1960; HDA, Collection 223, MUP NDH, 1101/II-A, 12483, which is confirmed by the parish office in Stenjevec—NAZ, group NDS 5285/1941.

90. HDA, Collection ZKRZ GUZ, no. 306, box 10, 93–94.

91. HDA, Collection ZKRZ GUZ, no. 306, box 10, 93; Collection 252, RUR, J. Section, 27319.

92. HDA, Collection ZKRZ GUZ, no. 306, box 10, 93.

93. JIM, Collection ŽOZ, without reg. no.

94. Lengel-Krizman, "Revolucionarni omladinski pokret u Zagrebu u toku rata," 141.

26. In the New Year

1. HDA, Collection MUP SRH, 013.0.65, 76–77.

2. *Dnevnik grofa Ciana* (Zagreb 1948), 500.

3. Testimony of Vera Zoričić, née Schwabenitz.

4. HDA, Collection 252, RUR, J. Section, 28836; *Popis žrtava.*

5. HDA, Collection 252, RUR, J. Section, 28522.

6. *Popis žrtava*; *Spiskovi preživelih.*

7. See list of prisoners by name, JIM, Collection ŽOZ, without reg. no.

8. HDA, Collection ZKRZ GUZ, no. 306, box 10, 86 (study *Zločini okupatora i njihovih pomagača*); box 15, 3732, 3817; according to the report, prisoners were first brought to the Zagreb Fairground, then taken to the Sava Road prison. It seems that this is a mistake, and must have been the reverse, as there are other reports that prisoners were transported by rail to Jasenovac from the Zagreb Fairground, see the case of Slavko Bril (Levental, "Sećanje na medicinski rad"; Ivanuša, "Židovi—likovni umjetnici"; JIM, Collection ŽOZ, reg. no. 4869, sign. K-66–4-1/1–17).

9. HDA, Collection 252, RUR, J. Section, 28189; JIM, Collection ŽOZ, without reg. no.; *Popis žrtava.*

10. Testimony of Vera Fischer.

11. JIM, Collection ŽOZ, without reg. no.; *Popis žrtava.*

12. NAZ, group NDS 1043/1942.

13. Testimony of Branko Polić.

14. JIM, Collection ŽOZ, reg. no. 4870, sign. K-65–2-1/1–48, 1–49; *Popis žrtava.*

15. JIM, Collection ŽOZ, reg. no. 4970, sign. K-63–3-2/1–1; reg. no. 4864, sign. K-63–1-1/1–200.

16. Ben-Sasson, *History of the Jewish People*, 1027–28.

17. *Narodne novine*, January 15 and 19, 1942.

18. Kisić-Kolanović, *Židovska imovina*, 440.

19. In detail, in: Kisić-Kolanović, "Hrvatski državni sabor NDH 1942."

20. *Ustaša, Dokumenti*, 245; *Brzopisni zapisnici*, 6.

21. *Narodne novine*, February 25, 1942; HDA, Collection 211, HDS, box 6; *Brzopisni zapisnici*, 30; HDA, Collection ZKRZ GUZ, no. 306, box 10, 287, 522.

22. *Narodne novine*, February 26, 1942; HDA, Collection 211, HDS, box 6; *Brzopisni zapisnici*, 38; HDA, Collection ZKRZ GUZ, no. 306, box 10, 287, 522.

23. *Narodne novine*, February 26, 1942; HDA, Collection 211, HDS, box 6; *Brzopisni zapisnici*, 150, do not mention these interruptions.

24. Kisić-Kolanović, "Hrvatski državni sabor NDH 1942," 563. It is not clear why N. Kisić-Kolanović thinks that this was parliamentary "opposition," as these members only demanded that laws should be consistently abided by. A real "opposition" should surely have demanded the repeal of laws allowing the seizure of Jewish and Serb Orthodox property.

25. HDA, Collection HDS, Predsjednički spisi 23, of 4/7/1942; Kisić-Kolanović, *Židovska imovina*, 431; quoted according to Sobolevski, "Zagrebačka židovska općina od 1941," 111–12.

26. Testimony of Berta Israel, née Švarcenberg.

27. Testimony of Berta Israel, née Švarcenberg; *Knjiga umrlih*.

28. *Hrvatski narod* (Zagreb), April 8, 1942.

29. HDA, Collection 252, RUR, J. Section, 28798.

30. *Hrvatska gruda* 94 (1942).

31. See exhibition catalogue, *Židovi–izložba o razvoju židovstva i njihovog rušilačkog rada u Hrvatskoj prije 10. IV. 1941. Rješenje židovskog pitanja u NDH, katalog izložbe*; see also HDA, Collection ZKRZ GUZ, no. 306, box 10, 288–295.

32. About the decree of Emperor Joseph II, "Systematica gentis Judaicae regulatio," which is usually called the Edict of Tolerance, see chapter 2.

33. This refers to the notorious lie that President Roosevelt of the USA was Jewish. The Nazis and their Ustashe followers probably thought this the easiest way to explain the strong resistance of the USA against anti-Semitism, Nazi ideology, and the Axis Powers in general.

34. *Nova Hrvatska*, April 14, 1942; April 17, 1942; May 5, 1942; see also HDA, Collection ZKRZ GUZ, no. 306, box 10, 295.

35. See, for example, *Spremnost* (Zagreb), May 3, 1942.

36. *Hrvatski narod*, September 9, 1942; Miletić, *Koncentracioni logor Jasenovac*, 1:440–44; Strčić, "Jasenovac i ratni zločin," 55, 92.

37. *Ustaša* 24, June 14, 1942.

38. *Ustaša* 18, May 3, 1942.

39. Soltikow and Schadewaldt, *Anglosaksonski sviet*. I could not find this text in the German original. It was probably written by Count Michael Alexander Soltikow, who wrote thrillers in the fifties, and said he was a member of the group around Admiral Canaris, head of the Abwehr (German military intelligence service). See Soltikow, *Ich war mittendrin*. It seems that Schadewaldt (1894–?) was a propagandist for the Auswärtiges Amt (Foreign Ministry); his 1940 book about the alleged persecution by Poles of the German ethnic minority in Poland was translated into French and English: Schadewaldt, *Polish Acts of Atrocity*.

40. HDA, Collection HDS, Treasury Affairs Committee, minutes from a meeting held on June 17, 1942; Kisić-Kolanović, *Židovska imovina*, 449; in 1942, Fran Milobar (1869–1945) spoke bravely in public several times; about him, see Stuparić, *Tko je tko u NDH*, 274–75; Matković, *Stjepan Radić*. He died in October 1945 in Zagreb of natural causes.

41. HDA, Collection: NDH, inv. no. 30062; Sobolevski, "Zagrebačka židovska općina od 1941."

42. HDA, Collection 252, RUR, J. Section, 28473.

43. *Popis žrtava*.

44. Testimony of Dr. Teodor Grüner.

45. *Židov* 1 (1938); JIM, Collection ŽOZ, sign. K-65-3-1/1–115.

46. HDA, Collection 252, RUR, J. Section, 29340, 29502.

47. HDA, Collection 252, RUR, J. Section, 29529, 29530.

48. HDA, Collection 252, RUR, J. Section, 28755.

49. HDA, Collection 252, RUR, J. Section, 29102, 29108, 29111, 29112, 29147, 29168, 29189, 29190, 29294, 29315, 29410, 29613, 29614, 29616, 29618, 29634, 29684; JIM, Collection ŽOZ, reg. no. 5382, sign. K-65–3-1/1–45 to 1–48, 1–108, 1–109.

50. HDA, Collection 252, RUR, J. Section, 29126, 29213, 29627, 29689; JIM, Collection ŽOZ, reg. no. 5382, sign. K-65–3-1/1–111, 1–113.

51. JIM, Collection ŽOZ, reg. no. 5382, sign. K-65–3-1/1–62 to 1–112.

52. HDA, Collection 252, RUR, J. Section, 29411, 29554, 29637, 29715.

53. JIM, Collection ŽOZ, reg. no. 5382, sign. K-65–3-1/1–1, 1–82.

54. JIM, Collection ŽOZ, reg. no. 5382, sign. K-65–3-1/1–116.

55. JIM, Collection ŽOZ, reg. no. 5382, sign. K-65–3-1/1–71, 1–72, 1–87.

56. *Popis žrtava.*

57. HDA, Collection 252, RUR, J. Section, 28967, 28968.

58. Miletić, *Koncentracioni logor Jasenovac*, 3:96; HDA, Collection 252, RUR, J. Section, 28996.

59. Peršen, *Ustaški logori*, 152.

60. HDA, Collection 252, RUR, J. Section, 29288, 29289.

61. HDA, Collection 252, RUR, J. Section, 29308, 29363, 29374, 29379.

62. HDA, Collection 248, UNS, folder I-A-II 377, file no. 11, file no. 12; HDA, Collection 252, RUR, J. Section, 29218, 29680; JIM, Collection ŽOZ, reg. no. 4973, sign. K-64–2-1/1–26.

63. For example, on July 21, only twenty-three women were sent away to Stara Gradiška, most of them housewives; HDA, Collection 252, RUR, J. Section, 29645, 29647, 29652–29654, 29657, 29670, 29696, 29698, 29701, 29702, 29704, 29725, 29726, 29737–29739, 29756, 29761, 29782, 29802, 29827, 29841.

64. See, e.g., HDA, Collection 252, RUR, J. Section, 29871.

65. HDA, Collection 252, RUR, J. Section, 29645, 29647, 29744; *Popis žrtava*; Kolar-Dimitrijević, "Sjećanja veterinara Zorka Goluba," 164; Romano, *Jevreji zdravstveni radnici Jugoslavije*, 83, 157; JIM, Collection ŽOZ, sign. K-65–4-1/1–231; JIM, Collection ŽOZ, without reg. no.; *Kartoteka židovskog znaka*; *Popis žrtava.*

66. HDA, Collection 252, RUR, J. Section, 29214, 29215.

67. According to Ljerka Magdić in *Novi Omanut* 49 (2001).

68. HDA, Collection 252, RUR, J. Section, 29390.

69. HDA, Collection ZKRZ GUZ, no. 306, box 10, 88–89; Miletić, *Koncentracioni logor Jasenovac*, 2:871; Kolar-Dimitrijević, "Sjećanja veterinara Zorka Goluba," 172; this report is confirmed by many independent sources, but the number of 3,208 killed could not be confirmed. Vasiljević, *Sabirni logor Đakovo*, 73–77, quotes many testimonies and claims that there were about 2,400 victims.

70. According to material from the archives of the Jewish Community in Split, Maričić, *Luka spasa*, 33.

71. According to material from the archives of the Jewish Community in Split, Maričić, *Luka spasa*, 33.

72. JIM, Collection ŽOZ, reg. no. 4869, sign. K-66–4-1/1–2, 1–4.

73. JIM, Collection ŽOZ, reg. no. 4858, sign. K-62–4-1/1–12.

74. JIM, Collection ŽOZ, without reg. no.; see also, JIM, Collection ŽOZ, sign. K-67–1-1/1–196.

27. Deportations in August 1942

1. For the entire report, see HDA, Collection ZKRZ GUZ, no. 306, box 10, 62–79.

2. See, Goldstein, *Croatia*, 147–49.

3. Lengel-Krizman, "Logori za Židove u NDH," 95.

4. HDA, Collection MUP SRH, 013.0.65, Part III, 223.

5. See, e.g., HDA, Collection 252, RUR, J. Section, 29836.

6. HDA, Collection 252, RUR, J. Section, 28322.

7. HDA, Collection 252, RUR, J. Section, 29876.

8. HDA, Collection 252, RUR, J. Section, 29833.

9. HDA, Collection 252, RUR, J. Section, 29059. On Kühnel, Collection ZKRZ, card index of war criminals, and chapter 11 in this book.

10. This was a major German-Ustasha operation on Mount Kozara (in northwest Bosnia), where there was a stronghold of Tito's Partisans. After they conquered this territory, they deported most of the captured civilians (including children), several tens of thousands, to camps.

11. HDA, Collection ZKRZ GUZ, no. 306, box 10, 283.

12. See, chapter 5.

13. *Hrvatski narod*, August 7, 1942.

14. *Hrvatski narod*, August 14, 1942.

15. HDA, Collection 252, RUR, J. Section, 29785; Collection ZKRZ GUZ, no. 306, box 10, 88–89; Collection ZKRZ GUZ, no. 306, box 15, 3817; Ristović, *U potrazi za utočištem, Jugoslovenski Jevreji*, 133.

16. Testimony of Professor Dr. Ivan Kampuš (son of Captain Ivan Kampuš).

17. *Kartoteka židovskog znaka*; *Knjiga umrlih.*

18. Testimonies of Radojka Ivančević-Tanhofer and Dr. Lea Prašek, née Neufeld.

19. See, e.g., HDA, Collection 252, RUR, J. Section, 29783, 28790, 29794, 29802.

20. Testimony of Ljerka Magdić.

21. HDA, Collection 252, RUR, J. Section, 29771, 29780, 29784, 29824, 29834.

22. HDA, Collection 252, RUR, J. Section, 29769, 29817, 29855, 29861.

23. HDA, Collection 252, RUR, J. Section, 29811.

24. Hilberg, *Destruction of the European Jews*, 714–15.

25. HDA, Collection 252, RUR, J. Section, 29877.

26. Testimony of Professor Dr. Ivan Kampuš (son of Captain Ivan Kampuš).

27. HDA, Collection 252, RUR, J. Section, 29769, 29817, 29855, 29861.

28. Miletić, *Koncentracioni logor Jasenovac*, 1:489; on Fra Mandić, see Pandžić, *Životopis Dr. fra Dominika Mandića.*

29. Steinberg, *All or Nothing*, 57–58.

30. Testimony of Dr. Teodor Grüner, according to his father, Chief Cantor Bernard.

31. Testimony of Branko Polić; *Popis žrtava.*

32. *Popis žrtava*; *Kartoteka židovskog znaka*; Dębski, *Sterbebücher von Auschwitz*, 2–3:123, 223, 792, 1069; *Jevrejska tribuna* 45 (1938).

33. Testimony of Mirko Mirković.

34. HDA, Collection ZKRZ GUZ, no. 306, box 15, 3876.

35. Prašek-Całczyńska, *Memoari*, 146.

36. Testimony of Professor Dr. Zdenko Šternberg.

37. HDA, Collection ZKRZ GUZ, no. 306, box 10, 88–89; box 15, 3768–69.

38. This is a list of just under 100,000 victims, which means that it hardly covers 10 percent of the people gassed in Auschwitz.

39. Dębski, *Sterbebücher von Auschwitz*, 2–3:223, 1274, 1311, 1319.

40. Dębski, *Sterbebücher von Auschwitz*, 2–3:58, 132, 223, 257, 258, 267, 269, 282, 290, 300, 308, 325, 363, 367, 371, 393, 792, 814, 857, 964, 1020, 1021, 1023, 1059, 1069, 1082, 1088, 1092, 1097, 1150, 1151, 1156, 1169, 1170, 1175, 1179, 1319, 1321.

41. Dębski, *Sterbebücher von Auschwitz*, 2–3:1071.

42. Testimony of Profesor Dr. Zdenko Šternberg.

43. JIM, Collection ŽOZ, reg. no. 4858, sign. K-62–4-1/1–18.

44. HDA, Collection 252, RUR, J. Section, 27915; *Popis žrtava*; estate of Dr. Miroslava Despot.

45. Hilberg, *Destruction of the European Jews*, 717, 1204.

46. Miletić, *Koncentracioni logor Jasenovac*, 1:489.

47. Sobolevski, "Židovi u kompleksu koncentracijskog logora Jasenovac," 112.

48. HDA, Collection 1076, Reconstruction, DKI Index, file Bertold and Malvina Jünker-546/2.

28. Saving the Children, Hiding in Hospitals

1. HDA, Collection 223, MUP NDH, III- 16, 1277–1282.

2. JIM, Collection ŽOZ, reg. no. 5386, sign. K-65–6-1/1–36 to 1–39, 1–137, 1–138, 1–142 to 1–144.

3. NAZ, group NDS 9808/1942; *Spiskovi preživelih.*

4. JIM, Collection ŽOZ, reg. no. 1909.

5. Magdić, "Prepoznala sam kolegice"; testimony of Ljerka Magdić.

6. Miletić, *Koncentracioni logor Jasenovac*, 1:489.

7. NAZ, group NDS 9805/1942.

8. NAZ, group NDS 10729/1942; *Popis žrtava*; *Spiskovi preživelih.*

9. NAZ, group NDS 9274/1942.

10. JIM, Collection ŽOZ, reg. no. 4872, sign. K-60–7-1/1–16; Šalić, *Židovi u Vinkovcima*, 255.

11. Testimony of Aleksandar-Saša Friedrich.

12. NAZ, Collection Prezidijalni spisi, 62/1943.

13. NAZ, group NDS 1536/1943; however, in January 1943, and probably even during 1942, *Katolički list* did not give precise instructions about converting to Catholicism in cases of this kind. Besides, no such instructions could have been given, only informal recommendations. Many articles encouraged conversion to Catholicism from other Christian communities, such as the series of articles by S. Banić,

"Obraćenja i obraćenici opravdavaju kršćanstvo" (Conversions and the Converted Justify Christianity), *Katolički list* 38, 39, and 44 (1942): 1; 2 (1943).

14. Archive of the Carmelite Convent on Vrhovac, Zagreb; testimony of Biserka Hirschl-Barac.

15. JIM, Collection ŽOZ, without reg. no.; Archive of the Carmelite Convent in Hrvatski Leskovac near Zagreb.

16. JIM, Collection ŽOZ, reg. no. 4872, sign. K-60–7-1/1–6.

17. Testimony of Ljerka Magdić.

18. JIM, Collection ŽOZ, without reg. no.

19. For more detail, see Ristović, *U potrazi za utočištem, Jugoslovenski Jevreji*, 320–24.

20. Krišto, *Katolička crkva*, 2:219; Shomrony, *Referat na simpoziju.*

21. HDA, Collection ZKRZ GUZ, no. 306, box 16, 4526–4687, 4771–4818, 4825, 4877; Carpi, "Diplomatic Negotiations," 112.

22. See lists of requests for passports: HDA, Collection ZKRZ GUZ, no. 306, box 16, 4500–4520.

23. JIM, Collection ŽOZ, sign. K-67–1-1/1–101; JIM, Collection ŽOZ, without reg. no.

24. HDA, Collection ZKRZ GUZ, no. 306, box 16, 4459–4476; Lengel-Krizman, "Prilog proučavanju terora u NDH," 8, 16–18.

25. JIM, Collection ŽOZ, without reg. no.

26. JIM, Collection ŽOZ, without reg. no.

27. JIM, Collection ŽOZ, without reg. no.

28. JIM, Collection ŽOZ, without reg. no.

29. JIM, Collection ŽOZ, without reg. no.

30. JIM, Collection ŽOZ, without reg. no.

31. HDA, Collection ZKRZ GUZ, no. 306, box 10, 92; Krišto, *Katolička crkva*, 2:242–43, 254, 280–81.

32. JIM, Collection ŽOZ, sign. K-65–4-1/1–106; HDA, Collection ZKRZ GUZ, no. 306, box 16, 4487–4492.

33. HDA, Collection ZKRZ GUZ, no. 306, box 16, 4487–4492.

34. Shomrony, "Kako su prodani certifikati."

35. JIM, Collection ŽOZ, sign. K-65–4-1/1–114.

36. Ristović, *U potrazi za utočištem, Jugoslovenski Jevreji*, 320, 324.

37. D. Mihalek, according to the testimony of Amiel Shomrony.

38. *Kartoteka židovskog znaka*; *Popis žrtava.*

39. JIM, Collection ŽOZ, without reg. no.

40. JIM, Collection ŽOZ, without reg. no. The list says that Lea Deutsch was born in 1933, although she was in fact six years older. The mistake was probably intentional because only children up to sixteen were eligible for this transport.

41. JIM, Collection ŽOZ, sign. K-65–4-1/1–114.

42. JIM, Collection ŽOZ, without reg. no. and sign.

43. HDA, Collection ZKRZ GUZ, no. 306, box 16, 4487–4492.

44. Carpi, "Diplomatic Negotiations," 115.

45. Isaić, *Put prognanih*, 42.

46. JIM, Collection ŽOZ, reg. no. 5993, sign. K-62–6-1/1–146, 1–159, 1–166, 1–171; JIM, Collection ŽOZ, without reg. no. and sign; Ristović, *U potrazi za utočištem, Jugoslovenski Jevreji*, 325–28.

29. The Agony on the Eve of the Last Deportation

1. "Načela," in *Ustaša, Dokumenti*, 76–77.

2. *Hrvatska gruda* (Zagreb), October 3, 1942.

3. *Spremnost* (Zagreb), September 13, 1942.

4. *Ustaša* 19, May 10, 1942; 26, June 28, 1942.

5. Pekić, *Postanak NDH*, 97, 116–17.

6. HDA, Collection 252, RUR, J. Section, 29907; the Bačićes are not in the indexes of the Jewish Community nor in *Imenik Ponove* (Economic econstruction directory), so, even if they were killed, they could not be entered on the list of Jewish victims.

7. Testimony of Boris Braun.

8. Krizman, *NDH između Hitlera i Mussolinija*, 558; Lengel-Krizman, "Prilog proučavanju terora u NDH," 20.

9. JIM, Collection ŽOZ, without reg. no.; Ristović, *U potrazi za utočištem, Jugoslovenski Jevreji*, 111, 126.

10. JIM, Collection ŽOZ, sign. K-65–4-1/1–37, 1–69, 1–79 to 1–82; JIM, Collection ŽOZ, reg. no. 5386, sign. K-65–6-1/1–64, 1–88 to 1–94; JIM, Collection ŽOZ, reg. no. 4850, sign. K-66–1-1/1–61 to 1–64; see also JIM, Collection ŽOZ, without reg. no.

11. JIM, Collection ŽOZ, reg. no. 5993, sign. K-62–6-1/1–46; JIM, Collection ŽOZ, without reg. no.

12. JIM, Collection ŽOZ, sign. K-65–4-1/1–30 to 1–33, 1–44 to 1–47, 1–49 to 1–55, 1–71 to 1–77; JIM, Collection ŽOZ, reg. no. 5386, sign. K-65–6-1/1–67, 1–95 to 1–103, 1–118; JIM, Collection ŽOZ, reg. no. 4850, sign. K-60–1-1/1–46 to 1–57, 1–65 to 1–78; see also JIM, Collection ŽOZ, without reg. no.

13. JIM, Collection ŽOZ, without reg. no.

14. JIM, Collection ŽOZ, without reg. no.

15. JIM, Collection ŽOZ, without reg. no.

16. *Kartoteka židovskog znaka.*

17. JIM, Collection ŽOZ, without reg. no.; JIM, Collection ŽOZ, reg. no. 4973, sign. K-64–2-1/1–26; *Kartoteka židovskog znaka.*

18. JIM, Collection ŽOZ, reg. no. 5386, sign. K-65–6-1/1–71, 1–72; JIM, Collection ŽOZ, without reg. no.

19. *Knjiga kontribucije.*

20. Testimony of Vlasta Urbić, née Deutsch-Maceljski.

21. *Jutarnji list* (Zagreb), December 9, 1929; Polić, "Humanitarni doprinos Aleksandra Frelića"; JIM, Collection ŽOZ, without reg. no.; JIM, Collection ŽOZ, reg. no. 4850, sign. K-66–1-1/1–58; HDA, Collection 252, RUR, J. Section, Index, 836; testimony of Branko Polić.

22. JIM, Collection ŽOZ, reg. no. 4973, sign. K-64–2-1/1–26.

23. Testimony of Branko Polić.

24. JIM, Collection ŽOZ, sign. K-65–4-1/1–36, 1–38 to 1–40; JIM, Collection ŽOZ, reg. no. 5386, sign. K-65–6-1/1–62, 1–66, 1–68, 1–76, 1–77, 1–79, 1–81 to 1–85, 1–87; see also JIM, Collection ŽOZ, without reg. no.

25. JIM, Collection ŽOZ, reg. no. 4850, sign. K-66–1-1/1–33.

26. JIM, Collection ŽOZ, sign. K-65–4-1/1–91; JIM, Collection ŽOZ, reg. no. 5386, sign. K-65–6-1/1–126, 1–132.

27. JIM, Collection ŽOZ, reg. no. 5386, sign. K-65–6-1/1–80, 1–139; JIM, Collection ŽOZ, reg. no. 5993, sign. K-62–6-1/1–26; JIM, Collection ŽOZ, without reg. no.

28. JIM, Collection ŽOZ, without reg. no.

29. JIM, Collection ŽOZ, sign. K-65–4-1/1–91, 1–82.

30. HDA, Collection 252, RUR, J. Section, 28841, 28849.

31. HDA, Collection ZKRZ GUZ, no. 306, box 16, 4481.

32. JIM, Collection ŽOZ, sign. K-65–4-1/1–110, 1–120, 1–155, 1–161 and elsewhere.

33. HDA, Collection 252, RUR, J. Section, 29867, 29869.

34. JIM, Collection ŽOZ, sign. K-65–4-1/1–9.

35. JIM, Collection ŽOZ, sign. K-65–4-1/1–10.

36. There is extensive documentation about this in JIM, Collection ŽOZ; see, for example, JIM, Collection ŽOZ, sign. K-65–4-1/1–92.

37. JIM, Collection ŽOZ, without reg. no.

38. JIM, Collection ŽOZ, sign. K-65–4-1/1–128; JIM, Collection ŽOZ, without reg. no.

39. JIM, Collection ŽOZ, without reg. no.

40. JIM, Collection ŽOZ, sign. K-65–4-1/1–108.

41. JIM, Collection ŽOZ, sign. K-65–4-1/1–187, 1–192–1-195, 1–200, 1–203, 1–204, 1–207, 1–230.

42. JIM, Collection ŽOZ, sign. K-65–4-1/1–218.

43. JIM, Collection ŽOZ, without reg. no.

44. JIM, Collection ŽOZ, sign. K-65–4-1/1–94.

45. JIM, Collection ŽOZ, sign. K-65–4-1/1–48, 1–139, 1–140, 1–152 to 1/154, and elsewhere, 1–201, 1–213, 1–240.

46. JIM, Collection ŽOZ, without reg. no.

47. JIM, Collection ŽOZ, reg. no. 5382, sign. K-65–5-1/1–54, 1–61, 1–74, 1–75, 1–80, 1–81.

48. JIM, Collection ŽOZ, reg. no. 5382, sign. K-65–5-1/1–93, 1–94, 1–101 to 1–106.

49. HDA, Collection ZKRZ GUZ, no. 306, box 10, 93.

50. JIM, Collection ŽOZ, reg. no. 5386, sign. K-65–6-1/1–125.

51. On the other hand, Miroslav Šalom Freiberger wrote in the letter to Osijek in January that 150 parcels were being sent a week, which means that parcels were sent with different intensities at different periods. The reasons for this are not known, but large numbers of parcels were in any case sent. HDA, Collection ZKRZ GUZ, no. 306, box 15, 3877, box 16, 4477–4480; Sobolevski, "Židovi u kompleksu koncentracijskog logora Jasenovac," 113.

52. JIM, Collection ŽOZ, sign. K-65–4-1/1–133, 1–179, 1–209.

53. JIM, Collection ŽOZ, sign. K-65–4-1/1–228.

54. JIM, Collection ŽOZ, without reg. no.

55. JIM, Collection ŽOZ, reg. no. 5993, sign. K-62–6-1/1–105, 1–106, 1–190.

56. JIM, Collection ŽOZ, without reg. no.

57. JIM, Collection ŽOZ, without reg. no.

58. JIM, Collection ŽOZ, reg. no. 4857, sign. K-62–3-1/1–1, 1–13, 1–17, 1–31.

59. JIM, Collection ŽOZ, reg. no. 5386, sign. K-65–6-1/1–57, 1–104, 1–152; JIM, Collection ŽOZ, reg. no. 5381, sign. K-66–5-1/1–72, 1–75; JIM, Collection ŽOZ, without reg. no.

60. See in various places in JIM, Collection ŽOZ, without reg. no.

61. JIM, Collection ŽOZ, sign. K-65–4-1/1–115; *Popis žrtava.*

62. JIM, Collection ŽOZ, sign. K-65–4-1/1–127, 1–130.

63. JIM, Collection ŽOZ, without reg. no.

64. JIM, Collection ŽOZ, reg. no. 4858, sign. K-62–4-1/1–68.

65. JIM, Collection ŽOZ, sign. K-65–4-1/1/179, 1–205, 1–211, 1–221.

66. JIM, Collection ŽOZ, sign. K-65–4-1/1–190, 1/191, 1–197, 1–202.

67. JIM, Collection ŽOZ, sign. K-65–4-1/1–115, 1–196, 1–217.

68. JIM, Collection ŽOZ, sign. K-65–4-1/1–177, 1–184.

69. JIM, Collection ŽOZ, without reg. no.

70. HDA, Collection ZKRZ GUZ, no. 306, box 16, 4489.

30. Final Annihilation

1. Sobolevski, "Zagrebačka židovska općina od 1941."

2. HDA, Collection ZKRZ GUZ, no. 306, box 15, 3732; Krizman, *NDH između Hitlera i Mussolinija*, 559–60; HDA, Collection MUP SRH, 013.0.65, part III, 223. About Crvenković, see Stuparić, *Tko je tko u NDH*, 74.

3. HDA, Collection ZKRZ GUZ, no. 306, box 10, 89.

4. HDA, Collection MUP SRH, 013.0.65, part III, 223–24.

5. Testimony of Branko Polić.

6. Testimony of Aleksandar-Saša Friedrich

7. Testimony of Vlasta Urbić, née Deutsch-Maceljski.

8. Lengel-Krizman, "Kronologija židovskog stradanja," 252.

9. HDA, Collection MUP SRH, 013.0.65, part III, 222.

10. JIM, Collection ŽOZ, sign. K-65–4-1/1–89, 1–92, 1–93.

11. Krišto, *Katolička crkva*, 2:257–65, 284.

12. HDA, Collection 223, MUP NDH, 8893, R. U. B.-III bb/43.

13. See, *Kartoteka židovskog znaka*; *Popis žrtava*; *Spiskovi preživelih.*

14. Geiger, "Saslušanje Branimira Altgayera," 625.

15. Geiger and Jurković, *Što se dogodilo s folksdojčerima*, 46–52.

16. The owner and manager of the sanatorium was Dr. Đuro Vranešić, a man described in a police report from 1943 as "without any political affiliation, who tries to be on a good footing with everyone . . ." (HDA, Collection MUP NDH, file 301941—Đuro Vranešić). On the one hand, Vranešić was a member of the Racial Political Commission of the Ministry of the Interior and was friendly with German representatives in Zagreb; on the other, he helped those who were persecuted in the

Kingdom of Yugoslavia and in the ISC. Despite many intercessions on his behalf, he was sentenced to death in 1945 and shot in January 1946. About Vranešić, see Stuparić, *Tko je tko u NDH*, 420.

17. Testimony of Vera Zoričić, née Schwabenitz.

18. Testimony of Branko Polić.

19. HDA, Collection MUP SRH, 013.0.65, part III, 196–98, 355–56, 360–61; *Popis žrtava.*

20. *Popis žrtava*; *Popis žrtava Zagreb.*

21. JIM, Collection ŽOZ, reg. no. 5386, sign. K-65–6-1/1–203, 1–204.

22. JIM, Collection ŽOZ, sign. K-65–4-1/1–10; *Popis žrtava*; *Kartoteka židovskog znaka.*

23. JIM, Collection ŽOZ, sign. K-67–1-1/1–204 to 1–207.

24. HDA, Collection ZKRZ GUZ, no. 306, box 15, 3732, 3759, 3760, 3823–3824; Krišto, *Katolička crkva*, 2:289–90.

25. Krizman, *NDH između Hitlera i Mussolinija*, 560, also wrote that about 1,700 Jews were caught, and that German intelligence had estimated about 1,500 Jews would be deported in the action. HDA, Collection ZKRZ GUZ, no. 306, box 15, 3732, says that about 1,200 Zagreb Jews were caught and deported in this action; according to the testimony of Josip Abraham, *ibid.*, 3817, the number was 1,300; the Apostolic Visitator in Zagreb, Marcone, reported that 600 Jews were deported at that time—Krišto, *Katolička crkva*, 2:284; about the action in detail, see Krizman, *NDH između Hitlera i Mussolinija*, 559–60.

26. HDA, Collection ZKRZ GUZ, no. 306, box 10, 89.

27. Testimony of Boris Braun.

28. Testimonies of Vlasta Urbić, née Deutsch-Maceljski, and Mirko Mirković.

29. Testimony of Aleksandar-Saša Friedrich.

30. JIM, Collection ŽOZ, sign. K-65–4-1/1–233, 1–234; JIM, Collection ŽOZ, reg. no. 5386, sign. K-65–6-1/1–220.

31. JIM, Collection ŽOZ, sign. K-65–4-1/1–238, 1–239; JIM, Collection ŽOZ, reg. no. 5386, sign. K-65–6-1/1–223.

32. JIM, Collection ŽOZ, sign. K-65–4-1/1–243, 1–244, 1–46, 1–247; JIM, Collection ŽOZ, reg. no. 5386, sign. K-65–6-1/1–221, 1–229, 1–230.

33. JIM, Collection ŽOZ, sign. K-65–4-1/1–242.

34. HDA, Collection MUP SRH, 013.0.65, part III, 48, 276.

35. *Popis žrtava.*

36. *Dotrščina projekt*, HDA, 23 and 24.

37. HDA, Collection ZKRZ GUZ, no. 306, box 10, 89, 149–150; *ibid.*, box 15, 3874; Shomrony, "Svjedočenja, Gdje je Freibergerova biblioteka?"; Goldstein, "Uz reprint."

38. About Lea, see Stuparić, *Tko je tko u NDH*, 89–90; NAZ, group NDS 5952/1941.

39. HDA, Collection ZKRZ GUZ, no. 306, box 10, 149–150.

40. Testimony of Ivana Forenbacher, née Rosskamp.

41. Testimony of Vlasta Urbić, née Deutsch-Maceljski.

42. Testimony of Ljerka Magdić.

43. Testimony of Ljerka Magdić.

44. Testimony of Vlasta Urbić, née Deutsch-Maceljski.

45. JIM, Collection ŽOZ, reg. no. 5993, sign. K-62–6-1/1–82, 1–91, 1–126 do 1–129, 1–134, 1–135, 1–144, 1–150 to 1–153, 1–155, 1–175 to 1–180, 1–202, 1–204, 1–215, 1–226, 1–227, 1–251 to 1–253; JIM, Collection ŽOZ, without reg. no.; *Popis žrtava*; *Spiskovi preživelih.*

46. JIM, Collection ŽOZ, reg. no. 4863, sign. K-62–5-1/1–422. According to this document, the Spillers were from Vinkovci, but they do not appear in the lists of Vinkovci Jews—see, Šalić, *Židovi u Vinkovcima.*

47. JIM, Collection ŽOZ, without reg. no.

48. JIM, Collection ŽOZ, without reg. no.; *Kartoteka židovskog znaka*; *Popis žrtava.*

49. Testimony of Boris Braun.

50. Lengel-Krizman, "Sudbina," 8.

51. Testimony of Boris Braun.

52. NAZ, group NDS 4716/1943; *Kartoteka židovskog znaka.*

53. Ristović, *U potrazi za utočištem, Jugoslovenski Jevreji*, 229–30.

54. Krišto, *Katolička crkva*, 2:294, 298–300.

55. HDA, Collection MUP SRH, 013.0.65, part III, 113, 114, 316, 317.

56. HDA, Collection ZKRZ GUZ, no. 306, box 10, 89.

57. Magdić, "Prepoznala sam kolegice."

58. Goldstein, "Uz reprint."

59. Krizman, *NDH između Hitlera i Mussolinija*, 557; the Apostolic Visitator Marcone also mentioned Himmler—Krišto, *Katolička crkva*, 2:284. Pečarić gave a completely wrong interpretation of Himmler's visit, *Srpski mit.*

60. JIM, Collection ŽOZ, sign. K-65–4-1/1–248.

61. JIM, Collection ŽOZ, sign. K-65–4-1/1–248.

62. JIM, Collection ŽOZ, sign. K-65–4-1/1–106.

63. Archive of the Carmelite Convent on Vrhovac, Zagreb.

64. JIM, Collection ŽOZ, sign. K-65–4-1/1–248.

65. Krizman, *Ustaše i Treći Reich*, 1:236.

31. Converting to Catholicism

1. About the Chetniks, see Tomasevich, *Chetniks.*

2. HDA, Collection 252, RUR, J. Section, 28481.

3. ŽOZ Archives for 1960.

4. HDA, Collection 252, RUR, J. Section, 27309.

5. HDA, Collection 252, RUR, J. Section, 27309.

6. HDA, Collection 252, RUR, J. Section, 27309.

7. *Hrvatski narod* 2 (1939); *Glasnik SJVO* 3 (1933): 196–200; *Židov* 18 (1936); 13 (1938).

8. NAZ, NDS group to number 5942/1941.

9. NAZ, NDS group to number 7254/1941.

10. NAZ, NDS group to about number 11000/1941.

11. NAZ, NDS group 10155, 10531, 10909/1941.

12. NAZ, Collection Prezidijalni spisi, 61/1941.

13. NAZ, NDS group to around number 12500/1941.

14. NAZ, NDS group to number around 16000/1941.
15. NAZ, NDS group to number 21953/1941.
16. NAZ, NDS group, protocols for 1942 and 1943.
17. ŽOZ Council Record 1941, ŽOZ Archives.
18. ŽOZ Council Record 1941, ŽOZ Archives.
19. JIM, ŽOZ Collection, reg. no. 5386, sign. K-65–6-1/1–80, 1–139; JIM, ŽOZ Collection, reg. no. 5993, sign. K-62–6-1/1–26; JIM, ŽOZ Collection, without reg. no.
20. NAZ, NDS group 8655/1943.
21. NAZ, NDS group 8890/1943.
22. NAZ, NDS group 3289/1944; testimony of Ivana Forenbacher, née Rosskamp.
23. NAZ, NDS group 5119, 5812/1944.
24. NAZ, NDS group 8723/1944.
25. Krišto, *Katolička crkva*, 2:145.
26. NAZ, NDS group 3864/1941.
27. NAZ, NDS group 158, 568, 1030, 1032, 1033, 2581, 2588, 2990, 2991, 3070, 3528, 3578, 4088, 5007, 5510, 5513, 9089, 9855, 9856, 10730, 12153/1942.
28. NAZ, NDS group 1029/1942.
29. *Codex iuris canonici,* paragraph 737 and throughout, and especially paragraph 745.
30. NAZ, NDS group 529/1942.
31. NAZ, NDS group 8046/1942.
32. NAZ, NDS group 1559/1942; *Popis žrtava.*
33. NAZ, NDS group 1035/1942; *Popis žrtava*; HDA, Collection ZKRZ GUZ, no. 306, box 15, 3732, 3761.
34. NAZ, NDS group 354/1942.
35. NAZ, NDS group 2038/1942.
36. NAZ, NDS group 1028, 1097/1942.
37. *Popis žrtava*; *Kartoteka židovskog znaka.*
38. NAZ, NDS group 4545/1942.
39. *Popis žrtava.*
40. *Istupi iz židovstva 1941*, Archive ŽOZ; *Popis žrtava*; testimony of Ljerka Abramović.
41. NAZ, NDS group 10645/1941; *Popis žrtava*; Jewish Insignia Index.
42. NAZ, NDS group 10503/1941; *Popis žrtava.*
43. NAZ, NDS group 989/1944.
44. NAZ, NDS group 9856/1942; *Popis žrtava*; *Spiskovi preživelih*; *Kartoteka židovskog znaka.*
45. NAZ, NDS group 1550/1942.
46. NAZ, NDS group 5051/1941; testimony of Zora Dirnbach.
47. Testimony of Ljerka Magdić.
48. NAZ, NDS group 7005, 9141/1941.
49. NAZ, NDS group 7466, 10072/1941.
50. NAZ, NDS group 7466, 10072/1941; testimony of Vlasta Urbić, née Deutsch-Maceljski.
51. HDA Collection ZKRZ GUZ, no. 306, box 11, 1048–1095.

52. NAZ, NDS group 4647–4657/1941.

53. NAZ, NDS group 3558, 3620, 3851, 4097, 4345, 4435, 4584/1941.

54. NAZ, NDS group 6634/1941.

55. NAZ, NDS group 1033, 2738/1942.

56. JIM, ŽOZ Collection, reg. no. 5382, sign. K-65–3-1/1–95 to 1–98, 1–132; *Popis žrtava*; *Popis žrtava Zagreb*; NAZ, NDS group 1654/1941.

57. NAZ, NDS group 190, 3802/1942; *Popis žrtava.*

58. NAZ, NDS group 3802/1942; *Spiskovi preživelih.*

59. NAZ, NDS group 5292/1942.

60. NAZ, NDS group 1043, 9274, 9805/1942.

61. NAZ, NDS group 7763/1941.

62. NAZ, NDS group 6682/1941.

63. NAZ, NDS group 9808/1942.

64. About Dockal, see HBL IV, 449.

65. NAZ, NDS group 4912/1942.

66. NAZ, NDS group to number 6693/1943; Oskar Rösler converted in July 1941—NAZ, NDS group 8722/1941.

67. NAZ, NDS group 4689/1941; *Popis žrtava*; JIM, ŽOZ Collection, reg. no. 4860, sign. K-60–5-1/1–30.

68. JIM, ŽOZ Collection, reg. no. 4860, sign. K-60–5-1/1–20 to 1–37, 1–50, 1–65, 1–66, 1–72 to 1–91, 1–98 to 1–163.

69. *Spiskovi preživelih*, 2:313–32.

70. JIM ŽOZ Collection, without reg. no.; NAZ, NDS group 7770/1945.

71. Registry office; Office of the Chief Rabbi in Zagreb.

72. JIM, ŽOZ Collection, reg. no. 5285, sign K-8a-1–2/7.

73. JIM, ŽOZ Collection, without reg. no.

74. NAZ, NDS group 5346/1941.

75. HAD, 252 Collection, RUR, J. Section, 27273.

76. *Popis žrtava*; *Kartoteka židovskog znaka.*

32. To Stay Put or Escape?

1. Shomrony, "Svjedočenja, Gdje je Freibergerova biblioteka?"

2. Testimony of Berta Israel, née Švarcenberg.

3. Testimonies of Berta Israel, née Švarcenberg, and Ljerka Magdić; *Kartoteka židovskog znaka*; *Popis žrtava.*

4. Shomrony, "Svjedočenja, Gdje je Freibergerova biblioteka?"

5. Carmon, "31. svibnja 1941."

6. Testimony of Drago Baum.

7. Testimony of Drago Baum, Albert's son and Geza's relative; testimony of Ljerka Magdić; testimony of Branko Polić and Dr. Lea Prašek, née Neufeld; *Popis žrtava;* JIM, Collection ŽOZ, sign. K-66–2-1/1. In Pavelić's detailed biography (Stuparić, *Tko je tko u NDH*, 306–10.) there is no mention of Geza Frank, only that Pavelić had been a junior clerk in Aleksandar Horvat's law office. It seems that Pavelić wanted to do all he could to cover up the fact that he had trained with a Jewish attorney.

8. Shomrony, "Svjedočenja, Gdje je Freibergerova biblioteka?"
9. Romano, *Jevreji zdravstveni radnici Jugoslavije*, 93, 156.
10. JIM, Collection ŽOZ, without reg. no.; *Kartoteka židovskog znaka*; *Popis žrtava*.
11. Testimony of Vera Zoričić, née Schwabenitz; *Popis žrtava*.
12. Testimony of Berta Israel, née Švarcenberg
13. Testimony of Vlasta Urbic, née Deutsch-Maceljski.
14. HDA, Collection 252, RUR, J. Section, 27664.
15. HDA, Collection 252, RUR, J. Section, 29860; *Knjiga umrlih*; JIM, Collection ŽOZ, reg. no. 4973, sign. K-64–2-1/1–26; reg. no. 5386, sign. K-65–6-1/1–113, 1–120.
16. Testimony of Andrija Duić; Romano, *Jevreji zdravstveni radnici Jugoslavije*, 178.
17. Testimony of Vera Fischer.
18. See, Kovačić, *Kampor 1942–1943*, 281–82.
19. Testimony of Alfred Pal
20. Testimony of Vera Fischer.
21. Testimony of Professor Dr. Stjepan Steiner.
22. Testimony of Vera Fischer.
23. Berger, *44 mjeseca u Jasenovcu*, 7.
24. Testimony of Professor Dr. Stjepan Steiner.
25. *Kartoteka židovskog znaka*.
26. Testimony of Professor Dr. Stjepan Steiner.
27. Levi, "Od pisma do pisma," 100.
28. *Popis žrtava*; *Kartoteka židovskog znaka*.
29. *Bilten ŽOZ* 39–40 (1994).
30. JIM, Collection ŽOZ, reg. no. 4872, sign. K-60–7-1/1–42.
31. HDA, Collection ZKRZ GUZ, no. 306, box 15, 3732, 3817–3818.
32. Testimony of Andrija Präger.
33. *bski, Sterbebücher von Auschwitz*, 3:1151; testimony of Branko Polić.
34. Plase is a village above Hreljin on the Zagreb–Rijeka railway line, at that time the last village in the ISC (in Zone B) before the Italian border.
35. Testimony of Ljerka Magdić.
36. Ristović, *U potrazi za utočištem, Jugoslovenski Jevreji*, 300; testimony of Branko Polić.
37. Kornfein, "I u paklu."
38. Testimony of Mira Altarac-Hadži-Ristić.
39. Jakovljević, "Putevi stradanja."
40. Perić, "Daljni rezultati," 19.
41. NAZ, group NDS 2467/1943; *Popis žrtava*; *Spiskovi preživelih*.
42. NAZ, group NDS 2255, 2792/1943.
43. *Popis žrtava*; *Spiskovi preživelih*.

33. Escape

1. Ristović, *U potrazi za utočištem, Jugoslovenski Jevreji*, 105. The estimate of 12,000 is very exaggerated, but it comes slightly closer to the truth if the Jews who fled to the Italian occupation zone in the ISC are included (about 5,000).

2. For a precise map, see on the fly leaf and endleaf of Krizman, *NDH izmedu*; Matković, *Povijest Nezavisne Države Hrvatske*, 138; on the fate of Jews in the First and Second Zone, see Romano, *Jevreji Jugoslavije*, 136–44; see, also, Tomasevich, "War and Revolution in Yugoslavia," 233 and throughout.

3. HDA, Collection 252, RUR, J. Section, 28270. Whatever the number of Jews, it was very many for Crikvenica, which, according to the 1931 census, had only 3,240 inhabitants.

4. HDA, Collection 252, RUR, J. Section, 29444.

5. HDA, Collection 252, RUR, J. Section, 29452.

6. HDA, Collection 252, RUR, J. Section, 28374.

7. Ristović, *U potrazi za utočištem, Jugoslovenski Jevreji*, 119.

8. HDA, Collection 252, RUR, J. Section, 29073, 29650, 29765, 29814.

9. HDA, Collection 252, RUR, J. Section, 29453.

10. HDA, Collection General Administrative Commission in the Headquarters of the Second Corps of the Italian Army, 13426; 2761/42.

11. Ristović, *U potrazi za utočištem, Jugoslovenski Jevreji*, 105.

12. HDA, Collection ZKRZ GUZ, no. 306, box 11, 1294–1299.

13. Vidi, JIM, Collection ŽOZ, without reg. no.

14. According to the letter of their son, Robert Veith, from Jerusalem, Archive ŽOZ for 1960.

15. HDA, Collection 252, RUR, J. Section, 28102, 28111; *Popis žrtava.*

16. *Dotršcina projekt*, 21.

17. Testimony of Vlasta Urbić, née Deutsch-Maceljski.

18. HDA, Collection 223, MUP NDH, 4276/I-A, 10521.

19. Hilberg, *Destruction of the European Jews*, 715.

20. Krizman, *NDH izmedu*, 558.

21. Hilberg, *Destruction of the European Jews*, 715–16; Krizman, *NDH izmedu*, 558; for more details on the whole course of the very complicated negotiations and correspondence about the fate of the Jews in Zone B, see Hilberg, *Destruction of the European Jews*, 714–18; and Krizman, *NDH izmedu*, 557–61; see also, Carpi, "Diplomatic Negotiations," 115–24; Steinberg, *All or Nothing*, 75–77; Born, "O talijanskim grijesima"; on the attitude of the Italians to the Jews, see a rather biased opinion in Šelah, "Kako su Talijani."

22. Krizman, *NDH izmedu*, 558.

23. Documents of Slavko Goldstein.

24. Hilberg, *Destruction of the European Jews*, 716–17.

25. Krizman, *NDH izmedu*, 558–59.

26. Testimony of Đorđe Ivković.

27. Testimony of Professor Dr. Stjepan Steiner.

28. Maričić, *Luka spasa*, 38–39.

29. Testimony of Đorđe Ivković.

30. Isaić, *Put prognanih*, 32.

31. Testimony of Vera Fischer.

32. Testimony of Đorđe Ivković.

33. Maričić, *Luka spasa*, 69.

34. Romano, *Jevreji Jugoslavije*, 144–51; Kečkemet, "Židovski sabirni logori," 122–25.

35. Konforti, *Od 6. aprila 1941*, 432.

36. Kečkemet, "Židovski sabirni logori," 126; *ZAVNOH*, 3:188.

37. HDA, Collection ZKRZ GUZ, no. 306, box 15, 3666.

38. Kečkemet, "Židovski sabirni logori," 129.

39. Goldstein, "Porto Re."

40. Romano, *Jevreji Jugoslavije*, 142.

41. HDA, Collection ZKRZ GUZ, no. 306, box 11, 1038–1095.

42. Polić, "Logor Kraljevica."

43. Polić, "Logor Kraljevica"; in July 1941, Vranić and his son, Mladen, converted from the Lutheran to the Catholic faith—NAZ, group NDS 10263/1941.

44. Testimony of Branko Polić.

45. HDA, Collection ZKRZ GUZ, no. 306, box 11, 1038–1095; Romano, *Jevreji Jugoslavije*, 145–47, 186; Ristović, *U potrazi za utočištem, Jugoslovenski Jevreji*, 125.

46. Goldstein, "Porto Re"; see also, Jurak, "Uspomene iz logora."

47. NAZ, Collection Caritas of the Zagreb Archbishopric 347/1943.

48. HDA, Collection ZKRZ GUZ, no. 306, box 11, 1038–1095; Romano, *Jevreji Jugoslavije*, 145–47, 186; Ristović, *U potrazi za utočištem, Jugoslovenski Jevreji*, 125.

49. HDA, Collection ZKRZ GUZ, no. 306, box 10, 121.

50. Testimony of Alfred Pal.

51. Testimony of Branko Polić.

52. HDA, Collection MUP SRH, 013.0.65, Part III, 229.

53. HDA, Collection MUP SRH, 013.0.65, Part III, 20–23, 37, 229, 256, 269, 306, 307, 309.

54. HDA, Collection MUP SRH, 013.0.65, Part III, 71, 72, 282, 283.

55. Testimony of Alfred Pal.

56. Kovačić, *Kampor 1942–1943*, 281–82.

57. Kovačić, *Kampor 1942–1943*, 281–82.

58. Isaić, *Put prognanih*, 64.

59. Testimony of Branko Polić.

60. Testimony of Branko Polić.

61. Kovačić, *Kampor 1942–1943*, 285–86.

62. Testimony of Vera Fischer.

63. Isaić, *Put prognanih*, 64–65.

64. Piliš, "Proljetna uvertira"; see also the photograph in *Bilten ŽOZ* 28–29 (1992).

65. HDA, Collection ZKRZ GUZ, no. 306, box 11, 1229–1256; Romano, *Jevreji Jugoslavije*, 149–51; Lengel-Krizman, *Koncentracioni logori*, 269–81; Kovačić, *Kampor 1942–1943*, 286.

66. Romano, *Jevreji u logoru na Rabu*; Knez, "Rab rujna 1943."

67. In greater detail on this subject, see Lengel-Krizman, "Sudbina."

68. Testimony of Vera Zoričić, née Schwabenitz.

69. Testimony of Ivan Pajalica from Baška on Krk, author's archives

70. Testimony of Branko Polić, from the statement of Ana Reich in 1945.

71. Lengel-Krizman, "Sudbina"; Romano, *Jevreji Jugoslavije*, 151; Magašić, "Iz logora"; Romano, *Jevreji u logoru na Rabu*; Kovačić, *Kampor 1942–1943*, 334 and throughout; Šelah, *Sudbina izbjeglica.*

72. Šelah, *Sudbina izbeglica*; Romano, *Jevreji Jugoslavije*, 283–85.

73. In more detail in Isaić, *Desant.*

74. Kovačić, *Kampor 1942–1943*, 337–39; Isaić, "Časno djelo"; testimony of Branko Polić.

75. HDA, Collection ZKRZ GUZ, no. 306, box 11, 1238–1253; Kovačić, *Kampor 1942–1943*, 336–37; Lengel-Krizman, "Sudbina."

76. Testimony of Branko Polić; *Spiskovi preživelih* (they give the three people mentioned, but not Mira Wollner); Lucy wrote the book *Mit meinen Augen: Botschaft einer Auschwitz Überlebenden* (Gerlingen 1983).

77. Miletić, *Koncentracioni logor Jasenovac*, 3:600–606.

78. Ristović, *U potrazi za utočištem, Jugoslovenski Jevreji*, 91. The statistics that Ristović took from Folino, *Ferramonti,* vol. 9 (an edition that was inaccessible to me) are doubtful. They state that fifty-six Jews were born in Ljubljana, eleven in Pula, six in Šibenik, twenty-two in Split, eighteen in Sušak, and thirteen in Vodice. This probably was neither their place of birth nor their place of permanent residence, as there were no Jews in Vodice and in Šibenik before the war, and there was no major Jewish community in any of the other places mentioned (except for Split). It is more likely that the statistics show the place of last residence, which means that those 126 Jews from six towns probably included some from Zagreb.

79. Levi, "Povodom 30-godišnjice oslobođenja–poslednji dani Feramontija."

80. Ristović, *U potrazi za utočištem, Jugoslovenski Jevreji*, 99; *Popis žrtava*; *Kartoteka židovskog znaka*; *Spiskovi preživelih*; testimony of Vlasta Urbić, née Deutsch-Maceljski.

81. Testimony of Pavel (Meir) Deutsch.

82. Bonardi, *Propaganda antiebraica*, in various places.

83. Konforti, *Od 6. aprila 1941,* 432–34.

84. Minutes from the Twenty-Seventh Meeting of the Executive Committee SVJOJ of 21.11.1940, JIM, Belgrade, 103.

85. In more detail, Itai-Indik, "Djeca"; Ristović, *U potrazi za utočištem, Jugoslovenski Jevreji*, 141, 328–30; *Ha-kol* 57–58 (1999); HDA, Collection 252, RUR, J. Section, 27266; Voigt, *Villa Emma.*

86. JIM, Collection ŽOZ, without reg. no. and sign.

87. Itai-Indik, "Djeca," 132; Ristović, *U potrazi za utočištem, Jugoslovenski Jevreji*, 176, 180, 182, 183, 237, 267, 288–89, 329, 330; extensively, Piccinini and Voigt, *I ragazzi ebrei.*

88. *Bilten ŽOZ* 37 (1994); JIM, Collection ŽOZ, reg. no. 4853, sign. K-62–1-1/1–77; testimony of Dr Lea Prašek, née Neufeld.

89. JIM, Collection ŽOZ, without reg. no. and sign; *Popis žrtava.*

90. Ristović, *U potrazi za utočištem, Jugoslovenski Jevreji*, 193, 197, 205; testimony of Mia Bernfest-Roth.

91. Ristović, *U potrazi za utočištem, Jugoslovenski Jevreji*, 261–263; HDA, Collection 252, RUR, J. Section, 28885.

92. Testimony of Branko Polić.

93. HDA, Collection ZKRZ GUZ, no. 306, box 10, 91.

94. See photograph in JP 7–8 (1976); Kadelburg, "Šta je značilo jevrejsko opredeljivanje."

95. JIM, Collection ŽOZ, reg. no. 5386, sign. K-65–6-1/1–55, 1–75; see also other letters, the same, 1–171, 1–179, 1–200, 1–211; and letters in German—JIM, Collection ŽOZ, without reg. no.

96. JIM, Collection ŽOZ, reg. no. 5386, sign. K-65–6-1/1–237; JIM, Collection ŽOZ, without reg. no.

97. Kadelburg, "Šta je značilo jevrejsko opredeljivanje."

98. JP 5–6 (1976).

99. Lebl, *Jevreji iz Jugoslavije*, 70–91; *Spiskovi preživelih*; testimony of Branko Polić.

100. Kočić, *Jugosloveni u koncentracionom logoru Buhenvald*, 199–258; Novak, *Buchenwald*, 165–79; Romano, *Jevreji zdravstveni radnici Jugoslavije*, 184; *Jutarnji list* (Zagreb), November 10, 2001; *Kartoteka židovskog znaka*; *Popis žrtava*; testimony of Professor Dr. Mirjana Gross; testimony of Mirko Mirković.

101. Testimony of Mirko Mirković.

102. HDA, Collection ZKRZ GUZ, no. 306, box 11, 1288–1321.

103. Testimonies of Branko Polić and Professor Dr. Zdenko Šternberg.

104. Testimony of Boris Braun.

105. Testimony of Boris Braun.

106. Testimony of Ljerka Magdić.

34. Joining the Partisans

1. See list in Romano, *Jevreji Jugoslavije*, 229–30.

2. Testimony of Vera Zoričić, née Schwabenitz.

3. Romano, *Jevreji Jugoslavije*, 277.

4. Dedijer, *Dnevnik*, 1:22.

5. HDA, Collection 252, RUR, J. Section, 27754.

6. JIM, Collection ŽOZ, reg. no. 4866, sign. K-66–1-1/1–67.

7. In more detail in Pavlović, "Narodni heroj Josip Engl."

8. HDA, Collection 252, RUR, J. Section, 28173, has a list of Jews in suburban settlements, with the remark beside the name of Stjepan Engel that he had "illegally traveled to Italy." This, of course, was not correct. Some sources say that the oldest brother, Đuro (1905), was also killed, but he had changed his surname to Pavlović earlier, and survived the war. He lived in Vela Luka for a time in 1941–1942; Maričić, *Luka spasa*, 46; *Spiskovi preživelih*, 290.

9. JP 9–10 (1966); 9–10 (1971); 9–10 (1984); Romano, *Jevreji Jugoslavije*, 228.

10. *Bilten ŽOZ* 6–7 (1988); JP 5–6 (1977); Švob, "Dr. Pavao Wertheim."

11. Romano, *Jevreji Jugoslavije*, 227.

12. Ivanc, *Nepokorena mladost*, 154–55, 164.

13. Đurić, "Naš komandant Vojko Hohšteter."

14. Romano, *Jevreji Jugoslavije*, 228.

15. Romano, *Jevreji Jugoslavije*, 357.

16. Romano, *Jevreji Jugoslavije*, 278.

17. Testimony of Professor Dr. Stjepan Steiner; *Popis žrtava.*

18. Romano, *Jevreji Jugoslavije*, 281.

19. Romano, *Jevreji Jugoslavije*, 205–6.

20. Testimony of Professor Dr. Stjepan Steiner.

21. Goldstein, "Židovi Hrvatske u antifašističkom otporu," 150.

22. Gizdić, *Dalmacija 1941*, 279.

23. Goldstein, "Židovi Hrvatske u antifašističkom otporu," 153.

24. Goldstein, "Židovi Hrvatske u antifašističkom otporu," 151–52.

25. Romano, *Jevreji Jugoslavije*, 282–284.

26. Kovačević, *Pod otvorenim nebom*, 408–9, and in other places; JP 3–4 (1986).

27. Lebl, "Četvrt veka od formiranja rapskog bataljona."

28. According to reports of the ZAVNOH Social Welfare Department from March and April 1944—*ZAVNOH*, 2:238, 529, 654.

29. *ZAVNOH*, 2:654.

30. *ZAVNOH*, 2:529.

31. *ZAVNOH*, 2:529.

32. Testimonies of Branko Polić and Slavko Goldstein.

33 *ZAVNOH*, 2:529.

34. *ZAVNOH*, 3:188, 248; Romano, *Jevreji zdravstveni radnici Jugoslavije*, 179.

35. *ZAVNOH*, 2:389–90; Romano, *Jevreji Jugoslavije*, 389.

36. JIM, Collection ŽOZ, reg. no. 4863, sign. K-62–5-1/1–276.

37. JIM, Collection ŽOZ, without reg. no. Branko Polić claims there were many more Jews in Glina, but there are no data about this.

38. Testimony of Mira Altarac-Hađiristić.

39. Romano, *Jevreji Jugoslavije*, 269–71, 284–85.

40. Goldstein, "Porto Re."

41. Testimony of Branko Polić.

42. Testimonies of Alfred Pal and Branko Polić. See also: Isaić, *Put prognanih,* 88. Witnesses found some grounds for accusations about "spying for" or "collaborating with" the Italians in the fact that the Partisans found many passes in Helga's name in the Italian administration offices after they entered Crikvenica in September 1943. However, if she really was guilty, why did they wait three or four months from September until the end of the year to accuse her? Alfred Pal proved that the accusations of "whoring" were completely groundless, stating that Dr. Eugen Miškolci did an autopsy on Helga Heim and established her to be "*virgo intacta*"; HDA, Collection 252, RUR, J. Section, *Kazalo,* 3295.

43. Testimony of Professor Dr. Stjepan Steiner; testimony of Lea Prašek, née Neufeld; Levental, *Sećanje;* of the four Partisan victims mentioned, only Helga Heim and Slavko Hirschl-Herak appear in *Popis žrtava*—under the heading *Crime Perpetrators*, it says "unknown."

44. Testimony of Slavko Goldstein, who learned in detail from the three members of the Supreme Command mentioned above about the relationships among the leaders of the NOV and KPJ.

45. Testimony of Alfred Pal; Šalić, *Židovi u Vinkovcima*, 67–68; *Bilten ŽOZ* 31–32 (1993).

46. Testimony of Branko Polić; Romano, *Jevreji zdravstveni radnici Jugoslavije*, 179.

47. Holjevac, *Zapisi*, 120–21, 232–33; Romano, *Jevreji Jugoslavije*, 506.

48. HDA, OZNA 30/50; on Dr. Julius, see Romano, *Jevreji zdravstveni radnici Jugoslavije*, 183.

49. HDA, OZNA 30/50. During the war, the Partisans merely criticized Dr. Julius, but the insinuations were renewed several years after the war, which led to his suicide.

50. HDA, OZNA 30/49.

51. HDA, OZNA 34/45; there is no information about anyone called Zina Pengov.

52. In Broz, *Sabrana djela*, 2, 324, it says only that "Breyer did not return from the Partisans"; compare also Sobolevski, *Bombaški proces Josipu Brozu*, 60 and throughout; Broz, *Sabrana djela*, 4, 97, 342; testimonies of Vera Zoričić, née Schwabenitz, and Slavko Goldstein.

53. Romano, *Jevreji zdravstveni radnici Jugoslavije*, 184; testimony of Mirko Mirković.

54. HDA, OZNA; there is no village called Rumljani in Croatia; the only similar name is Rimljani near Crikvenica, but there were no Jews there before the war.

55. *Dotrščina projekt*, HDA.

56. Testimony of Mira Altarac-Hađiristić.

35. The Languishing of the Remaining Jews

1. HDA, Collection MUP SRH, 013.0.65, Part III, 61, 278.

2. HDA, Collection MUP SRH, 013.0.65, Part III, 122, 318, 322; Gustović (1909), a lawyer, was sentenced to twenty years of prison in 1946 and released in 1951, see HDA, Collection MUP NDH, folder SDS no. 321308.

3. HDA, Collection ZKRZ GUZ, no. 306, box 10, 405.

4. Krišto, *Katolička crkva*, 2:348–49; *Popis žrtava.*

5. *Dotrščina projekt*, HDA, 26.

6. See chapter 24.

7. Testimony of Branko Polić; also about Sidonija Geiger in *HBL* 4, 634–35.

8. *Dotrščina projekt*, HDA, 26.

9. *Dotrščina projekt*, HDA, 26.

10. Testimony of Ljerka Magdić.

11. *Dotrščina projekt*, HDA, 23; testimony of Vera Zoričić, née Schwabenitz.

12. *Dotrščina projekt*, HDA, 23; testimony of Berta Israel, née Švarcenberg.

13. *Dotrščina projekt*, HDA, 24.

14. NAZ, group NDS 5106/1944; *Popis žrtava*; *Kartoteka židovskog znaka.*

15. HDA, Collection ZKRZ GUZ, no. 306, box 15, 3732, 3761.

16. Fuchs and Hafner paid the Community dues at the beginning of 1943; JIM, Collection ŽOZ, without reg. no.; *Popis žrtava*; *Dotrščina projekt*, HDA, 27; *Odmazde* 28 (1944); *Odmazde* 29 (1945).

17. Testimony of Aleksandar Tolnauer.

18. Brdovečko Prigorje Registry Office (near Zaprešić), Register of Deaths 1917–

1947, p. 148; see Ivić, "NOB na području općine Zaprešić," 129; testimonies of Viktorija Kocijan, Franjo Kocijan, and Drago Jančić.

19. See also HDA, Collection MUP SRH, 013.0.65, Part III, 343–345, 347–350.

20. HDA, Collection MUP SRH, 013.0.65, Part III, 48, 276.

21. HDA, Collection MUP SRH, 013.0.65, Part III, 48, 276.

22. HDA, Collection MUP SRH, 013.0.65, Part III, 176, 344.

23. HDA, Collection MUP SRH, 013.0.65, Part III, 276.

24. HDA, Collection MUP SRH, 013.0.65, Part III, 81–86,

25. HDA, Collection MUP SRH, 013.0.65, Part III, 81–86; *Kartoteka židovskog znaka*; *Filekovi preživelih.*

26. Testimony of Mila Kniewald-Mirković.

27. See, Krišto, *Katolička crkva*, 2:304; *Kartoteka židovskog znaka*; *Popis žrtava.*

28. HDA, Collection MUP SRH, 013.0.65, Part III, 79, 294.

29. HDA, Collection MUP SRH, 013.0.65, Part III, 80, 295.

30. HDA, Collection MUP SRH, 013.0.65, Part III, 92–95, 297–301; testimony of Branko Polić; National Archives, Washington D. C., declassified, Authority NND 007006.

31. Testimony of Professor Dr. Stjepan Steiner.

32. HDA, Collection MUP SRH, 013.0.65, Part III, 108–110, 312.

33. HDA, Collection MUP SRH, 013.0.65, Part III, 323.

34. HDA, Collection MUP SRH, 013.0.65, Part III, 157–160, 340–342; *Knjiga pokojnih* od 1955 (5715); Archive ŽOZ.

35. HDA, Collection MUP SRH, 013.0.65, Part III, 176, 344.

36. HDA, Collection MUP SRH, 013.0.65, Part III, 362.

37. HDA, Collection MUP SRH, 013.0.65, Part III, 343–345, 347–350.

38. HDA, Collection MUP SRH, 013.0.65, Part III, 180, 181, 347.

39. HDA, Collection MUP SRH, 013.0.65, Part III, 186–187, 348–350; *Spiskovi preživelih.*

40. JIM, Collection ŽOZ, reg. no. 5382, sign. K-65-3-1/1–62 to 1–65.

41. JIM, Collection ŽOZ, reg. no. 5382, sign. K-65–3-1/1–1.

42. NAZ, group NDS 8922/1941.

43. JIM, Collection ŽOZ, reg. no. 5382, sign. K-65–3-1/1–90, 1–91.

44. NAZ, group NDS 5927/1943.

45. JIM, Collection ŽOZ, reg. no. 5382, sign. K-65–3-1/1–62 to 1–78, 1–79.

46. JIM, Collection ŽOZ, reg. no. 5382, sign. K-65–3-1/1–3 to 1–6.

47. JIM, Collection ŽOZ, sign. K-67–1-1/1–262 to 1–264, 1–267 to 1–269, 1–271 to 1–276, 1–280 to 1/282, 1–285.

48. HDA, Collection ZKRZ GUZ, no. 306, box 10, 89, box 15, 3879.

49. After the war Korda lived in Rijeka—Korda, "Nikad dosta suza," 36; Korda, "Povratak iz Jasenovca," 47–48.

50. HDA, Collection ZKRZ GUZ, no. 306, box 10, 93.

51. JIM, Collection ŽOZ, reg. no. 5993, sign. K-62–6-1/1–270.

52. Prašek-Całczyńska, *Memoari*, 146–47.

53. JIM, Collection ŽOZ, without reg. no.; testimony of Alfi Kabiljo in *Obitelj*, edited by J. Domaš-Nalbantić, 150–53.

54. HDA, Collection 487, Ministry of the Armed Forces ISC, Department II, no. 1814/41, January 22, 1942.

55. HDA, Collection Courts of the Armed Forces ISC, Ukp. 2/43–1. HDA, Collection 252, RUR, J. Section, 27546, 29851; *Kartoteka židovskog znaka*; *Imenik Ponove*; *Knjiga kontribucije*; *Jevrejska tribuna* 45 (1938).

56. HDA, Collection ZKRZ GUZ, no. 306, box 15, 3874.

57. JIM, Collection ŽOZ, sign. K-67–1-1/1–223.

58. Krišto, "Katolička crkva i Židovi"; Krišto, *Katolička crkva*, 2:283–84.

59. About the Kišicky brothers, Oskar-Ašer and Norbert, both of whom survived the war, see Agmon, M. "Ličnosti iz naših desetkovanih općina." The third brother, Žiga, a dentist, was killed by the Chetniks in 1944 near Mrkonjić-Grad (in Bosnia), and his son, Cvi, was killed in Auschwitz; see *Popis žrtava.*

60. HDA, Collection: NDH, inv. no. 25109; HDA, Collection ZKRZ GUZ, no. 306, box 10, 89, box 15, 3876, 3877.

61. HDA, Collection ZKRZ GUZ, no. 306, box 10, 92.

62. JIM, Collection ŽOZ, sign. K-65–4-1/1–242.

63. JIM, Collection ŽOZ, reg. no. 5386, sign. K-65–6-1/1–235.

64. JIM, Collection ŽOZ, reg. no. 5386, sign. K-65–6-1/1–262, 1–263, 1–265 to 1–268, 1–275 to 1–279, 1–305.

65. JIM, Collection ŽOZ, reg. no. 5386, sign. K-65–6-1/1–309.

66. JIM, Collection ŽOZ, reg. no. 5993, sign. K-62–6-1/1–210, 1–212.

67. JIM, Collection ŽOZ, reg. no. 5993, sign. K-62–6-1/1–221.

68. JIM, Collection ŽOZ, without reg. no.

69. JIM, Collection ŽOZ, reg. no. 5386, sign. K-65–6-1/1–250, 1–294.

70. JIM, Collection ŽOZ, reg. no. 5386, sign. K-65–6-1/1–325.

71. JIM, Collection ŽOZ, reg. no. 5382, sign. K-65–3-1/1–34.

72. HDA, Collection MUP SRH, 013.0.65, Part III, 277, 278.

73. JIM, Collection ŽOZ, reg. no. 4855, sign. K-60–1-2/1–11, 1–19.

74. Ristović, *U potrazi za utočištem, Jugoslovenski Jevreji*, 80.

75. *Spomenica Saveza jevrejskih opština Jugoslavije 1919–1969*, 89.

76. JIM, Collection ŽOZ, sign. K-65–4-1/1–206.

77. JIM, Collection ŽOZ, reg. no. 5381, sign. K-66–5-1/1–26, 1–27, 1–53, 1–55; reg. no. 5386, sign. K-65–6-1/1–336 to 1–340.

78. JIM, Collection ŽOZ, reg. no. 5381, sign. K-66–5-1/1–9, 1–16.

79. *Kartoteka jasenovačkih zatočenika.*

80. JIM, Collection ŽOZ, sign. K-65–4-1/1–79 to 1–82, 1–91, 1–133, 1–179, 1–209.

81. *Kartoteka jasenovačkih zatočenika.*

82. JIM, Collection ŽOZ, reg. no. 4864, sign. K-63–1-1/1–249; the Friedländers lived in Vinkovci until 1941; from there, they were deported to Jasenovac, and then to Lepoglava.

83. Testimony of Vera Fischer.

84. NAZ, group NDS 9417/1944.

85. *Ustaša, Dokumenti*, 321–23.

86. *Enciklopedija Jugoslavije*, 6:498–99.

87. Miletić, *Miletić, Koncentracioni logor Jasenovac*, 1:434.

88. AHA, 153; it is not known when this poster was made, but the context shows that Tito's Partisans were already in Belgrade, and that Hebrang was "minister" and no longer Secretary of the Central Committee KPH, which dates it after October 1944.

89. *Hrvatski radnik* 25 (Zagreb), June 29, 1944.

90. Ristović, *U potrazi za utočištem, Jugoslovenski Jevreji*, 188; HDA, Collection ZKRZ GUZ, no. 306, box 10, 94–95; *Dotrščina projekt*, HDA, 28. Sources and literature from the days of Communism gave the impression that Gaon and Katan were in fact very active Communists, that they had "organized Communist groups and cells in Bosnia, Herzegovina, Dalmatia, Lika, Zagorje, and Posavina . . . and groups of saboteurs," etc. It seems that this was not true; about erecting a monument to Gaon and Katan, among others, see JIM, Collection ŽOZ, reg. no. 4863, sign. K-62–5-1/1–309, 1–317; JIM, Collection ŽOZ, without reg. no.

91. *Dotrščina projekt*, HDA, 27, 28, 29.

92. JIM, Collection ŽOZ, without reg. no. and sign.

93. HDA, Collection Ustasha Army, Reports Department, 853; there is no Adolf Binenfeld in *Kartotekai židovskog znaka*; he cannot be found in the book *Istupi iz židovstva 1941*, Archive *ŽOZ* either, nor in *Spiskovi preživelih*. It is possible that Barica Bulić was wrong about the name, that it was not Adolf; about Tomić, see Stuparić, *Tko je tko u NDH*, 401; about Bzik, see Stuparić, *Tko je tko u NDH*, 62–63.

94. *Ustaša, Dokumenti*, 341–43.

95. HDA, Collection 218, MPB NDH, Department of Justice, box 417, VI 8/1945.

96. *Narodne novine* 135, May 5, 1945; about this, see Jelić-Butić, *Ustaše i NDH*, 304.

97. Horvat, *Preživjeti u Zagrebu*, 227.

36. The Old People's Home

1. HDA, Collection ZKRZ GUZ, no. 306, box 10, 313, 542; Savez jevrejskih opština Jugoslavije, *Spomenica povodom pedesetogodišnjice Doma staraca Saveza jevrejskih opština Jugoslavije*, 13; *Zapisnici 1941*, Archive ŽOZ.

2. Novak, "Povijest Doma Zaklade Lavoslav Schwarz," 75; *Zapisnici 1941*, Archive ŽOZ.

3. JIM, Collection ŽOZ, without reg. no.

4. HDA, Collection ZKRZ GUZ, no. 306, box 15, 3876, box 16, 4477–4480.

5. JIM, Collection ŽOZ, sign. K-65–4-1/1–185.

6. JIM, Collection ŽOZ, sign. K-65–4-1/1–187, 1–192–1-195, 1–200, 1–203, 1–204, 1–225, 1–230, 1–237.

7. JIM, Collection ŽOZ, without reg. no.

8. JIM, Collection ŽOZ, sign. K-65–4-1/1–57 to 1–59, 1–61 to 1–66; JIM, Collection ŽOZ, reg. no. 5386, sign. K-65–6-1/1–105, 1–107 to 1–109.

9. JIM, Collection ŽOZ, sign. K-65–4-1/1–60; JIM, Collection ŽOZ, reg. no. 5386, sign. K-65–6-1/1–106; JIM, Collection ŽOZ, without reg. no.

10. JIM, Collection ŽOZ, without reg. no.

11. JIM, Collection ŽOZ, without reg. no.

12. JIM, Collection ŽOZ, reg. no. 5382, sign. K-65–3-1/1–70.

13. JIM, Collection ŽOZ, without reg. no.

14. JIM, Collection ŽOZ, without reg. no.

15. JIM, Collection ŽOZ, without reg. no.

16. JIM, Collection ŽOZ, without reg. no.

17. JIM, Collection ŽOZ, without reg. no.; *Popis žrtava*; testimony of Vera Fischer.

18. JIM, Collection ŽOZ, sign. K-65–4-1/1–30 to 1–33, 1–44 to 1–47, 1–49 to 1–55, 1–71 to 1–77; JIM, Collection ŽOZ, reg. no. 5386, sign. K-65–6-1/1–67, 1–95 to 1–103, 1–118; see also JIM, Collection ŽOZ, without reg. no.

19. JIM, Collection ŽOZ, without reg. no.

20. JIM, Collection ŽOZ, K-65–4-1/1–1 to 1–5.

21. JIM, Collection ŽOZ, reg. no. 5386, sign. K-65–6-1/1–124.

22. JIM, Collection ŽOZ, without reg. no.

23. JIM, Collection ŽOZ, reg. no. 5386, sign. K-65–6-1/1–73, 1–74.

24. Testimony of Vera Fischer.

25. JIM, Collection ŽOZ, without reg. no.

26. JIM, Collection ŽOZ, without reg. no.

27. JIM, Collection ŽOZ, sign. K-65–4-1/1–173, 1–174, 1–180, 1–203, 1–207, 1–225, 1–226; JIM, Collection ŽOZ, without reg. no.

28. JIM, Collection ŽOZ, sign. K-65–4-1/1–251.

29. HDA, Collection ZKRZ GUZ, no. 306, box 10, 91, 151.

30. HDA, Collection ZKRZ GUZ, no. 306, box 15, 3876. This report claimed that it was the SS that had "its eye on these buildings."

31. Benigar, *Alojzije Stepinac*, 395, incorrectly claimed that Stepinac, "when the German troops came to Zagreb in 1941, placed old and ill Jews under his personal protection and accommodated them in the small house at his summer villa in Brezovica, where they could live in peace." Benigar was not the only one to falsify these facts: Shomrony himself, in a paper at a symposium in 2001, gave a confusing report and maintained that the Archbishop "very quickly after the first anti-Jewish measures took in on his estate, at his own expense, old people who had been thrown into the street from the home in Maksimirska"—Shomrony, *Symposium Paper.* Shomrony's story about how the Ustasha authorities had tried to arrest him in May 1943, at the behest of Eugen Dido Kvaternik, shows that he can no longer be regarded as a valid source, because, after the fall of 1942, Kvaternik was no longer in power.

32. HDA, Collection ZKRZ GUZ, no. 306, box 10, 91, 151, box 15, 3876, i.e., the report about the work of the Jewish Community 1941–1945, says that the "Archbishop showed a lot of understanding for our troubles"; see also, Novak, "Povijest Doma Zaklade Lavoslav Schwarz," 75–76.

33. JIM, Collection ŽOZ, reg. no. 4865, sign. K-63–2-1/1–178.

34. Savez jevrejskih opština Jugoslavije, *Spomenica povodom pedesetogodišnjice Doma staraca Saveza jevrejskih opština Jugoslavije*, 14. In accordance with the adopted policy at that time, *Spomenica* does not mention Archbishop Stepinac at all, but, unlike the State Commission documents, which incorrectly (perhaps by mistake?) claim that this took place at the end of 1944, gives the exact date when the old people were relocated to Brezovica.

35. JIM, Collection ŽOZ, sign. K-65–4-1/1–249.

37. The Catholic Church, Archbishop Stepinac, and the Jews

1. Goldstein, "Beatifikacija kardinala Alojzija Stepinca."

2. So much has been written by now about the Catholic Church in the ISC, and especially about its relation to the crimes, that it has become almost overwhelming—compare, Strčić, "Jasenovac i ratni zločin," 39, 78–79.

3. Shirer, *Rise and Fall of the Third Reich*, 235.

4. Passelecq and Suchecky, *L'Encyclique cachée de Pie XI.*

5. Among major books, see, for example, Cornwell, *Hitler's Pope.*

6. Shirer, *Rise and Fall of the Third Reich*, 561.

7. Shirer, *Rise and Fall of the Third Reich*, 747.

8. Hilberg, *Destruction of the European Jews*, 1019.

9. Hilberg, *Destruction of the European Jews*, 672–73.

10. Jelić-Butić, *Ustaše i NDH*, 214.

11. NAZ, Collection Prezidijalni spisi 40/1941.

12. NAZ, Collection Prezidijalni spisi 59/1941; *Hrvatski glas*, May 1, 1941; Krišto, *Katolička crkva*, 2:34–35.

13. *Katolički list* 21–22 (1941): 245.

14. Although these words referred to a specific case, they are a good illustration of the Archbishop's general attitude toward the irregularities and crimes that were taking place—Krišto, *Katolička crkva*, 2:115.

15. *Katolički list* 17 (1941): 206; 21–22 (1941): 259; 33 (1941): 391; 37 (1941): 438. The church circles were in fact right—the "Marriages" column in Zagreb's *Jutarnji list* was full of offers placed by Jewish men and women, or offers to Jewish men and women. For example, on 27 November 1938 there were 15 such offers out of a total of 133, or more than 11 percent. Probably some other Jews also placed the ads but they did not write they were Jewish, which indicates that there were more than 11 percent Jewish men and women in this practice. One of the reasons was that the middle class, which sent ads to the "marriages" column, had a higher percentage of Jews, and that Jews were perceived as rich: "genius student, Roman Catholic, seeks for a Jewish woman who can help me financially, for which I offer a fixed guarantee, a sure livelihood and marriage."

16. Krišto, *Katolička crkva*, 2:269.

17. On this matter, see, for more detail, Petešić, *Katoličko svečenstvo*, 274–76.

18. NAZ, Collection Prezidijalni spisi 135/1941; *Katolički list* 34 (1941); 1 (1943); Ivančan, *Lončar,* 1175; Kožul, *Spomenica žrtvama ljubavi zagrebačke nadbiskupije*, 335–37; Maček, *Memoari*, 160.

19. Ciliga, *Sam kroz Europu u ratu*, 323. One must remember that Ciliga's claims should always be taken with some skepticism. Publicist and politician Ante Ciliga (1898–1992) lived in the USSR for ten years and was a Trotsky sympathizer, then he was a prisoner in Jasenovac, and after that contributed to Ustasha newspapers. He wrote the memoir *Sam kroz Europu u ratu 1939–1945*. In professional circles, he is known as a "writer of fables." He writes well, in places has a good literary style, but his lively imagination too often leads him to write falsehoods, usually of the kind that

justify some of his problematic actions or that show him as far-sighted, brave, and above all as extremely well informed in any situation. About this, and about Ciliga's attitude toward the Jews, see 530–33 in this book.

20. Stuparić, *Tko je tko u NDH*, 114–15. Goldhagen, *Moral Reckoning*, 87, wrongly says that "Pius XII neither reproached nor punished him or the other Croatian priest/executioners during or after the war."

21. Goldhagen, *Moral Reckoning*, 87, claims, based on the text of Shelah, *Catholic Church in Croatia*, 269; that "dozens, perhaps even hundreds of priests and monks shed their priestly apparel and donned Ustasha uniforms, in order to share in the 'sacred work' of murder, rape, and robbery." This quotation of Shelah is not only one-sided, it is untrue: of church people, only Filipović-Majstorović it is known to have directly engaged in killing, but he was ousted from the Franciscan Order. Some other priests and monks are also known to have donned Ustasha uniforms, but there is no proof that they directly took part in mass crimes.

22. Pandžić, *Životopis Dr. fra Dominika Mandića*, 80.

23. Pandžić, *Životopis Dr. fra Dominika Mandića*, 81–83.

24. The Križari (Crusaders) was the colloquial name for the Croatian Catholic Movement, whose foundations were laid at the beginning of the twentieth century on the model of similar movements in Europe (for example, the German Katolischer Verein). They championed the establishment of social relations based on Christian values. Their opponents, mostly liberals, later also the Communists, considered them extremely conservative and called them clerical.

25. *Katolički tjednik* 21–43 (1941).

26. *Katolički tjednik* 20 (1941).

27. *Katolički tjednik* 21 (1941).

28. *Katolički tjednik* 24 (1941).

29. *Katolički tjednik* 24 (1941).

30. *Katolički tjednik* 27 (1941).

31. *Glasnik sv. Ante* 7–8 (1942): 240.

32. Krišto, *Katolička crkva*, 2:34; HDA, Collection Ivo Politeo 416, 222.

33. Krišto, *Katolička crkva*, 2:50–51.

34. Krišto, *Katolička crkva*, 2:50.

35. Krišto, *Katolička crkva*, 2:34–35; Stepinac's formulation "reasons beyond our control" in the introduction to this letter is probably a phrase taken from conversations with representatives of the Ustasha authorities, who obviously tried to convince the Archbishop that the "racial laws" had to be passed because of the Germans, which was true only to a small degree.

36. Krišto, *Katolička crkva*, 2:51.

37. Krišto, *Katolička crkva*, 2:160.

38. HDA, Collection ZKRZ GUZ, no. 306, box 10, 146, 459–460.

39. Benigar, *Alojzije Stepinac*, 405–6.

40. NAZ, Collection Prezidijalni spisi 77/1941.

41. Krišto, *Katolička crkva*, 2:140; HDA, Collection Ivo Politeo, 416, 332.

42. HDA, Collection MUP SRH, 301886. Folder S. Kvaternik, Stenographic

record from the main hearing (evidence of Mario Maričić, 319). Maričić (1898) was a civil engineer who was in the Ustasha prison, but had connections among the Ustasha authorities—HDA, Folder SDS no. 301652; Kisić-Kolanović, *Židovska imovina*, 436.

43. Krišto, *Katolička crkva*, 2:77–78; Benigar, *Alojzije Stepinac*, 406–7, quotes the same document, but its content does not lead him to critical thinking about Stepinac.

44. Krišto, *Katolička crkva*, 2:136, 140; there are some doubts about the formulations in Stepinac's letter to Maglione, because the Croatian draft and the Latin translation that was sent to the Vatican differ greatly—see in the same source, 136, note 302.

45. NAZ, Collection Prezidijalni spisi 108/1941; HDA, Collection 252, RUR, J. Section, Kazalo, 5749, 6780; *Popis žrtava*.

46. NAZ, group NDS 318/1943; *Popis žrtava*.

47. Testimony of Professor Dr. Mirjana Gross.

48. Shomrony, "Svjedočenja, Gdje je Freibergerova biblioteka?"

49. Shomrony, *Referat na simpoziju*.

50. Shomrony, "Svjedočenja, Gdje je Freibergerova biblioteka?"

51. Krišto, *Katolička crkva*, 2:110.

52. Krišto, *Katolička crkva*, 2:300.

53. Krišto, *Katolička crkva*, 2:110.

54. Hilberg, *Destruction of the European Jews*, 559–67, 586, 641–42, 672.

55. Hilberg, *Destruction of the European Jews*, 738, 753.

56. HDA, Collection ZKRZ GUZ, no. 306, box 10, 114.

57. Although several families called Hahn lived in Trešnjevka, making it impossible to know exactly which Hahn was meant, it was probably Gustav Hahn; *Kartoteka židovskog znaka*; *Popis žrtava*; *Ha-kol* 49–50.

58. Shomrony, "Svjedočenja, Gdje je Freibergerova biblioteka?"

59. Miletić, *Koncentracioni logor Jasenovac*, 1:170.

60. Krišto, *Katolička crkva*, 2:160.

61. Krišto, *Katolička crkva*, 2:224–25.

62. NAZ, Collection Prezidijalni spisi 163/1942.

63. *Ustaša, Dokumenti*, 230–31.

64. Krišto, *Katolička crkva*, 2:149–50.

65. Krišto, *Katolička crkva*, 2:255.

66. Krišto, *Katolička crkva*, 2:258.

67. Krišto, *Katolička crkva*, 2:261.

68. When he mentioned the slaughters, Bishop Čule was referring to the massacres of the Serbs committed by the Ustashe in Herzegovina, in the surroundings of Mostar.

69. NAZ, Collection Prezidijalni spisi 101/1943.

70. Krišto, *Katolička crkva*, 2:119.

71. Krišto, *Katolička crkva*, 2:268, 271–72, 299.

72. Testimony of Berta Israel, née Švarcenberg.

73. Testimony of Professor Dr. Mirjana Gross.

74. Krišto, *Katolička crkva*, 2:91.

75. JIM, Collection ŽOZ, reg. no. 4866, sign. K-66–1-1/1–40 to 1–42.

76. Thus, there is no truth to the claim in Goldhagen, *Moral Reckoning*, 87, that "Pius XII supported the country's mass-murdering regime."

77. Krišto, *Katolička crkva*, 2:281–82, 290, 303.

78. Krišto, *Katolička crkva*, 2:216, 229, 235, 254, 259, 290, 298–99.

79. Excerpts from Masucci's diary were published in Boban, *Kontroverze* 3, 302–306.

80. Masucci, *Misija*, 53; Boban, *Kontroverze*, 305–6.

81. Krišto, *Katolička crkva*, 2:209.

82. It seems that the Church, despite its powerful intercessions, was not so successful, and it is not quite true that "families from mixed marriages were spared without exception"—Krišto, *Katolička crkva*, 2:214.

83. Krišto, *Katolička crkva*, 2:214, 219, 254.

84. Krišto, *Katolička crkva*, 2:298, 300–303.

85. This was suggested by a Partisan intelligence officer in April 1945—Krišto, *Katolička crkva*, 2:370; at that time, in July 1943, the relations between the Church and the state had obviously deteriorated—UNS reported that Apostolic Visitator Marcone and his secretary Masucci "are discretely supervising the public life in Croatia . . . when it is completely clear that there is a clerical movement in Croatia, headed by Archbishop Stepinac, who, under the guise of religious work, does work that is detrimental to the Croatian state."—Krišto, *Katolička crkva*, 2:304.

86. Krišto, *Katolička crkva*, 2:319, 321–22, 349.

87. Krišto, *Katolička crkva*, 2:348–49.

88. *Popis žrtava.*

89. JIM, Collection ŽOZ, reg. no. 4970, sign. K-63–3-2/1–1, reg. no. 4864, sign. K-63–1-1/1–200.

90. NAZ, group NDS 5106/1944; *Popis žrtava*; after the war, Borić was sentenced to four years in prison, but then the sentence was increased to five years for "aiding armed bandits . . . and hindering the authorities in finding them." See HDA, Collection of Documents SDS SRH, 001.44, box 6, folder no. 300218; see also Kožul, *Spomenica žrtvama ljubavi zagrebačke nadbiskupije*, 289–92.

91. NAZ, group NDS 5081/1943.

92. JIM, Collection ŽOZ, sign. K-65–4-1/1–248.

93. Goldstein, "Beatifikacija kardinala Alojzija Stepinca."

94. See *Suđenje Lisaku, Stepincu*; Alexander, *Church and State*, 95–120.

95. This position is based on Novak's book, *Magnum Crimen*, which essentially deals with clericalism and the negative acts of the Vatican in the Church in Croatia, and in Bosnia and Herzegovina.

96. Goldstein, "Beatifikacija kardinala Alojzija Stepinca."

38. Who Is Responsible?

1. Jareb, *Pola stoljeća*, 94.

2. HDA, Collection MUP SRH, 013.0.4, Folder Dr. Ante Pavelić, study of the Ustasha Movement and of Poglavnik of the ISC, Ante Pavelić, 189–90.

3. Ante Nikšić was at that time president of the Ustasha Office in Karlovac, later

Grand Prefect of the Grand County of Pokupje and Minister of the Interior; about Nikšić, see Stuparić, *Tko je tko u NDH*, 296.

4. HDA, Collection MUP SRH, 013.0.56, V. Židovec, *Moje sudjelovanje u političkom životu*, 138. An attorney by profession, Vladimir Židovec (1907–1948) was an enterprising participant and organizer of the Ustasha movement from the late thirties; later, he was the ISC ambassador in Bulgaria and a high official in the ISC Foreign Ministry. In the opinion of several competent researchers, his political autobiography, quoted above, written in 1947 in the investigative prison in Zagreb, is probably the most valuable testimony of a prominent participant about the political dilemmas and currents within the Ustasha movement in 1941–1945; about Židovec, see Stuparić, *Tko je tko u NDH*, 435.

5. HDA, Collection MUP SRH, 013.0.56, V. Židovec, *Moje sudjelovanje u političkom životu*, 32.

6. Ljubo Miloš at the UDB interrogation in Zagreb in 1947, in Miletić, *Koncentracioni logor Jasenovac*, 2:1012.

7. Broucek, *Ein General in Zwielicht*, 165.

8. HDA, Collection MUP SRH, 013.0.4, Folder Dr. Ante Pavelić, Ustasha Movement and the Poglavnik of the ISC, Ante Pavelić, 135–136; Ante Moškov (1907–1948), from 1933 an Ustasha émigré, and for many years one of Pavelić's very close collaborators and confidants. In the ISC, he was commander of the Poglavnik's Bodyguard and other elite Ustasha units. Only at the time of the second emigration, in 1946, did he part company with Pavelić; about Moškov, see Stuparić, *Tko je tko u NDH*, 283; Hrastović, *Ante Moškov*, 127–51.

9. HDA, Collection MUP SRH, 013.0.56, V. Židovec, *Moje sudjelovanje u političkom životu*, 31, 33; see Stuparić, *Tko je tko u NDH*, 424; *Hrvatski narod*, June 30, 1941.

10. HDA, KZ 569/45—306/ZKRZ-GUZ, District Court Zagreb, box 26, Record of the interrogation of Dr. Gjuro Vranešić, 3; Boris Zarnik (1883–1945) was from 1918 to 1942 professor of biology, histology, and embryology at the Faculty of Medicine in Zagreb. He published discussions on eugenics and racial matters during the second half of the twenties, as well as the book *O rasnom sastavu evropskog pučanstva* (On the racial composition of the European population). His students in the thirties remember him as a pronounced sympathizer of German Nazism—testimonies of Professor Dr. Stjepan Steiner and Professor Dr. Mirjana Gross. He died in January 1945 in Zagreb (*Hrvatski leksikon*, 2:699.).

11. *Hrvatska gruda* 43 (1941).

12. *Novi list* 2, April 30, 1941.

13. *Hrvatski narod*, May 1, 1941; *Narodne novine*, April 30, 1941; HDA, Collection ZKRZ GUZ, no. 306, box 10, 446–8.

14. HDA, Collection MUP SRH, 013.0.52, Folder Dr. Mile Budak, interrogation record, 16.

15. HDA, Collection MUP SRH, 013.0.65, Part II, 40.

16. HDA, Collection MUP SRH, 301886, Folder S. Kvaternik, Shorthand record from the main hearing (hearing of Mario Marižić), 319; Kisić-Kolanović, *Židovska imovina*, 436.

17. HDA, Collection MUP SRH, 013.0.2, *Historijat ustaškog pokreta i NDH*, edited by S. Kvaternik and V. Košak, 266.

18. HDA, Collection MUP SRH, 013.0.52, Folder Dr. Mile Budak, from the archives of H. Helm, 64.

19. Krizman, *Ante Pavelić i ustaše*, 416.

20. See chapter 34.

21. Stuparić, *Tko je tko u NDH*, 224–25; on the omnipotence of Dido Kvaternik and Pavelić's support, see the testimony of Stjepan Vukovac, who, in April and May 1941, was assistant minister of the interior—HDA, Collection MUP RH, 013.2.4, 70 ff.

22. HDA, Collection MUP SRH, 013.0.65, 419; Hory and Broszat, *Der Kroatische Ustascha-Staat*, 71.

23. Kvaternik, *Sjećanja i zapažanja*, 192, 291; see also, Krizman, *NDH izmedu*, 331–33 and elsewhere; also, HDA, Collection MUP SRH, 013.0.2, *Historijat ustaškog pokreta i NDH*, edited by S. Kvaternik and V. Košak, 281.

24. Broucek, *Ein General in Zwielicht*, 165.

25. HDA, Collection MUP SRH, 013.0.65, Part II, 41–43; Miletić, *Koncentracioni logor Jasenovac*, 2:1012.

26. See, HDA, Collection MUP SRH, 013.0.56, V. Židovec, *Moje sudjelovanje u političkom životu*, 139.

27. See, HDA, Collection MUP SRH, 013.0.56, V. Židovec, *Moje sudjelovanje u političkom životu*, 30, 138, 139.

28. Kvaternik, *Sjećanja i zapažanja*, 144 and throughout.

29. Kvaternik, *Sjećanja i zapažanja*, 284.

30. Kvaternik, *Sjećanja i zapažanja*, 286.

31. Kvaternik, *Sjećanja i zapažanja*, 143.

32. Kvaternik, *Sjećanja i zapažanja*, 96.

33. Kvaternik, *Sjećanja i zapažanja*, 76.

34. Kvaternik, *Sjećanja i zapažanja*, 255.

35. Kvaternik, *Sjećanja i zapažanja*, 289.

36. HDA, Collection MUP SRH, 013.0.4, Folder Dr. Ante Pavelić, Ustasha Movement, and the Poglavnik of the ISC, Ante Pavelić, 136.

37. HDA, Collection MUP SRH, 013.0.56, V. Židovec, *Moje sudjelovanje u političkom životu*, 139–140.

38. HDA, Collection MUP SRH, 013.0.56, V. Židovec, *Moje sudjelovanje u političkom životu*, 139, 140; Kisić-Kolanović, *Židovska imovina*, 435; Drago Čubelić, an émigré in Rome who died in Zagreb in 1994, was secretary to Eugen Dido Kvaternik—Kvaternik, *Sjećanja i zapažanja*, 255.

39. Maček, *Memoari*, 168; Jakovljević, *Konclogor na Savi*, 57.

40. *Hrvatski narod*, February 10, 1942; Kvaternik, *Sjećanja i zapažanja*, 284.

41. HDA, MUP RH, file II/91, box 150, USIKS 337/41, 738.

42. HDA, Collection MUP SRH, 013.0.65, Part II, 49; Miletić, *Koncentracioni logor Jasenovac*, 2:1013.

43. HDA, Collection MUP SRH, 013.2.86, 2; this was Ivica Matković, Director

of the General Department, Jasenovac Camp Command (nadstojniku Opceg odjela Zapovjedništva logora u Jasenovcu)—Stuparić, *Tko je tko u NDH*, 261.

44. Žalac, "Hrvatski Blagaj," unpublished manuscript in the possession of the author, pp. 47–55; Interrogation record A. Moškov of May 20, 1947—HDA, Collection MUP SRH, 013.0.4; Folder Dr. Ante Pavelić, Ustasha Movement, and the Poglavnik of the ISC, Ante Pavelić, 52.

45. Stuparić, *Tko je tko u NDH*, 240–42.

46. HDA, Collection MUP SRH, 013.0.2, *Historijat ustaškog pokreta i NDH*, edited by S. Kvaternik and V. Košak, 309; Collection MUP SRH, 013.0.49, Part II, 151, 169; Kisić-Kolanović, *Židovska imovina*, 437. *Omertà*, Italian: an oath of silence, specifically, the pact of silence of the Mafia.

47. HDA, Collection MUP SRH, 013.0.49, Part II, 179; Kisić-Kolanović, *Židovska imovina*, 440.

48. HDA, Collection MUP SRH, 013.0.52, Folder Dr. Mile Budak, interrogation record, 16.

49. HDA, Collection MUP SRH, 013.0.52, Folder Dr. Mile Budak, interrogation record, 22.

50. See, HDA, Collection MUP SRH, 013.0.56, V. Židovec, *Moje sudjelovanje u političkom životu*, 38.

51. HDA, Collection MUP SRH, 013.0.56, V. Židovec, *Moje sudjelovanje u političkom životu*, 30.

52. See, HDA, Collection MUP SRH, 013.0.56, V. Židovec, *Moje sudjelovanje u političkom životu*, 138. See also a detailed survey of the writing of *Hrvatska revija*, which shows that this émigré magazine discussed in detail many foreign and internal policy subjects from the history of the ISC, but not the genocide of the Jews—see Bednjanec-Vuković, "Prilozi."

53. Kisić-Kolanović, *Kvaternik*, 204.

54. HDA, Collection MUP SRH, 301886, Folder S. Kvaternik. Shorthand record from the main hearing, 995; Kisić-Kolanović, *Židovska imovina*.

55. HDA, Collection MUP SRH, 301886, Folder S. Kvaternik, Shorthand record from the main hearing (hearing of Mario Marižić), 319; Kisić-Kolanović, *Židovska imovina*, 436.

56. Shirer, *Rise and Fall of the Third Reich*, 824–25.

57. Krizman, *Ante Pavelić i ustaše*, 483–91.

58. HDA, Collection MUP SRH, 013.0.52, Folder Dr. Mile Budak, from the archives of H. Helm, 75.

59. HDA, Collection MUP SRH, 013.0.2, *Historijat ustaškog pokreta i NDH*, edited by S. Kvaternik and V. Košak, 276–277; the same, 013.0.4, Folder Dr. Ante Pavelić, 1400–1404. Kvaternik, *Sjećanja i zapažanja*, in various places.

60. HDA, Reconstruction, box 1810, personal files; Collection MUP SRH, 013.0.65, Part III, 202–218.

61. HDA, Collection MUP SRH, 013.0.2, *Historijat ustaškog pokreta i NDH*, edited by S. Kvaternik and V. Košak, 277.

62. HDA, Collection MUP SRH, 013.0.65, 419.

63. HDA, Collection MUP SRH, 013.0.65, 419.

64. HDA, Collection MUP SRH, 013.0.65, 416; in this context it is not clear whether it was Blaž or Mladen Lorković.

65. HDA, Collection MUP SRH, 013.0.65, 417.

66. HDA, Collection MUP SRH, 013.0.65, Part III, 48, 276.

67. HDA, Collection MUP SRH, 013.0.56, V. Židovec, *Moje sudjelovanje u političkom životu*, 31.

68. From the study by the later Ustasha official Vjekoslav Servatzy, *Razvitak ustaškog pokreta u inozemstvu*, in Krizman, *Ustaše i Reich*, 2, 424.

69. For a list of interned Ustashe in Italy, see Krizman, *Ante Pavelić i ustaše*, 564–74.

70. HDA, MUP RH, file II/91, box 150, USIKS 337/41, 814.

71. Berger, *44 mjeseca u Jasenovcu*, 42.

72. Kolar-Dimitrijević, "Sjećanja veterinara Zorka Goluba," 175; *Zložini fašističkih okupatora*, 93. The execution of Jewish camp foremen is also mentioned by Ciliga, *Sam kroz Europu*, 236, who claimed that it was a "junior second lieutenant whose name I have forgotten"; he remembered only that he was a Muslim from eastern Bosnia.

73. Many descriptions of these "atrocities" in the diaries of the German military representative in the ISC, General Glaise von Horstenau, can be found in Broucek, *Ein General in Zwielicht*, especially 165–69, and in many reports of his chief intelligence office, Captain Hefner, in Kazimirović, *NDH*, 111–29.

74. HDA, Collection MUP SRH, 013.0.65, Part II, 49; HDA, Collection ZKRZ GUZ, no. 306, box 279, 15539/45; Miletić, *Koncentracioni logor Jasenovac*, 2:1010–23, 1051–89; Kovačić, "Zapovjednici i dužnosnici jasenovačke," 104–7.

75. Jelić-Butić, *Ustaše i NDH*, 158.

39. Revisionism in Croatia

1. For example, Stern, *Holocaust Denial*, gives a comprehensive review of revisionist stands, and a bibliography of over 350 titles of books and articles of revisionist content, including the *Horrors of War* by Franjo Tuđman.

2. *Izvješće o radu Komisije za utvrđivanje ratnih i poratnih žrtava od osnutka*, tables on pp. 16, 17, and 20. The Commission adopted this report with a great majority of votes (with only one vote against and three abstentions) at its meeting on October 11, 1999, but the new session of the Croatian Parliament (after the opposition victory of January 3, 2000) neither adopted nor rejected it, returning it instead to the Commission with suggestions that it should be completed. This had not been done by the beginning of 2002 and it seems that it never will be.

3. About the idea of "reconciliation," see Goldstein, "Pomirenje," *Erasmus* 2 (1993): 13–18.

4. Ćosić, *Stvarno i moguće*, 27 and throughout.

5. *Večernje novosti* (Belgrade), September 24–25, 1986.

6. *Književne novine* 716 (Belgrade), September 15, 1986.

7. Žerjavić, *Population Losses and Manipulations*; Žerjavić, *Pertes de la population en Yougoslavie*.

8. S. Živanović in *Politika* (Belgrade), October 8, 1989.

9. Facsimile of the document is presented in Jurčević, *Nastanak jasenovačkog mita*, 165.

10. Bulatović, *Koncentracioni logor Jasenovac*, 413.

11. See in detail *Srpska strana rata*, 583–686; Anzulovic, *Heavenly Serbia*.

12. Tuđman, *Bespuća povijesne zbiljnosti*, 129, 158, 161

13. Tuđman, *Bespuća povijesne zbiljnosti*, 316.

14. Tuđman, *Bespuća povijesne zbiljnosti*, 160

15. Tuđman, *Bespuća povijesne zbiljnosti*, 148; Tuđman claims that Shoah ("catastrophe") means "sacrifice by fire," and on the basis of this completely wrong translation erroneously deduces that the Jews link the Holocaust with the cult of the victim in the spirit of the Biblical sacrifice by fire. In several places, Tuđman also misquotes or misinterprets the basic book about the Holocaust, Hilberg, *Destruction of the European Jews*—see, for example, Tuđman, *Bespuća povijesne zbiljnosti*, 318–19, note 496; see also the English edition.

16. Tuđman, *Bespuća povijesne zbiljnosti*, 316

17. For more detailed information, see chapter 21.

18. Miletić, *Koncentracioni logor Jasenovac*, 1:207–12.

19. Miletić, *Koncentracioni logor Jasenovac*, 1:213–54.

20. More detailed information, see chapter 21.

21. See letter by Milan Nedić, the chief of the Serbian quisling regime, to state adviser Neubacher, in Miletić, *Koncentracioni logor Jasenovac*, 3:123–24.

22. Miletić, *Koncentracioni logor Jasenovac*, 3:135–37

23. Miletić, *Koncentracioni logor Jasenovac*, 3:106–19.

24. Miletić, *Koncentracioni logor Jasenovac*, 3:115–16.

25. Tuđman, *Bespuća povijesne zbiljnosti*, 318

26. *Sećanja Jevreja na logor Jasenovac*, Belgrade 1972, 125

27. Miletić, *Koncentracioni logor Jasenovac*, 3:119.

28. Tuđman, *Bespuća povijesne zbiljnosti*, 318, note 492.

29. Tuđman, *Bespuća povijesne zbiljnosti*, 318–20.

30. Ciliga, *Sam kroz Europu u ratu*, 276–78.

31. Ciliga, *Sam kroz Europu u ratu*, 427–28.

32. Ciliga, *Sam kroz Europu u ratu*, 436.

33. Ciliga, *Sam kroz Europu u ratu*, 348–49, 390–92.

34. Ciliga, *Sam kroz Europu u ratu*, 232, 366–67, 370.

35. Ciliga, *Sam kroz Europu u ratu*, 304.

36. Ciliga, *Sam kroz Europu u ratu*, 280, 305.

37. Ciliga, *Sam kroz Europu u ratu*, 323, 344; Romano, *Jevreji zdravstveni radnici Jugoslavije*, 191; Luburić did not kill Spitzer or have him killed because, according to Ciliga, "brave himself, the cruel, bloodthirsty, and primitive Luburić seems to have respected only courage."

38. See Tuđman, *Bespuća povijesne zbiljnosti*; Tuđman, *Horrors*.

39. Hrženjak, *Rušenje antifašističkih spomenika u Hrvatskoj*, 346.

40. About these events in May 1945, see Tomasevich, "War and Revolution in Yugoslavia"; Goldstein, *Croatia*, 155–56.

41. Stuparić, *Tko je tko u NDH*, 241–42.

42. *Hrvatski leksikon*, 1:103, 416, 482, 507.

43. *Hrvatski leksikon*, 1:110, 535, 649.

44. Jareb, *Pola stoljeća hrvatske politike*, 90, 94.

45. Jareb, *Pola stoljeća*, 91–92.

46. Benigar, *Alojzije Stepinac*, 364–65.

47. Cota, *Slučaj Šakić*, 103. This author of extremely limited abilities was not only in conflict with basic historical facts, but with orthography as well—see note 334 on p. 611 in the Croatian edition of the book.

48. *Istina o Nezavisnoj Državi Hrvatskoj*, 28–29.

49. See, for example, in the works of L. Boban in the bibliography and Goldstein, *Croatia*, 199–202.

50. See, for example, Jurčević, *Nastanak*, 35, with an exaggerated, almost idyllic, description of the "intensive work" in the industrial plants and workshops of Jasenovac, while different testimonies of people who were there are simply rejected as "lacking the minimum of authenticity" (p. 39).

51. Jurčević, *Nastanak*, 135.

52. Pečarić published the first edition in 1998 in one volume, and the second in 2000 in two volumes—the first volume was the repeated first edition, while the second contained texts written later.

53. Pečarić, *Srpski mit*, 1:184; 2:33, 50, 61.

54. Pečarić, *Srpski mit*, 1:184.

55. See chapter 37 in this book.

56. Pečarić, *Srpski mit*, 2:132.

57. See for example, Hilberg, *Destruction of the European Jews*, 439 and 608.

58. Pečarić, *Srpski mit*, 2:25.

59. Pečarić, *Srpski mit*, 2:25–27. In 1940, about 13,000 Jews lived in the part of Serbia under the Nedić administration, 11,500 of whom were killed, so Gumzej's claim, on which Pečarić insists, that 45,000 Jews were killed in "Nedić's Serbia" is absurd.

60. Pečarić, *Srpski mit*, 2:130–32.

61. Pečarić, *Srpski mit*, 1:98; 2:17, 39, 42, 66, 87, 128, 186, 192.

62. Pečarić, *Srpski mit*, 2:17.

63. Pečarić, *Srpski mit*, 2:108–13. About what happened on the area of Jasenovac Camp after May 1945, see Goldstein and Goldstein, *Jasenovac i Bleiburg*, 107–15.

64. Pečarić, *Srpski mit*, 1:dust jacket.

65. Krišto, *Katolička crkva*, 1:293–98.

66. Krišto, *Katolička crkva*, 1:296.

67. Žerjavić, *Opsesije i megalomanije*, 170.

68. Paver, "Rezultati," 610; Krišto, *Katolička crkva*, 1:297.

69. Paver, "Rezultati," 611; I have tried to supplement the figures about the killing of Jews given in the Dotrščina Project.

70. Krišto, *Katolička crkva*, 1:294.

71. Krišto, *Katolička crkva*, 1:296.

72. There is the most about Pavelić's wife, Mara, in Lasić, *Autobiografski zapisi*, 174–78.

73. Krišto, *Katolička crkva*, 1:298.

74. Lengel-Krizman, "Logori za Židove u NDH," 102; Sobolevski, "Židovi u kompleksu koncentracijskog logora Jasenovac," 119.

75. Krišto, *Katolička crkva*, 1:298.

76. See chapters 10 and 31.

77. Krišto, *Katolička crkva*, 1:365.

78. Vučić, *Židovstvo i hrvatstvo*, 218–22.

79. Vučić, *Židovstvo i hrvatstvo*, 210–11.

80. Vučić, *Židovstvo i hrvatstvo*, 55–58, 208; Weininger, *Pol i karakter.*

81. Vučić, *Židovstvo i hrvatstvo*, 222.

82. Vučić, *Židovstvo i hrvatstvo*, 60.

83. Vučić, *Židovstvo i hrvatstvo*, 59–60.

84. Vučić, *Židovstvo i hrvatstvo*, 88.

85. Revisionism was also present in *Časopis za suvremenu povijest* that comes out in Zagreb. In number 2 for 2001, Z. Kantolić analyzed the work of the Inquiry Commission for Establishing Crimes Committed by Cultural Collaboration with the Enemy in 1945 in Zagreb. The author's *a priori* stand was that the Commission's work was motivated exclusively by ideology, and that the people under investigation were *a priori* innocent. They included Ivo Bogdan, without saying that he had been one of the "leading journalists, propagandists, and censors" in the ISC, director of *Hrvatski narod*, and director of the State Propaganda Directorate (Stuparić, *Tko je tko u NDH*, 43). There is no doubt about Bogdan's responsibility for spreading hate speech, characteristic of propaganda in the Ustasha state and of some papers that he edited. It is certain that any court in every democratic state would find Bogdan criminally responsible.

40. Jews in the Ustasha State Administration

1. Jelić-Butić, *Ustaše i NDH*, 19.

2. Stuparić, *Tko je tko u NDH*, 359.

3. HDA, Collection MUP SRH, 013.0.2, *Historijat ustaškog pokreta i NDH*, prepared by S. Kvaternik and V. Košak, 45, 151, 201–202, 310.

4. Kvaternik, *Sjećanja i zapažanja*, 131.

5. HDA, Collection MUP SRH, 013.0.4, Folder Dr. Ante Pavelić, the Ustasha movement and the Poglavnik of the ISC Ante Pavelić, 91–93.

6. Kvaternik, *Sjećanja i zapažanja*, 76.

7. HDA, Collection MUP SRH, 013.0.4, Folder Dr. Ante Pavelić, the Ustasha movement and the Poglavnik of the ISC Ante Pavelić, 91–93; about Pečnikar, see Stuparić, *Tko je tko u NDH*, 314; Maček, *Memoari*, 167. See Singer's report on his conversation with Maček in *Maček u Luburićevu zatočeništvu*, prepared by J. Mužić, Split 1999, 91–116,

8. HDA, Collection MUP SRH, 013.0.4, Folder Dr. Ante Pavelić, the Ustasha movement and the Poglavnik of the ISC Ante Pavelić, 92.

9. This was how Krišto listed them, *Katolička crkva*, 2:141.

10. About Bauer, see Stuparić, *Tko je tko u NDH*, 27–28.

11. HDA, Collection MUP SRH, 013.0.56, V. Židovec, *Moje sudjelovanje u političkom životu*, 138; see also Krišto, *Katolička crkva*, 1:296.

12. HDA, Collection MUP SRH, 013.0.2, *Historijat ustaškog pokreta i NDH*, prepared by S. Kvaternik and V. Košak, 266. See also Cota, *Slučaj Šakić*, 107.

13. HDA, Collection 1076, Reconstruction, DKM card index, Vilko Lehner file 697/3; HDA, Collection 252, RUR, J. Section, 29884.

14. Stuparić, *Tko je tko u NDH*, 183.

15. Stuparić, *Tko je tko u NDH*, 197–198.

16. Testimony of Professor Dr. Stjepan Steiner.

17. HDA, Collection MUP SRH, 013.0.55; *Narodne novine*, Zagreb, 76, July 15, 1941; 211, December 27, 1941; HDA, Collection 1209, Colonel Luburić's Staff; Kvaternik, *Sjećanja i zapažanja*, 175, 180, 183, 184, 292.

18. Kvaternik, *Sjećanja i zapažanja*, 210.

19. HDA, Collection MUP SRH, 013.0.4, Folder Dr. Ante Pavelić, the Ustasha movement and the Poglavnik of the ISC Ante Pavelić, 68, 72, 73.

20. HDA, Collection 252, RUR, J. Section, 29865, 29866; About Kremzir, see Stuparić, *Tko je tko u NDH*, 206–7; *Popis žrtava*.

21. Testimony of Dr. Dragutin Kremzir.

22. HDA, Collection MUP SRH, 013.0.4, Folder Dr. Ante Pavelić, 136.

23. Testimony of Branko Polić.

24. HDA, Collection MUP SRH, 013.0.52, Folder Dr. Mile Budak, interrogation record, 16.

25. They have already been mentioned in chapter 6.

26. HDA, Collection MUP SRH, 013.0.4, Folder Dr. Ante Pavelić, the Ustasha movement and the Poglavnik of the ISC, Ante Pavelić, 136. This A. Klein is not the same as A. Klein, secretary of the Jewish Religious Community of Zagreb, who survived the war.

27. *Novi list* 60, June 28, 1941.

28. HDA, Collection HDS, Praesidium Documents 23 of April 7, 1942; Kisić-Kolanović, *Židovska imovina*, 431.

29. HDA, MUP SRH 301886, Folder S. Kvaternik, Shorthand record from the main hearing, 551; Kisić-Kolanović, *Židovska imovina*, 436.

30. The investigator made a mistake, as Pavelić's wife was not Jewish—HDA, Collection MUP SRH, 013.0.65, part II, 40.

31. Testimony of Branko Polić.

32. Testimony of Branko Polić; Bauer also wrote his memoirs, *Život je kratak san uspomene, 1910–1985*.

33. HDA, Collection MUP SRH, 013.0.65, part II, 15; about Kuveždić, see Stuparić, *Tko je tko u NDH*, 223.

34. This is a sophistic exhibition and the assumptions are not based on any kinds of documents—people who use this approach ask the question "How could the Jews among the Ustashe have done this to their own people?" but they do not challenge the final numbers.

41. The Ustashe, the Croats, and the Jews

1. About this, Goldstein, "Iskustva."

2. Testimony of Professor Dr. Stjepan Steiner.

3. Prašek-Całczyńska, *Memoari*, 144.

4. HDA, Collection MUP SRH, 013.0.3, Dizdar, *Ustaštvo i NDH*, 55; see similarly HDA, Collection MUP SRH, 013.0.56, V. Židovec, *Moje sudjelovanje u političkom životu*, 138. Viktor Gutić was especially persistent in the persecution of Serbs, about which the Germans cautioned the authorities—see Stuparić, *Tko je tko u NDH*, 145.

5. JP 7–8 (1966).

6. According to the data in the ŽOZ library; see also the list, by name, of the first forty-three Righteous, *Bilten ŽOZ* 38 (1995).

7. *Bilten ŽOZ* 34–35 (1994).

8. JIM, Collection ŽOZ, without reg. no.

9. HDA, Collection ZKRZ GUZ, no. 306, box 15, 3733, 3762.

10. HDA, Collection 252, RUR, J. Section, 29059; about Kühnel, Collection ZKRZ, index (of war criminals).

11. HDA, Collection 252, Hans Helm, index-card V. Kühnel.

12. Testimony of Biserka Hiršl-Barac.

13. *Ustaše su ubijale javno*; about Vrkljan, see HDA, Collection ZKRZ ZH no. 12415, 14256, 20829, 33596, 42347; HDA, Folder SDS no. 062021, 312528.

14. HDA, Collection 223, MUP NDH, 1058/II-C, 9566.

15. HDA, Collection ZKRZ GUZ, no. 306, box 15, 3764–3766, 3770–3771; Collection ZKRZ, ZH. no. 2755, 8501, 12267, 42526; HDA, Folder SDS no. 316982, 319034, 319711.

16. HDA, Collection 248, UNS, Folder I-A-II 377, file no. 1653; *Kartoteka židovskog znaka.*

17. HDA, Collection 252, RUR, J. Section, 27999.

18. HDA, Collection 252, RUR, J. Section, 27238; Mirnik, *Obitelj Alexander*, 28, 107.

19. HDA, Collection 252, RUR, J. Section, 28451; *Kartoteka židovskog znaka*; *Popis žrtava.*

20. See, e.g., HDA, Collection 252, RUR, J. Section, 29872; *Popis žrtava.*

21. HDA, Collection 252, RUR, J. Section, 28794; *Popis žrtava.*

22. HDA, Collection 252, RUR, J. Section, 28033.

23. HDA, Collection 252, RUR, J. Section, 29278.

24. HDA, Collection 252, RUR, J. Section, 29432.

25. HDA, Collection 252, RUR, J. Section, 28431.

26. HDA, Collection 252, RUR, J. Section, 27238, 27311, 27332, 27593, 27601, 27611.

27. HDA, Collection 252, RUR, J. Section, 27545; *Popis žrtava.*

28. HDA, Collection ZKRZ GUZ, no. 306, box 10, 130.

29. HDA, Collection 252, RUR, J. Section, 28454.

30. HDA, Collection 252, RUR, J. Section, 27572; *Popis žrtava.*

31. *Ustaše su ubijale javno.*

32. HDA, Collection 223, MUP NDH, 1776/15883.

33. HDA, Collection 223, MUP NDH, 8897, III-A, 45072/41.

34. HDA, Collection 252, RUR, J. Section, 27673.

35. HDA, Collection 252, RUR, J. Section, 28026.

36. HDA, Collection 252, RUR, J. Section, 28237.

37. HDA, Collection 252, RUR, J. Section, 28293.

38. HDA, Collection 252, RUR, J. Section, 28338; *Kartoteka židovskog znaka.*

39. HDA, Collection 252, RUR, J. Section, 28704, 29099; *Popis žrtava.*

40. HDA, Collection 252, RUR, J. Section, 28264; about Hirschler, ME 2, 134; Vujović-Tonković, *Hirschler*; *Popis žrtava*; *Kartoteka Jasenovac.*

41. HDA, Collection 252, RUR, J. Section, 28134; Kolar-Dimitrijević, *Akcija povjesničara.*

42. HDA, Collection 248, UNS, folder I-A-II 377; *Popis žrtava.*

43. Testimony of Berta Israel, née Švarcenberg.

44. Prašek, *Memoari,* 147.

45. NAZ, group NDS 2675/1942.

46. JIM, Collection ŽOZ, without reg. no.; testimony of Ljubica Sakušek, widow of Vilko, and Ada Marhofer, widow of Vladimir; *Popis žrtava*; *Spiskovi preživelih.*

47. NAZ, Collection Prezidijalni spisi 108/1941.

48. JIM, Collection ŽOZ, reg. no. 4865, sign. K-63–2-1/1–178.

49. Testimony of Professor Dr. Zdenko Šternberg.

50. Goldstein, "Porto Re."

42. On the Number of Jewish Victims in Zagreb and Croatia

1. See, for example, the table about differences in Žerjavić, "Demografski pokazatelji."

2. *Spiskovi preživelih,* 264–332.

3. There is extensive archive material about the Holocaust—see Kolanović, "Holocaust in Croatia."

4. Kolanović, *Elektronska baza.*

5. Kolanović, *Elektronska baza.*

6. HDA, Collection ZKRZ GUZ, no. 306, box 15, 3871.

7. Goldstein, "Židovska općina."

8. About the project—Paver, "Rezultati," 609, 611.

9. HDA, Collection 252, RUR, J. Section, 28968, 28996.

10. Dębski, *Sterbebücher von Auschwitz,* 2:223.

11. *Kartoteka židovskog znaka*; *Spiskovi preživelih.*

12. *Ha-kol* 49–50 (1997).

13. JIM, Collection ŽOZ, without reg. no.; *Popis žrtava*; *Knjiga umrlih.*

14. Testimony of Berta Israel, née Švarcenberg; *Knjiga umrlih.*

15. HDA, Collection ZKRZ GUZ, no. 306, box 15, 3703–3717.

16. HDA, Collection ZKRZ GUZ, no. 306, box 15, 3732, 3817–3818.

17. HDA, Collection ZKRZ GUZ, no. 306, box 15, 3871.

18. About the Dotrščina locality, see Paver, "Rezultati," 608.

19. *Dotrščina projekt*, HDA, 27–29; the authors of the project recognized ninety people as Jews.

20. *Dotrščina projekt*, HDA, 24.

21. *Dotrščina projekt*, HDA, 23.

22. Such as Andrija Kraljević and Mirko Ilić.

23. Dębski, *Sterbebücher von Auschwitz*, 2:38, 123; HDA, Collection 1076, Reconstruction, Card Index DKM, 3418/2, 126/2; they do not appear in the list of the Community dues for 1941/2 either—Dora Bošan probably lived in the same household as Matilda Bošan—JIM, Collection ŽOZ, reg. no. 4973, sign. K-64–2-1/1–26.

24. Dębski, *Sterbebücher von Auschwitz*, 2:38, 223, 792, 1069.

25. *Popis žrtava*; *Kartoteka židovskog znaka.*

26. *Popis žrtava.*

27. *Popis žrtava*; Dębski, *Sterbebücher von Auschwitz*, 2:1151.

28. JIM, Collection ŽOZ, reg. no. 4863, sign. K-62–5-1/1–103.

29. HDA, Collection MUP, 27957; see also Lengel-Krizman and Sobolevski, "Hapšenje."

30. *Dotrščina projekt*, HDA, 26.

31. JIM, Collection ŽOZ, reg. no. 1909.

32. JIM, Collection ŽOZ, reg. no. 4864, sign. K-63–1-1/1–116; by mistake, *Popis žrtava* also includes Gizela.

33. *Jasenovac, koncentracioni logor.*

34. Zagreb can be found in the volume *Hrvatska 24*, p. 4631–4798.

35. *Kartoteka židovskog znaka*; *Popis žrtava Zagreb.*

36. Peršen, *Ustaški logori*, 101, says that eighty-seven Zagreb Jews were victims of the camp on Pag, as recorded in the Croatian State Archives; however, when the number of Zagreb citizens sent off from the Zagreb Fairground via Gospić to Pag in June and July 1941 is compared with the number of those who went from there to other camps, the total number of victims is much greater.

37. Gross, "Slike povijesti," 87.

38. Goldstein, "Genocid nad Židovima u NDH?"

39. Students in the course *Jews in Croatia, 1800–1945*, during the academic year 1999–2000 (Dijana Bolfek, Tanja Didak, Tatjana Margitić, Ivan Botica) helped count victims by place of death in the Dotrščina Project.

43. A New Beginning?

1. JIM, Collection ŽOZ, reg. no. 4864, sign. K-63–1-1/1–257.

2. JIM, Collection ŽOZ, reg. no. 4864, sign. K-63–1-1/1–8; *Popis žrtava.* See also other cases—JIM, Collection ŽOZ, reg. no. 4864, sign. K-63–1-1/1–67, 1–71, 1–72.

3. JIM, Collection ŽOZ, reg. no. 4864, sign. K-64–1-1/1–51.

4. JIM, Collection ŽOZ, reg. no. 4864, sign. K-63–1-1/1–70; see also other similar examples: 1–127, 1–128, 1–131.

5. JIM, Collection ŽOZ, reg. no. 4864, sign. K-63–1-1/1–73, 1–74.

6. JIM, Collection ŽOZ, reg. no. 4970, sign. K-63–3-2/1–3 of 1–5, see also 1–6, in the same place.

7. JIM, Collection ŽOZ, reg. no. 4863, sign. K-62–5-1/1–365.

8. JIM, Collection ŽOZ, reg. no. 4864, sign. K-64–1-1/1–56 do 1–60.

9. JIM, Collection ŽOZ, reg. no. 4864, sign. K-63–1-1/1–52. Ruben was killed as an Israeli soldier in the Sinai campaign in 1956. He was a talented young composer, and his music to the poems of the biblical *Song of Songs* is still played on Israeli radio.

10. JIM, Collection ŽOZ, reg. no. 4864, sign. K-63–1-1/1–76 do 1–79, 1–88, 1–91 do 1–93, 1–96, 1–100, 1–113 do 1–115, 1–117, 1–124, 1–133, 1–139, 1–140, 1–154, 1–157 to 1–161, 1–190, 1–193 to 1–195, 1–199, 1–206, 1–209, 1–212, 1–237, 1–238, 1–242, 1–244 to 1–248.

11. JIM, Collection ŽOZ, without reg. no.

12. JIM, Collection ŽOZ, without reg. no.

13. JIM, Collection ŽOZ, reg. no. 4864, sign. K-63–1-1/1–204.

14. JIM, Collection ŽOZ, reg. no. 4864, sign. K-63–1-1/1–243.

15. JIM, Collection ŽOZ, without reg. no.

16. JIM, Collection ŽOZ, reg. no. 1909.

17. JIM, Collection ŽOZ, reg. no. 4864, sign. K-63–1-1/1–94.

18. JIM, Collection ŽOZ, reg. no. 4970, sign. K-63–3-2/1–1.

19. JIM, Collection ŽOZ, reg. no. 4864, sign. K-63–1-1/1–200.

20. JIM, Collection ŽOZ, reg. no. 4863, sign. K-62–5-1/1–226; *Spiskovi preživelih.*

21. JIM, Collection ŽOZ, reg. no. 4864, sign. K-63–1-1/1–173 to 1–179.

22. JIM, Collection ŽOZ, reg. no. 4864, sign. K-63–1-1/1–148; JIM, Collection ŽOZ, reg. no. 4863, sign. K-62–5-1/1–230.

23. JIM, Collection ŽOZ, reg. no. 4864, sign. K-63–1-1/1–254.

24. JIM, Collection ŽOZ, reg. no. 4863, sign. K-62–5-1/1–212 do 1–214.

25. See *Ha-kol* 63–64 (1999–2000).

26. JIM, Collection ŽOZ, reg. no. 4864, sign. K-63–1-1/1–84.

27. JIM, Collection ŽOZ, reg. no. 4864, sign. K-63–1-1/1–134.

28. JIM, Collection ŽOZ, reg. no. 4864, sign. K-63–1-1/1–162.

29. JIM, Collection ŽOZ, reg. no. 4864, sign. K-63–1-1/1–187.

30. JIM, Collection ŽOZ, reg. no. 4864, sign. K-63–1-1/1–110.

31. JIM, Collection ŽOZ, reg. no. 4864, sign. K-63–1-1/1–118.

32. JIM, Collection ŽOZ, reg. no. 4864, sign. K-63–1-1/1–151.

33. JIM, Collection ŽOZ, without reg. no.

34. JIM, Collection ŽOZ, reg. no. 4863, sign. K-62–5-1/1–99.

35. JIM, Collection ŽOZ, without reg. no.

36. JIM, Collection ŽOZ, reg. no. 4969, sign. K-63–3-1/1–52.

37. JIM, Collection ŽOZ, reg. no. 4969, sign. K-63–3-1/1–55.

38. JIM, Collection ŽOZ, without reg. no.

39. JIM, Collection ŽOZ, sign. K-66–2-1/1–1 to 1–55.

40. JIM, Collection ŽOZ, without reg. no.

41. JIM, Collection ŽOZ, without reg. no.

42. JIM, Collection ŽOZ, without reg. no.

43. JIM, Collection ŽOZ, without reg. no.

44. JIM, Collection ŽOZ, reg. no. 4970, sign. K-63–3-2/1–171.

BIBLIOGRAPHY

Archives and Archival Collections Consulted

Arhiv samostana karmelićanki u Hrvatskom Leskovcu kod Zagreba (Carmelite Monastery Archive in Hrvatski Leskovac, near Zagreb)

Arhiv samostana karmelićanki na Vrhovcu, Zagreb (Carmelite Monastery Archive on Vrhovec in Zagreb)

Arhiv Židovske općine Zagreb (Archive of the Zagreb Jewish Community)

Državni arhiv u Zagrebu (State Archives in Zagreb)

Fond Gradsko poglavarstvo Zagreb (GPZ) (Collection of the Municipal Council)

Fond Gradsko poglavarstvo stambeni ured u Zagrebu (GPSUZ) (Collection of the City Council Housing Office in Zagreb)

Fond Odvjetnička pisarna Aleksandar Licht (Law office of Aleksandar Licht)

Hrvatski državni arhiv (HDA), Zagreb (Croatian State Archives, Zagreb)

Fond 144, Savska banovina, Upravno odjeljenje (SBUO) (Collection 144, the Banovina of Sava, Administrative Division)

Fond 155, Banska vlast Banovine Hrvatske (BVBN) (Collection 155, Ban's Office of the Banovina of Croatia)

Fond 211, Hrvatski državni sabor NDH (Collection 211, Croatian State Parliament of the Independent State of Croatia)

Fond 218, Ministarstvo pravosuđa i bogoštovlja NDH, Odjel za pravosuđe (Collection 218, the Ministry of Justice and Religion of the Independent State of Croatia, Department of Justice)

Fond 223, Ministarstvo unutrašnjih poslova Nezavisne Države Hrvatske (MUP NDH) (Collection 223, the Ministry of Internal Affairs of the Independent State of Croatia)

Fond 237, Državni izvještajni i promičbeni ured pri Predsjedništvu Vlade NDH (Collection 237, the State Information and Propaganda

Office of the Prime Minister of the Government of the Independent State of Croatia)

Fond OZNA, Odjeljenje za zaštitu naroda (Collection of the Department of National Security)

Fond 252, Židovski odsjek Ravnateljstva ustaškog redarstva (Collection 252, Jewish Section of the Directorate of the Ustasha Police)

Fond 306, Zemaljska komisija za utvrđivanje zločina okupatora i njihovih pomagača (Zemaljska komisija za ratne zločine—ZKRZ) (Collection 306, State Commission for Investigating the Crimes of the Occupying Forces and Their Supporters [State Commission for War Crimes])

Fond 416, odvjetnička pisarnica Ive Politea (Collection 416, Law Office of Ivo Politeo)

Fond 486, Poglavnikov vojni ured (Collection 486, Military Office of the Poglavnik)

Fond 487, Ministarstvo oružanih snaga NDH (MINORS) (Collection 487, Ministry of the Armed Forces of the Independent State of Croatia)

Fond 491, Opće upravno povjereništvo kod zapovjedništva II. armate talijanske vojske (Collection 491, General Governing Commission at the Headquarters of the Second Corps of the Italian Army)

Fond 493, Sudovi oružanih snaga NDH (Collection 493, the Military Courts of the Independent State of Croatia)

Fond 1076, Ponova (Collection 1076, Ponova [documents concerning the requisition of Jewish property])

Grupa Instituta za suvremenu povijest—grupa XXIV (Group of the Institute for Contemporary History—Group XXIV)

Zbirka dokumenata Službe državne sigurnosti RSUP-a SRH, inv. Br. 1547 (Collection of documents of the State Security Service of the Secretariat of the Interior of the Socialist Republic of Croatia, no. 1547)

Zbirka dosjea Službe državne sigurnosti (SDS), inv. Br. 1548 (Collection of the dossiers of the State Security Service, no. 1548)

Jevrejski istorijski muzej (JIM), Beograd (Jewish Historical Museum, Belgrade)

Fond Židovska općina Zagreb (Collection of Zagreb Jewish Community)

Nadbiskupski arhiv Zagreb (NAZ), Zagreb (Archdiocesan Archives in Zagreb)

Fond Nadbiskupski duhovni stol (NDS) (Collection of Archdiocesan Spiritual Committee [NDS is the central administrative and advisory body of the Archdiocese of Zagreb])

Fond Prezidijalni spisi (Collection of Praesidium Documents)

Fond Caritas zagrebačke nadbiskupije (Collection of the Archdiocesan Caritas of Zagreb)

Selected Primary Sources

Baza podataka o Židovima žrtvama Holokausta u Hrvatskoj, Arhiv Židovska općina Zagreb [Database of Jewish victims of the Holocaust in Croatia, Archives of the Jewish Community of Zagreb].

Bilten ŽOZ [Bulletin of the Jewish Community of Zagreb], 1–47. Zagreb, 1987–1996.

Brzopisni zapisnici prvog zasjedanja Hrvatskog državnog sabora u NDH godine 1942 [Stenographic minutes of the first session of the Croatian State Parliament in the Independent State of Croatia]. Zagreb 1942.

Codex iuris canonici [The code of canon law]. Freiburg 1919.

Danica, hrvatski obiteljski tjednik za grad i selo [Danica, Croatian family weekly for city and village]. Zagreb 1933–1938.

Dębski, J., and the State Museum of Auschwitz-Birkenau. *Sterbebücher von Auschwitz* [*Death Books from Auschwitz*], vols. 1–3. München and New Providence, 1995.

Dnevnik Alojzija Stepinca [The diary of Alojzije Stepinac], *Danas (tjednik)* (Zagreb), August 7, 1990–September 26, 1990.

Dnevnik Blaža Jurišića [The diary of Blaž Jurišić], edited by Biserka Rako. Zagreb, 1993.

Dnevnik Dijane Budisavljević [The diary of Dijana Budisavljević], edited by J. Kolanović. Zagreb 2003.

Dotrščina projekt [Dotrščina project], Hrvatski državni arhiv [Croatian State Archives]. Zagreb 1986.

Felicinović, J., *Lične uspomene – logor Slana na Pagu, neobjavljeni rukopis*, str. 20 [Personal memories: The Slana camp on Pag Island, unpublished manuscript, p. 20]. Photocopy in the possession of Ivo Goldstein, original in the possession of the heirs of Father Živko Kustić.

Friedländer, S., *Pio XII i Treći Reich: Dokumenti* [Pius XII and the Third Reich: Documents]. Zagreb, 1966.

Glasnik Saveza jevrejskih opština Jugoslavije [Voice of the union of Jewish communities of Yugoslavia]. Belgrade, 1919–1941.

Glasnik sv. Ante [Saint Anthony herald]. Visoko [central Bosnia], 1900–.

Ha-kol, glasilo židovske zajednice u Hrvatskoj [The Voice, organ of the Jewish Community in Croatia], 48– . Zagreb 1997– . See *Bilten ŽOZ* above for vols. 1–47.

Hrvatska gruda [Croatian soil]. Zagreb 1936, 1940–1945.

Hrvatska straža, tjednik za katolički dom [Croatian guard, weekly for the Catholic home]. Zagreb, 1933–1943.

Hrvatski dnevnik [Croatian daily]. Zagreb, 1936–1941.

Hrvatski list [Croatian journal]. Osijek, 1921–1945.

Hrvatski narod, glasilo hrvatskog ustaškog pokreta [Croatian people, organ of the Croatian Ustasha movement]. Zagreb, 1939–1945.

Hrvatski radnik [Croatian worker]. Zagreb, 1936–1945.

Imenik privatnika za grad i kotar Zagreb, Ponova, Predmetni spisi, Dosjei konfiscirane – imetak Židova [Address directory of individuals for the city and county of Zagreb, Ponovo, case files, dossiers of confiscated Jewish property].

Istupi iz židovstva 1941, Arhiv Židovska općina Zagreb [Departure from Judaism 1941, Archives of the Jewish Community of Zagreb].

Izvješće o radu Komisije za utvrđivanje ratnih i poratnih žrtava od osnutka (11. veljače 1992.) do rujna 1999. godine [Report on the work of the commission for establishing a list of wartime and postwar victims, from its founding on February 11, 1992, up to September 1999]. Zagreb 1999.

Jasenovac—Žrtve rata prema podacima Statističkog zavoda Jugoslavije [Jasenovac—victims of the war according to the data of the Statistical Institute of Yugoslavia]. Sarajevo and Zürich, 1998.

Jevrejski pregled [Jewish review]. Belgrade, 1950–.

Jevrejski život [Jewish life]. Sarajevo, 1925–1927.

Jevrejski glas [Jewish voice]. Sarajevo, 1928–1941.

Jutarnji list [Morning journal]. Zagreb, 1912–1941.

Kartoteka jasenovačkih zatočenika (*Kartoteka Jasenovac*) [Card file of the detainees in Jasenovac (card file Jasenovac)].

Kartoteka pripadnika židovske zajednice u Zagrebu, svibanj 1941 [Card file of the Members of the Jewish Community of Zagreb, May 1941].

Katolički list [Catholic journal]. Zagreb, 1849–1945.

Knjiga kontribucije, Arhiv Židovska općina Zagreb [Contribution Book, Archives of the Jewish Community of Zagreb].

Knjiga prijelaza, Arhiv Židovska općina Zagreb [Registry of Conversions, Archives of the Jewish Community of Zagreb].

Knjiga umrlih ŽOZ (*Hevra Kadiša*) [Registry of deaths among the members of the Jewish Community of Zagreb (burial society)].

Književne novine [Literary gazette]. Belgrade.

Mlada Hrvatska [Young Croatia]. Zagreb, 1936.

Načela hrvatskog ustaškog pokreta [Principles of the Croatian Ustasha movement], edited by D. Crljen. Zagreb, 1942.

Narodne novine [National gazette]. Zagreb, 1941–1945.

Nepotpuni spisak zatočenika sabirnog logora Jasenovac III, prema indeksu parketarnice iz 1944. godine, umnožio Jovan Živković [Incomplete list of the detainees in the Jasenovac III concentration camp, according to the index of the parquet floor works from 1944, compiled by Jovan Živković]. Zrenjanin, 1966.

Neue Ordnung in Kroatien, Kroatische Wochenschrift [New order in Croatia, German-language weekly]. Zagreb, 1941–1945.

Nezavisnost [Independence]. Zagreb, 1938–1940.

Nova Evropa [New Europe]. Zagreb, 1920–1941.

Nova Hrvatska [New Croatia]. Zagreb, 1941–1945.

Novi list [New journal]. Zagreb, 1941–1945.

Novi list [New journal]. Rijeka, 1900–.

Novi Omanut [New omnaut]. Zagreb 1993–.

Omanut [Omanut]. Zagreb, 1936–1941.

Opći šematizam katoličke crkve u Jugoslaviji 1974 [A general overview of the Catholic Church in Yugoslavia in 1974]. Zagreb, 1975.

Popis preuzetih stvari židovskih ordinacija, Arhiv Židovska općina Zagreb [List of goods confiscated from Jewish doctors' offices, Archives of the Jewish Community of Zagreb].

Popis žrtava lišenih života, Arhiv Židovska općina Zagreb [List of war dead, Archives of the Jewish Community of Zagreb].

Schwarz, Dr. Gavro. *Spomenica kuratorija doma zaklade Lavoslava Schwarza u Zagrebu prigodom tridesetgodišnjice opstanka 1909–1939* [Memorial of the trustees of the old age home of the Lavoslav Schwarz Foundation in Zagreb on the occasion of its thirtieth anniversary, 1909–1939]. Zagreb 1940.

Spiskovi preživelih Jevreja u Jugoslaviji, Autonomni odbor za pomoć Beograd [Lists of Jewish survivors in Yugoslavia, autonomous committee for aid, Belgrade], Savez jevrejskih vjeroispovjednih opština (općina) Jugoslavije [Association of Jewish Religious Communities in Yugoslavia], Belgrade 1946.

Spomenica Izraelske ferijalne kolonije u Zagrebu prigodom dvadesetpetgodišnjice opstanka društva 1914–1939 [Memorial of the Israelite vacation colony in Zagreb on the occasion of its twenty-fifth anniversary, 1914–1939]. Zagreb 1940.

Spomenica Saveza jevrejskih opština Jugoslavije 1919–1969 [Memorial of the Association of Jewish Communities in Yugoslavia (facsimile)]. Belgrade, 1969.

Spremnost, misao i volja ustaške Hrvatske [The readiness, thought, and will of the Ustasha Croatian]. Zagreb, 1942–1945.

Ustaša, viestnik hrvatskog ustaškog oslobodilačkog pokreta [Ustaša, herald of the Croatian Ustasha liberation movement]. Zagreb, 1941–1945.

Ustaša, Dokumenti o ustaškom pokretu [Ustaša, documents about the Ustasha movement], edited by P. Požar. Zagreb, 1995.

Zakoni, zakonske odredbe, naredbe NDH, I–IV [Laws, legislation, and orders in the Independent State of Croatia, I–IV]. Zagreb, 1941.

Zapisnici 1941, Arhiv Židovska općina Zagreb [Minutes 1941, Archives of the Jewish Community of Zagreb].

Zapisnik rasprave sa suđenja Dinku Šakiću—Županijski sud u Zagrebu—poslovni broj VK–242/98–190 [Court record from the trial of Dinko Šakić—The county court of Zagreb—registered no. VK–242/98–190].

Zbornik zakona i naredaba NDH, god. 1941, svezak I–XII, god. I [Almanac of the laws and commands in the Independent State of Croatia, 1941, vols. 1–12, year 1], edited by J. Junašević and M. Šantek. Zagreb, 1942.

Židov [The Jew]. Zagreb, 1917–1941.

Židovi—izložba o razvoju židovstva i njihovog rušilačkog rada u Hrvatskoj prije 10. IV. 1941. Rješenje židovskog pitanja u NDH, katalog izložbe [The Jews: Exhibition about the development of Judaism and its destructive work in Croatia prior to April 10, 1941. The solution to the Jewish question in the Independent State of Croatia, exhibition catalog]. Zagreb, 1942.

Židovska smotra [The Jewish festival]. Zagreb and Osijek, 1902–1914.

Published Sources

Abrahamsen, D. *The Mind and Death of a Genius.* New York: Columbia University Press, 1946.

Agičić, D. *Susreti Hrvata i Čeha koncem 19. stoljeća.* In *Zbornik Mirjane Gross,* edited by N. Budak and others. Zagreb, 1999.

Agmon, M. "Ličnosti iz naših desetkovanih općina, Ašer Kišicki, profil jednog općinskog službenika," *Jevrejski pregled* 9–10 (1973).

Albala, P. "Dr. David Albala kao jevrejski nacionalni radnik," *Jevrejski almanah 1957–1958* (1958): 94–108.

Altarac Hadji-Ristić, M. "Veliki humanist Adela Weisz," *Bilten ŽOZ* 43 (1995–1996): 9.

Alexander, S. *Church and State in Yugoslavia since 1945.* Cambridge: Cambridge University Press, 1979.

Ančić, M. "Ljetopis kraljeva Hrvatske i Dalmacije (Vrijeme nastanka i autorstvo Hrvatske redakcije Ljetopisa popa Dukljanina)," *Zbornik radova "Zvonimir kralj hrvatski"* (Zagreb, 1997): 271–303.

Anić, V. *Rječnik hrvatskoga jezika,* 3. izdanje. Zagreb, 1998.

Anzulovic, B. *Heavenly Serbia, from Myth to Genocide,* New York; New York University Press, 1999.

Arendt, H. *Antisemitism.* New York: Harvest Books, 1968.

Arendt, H. *Eichmann in Jerusalem.* 5th ed. New York: Viking Press, 1994.

Arendt, H., and K. Jaspers. *Correspondence, 1926–1969.* Edited by L. Köhler and H. Saner. New York: Harcourt, 1992.

Artuković, M. "Židovi u srpskom tisku u Hrvatskoj potkraj 19. stoljeća," *Časopis za suvremenu povijest* 3 (2001): 725–46.

Atijas, J. "Esperansa jevrejski sefardski studentski klub u Zagrebu," *Jevrejski almanah 1955–1956* (1956).

Banac, I. *Nacionalno pitanje u Jugoslaviji: Porijeklo, povijest, politika.* Zagreb, 1988.

Banac, I."'I Karlo je oš'o u komite'—nemiri u sjevernoj Hrvatskoj u jesen 1918," *Časopis za suvremenu povijest* 3 (1992): 23–43.

Banja, L. "Statistički dodatak o liečnicima Zavoda za suzbijanje endemijskog sifilisa i njihova služba," *Vjesnik Zavoda za suzbijanje endemijskog sifilisa* 4 (1942): 36–47.

Barbić, J., and Ž. Pavić. *Pravni fakultet u Zagrebu III, Nastavnici fakulteta,* vol. 3. Zagreb, 1998.

Bar-Chaim, Y. "Židovi i dezintegracija europskog društva: slučaj bivše Jugoslavije," *Novi omanut* (Zagreb).

Barle, J. "Još nekoliko priloga k povijesti Židova u Hrvatskoj," *Vjesnik arhiva* (Zagreb) 11 (1909): 124–33.

Baron, S. V. *A Social and Religious History of the Jews,* vols. 3–15. 2nd ed. New York: Columbia University Press, 1983.

Bauer, E. *Današnja Njemačka, izdanje MH.* Biblioteka Mala knjižnica, Zagreb, 1937.

Bauer, E. *Život je kratak san: uspomene, 1910–1985.* Barcelona and Munich, 1986.

Bauer, M. "Pionirstvo Keren Kajemeta," *Hanoar* 5–6 (1932): 136–42.

Bauer, Y. *American Jewry and the Holocaust: The American Jewish Joint Distribution Committee, 1939–1945.* Jerusalem and Detroit: Wayne State University Press, 1981.

Bedenko, V. *Domus judeorum u srednjovjekovnom Zagrebu.* In *Dva stoljeća povijesti i kulture Židova u Zagrebu i Hrvatskoj,* edited by O. Kraus, 59–68. Zagreb: Židovska Općina Zagreb, 1998.

Bedenko, V. *Zagrebački Gradec, kuća i grad u srednjem vijeku.* Zagreb, 1989.

Bedenko, V. *Društvo i prostor srednjovjekovnog Gradeca.* In *Zagrebački Gradec 1242–1850,* edited by I. Kampuš, L. Margetić, and F. Šanjek, 37–50. Zagreb: Grad Zagreb, 1994.

Bednjanec-Vuković, A. "Prilozi o NDH," *Časopis za suvremenu povijest* 1 (2000): 73–96.

Belicza, B., and S. Jevtović. *Udio Židova u medicini u Hrvatskoj i Zagrebu.* In *Dva stoljeća povijesti i kulture Židova u Zagrebu i Hrvatskoj,* edited by O. Kraus, 202–28. Zagreb: Židovska Općina Zagreb, 1998.

Beluhan, M. *Obraćenje dra: Hinka Hinkovića.* Židov, 1934.

Benigar, A. *Alojzije Stepinac, hrvatski kardinal.* Rome, 1974.

Ben-Sasson, H. H., and others, eds. *A History of the Jewish People,* Cambridge: Harvard University Press, 1976.

Berger, E. *44 mjeseca u Jasenovcu.* Zagreb, 1966.

Bernstein, S., and I. Altaraz. *Cijonizam, njegovo biće i njegova organizacija.* Zagreb, 1919.

Birin, A., and T. Jonjić. "Hrvatska vanjska politika 1939–1942 (recenzija)," *Časopis za suvremenu povijest* 1 (2001): 221–30.

Boban, B. *Demokratski nacionalizam Stjepana Radića.* Zagreb, 1998.

Boban, B. *Stjepan Radić—opus, utjecaji i dodiri.* Zavod za hrvatsku povijest Papers 22, 147–208. Zagreb, 1989.

Boban, Lj. *Hrvatska u arhivima izbjegličke vlade 1941–1943.* Zagreb, 1985.

Boban, Lj. *Kontroverze iz povijesti Jugoslavije 3.* Zagreb, 1990.

Boban, Lj. "Nekoliko izvještaja o povratku Mile Budaka iz emigracije," *Zbornik Historijskog instituta Slavonije* 7–8, Slavonski Brod (1970): 510–14.

Bobinac, M. "Satira, utopija, afera (O 'Ladanjskoj opoziciji' Marijana Derenčina)," *Republika* 7–8, god. 55 (1999): 213–27.

Boeckh (Völkl), K. "Židovska vjerska općina u Zagrebu do 1941. godine," *Časopis za suvremenu povijest* 1 (1995): 33–53.

Bon, S. "Le communità ebraiche nel Carnaro durante il fascismo," *Quaderni* 14 (2002): 127–47.

Bon, S. *Trieste e le leggi razziali, posebni otisak.* Trieste, 2003.

Bonardi, P. *Propaganda antiebraica sulla stampa parmense (1938–1945).* Parma, 1998.

Born, H. "O talijanskim grijesima i njemačkim vrlinama," *Bilten ŽOZ* 27 (1992): 14–15.

Bostanić, G. *Masonstvo.* Belgrade, 1928.

Bošković, M. "Magda Bošković," *Jevrejski almanah 1955–1956* (1956): 154–58.

Bošković-Stulli, M. "Pjesnikinja istrgnuta iz života—Magda Bošković (1914–1942)," *Bilten ŽOZ* 24 (1992): 9.

Bracher, K. D. *The German Dictatorship: The Origins, Structure, and Effects of National Socialism.* New York: Praeger, 1970.

Breyer, M. "Glas srca i savjesti: Jedna ispovijest," *Nova Evropa* (1922): 9–10.

Breyer, R. "Pravo građanstva." In *Obitelj*, edited by J. Domaš-Nalbantić, 107–12. Zagreb, 1996.

Broucek, P. *Ein General in Zwielicht.* Wien, Köln, and Graz, 1988.

Broz, J. T. *Sabrana djela.* Sarajevo, 1977.

Brozović, L. *Građa za povijest Koprivnice.* Koprivnica, 1978.

Buć, S. *Naši službeni povjesničari i pitanje podrijetla Hrvata.* Zagreb, 1941.

Buć, S. *Temeljne misli nauke Dra. Ante Starčevića.* Zagreb, 1936.

Budak, N., and others, eds. *Zbornik Mirjane Gross.* Zagreb, 1999.

Budak, M. *Rascvjetana trešnja.* Zagreb, 1939.

Bulatović, R. *Koncentracioni logor Jasenovac s posebnim osvrtom na Donju Gradinu.* Sarajevo, 1990.

Buntak, F. *Povijest Zagreba.* Zagreb, 1996.

Butmi, J., and M. Tomić. *Krvave osnove ili protokoli sionskih mudraca.* Split-Šibenik, 1929.

Carin, V. *Smrt je hodala četveronoške.* Zagreb, 1961.

Carmon, B. "31. svibnja 1941. u Zagrebu," *Novi omanut* (Zagreb) 21 (1997): 3.

Carpi, D. "The Diplomatic Negotiations over the Transfer of Jewish Children from Croatia to Turkey and Palestine in 1943," *Yad Vashem Studies* 12 (1977): 109–24.

Čepo, Z. *Zagreb u NOB-i i socijalističkoj revoluciji.* Zagreb: Institut za historiju radničkog pokreta Hrvatske, 1971.

Cesarec, A. *Na Ukrajini.* Zagreb, 1940.

Ciliga, A. *Sam kroz Europu u ratu.* Rome, 1978.

Cindrić, P. "Dr. Vilko Panac: nepravedno zaboravljeni pravednik," *Novi omanut* (Zagreb) 29–30 (1998): 9.

Cornwell, J. *Hitler's Pope: The Secret History of Pius XII.* New York: Viking, 1999.

Ćosić, D. *Stvarno i moguće.* Ljubljana and Zagreb, 1988.

Cota, M. *Slučaj Šakić, Dezinformiranost ili zlonamjernost.* Zagreb, 1999.

Cuvaj, A. *Građa za povijest školstva, II–III.* Zagreb, 1910.

Cvjetković-Kurelec, V. "Grci u Zagrebu." In *Zagrebački Gradec 1242–1850*, edited by I. Kampuš, L. Margetić, and F. Šanjek. Zagreb: Grad Zagreb, 1994.

Dawidowicz, L. S. *The War against the Jews, 1933–1945.* New York: Holt, 1975.

Decenij cionizma, separat. Zagreb, n.d.

Dedijer, V. *Dnevnik*, 3 vols. Beograd, 1970.

Delić, R. St. *Jevreji u Jugoslaviji.* Belgrade, 1939.

Derenčin, M. "Ladanjska opozicija." In *Pučki igrokazi XIX stoljeća*, edited by N. Batušić, 393–452. Zagreb, 1973.

Despot, M. *Industrija i trgovina građanske Hrvatske 1873–1880*. Zagreb, 1979.

Despot, M. "Jacques Epstein: život i rad," *Jevrejski almanah 1963–1964* (1965): 82–91.

Despot, M. "Jakob Weiss, zagrebački veletrgovac i manufakturista (1864–1935)," *Jevrejski almanah 1961–1962* (1962): 42–57.

Despot, M. "Protužidovski izgredi u Zagorju i Zagrebu godine 1883," *Jevrejski almanah 1957–1958* (1958): 75–85.

Despot, M."'Schabsel i Co.' kao zakupnici staklane na zagrebačkom kaptolskom posjedu Varaždinske Toplice 1784–1786," *Jevrejski almanah 1959–1960* (1960): 79–93.

Despot, M. *Josip Tömör, zagrebački trgovac, obrtnik i manufakturista, Iz starog i novog Zagreba III*. 107–16.

Despot, M. "Žak Epštajn (Jacques Epstein), Značajna ličnost u javnom i kulturnom životu Zagreba u prvoj polovini 19. stoljeća," *Jevrejski pregled* 7–8 (1973).

Diamant, J. "Najstarija židovska bogoštovna općina u Hrvatskoj," *Jevrejski almanah* 1 (Vršac, 1925): 127–32.

Dizdar, Z. "Logori na području sjeverozapadne Hrvatske u toku drugog svjetskog rata 1941–1945. godine," *Časopis za suvremenu povijest* 1–2 (1990): 83–110.

Dobronić, Lj. "Ignjat Granitz, hrvatski industrijalac, dobrotvor i mecena," *Povijesni prilozi* 15 (1996).

Dobronić, Lj. *Splet sudbina*. Zagreb, 2000.

Dojč, V. "100 godina organiziranog rada židovskih žena u Zagrebu." In *200 godina Židova u Zagrebu*, edited by M. Mirković, Jevrejska općina Zagreb, and Savez jevrejskih opština Jugoslavije, 53–61. Zagreb: Jevrejska općina Zagreb, 1988.

Dojč, V. "Utočište u Zagrebu," *Bilten ŽOZ* 4–5 (1988).

Dojč, V. "U sjeni Hrama." In *Obitelj*, edited by J. Domaš-Nalbantić, 89–94. Zagreb, 1996.

Domaš, J. "Zeev Glück (1912–1982), posljednji urednik tjednika 'Židov,'" *Bilten ŽOZ* 17 (1991).

Domaš-Nalbantić, J., ed. *Obitelj*. Zagreb, 1996.

Domljan, Ž., and Jugoslavenski leksikografski zavod Miroslav Krleža. *Likovna enciklopedija Jugoslavije*, vols. 1–4. Zagreb, 1966–1969.

Došen, M. *Ante Starčević, povodom 47. godišnjice smerti*. Zagreb, 1943.

Draganović, K. *Povijest Bosne i Hercegovine*, vol. 1. 2nd ed. Sarajevo, 1998.

Dr. Hinko Hinković i-istina. Zagreb, 1905.

Duffy, E. *Sveci i grešnici, povijest papa*. Rijeka, 1998.

Đurić, Lj. "Naš komandant Vojko Hohšteter," *Bilten ŽOZ* 4–7 (1988).

Đurić, T. "Utjecaj židovske etničke skupine na razvoj novčarstva u Hrvatskoj," *Bilten ŽOZ* 27 (1992): 10–11.

Elon, A. *The Pity of It All: A History of the Jews in Germany, 1743–1933*. New York: Metropolitian, 2002.

Enciklopedija Jugoslavije, t. 1–8. Zagreb, 1965–1971.

Encyclopaedia Judaica, sv. 1–17. Jerusalem, 1971–1972.

Erlih, J. "Sećanje na logor Jasenovac (Pre 31 godinu prestao je da postoji jedan od najzloglasnijih koncentracionih logora)," *Jevrejski pregled* 3–4 (1976): 5–7.

Etinger, Š, and others. *Istorija jevrejskog naroda.* Belgrade, 1996.

Eventov, J. *Istorija Jevreja Jugoslavije. I: Od davnine do kraja 19. vijeka.* Tel Aviv, 1971 (abstract in Serbo-Croatian, 370–98).

Favez, J.-C. *Das Internationale Rote Kreutz und das Dritte Reich. War der Holocausta aufzuhalten?* Munich, 1989.

Feldman, A. "Gospođica Ashkenazy žali. Intelektualni život Židova u međuratnoj Hrvatskoj." In *Zbornik Mirjane Gross,* edited by N. Budak and others, 353–58. Zagreb, 1999.

Ferrero, G. *Mlada Evropa,* II. Zagreb, 1918.

Fischer, V. "Židovska pučka škola u Palmotićevoj 16, Zagreb, šk. god. 1931–32., 1. razred," *Ha-kol* 49–50 (1997).

Fišer, D. *Židovi u Osijeku.* In *Dva stoljeća povijesti i kulture Židova u Zagrebu i Hrvatskoj,* edited by O. Kraus, 425–27. Zagreb: Židovska Općina Zagreb, 1998.

Frangeš, I. *Povijest hrvatske književnosti.* Zagreb and Ljubljana, 1987.

Freiberger, Š. M. *Molitvenik.* Zagreb, 1st ed. 1938, 2nd ed. 1994.

Freidenreich, H. P. *The Jews of Yugoslavia: A Quest for Community.* Philadelphia, 1979.

Freundlich, E. "Tragedija na Jadovnu ljeta 1941," *Novi omanut* (Zagreb) 34–35 (1999): 22–23.

Gabrijel, St. *Čivut i Talmud ili najveći neprijatelj svih Nežidova.* Osijek, 1941.

Gajić, E. B. *Jugoslavija i "jevrejski problem."* Belgrade, 1938.

Gavrilović, S. "O Jevrejima u Ugarskoj XVIII. i XIX. veka," *Jevrejski almanah 1971–1996* (2000): 123–36.

Geiger, V. "Nijemci Đakova i Đakovštine u Drugom svjetskom ratu (1941–1945)," *Časopis za suvremenu povijest* 3 (1996): 399–424.

Geiger, V. "Nijemci Đakova i Đakovštine u Kraljevini SHS/Jugoslaviji," *Kolo, Časopis Matice hrvatske* 4 (winter 1997): 178–215.

Geiger, V. "Saslušanje Branimira Altgayera, vođe Njemačke narodne skupine u NDH u Upravi državne bezbjednosti za NRH 1949. godine," *Časopis za suvremenu povijest* 3 (1999): 575–638.

Geiger, V., and N. Barić. "Odjeci i obilježavanje 5. prosinca 1918. u NDH," *Časopis za suvremenu povijest* 3 (2002): 833–52.

Geiger, V., and I. Jurković. *Što se dogodilo s folksdojčerima.* Zagreb, 1993.

Gero, A. "Liberals, Anti-Semites, and Jews at the Birth of Modern Hungary." In *Modern Hungarian Society in the Making: The Unfinished Experience,* 182–99. Budapest: CEU, 1993.

Gilbert, M., *Jewish History Atlas,* 2nd ed. London, 1976.

Ginsberg, D. "Strossmayer i Židovi," *Omanut* 10 (1938).

Giron, A. "Židovsko pitanje u općini Opatija (1938–1945)," *Problemi sjevernog Jadrana* (Zagreb-Rijeka) 7 (2000): 143–65.

Gizdić, D. *Dalmacija 1941.* Zagreb, 1957.

Gjalski, K. Š. "Feminalija," *Književnik* 2, no. 11 (1929): 401–7.

Glaessinger, L. *Ilirski pokret i Jevreji.* Zagreb, 1936.

Glavina, F. *Neobjavljeni novinski napis Joea Matošića iz 1941. godine, Pro historia croatica 1, zbornik uz 70. godišnjicu života Dragutina Pavličevića.* 358–69. Zagreb, 2002.

Glesinger, L. "Dr. Lavoslav Šik, 1881–1942," *Jevrejski pregled* 9–10 (1974).
Glesinger, L. "Gavro Schwarz, Povijest zagrebačke židovske općine od osnutka do 50-ih godina 19. vijeka (recenzija)," *Omanut* 10 (1939): 158–60.
Glesinger, L. "Hebraizmi u govoru zagrebačkih Jevreja i ne-Jevreja," *Jevrejski almanah 1957–1958* (1958): 9–28.
Glesinger, L. "Interesantan prilog povijesti Jevreja u bivšoj Vojnoj Krajini," *Židov* (1935–1936).
Glesinger, L. "Iz povijesti Jevreja u Hrvatskoj," *Jevrejski almanah 1954* (1954): 60–67.
Glesinger, L. "Jedna molba za dozvolu boravka u Zagrebu iz godine 1830," *Omanut* 10 (1939): 160–63.
Glesinger, L. "Moises Jakobsohn, prvi tolerirani Jevrejin u Hrvatskoj," *Židov* (1936): 24.
Glesinger, L. "Prvi jevrejski bolesnici u Zakladnoj bolnici u Zagrebu," *Jevrejski almanah 1965–1967* (1967): 92–97.
Glesinger, L. "Strossmayer i Židovi," *Židov* (1938): 27.
Goldhagen, D. J. *A Moral Reckoning: The Role of the Catholic Church in the Holocaust and Its Unfulfilled Duty of Repair.* New York: Knopf, 2002.
Goldstein, A. "Porto Re 1942/3, Kraljevica," *Bilten ŽOZ* 28–29 (1993): 12–13.
Goldstein, I. "Antifašizam—jučer, danas, sutra." In *Antisemitizam, Holokaust, Antifašizam*, edited by N. Lengel-Krizman and I. Goldstein, 285–89. Zagreb, 1996.
Goldstein, I. *Antisemitizam ustaškog pokreta, Spomenica Ljube Bobana.* Zagreb, 1996, pp. 321–332.
Goldstein, I. "Antisemitizam u Hrvatskoj." In *Antisemitizam, Holokaust, Antifašizam*, edited by N. Lengel-Krizman and I. Goldstein, 12–52. Zagreb, 1996.
Goldstein, I. *Croatia: A History.* London-Montreal, 1999.
Goldstein, I. "Genocid nad Židovima u NDH?," *Novi omanut* (Zagreb) (1996).
Goldstein, I. *Hrvatski rani srednji vijek.* Zagreb, 1995.
Goldstein, I. *Kako, kada i zašto je nastala legenda o nasilnoj smrti kralja Zvonimira.* Institut za hrvatsku povijest Papers 17, 35–52. Zagreb, 1984.
Goldstein, I. "Memorija i obitelj u povijesti." In *Obitelj*, edited by J. Domaš-Nalbantić, 11–26. Zagreb, 1996.
Goldstein, I. "Sisačka bitka u hrvatskoj povijesti i društvu u 19. i 20. stoljeću," *Zbornik radova "Sisačka bitka 1593"* (Zagreb-Sisak, 1994): 275–88.
Goldstein, I. *Stjepan Radić i Židovi.* Zavod za hrvatsku povijest Papers 29, 208–16. Zagreb, 1996.
Goldstein, I. "Upotreba povijesti," *Erazmus* (Zagreb) 1 (1993): 52–62.
Goldstein, I. "Zagrebačka židovska općina od osnutka do 1941." In *Dva stoljeća povijesti i kulture Židova u Zagrebu i Hrvatskoj*, edited by O. Kraus, 12–18. Zagreb: Židovska Općina Zagreb, 1998.
Goldstein, I. "Židovi na Gradecu od 14. stoljeća do 1848. godine." In *Zagrebački Gradec 1242–1850*, edited by I. Kampuš, L. Margetić, and F. Šanjek, 293–303. Zagreb: Grad Zagreb, 1994.
Goldstein, I. *Židovi u Zagrebu: 1918–1941.* Zagreb, 2004.
Goldstein, I., ed. *Kronologija, Hrvatska–Europa–svijet.* Zagreb, 1996.

Goldstein, I., and S. Goldstein. "Farma jugoslavenskih židovskih naseljenika u Palestini 1926–1928." In *Zbornik Mirjane Gross*, edited by N. Budak and others, 371–86. Zagreb, 1999.

Goldstein, I., and S. Goldstein. *Holokaust u Zagrebu*. Zagreb: Novi Liber, 2001.

Goldstein, I., and S. Goldstein. *Jasenovac i Bleiburg nisu isto*. Zagreb, 2011.

Goldstein, S. "Beatifikacija kardinala Alojzija Stepinca," *Ha-kol* 55–56 (1998): 15–16.

Goldstein, S. "Iskustva Holokausta u Hrvatskoj." *Bilten ŽOZ* 28–29 (1993): 4–5.

Goldstein, S. "Neprihvatljiva rehabilitacija ustaške NDH," *Bilten ŽOZ* 30 (1993): 2–3.

Goldstein, S. "Potomstvo naroda izabranog (Biblija i opstanak židovskog naroda)," *Kultura* (Zagreb) 12 (1970): 287–301.

Goldstein, S. "Uz reprint Freibergerova molitvenika iz 1938. godine." In *Molitvenik*, Š. M. Freiberger. Zagreb, 1994.

Goldstein, S. "Židovi Hrvatske u antifašističkom otporu." In *Antisemitizam, Holokaust, Antifašizam*, edited by N. Lengel-Krizman and I. Goldstein, 148–55. Zagreb, 1996.

Goldstein, S. "Židovska općina Zagreb od 1941. do 1997. godine." In *Dva stoljeća povijesti i kulture Židova u Zagrebu i Hrvatskoj*, edited by O. Kraus, 19–27. Zagreb: Židovska Općina Zagreb, 1998.

Golec, I. *Tiskarstvo, izdavaštvo i knjižarstvo Petrinje*. Zagreb, 1992.

Golubić, R. *Postoji li židovska opasnost (moj proces sa Židovima)*. Slavonski Brod, 1941.

Golubić, R. *Zašto propadamo ili Židovi i Nežidovi*. Brod n. Savi (Slavonski Brod), n.d.

Gordiejew, P. B. *Voices of Yugoslav Jewry*. Albany: State University of New York Press, 1999.

Grgec-Tusun, A. *Uspomena iz djetinjstva na mog dragog oca prof. P. Grgeca*. Marulić, 1992.

Gross, M. *Izvorno pravaštvo*. Zagreb, 2000.

Gross, M. *Počeci moderne Hrvatske*. Zagreb, 1985.

Gross, M. *Povijest pravaške ideologije*. Zagreb, 1974.

Gross, M. *Ravnopravnost bez jednakovrijednosti (Prilog pitanju mentaliteta i ideologije hrvatskih cionista na početku 20. stoljeća)*. In *Dva stoljeća povijesti i kulture Židova u Zagrebu i Hrvatskoj*, edited by O. Kraus, 106–26. Zagreb: Židovska Općina Zagreb, 1998.

Gross, M. "Slike povijesti." In *Obitelj*, edited by J. Domaš-Nalbantić, 85–87. Zagreb, 1996.

Gross, M. *Vladavina Hrvatsko-srpske koalicije 1906–1907*. Belgrade, 1960.

Gross, M. *Židovi u Habsburškoj Monarhiji u 19. stoljeću*. Gordogan 23–24. Zagreb, 1987.

Gross, M., and A. Szabo. *Prema hrvatskome građanskom društvu*. Zagreb, 1992.

Grossepais-Gil, J. "Bekstvo iz logora Jasenovac," *Jevrejski pregled* 1–2 (1982): 21–27.

Grothusen, K.-D. *Entstehung und Geschichte Zagrebs bis zum Ausgang des 14. Jhr.* Wiesbaden, 1967.

Gruden, Ž. "Fašizam je antifašizam, antifašizam je fašizam," *Bilten ŽOZ* 38 (1995).

Gruden, Ž. "Perači Endehazije," *Bilten ŽOZ* 41–42 (1995).

Gruden, Ž. "Što je na etiketama, a što ispod njih," *Bilten ŽOZ* 43 (1995–1996).

Gruden, Ž. "Židovi u novinarstvu u Hrvatskoj." In *Dva stoljeća povijesti i kulture Ži-*

dova u Zagrebu i Hrvatskoj, edited by O. Kraus, 253–59. Zagreb: Židovska Općina Zagreb, 1998.

Grünfelder, A.-M. "Manes Sperber i zagrebački ljevičarski intelektualci," *Jevrejski almanah 1971–1996* (2000): 166–72.

Hanak, P. "Tipovi židovske asimilacije u Habsburškoj monarhiji." In *Zbornik Mirjane Gross*, edited by N. Budak and others, 209–18. Zagreb, 1999.

Harviainen, T. "The Jews in Finland and World War II," *Scandinavian Jewish Studies* 21, 1–2 (2000): 157–66.

Hayden, Robert M. "Balancing Discussion of Jasenovac and the Manipulation of History," *East European Politics and Societies* 6, no. 2 (1992): 207–12.

Hayden, Robert M. "Recounting the Dead: The Rediscovery and Redefinition of Wartime Massacres in Late- and Post-Communist Yugoslavia." In *Memory, History, and Opposition Under State Socialism*, edited by R. Watson, 167–84. Santa Fe: School of American Research Press, 1994.

Herzig, M. *Viribus unitis: Das Buch vom Kaiser.* Budapest, Vienna, and Leipzig, 1898.

Hilberg, R. *The Destruction of the European Jews.* Revised, second edition. New York: Holmes & Meier, 1985.

Hinković, H. *Raj i pakao, Slike s onkraj groba.* Novi Sad, 1902.

Hinković, H. *Kradja kod kraljevičkih jezuita: Jedno pravosudno umorstvo.* Rieka, 1905.

Hirschmann, I. *Djevojačka gimnastika, priručnik.* Zagreb, 1906.

Hirschmann, I. *Kratki izvadak iz historije gimnastike.* Zagreb, 1906, 1914.

Holjevac, V. *Zapisi iz rodnog grada.* Zagreb, 1972.

Hoptner, J. B. *Yugoslavia in Crisis, 1934–1941.* New York: Columbia University Press, 1962.

Horvat, J. *Zapisci iz nepovrata—Hrvatski mikrokozam između dva rata 1919–1941.* Zagreb, 1983.

Horvat, J. *Preživjeti u Zagrebu, Dnevnik 1943–1945.* Zagreb, 1989.

Horvatić, F. "Logor Danica u Koprivnici," *Podravski zbornik* 8 (Koprivnica, 1975): 43–55.

Hory, L., and M. Broszat. *Der Kroatische Ustascha-Staat.* Stuttgart, 1964.

Hrastović, I. "Ante Moškov—uloga u stvaranju i propasti NDH (Ante Moškov's Role in the Creation and Dissolution of the ISC)," *Časopis za suvremenu povijest* 1 (1999).

Hrvatski biografski leksikon, I–V. Zagreb, 1983–2002.

Hrvatski leksikon, t. I–II. Zagreb, 1996–1997.

Hrženjak, J. *Rušenje antifašističkih spomenika u Hrvatskoj, 1990–2000.* Zagreb, 2002.

Huberband, S. *Kiddush Hashem: Jewish Religious and Cultural Life in Poland during the Holocaust.* New York: Yeshiva University Press, 1987.

Imenik prautemeljitah, utemeljiteljah i članovah zagrebačkog društva čovječnosti. Zagreb, 1868.

Isaić, V. "Časno djelo sestara franjevki na Rabu," *Bilten ŽOZ* 46–47 (1996): 6.

Isaić, V. "Njemački desant na otok Rab—operacija 'Illusion,'" *Bilten ŽOZ* 39–40 (1995): 10–11.

Isaić, V. *Put prognanih—od Mostara do Raba.* Split, 2003.

Istina o Nezavisnoj Državi Hrvatskoj. Buenos Aires, 1991.

Itai-Indik, J. "Djeca bježe," *Jevrejski almanah 1963–1964* (1965): 129–36.

Ivanc, E. *Nepokorena mladost.* Zagreb, 1961.

Ivančan, Lj. *Podaci o zagrebačkim kanonicima.* Kaptolski arhiv u Zagrebu.

Ivanuša, D. "Židovi—likovni umjetnici u antifašističkoj borbi i žrtve holokausta." In *Antisemitizam, Holokaust, Antifašizam*, edited by N. Lengel-Krizman and I. Goldstein, 156–85. Zagreb, 1996.

Iveković, M. *Hrvatska lijeva inteligencija 1918–1945.* Zagreb, 1970.

Ivić, V. "NOB na području općine Zaprešić," *Zaprešićki zbornik* 2 (1988).

Jakovljević, B. "Putevi stradanja, borbe i spasavanja Jevreja Jugoslavije, 1941–1945," *Jevrejski pregled* 1–2 (1982): 27–34.

Jakovljević, I. *Konclogor na Savi.* Zagreb, 1999.

Janjatović, B. *Stjepan Radić—progoni, zatvori, suđenja, ubojstvo, 1889–1928.* Zagreb, 2003.

Jareb, J. *Pola stoljeća hrvatske politike.* Zagreb, 1995.

Jareb, J. *Zlato i novac Nezavisne Države Hrvatske izneseni u inozemstvo.* Zagreb, 1997.

Jareb, M. "Ustaški pokret." PhD dissertation, Zagreb, 2003.

Jelić-Butić, F. *Ustaše i NDH.* Zagreb, 1977.

Jews in Yugoslavia. Zagreb: Muzejski prostor, 1989.

Johnson, P. *A History of the Jews,* London, 1987.

Joško. "Naša posljednja utakmica," *Bilten Hitahdut Olej Jugoslavija* (Tel Aviv) 8–10 (1972).

Jurak, R. "Uspomene iz logora u Kraljevici," *Bilten ŽOZ* 28–29 (1993): 13–14.

Jurčević, J. *Nastanak jasenovačkog mita.* Zagreb, 1998.

Kadelburg, L. "Jevrejska zajednica Jugoslavije (njen odnos prema jevrejskim organizacijama u inostranstvu)," *Kadima* 20 (March 1967).

Kadelburg, L. "Neka aktuelna pitanja," *Jevrejski pregled* 11–12 (1970): 2–6.

Kalezić, V. *NDH u svetlu nemačkih dokumenata i dnevnika Gleza fon Horstenaua 1941–1944.* Belgrade, 1987.

Kampuš, I., L. Margetić, and F. Šanjek, eds. *Zagrebački Gradec 1242–1850.* Zagreb: Grad Zagreb, 1994.

Kantolić, Z. "Djelovanje Anketne komisije 1945. u Zagrebu—'Utvrđivanje zločina kulturnom saradnjom s neprijateljem,'" *Časopis za suvremenu povijest* 1 (2001): 41–74.

Kečkemet, D. "Židovski sabirni logori na području pod talijanskom okupacijom." In *Antisemitizam, Holokaust, Antifašizam*, edited by N. Lengel-Krizman and I. Goldstein, 120–32. Zagreb, 1996.

Kevo, M. *Počeci logora Jasenovac.* Zagreb, 2003.

Kieval, H. J. *The Making of Czech Jewry, National Conflict, and Jewish Society in Bohemia, 1870–1918.* New York: Oxford University Press, 1988.

Kisić-Kolanović, N. "Hrvatski državni sabor NDH 1942," *Časopis za suvremenu povijest* 3 (2000): 545–65.

Kisić-Kolanović, N. "Podržavljenje imovine Židova u NDH," *Časopis za suvremenu povijest* 3 (1998): 429–53.

Kisić-Kolanović, N. *Vojskovođa i politika, Sjećanja Slavka Kvaternika.* Zagreb, 1997.

Klaić, N. *Zagreb u srednjem vijeku 1.* Zagreb, 1982.

Klein, R. "Sinagogalna arhitektura na tlu Hrvatske u kontekstu Austro-Ugarske Monarhije." In *Dva stoljeća povijesti i kulture Židova u Zagrebu i Hrvatskoj*, edited by O. Kraus, 156–65. Zagreb: Židovska Općina Zagreb, 1998.

Knez, J. "Rab rujna 1943," *Bilten ŽOZ* 31–32 (1993): 8.

Knežević, S. *Zagrebačka sinagoga.* Exhibition catalog. Zagreb, 1996.

Knežević, S. "Izbor dokumenata vezanih uz gradnju zagrebačke sinagoge," *Ha-kol* 65–66 (2000): 2–4.

Kobsa, L. "O organizaciji ustaškog aparata vlasti za provođenje terora u tzv. NDH." In *Zagreb u NOB-i i socijalističkoj revoluciji*, edited by Z. Čepo, 239–50. Zagreb: Institut za historiju radničkog pokreta Hrvatske, 1971

Kočić, D. M. *Jugosloveni u koncentracionom logoru Buhenvald, 1941–1945.* Belgrade, 1989.

Kolanović, J. "Holocaust in Croatia—Documentation and Research Perspectives," *Arhivski vjesnik* 39 (1996): 157–74.

Kolanović, M. *Elektronska baza podataka žrtava drugog svjetskog rata s područja grada Zagreba* (analiza projekta "Dotrščina"). Hrvatski državni arhiv, neobjavljeno, 12 str.

Kolar-Dimitrijević, M. "Akcija povjesničara dr. Rudolfa Horvata na spašavanju gradečkog Židova Arpada Sterna 1941. godine," *Novi omanut* (Zagreb) 26 (1998): 10.

Kolar-Dimitrijević, M. "Prvo dobrotvorno društvo Humanitaetsverein u Zagrebu: u povodu stopedesete obljetnice (1846–1996)." In *Dva stoljeća povijesti i kulture Židova u Zagrebu i Hrvatskoj*, edited by O. Kraus, 69–73. Zagreb: Židovska Općina Zagreb, 1998.

Kolar-Dimitrijević, M. *Prvo zagrebačko dobrotvorno društvo—Društvo čovječnosti 1846–1946.* Zagreb, 1998

Kolar-Dimitrijević, M. *Radni slojevi Zagreba od 1918. do 1931.* Zagreb, 1973.

Kolar-Dimitrijević, M. "Sjećanja veterinara Zorka Goluba na trinaest dana boravka u logoru Jasenovac 1942. godine," *Časopis za suvremenu povijest* 15, no. 2 (1983): 155–76.

Kolar-Dimitrijević, M. "Židovi u gospodarstvu sjeverne Hrvatske od 1873. do 1941. godine." In *Dva stoljeća povijesti i kulture Židova u Zagrebu i Hrvatskoj*, edited by O. Kraus, 127–41. Zagreb: Židovska Općina Zagreb, 1998.

Koledar zagrebačko društva čovječnosti. Zagreb, 1872.

Komarica, Z. *Kerestinečka kronika.* Zagreb, 1989.

Korda, I. "Nikad dosta suza," *Jevrejski pregled* 7–8 (1986).

Korda, I. "Povratak iz Jasenovca . . . koji to nije bio," *Jevrejski pregled* 11–12 (1986).

Kornfein, P. "Crno sjećanje na 'Zavrtnicu,'" *Jevrejski pregled* 11–12 (1974): 56.

Kornfein, P. "I u paklu ima anđela," *Novi omanut* (Zagreb) 21 (1997): 2–3.

Kosier, Lj. *Historija Jevreja u Jugoslaviji.* Zagreb, 1929.

Kosier, Lj. *Jevreji u trgovini Jugoslavije i Bugarske.* Zagreb, 1930.

Kosier, Lj. *Nacionalno-socijalna struktura Jugoslavije, II. Jevreji u Jugoslaviji.* Belgrade and Zagreb, 1936.

Koš, J. *Lavoslav Šik i njegova knjižnica.* In *Dva stoljeća povijesti i kulture Židova u Zagrebu i Hrvatskoj*, edited by O. Kraus, 78–83. Zagreb: Židovska Općina Zagreb, 1998.

Košutić, I. *Hrvatsko domobranstvo u drugom svjetskom ratu.* Zagreb, 1992.

Kovač, V. *Obnova židovskog tiska u Hrvatskoj.* In *Dva stoljeća povijesti i kulture Židova u Zagrebu i Hrvatskoj*, edited by O. Kraus, 92–101. Zagreb: Židovska Općina Zagreb, 1998.

Kovač, V., and J. Domaš. *Jewish Heritage in Zagreb and Croatia.* Zagreb, 1993.

Kovačec, A. *Bosanski Židovi u Zagrebu nakon okupacije Bosne 1878. do 1941. godine.* In *Dva stoljeća povijesti i kulture Židova u Zagrebu i Hrvatskoj*, edited by O. Kraus, 84–91. Zagreb: Židovska Općina Zagreb, 1998.

Kovačević, B. *Psihoanaliza i ljevica.* Zagreb, 1988.

Kovačević, B. *Slučaj zagrebačkih revizionista.* Zagreb, 1988.

Kovačević, V. *Pod otvorenim nebom.* Belgrade, 1985.

Kovačić, D. "Zapovjednici i dužnosnici jasenovačke skupine logora 1941–1945. godine," *Časopis za suvremenu povijest* 1 (1999): 97–112.

Kovačić, I. *Kampor 1942–1943: Hrvati, Slovenci i Židovi u koncentracijskom logoru Kampor na Rabu.* Rijeka, 1998.

Kovačić, I. "Pitanje broja umrlih zatočenika u koncentracijskom logoru Kampor Kraljevine Italije na otoku Rabu (1942–1943)," *Rijeka* 5, nos. 1–2 (2000): 107–18.

Kožul, S. *Spomenica žrtvama ljubavi zagrebačke nadbiskupije.* Zagreb, 1992.

Kramer, F. "Makabi 1913–1993," *Bilten ŽOZ* 39–40 (1994).

Kramer, T. "Udio Židova u športu u Hrvatskoj." In *Dva stoljeća povijesti i kulture Židova u Zagrebu i Hrvatskoj*, edited by O. Kraus, 263–67. Zagreb: Židovska Općina Zagreb, 1998.

Kraus, O., ed. *Dva stoljeća povijesti i kulture Židova u Zagrebu i Hrvatskoj.* Zagreb: Židovska Općina Zagreb, 1998.

Krišto, J. *Katolička crkva i Nezavisna Država Hrvatska 1941–1945*, vols. 1–2. Zagreb, 1998.

Krišto, J. "Katolička crkva i Židovi u vrijeme NDH." In *Antisemitizam, Holokaust, Antifašizam*, edited by N. Lengel-Krizman and I. Goldstein, 139–47. Zagreb, 1996.

Krišto, J. *Prešućena povijest, katolička crkva u hrvatskoj politici 1850–1918. godine.* Zagreb, 1994.

Krizman, B. *Ante Pavelić i ustaše*, 2nd ed. Zagreb, 1983.

Krizman, B. *NDH između Hitlera i Mussolinija*, 3rd ed. Zagreb, 1986.

Krizman, B. "O odjecima Oktobarske revolucije i zelenom kadru," *Historijski zbornik* (1957): 149–57.

Krizman, B. *Ustaše i Treći Reich, 1–2.* Zagreb, 1983–1986.

Krleža, M. *Balade Petrice Kerempuha.* Zagreb, 1946.

Krleža, M. *Deset krvavih godina.* Zagreb, 1971.

Krleža, M. "Donadini, Dostojevski i Ivan Nevistić," *Književna republika* 5, nos. 3–4 (1927): 219–24.

Kvaternik, E. D., and J. Jareb. *Sjećanja i zapažanja, 1925–1945.* Zagreb, 1995.

Kustić, Ž. "Dobri duh otoka Paga," *Glas koncila* 10 (1985): 10.

Lador-Lederer, Ž.-J. "Tri fragmenta o cionizmu." In *Dva stoljeća povijesti i kulture Židova u Zagrebu i Hrvatskoj*, edited by O. Kraus, 179–92. Zagreb: Židovska Općina Zagreb, 1998.

LaFarge, J. *Un Américain comme les autres*. Paris 1959.

Laqueur, W. *The Terrible Secret*. London: Holt, 1980.

Lasić, S. *Autobiografski zapisi*. Zagreb, 2000.

Lasić, S. *Krležologija III*. Zagreb, 1989.

Laszlo, A. "Croquis za urotu sjećanja," *Bilten ŽOZ* 12 (1989): 10–11.

Lebl, Aleksandar. "Četvrt veka od formiranja rapskog bataljona," *Jevrejski pregled* (1968): 7–8.

Lebl, Ana. "Židovstvo između prozelitizma i asimilacije." In *Dva stoljeća povijesti i kulture Židova u Zagrebu i Hrvatskoj*, edited by O. Kraus, 193–97. Zagreb: Židovska Općina Zagreb, 1998.

Lebl, Ž., ed. *Jevreji iz Jugoslavije ratni vojni zarobljenici u Nemačkoj, Spomen-album, pola veka od oslobođenja 1945–1995*. Tel Aviv, 1995.

Lengel-Krizman, N. "Kronologija židovskog stradanja 1938–1945." In *Antisemitizam, Holokaust, Antifašizam*, edited by N. Lengel-Krizman and I. Goldstein, 247–59. Zagreb, 1996.

Lengel-Krizman, N. "Logori za Židove u NDH." In *Antisemitizam, Holokaust, Antifašizam*, edited by N. Lengel-Krizman and I. Goldstein, 91–103. Zagreb, 1996.

Lengel-Krizman, N. "Narodnooslobodilački pokret u Zagrebu 1941–1945," *Zbornik radova "Zagrebu u NOB-u i socijalističkoj revoluciji"* (Zagreb, 1971): 33–61.

Lengel-Krizman, N. *O nekim pitanjima organizacije i djelovanja NOO-a i odbora JNOF-a u Zagrebu za vrijeme NOB-a*. Institut za hrvatsku povijest Papers 4, 197–222. Zagreb, 1973.

Lengel-Krizman, N. "Prilog proučavanju terora u NDH. Ženski sabirni logori, 1941–1942," *Povijesni prilozi* 4 (1985): 1–38.

Lengel-Krizman, N. "Revolucionarni omladinski pokret u Zagrebu u toku rata," *Zbornik radova "Zagreb u NOB-u i socijalističkoj revoluciji"* (Zagreb, 1971): 137–62.

Lengel-Krizman, N. "Sabirni logori i dječja sabirališta na području sjeverozapadne Hrvatske 1941–1942." In *Sjeverozapadna Hrvatska u NOB-u i socijalističkoj revoluciji*, edited by L. Boban and others, 30–48. Varaždin, 1976.

Lengel-Krizman, N. "Sudbina preživjelih Židova iz logora na Rabu 1943–1945," *Bilten ŽOZ* 46–47: 7–16.

Lengel-Krizman, N., and I. Goldstein, eds. *Antisemitizam, Holokaust, Antifašizam*. Zagreb, 1996.

Lengel-Krizman, N., and M. Sobolevski. "Hapšenje 165 židovskih omladinaca u Zagrebu u svibnju 1941. godine," *Novi omanut* (Zagreb) 31 (1998): 6–9.

Lessing, T. *Jüdischer Selbsthass*. Berlin: Jüdischer Verlag, 1930.

Levental, Z. "Još o Makabiju," *Bilten ŽOZ* 46–47 (1996).

Levental, Z. "Lekari na suzbijanju endemskog sifilisa u Bosni i Hercegovini i njihovo učešće u NOB-i," *Zbornik radova Naučnog društva za istoriju zdravstvene kulture Jugoslavije* (Belgrade, 1963).

Levental, Z. "Sećanje na medicinski rad u Jevrejskoj opštini u Zagrebu," *Bilten ŽOZ* 19–20 (1991).

Levi, D. "Četrdesetgodišnjica 'sarajevskog mira,'" *Jevrejski pregled* (1968): 7–8.

Levi, D. "Jedan nedoživljeni jubilej (povodom 100-godišnjjice osvećenja zagrebačke sinagoge)," *Jevrejski pregled* (1967): 8–9.

Levi, D. "Povodom 30-godišnjice oslobođenja–poslednji dani Feramontija," *Jevrejski pregled* (1975): 9–10.

Levi, M. "Od pisma do pisma." In *Obitelj*, edited by J. Domaš-Nalbantić, 99–101. Zagreb, 1996.

Levntal, Z. "Naš rad na istraživanju jugoslovenskih Jevreja, koncepcije i neki dosadašnji rezultati," *Jevrejski almanah 1957* (1958): 139–48.

Licht, Aleksandar (povodom 50. rođendana). Zagreb, 1934.

Licht, A. *O mržnji i o izbavljenju*. Biblioteka "Židov," knj. 9. Zagreb, 1937.

Licht, A. *Potrebe i zahtjevi*. Zagreb, ca. 1919.

Lipa, R. "Pomoć Jevreja Jugoslavije jevrejskim izbeglicama," *Bilten SJOJ* 1 (1987): 7–17.

Lipa, R. "Židovska općina u Zagrebu i njezino djelovanje za vrijeme NDH," *Ha-kol* 51–52 (1997).

Kadelburg, L. "Šta je značilo jevrejsko opredeljivanje," *Jevrejski pregled* (1981): 3–4.

Loker, C. *Začeci i razvoj cionizma u južnoslavenskim krajevima*. In *Dva stoljeća povijesti i kulture Židova u Zagrebu i Hrvatskoj*, edited by O. Kraus, 166–78. Zagreb: Židovska Općina Zagreb, 1998.

Loker, C. *Sarajevski spor i sefardski pokret u Jugoslaviji*, Zbornik JIM 7, Belgrade, 1997, pp. 72–79.

Lončarić, M., and V. Lončarić. *Židovi u Varaždinu*. In *Dva stoljeća povijesti i kulture Židova u Zagrebu i Hrvatskoj*, edited by O. Kraus, 358–77. Zagreb: Židovska Općina Zagreb, 1998.

Lönne, K.-E. *Il cattolicesimo politico nel XIX e XX secolo*. Bologna, 1991.

Lorković, M. *Narod i zemlja Hrvata*. Zagreb, 1939.

Lukas, F. *Dr. Ante Starčević: o 40. godišnjici smrti*. Zagreb, 1936.

Lukas, F. *Dr. Ante Starčević (govor dr. Filipa Lukasa, prigodom 41-godišnjice Starčevićeve smrti)*. Zagreb, 1937.

Lukas, F. *Hrvatski narod i hrvatska državna misao*. Zagreb, 1944.

Lukas, F. *Ličnosti–stvaranja–pokreti*. Zagreb, 1944.

Lukas, F. "Starčević." In *Dr. Ante Starčević: o 40. godišnjici smrti*, 3–13. Zagreb, 1936.

Macanović, H. "Ivana Hirschmann (1866–1943), Historija fizičke kulture," *Bilten* no. 2. Zagreb, 1966. Also published in *Jevrejski pregled* 5–6 (1974).

Macartney, C. A. *Hungary and Her Successors*. London: Oxford University Press, 1937.

Macartney, C. A. *National States and National Minorities*. London: Oxford University Press, 1934.

Maček, V. *Memoari*. Zagreb, 1992.

Magašić, M. "Iz logora na otoku Rabu I–II," *Bilten ŽOZ* 25 (1992): 10–11, 13, 26.

Magdić, Lj. "Prepoznala sam kolegice," *Ha-kol* 61–62 (1999).

Makanec, J. *Hrvatski vidici, nacionalno-politički eseji*. Zagreb, 1944.

Maričić, J. *Luka spasa–Židovi u Veloj Luci od 1937 do 1943*. Vela Luka, 2002.

Marjah-Johanan, B. B. *Trojanski konj ili Židovi među nama*. Zagreb, 1940.

Maštrović, Lj. "Karlo Brkljačić." In *Dom 16*. Zagreb, 1936.

Masucci, G. *Misija u Hrvatskoj. Dnevnik od 1. kolovoza do 28. ožujka 1946*, edited by M. Mikac. Madrid, 1967.

Matasović, J. "Dva prosvjeda proti konkurenciji u Zagrebu 1769 i 1780," *Narodna starina* 19 (1930): 107–9.
Matasović, J. "Knez Lenard kaptoloma zagrebečkog kramar," *Narodna prosvjeta* 32, (1933): 192.
Matić, S. "Bilješka o najstarijoj knjizi u Šikovoj biblioteci," *Bilten* 14 (1990): 7.
Matijević, Z. "Poticaji i organiziranje II. hrvatskog katoličkog kongresa (sastanaka) u Ljubljani i referat dr. Janka Šimraka o vjerskom jedinstvu Slavena (1913)," *Časopis za suvremenu povijest* 3 (2001): 707–23.
Matijević, Z. *Slom politike katoličkog jugoslavenstva. Hrvatska pučka stranka u političkom životu Kraljevine SHS (1919–1929)*. Zagreb, 1998.
Matković, H. *Povijest Hrvatske seljačke stranke*. Zagreb, 1999.
Matković, H. *Povijest Nezavisne Države Hrvatske*. Zagreb, 1994.
Matković, H. *Stjepan Radić i Hrvatski blok*. Zavod za hrvatsku povijest Papers 32–33, 267–76. Zagreb, 1999–2000.
Matković, S. *Čista stranka prava 1895–1903*. Zagreb, 2001.
Mayer, A. J. *Why Did the Heavens Not Darken?* New York: Pantheon Books, 1988.
Mažuranić, V. *Prinosi za hrvatski pravno-povijesni rječnik I–II*, 2nd ed. Zagreb, 1975.
McNeill, W. H. *Les temps de la peste*. Paris, 1978.
Mihailović, Milica, Andreja Preger, Jevrejski istorijski muzej, et al. *Jevrejska omladinska društva na tlu Jugoslavije, 1919–1941*. Exhibition catalog. Belgrade, 1995.
Miletić, A. *Koncentracioni logor Jasenovac, knj. 1–3*. Belgrade, 1986–1987.
Mirković, J. *Objavljeni izvori i literatura o jasenovačkim logorima*. Banja Luka and Belgrade, 2000.
Mirković, M. "Židovska zajednica u Zagrebu i njezin doprinos duhovnoj i materijalnoj kulturi grada." In *200 godina Židova u Zagrebu*, edited by M. Mirković, Jevrejska općina Zagreb, and Savez jevrejskih opština Jugoslavije. Zagreb: Jevrejska općina Zagreb, 1988.
Mirković, M., Jevrejska općina Zagreb, and Savez jevrejskih opština Jugoslavije, eds. *200 godina Židova u Zagrebu*. Zagreb: Jevrejska općina Zagreb, 1988.
Mirnik, I. *Obitelj Alexander ili kratka kronika izgubljenog vremena*. Zavod za hrvatsku povijest Papers 28, 96–127. Zagreb, 1995.
Mirnik, I. "Obitelj Alexander ili povijest jedne zagrebačke obitelji u pluskvamperfektu." In *Obitelj*, edited by J. Domaš-Nalbantić, 37–54. Zagreb, 1996.
Mitrović, A. "Nastanak moderne Srednje Evrope–prekretna jesen 1918." In *Zbornik Janka Pleterskega*, edited by O. Luthar, J. Perovšek, J. Pleterski, et al., 305–12. Ljubljana, 2003.
Montiljo, M. "43 godine uspješnog djelovanja mješovitog pjevačkoj zbora Lira iz Zagreba." In *Dva stoljeća povijesti i kulture Židova u Zagrebu i Hrvatskoj*, edited by O. Kraus, 249–52. Zagreb: Židovska Općina Zagreb, 1998.
Mosbacher, E. "Jugoslovenski Jevreji u svetlosti statistike," *Jevrejski narodni kalendar* 6 (1940): 130.
Moses, L. "Iz porodičnih papira–moj djed i baka," *Omanut* 4–5 (1939): 67–72.
Mošić, A. "'Židov' ili 'Jevrej'?," *Jevrejski pregled* 11–12 (1970): 8–9.
Muljević, V. "David Schwarz i njegov zračni brod," *Novi omanut* (Zagreb) 36–37 (1999).

Münster, L. "Proces zbog 'ritualnog ubistva' u Dubrovniku 1502. godine i tragična smrt lekara Moše Maralija," *Zbornik Jevrejski istorijski muzej* 1 (1971): 99–111.

Murgić, B. "Hrvatski nacionalizam Ante Starčevića." In *Dr. Ante Starčević, o 40. godišnjici smrti*, 44–52. Zagreb, 1936.

Mužić, I. *Masonstvo u Hrvata*, 5th ed. Split, 1997.

Najfeld, E. "Židovska akademska menza u Zagrebu." In *200 godina Židova u Zagrebu*, edited by M. Mirković, Jevrejska općina Zagreb, and Savez jevrejskih opština Jugoslavije, 69–73. Zagreb: Jevrejska općina Zagreb, 1988.

Najfeld, E."Sećanje iz vremena drugog svetskog rata," *Jevrejski pregled* 1–2 (1975).

Najfeld, E. "Sećanja na Židovsku menzu u Zagrebu," *Jevrejski pregled* 5–6 (1979): 29–33.

Nedeljković, D. *Rase i rasizam.* Skopje, 1937.

Nenezić, Z. D. *Masoni u Jugoslaviji (1760–1980).* Belgrade, 1988.

Neufeld, E. "Svjedočanstvo preživjelog," *Novi omanut* (Zagreb) 42–43 (2000).

Neustädter, J. *Ban Jelačić i događaji u Hrvatskoj od 1848. godine.* Zagreb, 1994.

Nevistić, I. *Ulderiko Donadini, studija o književnom razlomku.* Zagreb, 1925.

Nikolić, N. *Jasenovački logor.* Zagreb, 1948.

Nikolić, N. *Jasenovački logor smrti.* Sarajevo, 1977.

Nikolić, V. *Pred vratima domovine: Susret s hrvatskom emigracijom 1965.–dojmovi i razgovori, I–II.* Buenos Aires, 1966.

Nikoliš, G. *Korijen, stablo, pavetina–memoari.* Zagreb, 1980.

Novak, G. *Židovi u Splitu.* Split, 1920.

Novak, P. "Povijest Doma Zaklade Lavoslav Schwarz." In *Dva stoljeća povijesti i kulture Židova u Zagrebu i Hrvatskoj*, edited by O. Kraus, 74–77. Zagreb: Židovska Općina Zagreb, 1998.

Novak, T. *Buchenwald, svjedočanstvo.* Zagreb, 1996.

Novak, Z. *When Heaven's Vault Cracked.* Devon: Braunton, 1995.

Obad, V. *Slavonska književnost na njemačkom jeziku.* Osijek, 1989.

Obradović, M. *Kako da riješimo židovsko pitanje? Najpreča stvar–spas Hrvata i Hrvatske u zadnjem času.* 1920.

Obradović, M. *Kako su Židovi varali četrdeset godina jadne i neuke Hrvate, da su oni Hrvati Mojsijeve vjere.* 1909.

Obradović, M. *Kršćanski nemar i nehaj–propast Hrvatske i Slavonije.*

Obradović, M. *Myšpoka. Rodoslovje odabranoga naroda od Isusa do danas.*

Obradović, M. *Prva poslanica braći Srbima u Bjelovaru i njegovoj okolici.* 1912.

Obradović, M. *Zašto smo mi antisemiti i što hoćemo mi?* 1909.

Obradović, M. *Židovi u tajnim društvima i udruženjima.*

Oršanić, A. *Dr. Ante Starčević: 1896–1936.* Jastrebarsko, 1936.

Oršanić, A. *Duh starčevićanstva u svijetu europskog nacionalizam.* Zagreb, 1942.

Ostojić, B., and M. Sobolevski. "Pakao u kamenoj pustinji. Ustaški koncentracioni logor Slano na Pagu," *Novi list* (Rijeka, July–September 1985).

Palestina–Jevreji i Arapi u današnjem ratu. Belgrade, 1941.

Pallua, E. "Te sam ljude poznavao," *Bilten ŽOZ* 12 (1989).

Pandžić, B. *Životopis Dr. fra Dominika Mandića.* Chicago, 1994.

Parker, J. *The Jew in the Medieval Community*, New York: Hermon Press, 1976.

Parkes, J. *Antisemitism*. Chicago: Quadrangle, 1963.
Passelecq, G., and B. Suchecky. *L'Encyclique cachée de Pie XI*. Paris, 1995.
Pavelić, A. *Liepa plavka*, 3rd ed. Chicago, 1968.
Pavelić, A. *Strahote zabluda, Komunizam i boljševizam u Rusiji i u svijetu*. Zagreb, 1942.
Pavelić Ante (Dr. Ante Pavelić) riješio je Hrvatsko pitanje. Zagreb, 1942.
Paver, J. "Rezultati arhivskih istraživanja podataka o revolucionarima Zagreba–sudionicima NOB-a i žrtvama fašističkog terora." In *Oslobođenje Hrvatske 1945. godine, zbornik radova*, edited by M. Kolar-Dimitrijević, 608–11. Zagreb, 1986.
Paver, J., and P. Strčić. "Tisuću kilograma zlata," *Dalje* (1990): 188–52.
Pavličević, D. *Narodni pokret 1883. u Hrvatskoj*. Zagreb, 1980.
Pavličević, D. "Pojave antisemitizma u Hrvatskoj i Slavoniji 1883," *Bilten ŽOZ* 15 (1990).
Pavlović, Đ. "Narodni heroj Josip Engl, tvorac prve tajne radiostanice za NOB," *Jevrejski almanah 1957* (1958): 122–28.
Pečarić, J. *Srpski mit o Jasenovcu*, 2 vols. 2nd ed. Zagreb, 2000.
Pederin, I. *"Začinjavci," štioci i pregaoci*. Zagreb, 1977.
Pekić, P. *Postanak NDH, Borba za njeno oslobođenje i rad na unutrašnjem ustrojstvu*. Zagreb, 1942.
Pelesić, M. "Bliski istok 1940. godine u izvještajima Generalnog konzula Kraljevine Jugoslavije u Jerusalimu," *Prilozi* 28 (1999): 181–87.
Pelesić, M. "Palestina tridesetih godina u dokumentima Generalnog konzulata Kraljevine Jugoslavije u Jerusalimu," *Prilozi* 24 (1988): 183–207.
Perera, D. "Neki statistički podaci o Jevrejima u Jugoslaviji u periodu od 1938. do 1965. godine," *Jevrejski almanah 1968–1970*, 132–47.
Perić, M. "Daljni rezultati našeg demografskog istraživanja, U zagrebačkoj Opštini anketirana 1122 člana," *Jevrejski pregled* 1–2 (1973): 16–21.
Perić, M. "Posebno demografsko istraživanje jevrejske zajednice u Jugoslaviji," *Stanovništvo* 12–13 (1974–1975): 169–84.
Perić, M., and V. Drechsler. *Doživljaji jednog Španca*. Zagreb, 1963.
Perić, M., and V. Drechsler. "Jugoslovenski Jevreji-španski borci," *Jevrejski almanah 1963–1964*, 96–102.
Peršen, M. *Ustaški logori*. Zagreb, 1990.
Petešić, Ć. *Katoličko svećenstvo u NOB-u: 1941–1945*. Zagreb, 1982.
Petranović, B. *Istorija Jugoslavije 1918–1978*. Belgrade, 1980.
Petrić, H. *Imena u Drnju 1918–1977. godine*. Zavod za hrvatsku povijest Papers 32, 191–99. Zagreb, 1999.
Petrić, H. *Koprivnica na razmeđi epoha (1765–1870)*. Koprivnica and Zagreb, 2000.
Piliš, H. "Proljetna uvertira," *Bilten ŽOZ* 27 (1992): 15, 18.
Pinto, A. *Jevrejska društva u Sarajevu, Spomenica*. Sarajevo, 1966,
Polić, B. "Antun Švarc, prvi zagrebački židovski glazbenik," *Bilten ŽOZ* 22 (1992): 8.
Polić, B. "Humanitarni doprinos Aleksandra Frelića," *Bilten ŽOZ* 14 (1990): 8.
Polić, B. "Logor Kraljevica i njegova dječja kuhinja," *Bilten ŽOZ* 28–29 (1993): 14.
Polić, B. "Tragična kronologija zagrebačke Anc Frank," *Bilten ŽOZ* 12 (1989): 1–2.
Polić, B. "Uspomena na glazbena imena," *Bilten ŽOZ* 12 (1989): 14.
Polić, B. "Židovi u muzičkoj kulturi Hrvatske." In *Dva stoljeća povijesti i kulture Ži-*

dova u Zagrebu i Hrvatskoj, edited by O. Kraus, 239–48. Zagreb: Židovska Općina Zagreb, 1998.

Potrebica, F. "Doprinos Požeške gimnazije narodnom pokretu u Požegi 1848. Četvrti znanstveni sabor Slavonije i Baranje, svezak I," *Osijek* (1984): 178–88.

Prašek-Całczyńska, B. *Memoari jedne liječnice,* Zagreb, 1997.

Preger, A. "Sjećanje na omladinski klub 'Literarni sastanci.'" In *200 godina Židova u Zagrebu,* edited by M. Mirković, Jevrejska općina Zagreb, and Savez jevrejskih opština Jugoslavije, 64–66. Zagreb: Jevrejska općina Zagreb, 1988.

Premrl, N. "Salomon Berger, čuvar i sakupljač našeg narodnog blaga," *Bilten ŽOZ* 6–7 (1988).

Previšić, V. "Sociodemografske karakteristike srednjoškolaca i socijalna distanca prema nacionalnim i religijskim skupinama," *Društvena istraživanja* 25–26 (1996): 859–74.

Radej, S. "Hinko Gotlib," *Jevrejski almanah 1954*, 127–31.

Radeka, M. "Neka sjećanja na 1941." In *Ljetopis Srpskog kulturnog društva "Prosvjeta,"* edited by D. Kekanović and C. Višnjić, 15–70. Zagreb, 2000.

Radenić, A. "Bene berit u Srbiji i Jugoslaviji 1911–1940," *Zbornik Jevrejski istorijski muzej* 7 (1997): 3–71.

Radić, S. "Židovstvo kao negativni elemenat kulture," *Hrvatsko kolo* 2 (1906).

Radović, M. "Istaknuti Makabejci," *Bilten ŽOZ* 11 (1989): 8–9.

Radović, M. "Židovsko gombalačko i sportsko društvo Makabi u Zagrebu," *Povijest sporta* 4, no. 13 (1973): 1202–12.

Radović-Mahečić, D. "Slavko Löwy i hrvatska arhitektura, u povodu 90. rođendana," *Bilten ŽOZ* 37 (1994).

Rajčević, V. *Studentski pokret na zagrebačkom sveučilištu 1918–1941.* Zagreb, 1959.

Rajner, N. "Dom Lavoslav Švarc." In *200 godina Židova u Zagrebu,* edited by M. Mirković, Jevrejska općina Zagreb, and Savez jevrejskih opština Jugoslavije. Zagreb: Jevrejska općina Zagreb, 1988.

Rakić, L. *Jaša Tomić (1856–1922).* Novi Sad, 1986.

Rakić, L. *Radikalna stranka u Vojvodini (do početka 20. veka).* Novi Sad, 1975.

Raukar, T. "Cives, habitatores, forenses u srednjovjekovnim dalmatinskim gradovima," *Historijski zbornik* 29–30 (1976–1977): 139–50.

Rauschning, H. *Gespräche mit Hitler.* Zürich: Europa-Verlag, 1940.

Rauschning, H. *Moji povjerljivi razgovori.* New York: Europa-Verlag, 1940.

Reitlinger, G. *The Final Solution.* London: Sphere Books, 1971.

Ristović, M. *U potrazi za utočištem, Jugoslovenski Jevreji u bekstvu od holokausta 1941–1945.* Belgrade, 1998.

Roksandić, D. "Srbi u Zagrebu." In *Zagrebački Gradec 1242–1850*, edited by I. Kampuš, L. Margetić, and F. Šanjek. Zagreb: Grad Zagreb, 1994.

Romano, J. *Jevreji Jugoslavije 1941–1945: Žrtve genocida i učesnici narodnooslobodilačkog rata.* Belgrade, 1980.

Romano, J. *Jevreji u logoru na Rabu i njihovo uključivanje u narodnooslobodilački rat.* Zbornik Jevrejski istorijski muzej 2, 1–69. Belgrade, 1973.

Romano, J. "Jevreji u naprednom pokretu između dva svetska rata," *Jevrejski pregled* 7–8 (1971).

Romano, J. "Jevreji zdravstveni radnici Jugoslavije, 1941–1945: Žrtve fašističkog terora i učesnici u NOR-u," *Zbornik Jevrejski istorijski muzej* 2 (1973): 73–258.

Romano, J. "Jevrejke Jugoslavije u naprednom pokretu i Narodnooslobodilačkom ratu," *Jevrejski pregled* 1–2 (1971).

Rothmüller, C. *Židovska kolonizacija Palestine (pregled)*. Biblioteka Gideon No. 1. Zagreb, 1925.

Rudolf, Z. "O dječjem vrtiću." In *200 godina Židova u Zagrebu*, edited by M. Mirković, Jevrejska općina Zagreb, and Savez jevrejskih opština Jugoslavije, 67–68. Zagreb: Jevrejska općina Zagreb, 1988.

Ruppin, A. *The Jewish Fate and the Future*. London: Macmillan and Co., Ltd., 1940.

Sachar, H. M. *The Course of Modern Jewish History*. New York: Vintage, 1990.

Šalić, T. *Židovi u Vinkovcima*. Osijek, 2002.

Samokovlija, M. "Sjećanje na 'Hanigun' i 'Liru,'" *Jevrejski pregled* 9–10 (1979).

Šarić, A. "Sedamdeset godina od osnutka Makabija," *Bilten ŽOZ* 11 (1989): 8–10.

Savez jevrejskih opština Jugoslavije. *Sećanja Jevreja na logor Jasenovac*. Belgrade 1972.

Savez jevrejskih opština Jugoslavije. *Spomenica povodom pedesetogodišnjice Doma staraca Saveza jevrejskih opština Jugoslavije (Zaklade Lavoslava Švarca) u Zagrebu, 1910–1960*. Zagreb and Belgrade, 1960.

Savez židovskih omladinskih udruženja kraljevine Jugoslavije. *Naše omladinstvo, članci i govori*. Zagreb, 1930.

Savić, V. "Tuberkuloza." In *Socialna medicina*, vol. 3, edited by A. Štampar. Zagreb, 1926.

Scherer, A., and M. Straka. *Kratka povijest podunavskih Nijemaca*. Zagreb, 1999.

Schwarz, G. *Izraelitički molitvenik*. Zagreb, 1902.

Schwarz, G. "Iz starina zagrebačke izraelske općine," *Vjesnik Zemaljskog arhiva* 16 (1914): 102–16.

Schwarz, G. *Povijest zagrebačke židovske općine od osnutka do 50-ih godina 19. vijeka*. Zagreb, 1939.

Schwarz, G. *Molitve zadušnice u hramu izraelske općine zagrebačke*. Edited by Hevra Kadiša. Zagreb, 1922.

Schwarz, G. *Obredi izraelske vjere*, 2nd ed. Zagreb, 1924.

Schwarz, G. "Prilozi k povijesti Židova u Hrvatskoj, Iz starine zagrebačke općine (1806–1845)," *Vještnik Kraljevskog Hrvatsko-Slavonsko-Dalmatinskog zemaljskog arkiva* 5, no. 2 (1903): 89–104.

Schwarz, G. "Prilozi k povijesti Židova u Hrvatskoj u 18. st.," *Vjesnik Zemaljskog arhiva* 3, vol. 1 (1901), 185–94; *Vjesnik Zemaljskog arhiva* 4, vol. (1902), 189–92.

Šelah, M. "Kako su Talijani spašavali Židove," *Novi omanut* (Zagreb) 24 (1997): 6.

Šelah, M. "Sudbina jevrejskih izbeglica na otoku Rabu," *Zbornik Jevrejski istorijski muzej* 7 (1997): 190–97.

Seljan, D. *Zemljopis pokrajinah ilirskih iliti ogledalo zemlje*. Zagreb, 1843.

Šentija, J., et al. *Opća enciklopedija Jugoslavenskog Leksikografskog zavoda*, vols. 1–4. Zagreb, 1977–1982.

Shik, G. "Ratni zločinac i varalica ponovno na djelu," *Ha-kol* 49–50 (1997): 21.

Shirer, W. L. *The Rise and Fall of the Third Reich*. New York: Simon and Schuster, 1960.

Shomrony, A. "Kako su prodani certifikati," *Ha-kol* 51–52 (1997).

Shomrony, A. "Svjedočenja, Gdje je Freibergerova biblioteka?," *Bilten ŽOZ* 30 (1993): 10–11.

Šibl, I. *Zagreb 1941.* Zagreb, 1967.

Šidak, J. *Studije iz hrvatske povijesti za revolucije 1848.* Zagreb, 1979.

Šidak, J. "Sveučilište za vrijeme rata i okupacije od, 1941–1945." In *Spomenica u povodu proslave 300-godišnjice Sveučilišta u Zagrebu I,* edited by J. Šidak, et al., 174–84. Zagreb, 1969.

Šik, L. "Domus judaeorum, Židovski dom u Zagrebu," *Godišnjak Izraelske bogoštovne općine zagrebačke* 1 (1927): 8.

Šik, L. "Iz povijesti zagrebačkih Jevreja," *Židov* (1931): 37.

Šik, L. "Iz Siebenscheinove porodične kronike," *Židov* (1938): 12.

Šik, L. "O potrebi povjesnice Jevreja u Jugoslaviji," *Jevrejski almanah 1925* (1925): 89–102.

Šik, L. "Tragom prošlosti zagrebačkih Židova," *Židov* (1932): 16.

Šik, L. "Sedam generacija zagrebačke jevrejske porodice," *Židov* (1934): 5–6.

Šik, L. "Zagrebački Židovi u privredi," *Židov* (1927): 17.

Šik, L. "Židovi u slovenskim zemljama, nekad i sad," *Nova Evropa* (1922): 9–10.

Šimončić, Z. *Drvna industrija Hrvatske u gospodarskoj krizi 1930–1934. godine.* Institut za hrvatsku povijest Papers 8, 167–275. Zagreb, 1976.

Sinagoga i Zagreb. Katalog izložbe. Zagreb, 2001.

Sobolevski, M. *Bombaški proces Josipu Brozu.* Zagreb, 1977.

Sobolevski, M. "Zagrebačka židovska općina od 1941. do 1945. godine." In *Dva stoljeća povijesti i kulture Židova u Zagrebu i Hrvatskoj,* edited by O. Kraus, 28–46. Zagreb: Židovska Općina Zagreb, 1998.

Sobolevski, M. "Židovi u kompleksu koncentracijskog logora Jasenovac." In *Zagreb 96,* 104–19. Zagreb, 1996.

Sobolevski, M., and N. Lengel-Krizman. "Hapšenje 165 židovskih omladinaca," *Omanut* 31 (1998).

Soltikow, M. A. *Ich war mittendrin: meine Jahre bei Canaris.* Berlin: Paul Neff Verlag, 1980.

Šosberger, P. "Dvestapedeset godina jevrejske zajednice u Novom Sadu," *Jevrejski pregled* 1–2 (1968).

Spitzer, D. "Reminiscence (umjesto nekoliko nekrologa)," *Omanut* 4–5 (1939): 56–59.

Spomenica 1919–1969. Belgrade, 1969.

Šprajc, D. "Na putu prema novom židovskom identitetu." In *Dva stoljeća povijesti i kulture Židova u Zagrebu i Hrvatskoj,* edited by O. Kraus, 198–201. Zagreb: Židovska Općina Zagreb, 1998.

Srpska strana rata. Belgrade, 1996.

Šrenger, Ž. "Zagrebački Makabi." In *Dva stoljeća povijesti i kulture Židova u Zagrebu i Hrvatskoj,* edited by O. Kraus, 260–62. Zagreb: Židovska Općina Zagreb, 1998.

Staub, E. *The Roots of Evil.* Cambridge: Cambridge University Press, 1989.

Štefan, M. "Antisemitizam u Srbiji za vrijeme Drugoga svjetskoga rata," *Hrvatski iseljenički zbornik* (1995–1996): 308–19.

Štefan, M. *From Fairy Tale to Holocaust: Serbia–Quisling Collaboration with the Occupier during the Period of the Third Reich with Reference to Genocide against the Jewish People*. Zagreb, 1993.

Steinberg, J. *All or Nothing: The Axis and the Holocaust, 1941–1943*. London: Routledge, 1990.

Steinberg, J. *Deutsche, Italiener und Juden: Der italienische Wiederstand gegen den Holokaust*. Götingen, 1992.

Steiner, S. "Sjećanje na Židove liječnike u NOB," *Bilten ŽOZ* 11–12 (1989).

Stern, K. S. *Holocaust Denial*, 3rd ed. New York: American Jewish Committee, 1994.

Šternberg, Z. "Doprinos Židova u prirodoslovno-matematičkim znanostima i tehničkoj kulturi u Hrvatskoj." In *Dva stoljeća povijesti i kulture Židova u Zagrebu i Hrvatskoj*, edited by O. Kraus, 229–38. Zagreb: Židovska Općina Zagreb, 1998.

Strčić, P. "Jasenovac i ratni zločin," *Rijeka* 5, nos. 1–2 (2000): 33–105.

Strčić, P. "Pljačka zlata zagrebačkih Židova u NDH," *Ha-kol* 48 (1997).

Strčić, P. "Pljačka zlata (1.065,339 kg) zagrebačkih Židova (svibanj–listopad 1941)." In *Dva stoljeća povijesti i kulture Židova u Zagrebu i Hrvatskoj*, edited by O. Kraus, 47–58. Zagreb: Židovska Općina Zagreb, 1998.

Strecha, M. ". . . *Mi smo Hrvati i katolici* . . ." Zavod za hrvatsku povijest Papers 27, 127–62. Zagreb, 1994.

Strecha, M. *Katoličko hrvatstvo: počeci političkog katolicizma u Banskoj Hrvatskoj 1897–1904*. Zagreb, 1997.

Strecha, M. "'Sve za vjeru i domovinu,' idejna strujanja u katolicizmu u banskoj Hrvatskoj potkraj 19. stoljeća," *Croatica Christiana Periodica* 38 (1996): 73–132.

Strecha, M. "To je pravi škandal. Prilog pitanju ravnopravnosti Židova u banskoj Hrvatskoj u drugoj polovici 19. stoljeća." In *Zbornik Mirjane Gross*, edited by N. Budak and others, 219–36. Zagreb, 1999.

Stulli, B. *Židovi u Dubrovniku*. Zagreb, 1989.

Stuparić, D. *Tko je tko u NDH*. Zagreb, 1995.

Šufflay, M. *Hrvatska u svijetlu svjetske historije i politike*. Zagreb, 1928.

Šurmin, Đ. *Hrvatski spomenici*. Zagreb, 1898.

Šute, I. "Položaj i obilježje trgovine u Banovini Hrvatskoj (1939–1941)." Ph.D. thesis, Univ. of Zagreb, 2002.

Švarc, B. "Kako sam preživio," *Ha-kol* 69–70 (2001).

Švob, M. "Migracije i promjene u židovskoj populaciji," *Migracijske teme* 11 (1995): 231–89.

Švob, M. "Promjene u populaciji Židova u Hrvatskoj od XVIII. do XX. stoljeća." In *Dva stoljeća povijesti i kulture Židova u Zagrebu i Hrvatskoj*, edited by O. Kraus, 287–310. Zagreb: Židovska Općina Zagreb, 1998.

Švob, M. "Razvoj ženskih općih i židovskih dobrotvornih organizacija." In *Dva stoljeća povijesti i kulture Židova u Zagrebu i Hrvatskoj*, edited by O. Kraus, 268–82. Zagreb: Židovska Općina Zagreb, 1998.

Švob, M. "Židovi danas," *Novi omanut* (Zagreb) 9 (1995).

Švob, M. *Židovi u Hrvatskoj*. Zagreb, 1997.

Švob, M., C. Brčić, and S. Podgorelec. "Židovi u Hrvatskoj s posebnim osvrtom na grad Zagreb," *Migracijske teme* 10 (1994): 55–85.

Švob, T. "Dr. Pavao Wertheim (1911–1941), sjećanja i podaci o istaknutom biologu," *Novi omanut* (Zagreb) 21 (1997): 2.

Szabo, A. "Glavna zanimanja Židova u banskoj Hrvatskoj krajem 19. i početkom 20. stoljeća," *Bilten ŽOZ* 28–29 (1993): 23.

Szabo, A. "Židovi i proces modernizacije građanskog društva u Hrvatskoj između 1873. i 1914. godine." In *Dva stoljeća povijesti i kulture Židova u Zagrebu i Hrvatskoj*, edited by O. Kraus, 142–55. Zagreb: Židovska Općina Zagreb, 1998.

Tadić, J. *Jevreji u Dubrovniku do polovine 17. stoljeća.* Sarajevo, 1937.

Tolentino, E. *Fašistička okupacija Dubrovnika 1941–1945. godine i rješavanje "jevrejskog pitanja."* Zbornik Jevrejski istorijski muzej 1, 201–10. Belgrade, 1971.

Tomasevich, J. *The Chetniks: War and Revolution in Yugoslavia, 1941–1945.* Stanford: Stanford University Press, 1975.

Tomasevich, J. "War and Revolution in Yugoslavia, 1941–1945: Occupation and Collaboration," *Canadian Journal of History* 39, no. 1 (2004): 165–67.

Trninić-Šević, N. "Jom Kipur u logoru," *Jevrejski pregled* 5–8 (1989): 41–44.

Tuđman, F. *Bespuća povijesne zbiljnosti.* Zagreb, 1989.

Ukrainčik, E. *Erec Izrael (1921–1924).* Zagreb, 1934.

"Ustaše su ubijale javno, svjedočanstvo," *Ha-kol* 61–62 (1999).

Uzelac Schewendeman, S. "Krhotine iz povijesti židovske zajednice u Slavonskom Brodu." In *Dva stoljeća povijesti i kulture Židova u Zagrebu i Hrvatskoj*, edited by O. Kraus, 392–405. Zagreb: Židovska Općina Zagreb, 1998.

Vajs, A. "Jevreji u novoj Jugoslaviji," *Jevrejski almanah 1954* (1954): 45.

Vajs, M."Kada je broj zamijenjen zaboravljenim imenom (Sjećanje na oslobođenje iz logora 1. svibnja 1945)," *Jevrejski pregled* 3–4 (1983): 35–42.

Vajs, M. "Prethodni rezultati popisa Jevreja u Jugoslaviji," *Jevrejski almanah 1957* (1958): 162–68.

Vasiljević, Z. *Sabirni logor Đakovo.* Slavonski Brod, 1988.

Verber, E. *Kršćanstvo prije Krista.* Zagreb, 1972.

Verber, E. *Talmud.* Zagreb, 1982.

Vilimkova, M. *Die Präger Judenstadt.* Aventinum Prag, 1990.

Vincetić, L. "Antisemitizam u hrvatskoj katoličkoj štampi do Drugoga svjetskog rata." In *Antisemitizam, Holokaust, Antifašizam*, edited by N. Lengel-Krizman and I. Goldstein, 54–64. Zagreb, 1996.

Visković, V. *Sukob na ljevici, Krležina uloga u sukobu na ljevici.* Belgrade, 2001.

Völkl, K. "Die jüdische Gemeinde von Zagreb. Sozialarbeit und gesellschaftliche Einrichtungen in der Zwischenkriegszeit," *Münchner Zeitschrift für Balkankunde* 9 (1993): 105–54.

Völkl, K. "Zur Judenfeindlichkeit in Kroatien. Wieweit gab es Antisemitismus bis 1941?," *Südosteuropa* 1 (1993): 59–77.

Völkl-Boeckh, K. "Židovska vjerska općina u Zagrebu do 1941. godine," *ČCP* 1 (1995): 33–53.

Volner, Z. "EZRA–Jevrejska štedna kreditna zadruga." In *200 godina Židova u Zagrebu*, edited by M. Mirković, Jevrejska općina Zagreb, and Savez jevrejskih opština Jugoslavije, 80–81. Zagreb: Jevrejska općina Zagreb, 1988.

Vrgoč, A. "Iz povijesti farmacije za vrijeme bivše tako zvane hrvatsko-slavonske Vojne Krajine," *Apotekarski vjesnik* (1935): 7–11.

Vučić, P. *Židovstvo i hrvatstvo*. Zagreb, 2000.

Vujnović-Tonković, A. "Pisana riječ Žige Hirschlera," *Novi omanut* (Zagreb) 12 (1995): 5–7.

Vuković, T., and E. Bojović. *Pregled srpskog antisemitizma*. Zagreb, 1992.

Weininger (Vajninger), O. *Pol i karakter*. Belgrade, 1986.

Wertheim, P. "Sastanku omladine," *Hanoar* 3–4 (1930): 49–50.

Wertheim, P., and C. Rothmüller. *Ideologija cionizma*. Zagreb, 1928.

Žalac, T. "Hrvatski Blagaj." Unpublished manuscript.

Za spomen dra Aleksandra Lichta: U povodu prenosa njegovih posmrtnih ostataka na vječni počinak u zemlji Jisraela. Tel Aviv, ca. 1955–1956.

Zašto se Nemačka brani od Jevreja. Belgrade, 1933.

Zatezalo, Đ. *Jadovno: Kompleks ustaških logora 1941*. Belgrade, 2007.

ZAVNOH: Zbornik dokumenata i podataka, vols. 1–4. Zagreb, 1964–1985.

Zbirka Erich Šlomović. Katalog izložbe. Zagreb, 1989.

Zbornik Narodnih heroja Jugoslavije. Belgrade, 1957.

Zečević, D. "Polemička pučka književna pouka Antuna Kanižlića o Fociju kao uzročniku crkvenog raskola." In *Književni Osijek: Književnost u Osijeku i o Osijeku od početka do danas*, edited by S. Marijanović, 155–70. Osijek, 1996.

Zečević, D. *Pučki pamfleti Milana Obradovića*. Zavod za hrvatsku povijest Papers 30. Zagreb, 1997.

Zemljar, A. *Haron i sudbine*. Zagreb, 1988.

Zemljar, A. "Relativnost poznavanja konclogora Slana na Pagu," *Novi omanut* (Zagreb) 36–37 (1999): 21–22.

Žerjavić, V. "Demografski pokazatelji o stradanju Židova u NDH." In *Antisemitizam, Holokaust, Antifašizam*, edited by N. Lengel-Krizman and I. Goldstein, 133–38. Zagreb, 1996.

Žerjavić, V. *Gubici stanovništva Jugoslavije u Drugom svjetskom ratu*. Zagreb, 1989.

Žerjavić, V. *Opsesije i megalomanije oko Jasenovca i Bleiburga: Gubici stanovništva Jugoslavije u Drugom svjetskom ratu*. Zagreb, 1992.

Žerjavić, V. *Pertes de la population en Yougoslavie, 1941–1945*. Zagreb, 1997.

Žerjavić, V. *Population Losses and Manipulations with the Number of Second World War Victims*. Zagreb, 1993.

Židovec, V. *Moje sudjelovanje u političkom životu*. Hrvatski državni arhiv, Collection of Ministarstvo unutarnjih (unutrašnjih) poslova, Socijalistička Republika Hrvatska 013.0.56.

Židovi na tlu Jugoslavije. Katalog izložbe. Zagreb, 1988.

Židovi–izložba o razvoju židovstva i njihovog rušilačkog rada u Hrvatskoj prije 10. IV. 1941. Rješenje židovskog pitanja u NDH, katalog izložbe. Zagreb, 1942.

"Židovska masonerija (Prvi popis članova loža u Zagrebu, Osijeku, Sarajevu, Subotici, Novom Sadu i Beogradu)," *Moderna socijalna kronika* 2, no. 1 (1935).

Židovske narodne pjesme, ur. S. Löwy, glazbeno obradio Ž. Hirschler. Zagreb, 1921. Reprint, Zagreb, 2003.

Zlatković Winter, J. "Dijaspora i Židovi na području Jugoslavije," *Migracijske teme* 3 (1987): 161–75.

Zločini fašističkih okupatora i njihovih pomagača protiv Jevreja u Jugoslaviji. Belgrade, 1952.

Zovko, I. "Što narod u Herceg-Bosni priča o Jevrejima," *Zbornik za život i običaje Južnih Slavena* (1906): 293–97.

Žugaj, V. *Židovi novogradiškog kraja.* Zagreb, 2001.

INDEX